THUNDERBIRDS FOR PEACE
DIARY OF A TRANSPORT SQUADRON

Dedicated to all Thunderbirds past and present.

Laurence Motiuk

© Laurence Motiuk

Cover painting: Don Connolly
Editing: Charmion Chaplin-Thomas, Cecilia Blanchfield
Design and layout: Accurate Design & Communication, Inc.
Printing: Tri-Graphic Printing

Larmot Associates
39 Higwood Drive
Ottawa, Ontario K2E 5K9

ISBN: 0-9683431-1-2

TABLE OF CONTENTS

Preface v
Acknowledgements vii

Part I: Transition
    Chapter 1:   From Bombing To Transport,
                      25 April 1945–25 June 1945 1

Part II: Liberators
    Chapter 2:   Formation and Training,
                      26 June 1945–30 September 1945 13
    Chapter 3:   Trooping Operations, RAF Transport Command,
                      1 October 1945–6 January 1946 31

Part III: Dakotas
    Chapter 4:   Dartmouth, Nova Scotia, August–December 1946 59
    Chapter 5:   Dartmouth–Dorval, 1947 73

Part IV: North Stars
    Chapter 6:   Dorval, 1948 93
    Chapter 7:   Dorval, 1949 129
    Chapter 8:   Dorval, January–June 1950 157
    Chapter 9:   Dorval and McChord Air Force Base,
                      July–August 1950 179
    Chapter 10: McChord AFB, September–December 1950 209
    Chapter 11: McChord AFB, January–June 1951 241
    Chapter 12: Lachine, July–December 1951 273
    Chapter 13: Lachine, January–June 1952 301
    Chapter 14: Lachine, July–December 1952 331
    Chapter 15: Lachine, January–June 1953 353
    Chapter 16: Lachine, July–December 1953 375

Chapter 17: Lachine, January–June 1954 395
Chapter 18: Lachine, July–December 1954 419
Chapter 19: Lachine, 1955 439
Chapter 20: Lachine, 1956 473
Chapter 21: Lachine, 1957 513
Chapter 22: Lachine, 1958 543
Chapter 23: Lachine and Trenton, 1959 563
Chapter 24: Trenton, 1960 587
Chapter 25: Trenton, 1961 625

Part V: Disbandment
Chapter 26: St-Hubert, January–October 1962 651

Epilogue 663

Notes & References
  Notes 667
  References 721

Appendices
  Appendix A: Glossary 731
  Appendix B: Schedule of Operations 737
  Appendix C: RCAF-MATS Airlift Agreement 745
  Appendix D: Nominal Roll—*Operation HAWK* 749
  Appendix E: Korean Airlift—Schedule of Operations 761
  Appendix F: Squadron Commanders 779
  Appendix G: Honours and Awards 785

Index 787

PREFACE

The author took on a monumental task in researching and writing the history of No 426 (Thunderbird) Squadron, RCAF. His first volume, Thunderbirds At War, covers the history of the squadron from its formation as the seventh bomber squadron in the RCAF at Dishforth, Yorkshire, on 15 October 1942, to the end of the Second World War. That book is a remarkable record of the trials and tribulations overcome by the squadron as it converted to newer types of bombers and endured many aircrew casualties, not only on operations over enemy-held Europe, but also in accidents over England caused by weather or battle-damage to their aircraft. The heroism and valour displayed by these very young Canadians was acknowledged by the award of many honours and mentions in dispatches. No 426 was probably one of the best squadrons in No 6 (RCAF) Group, Bomber Command, which was formed on 1 January 1943 to bring all the Canadian bomber units operating from Britain under Canadian control. Fourteen of these squadrons were operational by the end of the war.

This second volume picks up the story in 1945, after the end of hostilities, when No 426 Squadron was re-formed as a transport unit for service in the post-war RCAF, which then totalled some 12,000 officers and airmen. The skills of both the flight crews and ground crews were needed to prevail over the many obstacles the squadron encountered flying for Canada in a multitude of operations all over the world, many of them carried out under United Nations aegis. At home, the squadron played an important role in opening Canada's North, particularly the high Arctic. On these missions, the ground crews had to keep the aircraft flying in the worst possible climatic conditions, and they maintained an extraordinarily high state of serviceability that permitted the squadron to complete its many operational tasks on time. It was then — and is now — a very proud unit, and a great asset to the RCAF and the Canadian Forces, and to Canada.

The author compiled this story from many sources, official and otherwise. Some people would consider this a tedious task, but for him it was an opportunity to make a detailed study of historically significant events in which he was personally involved. This is a great book to complement his first volume, and will be enjoyed by aviation enthusiasts and anyone who has ever had contact with No 426 Squadron.

Lieutenant-General R.J. Lane, DSO, DFC and Bar, CD

Acknowledgements

I am deeply indebted to many individuals and organizations for advice and assistance provided during the preparation of this postwar history of No 426 Squadron. I am especially grateful to the many members of the 426 (Thunderbird) Squadron Association, the relatives of those who served with the squadron after the Second World War, and to others for providing background material, anecdotes and log book entries; replying to letters; sending photographs and memorabilia; and reviewing and commenting on segments of the manuscript. In particular, I would like to thank the following individuals for significant contributions to the project:

Nova Scotia: S. Logan (Pictou), R. Lohnes (Lunenburg), and F. Sanford (Maitland).

Prince Edward Island: T. Richardson (New London), and Mary Sage and Barbara Wood (Charlottetown).

Quebec: G. Brassard and Phil Rodrique (Aylmer); J. Henry, L. Joron and J.-L. Denis (Baie d'Urfé); Y. Lafreniere (Boucherville); R. Nurse (Brossard); A. St. Laurent (Île Bizard); J. Bugdale (Kirkland); A. De Quoy (Laval); L. Leclair (Mont-St-Grégoire); C. Lalande (Plaisance); C. Binette (Racine); and A. Fullam (St-Jean-sur-Richelieu).

Ontario: J. Lambert (Ajax); E. Heikkila (Barrie); J. Moric (Bath); D. Cameron, R. Doucette, L. Halpin, Bob Hayes, J. Hutchinson, F. King, J. Lindgren, R. Longworth, J. Lynch, R. Rose, J. Santarelli, J. Sopaz and D. Yates (Belleville); D. Thompson (Bracebridge); C. Wenzel (Brampton); P. Tutt (Brantford); C. Bennett and J. Sare (Brighton); J. Bowers (Chesley); W. Luhtala (Clinton); G. Brogden (Consecon); J. Trethowan (Cumberland); R. Livock (Dalkieth); R. Lloyd (Elgin); C. Casson (Etobicoke); P. Major (Georgetown); D. Harrison and D. Kuhn (Guelph); R. Lupton, K. Reid and H. Smith (Kingston); R. Brown (Kitchener); Mac Morrison (Oakville); C. Empey (Osgoode); F. Bowman, D. Broadfoot, M. Brunotte, G. Bussières, A. Byford, C.G.W. Chapman, F.R. Cleminson, M. Darville, B. Davidge, P. Dragojevich, D. Eagles, M. Finklestein, J. Forest, K. Greenaway, B. Graves, E. Grose, R. Gurney, B. Hoy, Michaela Huard, C. Knight, T. Latham, L. O'Ray, P. Pawliuk, K. Roulston, D. Shade, J. Shipton, R. Sierolawski, Bob Smith, O. Stevens, P. Sutherland, Tim Timmins, C. Torontow, G. Webb, R.T. Whitman and R. Wilson (Ottawa); M. Gordon and D. Haire (Perth); J. Morfitt (Sharbot Lake); J. Beath (St. Catharines); LGen W.K. Carr and J. Maitland (Stittsville); Bill Swetman (Tottenham); E. Chevalier, W. Crosby, D. Jones, D. Scott, T. Sutton and S. Walton (Trenton); C. Mills and Ramona Parmelee (Toronto); R. Burn (Whitby); and N. Campbell (Williamstown).

Saskatchewan: B. Carss (Kamsack).

Alberta: R. Edwards, Marie Gee, B. Lahey and P. McDonald (Calgary); A. Ronning (Camrose); W. Lupton (Devon); G. Holmes and O. Milner (Edmonton); G. McCormick (Fort Saskatchewan); T. Charchuk (Leduc); and R. Langman, D. McBurney and L. Rodewolt (St. Albert).

British Columbia: L. Rushcall (Chilliwack); D. Woodman (Comox); D. Payne (Cowichan Bay); C. Baine and S. Quickfall (Delta); J. Ford (Fruitvale); Al Trotter (Kamloops); R. Husch and S. Olsen (Kelowna); T. Potekal (North Vancouver); D. Deeprose (Penticton); A. Gerding and B. Ingall (Richmond); A. Mackie (Sardis); H. Cram, W. Dick and G. McAninch (Sidney); J. Fabi (Vernon); and H. Filleul, LGen. R.J. Lane, M. Majocha, E. Miskiman, G. Reed and Dennis Smith (Victoria).

United States: L. Byrne (Port Angeles, Washington); J.H. Ralph (Enid, Oklahoma); R. Roane (Cape Coral, Florida); D. Schwanky (El Paso, Texas); G. Sweanor (Colorado Springs, Colorado); and H. Zbesheski (Riverside, California).

Many thanks are due to the following organizations and their staff for permitting me to work in their research facilities or use their copyright material in this publication:
1. Air Force Association of Canada, Ottawa, Ontario (Bob Tracy, Fred Aldworth)
2. Canada Aviation Museum, Ottawa, Ontario (Fiona Hale, Librarian; Ian Leslie, Library Assistant)
3. National Archives of Canada, Ottawa, Ontario (Tim Dubé and Greg McCooeye, Archivists)
4. Transport Canada, Ottawa, Ontario (Doug Mein, Air Navigation Services and Airspace)
5. Department of National Defence, Canada:
    5.1. Canadian Forces College, Toronto, Ontario (Cathy Murphy, Librarian)
    5.2. Canadian Forces Photographic Unit, Ottawa, Ontario (Janet Lacroix, Imagery Library)
    5.3. Directorate of History and Heritage, Ottawa, Ontario (Dr. Serge Bernier and Dr. Steve Harris, Historical Research Officers)
    5.4. Colonel Wade Hoddinott, NORAD Headquarters, Colorado Springs, Colorado (a former Commanding Officer of No 426 Transport Training Squadron)
    5.5. Lieutenant-Colonel Mario Fortin, Canadian Forces College, Toronto, Ontario (a former Commanding Officer No 426 Transport Training Squadron)
    5.6. Lieutenant-Colonel John Anderson, 8 Wing, CFB Trenton, Ontario (current Commanding Officer of No 426 Transport Training Squadron)
6. U.S. Department of the Air Force:
    6.1. Washington, D.C. (Douglas R. Thar, Public Communication Division)
    6.2. Air Force Historical Research Agency, Maxwell AFB, Alabama (Archie Di Fante, Archivist)
    6.3. Air Mobility Command Headquarters, Scott AFB, Illinois (Dr. Tommy R. Young, Historian)

I would also like to thank:
7. Don Connolly, artist (Sydenham, Ontario), for the cover design and permission to reproduce his Liberator, Dakota, North Star and Sabre paintings;
8. William Constable, cartographer (Ottawa, Ontario), for preparing the maps;
9. Hugh Halliday, historian (Ottawa, Ontario), for providing the documentation regarding honours and awards;
10. Larry Milberry, aviation historian (Toronto, Ontario), for making available his North Star research material;
11. Shirley Newell (Ottawa, Ontario) for typing the manuscript; and
12. Charmion Chaplin-Thomas and Cecilia Blanchfield, editors (Ottawa, Ontario), for converting a mass of notes into this second volume of the squadron history.

Finally, I wish to emphasize that I alone am responsible for any errors or omissions in the text of this book, its appendices or, indeed, this list of acknowledgements!

Ottawa, May 2004   Laurence Motiuk

Part I

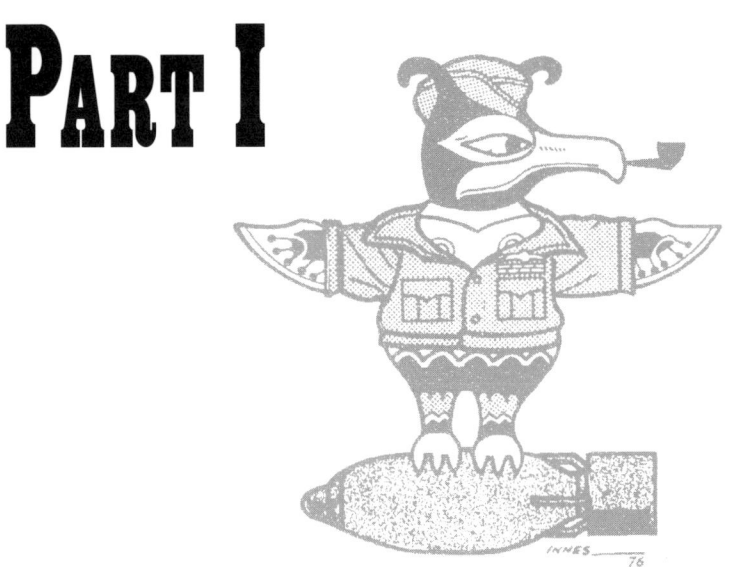

Transition

Chapter 1

From Bombing To Transport
25 April 1945–25 June 1945

At 1431 hours on Wednesday, 25 April 1945, Flight Lieutenant C.V. Rouse of Regina, Saskatchewan, lifted Halifax LW207/OW "K" off the runway at RCAF Station Linton-on-Ouse and headed east on the last bombing mission No 6 (RCAF) Group would ever undertake. The target was the group of coastal defence batteries located on Wangerooge, the northernmost island of the East Frisian chain, to protect the sea approaches to Bremerhaven and Wilhelmshaven. The Thunderbirds had twenty Halifaxes on the battle order for this five-and-a-half-hour operation, and No 408 (Goose) Squadron, which shared Linton-on-Ouse, contributed seventeen more. Ten squadrons of Spitfires escorted the Bomber Command attack force of 482 aircraft, 192 of them from No 6 Group. The only resistance encountered was heavy flak from Wangerooge. The weather was clear. The detail from No 426 Squadron took only two minutes to drop its bombs from 10,400 to 12,000 feet, and was heading home by 1718 hours.

The attack was considered a success, but it had tragic consequences. On the way to the target, a No 426 Squadron Halifax captained by Warrant Officer 2nd Class J.C. Tuplin of Summerside, Prince Edward Island, collided in mid-air with a Halifax from No 408 Squadron, piloted by Flight Lieutenant E.B. Ely of Toronto, Ontario. Both aircraft disintegrated and crashed into the sea. Five other aircraft were lost that day, one to enemy action and four to accidents. One Halifax from No 347 (Free French) Squadron, stationed at Elvington, Yorkshire, failed to return from the operation; two Lancasters from No 431 Squadron from Croft collided, killing members of both crews; and two Halifaxes from No 76 Squadron from Holme collided, killing one entire crew and all but one member of the other.[1]

At 2006 hours that evening, when Flying Officer J. Boyle of Toronto, Ontario, and his crew brought Halifax NP737/OW "N" home from Wangerooge, No 426 Squadron's service as a heavy bomber unit came to an end.[2]

Early in 1944, authorities in Canada began to consider increasing its participation in the Far East war when Germany was defeated. On 18 January 1944, the Honourable C.G. (Chubby) Power, Minister of National Defence for Air, advised his British counterpart, Sir Archibald Sinclair, that, for the rest of the war, Canadians should serve with Canadian units and, after the defeat of

Germany, Canada would seek prompt separation and repatriation of all Canadian personnel serving with RAF squadrons. All Canadians wishing to leave the service would be demobilized. The British received this proposal coldly.[3]

At a meeting on 18 February 1944, the Canadian Cabinet learned that as many as ninety-three RCAF squadrons might be needed to help bring the war to an end: forty-six to remain in Europe and forty-seven for the Far East. In May 1944, when Prime Minister Mackenzie King arrived in London for the Conference of Empire Prime Ministers, the Far East requirement remained at forty-seven RCAF squadrons, including fourteen heavy bomber units, but reducing the European requirement to eleven squadrons. On 14 June 1944, Cabinet accepted the proposal for a force of fifty-eight squadrons as a basis for planning commitments for the war's next phase (commonly called Phase Two). As Power indicated on 25 July to Air Marshal L.S. Breadner, Air Officer Commanding-in-Chief, RCAF Overseas, the aim was to create two or three RCAF groups commanded by one RCAF Headquarters; these formations would function under the operational direction of an American or British supreme commander.[4]

On 14 September 1944, while attending the Octagon Conference in Quebec, Marshal of the RAF Sir Charles Portal, the Chief of the Air Staff, informed the Canadian Cabinet that the RCAF was expected to contribute eighteen heavy bomber squadrons and fourteen fighter squadrons to the war in the Pacific. In his discussions with Canadian service chiefs later that day, Portal increased that estimate by ten transport squadrons, one air-sea rescue and one air-observation squadron — forty-four squadrons in all — plus fourteen squadrons to support the occupation forces in Europe.[5]

On 6 October 1944, Air Marshal Sir Douglas Evill of the Air Ministry wrote to Air Marshal Breadner regarding the place of the RCAF in RAF plans for the war in the Far East. At that time, the RAF intended to deploy thirty-six Lancaster squadrons supported by long-range fighters. The Lancasters' range would be increased by means of in-flight refueling. Evill suggested that the RCAF should field a similar force, comprising twelve heavy bomber squadrons (including six strike squadrons and six tanker squadrons) and six fighter squadrons. No difficulty was foreseen in organizing the eighteen squadrons as an RCAF formation.[6]

A firm decision on a commitment for Phase Two was finally made toward the end of 1944. On 11 December, the Cabinet and the Chiefs of Staff meeting in Ottawa to consider Evill's suggestions approved the proposed force of twenty-two squadrons (to include twelve heavy bomber squadrons, six long-range day-fighter squadrons, three transport squadrons and one air-sea rescue squadron) and up to 23,000 personnel, to be deployed in the Pacific under RAF command. To support the occupation force in Germany, they earmarked eleven more squadrons, to be grouped into Canadian Wings in Europe under the appropriate RAF functional command and linked to the RCAF Overseas Headquarters in London.[7]

The RAF dubbed the Far East very-long-range bomber formation Tiger Force, and one of its three groups was to be formed from the RCAF contingent of twelve heavy bomber squadrons and six fighter squadrons. Tiger Force planners did not expect to need the RCAF units for at least three months after the end of hostilities in Europe, which was forecast for June 1945; in the meantime, all RCAF heavy bomber squadrons would remain operational. Tentatively, the RCAF fighter component of Tiger Force was to include No 401, No 402, No 403, No 438, No 440 squadrons, as well as No 400 Squadron, an army-cooperation unit. Force planning also called for the creation of air transport units by converting No 422 Squadron and No 423 Squadron from flying boats, and No 407 Squadron from maritime reconnaissance. No 404 Squadron, a coastal fighter unit, would be assigned air-sea rescue duties.[8]

By December 1944, Tiger Force was assembled on paper. The first administrative outline for *Operation MOULD* (later renamed *Operation TIGER*), was completed on 23 November 1944. This document set out operational requirements for force composition, types of aircraft, maintenance organization, lines of communication, planning and intergroup coordination, and manpower and training. In February 1945, the designated commander of Tiger Force, RAF Air Vice Marshal Hugh Lloyd, visited Ottawa to discuss the Pacific deployment with Canadian officials. Air Commodore C.R. Slemon, previously the Senior Air Staff Officer at No 6 Group, was selected to command the Canadian contingent.[9]

In Ottawa, Air Force Headquarters decided that selection priority for Tiger Force should go to men who had yet to complete an operational tour or to serve overseas. In January 1945, Chief of the Air Staff Air Marshal Robert Leckie stated that the RCAF VLR Group would form and train in Canada. This decision was influenced by an RCAF Overseas Headquarters survey indicating that personnel would accept transfer to the Pacific only if they could take leave in Canada first. This finding was reinforced by a Cabinet decision that only volunteers would be sent to fight Japan. On 4 April 1945, the Prime Minister announced that no member of the armed forces who had served in Europe would be sent to the Pacific unless he or she had specifically volunteered to go, and had received thirty days of disembarkation leave in Canada. These provisions made it easier to organize and move the Canadian contingent to the Far East and permitted the creation of a self-sufficient RCAF force, a goal that would be easier to accomplish in Canada during the build-up phase.[10]

On 19 April 1945, RCAF Overseas Headquarters asked Air Force Headquarters in Ottawa to approve the selection of No 63 Base at Leeming and its four squadrons for the European force. Until then, the rationale for selecting RCAF squadrons for the post-VE Day phase of the war was based on seniority — the units with the longest service in Europe would go to the Pacific theatre, and the remaining squadrons would join the occupation force in Europe or be disbanded. However, the size of Canada's contribution to the Far East had yet to be decided, and four bomber squadrons were required immediately for the European force. Therefore, it was decided to post personnel willing to remain in Britain to these units, and to get on with organizing the occupation force.[11]

On 20 April, No 424 Squadron and No 433 Squadron at Skipton-on-Swale, and No 427 Squadron and No 429 Squadron at Leeming, received word that their assignment to the European force had been approved. With these four units flying the British-built Lancaster I and Lancaster III, No 63 Base constituted a self-contained operational organization already equipped with aircraft suitable for its European assignment. This left the selection of the squadrons for Tiger Force to be made from the other bomber units in No 6 Group. These units were armed with the Canadian-built Lancaster X and the British-built Halifax. Here preference was to be given to units flying the Lancaster X and to the squadrons with the longest service in the theatre, provided that the latter condition did not complicate the situation unduly.[12]

By the end of April 1945, the RCAF's Phase Two requirements had dropped to twenty-four squadrons: only ten heavy bomber squadrons and three long-range transport squadrons were now needed for Tiger Force, and the European force now required only four heavy bomber squadrons, four fighter squadrons and three medium-range transport squadrons. The Air Ministry did not wish to reduce its coastal forces until July, so No 407 Squadron, slated for conversion to transport, would be replaced by a unit from No 6 Group — No 426 Squadron.[13]

On 2 May 1945, Air Marshal G.O. Johnson, Air Officer Commanding-in-Chief, RCAF Overseas, met with Air Vice Marshal G.C. Pirie, the Air Ministry's Director-General, Organization, to discuss what the RCAF would do in Phase Two. Eight Canadian heavy bomber units — No 405,

No 408, No 419, No 420, No 425, No 428, No 431 and No 434 squadrons — were earmarked for Tiger Force, and the squadrons from No 63 Base (No 424, No 427, No 429 and No 433) were allocated to the European force. For the units based at RCAF Station Linton-on-Ouse, it was agreed that No 408 Squadron would rearm as soon as possible with the Lancaster X and that the ground crew assigned to No 426 Squadron would be transferred to RAF Transport Command for VLR service. No 415 and No 432 squadrons, stationed at East Moor, would disband.[14]

On 19 May 1945, Air Marshal Johnson advised Air Force Headquarters in Ottawa that new circumstances required the revision of some earlier recommendations regarding the disposition of RCAF squadrons overseas. At the same time, however, he confirmed that No 63 Base and its Lancaster squadrons would be included in the European occupation force, and that the accompanying fighter units would be No 401, No 402, No 411 and No 412 squadrons, at that time attached to No 126 Wing, 2nd Tactical Air Force. For medium-range transport, the European force would have No 435 Squadron, No 436 Squadron (withdrawn from southeast Asia) and No 437 Squadron.[15]

No 405 Squadron, still flying with the Pathfinders, was scheduled to move from Gransden Lodge to Linton-on-Ouse and, on 26 May 1945, convert to the Lancaster X. After this change, all eight Pacific-bound VLR squadrons would be flying the same type of aircraft. Meanwhile, all hands were engaged in preparing for the move by air to Eastern Air Command stations in Nova Scotia. As for the VLR transport units, No 426 Squadron was scheduled for transfer to No 4 Group, Transport Command, on 25 May 1945, and RCAF Overseas Headquarters expected that No 422 Squadron and No 423 Squadron (still flying Sunderland flying boats) to be transferred from Coastal Command to Transport Command and converted to the transport role. Of the heavy bomber squadrons, No 415 and No 432 had been disbanded on 15 May and No 413, already reduced to nil strength, was slated to be disbanded. The other nineteen RCAF squadrons still overseas — No 400, No 403, No 404, No 406, No 407, No 409, No 410, No 414, No 416, No 417, No 418, No 421, No 430, No 438, No 439, No 440, No 441, No 442 and No 443 — were ready to be disbanded or reassigned as directed by Ottawa.[16]

While the policy and command hierarchies were pondering its future, No 426 Squadron maintained operational readiness. On 26 April, Bomber Command ordered a follow-up to the daylight attack of 18 April on Heligoland. No 408 Squadron and No 426 Squadron each prepared fifteen aircraft and crews for the operation, which was cancelled just before take-off. The following day, the two squadrons were again ordered to put up fifteen Halifaxes each for an attack to complete the destruction of the guns on Wangerooge, and that operation was cancelled after the briefing. The rest of the month was spent training new crews fresh from the heavy conversion units.[17]

On 4 May, for the first time in a week, Bomber Command laid on an early-morning operation that precipitated a flurry of station activity before the mission was scrubbed — the enemy forces in Denmark, Holland and northwest Germany had surrendered.[18]

On 5 May, Linton was stood down from operations, and No 426 Squadron organized flying training to keep the crews busy. No 6 Group Headquarters had issued instructions to train wireless operators to handle loop antennae for the trip home. On 6 May, with no flying scheduled and the news media reporting that the surrender negotiations were nearly complete, the station's maintenance crews started stripping the Halifax aircraft of their guns, pyrotechnics and ammunition in anticipation of VE Day. On 7 May, routine activity almost ground to a halt as No 426 Squadron waited to hear whether it would be disbanded or reassigned — and, if reassigned, where it would be going. The Station Commander, Group Captain W.P. Pleasance, knew the VE Day announcement was imminent, so he ordered all aircraft immobilized, all operational supplies returned to stores, and all hangars and dispersal areas scrubbed down. These orders complied with Bomber Command's instructions to all stations, which were to immobilize motor transport and to guard aircraft and dangerous installations such as bomb dumps and fuel points.[19]

On the morning of 8 May, Group Captain Pleasance declared a general stand-down and informed all personnel that Prime Minister Churchill would announce VE Day at 1500 hours. Linton's security plan went into effect, and guards were posted at all strategic locations. After the Prime Minister's address, Group Captain Pleasance made a brief Tannoy broadcast to thank all hands for their hard work and cooperation and to give all non-essential personnel two days off. Announcements followed, detailing the entertainment arrangements for the evening. Additional stocks of beer and spirits — carefully hoarded for the occasion — were brought out, a gala station dance was held at the NAAFI, and the sergeants' and officers' messes organized parties. The celebrations continued until the early hours of the morning, and the holiday spirit prevailed into the next day.[20]

On 10 May, Group Captain Pleasance held a Commanding Officer's conference to plan "Linton-At-Home Day," scheduled for Sunday, 20 May. No 6 Group Headquarters instructed No 408 Squadron to convert to Lancaster Xs preparatory to joining Tiger Force.[21] And RCAF Overseas Headquarters began informing RCAF personnel in Bomber Command about options for their immediate future: they could volunteer for Tiger Force and serve in the Pacific Theatre of Operations; they could stay in Europe to serve with the occupation force; they could serve somewhere in the Western Hemisphere; or, if they were surplus to RCAF requirements, they could request release. This last option entailed waiting for repatriation to Canada and demobilization on a schedule based on length of overseas service.

By 12 May, No 426 Squadron still had no idea whether it would continue to exist, and its daily routine was at a virtual standstill. On Sunday, 13 May, an impressive church parade for the VE Thanksgiving service was held in No 3 Hangar — a less than liturgical but necessary setting, as more than 2,000 people attended, including all members of No 408 Squadron and No 426 Squadron. On 14 May, the Thunderbirds finally learned that they would be transferred from Linton to somewhere in No 4 Group, RAF Transport Command. Their space at Linton would be taken over by No 405 (Vancouver) Squadron, which would convert to the Lancaster X with No 408 Squadron and then return to Canada to join Tiger Force. Goose Squadron received nine Lancaster Xs with which to begin the changeover.[22]

On 15 May, at East Moor, No 415 (Swordfish) and No 432 (Leaside) squadrons were officially disbanded and their personnel were posted to No 62 (Beaver) Base Headquarters at Linton. The next day, No 426 Squadron received orders to move its ground personnel to RAF Station Driffield, thirty-three miles east of Linton, on 25 May. Like all Bomber Command squadrons, No 426 had only one non-flying member, the Adjutant; all its support and maintenance requirements were filled by ground staff on the base or station strength. Accordingly, an appropriate number of servicing, maintenance and repair staff from the stations at East Moor, Linton-on-Ouse and Tholthorpe were selected to form a servicing echelon for the reconstituted

Thunderbird Squadron. The Thunderbird aircrew were temporarily attached to RCAF Station Dishforth for reassignment to Tiger Force, occupation force duties, service in North America, or eventual demobilization.²³

On 18 May, RCAF Station Linton received instructions to the effect that the Halifax aircraft were now "surplus to requirements" and would be disposed of. That meant stripping them of all their communications, navigation and safety equipment. The ground staff did not take long to transfer twenty Halifaxes to the surplus list and write them off as spares and scrap. The next day, preparations for No 426 Squadron's move were well underway, but without aircrew, aircraft, tools or handling equipment, as the squadron was permitted to take only mechanical transport, equipment and publications specifically on its charge; however, at East Moor, Linton and Tholthorpe, more than 400 ground personnel were clearing out and preparing to transfer to the Thunderbirds. At this point, the squadron learned that, as it would be converting to Liberators, the RCAF had decided that the aircrews would be made up of Canadian personnel currently serving with RAF Coastal Command and Transport Command units.²⁴

On 20 May, to express their appreciation for the hospitality shown them by the people of Yorkshire, No 62 Base and RCAF Station Linton held Linton-At-Home Day. All service personnel were urged to invite their civilian friends and, at 1400 hours, the station was opened to visitors. The Lord Mayor of York and nearly 3,000 people from neighbouring communities enjoyed entertainments — tours of Halifax aircraft (the first time civilians not employed in war work were allowed anywhere near a bomber), boxing matches, roller-skating, children's movies and exhibition softball games. Refreshments were served in No 3 Hangar, and children received sweets donated by their hosts from parcels received from Canada.²⁵

On 23 May, the Officers' Mess threw a farewell party for the departing Thunderbirds; by all accounts, an excellent send-off. The ex-Thunderbird aircrew were due to report at RCAF Station Dishforth on 26 May, leaving Linton even as No 405 Squadron arrived.

On 24 May, No 426 Squadron put in its last official day as a bomber squadron as the ground staff packed up the last bits of useful equipment for the move from Linton. At 1000 hours on Friday, 25 May, now part of Transport Command, No 426 Squadron moved its 435 ground crew and administrative staff down the road to Driffield, in convoy under the command of the Adjutant, Flight Lieutenant A.F. MacKell. The next stage of the squadron's history was about to begin.²⁶

During its thirty-one months as a bomber squadron, No 426 Squadron participated in 268 missions and launched 3,240 sorties, including: seventy sorties from which the aircraft failed to return; twenty sorties devoted to sea searches; and 3,150 bombing and mining sorties. The bombing and mining sorties included: 2,870 that were completed; ten in which the aircraft crashed on return to base; and 270 in which the task was abandoned, 110 of these on instructions from the Master Bomber or the Operations Centre.

Of the squadron's aircraft, twenty Wellingtons, thirty-three Lancasters and thirty-eight Halifaxes — ninety-one in all — were lost to enemy action, crashes and accidents.

Between November 1942 and April 1945, the Thunderbirds sustained 579 aircrew casualties. This total includes: 426 dead (including 419 who were killed in action, two who died of injuries, three prisoners of war who died in captivity, and two evaders who were executed); 104 captured;

twenty-three evaders; eighteen injured; seven internees held in Sweden; and two who were rescued after their aircraft ditched, one of whom was later taken prisoner and is, therefore, counted as a prisoner-of-war.

While serving with the Thunderbirds, 191 squadron members received 198 decorations, including: two Distinguished Service Orders, two Bars to the Distinguished Flying Cross, 131 Distinguished Flying Crosses, one Conspicuous Gallantry Medal, twenty-five Distinguished Flying Medals, three British Empire Medals and twenty-two Mentions in Despatches. In addition, seven squadron members posthumously received the Belgian Croix de Guerre with Palm; three received the French Croix de Guerre with Silver Star; one received the American Distinguished Flying Cross; and one received the Norwegian Commemorative Medal.[27]

RAF Station Driffield lay two miles west of the small market town of Great Driffield, Yorkshire. First used by the Royal Flying Corps during the Great War and developed as a permanent aerodrome in 1918, it was deactivated shortly after the Armistice and not reopened until 1936, when it was rebuilt as a bomber station. In 1941, Driffield became part of No 4 Group, Bomber Command, accommodating No 614, No 462 and No 466 squadrons of the Royal Australian Air Force. The RCAF arrived at Driffield in February 1941, when No 401 Squadron, a fighter unit, was briefly stationed there. On 23 April 1941, No 405 Squadron (the first RCAF bomber squadron to form overseas) organized at Driffield and launched its first sorties against the enemy from that station.[28]

On 26 May 1945, No 426 Squadron's ground personnel were settling into their new home, establishing a daily routine under Flight Lieutenant MacKell's command and handing over the vehicles brought from Linton to the Driffield MT Section for servicing and control. They had comparatively little to do, however, so many airmen were sent on leave. The same day, Wing Commander D.R. Miller of Saskatoon, Saskatchewan (who had yet to report), was appointed the new Squadron Commander. He had joined the RAF in 1936 and, before transferring to the RCAF, was Commanding Officer of No 525 (Transport) Squadron at RAF Station Lyneham. The Liberators and the aircrews were expected to arrive soon to begin transforming No 426 Squadron into a heavy transport unit. The squadron expected to stay at Driffield until its transport training was completed, and then be transferred to No 47 Group.

On 28 May, Flight Lieutenant MacKell organized a sports program to occupy the few airmen still on the station. On 30 May, a Canadian YMCA opened at Driffield for RCAF personnel. The month ended with No 426 Squadron still awaiting its aircrew and its new Liberators.[29]

In early June, planners at RCAF Overseas Headquarters were still unable to set a firm date for the issue of new aircraft to No 426 Squadron. Their latest information was that Liberators should be available in July. By that time, crews should have been selected from RCAF units in Britain, and the squadron should have begun training them for their new job.

Although their immediate future had yet to be decided, No 422 Squadron and No 423 Squadron were also scheduled to transfer to Transport Command as very-long-range transport squadrons flying the "multi-engine" routes. These two squadrons would continue operating their Sunderland flying boats while awaiting delivery of their Liberators. RCAF Overseas Headquarters disagreed with this plan, and had already recommended to AFHQ in Ottawa that transport squadrons should be formed only when Liberator aircraft became available, that their crews should be trained in Canada, and that the three VLR squadrons (No 426, No 422 and No 423) should be organized into a Canadian Wing.[30]

On 8 June, at a meeting held at Transport Command Headquarters (Bushy Park, Teddington), it was announced that all but one of the RAF Liberator squadrons would be transferred to Transport Command, and that all Liberator Mk VI and Liberator Mk VIII aircraft would be modified for transport use. The Ministry of Aircraft Production was already modifying the Liberator VIs, but would not be able to install passenger seats, heating or oxygen equipment; Transport Command would add these amenities when the equipment kits became available. MAP had twenty aircraft ready for delivery and expected to complete forty more by 30 June, and Transport Command had undertaken to complete the modification program at a rate of fifteen Liberators per month. Some of this work was to be done at RAF Station Tempsford.

At the meeting it was recommended that, of the available Liberators (modified and unmodified), five each should be allocated to five RAF squadrons (No 53, No 59, No 86, No 206 and No 220) and fifteen should be immediately delivered to No 426 Squadron, which could obtain highly qualified transport aircrew and the ground crew required to service and maintain the Liberators from the RCAF. No 426 Squadron was scheduled to be the first of the new VLR units to be fully operational, so it would have first claim on fully modified aircraft designed for transporting passengers (in the military context, "trooping") and on accommodation at a trunk-route airfield.[31]

On 15 June 1945, Transport Command Headquarters issued an organization order transferring RAF Station Tempsford and its personnel, equipment and responsibilities from No 38 Group to No 47 Group. The organization order also announced that, once its members had completed conversion training, No 426 Squadron would move to Tempsford and join No 47 Group, and that Transport Command would equip the squadron with thirty Liberator VI aircraft as soon as Air Ministry authority to do so was received.[32]

On 18 June, the Canadian VLR transport squadrons were on the agenda of a meeting held at AFHQ in Ottawa and chaired by Air Marshal Robert Leckie, the Chief of the Air Staff. Air Marshal G.O. Johnson, Air Officer Commanding-in-Chief, RCAF Overseas, explained that two draft plans for employing the three VLR squadrons were under consideration. The first draft plan, proposed by the Air Ministry, had two of the squadrons based in the Philippines to serve the Philippines–Rangoon route and the third squadron operating on a trans-Pacific route between the Philippines and Canada. In the second draft plan, proposed by RAF Transport Command, all three squadrons would operate over main Transport Command routes. The consensus at the meeting was that Air Marshal Johnson should be free to negotiate with both RAF Transport Command and the Air Ministry the terms of the three squadrons' employment, including the selection of routes and the location of stations and Wing Headquarters. Air Marshal Johnson was also authorized to insist that RCAF units should not operate in Southeast Asia.[33]

On 22 June, Transport Command Headquarters authorized the transfer of No 426 (RCAF) Squadron from RAF Station Driffield in No 4 Group to RAF Station Tempsford in No 47 Group, effective 25 June. The same day, No 4 Group issued an administrative order authorizing the

squadron's 400 ground staff (the Adjutant and 399 junior ranks and senior NCOs) to move themselves, along with the vehicles and office equipment they had brought from Linton, from Driffield to Tempsford. A squadron movement order issued on 22 June spelled out precisely how this evolution would be carried out.[34]

On 26 June, the manning of RCAF transport squadrons was the main topic of discussion at a Phase Two Planning Committee meeting at RCAF Overseas Headquarters. A report presented by Group Captain G.S. McDougall, the RCAF Staff Officer in Transport Command, stated unequivocally that Transport Command (including its new squadrons recently transferred from Coastal Command) could produce the 104 five-man crews, each comprising a pilot, a co-pilot, a navigator, a wireless operator and a flight engineer, required for the VLR squadrons. In fact, if only forty crews could be produced by 31 October 1945, the VLR squadrons' initial staffing requirements would be met; however, after the initial postings were made, each VLR squadron would need four replacement crews per month. The meeting decided to recommend to Ottawa that the forty crews required immediately in Britain be trained at Canadian operational training units. It also recommended that potential VLR captains should have completed at least 700 flying hours, including 100 hours as captain, of which fifty hours should have been completed at night.[35]

The meeting learned that the formation of No 422 Squadron, No 423 Squadron and No 426 Squadron was ahead of schedule; in No 426 it was already under way, and No 422 and No 423 were expected to form by the end of July. The initial aircrews for these squadrons were to be RCAF personnel already in Transport Command, some from the units transferred from Coastal Command. The planners assumed that all aircrew posted to the VLR squadrons would have received their thirty days of leave in Canada by the end of 1945, and that most of the aircrew posted to No 422 Squadron and No 423 Squadron would volunteer for the Pacific, start their training on Liberators as soon as aircraft were available, and take leave using a rotation based on the length of their overseas service.[36]

Group Captain McDougall advised the meeting that thirty-six crews had already been posted to No 426 Squadron, and that the unit would shortly receive twenty Liberators and be manned at a rate of 2.4 crews per aircraft for a total of forty-eight crews. The computed wastage rate per month per squadron, assuming casualties and tour expiration (based on an eighteen-month tour) was three crews; however, to permit early screening of crews that failed to meet operational standards, the recommended monthly reinforcement rate would be four crews per squadron.[37]

Between 25 May and 25 June 1945, No 426 Squadron lay idle; without aircraft, tools or equipment, the ground staff could accomplish little during the month after their departure from Linton. In fact, all that remained of Thunderbird Squadron from its days as a bomber unit was its name and a cadre of airmen, some of whom had served with the squadron since the Wellington days at Dishforth. On 22 June, the instructions were issued for the move to Tempsford, where the ground staff would meet the new aircrew and receive their aircraft. On 25 June 1945, the move was successfully carried out by rail and road.[38]

Part II

Liberators

Formation and Training, 26 June 1945–30 September 1945

CHAPTER 2

FORMATION AND TRAINING

26 JUNE 1945–30 SEPTEMBER 1945

On 26 June, the new Thunderbird aircrew began arriving at Tempsford and, with the ground staff already in place, the reconstitution of the squadron could now commence in earnest. Wing Commander D.R. Miller, the new Squadron Commander, was on hand, soon to be joined by a colleague from No 525 Squadron, Squadron Leader J.T. McCutcheon DFC, to serve, first, as a flight commander and, later, as Officer Commanding Flying.

The squadron ground staff had a busy day settling into their new quarters, a process that required considerable adjustment to Tempsford's dispersed accommodations. Transport Command intended the ground staff to be on squadron strength for administration purposes, and to come under the station's Chief Technical Officer for duty and discipline. With aircrew and ground staff ready and waiting, the squadron continued to wait for delivery of their modified Liberators, which would permit training to start.[1]

RAF Station Tempsford lay in Bedfordshire, seven miles east-northeast of Bedford and a mile and a half north of Sandy. Built between late 1940 and the summer of 1941, Tempsford became part of No 3 Group, Bomber Command in March 1942. From that time until the end of the war, the station was involved in the support of Special Operations Executive operations. SOE agents came to Tempsford to be dressed and equipped for their missions, and to be flown out to their hazardous drops and daring landings into occupied Europe. Most of these clandestine activities were carried out by No 138 Squadron and No 161 Squadron, which flew a variety of aircraft out of Tempsford. Toward the end of the war in Europe, No 138 Squadron became a heavy bomber unit and left Tempsford; on 14 June 1945, No 161 Squadron was disbanded and replaced by No 1 Transport Aircraft Modification Unit, which was created to complete the modification of Liberators obtained from Coastal Command and Bomber Command into transport aircraft.[2]

On the morning of 27 June 1945, No 426 Squadron paraded all its ground staff to hear an address by the Station Commander, Group Captain Palmer, and a short talk from Wing Commander Miller in which he introduced himself. The crewing-up process began in the traditional, informal way. About 120 aircrew were withdrawn from the regular squadron roll to await reassignment to other operational areas; this group was not to train on the Liberators. Finally, Flying Officer A.M. Davison reported in from RCAF Overseas Headquarters in London, attached to the squadron as Education Officer.

The next morning, all ground staff began training courses on the Liberator aircraft, and crewing-up continued as new aircrew personnel trickled in. On 29 June, Wing Commander Miller attended a meeting at Station Headquarters to discuss the squadron's operational role with officers from Transport Command Headquarters. Posting notices to the Repatriation Depot at Torquay and a holding unit at Snaith, Yorkshire, came in for 120 ground staff awaiting return to Canada; after their disembarkation leave, they would go to the Far East or return to Europe for service with the occupation force. In the afternoon, their replacements arrived from No 3 RCAF Personnel Reception Centre at Bournemouth, along with the new Canadian chaplain, Squadron Leader D.R.L. Clarke. No aircraft arrived, so all aircrew received forty-eight hours' leave for the weekend.

By 30 June, squadron strength stood at 727 personnel, including 125 officers.[3]

On Sunday, 1 July, the Thunderbirds received a visit from Squadron Leader C.J. Fitzgerald, the Roman Catholic chaplain from No 3 RCAF District Headquarters. As the area's "mobile Padre," Squadron Leader Fitzgerald was expected to drop in frequently. The same day, Group Captain McDougall from Transport Command Headquarters met privately with Wing Commander Miller to discuss the squadron and its projected role, and with a large gathering of aircrew to address their concerns. All the vehicles brought from Linton-on-Ouse via Driffield were turned over to the Tempsford MT Section, which would handle No 426 Squadron's motor transport requirements from now on.[4]

On 2 July, the squadron continued sorting the aircrew, separating volunteers and non-volunteers and posting out everyone who did not wish to serve in the Pacific or in the European force. The next day, thirty-five aircrew arrived, and the non-volunteers among them were immediately sent on seven days' leave to await posting to holding units. On 4 July, four more aircrew reported in, and completed crews began departing on leave to ease the crowding in Tempsford's inadequate living quarters. Over the next few days, many ground staff who should have been training on the still-unavailable Liberators would also proceed on leave.

At a meeting of the Planning Working Committee held on 4 July at RCAF Overseas Headquarters in London, it was decided that the three VLR squadrons selected for Tiger Force would be based in Britain. The planners had only one reservation, that the RCAF might be asked to re-deploy perhaps as much as an entire squadron to meet trans-Pacific airlift requirements that should have been the responsibility of Tiger Force.[5]

On 6 July, Wing Commander Miller visited No 4 Group Headquarters at Heslington, Yorkshire, to enquire about plans for the squadron's future. Meanwhile, at Tempsford, No 426 Squadron received ten training spaces for pilots on Radio Range and Standard Beam Approach courses scheduled to begin on 11 July. The W-Debs, an RCAF concert party, staged a very entertaining show at the NAAFI that evening, and repeated it the next night to the delight of the audience.[6]

On 8 July, the Thunderbirds heard that three Liberators were finally available for pick-up at Prestwick, the large international aerodrome near Glasgow, and that No 47 Group would arrange to have them ferried to Tempsford. Aircrew training that day consisted of dinghy drills at the swimming pool in Tempsford village. The following day, a new flight commander, Squadron Leader McCutcheon, reported in, and an extensive shuffle of aircrew officers' quarters was undertaken to house as many No 426 Squadron crews together as possible. Auxiliary Services brought in a large truckload of furniture for the large Nissen hut dubbed "Canada House" and designated as a recreation centre.[7]

On 10 July, the squadron paraded all its ground staff to hear the Commanding Officer tell what he knew about plans for their future and to answer questions. Accommodations problems continued: the arrival of thirty-two new aircrew from RAF Station Bircham Newton, Norkfolk, precipitated a housing crisis because the forty-eight non-volunteers posted out to RAF Station Snaith were not due to leave for two days. Even the allocation to No 426 Squadron of five pilot vacancies on radio-range courses at Prestwick and Valley presented difficulties: the selected candidates had to be recalled from leave.

On 11 July, the Squadron Commander and two crews went to Prestwick by Dakota to pick up their first two Liberators, and Mr. R.G. LeBlanc, a supervisor from the Knights of Columbus, arrived at Tempsford to be the squadron's recreational and social organizer. On 12 July, five more of the Thunderbirds' promised Liberators were ferried in during the afternoon and early evening, and a small group of aircrew reported in. Still more were expected, and their arrival would bring No 426 Squadron up to strength. The forty non-volunteer aircrew posted to Snaith left Tempsford, and ten more would leave in a couple of days.[8]

On 13 July, six more Liberators arrived and the airfield finally began to take on an operational look. Flight Lieutenant H.E. Fleishman, an engineering officer from RAF Station Odiham, dropped in; the squadron expected him to be posted in soon. Twenty more aircrew showed up. The next day, the Thunderbirds acquired Flight Lieutenant J.H. Young, a medical officer fresh from sixteen months with a Canadian fighter wing in No 2 Tactical Air Force, and yet another Liberator — the inventory now stood at fourteen.[9]

On 14 July, Transport Command Headquarters asked the Thunderbirds to take one of their Liberators to RAF Station Northolt for inspection by Air Marshal Sir Ralph A. Cochrane, the Commander-in-Chief of Transport Command, and Wing Commander Miller and his crew departed accordingly for Northolt on the morning of 16 July. Meanwhile, at Tempsford, the squadron aircrew began ground training with a full day of lectures, Flight Lieutenant Fleishman the engineering officer reported in as expected, and Captain Fletcher from the Canadian dental clinic at No 5 District Headquarters in York visited to explore the possibility of establishing a dental unit on the station to look after Canadian personnel.[10]

On 17 July, ground training was in full swing, the Canadians double-banking with RAF ground staff to learn Liberator servicing routines. Wing Commander Miller attended a meeting convened by the Station Commander to discuss the overcrowding problem; with so many aircrew on the station, accommodations and messes were overtaxed. Visitors to the squadron included Group Captain G.G. Truscott and Wing Commander R.B. Middleton from the Organization Branch at RCAF Overseas Headquarters. The next day, Squadron Leader Edwards arrived from No 4 Group Headquarters to discuss training for flight engineers, who were both scarce and comparatively inexperienced on Liberators. As aircrew continued to report in, ten pilots left for radio-range courses at No 1513 BAT Flight in Bramcote and standard beam approach courses at No 1521 BAT Flight in Wymeswold. Two more Liberators were ferried in, bringing the squadron's inventory to sixteen.[11]

Now that the No 426 Squadron had enough aircraft, and ground instruction was under way, the next step was to get crews into the air. Flying training had to be individually tailored. A check ride with the Flight Commander or a check pilot established what each pilot needed to learn, and was normally followed by a couple of sessions of circuits and bumps, then day and night flying so crews could get to know the area. After completing local familiarization training, pilots who needed standard beam approach and radio-range training went to the appropriate schools. Each crew also made the four- to five-hour trip to Germany, ostensibly to learn the routine for picking up troops in Europe for transfer to the Pacific but actually to give crews a chance to see the sights and satisfy their curiosity. Ground staff were taken along on these flights as often as possible.

Later, the training schedule would take aircrews from Tempsford on a grand tour of the western Mediterranean by way of St. Mawgan, Cornwall, a major departure point for flights heading southeast. The Tempsford–St. Mawgan leg took about an hour and a half; then the crews headed across the Atlantic to Morocco, landing at Rabat-Salé Airport to spend the night after flying nearly seven hours. On the second day, they would leave the Rabat area to fly for six hours across north Africa to Castel Benito, a town near Tripoli in Libya, and then five and a half hours more across the Mediterranean to the south of France, to land near Marseilles at Istres-le-Tube, a large airfield soon to be an important diversion point on the trooping runs. On the third day, the crews would make the four-and-a-half-hour flight back to St. Mawgan, and then return to base. Each training flight carried two or three crews that alternated flying chores on the various legs of the trip. This arrangement gave the crews the experience they needed before tackling the real thing — flying the route to India. It also meant that the squadron did not have to position slip crews (relief crews) along the route.[12]

The Liberator was one of the Americans' leading heavy bombers of the Second World War. Consolidated Vultee Aircraft Corporation of San Diego, California, and, under subcontract, Douglas, North American and Ford, built more than 19,000 of them in several versions. Under the *Lend-Lease Act*, the United States transferred more than 2,000 early-model Liberators to the RAF and the Commonwealth air forces; later variants acquired by the RAF included the GR Mk VI long-range maritime reconnaissance airplane; the B–24J, which served as the Liberator B.Mk VI; the B–24L, which served as the Liberator B.Mk VIII; and the B–24M, which served as the Liberator GR Mk VIII. No 426 Squadron operated both the Mk VI and the Mk VIII.[13]

The Liberator B.Mk.VI was sixty-seven feet two inches long, eighteen feet high and had a 110-foot wingspan. Powered by four 1,200-horsepower Pratt and Whitney 14-cylinder two-row radial engines, its maximum speed was 270 miles per hour and it could climb to 20,000 feet in forty minutes. The aircraft had a service ceiling of 32,000 feet and a range of 990 miles fully loaded with 12,800 pounds of bombs; with a reduced bombload, its maximum range was 2,290 miles. Empty, it weighed 37,000 pounds, and its maximum take off weight was 62,000 pounds.[14]

The conversion of the RAF and RCAF Liberators from maritime-reconnaissance aircraft and bombers to passenger-carriers was done by Scottish Aviation at their Prestwick base. From a distance, the aircraft looked much as they always had, but up close the modifications were obvious: the gun turrets were gone, the resulting holes were closed in, the bomb-bay doors were bolted shut, and the fuselage had a large Perspex window installed on each side, just aft of the wing.

The bomb-bay now contained two rows of seats, bolted to the walls so the passengers faced inboard. The fuselage was so narrow that the passengers' knees almost touched in the middle, so moving between the rows was very difficult. The normal payload was twenty-six passengers and a total weight of about 6,500 pounds. Weight and balance requirements limited seating in the aft compartment to six places; consequently, passengers seated aft could look out the Perspex "picture windows," stretch out, lie flat on the floor, and generally enjoy themselves in their first-class accommodations. Passenger-control staff usually reserved these seats for officers.

To save time and money on converting the Liberators, Scottish Aviation did nothing to the crew positions. For a single type of aircraft, with two fixed positions — the pilots' position was always in the same place and the flight engineer usually sat in a jump seat behind the pilots — the Liberator had an incredible variety of crew layouts. In some, the navigator's position was in the nose; in others, it was on the flight deck behind the pilot, facing either forward or aft. Some aircraft had the astrodome in the nose, where the navigator and the pilots could see each other and gesticulate appropriately; other aircraft had the astrodome on the flight deck. Awkwardly, in some of No 426 Squadron's Liberators, the astrodome was in the nose and the navigator's position was on the flight deck, while in others the layout was reversed. The radio operator's position was usually on the flight deck behind the co-pilot, but in some aircraft it faced forward and in others it faced aft. In still other aircraft, the radio operator sat in a cramped cubbyhole located above the "first-class" aft passenger compartment, and sent messages to the flight deck paper-clipped to a pulley-mounted cable that ran the length of the fuselage.

During take-off and landing, the nose compartment was a dangerous place. Aircraft are most vulnerable to accidents at those times, and anyone occupying the nose would be in a most perilous situation in an accident. Also, any equipment not tied down could fall through the nose-wheel door. Finally, at specific times, the nose-wheel itself presented a threat — to the navigator.

After take-off, and before raising the undercarriage, the pilot braked all the wheels except the nose-wheel. This was done to reduce vibration in the fuselage and prevent accidental damage to the tires. The nose-wheel was a simple mechanism for which this precaution was not considered necessary, and it would still be spinning at 120 to 130 miles per hour as it was drawn up into the nose compartment. The navigator would wait on the flight deck until the pilots had trimmed the aircraft to normal flight mode and started to climb. Anxious to get his plot started, he would then lower himself into the little gap between the spinning nose wheel and the starboard side of the fuselage, and creep forward to the astrodome, pushing or pulling his navigation bag, sextant and astro-compass. If they were in the tropics, he would be wearing only a light shirt and shorts. The Liberator nose-wheel could run freely for an unbelievably long time, and a wheel revolving at high speed, seen up close in a relatively dark area, can look as if it is stationary. Under these circumstances, navigators sometimes failed to take sufficient care, and allowed parts of their anatomy to touch the spinning nose-wheel. The consequences were always painful.

The Liberator had other interesting features. One of these was the turbine in the exhaust stream of each engine that used the otherwise wasted force of the exhaust to drive the very efficient superchargers. With the turbochargers and the very-high-aspect-ratio Davis wing, which minimized induced drag, the Liberator had a remarkable capacity for high-altitude, long-range flight. These revolutionary features gave the Liberator a few special problems, however.

With the turbochargers consuming the exhaust, the usual source of space heat in aircraft, the designers of the Liberator had to come up with another way to keep the crew and passengers from freezing to death. Their solution was the "Southwind" system, a network of strategically located, gasoline-fired fan heaters that worked by means of a glow-plug in a closed combustion chamber. The Southwind system was reasonably efficient but dangerous; fuel flowed to the heaters from the main tanks through exposed lines that ran through the interior of the fuselage. Liberators were known to blow up in flight; rightly or wrongly, the Southwind system was sometimes blamed for explosions that could not be explained otherwise. The ban on smoking in military aircraft, sometimes overlooked in appropriate circumstances, was firmly enforced aboard Liberators. In the Liberator, no situation was appropriate, and only the foolhardy would smoke. Also, when heavily loaded and trimmed for level flight, Liberators tended to mush, or fly nose-up. In this attitude, the aircraft was less fuel-efficient, a problem corrected by lowering the flaps very slightly. The handling notes never included this technique, which pilots passed along by word of mouth. Finally, like other high-aspect-ratio aircraft, a Liberator in a steep turn built up stalling speed rapidly and, in an unusual situation, the pilot had to ensure that he could increase speed rapidly. The best solution to this problem was to avoid unusual situations.

Even with these quirks, the Liberator was a stable, quiet aircraft built for comfortable flying. Crews accustomed to British four-engine bombers found it quite delightful to work without leaks, freezing drafts or the howl of Merlin engines.[15]

On 19 July, two more Liberators arrived, bringing No 426 Squadron's total to eighteen; Squadron Leader G.E.F. Elliott from RCAF Overseas Headquarters visited to discuss Canadian medical issues with station staff; and Squadron Leader King of No 4 Group Headquarters discussed signals procedures and equipment with Wing Commander Miller.[16]

On 20 July, Transport Command Headquarters issued a detailed instruction on a trooping trial to be made with two Liberator VIs, one with seating from the Transport Command Development Unit at Harwell, Berkshire, and one without seating from No 426 Squadron. Forty-eight soldiers would be transported from RAF Station Merryfield in No 47 Group, located near Taunton, Somerset, to Mauripur, near Karachi in northern India, by way of Castel Benito, Libya, Lydda, Palestine and Basra, Iraq. On the return trip, retracing the same route, the aircraft would transport forty-eight more soldiers back to England. That same day, No 4 Group Headquarters instructed No 426 Squadron to send a Liberator to the Air Transport Tactical Development Unit at Netheravon, near Amesbury, Wiltshire, for about two weeks. No 426 Squadron selected Flight Lieutenant K. Warner and his crew for the trooping trial, but only four hours after leaving Tempsford, they were back, in another Liberator. The aircraft they left in needed considerably more modification before it could be used for a trooping trial, and the work was expected to take a week.[17]

On 21 July, No 426 Squadron received word of nine radio-range and SBA training vacancies. Aircrew ground training was advanced enough that flying training was scheduled to begin in two days. Tempsford's Canadian personnel were enjoying the newly opened Canada House, which offered amenities such as a lounge, a reading and writing room, games facilities, and a canteen, due to open on 22 July, with (among other delicacies) soft drinks imported from Canada.

On 23 July, No 426 Squadron launched flying training in excellent weather, and the unit's nineteenth Liberator, arrived. Wing Commander Miller was away, so Squadron Leader McCutcheon attended a section heads' meeting called by the Station Commander to discuss Tempsford's continuing snags, a list topped by messing and accommodations. The squadron spent the next day flying, and three Thunderbirds attended a lively meeting of the Airmen's Mess Committee at Station Headquarters at which dissatisfactions were clearly and forcefully discussed. Nothing dramatic occurred in consequence.

On 25 July, Squadron Leader Dinsmore, an RAF engineering officer, arrived at Station Headquarters as Tempsford's Chief Technical Officer, responsible for control and supervision of aircraft servicing, and No 426 Squadron adjusted its flying training program to allow aircrew to begin receiving inoculations in preparation for operations in Africa, the Middle East and the Pacific. That afternoon, thirty-nine cast and crew of the RCAF show *All Clear* arrived; they were scheduled to perform at the NAAFI Hall the next evening.[18]

On 26 July, Transport Command Headquarters directed No 426 Squadron to hand over four Liberators to No 59 Squadron, an unusual order considering that the Thunderbirds were supposed to be fully equipped with aircraft as soon as possible. Flying training continued on schedule despite bad weather, and the squadron received instructions from No 4 Group Air Staff to carry parachutes on all training flights – a new practice for Transport Command; sure enough, the instruction was countermanded within 24 hours. Finally, Group Captain W.V. McCarthy, the senior RCAF Roman Catholic chaplain overseas, visited the squadron to talk with its Roman Catholic members.

On 27 July, Wing Command Miller and Squadron Leader A.R. Holmes went to London for meetings at RCAF Overseas Headquarters, and dental officer Captain G.H. McKinney and two assistants reported in from RAF Station Snaith to set up a Canadian dental clinic; arrangements were made to establish them at the Station Sick Quarters.

On 29 July, a Sunday, the Thunderbirds got no stand-down, not with a full flying training program under way, with night flying for the first time since hostilities ended. However, their workload was lightened by the arrival of 500 long-awaited bicycles, very helpful for getting about Tempsford's widely dispersed facilities.[19]

On 30 July, the good weather returned, permitting No 426 Squadron to log a full day of flying training. The Squadron Commander and the Adjutant went to Station Headquarters to attend a meeting to hear the Station Commander outline a stricter working routine and recommend improvements to Tempsford airmen's general deportment; the war in Europe was barely over and a peacetime mentality was already setting in. No 426 Squadron received word that Flight Lieutenant J.A. Elviss, a pilot in A Flight, would receive the Distinguished Flying Cross.

On 31 July, bad weather curtailed flying, and the Adjutant, Flight Lieutenant A. MacKell, left for RAF Station Bassingbourn, near Cambridge, to become Station Adjutant after serving as Adjutant in No 426 Squadron since September 1944; he would be replaced by Flying Officer C.E. Glover. During the day, Wing Commander Miller, went to Bassingbourn to exchange opinions with the Station Commander, Group Captain K.L.B. Hodgson; the RCAF expected to take over Bassingbourn soon to accommodate two transport squadrons.[20]

July 1945 was No 426 Squadron's first full month as a transport unit. Despite the lack of tools and equipment, the ground crew were able to get enough aircraft serviceable to support an ambitious program of ground and flying training. In eight days of flying, the squadron flew 371 non-operational hours, including twenty-nine hours at night. By 31 July, squadron strength stood at 721 all ranks, including 224 officers and 497 non-commissioned officers and other ranks, and sixteen Liberator VIs.

On 1 August, all No 426 Squadron's ground crew — RCAF members — were posted to No 4426 Servicing Echelon, an RAF unit commanded by Squadron Leader Dinsmore, the station's Chief Technical Officer. The good weather continued, and flying training continued with it. Flight Lieutenant Warner and his crew left for Netheravon again, this time in a Liberator adequately modified for the Britain-to-India trooping trial scheduled to begin on 20 July, and the squadron delivered the last of the four Liberators that Transport Command ordered transferred to No 56 Squadron at RAF Station Tain. Squadron Leader Cook from No 4 Group Headquarters at York visited the Thunderbirds to discuss navigation problems and offer assistance to Navigation Section.[21]

The excellent weather held for the next several days, but flying training slowed down because No 426 Squadron lacked serviceable aircraft, the result of a shortage of tools and spares. The ground crew did the best they could with what they had, but the supply system was simply not responding to their original requisitions, let alone the follow-up inquiries.

While No 426 Squadron worked on in Britain, struggling to transform itself into a transport organization, the war raged on in the Pacific. On 6 August, a frightening new weapon made its début when the Americans flattened the Japanese city of Hiroshima with a single atomic bomb. On 8 August, they did it again, at Nagasaki, and on 15 August, the Emperor of Japan surrendered. The Second World War was over.[22]

At Tempsford, meanwhile, 6 August was the first of several days of frequent, heavy showers and thunderstorms. Three of a group of four flight engineer instructors arrived to join the squadron training program, and RCAF Overseas Headquarters gave formal permission — and supplied thirty stencils — to mark the nose of each Thunderbird aircraft with a maple leaf and the name of a Canadian city. On 7 August, training flights to Germany began, using several authorized routes that reached north to Kiel and south to Bonn; the squadron dispatched four aircraft, each carrying six ground crew passengers, while the continuing marginal weather at Tempsford restricted local flying.

On 8 August, despite the weather, the squadron launched another four aircraft on flights to Germany, and three flight engineers on loan to the Thunderbirds from No 422 Squadron went back to their own unit, aggravating No 426's shortage of flight engineers. The squadron now had forty-one complete crews, five partial crews, and a fighting chance of attaining the full complement of forty-eight operational crews. That evening, the *All Clear* show presented the first of two excellent performances at the NAAFI.[23]

On 9 August, the weather was worse; only radio-range exercises could be flown. The next day, No 426 Squadron received orders from Transport Command to ferry Liberators from Prestwick to Bassingbourn to equip No 422 Squadron, and ferried the first three of nineteen aircraft that afternoon. On 12 August, repatriation posting messages came in for fifty-eight ground crew, who were to be replaced shortly. While continuing bad weather kept the aircraft on the ground, the squadron received a visit from Air Commodore H.B. Godwin, the Deputy Air Officer Commanding in Chief, RCAF Overseas Headquarters, and Group Captain McDougall, the RCAF Liaison Officer in Transport Command, who toured the buildings and aircraft with Wing Commander Miller.[24]

On 13 August, the weather was still bad; during the day, only three training flights to Germany were possible and night flying training was scrubbed for the second night in a row. The squadron was able to ferry eight more Liberators from Prestwick to Bassingbourn, however. Grounded the next day because of the continuing bad weather, the squadron heard of the surrender of Japan shortly after midnight.

On 15 August, Wing Commander Miller attended a meeting called by the Station Commander where a decision was made to close down Tempsford until the morning of 18 August. All flying, including the Thunderbirds' training program, was cancelled. Four flight engineers arrived from No 422 Squadron to replace four scheduled to join No 423 Squadron on 18 August, and Flight Lieutenant Warner and his crew came home from the experimental trooping flight to Karachi.[25]

In a 16 August message, Air Marshal Johnson advised RCAF Headquarters in Ottawa that, with the collapse of Japan, the Tiger Force plan was abandoned and some staff allocated to Tiger Force might be assigned to occupation forces; he proposed to use some of the RCAF members of the Tiger Force staff in Germany and repatriate the remainder. The conversion of No 422 Squadron and No 423 Squadron to the very-long-range transport role was to be abandoned; however, the Air Ministry had asked the Canadian government to permit No 426 Squadron, now practically ready for operations, to operate on the United Kingdom-Karachi route until at least the end of 1945. With the end of hostilities in the Pacific, trooping flights were needed even more urgently, especially to repatriate prisoners of war recently recovered from Japanese captivity. When the most pressing requirements were met, No 426 Squadron could either return to Canada as a formed unit with their Liberators, or give the aircraft back to the RAF and repatriate only the personnel.[26]

On Saturday, 18 August, after their two-day break, No 426 Squadron was back at work, despite the lingering bad weather that continued to restrict flying. Squadron Leader Lingham from Transport Command visited the Thunderbirds to discuss navigation problems. The following morning, about 350 squadron personnel headed out onto one of the runways to attend services of thanksgiving for the end of the war. The weather was still bad enough to restrict local flying, but not, apparently, bad enough to prevent No 426 Squadron from flying its volleyball team to Linton-on-Ouse to represent No 1 District in the RCAF Overseas championship. A short meeting at Station Headquarters produced the information that, as of 21 August, No 4426 Servicing Echelon would be administered from Servicing Wing Headquarters at Tempsford.

On 20 August, the weather finally cleared and flying was on — trips to Germany as well as local and night exercises. Six new flight engineers reported in, and were immediately billeted and assigned to crews.[27]

On 21 August, the weather deteriorated again and flying was curtailed by No 4 Group Headquarters, which cancelled training flights to Germany. Five pilots left by rail for Bramcote to take a radio-range course, and seventeen aircrew drove off to Bassingbourn for yellow fever inoculations. On 22 August, flights to Germany were back on the training agenda, and the new Personnel Counsellor, Flight Lieutenant R.D. McLeod, reported in. The weather was still too bad for night flying, but it cleared up the next night.

On 24 August, Wing Commander Millar flew to RAF Station St. Mawgan to check out the facilities; St. Mawgan would be No 426 Squadron's departure point on training flights to Castel Benito. Back at Tempsford, training flights to Germany continued but night flying was off again — the weather. On Saturday, 25 August, the squadron received approval to fly to Castel Benito; the first trip was scheduled for Monday. The same day, No 4 Group Headquarters organized radio-range courses at Prestwick and Bramcote for nine more Thunderbird pilots.[28]

On 27 August, only one Castel Benito-bound flight got away; No 426 Squadron was out of serviceable aircraft. That afternoon, all the squadron's aircrew were on parade and, in the evening, Tempsford lost its first softball game to Bassingbourn. Captain K.A. Moore and a new dental team arrived to replace Captain McKinney and his people, and Flight Lieutenant E.P. Nonamaker, the new Squadron Medical Officer, arrived to replace Flight Lieutenant Young, who was posted to a Canadian general hospital. On 28 August, more long training flights were launched, to Castel Benito and other destinations, and Flying Officer F.T. O'Brecht reported in as Link Trainer Officer and assistant to the Squadron Training Officer in the ground instruction program.

On 29 August, the bad weather conspired with the continuing lack serviceable aircraft to keep the Thunderbirds on the ground. The long-awaited, much-requisitioned tools and spares still had not come, and without them, the ground crew could do little to keep the Liberators flying. Late in the evening, word came in that a squadron aircraft homeward-bound from Castel Benito had been damaged at RAF Station Merryfield; as it was taxiing, its nose-wheel had given way. The accident was rated Category AC — repairable beyond unit capability.[29]

On 30 August, Tempsford lay under a blanket of fog and flying was scrubbed, except for air-testing a converted Liberator for No 1 Transport Aircraft Modification Unit, a service routinely performed by No 426 Squadron.

On 31 August, the weather improved enough to permit flights to Castel Benito, although local flying was still cancelled, and Wing Commander Dixon from the training staff at No 4 Group Headquarters visited the Thunderbirds to discuss the squadron training program with the Squadron Commander. Messages came in saying that three more crews were being posted in from No 422 Squadron and No 423 Squadron, bringing aircrew strength up to the established level of forty-eight crews.

During August, No 426 Squadron logged 821 non-operational flying hours, including 110 hours at night. On 31 August, squadron strength stood at 273 all ranks, including 248 aircrew, with nineteen Liberator VIs on the inventory.[30]

The fair weather on 1 September permitted a modest flying program, and another Link Trainer instructor, Flight Lieutenant S.C. McLeod, arrived from No 3 PRC Bournemouth. On 2 September, the weather cleared enough by noon for long-distance training flights, one to

Germany and another to Castel Benito via St. Mawgan. As the squadron had little work for aircrew, many were sent on leave. On 3 September, three No 422 Squadron Liberators arrived at Tempsford from Bassingbourn, and RCAF Overseas Headquarters issued instructions about a new repatriation policy: all Canadian personnel were to be canvassed again to find out who wished to remain in Britain or Europe for an indeterminate period, and who wanted to return to Canada in accordance with the established repatriation schedule. That evening, the "RCAF Airscrews" variety show company opened a two-day stand at the NAAFI.[31]

On 4 September, Group Captain McDougall informed No 426 Squadron that a definite policy on its future had just been announced. From 1 October 1945 to 31 December 1945, the Thunderbirds would conduct trooping flights to and from India and, as of 31 December, they would be disbanded and returned to Canada in accordance with their Repatriation Group numbers. Ground crew repatriations would continue during the three months of trooping, but aircrew postings would cease. The same day, six more pilots left for Prestwick and Bramcote for radio-range courses.

On 5 September, Link Trainer instructor Flight Lieutenant McLeod, who arrived only four days before, was posted back to Bournemouth; Flight Lieutenant M. Greenway and the RCAF Trade Test Board came to assess Tempsford's Canadian personnel, and Flight Officer F.W. Stacey, of the Catering Branch at RCAF Overseas Headquarters, arrived to investigate the station's messing facilities and accommodations.[32] Now that No 426 Squadron was assigned to Tempsford at least until the end of the year, the lamentable state of the quarters assigned to ground crews had finally attracted official attention.

On 6 September, training flights to Germany were scheduled and the frequency of flights to Castel Benito was doubled, from one to two per day; local flying remained limited because most crews had completed that phase of training. On 7 September, the RCAF Trade Test Board finished its interviews after testing about eighty-five airmen, who seemed generally uninterested in improving their trade skills. Four more Liberators arrived at No 426 Squadron, bringing the unit inventory to twenty-three.

On 11 September, Wing Commander Miller learned that he had been awarded the Air Force Cross. The next day, the bad weather that had prevailed for several days let up enough to permit the departure of four aircraft to Castel Benito, and the despatch of No 426 Squadron's first India-bound training flight, carrying five crews: two to make the round trip and three slip crews, two to be positioned at Lydda and one to be positioned at Karachi. On 15 September, the squadron was supposed to start sending out one training flight to Karachi per day.[33]

On 14 September, deteriorating weather at St. Mawgan made it impossible for the Thunderbirds to start despatching flights to India trips as scheduled so, that evening, everyone was able to attend the first squadron party since leaving Linton-on-Ouse. About 600 people gathered at a Territorial Army drill hall in Biggleswade, a village seven miles from Tempsford, to dance to the Westernaires, an RCAF orchestra. By all accounts, everyone had a good time.

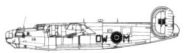

On 14 September, Transport Command issued Operation Order No 12/1945 on large-scale trooping operations stating that, as of 1 October 1945, the Liberator squadrons — No 53, No 59, No 86, No 206, No 220 and No 426 — and the Short Stirling squadrons — No 51 and No 158 — would have completed their training on the trunk routes and would be ready for trooping service

between Britain and India. The Thunderbirds would fly the Tempsford–Castel Benito–Lydda–Mauripur-and-return route on Schedule No 3, which had nine departures per week: two each on Monday and Friday, and one on each other day. This routine called for two departures on the Tuesdays of the third and fourth weeks of October, each Liberator carrying twenty-six passengers, leaving Tempsford at 0730 hours and returning to base six days later. The crews would be away from base for about two weeks.[34]

On 15 September, No 426 Squadron began an all-out effort to comply with Training Branch, Transport Command instructions to have all forty-eight crews operational by 1 October. Several crews had yet to complete the Britain-to-India route training, a high priority for the next two weeks. The same day, RCAF Overseas Headquarters informed the squadron that all seniority-based promotions from Flying Officer to Flight Lieutenant made after 8 May 1945 were cancelled; this ruling affected many Thunderbirds.

On 19 September, poor weather at St. Mawgan forced several training flights outward-bound for Castel Benito back to base. Squadron Leader A.R. Holmes, the acting Deputy Squadron Commander, was promoted to Wing Commander and posted to Odiham, Hampshire, to command No 437 (Husky) Squadron, accompanied by Squadron Leader M.S. Strange, who had reported in only three weeks before from No 422 Squadron. On 20 September, the squadron arranged to move six Liberators (recent property of No 422 and No 423 squadrons) to Tempsford to help get all forty-eight Thunderbird crews operational.

This crucial moment in the history of Thunderbird Squadron was also the occasion of a new kind of crisis — a work stoppage by ground crews to force action to improve the dreadful conditions in which they were forced to live. For four days, the only aircraft servicing performed in No 426 Squadron was done by flight engineers.[35]

The reaction was swift. On 21 September, in response to Servicing Echelon's fierce — and justified — complaints about Tempsford's messes and quarters, RCAF Overseas Headquarters sent Air Commodore Godwin and Group Captain F.A. Sampson, and No 47 Group Headquarters sent the Air Officer Commanding, Air Commodore Pressanges, and Air Commodore Harvey of the Engineering Branch. The ground crew were paraded before Air Commodore Godwin, who addressed them and heard their grievances. Tempsford's new Station Commander promptly set about correcting the problems.[36]

On 22 September, Air Commodore Godwin was back in London at RCAF Overseas Headquarters, informing a meeting of senior staff officers about his visit to Tempsford the previous day and what he, Group Captain Sampson and Air Commodore Pressanges learned during their investigation. The *casus belli* was filth, especially in the kitchens and wash-places, which were apparently innocent of cleaning equipment — no brushes for scrubbing sinks and pots, no brooms for sweeping floors. Godwin stated that RCAF Overseas Headquarters staff officers should get out of London more often, and should tour stations in Britain and in Europe to ensure that such conditions did not develop elsewhere. He also pointed out that Tempsford's Medical Officer should have brought the problems there to official attention — forcefully, if necessary. RCAF Overseas Headquarters would send a Nursing Sister and a Messing Officer to Tempsford for three months to help correct the situation.[37]

Formation and Training, 26 June 1945–30 September 1945

In its Operation Order No 13/1945 of 21 September, Transport Command elaborated on the instructions in its previous order: No 426 Squadron would prefix its flight numbers with the letters LTT, and Thunderbird aircraft would undergo a Route Inspection at each stop except Mauripur, where a Terminal Inspection would be done.[38]

On 23 September, the squadron accelerated its training program as instructed, and launched five training flights to India; the next day, another flight was dispatched to India and new crews were sent off to Germany. On 25 September, the squadron learned that Liberator KL625 flown by Flying Officer Cronje had a Category AC accident while being marshalled at Castel Benito, the first Britain-India-Britain flights began returning, and the Navigation Officer from No 47 Group Headquarters, Wing Commander Durant, visited to discuss navigation problems with the Squadron Commander. On 26 September, Wing Commander Miller took his OC Flying, Squadron Leader J.T. McCutcheon, and his three Flight Commanders, Squadron Leader J.F. Green, Squadron Leader H.V. Peterson and Squadron Leader D.D. Brownridge, to a conference on trooping at Transport Command Headquarters; and the Squadron Training Officer, Flight Lieutenant E.A. Allan, went to Waterbeach, Cambridgeshire, for a No 47 Group conference on teaching air-sea rescue techniques.[39]

On 27 September, Flight Lieutenant J.K. Meyer, the Radio and Public Relations Officer from RCAF Overseas Headquarters came to Tempsford to prepare for a trooping flight to India with the Thunderbirds. His assignment was research for a BBC radio feature on No 426 Squadron that would be re-broadcast later on the CBC. The same day, the squadron went to Bassingbourn to borrow two more Liberators for training, and the Link Trainer instructor, Flying Officer Leiskam, left for the Repatriation Depot at Torquay.

No 47 Group Headquarters Operation Order No 21/45 of 28 September 1945 outlined a new trooping operation (*Operation ANNEX*) and its execution. On top of the routine trooping responsibilities for October, Transport Command was required to airlift the 10,000 soldiers of the British 52nd Division from Brussels to the Middle East. This task would interrupt the planned trooping program, at least for the outward leg of the journey; Indian soldiers had to be transported from the Middle East to India, and other troops had to be repatriated to Britain from India. As well as airlifting the 52nd Division to the Middle East, Transport Command had to take 10,000 troops from the Middle East to India, and another 10,000 troops from the Far East to England.

No 426 Squadron was assigned to the Tempsford–Melsbroek, Belgium–Castel Benito–Shallufa, Egypt–Lydda–Mauripur–Lydda–Castel Benito–Tempsford route, with Rabat-Salé as a diversionary field and refuelling at RAF Station Melsbroek. The squadron's revised schedule called for forty-two trips every twenty-eight days, which meant either ten departures one week and eleven departures the next.[40]

On 28 September, as the squadron prepared to go operational, a training flight left for India, and Air Commodore Walker, the Senior Air Staff Officer at No 4 Group Headquarters, and Squadron Leader Higham from Training Branch at No 47 Group visited the squadron to discuss the state of training. On 29 September, No 426 Squadron despatched another training flight to India and put in some local flying.

Beginning at noon on 30 September, Tempsford went into a flap as it prepared for the Thunderbirds' first scheduled trooping flights to India. The departure of the two aircraft due to leave at 0430 hours on 1 October was moved up so they would reach Melsbroek as early as possible. Also, the route was changed; outbound aircraft were to land at Cairo West instead of Shallufa and skip Lydda, and returning aircraft were to land at Lydda and skip Cairo West. Despite the last-minute revisions to the flight plan, at 1830 hours on 30 September 1945, Flight Lieutenant K.W. Warner lifted Liberator KL641/A off the runway at Tempsford and set heading for Melsbroek, thus beginning No 426 Squadron's first trooping run, designated LTT 1. (Wing Commander Miller, the Thunderbirds' Squadron Commander, was aboard this flight, outbound for India.) At 1955 hours, Flying Officer H.E. Miskiman and his crew followed in Liberator KK341/P, as LTT 3 — outbound flights had odd numbers, inbound flights even numbers.[41]

After flying ninety minutes to Melsbroek, where the passengers boarded, the aircraft flew eight more hours to Castel Benito, where the crew changed. The next leg of the trip, to Cairo West, took nearly six hours, and the crew changed again for the twelve-hour flight to Mauripur. At this point in the trip, national borders became important. Palestine and Transjordan were British Mandated Territories and Iraq was under British military rule, but neither Saudi Arabia nor Syria permitted foreign military aircraft in their airspace. Therefore, British military aircraft had to fly either across Palestine and Transjordan to Iraq, or south along the Red Sea to Aden, then around the south coast of the Arabian Peninsula, and finally across the Arabian Sea to Karachi. The shorter, safer Iraqi route was chosen, but even then the total flying time from Britain to India was about twenty-seven hours.

From Cairo, the Liberators flew directly to a Transjordan airfield, known to the aircrews by the designation LGH4, that lay on the Mosul-Haifa pipeline near the Iraqi border. Long used by navigators as a visual reference for a turning point, LGH4 had been a military outpost since the Arab rebellions of previous generations; the airfield was originally built during the war as an emergency landing strip. From LGH4, the Liberators flew over RAF Station Shaibah, a large base near Basra, then past Bahrein and through the Persian Gulf and the Strait of Hormuz, then past Jask on the coast of Iran and Jivani just inside the Indian border, and on to Mauripur, one of several airfields around Karachi. On the return flight from Mauripur to Lydda, the crews retraced their outbound route.

Because of the detour around Arabia, the Cairo-to-Karachi leg of the trip could be beyond the safe range of the Liberator if very strong headwinds were encountered. Shaibah was the crews' designated alternate airfield, and they were briefed to make a refuelling decision on passing Shaibah in either direction.

The flight from Mauripur to Lydda took about eleven hours and, after a crew change, the aircraft left for Castel Benito, a seven-hour run. From Castel Benito, it usually was another nine hours back to Tempsford. The south of England and the north of France could easily be weathered in, so Istres le Tube was designated as the bad-weather diversion point. Since they could easily be required to land at Shaibah and Istres, the crews had visited both airfields during their training flights to learn the local facilities and flying conditions.

The return trip from India to England averaged twenty-eight hours flying time. The round trip averaged about fifty-five flying hours.

Plans for stopovers and refuelling had to cover housing and feeding the passengers. The airways between Britain and India were full of Liberators, Dakotas, Yorks, Stirlings and even Sunderlands, all belonging to squadrons based in Britain. Planners apportioned routes in accordance with the operational capabilities of the aircraft, the airfields available, and the logistical capacity of these airfields to support the aircraft, crews and passengers. No 426 Squadron was part of this grand plan.

Three of the four overseas bases — Cairo West, Lydda and Mauripur — had large, quite comfortable, tented camps — transit camps — for crews and passengers. Castel Benito had permanent transit quarters, formerly an Italian air force officers' brothel, next door to an officers' swimming pool. Theft was a major problem in all transit quarters, and great care had to be taken to defend personal belongings.[42]

On 30 September, Air Commodore Godwin and Group Captain Doyle from RCAF Overseas Headquarters visited Tempsford to find out whether the Canadian airmen's living conditions had improved. They had — a little.

During the month of September, the Thunderbirds logged 1,282 non-operational flying hours, including 354 hours of night flying. On 30 September 1945, squadron strength stood at 273 all ranks, including 262 aircrew, and thirty Liberator VIs, including six borrowed from Bassingbourn, on the inventory.

MAP 1: *Liberator Operations, September—December 1945*

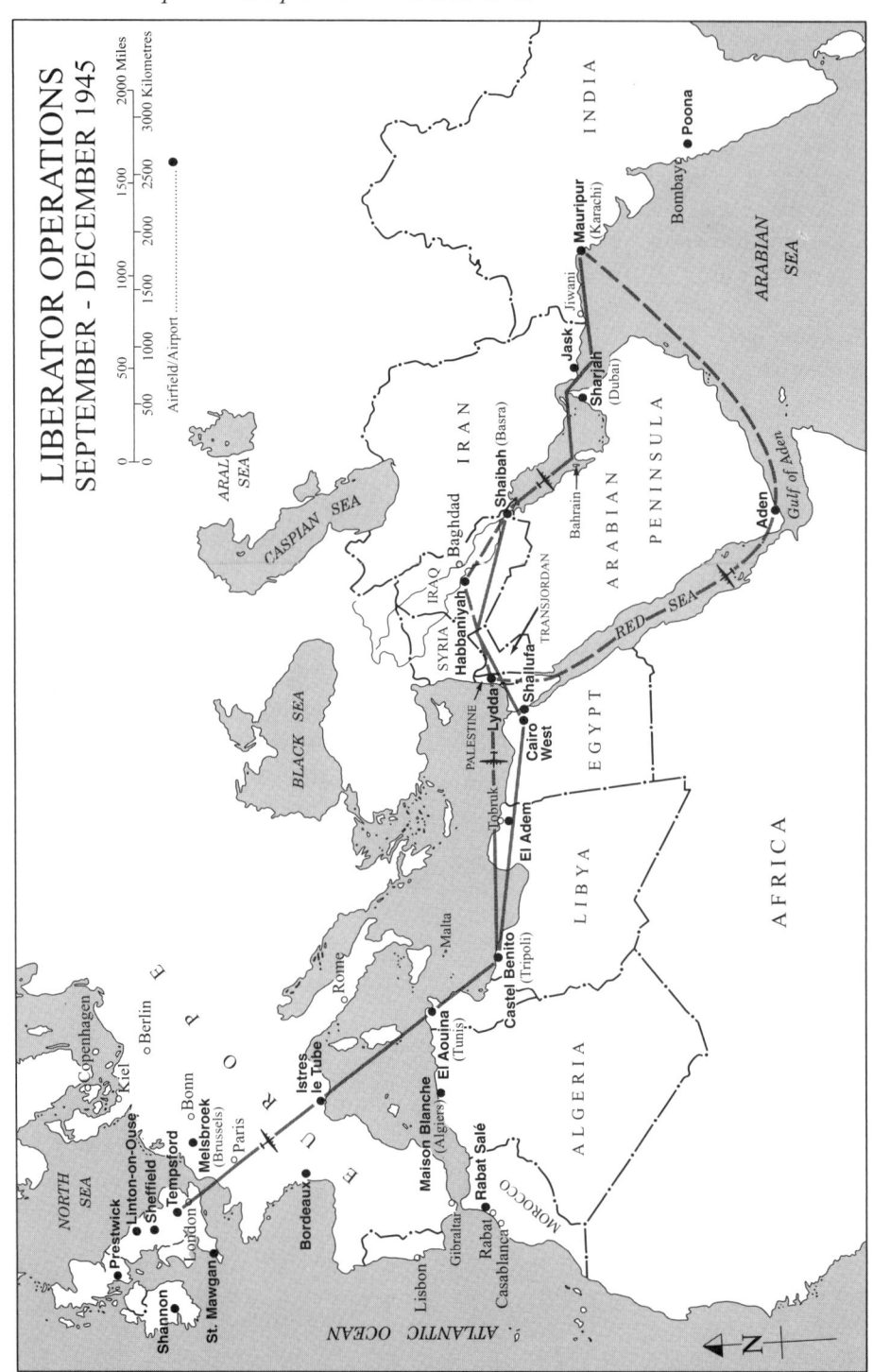

CHAPTER 3

TROOPING OPERATIONS, RAF TRANSPORT COMMAND
1 OCTOBER 1945–6 JANUARY 1946

Now operational as a transport unit, No 426 Squadron was officially transferred to No 47 Group (Transport Command) from No 4 Group (Transport Command), effective 1 October 1945.

On 1 October, Flight Lieutenant J.A. Badgley took the Thunderbirds' third trooping flight out of Tempsford and, with Wing Commander Miller on his way to India, Squadron Leader McCutcheon assumed command of the Thunderbirds.[1]

In the afternoon of 2 October, two more trooping flights under Flight Lieutenant G.W. Crawford and Flight Lieutenant D. Harrison departed for Melsbroek; the squadron Personnel Counsellor, Flight Lieutenant T.M. McLeod, was posted to No 3 Personnel Replacement Centre at Bournemouth; and a new pilot reported in: Squadron Leader B.B. Hodgkinson, formerly a Flight Commander with No 511 Squadron at RAF Station Lyneham. On 3 October, another trooping flight took off for Melsbroek, this one skippered by Flight Lieutenant R.J. Roach, and training flights were on again — the supply of serviceable aircraft was improving. That afternoon, RCAF Overseas Headquarters delivered five vehicles to Tempsford for No 426 Squadron to use until the end of the year. Until that time, the Thunderbirds had been making do with vehicles from the station's MT section.[2]

On 4 October, heavy fog blanketed the Tempsford area, preventing training flights but not the station parade at which the Station Commander spoke about the work to be done at Tempsford during the next three months. Despite the fog, the two scheduled passenger flights were able to leave for Melsbroek by 1600 hours. The fog persisted until late in the morning of 5 October, when it cleared in time to permit another trooping flight to depart for India. That afternoon, No 426 Squadron received a visit from Flight Officer Stacey and Flight Officer A.L. Campbell of the Catering Branch at RCAF Overseas Headquarters. Flight Officer Campbell stayed behind to be No 426 Squadron's Catering Officer and assist the station's RAF Catering Officer. The same day, a letter RCAF Overseas Headquarters arrived, saying that all Canadian personnel were to be canvassed again to find out who was willing to serve until 30 September 1946, the expected completion date for the new RCAF permanent force establishment.[3]

On 6 October, two more Liberators took off for India, at 1550 hours and 1555 hours. The next afternoon, the Thunderbirds' first two troopers, Liberator KK341/P with Flying Officer W.A. Craig and crew, and Liberator KK341/A with Flight Lieutenant L. Greenburgh and crew, which departed for Mauripur on 30 September, landed at Tempsford at 1350 hours and 1400 hours carrying forty-six British veterans of the fighting in Burma. The passengers must have been puzzled by the welcoming crowd — squadron personnel who turned out to greet the aircraft. The same day, 7 October, six crews came home from India, having completed their training flights; a variety of obstacles had delayed some of them for considerable periods along the route. Finally, a new squadron engineering officer, Flying Officer J. Morris, reported in from Skipton-on-Swale.[4]

On 8 October, the weather started warm and clear but turned cloudy in the afternoon. Flying training was in full swing and two aircraft departed for India. Squadron Leader J.F. Green, the officer in charge of the Squadron Loan Committee, went to RCAF Overseas Headquarters for a conference on organizing the Ninth Canadian Victory Loan; the overseas campaign was scheduled to start 22 October. On 9 October, one aircraft left for India, two returned from trooping runs, and a training aircraft came in with four crews who had been out on the route for some time. Also that day, Flying Officer W. Skinner (recently designated a Special Deputy Returning Officer) went to RCAF Overseas Headquarters for a special briefing on conducting the overseas military polls for the British Columbia general election, scheduled for 13 October and 15–16 October.

On 10 October, two flights departed for India and two came in, each carrying a full load of troops, and two RAF pilots reported in; as the Thunderbird aircrew (except for three RAF flight engineers) were all Canadian, the squadron asked Transport Command for an explanation. On 11 October, one trooping flight took off for India and none arrived; also, Flight Lieutenant Meyer, an RCAF Public Relations Officer, arrived to make the trip to Mauripur. Meyer was preparing a radio story on the Thunderbirds to be broadcast on the BBC and the CBC; he had intended to travel a fortnight earlier, but his journey was postponed so he could be appropriately immunized. The next day, 12 October, two aircraft left for India, one of them with Meyer attached to Flight Lieutenant H.A. Lutes' crew; one aircraft came in, and Wing Commander Miller went to Transport Command Headquarters to attend a conference with representatives of all the trooping squadrons.[5]

On 13 October, one Thunderbird Liberator left for India and three returned to base loaded with passengers. The next day, only one aircraft took off for Melsbroek; the other scheduled flight did not get away until the following morning. On 15 October, two aircraft made successful returns to Tempsford, and Liberator KL639/F, captained by Flight Lieutenant L. Greenburgh, broke down at Melsbroek, forcing crew and passengers to wait three days for repairs before resuming their journey to India. On 16 October, the squadron dispatched one flight and received two; one of the outbound flights, Liberator KL621/D, captained by Flying Officer W.A. Craig, was delayed at Melsbroek by dense fog and a malfunctioning auxiliary power unit.

On 17 October, heavy mist at Tempsford restricted flying except for the two scheduled troopers, and Wing Commander P.J. Grant, newly appointed RCAF Staff Officer at Transport Command Headquarters, arrived to observe the Thunderbirds' activities. On 18 October, the weather was still cloudy with low ceilings. One trooper arrived and two more took off; one of these, Liberator KK340/R captained by Flying Officer H.J. Oliver, went unserviceable at Melsbroek and came home after repairs; that flight was cancelled. Air Vice Marshal Stevens, Air Officer Commanding No 48 Group, visited the squadron to observe operational procedures, such as recording details of flights and maintaining contact with aircraft while they were on the route.

The same day, Transport Command warned the squadron to be prepared to move to another airfield, not yet named, on twenty-four hours notice.[6]

Flying weather was excellent on 19 October. At Melsbroek, outbound Liberator KK267/O, captained by Flying Officer G. Rubenck, developed a sump-oil leak on No 3 engine and, as the repairs would take four days, the flight was cancelled. (Normally, in such circumstances, the crew would stay with the aircraft until it was repaired, and the passengers would be assigned to another aircraft as soon as possible.) The day's only scheduled inbound flight was delayed at Castel Benito, first by a lack of ground transport that made the passengers arrive late at the airfield, and then by the time it took to load a casualty. The same day, Transport Command thought better of its inexplicable decision to give the Thunderbirds two RAF pilots and posted them out, and Captain Moore of the Canadian Dental Clinic left for Torquay and the Repatriation Depot. A new dental officer was expected later in the day.

On 20 October, one aircraft returned from a trooping run and two aircraft took off on the first leg of the route; both outbound flights were held up at Melsbroek, however, one by trouble with its No 3 engine and the other by late passengers. In the afternoon, the squadron's new dental officer, Captain Beaudet, arrived and, at 1900 hours, two squadron Liberators went up to perform a Verey light display to mark the opening of National Savings Thanksgiving week for the nearby town of Biggleswade.[7]

On 21 October, it drizzled most of the day, the first rain the area had received for some time. That day's one outbound flight, Liberator KL625/V captained by Flying Officer N.A. Noel, got as far as Melsbroek but developed mechanical problems that would take about a week to repair; the flight was cancelled and the Liberator was returned to Tempsford when the work was completed. That same day, word came in that, as of 24 October, the troop transport schedule was to change; passengers would board at Tempsford instead of Melsbroek, and the Indian terminus would be Poona, seventy-seven miles southeast of Bombay, instead of Karachi. Another message informed the squadron of two vacancies on the next radio-range course at St. Mawgan, and two vacancies on the runway localization courses at Bramcote. Finally, nine more squadron Liberators were to go to RAF Station Speke, near Liverpool, to be modified for trooping; so far, these aircraft had been used for training.[8]

The good weather continued on 22 October. Four aircraft arrived, two loaded with soldiers and two on completion of a training flight to India, and two trooping flights departed, only to be cancelled at Melsbroek. No passengers were ready for Liberator KH381/W, captained by Flight Lieutenant J.F. Lambert, so it returned to base; Liberator KL647/M, with Flying Officer J.S. Wright and his crew, had its No 2 engine overfilled with oil, so it came home once the problem was cleared up. The RCAF Overseas 9th Victory Loan Campaign opened that day, and the squadron's investment totalled $105,000, exceeding the unit quota of $80,000 by such a large margin that the campaign organizers decided that $150,000 could be raised before the campaign closed on 3 November.

On 23 October, the weather had deteriorated — strong winds and rain. Three aircraft returned from the India run and, as all the troops at Melsbroek had now been moved out, four aircraft returned to base from Melsbroek and no departures were scheduled. The next day, the first of the new trooping schedule, the weather continued very rough and unsettled. The first aircraft took off from Tempsford with a full load of passengers but, instead of heading for Poona, the Thunderbird crews were ordered to land at Karachi. At least one outbound crew did not get the word and landed at Poona after all. Also that day, Flight Lieutenant H.B. Timlick, a radar officer, arrived unexpectedly at the squadron from No 18 Group Headquarters; the Thunderbirds had to ask the exact nature of his duties at Tempsford.[9]

On 25 October, the unit was able to launch two flights to India before heavy rain showers and winds gusting to gale force hit Tempsford; no flights arrived, as the weather was unsuitable between north Africa and England. Transport Command Operation Order No 75 came in, announcing that the frequency of trooping flights between Britain and India would now increase; No 426 Squadron would dispatch two aircraft each day of the week except Wednesdays, departing from Tempsford daily at 1400 hours and returning within seven days.[10]

On 26 October, strong winds and heavy showers prevailed at Tempsford all day. In the afternoon, four aircraft landed within an hour and a half; all had been diverted to Rabat-Salé because of bad weather, and one had a malfunctioning No 2 engine. On 27 October, the weather moderated somewhat; three aircraft took off on the first leg of the trooping run, to Castel Benito, and four returned from India. The following day, 28 October, it was cloudy and hazy with poor visibility; one flight to Castel Benito went out and two Liberators loaded with passengers came in. A message came in from Transport Command, ordering No 426 Squadron to move to RAF Station Bassingbourn, ten miles down the road, as soon as No 466 Squadron's recently vacated accommodations could be made ready. No 47 Group would issue detailed instructions, first for dispatching an advance party, and then for the move itself.[11]

On 29 October, the weather was mild with light rain throughout the day; two trooping flights went out and one came in. Ten aircrew of various trades reported in to No 426 Squadron to replace members of the forty-eight regular trooping crews who were grounded for any reason. The following day, the weather was good, one flight to India went out, and Nursing Sister M.F. McBride reported in to assist the Squadron Medical Officer. On 31 October, fog closed Tempsford in the morning but lifted enough in the afternoon to permit two scheduled departures; no return flights came in. In the morning, Air Commodore Godwin arrived to meet Wing Commander Miller and go on to Bassingbourn to inspect the squadron's new accommodations.

By 31 October, No 426 Squadron logged 1,760 operational flying hours, including 793 hours flown at night, and 1,007 non-operational flying hours, including 448 at night, mostly spent in training; and dispatched forty-two aircraft that carried 1,043 passengers to various destinations on the trooping route, and five aircraft that halted at Melsbroek. Twenty-nine Thunderbird Liberators completed the round trip to India and brought 752 passengers to Britain. The serviceability rate of the squadron's twenty-four operational aircraft was 67 percent, and that of the seven non-operational aircraft was 56.4 percent. On 31 October, No 426 Squadron had 273 personnel on strength, including 261 aircrew.

From the beginning of the trooping operation, No 426 Squadron had maintained Transport Command's schedule of departures from Britain. Both aircrew and ground crew had applied themselves to the task diligently and enthusiastically. All opposed Transport Command's plan to move the squadron to Bassingbourn.[12]

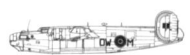

On 1 November, Transport Command performed yet another organizational shuffle that transferred No 426 Squadron to No 48 Group for administration but left it under the operational control of No 47 Group. No 48 Group Headquarters was at Milton Ernest Hall, four miles northwest of Bedford. Transport Command also introduced a new trooping schedule; aircraft would now stop at Castel Benito; Cairo West; Habbaniyah in Iraq, fifty miles west of Baghdad; and Mauripur, changing crews at Cairo. On the homeward leg of the route, aircraft would stop at Lydda, Castel Benito and Tempsford, and crews would change at Castel Benito.[13]

Habbaniyah was a new stop on the outbound leg of the route, and it did not seem to get much business from the trooping squadrons; most of their aircraft continued to fly direct to Mauripur from Cairo, landing at Shaibah when they needed fuel. Habbaniyah was about 120 miles off-track, and too far from Mauripur to permit crews making direct flights to India to make reliable fuel decisions. However, several squadron aircraft did stop at Habbaniyah, mostly on the return flight from Mauripur.[14]

On 1 November, the weather at Tempsford was misty and cold, and hazy in the afternoon. No 426 Squadron launched two India-bound aircraft close to the new departure time of 1400 hours, and some local training flights. Bad weather slightly delayed the one aircraft expected in from Castel Benito.

In November, the weather deteriorated over the entire route. Large-scale thunderstorm activity began to develop over Iraq, from the Persian Gulf along the Tigris and Euphrates rivers, making flying in this area both dangerous and uncomfortable. On one occasion, as Flying Officer J.S. Wright and his crew approached Bahrain, the sky to the northwest gradually filled with thunderheads and, as sunset approached, a spectacular display of lightning from a massive storm-line filled the darkening skies. Faced with such a daunting barrier, Wright and his crew could hardly stay on the route, and so had the choice of returning to Karachi, landing at Bahrain or Sharjah-Dubai, or flying across Arabia to Lydda. Because of the weather, Arabia — normally off limits — was the best option. The trip was uneventful, noteworthy only for the multitude of campfires the crew could see in a landscape that in daylight looked quite uninhabited. Later, Wright's crew learned that theirs wasn't the only aircraft to sneak across Arabia; others made the same decision on occasion. Bad weather usually lasted for several days over Iraq, and aircraft were either held at Mauripur until conditions improved or routed across the Arabian Sea by way of Aden and the Red Sea. Crews did not recommend the latter option.[15]

On 2 November, Tempsford's weather continued foggy, cold and not particularly suitable for flying most of the day. Two India-bound flights went out and two aircraft came in from the route. Flying Officer C.A. Grassi, the new Squadron Adjutant,, reported in to replace Flying Officer C.E. Glover, who was returning to Canada. Squadron Leader H.T. Lingham from No 120 (RCAF) Wing, Odiham visited the Thunderbirds to discuss the supply of Staff Navigation Officers.

On 3 November, despite the haze and mist that blanketed the airfield all day, No 426 Squadron dispatched two more trooping flights, one of them delayed for nearly four hours by an engine oil leak. The aircraft that left on time, KL658/B captained by Flight Lieutenant F.R. McGill, was diverted to Luqa, on Malta, by local conditions that kept them out of both Castel Benito and Cairo West. In North Africa and the Middle East, sandstorms occasionally disrupted flight schedules. A flight due in at Tempsford that day was held up, first, by the operations staff at Castel Benito because of fog in Britain, and then diverted to Holmsley South, Dorset, for the same reason. Finally, Tempsford's part in the Ninth Victory Loan campaign officially closed, with 647 subscriptions purchased by Canadians for a total of $179,200—a highly commendable response, as the original goal was $80,000.[16]

On 4 November, Transport Command issued a new schedule for *Operation ANNEX* flights; as of 9 November, aircraft would be expected to complete the round trip to India within four days, changing crews at Castel Benito, Cairo West and Lydda. Liberator KL647/M, with Flight Lieutenant J.A. Badgley and crew, left for India at 1430 hours, and Liberator KK255/Q, piloted by Flight Lieutenant G.E. Seward, took off at 1440 hours. Both refuelled at Bassingbourn and were diverted to Bordeaux, France, because of bad weather at Castel Benito. Badgely and his crew made it to Castel Benito the next day, but Seward's aircraft was diverted again, this time to El Aouina, near Tunis, where they had to wait for three days before resuming their journey.[17]

On 5 November, the weather was very misty and damp, and No 426 Squadron had no operational flights, either incoming or outgoing; they did some daytime flying training but night flying was scrubbed. Three autocycles came in from the RCAF Motor Transport Repair Unit at Warrington, lent to the squadron to help Servicing Section and Repair and Inspection Section ground staff get around the widely dispersed station buildings.

On 6 November, the weather at base remained cloudy and misty, keeping two outbound aircraft on the ground until mid-morning; a third was able to leave for Castel Benito early in the afternoon. The day's single arrival brought in twenty-six passengers. Despite the weather, No 426 Squadron conducted both day and night training exercises. The next day, three aircraft returned from India, one by way of Bordeaux, where it had been diverted the previous day, and the two scheduled departures were cancelled because no serviceable aircraft were available. Flying Officer Glover, the outgoing adjutant, caught the train for Torquay and repatriation, and Flight Lieutenant Meyer, the Public Relations Officer, interviewed the Squadron Commander for his radio feature. Finally, the squadron acquired an Airspeed Oxford MP354 from RAF Station Blakehill Farm to use as a communications and training aircraft.

On 8 November, two scheduled outbound flights were cancelled for lack of serviceable aircraft, and the day's four arrivals included Liberator KK374/T, which left Tempsford on 6 October and broke down at Castel Benito. Flight Officer Campbell, the Catering Officer, told the Squadron Commander that a consignment of fruit juice would arrive shortly from Canada for distribution to Canadian personnel, and a meeting of the Officers' Mess laid plans for a squadron party before the move to Bassingbourn.

On 9 November, the weather was clear with chilly, gusty winds. Two trooping flights went out during the afternoon; none arrived; and No 426 Squadron put in some daytime flying training. Transport Command's new schedule for *Operation ANNEX* went into effect, but with the original routing restored: Cairo–Karachi with an optional refuelling stop at Shaibah. Slip crews would be in place for one day at Castel Benito, two days at Mauripur and one day at Lydda; however, crews could count on frequent extra rest days when their flights were held up by bad weather (particularly in Britain) and equipment failures.[18]

That same day, Wing Commander Miller went on leave and Squadron Leader J.F. Green took over command of the squadron; Squadron Leader Hodgkinson left for Torquay and repatriation to Canada; and No 48 Group Headquarters assigned the squadron three training vacancies: two at Prestwick for radio-range courses (taken by Flight Lieutenant D. McIvor and Flying Officer D.H. Bjarnson), and one at St. Mawgan for a Standard Beam Approach course (taken by Flight Lieutenant K.W. Warner).

On 10 November, the strong winds of the past few days abated, it rained in the afternoon, and No 426 Squadron expanded its flying training schedule. No aircraft came in, and the day's two trooping flights to India departed on schedule. Engine trouble over continental Europe forced the return of Liberator KL670/G, which took off in the early afternoon; it landed at Holmsley South, where Flight Lieutenant G.R. Guess and his crew immediately took Liberator KL650/J to pick up the passengers and proceed to Castel Benito. The final tally of the Ninth Victory Loan campaign at Tempsford came to 756 purchases and $206,050; of this amount, $128,700 came from personnel using their War Services Gratuities. The Canadians on the station exceeded their quota of $80,000 by 258 percent.

On Remembrance Day, 11 November, the weather was clear and cold and the squadron was at work as usual: flying training continued, with both day and night exercises, two India-bound flights went out, and four aircraft came in. One of the arrivals, Liberator KH333/JW captained by Flight Lieutenant D. Harrison, was diverted because of weather to Maison Blanche, near Algiers, after leaving Castel Benito and, on leaving Maison Blanche, diverted again, this time to Rabat-Salé. After the second diversion, Harrison's crew and their load of passengers finally able to made it home to Tempsford.

The weather on 12 November was very dull and cloudy with intermittent rain. No troopers came in, and two India-bound flights went out; some flying training was carried out during the day but night flying was scrubbed. Flight Lieutenant H.W. Marriott from the Directorate of Equipment at RCAF Overseas Headquarters and Flight Lieutenant W.A. Morrison of the RCAF Motor Transport Repair Unit at Warrington arrived to discuss the motor transport situation; the squadron's was to receive three more vans. Flying Officer J.H. Thompson, the Flight Engineer Leader, learned that, as of 1 October, he had been promoted to the rank of Flight Lieutenant.[19]

On 13 November, one squadron aircraft departed on its overseas run and another returned to base. The weather was better, so more flying training was done. Squadron Leader Green went to Transport Command Headquarters to discuss personnel matters with Wing Commander P.J. Grant, the Canadian Staff Officer.

The morning of 14 November was foggy with low stratus cloud, but the weather improved later in the day; in the afternoon, the squadron handled four arrivals and dispatched two flights to India. One of the departures, Liberator KH333/JW captained by Flight Lieutenant W.J. Cameron, had engine trouble and diverted to Istres-le-Tube, near Marseilles, where the problem was rectified; the flight carried on to Castel Benito the next day. Flying Officer C.A. Hobbs of the RCAF Overseas Postal Service Headquarters arrived to make a routine inspection of the Squadron Post Office.

On 15 November, fog hung around Tempsford most of the day, but not enough of it to interfere with the scheduled flights: two departures and two arrivals, all in the afternoon. Flying Officer Grassi, the Squadron Adjutant, called a meeting with the Catering Officer and the Knights of Columbus Supervisor to organize the distribution of the eagerly anticipated Canadian fruit juice.

On 16 November, the squadron sent two aircraft overseas and handled two arrivals from India, and received a visit from Air Marshal Sir Ralph A. Cochrane, Air Officer Commanding-in-Chief, Transport Command. It seemed that the RAF might want the Thunderbirds to stay in the trooping business beyond the end of the year.

The first duty of the captain and crew of an aircraft is to protect it and its occupants from danger. Flight Lieutenant R.H. Fraser and his crew had an unpleasant brush with this responsibility on the homeward leg of their 26 October–16 November trip, between Lydda and Castel Benito. When flight engineer Flight Sergeant J.D. Geoffrion went aft for a normal post-take-off check, he caught a British Army colonel in the act of lighting a cigar. Having the Liberator's incendiary behaviour always in mind, Geoffrion politely informed the colonel that smoking was forbidden, but the colonel put on a show of authority and said, "It's okay, my boy, we smoke all the time in Far East aircraft." Geoffrion replied, "Well, you don't smoke on this aircraft. Put it out, sir!" and the colonel retorted, "You can't order me about; I'm a colonel in the British Army and I'll smoke if I want to!" Realizing that the situation was serious, Geoffrion immediately went to Fraser and repeated the conversation.

Fraser got out of his seat and went back to confront the colonel, who continued to argue that his rank gave him the right to do as he pleased, and he was not going to be intimidated by a mere flight lieutenant. Fraser quickly realized that he had to do something dramatic to get the man's attention, so he announced, "As captain of this aircraft, I am placing you under arrest. Now, put out the cigar!" The colonel responded, "I'll have you when we get to England," so Fraser replied, "We'll see about that," and stomped back to the cockpit.

El Adem, sixteen miles south of Tobruk, was a major airport and close to the aircraft's flight path to Tripoli. Fraser called the air traffic control tower and asked to be met by a Military Police escort and someone with the authority to take his prisoner in charge. He landed the aircraft El Adem, handed the colonel over to the provosts and promptly took off again for Castel Benito.

Back at Tempsford, Fraser explained that, if allowed to return to England, the colonel would probably have found a way to wiggle out of the situation. By dropping him off at El Adem, Fraser ensured that the colonel would be in the hands of RAF personnel likely to support Fraser's actions, and that the colonel would be highly embarrassed and seriously delayed in getting home. In honour of this occasion, and of a character in Al Capp's *Li'l Abner* comic strip, the rest of the squadron immediately dubbed the flight lieutenant "Fearless Fraser."[20]

On 18 November, two trooping flights arrived, but the two scheduled departures to India were scrubbed for lack of serviceable aircraft. The three vans promised by RCAF Overseas Headquarters arrived, each with a driver. The next day, despite marginal weather, two trooping flights went out, an early-morning flight from Castel Benito came in, and the squadron managed both day and night flying training exercises. Air Marshal Johnson, Air Officer Commanding-in-Chief, RCAF Overseas Headquarters, descended on Tempsford to discuss trooping operations with Canadian personnel.

On 20 November, Tempsford lay under a heavy blanket of fog that prevented all departures, but two aircraft made it in from Tripoli, one early in the morning and the other late in the afternoon. Much to everyone's delight, twenty-seven cases of grapefruit juice arrived.[21]

On 21 November, the continuing heavy fog meant the cancellation of two more scheduled flights to India. In the afternoon, the distribution of grapefruit juice to the Canadian squadron and echelon began at the Canada House Canteen. For most of the next day, the weather was marginal with persistent fog and showers, but the squadron managed to dispatch one trooper to India and squeeze in some flying training. Flight Lieutenant J.E. Cunningham of Auxiliary Services at No 1 District Headquarters in London made a routine visit to Tempsford, and Nursing Sister M.F. McBride was posted out to RCAF Station Tholthorpe in Yorkshire. That evening, the Thunderbirds' five-piece orchestra played for an all-ranks dance at Canada House.

The weather on 23 November was on the dull side with misty patches. It was a busy day operationally, with three departures for India and four aircraft returned from the route, including two that had been diverted to St. Mawgan because of Tempsford's bad weather the previous day, and one that had to stop over at El Adem when Castel Benito was weathered in, and then divert to Istres on the way back to Tempsford. The squadron also managed a full day and night flying training program. Wing Commander Miller returned from leave and Squadron Leader Green relinquished command.

On 24 November, two more flights to India departed and two aircraft came in from the route. The following day, only one flight went out because the second aircraft had engine problems; the day's only arrival came in from Castel Benito, with Flight Lieutenant A.J. Mackie and crew.

On 26 November, Tempsford's weather was generally fair and cool, and two flights bound for Tripoli went out. Flying Officer Miskiman and his crew departed on time at 1400 hours, but Flight Lieutenant J.A. Badgley and his crew were delayed by aircraft maintenance problems and left at 1630 hours. Delayed overnight, Flight Lieutenant F.R. McGill and his crew headed out on the first leg of the flight to India on 27 November at 0850 hours in Liberator KK341/P; the nose wheel in this aircraft collapsed at Castel Benito, just as the slip crew was taking off for Cairo West. No one was hurt, crew or passenger, and the damage was classed as Category AC, repairable at unit level. This Liberator remained at Castel Benito, fated to become a hangar queen and a source of spare parts. When a Thunderbird aircraft was held up by lack of a part, someone on the next flight through Castel Benito would remove the necessary item from KK341/P and take it where it was needed.[22]

Back at Tempsford, flight engineer Flying Officer R.W. Stocker departed for the Repatriation Depot at Torquay, and a message from the Air Ministry instructed Squadron Leader Green, Flight Lieutenant L. Greenburgh, Flight Lieutenant M.G. Jensen and Flight Lieutenant G.M. Goodman to appear on or about 11 December at Buckingham Palace for investiture.

On 27 November, two flights from Tripoli came in, the first at 0735 hours and the second at 1000 hours, and two Liberators left for India on schedule with a total of fifty passengers. The squadron received two visitors: Wing Commander P.J. Grant from Transport Command to discuss personnel matters, and Squadron Leader J.D. Mallinson from Training Branch at No 48 Group Headquarters to discuss general training issues.

On 28 November, Flight Lieutenant J.D. Matheson and his crew brought in Liberator KL618/K from Tripoli at 0130 hours — they had arrived late at Castel Benito — and two India-bound flights went out in the early afternoon. RCAF Overseas Headquarters notified the squadron that one member of its Ninth Victory Loan Committee was entitled to a one-week special-leave trip to Copenhagen, starting 3 December, and the lot fell to Squadron Leader Green.

Writing from Transport Command on 28 November, Wing Commander Grant advised RCAF Overseas Headquarters that Operations Branch had informed No 426 Squadron that its last outbound trooping run from Britain was to depart no later than 20 December, and that an Operational Organization Order to this effect was being prepared. He also stated that, after 20 December, the squadron should start "unscrambling" its personnel (gradually withdraw them from the operation) as conveniently and economically as possible. No 4426 Servicing Echelon could be unscrambled as soon as the last Thunderbird trooping flight took off from Tempsford. The objective was to have all RCAF personnel except a small rear party cleared and out of Tempsford by 2 January 1946.[23]

In a 28 November message from RCAF Overseas Headquarters to AFHQ in Ottawa, Air Marshal Johnson referred to direction he had received from the Chief of the Air Staff several days earlier, which stated that No 426 Squadron's employment with Transport Command was not to extend beyond 31 December 1945, and that the Air Ministry had been advised to this effect. Johnson also indicated that the squadron had performed exceedingly well throughout *Operation ANNEX*, carrying more passengers, keeping closer to the schedule, and operating more safely than any other trooping squadron in RAF Transport Command.

Air Marshal Sir Ralph A. Cochrane, Air Officer Commanding-in-Chief, Transport Command, had requested help from RCAF Overseas Headquarters, proposing that, because Transport Command was extremely short of Liberator crews, No 426 Squadron's aircrew should be asked to continue on operations until 31 March 1946. Replacing experienced RCAF crews with inexperienced RAF crews could be a bad idea, especially on the trooping operation. Cochrane saw no difficulty providing the Thunderbirds with ground crews after 1 January 1946.

In his message to Ottawa, Air Marshal Johnson explained that the RAF understood that it had given a firm commitment to relinquish No 426 Squadron at the end of the year, and that this question could be reconsidered only at a high level of government. Therefore, unless Air Marshal Leckie thought the RCAF would accept a change of date, the RAF would not initiate an approach to the Canadian government.

Wing Commander Miller had informed Johnson that, although the ground crew were anxious to be repatriated, about 80 percent of the aircrew were willing to continue operations for three more months; they found trooping an interesting job that gave them valuable experience. In the 28 November message, Johnson pointed out that main objective of trooping operations was to bring British personnel home for demobilization — a British priority — while the disbandment of No 426 Squadron, and the repatriation and demobilization of its personnel, were Canadian priorities. He recommended that the original plan for No 426 Squadron should remain in place.[24]

The weather on 29 November was cloudy, with extensive mist, haze and local fog patches. The squadron dispatched two India-bound flights on schedule, and two homeward-bound flights came in. That evening, Canada House scored a success with its second weekly dance; the Station Commander, Group Captain N.R. Buckle, presented the novelty prizes.

The last day of November was cloudy and cool, and flying training was limited to day exercises. At 1100 hours, a flight from Castel Benito came in, and two flights bound for Castel Benito went out on schedule. RCAF Overseas Headquarters advised Squadron Leader Green that his trip to Copenhagen had been cancelled for reasons beyond its control.

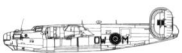

November was a busy month for No 426 Squadron. Forty-seven outbound flights were dispatched with 1,205 passengers, and forty-five inbound aircraft brought 1,134 passengers to Britain. The squadron logged 2,257 operational flying hours, including 917 hours at night, and 133 training hours. On 31 November, squadron strength stood at 287 all ranks, including 271 aircrew, and twenty-six Liberator VIs, two non-operational and twenty-four operational.

The operational Liberators had a serviceability rate of 76.6 percent, considered good; however, out on the route they had suffered several engine failures. Some of these failures could be attributed to overboosting, a technique for obtaining the power required to get the Liberator up to cruising altitude by using the turbo system to supercharge the engine induction system. The extra power thus obtained, called "boost," was controlled from the throttles. Maximum boost, or "overboost," damaged the engines if used at low altitudes or on take-off, but pilots needed it to get the Liberator off the ground with a full load in less-than-ideal conditions, such as high temperatures or a sandy runway. Ingested sand also helped reduce the life of Liberator engines. No 426 Squadron made every effort to keep the rate of engine failure as low as possible; the Squadron Commander even gave each captain a personal briefing on the subject.[25]

While operating on the route, the crews had to contend with extreme climatic conditions varying from the cold and wet of the British winter to the blistering dry heat of north Africa, the Middle East and southwestern Asia. Cairo West, for example, could report a runway temperature of 130°F. The Liberator was not the easiest aircraft to lift off at the best of times, and such heat made the task a decided challenge; just to get airborne, the pilot had to get the engines to deliver all the power they were capable of.

As if the temperature wasn't enough of a problem, the runway at Habbaniyah had two major obstacles. At the northeast end, pilots had to avoid a 100-foot-high sand barrier, and the southeast end featured a transverse section of railway track, where workers liked to park light rail cars in the path of fully loaded Liberators struggling for altitude.[26]

For most of 1 December, the weather was cloudy with poor visibility. Two flights to Tripoli went out on schedule and, early in the afternoon, a flight from India arrived after being diverting to Stoney Cross near Southampton because of the weather at Tempsford. No 426 Squadron received a new version of the trooping schedule, effective 3 December, that included a two-hour step-up in departure times, a stop at Habbaniyah rather than Shaibah on the outbound leg, a stopover at Shaibah instead of Habbaniyah on the homeward-bound leg, and a ninety-minute step-up in arrival times. Despite these orders, crews would continue to stop at Shaibah on both legs of the trip. The squadron also received a copy of Wing Commander P.J. Grant's 28 November letter to RCAF Overseas Headquarters on disbanding the unit.[27]

On 2 December, the only action at No 426 Squadron was two arrivals from overseas. One of these aircraft, Liberator KK267/O captained by Flight Lieutenant M.C. Butler, had diverted to Tunis because of mechanical problems that continued after they left, eventually forcing a land at Istres for repairs. Two squadron members, pilot Flight Lieutenant E.A. Allan and navigator Flying Officer V. Burns, were posted to the Repatriation Depot at Torquay to await return to Canada.

On 3 December, the squadron launched four outbound flights: two early in the morning and two more at noon, as required by the new schedule. During the afternoon, the RCAF Entertainment Committee met at Canada House.

It was thoroughly miserable on 4 December, very frosty with rain showers in the afternoon and a heavy haze that hung over the station most of the day. Flight Lieutenant J.A. Elviss and his crew departed at 1205 hours for Tripoli in Liberator KH381/W, but they were diverted *en route* to Istres because of bad weather at their destination. Back at Tempsford, Flight Lieutenant D.L. Palmer reported in to No 426 Squadron from RCAF Overseas Headquarters to help RCAF personnel organize their post-war plans.

On 5 December, it was cold and clear at Tempsford but bad weather over continental Europe caused the cancellation of two departures. In the late afternoon, two aircraft came in, one of them, Liberator KL224/NW captained by Flight Lieutenant C.E. Seward, held up on the route for two days by an unserviceable undercarriage. Flight Lieutenant Palmer began interviewing RCAF personnel in No 426 Squadron and the Servicing Echelon about the problems they might have in adjusting to civilian life.

In a 5 December message to Air Marshal Johnson at RCAF Overseas Headquarters, Air Marshal Leckie discussed the possibility that No 426 Squadron's aircrew might stay in Britain after the disbandment of the unit at the end of the year. Since it seemed impossible that all the squadron's RCAF personnel could be repatriated immediately on disbandment, Leckie was prepared to acquiesce to the RAF's request — on certain, very strict terms. First, No 426 Squadron must cease functioning as an RCAF unit on 31 December 1945; second, the RAF must take custody of all Thunderbird aircraft; third, all RCAF ground crew must leave the squadron on 1 January 1946; fourth, the new, reconstituted No 426 Squadron must employ only aircrew who volunteered for extended service; fifth, the Air Ministry must organize replacements for these aircrew as promptly as possible; and, finally, all RCAF aircrew must leave their assigned squadrons by 31 March 1946. Air Marshal Johnson was advised that, if the Air Ministry accepted these conditions, its request for No 426 Squadron's aircrew could be granted without reference to higher authority.[28]

On 6 December, bad weather in Europe forced the cancellation of overseas departures were cancelled for a second day, and there were no arrivals. Flying Officer J.H. Lyndon left the squadron for RCAF Overseas Headquarters and a flight home to Canada for compassionate reasons. On 7 December, the weather was cold and cloudy with a thick haze over the area most of the day, and again, bad weather across the Channel prevented overseas arrivals and departures. That evening, Air Marshal Johnson, Air Commodore Godwin and a contingent from RCAF Overseas Headquarters attended a farewell party at the Officers' Mess thrown for the Thunderbirds by RAF Station Tempsford.[29]

On 8 December, the weather continued cold and cloudy, but flying resumed: it was a very busy day for the squadron and the Servicing Echelon. Four overseas flights arrived, and four flights to Mauripur by way of Tripoli went out. The first to take off, Liberator KL658/B captained by Flight Lieutenant L.R. Pattee, diverted to Malta because of bad weather but, as it was not carrying passengers, the crew was able to bypass Castel Benito and stop at El Adem before carrying on to Cairo West. Also that day, the Service Police hauled away a Thunderbird pilot who was destined for Court Martial at RCAF Station Topcliffe. That evening, Canada House held a Bingo with many prizes of sweaters, socks and handkerchiefs.

The weather over the Mediterranean was now very difficult, forcing Liberator crews to operate at higher altitudes and thread their way through and around the cumulonimbus clouds that towered over Tunisia and Sicily.

On 8 December, pilot Flying Officer J.S. Wright, co-pilot Flying Officer T.H. Hubbard, navigator Flying Officer R.J. Gurney, wireless operator Warrant Officer A.P. Stitt and flight engineer Flight Sergeant M.M. Lyons all set out from Castel Benito, heading for home in Liberator KK340/R. Shortly after departing, an unserviceable No 1 engine forced them to turn back; three days later, they again took off for Tempsford, but the wireless transmitter failed and obliged them to divert to Istres-le-Tube. At Istres, Wright and his crew found some thirty more aircrew, all stranded by weather or mechanical problems.

It was, after all, the Mediterranean, so the crews expected warm sunshine, but no such luck — the *mistral*, a violent, cold, dry northerly wind, was streaming in full force out of the *Massif central*. This put a damper on any thoughts of sunbathing, but at least the crews could go to the harbour, where they found a sidewalk café, sunlit and sheltered from the wind, where they settled in to enjoy the local food and wine.

At 2130, a bus brought them to Istres' transient quarters, rows of wooden bungalows much like very basic summer cottages, lacking interior finishing, heat and much in the way of plumbing, and equipped with bedding suitable for high summer. Too cold to sleep, so the crews gathered in the street around a fire started by some enterprising individual who found an empty oil drum and some loose boards. The fire consumed wood faster than the chilly transients could collect it, so the siding from an unoccupied bungalow soon joined the battle against the cold. Some crews consolidated their blankets and took turns sleeping, one cocooned while the others sat up by the fire. By dawn, the plundered bungalow looked more like a bandstand, so no one dawdled; all the crews departed as early as possible, fully expecting the wrath of the authorities. The only defence anyone could think of was that they were all cold and, since the bungalows were originally for German troops, they did the community a favour by destroying one. Wright and his crew were airborne early, and never found out whether anyone complained.[30]

On 8 December, Air Marshal Johnson wrote to Air Marshal Leckie that so many berths were available in troopships plying the Britain–Canada route in January and February that RCAF Overseas Headquarters would have trouble filling its allocated space; therefore, eligible personnel

from No 426 Squadron would be repatriated in January 1946. If the Thunderbird aircrew were allowed to be rescrambled in Transport Command, then administrative services in proportion to their number would have to be retained, so retention of No 426 Squadron's aircrew would hinder the repatriation and demobilization scheme. In view of these circumstances, Johnson urged Leckie to reconsider the position set out in his message of 5 December.[31]

Leckie responded the same day, stating that he had no desire to interfere with Johnson's repatriation and demobilization and program. AFHQ in Ottawa estimated that about eighty aircrew were involved in the No 426 Squadron scheme, and Leckie failed to see how this number could add significantly to RCAF administrative problems when more than 18,000 Canadian personnel were overseas, only 9,000 of them eligible for repatriation after 1 January 1946. If the RAF request was important enough to warrant consideration of negotiation at the national government level, then the administration involved in retaining eighty aircrew for three months should not be an insuperable obstacle. Was it necessary to rescramble these crews in Transport Command? Could not arrangements be made to keep them in one or two squadrons if the Air Ministry did not intend to form a replacement squadron around a nucleus of No 426 Squadron personnel?[32]

On 9 December, no serviceable aircraft were available, so no trooping flights went out. One flight from Mauripur came in, and a training flight returned from Castel Benito with a full load of passengers. On 10 December, there were no arrivals or departures. Wing Commander Miller was posted to the command of RCAF Station Down Ampney effective 12 December, but then an amendment to the instruction came in saying that the posting was to RCAF Station Odiham as second in command. Another message said that, on 12 December, Squadron Leader J.F. Green, DFC, would assume command of No 426 Squadron and the rank of Acting Wing Commander, and that Flight Lieutenant A.J. Mackie was promoted to Squadron Leader as of 1 June 1945.[33]

On 10 December, Air Marshall Johnson wrote to Air Vice Marshal W.F. Dickson, the Assistant Chief of Air Staff – Policy at the Air Ministry, to say that he had communicated with the Chief of the Air Staff in Ottawa, who had given permission for No 426 Squadron's aircrew to continue in service with RAF Transport Command, subject to the following conditions:

1. No 426 Squadron ceased to function as an RCAF Squadron as of 31 December 1945, and all its aircraft were to be turned over to the RAF.
2. All RCAF ground crew were to be withdrawn from the RAF effective 1 January 1946.
3. Only aircrew who volunteered for extended service in an RAF squadron until 31 March 1946 were to be employed therein.
4. All No 426 Squadron aircrew were to be employed on the trunk route between Karachi and Britain. They were not to be employed on other services, or further east than Karachi.
5. All No 426 Squadron aircrew were to be employed in a single RAF squadron.
6. The Air Ministry was to arrange for progressive replacement of the No 426 Squadron aircrew as promptly as possible and, in any event, all were to be withdrawn from the RAF by 31 March 1946.

Johnson concluded by saying that, if the Air Ministry accepted these conditions, he would not have to refer the matter to higher authority, and that the volunteer aircrew would be available on 1 January 1946.[34]

That same day, Air Commodore Godwin wrote to Wing Commander Grant at Transport Command to inform him of the conditions under which the RAF might employ No 426 Squadron's Liberator aircrew, and to direct Grant to identify volunteers by rank, name and trade under the outlined conditions. Grant was also to point out to the volunteers that they would be working in an RAF squadron with RAF ground crew, probably under British flight commanders and a British squadron commander, living in RAF quarters and eating RAF rations. Godwin ended by stating that these conditions were on offer to the Air Ministry, and that the proposal was subject to Air Ministry agreement.[35]

On 11 December, No 426 Squadron dispatched three aircraft to Karachi and two aircraft returned to Tempsford with fifty passengers. Squadron Leader J.F. Green, Flight Lieutenant M.G. Jensen, Flight Lieutenant L. Greenburg and Flight Lieutenant G.W. Goodman went to Buckingham Palace for an investiture; Flight Lieutenant Greenburg received a Bar to his Distinguished Flying Cross, and the others each received the DFC. Squadron Leader J.B. Campbell of No 120 Wing Headquarters and Flight Lieutenant Doherty of Transport Command Headquarters arrived to form a Thunderbird Squadron Unscrambling Committee, charged with interviewing the Squadron Commander and all technical NCOs about extending their service in Britain.[36]

On 12 December, one India-bound flight went out and two aircraft returned to base, including Liberator KK340/R with Flying Officer Wright and crew, fresh from their adventure in the transient quarters of Istres-le-Tube. Wing Commander Miller left Tempsford for his new appointment, and the now Acting Wing Commander Green took command of the squadron. A consignment of tomato juice arrived from Aldershot, and Canada House began handing it out to RCAF personnel, who each received one forty-eight-ounce tin.

On 13 December, the sky over Tempsford was cloudy with gusty winds. Three aircraft departed for Mauripur by way of Tripoli, and three more returned from the route. At 1400 hours, all available aircrew assembled in the squadron Crew Room to hear Wing Commander Green explain options for continued service in the RCAF and to express their preferences. The three options were: repatriation and demobilization, service with an RAF Liberator squadron employed in passenger transport, and service with a Dakota squadron in No 120 (RCAF) Transport Wing, and the two latter options were open only to aircrew who waived their right to return to Canada under the Repatriation Group Number scheme and agreed to serve as long as the RCAF required them. Of the seventy-four personnel who completed documents that day, thirty-one asserted their right to repatriation, three applied for service with RAF Liberator squadrons, and forty applied for service with RCAF Dakota squadrons. Wing Commander Green did not neglect to praise the crews for their good work and encourage them to continue the squadron's enviable record.[37]

On 14 December, No 426 Squadron dispatched one flight to India and handled two arrivals from the route, and the administrative staff struggled with a huge workload caused by the pending disbandment of the unit and demobilization of its RCAF personnel. That evening, the RCAF Show troupe presented *Flying Home* to a packed, enthusiastic audience at the NAAFI.

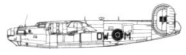

On 14 December, in his reply to Air Marshal Johnson's letter of 10 December, Air Vice Marshal W.F. Dickson of the Air Ministry confirmed that both Transport Command and the Air Ministry accepted Canada's conditions for employing volunteers from No 426 Squadron in the RAF. Dickson went on to ask that the definitive offer of volunteers, including their names, come from RCAF Overseas Headquarters. He also stated that Transport Command was in the process of choosing an RAF squadron to receive the RCAF volunteers.[38]

Trooping operations continued on 15 December with one departure for Karachi — two more outbound flights were cancelled for lack of serviceable aircraft — and two arrivals from the route. There should have been three, but Liberator KK255/Q with Flight Lieutenant R.J. Traill and crew, had departed Castel Benito on the last leg of the return journey when it began having mechanical problems; the crew diverted to El Aouina, Tunisia, and the aircraft was still there at the end of the month. Wing Commander Green spent the day in London discussing the disbandment of the squadron. Many aircrew who were absent from the meeting of 13 December completed the continuation-of-service documentation.

Tempsford had a clear day with gusty winds on 16 December; two India-bound flights went out and one aircraft came in from the route: Flight Lieutenant D.E. Merriam and his crew in Liberator KL647/M, who had started home the previous day but were diverted to Istres because of bad weather in Britain. Group Captain M.G. Doyle and Wing Commander Ashdown arrived from RCAF Overseas Headquarters to make the journey to India with Flying Officer W.A. Craig, but a maintenance problem delayed their flight. Wing Commander Green and Wing Commander Miller worked late, writing recommendations for honours and awards.

On 17 December, the squadron dispatched three overseas flights and handled two arrivals from Karachi. That afternoon, two mass meetings of RCAF personnel were held — ground crew in a hangar and aircrew in the Navigation Crew Room — to hear a farewell address from Wing Commander Miller, and an announcement from Wing Commander Green that personnel with high repatriation priority would head to the R Depot before Christmas, and everyone else would leave Tempsford between 28 December and the end of the month.

Bad weather over continental Europe halted trooping flights in and out of Tempsford on 18 December and 19 December. On 18 December, Wing Commander J.E. Cahill, the Principal Roman Catholic Chaplain, visited to inform the squadron that a Roman Catholic chaplain would arrive in Tempsford for the Christmas season in a few days. Flight Lieutenant W. Gill, a Public Relations Officer from RCAF Overseas Headquarters, arrived with a photographer to spend a few days with the squadron and prepare a news feature on its activities and now-imminent disbandment.

On 18 December, Transport Command Headquarters issued an Organization Order on employment of volunteer RCAF aircrew in RAF units. Up to fifteen crews were to be posted into establishment vacancies in No 102 (RAF) Squadron at Bassingbourn, and the aircrew displaced from No 102 Squadron by this decision would be distributed among the other squadrons in Transport Command. The RCAF crews serving with No 102 Squadron were to be posted out only for repatriation or release in March 1946, and they were not to operate east of Karachi.[39]

On 19 December, Wing Commander Green visited both RCAF Overseas Headquarters and Transport Command Headquarters to arrange all the aircrew postings involved in the plan for disbanding No 426 Squadron, and forty-nine airmen from the Servicing Echelon received orders to report to the Repatriation Depot at Torquay on 22 December. Squadron Leader E. Rhéaume, the promised Roman Catholic chaplain, arrived from RCAF Station Skipton to spend Christmas at Tempsford.

On 20 December, Tempsford was cold and frosty with poor visibility most of the day, and No 426 Squadron dispatched four Karachi-bound aircraft, the last operational flights to leave Tempsford, captained by Flight Lieutenant L. Greenburgh, Flying Officer G. More, Flying Officer H.J. Oliver and Flying Officer G. Rubenck. The aircraft were empty for the first leg of the trip, to Castel Benito, so they could climb above the bad weather over France and the Mediterranean. The squadron also handled three arrivals, each with ten passengers.

Two Thunderbird officers spent the day in London. Flying Officer A.M. Davison, the Squadron Educational Officer, attended a Department of Veterans' Affairs interview regarding application for a French government scholarship at the University of Paris, and Flying Officer B.S. Ballerini visited RCAF Overseas Headquarters for a briefing on being Tempsford's Deputy Returning Officer in the Manitoba provincial election. Finally, messages arrived that day from RAF Hospital Henlow to inform the squadron that Leading Aircraftsman R.E. Gardiner of the Servicing Echelon had died of natural causes, and that Flying Officer R.R. Wallace was on the seriously-ill list, after being injured on 30 November in a bicycle accident at Tempsford.

On 21 December, a non-operational flight (classed as a training flight) originally scheduled for the previous day took off for El Aouina, near Tunis, to pick up twenty-two soldiers stranded in North Africa, and the RCAF Farewell Smoker planned for that evening had to be cancelled because the organizing committee had trouble getting supplies.

On 22 December, five aircraft arrived, four of them after completing the entire route. The fifth was Liberator KH333/JW captained by Flight Lieutenant C.B. McDormund, home from El Aouina, with the soldiers and Flight Lieutenant R.J. Traill's crew, stranded since 15 December. Most squadron personnel were on leave, and the busiest place in camp was the squadron Post Office, which was inundated with Christmas mail — 105 bags of it. Flight Lieutenant J.H. Thompson, a flight engineer, departed for Torquay and repatriation to Canada.[40]

On 23 December, one overseas flight came in at noon with ten passengers, and the overflowing Squadron Post Office received another sixty bags of mail.

On 24 December, it rained most of the morning, but the weather cleared by evening. At midnight, Squadron Leader Rhéaume celebrated Mass in the Station Chapel, after which the Canada House canteen held Open House with music, food and drink.

The Thunderbirds celebrated their fourth Christmas in England quietly at Tempsford, with dinner at the Airmen's Mess, served to the junior ranks in the traditional way by the officers and senior NCOs, all organized magnificently by the Catering Officer, Flight Officer E.J. Campbell.

A signal came in with the sad news that Flight Sergeant McGovern's father had died and that his mother was seriously ill, and the Squadron Adjutant quickly tracked McGovern down at his leave address and pass on the arrangements made by RCAF Overseas Headquarters fly him home to Canada on 27 December.

On 27 December, Squadron Leader A.J. Mackie and Flying Officer A.V. Cronje and their crews completed the overseas route and returned to base. At noon, four training flights went out to pick up Thunderbird slip crews waiting at staging posts along the route; Liberator KH224/NW with Flight Lieutenant J.R. Ketcheson's crew and Liberator KN833/OW with Squadron Leader H.V. Peterson's crew headed for Mauripur, and Liberator KK374/T with Flight Lieutenant R.J. Roach's crew and Liberator KL641/A with Flight Lieutenant J.A. Badgley's crew went to Lydda. By 6 January 1946, all four aircraft were expected back at Tempsford.[41]

On 28 December, it rained and snowed for most of the day. At 1000 hours, all available squadron aircrew were gathered in the Navigation Crew Room and sorted into three groups: those wishing to be demobilized; those applying for service with in an RAF Liberator squadron, and those applying for service in RCAF Dakota squadrons. Anyone who had missed previous opportunities to choose one of these options was asked to do so immediately. For each volunteer, squadron administrative staff then organized the completion of a service history and the execution of the legal waivers and agreements. They then compiled three nominal rolls, which Wing Commander Green personally conveyed to Transport Command Headquarters.[42]

In the afternoon of 29 December, the squadron handled three inbound troopers, captained by Flight Lieutenant J.D. Matheson, Flying Officer G.S. Galley and Flying Officer D.T. Cook, and Flight Lieutenant Roach, bringing home nineteen members of Thunderbird slip crews. Posting instructions arrived for forty-two aircrew, due at the Repatriation Depot in Torquay on 2 January 1946.

In a letter to Air Commodore Godwin at RCAF Overseas Headquarters, Wing Commander Green wrote a summary of No 426 Squadron's progress toward disbandment. All personnel due for repatriation were to have left Tempsford by 31 December, and about fifty were already gone. Some 300 air and ground personnel destined for No 120 (RCAF) Wing were posted to Odiham effective 31 December and would report there on 3 January 1946. The last aircraft collecting slip crews from staging posts on the trooping route were expected back in Tempsford by 6 January 1946, bringing about thirty aircrew with them. With the Adjutant and the staff of the Squadron Orderly Room, Green thought he would need about two days after 6 January to write final training and performance reports, complete clearances, finish the Squadron Diary and pack up all the unit's files. He finished by saying that all aircrew still out on the route would be posted to their next unit destinations effective 31 December with their reporting dates contingent on date of return to Tempsford.[43]

On 29 December, the Canadian forces newspaper *Maple Leaf* ran a feature story about the Thunderbirds' reincarnation as a transport squadron, outlining their achievements and paying tribute to the aircrews and ground staff who established an enviable record in the short time they

worked together. For the ground staff, who spent endless hours working in open dispersals in the miserable English winter, the trooping assignment offered one small compensation: about thirty airmen made the round trip to Karachi, riding as supernumerary crew members, visiting the exotic stops on the route and, in the case of junior ranks, promoted Acting Sergeant for the trip so they could share the accommodation and amenities allocated to the regular aircrew.[44]

The Thunderbirds spent the last two days of December 1945 on the myriad of administrative and logistical details involved in disbanding a squadron. No overseas flights arrived until 1356 hours on New Year's Day, when the squadron's last operational flight — ten passengers with Liberator KL618/K, captained by Flight Lieutenant Hogarth from No 53 (RAF) Squadron at Merryfield — came in from Castel Benito.

On 31 December, several Thunderbird aircrew were still waiting for posting instructions. Transport Command was expected to keep thirteen or fourteen crews on trooping flights to India, about forty aircrew were to go to the Dakota squadrons in No 120 (RCAF) Wing, and the remainder were bound for Canada. The squadron received a letter from Air Marshal Johnson at RCAF Overseas Headquarters, stating that he had received the following message from Air Marshal Sir Ralph A. Cochrane, Air Officer Commanding-in-Chief, Transport Command:

> On completion by 426 (RCAF) Squadron of their Trooping Task, I would like to offer my congratulations on their fine record. They have done more than 100 round trips to India and back carrying over 5,000 troops. In some 5,000 hours flying on a trunk route, they have had one accident that could be attributed to pilot error and that a minor one. Grateful if you would convey to all ranks my appreciation of all they have done and my best wishes for their return to Canada. They have built up a great reputation and it is with genuine regret that we see them leave. Good luck to them all.

In closing, Air Marshal Johnson extended his congratulations and added, "…the outstanding record of your squadron has brought great credit to yourselves and to the Royal Canadian Air Force."[45]

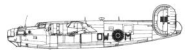

In December, No 426 Squadron logged 1,615 operational flying hours, including 606 at night, and 102 non-operational (mostly training) flying hours, including thirty at night. The unit transported 520 passengers on the run to Mauripur in twenty-eight passenger aircraft and one training aircraft, and handled forty return flights (including the aircraft brought back by a RAF crew on 1 January) that transported 820 passengers to Britain. On 31 December, three squadron aircraft were still out on the route, delayed by mechanical problems at El Aouina-Tunis, Cairo West and Shaibah-Basra and awaiting disposition by Transport Command. At disbandment, No 426 Squadron had two non-operational aircraft and twenty-eight operational aircraft that had a December serviceability rate of 76.6 percent. (Always reported as being on squadron strength, these aircraft were actually charged to Tempsford's Servicing Wing, which included No 4426 Servicing Echelon.)

On 30 December 1945, squadron strength stood at 280 all ranks, including fifteen ground crew. On 31 December 1945, No 426 Squadron was reduced to nil strength.⁴⁶

In its thirteen weeks as an operational long-range transport squadron, the Thunderbirds made 118 outbound flights and 114 inbound flights. They scheduled a total of 143 round trips, of which twenty were cancelled: eleven because of bad weather, seven for lack of serviceable aircraft, two because of mechanical failures. The squadron's other five cancellations included four Liberators that went unserviceable at Melsbroek and returned to Tempsford once repaired, and one Liberator directed back to base when Melsbroek was emptied of soldiers; on their return flights to Tempsford, these aircraft carried forty-two passengers. The four uncompleted homeward flights were Liberators that went unserviceable on the route; left behind at El Aouina, Cairo West, Shaibah and Castel Benito, they awaited repair and retrieval at Transport Command's leisure.

On the 232 completed flights, more than 5,500 passengers most of them British Army and RAF personnel, travelled to destinations between Tempsford and Mauripur. Only one woman was transported, on a mercy flight with her severely wounded husband.

The Thunderbirds' trooping operation involved more than 5,600 flying hours, about one million miles, no injuries to passengers or crew, and only one minor mishap. The Thunderbirds claimed the status of Transport Command's only squadron to complete all its operational assignments without a single fatal accident or injury of any kind to a passenger, a remarkable record attributable not only to the skill, experience and committed effort of the aircrews and ground staff, but also to the 3,700 hours of non-operational flying, mostly devoted to training, performed during the trooping period.⁴⁷

Wing Commander Green stayed at Tempsford with an RCAF rear party for nearly two weeks into the New Year, winding up the disbanded squadron's business. As the last aircraft returned to base, the slip crews were cleared and sent off to start the next phase of their lives. About seventy-five aircrew, designated as No 426 (RCAF) Flight, were dispatched to Bassingbourn to fly with No 102 (Liberator) Squadron of the RAF until the end of March. Wing Commander Green wrote to Mr. George Stronach of Toronto and Miss Lorna Fasken of the Ladies' Auxiliary in Regina, thanking them and their organizations for the cigarettes and other gifts they had sent to the squadron over the years of war.⁴⁸

One of the last hassles Wing Commander Green had to deal with was a query from RCAF Overseas Headquarters about the scanty flight details entered in the squadron's Operations Record Book; he replied that the instruction from No 48 Group Headquarters was to record only the first and last legs of round trips to India. Finally, Transport Command Headquarters issued instructions to distribute the aircraft made redundant by the disbandment of No 426 Squadron — thirty converted Liberators and one Airspeed Oxford — among the units of the command.

After an exchange of letters between the Air Ministry and RCAF Overseas Headquarters, No 426 Squadron's official date of disbandment was revised from 15 January 1946 to 31 December 1945. For the time being, officially at least, Thunderbird Squadron had ceased to exist. On 1 August 1946, it would reform again at Dartmouth, Nova Scotia, again as a transport squadron.⁴⁹

Trooping Operations, RAF Transport Command, 1 October 1945–6 January 1946

PHOTO 1
F/O Charles Labelle (radio officer); October 1945. (J.L. Bowers Collection)

PHOTO 2
No 426 Squadron Liberators at RAF Station Tempsford; September 1945. (DND PL 46845)

PHOTO 3
*Wright's crew; October 1945.
From left, standing: Sgt. L. Lyons
(flight engineer) and F/O J. Caton
(radio officer); seated:
F/O T. Hubbard (pilot),
F/O J.S. Wright (captain) and
F/O R.J. Gurney (navigator).
(R.J. Gurney Collection)*

PHOTO 4
*LAC J.P. Cadieux and
LAC F. Mancini at
work inside a Liberator;
autumn 1945
(DND PL 46850)*

Trooping Operations, RAF Transport Command, 1 October 1945–6 January 1946

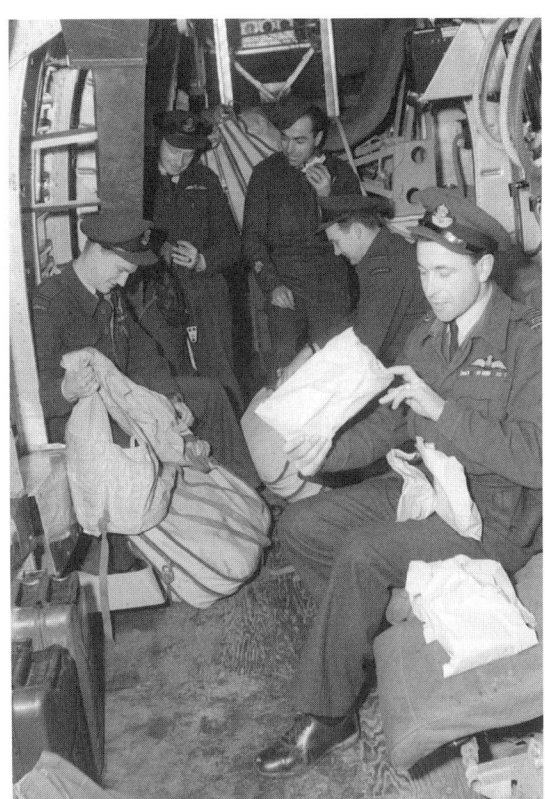

PHOTO 5
Checking rations before leaving for Africa; October 1945. From left: F/O J.A. Sime, F/O A.B. Wilson, WO1 A.J. Deschutter, F/L G.H. Ghent and F/L L. Greenburgh (captain). (DND PL 46848)

PHOTO 6
Galley's crew; October 1945. F/O J. Bowers (pilot), F/O C. Labelle (radio officer), F/O G. Galley (captain) and an unidentified flight engineer and navigator. (J.L. Bowers Collection)

PHOTO 7
Rigger LAC F. Howard looks up at the Liberator that will take him to India; RAF Station Tempsford, December 1945. (DND PL 46853)

PHOTO 8
Fitters LAC J. Hawkes and LAC P. Kavanagh work on the engine of a Liberator; RAF Station Tempsford, October 1945. (DND PL 46852)

Trooping Operations, RAF Transport Command, 1 October 1945–6 January 1946

PHOTO 9
*Aircraft and passengers being readied for departure; RAF Station Tempsford, October 1945.
(J.L. Bowers Collection)*

PHOTO 10
The crew of the Liberator Ottawa *watch another squadron aircraft take off; October 1945.
From left: F/O G. More (captain), F/O H.A. Norton (navigator), F/L G.N. Goodman (flight engineer), F/O H.A., Rawlinson (radio officer), WO1 J.V. Boyczuk (pilot). (DND PL 46847)*

PHOTO 11
The crew of the Liberator Winnipeg *show a WAAF driver where they have just returned from; RAF Station Tempsford, November 1945. From left: WO2 A. Stilt (radio officer), F/O T.H. Hubbard (pilot), LAW S. Holmes, F/O R. Gurney (navigator), F/O J. Wright (captain). (DND PL 46846)*

PHOTO 12
Servicing the Liberator Toronto; *Castel Benito (Tripoli), November 1945. (J.L. Bowers Collection)*

PHOTO 13
F/O J. Bowers (pilot) and the Liberator Fredericton, *November 1945. (J.L. Bowers Collection)*

PHOTO 14
F/O H.J. Oliver (captain) at the controls of a Liberator, December 1945. (DND PL 46851)

PHOTO 15

The morning conference of No 426 Squadron's section heads in the Squadron Commander's office; RAF Station Tempsford, December 1945. From left, back row: S/L D.D. Brownridge, S/L H.V. Peterson, F/L P.F. Someville and F/O A. Atken; front row: F/O R.J. Gurney, F/L K.A. McRoy, S/L R.A. Dinsmore, F/L G.H. Thomson and W/C J.F. Green. (DND PL 46849)

Part III

Dakotas

Chapter 4

Dartmouth, Nova Scotia
August–December 1946

At the beginning of the Second World War, the air transport capability of the RCAF amounted to a single flight of small passenger aircraft based at RCAF Station Rockcliffe, on the northeast fringe of Ottawa. On 30 August 1940, this flight was expanded to become No 12 (Communications) Squadron,[1] for employment in general communications and light transport — especially flying senior officers from AFHQ in Ottawa to the various Command Headquarters across Canada. No one seriously considered expanding this modest operation until the summer of 1942, when the RCAF accepted the task of developing an aerodrome at Goose Bay, Labrador. Construction materials could be brought in by sea during the summer, but Goose Bay was accessible only by air during its long, harsh winter.[2]

With this immediate problem to solve and others looming, Squadron Leader Z.L. Leigh (a former bush pilot and Trans-Canada Airlines flying instructor) was hastily transferred in July 1942 to AFHQ from the command of No 13 (Operational Training) Squadron at Sea Island, near Vancouver. During the fall of 1942, as Leigh set about organizing a specialized transport service with the ultimate goal of creating an Air Transport Command, pressure increased to get Goose Bay operational as a military aerodrome as soon as practicable. Completing the project before spring meant flying in huge quantities of materiel, and the construction site had only a temporary airstrip. For this task (and other purposes), No 164 (Transport) Squadron was formed on 23 January 1943. Based at Moncton, New Brunswick, No 164 Squadron started out flying the Lockheed Lodestar and later re-equipped with the Douglas Dakota. During the war, No 164 Squadron carried out a wide range of transport assignments in the Atlantic region and, in peacetime, became a cornerstone of the RCAF air transport service, supplying trained crews for the new transport squadrons formed in Canada and overseas.[3]

Early in 1943, the Air Staff in Ottawa realized that another transport squadron was needed to serve western Canada, especially the North-West Staging Route through the Yukon Territory to Alaska; consequently, No 165 Squadron, based at Sea Island, was formed on 13 July 1943. Although the Chief of the Air Staff, Air Marshal L.S. Breadner, succeeded in obtaining approval for No 165 Squadron, he failed to convince the Cabinet that the RCAF should have a Transport Command; therefore, he took a different approach to the achievement of this long-term goal.[4]

On 5 August 1943, the Directorate of Air Transport Command was formed at Air Force Headquarters, with the newly promoted Wing Commander Z.L. Leigh in charge. Functioning exactly like a Command Headquarters, the directorate controlled the operational activities of air transport units through three wings: Domestic Transport Wing, Ferry Wing and Overseas Transport Wing.[5]

Domestic Transport Wing, which tasked No 12 Squadron, looked after the communications and service flights in Canada. Ferry Wing moved aircraft from the factories and overhaul bases to training schools and operational squadrons in Canada. This task was initially handled by the Rockcliffe-based No 124 (Ferry) Squadron, formed on 1 January 1942 with a detachment in Winnipeg that, on 1 March 1944, became No 170 (Ferry) Squadron serving RCAF units in western Canada. Ferry Command of the RAF, based in Montreal, moved aircraft to Europe.[6] Overseas Transport Wing was responsible for airlifting high-priority passengers and freight, and for the trans-Atlantic "Bomber Mail" service. To achieve Air Marshal Breadner's objective of launching Bomber Mail in time for Christmas, No 168 (Heavy Transport) Squadron was formed at Rockcliffe on 18 October 1943, and equipped with Consolidated Liberators and specially modified Boeing B–17 Flying Fortresses.

On 5 February 1945, the Directorate of Air Transport Command was redesignated an autonomous headquarters under the title No 9 (Transport) Group, and moved to Rockcliffe with Z.L. Leigh, now a Group Captain, in command. On 1 April 1948, No 9 Group finally became Air Transport Command; on 9 August 1951, it moved to Lachine, Quebec, west of Montreal; and on 1 September 1959 it finally settled at RCAF Station Trenton.[7]

On 1 October 1945, No 164 (Transport) Squadron and its Dakota aircraft moved from Moncton, New Brunswick, to Dartmouth, Nova Scotia. The unit comprised a Squadron Headquarters at Dartmouth; two transport flights at Dartmouth; and a detachment at Edmonton, Alberta, which had its own sub-detachment at Stevenson Field, Winnipeg. The Winnipeg sub-detachment took over the parachute-training-support task from the Rivers, Manitoba, detachment of No 165 (Transport) Squadron, which was disbanded on 1 November 1945.[8]

In the spring of 1946, AFHQ decided to reorganize No 9 (Transport) Group to save money and facilitate the control, operation and administration of several miscellaneous units. At that time, No 9 (Transport) Group comprised the following units:

1. At Rockcliffe, Ontario:
   - No 9 (Transport) Group Headquarters
   - No 12 (Communications) Squadron
   - No 124 (Ferry) Squadron
   - No 168 (Heavy Transport) Squadron (to be disbanded 21 April 1946)
2. At Dartmouth, Nova Scotia:
   - No 164 (Transport) Squadron
3. At Kapuskasing, Ontario:
   - a detachment of No 124 (Ferry) Squadron
4. At Winnipeg, Manitoba:
   - a detachment of No 124 (Ferry) Squadron)
   - a sub-detachment of No 164 (Transport) Squadron
5. At Edmonton, Alberta:
   - a detachment of No 164 (Transport) Squadron

When the reorganization of No 9 Group took effect on 1 April 1946, No 9 (Transport) Group would look like this:[9]
1. At Rockcliffe, Ontario:
   - No 9 (Transport) Group Headquarters
   - RCAF Station Rockcliffe
   - No 12 (Communications) Squadron
   - No 124 (Ferry) Squadron
   - No 168 (Heavy Transport) Squadron (to be disbanded 21 April 1946)
   - No 7 (Photographic) Wing, comprising:
     - No 13 Photographic Squadron
     - No 14 Photographic Squadron
     - No 1 Photographic Establishment
2. At Dartmouth, Nova Scotia:
   - No 164 (Transport) Squadron
3. At Kapuskasing, Ontario:
   - a detachment of No 124 (Ferry) Squadron
4. At Winnipeg, Manitoba:
   - a detachment of No 124 (Ferry) Squadron
   - a sub-detachment of No 164 (Transport) Squadron
5. At Gimli, Manitoba:
   - No 1 Air Supply Unit
6. At Edmonton, Alberta:
   - a detachment of No 164 (Transport) Squadron

This multi-functional, far-flung formation was to be commanded by Air Commodore L.E. Wray.

On 31 May 1946, the Minister of National Defence for Air, Colonel Colin Gibson, announced the formation of two auxiliary squadrons — No 438 (Wildcat) Fighter Bomber Squadron, and No 401 (Ram) Fighter Squadron, both to be based at St-Hubert, Quebec, a suburb of Montreal located on the south shore of the St. Lawrence River — and one regular squadron — No 426 (Thunderbird) Transport Squadron, which would be based at Dorval, Quebec, located on the western fringe of Montreal. No 426 Squadron would fly a Canadian version of the Douglas C-54, a four-engine heavy transport aircraft[10] that would make its first flight at Cartierville Airport on 15 July 1946.

RCAF postwar plans called for reorganizing the transport squadrons so one would be based in Edmonton, and a policy decision had been made to perpetuate the squadrons that served overseas during the war by giving their numbers to peacetime RCAF units. To satisfy these needs, the western elements of No 164 (Transport) Squadron — a detachment in Edmonton and a sub-detachment in Winnipeg, both flying the Douglas Dakota — were to be reorganized as No 435 (Transport) Squadron, based in Edmonton with a detachment at Winnipeg. The eastern elements of No 164 Squadron based at Dartmouth became No 426 Squadron, which moved to Dorval in 1947, and re-equipped with the Douglas C-54. All these organizational changes came into effect on 1 August 1946.[11] When the Dartmouth element of No 164 Squadron officially became No 426 Squadron, its commanding officer, Wing Commander C.A. Willis, DFC, took over the new unit. In command of No 164 since 30 April, he was a veteran of the war in Europe, having commanded No 404 Squadron, a coastal fighter unit, until he was shot down and taken prisoner in March 1944.

On 1 August 1946, No 426 Squadron's strength was 139 air force and civilian personnel, and seven Dakota aircraft. The squadron came under No 9 (Transport) Group (headquartered at RCAF Station Rockcliffe) for functional control, and Eastern Air Command (headquartered at Halifax) for discipline and administrative control. Its mission was to transport freight and personnel, operating mainly between Dartmouth, Nova Scotia, and Goose Bay, Labrador.

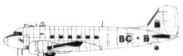

The first Douglas Dakota military transport (called the C-47 by the Americans) entered service with the RCAF on 29 March 1943, when No 12 (Communications) Squadron at Rockcliffe took delivery of Aircraft No 650, which moved on to No 164 Squadron at Moncton within a month. Over the years, Douglas Aircraft of Santa Monica, California, built nearly 11,000 copies of the Dakota in several variants, and the RCAF purchased about 570.

Of all-metal, stressed-skin construction, the Dakota was 64 feet 5.5 inches long and 16 feet 11 inches high, with a wingspan of 95 feet. Fitted with two 1,200-horsepower Pratt and Whitney R-1830-92 fourteen-cylinder, two-row, radial engines, its top speed was 230 miles per hour, with a service ceiling of 24,000 feet and a range of 1,600 miles. The Dakota could carry twenty-eight passengers, or fourteen litter patients with three attendants, or 10,000 pounds of freight, and its maximum take-off weight was 31,000 pounds. The normal crew was two pilots and a crewman, with a wireless operator and a navigator when required.[12]

August

The first day of Thunderbird Squadron's second lease on life passed quietly. On 2 August, Wing Commander Willis took a special flight to Goose Bay, three and a half hours away, with a load of freight. On 5 August, Flight Lieutenant A.J. Boyce took Service Flight 21 ("SF21") to Goose Bay, and delayed the return flight until a litter patient, a sick Hudson's Bay Company employee, was able to travel. Flight Lieutenant C.F. Sanford and Flying Officer H.T. Giles proceeded to Torbay, near St. John's, Newfoundland, to pick up some special equipment for delivery to Goose Bay. When Boyce returned at 0500 hours the following morning, he was kept waiting at the terminal — although he managed to get the patient off to hospital — because the Customs officers were off duty. Sanford and Giles returned from Goose Bay later in the day, only to be sent right back to Goose Bay on a special transport run.[13]

The next morning (7 August), Sanford and Giles left Goose Bay for Gander, with the Governor of Newfoundland aboard. The weather was bad at Gander and, after circling the airport for a while waiting for a break in the clouds, they managed to land at Torbay. Flight Lieutenant H. Hale took SF21 to Goose Bay, where the aircraft went U/S, compelling him to stay overnight. Flight Lieutenant T.S. Forbes and Flight Lieutenant W.J. Johnston departed on *Operation BEEFSTEAK*, transporting 9,000 pounds of beef from Montreal to Goose Bay.[14] When *Op BEEFSTEAK* returned to base on 12 August, Flight Lieutenant R.S. Clements was the co-pilot because Flight Lieutenant Forbes was in hospital at RCAF Station Rockcliffe with appendicitis.

On 14 August, Flight Lieutenant H. Hale took out SF21 for Goose Bay, only to hit a flock of gulls soon after take-off. After a safe landing in the extensively damaged Dakota, he headed out again in another aircraft.[15]

On 17 August, Flight Lieutenant Hale again took SF 21 to Goose Bay and, on the return leg, diverted to Sydney because Dartmouth was closed by bad weather. Flying Officer T.J. Derbyshire captained a special freight run to Goose Bay, where one of the tires went flat; the return leg of the flight was delayed until the next morning, when a new tire was replaced with one obtained from a USAAF unit that shared the station. Back in Dartmouth, he had to pay import duty on the tire.

On 26 August, Field Marshal Sir Bernard Montgomery of the British Army visited RCAF Station Dartmouth, to be greeted by airmen lining the road from the Marine Dock to the tarmac, where he inspected the Guard of Honour. After the Field Marshal was gone, Wing Commander Willis took an aircraft to Toronto with a load of spare parts for a Fleet Air Arm contingent that was participating in the Toronto Air Show. At the end of the month, Flying Officer D.E. Piette took over as Squadron Adjutant.[16]

During August, No 426 Squadron made fourteen scheduled flights and twelve special flights, amounting to 267 operational flying hours, during which 436 passengers, 110,971 pounds of freight and 4,222 pounds of mail were transported to destinations including Goose Bay, Labrador; Torbay, Newfoundland; Montreal, Quebec; and Ottawa (Uplands and Rockcliffe), Toronto and Kapuskasing in Ontario. The squadron also flew twenty-two training hours and spent nine hours in test flights. The serviceability rate of the squadron's seven Dakota aircraft was 92.7 percent.[17]

September

September continued the pattern set in August; No 426 Squadron making scheduled flights to Goose Bay and special runs as tasked by No 9 Group Headquarters.

On 7 September, Wing Commander Willis flew a planeload of perishable food to Goose Bay. On 8 September, a Sunday, many members of the squadron turned out for a large church parade in Halifax. On 9 September, the airmen's barracks were equipped with single cots and the old double-decker bunks were removed. On 11 September, the Sergeants' Mess held a gala evening party that was well-attended and considered a huge success. On 18 September, when the Cunard liner *Queen Mary* put into Halifax instead of New York, where the dock workers were on strike, the Squadron Commander flew the Chairman of the Bank of England to New York.

At about 1500 hours on 22 September, Flight Lieutenant H. Hale and crew were taking off with a load of passengers from Gander, Newfoundland, when the starboard engine of Dakota 967 caught fire, causing it to crash; the aircraft was badly damaged but no one was hurt. Dartmouth was fogged in for several days, and Flight Lieutenant A.J. Boyce had to wait until September 26 to fly the squadron's Chief Engineering Officer and Group Captain F.H. Watkins from Ottawa to Gander and pick up the stranded crew and their passengers.

Squadron Leader C.N. McVeigh left Halifax aboard the Cunard liner *Aquitania* for two months of temporary duty in Britain, flying VIPs around Europe. On 27 September, all airmen in the squadron who wished to remain in the RCAF for the next five years were re-attested, and those who did not wish to remain received their clearance forms.

On 28 September, Flight Lieutenant C.F. Sanford took out the scheduled flight to Goose Bay, and Flying Officer T.J. Derbyshire made an air tour of the Annapolis Valley and Prince Edward Island, accompanied by a National Film Board crew shooting scenes for the *Canada Carries On* series. On 30 September, the film team went on to locations in Newfoundland.

During September, No 426 Squadron made thirteen scheduled flights and twenty-one special flights, amounting to 231 operational flying hours, during which 416 passengers, 79,821 pounds of freight and 4,330 pounds of mail were delivered. The squadron also flew fifty-three training hours and spent fifteen hours on test flights. The serviceability rate of the squadron's seven Dakota aircraft was 81.1 percent. On 30 September 1946, the strength of No 426 Squadron stood at 125 all ranks, including forty-two officers (thirty-nine aircrew), seventy–three airmen and ten civilians.[18]

October

As in the other Canadian armed services, 1 October was observed in the RCAF as R-Day, the day of "reversion" to peacetime establishment. For many officers, senior NCOs and airmen, the only observable effect of R-Day was that they each lost at least one rank.

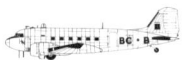

On 1 October, the Europe-bound Liberator carrying General Crerar unexpectedly landed at Dartmouth with an engine malfunction, and No 426 Squadron began preparing for the arrival of the new Douglas C-54 aircraft by picking out the four best Dakotas — 661, 664, 657 and 658 — and requesting transfer orders for the others — 965 and 967 at Dartmouth, and 967 still unserviceable at Gander. During the evening, Flying Officer Derbyshire returned from Gander, bringing Group Captain F.S. Wilkins in from Stephenville, where he had been investigating a crash. On 4 October, Flight Lieutenant C.F. Sanford flew to Gander, taking Wilkins on the first leg of his journey back to Stephenville to finish the investigation, and Squadron Leader C.D. McLean, who was going to cannibalize Dakota 967 for parts. Sergeant W.A. Westell left for Hartford, Connecticut, where he was scheduled to attend a propeller course. This training assignment set the squadron to speculating that the arrival of the Douglas C-54s could be imminent.

On 8 October, winter started in Dartmouth and No 426 Squadron could not get heat in its hangar. On 11 October, after changing an engine on Dakota 664, Flight Lieutenant A.J. Boyce took it to Rockcliffe on a training flight, with an extra crew to bring back Dakota 661 which had been left there for repair. On 18 October, the squadron held a Commanding Officer's parade and inspection, executed with the usual fine turn-out and excellent drill. By 22 October, the hangar was still unheated and the administrative staff were complaining about the difficulty of typing with gloves on.

During October, No 426 Squadron logged 167 operational flying hours, during which 154 passengers, 47,396 pounds of freight and 3,114 pounds of mail were delivered. The squadron also flew thirty training hours and spent twelve hours on test flights. The serviceability rate of the squadron's four Dakota aircraft was 70 percent. On 31 October 1946, the strength of No 426 Squadron stood at 157 all ranks, including forty-five officers.[19]

November

Despite engine problems, spells of bad weather, and an increase from three scheduled runs to Goose Bay per week to five, No 426 Squadron was able to carry out most of its flying assignments in November. On 7 November, Air Vice Marshal A.L. Morphee, Air Officer Commanding Eastern Air Command, visited Dartmouth to inspect the squadron and its facilities, and found everything in good order. On 11 November, the Remembrance Day ceremony was marked by an awkwardness when the Thunderbirds found themselves empty-handed when the time came to lay a poppy wreath for the air force; the squadron had come on parade believing that a Dartmouth veterans' group had brought the wreath, while the veterans assumed that No 426 Squadron would bring it.

On 12 November, Flying Officer T.J. Derbyshire was lined up ready to take off for Goose Bay when one of his engines failed and, by the time he changed aircraft, the weather had deteriorated enough that the flight had to be cancelled. On 18 November, Flight Lieutenant C.F. Sanford had an engine conk out over Charlottetown on the way to Goose Bay, and made it back to base on one engine. On 25 November, also en route to Goose Bay, Flying Officer C.R. Johnson's port engine packed up; with the aircraft struggling to maintain altitude, he feathered the propeller to reduce drag on the aircraft and had the crew jettison ten large containers of milk near Truro, Nova Scotia. After returning to base on one engine, he had the remainder of his load transferred to another aircraft, but by that time the weather was too bad for flying and the trip was off. On 30 November, the Squadron Commander was twenty-five miles out of Goose Bay on the way home when his port engine failed; he turned back to Goose Bay and touched down safely with the starboard engine leaking oil.

During November, No 426 Squadron made thirty-one flights, amounting to 245 operational flying hours, during which 176 passengers, 82,268 pounds of freight and 5,393 pounds of mail were delivered. The squadron also flew twelve training hours and spent eleven hours on test flights. The serviceability rate of the squadron's four Dakota aircraft was 73.4 percent. On 30 November 1946, the strength of No 426 Squadron stood at 152 all ranks, including forty-five officers.[20]

December

During December, engine problems and bad weather continued to plague squadron operations. On 2 December, Wing Commander Willis and his crew came home as passengers, leaving Dakota 658 in Goose Bay for an engine change. Two days later, on the way to Goose Bay with SF 21, Flight Lieutenant P.L. Michel lost one engine and had to fly the last fifty miles on the other.

On 5 December, Squadron Leader W.H. Lewis arrived from No 9 Group Headquarters to help Wing Commander F. Lund of Eastern Air Command and Squadron Leader C.D. McLean, the squadron Chief Engineering Officer, investigate the engine failures. On 6 December, the three senior officers concluded that the problem did not originate in any negligence or carelessness by any member of the squadron — a conclusion they could have reached without bothering to meet, according to the Daily Diary. On the same day, Dakota 368 and Dakota 602 were ferried in from Rockcliffe on temporary loan to the squadron.

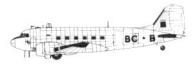

With Christmas in the offing, No 426 Squadron was tasked with transporting holiday necessities to Goose Bay, and bringing personnel back to Canada for leave. On 2 December, Flight Lieutenant C.F. Sanford and his crew battled bad weather all the way to Goose Bay to deliver a load of Christmas supplies and, on 20 December, the Squadron Commander got only as far as Truro with a similar load when one of his engines failed, forcing him back to base.

On 24 December, low ceilings, fog and rain scrubbed all flying activity out of Dartmouth, and Midnight Mass was celebrated at the Chapel. On Christmas Day, the squadron's fifth Christmas and first in Canada, the Officers' Mess entertained the senior NCOs at noon and, in the evening, the officers proceeded to the Airmen's Mess where they served up a sumptuous dinner. Everything was sharply different from the austere celebrations of the wartime Christmases in England.

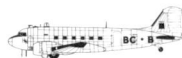

On 26 December, Wing Commander Willis and Flight Lieutenant Sanford each made a flight to Goose Bay; despite some concern over one of the Squadron Commander's engines, both aircraft made the round trip without trouble. On 27 December, Willis made the Goose Bay run again and this time had no problems at all. On 28 December, Dartmouth was socked in again, and all flying was scrubbed. On 29 December, a Sunday and normally a day of rest, the squadron dispatched two Goose Bay flights, primarily to take personnel returning from Christmas leave to their duty stations and to bring personnel proceeding on New Year's leave back to Dartmouth. On 30 December, bad weather again cancelled flying, so Flying Officer T.J. Derbyshire and Flying Officer H.T. Giles and their crews made the freight run and a special flight to Goose Bay the following day, hurrying back to Dartmouth for the station's New Year's Eve celebrations.

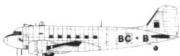

During December, No 426 Squadron made thirty-six flights, amounting to 268 operational flying hours, during which 250 passengers, 105,820 pounds of freight and 3,617 pounds of mail were delivered. The squadron also flew thirty-two training hours and spent four hours on test flights. The serviceability rate of the squadron's five Dakota aircraft was 56 percent. On 31 December 1946, the strength of No 426 Squadron stood at 141 all ranks, including forty-two officers.[21]

Dartmouth, Nova Scotia, August–December 1946

MAP 2: *Dakota Operations, 1946–1948*

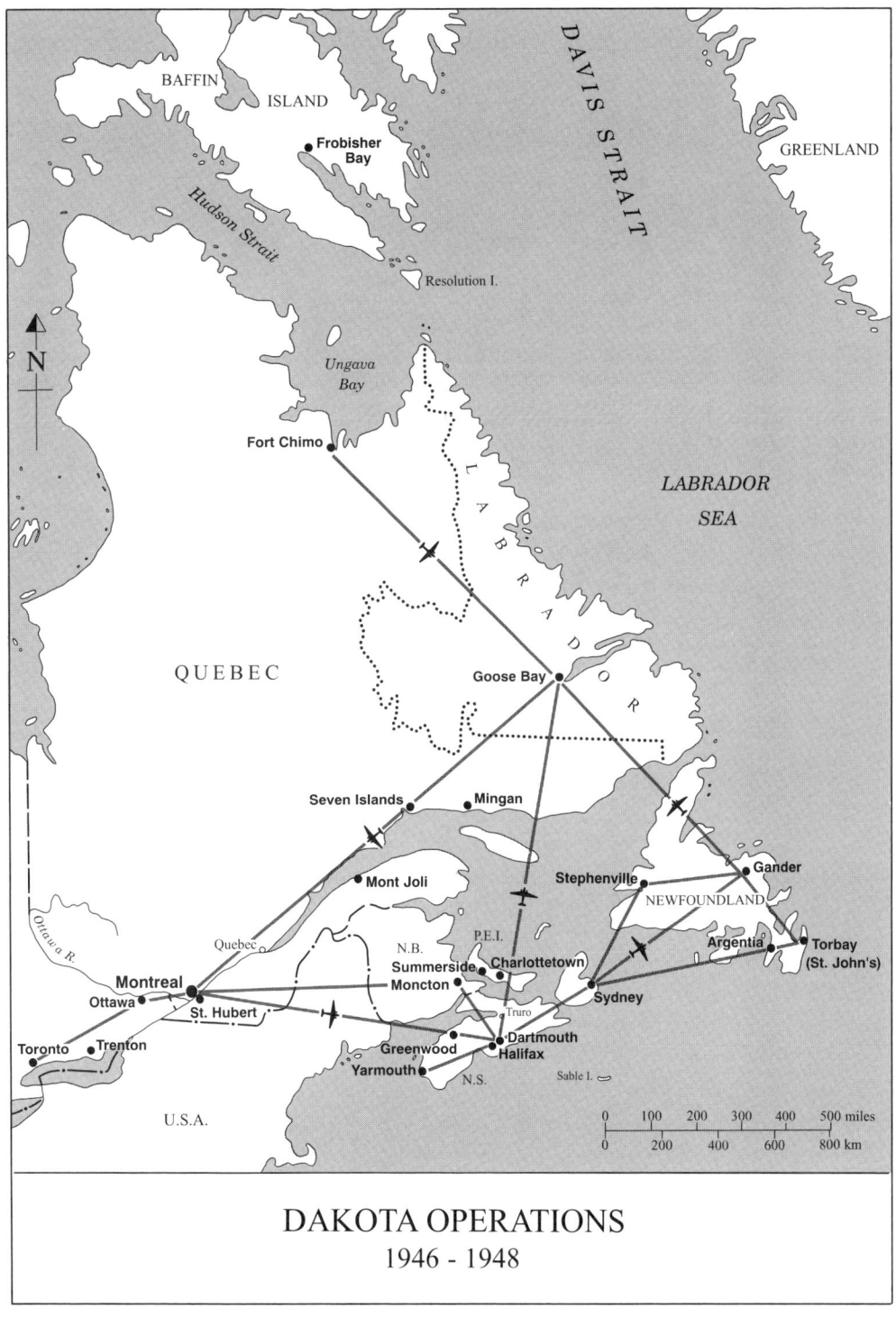

Maps by: Wm. Constable

PHOTO 16
Canadair unveils the North Star at Cartierville Airport, 20 July 1946. (Public Archives of Canada, PA 129328)

Dartmouth, Nova Scotia, August–December 1946

PHOTO 17

The newly re-formed No 426 (Transport) Squadron; RCAF Station Dartmouth, November 1946. From left, front row: Cpl. Epp, Miss Patterson, F/O Culligan, F/O Clough, F/O Banks, F/O Broun, F/O Bell, F/L Michel, F/L Watt, S/L McLean, W/C Willis, F/O Payette, F/L Sanford, F/O Derbyshire, F/O Bishop, F/O Spratt, F/O Fleming, F/O Johnson, F/O Whittington, F/O King and LAW Lins; second row: F/L Brodeur, F/O Chambers, F/L Publicover, F/O Smith, F/L Bourbonnais, WO2 Stevens, F/S Hill, Sgt. Westall, F/S Sollows, F/S Grant, Sgt. Tolland, Sgt. Zdan, F/O McDonald, F/O Carling, F/O Cairns, F/L Campbell-Rogers, F/O Forbes and F/O Jolicoeur; third row: Sgt. Geldart, Sgt. Kennedy, Sgt. Gowda, Sgt. Ruffell, WO2 Bell, Cpl. Vasseur, Cpl. Forbes, LAC Rix, Cpl. James, Cpl. MacLean, Cpl. Purcell, LAC Thorson, LAC Widger, Sgt. Moores, LAC Zimmer, Sgt. Siggens, Sgt. Terrio and WO2 Graves; fourth row: WO2 McCarrol, LAC Wilson, LAC Davies, LAC Sharp, LAC Kelly, LAC Taylor, LAC Ellery, LAC Hagen, LAC Tian, LAC Cook, LAC Moore, LAC Wilson, LAC Shane and LAC Mancuse; fifth row: LAC Burns, LAC Millette, LAC Pearson, LAC Thompson, LAC MacKay, LAC Bingham, LAC Cockerton, LAC Doyle, LAC Jaquish, LAC Scott, LAC Stripchuk, LAC Noonan, LAC Ferguson, LAC Payne, Sgt. Farmer and LAC McCoy. (E. Grose Collection)

Chapter 5

Dartmouth–Dorval, 1947

On New Year's Day 1947, Service Flight 1 departed Dartmouth on schedule for Montreal and Rockcliffe. The next day, a heavy snowstorm hit Dartmouth, scrubbing all flying. On 3 January, Flying Officer Giles took out SF 21 to Goose Bay, and had to stay for twenty-four hours, delayed by engine problems. On 7 January, the Squadron Commander set out for Goose Bay but turned back to base when the weather closed in, not only at Goose itself, but also at all the other airports in the Atlantic region. After that, the weather co-operated for a week, permitting No 426 Squadron to make all its scheduled and special flights.

On 15 January, Flight Lieutenant G.L. Sheahan and his crew were heading home when they found that the ceiling was well below landing limits. After trying twice to land, they were diverted to Moncton, which was also below limits. Low on fuel and out of options, Sheahan made three attempts before finally landing with the ceiling and visibility down to zero.

The next day, Flight Lieutenant P.L. Michel and his crew had to abort their run to Goose Bay at Truro, where their port engine failed completely. They returned to Dartmouth on one engine, moved their cargo to another aircraft, and set off again for Goose Bay. On 20 January, Michel took Dakota 657 out for an air test and had a runaway propeller. On his return to base on one engine, he found that he was rapidly acquiring a reputation as the only single-engine transport pilot in the RCAF.

On 21 January, the flight from Rockcliffe brought Squadron Leader C.R. Knowles and Squadron Leader A.J. Mackie from No 9 Group Headquarters, Squadron Leader J.C. McCarthy from the Experimental and Proving Establishment, and Flight Lieutenant J.G. Mills from No 12 Communications Squadron, all to be checked out on a Douglas C-54 on loan from the USAAF.

On 24 January, in marginal weather, the two-man crew of a United States Navy transport lost sight of the field during their final approach and crashed into a hill three miles from the end of the runway. Incredibly, both pilots survived.

During January, No 426 Squadron logged 288 flying hours, including 281 operational hours during which 149 passengers, 99,617 pounds of freight and 3,180 pounds of mail were delivered. The serviceability rate for the squadron's five Dakotas stood at 62.3 percent. On 31 January 1947, squadron strength stood at 102 all ranks, including thirty-four officers.[1]

February

During February, the weather in the Maritime provinces varied from poor to bad, compelling No 426 Squadron to curtail flying or cancel it outright on fifteen days. Service flights and freight runs to Goose Bay were most affected.

On 11 February, Squadron Leader A.J. Mackie arrived from No 9 Group Headquarters to take over as Squadron Commander while Wing Commander C.A. Willis took leave. On 13 February, Flight Lieutenant A.A.S. Law and Flying Officer H.T. Giles were outward bound for Goose Bay when they had to divert to Moncton — Goose Bay was weathered in. On 15 February, on their way home from Goose Bay, both pilots had to land at Moncton again, this time because the weather at Dartmouth was below limits. On 26 February, the squadron tried to make up for the cancelled flights to Goose Bay by sending out three aircraft in marginal conditions; by the time they reached the north shore of the St. Lawrence, the weather had closed Goose Bay and the aircraft were diverted to Mingan and Seven Islands, on the north shore of the St. Lawrence River.

The weather was much better to the west, so Squadron Leader C.D. McLean was able to take the service flight to Dorval for a meeting with Air Commodore L.E. Wray, Air Officer Commanding No 9 Group. The main agenda item was No 426 Squadron's impending move to Dorval. Hangar space and offices would be found at the airport, and squadron personnel would live at the former RCAF Station Lachine, which closed on 1 December 1946. Like every Canadian city, Montreal had a severe housing shortage at this time — during the war, people flocked to urban areas to work in the expanding industries, but domestic construction ceased for lack of building materials. Therefore, No 426 Squadron would have to share the accommodations at Lachine with civilian families settled there by the Department of Public Works.[2]

On 27 February, three more Goose Bay flights were scheduled. Two aircraft captained by Flight Lieutenant G.L. Sheahan and Flying Officer J.A. Jolicoeur got away, but were soon recalled when Goose Bay closed down because of the weather. Air Commodore Wray arrived from Rockcliffe for more discussions regarding the squadron's relocation to Dorval.

During February, No 426 Squadron logged 210 flying hours, including 192 operational hours on twenty-five trips, during which eighty-seven passengers, 71,008 pounds of freight and 6,047 pounds of mail were transported. The serviceability rate for the squadron's five aircraft was 65 percent. On 28 February 1947, squadron strength stood at ninety-nine personnel, including thirty-four officers.[3]

March

During March, better weather across the Atlantic region permitted the Thunderbirds to attain a degree of operational normality, although the imminent move to Dorval required a gradual shift of operations from Dartmouth to the new base. For a short time, Goose Bay flights went out from both Dartmouth and Dorval, but operations were consolidated at Dorval by the end of the month.

On 1 March, bad weather at Goose Bay meant that all the morning flights to that destination had to be cancelled; however, in the late afternoon, conditions improved enough for Air Commodore Wray to take a party of six on an inspection tour to Goose Bay.

On 7 March, Wing Commander C.G.W. Chapman, DSO (the incoming Squadron Commander), reported in from the RCAF Staff College in Toronto. (During the war, Wing Commander Chapman commanded No 162 Squadron, an RCAF Home War Establishment unit that flew the Consolidated Canso flying boat on anti-submarine operations.) On 8 March, he flew to Goose Bay as a passenger on a morning flight captained by Flying Officer H.T. Giles. On 10 March, Wing Commander Willis returned from leave, resuming command of the squadron. On 12 March, Wing Commander Chapman flew to Dorval from Dartmouth, while Squadron Leader Mackie, who had commanded the unit in Wing Commander Willis's absence, returned to Rockcliffe.

On 13 March, the Maintenance Hangar at Dartmouth was a hive of activity as equipment and tools were packed for shipment to Dorval.

On 15 March, Wing Commander Chapman, Squadron Leader C.R. Knowles, Flight Lieutenant E. Anderson, Flight Lieutenant E.J. Grosz and Flight Lieutenant J.G. Mills were officially posted to the squadron, with Chapman as Squadron Commander and Anderson as Adjutant. Also that day, the squadron's advance party departed for Montreal, travelling by road and rail, and the Airmen's Mess at Lachine opened to serve Thunderbird personnel their first meal in their new home. Meanwhile, bad weather at Dartmouth prevented Flight Lieutenant C.F. Sanford from departing for Goose Bay until early afternoon.

On 17 March, all personnel available at Lachine started cleaning the station buildings, and the Airmen's Canteen opened for business. At Dorval, the advance party reported in from Dartmouth, and Flying Officer Smith, one of the squadron's engineering officers, took a crew of airmen and started building tool cribs in No 6 Hangar.

Over the next few days, the elements of No 426 Squadron remaining at Dartmouth sent out the regular flights to Goose Bay as well as nearly 18,000 pounds of equipment to Montreal. On 21 March, Flight Lieutenant G.L. Sheahan and Flying Officer C.R. Johnson brought about 4,200 pounds of equipment, nine squadron personnel and two Dakotas — 658 and 965 — to Dorval. The next day, still more personnel reported in at Dorval from Dartmouth and Rockcliffe.

On 24 March, No 426 Squadron officially began operations from Dorval with a round trip to Goose Bay via Dartmouth, made by Flight Lieutenant G.L. Sheahan in Dakota 965. Flying Officer J.A. Jolicoeur captained that day's direct flight to Goose Bay. On 27 March, the Squadron

Commander went to Dartmouth to meet with the Air Officer Commanding No 10 Group and the Station Commander of RCAF Station Dartmouth to make the final arrangements for No 426 Squadron's departure. For the rest of the month, new Thunderbird personnel reported in at Dorval from locations as diverse as Vancouver, Edmonton, Winnipeg, Trenton and Rockcliffe.

During the month of March, No 426 Squadron logged 310 hours on thirty-one service flights to deliver 120 passengers, nearly 90,000 pounds of freight and 3,200 pounds of mail. In six flights to Dorval, the squadron transported 21,880 pounds of its own equipment from Dartmouth. On 31 March, squadron strength stood at 228 all ranks, including forty-eight officers (of whom forty-three were aircrew), 148 other ranks, thirty-two civilians, and six Dakotas (657, 658, 659, 661, 664 and 965).[4]

April

As a self–accounting unit, No 426 Squadron was responsible for its own financial, logistical and technical affairs. This arrangement meant that the squadron had to find the resources to do a great deal of work and correct many problems in their first days in Montreal.

Getting established required considerable initiative and hard work of everyone. First and foremost, No 426 Squadron had two sites almost five miles apart. At Lachine, they were assigned to buildings constructed for No 5 Manning Depot and last used by No 1 Y (Embarkation) Depot. Vacant for months, they had to be thoroughly cleaned and renovated to provide administrative offices, quarters, messes and recreational areas. At Dorval Airport, the squadron took over No 6 Hangar, which was also vacant and in need of overhaul. Also, an Operations Centre and Technical Stores had to be set up; and technical, maintenance and servicing areas had to be laid out. Finally, communications facilities were inadequate, and this problem took some time to rectify. With all this extra work to be done, the squadron still had to keep the service flights coming and going on schedule.[5]

April began with good weather and, throughout the month, weather held up flight operations on only three occasions; two more delays were caused by serviceability problems with aircraft. Settling-in activities and efforts to improve the squadron's domestic arrangements dominated the beginning of the month. Unit morale was high, but not so stratospheric that entertainment and recreational facilities, and some relief on the housing front, could not enhance it.

On 8 April, squadron personnel cleaned the barracks, buildings and grounds at Lachine, and unloaded three boxcars of equipment just in from Dartmouth. On 9 April, Flying Officer W.H. Smith took a party of airmen to RCAF Station Uplands, south of Ottawa (now the Macdonald-Cartier International Airport), to dismantle and move to Lachine a significant haul of recreation equipment — pool tables and an entire bowling alley. The job of moving the equipment and placing it in temporary storage at Lachine took only four days. On 14 April, Thunderbird personnel made their applications for married quarters, hoping for fast action because of the serious local housing shortage.

In the morning of 11 April, Wing Commander Chapman held his first Squadron Commander's parade at Lachine, and inspected the station's barracks and messes with the Adjutant. The parade produced a fine turn-out, but the two officers concluded that a lot more work would have to be done on the buildings before they would attain first-class standard.[6] On 15 April, Wing Commander Chapman went to Ottawa to visit No 9 Group Headquarters and AFHQ. His agenda included unit welfare and married quarters as well as maintenance problems.

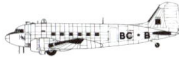

While this domestic and administrative labour was going on, the squadron was also working on operational improvements. On 10 April, Flying Officer L. Chambers and a party of six airmen left for Churchill, Manitoba for four weeks of temporary duty at the Combined Experimental and Training Station.

On 15 April, Flying Officer Smith and the Squadron Equipment Officer, Flight Lieutenant E.J. Grosz, went to Cartierville, Quebec to visit the Canadair plant to discuss supplies and spares for the North Star transport that the squadron was planning to acquire. (On 15 July 1946, the first North Star prototype built at this plant flew for the first time.)[7] On 16 April, Grosz and Smith went to the Pratt and Whitney plant at Longueuil, Quebec to discuss North Star propeller maintenance and spares with a Mr. Drummond.

With the Flight Controller's office now on the upper level, all offices and sections were permanently established at Dorval in No 6 Hangar and its Annex. On 16 April, the squadron's ancient shuttle bus died, and many airmen got an unexpected afternoon off; without the bus, they couldn't get to work from the quarters at Lachine.

On 17 April, No 426 Squadron's communications problems were partially solved by the arrival of a Teletype machine and, temporarily (until a Teletype operator could be posted in), Sergeant Martin from RCAF Station St-Hubert to operate it. With the teletype up and running, No 426 Squadron found itself handling all government message traffic to the Montreal area — for other federal departments and agencies as well as for DND offices and units of all three armed services. The same day, Flying Officer T. Alliston was appointed the squadron's Signals Leader.

The next morning, the Squadron Commander's parade was called off on account of rain, and maintenance problems forced cancellation of the service flight to Goose Bay.

On 21 April, the squadron received its first "radio navigators," Flying Officer J.H.C. Boby and Flying Officer C.R. Gates, posted from in the Radio and Communications School at RCAF Station Clinton, Ontario.

On the morning of 23 April, the Squadron Commander held his parade and inspected the squadron's buildings at Lachine — again, the parade well turned out, but the buildings less than satisfactory, despite considerable progress since the last inspection. On 25 April, Wing Commander Chapman went to Ottawa for a conference at No 9 Group Headquarters. The next day, Flight Lieutenant P.L. Michel and a contingent of sixty-three squadron personnel went to Montreal to take part in a parade at the Cenotaph. Marshal of the RAF Sir Arthur Harris, former head of Bomber Command, laid a wreath.

On 28 April, Flight Lieutenant C.F. Sanford took a special flight to Goose Bay with two tons of freight, including 965 pounds of sulphuric acid. On 30 April, the weather was so bad that all flying had to be cancelled; however, the squadron was busy enough receiving Air Vice Marshal C.R. Slemon from AFHQ, who inspected both the hangar at Dorval and the domestic site at Lachine.

During the month of April, No 426 Squadron logged 388 flying hours, including 332 hours on operations, forty-three hours on training and thirteen hours on flight testing, and completed thirty-seven service flights and special flights to transport ninety-three passengers, 95,160 pounds of freight and 3,567 pounds of mail. On 30 April 1947, squadron strength stood at 206 all ranks, including fifty officers, with six Dakota aircraft on the inventory.[8]

May

May began with weather bad enough to curtail flying operations. On 2 May, Squadron Leader C.R. Knowles returned from Goose Bay after extensive discussions with the Station Commander, Group Captain Z.L. Leigh, on local air-traffic control problems. On 3 May, Flight Lieutenant C.F. Sanford departed for Selma, Alabama by way of Toronto, where he stopped to pick up staff and students from the RCAF Staff College who were to hold joint study sessions with their American counterparts. The same day, Flight Lieutenant J.D. Dickson proceeded on temporary duty with No 412 Squadron at Rockcliffe, where he would captain a VIP flight touring the Northwest Territories, Yukon Territory and Alaska. On Sunday 4 May, Squadron Leader M.W. Williams held a Protestant service in the newly reopened station chapel.

On 5 May, a service flight to Goose Bay captained by Flying Officer C.R. Johnson returned to base with a malfunctioning engine; the ground crew soon corrected the problem and sent him on his way. The same day, Flight Lieutenant P.L. Michel took a special flight to RCAF Station Rockcliffe to transport ex-members of No 168 Squadron to a ceremony in the station chapel. Dr. A. Frederkiewicz, Polish Minister to Canada, was to unveil a plaque commemorating the crew of a No 168 Squadron B–17 "Flying Fortress" who died trying to transport medical supplies to Warsaw.

Back at Lachine, everyone was at work on the refurbishing operation, with a crew of airmen painting the airmen's dining hall, civilian contractors painting the airmen's quarters and officers spending their off-duty hours getting their own dining hall into shape. Meanwhile, the Squadron Sports Officer, Flight Lieutenant S.F. Cowan, addressed himself to getting Lachine's recreation hall and cinema into action.

On 7 May, Wing Commander Chapman checked progress toward his objective of making Lachine the showplace of the RCAF — he held another Commanding Officer's parade and inspection. Marked progress was noted in personal appearance and drill, and a less-dramatic improvement in buildings and messing facilities due to the daily cleaning and painting activities.

Also on 7 May, two service flights to Goose Bay were held back by a delay in obtaining customs clearances, and Flight Lieutenant P.W. Holloway, previously one of the squadron's flight controllers, reported in from Clinton as a fully qualified radio navigator. That evening, Flight Lieutenant

S.F. Cowan, Flying Officer W.H. Smith and a working party of airmen moved the bowling alley components, which weighed 1,500 pounds each, out of temporary storage in No 1 Drill Hall to No 2 Drill Hall, where the bowling alley would be assembled and installed.

The second anniversary of VE Day, 8 May, passed quietly. Flight Lieutenant L.M. Bishop and Flight Lieutenant C.E. Snider took flights to Goose Bay, and both reported heavy icing on the way. The officers' dining hall opened without fanfare. On 9 May, Air Commodore Wray visited, and was impressed by the squadron's progress in getting established at its sites in Lachine and Dorval. On 10 May, Wing Commander Chapman and Flight Lieutenant J.G. Mills flew to Mountain View, Ontario, a BCATP station near Trenton, Ontario, where they collected projection equipment sufficient to re-equip the cinema at Lachine. That evening, the Sergeants' Mess re-opened with a bang-up party.

On 13 May, Flying Officer J.A. Jolicoeur got stuck at Dartmouth with a flat tire on Dakota 658; the next day, the squadron had to fly out a spare wheel, a jack and several airmen to change the wheel. Flying Officer H.T. Giles left for Selma, Alabama via Rockcliffe to pick up the RCAF Staff College contingent after their joint exercise with the Americans. He returned to base on 17 May.

On 19 May, a Pratt & Whitney representative came to Dorval to visit Maintenance Section to find out what was causing high cylinder-head temperatures in Dakota 657 and Dakota 664. At the same time, Dakota 661 was undergoing a major inspection and Dakota 659 was being prepared for transfer to No 6 Repair Depot at Trenton for modifications. The same day, Flight Lieutenant E. Anderson was transferred to No 9 Group Headquarters, for duties in the Personnel Branch, and Flight Lieutenant W.P. Casey, the new Squadron Adjutant, reported in from RCAF Station Rockcliffe.

On 21 May, a dull, cloudy day with intermittent rain, a Commanding Officer's parade and inspection were held in the morning, and two flights departed for Goose Bay. One of these aircraft, captained by Flight Lieutenant C.F. Sanford, delivered three cases of dynamite. The next day, Flight Lieutenant Bishop's freight run to Goose Bay carried nine more cases of dynamite; also, Flying Officer H.T. Giles ferried Dakota 659 to No 6 RD Trenton, and Flying Officer Johnson brought its replacement, Dakota KG350, to Dorval from No 412 Squadron at Rockcliffe. On 23 May, Service Flight 21 was diverted to RCAF Station Greenwood with Air Vice Marshal A.L. Morfee aboard; the ceiling at Dartmouth had dropped below 100 feet.

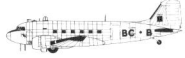

Now that No 426 Squadron was more or less settled into the Montreal area, the social calendar began to perk up. In the afternoon of 23 May, the Thunderbirds received a visiting party of officers from Chiang Kai-Shek's air force, members of China's delegation to the International Civil Aviation Organization (ICAO). That evening, the first dance was held at the restored Airmen's Canteen. On 24 May, Victoria Day, the Officers' Mess opened with a dance and seafood party. On 26 May, the United Benevolent Fund Committee formed with six members and Wing Commander Chapman as President; that afternoon, the Officers' Mess Committee held its monthly meeting. The next day, Flight Lieutenant P.L. Michel and Flight Lieutenant G.L. Sheahan took two aircraft to Toronto to transport the RCAF Central Band to Goose Bay. On 29 May, Wing Commander

Chapman went to No 9 Group Headquarters at Rockcliffe on temporary duty, leaving Squadron Leader C.R. Knowles in temporary command of the squadron.

On 30 May, payday, the weather was cold, wet and miserable at Dorval and even worse in Atlantic Canada, so the service flights to Dartmouth and Goose Bay were cancelled. Squadron Leader Knowles took Dakota 658 up for a test flight and had to land it on one engine when the starboard engine conked out.

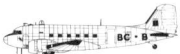

During the month of May, No 426 Squadron logged 476 flying hours, including twelve hours on tests, twenty-six training hours and 438 operational hours, during which nearly 95,000 pounds of freight, 4,056 pounds of mail and 160 passengers were transported. On 31 May 1947, squadron strength stood at 238 all ranks, including forty-nine aircrew, four ground officers, 151 other ranks and thirty-four civilians, with six Dakota aircraft on the inventory.[9]

June

On 2 June, the squadron despatched three flights to Goose Bay and half the aircrew to the Trans-Canada Airline Lecture Rooms to begin a six-day ground course on the North Star aircraft. On 3 June, Flight Lieutenant L.M. Bishop and Flight Lieutenant S.F. Cowan took two aircraft to Goose Bay to transport the RCAF Central Band back to Toronto, and Dakota 664 was brought in for a major inspection. On 4 June, Dakota 661 was also hauled in for a major inspection and, by 6 June, the squadron had only three serviceable — the starboard propeller had failed on Dakota 661.

On 7 June, the aircrew on the North Star Ground Course finished classes, and Flight Lieutenant P.L. Michel test-flew Dakota 350 and Dakota 661. The other three Dakotas — 664, 657 and 965 — were all in for inspection, so no operational flying was going on. Monday, 9 June, was the King's birthday, so the squadron was on Sunday routine, and the rest of the aircrew went to TCA to start the North Star Ground Course.

In the morning of 11 June, a very hot day in Montreal, the Commanding Officer's parade and inspection was held, followed by a drill period. Flight Lieutenant C.E. Snider ran into engine trouble on the way home from Goose Bay and made a successful single-engine landing at Mont Joli. This was the squadron's first major unserviceability in the air since the move to Montreal.

On 13 June, Service Flight 21 to Goose Bay was despatched, and a detail of airmen left for Mont Joli, where they would change the engine on Dakota 658. Dakota 664 and Dakota 965 were still undergoing inspection. That evening, the Airmen's Mess hosted a squadron dinner and smoker, featuring cocktails, turkey and a variety of entertainment. The next day, Wing Commander Chapman and Flying Officer H.T. Giles flew a party of scientists from McGill University and about 3,100 pounds of marine and hydrographic equipment to Fort Chimo, and Flight Lieutenant C.F. Sanford went to Mont Joli in Dakota 965 with the new engine for Dakota 658. On 17 June, an RAF Lincoln transport (a variant of the Lancaster), captained by Flight Lieutenant Woods, arrived from Edmonton en route to Prestwick, Scotland. The Lincoln and its crew were delayed in Dorval for a week with engine problems.

On 18 June, equipment was the priority. No 5 Equipment Depot in Moncton, New Brunswick delivered a twenty-seven-passenger bus to replace the squadron's ancient, creaking trailer bus. Dakota 664 was still undergoing a major inspection, and Flight Lieutenant Sanford flew Flying Officer Giles to Mont Joli to give Dakota 658 a rigorous air test and ferry it back to Dorval.

On 20 June, Flight Lieutenant C.E. Snider turned back to base with engine trouble eighty minutes after taking off for Goose Bay; after switching aircraft, he was able to complete the service flight. Three days later, Snider had engine trouble again during a test flight, and made a successful single-engine landing. He was rapidly building a reputation as a single-engine transport pilot.

On 24 June, with only three serviceable aircraft, the Thunderbirds received orders from No 9 Group Headquarters to ground all their Dakotas, inspect them for "sludge," and send the findings to the National Research Council in Ottawa. The next day, the Squadron Commander's parade was called on account of continuous light rain; however, the weather did not hamper the inspection of barracks and buildings, which went ahead as planned. On 28 June, only Dakota 350 (which seemed clear of problems) was still flying; all the other aircraft were grounded until special inspections could be carried out. Also that day, the first squadron wedding was held at the Lachine station chapel — Corporal R.J. Brown of Motor Transport Section and Miss Anna Petrakes were married by the padre, Squadron Leader M.W. Williams. That evening, the Airmen's Canteen hosted the wedding reception and dance.

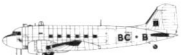

During the month of June, despite problems keeping the aircraft serviceable, No 426 Squadron logged 384 flying hours, including forty training hours and 344 hours on operations, transporting 470 passengers, 117,843 pounds of freight and 4,911 pounds of mail. On 30 June 1947, squadron strength stood at 239 all ranks, including fifty officers, 156 airmen and thirty-three civilians.[10]

July

For the first two weeks in July, No 426 Squadron had only one serviceable Dakota, which did yeoman service between Dorval and Goose Bay; the other five aircraft remained grounded for special checks.

On 3 July, the squadron opened a radio link between Operations at Dorval and its quite unauthorised ground receiving station at Lachine. Until this point, flights to Goose Bay were not heard from until the aircraft returned to base; now, the Flight Controller could be kept informed of the movements of aircraft away from home. The radio installation was Wing Commander Chapman's idea. On his own initiative, he acquired a spare transmitter and receiver from Goose Bay and, from RCAF Station St-Hubert, some seventy-foot poles for mounting the antennae at Lachine. The radios, manned by aircrew, found a home in the NCOs' quarters at Lachine.[11]

When the Telecommunications Branch got wind of the radio, No 426 Squadron received a stern message from No 9 Group Headquarters that the radio installation was not authorised, to which Wing Commander Chapman responded that it was built at no cost to the Crown. No 9 Group Technical Branch then got into the act, ordering the installation shut down because it did not meet RCAF technical standards, and Wing Commander Chapman told them that he would shut the radio down only if a technically adequate alternative was provided. No 9 Group Headquarters had nothing to offer, so the Thunderbirds kept their radio.

From this modest beginning, No 426 Squadron gradually developed the capacity to maintain contact with its aircraft, first, throughout North America and, later, around the world.[12]

On 5 July, Dakota 965 and Dakota 661 underwent engine changes. On 7 July, at Goose Bay, a truck hit the squadron's only serviceable aircraft, puncturing the fuselage; the next day, the aircraft had to be ferried back to Dorval and repaired, which meant cancelling a service flight. Also on 6 July, No 9 Group Headquarters requested a ferrying job, so Flight Lieutenant C.E. Snider and crew took the train to Nova Scotia to pick up a Dakota at RCAF Station Greenwood and deliver it to RCAF Station Centralia. At Dorval, the Wireless Section finished installing an inter-office communication (intercom) system, so all sections could be in direct contact.

On 9 July, a Beechcraft with Air Vice Marshal Carnegie aboard had landing gear trouble, and had to make an emergency landing at Dorval. Flight Lieutenant G.L. Sheahan in the control tower talked the pilot through the emergency landing procedures until he eventually managed to lock the Beechcraft's wheels and land safely.

On the morning of 11 July, during a flight to and from Rockcliffe, check pilot Flight Lieutenant H.J. Galen from RCAF Station Trenton tested Flight Lieutenant W.J. Johnston and Flying Officer E.L. Banks for the "Green Ticket" that authorized a pilot to fly under prescribed instrument conditions.

On 14 July, the squadron got a second Dakota into serviceable condition for service flights to Goose Bay, and the Wireless Workshop at No 6 Hangar at Dorval went into full operation with the arrival of long-awaited equipment. On 16 July, the Commanding Officer's parade was called on account of rain but, again, the inspection of barracks and buildings went ahead. On 18 July, with a third Dakota back in service and the fleet at half strength, the squadron was able to get back on schedule. During the week, the Lachine transmitter room was enlarged to accommodate more radio equipment — apparently, No 9 Group Headquarters had decided to leave well enough alone.

On 24 July, thanks to Flight Lieutenant S.F. Cowan, the Sports and Recreation Officer, the squadron held a Field Day, with a track meet in the afternoon and a challenge softball game against RCAF Station St-Hubert in the evening. After the ballgame, an all-ranks gala dance with the RCAF Central Band was held in the Drill Hall. The Thunderbirds won the ballgame and, at the track meet, the officers' team won the trophy, the Squadron Headquarters team came in second, and the Squadron Engineering Officer, Flying Officer W.H. Smith, was the leading point

winner. Also that day, Wing Commander Chapman went to Windsor Station in Montreal to meet an advance party of Air Cadets heading for the United Kingdom on an exchange program with British cadets.

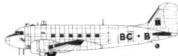

On 25 July, Flight Lieutenant J.A. Watt, the Squadron Senior Traffic Officer, went to Moncton to set up air traffic facilities at No 5 Equipment Depot in preparation for a new flight schedule to be implemented on 1 August. The next day brought more Air Cadets and the officers in charge of the exchange program, Wing Commander W.F.M. Newson and Flight Lieutenant A.G. Dagg from AFHQ. All afternoon, the Equipment Section at Lachine was kept busy issuing the cadets with clothing and equipment.

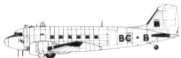

On 27 July, Flight Lieutenant Watt left for No 1 Equipment Depot at Weston, Ontario and Malton Airport in Toronto, by way of RCAF Station Rockcliffe. At Malton, he set up air traffic facilities like the new arrangement at Moncton.

On the morning of 29 July, the first of two RAF York transports arrived at Dorval from the United Kingdom (by way of the Azores and Gander) to deliver twenty-four British air cadets to a large welcoming committee, including Air Vice Marshal E.E. Middleton, Air Officer Commanding, Central Air Command; the Central Air Command Band; an Air Cadet guard of honour; and the press. Another RAF York was held over at Gander with radio trouble. On a more mundane note, the Squadron Signals Officer finally managed to have his précis on the North Star radio system for circulation to squadron members. He had spent weeks entreating the Orderly Room staff to type the document and get it printed.

On 30 July, after another impressive ceremony in which the British cadets made up the guard of honour, the RAF York and two RCAF Dakotas took off for Gander with the Canadian Air Cadets on the first stage of their trip to Britain. Flight Lieutenant L.M. Bishop and Flying Officer W.C. Chrismas captained the RCAF Dakotas as far as Gander, and returned to Dorval with the rest of the British cadets, who had been stranded there by the radio failure in the other RAF York. Meanwhile, three RCAF Dakotas arrived from the west to pick up the British cadets. The next day, they departed for Rockcliffe on the first leg of their Canadian tour.

During the month of July, although most of the aircraft were unserviceable much of the time, No 426 Squadron managed to log 307 flying hours, including eleven hours on air tests, twenty-five hours on training and 271 hours on operations, carrying 224 passengers, 52,343 pounds of freight and 3,456 pounds of mail. On 31 July 1947, squadron strength stood at 209 all ranks, including forty-eight aircrew and five ground officers.[13]

August

On 1 August, a new service flight schedule came into effect. The outbound leg of the Goose Bay flight routed through Moncton and Dartmouth would be designated SF31; the return leg would be designated SF32. The direct flight to Goose Bay — the Goose Bay Express — became SF33 on the outbound leg and SF34 on the return leg. The service flight to Winnipeg by way of Rockcliffe and Toronto became SF35 (outbound) and SF36 (return). Added to the squadron's workload was SF37/38, a regular run to Churchill, Manitoba via Winnipeg.

On 1 August, Flying Officer H.T. Giles took Dakota 664 out on the first SF31 to Goose Bay carrying a mix of passengers, mail and freight. On the morning of 4 August, Flight Lieutenant P.L. Michel departed base on the initial run of SF35/36 to Winnipeg. On 6 August, the first SF37/38 to Churchill left Dorval with Flight Lieutenant J.D. Dickson in Dakota 661.

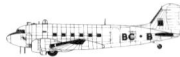

On 6 August, Flight Lieutenant G.L. Sheahan and Flying Officer G. Fisher completed a survey of the living accommodation available to squadron personnel, especially married men, confirming reports that the Montreal-area vacancy rate was at an all-time low, and members of the unit were having trouble housing their families.

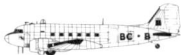

Early in the morning of 10 August, Wing Commander Chapman warned the stand-by crew for a special flight to Washington, D.C. Sir William Strang and the British Coal Mission, travelling in an RAF Lancaster, were on their way to Washington from the Ruhr Valley when their aircraft went unserviceable at Goose Bay. A USAAF Dakota delivered the party to Dorval, where Wing Commander Chapman and Flight Lieutenant I.F. Campbell-Rogers met them. After the Coal Mission cleared Customs and lunched at the TCA terminal, Flight Lieutenant C.E. Snider and his crew flew them to Washington in Dakota 661.

Later that afternoon, Flight Lieutenant J.E. Creeper of No 10 Communications Flight at RCAF Station Dartmouth flew in a seriously injured naval rating attended by an RCN surgeon and nursing officer. With the help of squadron personnel to move the patient and summon an ambulance, the sailor and the navy medical team were rushed to the Victoria General Hospital in downtown Montreal.

On 11 August, four Beechcraft arrived during the afternoon from No 1 Instrument Flight School at Centralia, one of them flown by Flying Officer R.J. Brown, a Thunderbird and a student at the school. The same day, Air Commodore Wray received a letter about the air cadet tour from Air Vice Marshal Middleton:

> Would you please pass on to Wing Commander Chapman my sincere thanks for the efficient manner in which he and his squadron handled the operational requirements of the arrival and also the courtesies which he extended to both groups of Cadets during their stay at Lachine. He should be highly commended for the job which he did.

On the morning of 12 August, the squadron received an RAF Lancaster Aries II that stopped at Dorval during a navigation liaison trip. (As the only permanent RCAF unit at Dorval, No 426 Squadron usually got to handle the servicing and maintenance requirements of visiting military aircraft.) The crew of the RAF Lancaster, captained by Squadron Leader Churcher, included Air Commodore D'Aoth and Group Captain Chilton.

During the next several days, Montreal was very hot and humid, and keeping cool was the preoccupation. Unpleasant as it was for humans, the weather did not affect the aircraft, and the squadron had no trouble maintaining the schedule of service flights.

On 15 August, Flying Officer E.L. Banks on his first scheduled flight as senior captain, had an uneventful trip as far as Dartmouth; however, on the way to Goose Bay, he encountered violent thunderstorms and had to turn back to Dartmouth. The same day, Flight Lieutenant P.L. Michel came in from Goose Bay with several passengers, including a member of the Grenfell Mission who needed medical treatment in Montreal.

On 16 August, Dakota 350 came out of Maintenance with two new engines, and requiring at least ten hours of test flight before it could be used on operations.

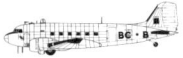

On 18 August, the squadron received authority to spend $3,400 on converting unused barracks into emergency quarters for seventeen families, a project led by the squadron's Chief Administrative Officer, Flight Lieutenant W.G. Pate. To meet the squadron's long-term need for family housing, Flight Lieutenant Pate formed a Board of Officers comprising Flight Lieutenant W. Loynes from Rockcliffe and Flight Lieutenant E.J. Grosz, the squadron's Supply Officer, as well as himself to handle the transfer of four buildings at Lachine from the Department of Public Works to DND. Over time, teams of airmen (relieved of their regular duties by the Squadron Commander) converted these buildings into housing for 150 families. Under the "self-help" principle, those with building and decorating skills, or willing to learn, created quarters for themselves and their families. In similar fashion, the former station hospital was later turned into thirty-eight apartments. The squadron also obtained two Canadian Arsenals Ltd. "staff houses" (barracks for civilian munitions workers) in Nitro, a village near Valleyfield, about twenty miles southwest of Dorval. After conversion and renovation, each staff house provided eighteen apartments.[14]

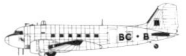

On 17 August, the British air cadets finished their tour of Canada and arrived back at Dorval, where they were met by Mr. G. Ross and Mr. L. Bouchard of the Air Cadet League.

On 18 August, Flight Lieutenant Grosz launched the married quarters project by starting a round-up of construction materials and equipment — very scarce items, after years of wartime production controls.

On 21 August, the Squadron Commander returned from several days of temporary duty in Ottawa and Toronto to preside over the weekly Section Heads' meeting.

In the evening of 21 August, two RAF Transport Command Yorks brought the Canadian air cadets home, to be greeted by Air Vice Marshal Middleton of Central Air Command and Mr. D. Taylor, Mr. G. Ross, Mr. L. Bouchard and Mr. G. Kennedy of the Air Cadet League of Canada. The reception was broadcast on radio station CJAD under the direction of Ron Morrier, and followed by a civic dinner atop Mount Royal given by Mayor Camille Houde. An excellent time was had by all.

The next day, 22 August, No 426 Squadron bade the Canadian air cadets farewell, having organized their airlift across Canada as far as Edmonton in Edmonton-based Dakotas captained by Flight Lieutenant C. Torontow and Flying Officer Charles Buxton. On 23 August, before dawn, the forty-six British cadets left for home in the two RAF Yorks (captained by Flying Officer J. Boyd and Flight Lieutenant T. Sloan) that brought the Canadian cadets home. Air Vice Marshal Middleton and the Air Cadet League representatives waved goodbye, and Ron Morrier was there to cover the departure for CJAD.

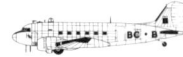

On 25 August, Flight Lieutenant J. Mills was *en route* to Winnipeg in Dakota 350 when engine trouble forced him to land at Sault Ste. Marie. The next day, while preparations to fly an engine to the Sault were under way, the squadron learned that an aircraft from No 7 Photographic Wing at Rockcliffe could take it. At Lachine, ground was broken for gas tanks — a new gas station! People with cars could hardly wait.

On 26 August, an important day for the unit, Squadron Leader C.R. Knowles went to the Canadair plant at Cartierville with Squadron Leader J.C. McCarthy of the Experimental and Proving Establishment to test-fly and conduct the acceptance check on NS17501, which first flew on 14 July. The aircraft performed as expected, and Flight Lieutenant Grosz went to Canadair on 27 August to check the equipment in the North Star for Maintenance Command in Ottawa. Flying Officer W.H. Smith from Engineering Section was a passenger on another test flight in the North Star so he could report on the aircraft's instruments and performance.

On 28 August, Squadron Leader McCarthy accepted North Star 17502 (which flew for the first time on 10 July) and North Star 17501 as airworthy, subject to successful completion of equipment checks. The squadron could now count the days to delivery of their new aircraft.[15]

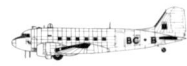

On 29 August, Flight Lieutenant J.G. Mills went to Sault Ste. Marie to air-test Dakota 350 after its engine change and give it the usual flying check required before it could be certified serviceable for operations. He returned to Dorval that evening.

During the month of August, No 426 Squadron logged 383 flying hours, including eleven training hours, fifteen hours on test flights, and 357 operational hours.[16]

September

On 3 September, Wing Commander Chapman inspected the squadron's buildings at Lachine and received many suggestions for improvements. At the Section Heads' meeting the following day, he discussed many of these suggestions, along with plans to decorate the Drill Hall.

On 5 September, ten families moved into the new married quarters created in the Canadian Arsenals Ltd staff houses at Nitro — total elapsed time less than three weeks. At Lachine, however, progress on the housing front was glacial.

The officers made plans for a party on 4 October, the same evening the airmen had arranged to hold a dance at the Airmen's Canteen.

With good weather and serviceable aircraft, No 426 Squadron had no trouble making the scheduled service flights in September. On 12 September, a milestone in squadron history, Squadron Leader C.R. Knowles and Flying Officers H.T. Giles and W.H. Smith ferried NS17501 the eight miles between the Canadair plant at Cartierville and Dorval. The squadron lacked handling equipment for the North Star, however, so a full flying program was still in the future. Until the equipment could be obtained, the new aircraft was used for ground training and familiarization for both aircrew and ground staff. On 25 September, the squadron's second North Star arrived from the factory with Squadron Leader C.R. Knowles, Flight Lieutenant J.G. Mills, Flight Lieutenant E.A. Alliston and Flying Officer W.H. Smith aboard.

Another technical advance made during September was the erection at Lachine of three seventy-foot aerial masts and a transmitter shack for a CT27 radio. All the squadron's officers, especially the radio navigators and wireless operators, invested much time and effort in this project.

On 20 September, Flight Lieutenant S.F. Cowan announced that the squadron's excellent bowling alleys (now in Drill Hall No 2) and badminton courts were open Monday to Friday until 2130 hours. About this time, Flying Officer R.J. Brown returned to the squadron from the Instrument Flying Course at Centralia.

During the month of September, No 426 Squadron logged 375 flying hours, including thirty-two hours in training and air tests, and 343 operational hours carrying 823 passengers, 166,733 pounds of freight and 5,526 pounds of mail.[17]

October

On 9 July 1947, the Minister of Defence, the Honourable Brooke Claxton tabled his departmental estimates in the House of Commons with the following statement (quoted in part):

> On June 17, 1947, P.C. 2372 was adopted providing that the members of the armed forces shall cease to be on active service as at September 30, 1947. At that time, the formal change from a war footing to a peace footing for the armed services will be related to the inauguration of a campaign to obtain recruits for the active and reserve forces.[18]

October, therefore, was Thunderbird Squadron's first month formally at peace, but it was still busy for the Dakota fleet. Most scheduled flights took off on time, but progress on the North Star was painfully slow. Part of the reason was that AFHQ had lent the first six production aircraft (destined for No 426 Squadron) to Trans-Canada Airlines, which was developing its North Atlantic route. Getting the North Star operational as a civil airliner was a high political and commercial priority at the time, so the early production and support effort was channelled to TCA.

On 2 October, the first Thunderbird aircraft landed at The Pas, Manitoba — SF37 en route from Winnipeg to Churchill. On 4 October, the officers held their first formal dance of the fall season, a well-organized and very successful affair. On 8 October, a successful stag party was held at the Officers' Mess to present gifts to the recently married Flying Officer J. Galipeau and the soon-to-be-married Flying Officer K.A. McCoy. On 10 October, a helicopter, the first most of the Thunderbird aircrew had ever seen, dropped in at Dorval on its way from Trenton to Dartmouth, where it was to be employed in search and rescue.

On 15 October, the Canada Savings Bond drive opened, with Flying Officer R.J. Brown in charge of the squadron sales effort. The same day, the squadron began a series of lectures for North Star maintenance personnel, and Squadron Leader C.R. Knowles flew one of the North Star aircraft to Trenton for temporary storage, with an extra crew aboard for the experience. On 16 October, Squadron Leader Knowles and another extra crew repeated the Trenton trip to deliver the squadron's other North Star to storage.

On 19 October, Squadron Leader M.W. Williams officiated at church services and a group christening at the station chapel. The Officers' Mess hosted a reception for the families of the newly baptized.

On 20 October, No 426 Squadron again sent out two Dakotas to transport the RCAF Central Band, picking them up in Toronto and delivering them to Goose Bay. Squadron Leader E.E. Parks, Squadron Leader E.C. Miller and Flight Lieutenant W. Loynes arrived from No 9 Group Headquarters at Rockcliffe on an inspection tour, and managed to solve many of the squadron's administrative and operational problems before they moved on to their next stop. On

22 October, the RCAF and Shell Oil signed a new fuel contract for the Goose Bay run; gas and oil would be available at Moncton, and the service flights would not have to go to Dartmouth to refuel any more.

On 26 October, the Thunderbirds and RCAF Auxiliary units based at St-Hubert put on a formation flying display scheduled to coincide with a huge tri-service recruiting parade in downtown Montreal. The next day, Wing Commander P.J. Grant, the Commanding Officer of No 435 Transport Squadron, made a visit, and used the occasion to renew his acquaintance with former members of his squadron. On 30 October, the service flight from Goose Bay brought out a meteorologist based at Resolution Island who had been badly mauled by a polar bear. The next day, Flying Officer R.J. Brown made his first trip as captain on the service flight to Goose Bay. The month ended with a successful station dance at Lachine featuring a Halloween motif.

During the month of October, No 426 Squadron logged 507 flying hours, including eleven hours on testing, seventy-one hours on training, and 423 hours on operations, carrying 577 passengers, 125,831 pounds of freight and 5,742 pounds of mail. On 31 October 1947, squadron strength stood at 258 all ranks, including forty-one officers, 186 airmen and thirty-one civilians.[19]

November

The squadron had another busy month in November. Despite some maintenance problems and weather delays, the squadron was able to maintain its operational schedule. More important, it also finally managed to train on the new North Stars. The immediate objective was to have three crews trained up to day-solo standard by the end of the year.

On 1 November, the focus — apart from despatching service flights — was the beginning of the renovation of the Operations Room at Dorval. Plans called for a counter-type cupboard unit made in six sections designed to be bolted together for use and taken apart when the squadron had to move. In preparation for briefings, two walls of the operations room were to be panelled with dismountable plywood map boards. As usual, all structural and finishing carpentry would be done by members of the squadron — in this case, aircrew officers who were not actually flying. The guiding genius behind the project was Flight Lieutenant Johnson.

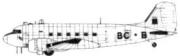

On 4 November, Wing Commander Chapman accepted recommendations from several committees and set aside Wednesday evenings as "guest nights" at the Drill Hall, where squadron personnel could bring their friends to bowl and play badminton and other sports. On 5 November, the Signals Officer, Flight Lieutenant D.G. Forrest, reported that enough construction material had been found to start making work benches and storage for wireless equipment in the Signals Training Room. The next day, work on the Operations Room started with hammers clattering in a cloud of sawdust.

On 8 November, it was announced that pilots from other units would come to No 426 Squadron for week-long sessions of Link training, formalizing an established ad hoc practice. On the sports front, a squadron bowling league formed on 10 November, with teams entered from all sections. Each team would bowl one night a week, and league play would dominate the bowling alley four nights a week.

On 11 November, Remembrance Day, the squadron maintained only a skeleton staff, although Flight Lieutenant C.F. Sanford took out the scheduled run to Goose Bay. Two flights of Thunderbird airmen were in downtown Montreal taking part in the tri-service parade that formed up in Dominion Square, and Flight Lieutenant W.J. Johnston was assigned to fly over the parade in a Dakota from which poppies were dropped. He made an excellent job of swooping low between the Sun Life Building and the Windsor Hotel, but a strong crosswind blew some of the poppies away from the target zone.

On 13 November, the squadron maintenance staff was finally able to get NS17502 serviceable, and flying training commenced. Pilots limited themselves to circuits and bumps while wireless operators tried out the new equipment with the squadron's practice frequency. Both the pilots and wireless operators liked operating the aircraft and its equipment, but thought that passengers would find it uncomfortably noisy, especially in the middle of the fuselage opposite the engines. The following day, Dakota 664 came in for a major inspection, and NS17501 and NS17504 were still unserviceable, awaiting acceptance checks. On 15 November, more flying training on the North Star was done, with Flying Officer H.T. Giles in charge of the flying program and Squadron Leader C.R. Knowles giving the crews their final solo check.

On 17 November, NS17502 went unserviceable with burnt-out brakes, bringing flying training to a halt. In the Signals Training Room, Masonite work benches now circled the room, but the squadron did not have enough North Star wireless equipment to install it in the training facility. Only one demonstration bench was fitted out with equipment: a "long range radar fixing aid" (i.e., Loran) trainer and a Rebecca (radar homing aid) installation. The goal was to stock the room with a complete set of North Star radio and radar equipment.

On 19 November, the Squadron Sports Officer, Flight Lieutenant Cowan, captained SF33 to Goose Bay and broke his ankle playing volleyball during his layover. On 20 November, Flight Lieutenant P.L. Michel took SF37 from Winnipeg to Churchill with Wing Commander Chapman aboard. Flight Lieutenant J.D. Dickson and navigator Flying Officer R.C.M. Bayliss went with them as far as Winnipeg to fly a No 412 Squadron Dakota on a northern tour, to Churchill, Baker Lake and Coral Harbour. The next day, Dickson and Wing Commander Chapman made the return run to Baker Lake; Michel was delayed at Churchill for eight hours by bad weather before he could leave for Winnipeg. On 22 November, Dickson made the return run to Coral Harbour and then left for Winnipeg on the first leg home, arriving the following day.

On 24 November, NS17504 was declared serviceable after an acceptance check, and plans were made to resume flight training. Flying Officer A.G. Brunet arrived from No 412 Squadron for a week of Link training. The next day, NS17504 was grounded again — temporarily — with an unserviceable actuator strut; the repairs were completed and flying training resumed on 26 November. Bad weather halted flying training again on 28 November, and when it resumed the next morning NS17504 went unserviceable again with throttle cables out of alignment. The same day, two of the squadron's Dakotas were pulled in for inspections.

With the aircraft on the ground so much, the aircrew were available to volunteer for construction work. Considerable progress was made in the Operations Room and the Signals Training Rooms.

During the month of November, No 426 Squadron logged 396 flying hours, including five hours on air tests, thirty-five hours on training and 356 hours on operations, carrying 383 passengers, 111,546 pounds of freight and 5,833 pounds of mail. On 30 November 1947, squadron strength stood at 241 all ranks, including forty-two officers, 193 other ranks and thirty-six civilians.[20]

December

December was a typically busy month for the squadron. The service flights to Goose Bay, Winnipeg and Churchill went out and came home despite occasional delays caused by marginal weather and aircraft serviceability problems. At Dorval, as the ground crews gained experience on the North Star, the squadron managed flying training on sixteen days during the month.

At Lachine, the repainting of the Officers' Mess began on 15 December and, on 17 December, Flight Lieutenant J.G. Mills received the Croix de Guerre for distinguished service in co-operation with the French armed forces. The following day, the Group Commander, Air Commodore L.E. Wray, arrived to make his annual inspection. At the parade, held in No 6 Hangar at Dorval, Air Commodore Wray presented the Air Force Cross to Flying Officer E.A. Alliston, a certificate stating that he had been Mentioned in Despatches to Flight Lieutenant G.L. Sheahan, and the British Empire Medal to Corporal Widger. After the parade, Wing Commander Chapman and Squadron Leader Knowles proudly escorted Air Commodore Wray through the squadron's sections and facilities; the highlight of the tour was the new Operations Room. That evening, the Group Commander and his party were entertained at the Officers' Mess.

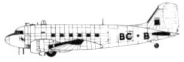

Operations continued even through the AOC's inspection. Flying Officer J.A. Jolicoeur headed out for Goose Bay with the previous day's service flight, which had been delayed by weather, and Flying Officer H.T. Giles took out that day's scheduled flight to the same destination. Meanwhile, Flying Officer R.J. Brown was in Goose Bay flight testing Dakota 659 after an engine change. On 19 December, Flight Lieutenant J.D. Dickson was an hour out of Churchill when he lost an engine and had to turn back. The next day, Flight Lieutenant J.G. Mills set out for Churchill with a new engine for Dickson but had to return to Dorval with engine trouble of his own. He finally got away on the morning of 21 December, and arrived at Churchill nine and a half hours later.

Back at base, Christmas plans were in full swing, and a large New Year's Eve party was in the works. Flight Lieutenant Dickson and Flight Lieutenant Mills returned from Churchill on 23 December, with compliments for the Churchill maintenance crew that performed a speedy engine change in most unpleasant working conditions.

The squadron's second Christmas Day in Canada and first in Montreal dawned bright and clear with no flying scheduled. After church services, the officers entertained the senior NCOs in the Officers' Mess at 1100 hours, and later, in keeping with Air Force tradition, served Christmas dinner in the Airmen's Mess.

On Boxing Day, 26 December, it was back to work with two scheduled runs to Goose Bay. For the rest of the month, the squadron concentrated on maintaining the flight schedule and getting aircrew checked out on the North Star.

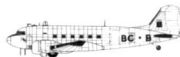

During the month of December, No 426 Squadron logged 539 flying hours, including 456 hours on operations and eighty-three hours on other activities, mostly devoted to training on the North Star. On 31 December 1947, squadron strength stood at 291 all ranks, including fifty officers, 200 airmen and thirty-eight civilians.[21]

PHOTO 18
The Canadian Arsenals Ltd. "staff houses" converted to emergency married quarters; Nitro, Quebec, August 1947. (D. Shade Collection)

Part IV

North Stars

Chapter 6

Dorval, 1948

The North Star had its origins in the early days of Trans-Canada Airlines. Established in 1937 as a Crown corporation, TCA dominated the Canadian civil aviation scene by 1940, when its planning team drew up specifications for a post-war airliner. Understanding that what you don't ask for, you don't get, TCA's planners started with a wish list comprising the best features of the era's most advanced commercial aircraft: the Douglas DC-4, the Boeing Stratoliner and the Curtiss CW-20. Throughout the war, while the Allied forces flew huge numbers of aircraft of continuously improving quality for longer and longer distances, TCA regularly updated its airliner specifications to include the most successful innovations.[1]

TCA was not Canada's only Crown-supported air-transport enterprise. The constant wartime requirement for delivery to Britain of new aircraft built in North America led to the creation on 20 July 1941 of RAF Ferry Command, based at Dorval and headed by Air Chief Marshal Sir Frederick Bowhill. On the civil side, the Canadian federal Minister of Munitions and Supply, Clarence Decatur Howe, recommended to the Cabinet War Committee on 21 October 1942 that the federal government should operate a trans-Atlantic air transport service for passengers and mail.

Howe hoped to start the operation with four-engine transport aircraft obtained from the United States[2] but, when the Americans had none to offer, he turned to the British. In August 1942, when ferry pilot Captain Clyde Pangborn of the Air Transport Auxiliary brought Lancaster R5727 (a Mk III belonging to Bomber Command) to Canada for demonstration purposes, Howe arranged to keep it in Canada so TCA pilots could obtain first-hand experience operating four-engine aircraft. With its military equipment removed by Victory Aviation of Toronto, Lancaster R5727 started moving freight to Goose Bay in March 1943. In May 1943, with Howe aboard, the Lancaster returned to Britain so AVRO could fit it with new engines, long-range fuel tanks and a pointed plywood nose, thus extending its range to 4,000 miles. With these modifications, Lancaster R5727 became TCA-100, registered as CF-CSM.[3]

On 16 June 1943, Howe rose in the House of Commons to announce the launch of the Canadian Government Trans-Atlantic Air Service (soon better known as Bomber Mail), a temporary, non-commercial service operated by TCA to transport armed forces and government mail and official passengers to and from Britain. To help the CGTAS get off the ground, Ferry Command offered training for TCA pilots, and the RCAF provided navigators. On 22 July 1943, TCA-100 made the inaugural flight from Dorval to Prestwick with a few passengers and several thousand pounds of mail. In the fall of 1943, the service acquired two transport-type Lancaster Xs built by Victory Aircraft in Toronto and, during the last year of the war, four more aircraft.

The CGTAS had a military counterpart: No 168 (Heavy) Transport Squadron of the RCAF, formed in October 1943 and operational by the end of that year. No 168 Squadron, which was based at Rockcliffe, used modified Flying Fortresses and Liberators to cross the Atlantic, and Dakotas in Europe.[4]

During 1943, a TCA team seeking aircraft designs for post-war use made several visits to Boeing, Consolidated, Douglas and Lockheed plants in the United States. The TCA team discovered that the big American manufacturers had no large transport aircraft on the drawing boards that were suited to the company's needs and likely to be available soon. Of the aircraft types studied (including the York, built by AVRO of Britain), only the Douglas DC-4 (TCA did not know that Douglas was developing the larger DC-6) and the Lockheed Constellation qualified for serious consideration. In the end, TCA chose the DC-4 as the base model for its new airliner; the company's experience with Lockheed aircraft suggested that, if they based their design on the Constellation, eliminating minor maintenance deficiencies would take a long time.[5]

In the fall of 1944, the Canadian government and Douglas Aircraft entered into a licence agreement under which Douglas would furnish Canada with the plans for the DC-4 (in service) and the DC-6 (in development). Douglas would also assist in the design, development and construction, in Canada, of an aircraft based on the DC-4 and the DC-6 and fitted with Rolls-Royce engines. (The Rolls-Royce Company co-operated fully in this arrangement.)[6]

Design work on the DC-4 began at Douglas Aircraft in February 1936, and the prototype flew for the first time on 7 June 1938. After selling this aircraft to Japan, Douglas started working on a second model. The new version (called the DC-4A) made its maiden flight on 14 February 1942 and, as the United States had just entered the war, production was diverted to the USAAF. Douglas quickly modified the aircraft to meet military requirements, increased its fuel capacity and redesignated it as the C-54; it entered service with the USAAF in June 1942 and, by the end of the war, 1,163 C-54s had been built in several series. At the same time, Douglas continued work on the civilian version, the DC-4-1009, of which seventy-nine were built.[7]

C.D. Howe was in the habit of having people of his choice appointed to key managerial positions in companies with major defence contracts. When the time came to develop the Canadian aircraft industry, he had Benjamin Franklin brought in at Canadian Vickers to manage production there. One of Franklin's chief assistants was Ralph G. Stopps, who had been with the Vickers aircraft division since 1936; by 1942, Stopps was production manager of Vickers' Montreal plant, which was then building the Consolidated PBY patrol bomber. In June 1942, Franklin sent Stopps to supervise the construction of Vickers' new factory at Cartierville and to stay on there as plant engineer. When the Cartierville facility opened, Vickers phased out PBY production in Montreal, and moved PBY flight-testing from St-Hubert to Cartierville.[8]

As well as aircraft, Canadian Vickers was building ships, not only for Allied navies but also for private shipping companies. The shipbuilding program involved heavy financial commitments and, important as the aircraft were, the ships were crucial to the convoy systems that supplied

Britain and the Allied forces. Toward the end of 1944, the federal government asked Vickers to give up its managerial responsibilities at Cartierville and increase its focus on shipbuilding. At the same time, the Department of Munitions and Supply entered into a agreement with a group headed by Benjamin Franklin, which had formed a private management company called Canadair Limited to operate the Cartierville plant, on a management-fee basis, as agents of the Crown.[9]

About this time, Franklin and his colleagues at Canadair became aware of the government's plan to build a large transport aircraft for post-war commercial use as well as for immediate military use. Once the Air Ministry approved the release of Cartierville from war production, Canadair was able to secure the contract to build this aircraft.

With the contract signed, Canadair sent R.G. Stopps to the Douglas plant in Santa Monica to study the DC-4 production line. While there, Stopps learned that Douglas was about to dispose of most of its C-47 and DC-4 assets, including a plant in Oklahoma City, the C-54 plant at Parkridge, Illinois, and the C-47 wing-production facilities at the Pullman sleeper-car factory in Chicago. On his return to Montreal, Stopps met with Howe and Franklin to tell them that Douglas assets worth more than US$120 million could be acquired at very low cost; he was immediately designated Canadair's representative and sent back to the United States to buy what he could. He immediately set about bidding on the basis of US$200 a ton for aircraft parts and US$40 a ton for tools, and eventually purchased almost everything on offer, including nearly-completed C-47s and C-54s. The Parkridge and Pullman plants alone yielded about 600 carloads of material, including more than sixty C-54 fuselages; Douglas also sold the original C-47/DC-3 engineering drawings. In a separate acquisition, more than 200 surplus C-47s were purchased in the United States and Britain. The aircraft purchase positioned Canadair to prepare early for post-war operations by launching a major program to convert them to commercial use. The C-47 conversion program alone allowed Canadair to manufacture and sell C-47 parts for more than twenty years.[10]

In 1944, work accelerated on the redesign of the C-54/DC-4 into a new airliner, dubbed the DC-4M (M for Merlin). As well as the Canadair plant at Cartierville, which spent most of 1945 tooling up for production, the project involved the TCA engineering facilities in Winnipeg and Dorval. Staff at Winnipeg built a wooden mock-up of the cabin and cockpit that was used to generate ideas for the production model. The project was a major undertaking for TCA, Canadair, Douglas and Rolls-Royce, involving constant, very close liaison among all the principals to ensure that TCA ended up with an aircraft engineered to the airline's requirements that also met the well-known Douglas standards. Throughout the development process, the RCAF—mindful of its post-war plans for a heavy transport—stayed in close touch with the project.[11]

In responding to questions in the House of Commons on 20 March 1947, C.D. Howe stated that, early in 1944, it was apparent that Vickers would not receive enough orders for PBY-type aircraft to operate the Cartierville plant; it was imperative to make plans either to close it, and lay off some 8,000 skilled workers, or to build another type of aeroplane. He went on to say that the RCAF fighter plane requirement was well in hand, but both the RCAF and Trans-Canada Airlines had substantial estimated requirements for long-range transport aircraft—stated to be at least fifty for the RCAF and at least twenty-five for TCA—that were still under consideration. Later in his statement, Howe mentioned that, after extensive negotiations, the Electric Boat

Company of New London, Connecticut, acquired most of the stock of Canadair Limited and had entered into an agreement with the Canadian government, effective 14 September 1946, covering the Crown facilities and contracts at Cartierville. One of the agreement's most important clauses stated that Canadair would sell thirty-four unpressurized aircraft to the government for the RCAF, and twenty pressurized aircraft to TCA. Howe concluded his remarks by saying that, after V-J Day, the RCAF requirement was cut to twenty-four aircraft, and the TCA requirement was cut to twenty.[12]

The first new Canadair airliner left the assembly line in June 1946, less than two years after the program began. Its original civil registration was CF-TEN-X, to be changed to 17525 in 1950, when the RCAF acquired it. The first aircraft off the production line were originally destined for the RCAF, as they were the unpressurized C-54 GMs and DC-4Ms fabricated largely from the components Canadair had bought from Douglas. However, TCA's need was so urgent that the RCAF lent the company six of these unpressurized aircraft for use on the North Atlantic run. By mid-July, following a series of ground tests and taxi trails, the airliner was ready for its maiden flight.[13]

Before the new aircraft could take flight, however, it had to have a name. According to Ron Baker of TCA, a few people (including Jim Bain, head of the DC-4M project, who was on secondment from TCA to Canadair; project secretary Joan Paul; Frank Rousseau of TCA, and TCA engineer Clayton H. Glenn) were discussing names as they waited around the flight-test hangar at Cartierville. Baker, who was interested in celestial navigation, came up with Polaris, and someone else eventually said, "Let's call it the 'North Star.'" The name stuck.[14]

The first flight of the prototype North Star took place during the late afternoon of 15 July 1946, after CF-TEN-X had been on the runway at Cartierville doing high-speed taxi trials for several days. When Canadair pilot Al Lilly suggested to Robert R. Brush, chief test pilot from Douglas in Santa Monica, that it was as good a time as any to fly the North Star, the decision was made to go, and the North Star was away on its first flight, which lasted twenty-five minutes, with engineers W.L. Harris and Clayton Glenn aboard. Two days later, the North Star was back in the air and, on 20 July, it was ceremonially unveiled at Cartierville.[15]

The North Star delivered to No 426 Squadron was a low-wing monoplane with full-cantilever wing and tail surfaces, semi-monocoupe fuselage and fully retractable tricycle landing gear. It could be configured to carry passengers, bulk cargo or medical patients on litters. Its four engines were 1,760-horsepower, 12-cylinder, liquid cooled, V-type 620/622 Rolls-Royce Merlins, fitted with two-stage, two speed superchargers and Hamilton Standard Hydromatic three-bladed, quick-feathering propellers.

The North Star was 93 feet, 5 inches long (94 feet, 9 1/2 inches counting the nose radar) and 27 feet 6 inches high, with a wingspan of 117 feet, 6 inches. Its operating empty weight was 44,000 pounds, its maximum gross take-off weight was 76,500 pounds, and its maximum landing weight was 67,000 pounds The aircraft carried 2,950 imperial gallons (21,240 pounds) of fuel and 101.2 imperial gallons of oil. Its normal cruising speed was 230 miles per hour, its service ceiling was 36,000 feet, and its maximum range was 3,060 miles.

The main cabin had cargo-stowage fittings, troop benches for forty-five (normal load) to fifty-five (maximum load) passengers, and litter supports for thirty-two patients. Between the cabin and the two cargo compartments in the belly of the fuselage, the aircraft had a freight load-limit 18,970 pounds The flight and crew compartments included accommodations for the basic crew—pilot, co-pilot, navigator, radio operator, flight engineer and "air traffic assistant" (better known as the loadmaster)—plus four seats and an upper bunk for the extra crew members required for very long flights.[16]

January

No 426 Squadron opened the New Year on a social note. In the morning, the senior NCOs entertained the officers at the Sergeants' Mess; at noon, the officers and senior NCOs carved and served dinner to the airmen; and, after dinner, the officers returned to their own mess, which was open to members of all the other messes in the Montreal area.

On 3 January, Flight Lieutenant R.J. Brown captained a special flight to transport oxygen to Goose Bay for Glenda Roberts, who was critically ill with pneumonia; three days later, Flying Officer E.L. Banks made another special flight to Goose Bay with oxygen for Miss Roberts, plus the squadron medical officer, Squadron Leader W.L. Orr, and an oxygen technician from the military hospital at Ste-Anne-de-Bellevue, as well as an iron lung that they did not have to use.

The RCAF was planning a Montreal-area recruiting drive to run between 5 January and 11 January, and tasked No 426 Squadron and RCAF Station St-Hubert to contribute air displays and a Guard of Honour. On the first two days of the drive, a Thunderbird flight demonstrated formation flying in two North Stars and three Dakotas and, on 8 January, Flying Officer S.E.M. Milliken from the Experimental and Proving Establishment at RCAF Station Rockcliffe caused quite a stir by bringing a helicopter to Montreal and putting on a series of flying demonstrations. The Thunderbirds also provided the Guard of Honour, under the command of Flight Lieutenant J.G. Mills, that appeared at the Craig Street Armoury to be inspected by Air Vice Marshal C.M. McEwen, who had commanded No 6 (RCAF) Group during the war. The display flights over Montreal halted on 9 January because of bad weather, but resumed on 10 January, while Flying Officer Milliken dropped in on parks and playgrounds around the city to demonstrate the marvellous versatility of his helicopter. On 11 January, the last day of the drive, a formation of squadron Dakotas were over Montreal to rendezvous with Harvards from No 401 (Fighter) Squadron led by Squadron Leader Bud Malloy, and more appearances by Flying Officer Milliken with the helicopter.

On 14 January, No 9 Group Headquarters advised No 426 Squadron that the contract to convert the station hospital building at Lachine to married quarters would be let before the end of the month—for many married personnel, the first sign that their very long wait might be coming to an end. The same day, the squadron received a visit from Wing Commander W.R. Franks from the Institute of Aviation Medicine in Toronto, the leader of the RCAF–University of Toronto team that, during the war, built a "human centrifuge"—a device for testing potential aviators for susceptibility to G force—and developed the first effective anti-G flying suit.[17] In the evening, the

squadron held a very successful badminton tournament in the Drill Hall, organized by Flight Lieutenant Stu Cowan and hosting members of the Dominion Bridge club.

On 16 January, the Officers' Mess held an evening party to say goodbye to several squadron stalwarts: Flying Officer W.J. Clough, who was leaving the RCAF to join TCA; Flying Officer T.S. Forbes, who was posted to the Central Flying School at RCAF Station Trenton, Ontario; and Flight Lieutenant P.W. Holloway, who was posted to the staff at Air Force Headquarters in Ottawa. Squadron Leader C.R. Knowles, the President of the Mess Committee, made the presentations and wished the departing members every success in their new endeavours.

On 19 January, No 412 Squadron at RCAF Station Rockcliffe took over the western service flights to give the Thunderbirds time to train on the new North Star.

On 20 January, No 426 Squadron threw a surprise party for Flight Lieutenant E.A. Alliston and his wife, who were celebrating their eighth wedding anniversary.

On 21 January, Flight Lieutenant P.L. Michel diverted to Québec City on the way home from Goose Bay to transfer a stretcher patient— Mrs. Forsythe, the wife of a doctor at the Grenfell Mission in Labrador—to the Jeffrey Hale Memorial Hospital.

On 23 January, with four crews assigned full-time to train on the North Star, the squadron conversion program produced its first graduates: Flight Lieutenant J.D. Dickson, and Flight Lieutenant R.J. Brown. On the same day, the RCAF accepted delivery of its first jet aircraft: the DH-100 Vampire Mk I, a fighter built by De Havilland.

On 26 January, several of the squadron's pilots began writing examinations for the "green ticket"—the instrument rating that permitted pilots to fly within prescribed limits. Flight checks would follow.

On 27 January, the Thunderbirds completed yet another "quality of life" project at Dorval—this one managed by Flight Lieutenant R.J. Brown and Corporal Landreville—with the opening of an attractively furnished airmen's lunchroom in No 6 Hangar.

Wing Commander Jeffs of the RAF detachment in Washington picked 28 January, one of the winter's coldest days, to visit the squadron to discuss installing a liquid oxygen system in the North Star. His very interesting presentation to the Thunderbird aircrew was followed by a lively question and answer period.

Flight Lieutenant J.G. Mills received a posting overseas much to his surprise. Flying Officer J. Goldsmith was transferred to No 413 (Photo) Squadron in Rockcliffe. Squadron Leader C.H. Mussells paid the unit a visit from AFHQ. He became the unit commander the following year.

During January, No 426 Squadron's five Dakotas logged 363 operational flying hours on fifty-three service flights and six special flights; the four North Stars logged ninety-two training flying hours over seventeen days. A further thirty-eight hours were spent on other flying activities, mostly associated with the recruiting drive. On 31 January 1948, squadron strength stood at 308 all ranks, with fifty officers (including an exchange officer from the USAF), 218 airmen and forty civilians.[18]

February

On 4 February, Central Air Command sent two Dakotas to help No 426 Squadron haul freight from St-Hubert to Goose Bay. On 6 February, the North Star training program had

Flight Lieutenant J.G. Mills and Flying Officer H.T. Giles practising three-engine takeoffs with the Squadron Commander aboard. On 8 February, word came in from St. Moritz, Switzerland that the RCAF hockey team, the Flyers, had won the gold medal at the Winter Olympic Games, signifying the world championship of amateur ice hockey. That evening, the Officers' Mess attained its highest attendance at Sunday dinner since opening day.[19]

On 11 February, Flight Lieutenant J.G. Mills and Flight Lieutenant W.J. Johnston went to Canadair at Cartierville and collected North Star 17510, which they ferried to Dorval. At the same time, Flight Lieutenant E.A. Alliston, Flight Lieutenant C.E. Snider and Flying Officer H.T. Giles were flying a North Star in an air display at RCAF Station Rockcliffe. The Squadron Commander had gone with them to attend a meeting at No 9 Group Headquarters. On 13 February, the Squadron Commander met with his Section Heads to discuss taskings; once the Thunderbirds were fully proficient on the North Star, the RCAF would have a global airlift capability, and they could expect significant operational consequences. Later in the day, Air Commodore Wray and a party from No 9 Group arrived for a staff visit. That evening, the airmen held one of their successful bi-monthly dances. The next evening, the Officers' Mess held a well attended St. Valentine's party and dance.

On 17 February Wing Commander Chapman and Flight Lieutenant J.G. Mills went to Cartierville to accept NS17511 from Canadair. On 18 February, after the Commanding Officer's parade, two sales representatives from Blue Cross gave the squadron a presentation on the company's hospital insurance plan. Later the same day, a team arrived from USAF Tactical Air Command Headquarters at Langley Field, Virginia to meet with the Squadron Commander and his staff.

On 20 February, the section heads completed R211s (RCAF annual performance evaluation form) on all the squadron's senior NCOs, and, on 24 February, all the Flying Officers in the squadron began promotion examinations—three days of them—while the Flight Lieutenants did their work.

On 26 February, the squadron received a visit from Air Commodore Wray, who used the occasion to outline No 9 Group's plans for expanding RCAF transport operations. For the rest of the month, on top of its regular schedule of service flights, the squadron prepared to conduct its first long-range training flight—to Edmonton, about eight flying hours away.

During February, No 426 Squadron's five Dakotas earned their keep, flying a total of 378 hours, including 359 operational hours on sixty-nine service flights and special flights, twelve hours on training flights, and seven hours on test flights. Training on the North Stars was carried out on twenty-four days of the month, and the seven North Stars available to the squadron flew a total of 121 hours on a variety of training exercises and three hours on test flights.[20]

March

March was to be the last month in which No 426 Squadron would fly the Dakota as its principal aircraft but, although it was being phased out of operations, the squadron's Dakotas made a total of fifty-four service flights and special flights, comprising 293 operational flying hours, during the month.

On 1 March, a North Star captained by Flying Officer H.T. Giles left Dorval on the first long-range training flight to Edmonton. As well as the training crew, the aircraft carried the Squadron Equipment Officer, Flight Lieutenant E.J. Grosz; Squadron Leader W.L. Orr of the Institute of Aviation Medicine in Toronto, who joined the flight to monitor noise levels in the aircraft; Flight Lieutenant N. Bray from E&PE Rockcliffe; and Flight Lieutenant J.A. Watt from No 901 ATHU Rockcliffe. The flight was carried out at 10,000 feet and, eight and a half hours after departure, the aircraft arrived at Edmonton without incident.

On 2 March, Flight Lieutenant Frank Sanford, one of the squadron originals, married Miss Jean Lafurgey at Grace United Church, with Squadron Leader M.W. Williams officiating. After the reception at the Officers' Mess, the newlyweds left by air for a honeymoon in Bermuda.

On 3 March, Flying Officer H.T. Giles and his crew brought their North Star home from Edmonton. Although the aircraft lost an engine near Winnipeg and completed the flight on three engines, the return trip took only six and a half hours.

On 15 March, a second Edmonton flight departed with Wing Commander Chapman on board and Flight Lieutenant W.J. Johnston in command. This trip was completed in eight and a half hours. On the same day, Air Marshal W.A. Curtis, the Chief of the Air Staff, arrived at Dorval from Air Force Headquarters; he and his party took a guided tour of the squadron's aircraft and facilities at Dorval. That evening, Air Marshal Curtis was the guest speaker at the United Services Institute in Montreal.

The next day, Squadron Leader the Reverend Father W.H. Dunphy, the Roman Catholic chaplain at Central Air Command in Trenton, arrived to spend a few days at Lachine with Father Trottier, the squadron's part-time Roman Catholic padre.

On 18 March, Flight Lieutenant Johnston returned to base from Edmonton via Rockcliffe, making the trip in seven hours and fifty minutes.

On 19 March, airframe mechanic Aircraftsman 1st Class Emery of No 426 Squadron received the Bronze Medal as an honour student on No 6 Course at Camp Borden. The same day, the married quarters at Lachine were close enough to completion for the Squadron Commander to address the issue of deciding how houses were to be allocated: eligibility criteria would be developed and applied by the Unit Housing Committee, which comprised members of all ranks and representating all sections of the squadron.

On Sunday, 21 March, Wing Commander Chapman took a prominent place on the reviewing stand for the St. Patrick's Day parade in downtown Montreal. Despite the rain, three Thunderbird Dakotas did a fly-past.

On 22 March, Flight Lieutenant A.L. Michel captained a third long-range training flight, with Squadron Leader J.T. McCutcheon aboard; after nine hours and fifty-five minutes in the air, battling headwinds most of the way, the North Star arrived at Edmonton.

On 23 March, Wing Commander Chapman worked with the squadron's Chief Technical Officer on the allocation of married quarters, narratives for the Officers' Promotion Board, and the R211s on the squadron's Flight Lieutenants. The same day, two Link trainers were delivered to Dorval, where they were installed in the Navigation Officer's office—displacing the occupant, Flight Lieutenant J.H.C. Boby.

For the rest of the month, except for 24 March, when Flight Lieutenant J.D. Dixon lost an engine shortly after departing base for Goose Bay, the Thunderbirds occupied their time getting out the service flights and training on the North Stars.

During March, No 426 Squadron logged 546 flying hours, including 236 hours of North Star training flights. On 31 March, squadron strength stood at 314 personnel, including fifty officers, 222 other ranks and forty-two civilians, and twelve aircraft: seven North Stars and five Dakotas.[21]

April

On 1 April 1948, the Royal Canadian Air Force celebrated the twenty-fourth anniversary of its formation and made an organizational change to upgrade No 9 (Transport) Group to Command status as Air Transport Command, with Air Commodore L.E. Wray, the Group Commander since 5 February 1946, as Air Officer Commanding.[22]

That day, as part of a training exercise, Flight Lieutenant C.F. Sanford and Flying Officer H.T. Giles reached 32,000 feet in a North Star during a local height test, and the first scheduled service flight in a North Star departed from Montreal to Goose Bay via Moncton and Halifax, a two-day trip with Flight Lieutenant J.G. Mills as captain. On 3 April, Squadron Leader C.R. Knowles took the first North Star run to Whitehorse with a stopover at Edmonton.

On 6 April, the squadron's Flight Lieutenants started writing three days' worth of promotion examinations. On 7 April, Dr. O.M. Solandt of the National Research Council made a brief visit to Dorval and was shown around the squadron facilities. On 11 April, formation flying over Montreal in support of Air Cadet Week was cancelled because of poor weather.

On 15 April, No 426 Squadron despatched a North Star captained by Flight Lieutenant C.E. Snider to Maxwell Air Force Base in Montgomery, Alabama to bring students from the RCAF Staff College back to Toronto from their visit to the Air University.

Meanwhile, the squadron was making significant progress on the domestic front. On 14 April, Wing Commander Chapman took Group Captain R.F. Gibb, Chief Staff Officer at Air Transport Command Headquarters, on an inspection tour of single and married quarters at Lachine and married quarters at Nitro, near Valleyfield. (To celebrate, the Officers' Mess threw a cocktail party that evening with Gibb as guest of honour.) Recreation facilities were also expanding; a voluntary labour crew under the guidance of Flight Lieutenant J.G. Mills had a new swimming pool well under way next door to the Officers' Mess. On 16 April, the squadron received official word that the project to convert the hospital at Lachine to married quarters had at last been approved.

On 16 April, Squadron Leader C.R. Knowles met with the squadron's section heads to discuss trans-Atlantic flight training. TCA's Dorval-to-Prestwick service with North Stars was already a year old, and route information flowed freely between TCA and Thunderbird flight crews, who were all based at Dorval. The TCA crews even used the squadron's Link trainers.[23]

On 24 April, an RAF Lancastrian captained by Flight Lieutenant Boyd from No 24 (Commonwealth) Squadron arrived at Dorval from Britain on a long-range training mission. Wing Commander McAllard was in charge of the visitors. Next day, Air Commodore Busk and Group Captain Robertson of the United Kingdom Air Liaison Mission in Ottawa came to Dorval to meet with McAllard and the Lancastrian crew.

On 26 April, a Commanding Officer's Parade was held at Lachine in honour of the 25th wedding anniversary of King George VI and Queen Elizabeth. The following day, the RAF Lancastrian left for home; two Dakotas were ferried out, having been taken off the squadron establishment; and Flying Officer H.T. Giles ferried in a new North Star to Camp Borden by way of Rockcliffe, Trenton and Toronto.

On 29 April, Squadron Leader Knowles and Flight Lieutenant S.F. Cowan took two North Stars to Winnipeg, loaded with 50,000 sandbags for use by crews working to hold back flooding rivers in Regina and Winnipeg. The next day, Flight Lieutenant G.L. Sheahan and his crew took another load of sandbags to Winnipeg.

April saw the North Star taking over operations from the Dakotas and, by the end of the month, the squadron inventory included ten North Stars and only one Dakota. During the month, No 426 Squadron logged 477 flying hours, including 382 operational hours on sixty-six service flights and special flights; fifty-two hours on training flights; thirty hours on test flights; and thirteen hours on ferry flights. On 30 April, squadron strength stood at 316 personnel, including fifty-two officers, 223 airmen and forty-one civilians.[24]

May

In May, No 426 Squadron hit its stride on domestic flight operations. On 1 May, Flight Lieutenant J.G. Mills and his crew completed their preparations for *Operation CARIBERG*, a five-day tour of the sub-Arctic that would take them to Churchill, Manitoba, then to Fort Nelson, British Columbia, back to Churchill, and then to Goose Bay before returning to Dorval; on 3 May, Mills and his crew took off for Churchill. On the same day, Wing Commander W.H. Swetman of No 412 Squadron dropped in; his unit was slated to acquire two North Star soon, with training to be provided by No 426 Squadron.

On 6 May, the officers held their first mess dinner, and many showed up in the new RCAF mess kit.

On 9 May, Flight Lieutenant E.H. Shaw, captain of an Air Sea Rescue aircraft, brought in a seriously injured child from Goose Bay, and Squadron Operations staff arranged for an ambulance to transport the patient to the Royal Victoria Hospital in Montreal. On 10 May, a Public Relations Officer from the Army, one Major Duccett, brought Frank Lowe of the Montreal *Star* and Al Crawley of radio station CJAD to Dorval and Lachine to tour the squadron's operational and domestic facilities and gather material for a *Star* feature and a broadcast.

On 11 May, Flight Lieutenant C.F. Sanford went to Rockcliffe to pick up the students of the National Defence College for a tour of the Canadian North.

On the international scene, General Sir Allan Cunningham, the last British High Commissioner to Palestine, closed his legation on 14 May, and a new Jewish state to be called "Israel" was proclaimed in Tel Aviv by the Jewish National Council and the General Zionist Council, which promptly set up a provisional government.[25]

On 20 May, the newspapers were full of reports on the death of the RCAF fighter ace G.F. "Buzz" Beurling in the crash of a Canadian-built Norduyn Norseman transport aircraft at Fiumicino Airport near Rome. With his co-pilot, Leonard Cohen, who also died in the crash, Beurling was ferrying the Norseman to Israel.[26]

On 15 May, before the evening's big event, the squadron dance, Wing Commander Chapman threw a cocktail party at the Officers' Mess at which he announced his engagement to Miss Yvonne Cournoyer. The squadron dance (music by the RCAF Central Band) was a well-attended success, much to the credit of the organizer, Flight Lieutenant Stu Cowan.

A number of transfers from the unit were announced on 25 May. Flight Lieutenant J.G. Mills was going to Britain. Flight Lieutenant R. Murray was posted to RCAF Station Centralia in southern Ontario, and Flying Officers J.A. Jolicoeur and C.R. Johnson were assigned to E&PE Rockcliffe.

The same day, Air Vice Marshal Middleton arrived at Dorval en route for Montreal to attend the funeral of Colonel the Honourable James Layton Ralston, the Great War veteran and long-serving Member of Parliament who was twice Minister of National Defence—from 1926 to 1930, and from 1940 to 1944, when he was forced out of office because of his outspoken support for conscription for overseas service. Flying Officer Jolicoeur was the Air Vice Marshal's Personal Staff Officer while he was in Montreal.

On the evening of 26 May, the Officers' Mess held a combined stag party for Wing Commander Chapman, organized by Squadron Leader W.L. Orr and Flight Lieutenant R. Murray.

Two days later, Air Transport Command Headquarters advised No 426 Squadron of another sandbag-delivery mission, this time to Vancouver, where the Fraser River was reaching record high levels. On the morning of 29 May, Flight Lieutenant Murray and Flight Lieutenant W.J. Johnston and their crews left Dorval in two North Stars, lugging 40,000 sandbags destined for Vancouver, by way of a refuelling stop in Winnipeg.

That afternoon, Wing Commander Chapman married Miss Yvonne Cournoyer at Grace United Church, with Squadron Leader M.W. Williams officiating. The bride's parents held a reception for about 200 guests at the Officers' Mess, and the newlyweds departed on a motor trip through the eastern United States.

On 30 May and 31 May, No 426 Squadron despatched a total of five North Stars, each fully loaded with about 20,000 sandbags, outward bound from Dorval to Vancouver via Winnipeg, their refuelling stop. During the day on 30 May, it was Flight Lieutenant C.F. Sanford; at midnight, Squadron Leader C.R. Knowles; between midnight and dawn, Flying Officer H.T. Giles; and by mid-morning on 31 May, Flight Lieutenant S.F. Cowan and Flight Lieutenant A.B. Hammond. Thunderbird ground staff at Dorval also handled the passage to Vancouver of two Lancasters from a search-and-rescue unit at Greenwood, Nova Scotia: Flight Lieutenant Moss with 9,600 sandbags, and Flight Lieutenant E.H. Shaw with 14,700 sandbags. Six of these seven aircraft completed their missions except that of Squadron Leader Knowles, whose North Star made it only as far as Winnipeg; after refuelling, he lost an engine and had to turn back. Knowles transferred his load to another westbound aircraft, obtained permission for a three-engine take-off from Air Transport Command Headquarters and brought his aircraft back to Dorval.

The Thunderbird servicing and maintenance crews worked round the clock, some without sleep for more than forty-eight hours. They earned their commendations for dedication and vital contribution to the flood-relief operation.

During May, No 426 Squadron logged 589 flying hours, including 551 operational hours on seventy-six scheduled flights and special flights, nineteen training hours and nineteen hours on flight tests. On 31 May 1948, the squadron had ten North Stars on the inventory.[27]

June

On 1 June, Squadron Leader Knowles visited Air Transport Command Headquarters at Rockcliffe to discuss No 426 Squadron's plans for a series of trans-Atlantic training flights—the next step toward developing the expertise required to operate around the world.

Late in the afternoon of 2 June, the squadron received a request to deliver 10,000 pounds of communication cable to the flooded areas of British Columbia; by noon on 3 June, Squadron Leader Knowles and his crew were on their way to Vancouver with the cable. The next day, Knowles notified Squadron Operations that his aircraft was delayed in Calgary with an unserviceability.

On 4 June, the cement of the squadron swimming pool was dry and cured, so a group of officers began dismantling the forms; everyone expected the pool to be ready for use in a week.

On 5 June, Flight Lieutenant A.B. Hammond took out a special run to Vancouver via Winnipeg and Calgary, and Flying Officer J.A. Jolicoeur captained the scheduled run to Edmonton via Rockcliffe and Winnipeg.

On 6 June an RAF York arrived at Dorval with members of No 125 Squadron aboard, and the Thunderbirds entertained the visitors suitably; the next morning, Flight Lieutenant Long from the British High Commission in Ottawa held a pay parade at Dorval for the visiting RAF personnel.

On 7 June, two scheduled runs went out: one to Edmonton, captained by Flight Lieutenant S.F. Cowan, and the other to Goose Bay, with Flight Lieutenant R. Murray in command. On 8 June, Cowan went on to Whitehorse, while Murray returned to base by way of Buchans, Newfoundland. Of the rest of the squadron, as many personnel as possible were busy helping Flying Officer J.A. Smith, who was co-ordinating Thunderbird input to Air Force Day.

On 9 June, Flight Lieutenant Arthur W. Bishop of Air Transport Command Headquarters visited to discuss problems related to the proposed trans-Atlantic training program, which was scheduled to start on 15 June.

On 10 June, as well as the scheduled service flights to Goose Bay and Edmonton, the squadron sent out a special flight, captained by Flight Lieutenant J.D. Dixon, to Toronto to pick up a group of officers and then tour the North. From Toronto, this flight proceeded to Winnipeg, Edmonton, Whitehorse, Fairbanks, Burwash Landing, Sawmill Bay, Churchill and Goose Bay before returning to Toronto to drop off the officers, and then back to Dorval.

On 10 June, RCAF veterans of the Second World War formed the Air Force Association. The next day, the new association held a celebratory dinner at the Windsor Hotel in Montreal, with special guests the Honourable Brooke Claxton, Minister of National Defence; the Honourable

Colin Gibson, former Minister of National Defence for Air; Air Marshal W.A. Curtis, the Chief of the Air Staff; and Air Vice Marshal E.E. Middleton; and featured speaker Major Paul de Seversky. Wing Commander W.H. Swetman, Wing Commander W.F.M. Newson and Squadron Leader E.A. Wilson all came from Rockcliffe for the dinner.

On 12 June, RCAF Station St-Hubert celebrated Air Force Day, with ceremonies and displays presented before a large, appreciative crowd.

On 14 June, Wing Commander Chapman returned from his honeymoon leave just in time for a squadron mess dinner for Air Vice Marshal J.L. de Niverville from the Department of Transport; Air Commodore Wray from Air Transport Command Headquarters; Group Captain MacDougall of the British Overseas Airways Corporation; Lee Capreol, manager of Dorval Airport; Lieutenant-Colonel P.M. Desautels of the Royal Canadian Army Service Corps; Wing Commander J.A.D.B. Richer, Officer Commanding RCAF Station St-Hubert; Squadron Leader Vinnicombe of RCAF Station St-Hubert; and Mr. Langlois, the Director of the Montreal Police Force. Air Commodore Wray delivered an interesting and informative after-dinner address, and Squadron Leader C.R. Knowles presented him with a silver stein, a gift from the squadron.

On 15 June, the Thunderbirds despatched their first trans-Atlantic training flight, captained by Flying Officer H.T. Giles and carrying Wing Commander Chapman. The four-day flight (35 hours, 35 minutes flying time) was routed to RAF Station Lyneham via Gander, Newfoundland and Lajes in the Azores on the outward-bound leg, returning via Keflavik, Iceland and Goose Bay, Labrador. In this enterprise, the RCAF was profiting from TCA experience—TCA made its first trans-Atlantic flight, from Dorval to Prestwick, on 15 April 1947 and, since then, had completed about 1,200 Atlantic crossings with the North Star aircraft.[28]

On 16 June, Flight Lieutenant Gordie Miller, Flying Officer Ron Gilmour and Mr. Eckblow, a representative of Raytheon, the radar manufacturer, met at the Thunderbird offices at Dorval to discuss setting up ground-controlled approach equipment at the airport; the personnel to operate it would be attached to No 426 Squadron.

On 17 June, the Officers' Mess held an informal party for Flight Lieutenant J.G. Mills, the ramrod of the swimming pool project, who was departing by ship for Britain the following day. With the swimming pool finally filled and ready for use, the guest of honour received the privilege of being the first in the water.

On 19 June, Flight Lieutenant R. Murray took off with a group of officials for Suffield, Alberta, home of the Chemical Warfare Experimental Station, and Flight Lieutenant W.J. Johnston captained a special flight to Goose Bay carrying tires for a RAF Lancaster.

On 21 June, a Board of Officers was convened at Lachine to take over Building 17 and Building 18 and convert them to airmen's married quarters.

Dorval, 1948

On 22 June, the western world woke up to a new stage in the growing international tension that would soon be called the Cold War. During the night, the Soviet Union placed a full blockade on land and water connections to the British-, French- and American-occupied sectors of Berlin— the capital city being a four-party enclave completely surrounded by the Soviet sector of occupied Germany. This action followed weeks of Soviet-initiated delays in the rail and road traffic between Berlin and the British, French and American sectors of occupied Germany.

While the Soviets were tightening the screws on Berlin, the other occupying powers planned for the inevitable show-down. The main strategy was a British-American airlift to supply the non-Soviet sectors of Berlin. The airlift began immediately, using cargo aircraft and converted bombers to deliver food and fuel around the clock to the Berlin airports at Tempelhof, Gatow and Tegel, and, when the weather permitted, Sunderland flying boats to deliver loads to Havel Lake. While Australia, New Zealand and South Africa all contributed aircraft and crews to the collective effort, Canada dithered about participating at all.[29]

On 26 June, No 426 Squadron received two groups of visitors: Squadron Leader J.T. McCutcheon and Squadron Leader W.H. Lewis from Air Transport Command Headquarters in Rockcliffe, who came to discuss the squadron's personnel and engineering problems; and Wing Commander Shelfoon, Wing Commander Barrett, Lieutenant-Colonel Poling and Flying Officer Pary of the Air Ministry in London, who were in Montreal to discuss all-weather trans-Atlantic flying problems with several agencies based in the area.

On 27 June, the second of Thunderbird trans-Atlantic training flight departed. This operation—a round trip from Dorval to Britain—was completed in 37 hours and 45 minutes.

On 30 June, squadron members returned to base from all over the country—Wing Commander Chapman from two days in Rockcliffe, spent in meetings at Air Transport Command Headquarters; Flight Lieutenant S.F. Cowan from Frobisher Bay and Goose Bay, completing a scheduled run; and Flying Officer H.T. Giles from the scheduled western run to Edmonton. On the same day, Lieutenant-Colonel Cardy of the United States Air Force arrived for an overnight visit with five of his pilots from Dow Field in Maine.

During the month of June, No 426 Squadron logged a total of 714 flying hours, including 602 operational hours on sixty-eight scheduled flights and special flights, seventy-six training hours, and thirty-six hours on test flights. On 30 June, squadron strength stood at 340 personnel, including fifty-three officers, 248 airmen and thirty-nine civilians, and ten North Star aircraft.[30]

July

On 1 July, Dominion Day, the crews were briefed for the next trans-Atlantic training flight: Squadron Leader C.R. Knowles and Flying Officer H.T. Giles worked with the pilots, Flight Lieutenant J.H.C. Boby with the navigators and Flight Lieutenant E.A Alliston with the radio operators. Flight Lieutenant G.L. Sheahan, a member of the training crew, then ran their assigned aircraft through a vigorous air test. The day's scheduled flights to Goose Bay and Edmonton departed on time.

On the same day, Air Transport Command Headquarters sent word that thirty-eight electric stoves for the new married quarters at Lachine were on their way, and the first other-ranks tenants, Corporal Perry and his family, moved in.

On 2 July, Squadron Leader C.R. Knowles and his crew left Dorval at 1115 hours on the third overseas training flight, to RAF Lyneham by way of Gander and Lages, a flight of seventeen hours and fifteen minutes. The passengers included Canadian shooters bound for Bisley.

Flight Lieutenant R.J. Brown had engine problems on the outbound leg of SF36 (Dorval to Edmonton and Whitehorse and return), and had to land at Port Arthur; on 5 July, Flight Lieutenant S.F. Cowan joined him with spare parts for Brown's aircraft and, after transferring the cargo to his aircraft, went on to complete SF36. Brown spent two more days trying to repair his aircraft before returning to base on three engines.

On 5 July, Squadron Leader Knowles and the overseas training crew flew from RAF Station Lyneham to London and back to familiarize themselves with air traffic control in the London area.

On 7 July, Squadron Leader B.G. Miller and Squadron Leader J.D. McCallum arrived at No 426 Squadron for a conference on establishing a GCA facility, to be attached to the squadron, at Dorval. On the same day, SF33 to Goose Bay (commanded by Flight Lieutenant P.L. Michel) went on to Frobisher Bay to deliver two Dakota engines to the local detachment of No 414 (Photographic) Squadron. On 8 July, Flying Officer H.T. Giles took SF31 (destination Goose Bay) on to Fort Chimo to deliver stores for No 414 Squadron.

On 9 July Flight Lieutenant C.F. Sanford lost an engine while arriving at Edmonton with SF35. The next day he returned to base on three engines. Squadron Leader Knowles arrived back from the United Kingdom on 12 July via Keflavik and Goose Bay. The return trip took 16 hours and 40 minutes. Flight Lieutenants S.A. Bascomb and W. Loynes formed a Board of Officers on 14 July to take over Buildings 19 and 28 at the Lachine site as married quarters for Senior NCOs and Officers. On operations, SF31 was again extended from Goose Bay to Frobisher Bay. On this occasion it was to again airlift supplies for No 414 Squadron.

On 14 July, the first east-west transit of the Atlantic by jet aircraft was made by an RAF flight of six Vampire fighters led by Squadron Leader R.W. Oxspring of No 54 Squadron from

RAF Station Odiham. They flew from Stornoway in the Hebrides to Goose Bay, Labrador via Keflavik, Iceland and Narsarssuak, Greenland (known as Bluie West 1) in a total flying time of eight hours and eighteen minutes. On 15 June, after staging an air show at Goose Bay, the RAF Vampires flew on to St-Hubert and Trenton, where they put on another air show on 21 July. The six aircraft and their crews then spent a month in the United States before heading home in late August.

On 16 July, a large formation of USAF F-80s left Goose Bay on the first west-east Atlantic crossing by jet aircraft. Their destination was Munich, to bolster American defences as the Berlin airlift continued and relations between the Soviet Union and the western powers grew steadily chillier.[31]

On 17 July, Flight Lieutenant C.E. Snider and Trans-Atlantic Training Flight No 4 took off for Britain, and Flight Lieutenant G.L. Sheahan brought the Whitehorse service flight back to base. Flight Lieutenant I.F. Campbell-Rogers left the squadron for RCAF Station Rockcliffe to serve at Air Transport Command Headquarters.

On 19 July, Wing Commander D.A. Willis from Air Force Headquarters and Squadron Leader J.V. Watts from Air Transport Command Headquarters visited No 426 Squadron to discuss staffing issues and qualifications for navigators; meanwhile, Wing Commander Chapman was in Valleyfield trying to solve the problem of delivering sufficient heat to the married quarters there, and the service flights to Goose Bay and Whitehorse departed on schedule.

The next day, several officers rewrote their "green ticket" examinations, and Wing Commander Chapman toured the Lachine site, focusing on the cleanliness of the grounds, the married quarters, the drill hall and the sports areas. In England, Flight Lieutenant Snider and his crew took Trans-Atlantic Training Flight No 4 to Heathrow Airport from RAF Station Lyneham to familiarize themselves with London-area air traffic control procedures.

On 22 July, the squadron selected a crew—pilots Flying Officer H.T. Giles and Flight Lieutenant P.L. Michel, navigator Flight Lieutenant J.H.C. Boby and radio officer Flight Lieutenant E.A. Alliston—for take the first Air Cadet flight to Britain. The next day, a line of thunderstorms moved through the Montreal area, forcing the RAF trans-Atlantic flying team to cancel the Vampire flying display they were scheduled to put on at RCAF Station St-Hubert. At 0500 hours on 24 July, Trans-Atlantic Training Flight No 4 returned to base.

On 24 July, as a result of Wing Commander Chapman's visit to Valleyfield, plans were made to close Staff House No 1 and install a boiler in Staff House No 2, which would thus become fit accommodations for fourteen more Thunderbird families.

On 26 July, Wing Commander Chapman departed for Goose Bay, leaving Squadron Leader C.R. Knowles in command of the squadron, and the Chief of the Air Staff dropped in,

to be met by Knowles. Flight Lieutenant B.C. Denomy reported in to the squadron for duties as the Squadron Chief Administrative Officer.

On 28 July, the squadron flew three stretcher patients to Montreal for emergency treatment: Sergeant Fulton and Leading Aircraftsman McLeod from Coral Harbour, who were seriously injured in a jeep accident, and a civilian engineer from Goose Bay, whose arm was mutilated in an accident with a steam shovel. Flight Lieutenant J.D. Dickson brought in the Whitehorse flight while Flight Lieutenant R.J. Brown completed the Goose Bay run.

The end of the month was committed to arrangements for receiving and transporting a group of Air Cadets.

During July, No 426 Squadron logged 553 flying hours, including 441 operational hours on fifty-one service flights and seven special flights, seventy-three training hours and thirty-nine hours on flight tests. On 31 July, squadron strength stood at 340 personnel (fifty-three officers, 247 airmen and forty civilians), with eight North Star aircraft on the inventory.[32]

August

August in Montreal is usually hot and humid, and so it would prove in 1948. August 1 was a Sunday, so work was limited to the usual air tests and all ranks concentrated on relaxing: a group of airmen went by squadron bus to swim at Crystal Beach, and the Officers' Mess organized something similar, followed by a cold-plate dinner.

On 2 August, Flight Lieutenant H.E. Carling, the squadron Adjutant, departed on two weeks annual leave, leaving his job to Flying Officer R.M. Kennedy for the duration. With Squadron Leader Knowles away on a service flight, Flight Lieutenant C.F. Sanford, as Acting Flight Commander, chaired an aircrew meeting at which the usual number of beefs were discussed and settled to the satisfaction of all.

At 1020 hours on 3 August, two Dakotas from No 435 Squadron arrived at Dorval, bringing a contingent of Canadian Air Cadets to a warm welcome that included Tim Derbyshire, formerly a Thunderbird pilot and now representing the CBC, and Air Vice Marshal Middleton, who just happened to be in Dorval on his way to Goose Bay. After lunch at Dorval, the Cadets departed at 1300 hours for Britain via Goose Bay, flown by Flying Officer H.T. Giles in a squadron North Star.

Among his activities at Dorval that day, Tim Derbyshire interviewed Wing Commander Chapman extensively about the Thunderbirds' domestic and international flying operations, recording the conversations for international broadcast.

On 4 August, Wing Commander Chapman convened a staff meeting to discuss plans to build a children's playground at Lachine. On the operational side, the Edmonton service flight returned to base, and considerable time was spent flight testing an aircraft following an engine change.

On 6 August, Wing Commander Chapman and the Equipment Officer spent the morning discussing squadron requirements, and making progress on the problem of acquiring the large loading crane that was urgently needed at Dorval. Two airmen left the squadron, voluntarily released from the RCAF; with their departure, the Thunderbirds had lost four qualified technicians in three weeks.

On August 7, Flying Officer Giles returned to base with a full load of British Air Cadets, who were greeted by a Guard of Honour mounted by the Air Cadet Squadron in nearby Verdun, Quebec. The formal welcome included Air Vice Marshal Middleton, members of the Air Cadet League, and members of the Air Liaison Mission at the British High Commission in Ottawa, and was covered by the news media.

On 9 August, Wing Commander J.H. Roberts, commanding officer of No 1 Instrument Flying School at RCAF Station Centralia, visited No 426 Squadron with one of his students, Squadron Leader H.A. Morrison, who would become the Thunderbirds' new Flight Commander.

On 11 August, Wing Commander Chapman concluded an agreement with the Canadian Corps of Commissioners under which the Corps would supply four hangar guards to keep No 6 Hangar under 24-hour surveillance. At this time, at least four investigations of petty thefts and motor vehicle accidents were under way. On 12 August, Leading Aircraftsman Perkins learned that he had passed the aircrew-qualification examination and was selected for aircrew training. His was the squadron's first such appointment.

Wing Commander Chapman spent 13 August at Air Transport Command Headquarters. After a day of meetings, he attended the farewell party for Air Commodore Wray, who had been appointed to the command of the RCAF Staff College in Toronto and would leave Air Transport Command on 16 August. His replacement as Air Officer Commanding, Air Transport Command, was Air Commodore A.D. Ross, who had commanded the Thunderbirds' wartime home, No 62 (Beaver) Base, Linton-on-Ouse, and had earned the George Cross in his effort to rescue an air gunner from the rear turret of a burning Halifax that was fully loaded with bombs.

On 14 August, two senior officials of the Canadian Corps of Commissionaires, Colonel Ross and Major Allister, visited No 426 Squadron to study the security situation and fire precautions at the RCAF facilities at Dorval, and make a report with recommendations to Wing Commander Chapman. During the morning, Air Vice Marshal Middleton and Group Captain H.H.C. Rutledge arrived at Dorval; they were on their way to catch the liner *Empress of Canada*, outward bound for Britain.

On 17 August, GCA operations at Dorval Airport were discussed. On 18 August, Dr. Kelly and Dr. Pody of McGill University arrived to discuss installing equipment in the North Star aircraft to obtain an in-flight bacteria count. On 19 August, Wing Commander Chapman appointed a Court of Inquiry to investigate the case of an airman who had been absent without leave for several weeks.

On 21 August, Flight Lieutenant J.D. Dickson lost an engine on the homeward leg of a scheduled run to Edmonton; after leaving his passengers in Winnipeg, he completed the journey to Dorval on three engines.

On 23 August, the British Air Cadets finished their tour of Canada and headed for home (by way of Goose Bay and Keflavik) in a North Star captained by Flight Lieutenant C.F. Sanford, with Wing Commander Chapman and a delegation of officials to see them off. The aircraft departed Dorval at 1610 hours. On the same day, Squadron Leader H.A. Morrison reported in to take over as Flight Commander from Squadron Leader C.R. Knowles, who was posted on course to the RCAF Staff College in Toronto.

On 24 August, Wing Commander Chapman held a Section Heads' meeting in the morning and, in the evening, hosted (with his wife) a cocktail party in honour of Squadron Leader Knowles and Mrs. Knowles.

On 26 August, Montreal suffered under a blanket of extraordinary heat—it was 112° Fahrenheit, and the squadron had no air conditioners—so a stand-down was declared at noon. Despite the weather, the squadron officers held a Mess Dinner that evening, at which they entertained Air Commodore Ross from Air Transport Command Headquarters, Commander Holmes from HMCS *Donnacona*, Lieutenant Colonel Cunnington from Quebec Command, Wing Commanders W.F.M. Newson from Air Force Headquarters, Wing Commander W.H. Swetman from No 412 Squadron, and Wing Commander J.A.D.B. Richer from RCAF Station St-Hubert.

On 27 August, Flight Lieutenant C.F. Sanford (who had returned only the previous day from an overseas run) captained the direct run to Goose Bay. Flying Officer H.T. Giles and his crew went to Whitehorse from Edmonton, while Flight Lieutenant S.F. Cowan returned to Dorval from Goose Bay via Halifax and Moncton. On 30 August, the squadron's AWOL airman, now eighty-five days adrift, turned himself in to the Service Police at Lachine.

During August, No 426 Squadron logged 471 flying hours, including 432 operational hours on forty-three scheduled flights and special flights, and thirty-nine hours on flight tests. On 31 August, unit strength stood at 334 personnel, including forty-five officers, 250 airmen and thirty-nine civilians.[33]

September

On 1 September, the RCAF was authorized to form a Fighter Operational Training Unit at RCAF Station St-Hubert. In the Thunderbird facilities at Dorval, as Squadron Leader C.R. Knowles was leaving for the RCAF Staff College, Air Commodore A.D. Ross, Wing Commander W.P. Pleasance and Squadron Leader W.H. Lewis from Air Transport Command Headquarters, and a party of officers from Air Force Headquarters, including Wing Commander D.A. Willis, met with TCA officials to discuss how and when TCA would hand over a group of DC-4M aircraft to the RCAF.

On 3 September, the squadron's section heads met with the Housing Committee to allocate married quarters at Lachine. The next day, the Saturday before Labour Day, many squadron members were told to cancel any holiday plans—too many aircraft required servicing and flight testing. On 5 September, the swimming pool at the Officers' Mess was full of people enjoying the last day it would be open before being drained for the winter.

On 7 September, the married quarters were alive with Thunderbird families getting their children into school for the new academic year, and Wing Commander Chapman met with representatives of J.L.E. Price & Co. about painting the former hospital, which was now married quarters for the squadron officers. Amid all this domestic activity, the squadron despatched a trans-Atlantic training flight to Britain with Flight Lieutenant A.B. Hammond as captain.

On 9 September, Wing Commander Chapman appointed Flight Lieutenant G.L. Sheahan to take a Summary of Evidence in the case of the squadron's AWOL airman, and took the squadron's Chief Administrative Officer on an inspection of the Valleyfield married quarters. Flight Lieutenant J.D. Dickson took over as Flight Commander from Squadron Leader Morrison, who was on the trans-Atlantic training flight.

On 11 September, Flight Lieutenant J.H. Gilmour and Flying Officer C. Lee arrived from Edmonton, ferrying two Harvard single-engine trainers bound for the Canadair plant at Cartierville, where they would be modified for use at the GCA School. Wing Commander Chapman had a busy day; in the morning, he received Flight Lieutenant Sheahan's Summary of Evidence and remanded the AWOL airman for trial by Court Martial and, in the afternoon, he and Mrs. Chapman moved into married quarters.

On 13 September, Flight Lieutenant D.G. Forrest left for Rockcliffe, the first stage of his journey to Washington where he was to attend a conference held by the Military Air Transport Service. At Dorval, squadron officers met with Wing Commander R.S. Turnbull and Squadron Leader L.A. Rosenthal from Air Transport Command Headquarters to discuss transport operations, and with Flight Lieutenant G.W. Patrick and Flying Officer D.F. Robertson from Central Air Command to discuss allocating space for the GCA School in No 3 Hangar at Dorval. At the section heads' meeting on 14 September, the main issue was participation in services to mark Battle of Britain Sunday.

On 16 September, Wing Commander Chapman heard the case of an airman charged with being absent without leave, and sentenced him to twenty-eight days in detention. Very early in the morning, the trans-Atlantic training flight returned to base carrying a party headed by Major-General Foster. Later in the day, Wing Commander G. Keefer visited briefly on behalf of the Air Cadet League.

The Battle of Britain Sunday parade was held in downtown Montreal on 19 September, with Wing Commander Chapman as Parade Commander, Squadron Leader W. Grant of No 11 Technical Service Unit as No 1 Squadron Commander, Squadron Leader H.A. Morrison as No 3 Squadron Commander, and Flying Officer Bion in command of the Air Cadet contingent. A fourth squadron of RCAF veterans was expected, but failed to show up.

On 20 September, the squadron's last trans-Atlantic training flight departed for Britain with Flying Officer E.L. Banks in command; scheduled flights to Edmonton and Goose Bay left on time; and Wing Commander Chapman chaired his weekly section heads' meeting. In the evening, the Officers' Mess held a small party to celebrate the award of long-service commissions to several squadron personnel.

On 22 September, Group Captain R.F. Gibb, the Chief Staff Officer at Air Transport Command Headquartes, and his colleague Squadron Leader W.H. Lewis, the Senior Technical Staff Officer, went to Air Force Headquarters to discuss the Berlin Airlift—the resources available, and the costs of contributing. On 25 September, the conference moved to Maintenance Command Headquarters in Ottawa, and Senior Supply Officer at Air Transport Command, Squadron Leader L.A. Rosenthal, arrived to take part. During the next two days, Flight Lieutenant P.A. Jones of the supply staff at Air Transport Command and Flight Lieutenant E.J. Grosz, the Squadron Supply Officer at No 426 Squadron, joined the conference. Discussion centred on the supply problems the RCAF would encounter if it were to participate in the Airlift.[34]

On 27 September, radio officer Flying Officer J. Santarelli transferred in, and Squadron Leader J.H. Hollies arrived to defend the airman facing Court Martial the next day. The accused was found guilty as charged and sentenced to fifty-five days detention.

On 29 September, Air Transport Command Headquarters issued advice on promotions for airmen; Squadron Leader H.A. Morrison headed for Ottawa, where his wife was in labour with their second son; and Flight Lieutenant C.F. Sanford went to Air Transport Command Headquarters to find out how his ear troubles would affect his career. The next day, he and Squadron Leader Morrison returned to Dorval in time to write the narrative reports for the officers' promotion board.

Dorval, 1948

The squadron's personnel strength at the end of September stood at 344 comprised of forty-six officers, 259 airmen and thirty-nine civilians. The unit carried out forty-nine scheduled and special flights putting in a total of 492 flying hours. Thirty-seven hours were spent on flight testing aircraft, fifty-two on training and the remaining 403 hours were devoted to operations.[35]

October

On 1 October, No 426 Squadron received word that the GCA School's move from London, Ontario to Dorval was approved and would take place immediately, and relinquished Flight Lieutenant P.V. Brodeur to the Fighter Operational Training Unit at RCAF Station St-Hubert to be its Navigation Officer.

On 2 October, an RAF Hastings arrived at Dorval on its way to the Winter Experimental Establishment at Edmonton. At Maintenance Command Headquarters in Ottawa, discussions on Canada's possible contribution to the Berlin Airlift continued, with input from No 426 Squadron.

On 5 October, Wing Commander Chapman held his weekly section heads' meeting, and Department of Transport staff started painting the squadron's offices in No 6 Hangar, brightening the work environment considerably. On the evening of 6 October, both the Sergeants' Mess and the Officers' Mess held stag nights with oysters and lobster on the menu.

On 7 October, Squadron Leader C.D. McLean, Flight Lieutenant E.J. Grosz and Flying Officer W.H. Smith returned from the Berlin Airlift conference in Ottawa and briefed the squadron section heads, whom the Commanding Officer had convened.

On 8 October, the squadron marked Fire Prevention Week with a parade in the hangar at Dorval, at which the airport Fire Chief addressed the flights, and. at Lachine, a talk on local fire prevention problems by Lieutenant E. Endersby of the Corps of Commissionaires.

On 9 October the Chief Technical Officer, Squadron Leader C.D. McLean and Flight Lieutenant Grosz, the Squadron Supply Officer, met with Flying Officer W.H. Smith and Squadron Leader W.H. Lewis from Air Transport Command Headquarters to discuss supply and maintenance problems that would arise if the squadron took part in the Berlin Airlift. Elsewhere in the squadron's facilities, Air Cadets from the Royal Montreal Squadron began reporting in for weekend contact training.

On 12 October, Wing Commander Chapman's meeting with the section heads was followed by an Officers' Promotion Board; the airman sentenced to detention by Wing Commander Chapman was released from detention after twenty days; and the airman sentenced by District Court Martial was shipped to the detention barracks at RCAF Station Camp Borden to serve his fifty-five-day sentence. On 13 October, a board assembled in Wing Commander Chapman's office to make promotion recommendations on squadron officers.

On 15 October, the Berlin Airlift dominated the squadron agenda; Wing Commander Chapman took Squadron Leader H.A. Morrison, Flight Lieutenant C.F. Sanford, Flight Lieutenant J.H.C. Boby, Flight Lieutenant E.A. Alliston and Flying Officer H.T. Giles to Air Transport Command Headquarters at Rockcliffe to attend another Airlift conference. On 16 October, administrative preparations for Airlift duty began: an augmentation posting plan went into effect, and Flight Lieutenant Sanford was directed to start planning mission-specific training.

On 18 October, the installation of the GCA School's equipment began at Dorval. The next day, Colonel Bond of the USAF and Wing Commander Bocking from Air Force Headquarters arrived at the Thunderbird facilities to discuss a GCA installation at the airport.

On 20 October, aircrew from No 412 Squadron in Rockcliffe reported for training on the North Star, and the squadron received a routine accounts inspection by Wing Commander M.J. Noland, the Staff Officer Accounts and Finance at Air Transport Command Headquarters. Three squadron officers, Flight Lieutenants H.E. Carling and A.B. Hammond and, Flying Officer G.W. Webb wrote the examination for their "green ticket". That evening, the Officers' Mess hosted Mr. McLeod of the Trans-Atlantic Meteorological Department, who presented an interesting talk on precipitation, icing and thunderstorm activity.

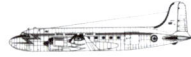

Despite planning for the Berlin Airlift and implementation of the GCA project at Dorval, regular flying operations continued, and routine RCAF administration droned on. On 23 October, applications for commissions from the ranks received priority attention. On October 25, the Squadron Promotion Board finished its work and Wing Commander Chapman personally delivered the results to Air Transport Command Headquarters; on the same day, at RCAF Station Summerside, Prince Edward Island, the first post-war course for Specialist Navigators was beginning. On 26 October, the morning program included a squadron parade followed by drill and an inspection of the Lachine messes and single quarters by Wing Commander Chapman; during the afternoon, he inspected the squadron facilities at Dorval. The next day, he gave the Lachine married quarters the same attention.

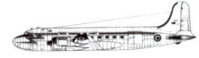

On 28 October, Air Commodore Ross brought several staff officers from Air Transport Command Headquarters to Dorval to discuss supply matters at the squadron and attend the official handover of a North Star from TCA to the RCAF. The next day, Squadron Leader A.P. Blackburn and Flight Lieutenant S.A. Bascom of Air Transport Command Headquarters studied the possibility of converting the Lachine detention barracks to single airmen's quarters, a project that would include transforming the guard house into an administrative building.

On 30 October, Squadron Leader H.A. Morrison and Flight Lieutenant A.B. Hammond took two North Stars to RCAF Station Trenton to pick up the staff and students from the National Defence College (located at Tête du Pont Barracks in Kingston, Ontario) and the RCAF Staff College in Toronto and take them to Elgin Field, Florida.

During October, No 426 Squadron logged 410 flying hours, including 391 operational hours on fifty-eight scheduled flights and special flights, and 19 hours on flight tests. On 31 October, squadron strength stood at 354 personnel, including fifty-four officers, 260 airmen and forty civilians.[36]

November

The monthly RCAF magazine *Roundel* first appeared in November 1948, and rapidly became integral to service life. As the year waned, the Thunderbirds kept busy maintaining the flight schedule and making special flights, while planning for participation in the Berlin Airlift and other far-flung operations.

On 2 November, Squadron Leader J.V. Watts, the Command Navigation Officer for Air Transport Command, and his colleague Squadron Leader H.R.R. Trepanier, the Command Signals Officer, went to Air Force Headquarters for a meeting the discuss the immediate requirement for modifications on North Star aircraft for operations over the North Atlantic and the Arctic. The next day, Watts visited the squadron to address re-enrolled navigators training at Dorval.

On 5 November, Flight Lieutenant J.D. Dickson captained the North Star sent to pick up the members of the National Defence College–RCAF Staff College tour at Lawson Field, Fort Benning, Georgia.

On the same day, the Squadron Accounts Officer, Flight Lieutenant J.B. Campbell, heard that he had received a permanent, regular commission in the RCAF. On 6 November, Wing Commander Chapman was ordered to go to RCAF Station Trenton on 14 November attend a three-week business-management course. On 8 November, the Chief of the Air Staff, Air Marshal W.A. Curtis, dropped in on the squadron on his way through Montreal. The next day, navigator Flying Officer J.A.L.P. Rodrigue reported in.

On 11 November, No 426 Squadron paraded 215 officers and airmen for Remembrance Day observances in downtown Montreal, during which Flight Lieutenant R.J. Brown, Flying Officer E.L. Banks and Flying Officer H.T. Giles carried out a formation fly-past in North Stars. Squadron Leader Vinnicome of RCAF Station St-Hubert was in charge of the parade, and Flight Lieutenant Gilmour, the commanding officer of the GCA School, acted as Squadron Commander for the occasion.

Also on Remembrance Day, at Air Transport Command Headquarters, Air Commodore Ross called a meeting of his senior staff officers to discuss sending a special flight to Nanking, China, to rescue Canadian diplomats and their families from the advancing Red Army. No 426 Squadron was alerted to stand by for the mission.

On 12 November, Mr. Hamsley of the Department of External Affairs advised Air Transport Command Headquarters that the China flight would soon be needed, and Air Transport Command Headquarters warned No 426 Squadron accordingly. At Dorval, the aircrew were selected and arrangements were made to obtain passports for them, and Maintenance Section prepared an aircraft.

On 13 November, Squadron Leader H.A. Morrison flew to Rockcliffe for a meeting on the China operation, now called *Operation ORIENT*, which had already consumed huge quantities of staff effort at Air Transport Command Headquarters.

On 14 November Wing Commander Chapman left for his management course in Trenton, leaving Squadron Leader H.A. Morrison as Acting Commanding Officer and Flight Lieutenant Dickson as Acting Flight Commander.

On 15 November, Louis St. Laurent was elected Prime Minister of Canada.

On 16 November, *Operation ORIENT* was cancelled.

On 16 November, Squadron Leader L.A. Rosenthal and Squadron Leader W.H. Lewis arrived from Air Transport Command Headquarters to discuss supply and engineering problems that could arise if the squadron's North Stars were deployed on *Operation BEETLE*.

After the war, the tension between the Soviet Union and the western powers quickly increased to the point that the lack of navigation aids in the Arctic became a serious tactical and strategic problem. The USAF held that Loran coverage could be extended if the frequency of the Standard Loran were lowered to 180 KHz. By late 1945, Canada was operating the Musk Calf Chain, a temporary 180-KHz Loran chain with a master station near North Battleford, Saskatchewan and slave stations at Gimli, Manitoba and Dawson Creek, British Columbia. The Musk Calf Chain project was directed by the Combined Low-Freqeuncy Loran Committee Canada–USA, and system tests (conducted mainly by the Americans) were promising enough that the Combined Committee try it again, this time farther north. The Beetle Chain had its master station at Kittigazuit, Northwest Territories, its western slave station at Skull Cliff, just west of Barrow, Alaska, and its eastern slave station at Cambridge Bay, a hamlet on the south coast of Victoria Island in the Arctic Archipelago. Construction was finished late in 1947, and the Beetle Chain was ready for testing by summer 1948. Before these tests could begin, however, control stations to assist in signal synchronization had to be established at two locations: Barter Island, Alaska and Sawmill Bay, Northwest Territories. (The low-frequency Loran program was abandoned early in 1950.)[37]

On 18 November, Wing Commander W.H. Swetman and Squadron Leader W.D. Reeves of No 412 Squadron visited the squadron to check on the serviceability of a North Star assigned to them for training.

On 22 November, Squadron Leader H.A. Morrison and Flight Lieutenant B.C. Denomy inspected the Valleyfield married quarters and visited Captain Heron of Canadian Arsenals, the company that owned the buildings. On the same day, Flight Lieutenant R.J. Brown and Flight Lieutenant J.D. Dickson made the scheduled runs to Goose Bay and Whitehorse. Flight Lieutenant Grosz, the Squadron Supply Officer, joined Squadron Leader L.A. Rosenthal of Air Transport Command Headquarters at Maintenance Command Headquarters for a meeting on the shortage of North Star spares.

On 23 November, Flight Lieutenant P.L. Michel, Flight Lieutenant A.J. Bradford and Flight Lieutenant C.E. Snider were notified that they were to be posted out of the squadron. On 24 November, Group Captain R.F. Gibb of Air Transport Command Headquarters sent word that Air Force Headquarters had revived *Operation ORIENT* and crews should stand by. On 25 November, Flying Officer Bob Clark took a No 10 Group Dakota to fly a badly injured pilot, Lieutenant Hopkins of the RCN, from Dartmouth to Montreal, accompanied by Surgeon Lieutenant-Commander Alford, for treatment at the military hospital in Ste-Anne-de-Bellevue.

On 28 November, the trainee specialist navigators from Summerside arrived at Dorval for an overnight stay. On 29 November, the squadron bowling league was hard at it, and the hockey season opened with the first RCAF–RCN game; the first puck was thrown in by Squadron Leader Morrison (for No 426 Squadron) and Commander Holmes (for HMCS *Donnacona*).

During November, No 426 Squadron logged 329 flying hours, including 294 operational hours on forty-five scheduled flights and special flights, and thirty-five hours on flight tests. On 30 Novemeber, the Thunderbird inventory included eight North Star aircraft.[38]

December

In December 1948, the RCAF replaced its Unit Daily Diary (a reporting document modelled on the RAF's Operational Record Book) with a Semi-Annual Historical Record. Consequently, unit-level activity—especially operational activity—ceased to be recorded in fine detail.

On 1 December, No 1 Air Defence Group was formed at Air Force Headquarters in Ottawa, with Group Captain W.R. MacBrien in command. On the same day, No 410 (Fighter) Squadron, Canada's first post-war permanent-force fighter unit, was formed at RCAF Station St-Hubert, with Squadron Leader R.A. Kipp in command and flying the De Havilland Vampire Mk III.[39]

On 4 December, No 426 Squadron lost one of its longest-serving captains, Flight Lieutenant W.J. Johnson, who was posted to RCAF Station Greenwood as a flight controller. The next day, the squadron launched a Sunday-evening bridge tournament for airmen and their wives, each session of play to be followed by refreshments and more general entertainment.

About this time, Squadron Headquarters issued occupants of the married quarters with formal permission to erect Christmas trees, the substantial fire hazard to be off-set by strict compliance with detailed instructions on installation, maintenance and disposal. Wing Commander Chapman undertook to visit all the married quarters with an electrician to inspect Christmas trees for faulty electrical apparatus.

On 15 December, the RCAF Survival Training School was established at Fort Nelson, British Columbia, to conduct one-week courses in summer and winter survival in the bush. The school later expanded to include Arctic survival training, using a site in the barrens near Cambridge Bay. No 426 Squadron's flight crew members generally completed at least one of these training programs.[40]

On 23 December, half of the squadron's personnel were on leave for Christmas. On Christmas Eve, the sections gathered to exchange of Christmas greetings. After church on Christmas Day, the Sergeants' Mess entertained the officers; then, Wing Commander Chapman led the officers to the Airmen's Mess to serve the traditional Christmas dinner in the traditional manner. On 28 December, those on Christmas leave returned to duty, and the other half of the squadron proceeded on leave to enjoy New Year celebrations unencumbered by work.

On 28 December, Minister of National Defence Brooke Claxton made a major speech in which he announced a significant increase in DND activity. Manning levels would increase, RCAF stations would be reconditioned, and a program to develop and produce jet fighters would begin immediately. On 30 December, the government announced a pay raise for all members of the armed forces, retroactive to 1 October 1948.

On 31 December, the strength of No 426 Squadron stood at 380 personnel, including sixty officers, 272 airmen and thirty-eight civilians, with eight North Stars on the inventory.[41]

Dorval, 1948

PHOTO 19
F/L C.F. Sanford and crew take out one of the first North Star service flights from Dorval to Goose Bay on 22 March 1948. From left: Bob Kennedy, John Hickey, Gerry Reed, Frank Sanford and Cam Whittington. (G. Reed Collection)

PHOTO 20
An aerial view of Lajes Airport, Azores; spring 1948. (Sperling Clay/National Archives of Canada, PA129310).

PHOTO 21
W/C C.G.W. Chapman on his wedding day with his best man, S/L H.C. Vinnicombe; Lachine, 29 May 1948. (R.J. Brown Collection)

PHOTO 22
Vampires of No 54 Squadron, RAF at Goose Bay after completing the first east-west transit of the Atlantic by jet aircraft; 15 July 1948. (E. Grose Collection)

Dorval, 1948

PHOTO 23
NS17517 at Lajes, Azores, during a training flight to Britain; July 1948. (R.J. Brown Collection)

PHOTO 24
At the British end of a trans-Atlantic training flight; RAF Station Lyneham, July 1948. From left: Cpl. McKnight, Sgt. Vassar, WO2 Graves, and F/S Reny. (R.J. Brown Collection)

PHOTO 25
An aerial view of Frobisher Bay, NWT; 1948. (DND REA 478–23)

Dorval, 1948

PHOTO 26
Engineering, Maintenance and Support staff of No 426 Squadron; Dorval, summer 1948. In the centre row, the sixth from left is Sgt. Gus Chalin and the eighth is S/L C.D. McLean. (G. Chalin Collection)

Dorval, 1949

CHAPTER 7
DORVAL, 1949

The squadron entered its fourth year as a Regular Force peacetime unit with an extension of Christmas celebrations to New Year's Day for those who had been on leave at Christmas: after serving dinner in the Airmen's Mess, the officers entertained the Senior NCOs in the Officers' Mess. At the same time, the traditional New Year levée visits were going on, with a team of Thunderbird officers travelling around the Montreal area to call at each mess that had sent No 426 Squadron an "At Home" invitation.

The theme of 1949 would be expansion in the RCAF establishment to accommodate its growing list of commitments. On 1 January, the first post-war commissions from the ranks took effect. On 5 January, No 426 Squadron lost three of its longest-serving captains, Flight Lieutenant P.L. Michel, Flight Lieutenant C.F. Sanford and Flight Lieutenant C.E. Snider, all posted to RCAF recruiting centres. On 10 January, the RCAF re-activated No 408 (Goose) Squadron as a photographic squadron to be based at RCAF Station Rockcliffe. During the war, Goose Squadron was based at RCAF Station Linton-on-Ouse in Yorkshire with the Thunderbirds. On the same day, the squadron's officers began writing examinations to qualify for promotion.

On 14–15 January, while conducting fuel-consumption tests on North Star 17512, Flying Officer J.A. Jolicoeur (recently posted from No 426 Squadron) and a fourteen-man crew from the Experimental and Proving Establishment at RCAF Station Rockcliffe made the first coast-to-coast non-stop flight in a North Star. Using the Great Circle route, the 2,785-mile trip from Vancouver to Halifax was made in the record time of eight hours and thirty-two minutes, at an average speed of 326 miles per hour. (One year later, Flying Officer G.W. Webb and his crew from No 426 Squadron would use the same aircraft to shave seven minutes off Jolicoeur's time.)[1]

On 16 January, Air Commodore Ross and members of his staff stopped in Winnipeg on their way to tour northern bases. During their stopover, they visited the TCA facilities to inspect the North Star aircraft that were on loan to the airline and due to be returned to the RCAF.

February

On 1 February, the USAF withdrew from *Operation BEETLE*, the re-supply airlift to the Loran sites in the Arctic, and Air Transport Command took over this commitment. Consequently, No 435 Squadron, based at Edmonton, suspended all its other operations to concentrate on the task of hauling 8,000 tons of supplies per week to the Beetle sites. The airlift would continue during and after the spring thaw, which would destroy the ice landing strips at the Beetle sites, by means of air drops from Dakota transports and the Canso flying boats, which could not touch down on the water because of the ice pans.

At the same time, Air Transport Command Headquarters introduced a new Inter-Command service schedule that had No 426 Squadron making two trans-Canada flights to Whitehorse per week, and No 412 Squadron conducting a weekly run to Churchill via Winnipeg with extensions, as necessary, to Baker Lake and Coral Harbour.[2]

On 7 February, the RCAF Regional Trade Test Board arrived at No 426 Squadron for three days of administering trade tests to all non-commissioned personnel eligible for promotion.

On 11 February one of the GCA School's most important vehicles broke down, and had to be taken to the RCEME Workshops at Longe Pointe for repair; while it was in the shop, the GCA School was allowed to use an Army vehicle as a replacement. On 14 February, four officers and a sergeant reported to the GCA School for the GCA Operator Course, and one sergeant and seven aircraftsmen started the GCA Technician Course. On 16 February, Mr. J.S. House of Marconi Limited in England visited the GCA School to inspect the installation and discuss training problems. The next day, Flight Lieutenant S.A. Bascomb of Air Transport Command Headquarters inspected the offices and classrooms at the GCA School, and reported that the building contract had been properly carried out.

On the morning of 18 February, a Commanding Officer's Parade and Change of Command ceremony were held in No 6 Hangar at Dorval. After inspecting the parade, Wing Commander C.W.G. Chapman DSO turned over No 426 Squadron to its new Commanding Officer, Wing Commander C.H. Mussells DSO, DFC. During the war, the new Squadron Commander had served with No 405 (RCAF) Squadron and had completed two tours of operations with the Pathfinder Force of Bomber Command. On dismissing the parade, Wing Commander Mussells stood down the squadron for the rest of the day.

Wing Commander Chapman was posted to the directing staff of the RAF Staff College at Bracknell, Berkshire and, on 24 February, he left for New York to take ship for Britain.

On 25 February, the new Squadron Commander paid his first official visit to the GCA School (with four officers and nine airmen under training) and its commanding officer, Flight Lieutenant R.A. Gilmour.

During a local flight on 28 February North Star 17516 lost an engine, thus terminating a training exercise. The serious damage to the engine was attributed to an inoperative sump pump.

On the last day of the month, No 426 Squadron had sixty-one officers, 266 airmen and thirty-seven civilians on strength.

March

In March, No 426 Squadron completed its first year of transport operations with the North Star. Its gradually expanding range of assignments would soon include missions to the high Arctic and, with the North Atlantic training exercises completed, Air Transport Command and the squadron were planning training flights to the South Atlantic area and South America.

On 1 March, radio navigator Flight Lieutenant P.F. Lee was posted in from RCAF Station Trenton. On 2 March, the editor of *Canadian Aviation*, L.A. Keith, visited the GCA School and interviewed the staff and students for an article on GCA training and developments that appeared in the July 1949 issue of the magazine.[3]

On 13 March, No 426 Squadron formed a Housing Committee (with Wing Commander Mussells as President) to assess all applications for married quarters, the allocation of which was determined on a sliding point scale. Housing Committee meetings were scheduled for the second Thursday of each month.

On 14 March, four officers began a GCA Operator Course, and Wing Commander Mussells went to Air Force Headquarters in Ottawa for a conference on special commitments for summer 1949 with Wing Commander W.F. Parks of No 435 Squadron and Air Commodore Ross and Wing Commander W.P. Pleasance of Air Transport Command Headquarters.

On 15 March, Wing Commander V.R. Hill was transferred from Cartierville, where he had been serving as the resident RCAF engineer at the Canadair plant, to North West Air Command Headquarters in Edmonton.

On 21 March, two District Courts Martial were held at Lachine, with Squadron Leader E. Miall from E & PE Rockcliffe presiding. The next day, a Commanding Officer's Parade, with the usual inspections of personnel and facilities, was held at Dorval and Lachine.

On 28 March, the first DC–4M Argonaut (a North Star variant) built by Canadair for the British Overseas Airways Corporation left Dorval for Britain, captained by Canadair test pilot A.J. Lilly. Twenty-one more Argonauts would eventually follow.[4]

On 29 March, in addition to his navigation duties, Flying Officer J.A.L.P. Rodrique took on the job of Unit Housing Officer. His new responsibilities included advertising in the Montreal-area newspapers for accommodation suitable for squadron families; keeping records of available housing; and notifying squadron members who needed housing about available rentals and how much they would have to pay in rent.

On 31 March, No 426 Squadron had 335 personnel on strength, twenty-one pupils in training at the GCA School, and eight North Stars on the inventory.[5] On the national scene, the Crown Colony of Newfoundland became the tenth Canadian province, following the passage of a plebiscite on 11 December 1948.

April

On 1 April, the RCAF celebrated the 25th anniversary of its formation with several major organizational changes. Central Air Command, headquartered at RCAF Station Trenton, was disbanded and Training Command was formed in its place, with Air Vice Marshal E.E. Middleton remaining in command until his retirement on 31 August 1949. No 10 Group, Central Air Command, which was based at Halifax, was renamed Maritime Group with Air Commodore F.G. Wait remaining as the Air Officer Commanding. Maintenance Command was renamed Air Materiel Command and moved from No 8 Temporary Building in downtown Ottawa to RCAF Station Rockcliffe; Air Vice Marshal R.E. McBurney continued in command until his retirement in 1951. No 11 Group, North West Air Command, based in Winnipeg, was renamed Tactical Air Group; Air Commodore M. Costello remained as Air Officer Commanding.[6]

RCAF plans for 1949–50 included transferring RCAF Station Goose Bay from Central Air Command to Air Transport Command, and this change, too, was made effective 1 April 1949.

No 426 Squadron celebrated the RCAF Silver Jubilee with a Commanding Officer's Parade in the morning, at which Wing Commander Mussells presented the Long Service Medal to Squadron Leader C.D. McLean, Flight Lieutenant R.A. Gilmour and Flight Sergeant F.J. Hill, each of whom heard the history of his RCAF career read to those present on parade. The parade ended with a squadron march-past, with the medal recipients taking the salute, and was followed by refreshments at the Airmen's Canteen and a dinner "fit for a king" for all ranks. During the afternoon, squadron personnel and their guests were treated to a movie at the Station Theatre, and the guests were then taken to Dorval for a tour of No 6 Hangar and the North Star aircraft. The day's celebrations closed with a huge station dance in the Drill Hall, with music by the RCMP Band.

On 4 April, delegates of twelve nations—including Norman Robertson for Canada—signed the North Atlantic Treaty at a ceremony in Washington, D.C.. Parliament ratified the treaty on 29 April.[7]

On 8 April, the GCA School received a visit from a party of nine officials of the International Civil Aviation Organization, a Montreal-based agency of the United Nations, led by a Mr. Cooper. They toured the entire school, with particular attention to the Demonstration Laboratory, and watched a practical demonstration of ground-controlled approach in action.

On 11 April, No 426 Squadron despatched a North Star to Britain to pick up a load of badly needed spare parts for the British-built Vampire aircraft in RCAF service; the flight returned to base on 15 April. On 12 April, Mr. E.F. Reedy of the Sperry Gyroscope Company arrived at the GCA School for talks with the staff on the school's acquisition of specialized equipment. On 13 April, students on the second GCA Technician Course started writing theory examinations.

North West Air Command Operation Order 7/49, dated 12 April 1949, initiated RCAF involvement in *Operation EAGLE*, scheduled for August. *Op EAGLE* was a combined exercise mounted by the Army's Western Command and North West Air Command for the RCAF to test the Calgary-based battalion of Princess Patricia's Canadian Light Infantry in its new role as an airborne and air-transportable unit. The RCAF would provide the airlift, and North West Air Command would exercise all its forces in the air-reconnaissance, close-support and air-transport roles. The exercise forces required considerably more air transport than North West Air Command could provide, so Air Transport Command was tasked with providing a large portion of the *Op EAGLE* Transport Wing, including its commander, Wing Commander W.H. Swetman, who was not only an experienced transport commander—he had completed the Transport Support Course given by the Canadian Joint Air Training Centre, at Rivers, Manitoba—but also an ex-Thunderbird, one of the squadron's most successful wartime commanders.[8]

Good Friday and Easter Monday were statutory holidays so all squadron personnel not employed on essential duties were stood down from 1700 hours on Thursday 14 April until 0800 hours on Tuesday, 19 April. The flight with the Vampire spares came in from Britain on Good Friday, and another, similar flight departed for Britain to pick up another load. It was delayed overseas and did not return until 2 May.

On 19 April, a Canadian Pacific Airlines flight departed Vancouver for Anchorage, Alaska, the first stop on the airline's first survey run to Hong Kong.

Canadian Pacific Airlines started life as an off-shoot of the Canadian Pacific Railway. In 1940, when the RCAF was recruiting every bush pilot it could get, the CPR started buying up northern bush-flying operations, most of which were in dire financial straits. On 1 July 1942, a new CPR subsidiary, Canadian Pacific Airlines, formally commenced operations in a market clamouring for air-transport services, flying the bush routes, conducting operations for RAF Ferry Command, and carrying out RCAF contracts for aircrew training, and aircraft maintenance and overhaul. The airline's days as a CPR subsidiary were numbered, however; under an Order-in-Council, the railway was compelled to divest itself of the airline as soon as hostilities ended.

In 1947, the newly independent Canadian Pacific Airlines under President Grant McConachie started opening air routes around the Pacific Rim, and decided to buy four North Stars (at that time still known as "Canadair Fours") to service them. By April 1949, CP had extended its reach north to Alaska and south to California, and time had come to develop trans-Pacific routes. The 19 April survey flight was planned to include several airports that could serve as alternates for Anchorage, and the CP crew visited Northway, Big Delta and Fairbanks before they departed for for Shemya, a tiny island near the end of the Aleutian chain, with a USAF base. After some local training, the CP flight pressed on to Tokyo, where the crew practised approaches and landings at Haneda Airport. From Tokyo, the CP crew proceeded to Osaka, Hiroshima and Fukuoka before heading out for Shanghai and Hong Kong. The return trip included stops at Okinawa, Tokyo, Misawa, the Aleutian island of Adak, and Anchorage before arriving at Vancouver on 1 May. In fifteen months, this North Pacific route would become very familiar territory to No 426 Squadron crews engaged in the Korean airlift.[9]

On 21 April, Mr. G. Dekoyer, Gilfillian Technical Representative and advisor to the USAF GCA Unit at Edmonton (part of the North West Staging Route), arrived at Dorval for a liaison visit to the GCA School. On 26 April, the Squadron Adjutant, Flight Lieutenant H.E. Carling, was posted to Air Force Headquarters; he was replaced by Flight Lieutenant P.E. O'Neil, who reported in on 2 May.

On 27 April, a Commanding Officer's Parade was held in No 6 Hangar, which Wing Commander Mussells inspected after he was finished with the squadron. On 29 April, a special flight was despatched to Frobisher Bay and Arctic Bay (it returned on 1 May).

On the same day, Air Transport Command Headquarters announced the transfer to ICAO in Montreal of Wing Commander W.P. Pleasance, Senior Air Staff Officer; during the last months of the war, Pleasance was the Station Commander at RCAF Station Linton-on-Ouse in Yorkshire. His replacement at Air Transport Command Headquarters was none other than Wing Commander W.H. Swetman, Commanding Officer No 412 Squadron at Rockcliffe and a wartime commander of the Thunderbirds. The transfers were to take place in August.

On 30 April, No 426 Squadron had 393 personnel on strength, including seventeen GCA School pupils, and eight North Stars on the inventory.[10]

Dorval, 1949

May

In May, the GCA School was the focus of considerable activity. On 3 May, Flying Officer A.T. Mather, the commandant of the GCA Unit in Edmonton, reported in on temporary duty to spend a week collecting copies of examinations, checking on equipment modifications and discussing operating procedures. On 5 May, Squadron Leader Webber and Flying Officer L.J. Lomas arrived in a B-25 Mitchell bomber from the Central Flying School at RCAF Station Trenton. They spent the next two days at Dorval making GCA runs so the school staff could test the students on GCA Operator Course No 2. On 10 May and 12 May, Trenton sent more Mitchells so the student controllers could complete their twin-engine requirement. To give the student operators enough time for their practical training, the GCA Operator Course was extended until 3 June. On 17 May, Wing Commander A.L. Bocking and Wing Commander D.E. Galloway arrived from Air Force Headquarters during the evening to make four night GCA runs in a Beechcraft, and reported that they were quite satisfied with the performance of both the controllers and the GCA equipment. On 19 May, the Air Armament School at Trenton despatched a Lancaster to give the student controllers practical experience with four-engine aircraft.

On 6 May, a special committee was appointed at the Lachine site to allocate garden plots to married personnel who might like to save some money on vegetables, or perhaps to take a little light exercise. On 11 May, about 90 percent of the squadron personnel turned out in response to a call for volunteers to give blood at a Red Cross clinic at Lachine.

At the United Nations, Philip Jessup, the American representative on the Security Council, and his Soviet counterpart, Yakov Malik, held discussions that resulted in the removal on 12 May of the blockade on Berlin. Despite this landmark agreement, the airlift continued until October.[11]

When selecting the route for an overseas airlift operation, planners had to consider several factors. The first factor to be considered was the maximum load the aircraft could carry, usually determined by the distance to be flown on the longest stage of the trip. The next priority, particularly for routes with many stopover points, was the availability of suitable "airports of entry" (usually abbreviated AOE), including alternative airports for use in emergencies. For each airport, route planners checked and carefully analyzed details such as the length and strength of the runways, the availability and quality of local supplies of POL (Petrol, Oil and Lubricants), the quality of servicing facilities, and the availability of navigational and landing aids. Typical weather conditions for the entire route had to be considered because of the effect of weather on flight safety, crew fatigue and passenger comfort.

As a general principle, as few stops as possible were included; the more stops, the higher the costs of personnel (slip crews, maintenance crews), facilities, spares and handling equipment. For each stopover point, planners had to evaluate access to air services (meteorology, communications, flight-following), and the availability and quality of housekeeping facilities (accommodation for slip crews, maintenance crews and liaison personnel), in-flight food services, fleet services (cleaning of aircraft), emergency medical and dental services, and government services such as Customs and Immigration. Emergency accommodation for delayed passengers and crews had to be organized.

RCAF planners also had to pay close attention to political considerations, such as restrictions on entering another country's territorial airspace, or using communications and navigation services at foreign airports. To ensure that RCAF aircraft and crews would not encounter problems, the planners at Air Force Headquarters had to maintain close contact with their counterparts in the Department of External Affairs, who would handle the diplomatic arrangements.

Finally, any unit involved in an airlift operation had to ensure that all deployed personnel were suitably immunized against disease, issued with environmental clothing, and provided with travel documents and cash in the appropriate currencies.

At 0450 hours on 23 May, No 426 Squadron launched NS17516 on the first of several training flights across the South Atlantic to collect information on routes and airfields in case of an as yet unforeseen operational requirement. This trip had a practical side, too; the flight was scheduled to stop in Britain to pick up two Vampire engines purchased by the RCAF. As one object of the exercise was to familiarize as many personnel as possible with conditions along the route, the manifest included two complete crews plus eight ground-crew airmen and Squadron Leader G.G. Wright, the Staff Officer Training Operations from Air Transport Command Headquarters.

The flight headed first to Ramey Air Force Base in Puerto Rico, then to Atkinson Field in British Guiana (now Guyana), and then to Natal, Brazil. The hop across the South Atlantic was made from Natal to Dakar, French West Africa (now Senegal) and, from there, the flight headed north to Gibraltar and then to Britain, stopping first at RAF Station Lyneham, near Swindon, Wiltshire, and then arriving at the De Havilland plant in Hatfield, Hertfordshire, just north of London, at 1650 hours on 31 May.

During the journey, the cargo to be picked up in England had changed slightly; at Hatfield, the last stop before departing for home, 7,100 pounds of Vampire spares were loaded. The flight left Hatfield at 0605 hours on 4 June, stopped briefly at RAF Lyneham, and then flew directly to Dorval with only brief refuelling stops at Keflavik, Iceland and Goose Bay, arriving at base at 2340 hours on 4 June after flying a total of 60 hours and 50 minutes. The entire training mission was completed without a hitch, an achievement attributed to excellent planning and the competence of the crew, which included Wing Commander C.H. Mussells (Commanding Officer, No 426 Squadron), Flying Officer H.T. Giles (captain), Flight Lieutenant G.L. Sheahan (pilot), Flying Officer J. Calipeau (pilot), Flying Officer R.M. Edwards (pilot), Flying Officer J.C. Hickey (navigator), Flying Officer A. Glustien (navigator), Flying Officer G.C. Whittington (wireless operator), Flying Officer R.W. Nymark (wireless operator), Flight Lieutenant W.H. Smith (Engineering Officer, No 426 Squadron), Sergeant R.T. Smith (flight engineer), Sergeant A.A.

Drackley, (flight engineer), Corporal K.F. Chabot (aero-engine technician), Leading Aircraftsman C.W. Brown (airframe technician), Corporal J.H. Belanger (electrical technician), Warrant Officer Second Class J.S.L. Coates (instrument technician), Corporal P. Zimmer (radio technician), and Leading Aircraftsman L.M. Flemming (air traffic assistant).[12]

On 23 May, an RAF Lincoln on an overseas run from the Britain arrived at Dorval. The crew spent the next two days touring the squadron facilities, and being briefed on the North Star aircraft and the GCA School and its programs.

On 28 May, Canadian Pacific Airlines sent out a second Pacific survey flight, this time to Australia, using their new North Star aircraft, Empress of Vancouver, registered as CF-CPR. The CP flight departed from Vancouver, refuelled in San Francisco, and then proceeded to Honolulu, where the crew completed some local flight training. From Honolulu, the flight continued to Palmyra Island, Canton Island (where they refuelled), Nandi in Fiji and, finally, Sydney, Australia. In Australia, they visited CP's registered alternate airports at Williamstown (near Melbourne), Brisbane and Dubbo (northwest of Sydney). From Sydney, the flight departed for Auckland, New Zealand with a stop at Ohakea, a possible alternate airport southeast of Wanganui. The return to Vancouver from New Zealand was routed by way of Nandi, Tongatabu, Canton Island, Honolulu and San Francisco, and arrived at base in Vancouver on 11 June. CP service from Vancouver to Australia began on 10 July with a "pre-inaugural" flight; the first scheduled run departed three days later.[13]

June

On 1 June, two No 426 Squadron aircraft, captained by Flight Lieutenant A.B. Hammond and Flight Lieutenant E.L. Banks, escorted the Constellation airliner carrying Prince Bernhardt of the Netherlands to Dorval. While touring the Thunderbird facilities, the Prince, a capable pilot, expressed a desire to fly in a North Star, so he was taken up for a short orientation flight during which he took the controls.

At Lachine, work began on the conversion of Building No 14, formerly a detention barracks, into transient accommodation for twenty personnel. When completed, the project helped alleviate the congestion that often prevailed in the Airmen's Barracks.

On 4 June, North Star 17516 and its crew returned to base, having completed their very successful South Atlantic training flight. To publicize and commemorate Air Force Day on 11 June, two squadron aircraft captained by Flight Lieutenant H.T. Giles and Flight Lieutenant A.B. Hammond visited the RCAF stations at Camp Borden, Aylmer, Centralia and Trenton (all in southern Ontario), and made a fly-past at each station. On the same day, chaplains Air Commodore D.E. MacKell from Air Force Headquarters and Squadron Leader N.J. Gallagher from Air Transport Command Headquarters departed Dorval in NS17514 captained by Flight Lieutenant R.J. Brown for France, by way of Britain; they were to represent the RCAF at the Eucharistic Congress in Paris.

On 13 June, Major Kotze of the Royal South African Air Force visited the squadron to learn how a RCAF transport unit and its aircraft functioned. On 18 June, personnel from the Maintenance Branch at Air Transport Command Headquarters arrived in Dorval to study the condition and availability of North Star ground handling equipment. Their mission was part of the preparations for the proposed re-equipping of No 435 Squadron with the North Star.

On 20 June, Group Captain R.F. Gibb, Wing Commander D.G. Nelson and Squadron Leader Duncan arrived from Air Transport Command Headquarters to inspect No 426 Squadron's administrative offices and maintenance workshops. On the same day, North Star 17520, captained by Flight Lieutenant J.D. Dickson, left Dorval for Rockcliffe carrying members of the Joint Defence Board on their way to begin a tour of the Canadian North. The passengers included General A.G.L. McNaughton, Rear Admiral F.L. Houghton, Major General H.D. Graham and Air Vice Marshal C.R. Dunlap, plus assistants and advisors. At Winnipeg, the first stop on the tour, they picked up the American members of the Joint Defence Board—General Henry, General Walsh, General Bolte and Admiral Libby, plus *their* assistants. The flight then proceeded to Edmonton, Whitehorse, Teslin, Watson Lake, Norman Wells, Fort Norman, Sawmill Bay, Port Radium, Churchill and then to Toronto. The aircraft returned to base on 27 June.

During June, plans were made at Air Transport Command Headquarters to carry out *Operation MOBILITY*, an exercise to test the rapid deployment capability of No 426 Squadron and No 435 Squadron. Not much deployment training had been done since the end of the war, and the goal was to have all squadrons in Air Transport Command trained and equipped to deploy anywhere in North America on six hours of notice, and to be able to operate essentially from their own resources for up to two weeks. The plan was to run the exercise on a weekend so both squadrons could be back at work on their regular operations on Monday.

On 30 June, No 426 Squadron had 399 personnel on strength, including seventeen GCA school students, and eight North Stars on the inventory.[14]

July

On 1 July, Flight Lieutenant A.B. Hammond, captain of NS17520, departed base for Rockcliffe, where he picked up a party of senior Air Force officers and officials bound for Gander (by way of Torbay) to attend a conference. The following day, Flight Lieutenant H.T. Giles captained NS17511 on a special run to Vancouver and Edmonton to airlift auxiliary and summer employment personnel to a camp at RCAF Station Gimli. After making the trip from Edmonton to Gimli twice, the aircraft proceeded to Kinross, Michigan to pick up a group of Army personnel bound for Trenton. The aircraft returned to base on 4 July.

On 5 July Flight Lieutenant J.D. Dickson and his crew flew NS17517 to Rockcliffe, where they took on fifteen passengers and 4,512 pounds of freight, and then proceeded to Resolute Bay by way of Lansdowne House and Trout Lake, with an overnight stopover at Churchill and a direct return to base with only a brief stopover at Rockcliffe. On this trip, the crew used the grid navigation technique essential for safe flying in the Arctic. On 9 July, Flight Lieutenant E.L. Banks captained NS17516 on a special run to Trenton to pick up a load of soldiers bound for Kinross, Michigan to attended a course run by the US Army. The aircraft returned to base the following day.

On 11 July, the squadron despatched another South Atlantic training flight, using the same stop-overs and airports on the same route used on the first exercise. The crew included the following members: Flight Lieutenant J.D. Dickson (captain), Flight Lieutenant A.B. Hammond (pilot), Flight Lieutenant A.J.P. Byford (pilot), Flight Lieutenant J.A. Watt (pilot), Flight Lieutenant J.H.C. Boby (navigator), Flight Lieutenant L.W. Queale (navigator) and Flying Officer H.J. Weeden (navigator), Flight Lieutenant C.E. Endersbe (wireless operator), Flying Officer J.W. Santarelli (wireless operator) and Flying Officer W. Smith (wireless operator). The trip terminated successfully at Dorval on 22 July.

On 15 July, Flight Lieutenant H.T. Giles in NS17520 and Flight Lieutenant J.R. Bell in NS17507 left Dorval for Winnipeg, Gimli, Edmonton and Vancouver to take the personnel attending the summer camp at Gimli back to their respective bases.

On 20 July, fifty airmen from No 426 Squadron maintenance section toured No 202 Base Workshops, the enormous RCEME operation at Longue Pointe, in an effort to improve liaison between RCAF and Army personnel, and to learn how the Army ran a large maintenance operation.

On the same day, a Thunderbird aircraft captained by Flight Lieutenant G.W. Allen flew to Rockcliffe, where two passengers and 5,000 pounds of freight were loaded, and then proceeded to Churchill, the next stop on the run terminating at Resolute Bay. Although the outward flight was routine, the aircraft had to spend the night in Churchill because the weather at Resolute Bay was below limits. The Resolute Bay leg was completed the next day at 19,000 feet instead of the normal 6,000 to 8,000 feet; the aircraft had to fly above the overcast to permit the navigator to obtain heading checks on the sun to rate the aircraft's directional gyro indicator and maintain his grid-navigation plot. Three hours after arriving in Resolute, the crew turned back to base, making only brief stops at Churchill and Rockcliffe.

On 22 July, the Air Staff at Air Transport Command Headquarters was reorganized, and Squadron Leader F.Y. Craig assumed the position of Staff Officer Navigation (SO Nav), replacing Squadron Leader J.V. Watts, who was posted to the RCAF Staff College on course.

On 25 July, another south Atlantic training flight departed base in NS17514 with the following crew members: Flight Lieutenant J.R. Bell (captain), Flight Lieutenant R.J. Brown, Flight Lieutenant B.C. Denomy, Flight Lieutenant K.A. McCoy, Flight Lieutenant R.E.D. Ratcliffe, Flying Officer A.A. Gilbert, Flying Officer J.A.L.P. Rodrique, Flying Officer G.G.D. McIntosh and Flying Officer E.R. Wolkowski. After an uneventful trip, NS17514 returned to base on 6 August.[15]

On 28 July, Flight Lieutenant E.L. Banks and his crew departed Dorval in NS17520 for RAF Station Northolt, Middlesex, via Gander for refuelling. The passenger list included Air Vice Marshal C.M. McEwen and the model aircraft team representing Canada in a British competition. The aircraft and crew returned on 1 August with a load of passengers from the Imperial Defence College, headed by Major-General Oliver.

July was one of the year's most active flying months; No 426 Squadron's fleet of eight North Stars put in a total of 721 flying hours. On 31 July, squadron strength stood at 408 personnel, including sixty-eight officers, 278 airmen, fifteen airmen training at the GCA school, and forty-seven civilians.

August

The main event of the summer for No 426 Squadron was *Operation EAGLE*, scheduled to run from 5 August to 8 August. *Op EAGLE* was a combined exercise designed to test the Calgary-based battalion of Princess Patricia's Canadian Light Infantry in its new airborne, air-transportable role, and to give the RCAF practice in supporting an airborne operation. It was also to give the Army and Air Force staffs practical experience in developing and conducting a combined operation, and an opportunity for RCAF Station personnel to practise airfield defence. The exercise area was on the North West Staging Route, served by airports in Grande Prairie, Alberta and Fort St. John, British Columbia. Most of the Transport Wing, commanded by Wing Commander W.H. Swetman, came from Air Transport Command units: No 435 Squadron from Edmonton, augmented by Dakotas from No 412 Squadron in Rockcliffe and North Stars from No 426 Squadron. Air Commodore A.D. Ross and several senior officers from Ottawa were present to observe the exercise.[16]

On 2 August, No 426 Squadron deployed its first aircraft for *Op EAGLE*: NS17517, captained by Squadron Leader H.A. Morrison. On 4 August, Flight Lieutenant A.B. Hammond with NS17512 and Flight Lieutenant E.L. Banks with NS17520 departed Dorval, Banks' crew to deliver observers and umpires to Grande Prairie and Fort St. John, and the other two crews to airlift troops to the exercise area. All the Thunderbird aircraft were back at by 9 August.[17]

Operation EAGLE revealed that all of Canada west of the Lakehead and north to the Arctic was defended by a fighter force comprising only six obsolete North American P-51 Mustangs and a few De Havilland Vampires flown by reserve squadrons. Despite the Air Force participants' limited resources, they achieved the objectives of the exercise, indicating that Canada's peacetime forces were maintaining a high level of skill and spirit.[18]

Several staff changes took place at Air Transport Command Headquarters during August. Wing Commander R.J. Lane was posted from Air Force Headquarters on 8 August to take over as Senior Personnel Staff Officer (SPSO) from Group Captain R.S. Turnbull, who became the new Director of Selection and Manning at Air Force Headquarters. On 15 August, Wing Commander W.H. Swetman left No 412 Squadron to become the Senior Air Staff Officer, replacing Wing Commander W.P. Pleasance, who was assigned to ICAO in Montreal. On 18 August, Squadron Leader G.J. Bury from RCAF Station Centralia took over the position of Chief Signals Officer from Squadron Leader H.R.R. Trepanier, who departed for Air Material Command.

On 10 August, the AVRO C.102 Jetliner made its first flight at Malton Airport near Toronto. The C.102 Jetliner was the first North American-built jet transport, and it performed admirably on hundreds of flights, but AVRO built only one; neither the Canadian government nor the airlines would back the project, and the manufacturer eventually scrapped it.[19]

On 10 August, NS17514 captained by Flight Lieutenant R.J. Brown departed base on another special flight to Resolute Bay by way of Rockcliffe, where passengers and freight were loaded, and Frobisher Bay. The aircraft returned to base the following day after stopping at Rockcliffe again. On 12 August, Flight Lieutenant A.B. Hammond in NS17517 made another run to Resolute Bay, this time via Rockcliffe and Churchill; Hammond returned the next day.

On 14 August, Flight Lieutenant J.R. Bell and his crew in NS17520 departed Dorval for RAF Station Northolt with thirty-two army veterans bound for France for a ceremony marking the seventh anniversary of the Dieppe Raid. Routed via Goose Bay and Keflavik, the overseas run was uneventful, as was the return flight on 24 August.

On 15 August, the squadron launched another south Atlantic training flight, including all the stopovers and landings used on previous flights, and transporting twenty-seven Imperial Defence College students from Gibraltar to RAF Station Lyneham. The flight crew included Squadron Leader J.H.C. Lewis, Squadron Leader F.Y. Craig, Flight Lieutenant R.C.M. Bayliss, Flight Lieutenant E.J.J. Boland, Flight Lieutenant J.T. Dalton, Flying Officer R.J. Bayne, Flying Officer R.S. Reid, Flying Officer J.W. Rodger, Flying Officer D.G. Selby and Flying Officer G.W. Webb.

On 17 August, two more squadron aircraft were despatched to Resolute Bay by way of Rockcliffe, where they loaded passengers and freight. These special summer flights were giving both air and ground crews invaluable experience in operating into the high Arctic, which would stand them in good stead in the winter to come. At Dorval, the squadron started active training in formation flying to prepare for the RCAF display and fly-pasts scheduled for the Canadian National Exhibition in Toronto.

On 22 August, the Squadron Engineering Officer attended meetings at Air Transport Command Headquarters regarding completing the winterization of all squadron aircraft, and Pilots' Notes and Procedures were amended accordingly. The Engineering Officer submitted a list prepared by the Supply Officers of recommended winter operations equipment to be procured.

On 25 August, five squadron aircraft departed for RCAF Station Trenton to spend two weeks performing daily at the CNE, and returning once each week to Dorval for maintenance inspections and crew changes. This arrangement was devised to give as many pilots as possible the chance to gain formation flying experience.

On 24 August, HMCS *Swansea*, a Royal Canadian Navy frigate, departed Halifax for Frobisher Bay, the first stop of a month-long Arctic cruise. The RCAF had agreed to provide ice-reconnaissance services for the first ten days of September, and No 426 Squadron had orders to have a North Star in Frobisher Bay by 29 August. Flight Lieutenant J.D. Dixon and his crew in NS17517 departed as scheduled, and stopped at Fort Chimo on the way.

On 31 August, a tragic accident happened at Lachine: the two-year-old son of Flying Officer Jack Richardson accidentally fell into the Officers' Mess swimming pool and drowned.

September
On the morning of 1 September, Flight Lieutenant E.L. Banks and his crew departed base in NS17520 for Rockcliffe, where they embarked Prime Minister Louis St. Laurent and a party bound for Banff, Alberta for the annual convention of the Canadian Bar Association. The Prime Minister and his party returned to Ottawa on 6 September.

On 4 September, the final South Atlantic training flight departed base with Flight Lieutenant R. Coates of the RAF, an exchange officer, as captain. The same route was used as on the previous flights, and the crew included Squadron Leader J.H.C. Lewis, Squadron Leader D.W. Henry, Flight Lieutenant G.W. Allen, Flying Officer N.E. Bohn, Flying Officer R.J. Cumming, Flying Officer J.W. Michaud and Flying Officer A.L. Quickfall.

On 10 September, No 426 Squadron received a delegation of senior officers from Air Materiel Command Headquarters, the RAF and executives of several American manufacturers of oxygen equipment, who came to inspect the liquid oxygen system installed in the squadron's North Star aircraft. On the same day, squadron crews took seventy-five seamen from HMS *Glasgow*, which was making a port visit during a training cruise, for a flight over Montreal. The matelots greatly enjoyed their aerial tour.

On 15 September, No 421 (Red Indian) Squadron was reformed at Chatham, New Brunswick as the second RCAF jet fighter squadron, equipped with the DH-100 Vampire. In January 1951, this squadron moved to the United Kingdom.[20]

On Friday, 16 September, Air Transport Command Headquarters signalled a warning order to No 426 Squadron and No 435 Squadron, initiating *Operation MOBILITY*. At 1200 hours, the Squadron Commander opened the sealed orders he received ten days before, and learned that No 426 Squadron at Dorval and No 435 Squadron at Edmonton were to swap bases and duties, except for the service flights from Edmonton to Whitehorse and back, which would remain a squadron responsibility.

Op MOBILITY was designed to test the speed with which both squadrons could mobilize and to identify supply and maintenance problems likely to arise when mobilizing in response to a national emergency. Movement began on Saturday, and 196 squadron personnel were operationally ready at Edmonton on the following Monday morning. The last Thunderbird aircraft departed Dorval only nine hours after the first, and the first aircraft despatched from Edmonton took off about twenty-one hours after the movement order was received.

On Saturday, 17 September, five Dakotas from No 435 Squadron flew in to Dorval with 102 personnel to carry out their part of *Op MOBILITY*; fortunately, the quarters at Lachine had room for all the visitors. *Op MOBILITY* finished on 1 October, when both squadrons returned to their home bases, and was judged extremely successful from the operational point of view.[21]

On 18 September, Air Commodore D.E. MacKell and several senior officers from Air Force Headquarters arrived at Dorval to inspect the squadron briefly and receive a briefing on the progress of *Op MOBILITY*. At Lachine, Motor Equipment Section finished installing a hydraulic vehicle hoist, a job that involved taking the roof off the building—a worthwhile effort, when weighed against the maintenance time and effort the hoist would save.

Great social and political changes taking place around the world would soon bring No 426 Squadron into a new phase of operations.

On 21 September, following parliamentary elections in August, the new Federal Republic of Germany, established on 8 May 1949 from the American, British and French occupation zones, received its first democratically elected government under the leadership of Chancellor Konrad Adenauer. On 7 October, the Soviet occupation zone became the German Democratic Republic; in 1950, a single list of candidates would be "elected" to form its government.

In the Far East, the late summer of 1949 saw the Red Army in control of almost all of mainland China. On 21 September, the Communist Party declared a People's Republic of China; at the end of the month, Mao Tse-Tung, the leader of the Communist Party, was proclaimed head of state with the title of Chairman of the People's Consultative Council; and on 1 October, the Central Government of the People's Republic of China was proclaimed in Beijing.[22]

On 23 September, President Harry S. Truman of the United States made a public statement, without details, to the effect that an atomic explosion had recently taken place in the Soviet Union, and that an effective and enforceable international control of atomic energy was required. In October 1951 the United States confirmed that two more nuclear explosions had taken place in the Soviet Union; the Soviet government's claim that it had conducted a test involving thermo-nuclear reactions was verified by the United States in August 1953. In September 1954, the Soviet government announced that it had set off yet another atomic explosion.[23]

On 28 September, a Dakota from No 412 Squadron arrived in Dorval from Rockcliffe, with Minister of National Defence Brooke Claxton aboard, accompanied by Sir Arthur Henderson, the British Minister for Air; the Chief of the Air Staff, Air Marshal W.A. Curtiss; Air Chief Marshal Hollinghurst of the RAF; Air Commodore J.L. Hurley and Mrs. Hurley; and several personal staff officers and advisors. After a short inspection of the squadron facilities, the Minister and his party departed for Cartierville and a tour of the Canadair plant.

On 30 September, RCAF Station Trenton was the scene of a major presentation ceremony, the unveiling of the Memorial Gates, presented to Canada by Australia, New Zealand and the United Kingdom in gratitude for the British Commonwealth Air Training Plan, which produced tens of thousands of trained aircrew during the Second World War. In October 1940, the first BCATP graduates to proceed overseas—a class of "observers" (later called navigators)—received

their wings. Trenton later became the hub of an enormous Canada-wide system of schools producing pilots, navigators, bomb aimers, air gunners and wireless operators.

The distinguished guests—200 in all—included the Governor General of Canada, Field Marshal Viscount Alexander of Tunis; Prime Minister Louis St. Laurent; the former Prime Minister, William Lyon Mackenzie King; Minister of National Defence Brooke Claxton; the former Minister of National Defence for Air, C.G. Power; the Chief of the Air Staff, Air Marshal W.A. Curtis; Sir Arthur Henderson, the Minister for Air in the British government; the Australian High Commissioner, F.M. Forde; the High Commissioner for New Zealand, James Thorn; and many senior civil servants and service personnel. The guests assembled in Ottawa, and were flown to and from Trenton by Air Transport Command. No 426 Squadron contributed NS17520 to the airlift.[24]

October

In Ottawa, plans were going forward to mount *Exercise SWEET BRIAR*, a major "joint and combined force" exercise, scheduled for early 1950 and designed to develop procedures, doctrine and techniques for Arctic deployment of American and Canadian land and air forces, including No 408 Squadron, No 426 Squadron and No 435 Squadron. Air Transport Command alerted its participating squadrons to prepare lists of the technical spares and ground-handling equipment they would need, and to submit all outstanding weatherizing requirements for their respective aircraft. All this information was to be passed to Air Transport Command Headquarters in time for a meeting at Air Material Command on 6–7 October to finalize the RCAF technical requirements for *SWEET BRIAR*.

On 1 October, No 426 Squadron was advised that sixteen of its airmen had been promoted and, with *Operation MOBILITY* completed, the aircraft and crews of No 435 Squadron departed for Edmonton while the Thunderbirds and their aircraft returned to Dorval and Lachine.

The next day, Flight Lieutenant Sheahan and his crew in NS17520 departed for Rockcliffe, where they embarked several senior British civil servants and RAF officers bound for the United Kingdom, most of whom had been in Canada for the Memorial Gates presentation at Trenton. The group included Lord Robb, Secretary of State for Air, and Lady Robb; Air Chief Marshal Hollinghurst; Air Commodore J.L. Hurley, the Air Member of the Canadian Joint Staff in London, and Mrs. Hurley. During the war, Air Commodore Hurley commanded No 62 Base at Linton-on-Ouse where No 426 Squadron was stationed. Except for a five-hour delay at Keflavik, the overseas flight was routine. The aircraft returned to Dorval on 7 October with twenty-one Army and Air Force passengers.

On 4 October, Squadron Leader H.A. Morrison and his crew made the freight run to Resolute Bay, with the usual stops at Rockcliffe and Churchill on the way. On 8 October, Flying Officer G.W. Webb and his crew took out NS17520 for a special flight; after stopping at Rockcliffe to pick up a small party of senior officers that included Lord and Lady Tedder and Air Marshal W.A. Curtis, they flew the group to Edmonton, Norman Wells and Grande Prairie, returning to Rockcliffe and Dorval on 14 October.

During the first week in October, discussions were held at Air Transport Command Headquarters regarding TCA's Link Trainer facility at Dorval. After comparing the number of hours of Link Trainer time used by No 426 Squadron and other RCAF units since 1947 with Air Transport Command requirements for 1950, Air Force Headquarters had decided to review the arrangement with TCA. Air Transport Command considered the Link Trainer essential to keep current with all domestic, American and trans-oceanic instrument flying procedures.

Interest had been expressed at Air Force Headquarters in the possibility of acquiring the American-built APS42 search radar, or other equipment of similar performance. The APS42 was then in the pre-production stage of development and was reported to have an excellent search range. It would be at least seven years before No 426 Squadron's North Star aircraft were fitted with this equipment.

On 10 October, Squadron Leader H.A. Morrison again captained a freight run to Resolute Bay with the usual stops en route and on the return two days later.

On 14 October, Air Commodore Ross (AOC Air Transport Command) wrote to Air Force Headquarters seeking approval for his training proposal, arguing that Air Transport Command had to be prepared for two crucial war-time roles: providing strategic transport, as needed, anywhere in the world, and providing and supervising air ferry services to any theatre of war. (This argument was both realistic and prophetic; before long, the RCAF would be conducting airlift operations to the Far East, the Middle East and Africa.) Air Commodore Ross went on to say that, if they were to carry out those tasks, transport squadrons and Air Transport Command staff would need a good knowledge of operating conditions along any air route that was or could be available. Air Transport Command could perform some aspects of both roles already, partly because of the long range training conducted over the preceding year and a half, and Ross was proposing that this training continue.

Air Commodore Ross pointed out that, at the beginning of 1948, Air Transport Command had almost no aircrew qualified to fly across either the Atlantic or the Pacific; several units had individual aircrew members with long-range flying expertise, but no RCAF squadron had been in a position to give even a single formed crew any experience in trans-oceanic flying. To create a nucleus of trained aircrew, No 426 Squadron had made five training flights across the North Atlantic to Britain, followed by six more flights to Britain by the South Atlantic route. At the time of writing, the squadron had eleven captains, nine co-pilots, fourteen navigators and eight radio officers fully qualified on routes that included the West Indies, the east coast of South America, West Africa, Gibraltar, the Azores, the United Kingdom and Iceland as well as domestic routes around North America. A considerable fund of knowledge of operating conditions over these regions had been acquired.

Air Commodore Ross's letter also advised Air Force Headquarters that No 426 Squadron was now required to make one trip per month to Resolute Bay, and planned to use this airfield as a base for High Arctic training. Some of the Resolute Bay flights would return to Dorval by way of Whitehorse to give the crews—especially navigators—yet more Arctic flying experience.

The feeling in Air Transport Command was that the time had come to expand the training effort to the Pacific and, eventually, around the world. After careful study of world air routes, available bases, weather on the various routes through the seasons, navigation facilities and related issues, the Staff Officer Navigation at Air Transport Command Headquarters had prepared an outline of a long-range training program for No 412 Squadron and No 426 Squadron. It covered most of the world's airways with four routes labelled Global, Pacific, Resolute and SAFAM (for South Africa–South America), as well as the South Atlantic route. Air Transport Command proposed ten long-range training flights per year—one per month, except in months when major exercises would require airlift support from No 426 Squadron.

Ross concluded that, to be of maximum benefit to crews, long-range training flights should be planned to include unfavourable weather, operations at oxygen heights, and practice in cruise-control, and that by giving such training, No 426 Squadron would produce world-class aircrews for Air Transport Command. In recommending approval of the proposed training program, Ross was confident that it would put Air Transport Command in a position to carry out its strategic roles well before the end of 1950.[25]

On 15 October Lord and Lady Tedder embarked for Britain in an RAF York for which No 426 Squadron had provided servicing facilities. On 17 October, Flight Lieutenant H.T. Giles captained NS17517 on the short hop to Mitchel Field, just to the east of New York City, to be briefed (with his squadron colleagues) on *Operation METROPOLIS*, a joint American–Canadian air-defence exercise being launched at the end of the week.

On the morning of Saturday, 22 October, the squadron despatched six North Stars to St-Hubert to airlift a large load of special equipment and personnel to Mitchel Field, where three RCAF Reserve units—No 401 (Fighter) Squadron, No 438 (Fighter) Squadron and No 1 (Radar and Communications) Unit—were going to participate in *Operation METROPOLIS*. By 1430 hours, the two fighter squadrons, with five Vampires each, would be flying from Mitchel Field, carrying out interceptions. Two of the North Stars returned to Dorval later in the day; the other four aircraft came back on 23 October.[26]

North Stars 17512 (Flight Lieutenant R. Coates) and 17516 (Flight Lieutenant G.W. Allen) flew to Trenton to pick up staff and students of the National Defence College from Kingston, and take them to Churchill and Rivers, Manitoba. Coates returned to base on 28 October and Allen a day later.

On 24 October, Flight Lieutenant J. Bell and his crew took the run to Resolute Bay in NS17514 with the usual stops at Rockcliffe and Churchill to pick up freight and passengers. They returned home four days later.

On 27 October, Major General L.P. Whitten, Commanding General, Newfoundland Base Command, USAF made the trip from St. John's to Ottawa to pay a visit to Air Transport Command Headquarters to discuss arrangements for transferring the bases at Fort Chimo, Mingan and Frobisher Bay from the USAF to the RCAF. As of 1 October, Air Transport Command had become the official custodian of Fort Chimo and Mingan, the officers stationed there as RCAF representatives had become Detachment Commanders, and the civilian positions were filled by those who had been employed by the Americans. The Air Transport Command detachments at all three locations were placed under the control of RCAF Station Goose Bay, which was charged with the responsibility of maintaining the buildings, installations and equipment at each site.[27]

On 29 October, Squadron Leader H.A. Morrison captained NS17512 on a special flight to Greenwood to pick up some urgently needed equipment for delivery to Torbay. He returned to base the same day. Resolute Bay was again the destination on 31 October; Flight Lieutenant A.B. Hammond and his crew successfully completed their assignment, returning to Dorval two days later.

November

On 1 November, the Air Defence Group commanded by Group Captain W.R. MacBrien moved from Air Force Headquarters to St-Hubert; declared operational on 23 November, Air Defence Group was elevated to command status on 1 June 1951.[28]

At Lachine, November opened with the launch of a painting campaign, in which the Station Theatre, the Airmen's Quarters and the Officers' Quarters received special attention. The appearance of the quarters, previously in a sorry state, improved considerably.

On 6 November, Flying Officer G.W. Webb in NS17507 flew to Trenton to embark a load of passengers for Dorval. The next day, Flight Lieutenant A.B. Hammond captained a special flight to Moncton and Torbay delivering passengers and freight.

On 8 November, the Officers' Mess was spruced up with rug-cleaning, new paint and curtains, and a host of sorely needed minor improvements. The face-lift came at an opportune time, as Air Commander Ross was due to make an inspection visit on 17 November. Building 6, which housed the Combined Mess, was also under construction, with additions to the building as well as renovations to the wet and dry garbage rooms, vegetable room, bake shop, staff dining room and a pot-storage room. Work on this project was expected to be completed by Christmas.

At 1300 hours on 17 November, when Air Commodore A.D. Ross and several staff officers alighted from their aircraft at Dorval for the AOC's annual inspection of No 426 Squadron, all ranks were at attention on the tarmac. During the ceremonial inspection parade, Air Commodore Ross presented Flight Sergeant H. Hogarth with the Long Service and Good Conduct Medal; after the parade, he conducted his inspection of the Dorval facilities; and that evening, he was the guest of honour at a formal mess dinner. The next morning, the AOC inspected the Lachine site; in the afternoon, he held a conference in the office of the Commanding Officer. At 1730 hours on 18 November, the AOC and his party departed for Rockcliffe.

On 24 November, at an impressive investiture at Alexander Hall, in the Canadian Legion Memorial Building in Montreal, the Governor General, Viscount Alexander of Tunis, presented decorations and awards to a large group of deserving Canadians, including several members of No 426 Squadron: Wing Commander C.H. Mussells, who received the DSO and DFC; Flight Lieutenant A.B. Hammond, who received the DFC and Bar; Flight Lieutenant H.T. Giles and Flight Lieutenant G.W. Williams, who each received the DFC; and Flying Officer A. Glustien, Flying Officer A.S. Logan, Flying Officer D.M. Payne, Flying Officer D.G. Selby and Flying Officer G.J. Weeden, each of whom also received the DFC.[29]

On 30 November, squadron strength stood at 420 all ranks, comprising seventy-five officers, 283 airmen, eleven airmen under training and fifty-one civilians, and eight North Stars on the inventory.

December

On 2 December, Flight Lieutenant J.D. Dickson was in Europe with NS17520, having taken the Minister of National Defence and his party to an Atlantic Pact Conference at the Hague. Dickson was making a training flight from Amsterdam to Brussels when he was recalled to Paris and directed to return immediately to Canada with Lieutenant-General Charles Foulkes and Brigadier J.D.B. Smith as passengers.

On 6 December, NS17520 again crossed the North Atlantic to RAF Station Northolt to pick up the Minister of National Defence who had arrived from the Hague in the Dakota transporting the Canadian Joint Staff. On the return flight, NS17520 stopped at Dublin, where the Minister conferred with the Prime Minister of Ireland. The return journey to Rockcliffe and Dorval was made via the Azores.

During the first week in December, arrangements were made for No 435 Squadron's radio officers to be trained and qualified on the North Star so No 435 Squadron could provide replacements should their Thunderbird counterparts be side-lined for any reason during the Edmonton–Whitehorse service flight or *Exercise SWEET BRIAR*.

On 9 December, all engineering officers in Air Transport Command units participating in *Exercise SWEET BRIAR* were advised to start training ground personnel in cold-weather maintenance, and to select key personnel for a short period of contact training at the Winter Experimental Establishment at Edmonton.

On 17 December, Santa Claus made a slightly premature appearance at the Station Drill Hall in Lachine, distributing presents to the dependants of all RCAF personnel at the squadron Christmas party. On 19 December, the squadron flew the RCAF Central Band to Goose Bay and Summerside to play Christmas concerts for the personnel serving there. At Lachine, the contractor officially handed over the new Airmen's Canteen and Lounge, a strikingly attractive facility that would soon be considerably enhanced by new furniture.

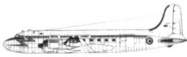

Air Materiel Command was asked to arrange with Canadian Wright to supply No 426 Squadron with four fully modified Merlin 620 engines, complete with power plant accessories, to be installed in a North Star aircraft and flown for 1000 hours with block changes at 500 hours. On completion of the test, the engines would be returned to Canadian Wright for strip inspection.

As the festive season was fast approaching, Maintenance Section held its Christmas party in the Station Drill Hall on 22 December. Reports indicated that a great time was had by all. The Combined Mess opened the following day, although much of the renovation had yet to be completed. The contractor estimated that the project would be finished by mid-January 1950.

Christmas Day 1949 dawned bright and cheery. After church, all available officers (as custom dictated) took leave of their personal Christmas festivities and proceeded to the Airmen's Mess to serve the airmen their Christmas dinner with all the trimmings. On 31 December dances were held at all three messes to welcome in the New Year.[30]

PHOTO 27
W/C C.G.W. Chapman cedes the command of No 426 Squadron to W/C C.H. Mussells; Dorval, 18 February 1949. (C.G.W. Chapman Collection)

PHOTO 28
W/C C.H. Mussells, A/C A.D. Ross and W/C C.G.W. Chapman at the mess dinner held in honour of the change of command; Lachine; 18 February 1949. (C.G.W. Chapman Collection)

PHOTO 29
An aerial view of Coral Harbour, NWT; spring 1949. (DND REA 488–7)

Dorval, 1949

PHOTO 30
LAC Frappier, LAC Logan and LAC Wood; Frobisher Bay, September 1949 (Barbara Wood Collection)

PHOTO 31
NS17517 at Ramey AFB during a South Atlantic training flight; July 1949. (D. Shade Collection)

PHOTO 32

The crew of NS17514 during a South Atlantic training flight; Natal, Brazil, 27 July 1949. From left, back row: Cpl. Mancusco, Sgt. Little, Cpl. Marshall and Sgt. Sigurdson; front row: LAC Grose, Cpl. O'Ray, LAC Brodie and Sgt. Reid. (DND, No 426 Squadron)

PHOTO 33

K. Morrow, D. Shade and G. West in the No 426 Squadron engine bay; Dorval, autumn 1949. (D. Shade Collection)

Dorval, 1949

PHOTO 34
The Schiphol Airport control tower—elevation 13 feet below sea level; Amsterdam, December 1949. (E. Grose Collection)

PHOTO 35
Nov. 26 1949, 426 Sqn takes Hon Brooke Claxton MND to NATO Conference in Paris. W/C Mussells observes F/L Dickson introducing crew of North Star 17520 (L-R) F/L Queale, F/O MacIntosh, F/O Broadfoot, F/L Endersbe, WO2 Bell, F/S Baine, Cpl Jacquish, LAC Grose. (E. Grose Collection)

PHOTO 36

The Certificate of the Winged Order of Neptunus Rex (designed by Gord and Audrey Webb) presented to LAC G.R. Reed on 7 September 1949. (G.R. Reed Collection)

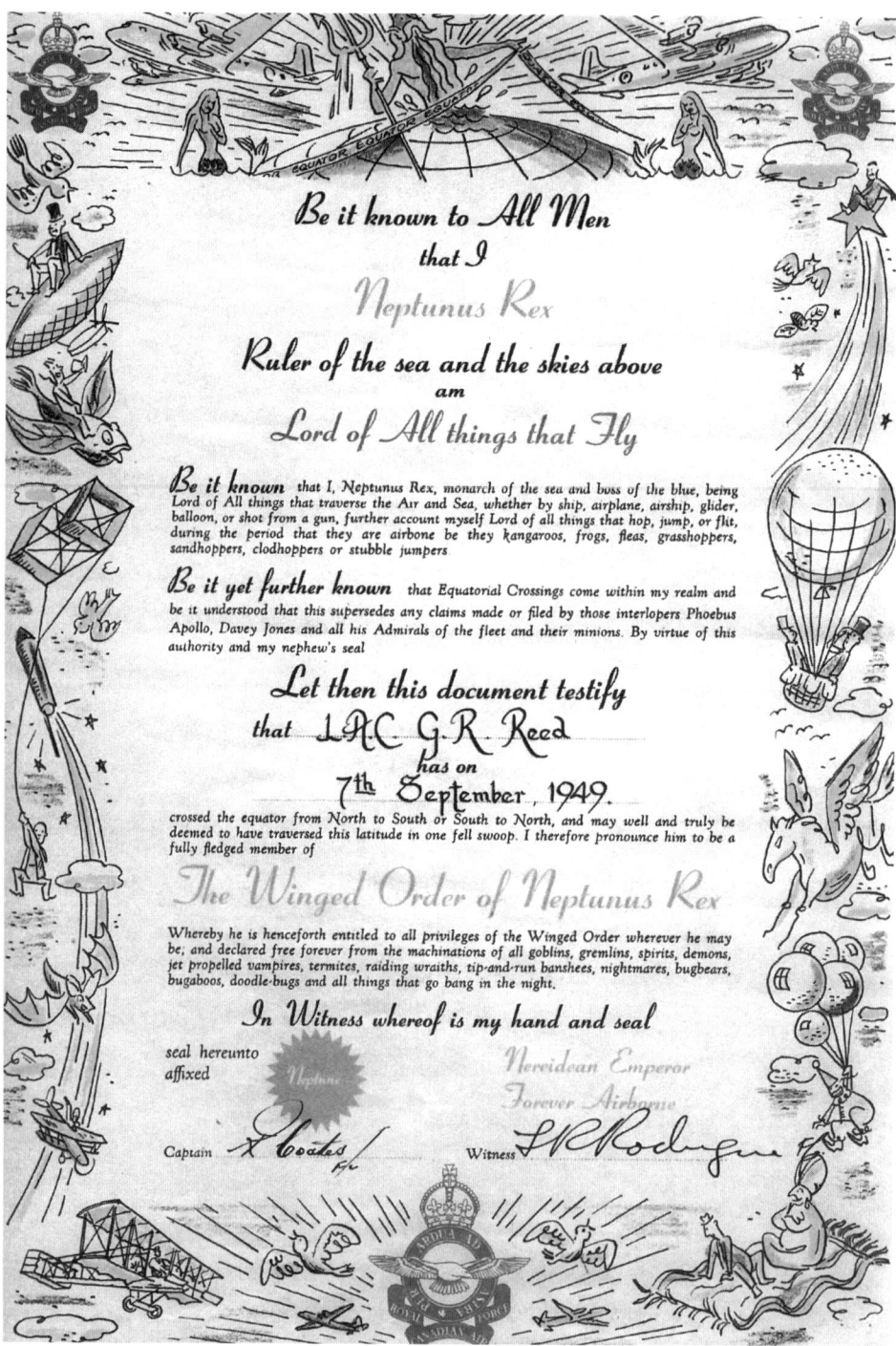

CHAPTER 8

DORVAL
JANUARY–JUNE 1950

On 1 January, No 426 Squadron entered its fifth year as a peacetime Regular Force unit based in Canada. By mid-year, the Thunderbirds would find themselves in another war zone, this time as a long-range transport squadron.

January

New Year's Day fell on a Sunday, and the Officers' Mess held Open House for the squadron senior NCOs from 1100 to 1200 hours. The officers then proceeded to the Composite Mess to serve dinner to the airmen. The next day being a statutory holiday, the Officers' Mess hosted the members of all Montreal-area RCN, Army and Air Force messes who cared to partake of squadron hospitality, which was noted for "moose milk," an eggnog heavily laced with rum. The Thunderbirds sent out several four-man teams specifically to visit the Montreal-area units that had issued New Year invitations of their own.

On the morning of 2 January, Squadron Leader Morrison, DSO, DFC (the squadron's Chief Operations Officer) flew to Rockcliffe, where he joined the crew of NS17518 from No 412 Squadron, captained by Flight Lieutenant E.W. Smith, DSO. They were tasked to transport the Secretary of State for External Affairs, the Honourable Lester B. Pearson, and his advisors to Columbo, Ceylon, to attend the Commonwealth Foreign Ministers' Conference set to begin on 9 January — a golden opportunity for the RCAF to conduct its first west-to-east flight around the world. The Conducting Officer for the mission was Group Captain R.J. Lane DSO, DFC from Air Transport Command Headquarters.

The flight was routed through Gander, Newfoundland; Lajes in the Azores; Gibraltar; and Luqa Airport in Malta. The stop after Malta was supposed to be Habbaniyah, Iraq, but the crew received reports of severe sandstorms in the Arabian desert and decided to divert to Fayid, a town on the west side of the Great Bitter Lake. From Fayid, the flight proceeded first to Karachi and then to Negombo, Ceylon. After the conference, the aircraft returned to Karachi for a short visit and then headed east to Rockcliffe, Ontario by way of Palam Airport in Delhi, India; Mingaladon Airport in Rangoon, Burma; Kallang Airport in Singapore; Kai Tak Airport in Hong Kong; Haneda Airport in Tokyo, Japan; Wake Island and Hickam Field on Oahu in the Hawaiian Islands; and Fairfield-Suisun Air Force Base near San Francisco, California. NS17518 arrived back at Rockcliffe on 9 February.[1]

On 3 January, Flight Lieutenant H.T. Gilles captained NS17520 on a special flight to Newfoundland, to visit Argentia and to deliver General A.G.L. McNaughton to Harmon Field (near Stephenville) for a meeting of the Joint Chiefs of Staff. Before leaving Dorval, General McNaughton toured the squadron facilities. On 6 January, the squadron despatched NS17517, captained by Flight Lieutenant R. Coates, to Britain to pick up spare parts urgently required for Vampire aircraft scheduled to deploy to Whitehorse for *Exercise SWEET BRIAR*.

On 7 January, Flight Lieutenant A.B. Hammond and his crew were in NS17511 on a routine flight from Edmonton to Whitehorse, about five minutes east of Watson Lake, Yukon Territory. At about 1210 hours local, Flight Lieutenant Hammond received a radio message from Watson Lake asking the crew to initiate a search for a USAF F-84 Thunderjet fighter that had just gone down in the vicinity. To help them fix a probable position for the downed aircraft, the radio operator in Watson Lake relayed the content of the F-84 pilot's last message, including his speed and direction, and his intention to attempt a crash landing on a lake beside the Alaska Highway.

After only about fifteen minutes of searching, Hammond and his crew spotted orange smoke that, on closer investigation, turned out to be coming from a smoke-pot lit by the downed pilot, who had crash-landed the F-84 west-northwest of Watson Lake. When Hammond did a low pass over the crash site, the crew could see the pilot waving excitedly, apparently uninjured, beside his aircraft. Hammond made another low pass and fired a green Verey light to inform the downed pilot that he had been seen.

In the meantime, members of the crew relayed the position of the crash site to the Watson Lake radio operator, prepared emergency equipment and winter clothing to be free-dropped to the F-84 pilot with a note saying that a truck was on its way from Watson Lake. At 1258 hours, the drop was made from 200 feet, and when Hammond turned back over the crash site his crew could see the pilot carrying one of the equipment packs up a nearby road. Hammond circled NS17511 over the crash site until an approaching vehicle was seen about five miles away. At that point, Hammond set course for Whitehorse.[2]

The Air Force Headquarters directive of 18 November 1949 on *Exercise SWEET BRIAR* authorized Air Transport Command to employ six Dakota aircraft from the Canadian Joint Air Training Centre in Rivers, Manitoba, and to second six North Stars, three Lancasters and six Dakotas, together with all aircrew and ground crews required to operate them, to the command and control of the Air Force Commander, *Exercise SWEET BRIAR*, for the duration of the exercise. On 11 January, Air Transport Command issued its Operation Order 1/50 setting out the details of these secondments.

No 426 Squadron's commitments were as follows:
- 23 January: Two North Stars arrive at St-Hubert, Quebec.

- 24 January: Each aircraft takes twenty-five passengers and 5,000 pounds of freight belonging to No 410 (Fighter) Squadron to Edmonton via North Bay and Lakehead (the airport at Fort William, Ontario), and Rivers, Manitoba; and provide air transport support to No 410 Squadron's twelve Vampire fighters en route to the exercise area.
- 25 January: Two more North Stars go to Rockcliffe to pick up ten members of No 408 (Photographic) Squadron and 16,000 pounds of freight bound for Edmonton.
- 26 January: The two North Stars that went to Rockcliffe arrive in Edmonton, where they spend the night with their cargo and passengers; in the morning, they fly to Whitehorse, unload, and then return to Edmonton.
- 27 January: The two North Stars that went to Whitehorse on 26 January go to Edmonton and embark sixty-five umpires and fly them to Whitehorse. One of these aircraft stays in Whitehorse to support the exercise, and the other returns to Dorval via Edmonton and Winnipeg as Service Flight 36.
- 28 January: The North Star that just returned as Service Flight 36 proceeds from Dorval to St-Hubert to embark fifteen members of No 408 Squadron, and any remaining No 410 Squadron personnel equipment, and transport them first to Edmonton and then to Whitehorse.
- 30 January: All six No 426 Squadron aircraft to be in position at Edmonton, ready for secondment to the Air Force Commander for employment as directed on *Exercise SWEET BRIAR*.
- On completion of the exercise, the six North Stars reverse the airlift process, and escort the No 410 Squadron Vampires to St-Hubert. On release, five aircraft return to Dorval, and one remains in Edmonton to provide logistics support for Operation BEETLE.³

On 11 January, a Wednesday, Flying Officer G.W. Webb and his crew departed Dorval on Service Flight 35, the Whitehorse run. They stopped briefly at Rockcliffe to take on passengers and cargo, and proceeded to Stevenson Field in Winnipeg, where the CSU (constant speed unit) failed on one engine as they taxied to the terminal building. Trans-Canada Airlines maintenance staff obliged with repairs and the aircraft was judged to be ready to continue the flight. However, as Flying Officer Webb was taxiing to the takeoff point, another CSU went unserviceable, which meant more delay for another round of repairs. Service Flight 35 finally got out of Winnipeg about four hours behind schedule, demonstrating the validity of the service maxim: "Time to spare? Go by air!"

On 12 January, Service Flight 35 was becalmed in Edmonton: its departure for Whitehorse was quite out of the question as the entire area lay under a blanket of ice-crystal fog. The next day was much the same in Edmonton, but worse elsewhere: a major storm had hit eastern Canada. Flying Officer Webb and his crew studied the weather charts, noting that the upper-level winds were quite strong, with a generally easterly flow across the continent. As it was almost precisely a year since Flying Officer J.A. Jolicoeur set a record for the Vancouver-Halifax run, and the weather conditions looked promising, Webb signalled the Squadron Commander at Dorval requesting permission to try for a new record. The next day, he had his answer from Wing Commander Mussells: "Proceed at your own discretion."

The ice fog persisted on 14 January, so take-off conditions were marginal at best when Webb lifted NS17512 off the runway. At 500 feet, the aircraft broke into the clear and the crew set course for Vancouver; arriving at Sea Island two and a half hours later. Arrangements were made to take sixteen Navy personnel as passengers on the trans-Canada run to Halifax and, shortly after 1800 hours on Sunday, 15 January, Webb took off and started his climb to 26,500 feet. All his passengers were soon on oxygen. Special clearances had been obtained to fly south of the airways, and the flight headed for its first checkpoint over Butte, Montana. Based on the forecast, the crew had hoped to catch a stiff tailwind, but instead hit a 70-mph headwind. Shortly after passing Butte, the aircraft entered the jet-stream with tailwinds at times reaching speeds of more than 120 mph.

The navigator, Flight Lieutenant L.W. Queale, had his work cut out for him. At their altitude, the aircraft was mostly in cirrus cloud, which limited his visibility and, therefore, his capacity for celestial navigation. Atmospheric conditions and static interfered with radio reception, making it very difficult to take usable radio-compass bearings. Also, the oxygen supply was rapidly running out, and the squadron's Oxygen Technician, Leading Aircraftsman Kirchenner (a member of the crew), regulated the flow to stretch the supply. His efforts were sufficient to allow the crew to maintain altitude until they were past Montreal, when they had to descend below oxygen level, thus losing the tail wind they had enjoyed for much of the trip.

Incidentally, while Webb and his crew winged their way across the country, their squadron mates at Lachine were tracking their progress during an impromptu party at the Officers' Mess.

Having flown all night, NS17512 arrived at Halifax shortly before dawn, eight hours and twenty-five minutes after take-off at Vancouver — seven minutes off the previous record. After disembarking their passengers and refuelling the aircraft, Webb and his crew returned to Dorval, arriving mid-morning on Monday, 16 January to a welcome by Air Commodore Ross and Wing Commander Mussells. As well as Webb, Queale and Kirchenner, the crew on this record-breaking flight included Flying Officer A.L. Quickfall (co-pilot), Flying Officer G. Fisher (radio operator); Corporal P. Leblanc and Leading Aircraftsman Guennette (flight engineers), and Leading Aircraftsman Beko (air movements assistant).[4]

Air Commodore Ross was at Dorval that day with a group of staff officers from Air Transport Command Headquarters to discuss a wide range of topics, including the squadron's heavy commitments during *Exercise SWEET BRIAR*, its establishment deficiency (short fifty-four airmen), aircraft modifications, and participation in operations to keep the Arctic weather stations supplied. Following a short tour of the newly renovated Airmen's Mess, canteen and grocery store in the afternoon, the Headquarters party returned to Rockcliffe.

On 15 January, Flight Lieutenant A.B. Hammond captained a special run from Rockcliffe to Washington, D.C., to transport the Chiefs of Staff to a joint defence conference.

On 17 January, Wing Commander W.H. Swetman submitted a detailed long-range training proposal for North Star aircraft to Air Force Headquarters, giving priority to Arctic training flights

to be co-ordinated with northern re-supply missions, and four overseas routes focussed on the North Atlantic, the South Atlantic and the Middle East. Air Transport Command wanted to launch the training program in April, and Air Force Headquarters would have to initiate the processing of diplomatic clearances by the Department of External Affairs.[5]

On 19 January, after a series of ground handling trials, AVRO's first CF-100 (serial number 18101) made its maiden flight at Malton Airport near Toronto, with Squadron Leader W.A. Waterton of the RAF at the controls. Waterton, the chief test pilot for Gloster Aircraft in Britain, had been brought in to help conduct the flight tests.[6]

On 17 January, Air Force Headquarters issued Operational Directive AOT 1/50 regarding the spring re-supply of four weather-reporting stations operating under joint Canadian-United States control in the Arctic Archipelago: Resolute Bay on Cornwallis Island, Eureka on the Fosheim Peninsula of Ellesmere Island, Isachsen on Ellef Ringnes Island, and Mould Bay on Prince Patrick Island. Until now, these weather stations had been supported by the USAF.

In 1949, three RCAF aircrew officers served with the USAF re-supply crews to gain experience. In 1950, the RCAF was to participate more fully, with even greater involvement in 1951 and complete takeover in 1952. In 1950, the RCAF contribution was to maintain one North Star "on the line" in the re-supply area, complete with flying and maintenance crews.

On 23 January, Air Commodore Ross chaired a meeting at Air Transport Command Headquarters to discuss North Star participation in the re-supply operation. The agenda was long and comprehensive. Wing Commander Mussells proposed that the operation would require nineteen No 426 Squadron personnel, including seven aircrew, two flight engineers, seven ground crew, two air traffic assistants, and one communications operator. After some discussion, it was decided to reduce the proposed squadron commitment by one air traffic assistant, and to obtain an air traffic NCO and a Movements Officer from Air Transport Command.

On 27 January, Air Commodore Ross chaired another meeting at Air Transport Command Headquarters, this time with five senior USAF officers from Newfoundland Base Command, Military Air Transport Service (MATS), and USAF Headquarters in Washington. Ross advised the Americans that, during the re-supply period, the USAF Detachment Commander would have operational control of RCAF aircraft and crew. The USAF advance party would move in at Resolute Bay on 15 March to get the camp ready, and the main party would arrive by 23 March. Operations would begin on 1 April with supply flights from Resolute to Mould Bay and Isachsen, and then the locus of the operation would move to Thule, Greenland, to establish a station at Alert Bay on the northern tip of Ellesmere Island and to supply Eureka. The entire operation was expected to last eight weeks.

When Wing Commander Mussells made it clear that No 426 Squadron was permitted to operate on three engines in emergencies, the Americans asked that the minutes of the meeting be amended to read: "RCAF three-engine take-offs would not be under US control, the authority to be left to the RCAF Detachment Commander without interference from US authorities."[7]

On 23 January, eleven of the squadron's Flying Officers started writing their qualifying examinations at Lachine, and some of the North Stars scheduled to depart for *Exercise SWEET BRIAR* were delayed because of fog at Dorval.

There were fears that a flood might develop in the Fraser Valley in the spring, and Air Transport Command Headquarters thought it best to do some contingency planning. If Air Transport Command resources were called upon, it was proposed to employ North Stars on any emergency operation, and to house them at Calgary Municipal Airport. This location was considered most convenient as it was big enough and properly equipped to provide adequate accommodation, and close to transport links for Army personnel and supplies. On 25 January, No 426 Squadron received the warning order to be prepared to move and, after *Operation MOBILITY*, everyone expected it to go smoothly.

The logistical airlift in support of No 408 Squadron, which was contributing three Lancasters to *Exercise SWEET BRIAR*, began on 24 January, and the Lancasters actually left for the exercise area on 28 January. On 26 January, the twelve Vampire fighters, mothered by the No 426 Squadron's North Stars, started to move west; after experiencing various difficulties along the way, they arrived at Edmonton on 31 January.

On 27 January, as Air Transport Command and much of the Canadian Army were gearing up for *Exercise SWEET BRIAR*, a USAF C-54 Skymaster with forty-four passengers went missing during a routine flight from Anchorage, Alaska to Great Falls, Montana. Air Transport Command Headquarters Operations staff put six aircraft and crews from RCAF Station Rockcliffe on immediate alert in response to a request from Search Headquarters in Edmonton; all the aircraft took off the following morning and participated in a large-scale search for the missing C-54. By the end of the month, the search involved fifty-four Canadian and American aircraft and about 7,000 military personnel, many assigned to *SWEET BRIAR*, but it proved fruitless.[8]

On 28 January, the governments of the United States and Canada reached an agreement on American bases in Canada. The RCAF would take over Frobisher Bay from the USAF and operate it in conjunction with the Department of Transport as a staging base on the route to the principal Arctic re-supply points. RCAF Unit Frobisher Bay would form on 1 September under the functional

and administrative control of the Air Officer Commanding, Air Transport Command, through the Commanding Officer of RCAF Station Goose Bay.⁹

On 28 January, a Goose Bay Dakota arrived at Dorval carrying six polio patients on stretchers, who were collected immediately by civilian ambulances for transport to the Children's Memorial Hospital in downtown Montreal. The entire effort was co-ordinated through the Operations Centre at No 426 Squadron.

On 31 January, President Harry S. Truman of the United States, released the following statement:

> It is part of my responsibility as Commander in Chief of the Armed Forces to see to it that our country is able to defend itself against any possible aggressor. Accordingly, I have directed the Atomic Energy Commission to continue its work on all forms of atomic weapons, including the so-called hydrogen or super-bomb …¹⁰

February

At the domestic site at Lachine, J.R. Trojan opened a barbershop in Building 9 on 1 February. The squadron charged him a monthly rent of $15, and his price for an RCAF-standard haircut was 35 cents, considerably less than the rates prevailing in downtown Montreal or even in Lachine.

On 6 February, Flight Lieutenant J.D. Dixon (captain) and Flight Lieutenant L.W. Queale (navigator) were assigned to take NS17502 on a hurry-up flight to Resolute Bay to deliver urgently needed supplies, and return within forty-eight hours. The round trip totalled more than 4,000 nautical miles, which meant a workday of more than thirty hours, with twenty-four hours spent in the air.

On 7 February, Flying Officer G.W. Webb and his crew departed for San Francisco in NS17520, conducting something of a rescue mission; NS17518, which belonged to No 412 Squadron, had lost its No 3 engine only thirty minutes out of nearby Fairfield-Suisun AFB. The aircraft was on the homeward leg of a round-the-world flight with Lester B. Pearson, the Secretary of State for External Affairs. The returning crew took over NS17520 and departed early in the evening of 8 February, arriving at Rockcliffe the following morning after a flight of ten hours and fifteen minutes. A couple of days later, Webb and his crew ferried NS17518 to Rockcliffe on three engines.

Wishing to see and talk to the aircrew who accompanied him on his round-the-world flight — a group that included Squadron Leader H.A. Morrison of No 426 Squadron — Mr. Pearson invited them all to a meeting in his office in the East Block of the Parliament Buildings in Ottawa. On 10 February, Squadron Leader Morrison went to Ottawa to attend this meeting.

Exercise SWEET BRIAR was conducted along the Northwest Staging Route between Whitehorse, Yukon Territory, and Fairbanks, Alaska from 13 February to 23 February 1950. The RCAF's first major exercise involving jet fighters, it was designed to develop joint service doctrine for Arctic deployment of the Canadian and American air and land forces. It gave USAF and RCAF units valuable experience in harsh-weather operations in support of land forces, providing services such as air transport, close tactical support, air evacuation, air supply, and visual and photographic reconnaissance. They also practised defending traffic on the Northwest Highway System (the Alaska Highway) from simulated enemy attacks.

In the exercise scenario, an aggressor force invaded Alaska from Siberia and captured both Anchorage and Fairbanks. A defending force of U.S. and Canadian soldiers and airmen was to hold back the invaders and attempt to drive them off. The RCAF contingent of 800 personnel and forty-five aircraft was headed by the Chief of the Air Staff, Air Marshal W.A. Curtis, and the 1,100 Canadian soldiers and their 471 vehicles were commanded by the Chief of the General Staff, Lieutenant-General Charles Foulkes. The Americans were represented by 1,300 US Army soldiers and 475 USAF personnel with about fifty aircraft, including fighter, reconnaissance and transport types.

Exercise SWEET BRIAR stretched the RCAF's limited resources quite thin. About 650 personnel and large quantities of equipment had to be moved to Edmonton before the exercise, the exercise involved considerable traffic between Edmonton and Whitehorse, and then the personnel and equipment all had to be hauled back to eastern Canada when the whole thing was over. During the exercise, the RCAF worked even harder, providing the Army with airborne assault, air cover, tactical support and logistics support, establishing Air Observation Posts and handling medical evacuations.[11]

On 13 February, eight of the squadron's Flight Lieutenants began several days of written examinations to qualify for promotion.

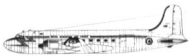

On the night of 13–14 February, just as *Exercise SWEET BRIAR* was getting under way, a search-and-rescue operation code named *BRIX* began on the Pacific coast. At 1627 hours, one of Strategic Air Command's heavy bombers, B-36 No 44-92075, left Eielson AFB near Fairbanks, Alaska with a 10,000-pound Mk IV atomic bomb, with a yield equivalent to that of Fat Boy, the bomb dropped on Hiroshima. According to its flight plan, the aircraft was to fly south along the Canadian coastline, carry out a simulated attack on San Francisco, and return to its home base at Carswell AFB near Fort Worth, Texas.

After nearly six hours in flight, when the aircraft was approaching the coast of British Columbia, the crew reported an encounter with severe icing conditions at 17,000 feet; two of their six engines were on fire, the propeller on a third engine was feathered, and many of their instruments had failed. Minutes later, another bomber received a message from the troubled B-36: it was letting down and might have to ditch, and the crew had been alerted to bail out. Within minutes of receiving this last distress call, RCAF Station Sea Island dispatched two rescue aircraft. Two American helicopters from Princess Royal Island promptly joined the search.

At 8,000 feet, just minutes before bailing out, the crew jettisoned the atomic bomb (which was not armed) in Hecate Strait, about twelve miles off the southern tip of Banks Island. The bright flash seen on impact was the bomb's conventional high-explosive charge detonating. As the crew bailed out near and over Princess Royal Island, the B-36 was seen circling over the island once and then turning inland. Within the next two days, eleven of the sixteen crew members and one passenger were rescued by the destroyer HMCS *Cayuga* and a fishing vessel, the *Cape Perry*. The other five crew members probably drowned when they were blown out to sea.

The wreckage of the B-36 was found in September 1953, during a search for another missing aircraft. After the crew bailed out, it continued flying another 160 miles to the northeast and finally struck Kispiox Mountain at the 6,000-foot level; the crash site is about thirty miles west of Hazelton, in the interior of British Columbia. This occurrence is the first item in a US Department of Defense summary of accidents involving nuclear weapons between 1950 and 1980. The Americans listed it as a "Broken Arrow" — the codeword means an incident involving any part of a nuclear weapon.[12]

Air Transport Command Operation Order 9/50, dated 16 February, gave No 426 Squadron detailed instructions for the re-supply of Arctic weather stations. All RCAF participants would be under squadron command, but the USAF Detachment Commander would control the RCAF aircraft while they were actively engaged in the re-supply operation. As well as the North Star to be in position at Resolute Bay by 22 March, No 426 Squadron would provide a backup freighter aircraft to be kept on continuous standby at base throughout the operation.

For personnel, No 426 Squadron would contribute twelve maintenance technicians, one cook, and an augmented flight crew of nine, comprising two pilots, two navigators, two radio officers, two flight engineers and one air traffic assistant; halfway through the operation, the squadron could replace this crew to give a second, similar flight crew valuable Arctic experience. No 901 Air Traffic Handling Unit (based at RCAF Station Rockcliffe) would send one air transport officer and one NCO air traffic assistant, and RCAF Station Rockcliffe would contribute one NCO senior communications operator and one mess orderly.

Op Order 9/50 specified that North Stars going in and out of Resolute Bay would stage through Goose Bay and Frobisher Bay to facilitate the movement of cargo to and from Goose Bay. Night landings were permitted at Resolute Bay but not at the satellite stations. The USAF would provide initial training at Goose Bay, to begin on 13 March, and to ensure that the entire RCAF detachment could attend, all members would assemble at Dorval and depart for Goose Bay on 11 March. The entire USAF/RCAF party for the operation would be in place at Resolute Bay by 22 March, and the re-supply airlift to Mould Bay and Isachsen would start on 1 April. When this phase of the operation was complete, the re-supply of Eureka and the establishment of Alert Bay would begin from Thule.[13]

On 20 February, the Minister of National Defence, the Chief of the Air Staff and several VIPs were airlifted in NS17520 to Edmonton and Whitehorse to observe *Exercise SWEET BRIAR.*

On 24 February, Flying Officer J.B. Miller captained NS17507 on a special run to Dartmouth to airlift reserve equipment to Torbay, Newfoundland. The aircraft returning to Dorval the following day.

On 25 February, more polio patients arrived from Goose Bay in the Dakota based there, and No 426 Squadron's ops staff repeated their co-ordination routine with the civilian ambulances to take the patients to the Children's Memorial Hospital in Montreal.

On 27 February, the last day of *Exercise SWEET BRIAR*, all personnel employed full-time in an active capacity in the exercise received seven days' special leave by direct order of the Minister of National Defence. No 426 Squadron wound up its participation in *Exercise SWEET BRIAR* with the return of its six North Stars to Dorval on 1 March.[14]

March

On 1 March, Squadron Leader H.A. Morrison took off from Trenton in NS17520 with a group of cadets from the Royal Military College bound for Vancouver for the Claxton Trophy sports competition.

On 2 March, a dental clinic opened in the No 6 Hangar Annex at Dorval, relieving squadron personnel of the ten-mile journey to Montreal to see the dentist. The next day, the redecoration of the Combined Mess Dining Hall and washrooms at Lachine was finished.

On 3 March, Air Transport Command Headquarters convened a meeting to discuss North Star engine failures with representatives from No 426 Squadron, Rolls-Royce, and Air Materiel Command. No 426 Squadron had taken independent preventive action as an interim measure, as new modifications had not been completed on unit aircraft.

On 4 March, Flight Lieutenant J.D. Dixon and Flying Officer J.B. Miller went to Westover AFB, near Springfield, Massachusetts, for three days of instruction on USAF transport procedures. Two days later, navigator Flight Lieutenant L.W. Queale and two radar technicians arrived at Westover for a two-week course on the APS-10 radar, which the RCAF intended to use in the Arctic when it was installed in some of the North Stars.

On 11 March, Flying Officer D.M. Payne departed for Goose Bay in NS17507, carrying a troupe of Montreal entertainers who put on a vaudeville show for the station's RCAF and civilian personnel. This special presentation at Goose Bay was the first in a series of four performances by different vaudeville troupes.

Also on 11 March, AV Roe Canada Limited and the RCAF organized the first official flight demonstration of a new twin-engine jet fighter, the CF-100 Canuck. The dignitaries in attendance at

RCAF Station Rockcliffe included HRH Prince Bernhardt of the Netherlands, who was in Canada on an official visit.[15]

On 12 March at Dorval, Wing Commander Mussells paraded the squadron for inspection and to present Sergeant Tremblay with the Efficiency Medal.

On 15 March (several days late, according to Op Order 9/50), the squadron personnel selected for *Operation RE-SUPPLY* went to Goose Bay for the USAF Winter Bush Survival Course.

Saint Patrick's Day, 17 March, was marked by parties at all squadron messes.

Beginning 20 March, Air Vice Marshal A.L. James, the Acting Chief of the Air Staff, chaired a two-day conference of Air Officers Commanding and Group Commanders in Ottawa. Minister of National Defence Brooke Claxton addressed the gathering, touching on the North Atlantic Treaty and what he saw as a marked improvement in Europe's political situation attributable mainly to the Americans' strong support for the Treaty. He also mentioned the government's comparatively lavish defence spending — the Department of National Defence was receiving about 40 percent of the controllable portion of the national budget. Since the three armed services would be subject to careful scrutiny by other government departments and the public, the Minister emphasized the importance of reducing overhead costs.

The conference also included an intelligence briefing in which current estimates of the capabilities and intentions of potential enemies were outlined. Although he did not say that war was imminent, the briefer did say that the strength of at least one potential enemy was increasing—the Soviet Union had exploded an atomic bomb.

Within four months, Canada would again be sending troops to war.[16]

On 20 March, Flying Officer G.W. Webb and his crew took off for Churchill and Resolute Bay in NS17507 carrying passengers and freight. The aircraft returned to base two days later.

The first phase of *Operation RE-SUPPLY* began on 22 March with flights to Mould Bay and Eureka. Back at base, an Air Transport Command staff officer from Rockcliffe accompanied Wing Commander J.A. Richer from Air Force Headquarters on a tour of the Dorval and Lachine sites, which were under consideration for the new home of Air Transport Command Headquarters.

On 25 March, Flight Lieutenant A.J.P. Byford and Flight Lieutenant E.L. Banks took NS17520 to Rockcliffe to pick up Mr. Claxton and his entourage, who were bound for a North Atlantic Pact conference in Europe. Their destination was Schiphol Airport near Amsterdam.

On 27 March, Squadron Leader H.A. Morrison captained NS17503 on the regular service flight to Goose Bay. The passengers included three former polio patients heading home, fully recovered.

On 28 March, a tragic accident happened at RCAF Station Rockcliffe: a Dakota operated from the station by the American Embassy crashed a few minutes after take-off. The United States Ambassador, L.A. Steinhardt, and four other passengers were killed instantly.[17]

On 31 March, No 405 Squadron was reformed at Greenwood, Nova Scotia, as a Maritime Reconnaissance unit flying the AVRO 683 Lancaster 10MR and commanded by Wing Commander D.T. French, DFC. During the Second World War, No 405 Squadron had seen action with No 8 (Pathfinder) Group in RAF Bomber Command.[18]

March saw the completion of several construction projects, including the alterations and additions to the Sergeants' Mess (including a large new sun verandah); waiting rooms for all ranks in A Bay of No 6 Hangar; the insulation of exposed steam pipes in the married quarters to prevent heat loss and injuries; a huge walk-in refrigerator in No 6 Hangar for perishables awaiting shipment to Goose Bay; and adapting Building 30 at Lachine to accommodate both the Protestant and Roman Catholic chapels.

April

On 1 April, Flight Lieutenant J.R. Bell took NS17507 to Goose Bay on the last of the four special flights for vaudeville troupes, which had entertained the station personnel at Goose Bay and their families each weekend since 11 March.

The same day, Air Commodore Ross and Wing Commander Mussells planned to depart by North Star for Resolute Bay by way of Churchill to inspect the Resolute Detachment on *Operation RE-SUPPLY*, followed by a trip to Goose Bay on 4 April to spend the day before returning to Rockcliffe and Dorval. The North Star went unserviceable, and the inspection party did not get away until 6 April.

On 3 April, work resumed on the swimming pool located next door to the fire station at Lachine. The pool was scheduled to open on 1 June.

On 13 April, Flying Officer D.M. Payne and his crew in NS17520 departed for Rockcliffe, where they picked up the students of the National Defence College, who were outward bound on a sixteen-day familiarization tour of southern Canada, the North West Staging Route, Alaska and northern Canada. Group Captain W.I. Clements was their Conducting Officer.

By this point, it was established Air Transport Command policy that as many of its personnel as possible should be familiar with airborne operations. On 15 April, to consolidate the lessons learned on *Exercise SWEET BRIAR*, No 435 Squadron conducted *Exercise BUCKREADIE,* an airborne assault exercise, with the 1st Battalion, Princess Patricia's Canadian Light Infantry, from Sarcee Barracks in Calgary. At the same time, Wing Commander R.O. Shaw (Staff Officer Operations at Air Transport Command Headquarters) and three other officers were selected to go to the Canadian Joint Air Training Centre in Rivers, Manitoba to Rivers for the Army/Air Indoctrination Course beginning 13 May.

On 17 April, at the National Research Council Fuel and Oil Laboratories, representatives from Air Force Headquarters, Air Materiel Command, Air Transport Command and No 426 Squadron met to discuss feasibility testing of the aviation oils used in North Star aircraft. NRC agreed to perform oxidation tests on the various brands of oils that met service specifications and analyze samples of the sludge taken from engines undergoing overhaul.

On 18 April, No 426 Squadron issued Ice Worm certificates to all members who had flown across the Arctic Circle on duty — a large number. Each certificate was signed by both the captain and the navigator of the relevant flight.

On 24 April, a gala all-ranks dance was held at the Lachine drill hall, with music by the Training Command Dance Band. Two days later, Flight Lieutenant R. Coates in NS17511 flew the Brass and Dance sections of the Training Command Band to Torbay, Newfoundland, for a series of performances in St. John's.

On April 26, Air Commodore Ross summoned all commanding officers in Air Transport Command to Rockcliffe for a meeting on activities planned for fiscal year 1950–51. At this meeting, the squadron commanders learned the following:
- the RCAF's main priority for the next several years was to build up its air-defence capability (fighters and radar units);
- the manpower ceiling would remain at 17,000 all ranks;
- No 413 (Survey Transport) Squadron and No 414 (Photo) Squadron would be disbanded on 1 November;
- the School of Photography would close on 1 August;
- Air Transport Command would assume control of Frobisher Bay on 1 September;
- No 408 Squadron would remain a photographic unit;

- No 412 Squadron's establishment was to be set at eight Dakotas and two Grumman Goose aircraft, effective 1 November, when it would inherit four Norduyn Norseman aircraft and some Dakotas from No 413 Squadron; it would also cease operating the passenger-configured NS17518, which would be placed in storage.

No 426 Squadron would continue operating with eight North Stars, each flying seventy hours per month. Effective 1 November, the squadron would receive two more aircraft, a North Star freighter and the Canadair C-5, a unique VIP-configured North Star with radial engines, which would be ready for test-flying in early May. Twenty-three ground crew were to be trained on the aircraft, and the courses would begin on 15 May and 1 June. Finally, No 426 Squadron was committed to supplying three North Stars for *Operation RE-SUPPLY* in 1951; it was suggested that Resolute Bay become a squadron responsibility, with a regular schedule of service flights.

Air Commodore Ross also announced changes in senior appointments, including the following:
- Group Captain R.J. Lane from Air Transport Command Headquarters to RCAF Station Edmonton as Commanding Officer;
- Wing Commander J.K.F. MacDonald from North West Air Command Headquarters in Edmonton to Air Transport Command Headquarters as Senior Personnel Staff Officer;
- Group Captain J.A. Verner from RCAF Station Goose Bay to Air Force Headquarters;
- Group Captain L.J. Birchall from Canadian Joint Staff, Washington, to RCAF Station Goose Bay as Commanding Officer;
- Wing Commander W.A. Parks from No 435 Squadron in Edmonton to Air Force Headquarters;
- Wing Commander M.E. Pollard from the RCAF Staff College in Toronto to No 435 Squadron as Commanding Officer;
- Group Captain N.J. Boyle from RCAF Station Rockcliffe to Air Force Headquarters;
- Wing Commander J.R. Frizzle to take command of RCAF Station Rockcliffe until the arrival of Group Captain R.A. Cameron;
- Squadron Leader A.W. Bishop from Air Transport Command Headquarters to RCAF Station Centralia; and
- Squadron Leader H.A. Morrison from No 426 Squadron to Air Transport Command Headquarters.[19]

On 27 April, No 426 Squadron received a brand-new Plymouth staff car—a big improvement over the superannuated 1941 model the squadron was previously saddled with.

The squadron launched its first training trip of the new fiscal year on 28 April with a double crew and some observers on board. The flight was routed via Goose Bay, Lyneham, Nice, Cairo, Malta, Gibraltar, Dakar, Natal, Port of Spain and Bermuda before returning to base.

May

On 3 May, on the homeward leg of Service Flight 36 from Edmonton, Flight Lieutenant J.D. Dickson in NS17503 touched down at Saskatoon to pick up some University Flight Cadets travelling to RCAF Station Centralia for summer training as pilots. On another service flight,

Flight Lieutenant R. Coates deposited his passengers and freight at Churchill and proceeded to Vancouver to pick up more Centralia-bound University Flight Cadets.

On 5 May, Air Transport Command Headquarters submitted the itineraries for six long-range training trips by No 426 Squadron to Air Force Headquarters. The itinerary had been expanded to include more airfields in the Caribbean area to increase the squadron's knowledge of operating conditions and procedures in that region.[20]

As Canadair was expected to deliver the C-5 to the RCAF in about six weeks, Air Transport Command Headquarters sent Air Force Headquarters two letters about it on 5 May. The letters dealt with preparing the handling notes, testing the aircraft, training the flight and ground crews, accepting the C-5, and delivering it to No 426 Squadron. The letters also informed Air Force Headquarters that tentative arrangements had been made for twelve aero-engine technicians (in two groups of six) to go to the Pratt and Whitney Aircraft plant at Hartford, Connecticut for a two-week course on the R2800 radial engine with which the aircraft was equipped. These courses were scheduled to start 15 and 29 May. Canadair would train forty more ground staff in two intakes timed to coincide with the Hartford courses. Eight pilots would also receive ground training at Canadair.[21]

On 13 May, several squadron aircrew and ground staff went to Cartierville for the Canadair conversion course on the C-5, which would soon go through acceptance testing. (The acceptance testing was completed as planned, but the anticipated hand-over to No 426 Squadron never took place. The C-5 spent its operational life with No 412 Squadron.)

On 6 May, *Operation RE-SUPPLY* ended with the return to Dorval of two special flights from Resolute Bay and Thule. The same day, No 426 Squadron was brought into *Operation RED RAMP,* which provided assistance to the flood-stricken city of Winnipeg. Five and a half hours after receiving the executive order, the squadron had four North Stars loaded with 100,000 sandbags on their way to Manitoba. The next morning, shortly after departing base for Harmon AFB near Stephenville, Newfoundland, where the Training Command Band was awaiting pick-up, Flight Lieutenant J.D. Dickson in NS17517 was recalled for flood operations, leaving the bandsmen stranded at Harmon until 11 May, when a USAF C-54 based at Goose Bay took them to Trenton.

The city of Winnipeg faced a major disaster; by 9 May, the Red River had flooded parts of the city and much of the surrounding area. All Air Transport Command's available aircraft were drawn into the relief effort, transporting sandbags and water pumps to Winnipeg with soldiers to use them. The struggle to save the city would be long and difficult, and special organizational measures were necessary to mobilize, centralize and control aircraft sources in support of flood control operations. Brigadier J.P.E. Bernatchez, the General Officer Commanding, Prairie Command, was appointed Flood Relief Controller with responsibility for assessing requests for airlift assistance, and the Red Ramp Airlift Agency was organized under Air Commodore M. Costello of RCAF Tactical Group. All Commands involved in *Operation RED RAMP* were instructed to produce a daily report of aircraft availability, including all transport aircraft.

Squadron Leader E.A. Wilson from the Operations Staff at Air Transport Command Headquarters was appointed Winnipeg Liaison Officer, and Air Commodore Ross arrived for a two-day visit to the flood area on 12 May.[22]

At one point during the flood, the mass evacuation of Winnipeg was considered, and all of No 426 Squadron was alerted for *Operation BLACK BOY*. *Operation RED RAMP* increased the squadron's workload considerably — from 9 May to 13 May, every squadron aircraft that could fly was fully tasked, and the squadron made eleven round trips between Montreal and Winnipeg, six round trips between Winnipeg and Minneapolis, two round trips between Rockcliffe and Trenton, and one trip from Toronto.

On 14 May, a report on airlift activities in and out of Winnipeg in support of flood-relief operations showed the following totals:

Winnipeg Airlift Statistics[23]		
Payload	ATC aircraft	Other aircraft
Sandbags (pounds) to Winnipeg	391,120	139,573
Freight (pounds) to Winnipeg	57,335	130,156
Passengers to Winnipeg	220	243
Patients from Winnipeg	138	4

On 15 May, following up on information received from Air Force Headquarters, members of the squadron went to Montreal to visit ex-Sergeant Thomas Plunkett, the squadron's wartime Orderly Room clerk. The visit was not social, but neither was it exactly operational; Sergeant Plunkett had custody of the No 426 Squadron wartime scrapbook, which he had rescued in December 1945 when the squadron was disbanded. The retired sergeant handed it over, satisfied that it would be conspicuously displayed by the squadron for the benefit of all its members; unfortunately, the scrapbook was lost with other priceless squadron records in a hangar fire on 19 March 1956.[24]

With flood-relief activities in Winnipeg winding down, the operational tempo slackened somewhat and the squadron could pay some attention to the social and sporting aspects of service life. On 19 May, the Officers' Mess held a formal mess dinner, with Air Commodore Ross, several staff officers from Air Transport Command Headquarters and the Station Commander from St-Hubert were honoured guests. On 22 May, a house softball league got under way with seven teams, six of them determined to unseat Maintenance Section, the 1949 champions. On 26 May, in partial compensation for a winter of hard work, an all-ranks squadron stag was held in the Station Theatre at Lachine, with food and drink paid for from a special fund established for the purpose and the entertainment by the squadron's more talented members.

On 27 May, the squadron provided a special flight to transport the Governor General, Viscount Alexander of Tunis, to Mont-Joli, Quebec. The flight returned the following day.

On 31 May, the GCA School in No 4 Hangar at Dorval was officially disbanded after eighteen months of producing ground control approach operators for the RCAF.[25] The same day, Air Transport Command released all its units from duties relating to *Operation RED RAMP*. During the operation, Air Transport Command aircraft airlifted more than 500 tons of cargo into Winnipeg and 617 passengers, including 264 patients and sixty-four medical attendants flown from Winnipeg to locations in the prairie provinces.

The results of No 426 Squadron's participation in *Operation RE-SUPPLY* were summarized by Air Transport Command Headquarters at the end of May. The operation took thirty-nine days to complete from 24 March, when the first load was delivered to Isachsen, to 2 May, when the last load was delivered to Alert. During this period, only eight days were lost due to bad weather or runway conditions. The satellite weather stations received a grand total of 715 tons, of which No 426 Squadron delivered 171 tons. Unit maintenance during the Isachsen-Mould Bay phase of the operation was excellent, and no flights were delayed because of breakdowns. On 9 April, a replacement aircraft and crew arrived at Thule AFB from Montreal to take part in the re-supply of Eureka and the establishment of Alert.[26]

June

On 1 June, Flight Lieutenant J.E. McNeely from Air Transport Command Headquarters arrived at Dorval with Flying Officer G.C. Hodgins, Warrant Officer 1st Class Hill and Flight Sergeant Silverman from Air Materiel Command Headquarters to conduct the annual inspection of Supply Section. On 7 June, Flight Lieutenant A.C. McKnight and Corporal Cronk from Air Materiel Command came for data on the consumption of North Star spares. On 10 June, the squadron's Supply Section started a complete review of all instruments used in North Star aircraft, an enormous task.

On 5 June, Viscount Alexander, the Governor General of Canada, presented the RCAF with new colours at an impressive ceremony held in Ottawa.

On 18 June, No 426 Squadron despatched its second long-range training flight to destinations in Europe, Africa, the Middle East, South America and the Caribbean. Apart from some minor changes to the Mediterranean section of the itinerary, the flight schedule was similar to that of the first training flight, which had returned to base two weeks before.

By 19 June, the Fraser River was beginning to flood — in fact, south coastal British Columbia was developing conditions like those that had devastated Winnipeg. At Dorval, all equipment required for field operations was prepared and packed in case No 426 Squadron was called out again for flood relief; after nine days, the unit was advised that the threat was not as serious as first thought, and its services would not be required.[27]

On 21 June, Squadron Leader H.J.C. Lewis, the President of the Mess Committee, and Flight Lieutenant V.W. Duke, the Squadron Supply Officer, flew to No 1 Supply Depot in Toronto to arrange the procurement of new furniture for the station's Roman Catholic and Protestant chapels and for the Officers' Mess.

The squadron's peacetime routine was about to be abruptly shattered by events occurring half a world away: on Sunday, 25 June, the army of North Korea crossed the 38th parallel into South Korea. The United States promptly brought the news to Trygve Lie, the Secretary-General of the United Nations, and requested an emergency meeting of the UN Security Council. When the Security Council met that afternoon, a report on the gravity of the situation had arrived by telegram from the United Nations' Korean Commission.

Yakov Malik, the Soviet delegate, was not present to veto decisions by the Security Council; about six months before, he had walked out in protest when he failed to get Communist China seated in place of Nationalist China.[28]

At its Sunday meeting, the Security Council termed the attack on the Republic of Korea a "breach of the peace", and demanded an immediate cease-fire and the withdrawal of North Korean forces. Meeting again on 27 June, the Security Council called upon member states to furnish such assistance to the Republic of Korea as might be necessary to repel the invading Communist forces. That day, acting with the sanction of the United Nations, President Harry S. Truman of the United States ordered General Douglas MacArthur, Commander-in-Chief US Far East Command, to send all air and naval forces at his disposal to defend South Korea. At the end of the month, Truman authorized MacArthur to send in American ground forces as well.[29]

On 29 June, Trygve Lie asked the members of the United Nations to state what help they could give in compliance with the Security Council resolution of 27 June, and the first offer of military assistance came from the United Kingdom. On 28 June, Prime Minister Clement Attlee announced that Royal Navy ships in Japanese waters were being placed at the disposal of the American authorities to operate on the UN's behalf in support of South Korea. Australia offered an RAAF squadron based in Japan and two warships, and New Zealand despatched two frigates. The government of Nationalist China offered three army divisions but, on the advice of the Unified Command, the UN did not accept. France and the Netherlands each sent a naval vessel and Bolivia offered thirty army officers. Other countries responded with pledges of medical assistance, transportation and various commodities.[30]

In Canada, statements on the Korean situation were made in the House of Commons on 29 June by Secretary of State for External Affairs Lester B. Pearson and on 30 June by Prime Minister Louis St. Laurent. In his speech, the Prime Minister announced that Canada was prepared to send three destroyers based in Esquimalt, British Columbia to operate in the Far East under UN command.[31]

When the Korean War broke out, No 426 Squadron was engaged in routine flights, mainly of a domestic nature, including scheduled runs to Whitehorse and Goose Bay. Apart from flights to northern destinations, most of the squadron's special flights involved moving Air Force and Militia personnel to and from summer training camps. The squadron's training agenda included a series of long-range overseas trips.

The squadron started preparing for war on hearing the official announcement that the United States would fight in Korea. No official notice had been given of any pending involvement, but No 426 was Canada's only long-range transport squadron, so it was highly likely to be employed in some capacity in support of UN forces; therefore, Wing Commander Mussells and his senior officers quickly made plans to deploy from Dorval; all Section Heads were instructed to be ready to move their people and equipment on short notice. These initial plans were mainly routine, since the squadron was well prepared for any move and had learned a great deal from *Operation MOBILITY, Exercise SWEET BRIAR, Op RE-SUPPLY* and *Op RED RAMP*.

Supply Section built boxes to transport all types of equipment. Lists were prepared for all equipment and spares the squadron would need while operating away from Dorval. These lists were prepared on the assumption that the squadron could be operating in the field for periods varying from two weeks to one year.

Maintenance Section accelerated its modification program to bring all aircraft to the same standard as quickly as possible. Personnel who would go to the field were listed and advised that the squadron might move on short notice. Accounts Section began getting the pay records ready to move, and updating squadron inventories to cover equipment that might be moved to a new base of operations. Medical Section began examining and inoculating all unit personnel.

Squadron planning was based on the assumption that six aircraft and twelve crews would move to a forward base. Crews were tentatively selected and advised to update their knowledge of the Pacific region and to think of operating in that area. Publications and maps were requested through Air Transport Command Headquarters, and Navigation Section began to study trans-Pacific routes. As the conflict in Korea intensified, so did squadron preparations. By the time the Canadian government offered No 426 Squadron for UN service, the unit was already in an advanced state of readiness.[32]

PHOTO 37
F/O G.W. Webb and crew on their return to Dorval in NS17512 after their record-setting non-stop trans-Canada flight of 15–16 January 1950: eight hours and 25 minutes from Vancouver to Halifax. From left: F/O Quickfall, F/O Fisher, F/L Queale, W/C Mussells, A/C Ross, F/O Webb, LAC Gennette, Cpl. Leblanc, LAC Guenet and LAC Kirchenner. (National Archives of Canada, PA 129602)

PHOTO 38
Re-supplying Resolute Bay; March 1950. (P.M. Tutt Collection)

PHOTO 39
F/L Art Byford (second from left) and the crew that flew Minister of National Defence Brooke Claxton to the Netherlands; Dorval, March 1950. (A.J.P. Byford Collection)

CHAPTER 9

DORVAL AND McCHORD AIR FORCE BASE
JULY–AUGUST 1950

On 1 July, while preparations were being made for a possible deployment, the squadron despatched the third of its long-range training flights. Captained by Flight Lieutenant G.W. Webb, NS17507 had twenty-four personnel on board, including two complete flight crews (The second crew was captained by Flying Officer M.D. Broadfoot.) The routing was similar to that of the first two flights, except for a one-week visit to England scheduled at the request of British civil aviation authorities, who wanted to see the North Star go through its paces at the Farnborough Air Show. As the Air Show began on the date when the training flight was originally scheduled to depart, the departure had to be advanced by a week.

During their stay in England, the two squadron crews operated out of RAF Station Bassingbourn, eleven miles southwest of Cambridge. Each day from 4 July to 8 July, they flew the North Star to RAF Station Abingdon, four miles southwest of Oxford, to join RAAF, RAF and RNZAF crews in flypasts and demonstrations over the Royal Aircraft Establishment at Farnborough. The training flight left England on 11 July, returning to base twelve days later via the South Atlantic and the Caribbean.

Meanwhile, the squadron's second long-range training flight ended successfully when it returned to base on 3 July[1]

On the morning of 6 July a squadron crew, captained by Flying Officer Bert Miller, went to the Canadair plant at Cartierville. There they joined the company's Chief Pilot, Captain Al Lilly, and his crew to fly a new aircraft, the C-5, to Rockcliffe. The Canadair C-5 VIP passenger transport was a unique hybrid, comprising a pressurized DC-4 fuselage equipped for twenty-four passengers, four comparatively quiet Pratt and Whitney R–2800 "Double Wasp" radial engines, a DC-6 undercarriage and reversing propellers. Under the registration number 17524 (subsequently changed to 10000), the C-5 had made its first flight on 15 May, with Captain Lilly at the controls.

During the landing at Rockcliffe, the engines produced a loud roar as the aircraft started to decelerate, rattling one of the squadron's airmen so badly that he pulled the arm off his seat. None of the RCAF crew had ever been aboard an aircraft with reversing propellers before.

On 7 July, after embarking Prime Minister St. Laurent and his party in the morning, Captain Lilly took the C-5 on to Saskatoon where it remained overnight. The next day, the Prime Minister and his party proceeded to Calgary for the opening of the Stampede. On 11 July, the C-5 arrived at Rockcliffe to disembark the VIPs, and then returned to Dorval.

Within weeks, the Canadair C-5 was transferred to No 412 (Transport) Squadron, where it served out its seventeen-year career in the RCAF.[2]

On 7 July, the Security Council of the United Nations passed its third resolution concerning the growing crisis in Korea, recommending that all member nations contributing military forces and other assistance to operations against North Korea should make them available to the Unified Command led by the United States under the blue UN flag. In conformity with this resolution, President Harry S. Truman appointed General Douglas MacArthur to the command of all UN forces operating in Korea. On 12 July, Canadian UN delegate John Holmes informed Trygve Lie, the Secretary-General of the UN, that the Canadian destroyers *Athabaskan*, *Cayuga* and *Sioux* had arrived in Pearl Harbor on their way to the western Pacific (having departed Esquimalt at 1500 hours on 5 July), and would soon be available for UN service.[3]

The Canadian flotilla was commanded by Captain J.V. Brock, DSC, in HMCS *Cayuga*, fresh from his recent appointment as Commander, Canadian Destroyers, Pacific. On arrival in Pearl Harbor, Captain Brock received orders to report by message to General MacArthur in Tokyo, which he did the following morning. On July 14, after taking on fuel and supplies, the Canadian flotilla set off for Kwajalein, where they arrived on 21 July and refuelled again. They then sailed to Guam, where they received orders to proceed directly to Sasebo, Japan, a port twenty-five miles north of Nagasaki on the island of Kyushu. Leaving Guam on 27 July, the Canadian flotilla arrived at Sasebo Harbour at 1530 hours local time on 30 July, ready for operational tasking.[4]

On 12 July, the Chief of the Air Staff, Air Marshal Curtis, wrote to the Air Officers Commanding, Air Materiel Command and Air Transport Command regarding RCAF support to UN forces in Korea. In view of the political embarrassment if the RCAF plans leaked prematurely, the subject was classified "secret and discreet." Air Marshal Curtis wrote that the USAF did not have enough air transport to meet the requirements of the Korean situation and would welcome RCAF assistance, and set the parameters for further planning.

Essentially, the RCAF would offer as many North Stars as it could, including stored reserves, withholding only the aircraft needed to meet high-priority domestic transport requirements such as re-supplying northern bases and training replacement crews. As soon as possible, the two AOCs were to produce an implementation plan with an estimate of the minimum time required to put No 426 Squadron into initial operation under the operational control of the Military Air Transport Service (MATS, part of the USAF), and to complete its build-up to planned final size.[5]

When the Berlin Airlift ended in the fall of 1949, the American air transport fleet needed extensive overhaul, not only because of the wear and tear caused by the exacting flying conditions, but also because coal dust and flour had sifted into the seams of every participating aircraft.

Consequently, flying hours were cut as much as possible, and the USAF, especially MATS, was cut back to core level, from which it was to be expanded in the event of war. Between August 1945 and June 1950, more than three-quarters of MATS airlift capability had been either demobilized, mothballed or placed in reserve. Although MATS was responsible for providing strategic airlift for the war in Korea, at the time it was ill-equipped for the mission.[6]

On 14 July, in his reply to John Holmes' communication of 12 July, the UN Secretary-General drew attention to the urgent need for effective assistance. The governments of Canada and other member nations were asked to consider providing more combat forces, particularly ground troops. The military situation in Korea was serious: American and South Korean forces were desperately trying to hold the Kum River line above Taejon.[7]

Trygve Lie's request did not seem to make much of a stir in official Ottawa circles. Minister of National Defence Brooke Claxton was in Newfoundland, discussing continental defence matters with US military officials, and the Prime Minister had gone fishing for the weekend.

On the evening of 14 July, No 426 Squadron despatched Flight Lieutenant Art Byford and his crew in NS17520 to bring Mr. Claxton back to Ottawa. They took off just before midnight and arrived in Gander early on Saturday morning — but the Minister was not to be found. After some inquiries, Byford learned that Mr. Claxton was at a remote fishing camp near Stephenville, so he flew to Harmon AFB, the airfield closest to the camp. With the Minister finally aboard, the aircraft departed Newfoundland late in the afternoon of 16 July, and landed at Rockcliffe that evening.[8]

On receipt of the 12 July letter from Air Marshal Curtis, the planning staff at Air Transport Command Headquarters met with Wing Commander Mussells and Squadron Leader Bill Lord, the Chief Technical Officer of No 426 Squadron, who then worked all weekend and were ready to present an outline plan of operations by 16 July. This plan stated how the squadron could support the UN effort in Korea with a unit establishment of eight freighter aircraft. Initially, six North Stars and twelve crews would be made available, and the rest of the squadron — two aircraft and three crews — would remain at Dorval to handle domestic missions such as the supply commitment at Resolute Bay, to form a nucleus from which the squadron would expand, and to train replacement crews.[9]

Wing Commander Mussells' plan of operations assumed that No 426 Squadron would be based in one of the western states of the U.S., and would be required to sustain airlift operations for one year. Six North Stars and twelve crews implied an operational element of fifty officers and 200 airmen, who would need to take 100,000 pounds of aircraft spares and ground-handling equipment with them. Within eighteen hours of notification, the six aircraft could be at their west-coast base with limited support and, with crew rest and briefings taken into account, the squadron could sustain its current flying rate of 70 hours per aircraft per month for at least two weeks without the support of a supply line. Within forty-eight hours of notification, the complete operational element could reach the west-coast base, and the squadron could then operate at its current flying rate for three weeks without a supply line. Thirty-six hours after notification, five North Stars of the operational element could be available for MATS operations from the west coast — again, allowing for crew rest, special briefings and handling a host of other issues. The sixth North Star would be used to provide the rest of the squadron with logistical support. Finally, the plan stated that, with unlimited logistical support, the squadron could operate over designated Pacific routes for up to 200 hours per aircraft per month without an increase in aircrew or subjecting squadron personnel to abnormal fatigue.[10]

Air Transport Command Headquarters endorsed Wing Commander Mussells' plan of operations, which went forward to the Chief of the Air Staff on 18 July with a detailed covering letter emphasizing that, at first, only six North Stars could be made available, and that the maximum flying rate for each North Star must be kept at seventy hours per month until logistical support could be increased. Most of the comments from Air Transport Command dealt with personnel, aircraft maintenance and logistics issues.[11]

The Chiefs of Staff Committee met on 18 July. On 19 July, the Cabinet Defence Committee met with the rest of the Cabinet and the Minister of National Defence advised the other ministers that the two committees had concluded that Canada was not prepared to send ground forces to Korea because the only available troops were in the Airborne Brigade Group, which was required for the defence of Canada. Consequently, the Cabinet decided to offer an air transport squadron equipped with North Stars to help supply and reinforce UN forces in Korea. At the same time, Cabinet increased the Defence budget by up to $50 million in the current fiscal year and authorized an expansion of the armed forces by 5,000 to 6,000 personnel.[12]

After the Cabinet meeting, Prime Minister St-Laurent issued a statement on Trygve Lie's request for additional assistance, emphasizing Canada's obligations as a member of the UN, as a signatory to the North Atlantic Treaty, and as a partner with the United States in the joint defence of North America. He mentioned the deployment of HMC ships *Athabaskan*, *Cayuga* and *Sioux*, and stated that the destroyers required continuing support. Since air transport was needed, the Government had decided to provide one RCAF long-range transport squadron immediately for service in the Pacific airlift. Since the Canadian Army had other obligations, the Cabinet had concluded that it could not despatch its first-line elements to Korea.[13]

On 20 July, on receiving formal notice of the Cabinet decision, the Chief of the Air Staff issued the following directives:

1 Immediate action is to be taken to integrate No 426 Transport Squadron operations with those of United States Military Air Transport Service (MATS, USAF) in support of the United Nations campaign in Korea.

2 No 426 Transport Squadron aircraft allocated to this task will be placed under the operational control of MATS insofar as operations directly applicable to Korean Airlift are concerned. RCAF Air Transport Command will maintain administrative control throughout and operational control in domestic operations or on those flights not immediately concerned with MATS operations.

3 All domestic operations of No 426 Transport Squadron are to be curtailed, except those given special authorization.

4 No 426 Transport Squadron is to be brought up to war strength [a unit establishment of twelve aircraft] as soon as possible with such additional personnel as may be required in accordance with the extended nature of the operations.

5   RCAF aircraft are not to operate into Korea.

6   It is anticipated that arrangement with other nations for logistic or other support will be on a CAN. PAY basis.

7   The planning and implementation of all financial, logistics, personnel, organizational and other matters in respect to this operation are to be given the highest priority.[14]

The Prime Minister's statement set off a flurry of activity in Air Transport Command. On 19 July, a Grumman Goose was despatched to Muskoka to fetch Air Commodore Ross back from leave at his cottage, senior officers from No 426 Squadron were summoned to Rockcliffe for a meeting that afternoon, and arrangements were made for a meeting with MATS officials in Washington the next day.

On 20 July, the squadron was officially alerted for the move to the west coast. Air Commodore Ross flew to Andrews Air Force Base (near Washington, DC) with Wing Commander Swetman, Wing Commander Mussells and Squadron Leader Lord for a all-day meeting with Major-General Laurence S. Kuter, the MATS Commander, and members of his staff at their headquarters. Among other things, they decided that No 426 Squadron would depart Dorval on 25 July, and that their west-coast base would be McChord AFB near Tacoma, Washington.[15]

After this meeting, an operational agreement on RCAF participation in the Far East airlift, dated 28 July (see Appendix C), was drawn up at MATS Headquarters and forwarded to Air Transport Command Headquarters at Rockcliffe. On receipt, two copies of the agreement were forwarded to Air Force Headquarters in Ottawa on 4 August by Wing Commander W.H. Swetman, the Senior Air Staff Officer. The accompanying letter stated that Air Commodore Ross had concurred in the agreement, and that Air Transport Command Headquarters was seeking to clarify one point with MATS Headquarters: the provision of a field-grade RCAF officer to act as liaison with the Continental Division of MATS. This liaison position was never established.[16]

With No 426 Squadron committed to the Pacific airlift, Air Transport Command cancelled all scheduled operations and special commitments for North Star freighters, except for supply runs to Resolute Bay, effective 23 July. No 412 Squadron, No 435 Squadron and aircraft from Goose Bay took over the scheduled services on 24 July.

The personnel of No 426 Squadron were officially informed on 23 July, a Sunday, that McChord AFB would be their new base of operations, and that they would leave Dorval on 25 July. That morning, Flight Lieutenant Webb brought the third long-range training flight back to base with ten of the twelve members of the flight crew unaware that they had 48 hours to put their affairs in order for an indefinite period of duty on the other side of the continent.

Monday, 24 July was extremely busy for those involved in preparing the squadron for departure. While the servicing and maintenance crews worked on the aircraft, Air Movements personnel supervised the packing and loading of tools, spares and ground-handling equipment. Meanwhile, from the first announcement of the squadron's participation in the Korean war effort, a plague of print and broadcast reporters descended on Dorval and Lachine, demanding interviews from Wing Commander Mussells and other squadron personnel until two Public Relations Officers arrived from Air Force Headquarters to handle all media contacts.

On 24 July, Air Force Headquarters issued two organization orders. The first authorized No 426 Squadron to move to McChord AFB on 25 July and to provide air transport services in co-operation with MATS for operations related to the invasion of South Korea only, as directed by the Air Officer Commanding, Air Transport Command, RCAF, who retained functional and administrative control of No 426 Squadron. The AOC was to direct personnel of No 426 Squadron to obey orders issued by the Commanding Officer, McChord AFB, on behalf of the Commanding General, Continental Division, MATS, only in respect of transport operations related to the invasion of South Korea, and matters affecting their occupancy and use of McChord AFB facilities. The second organization order, effective 25 July, re-created RCAF Station Lachine, which had been disbanded on 2 December 1946, to resupply Resolute Bay, and to provide No 426 Squadron with logistical support and trained replacement flight crews.

At the same time, Wing Commander Mussells issued an organization order, effective 25 July with the squadron's departure, establishing a Squadron Rear Party comprising the Thunderbird personnel who were not going to McChord AFB. Until they received further direction from Air Transport Command Headquarters, the Squadron Rear Party would provide an Operational Training Unit and ensure that essential services continued at Dorval and Lachine (see organization chart below). The Squadron Rear Party would be headed by the unit's Chief Administrative Officer, Squadron Leader Doug Henry.[17]

426 Squadron Rear Party

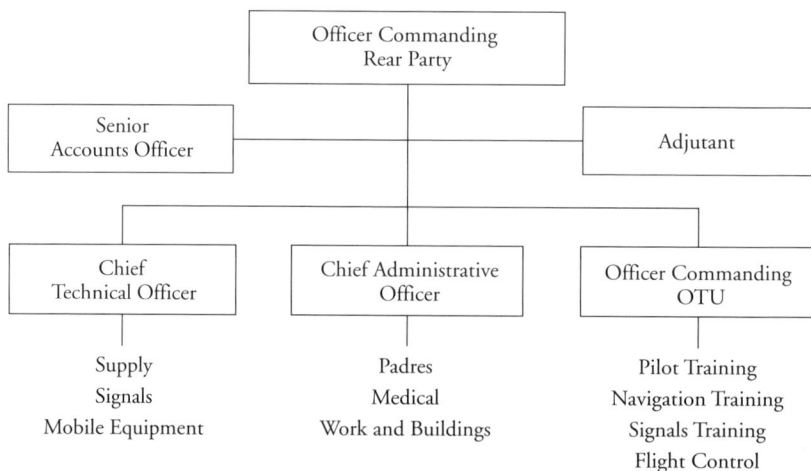

On 24 July, while departure preparations went on at Dorval and Lachine, Wing Commander M.B. McKinnon chaired a meeting at Air Materiel Command Headquarters in Ottawa on the squadron's deployment with supply and technical specialists from Air Material Command and Air Transport Command, and Rolls-Royce representatives from Montreal. He informed the meeting that No 426 Squadron would depart the next day for McChord AFB, from which location the squadron would conduct transport operations to Japan using the Great Circle Route. Transient bases had not yet been chosen. The squadron would begin operations using six North Stars and build up to eight, with four more based at Dorval for use in re-supplying northern bases, training replacement flight crews, and supporting the operational element of the squadron at McChord. Initially, each aircraft assigned to the airlift would be operated at a monthly flying rate of sixty hours, to be increased within two weeks to a monthly rate of eighty to ninety hours.

Wing Commander McKinnon also announced the immediate formation of RCAF Station Lachine, with responsibility for re-supply, flight crew training and airlift support and status as a supply sub-depot for No 426 Squadron's operational element. He revealed that arrangements had been made with MATS to supply spares that were common to both the C-54 and the North Star; MATS would also provide fuel, handling facilities, and housekeeping, health care, messing and accommodation services on a cost-recovery basis.

The Air Transport Command officers at the meeting presented the following supply lists for review: equipment being taken to McChord AFB by the squadron; spares support required by six North Stars for one month; estimated monthly consumption of spares; and engine, power plant and engine block requirements. The final item on the agenda was training, which would be carried out at Dorval, and would include weekly training flights to and from McChord AFB that would also be used as much as possible to re-supply the operational element of No 426 Squadron and to bring repairable equipment back to Dorval. The capacity of this weekly shuttle was estimated at 10,000 pounds of cargo each way.[18]

Air Transport Command Operation Order 17/50 issued on 24 July officially launched the RCAF's only long-range transport squadron on an airlift mission that was to last nearly four years.

No 426 Squadron was ordered to depart Dorval on 25 July at 1900 hours local time for Vancouver via Winnipeg, and to arrive at McChord AFB near Tacoma, Washington on 26 July. The USAF would direct the routing for the airlift to and from Japan. This routing would normally follow the Great Circle track to Tokyo, with regular stops at Anchorage, Shemya, at the end of the Aleutian chain, and Misawa, an airfield on the northeast coast of Honshu. The order specifically forbade RCAF to operate into Korea. If refuelling was necessary, the logistical support route to and from Dorval would be through Winnipeg.

The group from No 426 Squadron scheduled to leave for McChord AFB on July 25 comprised six North Star freighters with twelve complete crews and enough ground staff for squadron maintenance, with more to be added as personnel and logistics support became available. The Thunderbird crews included three exchange officers: pilot Captain T.J. Upton of the USAF, and pilot Flight Lieutenant R. Coates and navigator Flight Lieutenant A. Knapper of the RAF. (See Appendix B for the complete list of personnel who left for McChord AFB from No 426 Squadron on 25 July and RCAF Station Rockcliffe on 5 August.) The mission also included one officer, Flight Lieutenant H. Brisebois, and twelve air traffic assistants from the Dorval detachment of No 901 Air Traffic Handling Unit. MATS personnel would prepare the manifests and load the aircraft, the primary responsibility for the correct distribution of the load in each RCAF aircraft lay with the captain of the aircraft and the RCAF air traffic assistants.

The Canadian code word for the Korean airlift was *Operation HAWK*.[19]

At 1400 hours on Tuesday, 25 July, North Stars 17502, 17504, 17507, 17511, 17514 and 17517 — each sporting a freshly stencilled UN flag on its tailfin — were loaded, checked and lined up in front of the squadron hangars in two rows of three, and the entire squadron was on parade for a final inspection by Wing Commander Mussells. Messrs W. Gardner and C. Cowell of the Montreal Camp of the Gideons were also present to invite each member of the squadron to pick up a personal miniature copy of the New Testament. At 1815 hours, the flight crews and technicians were lined up in front of their aircraft, facing more than 500 family members and friends who had gathered at Dorval to say goodbye.

The formal farewells were delivered by Air Vice Marshal A.L. James, the Air Member for Air Plans at Air Force Headquarters, who had come from Rockcliffe that day with a party of senior officials. The message from Minister of Defence Brooke Claxton read as follows:

> Events will prevent my coming to Dorval as I had hoped. Accordingly, I have asked Air Vice Marshal James, in my name, to wish you Godspeed on your departure. You will be carrying with you the good name of Canada and the fine record of the RCAF. I know you will bring credit to both and will successfully carry through your important mission.
>
> Brooke Claxton

Air Vice Marshal James also relayed a message of warmest greetings and good wishes from Air Marshal Curtis, the Chief of the Air Staff "on this, another memorable day in the history of the RCAF". A/M Curtis's message concluded with "good luck, Godspeed and happy landings."[20]

The party accompanying Air Vice Marshal James included the following senior officers from Air Force Headquarters: Air Vice Marshal F.R. Miller, Air Member for Operations and Training; Air Vice Marshal J.L. Plant, Air Member for Personnel; Air Commodore F.C. Wait, Deputy Air Member for Personnel; Group Captain Z.L. Leigh, Director of Air Operations; and Group Captain J.G. Stevenson, Director of Postings and Careers; and the following senior officers from Air Transport Command Headquarters: Air Commodore A.D. Ross, the Air Officer Commanding; and Wing Commander W.H. Swetman, the Senior Air Staff Officer and a previous commanding officer of No 426 Squadron. The Army was represented by Major-General R.O.G. Morton, General Officer Commanding; and Lieutenant-Colonel P.M. Desautels of Quebec Command. The Royal Canadian Navy was represented by Lieutenant D.B. Daines of HMCS *Donnacona*.

To end the farewell ceremony, Air Vice Marshal James shook hands with each member of the flight and ground crews assigned to NS17502 and wished everyone "bon voyage." Then Wing Commander Mussells stepped up to the microphone and ordered, "Captains, have your crews board your aircraft," and the airmen clambered up the ladders into their designated aircraft and swung the doors shut as onlookers wept and waved handkerchiefs. Twenty-four Merlin engines rumbled through their warm-up as the cockpit crews ran through their checklists and then

NS17514 (captained by Wing Commander Mussells) headed down the taxiway to the active runway, followed by the others. On the taxiway, Mussells received the following message from Air Commodore Ross:

> I am proud of your selection as RCAF representatives in the UN Forces. I am confident that you will maintain your high standard of operational efficiency on your new assignment and will bring credit to this Command and to the RCAF as a whole. On behalf of Air Transport Command I send best wishes for your success and the speedy completion of your operation.

The other five captains (in order of departure) were Flight Lieutenant J.A. (Johnny) Watt, Flying Officer M.D. (Dean) Broadfoot, Squadron Leader H.A. (Howie) Morrison, Squadron Leader J.H.C. (Coach) Lewis, and Flight Lieutenant A.J.P. (Art) Byford.[21]

The RCAF contingent assembled for *Operation HAWK* included both veterans of the Second World War and men who had enlisted after 1945. Of the twenty-four pilots, eight had won their wings since 1948, and two — Flying Officer M.D. Broadfoot and Flying Officer R.M. Edwards — were qualified as captains on North Star aircraft. The other six pilots — Flying Officer J.C. Henry, Flying Officer D.H. Kuhn, Flying Officer P.M. Lemieux, Flying Officer D.G. Scott, Flying Officer A.L. Quickfall and Flying Officer E.R. Wolkowski — started out flying as first officers and qualified as captains in a few months. Of the navigators, Flying Officer J.A. Gauthier and Flying Officer E.H. Moberg had qualified after the war, and five of the radio officers — Flying Officer A.F. Fieldman, Flying Officer J.M. Latter, Flying Officer T.E. Richardson, Flying Officer J.S. Shipton and Flying Officer A.J.S. Timmins — were also of the postwar vintage.

At 1902 hours, a rain squall hit Dorval just as Wing Commander Mussells lifted NS17514 off the runway, closely followed by the rest of the squadron detail. As they headed northeast after takeoff, the pilots sorted themselves into two vics of three aircraft, the first led by Wing Commander Mussells with Broadfoot on his starboard wing and Watts to port, and the second led by Howie Morrison. As Mussells slowed down to let his wingmen catch up, Broadfoot's aircraft surged ahead, prompting Mussells to radio a reminder as to who was supposed to lead the formation.

Formation flying is not a high-priority skill for transport pilots, so the Thunderbird detail was near Trois-Rivières by the time it was formed up and ready to head west. When they reached Montreal, the six aircraft descended to 1,200 feet to overfly the city and then the base at Dorval, where friends and relatives stepped out of the hangars into the rain for a last wave good-bye. The aircraft dipped their wings and disappeared.

The next destination was Ottawa, where the six North Stars arrived at 2000 hours to fly past Parliament Hill and dip their wings again, for the flag on the Peace Tower was flying at half-mast in honour of former Prime Minister Mackenzie King, who had died on 22 July and was lying in state in the Hall of Honour. Their salute delivered, the aircraft flew on to Kingston, and then along the north shore of Lake Ontario to Toronto, where they arrived at dusk, just after 2100 hours, passing over the waterfront with their navigation lights on. The formation then broke up, and the aircraft climbed to their assigned altitudes between 6,000 and 8,000 feet for the flight to Winnipeg, their first refuelling stop.[22]

At 0050 hours local time, seven hours and ten minutes after taking off from Dorval, Mussells and his crew arrived at Stevenson Field, Winnipeg, closely followed by the rest of the detail. After a two-and-a-half-hour stopover, five North Stars were outward bound from Winnipeg to Vancouver, while Squadron Leader Lewis, the captain of the sixth aircraft, dealt with a faulty fuel pump that kept him and his crew on the ground for four hours. The journey to Vancouver took five hours and forty minutes, and the first aircraft arrived at Sea Island Airport shortly after 0600 hours local time. The stopover there was nearly three hours, which gave Lewis time to catch up. On Wednesday, 26 July, Wing Commander Mussells led the departure from Vancouver at 0845 hours and set down at McChord AFB, the squadron's new operational home, at 1005 hours; by noon, only eighteen hours after leaving Dorval, the rest of the detail had arrived, and the operational element of No 426 Squadron—258 personnel, including seventy-two flight crew—was in place.

On arrival at McChord, the Thunderbird aircraft were marshalled into an open field where the grass had recently been burned off. Nobody but a few romantics weaned on Hollywood movies expected to be greeted by brass bands, but Wing Commander Mussells (who was wearing his best uniform in anticipation of an official welcome) certainly did not expect a Second Lieutenant calling to him from a jeep to get his men off the aircraft as the buses would soon arrive.

Wing Commander Mussells was soon joined by the Base Commander, Colonel T.A. Bennett of Wilmington, Delaware, who waited with him to meet the other aircraft. As each North Star arrived, the flight crews were hustled off to their quarters and the ground staff, under the supervision of Squadron Leader Bill Lord, the Chief Technical Officer, supervised as squadron personnel unloaded their equipment and supplies into tents erected in the dispersal area — a temporary measure that lasted several weeks. Squadron Leader Lord was assisted by the Supply Officer, Flight Lieutenant V.W. Duke; the Signals Officer, Flight Lieutenant A.B. Stuart; and the squadron's two Engineering Officers, Flying Officer H.G. Graves and Flying Officer G. Kreklewetz.

The conditions the Thunderbird contingent found at McChord can best be described as chaotic. Before transport aircraft began flocking in, McChord AFB was the home of an All-Weather Fighter Group equipped with the F–82B Twin Mustang. When the Thunderbirds arrived, three squadrons of the 61st Troop Carrier Group had just flown in from Germany with thirty-six C-54 Skymaster transports, and the base was expecting three more squadrons (with thirty-six more C-54s) from Texas. The sudden influx of heavy transport aircraft into a fighter base had created an acute problem as far as accommodation, messing and maintenance facilities were concerned.[23]

Colonel Bennett said he would give No 426 Squadron one week to settle in before beginning operations. Wing Commander Mussells countered that, if loads were available, three of his aircraft could be ready to depart for Japan within thirty-six hours — consistent with the plan he submitted to Air Transport Command Headquarters on 16 July.[24]

Through a lot of improvisation by McChord base personnel, the RCAF contingent was fed and housed, a corner of a hangar was found for the squadron's maintenance and supply sections, and the servicing crews were moved into an old Quonset hut beside the dispersal area. Flight Lieutenant J.P. McDonald, the squadron's Operations Officer, set up shop in a little shack in the northeast corner of the airfield. The accommodations for the airmen were in a shabby two-storey wooden barrack that did not come close to RCAF standards; however, when Wing Commander Mussells informed Colonel Bennett that he was prepared to move the airmen off the base into civilian accommodation, conditions improved in days. Attention could be focussed on the task at hand.[25]

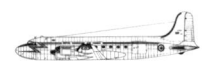

On 27 July, as the Thunderbirds were settling in at McChord, preparations were made to despatch three aircraft on their first airlift flight, and one aircraft back to Dorval for a load of equipment and spares. By the afternoon, Flying Officer Broadfoot and his crew were eastbound; they arrived at Dorval well after midnight, only to find no Customs officers present to clear the aircraft. After waiting a considerable time, Broadfoot gave up and taxied the aircraft to the No 426 Squadron dispersal area and, with the crew, proceeded to Lachine and bed. Several hours later, Broadfoot awoke to find two RCMP officers demanding to know why he had failed to clear Customs. When he explained that the crew had arrived late the previous night with an empty aircraft, that the Customs officials had not appeared, and that they were due to return to McChord later that day, the Mounties went on their way, apparently satisfied. Nothing more was heard.[26]

At 1945 hours local on Thursday 27 July, Squadron Leader Harry Lewis and his crew were airborne in NS17511, carrying a full load of US Army personnel on the first of 599 departures from McChord on *Operation HAWK*. Their first stop was Elmendorf AFB in Anchorage, Alaska. Besides Lewis, the other crew members on this epic first flight were: Flying Officer A.L. Quickfall (first officer), Flying Officer B.L. Ray (navigator), Flying Officer J.W. Santarelli (radio officer), Sergeant F.S. Bowman (flight engineer) and, Leading Aircraftsman H.R. MacDonald (air traffic assistant). An hour and a half later, Squadron Leader Don Dickson in NS17507 was also heading for Elmendorf AFB, also with a load of US Army personnel. Dickson's crew consisted of: Flight Lieutenant W.R. Lloyd (first officer), Flight Lieutenant R.E. Ratcliffe (navigator), Flying Officer W. Smith (radio officer), Warrant Officer C.W. Baine (flight engineer) and Leading Aircraftsman E.C. Grose (air traffic assistant). On both flights, the passengers seemed rather apprehensive about the journey, with reason: they were reservists who had just been called up and were heading for a war in a strange land, and they were being transported there by a foreign air force!

Two hours after Dickson's departure, the squadron had a third aircraft on its way to Tokyo with yet more American soldiers. NS17502 was captained by Flight Lieutenant Art Byford with Flying Officer D.H. Kuhn (first officer), Flying Officer E.J. Boland (navigator), Flying Officer N.E. Bohn (radio officer), Sergeant E.S. Barber (flight engineer) and Leading Aircraftsman J.A.A. St. Laurent (air traffic assistant).

In a little more than thirty-six hours, No 426 Squadron had moved to a new base of operations and despatched four aircraft: three to Tokyo and one to Dorval.

The three Tokyo-bound aircraft followed the North Pacific route to Japan. On average, a flight to Elmendorf AFB took seven hours and forty-five minutes, followed by about ten hours of crew rest. The next leg was to Shemya AFB, on an island near the western end of the Aleutian chain, a distance usually covered in eight hours, followed by two hours on the ground to refuel, feed the passengers and file flight plans to Misawa, on the northeast coast of Honshu. The ocean crossing generally took the North Star aircraft nine and a half hours and, after a brief stop at Misawa, the aircraft went on to Haneda AFB at Tokyo, a flight of two hours and fifteen minutes. After eighteen hours of crew rest, Lewis and Dickson returned to McChord by way of Adak in the Aleutians, where they refuelled. After nearly fifty hours of flying, and an elapsed time of about eighty-two hours, both aircraft were back at base by the morning of 31 July. Byford and his crew spent twenty-four hours in Tokyo and returned to McChord via Shemya and Elmendorf, where the crew stopped for seventeen hours; Byford was back at base early in the morning of 1 August, having been away for 103 hours, of which fifty were spent in the air. These three proving flights helped establish the North Pacific route to Japan used by the squadron on most of its runs during the Korean airlift.[27]

Apart from delivering their loads of troops and high-priority cargo, the squadron's most pressing operational planning issue was to determine where to put the slip crews and servicing crews. The servicing crews were initially positioned in Tokyo and Elmendorf AFB. On the run to Tokyo from Elmendorf, with a refuelling stop at Shemya, the flight crews faced a workday of about twenty-four hours. Flights from McChord to Elmendorf with a crew rest at Shemya tended to shorten duty time by about four hours. Wherever crew rests were taken, the workday often involved many hours of overtime. Delays on the ground were caused by local weather problems, cargo loading and equipment malfunctions. Delays in the air arose from engine problems, icing conditions, strong head winds, and deteriorating weather at the destination that forced crews in flight to divert to an alternate airport.

On a more mundane note, by the end of July, the squadron had a functioning account at the Tacoma branch of the Bank of California, based on an initial advance cheque signed by the Chief Treasury Officer, Department of National Defence, in the amount of $40,000 in American funds. Once the pay records arrived from RCAF Station Lachine, basic financial operations could begin.

August

On 1 August, a fourth squadron aircraft left for Tokyo in the evening, carrying two crews, one captained by Flying Officer J.B. Miller (who took the aircraft to Elmendorf), and the other skippered by Wing Commander Mussells (who flew on to Shemya). An extra captain, Flying Officer D.M. Payne, worked the leg to Tokyo, which was routed over Matsushima on the eastern coast of Honshu. This landfall was about an hour's flying time to the north of Tokyo's Haneda airport. The crew arrived at Haneda late in the evening of 3 August.

During the next four days, Wing Commander Mussells made local arrangements with MATS for the handling of the squadron's aircraft. With the help of the Canadian Embassy in Tokyo, he also arranged quarters for squadron personnel. Airmen and, sometimes, officers would stay in the outskirts of Tokyo at Ebisu Camp, a Japanese base previously used for developing midget submarines and now operated by the very co-operative Australian Army. Routine quarters for officers were arranged in downtown Tokyo at the Marunouchi Hotel, an establishment used by the British and Australian occupation forces to accommodate Commonwealth officers on leave or temporary duty.[28]

On 7 August, three more North Star captains, Flight Lieutenant Allen, Flight Lieutenant Bell and Flight Lieutenant Webb, arrived at McChord with navigators Flight Lieutenant Spector and Flying Officer Glustien.

The American authorities at McChord informed the Thunderbirds that they would receive a share of the profits of the Consolidated Non-Appropriated Welfare Fund (USAF) to the extent of forty cents per man per month, to be made available to the Squadron Fund Committee to pay for entertainment and sports activities.

On the same day, in Ottawa, Prime Minister Louis St-Laurent announced that, in addition to the three destroyers despatched to the west Pacific and the long-range transport squadron operating on the Korean airlift, Parliament had authorized the increase of the Canadian Army by a full brigade, to be known as the Canadian Army Special Force, and to be trained and equipped to carry out Canada's obligations under the United Nations Charter and the North Atlantic Pact. The infantry units selected for the Canadian Army Special Force were to be organized as second battalions of The Royal Canadian Regiment, Princess Patricia's Canadian Light Infantry and The Royal 22ᵉ Régiment. [29]

On 8 August, a duplex teletype landline opened between McChord AFB and the RCAF's No 12 Group Headquarters in Vancouver, so No 426 Squadron could stop using commercial systems to send operational message traffic, and seventy-two airmen from various RCAF units reported in to No 426 Squadron's McChord detachment. The next day, eighty more airmen arrived. The squadron's ground staff was being built up to cope with the increasing flying commitments and the corresponding step-up in maintenance.[30]

Also on 8 August, Wing Commander Mussells and his crew left Haneda, and made it back at McChord in thirty-three hours, which included ten hours of crew rest at Adak. Flying Officer Miller stayed in Tokyo as the captain of the first eastbound slip crew.

Early that morning, Flight Lieutenant Bob Coates brought NS17511 into Haneda, and the aircraft was serviced and prepared for Flying Officer Miller and his crew to take it back to McChord. When it was time to leave, Miller taxied out to the end of the runway, braked, and gunned his engines as he waited for the tower to give him permission to take off. On receiving clearance, he released the brakes but, as the aircraft started to roll forward, all four engines quit at once — a close call, as the malfunction could have happened in the air. The aircraft was immediately towed off the runway to a hangar for a thorough inspection.

Wing Commander Mussells sent Flying Officer Graves out from McChord to Haneda on the next available flight to investigate. Graves discovered that NS17511 had been filled with 115/145-octane fuel, appropriate for American-built radial engines, instead of the 100/130-octane fuel required by the Rolls-Royce Merlins with which the North Stars were equipped. The engines had quit because the spark plugs had leaded up.[31]

On 9 August, Canadair's test pilot, A.J. Lilly flew the Canadian prototype 191-010 of the North American F-86 Sabre 1 at Dorval. The aircraft had been towed there from Cartierville, where the runways were not yet ready for jet operations. 191-010 was the first of 1,815 Sabres that Canadair would build, and the squadron would soon be involved in providing logistics support for their overseas deployment.[32]

On 11 August, in a diplomatic note to the UN Secretary General, Canadian Acting Permanent Delegate John Holmes offered the UN the complete passenger facilities of Canadian Pacific Airlines' regular commercial service between Vancouver and Tokyo for the Korean airlift, courtesy of the Government of Canada and Canadian Pacific Airlines. This contribution amounted to two westbound flights per week and the equivalent of one eastbound flight per week. Unified Command would handle arrangements to integrate the CPA flights into the airlift schedule.[33]

Between 4 August and 14 August, No 426 Squadron sent out one Tokyo-bound aircraft every second day. MATS directed that, as of 14 August, the squadron would despatch one Tokyo-bound flight per day, to meet the urgent need for troops, anti-tank weapons and ammunition, and medical supplies, especially plasma. The military situation in South Korea was deteriorating badly.

The task of returning NS17511 (the aircraft with the leaded-up spark plugs) to service fell to the squadron's newly arrived Tokyo-based servicing detachment, headed by crew chief Flight Sergeant Bert Ruffell of Victoria, British Columbia. While servicing the other aircraft as they came in, the detachment also managed to get NS17511 back into the operational stream on 19 August. As well as Flight Sergeant Ruffell, the Tokyo ground crew included Corporal Pat Magdalinski of Guernsey, Saskatchewan; Corporal Maurice Soame of Ottawa, Ontario; Leading Aircraftsman Harry Rizum of Vegreville, Alberta; Leading Aircraftsman Red Bell of Saskatoon, Saskatchewan; Leading Aircraftsman T.G. Thompson of Winnipeg, Manitoba; Leading Aircraftsman Bert Ferguson of Norwood, Ontario; Leading Aircraftsman J.P. Thompson, Leading Aircraftsman Don Stead and Leading Aircraftsman Lionel Pelletier of Montreal, Quebec; and Leading Aircraftsman René Claveau of Québec City, Quebec.[34]

On 23 August, the squadron at McChord welcomed Mr. Paul Durand, the Rolls-Royce representative with the squadron at Dorval, who quickly contributed to squadron folklore. Having brought his wife from Montreal, Durand moved into at a motel about a mile from the main gate of the base, and soon found a hole in the fence that provided him with a marvellous short cut to the squadron's maintenance area. One morning, as he completed the manoeuvre of squirming under the fence, he found himself staring at the business end of a carbine wielded by a very determined military policeman. Unfortunately, he was carrying the drawings for the North Star engine mountings, but not his identification documents. Worse, English was not his first language, and his excited explanations in French and accented English convinced the MP that he had collared a spy or a saboteur. The MP promptly marched Durand off to the guardhouse and contacted Wing Commander Mussells. Lacking any form of supporting paperwork (such as orders), the squadron commander then had to convince Colonel Bennett, the Base Commander, that Durand belonged to the squadron. Wing Commander Mussells let Mr. Durand sit in cells for long enough to absorb the lesson, and then had him released from custody with strict instructions to carry his identification at all times and to enter the base only by the main gate. The perimeter fence was then checked and repaired.[35]

The supply flow to McChord tapered off toward the end of the month, and the squadron decided on 26 August to start a weekly supply run from RCAF Station Lachine, departing Dorval in time to arrive at McChord each Wednesday and return to Dorval each Thursday.

On Sunday, 27 August, the USAF airmen at McChord AFB held a welcoming dinner and dance in the Airmen's Recreation Club. Several of No 426 Squadron's officers also attended, at the express invitation of the Base Commander.

Briefings for the early runs to Tokyo were sketchy at best, and the first crews practically had to feel their way around the route. During the early stages of airlift operations out of McChord, the squadron's senior navigators played a key role in developing the briefing format used, not only by RCAF crews, but by American crews as well. During their first month at McChord, they essentially organized the briefing procedures and conducted a large part of the briefings.[36]

Shortly after the squadron's arrival, the USAF launched a large-scale base-rehabilitation program at McChord, including new buildings and an enormous (400 feet by 1000 feet) stretch of new pavement in the southwest sector of the airfield for aircraft parking and servicing. During the early weeks, the maintenance and supply sections lacked staff, equipment and spares, a situation that was eased by the timely arrival of 152 officers and airmen and a freight car full of spares. With this infusion, the squadron managed to sustain operations at one departure per day.

Squadron Leader Lord's maintenance organization at McChord comprised Maintenance Headquarters, Repair Flight, Servicing Flight and two servicing detachments, initially established at Elmendorf AFB and Haneda AFB. Repair Flight probably had the most trouble. The squadron's hangar space could accommodate only one aircraft, which meant doing practically all maintenance and repairs in the open. It was summer, so the weather was good and the ground crews could work with a minimum of inconvenience.

Eventually, Squadron Leader Lord acquired a building to house the tire and hydraulic shop, the instrument shop, and the Electrical, Wireless, and Safety Equipment sections, while personnel from the squadron's metal and carpentry shops worked with the corresponding USAF sections. A Nissen hut was procured and partitioned at one end to provide the Chief Technical Officer and the Engineering Officers with office space; the rest of the building accommodated the clerks of Maintenance Control Section. The motor transport provided to the squadron included three jeeps, three large trucks, a one-ton truck and an M2 Caterpillar tractor. A panel truck, a station wagon, six bicycles, a staff car and two stake trucks were requested from the RCAF, and the panel truck and the station wagon soon arrived.

During the month of August, No 426 Squadron despatched twenty-five Tokyo-bound aircraft, of which eighteen went out after 14 August. This effort taxed the energies and expertise of both the flight crews and ground crews, who had to keep the aircraft moving. The flight crews, who logged about 150 hours of airtime per month, relied for serviceable aircraft on the dedication and devotion of the servicing and maintenance staff stationed at McChord and at stops along the route. Only one engine problem arose after 14 August, in a North Star that had to return to Haneda after two and a half hours in flight. It was soon repaired and headed back to McChord.

During that first month, despite shortages of staff and supplies, the squadron's maintenance organization at McChord handled five engine changes, eighteen block changes, ten minor inspections and six major inspections. During the same period, the squadron's eight aircraft logged nearly 1,500 hours flying time —close to 200 hours per aircraft, and a far cry from the planned flying rate of seventy hours per aircraft per month.[37]

At Air Transport Command Headquarters in Rockcliffe, Group Captain R.F. Gibb was transferred to the station's Release Unit, pending retirement, on 13 August. On 14 August, Group Captain W.I. Clements was transferred from the National Defence College in Kingston to Rockcliffe to assume the duties of Chief Staff Officer, Air Transport Command Headquarters. On 16 August, Clements wrote to Air Force Headquarters to recommend that the wartime AN/APN4 Loran sets on the North Star aircraft be replaced by the more accurate and reliable AN/APN9 equipment used by the USAF, as navigators were complaining about the exceedingly poor utility and serviceability rate of the AN/APN4. No one at either headquarters was aware that enterprising individuals at No 426 Squadron had already fitted all the North Stars operating out of McChord with AN/APN9 sets borrowed from the Americans.

With No 426 Squadron fully occupied on the Korean airlift, the rest of Air Transport Command was called on to handle urgent requirements arising from the Canada-wide railway strike, which lasted from 22 August to 5 September.

On 23 August, the schedule for the AOC's Annual Inspection was made known. No 426 Squadron's operational element at McChord would receive a two-day visit, beginning 6 September.[38]

MAP 3: Operation Hawk, *July 1950–June 1954*

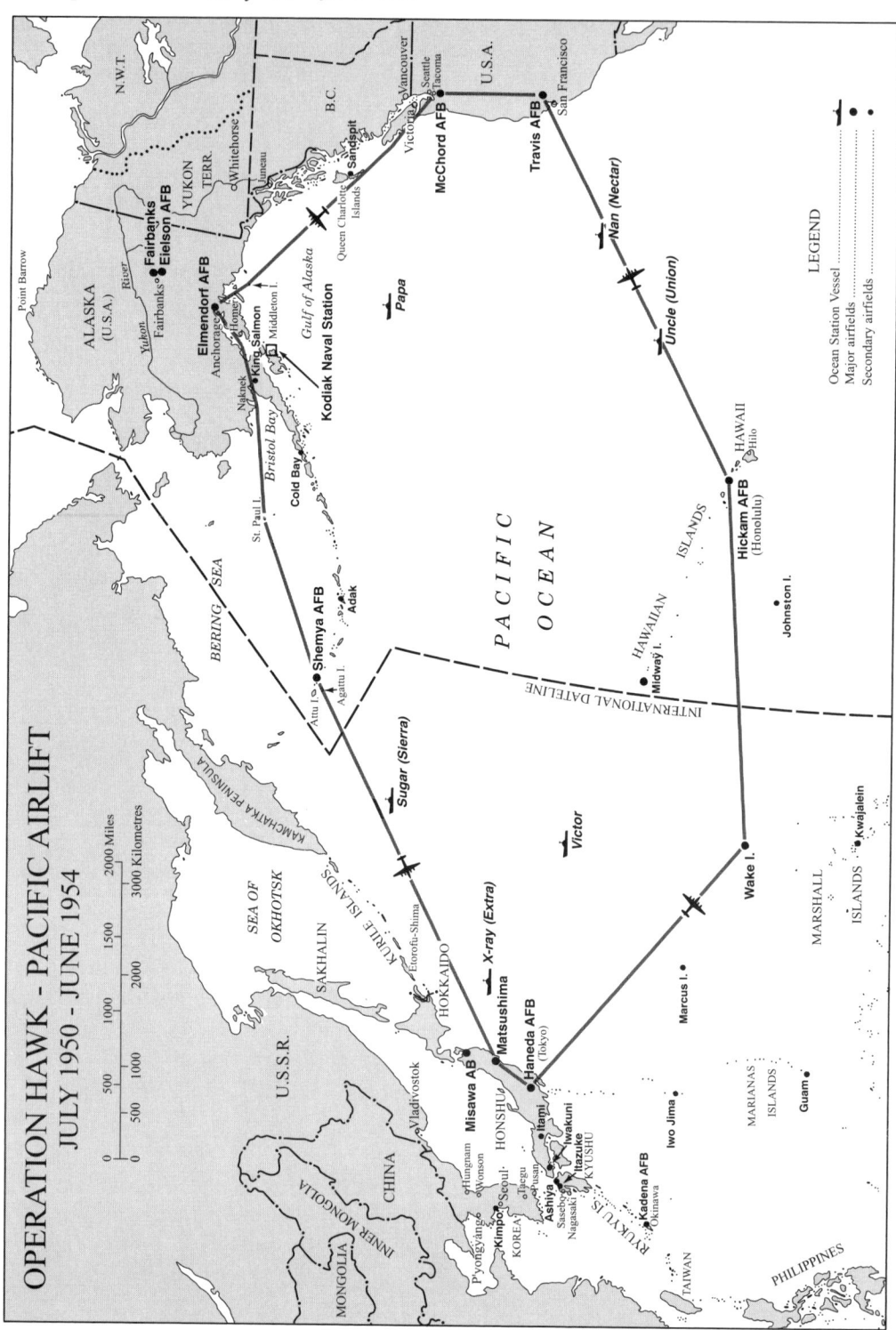

Maps by: *Wm. Constable*

Dorval and McChord Air Force Base, July–August 1950

PHOTO 40
F/L G.W. Webb and his crew take time out from a long-range training flight to visit the pyramids; Gizeh, July 1950. Back row, third from left: Tim Timmins; front row, third from left: Phil Rodrigue; and front row, fifth from left: Gord Webb. (G.W. Webb Collection)

PHOTO 41
S/L J.H.C. Lewis, W/C C.H. Mussells and S/L H.A. Morrison study the map of the Far East terminus of the Korean Airlift route in Japan; Dorval, July 1950. (DND PL 48866)

PHOTO 42
LAC J.D. Hagan, LAC P. Trudel and F/S J. Loucks check an engine on an aircraft slated for Operation HAWK; Dorval, July 1950. (DND PL 48887)

PHOTO 43
W/C C.H. Mussells briefs squadron officers on the eve of their departure for McChord AFB; Dorval, 24 July 1950. (DND PL 48904)

Dorval and McChord Air Force Base, July–August 1950

PHOTO 44
Shortly before No 426 Squadron's departure for McChord AFB, F/L R.E. Ratcliffe and S/L J.H.C. Lewis discuss last-minute routing details; Dorval, July 1950. (DND PL 48897)

PHOTO 45
Sgt. L.G. McLeod and Cpl. H.W. Wilson touch up the totem pole for its move to McChord with the squadron; Dorval, July 1950. (DND PL 48871)

PHOTO 46

F/L G.W. Webb brings squadron members up to date on latest deployment developments; Dorval, July 1950. From left: Sgt. B. Fisher, LAC T. Bryant, LAC J. Rouleau, LAC W.A. Nicholson, F/O L.P. Rodrigue and F/L Webb. (DND PL 48884)

PHOTO 47

CBC announcer Ken Davey interviews W/C C.H. Mussells during the wait for orders to move to McChord AFB for Operation HAWK; *Dorval, July 1950. (DND PL 48873)*

Dorval and McChord Air Force Base, July–August 1950

PHOTO 48
Relatives and friends of squadron members after the unit's departure for McChord; Dorval, 25 July. (DND PL 48914)

PHOTO 49
W.M. Gardiner of the Gideon Bible Society gives a Bible to each member of No 426 Squadron as they prepare to leave for McChord AFB; Dorval, 25 July 1950. (DND PL 48895)

PHOTO 50

A/C A.D. Ross and Air Vice Marshal A.L. James, the acting Chief of the Air Staff, wish members of No 426 Squadron Godspeed on the departure from Dorval, 25 July 1950. (DND PL 48898)

PHOTO 51

Air Vice Marshal A.L. James sees squadron members off to McChord; Dorval, 25 July, 1950. (DND PL 48906)

Dorval and McChord Air Force Base, July–August 1950

PHOTO 52
Pilots F/O A.L. Quickfall, Captain T.J. Upton (a USAF exchange officer) and F/O R.M. Edwards chat before boarding their aircraft for the flight to McChord AFB; Dorval, 25 July 1950. (DND PL 48893)

PHOTO 53
Rose Thompson bids her husband LAC T.G. Thompson a fond farewell on his departure for the west coast; Dorval, 25 July 1950. (DND PL 48900)

PHOTO 54

The No 426 Squadron totem pole boards the aircraft for the trip to McChord AFB; Dorval, 25 July 1950. From left: LAC K.O. Swollows, LAC F.J. Smith, LAC R.W. Gray and (in the aircraft with his hand on the totem pole) LAC W. Blotniuk. (DND PL 48901)

PHOTO 55

North Stars of No 426 Squadron over-fly the Peace Tower on their way to McChord AFB; Ottawa, 25 July 1950. (DND, No 426 Squadron)

Dorval and McChord Air Force Base, July–August 1950

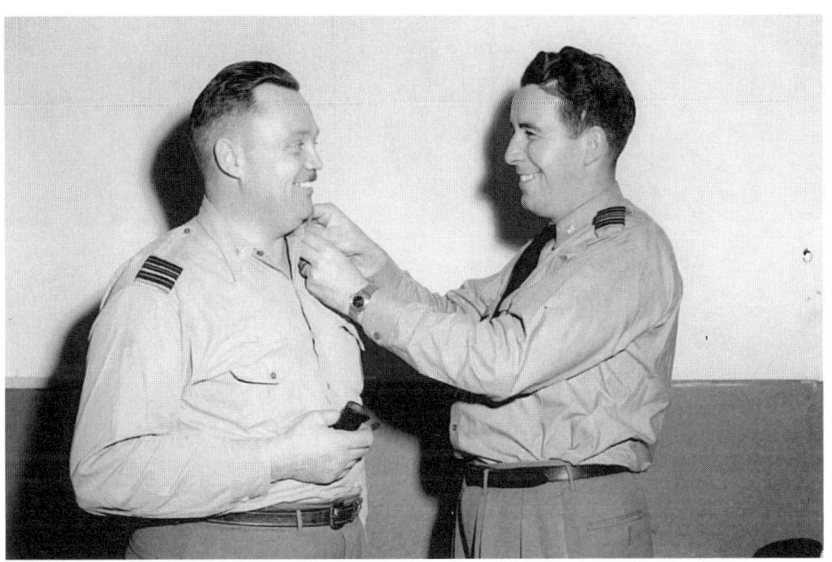

PHOTO 56
S/L J.D. Dickson pins USAF rank badges on S/L W.H. Lord, No 426 Squadron's Chief Technical Officer; McChord AFB, July 1950. (DND PL 48963)

PHOTO 57
F/S E.E. Brason gets directions to his quarters; McChord AFB, 26 July 1950. (DND PL 48951)

PHOTO 58
The Traffic Office at McChord AFB, July 1950. From left: LAC Don Towe and LAC E. Grose. (E. Grose Collection)

PHOTO 59
S/L W.H. Lord, Chief Technical Officer of No 426 Squadron, at the Maintenance Control Office; McChord AFB,; July 1950. (DND PL 48968)

Dorval and McChord Air Force Base, July–August 1950

PHOTO 60
F/L A.J.P. Byford (captain) and F/O D.H. Kuhn (first officer) at the controls of NS17502 on their way to Tokyo; 28 July 1950. (DND PL 48929)

PHOTO 61
Navigator F/L E.J. Boland works out a course for the pilots to fly to Japan; July 1950. (DND PL 48940)

PHOTO 62
F/L A.J.P. Byford and his crew arrive at Haneda AFB, July 1950. From left: F/L E.J. Boland, F/L Byford, F/O N.E. Bohn, F/O D.H. Kuhn and (handing down luggage) LAC Andy St. Laurent. (DND PL 50716)

McChord AFB, September–December 1950

CHAPTER 10

McCHORD AFB
SEPTEMBER–DECEMBER 1950

With the airlift in full swing, each leg on the North Pacific route presented the crews with its own characteristic challenges and hazards.

On departing McChord for Elmendorf AFB, a 1,490-mile flight, the crews would take the unpressurized North Star to its cruising altitude, usually 8,000 feet, as it flew over Puget Sound. At this altitude, the aircraft generally travelled at 200 knots (230 mph) and consumed 200 gallons of fuel per hour. With a full fuel load of 2,950 gallons, the aircraft had an endurance of approximately fifteen hours.

Heading north, the flight passed Vancouver and followed the airway along the eastern coast of Vancouver Island to the radio beacon at Sandspit on Moresby Island in the Queen Charlotte group. Next was a 705-mile over-water stretch to Middleton Island off the south coast of Alaska. From there, it was 161 miles over the very rugged coastal mountains to the river basin that sheltered Anchorage and Elmendorf. Navigation facilities were considered adequate on this leg of the route; navigators could use the radio range stations to get bearings, take astro sights and calculate pressure drifts, and use Loran when they were able to coax readings from their sets. If they needed to divert, they could use Fairbanks and Kodiak in Alaska as alternates.

In summer, along the west coast of Canada and the United States, there is often a lot of low stratus cloud, which develops as warm Pacific air is chilled as it passes over the cooler coastal waters. This low cloud can frequently stretch from the California coast to the Hawaiian Islands. For pilots, this can mean low ceilings and poor visibility along the coast during the morning hours, with an onshore wind effect. As winter comes on, the sub-tropical high-pressure areas break down, leading to the development of mid-latitude frontal systems. There is frequent frontal weather along the coasts from northern California to British Columbia.

The interior of Alaska has a continental climate similar to that of the Yukon Territory. Arctic to semi-Arctic conditions prevail during the winter months, with periods of extreme cold and blowing snow in places like Fairbanks. The Alaskan coast is frequently battered by intense frontal depressions. These are often characterized by heavy cloud layers with associated icing conditions and turbulence. In these situations, pilots were sometimes forced to change their airspeed or altitude.

At the time, little was known about the problem of the low-level jet stream.

Periodically, the jet stream dips to 8,000 feet or even lower in the Gulf of Alaska area. Navigators calculated westerly winds of 120 knots (140 mph) and sometimes higher. The crews found this phenomenon quite disconcerting, as it was not mentioned in their meteorological briefings. An encounter with the jet stream could be dramatic, causing the aircraft to suddenly veer off track by thirty or more degrees. After struggling to compensate for the wind, navigators would suddenly discover they had passed through the jet stream and would have to correct the aircraft's heading again, quickly. When it was cloudy, navigators tried to keep their aircraft at a respectable distance out to sea, and watched closely for abrupt changes in wind speed and direction. The low-lying jet stream could be deadly: a number of USAF and other aircraft are believed to have been blown off course and lost in the mountains after being caught up in its effects.

The 1,537-mile flight from Elmendorf to Shemya was usually routed south and then westward to Naknek at the head of Bristol Bay in Alaska. The next leg, over the Bering Sea, took the aircraft by St. Paul Island in the Pribilof group and then to Shemya, one of the Semichi group of islands. Agattu, a large uninhabited island, lay thirty miles to the southwest of Shemya. Attu, the last island in the Aleutians and the site of a US naval base, was located forty-six miles to the west. The closest alternate to Shemya was Adak, 395 miles to the east in the Andreanof group. The next nearest alternate was Cold Bay at the western end of the Alaskan Peninsula, 950 miles east of Shemya.

During the Elmendorf–Shemya run, the navigators could get bearings from the various radio beacons, take astro sights and use Loran. En route, the weather presented few undue difficulties, and, at 8,000 feet, the aircraft were generally above the clouds.

Landing conditions, both at their destinations and at the alternates, were another matter.

The Aleutians are rugged volcanic islands that rise in places to 9,000 feet. The region has a maritime climate, as the surrounding waters are at least five degrees above freezing. Generally, the weather in the Aleutians is cool, humid and cloudy. The region is subject to frequent cyclonic depressions, however, with squalls, snow, rain and fog. Winds in all seasons are predominantly from a south to south-westerly direction, and channelled by the topography.

In winter, Arctic outbreaks bring heavy snow squalls, creating very poor conditions along the windward slopes. On the smaller islands, the weather is only slightly better in the lee of the mountain peaks. Depressions are frequent in winter and, coupled with the rugged terrain, produce periods of low ceilings and gusty winds. The strong winds of passing depressions often trigger a "williwaw", which is a fierce, short-lived, down-slope wind.

During the summer months, fog is very prevalent, especially during periods of southerly flow when warm air is transported over the relatively cold ocean. The worst period for fog is June to August, with some weather stations reporting visibility of less than a mile about a quarter of the time. Locations where the prevailing drift is offshore enjoy slightly better conditions than those where the drift is from the sea. The airfield at Shemya lies along the south coast of the island, which is small and not very mountainous. There is no appreciable lee-side clearing unless the surface winds are more than ten miles per hour.

Crews arriving at Shemya would have been on the go the better part of a full day and were not at the peak of their performance. Landings were almost always handled by the GCA unit, whose controllers were considered to be the best in the world. Their expertise enabled the crews to file Shemya as a destination even when the weather forecast called for a 200-foot ceiling and a half-mile of visibility, which coincided with the GCA limits. In many instances, landings were made under GCA control even when the ceiling and visibility were in fact below stated limits.

Usually, a crew would make one attempt to land before deciding to push off for the nearest alternate. At Shemya, crews had the decided advantage of a large runway: it was 10,006 feet long and 200 feet wide, with each side marked with runway lights at 200-foot intervals and augmented by a 150-foot paved strip that gave the runway an effective width of 500 feet. When weather conditions were marginal, an important activity in the cockpit during the final stages of a GCA approach was looking for the runway lights. Once they were spotted, the captain quickly positioned the aircraft so it straddled the lights, then reduced power and landed. This technique usually worked but, from time to time, an aircraft would knock out a few lights in the process. You could sometimes get take-off clearance by telling the tower how many runway lights were visible from the cockpit.

An additional landing hazard at Shemya was the high surface wind that frequently swept the island. Pilots could face severe crosswinds coupled with turbulence, a combination that fully taxed their aircraft-handling skills. Landings with winds on the order of 100 mph, though infrequent, were not unknown.

The final leg, a distance of 2,104 miles, from Shemya to Tokyo, with landfall at Matsushima, Japan, took an average of ten and a half hours to complete. Matsushima was 212 miles (about an hour's flying time) north of Tokyo. The routing over the North Pacific took the flight past Attu, across the International Date Line, and by Ocean Station Sugar, a weather ship stationed at 48°N 162°E in the middle of the ocean, about two and a half hours flying time from Shemya.

The flight path of the aircraft roughly paralleled the Kuriles, coming to within eighty miles of the islands at the southwestern end of that chain. Six of these islands, from just off the northeast coast of Hokkaido to Etorofu-Shima, had been Japanese territory until they were occupied by the Soviet Union in 1945. The Soviets strictly prohibited any flights in the airspace they controlled. Since the consequences for intruders could be fatal, navigators took great care to ensure that their aircraft did not stray into this forbidden territory.

The distance from Shemya to Misawa was 1,733 miles, and the flight path was much closer to the Kuriles than the one that went over Matsushima. The flight time from Shemya to Misawa averaged about nine hours and took approximately thirty minutes less going in the opposite direction. Tokyo, which was 371 miles from Misawa, was frequently used as a fuelling stop on the return flight to Shemya when the winds were unfavourable and the added endurance was needed. It also served as an alternate for Haneda.

The North Pacific is a region of very extensive storm activity. Gales associated with deep and extensive low-pressure systems result in wide areas of cloud and attendant flight problems. These cloud areas often stretch from the Aleutians to the coast of Japan. The oceanic exposure and mountainous terrain of the Japanese islands create climatic conditions quite unlike those of continental Asia. In winter, frontal lows develop and move across the islands. During the summer months, a weak monsoon and the occasional typhoon create other weather problems. There is no real dry season.

The Shemya-to-Tokyo leg was perhaps the stiffest test of a navigator's skill on the whole route. Apart from the challenge of avoiding Soviet airspace, the navigator often had to face solid cloud at the aircraft's assigned altitude (usually 8,000 feet outbound, 9,000 feet inbound) for most of the flight. Navigators were forced to rely heavily on the most basic of navigation methods, that of dead reckoning (DR). They also practised "pressure-pattern navigation", a new technique at the time, in which the navigator used changes in pressure and radar altimeter readings to calculate the aircraft's displacement either to port or starboard of track. He would make calculations based on readings taken every half hour and these were reliable enough to keep the aircraft from straying too far off track. One disadvantage of the technique was that it gave no check on ground speed and was not very useful when going through fast-moving pressure systems.

Navigators could get bearings from the Radio Range Stations at Shemya and Attu on departure, and from Misawa, Matsushima and Tokyo at the destination end of the flight. Usable bearings could be obtained at a range of 100 miles, sometimes further. It was also possible to fix one's position by taking a series of bearings going by Ocean Station Sugar. However, with the stormy conditions prevailing in the North Pacific, the weather ship had a hard time maintaining its "on station" position or determining its location on a grid when it was "off station". If the aircraft was above the cloud layer, astro sights became the principal navigation aid.

As the flight neared the Kuriles, the Soviets would resort to electronic interference, complicating life for the crews. The Soviets transmitted powerful signals on the same frequency and broadcast the same identification letters as stations in Japan. These transmissions and false bearings were readily picked up on the aircraft's radio compasses. Soviet radio operators also answered the aircraft's HF (high frequency) radio transmissions. This would happen when the radio officers called Tokyo or Shemya Airways in Morse code to send their hourly position reports or to request the weather for destination or alternate airports.

TABLE 1: NORTH PACIFIC AIRLIFT ROUTE		
PRIMARY DESTINATIONS		
From	To	Distance (miles)
McChord AFB (Tacoma, Washington)	Elmendorf AFB (Anchorage, Alaska)	1,490
Elmendorf AFB	Shemya AFB	1,537
Shemya AFB	Haneda AFB (Tokyo, Japan)	2,104
Shemya AFB	Misawa Air Base	1,733
Shemya AFB	Matsushima	1,892
Misawa Air Base	Haneda AFB	371
Matsushima	Haneda AFB	212
Haneda AFB	Adak Naval Station	2,446
Adak Naval Station	McChord AFB	2,415
ALTERNATE AIRFIELDS AND OTHER DESTINATIONS		
From	To	Distance (miles)
Elmendorf AFB	Adak Naval Station	1,247
Elmendorf AFB	Fairbanks, Alaska	254
Elmendorf AFB	Kodiak Naval Station	265
Elmendorf AFB	Cold Bay	670
Shemya AFB	Adak Naval Station	395
Shemya AFB	Cold Bay	950
Shemya AFB	Kodiak Naval Station	1,339

The Soviets did not interfere with the Loran stations, but use of these stations was very limited on this particular leg because the aircraft were operating on or near the stations' baseline extensions so, even when readings could be obtained, they were not very reliable. As well, precipitation static usually cluttered the screens of the AN/APN9 Loran sets on loan to No 426 Squadron from the USAF.[1]

September

On 1 September, by way of preparation for the AOC's annual inspection, No 426 Squadron inaugurated a paint-up, spruce-up program in all the areas it was using at McChord. On 6 September, due to a shortage of both aircraft and crews, trips were cancelled for the day and the despatch of a flight every twenty-four hours was temporarily discontinued.

On the morning of 9 September, the AOC, Air Commodore Ross, and his party of staff officers arrived at McChord from Edmonton in No 412 Squadron's C-5 aircraft. After inspecting the squadron, they were accorded a brief tour of USAF installations, followed by a conference with the senior USAF officers at the base. In the evening, a cocktail party was held at the Officers' Club in honour of the AOC's visit, with many USAF officers in attendance. Ross continued his inspection of the squadron on 7 September, addressed all ranks at the Base Theatre in the afternoon, and departed for Rockcliffe that evening.[2]

On 9 September, Wing Commander Mussells and his crew left McChord for Elmendorf in NS17515, which was making its first flight after several power-plant changes. The aircraft was carrying both passengers —a draft of US Army personnel not at all enamoured of the prospect of going to Korea — and cargo: the space between the side rows of seats was filled with boxes of anti-tank ammunition urgently needed to stop the North Korean armour.

About three hours out of McChord, the crew noticed that one of the engines had lost a lot of its coolant. When the engine began to overheat, Mussells shut it down and feathered the propeller. Just as he began his turn to head back to base, a second engine on the same side had to be shut down for the same reason. Mussells decided to make an emergency landing at Sandspit on Moresby Island. Because of the need for ammunition in Korea, the aircraft was operating at a permitted overload. This, combined with a heavy fuel load, put the North Star way over an allowable landing weight. It was not a good situation.

Mussells decided to dump some of his fuel, and it spewed out below and behind the wing in a fine mist that looked a lot like smoke. Some of the passengers panicked and started to move to the rear of the aircraft — where they expected to go was unclear! Mussells was having enough trouble getting the aircraft on the ground safely without having to continuously adjust trim, so he sent a member of the cockpit crew back to restore order and get the passengers back in their seats. To add to the excitement, the final approach to Sandspit was over a wrecked USAF aircraft with its tail sticking out of the water. Luckily, the landing was successful.

A MATS C-54 from McChord retrieved the cargo and passengers and continued on to Elmendorf. These passengers included Leading Aircraftsman D.I. Shade from Coventry, England, who was en route to Haneda to replace one of the ground support staff. He had to stand in the crew compartment almost all the way to Tokyo.

Some minor repair work on NS17515 enabled Mussells and his crew to make a three-engine take-off from Sandspit and return to McChord early in the afternoon of 10 September. They were able to take their aircraft back out on the Tokyo run the following day.³

At McChord, progress was being made on the construction of two "nose-docks" for the squadron maintenance organization. In addition, four twenty-by-sixty-foot huts were being built to house the unit's various technical sections. These were expected to be ready in three to four weeks.

On 11 September, the RCAF flight schedule was altered: there were now departures only every forty-eight hours. This schedule continued in effect until 17 September, when it was again possible to send out five trips a week.

The unit received the first shipment of the airmen's work dress on 12 September. A clothing parade was immediately arranged and USAF personnel had many favourable comments when they saw squadron members in their new uniform.

On 8 September, following his return from McChord, Air Commodore Ross briefed the Deputy Minister of National Defence, the Chief of the Air Staff, and members of the Air Council on the RCAF participation in the Korean Airlift. He followed up his briefing with a detailed report that was submitted to the CAS on 12 September.

The report informed Air Marshal Curtis that, at the beginning of the strategic airlift to Japan, the operation was controlled by the Continental Division of MATS; toward the end of August, however, Continental Division handed it over to a new offshoot organization called the Far East Airlift Task Force (FEALTF). FEALTF headquarters was being established at Fairfield-Suison AFB (later renamed Travis) and, thus, Fairfield and McChord AFB were the Airlift's two operating bases in the United States. The FEALTF Commander was Brigadier-General Henry C. Kristofferson, a USAF reservist who had been the chief pilot at Pan-American Airways in civil life.

The report listed the operational formations and units located at McChord: in addition to the transport elements, which came under the 1705th Air Transport Wing, there was a Support Squadron operating C-54 and B-17 aircraft, an All Weather (Air Defense) Fighter Group equipped with F-82 Twin Mustangs, and three other groups of an administrative nature. As well as logistics airlift between depots, the Support Squadron provided search and rescue services using B-17 aircraft. The 1705th Air Transport Wing, activated on 24 August 1950, was commanded by Colonel Richard F. Bromiley and included the following units: the 4th, 7th and 8th Squadrons of the 61st Troop Carrier Group; the 14th, 15th and 53rd Squadrons of the 62nd Troop Carrier Group; No 426 Squadron, RCAF, with its North Stars; the 1726th Support Squadron; and a Wing Headquarters. Each Troop Carrier Squadron was equipped with twelve C-54 aircraft. At the time of Ross's visit, there were 5,500 personnel on strength at McChord.

Ross related that No 426 Squadron was one of seven engaged in the airlift from McChord and the unit was fitting in well with the rest of the MATS organization. The squadron was self-accounting and carried out all its own maintenance at McChord. The USAF was providing living quarters, messing, a limited amount of hangar space and some vehicles. No 426 Squadron had detachments at Elmendorf AFB and Haneda AFB to maintain North Star aircraft on the Tokyo run.

Ross pointed out that, although the 62nd Troop Carrier Group at McChord had been switched to the mid-Pacific route on 4 September, he had learned from Brigadier-General Kristofferson that the 61st Group and No 426 Squadron were to remain on the North Pacific route until the end of September. When Ross asked the MATS Commander what he intended No 426 Squadron to do after that date, because any change would affect RCAF logistics and personnel plans, he was told that no change of route was anticipated.

Touching on the scale of effort, Ross stated that 200 trips per month were scheduled to depart from McChord, of which thirty were allotted to the RCAF. All the squadrons began operating on a trip-a-day basis effective 13 August and, as of 8 September, No 426 Squadron had completed thirty-five round trips. MATS had set a target daily utilization rate of six hours per aircraft and, of the units working the Far East Airlift, only No 426 Squadron had met this target — since 13 August, its daily utilization rate had been seven hours per aircraft. The faster North Stars averaged 3.5 days for a round trip, where the average for the USAF C-54s was 4.5 days. Assuming no unserviceabilities on the route, three of the North Stars were usually away from base at any one time.

Regarding cargo, he reported that the squadron carried mainly US Army personnel and a small amount of freight on each trip. The critical leg on the route was from Shemya to Japan and the loads varied from 7500 to 7800 pounds, depending on weather and the fuel required. On the McChord to Elmendorf run the North Stars could carry 10,000 pounds, and MATS took advantage of this extra capacity to provide logistic support for the Alaskan Command. Two of the special loads taken by the squadron consisted of 3.5-inch bazookas and ammunition. On nearly every trip, the squadron also carried mail for the three RCN destroyers deployed in Korean waters.

With respect to personnel, as of the AOC's visit, the squadron had twelve complete crews and several spare aircrew members with which to meet the squadron's operational commitments. Each crew flew approximately 155 hours per month. This workload was considered excessive, particularly since MATS scheduled its own crews to fly at a rate of only 110 hours per month. The AOC therefore planned to increase the unit's crew complement to sixteen, exclusive of the Commanding Officer, the Flight Commanders and the Aircrew Leaders. The squadron's airman strength stood at 379 against an establishment figure of 314. The original establishment had been drafted to meet a flying commitment of 800 hours per month, and the actual commitment had more than doubled since the middle of August. An establishment review had found that 451 airmen were needed to maintain operations at the current level. There were twenty-two airmen on detachment in Haneda and a further eleven at Elmendorf. The unit was planning to increase the strength of its detachment in Elmendorf before the onset of winter.

The squadron had eight North Stars at its disposal. Operating at the rate of one trip per day, every aircraft was tied up and any unforeseen unserviceability played havoc with the schedule. The flying rate of more than 1,600 hours per month made it necessary to carry out one major and three or four minor inspections every week. Engines also required block changes or removals, but the Rolls-Royce engines were performing well, with only two unscheduled changes in more than 1,300 flying hours

Air Commodore Ross noted that, during his visit, three aircraft were out on the route, one was in the hangar for a major inspection, two were outdoors for minor inspections, one was outdoors for engine removal and one was outdoors having replacement engines installed so that it could depart the following morning. In the AOC's view, this was too tight a schedule; he thought the squadron needed twelve North Stars at McChord to meet the commitment.

Ross concluded his report by stating that the squadron had settled down very well at McChord, considering the lack of facilities and the rapid expansion of the base. The unit was more than holding its own with the USAF units engaged in the same operation. The squadron was a distinct credit to the RCAF and with the backing being given by supporting agencies, there should be no trouble maintaining the existing scale of effort.[4]

On 15 September, in a brilliant (if controversial) move, General Douglas MacArthur launched a daring amphibious assault on the Korean port of Inch'on, using the operationally independent US X Corps, assembled in Japan and commanded by Major General E.M. Almond. Inch'on had one of the finest harbours in Korea and was located twenty-five miles from the capital city of Seoul. That city was important from both the political and strategic standpoints. Situated nearby was Kimpo, the best-surfaced airfield in Korea. Seoul was also the transportation hub where the peninsula's main railways and roads converged.

The landing, well to the rear of the enemy positions, was intended to sever the North Korean lines of communication.

Because of the extreme tides, the US Marine Corps carried out their assault in two phases. In the first phase of the assault, during the early daylight hours of 15 September, the Marines succeeded in taking the island of Wolmi-do. The island dominated the approaches to the harbour and was linked by a causeway to Inch'on. Late that afternoon, the Marines carried out further successful landings to the north and south of the island. Pushing inland the following day, they advanced to Kimpo airfield, which they captured on 18 September. This gave American air support a base on land. MacArthur issued a communiqué on 26 September announcing the capture of Seoul, but it was several more days before his troops could finish mopping up pockets of resistance.

MacArthur's master plan for ending the Korean conflict called for a massive offensive by the Eighth Army, which was bottled up in the Pusan Perimeter. On breaking out, the Eighth, commanded by Lieutenant General Walton H. Walker, was to drive north and link up with the UN forces that had taken part in the assault on Inch'on. To take advantage of a boost in the Army's morale when word was received of the successful landing, the breakout was delayed until the morning of 16 September. It was hoped that the news of the landing would also demoralize the enemy. In fact, it took several days for the North Korean line to begin to fall apart. The United Nations forces from Inch'on and the Pusan Perimeter were able to link up on 26 September.[5]

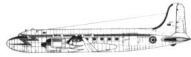

Back at McChord, Wing Commander Mussells decided on 17 September that, rather than have servicing personnel remain on detachment indefinitely, they should rotate. Henceforth, all servicing personnel would return to base after six weeks on detachment.

The following day, Squadron Leader Morrison went to Victoria to address the Air Force Officers' Association on the topic of the Korean Airlift.

On 24 September, Flying Officer Broadfoot and his crew departed on a regular run to Japan. From Tokyo the crew conducted a proving flight along the southern Pacific route with stops at Iwo Jima, Wake Island, Honolulu and San Francisco. Squadron Leader Morrison, who was being reassigned to the Operations Branch at Air Transport Command Headquarters, accompanied the crew on this flight, which returned on 5 October.

With the onset of cooler weather, the squadron needed heating units for its various maintenance sections. On 27 September, three rail cars of equipment arrived from Canada and threatened to over-tax the existing supply facilities. The situation was alleviated at the end of the month when the unit got another storage building.

On 29 September, the first of five North Stars to have their vertical and horizontal stabilizers reinforced was flown to Vancouver. This work was being carried out by a combined team of squadron personnel and civilian tradesmen from the Canadair plant at Cartierville.

On the same day, twelve of the squadron's officers learned that they were being offered long-service commissions in the RCAF. The event was celebrated in typical service fashion.[6]

On 2 October, Flying Officer Payne and his crew were on layover at Elmendorf when they took over NS17504 for the run to Tokyo with a heavy load of ammunition. The leg to Shemya was routine; they took on fuel there and filed a flight plan for Haneda. Payne departed Shemya at 0520 hours local, climbed out to 8,000 feet and set course for Matsushima. The flight progressed normally until it was about 700 miles from its departure point. Then there was a sudden loud bang as the reduction gear case on No 3 engine (starboard inner) cracked and the propeller ran away.

Payne shut down the engine by cutting off the fuel flow, but the propeller, which was in fine pitch, could not be feathered. The propeller free-wheeled and started to wobble with its spinner. At any moment, the propeller could fly loose and take out the outer starboard engine or cut into the fuselage. To lessen the risk of this occurring, Payne reduced airspeed to an average of 120 to 130 mph. This led to some loss of altitude, with the aircraft being brought down to about 5,000 feet. Repeated attempts to feather the propeller were unsuccessful. On the positive side, however, the lower speed kept the propeller jammed back in the casing, although some hydraulic fluid was lost.

Since the flight had yet to reach its critical point (CP), Payne chose to go back to Shemya. He considered jettisoning some of the ammunition but, since the boxes were quite heavy and releasing their tie-down straps on an unstable platform could create other problems, he decided against it. Ocean Station Sugar, Shemya and Tokyo Airways were all alerted to the predicament aboard the aircraft.

During the Second World War, Payne had spent eleven days in a dinghy after ditching a Lancaster in the North Sea. He was not looking forward to another dunking.

Flight Lieutenant Torchy Weeden, the navigator, had his hands full fixing the aircraft's position, as they were in cloud most of the time. Fortunately, the weather at the airfield held and, nearly six and a half hours after turning back, Payne made a successful landing at Shemya. For his skill and resourcefulness in bringing his aircraft and crew back safely, he would receive the Air Force Cross.

On 4 October, Payne and his crew took NS17511 to Tokyo, returning to McChord three days later. NS17504 was repaired and ferried back to base by Flight Lieutenant Allen on 9 October.[7]

During the month of September, No 426 Squadron despatched twenty-four trips to Japan, of which twenty-one were completed. One trip was aborted when it landed at Sandspit with engine problems, another made it only as far as Shemya, and a third was rerouted from Tokyo without cargo to conduct a proving flight along the southern route. At the end of the month, the squadron had thirteen line crews available, of which one was on leave, two were positioned at Haneda and another was at Elmendorf; the plan was to bring the squadron up to sixteen line crews as soon as practicable. The squadron maintenance organization had two detachments in the field on six-week assignments: twenty-four personnel at Haneda under Warrant Officer 1st Class E. Edey, and seventeen at Elmendorf under Flight Sergeant Swift.

On 29 September, Air Transport Command Headquarters at Rockcliffe issued Operation Order 20/50, initiating RCAF participation in the re-supply of the Arctic weather stations at Isaachsen and Mould Bay between 1 October and 15 October. The operation would be carried out from Resolute Bay, and would be controlled by Major McGovern, the USAF Project Manager. RCAF Station Lachine would provide one North Star freighter, and the USAF, which would assign two C-54s and a C-82, was responsible for re-supplying the weather stations at Alert and Eureka.[8]

October

On 1 October, General MacArthur sent a message to Kim Il Sung, the Commander-in-Chief of the North Korean forces, demanding their surrender, and received no reply. On the same day, Chairman Mao Tse-Tung announced, "The Chinese people will not tolerate foreign aggression and will not stand aside if imperialists wantonly invade the territory of their neighbour."

On 9 October, MacArthur's second message to Kim Il Sung calling for a North Korean surrender also went unheeded. On 15 October, as the American and UN forces continued their northward advance, MacArthur and President Truman held an historic meeting on Wake Island to discuss the final phases of the war. When the President asked whether there was any chance the Soviets or the Chinese would intervene in the conflict, MacArthur replied, "Very little"; in fact, 120,000 Chinese troops were already in North Korea. Despite growing indications to the contrary, MacArthur's Tokyo headquarters held to the view that the Chinese would not dare to intervene.[9]

At McChord, October was another busy month for the squadron. Twenty-six trips were despatched to Japan, and a crew was sent to Shemya to ferry NS17504 back to base. Another crew ferried NS17517 to Elmendorf, returning to McChord with the USAF.

Crews faced a number of technical difficulties. On 1 October, Flying Officer Miller had hydraulic problems shortly after leaving base in NS17504. This was the aircraft Flying Officer Payne would pick up at Elmendorf. Two hours after returning to base, Miller was on his way to Alaska.

Flying Officer Broadfoot was an hour and a half out of Elmendorf heading for Shemya on 9 October, when he had to shut down an engine. He returned to point of departure, where the engine was repaired, and resumed the flight the following day.

Two hours after leaving Tokyo on 20 October, Squadron Leader Lewis returned with an unserviceable radio. It was repaired and the flight again departed for Shemya.

Two days later, Flight Lieutenant Bell and his crew were on their way from Shemya to Tokyo in NS17507 when they encountered severe weather and icing conditions. Their attempts to climb above the cloud were unsuccessful and, at one point, they were down to 500 feet. The weather system most likely carried them westward over the Kuriles and to the vicinity of Sakhalin Island, as Flying Officer Shipton had to take a series of radio bearings to bring them to Misawa. A flight that normally took nine hours ended up lasting twelve hours and five minutes.[10]

On 2 October, while in Ottawa for a weekend conference of senior Air Transport Command officers, Wing Commander Mussells announced that No 426 Squadron was now operating with twelve North Stars over the North Pacific route to Japan. This was six more than the squadron had when *Operation HAWK* began in late July. The additional aircraft had eased the maintenance situation considerably, since all repairs to the North Stars were made outdoors, regardless of weather conditions.[11]

On 7 October, the squadron was advised that personnel serving on the Korean Airlift would begin receiving Special Supplementary Allowances — $45 per month for officers and $30 per month for airmen, effective the date they arrived on the squadron. They were also granted an allowance for accommodation and meals: $135 per month for each officer while actually based at McChord, and $120 per month for each airman on detachment at either Elmendorf or Haneda. A per diem allowance for personnel flying the Northern Route to Japan was also approved. This clarification of the pay and allowance situation was long overdue and it was a definite moral booster for the squadron.[12]

On 10 October, Squadron Leader R.H. Lowry of the Institute of Aviation Medicine in Toronto arrived at McChord to fly with the squadron crews on the Airlift and report to the Institute on the facilities, equipment and procedures in place to meet their medical needs.

The following day, Squadron Leader Morrison, the Chief Operations Officer, left for Rockcliffe to take up his new posting in the Operations Branch at Air Transport Command Headquarters. Squadron Leader Dixon, the squadron's check pilot, took over as Chief Operations Officer.

On 11 October, Air Commodore Ross went to RCAF Station Lachine with a party of staff officers to carry out its first AOC's Annual Inspection since its formation as an Air Transport Command unit. He inspected a ceremonial parade under the command of Wing Commander R.W. McNair, and was given a tour of the housekeeping facilities at the Lachine site. That evening, the visitors were guests at a mess dinner hosted by the officers. The AOC and his party inspected the Dorval site the next morning, and returned to Rockcliffe in the afternoon.

On 14 October, Flight Lieutenant Beach, the Senior Medical Officer at Lachine, arrived at McChord to solve several minor medical problems that had arisen at No 426 Squadron. He was accompanied by Flying Officer S.R. Marshall, a Public Relations Officer from Air Transport Command Headquarters, who was to write a news feature about the squadron and the Korean Airlift.

No 426 Squadron had now been in existence for eight years.

On 15 October, Wing Commander Mussells released a statement for broadcast by the CBC, announcing that several squadron aircraft would be making the homeward leg of the "UN Pacific Airlift" by the southern route, through Iwo Jima, Guam, Kwajalein, Johnson Island and the Hawaiian Islands, to San Francisco and McChord. Plans called for one round trip in five to return from Japan by way of Wake Island and Hawaii, a route that added 1,150 miles to the 12,000-mile McChord-Haneda round trip and brought it to fifty-seven flying hours, on average. The southern route would not interfere with the squadron's commitment of one round trip per day to Japan, however, and it provided opportunities for valuable training in a different operational setting.

A dramatic improvement in the war situation in Korea gave rise to persistent rumours that No 426 Squadron might shortly be returning to the Montreal area. On 17 October, MATS advised the unit that, unless they received other instructions, they were not to send any loads to Japan after the 25th of the month. In view of this advice, the squadron made preliminary plans to move back to Montreal.

Winter was coming, and the shortage of hangar space at McChord meant that the squadron had to find somewhere else to carry out major inspections on the North Star aircraft. On 18 October, Air Transport Command Headquarters issued Organization Order 3/50, creating a detachment of No 426 Squadron at RCAF Station Sea Island near Vancouver, with technical services personnel from No 426 Squadron who would be attached to RCAF Station Sea Island for rations and quarters, pay and discipline. The special allowances and pay procedures applicable at McChord did not apply to this detachment, and technical control remained in the hands of the squadron. The station would provide ground handling and shop facilities, and the squadron would provide special ground handling equipment, aircraft spares and special tools.[13]

On 20 October, the US Armed Forces Information Office in Seattle issued a press release describing the first embarkation of Canadian troops for Korea. It stated that the advance party of the Canadian Army Special Force had boarded a ship operated by the Military Sea Transportation Service from Pier 39, Seattle Port of Embarkation. The Canadian force was organized as a brigade with service support units and attached weapons. The advance party comprised representatives of all units in the brigade, and its purpose was to establish a reception camp at an overseas base.[14]

On 22 October, No 426 Squadron was invaded by a contingent of Canadian newspaper correspondents and radio announcers intent on writing or recording stories on the unit's participation in the Korean Airlift.

The next day, in response to an invitation extended by the management, an RCAF contingent visited Sick's Brewery, where they were well entertained and treated to a buffet luncheon and liquid refreshments. As his guests left, the brewery manager commented that the squadron's airmen were the best-behaved organization that had ever visited his establishment.

On 24 October, the fifth anniversary of the United Nations, Colonel Bennett, the Base Commander, welcomed press and radio representatives from Canada and the US to McChord AFB for a briefing on the Airlift and a tour of the base facilities. The journalists interviewed the crew of a North Star departing for Japan with a load of American troops, and met a C-54 coming in from Tokyo to interview the crew.

It was inspection time again for No 426 Squadron. On 27 October, Wing Commander Mussells, Colonel Bennett and Colonel Bromiley, the commander of the 1705th Air Transport Wing, conducted a thorough inspection of the RCAF facilities at McChord. Both USAF commanders expressed a high degree of satisfaction with their findings.

The next day, letters of thanks went out to the *Vancouver Province* and the Montreal papers *La Patrie*, *La Presse*, the *Ensign* and the *Daily Star*, which had all sent copies to be distributed free to squadron personnel.

Despite talk of the impending end of the war, No 426 Squadron received further operational commitments for the month of November. The unit was tasked to assist in the movement of a Bomber Group from Yokota AFB, just to the west of Tokyo, to Spokane, Washington. Thirty trips were authorized for the month, including the movement of the Bomber Group. Six training trips, to be carried outbound by the southern or mid-Pacific route, were included as part of the thirty trips. At the end of the month, a party of officers from Air Transport Command Headquarters and Lachine arrived at McChord to take familiarization flights to Japan and get first hand information regarding operational problems facing the squadron. In the group were Wing Commander McNair, the Commanding Officer at Lachine, Mr. B. Boville, Meteorologist at Station Rockcliffe and Mr. John McLean, a reporter for the *Toronto Telegram*. MacLean was working on stories about the squadron's activities at McChord and those of the 25th Canadian Infantry Brigade situated at Fort Lewis, some eight miles from the air base.

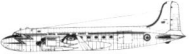

At the end of October, No 426 Squadron had fourteen front-line crews, of which one was on leave, two were in slip positions at Haneda, and one was at Elmendorf. The duration of the average trip was seven days per crew and nearly four days per aircraft. In October, round trips to Japan averaged fifty-one hours.

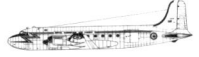

One advantage of operating through USAF bases was that squadron members could occasionally attend the excellent shows put on by American stars of stage, screen and radio. Flight Lieutenant Wallace and his crew, which included Flying Officer Finkelstein, Flying Officer Kuhn, Flying Officer Tutt, Flight Sergeant Barber, Sergeant McKnight and LAC Walt, were among the lucky ones. They arrived at Elmendorf from McChord on the afternoon of 31 October, to find that comedian Bob Hope and his troupe, who were winding up a whirlwind tour of Korea and the Pacific tour, were performing that evening at Eielson AFB, about twenty-six miles from Fairbanks, and the following night were scheduled to play Elmendorf. On 1 November, the troupe entertained an enthusiastic crowd of some 10,000 servicemen (including a small party of Canadians) in Elmendorf's huge No 2 Hangar, which could comfortably house several B-29 bombers. Apart from Bob Hope, the troupe included singer Marilyn Maxwell, Les Brown and his band, cowboy singer Jim Wakely, dancer Judy Kelly, and the song and dance teams the Taylor Maids and the High Hatters. The show was sponsored by the Chesterfield Tobacco Company and everyone entering the hangar received a ten-pack of cigarettes.[15]

November

On 1 November, almost as soon as they were approved for squadron personnel, the Special Supplementary Allowances were reduced by 5 percent because the rate of exchange had altered slightly in favour of Canadian currency.

Despite several flight cancellations, the month of November saw the beginning of a new phase in the airlift. On 2 November, No 426 Squadron was committed to eight return trips from Yokota AFB to Spokane, a tasking that involved moving personnel and equipment of the 92nd Bombardment Group back to the United States.

On 5 November, a group of staff officers from Air Transport Command Headquarters arrived at McChord to familiarize themselves with the Airlift operation and fly the route to Japan. The group included Wing Commander J.K. MacDonald, who was to succeed Mussells as the Commanding Officer of the squadron, and Wing Commander McNair, the Station Commander at Lachine.

As there was a temporary lull in taskings, the squadron obtained approval for a series of six training flights along the Mid-Pacific route to Tokyo. The first of these flights departed on 6 November in NS17502 with Wing Commander MacDonald and Wing Commander McNair and two crews: one captained by Flight Lieutenant Bell and the other by Flying Officer Edwards. The aircraft was routed to Haneda through San Francisco, Honolulu, Johnston Island, Kwajalein, Guam and Okinawa. Bell returned to base on 17 November in the same aircraft via Shemya, King Salmon and Kodiak; Edwards returned to McChord in NS17505 on 19 November after staging through Shemya and Elmendorf.[16]

Acting on the assumption that the Korean War was about to end and the Airlift with it, on 6 November Air Transport Command Headquarters made a proposal to Air Materiel Command for the reallocation of the North Star fleet. Wing Commander W.P. Gouin, the Senior Technical Staff Officer, recommended that twelve North Star C-54 GM aircraft — NS17502, 04, 05, 06, 07, 09, 11, 12, 14, 15, 16 and 17 — be allocated to No 426 Squadron, which would move to RCAF Station Lachine. North Stars 17518 and 17524 (the C-5) would stay with No 412 Squadron, and

NS17513 (the Ice Wagon) would remain with the Experimental and Proving Establishment at Rockcliffe. Of the eight remaining North Stars, Gouin recommended that six (NS17503, 08, 20, 21, 22, 23) be placed in reserve storage; that NS17501 be returned to E&PE; and that NS17510 be assigned to the Winter Experimental Establishment at Edmonton.[17]

On 8 November, a second mid-Pacific flight left McChord in NS17512. Again there were two crews aboard: one captained by Flight Lieutenant J.A. Watt and the other by Flying Officer J.B. Miller. The route followed was the same as that taken by Bell and Edwards to Tokyo, and both crews returned from Tokyo in the same aircraft on 18 November.

By 9 November the Airlift had resumed its previous momentum as the result of reversals on the war front. No 426 Squadron cancelled the rest of the training flights.

On 20–21 November, a Commanding Officers' Conference was held at Air Transport Command Headquarters in Rockcliffe, and several matters affecting No 426 Squadron were discussed. On its (presumably early) return from *Operation HAWK*, the squadron would resume its weekly scheduled runs from Montreal to Edmonton, and the three flights a week via the Maritimes to Goose Bay.

As part of Canada's contribution to the build-up of NATO forces in Europe, a decision had been made to move the Vampire-equipped No 421 (Red Indian) Squadron from Chatham, New Brunswick to Odiham, Hampshire by 15 January 1951 for operational training with the RAF. No 421 Squadron was not taking its aircraft overseas, so the move could be accomplished with only six North Star trips. If No 426 Squadron was not available at the time, Station Lachine aircraft would carry out the required airlift. In fall 1951, No 410 (Cougar) Squadron, based at St-Hubert, was slated to move to North Luffenham, Leicestershire with its Canadair Mk II Sabres with them. Again, North Star aircraft would be required to provide airlift.

To re-supply the Arctic weather stations, approximately one trip a month to Resolute Bay was required, until the re-supply of the stations at Mould Bay and Isachsen took place, around March 1951. About 180 tons of supplies destined for the weather stations still had to be airlifted from Resolute Bay. At the meeting, it was decided that the responsibility for the control of Resolute Bay be re-allocated from Station Rockcliffe to Station Lachine. Since the aircraft were flown from Dorval to supply this Arctic base, it was thought that Lachine could handle control better than Rockcliffe.

The meeting then turned to long-range training exercises were discussed, which depended mostly on the return of No 426 Squadron to Montreal, when a program would be submitted to Air Force Headquarters for training flights around the South Atlantic, South Pacific and for one "round the world" flight.

Wing Commander Mussells asked that a policy be established with respect to requests from the Canadian Army at Fort Lewis for air transport. Air Commodore Ross said Air Transport Command had not received any such requests, and that the squadron was to notify Air Transport Command Headquarters when any such requests were received. Wing Commander R.O. Shaw,

Staff Officer Operations, was directed to notify the Army through Air Force Headquarters that airlift requests were to be forwarded to Air Transport Command.

The issue of establishing a North Star Operational Training Unit at Station Lachine, separate from No 426 Squadron, was fully aired. Wing Commander R.W. McNair, the station commander, thought it was desirable to create a North Star, Dakota and Lancaster OTU for Air Transport Command; with such a unit, any special commitments could be met with a reserve of trained personnel. It was also considered essential to keep the OTU separate to prevent training aircraft from being pressed into service to cover operational commitments. Wing Commander Mussells stated that an OTU was necessary but, at that moment, No 426 Squadron was set up to handle operational training within its own organization.

The AOC said he had recognized the need for such an establishment for some time. A start had been made with a small unit, which would be maintained for North Stars and not considered for other aircraft because of a shortage of personnel. When No 426 Squadron returned to Dorval, the intention was to set its establishment at twelve aircraft, nine for operations and three for training. A decision was made to keep training as it was. When the unit returned, it was to have three training aircraft and was to be responsible for all conversion to North Stars.

Mussells proposed that the squadron be reorganized so that it could maintain its mobility and operational efficiency. He thought it imperative that No 426 Squadron be organized so that the unit was self-sufficient in everything except domestic household facilities. This was to include ground and aircrew training with the unit directly responsible to Air Transport Command Headquarters for its functional control regardless of the squadron's disposition. Air Commodore Ross pointed out that the organization, upon the return of the squadron, called for operational control through a Chief Operations Officer (COpsO). However, with one squadron at RCAF Station Lachine, this position was to be filled by the Squadron Commander, who would be responsible to the Station Commander. Should the squadron move away from the station all the extra personnel required were to move with the unit, making it self-sufficient. The operational link would be directly with Air Transport Command Headquarters, but for functional control, Ross stated that the squadron must be responsible to the Commanding Officer of Station Lachine.[18]

On 22 November, the Minister of National Defence, Brooke Claxton, and the Chief of the Air Staff, Air Marshal Curtis, arrived at McChord in the afternoon, after an inspection and luncheon at Sand Point Naval Air Station in Seattle, where they had been the guests of Rear Admiral D.E. Barbey, Commander of the 13th Naval District of the US Navy. Besides Air Marshal Curtis, the Minister's party included Brigadier H.L. Cameron, his Defence Secretary; Mr. Paul Pare, the Ministerial Secretary; Squadron Leader T.J. McKinnon, the Air Marshal's personal aide; and Air Commodore M.M. Hendrick, the Canadian Air Attaché in Washington. The visit was officially described as "informal".

At the Officers' Club, the Minister's party was briefed on the squadron's role in the Korean Airlift by Wing Commander Mussells, who had just returned from the Air Transport Command conference in Rockcliffe. After the briefing, the Minister's party spent what turned out to be a wet and foggy afternoon inspecting all the RCAF facilities at McChord, which were spread out over two miles of the sprawling base's perimeter.

At 1730 hours, the Minister and Air Marshal Curtis addressed the squadron at the Base Theatre. In his introductory remarks, Wing Commander Mussells informed Mr. Claxton that the unit was able to fly so efficiently for one reason: the competence of its ground crew, who were the backbone of the Airlift operation.

Speaking in both English and French, the Minister enthusiastically praised the job No 426 Squadron was doing on the Airlift. When an airman asked when the squadron might be withdrawn, Claxton explained that it was operating under the direction of the American Joint Chiefs of Staff for the United Nations, and they would make that decision. Air Marshal Curtis spoke next, saying he had been agreeably surprised when the UN authorities asked the RCAF to provide a heavy transport unit for the airlift operation; the RCAF expected only fighter or bomber squadrons to be sought for the Korean campaign. The request for transport units had given immediate stimulus to some of the less glamorous, yet vital services provided by the RCAF.

On leaving the Base Theatre, the Minister and his party proceeded to the army base at Fort Lewis, where they spent the night as guests of the Commanding General. The following morning, the Minister inspected the 5,000 men of the Canadian Army Special Force, better known as the 25th Canadian Infantry Brigade, and returned to McChord, where No 426 Squadron held a cocktail party in the Minister's honour. The VIPs departed late in the afternoon for Los Angeles in NS17518, operated by No 412 Squadron; in Los Angeles, the Minister and Air Marshal Curtis inspected Canada's powerful new Orenda jet engine, which was being tested in a North American F-86 Sabre fighter. According to the CAS, the tests conducted up to then had been very promising, and plans had been made to use the Orenda engine in both the Canadair-built CF-86 and the AVRO CF-100 Canuck.[19]

During the Minister's visit, the first, long-awaited shipment of Canadian cigarettes made it to McChord and were distributed immediately. Another visit of note was the arrival of the Northwest Air Command Band from Edmonton for a short visit during which it played for three dances and two concerts and were highly appreciated by both RCAF and USAF personnel. On 25 November, three more staff officers from Air Transport Command Headquarters reported to the squadron for familiarization flights to Tokyo.

On 25 November, RCAF Station Lachine dispatched NS17503 on a logistics run from Dorval to McChord with three Rolls-Royce engines for No 426 Squadron and Mr. Paul Durand, the Rolls-Royce technical representative at McChord. The flight was to stop at Lethbridge to refuel and at Vancouver to obtain Customs clearance for the cargo. The crew included Flight Lieutenant Earle Banks as Captain, Flight Lieutenant Gordie Stuart as First Officer and Flying Officer J.L. Denis, a recent arrival at Lachine, as navigator.

The flight took eight hours and fifteen minutes to reach Lethbridge, where the crew was briefed on the flight conditions they could expect on the leg to Vancouver. Ahead was a weather system with moderate to severe icing conditions in cloud and headwinds of nearly 60 mph at the 12,000-foot level. At 14,000 feet they would be in the clear, but the headwinds were forecast to be over 90 mph. Instead of battling the heavier headwinds and prolonging the flight, the Captain elected to proceed at 12,000 feet. The route over the Rocky Mountains to Vancouver was along the Green 1 Airway, which paralleled the American border about thirty miles to the north.

According to Denis, as the crew members were settling in their positions on the flight deck, the First Officer took off his jacket and said, "We're going to sweat this one." Shortly after leaving Lethbridge, the aircraft started to pick up ice and the situation started to get serious very soon. The true airspeed had dropped from 225 to 145 mph and the aircraft started to shudder. It came close to stalling at least five times.

Durand heard the engines straining and came forward. He advised the pilots to apply full power to avoid a stall, adding that the engines were up to the task. At the time the aircraft was in the vicinity of Penticton, BC, about 160 miles from Vancouver. Keeping the engines at full power, the pilots slowly and painfully inched the aircraft up until they broke clear and were flying above the cloud layer. The North Star was carrying a tremendous load of ice if the amount on the antennas was any indication. On arrival at Vancouver the pilots circled the airport for about an hour trying to shed as much of the ice as possible in the warmer air.

The crew spent the night in Vancouver and continued on to McChord the following morning. About three years later, NS17503 would come to a sticky end at Vancouver because of icing.[20]

On 25 November, three days after Brooke Claxton inspected the 25th Canadian Infantry Brigade on the great North Camp parade square at Fort Lewis, the 927 men of the 2nd Battalion, Princess Patricia's Canadian Light Infantry left Seattle aboard the USNS *Private Joe P. Martinez*, which delivered them in Yokohama on 14 December. When they left Seattle, the war in Korea seemed to be drawing to a close. By the time they arrived, however, the picture had changed completely. The day after 2 PPCLI sailed, the Communist Chinese forces launched a massive series of attacks on UN formations in North Korea. The troops defending South Korea found themselves facing more than 300,000 enemy soldiers.[21]

In its northward advance, the U.S. Eighth Army had taken P'yongyang, the North Korean capital, on 19 October, at which time it relieved the US X Corps, which had captured Inch'on and Seoul in late September. X Corps was then embarked on ships and transported to the port of Wonson on the east coast of the Korean peninsula; on 26 October, it began landing at Wonson, which had been captured by the 3rd Republic of Korea Division two weeks earlier. From 10 to 26 November, U.S. X Corps in the east and the U.S. Eighth Army in the west advanced towards the Yalu River, which was the border between North Korea and the Peoples' Republic of China.

On 24 November, General MacArthur opened a new offensive, employing all the resources of X Corps and the Eighth Army. Within two days, however, superior Chinese forces struck the Eighth Army along the Ch'ongch'on River and X Corps at the Chosin Reservoir. Between 26 November and 1 December, major elements of the Eighth Army were soundly defeated and forced to retreat; between 27 November and 10 December, X Corps was forced to fight its way back towards the port of Hungnam where it was to be evacuated.[2]

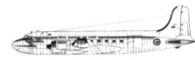

By the end of November, No 426 Squadron had launched 101 round trips to Tokyo, carrying a total of 2,169 passengers and 818,000 pounds of mail and freight. The squadron had twelve aircraft and fifteen line crews, of which three were in the slip positions at Elmendorf, Shemya and Haneda and one was on leave. Plans called for a route change that would take Thunderbird aircraft to Travis, Hickam, Wake Island, Haneda and Adak and then back to base; the Maintenance Section already had personnel selected for the detachment at Hickam. The detachment at Haneda would remain where it was, and the Elmendorf detachment would move to Adak; later it would move to Shemya.[23]

December

To give the squadron a Christmas break, all sections accelerated their activities to try to meet their December commitments early: the objective was to complete twenty flights by 19 December, and bring Shemya, Haneda and Hickam detachments and the slip crews back to McChord by 23 December. Nine of December's runs would turn out to be medical evacuation (medevac) flights.

On 1 December, MATS issued instructions to No 426 Squadron to start using the Mid-Pacific route. Late that afternoon, Flight Lieutenant Hammond departed for Travis in NS17516 with two other crews captained by Squadron Leader Lewis and Flight Lieutenant Webb and the maintenance crew for the detachment at Hickam. While getting to Travis was not a problem, the flight to Hickam took fourteen hours and ten minutes, which was really stretching the North Star's endurance envelope. Lewis and Hammond and their crews spent a week in Wake Island as slip crews. It was here the unit incurred its first casualty. Hammond slipped off a bar stool at the Drifter's Reef, the Island's only social centre, and fractured his ankle.

Both crews returned to base through Honolulu on 12 December. Webb and his crew carried on to Tokyo, returning to McChord via the mid-Pacific route on 14 December.

The serious reverses suffered by the United Nations forces in Korea raised the possibility of an air evacuation operation. On 6 December, the squadron was told that the Canadian government had authorized them to move to Japan and to operate into Korea should their services be required. Three days later, Air Transport Command Headquarters informed the squadron that MATS Headquarters had directed that there was to be no change in mission, and No 426 Squadron would not move.[24]

Since December 1, only one Thunderbird aircraft had succeeded — just barely, as it turned out — in making the crossing from Travis to Hickam. By the time the other squadron aircraft arrived in Travis, the head winds were so constant from the southwest at nearly 50 mph that MATS was forced to revise its operational plan. On 8 December, the aircraft waiting for more favourable winds at Travis were recalled to McChord for reloading, and despatched by the North Pacific route to return by the Mid-Pacific route. Several valuable days had been lost and, to make up for lost time, the squadron went into high gear.

Since the aircraft were now to stage through Shemya, the maintenance crew at Adak was moved there. Three aircraft were sent to Japan on 8 December and another five the next day, including the two that had returned from Travis. By the middle of the month, the unit had caught up on its commitments for December.

Earlier in the week, on 5 December, when Flight Lieutenant Rolly Lloyd brought in NS17516, the unit had completed its 100th flight of the Korean Airlift.[25]

On 19 December, Air Commodore Ross arrived with thirteen staff officers from Air Transport Command Headquarters for several days of thorough inspections of all the RCAF facilities at McChord. The AOC and his party were welcomed by Colonel Bromiley and brought up to date with squadron activities at a briefing in the Officers' Club by Wing Commander Mussells. Considerable time was spent in full and frank discussions with the visiting staff officers regarding a wide range of operational, technical, personnel and financial issues of concern to the unit. While at McChord, Air Commodore Ross and his officers were given a tour of the USAF radar installations.

Air Commodore Ross addressed all the squadron personnel at the Base Theatre and extended his Christmas greetings and best wishes for the coming year. Two RCAF chaplains, members of the staff party, conducted church services for squadron members. Some USAF personnel commented favourably on the thoughtfulness of the RCAF in having its chaplains come more than 3,000 miles to hold Christmas services. Ross and his party left for home on 22 December.[26]

Departing shortly after midnight on 17 December for Elmendorf in NS17510, Flying Officer Broadfoot had to shut down an engine about forty minutes into the flight and return to base for repairs. He and his crew took off again at 0910 hours but it happened again: he had to shut down the same engine and return to base after being airborne for only forty minutes. After working on NS17510 for nearly five hours, the maintenance section had the aircraft serviceable and Broadfoot was able to depart for the third time at 1615 hours. This time everything worked perfectly.

Three aircraft were sent out on the route on 19 December, the last flights before the squadron took a seven-day Christmas break. These and other returning aircraft brought the slip crews and the detachment personnel back to base. It was hoped to allow about 70 percent of the squadron's personnel to join their families for Christmas. Two aircraft returned from the route on 21 December, one on 22 December and one on 23 December; meanwhile, three North Stars, each with a full load of squadron personnel, made it back to Dorval on 22 December. Another aircraft followed the next day.

Squadron morale was high: a pay raise had just come into effect, they were going home for Christmas, and they had better facilities for working on the aircraft. Everyone went about their duties cheerfully. This would be the fifth Christmas the squadron spent out of Canada since its formation eight years earlier.[27]

The day after Christmas, Wing Commander Mussells, accompanied by Colonels Bromiley and Brown, flew to Kelly AFB near San Antonio, Texas, to find out the squadron's commitments for January at MATS Continental Division Headquarters.

The year ended with Flight Lieutenant Bell and Flight Lieutenant Lloyd heading out on the route on 30 December. Part of their task was to position slip crews and detachment personnel.

Air Transport Command Headquarters sent a letter to Air Force Headquarters recommending a renewal of the Link instruction contract with Trans-Canada Airlines for another year. ATC Operation Order 24/50 directed the Commanding Officer of Station Lachine to assign two North Star aircraft to bring personnel of No 421 Fighter Squadron from Chatham, New Brunswick to the Britain. The departures were to take place on 16 January, 22 January and 28 January.

At Air Transport Command Headquarters, Wing Commander W.H. Swetman was posted on course to the RCAF Staff College. He was replaced as the Senior Air Staff Officer by Wing Commander R.I. Thomas from RCAF Station Rockcliffe.[28]

A number of changes took place at Station Lachine in December. Flight Lieutenant Art Byford arrived from McChord to replace Flight Lieutenant Sandy Sanford as head of the Operations Section; Sandford joined the squadron at McChord. Flying Officer Tim Timbrell took over as Adjutant from Flying Officer Doug Souchen, who became the Senior Flight Controller. Flight Lieutenant Ted Ratcliffe arrived from McChord to head the Navigation Section. Flight Lieutenant C.E. Snider joined the squadron, replacing Flight Lieutenant Giles who returned to the Station. Flying Officer Johnny Middleton was selected to replace Flight Lieutenant Hammond, who had fractured his ankle at Wake Island.[29]

On 17 December the Christmas run to Resolute Bay was made by Wing Commander Buck McNair and Flight Lieutenant Earl Banks. Their cargo included parcels and Christmas cheer for the personnel based at this bleak Arctic outpost. This was followed up the next day by drops of mail, food and supplies to government weather personnel at Arctic Bay, located some 900 miles north of Churchill on Baffin Island. This operation was carried out during a thirty-minute period of poor twilight, under a three-quarter moon. The crew included navigators Flight Lieutenant Ed Boland and Flight Lieutenant Art Knapper, radio officer Flying Officer Art James, flight engineer Sergeant H.F. Smith and air traffic assistant Leading Aircraftsman J.L. Lanteigne. Earlier in the month another North Star captained by Flight Lieutenant Byford made the Christmas mail runs to Goose Bay and Frobisher Bay.[30]

A 1705th Air Transport Wing Historical Record Report covering the November and December 1950 comments on the abilities of the RCAF to perform its mission. The RCAF was told to inspect all engines of the North Star aircraft for a particular mechanical defect. The defect was so located that, to carry out the inspection, it was necessary to disassemble the engines completely. With the assistance of a mobile repair party, RCAF personnel at McChord completely disassembled, inspected and reassembled forty-two engines in five days. At the same time, six more engines were inspected at the Sea Island detachment. What had happened was that the RCAF had sent its engines for overhaul to the Rolls-Royce plant in Montreal. One of the over-conscientious workers at the plant not only cleaned the pistons but, as an added touch, polished them. This caused some aircraft to have piston failures. Since the magnitude of the problem was unknown, all the engines of the North Star fleet had to be checked. The Rolls-Royce worker was fired for his efforts.[31]

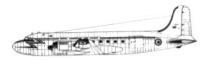

On 22 December, Lieutenant General Walker, Commander of the Eighth Army, was killed in a vehicle accident in Korea. He was replaced by Lieutenant General Matthew B. Ridgeway. X Corps, which had fought its way back to the port of Hungnam, was evacuated from North Korea on 24 December.[32]

PHOTO 63

No 426 Squadron's Maintenance Control Hut; McChord AFB, October 1950. (B. Nurse Collection)

PHOTO 64

Maintenance Control, No 426 Squadron; McChord AFB, October 1950. (H.G. Graves Collection)

McChord AFB, September–December 1950

PHOTO 65
Changing an engine on a North Star; McChord AFB, October 1950. (H.G. Graves Collection)

PHOTO 66
No 426 Squadron's aircraft tractor; McChord AFB, October 1950. (H.G. Graves Collection)

PHOTO 67
Resolute Bay, NWT; October 1950. (DND RT–10–1)

PHOTO 68
No 426 Squadron North Stars at Resolute Bay; October 1950. (DND RT–10–2)

PHOTO 69
F/L G.W. Webb and crew before a departure for Tokyo; McChord AFB, 8 September 1950. From left: F/O Paul Lemieux (pilot), F/O Tim Timmins (radio officer), F/O Harold Spector (navigator), LAC Gerry Reed (flight engineer), F/L Webb (captain), LAC Willie Verch (air traffic assistant). (Tim Timmins Collection)

PHOTO 70
Flight plan preparation; McChord AFB, September 1950. From left: F/L C.E. Emond, F/O R.M. Edwards, F/O M. Latter, F/L A. Knapper (an RAF exchange officer) and an unidentified USAF officer. (J.S. Shipton Collection)

PHOTO 71

F/L W.R. Lloyd and his crew at Misawa after a long flight from Shemya; October 1950. From left: LAC Grose, F/L Flemming, F/O Smith, F/L Lloyd, an unidentified officer and F/O Quickfall. (E. Grose Collection)

PHOTO 72

Flight engineer Sgt. F.S.M. Bowman takes a lunch break at the navigator's work station on the way to Japan; autumn 1950 (J. Henry Collection)

McChord AFB, September–December 1950

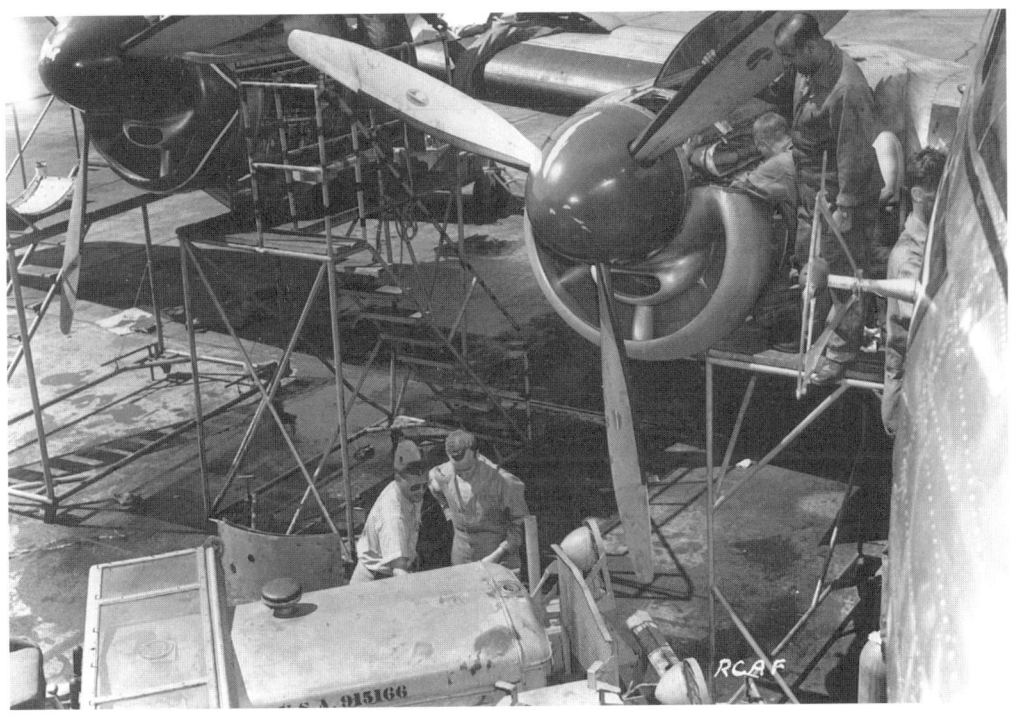

PHOTO 73
No 426 Squadron maintenance staff at work on North Star engines; McChord AFB, September 1950. (DND PL 50136)

PHOTO 74
LAC J.P. Thompson, LAC T.G. Thompson and LAC J.L. Claveau, of No 426 Squadron's detachment at Haneda AFB, Tokyo, at work on North Star engine. (DND PL 50035)

PHOTO 75

The Honourable Brooke Claxton, Minister of National Defence, enters the Officers' Club at McChord AFB with W/C C.H. Mussells for a briefing on Operation HAWK; *22 November 1950. (DND No 426 Squadron)*

PHOTO 76

Minister of National Defence Brooke Claxton arrives at the base theatre to address members of No 426 Squadron; McChord AFB, 22 November 1950. (DND 426 Squadron)

McChord AFB, September–December 1950

PHOTO 77
*Flight Control Officer F/L J.P. McDonald briefs Brooke Claxton and Air Marshal W.A. Curtis, Chief of the Air Staff, on No 426 Squadron's flying operations; 22 November 1950.
(DND 426 Squadron)*

PHOTO 78
*Engineering Officer F/O G. Kreklewetz briefs Brooke Claxton during his inspection of the squadron's hangar; McChord AFB, 22 November 1950.
(DND 426 Squadron)*

PHOTO 79
Minister of National Defence Brooke Claxton and Air Marshal W.A. Curtis, Chief of the Air Staff, visit the airmen's quarters at McChord AFB; 22 November 1950. (DND 426 Squadron)

PHOTO 80
Air Marshal W.A. Curtis and W/C C.H. Mussells chat during an Officers' Club reception; McChord AFB, 22 November 1950. (DND No 426 Squadron)

PHOTO 81
W/C Mussells introduces Air Commodore A.D. Ross during a social evening at the Airmen's Club; McChord AFB, 19 December 1950. (Pat Sterr Collection)

PHOTO 82
A/C A.D. Ross, AOC Air Transport Command, addresses squadron members at the Airmen's Club; McChord AFB, 19 December 1950. (Pat Sterr Collection)

McChord AFB, January–June 1951

CHAPTER 11

McCHORD AFB
JANUARY–JUNE 1951

As the New Year began, United Nations forces continued to withdraw as the Communist Chinese army pushed south. On 4 January, Seoul fell to the enemy for the second time, but by 14 January, the UN lines in South Korea had stabilized roughly along the 37th parallel. On 24 January, having stopped the enemy advance, the UN went on the offensive.[1]

Meanwhile, in an area along the banks of the Miryang River some fifty miles north of Pusan, 2 PPCLI was being brought to a state of operational readiness; as part of this activity, the battalion began anti-guerrilla operations on 16 January. 2 PPCLI left for its front-line positions on 17 February and three days later was in action against the enemy.[2]

January

Following its Christmas break, No 426 Squadron lost no time in repositioning its slip crews, servicing crews and detachment commanders along the route. In January, the unit completed eighteen of the twenty-one runs despatched to Japan during the month; on 31 January, three runs were still on their way back to base. All flights took the northern route to Tokyo, returning from Japan via Wake Island, Honolulu and San Francisco. Eight of the return flights were scheduled via Itami, near Osaka, and carried wounded soldiers back to the United States. One special flight was despatched to Honolulu and four logistics runs were made to Montreal.

During the month, four crews encountered equipment problems along the route. On 7 January, nearly an hour after leaving Haneda for Wake Island, Flying Officer Edwards in NS17516 had to return to his point of departure: the Radio Officer, Flying Officer D.C. Farrell, had been unable to establish HF contact with Oceanic Control after flying beyond VHF range from Japan. The servicing crew at Haneda worked on the radio set and four hours and fifteen minutes later Edwards was able to set off again. An hour and a half into the flight, the radio problem cropped up again, forcing Edwards to return to Haneda. This time, the squadron's technicians spent some nine hours working on the radio equipment, whose serviceability was finally confirmed by an air test. Twenty-one hours after their first take-off, Edwards and his crew got back on track for Wake Island. This time they completed the eight hour and fifty minute leg successfully.

Flying Officer Broadfoot had engine problems on 13 January. About a half hour after leaving Honolulu for San Francisco in NS17506, he had to shut down the starboard inner engine, dump fuel and return to Hickam AFB. After the servicing crew had worked on the aircraft for more than nine hours Broadfoot again left for San Francisco. Thirty minutes into the flight the port inner engine malfunctioned, forcing him to double back. The next morning, Broadfoot and his crew took out NS17507, which arrived from Wake Island. NS17506 was left in the capable hands of the servicing detachment and was returned to base several days later.

On 15 January, about an hour after leaving Shemya for Tokyo in NS17510, Flight Lieutenant Sanford had to turn back because of a malfunctioning starboard inner engine. After seven hours, the servicing detachment had the problem fixed and Sanford and his crew were on their way to Haneda.

On 26 January, Flight Lieutenant Webb departed Wake Island in NS17510 for Honolulu; some seventy minutes into the flight, he had to shut down the starboard inner engine and return to Wake. Fifteen hours later, Webb and his crew took out NS17506, which had arrived from Haneda. NS17510 was repaired and on its way back to base the next day.³

In January, the squadron had to cope with several visitors. Mr. J.E.D. McCord from Air Force Headquarters arrived to conduct an operational research study on long-range transport operations. Mr. G.B. Thornton from the Defence Research Medical Laboratories (DRML) in Toronto came on a similar mission, including a route tour. Dr. Whillans from DRML spent several days with the squadron conducting a study of its flying statistics. Five officers from Air Transport Command and other RCAF units came for familiarization flights along the route. Mr. J.G. Hannifan, the western US representative of *Time* and *Life* magazines, visited while preparing an illustrated story on the squadron's participation in the Korean airlift. Leading Aircraftsman Nakamura, a photographer from the Directorate of Public Relations at Air Force Headquarters, came with instructions to produce a complete picture story of the squadron and all its activities.

On 11 January, with little advance warning, the National Defence College arrived in a No 412 Squadron North Star from Seattle, where they had toured the Boeing aircraft plant and the giant US Navy yards. While they were at McChord, they visited the RCAF facilities and, courtesy of the USAF, toured the base's other installations, including the radar site and the flight line.

John Foster Dulles, US Ambassador-at-Large, arrived at McChord on his way to Japan, where he would take part in peace treaty discussions. When he asked to meet RCAF personnel employed on the airlift, he was introduced to several squadron members.

On 8 January, Wing Commander Mussells went to Ottawa to meet Air Commodore Ross, whom he them accompanied to Washington for a conference at which No 426 Squadron's commitments were discussed with senior MATS officers, including Colonel Brown (commanding officer of the 62ⁿᵈ Troop Carrier Group) and Colonel Bromiley from McChord. On 16 January, Mussells and Brown left McChord in NS17509, captained by Flight Lieutenant Emond, for an inspection tour of the RCAF detachments on the airlift route.⁴

Several days earlier, the detachment commander at Shemya, Flying Officer L.-P. Rodrique, had written to Mussells about the messing situation at this island outpost. A senior USAF officer had summoned Rodrique to inform him that his people were cooking in their quarters, which was against regulations. The RCAF airmen had good reasons: a nauseating odour pervaded the mess hall, and the food was doled out on stamped aluminum mess trays—known as "engine cowlings"—that were often greasy. At the best of times, Shemya cuisine left much to be desired.

Wing Commander Mussells investigated this problem during his visit to Shemya and, in his usual forthright manner, reported his findings to Colonel Bromiley, who advised him to take the matter up with Brigadier-General Kristofferson, the FEALTF Commander at Travis AFB, on his way back to McChord. Despite a bit of pique on Kristofferson's part at what he perceived as negative comments about the USAF, it wasn't long before the messing areas at Shemya were cleaned up and treated to the standard service cure-all, a new coat of paint. Food preparation, alas, remained unimaginative.[5]

The inspection tour of Wing Commander Mussells and Colonel Brown along the airlift route was both rapid and, in terms of transportation, varied. They flew to Tokyo by RCAF North Star and then on to Korea by USAF C-54. While at Ashiya, Mussells had an opportunity to fly the Fairchild C-119, more commonly known as the Flying Boxcar. The trip from Tokyo to Honolulu was made in a C-97 Stratofreighter and they returned to McChord via Travis AFB in a C-124 Globemaster.[6]

Toward the end of the month, the squadron subjected the RCAF facilities at McChord to a clean-up, paint-up campaign in preparation for a series of inspections: by Colonel Bromiley on 23 January, then by Colonel Bennett on 24 January, and finally by Lieutenant-General Kuter, the MATS Commander, during a visit to McChord on 25 January.

On 26 January, to mark the unit's first six months at McChord, a squadron stag was held at the Benbow Lodge at Lake Tanwax, some twenty-two miles from the base. The lodge had been recently donated by a philanthropist as a recreational site for personnel assigned to McChord, and No 426 Squadron had the privilege of opening it officially. By all accounts, the event was a great success.

During the month of January, the squadron's maintenance and servicing crews carried out seven engine changes and nineteen block changes, and completed six major and nine minor aircraft inspections. Several other equipment snags were handled routinely.

All squadron aircraft were now equipped with the APN-9 Loran set, a vast improvement over the obsolete APN-4. The APN-9 was simpler to operate, had a much higher serviceability rate and was a useful navigational aid, particularly for aircraft flying the mid-Pacific route.

The leave plan organized by the Squadron Commander shortly after arriving at McChord was working well, and proving to be a definite morale booster.

Arriving from Lachine in January for flying duties were Flight Lieutenant Bob Brown and Flight Lieutenant Phil Michel, pilots; Flying Officer Jean-Louis Denis, a navigator; and Flying Officer

Art James and Flying Officer R.J. MacNeil, radio officers. Flight Lieutenant P.F. Greenway reported in as the new Air Movements Officer.[7]

The four North Stars at Lachine were being used in operations as well training. On 15 January, Flying Officer Payne and his crew made a hurried trip to Keflavik in NS17520 to pick up the Prime Minister and his party, whose aircraft had gone unserviceable; on arrival, however, the crew discovered that the Prime Minister had already flown with Trans-Canada Airlines to Dorval, where the Station Commander and Squadron Leader Byford, the Squadron Operations Officer, were on hand to meet him. A No 412 Squadron Dakota was standing by to take the Prime Minister to Rockcliffe.

Immediately after the Prime Minister's departure, everyone concentrated on despatching a North Star to Chatham, New Brunswick. Pursuant to Air Transport Command Operation Order 24/50, dated 20 December 1950, RCAF Station Lachine was to provide two aircraft per day on 16 January, 22 January and 28 January to airlift No 421 (Fighter) Squadron to Odiham, Hampshire, where it was being transferred for training with the RAF — thus becoming the first RCAF squadron to go overseas in peacetime. The eastbound routing from Dorval was to Chatham and then via Goose Bay and Keflavik to Odiham, and the aircraft were to return to base by way of Keflavik and Goose Bay.

Flight Lieutenant Banks and his crew took out NS17522 on the first run to Odiham with Wing Commander R.W. McNair aboard. On 22 January, crews captained by Flight Lieutenant Giles in NS17514 and Squadron Leader Byford in 17521 made the next two runs. The last two flights on 28 January were assigned to Flying Officer Payne in NS17523 and Flight Lieutenant Watt in 17514. Mechanical problems forced Watt back to Dorval for repairs twice; finally, on 30 January, he was able to get away to Britain. The sixth and final group of No 421 Squadron personnel made the trip from Chatham to Britain in an RAF Hastings that had brought a group of air cadets to Canada.[8]

On 5 January, Air Transport Command issued its first operations order of the year. It dealt with a possibility the Department of National Defence was seriously considering, that an unfriendly nation might establish caches of fuel and other supplies in the Canadian Arctic, especially the Arctic islands, with the purpose of setting up weather stations or staging bases for bombing attacks on Canada and the United States.

Such caches could be established by sea in summer or by air at any time, but especially in winter. DND concluded that steps should be taken to prevent or discover any such action. RCAF Station Rockcliffe was directed to provide Lancaster X aircraft from No 408 (Photographic) Squadron to perform visual and photographic air reconnaissance of specific areas in northern Canada and the Arctic Archipelago, operating from Goose Bay, Frobisher and Resolute Bay. This reconnaissance was to be conducted on a monthly basis from January through May, stop for the summer while air-survey operations took priority, and then resume in September to continue until the following January.

On 11 January, control of Resolute Bay was transferred from RCAF Station Rockcliffe to RCAF Station Lachine. The same day, a joint meeting of civil, military and police officials from Canada and the United States was held at National Defence Headquarters. It was the fourth such meeting held to discuss plans for the establishment and operation of the Joint Arctic Weather Stations. Air Commodore Ross and several senior staff officers from Air Transport Command Headquarters attended. The next day, at Rockcliffe, staff officers from Air Transport Command Headquarters met with representatives of North East Air Command, the USAF formation based at St. John's, Newfoundland, to discuss how they would carry out the spring 1951 re-supply of the weather stations.

The second Air Transport Command operation order of the year was issued on 22 January. It spelled out the Command's participation in *SUNDOG II,* a joint Canadian Army–RCAF exercise to be conducted in the Rivers-Churchill-Nunalla area in February and early March 1951. The Royal Canadian Regiment was to be the main Army force, and the RCAF would supply aircraft for transport and photo reconnaissance. Troop transport would be provided by No 435 Squadron, with eight Dakota aircraft, and No 412 Squadron, with four Dakotas. Photo reconnaissance would be provided by No 408 Squadron, with two Lancaster Xs. Additional airlift would be provided by one North Star from RCAF Station Lachine and a Dakota from RCAF Station Rockcliffe.[9]

The return to base from Japan by the mid-Pacific route involved three long over-water legs followed by a flight of three hours and fifteen minutes up the Pacific coast from San Francisco. The flight time from Tokyo to Wake Island, a distance of 1,985 miles, averaged nine hours. It was forty minutes longer if the flight originated in Itami, which involved a two-hour positioning run from Tokyo.

Once an aircraft was well away from the Japanese mainland, there was only one point of land to be found before Wake Island: Marcus Island, which lay half-way between Japan and Wake, some 200 miles south of track. The flight stopped at Wake Island to change the crew and refuel the aircraft; the facilities at Wake were managed by Pan-American Airways under a contract with the United States government. After a briefing on the status of the North Star and its equipment, the outbound crew was usually on their way to Honolulu within a couple of hours.

Wake Island is actually an atoll of three coral islands — Wake, Peale and Wilkes — perched on the rim of an extinct underwater volcano; the central lagoon is the former crater. The total area of the three islands is less than three square miles, with about nine miles of total perimeter, and the land averages only twelve feet above sea level. The highest terrain is only fifteen to twenty feet above sea level, and it consists of coral rock and shell ridges that run parallel to the shore between ten and fifty feet from the sand beaches. The terrain slopes gently from the ridges to the lagoon, which in places has tidal flats. Wake's maritime climate is chiefly controlled by the easterly trade winds that blow throughout the year, and frequent tropical disturbances approach from the southeast during the late summer and early fall. These systems bring periods of light wind, high temperature and humidity, and moderate to heavy rain showers. Most of the cloud is of the cumulus type with little variation in amount from day to night; the sky is seldom completely overcast, but neither is it often completely clear. The showers that account for most of the Wake's precipitation occur most frequently between midnight and sunrise. Thunderstorms are infrequent but do occur with tropical disturbances.

The arrival crew would soon settle into their rather spartan quarters for a stay that could vary from twelve hours to two or three days. The food was nothing to write home about. For recreation one could swim in selected spots or relax on the beach, taking care not to get too much exposure to the blistering sun. For variety, crew members explored the rusting hulks of tanks, coastal battery emplacements, bunkers and other fortifications left over from the Second World War. Then there was the Drifter's Reef, a Quonset hut converted to a bar that was Wake's principal social centre.

The main determinants of the climate in the Hawaiian group are the prevailing northeast trade winds coming over cool ocean currents, and the mountainous nature of the terrain; as a result, the climate is cooler in the Hawaiian Islands than in other places at the same latitude. These islands have plenty of sunshine, uniform temperatures and very few tropical storms. There is no distinct rainy or dry season, but more rain generally falls during the winter than in the summer. At Hickam Field, near Honolulu on the island of Oahu, brief showers can occur at any time, but heavy downpours are generally limited to the winter months. The same weather conditions apply to the alternate to Hickam, General Lyman Field, 220 miles away at Hilo on the island of Hawaii.

The 2,305-mile run to Honolulu averaged eleven hours. About halfway along this leg, and some 500 miles to the north, is Midway Island, which could be used as either an alternate field or a refuelling stop. Crews could also land at Johnston Island, 340 miles south of track and two thirds of the way to Honolulu. On arrival at Hickam, a fresh crew would be standing by to take the aircraft out, and the technicians of the squadron detachment would swarm over the aircraft, rectifying any reported snags. Typically, the North Star would be serviced and ready to go in two hours.

Having handed over their aircraft, the incoming crew would head for the lodgings arranged for transient RCAF personnel: the Moana Hotel on Waikiki Beach, where a single room cost five dollars a night. Stopovers ranged from twelve hours to several days, depending on operational conditions along the route, but crews were always on a short leash.

The 2,459 miles from Hickam to Travis AFB near San Francisco took eleven hours and thirty-five minutes, on average. Two important features of the flight path were Weathership Uncle, located one third of the way across at 28°N and 145°W, and Weathership Nan, two thirds of the way to the mainland at 33°N and 135°W; the navigators obtained bearings on the weatherships' radio beacons to fix their positions. On all the long over-water legs, the basic navigation tool was dead reckoning with astro as the main fixing aid, supplemented by Loran readings and radio bearings.

The southern run offered a pleasant contrast to the dismal weather frequently encountered on the first half of the route, but the mid-Pacific presented its own challenges and flight hazards. The northwest Pacific — the area west of the International Date Line, north of the equator and south of 30°N — is probably the world's most complex weather region, with the northeast Trade Winds merging with the Asiatic monsoons, and intense tropical storm and typhoon activity.

The ITC (intertropical convergence zone), where the northeast and southeast Trade Winds meet, is a zone of weather that varies from twenty to four hundred miles in width and extends for hundreds of miles. It oscillates between the two hemispheres in a well-defined annual cycle, advancing northward at the beginning of summer; the resulting increase in weather activity comprises overcast cloud layers with embedded severe thunderstorms, icing, turbulence, hail, and heavy continuous rains. These conditions constitute a major flight problem for piston-powered aircraft.

By mid-summer, with the monsoon season well established, ITC weather activity is at maximum, with heavy summer rains and destructive typhoons tracking through the Marianas (Guam) area. In the cooler season, frontal depressions that develop off the east coast of Asia, between Taiwan and Japan, move east across the North Pacific into the Aleutian Islands. Although winter is supposed to be the quieter season for weather in the northeast flow of the Trades, typhoons and tropical storms can happen there at any time of the year.[10]

TABLE 2: MID-PACIFIC AIRLIFT ROUTE

PRIMARY DESTINATIONS

From	To	Distance (miles)
Haneda AFB (Tokyo)	Wake Island	1,985
Itami Air Base (Osaka)	Wake Island	2,188
Wake Island	Hickam AFB (Honolulu)	2,305
Hickam AFB	Travis AFB (San Francisco)	2,459
Travis AFB	McChord AFB (Tacoma)	614

OTHER DESTINATIONS

From	To	Distance (miles)
Wake Island	Johnston Island	1,588
Wake Island	Midway Island	1,186
Johnston Island	Hickam AFB	823
Midway Island	Hickam AFB	1,310
Hickam AFB	McChord AFB	2,705
Johnston Island	Kwajalein Island	1,635
Guam	Kadena AFB (Okinawa)	1,420
Kadena AFB	Haneda AFB	935
Haneda AFB	Iwo Jima	754
Iwo Jima	Wake Island	1,664
Haneda AFB	Ashiya AFB	526
Haneda AFB	Itami Air Base	248
Haneda AFB	Itazuki AFB	544
Haneda AFB	Iwakuni AFB	437
Haneda AFB	Kimpo Air Base	734
Ashiya AFB	Pusan	122
Ashiya AFB	Kimpo Air Base	335
Itazuki AFB	Kimpo Air Base	344
Iwakuni AFB	Kimpo Air Base	383
Pusan	Taegu	58

In his report to the Cabinet Defence Committee in December 1950, Brooke Claxton stated that NATO's planners had come to consider the probability of war in Europe to be much greater than they had estimated six months before. Mr Claxton recommended that Canada contribute a brigade group to NATO's Integrated Force, and make it known that the RCAF fighter squadrons going to the Britain (with others to follow) could be made available to SHAPE (Supreme Headquarters, Allied Powers in Europe).

These recommendations were accepted by the Cabinet Defence Committee on 28 December, and by the Cabinet the following day; in the Speech from the Throne on 30 January, it was officially announced that Canadian armed forces would return to Europe for peacetime service. Meanwhile, after weeks of consultation and discussion at the United Nations, the General Assembly passed a key resolution on 1 February, stating that the United Nations still intended to bring about a cessation of hostilities in Korea and the achievement of its objectives there by peaceful means.[11]

February

In February, No 426 Squadron launched seventeen flights to Tokyo. The detachment commanders, all Flying Officers, had completed their five- to six-week assignments in the field and were rotated back to the squadron. Phil Rodrique was replaced by Harvey Knight at Shemya; Tom Richardson drew the hardship post at Honolulu, replacing Dick Spratt; and Ben Budgeon took over from Abe Finkelstein at Haneda.

In the Air Force, transport flying is traditionally described as hours and hours of boredom interspersed with seconds of stark terror, and the experience of Flying Officer Bob Edwards is consistent with this impression. On 12 February, Edwards was captain of NS17504, en route from Itami to Wake Island with twenty-four litter patients, all American soldiers wounded in Korea. When the aircraft reached its cruising altitude of 9,000 feet, Edwards went back to the crew rest position to get some sleep, leaving instructions with his first officer, Flying Officer Montgomery, to wake him well before they ran into the weather front they expected to find about 400 miles from Wake Island.

Ever since it left the Japanese coast, the aircraft had endured a fair amount of turbulence and, as the trip progressed, Montgomery tried his best to thread a path around the thunderstorms that could be seen along the track, frequently illuminated by flashes of lightning. As the aircraft weaved all over the sky, the navigator, Flying Officer J.-L. Denis, tried to maintain a manual plot of their position — weather radar for North Stars was still a few years away.

Edwards never got his wake-up call, as he was jarred back to the real world by the crash of a lightning strike and the pounding of hail on the fuselage: the aircraft had flown into what they described later as a "grand-daddy" of a cumulo-nimbus storm cloud. When Denis saw the contents of his ashtray rise above his head, he concluded that the aircraft's wings had been torn off and glanced at the altimeter, expecting it to start unwinding rapidly. Edwards, in his rush to get forward, found himself momentarily pinned to the ceiling between the navigator's position and the radio operator's; on his way down, he grabbed all four throttles and pulled them back. (It was standard practice to reduce speed while going through a thunderstorm; it helped decrease the effects of turbulence and the risk of structural damage.) In seconds, before the crew fully realized what was going on, the aircraft was on the other side of the storm cloud and flying into a beautiful tropical sunrise.

If all was restored to serenity in the crew area, it was chaos in the passenger compartment. It all happened so fast there was no time for a warning, so the litter patients had not been strapped in, and they lay scattered about the cabin floor along with coffee cups, blankets and loose equipment. As the accompanying nursing officer and medical assistant were both helplessly air-sick, the job of calming the patients and getting them back into their litters was taken on by the flight crew. Luckily, the rest of the flight to Wake was smooth.

On arrival at Wake, the crew saw to the comfort of their passengers and then surveyed the damage to their aircraft. The nose and the leading edges of the wing were badly pock-marked right through the de-icer boots, a high-frequency aerial was missing, and the radiator fins of the liquid-cooled Merlin engines were all bent and flattened by hail. Normally, the stopover at Wake for refuelling and minor maintenance took about two hours; this time, it took several members of the crew working with screwdrivers for the better part of two hours just to open all the radiator fins.

Flight Lieutenant Cy Goodwin, the captain of the slip crew, asked Edwards one key question: Did the engines overheat? As the answer was No, Goodwin decided to carry on to Honolulu where any extended repairs could be made by the squadron's detachment. Departure was briefly delayed when two of the wounded American soldiers refused to continue the flight in the North Star, and insisted on completing the trip to the United States by sea. One was eventually convinced to get back on board, and the other caught a plane for Honolulu two days later.[12]

NS17504 arrived at Hickam eleven and a half uneventful hours after leaving Wake Island, and the squadron detachment had the aircraft serviced and ready in just under four hours. The Hickam slip crew, captained by Flying Officer Miller, flew the aircraft to the mainland and then back to base; on arrival at McChord, they had completed the 750th round trip on the Korean Airlift carried out by the McChord-based 1705th Air Transport Wing.[13]

Early in the afternoon of 14 February, Flight Lieutenant Snider brought in NS17510 from Shemya, and the slip crew, captained by Flying Officer Broadfoot, prepared to take the aircraft on to Wake Island as the detachment personnel serviced and readied the North Star for departure. It was dusk before the aircraft was ready, and it had begun to snow, an uncommon occurrence for the Tokyo area. As Flying Officer Broadfoot and his crew made their way to the aircraft, they noticed that the winds had picked up considerably; as Broadfoot taxied to the take-off position, the snowfall intensified along with the winds, which were now gusting up to sixty miles per hour.

The air traffic controllers told the captain that he could take off if he wished to, but they were abandoning the tower, an item of wartime construction; they were evidently concerned that its bamboo supports might collapse. Broadfoot opened the throttles, but the slippery runway and a bad crosswind quickly convinced him to pull power and abort the takeoff. By then the airfield was in nearly whiteout conditions, and Broadfoot had a hard time finding his way to a suitable parking spot near the terminal; the flight engineer, Sergeant Blowers, had to climb down the crew ladder and guide him with a flashlight. The crew then had to make their way through the blizzard to the terminal building where they spent the night. The air traffic controllers later told the crew that they were concerned about the aircraft because it hadn't called up on the en-route frequency.

In the morning, the airfield was under about a foot and a half of wet snow. As there was no snow-removal equipment at Haneda, hundreds of Japanese labourers were enlisted to shovel off the runways and taxiways. The field remained closed for nearly two days.

Broadfoot and his crew finally left for Wake Island on the afternoon of 16 February. Snider and his crew were bussed to Tachikawa Air Force Base, some twenty miles northwest of Haneda, where NS17505, captained by Flight Lieutenant Brown, had been redirected after leaving Shemya. Snider proceeded to Itami, picked up a load of wounded soldiers and headed for Wake Island.[14]

The weather continued to hamper the airlift operation. Toward the end of the month, aircraft heading for Elmendorf from McChord encountered severe icing conditions that caused serious problems. The southern end of the route featured thirty-mph headwinds for the first half of the run from Honolulu to the mainland, and winds blasting the beam at sixty mph for the latter half. This combination held up two squadron flights at Hickam.

By the end of February, No 426 Squadron had launched 163 flights on the airlift, comprising nearly 10,200 hours. The unit had fourteen flight crews available with four in slip positions and three on leave. The month's passenger list included 111 Canadian soldiers transported from McChord to Japan, 236 litter patients flown from Itami and Haneda to Hickam, and 48 patients carried from Hawaii to Travis AFB.

On 3 February, Sergeant H.T. MacDonnell, the NCO in charge of the clothing stores at McChord, suffered a cerebral haemorrhage and was immediately taken to the base hospital. After ten days, his condition had improved enough for his doctor to allow him to be airlifted to Montreal, where he was admitted to the military hospital.

On 6 February, Rear-Admiral John P. Whitney, Vice Commander-in-Chief of MATS, visited McChord with Rear-Admiral Hugh H. Goodwin, his successor, who was making a familiarization tour of MATS units. Both Admirals took the time to visit the Thunderbirds. Other visitors to the unit on 21 February were Guy De Merlis and Pierre Normandin, the military editor and Chief Photographer respectively of the Ottawa newspaper *Le Droit*. When they had amassed enough information on the squadron, they proceeded to Fort Lewis to get material on the 25th Canadian Infantry Brigade.

On 8 February, the squadron received a memorandum prepared at 1705th Air Transport Wing Headquarters in which its roles and responsibilities were set out thus, in part:

> **Mission.** The mission of the 426(T) Squadron RCAF is to provide, in accordance with policies and procedures by this and higher headquarters, airlift in support of the United Nations' efforts in Korea over Pacific Air Routes to Japan; to maintain the capability for strategic concentration, deployment and continued support of the United Nations' Forces in Korea; to train all flight and ground personnel assigned to the Squadron for the accomplishment of this assigned mission; to obtain necessary supplies and equipment and personnel from appropriate sources to carry out the assigned mission. Detailed and specific mission and workload data will be supplied from time to time by this headquarters.[15]

By early February, the unit had established a training program that involved a variety of flights in the McChord area. Circuits and bumps and GCA runs became so routine that the North Star ceased to be a curiosity in the skies around McChord, even at night.

On 24 February, Air Transport Command Headquarters issued Operation Order 6/51 concerning the air evacuation of Canadian Army casualties. The Canadian Army had completed negotiations with the USAF for the evacuation of casualties from the Korean theatre to McChord. Arrangements had also been completed to send these personnel to Canadian military hospitals near their homes. No 435 Squadron, based in Edmonton, was tasked with providing Dakota aircraft suitably equipped with cabin oxygen and litter fittings for the transfer of the wounded. It was stipulated that a maximum of fourteen litters be carried on each flight as well as a number of RCAF Flight Nurses and Flight Medical Assistants.

Station Lachine received some disheartening news during the month. The fourteen families occupying Emergency Married Quarters in a Canadian Arsenals building near Valleyfield, Quebec, were served with eviction notices. The Station had no alternative accommodation to offer the airmen and their families. The housing situation in the Montreal area was bleak at best and showed no sign of improving in the immediate future.

At the end of February, Wing Commander J.K. MacDonald left his position as Senior Personnel Staff Officer at Air Transport Command Headquarters at Rockcliffe and reported in at RCAF Station Lachine for conversion training on the North Star followed by familiarization trips along the airlift route. MacDonald was slated to replace Wing Commander Mussells in command of No 426 Squadron commander early in June. Mussells, in turn, would take up the SPSO position at Air Transport Command Headquarters.

In Korea, United Nations forces blunted a Communist counteroffensive on 15 February at the road junction village of Chipyong-ni. Two days later, the UN offensive resumed and, on 15 March, the 1st R.O.K. Division liberated Seoul.[16]

March

In March, No 426 Squadron instituted a system to rotate squadron personnel back to units in Canada and replace them with airmen posted in from RCAF units. This helped broaden the experience of RCAF ground crew by giving them opportunities for on-job training in an operational unit. The rotation system, which was fully endorsed by both Air Force Headquarters and Air Transport Command Headquarters, would serve the RCAF well in the months ahead. The first draft of thirty-eight airmen rotating back to Canada departed McChord on 3 March, and about the same number of replacements arrived two days later and reported in for duty with the squadron. The twenty-five airmen of the second rotation draft left McChord on 31 March, and their replacements reported in on 2 April.

During March, No 426 Squadron saw its fair share of visitors. C.A. Carroll, a correspondent for the Montreal *Standard*, came to do a feature story on the Korean Airlift. Pierre Berton of *Maclean's Magazine* departed McChord for Tokyo on 12 March in NS17504, captained by Flying Officer Broadfoot; his account of the trip appeared in *Maclean's* a couple of months later.[17] On 18 March, Lieutenant-General Guy Simonds, the newly appointed Chief of the General Staff, came through McChord on his way to Fort Lewis to visit the 25th Canadian Infantry Brigade; the next day, after his departure, his Dakota turned back with an unserviceable fuel pump and squadron personnel repaired the aircraft. Lieutenant-General Simonds was finally able to leave for Ottawa on the morning of 20 March.

On 25 March, the first Canadian Army casualty of the Korean War to be returned to North America arrived at McChord. He was met by a Canadian Army ambulance and taken to Madigan General Hospital at Fort Lewis for a short period of convalescence before being airlifted to Vancouver.

On 30 March, the officers of No 426 Squadron organized a party at the McChord Officers' Club to foster good relations between the USAF and the Canadian Army, and about 120 guest officers attended, sixty from each service. All squadron officers who could make themselves available also attended, and the evening turned out highly convivial.

At the end of March, No 426 Squadron sent two aircraft from McChord AFB to RCAF Station Greenwood, Nova Scotia, in accordance with Air Transport Command Operations Order 7/51 of 6 March 1951, which directed the squadron to provide airlift support for a one-month deployment of No 405 (MR) Squadron from Greenwood to Sea Island, British Columbia, near Vancouver, for *Exercise SEA GREEN*. The North Stars were to airlift fifty-four personnel with their baggage, and 5,400 pounds of cargo.

With a favourable forecast for upper-level winds, the No 426 Squadron crews, which were captained by Flight Lieutenant Sanford and Flight-Lieutenant Webb, planned to challenge the record for a trans-continental flight from Vancouver to Halifax. (Webb had captained the squadron crew that set the current record of eight hours and twenty-five minutes on 15–16 January 1950.) The navigation duties fell to Flying Officer Don Connolly and Flying Officer Paul Gagnon, both new arrivals at McChord and recent graduates of the Air Navigation School at RCAF Station Summerside, Prince Edward Island. This was to be their first mission with the squadron and, as it was a domestic run, no check navigators were assigned. When Connolly prepared his flight plan after the weather briefing, he accidentally left out a leg of the flight, so his calculations (which were at least two hours out) showed that the crews had a good chance of breaking the record. When Connolly finished his figures, Gagnon simply copied the erroneous flight plan.

On leaving McChord, the two North Stars headed for Vancouver, where they climbed to 23,000 feet and set a heading for Halifax. Shortly after reaching altitude over the Rockies, Connolly (who was with Webb's crew) began to feel the effects of anoxia — his oxygen hose was torn. To make things worse, the jet-stream they were counting on to give them a helpful push from behind had snaked over to the starboard beam. Suffering from the lack of oxygen, Connolly could not complete the simplest calculations, let alone produce timely position reports. Flying Officer Brooks, the crew's new and inexperienced Radio Officer, spent much of his time during the flight trying to keep Connolly awake and aware.

Despite the effect of the jet-stream, which blew them considerably north of track, Webb managed to bring the aircraft into Montreal before the situation got critical. They arrived at Dorval eight hours and twenty-five minutes after leaving McChord.

Gagnon in the second North Star also had to deal with the jet-stream on his starboard beam as well as the flawed flight plan. Instead of Calgary, the aircraft over-flew Edmonton, some 200 miles north of track. Sanford altered course southward as they passed well north of Winnipeg, but the change of heading was not drastic enough to bring them back on course. Gagnon could not fix their position by astro, because the aircraft was in the twilight period just before dawn. When Sanford heard a BOAC aircraft heading for Montreal pass a position report to Sept-Îles, he realized they must be somewhere over northern Quebec. He altered course to 240° and hoped it would take them to Montreal.

Although he didn't hear Québec City's radio as they went by some time later, he picked up the north leg of the Montreal Radio Range station and began his descent to Dorval at that point; the weather reports at Dorval called for a 400-foot ceiling and half a mile of visibility. Sanford's troubles were not over, however; as he made his approach, the flight engineer advised him that all fuel tanks were registering empty. Sanford set the aircraft down just in time, thirteen hours and ten minutes after leaving McChord — two engines quit as he taxied to the hangar area.

Both North Stars then proceeded to Greenwood, whence they departed on 1 April for Vancouver, where they arrived the same day after a refuelling stop at Winnipeg. After unloading their passengers and cargo, both aircraft returned to base at McChord.

With this, their first operational flight, behind them, both navigators thought it best to keep their profile very low, studiously avoiding the Commanding Officer in particular. After being checked out on the Tokyo run, however, both soon took their places among the squadron's operational crews.[18]

Of the seventeen aircraft No 426 Squadron despatched on the Korean run in March, only one had mechanical trouble. On 23 March, Flying Officer Broadfoot, captain of NS17516, returned to Honolulu fifty minutes after leaving with an unserviceable starboard outer engine. After some rapid repair work, the aircraft was test flown, and the crew finally took off for San Francisco only four and a half hours after their first departure for that destination.

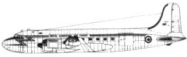

Several days of unexpectedly heavy snowfall at McChord during the first week of March presented the maintenance personnel with several problems. Because the squadron did not have enough hangar space, the ground crews had to put wing covers on the North Stars; even so, only one late departure could be attributed to the weather. The snow meant not enough traction for the towing gear, a great nuisance, and on one occasion tandem Cletracks had to be used to move aircraft.

During the month of March, the squadron's twelve aircraft flew 1,367 hours, counting training as well as airlift and logistics runs. As well as the seventeen airlift departures, the squadron despatched five flights to Montreal, two to Greenwood and one to Calgary. Toward the end of the month, strong headwinds delayed flights scheduled to return to base from Honolulu.[19]

At this stage of the airlift, navigators came to the squadron at McChord from RCAF Station Lachine, where they received an intensive three-week ground course in long-range navigation. Previously, training for new arrivals had consisted of check trips with an experienced navigator and a brush-up on navigation aids and techniques. In March, a Navigation Training Section separate from the squadron's operational flights was established, staffed by aircrew intimately familiar with the problems to be encountered along the route. The first group of squadron navigators temporarily detached for training duties comprised Flight Lieutenant Spector, Flying Officer Finkelstein, Flying Officer Logan, Flying Officer Rodger and Flying Officer Rodrique. Although it worked closely with the Senior Navigation Officer, the Navigation Training Section relieved him of the burden of assessing and integrating new arrivals while dealing with the higher-priority operational and administrative aspects of his job.

A further innovation at McChord was the inclusion, whenever possible, of American navigators in No 426 Squadron crews on the Korea run. Previously, the only second navigators carried on Thunderbird flights were new arrivals and visitors from other RCAF units. At the same time, the 61st and 62nd Troop Carrier Groups at McChord had such a surplus of navigators that, although two were carried on each trip, they still had trouble getting enough flying time to maintain their trade skills. Therefore, the Thunderbirds made a tacit agreement with their American colleagues to carry a USAF second navigator whenever a crew did not have an RCAF second navigator. This arrangement was popular with the Americans, and several who flew with the Canadians intimated that, should exchange postings become available, they would be more than pleased to be attached to the Thunderbirds. Eight months into the Korean Airlift, several navigators from Air Transport Command Headquarters and various RCAF squadrons had flown the route. The navigators from No 426 Squadron let their visitors do as much of the actual navigation work as circumstances allowed.

The new navigators reporting in from Lachine in March were Flying Officer Don Connolly, Flying Officer Paul Gagnon and Flying Officer Vince Kunce, all recent graduates of the Air Navigation School in Summerside.

The squadron at McChord also acquired three new radio officers in March: Flying Officer Brooks, Flying Officer Chuck Gauthier and Flying Officer Jack Munnock. Flight Lieutenant Ted Endersbe left to be an instructor at No 1 Radio Communications School at RCAF Station Clinton, Ontario. Flying Officer Jim Shipton returned to Lachine to await a posting to Summerside to train as a navigator. Like the new navigators, the new radio officers had completed 120 hours of ground instruction at Lachine and were flight-checked on the route by an experienced radio officer.[20]

For the four Thunderbird North Stars at RCAF Station Lachine, March was a busy month, with more than 400 hours of flying on operations and training. Six trips went to Resolute Bay via Churchill, and on one of these Arctic runs the RCAF suffered its first loss of a North Star aircraft.

NS17523 was lent to Trans-Canada Airlines in March 1947 and returned to the RCAF on 25 June 1949. On 16 March, Flight Lieutenant E.L. Banks, as captain, was attempting a take-off in this aircraft, in restricted visibility conditions on an icy runway with a high crosswind. Banks instructed his first officer to help him with the controls during take-off; the first officer, in turn, instructed the flight engineer to handle the throttles. During the take-off run, the aircraft veered to the right, and Flight Lieutenant Banks ordered, "Pull it off!" when the aircraft was ready to become airborne. The flight engineer misinterpreted the order and pulled *back* on all the throttles. The aircraft swung off the runway, crashed, caught fire and burned. Luckily, no-one on board was injured: there were eight crew and ten passengers.[21]

In addition to its operational tasks, particularly the trips to northern destinations, Lachine had launched an ambitious training program, albeit with modest resources. The training staff consisted of Squadron Leader Wilf Baynton as Chief Training Officer; Flight Lieutenant Joe Gilles and Flight Lieutenant Gordie Stuart as pilot instructors; Flight Lieutenant Ted Lee and Flight Lieutenant Ed Boland to look after navigation; and Flying Officer Gordie Fisher to instruct radio officers. The second formal OTU course started at the beginning of the month with the following pupils: pilots Wing Commander J.K. MacDonald, Flying Officer Phil Chandler, Flying Officer Arnold Gerding, Flying Officer Johnny Grant, Flying Officer Jean-Marie Robert, Flying Officer Doug Silver and Flying Officer Bill Strathy; navigators Flying Officer Ray Langman, Flying Officer A.L. Rosengren, Flying Officer Ted Walshe and Flying Officer Fred Wortman; and radio officers Flying Officer Pete Bilik, Flying Officer Hank Buechler, Flying Officer Larry Burns, Flying Officer A.L. Charters, Flying Officer D'Arcy Henry, Flying Officer Eric Snelling, Flying Officer Archie Tompkins and Flying Officer Johnny Wilson. Wing Commander MacDonald was posted to No 426 Squadron for flying duties on 26 March.

The students on the first course, which had finished the previous month, were: pilots Squadron Leader Gordie Fisher and Flight Lieutenant George Kightley; navigators Flying Officer Ted Simkins and Flying Officer Warner Unruh; and radio officer Flying Officer Terry Creteau. Their long-range training flights, conducted in March, took them to Goose Bay, Frobisher Bay, Moncton and Bermuda. Fisher, Creteau and Simkins were assigned to Operations at RCAF Station Lachine, while Kightley and Unruh were posted to the squadron at McChord.[22]

With the entry of Communist Chinese forces into the Korean War, a new element was introduced to air combat. On 1 November 1950, six MiG-15 swept-wing jet fighters crossed the Yalu River and attacked a flight of F-51 Mustang fighter-bombers. The MiG-15 was the Soviet Union's most advanced fighter, superior to every plane the UN forces had in Korea; the only comparable aircraft in western service was the F-86 Sabre, a swept-wing fighter built in the United States by North American and in Canada by Canadair. To counter the threat posed by the MiG-15, the USAF moved the Sabre-equipped 4th Interceptor Wing from the United States to Korea later in November.

With it went exchange officer Flight Lieutenant J.A. Omer Levesque of the RCAF, a veteran fighter pilot and the first Canadian to fly the Sabre. He was assigned to the detachment sent to Kimpo Airfield, near Seoul. In January 1951, the advancing Chinese Communist armies forced the Sabre unit to withdraw to Japan, but the UN counter-offensive launched at the end of the month took the Sabres — and Levesque — back to Korea.

On 30 March, Levesque was one of several Sabre pilots escorting a formation of B-29 bombers assigned to destroy the bridges over the Yalu at Sinuiju. The target was close to an enemy fighter base at Antung in Manchuria, and the MiG-15s came up to challenge the intruders. In the ensuing action, Levesque shot down one of the MiGs, his fifth victory in two wars. (In Europe, during the Second World War, he had shot down four German fighters before being downed himself and captured in February 1942.) For this achievement, he received the Distinguished Flying Cross from Canada and the Air Medal from the United States. Levesque's tour of duty with the Fighter Wing ended in May 1951, when he returned to Canada. Some time later, he was followed by twenty-one other RCAF pilots who were attached to USAF units to fly Sabres in Korea.[23]

As the United Nations forces advanced northward (Seoul was liberated on 15 March), the question of crossing the 38th Parallel became an issue again in the upper levels of command and among the members of the United Nations. If UN forces were to remain in Korea, the UN had two courses of action to choose from. The first was to try again for complete victory, but to do that, the UN forces would need not only considerable reinforcement, but also authorization to conduct operations beyond the Korean border, for this option would have to include strategic air strikes against the Chinese bases in Manchuria. The second option was to accept a stabilization of the military position — in effect, a stalemate — in the hope that subsequent negotiation by the UN would bring the conflict to an end.

General MacArthur had established himself as the leading advocate of the first option, which had little support among the members of the United Nations. President Truman wanted the situation stabilized, fearing that General MacArthur's favoured "victory" option would lead to war with Communist China and could spark a third world war. When MacArthur attempted to influence the decision, President Truman abruptly recalled him.

The General had made several statements regarding relations with China, implying criticism of the policy that restricted him to action in Korea. He had also issued an ultimatum to the Chinese by offering to discuss peace terms on the battlefield — something he was not authorized to do. In President Truman's opinion, General MacArthur had entered the field of foreign policy, thus challenging the President's authority and questioning the aims of the United Nations. On 11 April 1951, therefore, President Truman announced that MacArthur would be replaced as Commander, Far East Command by Lieutenant General Matthew B. Ridgeway, who would be replaced as Commander, Eighth U.S. Army, by Lieutenant General James A. Van Fleet.[24]

On 31 March, Flight Lieutenant Watt and his crew arrived at Honolulu in NS17502, on their way home after eleven days on the airlift route. They were the first of five squadron crews to be stuck in the Hawaiian Islands until 11 April, delayed by stiff headwinds. To fill the time, they did some local flying training; Flying Officer Quickfall, who brought in NS17511 on 2 April, managed to get in three training sessions while waiting for the winds to moderate.

The next to arrive, on 6 April, was Flying Officer Miller in NS17517, which had had mechanical difficulties en route. After leaving Itami, Miller had to return to Haneda for repairs to the synchronization box, which synchronized the revolutions of North Star's engines. After a successful air test, Miller flew to Wake Island but, shortly after leaving Wake, he had to turn back again, this time with radio problems; when these were rectified, the rest of the trip to Honolulu was routine. On 7 April, Flight Lieutenant Olsen and his crew arrived in NS17510, to be followed on 8 April by Squadron Leader Dickson in NS17507.

By the afternoon of 11 April, the winds had slackened enough that the crews could file flight plans for the mainland. At 1440 local time, Flight Lieutenant Watt left Hickam for Travis in NS17502. An hour and forty minutes later, all five squadron North Stars were winging their way back to base. The aircraft were home at McChord by the early evening of 12 April.

April

During the month of April, sixteen squadron aircraft were despatched to Tokyo.

When the USAF decided to expand Thule from a gravel strip to a full-scale airport, its navigators were required to be checked out on grid-navigation techniques if they were to fly north of the Arctic Circle. At USAF request, No 426 Squadron arranged a special training flight for USAF navigators based at Fairbanks. On 5 April, Flight Lieutenant Lloyd took NS17502 to Fairbanks, Alaska. The next day, he picked up several USAF navigators and took them on a ten-hour grid-navigation training run under the guidance of Flying Officer Stewart Logan, from Fairbanks, overflying Mould Bay and back to Fairbanks. Lloyd and his crew returned back to McChord on 7 April.[25]

Several aircraft ran into difficulties in April.

On 10 April, Flight Lieutenant Brown was an hour and a half into a flight in NS17506 when he had to shut down the port outer engine and return to base. The aircraft was repaired and he was able to depart for Elmendorf the following day.

On 30 April, Flight Lieutenant Michel returned to McChord in NS17510 an hour after departing for Elmendorf. His unserviceable No 1 engine was repaired and the aircraft was on its way again ninety-five minutes later.

On 19 April, the squadron came close to losing one of its North Stars. Over the previous few weeks there had been some talk in official circles about winding down the Korean Airlift and, to take advantage of the squadron's presence in the Far East, Air Transport Command Headquarters approved a special long-range training flight from Tokyo southeast through Asia, south to Australia and New Zealand, and then northeast across the Pacific and back to McChord. As well as two crews under captains Flight Lieutenant Johnny Watt and Flying Officer Bob Edwards, the roster comprised maintenance staff and several senior officers, including Wing Commander Mussells, the out-going squadron commander, and his successor Wing Commander J.K. MacDonald, who was in Flying Officer Edwards' crew as First Officer.

NS17509 captained by Flight Lieutenant Watt departed Tokyo at 1020 hours local time on 19 April for the 526 mile flight to Ashiya. The navigator on this leg was Flying Officer Logan. At take-off, the sky at Haneda was overcast with a ceiling of 1,200 feet, and the same conditions were forecast for Ashiya, a city 13 miles northwest of Osaka in Hyogo Prefecture.

Watt climbed to 12,000 to get above the cloud, and arrived over the Ashiya Non-Directional Beacon (NDB) nearly three hours later. He then proceeded to conduct a letdown and beacon approach to the airfield. Logan heard Watt's voice yelling "Full power!" and then "Pull 'er up!" — followed by a tremendous crash, as air rushed into the cockpit along with a shower of leaves and bits of tree branches. It took only seconds for the crew to realize they had hit some trees on top of a hill, and several more seconds to appreciate that the aircraft was still airborne and slowly gaining altitude. Fortunately for everyone aboard, the landing gear was up and the overshoot sequence had begun before the aircraft struck the trees. Wing Commander Mussells came back from the flight deck to the passenger cabin where he surveyed the scene from the side windows and then returned to the flight deck. A little later, he came back to the passenger cabin and instructed Flying Officer Edwards and Wing Commander MacDonald to go forward and take over the flying.

When they reached the cockpit area, Edwards and MacDonald noted that a tree branch — which had entered through the nose-wheel compartment — was lying practically in the lap of the First Officer, Flight Lieutenant Haley, and both Watt and Haley were visibly shaken. Edwards and MacDonald quickly took over the controls and continued the climb to a safe altitude. By this time, Logan had calculated a heading for a return to Haneda; however, both the inboard coolant-loss lights came on, and No 2 engine had to be shut down and the propeller feathered. No 3 engine was kept running at idle power to provide the hydraulic pressure for lowering the flaps and undercarriage. At this point, all thoughts of returning to Haneda were abandoned.

As the aircraft broke out above the clouds, the navigator suggested that Edwards head southwest, well out over the Sea of Japan, and a flat return on the radar altimeter told Logan when they had crossed the coast. They continued flying out to sea before beginning a slow descent to get below cloud level. After a long tense time, during which Logan kept his eyes glued to the radar altimeter, the aircraft broke cloud at 1,200 feet above the sea. The crew were relieved to get out of cloud without hitting anything, but they still had to get safely back on the ground.

The collision with the trees had destroyed both the loop antennae for the radio compass, rendering that navigation aid unavailable. It also damaged the pitot head, so there was no indication of airspeed. The pressure altimeters were unreliable at best. Fortunately, the Radio Officer found out that one of the radio sets would work through an antenna on top of the fuselage, and managed to re-establish VHF contact with Ashiya. They reversed course and headed back where they thought the airport should be; the heading proved accurate and Ashiya eventually came back into view. In the meantime, they established contact with GCA, which lined the aircraft up with the runway and advised the pilots about the glide slope.

Edwards had one last, crucial task: guessing the airspeed. With all four engines operating, it was simple to maintain a safe airspeed because the pilots could see with every landing what speeds were produced by normal power settings in combination with normal rates of descent. But few squadron pilots had ever practised two-engine landings, let alone done one for real. Fortunately, the landing gear came down normally. The flaps were selected down more slowly because the pilots decided that, if they were going to make a mistake in estimating speed, they would prefer to err on the high side. As it turned out, they were very much on the high side. As the aircraft neared the runway, Edwards realized that they were coming in very fast, so he pulled all power off well before reaching the runway threshold; fortunately, the aircraft came to a full stop before it ran out of runway. Assured that the undercarriage was not going to collapse, Edwards then taxied the aircraft to the terminal.

The Americans (who operated the airfield) sensed the drama of the situation, and took the Canadians to their Operations Building for debriefing. The process got under way as soon as the USAF colonel in charge had produced six bottles of bourbon, which were rapidly consumed without ice or mix. Thus began a marathon party that was vividly remembered by everyone present.

While the flight engineers and maintenance staff were busy with the emergency repairs to NS17509, many of the RCAF personnel accepted invitations from the USAF to fly with them to Pusan, Suwon and Taegu in Korea. Logan, for example, accompanied a USAF C-54 crew to deliver diesel fuel to a strip near Taegu: they landed on a dried-out rice paddy, shut down only the two port engines, opened the rear door and dropped out a huge inner tube, which they then inflated. Each fuel drum was then dropped onto the tube, which bounced them away from the aircraft safely — the whole load was out the door in minutes. The crew then distributed their flight lunches to the Korean children who swarmed about, restarted the two port engines, and immediately took the C-54 back to Ashiya.

On 23 April, with the emergency repairs in Ashiya completed, Flight Lieutenant Watt flew NS17509 back to Haneda. In Tokyo, the squadron detachment needed four hours to ready the aircraft for departure. It then left for Wake Island and made its way back to McChord two days later. The training trip to Australia was cancelled.

Subsequent investigation determined the cause of the incident to be a flawed approach chart, and no blame was attached to the flight crew. For his courage and display of skill, Flying Officer Edwards received the Air Force Cross.[26]

On a record flight for MATS aircraft in the Pacific Airlift at the end of April, No 426 Squadron demonstrated how maintenance can contribute to maximum use of aircraft. At 1105 hours local time on 28 April, Flight Lieutenant Snider left McChord in NS17505 for Elmendorf and Shemya. The aircraft made its way around the route in short order. Flight Lieutenant Goodwin and his crew picked up the North Star at Honolulu and flew directly to McChord, a 2,705-mile flight, in twelve hours. The aircraft was back at base at 1035 local time on 1 May. Elapsed time between departure and return to base: seventy-one hours and thirty minutes, or just under three days. This aircraft spent only thirteen and a half hours on the ground in five stops on its 12,097-mile flight to Tokyo and back to McChord. The shortest stop was at Wake Island, where the North Star was turned around in just thirty minutes. Although the aircraft was in the air for fifty-eight hours, no maintenance difficulties were encountered en route. This particular aircraft would come to an ignominious end on the route thirty months later, however.[27]

At McChord, 1 April was a happy day for thirty-four Thunderbird airmen who received well-deserved promotions. On 6 April, a squadron promotion party was held at the Benbow Lodge, where justice was done to seventy-nine cases of ale generously donated by Labatt's of London, Ontario, and delivered from RCAF Station Centralia by a squadron aircraft returning from a logistical support run to Montreal.

Early in the month, Group Captain V.S.J. Millard arrived at McChord from Air Force Headquarters to review supply procedures in effect and to complete a familiarization flight on the route. He was followed by Group Captain G.M. Fawcett from Air Materiel Command, who met with the staff of the Telecommunications Section and flew with the squadron to Tokyo. On the specific invitation of the RCAF Staff College, Wing Commander Mussells proceeded to Toronto on 10 April to speak on the Korean Airlift.

By now, No 426 Squadron was used to a passing stream of visitors, some quite high in rank, but the pending visit of the Governor General was especially significant. Preparations for such occasions generally evoked the hoary service adage "If it moves salute it; if it doesn't, paint it," and the squadron's ground personnel ensured that all facilities at McChord occupied by the RCAF were spruced up and gleaming with fresh coats of paint.

His Excellency, Governor General the Viscount Alexander of Tunis arrived early in the afternoon of 14 April in NS10000, captained by Flight Lieutenant Vrooman of No 412 Squadron, accompanied by Brooke Claxton, the Minister of National Defence, and his Parliamentary Assistant, Ralph Campney; Air Commodore A.D. Ross; and a group of senior officials. Viscount Alexander's visit had two purposes: to pay his respects to and conduct an inspection of No 426 Squadron, and to bid farewell to the 25th Canadian Infantry Brigade, commanded by Brigadier J.M. Rockingham, which was scheduled to leave soon for Korea.

On arrival, Viscount Alexander was greeted by the Governor of the State of Washington, A.B. Langlie, and several USAF and U.S. Army dignitaries. The vice-regal party then departed for Fort Lewis, where the Viscount was greeted by a U.S. Army guard of honour and a twenty-one gun salute. The obligatory cocktail party and reception at the main Fort Lewis Officers' Club was followed by a Mess Dinner with Brigadier Rockingham and the officers of the 25th Canadian Infantry Brigade. The next day, the Viscount was the guest of honour at a parade and march-past of the Brigade, at which he presented Brigadier Rockingham with a Canadian Red Ensign.

Immediately after the march-past of the 25th Canadian Infantry Brigade, the vice-regal party departed Fort Lewis for McChord AFB, where they arrived at the Officers' Club for a reception at which all the officers of No 426 Squadron were formally presented to the Governor General. The reception was followed by a formal luncheon attended by Colonel Bromiley, members of his staff, and the officers of No 426 Squadron. During the luncheon, the Viscount made a short speech of congratulations to the squadron for its fine record on the Korean Airlift. After lunch, the Governor General conducted a brief inspection of some of the RCAF installations and a tour of the base radar unit. His visit over, the Governor General then prepared for his departure by inspecting the composite Canadian Army–RCAF guard of honour commanded by Flight Lieutenant J.P. McDonald, and receiving a 21-gun salute fired by a battery from the 2nd Regiment, Royal Canadian Horse Artillery. He left for Ottawa at 1520 hours.

The 25th Canadian Infantry Brigade sailed for the Far East in three troopships operated by the Military Sea Transport Service: the USNS *Marine Adder*, which departed on 19 April; the USS *General Edwin P. Patrick* (20 April); and the USS *President Jackson* (21 April).[28]

Group Captain R.C. Hawtrey arrived at McChord from Training Command HQ for a route familiarization flight on 16 April. A week later, Group Captain M.P. Martyn, Senior Air Staff Officer at North West Air Command Headquarters in Edmonton, reported in for the same purpose. On 26 April, Mr. J. Nightingale, a reporter for the Edmonton radio station CKVA, visited McChord to tape conversations with squadron members from Alberta.

On 3 April, Air Transport Command Headquarters issued Operation Order 9/51on the 1951 edition of *Operation RE-SUPPLY*, the airlift program to the Canadian-U.S. weather stations in Arctic Canada. As in 1950, the RCAF would supply Isachsen and Mould Bay from Resolute Bay, while the USAF would handle Eureka and Alert with some flights from Resolute Bay and the rest from Thule. RCAF Station Lachine would be in command of the RCAF contribution, while the USAF detachment commander would control the two North Star aircraft assigned to the operation. On the same day, Air Transport Command submitted a proposal to Air Force Headquarters for the installation of runway and approach lights at Resolute Bay.[29]

On 14 April, three crews, twenty-seven technicians and two North Stars from Lachine arrived at Resolute Bay for *Operation RE-SUPPLY*. The USAF provided two C-54s and accompanying ground staff and flight crews. With everyone working around the clock, the airlift was completed in five days, with a total of 368,000 pounds of freight and eighty-four passengers delivered to various destinations from Resolute Bay. The North Stars transported 231,000 pounds of cargo in twenty-eight shuttle trips.[30]

At the end of April, No 404 Squadron was re-formed at RCAF Station Greenwood, Nova Scotia, as a maritime patrol unit equipped with the marine reconnaissance variant of the Lancaster, AVRO's 683 Lancaster X.

May

May 1951 was a landmark month for the RCAF for several reasons. First, recruitment of women resumed, this time directly into the RCAF and not into a separate Women's Division as was done during the Second World War. On 4 May, No 1 Air Navigation School at RCAF Station Summerside, Prince Edward Island, graduated its first class of navigators from NATO countries. On 19 May, No 410 Squadron began re-equipping with the Canadair F-86 Sabre Mk II fighter, and thus became the first RCAF squadron to fly the new aircraft.

In No 426 Squadron, May was another busy month of operations: the squadron's eleven North Stars logged 1,300 flying hours, and seventeen aircraft were despatched on the airlift. Two North Stars flew to Vancouver on 2 May for the final phase of *Exercise SEA GREEN*, the airlift of No 405 (M) Squadron back to RCAF Station Greenwood; on this mission, refuelling stops were made at Winnipeg on both the outbound and return legs. On 18 May, a special flight went to Honolulu to deliver a spare engine for NS17502, which had gone unserviceable. On another training exercise organized for USAF navigators, a North Star was flown to Fairbanks on 22 May and, the next day, taken on a ten-hour grid-navigation flight that over-flew Mould Bay and returned to Fairbanks. That aircraft was back at McChord on 24 May.

On 8 May, Flying Officer Miller and his crew left McChord in NS17510 bound for Elmendorf and Shemya with Air Commodore Ross of Air Transport Command and Group Captain McCormick of Air Materiel Command Headquarters aboard for a route familiarization flight. With them as escort was Wing Commander Mussells, making one of his last trips as Squadron Commander. From Shemya, Flight Lieutenant Sandford and his crew in NS17517 flew the three senior officers to Haneda, where they arrived in the early afternoon of 10 May.

The next day, Flight Lieutenant Emond flew the same aircraft to Ashiya — where NS17509 clipped the trees on 19 April — before returning to Haneda and then proceeding to Itami. The next stop was Ashiya again, where the crew conducted a thirty-minute local flight and then returned to Tokyo via Itami. The records are not clear on this point, but it is highly likely that Ross, McCormick and Mussells remained aboard throughout this itinerary, which included brief stops at each destination.

On 12 May, Flight Lieutenant Sanford left Tokyo for Pusan, Korea, in NS17517 shortly after noon, with Ross, McCormick and Mussells aboard. While in Pusan, Air Commodore Ross met with Brigadier J.M. Rockingham, commanding officer of the 25th Canadian Infantry Brigade, whose troops had arrived on 4 May. Three hours and fifteen minutes after arrival, NS17517 was on its way north, over-flying Taegu.

During their stop at Pusan, Wing Commander Mussells obtained a vague sort of clearance from the Americans at Taegu to continue the flight north towards the 38th Parallel. As the aircraft approached the front lines, Sanford and his crew started having serious misgivings about going any farther in an unarmed transport — a strange four-engine aircraft was an unusual and, therefore, suspect sight in the combat zone. But Mussells wanted to see where the fighting was.

Suddenly the radio crackled to life and two North American Yale spotter aircraft appeared on the scene. Their message was clear: the area was dangerous and the North Star had to leave. When Wing Commander Mussells tried to debate the point, the Yale pilot briskly told him, "Get the hell out of here." At this point, Sanford advised the Squadron Commander that, as captain of the aircraft, he had signed it out and was responsible for it and everyone aboard, and the Wing Commander let him turn the aircraft around and head for Tokyo, where they arrived at 2225 hours local time.[31]

All month, the squadron at McChord heard persistent rumours that they were soon to return to Montreal. The speculation arose from several sources. First, the build-up in the Far East for the fighting in Korea had progressed enough that critical supplies were not needed urgently any more. Second, the USAF needed expansion space at McChord. Third, as well as *Operation HAWK*, No 426 Squadron had other operational commitments that would be best handled from Dorval. Despite the rumours, the airmen's rotation program continued in May, with thirty-three technicians returned to units in Canada, but the program ended at this point.

On 19 May, two important events occurred at McChord. The squadron was involved in the culmination of Armed Forces week in the United States, which ended with a joint Canadian-American parade in Tacoma featuring a marching contingent of fifty airmen under the command of Flight Lieutenant J.P. McDonald. This was probably the only time an RCAF unit ever marched "seven deep" in the American style. A particularly effective touch was the contingent's RCAF pennant, which was made for the occasion by Squadron Leader Queale and his wife. As far as the RCAF was concerned, however, marching seven deep and flaunting a home-made pennant were unorthodox acts, but this was neither the first nor the last time the Thunderbirds would adapt to a challenging situation.

The second main event of the day was the official opening of the Thunderbird Club, with Air Commodore Ross — back from his route familiarization flight — to do the honours. The product of Squadron Leader Queale's untiring efforts to provide a gathering place for the squadron's airmen, the club featured a Thunderbird totem pole carved by Chief Mathias of Victoria, British Columbia. Although its life was destined to be short, the club served as a home away from home for the airmen at McChord.

On 21 May, Group Captain Van Camp from North West Air Command Headquarters in Edmonton reported in for a route familiarization flight.

On 27 May, the squadron was saddened by the accidental death in a car accident of Leading Aircraftsman M.D. MacIntyre. Chaplain Currie held a funeral service for him at McChord's Protestant chapel, and his sister came from San Francisco to attend. The coffin was airlifted by the logistical flight to Rockcliffe, and then moved to Williamstown, Ontario, for interment.

On 31 May, Wing Commander Mussell's last day in command of No 426 Squadron was celebrated with a farewell party at the Firs Cabaret, about twelve miles from McChord. During the evening, Mussells thanked everyone for the co-operation he had received during his twenty-eight months with the unit, and Wing Commander MacDonald, who would take command on 1 June, assured the assembled company that he would do his utmost to ensure that the squadron maintained its high standard of operations. During the Second World War, MacDonald had commanded No 432 Squadron in Bomber Command, survived being shot down, and successfully evaded capture.[32]

At about this time, the Minister of National Defence approved lowering the ages at which officers and airmen could draw marriage allowance: for officers, the age was now twenty-three, and for airmen it was twenty-one. To attract more skilled men into the service, Air Force Headquarters decided to offer prospective trade-qualified recruits immediate NCO rank on enrolment. The RCAF was expanding, and this action was necessary to prevent the ratio of unskilled to skilled airmen from increasing to an intolerable level.[33]

On 15 May, Air Transport Command Headquarters issued Operational Order 13/51, directing RCAF Station Lachine to provide two North Stars to airlift No 405 (MR) Squadron from Greenwood to Britain. No 405 was being deployed to St. Eval for a thirty-day joint exercise with RAF Coastal Command. The two aircraft were to be in position at Greenwood on 25 June.

On 31 May, *Operation RE-SUPPLY* was the subject of a meeting at Air Transport Command Headquarters. The RCAF was to get operational control of the re-supply mission to the Arctic weather stations, and the Thunderbirds would take the brunt of the task.[34]

June

No 426 Squadron was affected by several changes in June. Wing Commander MacDonald took over as Commanding Officer on the first of the month. In anticipation of the unit's move back to Dorval, the squadron made daily departures from McChord from 2 June until 13 June, all flights returning by the mid-Pacific route; with the return to base of two aircraft that had left at the end of

May, these flights made up the squadron's fifteen-trip commitment for June. All the slip crews and servicing detachments were then withdrawn from Shemya, Tokyo, Wake and Honolulu, and the squadron personnel were relocated to Montreal.

When the unit resumed airlift operations at the end of the month, it would be from Dorval, and would include a scheduled transcontinental service between Dorval and Vancouver, with stops at Winnipeg and Edmonton, before going on to McChord, where the aircraft were positioned for the Korean airlift. From this point until the end of *Operation HAWK* three years later, the squadron would operate only on the northern route. Accordingly, slip crews were located at McChord, Shemya and Tokyo. Unit detachments remained at Haneda and Shemya and one was placed at McChord.

During the month, several crews encountered operational problems along the route. On 1 June, Flight Lieutenant Watt returned to Shemya in NS17504 with an unserviceable port outer engine; the detachment had the problem rectified within an hour and the aircraft was on its way to Tokyo. Five days later, Watt and his crew were on their way to San Francisco from Honolulu in NS17506 when their aircraft was recalled, and unexpected headwinds slowed their progress so much on the way back that they almost ran out of fuel. After thirteen and a half hours in the air, they were safely back at Hickam.

On 2 June, Flying Officer Quickfall and his crew had to return to Shemya in NS17512 twenty minutes after departing for Tokyo; his malfunctioning radar altimeter was quickly replaced and they were heading out again in forty-five minutes. On 7 June, fifteen minutes after taking off from Shemya, the flight instruments in NS17504 went unserviceable, forcing Flight Lieutenant Nelles to turn back. The technicians of the squadron detachment had to work 24 hours on the problem before it was corrected and the aircraft could depart for Tokyo. Several mechanical problems encountered by Flying Officer Quickfall on 14 June necessitated a return to base an hour after leaving McChord; in this case, the squadron's maintenance staff had the problems fixed in short order and Quickfall and his crew left for Elmendorf two hours later. NS17505 was delayed in Honolulu for four days with serviceability problems; Major Upton, a USAF officer serving on exchange with the squadron, had to conduct air tests on 17 June and 18 June before the flight crew and the squadron detachment were satisfied that the aircraft was fully serviceable.

On 7 June, Flight Lieutenant Brown flew NS17517 from Haneda to Kimpo to deliver Group Captain Clements, Chief Staff Officer at Air Transport Command Headquarters, to Seoul for discussions with senior USAF officers. After a four-hour stay, the aircraft returned to Haneda.

On 1 June, six North American Mk IV Mustangs from No 416(F) Squadron at RCAF Station Uplands launched a "surprise attack" on McChord to test its radar defences.

In early June, No 426 Squadron received several visitors: aircrew taking route familiarization flights and specialist officers from Air Transport Command Headquarters come to discuss the squadron's move back to Montreal. On 12 June, the squadron received a warning order by signal approving the move, and Wing Commander MacDonald formally announced it the next day at an all-ranks meeting of squadron personnel.

Between the 16 June and 22 June, most of the squadron's personnel and equipment were moved to Lachine. Several airmen from each section were left behind with the rear party commanded by the Senior Accounts Officer, Squadron Leader M.J. Leboldus.

On 22 June, Wing Commander MacDonald departed McChord AFB for RCAF Station Lachine. On 25 June, on Wing Commander McNair's departure for Air Force Headquarters on temporary duty, he assumed command of the station. On 28 June, Air Commodore Ross made an informal visit to the squadron to meet the section heads, and two crews under Flight Lieutenant Brown and Flight Lieutenant Snider left for McChord to prepare for the July airlift commitment. Brown and his crew flew to Shemya in a MATS C-54 to be a slip crew. Snider and his crew flew to Tokyo by North West Airlines to await the first squadron aircraft out of McChord. Two days later, Flight Lieutenant Buchan, Flight Lieutenant Wallace and Flight Lieutenant Watt left Dorval with their crews in NS17507 for McChord and airlift duties on the northern route.[35]

PHOTO 83
NS17506 being serviced at Hickam AFB; Honolulu, February 1951. (DND PL 52073)

PHOTO 84

(From left) J. Gallipeau, S. Talbert, E. Grose and Cam Baine at Hickam AFB; Honolulu, spring 1951. (E. Grose Collection)

PHOTO 85

Casualties from the fighting in Korea being loaded aboard a North Star for transit to the United States; Tokyo, 17 February 1951. From left: F/O B. Budgeon (Detachment Commander, Haneda AFB), Lt. Mary Orichella, USAF (flight nurse) and F/L R.J. Brown (captain of the aircraft). (DND PL 51140)

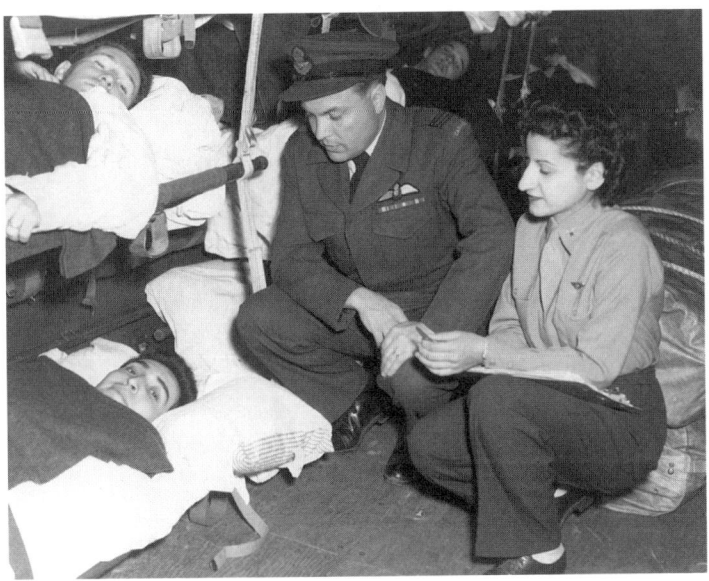

PHOTO 86
F/L R.J. Brown checks the comfort of his passengers with flight nurse Lt. Mary Orichella before leaving Haneda AFB for Wake Island, 17 February 1951. (DND PL 51133)

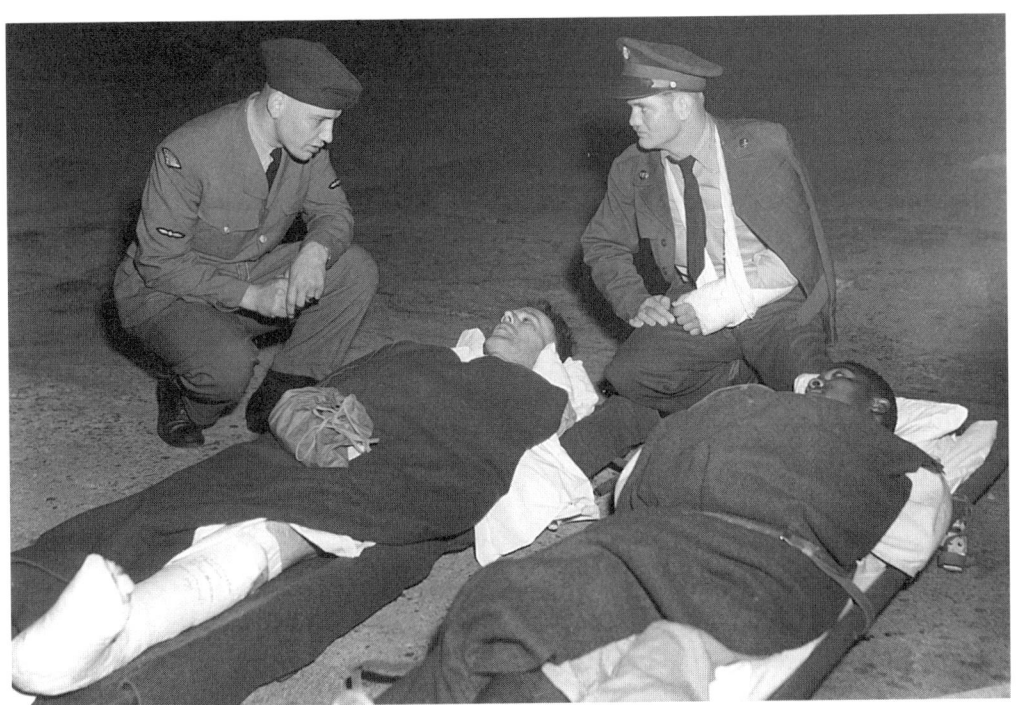

PHOTO 87
LAC P. Pawliuk talks to wounded soldiers waiting to board a North Star for transit back to the United States; Itami, March 1951. (DND PL 52303)

PHOTO 88

W/C C.H. Mussells chats with the squadron's detachment commander, F/O B. Budgeon, during an inspection trip along the Korean Airlift route; Haneda AFB, January 1951. (DND PL 51178)

PHOTO 89

F/L J.A. Watt and his crew before a familiarization trip to Korea in a USAF C–54; Ashiya, 26 March 1951. From left: Cpl. W.L. O'Ray, LAC B. Rogers, F/L Watt, F/O R.A. Spratt, F/O E.H. Moberg, F/O C.G. Jessup and Lt. Orlin D. Lewis, a USAF navigator training with No 426 Squadron. (DND PL 51396)

McChord AFB, January–June 1951

PHOTO 90
Brigadier J.M. Rockingham (Commander, 25th Canadian Infantry Brigade) shakes hands with W/C C.H. Mussells as A/C A.D. Ross looks on; Pusan, 12 May 1951. (DND PL 52319)

PHOTO 91
Members of No 426 Squadron's Tokyo detachment; Spring 1951. From left: Strilchuk, Wood, Black, Emms, Myers, an unidentified USAF airman and Calvin. (Barbara Wood Collection)

PHOTO 92
North Stars in "nose hangars" built to shelter maintenance personnel working on the aircraft; McChord AFB, autumn 1950. (DND PL 50474)

PHOTO 93
NS17517 (F/L R.J. Brown, captain) parked at Kimpo Air Base; 7 June 1951. (P.M. Tutt Collection)

McChord AFB, January–June 1951

PHOTO 94
F/O P.M. Tutt in front of the bombed-out Administration Building at Kimpo Air Base; 7 June 1951. (P.M. Tutt Collection)

PHOTO 95
Korean women filling in bomb craters under the supervision of an American sergeant; Kimpo Air Base, 7 June 1951. (P.M. Tutt Collection)

PHOTO 96
Roadside market on the perimeter of Kimpo Air Base; 7 June 1951. (P.M. Tutt Collection)

Lachine, July–December 1951

CHAPTER 12

LACHINE
JULY–DECEMBER 1951

On May 1951, the United Nations forces in Korea finally managed to halt a Communist offensive. They then advanced north and, by the middle of June, were back on the 38th Parallel. On 23 June, the Soviet member of United Nations Security Council, Yakov Malik, made a radio address containing a significant overture: a proposal that the warring parties should begin to discuss a cease-fire and armistice that would provide for a mutual withdrawal from the 38th Parallel.

President Truman instructed General Matthew Ridgeway, the UN force commander, to make preliminary arrangements for the proposed armistice talks. On 8 July, after an exchange of messages between their headquarters, representatives of the opposing commanders met at Kaesong, a town located just south of the 38th Parallel and about thirty-six miles northwest of Seoul. At this meeting, arrangements were made for the first cease-fire conference, which was scheduled for 10 July.

The area around Kaesong had been no man's land, but its neutral status disappeared on 9 July when Communist troops moved in. The UN Command suspended discussions from 12 July to 15 July until the Communists could be brought to agree that the conference site should be neutral. The issue came up again in August, with another Communist advance into the neutral zone and, after another suspension of the talks, this time for five days, the Communists again agreed to respect the neutrality of the conference site. Negotiations halted again on 23 August, when the Communists alleged that UN aircraft attacked the conference site. The UN refuted these allegations, but the talks remained in suspension until 25 October; meanwhile, the UN forces conducted a series of limited attacks to eliminate salients in their lines. Following prolonged discussions, both parties agreed to shift the conference site to Panmunjom, where truce talks resumed on 27 November. The cease-fire line eventually decided upon followed the line of contact established between the two armies at this time.[1]

July

On 3 July 1951, the RCAF's first group of post-war women recruits arrived at the Manning Depot in St-Jean-sur-Richelieu, Quebec. At the end of the month, a Canadian Pacific Airlines DC-4 disappeared on the way from Vancouver to Anchorage while en route for Tokyo. The RCAF and the USAF mounted an extensive search, but neither the aircraft nor any of its passengers or crew were found. Thirty-eight people perished: seven crew members, two RCN sailors and twenty-nine American servicemen.

On 1 August, the RCAF launched a series of significant structural changes with the merger of Tactical Group, based at Edmonton, and North West Air Command to form Tactical Air Group;

the formation of No 14 (Training) Group at Winnipeg to administer and control training facilities that had been reactivated in the Prairie provinces, and to train aircrew from other NATO countries; and reactivation of No 413 (Tusker) Squadron at RCAF Station Bagotville, this time as a fighter unit equipped with the De Havilland Vampire Mk III. In September, No 439 (Fighter) Squadron was established at RCAF Station Uplands and armed with the Canadair Mk II Sabre, and No 443 "City of New Westminster" Squadron (Auxiliary) formed at Vancouver; this latter unit would successively fly the Mustang, the Vampire and then the Sabre. On 15 October, as part of the expansion of Canadian air defences, the Ground Observer Corps was formed.

On 1 November, the RCAF formed No 1 Fighter Wing in England; two weeks later, RAF Station North Luffenham was transferred to the RCAF to accommodate the Wing, and No 410 (Cougar) Squadron arrived with thirty-five Sabres, having crossed the Atlantic in HMCS *Magnificent*, the Royal Canadian Navy aircraft carrier. The Sabres were flown from St-Hubert to Norfolk, Virginia, where the expert technicians of the U.S. Navy "cocooned" them for the voyage and loaded them into *Magnificent*. (Early in 1952, the RCN would deliver aircraft to Britain for one more RCAF squadron but, after that, fighter squadrons proceeding to Europe flew the Atlantic with logistic support from No 426 Squadron.) In mid-December, their training with the RAF completed, No 421 Squadron returned from Britain, settled at St-Hubert, and re-equipped with the Sabre Mk II.[2]

On 20 October, the NATO commitment took Canada into uncharted waters with the departure of the advance party of the 27th Canadian Infantry Brigade for northern Germany, where a Canadian brigade would be maintained in the British Army of the Rhine until 1970, when it would move to Lahr in Baden-Württemberg for another twenty years of service. This overseas commitment was the requirement that led to the conversion of Canada's armed services from Reserve-based organizations built around small professional cadres to a modern standing Army, Navy and Air Force.

On 22 October, NATO admitted Greece and Turkey as full members, a strategically important expansion that forestalled any possibility that they might become client states of the Soviet Union, which would thus obtain direct access to the Mediterranean Sea.

The effective date for the Thunderbirds' move back to the Montreal area was 1 July 1951. As directed by the Air Officer Commanding, Air Transport Command, the squadron was to provide air transport in co-operation with USAF/MATS for operations associated with the Korean Airlift, and such other air transport services as the AOC ATC should order. The AOC ATC would exercise functional control over No 426 Squadron through the commanding officer of RCAF Station Lachine, who would also command No 426 Squadron. As of 1 July, Wing Commander MacDonald assumed this dual role.

The squadron's command and control relationships with respect to the Korean Airlift were complex. Under a directive from Air Transport Command, No 426 Squadron personnel were to take orders and instructions from the Commander of the 1705th Air Transport Wing with respect to airlift operations and, in matters related to the occupancy and use of USAF facilities, comply with the orders and instructions of the Base Commander at McChord. The Squadron Commander was authorized to establish and control unit detachments at McChord and anywhere else he considered necessary to the squadron's efficient conduct of *Operation HAWK*.

On 1 August 1951, the squadron establishment was amended to authorize an aircraft strength of twelve North Stars (including three to be used exclusively for training), to be operated at a flying rate of 120 hours per month. The organization order of 1 November 1950 had authorized twelve aircraft at a flying rate of eighty hours per month. On 1 December 1951, the establishment was amended again to increase aircraft strength to fifteen North Stars, including three for crew training. The twelve aircraft on operations were to be flown at a rate of 130 hours per month, and the three assigned to training were to be flown at a rate of at 100 hours per month.[3]

No 426 Squadron didn't take long to settle back into the familiar surroundings of Dorval and Lachine. From this point on, squadron aircraft that flew the airlift were often given domestic air transport assignments for the trips between Dorval and McChord, which usually entailed stops at Winnipeg and sometimes Edmonton and Vancouver. This ad-hoc practice evolved into the scheduled cross-country service flights designated SF7 (westbound) and SF8 (eastbound).

Domestic operations in July included ration runs to Goose Bay; passenger and freight runs to Resolute Bay; carrying a backlog of freight to Frobisher Bay; transporting Air Cadets back and forth between Newfoundland and Greenwood, where they were attending summer camp; flying Militia soldiers home to Winnipeg from training at Abbotsford, British Columbia; and airlifting No 408 Squadron's personnel and equipment from Rockcliffe to Churchill, Manitoba, and Coral Harbour on Southampton Island.

The squadron's Korean Airlift commitment for July called for sixteen departures from McChord. These commitments were met, six shuttle runs carrying passengers and freight between McChord and Travis AFB were also done. All sixteen of the flights to Tokyo encountered delays because of mechanical problems, bad weather, or both. Minor technical troubles that caused delays of one to nine hours included: changing a wheel; fixing a leaking fuel tank; rectifying a problem in an aircraft's electrical system; repairing a defective radio compass; changing a magneto; and dealing with an unserviceable emergency air brake. Most of the maintenance and repair chores fell to the Shemya detachment, which handled four engine changes in July.

Flight Lieutenant Watt (whose aircraft and crew were already in position at McChord) departed for Tokyo on 1 July, and subsequent departures were scheduled for the odd-numbered days of the month. The next day, Flying Officer Broadfoot and his crew left Dorval for McChord by way of Winnipeg in NS17505 and positioned at McChord for a 5 July departure. NS17510, which Flight Lieutenant Watt had taken as far as Shemya, made a rapid run to Tokyo and was back at McChord in sixty-seven hours, including fifty hours and ten minutes of flight time. On 3 July, NS17507 was the next aircraft out. It arrived in Haneda without a hitch, but was delayed there for four days by terrible weather along the Aleutian chain; while the weather en route was far from good, the actual and forecast ceilings and visibilities for Shemya and alternate fields were consistently below landing limits. The slip crew from Tokyo, which was captained by Flight Lieutenant Brown, brought the flight in to Shemya on 9 July, and it continued on to McChord with Flight Lieutenant Snider's crew.

On 6 July, Flying Officer Broadfoot and his crew brought NS17505 into Shemya at 0120 hours in landing conditions that were marginal at best. The GCA team guided the aircraft down far enough so Broadfoot could just see several runway lights; by straddling the lights, he then managed to land[4] and, after an hour's delay to fix a fuel tank leak, the aircraft was on its way again, heading to Tokyo with Flight Lieutenant Wallace at the controls. Bad weather in the Aleutians delayed NS17505 at Haneda for two days before the return trip to Shemya could be made, and then on to McChord.

On 7 July, the next crew set out from McChord, captained by Flight Lieutenant Olsen in NS17517. At Elmendorf, after a routine eight-hour flight, the aircraft was refuelled and the crew briefed for their next leg to Shemya. As the destination weather forecast was "below limits", a flight plan was filed for Cold Bay, about halfway to Shemya, so the crew could use Elmendorf as an alternate if Shemya was shut down. The four-hour flight to Cold Bay was conducted at night and in instrument weather, and when they arrived the crew had been up for sixteen hours. Olsen made a GCA landing in the rain along an approach path bordered by mountainous terrain. Forty minutes later, despite a briefing that indicated continuing bad weather at Shemya, Olsen took off again into the darkness and overcast. By this point, everyone in the crew had been up for more than twenty hours and were very tired; Olsen recalls falling asleep in the captain's seat with the autopilot engaged — not unusual behaviour as the first officer and the flight engineer were there to keep an eye on the instruments. Such impromptu catnaps usually lasted only a minute or two, but Olsen woke up this time to find both the flight engineer and the first officer also dozing. There were guilty smiles all round, but the crew were too tired to worry about it.

Five hours out of Cold Bay, NS17517 arrived over Shemya where the weather, as forecast, was on the deck. Not wishing to return to Cold Bay or Elmendorf, Olsen chose to attempt a GCA landing — the Shemya GCA team was one of the USAF's most professional and most practised, as just about *all* landings at Shemya were conducted by GCA. This also applied to the aircraft crews.

Following the calm directions of the GCA controller, Olsen entered the final approach and came down the glide slope as instructed. He didn't want to overshoot, as this would mean a long trip back to an alternate. The first indication Olsen had of the runway was the red glow of the approach lights and, right on cue, the controller coolly called out, "You are passing over the end of the runway." At the same moment, the captain saw an amber light on each side and called "Power off." As the aircraft was crabbing at about 30° into a crosswind, the engineer (who sat in a jump seat a little lower than both the pilots) had seen nothing but fog to this point and he hesitated to act, but with a little help from the skipper's hand, the power came off and the aircraft touched down. The strong crosswinds for which Shemya was noted then seized the aircraft, blowing it to the right so its wheels took out two runway lights; fortunately, the runway was so wide that the lights were inset 150 feet from the edge. Olsen straightened out the aircraft, but it then careened to the left and knocked out a couple more lights. Luck was still with them: the tires did not blow out on contact with the lights, and the crew were able to bring the aircraft under control. As they came to a stop, the voice from the tower asked, "Did you make it, 17517?" Replying that they had indeed landed, first officer Flying Officer John Grant requested a "follow-me" jeep to lead them through the swirling fog to the parking area. The tower voice replied, "The jeep can't find you!"

Things were sorted out in short order and, in keeping with squadron routine, Olsen's crew retired to the Shemya Hotel (the station's Second World War-era barracks) and someone broke open a bottle of Canadian Club and passed it around. Next on the agenda was a hot meal and some sleep.

Reflecting on the squadron's airlift routine, an amateur psychologist has mused that it was probably healthy for the crews to unwind in this way, as disturbance of sleep patterns is as dangerous in its way as sheer fatigue. Many crew members on the airlift were in their twenties and able to cope fairly well — they could sleep anytime, day or night — but the older members of the flying fraternity had some difficulty in this regard. It would take several years for the RCAF to address the crew fatigue problem seriously.[5]

Eleven hours after NS17517 arrived at Shemya, the weather had lifted sufficiently for Broadfoot and his crew to take the aircraft on to Haneda. Once there, the aircraft's return trip to McChord was delayed for twelve hours by electrical problems and bad weather in the Aleutians.

The next aircraft to join the Tokyo run was NS17510, which was brought out to Shemya on 9 July by Flying Officer Quickfall; despite a minor technical delay, NS17510 made the round trip in sixty-eight hours. Flying Officer Miller was next to start out, two days later, in NS17505. With an hour's delay in Shemya for a magneto change, the aircraft was back in McChord in just under sixty-eight hours.

At this point in the operation, technical problems conspired with the weather to create some serious delays. On 13 July, Flight Lieutenant Lloyd and his crew departed McChord for Shemya in NS17511; on arrival, the crew reported mechanical difficulties and the aircraft was found to require a Corliss throttle and engine change. After a fifty-three hour delay for repairs, Miller took the aircraft to Haneda, where Quickfall took over to fly it to Shemya by way of Matsushima, where they stopped for fuel. At Shemya, Olsen and his crew took over for the return flight to McChord, where they arrived on 18 July.

The next aircraft out on the route was 17517, captained by Flight Lieutenant Herbert, which departed McChord on 15 July after an hour's delay due to loading problems. Shortly before arriving at Shemya, Herbert lost his No 3 engine, which had to be replaced, causing a delay of thirty-four hours. After the repairs were done, Lloyd and his crew took the aircraft on to Tokyo, where the slip crew, captained by Miller, were held up for seven hours by a refuelling delay. Then, on reaching Misawa, the Miller and his crew sat out the Aleutian weather for three and a half days, and at Shemya, they had to wait thirty-six hours more before take-off limits permitted Miller to carry on to McChord.

On 18 July, NS17515 captained by Flight Lieutenant Allen arrived at Shemya with an unserviceable engine that had to be replaced, delaying them for several days. The next squadron aircraft into Shemya from McChord was NS17511, captained by Flight Lieutenant Payne, which arrived on 20 July; after a twelve-hour weather delay, it was on its way to Haneda with Herbert and his crew. On a "first crew in, first crew out" basis, Allen left for Haneda next, on 21 July in NS17506, which was brought in by Flight Lieutenant Buchan and his crew. NS17515 was ready to go on 22 July; Flight Lieutenant Payne took it to Japan and was forced to land at Misawa and wait two days for the weather at Haneda to clear. On 24 July, NS17515 was flown back to Shemya via Misawa by Allen and his crew, and Herbert then took it on to Elmendorf and home, but had to return to Shemya with a stuck throttle; after a seventeen-hour delay while the stoic and overworked squadron detachment repaired the throttle, he was able to head out for McChord again and complete the mission on 26 July.

NS17506 made it around the route in four and a half days, including a twenty-seven hours at Haneda waiting for the weather to clear in the Aleutians, and twenty hours at Shemya while airfield conditions improved to take-off limits.

When NS17511 reached Haneda, Flight Lieutenant Lloyd and the slip crew were able to take it only as far as Misawa, where they waited thirty-six hours for the "below limits" forecast at Shemya to improve. Quickfall and his crew waited patiently at Shemya for nearly a week, and finally made it back to McChord with NS17511 by noon on 24 July.

The squadron launched five more flights in July. Flight Lieutenant Stuart set out for Tokyo in NS17512 on 25 July, two days behind schedule because of oil leaks that had to be fixed, and propeller repairs that had to wait for the tools to be returned from Shemya, where they had been sent for the engine change on NS17515. This was the only delay NS17512 encountered, however, and its run was completed in seventy-seven hours. On 27 July, Flying Officer Broadfoot (making his second trip in three weeks) took NS17506 to Shemya after a twenty-four hour delay at McChord caused by defective de-icer boots. After a nine-hour delay at Shemya for repairs to an emergency air brake, Stuart and his crew took off in NS17506 for the next leg of the trip, to Haneda, only to turn back after an hour with a malfunction in the No 3 engine, which had to be shut down and the propeller feathered. The engine change, the fourth handled by the sorely stretched squadron detachment at Shemya, took nearly four days.

The next outbound crew was captained by Flying Officer Wolkowski, who brought NS17515 in to Shemya on 29 July; as Stuart's was the first crew in, they took the aircraft on to Haneda. Within eight hours of arriving, NS17515 was on its way back to Shemya with Buchan's crew. From Shemya, Payne and his crew took it to McChord where it arrived on the morning of 1 August. Also on 1 August, the squadron detachment at Shemya finished working on NS17506 and Wolkowski and his crew took it out for a forty-five minute air test to ensure that everything checked out on the aircraft, and then were on their way to Haneda ninety minutes later. In ten hours, NS17506 was turned around and heading back to Shemya with Broadfoot's crew; at Shemya, it was handed over to Stuart, who had it back at McChord shortly before midnight on 3 August.

The last two departures for Japan in July were NS17504 captained by Flight Lieutenant Watt on 29 July, and NS17512 captained by Flying Officer Edwards on 31 July. Each aircraft was held up in Haneda for twenty hours by bad weather in the Aleutians.

When Flying Officer Broadfoot and his crew left Dorval for McChord on 23 July in NS17512, the passenger list included a journalist named René Lévesque, who was going to Korea for the CBC to record radio features about the Royal 22ᵉ Régiment — the Van Doos — for broadcast in Canada. Lacking enthusiasm for his assignment, Lévesque was even less keen on going to Tokyo by North Star. Among the disparaging remarks in his memoirs about that trip, he wrote that he nearly decided not to board for the Shemya-bound leg when he saw the captain weaving towards the aircraft after a binge that had lasted into the early hours of the morning, and noted that the navigator was in scarcely better shape and the first officer just looked tired.

The most charitable way to interpret this account, which was written some thirty-five years after the event, is to attribute it to journalistic licence. The captain on Lévesque's flight — NS17512 on 31 July 1951 — was Flying Officer Bob Edwards, who had been put up for the Air Force Cross and would be chosen to fly Princess Elizabeth and the Duke of Edinburgh during their forthcoming visit to Canada. He was hardly the officer to be so unprofessional as to stay up drinking most of the night before a twenty-hour workday. The navigator on that flight was of similarly high quality: Flight Lieutenant R.E.D. Ratcliffe, DFC, the squadron's Navigation Leader, who had also held that position with the squadron during the war. The North Star was a comparatively forgiving aircraft, but it was a complex machine that needed a highly skilled crew if it was to ply the difficult North Pacific route.

Lévesque made the trip in the main cabin of the North Star, which he shared with an RCAF sergeant, a spare engine and some parts destined for Shemya, and boxes of freight bound for Tokyo. The arrival at Shemya, where they stayed only three and a half hours, was probably unnerving to the uninitiated, as Edwards had to overshoot on his first attempt at a GCA landing. Flight Lieutenant Watt took over the flight for the Tokyo-bound leg, with Flying Officer Denis as navigator. Denis recalls being interviewed by Lévesque the following day in the basement of the Marunouchi Hotel, and then hearing it broadcast on 9 August, on CBM, the CBC station in Montreal.[6]

On 16 July, Wing Commander MacDonald and Squadron Leader Dickson positioned their North Star at RCAF Station Greenwood; the next day, they airlifted twenty-five personnel and 5,000 pounds of equipment from No 405 (MR) Squadron to Frobisher and Resolute Bay.

On 17 July and 21 July, the first fighter-affiliation exercises were held in the Montreal area, with the squadron's North Stars playing "enemy" bombers for the Mustang fighters of Air Defence Command.[7]

On 26 July, the personnel of 1705th Air Transport Wing and No 426 Squadron at McChord celebrated the end of the Korean Airlift's first year on 26 July. Coincidently, Flight Lieutenant R.G. Herbert completed the squadron's 232nd run to Japan when he brought in NS17515 at 0620 hours, and an American C-54 left for Japan at about the same time as the first North Star took off for Tokyo a year earlier.

A much more elaborate ceremony was staged at Dorval the next day, with all forty-four members of the Central Band of the RCAF (flown in that morning from Rockcliffe) and, in front of the squadron hangar, a dais hung with the United Nations flag, the RCAF Ensign, the Union Jack and the Stars and Stripes. Between the flags stood two five-man airlift crews, representing the RCAF and the USAF, and in front of the dais were three flights of airmen in their dress uniforms (5As) and medals formed up in a hollow square. After an inspection by C.M. (Bud) Drury, the Deputy Minister of National Defence, Wing Commander MacDonald read greetings from senior military and government officials from both Canadian and the U.S. Congratulatory remarks were then delivered by Deputy Minister Drury, Colonel Wentworth Goss (the Chief of Staff at MATS Headquarters), and Air Commodore Ross from Air Transport Command, who took this opportunity to make his farewell speech as he would soon be taking up as new position as Commander, Maritime Group, based in Halifax. The ceremony attracted a large civilian audience and extensive media coverage.

After thanking the speakers, Wing Commander MacDonald presented Colonel Goss with a hand-painted copy of the Thunderbird badge of No 426 Squadron and, in return, Goss gave the Squadron Commander a silk banner bearing the MATS insignia.[8] Air Commodore Ross then took the salute for the march past, which was led by the Central Band. The reception that followed the ceremonial parade was held at the RCAF Station Lachine Officers' Mess.

The guest list for this ceremonial parade included the following senior officers: Air Vice Marshal F.R. Miller, Vice Chief of the Air Staff; Major General R.O.G. Morton, General Officer Commanding, Quebec Command; Group Captain W.I. Clements; Wing Commander W.P. Gavin, Wing Commander C.H. Mussells and Wing Commander R.I. Thomas from Air Transport Command Headquarters; Air Commodore A.P. Revington, Senior Air Liaison Officer, United Kingdom Service Liaison Staff in Ottawa; Lieutenant-Colonel Green, the Assistant Air Attaché at the U.S. Embassy in Ottawa; Lieutenant-Colonel Max E. Van Benthuysen of the 1705th Air Transport Wing, Continental Division of MATS; and Lieutenant-Commander John Buzden of HMCS *Donnacona* in Montreal.[9]

August

The August commitment on the Korean Airlift was fifteen trips scheduled to depart from McChord on even-numbered days. Effective 1 August, the runways at Shemya were to be used during daylight hours only in emergencies because they were occupied by construction crews and equipment doing extensive repairs. Despite delays caused by weather problems and minor unserviceabilities, No 426 Squadron found it much easier than in July to complete the commitment.

On 1 August, the squadron personnel at McChord hosted Flying Officer V.M. Deneau and Flying Officer D.L. Thompson, RCAF nursing sisters who had been serving with the USAF air evacuation squadron at Hickam AFB in Honolulu, as they passed through on their way home to Canada. On the same day, a North Star departed from Dorval with thirty-two air cadets bound for Britain on an exchange visit, part of a program to promote co-operation and goodwill across the Commonwealth. When it returned, the aircraft brought thirty-one British cadets who went on to RCAF Station Centralia. On 4 August, the squadron airlifted thirty-seven air cadets from summer camp at RCAF Station Greenwood to Gander for a tour of the area and an over-night stay, and then brought them back to Greenwood the next day. On 18 August, a squadron North Star departed RCAF Station Rockcliffe for Britain with another group of forty air cadets. On 20 August, the Air Cadet International Drill Team was flown from camp at Greenwood to St. John's, Newfoundland, where they presented a display of precision drill, and brought them back to Greenwood.

As the Korean Airlift progressed, the squadron continued taking officers on familiarization trips. On 4 August, Squadron Leader W.M. Garnett from Tactical Air Group Headquarters in Edmonton departed McChord with Flight Lieutenant Olsen and his crew. On 16 August, Air Commodore W.C. Kennedy from Air Materiel Command Headquarters in Ottawa left McChord for Tokyo in NS17517, captained by Flight Lieutenant Allen.

On 4 August, Air Commodore R.C. Ripley became the new Air Officer Commanding, Air Transport Command; his previous posting was as Assistant to the Chief of the Air Staff at Air Force Headquarters in Ottawa. On 5 August, the newly promoted Squadron Leader Cy Torontow reported to No 426 Squadron for flying duties, his last posting having been in the Personnel

Branch at Air Transport Command Headquarters. On 9 August, Air Transport Command Headquarters moved from RCAF Station Rockcliffe to RCAF Station Lachine.

On 5 August, the squadron airlifted forty-four soldiers of the 60th Observation Regiment, Royal Canadian Artillery, from Montreal, and the 40th Observation Regiment from Malton Airport near Toronto to Rivers, Manitoba, for an exercise; they were returned to Malton and Montreal a week later.

On 8 August, having completed their run to Tokyo the previous day, Flight Lieutenant Watt and his crew positioned their aircraft at Vancouver, where they picked up a detachment of soldiers from The Seaforth Highlanders of Canada and transported them to Dorval.

On 20 August, Flight Lieutenant Jim Morrison captained NS17514 on the 1,000th military airlift flight to depart McChord AFB for Tokyo. The crew on this milestone run, which received an official USAF send-off, included first officer Flying Officer Russ Roane, navigator Jean-Louis Denis, radio officer Tom Richardson, flight engineer Sergeant Bill McKnight, and air traffic assistant Leading Aircraftsman Walt.

On 20 August, Flight Lieutenant Olsen and his crew departed Dorval at 0850 hours in NS17522 for Churchill, the first stop on the month's third logistics run to Resolute Bay. The 1,250-mile flight, conducted at 6,000 feet, took six hours and twenty minutes, and the route took the aircraft by Moosonee at the base of James Bay and along the western shore of Hudson Bay. After a stop of one hour and twenty-five minute to unload passengers and cargo, refuel and file a new flight plan, the aircraft left Churchill at 1535 hours local time, climbed to 8,000 feet and headed north.[10]

For flying in areas where the magnetic compass is not reliable enough for navigation (north of Churchill, for example), the RCAF had adopted the ASCO-GYRO system, which involved establishing the aircraft's heading by astro compass and maintaining direction by means of a gyro. The property of rigidity in space makes the gyro ideal for steering a grid direction or a true direction, but the gyro is subject to two types of precession or "drifting" from alignment. The first type is astronomical precession, caused by the earth's rotation, for which can be almost wholly compensated for. The second type is functional or random precession, which can change frequently. By 1951, manufacturing improvements had reduced but not eliminated functional precession in gyros, so the functional precession that remained had to be allowed for when steering a gyro heading.

The standard instrument used to provide a stabilized directional reference for both maintaining a heading and turning on to a new heading was the directional gyro indicator or DGI. The gyros' rate of precession was calculated by the navigator, who used the astro compass every twenty minutes to check the aircraft's true heading, and passed revised headings to the pilot to compensate for precession and to maintain track. The navigator kept a "gyro log" for use when a heading check was not available because of cloud cover or twilight; heading corrections could still be made based on the gyro's calculated precession rate. This technique served the purpose over a short period of time, but the precession rates of gyros could be erratic, which could be stressful for the navigator, let alone the other members of the crew.[11]

The true direction of any line drawn on a map is the angle measured clockwise between the line and the north end of a meridian of longitude. It's easy to measure true direction in the latitudes between 65° North and 65° South on plotting maps, as the meridians are nearly parallel straight lines, but in polar projections the true direction of a straight line changes rapidly as the meridians converge. Therefore, true-direction measurements are useless for navigating in the polar regions. To overcome this directional problem, a grid navigation system was developed.

A suitable meridian was selected as a reference and its true direction was called "Grid North". All lines drawn parallel to the reference meridian point to Grid North. General practice was to draw several lines to form a grid, and the grid direction of any line is defined as the angle measured clockwise between it and the direction of Grid North. Plotting charts in general use by the RCAF had an overprint using the Greenwich meridian as the reference meridian, so the angular difference between Grid North and True North on these charts was equal to the change of longitude. The formula for arriving at grid direction was to take true direction, as determined by astro compass, and add longitude, if west at place of measurement, or subtract longitude, if east.[12]

Resolute Bay is 1,105 miles almost due north of Churchill. Despite some stiff headwinds, NS17522 stayed above the cloud for most of the trip, which was also in daylight since the high latitudes experience extended periods of twilight in August. As Olsen and his crew approached Resolute, they were advised that the low-frequency beacon (a temperamental device) was off the air, and the airfield weather was deteriorating, with both ceiling and visibility coming down. As this was the first trip to Resolute Bay for the author, he turned on the AN/APN2 Rebecca set (an airborne radar-homing device), which triggered a Eureka beacon that enabled the operator to obtain range and bearing indications. Readings were obtained at the Eureka beacon's maximum range of ninety miles, and heading alternations were made as the aircraft neared Resolute Bay.[13]

Olsen chose to begin his descent over Somerset Island, as the area was clear and he was able to get below cloud over Barrow Strait. The weather at the airfield was closing in fast and, by the time the captain saw the runway, it was too late to land safely. Turning rapidly to port, Olsen brought the aircraft around at 200 feet for another approach to the runway from the south, while the crews of two Lancasters from No 408 Squadron fired flares so Olsen could see the end of the 6,500-foot gravel runway in time and make a smooth landing. Within minutes, the field was socked in.

Under normal circumstances, the cargo (which included a grader) would have been unloaded, the aircraft refuelled and loaded with any items to be taken back to Dorval, a new flight plan filed, and NS17522 would have been winging its way back to Churchill within two hours. But With the field closed, the crew had to rely on the hospitality of this spartan northern outpost, and after the seven-hour flight from Churchill they had been on duty for nearly seventeen hours. Although it was almost 2300 hours local, the station personnel provided hot meals and bunks for the night. By 0730 hours next day, the weather had cleared and the aircraft was readied for departure.

Part of the pre-takeoff cockpit drill involved setting the DGI to the Grid direction of the runway. Since the true direction of the departure runway was 167° and the longitude at Resolute Bay is 95° West, the Grid direction to be set on the DGI was 262°. After departure, the heading was altered slightly to compensate for drift and to make good a Grid track of 273° to Churchill. (A few months later, a squadron aircraft was nearly lost because the navigator mistakenly set the DGI to the departure runway's true direction of 167° instead of its Grid direction of 262°. As a result, after take-off, the aircraft turned more than 95° to starboard and headed west instead of south to Churchill.)

NS17522 departed Resolute Bay at 0855 hours local and arrived at Churchill five hours and ten minutes later. After a forty-five minute stop, the crew returned to Dorval following a six hour and forty-five minute flight.¹⁴

On 22 August, the squadron airlifted the No 401 "City of Westmount" Squadron Pipes and Drums from St-Hubert to Britain for a British Empire-wide pipe band competition in which they placed second. The band was flown back to Canada four days later along with 1,200 pounds of special equipment for the National Research Council in Ottawa.

On 24 August, in immediate response to a disastrous hurricane in the British West Indies, the squadron despatched an aircraft captained by Flight Lieutenant Olsen to airlift two representatives of the Canadian Red Cross and 9,000 pounds of clothing and supplies from North Bay and Toronto to Kingston, Jamaica.

On 28 August, a squadron aircraft departed base to take Air Commodore Ripley and several staff officers from Air Transport Command Headquarters on a five-day tour of northern bases. On 30 August, the Right Honourable Arthur Henderson, Britain's Secretary of State for Air, arrived at Dorval for a tour of the hangar areas, and informal discussions with squadron personnel. He was entertained later at the RCAF Station Lachine Officers' Mess.¹⁵

September

In September, the squadron was committed to fifteen flights on the Korean Airlift, with departures from McChord set for the odd-numbered days of the month. The runway at Shemya was still off limits in daylight except in emergencies. Most of the Pacific flights made their way around the route without undue delay, but four major equipment failures occurred during the month.

NS17506, captained by Flying Officer Scott, arrived at Shemya on 16 September with a blown intercooler unit on No 2 engine. As the detachment had no spares, the flight had to wait four and a half days while the parts were obtained and the aircraft was repaired. On the return trip, the daylight landing restriction delayed the departure from Haneda for another sixteen hours.

Two hours after leaving McChord in NS17509 on 21 September, Flight Lieutenant Miller had to turn back to McChord because the compass system had malfunctioned. They were then assigned NS17504, but it was delayed by an unserviceable CSU (constant speed unit) and radios. The flight finally got under way on 24 September, but the aircraft was held up again at Shemya for nearly three days, this time by an unserviceable phasing transformer.

Shortly after taking off from Dorval for McChord on 29 September in NS17514, Flying Officer Broadfoot had an engine failure; after feathering the propeller, he made a quick circuit and a smooth three-engine landing. An hour later, the crew were on their way to McChord via Winnipeg and Calgary in NS17511.

During the month of September, NS17522, NS17518, NS17508 and NS17502 all received extensive work from both the squadron maintenance crews and Canadair personnel so they would be ready for the Royal Tour.

The squadron completed a variety of domestic flights in September, including five ration runs to Goose Bay and four runs to Resolute Bay with freight, mail and passengers. A fifth flight that departed for Resolute Bay on 26 September also took part in the re-supply of the Arctic weather stations at Mould Bay, Eureka and Isachsen. On 10 September, the squadron conducted special runs from Dorval to RCAF Station Centralia to deliver eighty-two RAF trainees who had arrived by air from Britain for NATO-sponsored aircrew training.

In September, fifteen officers from various RCAF units reported to the squadron and proceeded to Japan on familiarization flights. On 16 September, Squadron Leader J.D. Dickson commanded the No 426 Squadron contingent marching in Montreal's Battle of Britain Sunday parade, and Wing Commander MacDonald returned to McChord from his inspection tour of the airlift route. On 17 September, Air Commodore Ripley departed McChord with Flying Officer Ed Wolkowski's crew in NS17509 to see the airlift operation for himself; as well as the squadron detachments at Shemya and Ebisu Camp in Tokyo, Ripley visited Canadian units in Korea.

October

The squadron's airlift commitment for October was fifteen flights to Japan, with departures scheduled for the odd-numbered days of the month; the first flight out, on 1 October, was Flight Lieutenant Stuart in NS17504. Most flights were conducted as scheduled. One had to divert to Tachikawa as weather had closed down Haneda, and two aircraft returning to base had to land at Larson AFB, 135 miles east of McChord, as McChord itself was below landing limits when they arrived.

Flight Lieutenant Bell departed McChord on 5 October with the extra task of a run to Kimpo near Seoul. Among his passengers was a senior USAF officer responsible for assessing Kimpo's potential as a base for transport operations.[16]

Apart from the engine failure at Dorval, Flying Officer Broadfoot and his crew (which included the author as navigator) had an uneventful trip from McChord to Shemya, where they arrived shortly after midnight on 4 October. NS17511 went on to Tokyo with Flying Officer Stuart's crew, and Broadfoot's crew took a two-day layover at Shemya.

The next outbound aircraft was NS17505, which arrived at 0100 hours on 6 October captained by Flight Lieutenant Bell, and Broadfoot and his crew received their weather briefing as NS17505 was being prepared for the Tokyo leg of its journey. While preparing the flight plan, the author decided to use the new single-heading pressure-pattern navigation technique for the flight from Shemya to Matsushima, as the weather systems across the North Pacific looked relatively stable. Broadfoot agreed, and the author calculated the forecast displacement (to starboard of track) and the drift over the eight-hour leg, determined a true heading to make good the track to Matsushima, and applied the average variation over the entire leg to give the pilots a single magnetic heading to steer.

NS17505 was away at 0615 hours local and climbed to its assigned altitude of 8,000 feet on the calculated single heading, entering cloud soon after departure and still in cloud at the top of the climb. There was nothing unusual about this situation and the crew settled into their usual routine; the captain got out of his seat and went back to the crew rest position. The author calculated pressure-pattern position lines every half hour and used them to establish the "most probable position" or MPP, of the aircraft. (This method indicates track-keeping well, but falls far short of providing a ground-speed check.) The Loran readings available in that remote area were not reliable enough to be useful, and two and a half hours of flying had elapsed before the aircraft passed Ocean Station Sugar, and a radio fix could be obtained. The radio fix indicated that the aircraft was on track (although still in cloud) and proceeding according to flight plan.

About an hour and a half later, the North Star began to pick up clear ice, which accumulated slowly but steadily. As the ice thickened, the airspeed began to decline and the aircraft began to lose altitude. The de-icer boots did not keep the wings clear, and the propeller blades (to which alcohol was being fed) were throwing off hunks of ice that clattered against the fuselage. Eventually the engines began to labour, and when the true airspeed was at 150 mph (the aircraft normally cruised at 230 mph) and the altimeter indicated only 500 feet, the author went to the crew rest and asked the captain to come forward. With the landing lights on, the crew could see the turbulent waters churning up whitecaps, which were definitely too close for comfort.

Knowing that the clear ice indicated warm air at some higher altitude — rain originating there in liquid form was being super-cooled on its way through colder layers — Broadfoot told the first officer and the flight engineer, "Now that you've got us into this situation, I'll show you how to get out." On his instructions, they increased power, and the aircraft gradually gained altitude as the airspeed built up. At 1,000 feet, about halfway across the North Pacific, the aircraft entered a layer of warmer air and the ice was soon peeling off with a vengeance, striking the fuselage with a noise like shrapnel.

As the ice came off, the aircraft returned to its normal cruising speed and altitude, but remained in cloud. The single heading had been maintained and the author continued to determine an MPP every half-hour using a pressure-pattern position line, and he was reasonably certain the flight was on track although he had not been able to check the ground speed since passing Ocean Station Sugar. Seven and a half hours into the flight, the radio compass picked up the Matsushima beacon, and a little later, when the captain asked for an ETA for landfall, the author responded, "Three minutes;" seconds later, NS17505 broke out of cloud and the crew could see that Matsushima and the Japanese coastline lay only about ten miles ahead. Eight hours on the same heading, and the flight plan estimate for Matsushima was off by only a minute! An hour later, the aircraft was safely on the ground at Haneda.[16]

This was not your typical single-heading flight; a unique set of circumstances led to the favourable result, and the only special skill involved was reliable dead-reckoning navigation. Navigators generally used the pressure-pattern technique for track-keeping, and single-heading flying produced mixed results — although it must be said that navigators' faith in the technique was reinforced by the occasional dramatic success.

The layover in Tokyo lasted two days, and Broadfoot's crew returned to Shemya in NS17502 at 0655 on 9 October after an eight hour and forty-five minute flight. Broadfoot skilfully battled a 65 mph crosswind to bring the aircraft down. Since NS17507 had been diverted to carry out a trip to Korea, the stay in Shemya was extended from two to nearly four days.

At this stage of the Korean Airlift, life for the outbound and inbound slip crews followed a predictable routine. Weather permitting, they walked along the cliffs and explored Shemya Island; they could sleep, read or play cards — "stook", a variant of blackjack, was popular; they could while away the hours in the Tank, as the Officers' Bar was affectionately called; or they could take in one of the nightly movies. Shemya's cuisine was not a highlight of anyone's stay.

A particular pleasure available to the denizens of Shemya was the practical joke, especially when the target was a newcomer to the squadron or someone on a familiarization trip. One of the more elaborate hoaxes dreamed up on the Airlift was the fictitious Saturday-night dance on the neighbouring island of Agattu, twenty miles away. The story was that a large fish cannery on the island had a workforce consisting mostly of Russian women, and servicemen from Shemya were, therefore, most welcome at the dance they held each week. Should anyone from Shemya be interested, they were advised to show up at the dock where they could catch a landing craft that would take them to Agattu — for a modest fee, of course.

The hoax depended on the fact that most newcomers to Shemya did not know that Agattu was uninhabited, and the instigators would make elaborate excuses as to why they could not go even as they arranged a jeep to transport the gullible to the dock. The USAF were in on the joke: on one occasion, a newly arrived American second lieutenant who had the duty as Officer of the Day was despatched to the dock to sell return tickets for the fictional landing craft. Those who had been duped usually returned tight-lipped and eager for their chance to entrap other unwary newcomers.

In 1943, during the battle for the Aleutians (which eventually coalesced at Attu), the Americans planned to build several airfields at the western end of the Aleutian chain. The reconnaissance of Shemya on 28 May 1943 found the island uninhabited, although Japanese troops had visited the island the previous November with a view to constructing an airstrip, a project they evidently abandoned. The American engineers developed a site plan for the construction on Shemya of a 3,000-foot fighter strip that could be extended to 10,000 feet to handle bombers. By 21 June 1943, the fighter strip was operational and, by mid-August, the runway had been sufficiently extended to permit B-24 Liberators to operate from Shemya. However, it wasn't until August 1944 that the runway surface was ready to be paved.

The worst hazard to aviation in the Aleutians was (and is) weather, especially fog. In England, the RAF had some success with landings in fog in February 1943 using "FIDO" (Fog Investigation Dispersal Organization), a technique for dispelling fog that involved warming the air by means of burners fed with gasoline stored under pressure and distributed by pipeline. Profiting from the British experience, the Americans installed an experimental FIDO unit on Amchitka, with which successful trials were conducted in June and July of 1944. The fog dispersal system planned for Shemya never got past the survey stage, however.[18]

Flight Lieutenant Bell landed NS17507 at Shemya at 0110 local time on 13 October; at 0455 hours, Broadfoot lifted the aircraft into the overcast and began to climb to the assigned altitude of 9,000 feet. During the climb, the "synch-box" went unserviceable, a problem as the box synchronized the revolutions of the engines and acted as the master control for the propellers, which ranged in pitch from full fine to full coarse. Since conditions at take-off had been marginal at best, Broadfoot chose to carry on to Anchorage, with the unsynchronized engines producing a discordant sound that distressed the passengers, American soldiers returning from Korea. Broadfoot sent the navigator (the author) back to the main cabin to flash a Pepsodent smile at the soldiers and assure them that the situation was under control. The flight to Anchorage took seven hours and, once arrived, the crew waited three days for the aircraft to be repaired and declared serviceable again.

At 1515 hours local time on 17 October, NS17507 departed Elmendorf for the seven-and-a-quarter-hour flight to McChord, with the main cabin occupied by several U.S. servicemen, boxes of freight bound for McChord, and four coffins containing the bodies of the crew of a USAF Dakota that flew into a box canyon in a storm and crashed. NS17507 climbed to 9,000 feet, where it entered cloud and picked up some ice in the process. When the aircraft passed Middleton Island and headed out over the Gulf of Alaska it was still in cloud, which made it impossible to take astro sights. Precipitation static affected both Loran and the reception from radio-range stations along the coast. If that weren't enough, the synch-box was malfunctioning again, and both pilots and the flight engineer were concerned about the starboard inner engine. The flight was an hour and a half past Middleton Island before a definite radio fix could be obtained, and it put the aircraft just off Sitka, some ninety miles to port of track — the speed of the westerly wind that had carried the aircraft towards the coast was calculated at 120 mph. The navigator submitted a rather generous alteration of heading to starboard to the pilots, who raised their eyebrows but asked no questions; thirty minutes later, a new fix placed the aircraft twenty miles to starboard of track, as it had passed through the low-level jet stream. Course was altered for Sandspit and the rest of the flight was almost routine. During the approach to McChord, two jet fighters on a night exercise intercepted the aircraft, positioned themselves off its wing tips and escorted it to the airport before breaking away.

The crew were treated to a four-day stay in McChord because of schedule changes, before departing for Montreal in NS17506 at 1100 hours on 21 October. After stops at Edmonton and Winnipeg, they arrived at Dorval at 0600 hours local time the following morning, having been away twenty-three days on a trip that should have taken only two weeks.[19]

During the month of October, No 426 Squadron had nineteen available flight crews, of which four were in slip positions: one at McChord, two at Shemya and one at Tokyo. The unit logged nearly 1,600 hours of flying time that month, including 1,017 hours on the Korean Airlift, 408 hours on domestic operations, and the rest on training and test flights.

Seven officers reported to the squadron and proceeded on familiarization trips to Japan during October.

On 1 October, two North Stars airlifted seventy-seven RAF trainees from Dorval to Centralia. Three weeks later, 107 more British trainees were flown to Centralia for integration into RCAF aircrew training programs. Two scheduled flights were made to Resolute Bay, the weekly ration runs to Goose Bay were carried out, and the aircraft and crew assigned to the re-supply of the northern bases returned to Dorval on 10 October. Two special runs were made to Britain, one on 1 October to Heathrow and then on to Le Bourget, near Paris, carrying jet engines for testing. The other flight picked up the dependants of No 421 Squadron personnel on 23 October and brought them home to Canada. On 30 October, personnel of No 416 Squadron were airlifted from RCAF Station Uplands, near Ottawa, to Minneapolis for training with the USAF. The return airlift was carried out two days later.

During the first week of October, the squadron hangar area at Dorval was abuzz with activity as newspaper reporters, telephone workers, wire picture services and teletype operators literally took the place over, disrupting maintenance work to install a whole range of communications equipment with which to cover the arrival of Princess Elizabeth and Prince Philip for their tour of Canada

On 8 October, a large crowd gathered at Dorval Airport, including Governor General Viscount Alexander and Prime Minister Louis St. Laurent, who greeted the royal couple when the BOAC Stratocruiser landed. On 12 October, three of the aircraft selected for the royal tour departed for Rockcliffe, Trenton and Toronto to deliver members of the royal entourage, the press and their baggage. During their visit, the Prince and Princess and their aides and assistants travelled with No 412 (VIP) Squadron.

On 14 October, a North Star from No 426 Squadron went to Winnipeg to support the royal tour, and the next day another squadron transported reporters from Windsor to Winnipeg to cover the royal visit there. On 26 October, Flying Officer Quickfall and his crew made a rather hurried trip to Saskatoon and Edmonton with Plexiglas coupé tops for convertibles to be used for the royal tour; the aircraft then returned to base via Winnipeg as a scheduled flight. Aircraft supporting the tour proceeded to Rivers, Manitoba, and Winnipeg on 28 October, and delivered reporters to Fort William and North Bay, returning to Dorval the following day. On 31 October, the royal couple proceeded to Washington, D.C., and and No 426 Squadron transported the press corps from Montreal to cover the visit to the United States, and airlifted the RCAF Central Band from Rockcliffe to Washington to play at several ceremonies.[20]

On D-Day, 6 June 1944, the soldiers of the 3rd Canadian Infantry Division, commanded by Major-General R.F.L. Keller landed on Juno Beach and advanced inland. Within the first few days, they came into contact with the 12th SS Panzer Division (Hitler Jugend) commanded by Brigadeführer Fritz Witt, a formation that included the 25th Panzer Grenadier Regiment, commanded by Standartenführer Kurt Meyer. When Witt was killed during an artillery barrage on 14 June, Meyer succeeded to his command.[21]

Within weeks of D-Day, both the British and Canadian headquarters began picking up rumours about Germans shooting unarmed Allied prisoners of war. Most of these reports originated in an area northwest of Caen that was held by the 12th SS Panzer Division, and were later corroborated by French civilians and surviving Canadian prisoners. When German-occupied territory was retaken, Canadian bodies — both buried and unburied — were found with suspicious wounds. Investigations carried out by SHAEF (Supreme Headquarters Allied Expeditionary Force) and Canadian Army authorities between 7 June and 17 June, 1944, established that at least 156 Canadian prisoners of war had been murdered by members of the 12th SS Panzer Division, and witnesses — including three Canadians who had been wounded and left for dead — were available to testify to the wrongful deaths of twenty-seven members of the North Nova Scotia Highlanders, the Fusiliers de Sherbrooke, the Royal Winnipeg Rifles and the Queen's Own Rifles of Canada.[22] The Americans captured Meyer near Liège, Belgium, on 7 September 1944, and he ended up in England in British hands. He would be the first and most senior German officer charged with war crimes against Canadians.

Major-General Chris Vokes, in command of the Canadian Occupation Forces headquartered in Bad Zwischenahn, Germany, convened a General Court Martial with Major-General H.W. Foster as President. Meyer was transferred to Canadian custody and the trial took place at the German Naval Barracks at Aurich, near Emden. The trial began on 10 December 1945, and on 28 December the accused was found guilty of war crimes and sentenced to death by firing squad; for reasons of his own, never stated, Major-General Vokes then stayed the execution and commuted the sentence to life imprisonment. Kurt Meyer was then flown to England by RCAF Dakota and incarcerated, first at the Canadian military prison in Reading and, later, at Hedley Down, near Aldershot. In late April 1946, Meyer's transfer to Canada was ordered, and he was shipped across the Atlantic in great secrecy on the Cunard liner *Aquitania*. On arrival at Halifax, he was whisked to Dorchester Penitentiary in New Brunswick.[23]

Meyer spent less than six years in Dorchester; when it became apparent that he was the only war criminal not serving his sentence in Germany, the Canadian government decided to repatriate him. There he would be imprisoned in Werl, fifteen miles east of Dortmund, with the rest of the condemned war criminals under British jurisdiction. On 17 October, therefore, No 426 Squadron was called on for an unusually secretive operation that could have had serious consequences.

An eleven-man crew comprising three pilots, two navigators, two radio operators, two flight engineers, an air traffic assistant and a steward was assembled and told they were going on a hush-hush trip, and that they would have to barrel on through to their destination without stopping for a crew rest. Flight Lieutenant Forbes Nelles, the designated Crew Commander, was the only member briefed on the purpose of the trip.[24]

Departure in NS17521 from Montreal was delayed until 18 October, as Moncton, the first stop, was fogged in. On arrival, several members of the Canadian Provost Corps came aboard. The next stop was RCAF Station Greenwood, where several Army vehicles showed up with Meyer, wearing Canadian Army battledress, and a Military Police escort. On departure from Greenwood, the North Star was routed via Goose Bay where it was refuelled, to RAF Station Lyneham, west of London, where it was refuelled again and the crew and passengers had a quick hot meal. Nelles filed a flight plan for RAF Bückeburg, thirty miles southwest of Hannover, and the flight was obliged to continue on into Germany even though the weather at destination was below limits. Evidently, Canadian authorities did not want any news of Meyer's return to Germany to leak out; they probably feared repercussions from veterans' organizations.

A weather report obtained over Holland confirmed that Bückeburg was still below limits and the flight was redirected to RAF Wünstorf, the "master aerodrome", fifteen miles northwest of Hannover, which was said to have the latest in bad weather landing aids. As they circled overhead, the crew could see the runway lights when they were looking down through the haze, but it was a different matter on the landing approach: horizontal visibility was so bad that the lights were invisible. Not wishing to commit himself too early, Nelles kept his airspeed up; unfortunately, when the runway came into view, the aircraft was still moving too fast. Tired and reluctant to try another approach, Nelles decided to land anyway, and the aircraft touched down hot about halfway down the runway. When he saw the lights streaking by, first officer Flight Lieutenant Olsen realized there couldn't be much runway left and started to meter the emergency brakes. The aircraft gave no sign of slowing down as it passed over the end of the runway, careering over bare ground, taxi strips and more bare ground before finally coming to a halt. The cockpit crew then shut down the engines and sat in complete silence for a few moments while fog swirled around the wingtips. Warrant Officer Cam Baine and Sergeant Wally Hoehn, the flight engineers, then got out and walked around the aircraft, one of them calling out, "Sir, all your tires are blown." A few minutes later, an RAF jeep emerged from the darkness and fog, and a voice called out, "Blimey! Do you chaps know where you are? About 100 yards ahead of you is a quarry 100 feet deep and 200 yards across!"

This hair-raising arrival called for some liquid therapy and the Canadians were well entertained by the RAF. Meyer was taken to the Officers' Mess and looked after by the Air Force until his escort arrived from Bückeburg. He was then driven to the military prison at Werl. Meyer would later tell the press that the RCAF had landed him in a ploughed field.

His sentence was examined by the joint British-German Reviewing Authorities and, with the concurrence of the Canadian government, reduced to fourteen years. With allowances made for good conduct, he was released in September 1954 after having been imprisoned for approximately nine years. Not much later, personnel at RCAF bases in Germany were surprised to discover that the affable liquor salesman calling on their messes was none other than the former SS General Kurt Meyer.[25]

All the aircraft needed to get going again was a new set of tires. A hurried message was sent to the Canadian Defence Liaison Staff in London, who arranged for BOAC to deliver four wheels with tires mounted to Wunsdorf the next day. (At that time, BOAC was flying the Argonaut, which was their name for the Canadair-built North Star.) Baine and Hoehn, the flight engineers, supervised the wheel changes and did their best to ascertain whether there was any structural damage to the aircraft, and on 20 October in the afternoon, Nelles and his crew set off for London, flying all the way to the Heathrow BOAC facility with the undercarriage down. Over the next four days, the undercarriage was fully tested and, having confirmed that the aircraft was airworthy, the crew returned to Dorval via Keflavik, Goose Bay and Rockcliffe on 25 October.[26]

There was some shuffling of personnel at the squadron towards the end of October and early November. Flight Lieutenant Ray Churchill was to be posted to Rivers, Manitoba and Flight Lieutenant Bert Miller drew an Air Force Headquarters assignment. Flight Lieutenant Ted Ratcliffe proceeded to RCAF Station Summerside to attend the lengthy and prestigious Specialist Navigation Course. Flying Officer Dean Broadfoot took over the RCAF detachment at Resolute Bay from Flight Lieutenant J.C. Fleming for a six-month stint at what was becoming the aviation hub of Canada's High Arctic. Flying Officer John Lindgren replaced Flying Officer Tim Timmins as Detachment Commander at Haneda, and Timmins was posted to Summerside to take the Navigation Officers' Course. He would eventually return to the squadron.

Flying Officer Warner Unruh filled the post of Detachment Commander at Shemya and Flying Officer Stuart Logan was assigned to hold the fort at McChord. The new navigators reporting to the unit were Flying Officer J.W.J.P. Camire, Flying Officer E.W. Norton and Flying Officer R.K. Wilson. Flying Officer J.J.C. Binette and Flying Officer G.F.T. Griffiths, fresh from 1R&CS Clinton, joined the Radio Officer Section. Flight Lieutenant Rolly Lloyd, Flight Lieutenant Doc Payne and Flight Lieutenant Stu Olsen went to RCAF Station Centralia for a three-day check-pilots' course with Flying Officer J.S. Middleton and Flying Officer R.A. Spratt, who were attending the Instrument Flying Course.

The main event of the month for the squadron was the royal tour. The maintenance crew selected to service the assigned North Stars were Sergeants Banks and Barlow; Corporals Baker,

Carl, Courrier, Coutts, Dupuis, Moberly, Stranks, Taylor, Tigges and Pinsonneault; and Leading Aircraftsmen Price and Guillet. Thanks to their dedication and professionalism, no major unserviceabilities occurred in any of the aircraft under their care during the visit.[27]

November

While most of the squadron's tasking was still devoted to the Korean Airlift, domestic commitments continued to grow, particularly in the Arctic. With the Canadian military build-up in Europe, transatlantic traffic was also increasing, and the squadron was developing a genuine global reach. The rising demand for their services taxed the professionalism of the flight and ground crews operating thousands of miles from home in all kinds of climatic conditions.

In November, the squadron flew a total of 1,715 hours, including 947 on the Korean Airlift (meeting the monthly quota of fifteen trips to Japan), 599 on domestic operations, and 169 hours for other purposes, mostly training. There were only two minor delays for aircraft unserviceabilities. On two occasions, departures from Elmendorf were delayed for twelve hours by bad weather at McChord; and on one occasion, bad weather at Shemya delayed one aircraft at Elmendorf for seventeen hours and a scheduled departure from Haneda for twelve hours. During the month, twelve individuals, both officers and others, made familiarization flights with the squadron.

Only one aircraft had serious mechanical problems during November. On 9 November, Flight Lieutenant Churchill brought NS17506 into Haneda in need of an engine change, a process that took five days because a spare engine had to be flown in. When it was finally ready to fly, the aircraft was diverted from Haneda for a special trip to Korea, which delayed its return another four days. To make the Korea flight, to Kimpo, Flight Lieutenant Herbert and his crew positioned at Itazuki, south of Ashiya, on 15 November, and made the run the next day; the crew returned to Japan on 18 November, landing at Iwakuni, south of Hiroshima, where they stayed overnight. Herbert then took NS17506 back to Haneda for a fast turnaround before it was taken on to Shemya by Flying Officer Scott. On arrival at Shemya, the aircraft required another engine change, which delayed its return yet again, this time by four days. Herbert finally brought it back to McChord on 23 November.

On 26 November at 0925 hours, Air Commodore Ripley and Wing Commander MacDonald witnessed the departure of NS17507 from Dorval on the squadron's 300th round trip on the Korean Airlift, with Major R.H. Ralph of Cuba City, Wisconsin, a USAF exchange officer, at the controls. The other members of the crew were first officer Flying Officer G.H. Knight of Toronto; navigator Flying Officer D.J. Connolly of Kingston, Ontario; radio officer Flying Officer F.L. Pearson of Toronto; flight engineer Corporal J.G. Thompson of Montreal; and air traffic assistant Leading Aircraftsman J.A. St. Laurent of Lévis, Quebec. The crew returned to base on 10 December.

On 27 November, a North Star flew to Toronto and returned to Dorval with three representatives of the Canadian Red Cross and a full load of relief supplies for victims of flooding in the valley of the Po River in Italy. The next day, two aircraft with augmented crews (captained by Flight Lieutenant Brown and Flight Lieutenant Stuart) departed for Rome with the Canadian medical and humanitarian aid shipment. Wing Commander G.S. Austin, the Station Commander at Lachine, accompanied Stuart's crew on this mission, and the passengers included the three Red Cross officials, an RCAF Public Relations Officer, and an RCAF cameraman. The route to Rome was via Gander, the Azores and Gibraltar.

On 29 November, Air Commodore Ripley inspected the Squadron Detachment at McChord. The following day, he flew to Nellis AFB with Flight Lieutenant Nelles' crew in NS17507 for a meeting with senior MATS officials. Later the same day he was flown to MATS Continental Division Headquarters at Kelly AFB near San Antonio, Texas. After a morning meeting on 1 December, Ripley returned to Montreal.

On 30 November, Flight Lieutenant Trotter and his crew in NS17505 had an experience that could have had tragic consequences. At 1000 hours local, they took off from McChord for Elmendorf and climbed to 10,000 feet while tracking north up Puget Sound, then turned west to Port Angeles and followed the Straits of Juan de Fuca to Neah Bay, where they set a heading for Sandspit. Their briefing had mentioned that they might encounter moderate icing conditions in cloud along the west coast of Vancouver Island and, in fact, the aircraft picked up some rime along the way. As the aircraft neared Tofino, it was in cloud when it was suddenly hit by severe clear icing like nothing the flight crew had ever experienced. Ice piled up on the nose, the propellers, the spinners, the windshield and the leading edges of the wings so rapidly that the de-icing equipment was useless. Despite efforts to increase engine power, the airspeed dropped, finally decreasing so much that the aircraft stalled and started to plunge through the cloud.

At about 6,000 feet, Trotter was able to restore level flight, but only temporarily; because of the weight of the ice and the loss of lift (result of the ice packed on the leading edge of the wings) the aircraft was soon losing airspeed and altitude again. While the aircraft was still in cloud, the author asked the captain to alter heading to port to avoid the high ground along the coast; it was only too possible that the aircraft would pile up on the rocks or hit the water. Of these alternatives, the latter, which offered the option of ditching, was the less unattractive.

When the aircraft broke cloud at 3,000 feet over the ocean and about two miles off the coast, Trotter again managed to level off, and the ice slowly began to dissipate, helped by warmer air and rain. After about forty minutes spent paralleling the coast at 3,000 feet, the captain called for climbing power and pushed the aircraft through the various cloud layers until it broke out into the clear at 14,000 feet. Having passed by Port Hardy, the crew altered their heading again for Sandspit, and the rest of the flight to Elmendorf was routine, as was the remainder of the run to Tokyo and the return to Dorval on 14 December.[28]

Domestic operations in November involved four trips to Washington in connection with the royal tour. On 2 November, the royal party arrived at Dorval from Washington in a blinding snowstorm, and a gathering was held for the squadron aircrew who had worked on the tour so they could meet Princess Elizabeth. After the introductions, Air Commodore Ripley entertained everyone at a cocktail party held in the TCA offices.

As the tour continued into the Atlantic provinces, No 426 Squadron provided support flights. The RCAF Central Band was flown from Dorval to Torbay, Newfoundland, on 7 November and back to Uplands on 13 November. On 9 November, a support flight went to Summerside and, the next day, continued on to Sydney and Torbay. On 12 November, as the tour concluded, these aircraft returned to Ottawa and Montreal with government officials and members of the press.[29]

In November, the squadron conducted five ration runs to Goose Bay, two freight runs to Frobisher Bay via Goose Bay, and three freight runs to Resolute Bay, two via Churchill and one by way of Coral Harbour. The 4 November run to Resolute Bay carried Wing Commander G.S. Austin and several senior officers from RCAF Station Lachine on an inspection and improvement tour of that installation. (Austin had been appointed Station Commander at Lachine in October, and Resolute Bay was in his area of responsibility.). On 11 November, two North Stars departed Trenton with seventy-two students from the Army Staff College on a tour of Northern bases.

On 3 November, the squadron took part in a mobility exercise that involved airlifting thirty-five personnel from No 400 (Fighter) Squadron and their equipment from Toronto to Trenton, with the reverse airlift the next day. On 4 November, two North Stars transported fifty-one Royal Canadian Navy personnel and 12,000 pounds of freight from Dartmouth to Rivers, Manitoba; the sailors and their gear were returned to Dartmouth two weeks later. Three flights were made to Britain on 9 November, 16 November and 23 November to airlift No 421 Squadron personnel with their equipment and dependants to Canada; on the outbound leg, the 23 November flight also carried personnel assigned to No 1 Fighter Wing Headquarters at North Luffenham. In another mobility exercise held on 24 November, forty personnel and 1,500 pounds of equipment from No 420 (F) Squadron in London and No 424 (F) Squadron in Mount Hope were transported to RCAF Station Uplands; the personnel and equipment were returned to their home bases the following day.[30]

On Remembrance Day, 11 November, a large squadron contingent went to Montreal for church services and to march in the city parade. On 14 November, the squadron had the privilege of entertaining Colonel Bennett, the Base Commander of McChord AFB, who was on leave in Montreal with his wife.

December

In December, No 426 Squadron put in 1,009 flying hours on *Operation HAWK* and completed sixteen flights to Tokyo. Korean Airlift crews spent an average of sixteen and a half days away from Montreal, and the average length of trip per aircraft from McChord to Haneda and back was seventy-seven hours, of which sixty-seven hours was flying time.

The squadron detachments along the route turned each aircraft around in minimum time, and there were only two delays caused by mechanical problems. On 8 December, Flight Lieutenant Michel had to return to Haneda with unserviceable hydraulics shortly after departing for Shemya in NS17505, and the aircraft was repaired and on its way again in under four hours. On 12 December, Flight Lieutenant Stuart and his crew in NS17509 were on their way from McChord to Elmendorf when they lost an engine as they passed Sandspit; they returned to McChord on three engines. Sixteen hours later, the unserviceable engine was changed and they were on their way to Tokyo.

Squadron Leader Torontow and his crew, who had arrived in Haneda on 8 December, were detailed to make a special run to Korea, and on 10 December, Torontow positioned NS17512 at Iwakuni to pick up several soldiers and the Christmas mail shipment for Canadian troops in Korea. The next day he flew to Kimpo, dropped off his passengers and mail, and an hour and forty minutes after arrival was on his way back to Haneda.[31]

As well as the detachment personnel at McChord, Shemya and Tokyo, seven flight crews would spend Christmas 1951 away from home; five of these crews would also be away for New Year's. Wing Commander MacDonald was on Flying Officer Edward's crew when they departed McChord on 19 December, and he visited all the detachments during the Christmas season. On 23 December, he arrived at Shemya, where he would spend the next two days. On Christmas Eve, after enjoying a show by Bob Hope and his troupe, the Canadians went to the Officers' Club to socialize with their American colleagues. Shortly after midnight, Flight Lieutenant Nelles came in from Elmendorf, and Wing Commander MacDonald suggested that Edwards delay his departure for Haneda for twenty hours so he and his crew could spend at least part of Christmas Day with the squadron detachment at Shemya. On a normal day, Edwards and his crew would have left at about 0400 hours, but they would have missed most of Christmas Day on crossing the International Date Line, so they departed for Tokyo at 0005 Shemya time on 26 December, arriving at destination eleven and a half hours later.[32]

At Montreal, preparations were made in early December not only for Christmas but also for the first annual inspection of Dorval and Lachine, on 17 December and 18 December respectively, by Air Commodore Ripley as Air Officer Commanding, Air Transport Command. On 11 December, the squadron despatched a re-supply run carrying mail, Christmas comforts and spare parts to the Arctic weather stations, and Flight Lieutenant Churchill and his crew carried out many of the air-drops at Arctic posts that were previously performed by American crews.

In December, the squadron logged 414 flying hours on domestic operations, including 175 training hours. Eight runs were made to Goose Bay, from which point two flights went on to Fort Chimo, two to Frobisher Bay and one to Torbay. Three trips were made to Resolute via Churchill. Other domestic flying included: two flights to carry RAF trainees from Dorval to Centralia; two runs from St-Hubert to Trenton for Air Defence Command; and two special logistics trips to Toronto. A special flight was conducted for Maritime Group from Greenwood to Keflavik, and another airlifted Fighter Wing Headquarters personnel to Britain.[33]

On 16 December, the families of squadron personnel engaged in the Korean Airlift held a "white gift" service at the Protestant Chapel at RCAF Station Lachine to collect food and Christmas presents for the children of Korea. On 19 December, No 426 Squadron held an evening smoker to entertain their colleagues on the strength of RCAF Station Lachine, and the event was a rare chance for people to mingle informally — in a unit with half its flight crews away on trips and about fifty of its ground personnel on detachment, such social occasions were important opportunities to get acquainted. On 21 December, Santa Claus arrived at the Lachine Drill Hall in a brightly decorated jeep, bringing Christmas gifts and treats for all the children of squadron and station personnel.

Christmas was celebrated in traditional Air Force style — after church, the officers and senior NCOs served the airmen their customary Christmas dinner, and then repaired to their own messes or went home to their families. On New Year's Eve, the Officers' Mess held a ball for the members, their wives and sweethearts, and guests from the naval and military community of the Montreal area. The Sergeants' Mess and Airmen's Canteen also threw parties to ring in the New Year.

On 27 December, Minister of National Defence Brooke Claxton left Rockcliffe with a group of officials in No 412 Squadron's C-5 VIP aircraft, captained by Flight Lieutenant L.W. Hussey. The Minister and his party were going to Korea (by way of Japan) to visit Canadian troops at the front, and the flight was routed to Haneda via Edmonton, Anchorage and Shemya. On reaching Tokyo, the C-5 needed an engine change, and No 426 Squadron was detailed to come to the rescue; at 0500 hours on Sunday, 30 December, the author was told by telephone that he would be picked up in two hours for a special mission to Japan. On reporting to the Squadron Operations Centre at Dorval, he learned that he would be part of an augmented crew captained by Flight Lieutenant Trotter that had been assigned to deliver the spare engine and parts to the No 412 Squadron crew marooned in Tokyo. On the drive from Lachine to Dorval, he saw that the fog was so thick that the airfield would be closed to air traffic; nevertheless, a flight plan was prepared for the first stop at Edmonton, although the crew had to cool their heels at Dorval for most of the day waiting for the fog to lift. The sense of urgency increased even more when Air Commodore Ripley himself arrived to wait with Trotter and his crew.

By late afternoon, the airfield was still below limits although the fog had lightened a little, but Trotter decided to give it a try. The crew climbed into NS17514, and Trotter started it up and taxied to the take-off point on the active runway. The forward visibility was not very good, but several runway lights were visible and Trotter received clearance to take off at his own discretion. He gunned the engines and the aircraft was airborne at 1820 hours; seconds later, it broke into the clear at 200 feet. The flight took nine hours and thirty-five minutes, arriving in Edmonton at 0155 hours local, so late that there was some delay in servicing the aircraft, and it finally got away three hours and fifteen minutes after arrival. The navigation chores on the trip were shared with Flying Officer Don Connolly, who worked the nine-hour-and-twenty-minute leg to Anchorage, where the weather was marginal on arrival so the aircraft came in on GCA at 1130 hours local, 31 December.

Servicing at Anchorage took just under three hours, and the aircraft took off for Shemya, a journey of nine hours and twenty minutes. NS17514 arrived at 2245 hours Shemya time, and the crew had all of seventy-five minutes to see the Old Year out before taking their twelve-hour rest before going on to Tokyo. Trotter took off at 1125 hours on New Year's Day, and the crossing to Tokyo took just under twelve hours, battling head-winds that averaged nearly sixty miles per hour. NS17514 finally arrived at Haneda at 1920 hours local on 2 January, much to the relief of the No 412 Squadron crew.[34]

PHOTO 97
F/O R.M. Edwards at the controls of North Star; McChord AFB, autumn 1950. (DND PL50553)

PHOTO 98
W/C J.K. MacDonald, Commanding Officer of No 426 Squadron, accepts a silk flag bearing the insignia of the US Military Air Transport Service from Colonel Wentworth W. Goss, the MATS Chief of Staff, to mark the first anniversary of the squadron's participation in Operation HAWK; Dorval, 27 July 1951. (DND PL52255)

Lachine, July–December 1951

PHOTO 99
Sgt. Jim Ward of Princess Patricia's Canadian Light Infantry, serving at the Canadian Military Mission in Japan, meets PPCLI reinforcements on their arrival in Japan aboard a North Star. From left: Cpl. Harvey Canuel (air traffic assistant, No 426 Squadron), and (descending the ramp) Private Francis Young, Private E.B. MacDonald, Private Archie Hearsey and Private Ian Baker; Haneda AFB, summer 1951. (DND PL51410)

PHOTO 100
US troops arriving at Haneda AFB by North Star; summer 1951. (DND PL51074)

PHOTO 101
Colonel Richard T. Bromiley, Commander of the 1705th Air Transport Wing, congratulates F/L J.R. Morrison and his crew on completion of the 1,000th Korean Airlift mission despatched from McChord AFB; 30 August 1951. (J.–L. Denis Collection)

PHOTO 102
During a tour of Canada and the US, Her Royal Highness Princess Elizabeth signs the guest log book aboard No 412 Squadron's C–5 transport; October 1951. (DND PL52800)

PHOTO 103
LAC Doug Wood; Itazuke AFB, November 1951. (Barbara Wood Collection)

PHOTO 104
W/C J.K. MacDonald and A/C R.C. Ripley congratulate Major John H. Ralph (pilot, USAF exchange officer) on completion of No 426 Squadron's 300th trip on the Korean Airlift; Dorval, December 1951. (LCol. J.H. Ralph Collection)

Chapter 13

Lachine
January–June 1952

During the early months of 1952, while the truce talks continued at Panmunjom, a stalemate developed along the Korean battlefront. In May, General Mark W. Clark succeeded General Matthew B. Ridgeway as Commander-in-Chief, United Nations Command.

In 1951, Lieutenant-General G.E. Stratemeyer, Commander of Far East Air Forces, had offered to rotate Commonwealth pilots through USAF units to give them combat experience. The RCAF was not then in a position to accept, but Air Marshal W.A. Curtis, the Chief of the Air Staff, instructed Air Commodore M.M. Hendrick, the Canadian Air Member in Washington, to initiate discussions with the USAF to lay the basis for a future exchange program.[1]

These talks led to a rotation plan that was implemented in 1952–1953. The terms were that RCAF pilots with at least fifty flying hours on Sabre aircraft could be selected for attachment to a USAF fighter-interceptor wing operating in Korea for a tour of duty that consisted of fifty completed combat missions or six months in theatre, whichever came first. To start the rotation, Flying Officers S.B. Fleming and G.W. Nixon were posted to Korea on 10 March.[2]

On 2 January 1952, a planning team was assembled in Paris to prepare for the establishment of RCAF Air Division Europe. The work of the planning team led to the formation of No 1 Air Division on 1 October 1952 as an operational NATO command with temporary headquarters in Paris. In April 1953, the headquarters would be moved to Metz, France.

The build-up of No 1 Air Division included the establishment of an Air Materiel Base to provide logistics support for twelve RCAF fighter squadrons. RAF Station Langar, eleven miles southeast of Nottingham (and twenty-four miles northwest of RCAF Station North Luffenham), and closed since December 1946, was selected as the site. Air Force Headquarters Organization Order 30/52, dated 15 April 1952, authorized the formation of No 30 Air Materiel Base, comprising No 30 Air Materiel Base Headquarters; No 312 Supply Unit (later No 312 Supply Depot) and No 314 Technical Services Unit, to form at Langar on 1 June 1952, and No 137 Transport Flight, to form at Dorval on 1 August 1952 and operate under RCAF Station Lachine until it proceeded overseas.

At Langar, construction was due to begin in the first week of April: existing buildings had to be reconditioned, new ones had to be built, and the runways had to be resurfaced. During the base's early stages, support services such as accommodation and administration were provided by No 1 Fighter Wing at North Luffenham.³

No 441 (Silver Fox) Squadron, formed as a fighter unit on 1 March 1951 at RCAF Station St-Hubert and commanded by Squadron Leader A.R. MacKenzie, DFC, left St-Hubert on 12 February 1952 to join No 1 Fighter Wing. While the aircraft carrier HMCS *Magnificent* transported their aircraft to Britain, the squadron's personnel travelled in the liner *Empress of France*. All other RCAF fighter units despatched to Europe would fly over, with logistics support by No 426 Squadron.⁴

An Air Force Headquarters organization order of 1 March 1952 approved the creation of No 4 (Transport) Operational Training Unit at RCAF Station Lachine, in effect formalizing the *ad hoc* training organization operated by No 426 Squadron. Reporting to the Commanding Officer of RCAF Station Lachine, No 4 (T) OTU would be responsible for conversion and continuation training of flight crews assigned to operate heavy and medium transport aircraft in Air Transport Command. The plan was for No 4 (T) OTU to become the nucleus of a larger, permanent organization at RCAF Station Namao near Edmonton, Alberta,⁵ but plans changed again in January 1954, and and No 4 (T) OTU finally settled at RCAF Station Trenton.

To meet the RCAF need — and that of the Canadian Army — for a heavy tactical transport, an evaluation was conducted of the twin-engine Fairchild C-119. Nicknamed the Flying Boxcar, the C-119 was developed from the C-82 Packet, an aircraft that saw service toward the end of the Second World War. In October 1950, the USAF delivered a C-119 to the Canadian Joint Air Training Centre at Rivers, Manitoba for extensive trials, which produced a very positive report that recommended taking the aircraft to Ottawa for demonstrations before an audience of politicians, senior military officers and senior government officials. The trials and demonstration convinced the government to place an order for thirty-five aircraft with Fairchild's Hagerstown, Maryland plant in 1952. Most of the new aircraft would go to No 435 Squadron, based at Edmonton, and No 436 Squadron, which was to form at Dorval on 1 April 1953; three would go to No 4 (T) OTU.⁶

In spring 1951, Flight Lieutenant G.W. Webb left the Thunderbirds for an exchange assignment with MATS Continental Division, based at Kelly AFB near San Antonio, Texas. Webb had been checked out as a C-97 Stratofreighter captain and had flown a wide variety of long-range transport missions. His duties included a quarterly report to Air Force Headquarters about his activities with the USAF, for which he usually received only a polite acknowledgement. In February 1952, however, while confirming the receipt of his latest report, Headquarters asked Webb for operational information on the C-119. The RCAF had basic performance data on the aircraft, but Air Force Headquarters was interested in how the C-119 performed on operations.

Letter in hand, Webb (accompanied by his Squadron Commander) went to see the Division Chief of Staff. In short order, they were ushered into the Division Commander's office for a brief discussion on the best places to get the requested information. The obvious answer was the combat zone in Korea, where the C-119 was used extensively in a variety of roles. It was decided that Webb would fly with MATS to Japan, where arrangements would be made with Tactical Air

Command for him to fly with a C-119 squadron based in Korea. Before leaving for the Far East, he was to go to Mountain Home AFB in Idaho for familiarization training on the C-119.

After a fast and furious eight-day introduction to the Boxcar, Webb found himself at Itami and then in Korea, where he flew for three weeks with a troop-carrier squadron, mostly as an observer but also a few times as co-pilot, transporting passengers, cargo, mail and medical supplies, including plasma. During his time in Korea, Webb discussed the aircraft's performance in detail with some of the most experienced C-119 pilots in the USAF.

On his return to Kelly AFB, Webb reported his findings to Air Force Headquarters, saying that American flight crews were generally quite happy with the C-119 and that it was doing a great job in Korea. He also drew attention to some of the aircraft's less attractive features, which he had learned about from personal observation and conversations with pilots.

The C-119 was equipped with Hamilton Standard propellers, which were hollow. To add strength without adding much weight, the cavity was filled with a material that was supposed to adhere to the inside wall. Every once in a while, however, some of the filling material would come loose, and centrifugal force would push it into a blade tip, turning the blade into something more like a baseball bat than the nicely aerodynamic airfoil required for smooth operation. Almost immediately after a shift of filling material, the propeller would start a vibration that could — and sometimes did — cause the engine to break away from its mount, which usually meant the loss of the aircraft. These propellers could also develop cracks, which were not nearly as serious as loose filling material because the progress of a crack was fairly predictable, so the propellers could be changed before the situation got critical.

The C-119 had two generators, one on each engine, that provided ample electrical power but with one crucial weakness. If an engine failed in circumstances that called for high amperage, such as icing conditions, the electrical load would be transferred immediately to the remaining generator, and the added load could cause the generator shaft to shear. The only electrical source left would be the battery, which, if fully charged, could deliver reduced amperage for a period of thirty minutes. This power was directed to the critical flight instruments, which were all electrically driven. There was no air-driven backup for the battery.

Webb detailed some twelve other factors that a prospective purchaser of the C-119 would have to consider seriously. He heard no more about the matter from Air Force Headquarters.[7]

The squadron met its January commitment of fifteen round trips to Tokyo in a total of 976 flying hours, with nine major delays of ten to seventeen hours: three for mechanical problems and six for weather-related reasons.

On 2 January, when Flight Lieutenant Trotter and his crew arrived at Haneda in NS17514 with an engine to replace the unserviceable one on the C-5, the No 426 Squadron personnel of the Tokyo detachment worked with the No 412 Squadron crew to complete the engine change as quickly as possible, and Trotter and his crew were slotted into the slip system for their return to Montreal via McChord.

On 7 January, after a visit with the Tokyo detachment, Mr. Claxton and the C-5 departed at 2000 hours for Canada by way of Wake Island, Honolulu and San Francisco, arriving at Rockcliffe at 1005 hours on 10 January.

On 4 January, Flight Lieutenant Morrison brought NS17515 into Haneda from Shemya late in the afternoon, but the return flight was delayed for twelve hours as Shemya and Adak were forecast to be below limits. The next morning, after the Detachment Commander had established that the weather at Shemya had improved, Trotter and his crew were alerted for the return trip. At the weather briefing, they were told that the forecasters were predicting 150-mph winds at 20,000 feet in a strong westerly flow that stretched across the North Pacific from Japan to Alaska. This was to be a freight run, so Trotter decided to try for a record crossing to Shemya at 20,000 feet. Based on the forecast, the author (whose turn it was to navigate) calculated that the flight to Shemya should take only six and a half hours, some three hours less than the average for the crossing.

Trotter lifted NS17515 off from Haneda at 0930 local and climbed to 20,000 feet with the crew on oxygen. To put the flight in a better position to catch the jet stream, it was routed north to Misawa before heading was set for Shemya, and the flight path took the aircraft close to the Kurile Islands. The winds were strengthening, although they were more southerly than westerly, and as the flight passed Nemuro, on the eastern tip of Hokkaido, the USAF radar facility there signalled "See you in the Red", a warning that the North Star was heading into Soviet airspace. A course correction was made, the aircraft entered the jet stream, and before long the flight had a 135-mph tail wind and a ground speed of 385 mph.

By the time NS17515 passed Ocean Station Sugar, the crew had decided they could bypass Shemya and make it safely to Anchorage, but when they informed Shemya, they received strong objections, particularly from the inbound slip crew who wanted to go home. Trotter decided to abandon the overflight notion and began to descend to 9,000 feet, the aircraft rapidly losing its strong tail wind on the way. Arriving over Shemya seven and a half hours after departing Tokyo, the crew were advised on the approach that the winds on the ground were over 100 mph, although — fortunately — only about ten degrees off the runway heading. After a bumpy ride around the circuit, Trotter brought the aircraft in on GCA, and as he chopped power and landed, one engine cut out and the propeller had to be feathered. With the wind howling over the aircraft, he decided to taxi into one of the large hangars, which was not exactly standard operating procedure, as it meant a lot of manoeuvring and considerable use of brakes. (When the crew got out of the aircraft, they could smell the hot rubber of the tires, and found the wheel rims too hot to touch.) While the North Star manoeuvred into the hangar, the captain of a USAF C-54 — who had been parked in the dispersal area for more than six hours, pointed into the wind with his engines running — finally decided to move his aircraft into a hangar.

The drive to the crew quarters was almost as exciting; with six people and their luggage packed into a covered jeep, it was all the driver could do to hold the vehicle on the road in the high wind.

NS17515 needed an engine change, which took eight and a half days as a spare engine had to be brought out from McChord. Flying Officer Wolkowski and the inbound slip crew, who had spent Christmas and New Year's away from home, were finally able to leave for McChord and Montreal on 7 January. After four days at Shemya, Trotter and his crew left on 9 January, arriving back at Dorval shortly after midnight on 12 January.[8]

On 18 January, Flight Lieutenant Allen and his crew in NS17512 made it to Elmendorf, where the aircraft was delayed by several maintenance problems that took nearly two and a half

days to rectify. On 21 January, shortly after the aircraft departed for McChord, an oil-pressure failure occurred in the starboard outer engine, and Allen had to return to Elmendorf, where the problem was quickly corrected and the flight was away again in seventy minutes. Flight Lietenant Edwards arrived at Shemya on 20 January with an unserviceable nose wheel, and the aircraft was delayed for four days before parts arrived and the detachment personnel could make the necessary repairs.

In January, No 426 Squadron logged 428 flying hours for domestic operations, of which nearly 100 hours also included a training component. Another 153 flying hours were logged as training time. Domestic operations included eleven trips to Goose Bay on ration runs and backlog specials, of which one went on to Frobisher Bay and another went on to Fort Chimo, and four freight runs to Resolute Bay with stopovers at Churchill. One Resolute Bay run involved a para-drop at Arctic Bay. A special trip was made to Toronto to pick up an Orenda engine and spare parts and take them to Churchill for cold-weather trials. On 6 January, a North Star was assigned to take National Defence College staff and students on a tour of the United States and Canada that included stops at Trenton, Ontario; Washington; Detroit; Rivers, Manitoba; Vancouver, Patricia Bay and Burwash Landing in British Columbia; Yellowknife, Northwest Territories; Churchill, Manitoba; and Bagotville, Quebec.

The freight run to Frobisher Bay was made on 17 January in NS17507 with Flight Lieutenant Trotter as captain. Leaving Dorval at 0650 local, the aircraft covered the leg to Goose Bay in four hours and fifty-five minutes. After a brief stopover to refuel, file a new flight plan, and change some of the cargo, the aircraft was on its way to Frobisher Bay, arriving four hours and thirty-five minutes later to face a temperature of -50°F. While the cargo was being unloaded and the aircraft refuelled, the captain and the author went to the Operations Building to file a flight plan for Dorval. The teletype circuits were out and the best meteorological information available for the return to base was more than eighteen hours old. There was nothing for it but to use the data available and hope for the best. A flight plan was prepared, and eighty-five minutes after arrival NS17507 was off on the 1,276-mile leg to Montreal.

The weather was clear as the aircraft climbed to 9,000 feet over Baffin Island and crossed Hudson Strait. The author got a fix as the flight paralleled the western coastline of Ungava Bay but, by the time it had passed Fort Chimo, the aircraft was in cloud. Apart from astro, fixing aids over northern Quebec were few and far between. Four hours into the flight, the last two using DR navigation, the decision was made to climb above cloud to get an astro fix. The aircraft broke clear at 18,000 feet and the author had time to take a moon shot and calculate a most-probable position.

One of the engines was malfunctioning, and Trotter thought it best to get back down to 9,000 feet. The weather report for Montreal obtained by the Radio Officer was far from encouraging: a storm was passing through the area with freezing rain and low ceilings. For the next three hours, the flight proceeded in a southerly direction, maintaining a DR plot. Finally, the crew was able to pick up the Montreal radio range on the radio compass, and they homed on in on the beacon. Trotter made three instrument approaches before landing. The runway was a sheet of ice made slick by rain and, as the aircraft landed and started to slow down, a crosswind caught it and inexorably pushed it off the runway until the nose-wheel embedded itself in a snow bank. As the crew came down the emergency ladder, Trotter gave way to frustration and kicked the nose-wheel. He had to be helped into the crew bus.

Thus ended a twenty-four-hour day. What should have been a six-hour flight from Frobisher Bay had taken eight hours.

On 5 January, Group Captain Leigh departed for Britain to inspect the DeHavilland Comet with Wing Commander Lewis and Squadron Leader Anderson of Air Transport Command Headquarters. Several No 426 Squadron personnel were candidates for the proposed RCAF Comet flight. On 13 January, the squadron transported a contingent of NATO trainees from Dorval to RCAF Station Centralia. Between 18 January and 22 January, the squadron completed one trans-Atlantic flight to Britain, and, from 19 January to 23 January, they were kept busy shuttling Air Cadets between Dorval and Rockcliffe for a program of inter-city exchange visits.

On 24 January, the squadron welcomed Sir Anthony Eden, Britain's Minister of Foreign Affairs, as he passed through Dorval on his way home. Eden had been in Ottawa since 13 January for talks with Lester Pearson, Secretary of State for External Affairs, and other Canadian officials.

On 27 January, a squadron aircraft left Rockcliffe carrying thirty military attachés from embassies in Ottawa on a tour that took them to Churchill, Whitehorse, Vancouver and Rivers, Manitoba.[9]

February

In February, No 426 Squadron logged 1,613 flying hours, including 982 hours on the Korean Airlift, 481 on domestic operations, and 150 on training and aircraft testing. Sixteen crews were available that month, including four in slip positions and two on leave. The month's commitment of fifteen flights to Tokyo was fulfilled, with an average trip per aircraft of eighty-eight hours, including sixty-five flying hours.

There were three major delays during the month. On 1 February, Flight Lieutenant Trotter brought NS17505 back to McChord after an engine failure some forty minutes after departing for Elmendorf; the engine was repaired within twenty-four hours and, after an air test, the flight resumed its schedule. Having left McChord on 17 February, NS17511 was stuck in Shemya for six days, while inbound, with unserviceable nose-wheel doors. The Shemya detachment made the necessary repairs when spare parts were flown in, and Squadron Leader Kightley and his crew took the aircraft on to McChord on 26 February. On 23 February, NS17503 was found to have a fuel leak during a stopover at Elmendorf, where the flight was delayed for sixty-seven hours before the problem was rectified and Flying Officer Quickfall and his crew could continue on to Shemya. Finally, bad weather at Shemya caused two delays, one of fourteen hours and the other of eighteen hours.[10]

During the month, the squadron conducted six ration runs to Goose Bay from Dorval, and four trips to Goose Bay from Moncton, New Brunswick, in support of *Exercise SUN DOG III*, which involved dropping a company of paratroopers from Dakota aircraft at Fort Chimo, 454 air miles from Goose Bay. When the exercise was completed, the North Stars made seven trips to Fort Chimo to bring the soldiers and their equipment home.[11]

Two trips were made to Resolute Bay during the month. The first, on 6 February, included stops at Churchill and Coral Harbour. On the first trip, the crew were enlisted by Flight Lieutenant Broadfoot, the Detachment Commander, to help raise a 100-foot trylon mast, which had more guy wires than Broadfoot had people to handle them. The mast was the antenna of Resolute's new high-powered medium-frequency (530 kilocycles) radio beacon, which extended the extreme range at which aural or null bearings could be taken to 800 miles, and the range at which automatic radio bearings were obtainable to 450 miles. The second trip, on 19 February, was conducted to deliver a Department of Transport official to be the new Officer in Charge of the Joint Arctic Weather Station at Resolute, and to bring out the body of his predecessor, who had committed suicide.

The death of King George VI at Sandringham on 6 February affected all RCAF units: all officers had to wear mourning bands and swear an oath of allegiance to the new Sovereign. On 13 February, No 426 Squadron airlifted the band of HMCS *Cornwallis*, the Royal Canadian Navy recruit training depot near Digby, Nova Scotia, from RCAF Station Greenwood to Rockcliffe so it could march in the memorial parade conducted in Ottawa on 15 February, the day of the King's funeral. Similar parades were held in cities and towns across Canada.[12]

On 16 February, a special run was despatched to airlift the *Cornwallis* band back to Greenwood, and then continue on to Washington, D.C., and Johnsville Naval Air Station near Philadelphia to pick up 7,400 pounds of naval equipment. After Johnsville, the aircraft's next stop was Mitchel AFB near New York, where the crew spent the night before flying to Halifax on 18 February to deliver most of the equipment. From Halifax, the flight proceeded to RCAF Station Rockcliffe to drop off the remainder of its load, and then returned to Dorval.

Two aircraft were despatched to RCAF Station Greenwood on 20 February to airlift 125 personnel from the maritime patrol units No 404 Squadron and No 405 Squadron, with their equipment, to Key West, Florida, for *Operation CONVEX*, a month-long exercise with the RCN and the US Navy. A third aircraft, NS17507, captained by Flight Lieutenant Morrison, completed a supply run to Goose Bay and flew to Halifax before positioning at Greenwood.

Late in the afternoon of 22 February, Morrison and his crew left for the eight-hour and forty-minute flight to Key West carrying No 405 Squadron personnel. Having left below-zero temperatures in Nova Scotia, the crew spent nearly three hours in the sweltering heat of Key West before making the seven-hour forty-five minute trip back to Greenwood. After dropping off personnel and cargo the flight returned to base.[13]

On 15 February, Group Captain Z.L. Leigh, the Chief Staff Officer at Air Transport Command Headquarters, departed Dorval for a tour of the Korean Airlift route with Flight Lieutenant Edwards' crew, which included, as First Officer, Wing Commander G.S. Austin, the Station Commander from Lachine. On 21 February, Wing Commander MacDonald went to Waterloo, Ontario, to speak to No 404 Wing RCAF Association on the Korean Airlift. At the end of the month, Air Commodore Ripley departed Dorval for an inspection tour of Air Transport Command units at Resolute Bay, Frobisher Bay and Goose Bay.

The squadron was tasked with three other special flights in February, and a flight to Britain. On 11 February, personnel from No 413 (F) Squadron and their luggage and equipment were airlifted from Bagotville to Ottawa, with a reverse airlift three days later. Forty-four cadets from the Royal Military College in Kingston were flown from Trenton on a tour that took them to Winnipeg and Patricia Bay near Victoria; they were returned to Trenton on 24 February. On that date, two North Stars departed Trenton with eighty-eight directing staff and students from the Army Staff College in Kingston for an eight-day tour of military and other installations in northwest Canada.

March

In March, the squadron had eighteen line crews, available with four in slip positions and two on leave. Fifteen trips were completed to Tokyo during the month. On average, each trip on the Airlift took crews away from Dorval for seventeen days, and aircraft away from McChord for eighty-six and a half hours, including sixty-four flying hours. Weather at Shemya delayed five flights for periods ranging from thirteen to twenty-nine hours. Two aircraft required engine changes.

On the morning of 2 March, Flying Officer Kuhn and his crew left McChord in NS17503 and arrived at Elmendorf with an unserviceable engine. It took nearly three days to replace the engine, and the crew made it to Shemya at 1945 hours local on 5 March. The aircraft was then turned over to Flight Lieutenant Buchan's crew, who had spent the previous five days on the island. Three hours later, NS17503 was in the air and on its way to Tokyo.

At 8,000 feet, the aircraft was levelled off and the crew settled down to their tasks. Buchan got out of the left-hand seat, turned the flying over to Flying Officer Bob Husch, who was making his first trip on the Pacific run, and went to the crew rest position. The cockpit lights were dimmed; it was a clear night. The author was in the astrodome shooting a three-star fix when suddenly all four engines quit — the flight engineer had fallen asleep while transferring fuel from the auxiliaries, but unfortunately the engines were also running off the auxiliaries, which were now empty. After a flurry of activity, the proper tanks were quickly selected and, after some backfiring, all four engines were running perfectly, as if nothing had happened.

A few remarks were directed to the embarrassed engineer and, with the skipper back in the left-hand seat, the situation was rapidly assessed. Some 400 gallons of fuel — most of the reserve — had gone out the overflow, which meant a loss of two hours of endurance. The aircraft was about halfway to the coast of Japan and, as long as the winds stayed as forecast, there would be no problem making landfall. Fortunately, the winds did hold and, when the aircraft reached Matsushima, it was determined that the flight could continue on to Tokyo safely. Ten hours and five minutes after leaving Shemya, NS17503 was safely on the ground.[14]

On the morning of 4 March, NS17512, with a crew captained by Flying Officer Don Harrison, departed McChord for Elmendorf, a flight of seven hours and fifty-five minutes. They stopped for two hours and then took off for Shemya, where they found the field socked in. Harrison made the usual attempt at a GCA landing, then overshot and headed for Cold Bay, the nearest alternate, where they landed after being airborne for twelve hours and five minutes and on duty for more than twenty-four hours. After a ten-hour rest, Harrison and his crew set off again for Shemya, where they landed nearly five hours later.

Shortly after Flight Lieutenant Morrison's crew arrived at Shemya with NS17506, early in the morning of 11 March, it was determined that the aircraft needed an engine change. This meant bringing a spare engine from McChord, so the repair took three and a half days. On 15 March, after an air test, Morrison and his crew resumed their trip to Tokyo. On the morning of 17 March, they were back in Shemya flying NS17517, and when Flight Lieutenant Stuart's crew brought in NS17504 in the early hours of 18 March, Morrison and his crew prepared to head back to McChord.

At the weather briefing, the briefing officer asked why they were headed for Anchorage if their final destination was McChord, and they replied that the 2,810-mile distance from Shemya to McChord was beyond the safe range of the North Star. The briefing officer assured them they really did not need to go via Anchorage as they could count on a stiff tail-wind. The navigator, Flight Lieutenant Bob Burn, calculated that the flight time to McChord would be ten and a half hours and, with a 10-percent en-route fuel reserve, forty-five minutes for holding at McChord, and the time required to reach an alternate, by-passing Anchorage looked feasible.

Morrison and his crew departed Shemya at 0605 hours local, climbed to 9,000 feet, and headed east towards McChord. By the time the flight had passed Adak and cleared the Aleutian Islands, there were indications that the forecast tail-wind was not materializing. About six hours into the flight, Burns, who had been fixing the aircraft's position using astro and pressure pattern, determined that the aircraft was actually bucking headwinds in the order of 75 mph. To conserve fuel and extend range, Morrison had initially elected to go on cruise control by reducing power, which dropped the true air-speed from 235 to 200 mph. After some discussion, it was agreed to take the opposite tack. Power was increased, bringing up the air-speed to reduce the time spent in a headwind. The penalty, of course, was increased fuel consumption, which would be offset by a faster transit through the area with unfavourable winds. By the time the flight had passed Ocean Station Papa, the winds were mainly on the beam.

Meanwhile, Radio Officer Sullivan was getting reports that most of the airfields along the west coast were down. Fortunately, McChord stayed open. Shortly after Morrison touched down, after thirteen hours in flight, two engines quit, and the aircraft had to be towed off the runway to the dispersal area.

A MATS check pilot had made the trip with them, and he ordered the crew to stay in the aircraft at first. Later, the check pilot asked them to wait in a security area while he discussed the flight with the Base Operations staff and, after a while, the crew were allowed to go to their quarters. Nothing more was heard of the matter — although, when the tanks of NS17504 were dipped, the servicing crew found less than forty gallons of fuel remaining.[15]

During March, the broadcaster and women's issues advocate Kate Aitken flew to Japan with the squadron at the request of the Canadian government. When she arrived at McChord on 28 March to board NS17509 with Flying Officer Harvey Knight's crew, a delegation of Tacoma women was there to see her off and present her with an armload of flowers. She was very gracious and friendly to the flight crews and detachment personnel, giving each detachment commander a bottle of Scotch. She also wrote to the families of all the men of the Shemya detachment, enclosing with each letter a copy of a photograph of the group taken during the seventeen hours she had to wait for the weather to clear so she could continue her trip to Tokyo with Flying Officer Harrison's crew. The author was with an inbound crew that happened to be at Shemya when Knight brought NS17509 in with Miss Aitken aboard.[16]

During the month of March, No 426 Squadron logged 1,509 flying hours, including 959 hours on the Airlift and 520 hours on domestic operations, of which 160 hours was also training time. Most of the remaining thirty hours were spent on aircraft testing. Goose Bay was a popular destination; ten (mostly freight) runs went to that station during the month. The first of these trips delivered the RCAF Station Lachine hockey team and a troupe of entertainers from Montreal to provide the station personnel and their families with an evening's distraction from the harsh Goose Bay winter.

Four freight trips were made to Resolute Bay in March, and two aircraft were assigned to take the National Defence College students and directing staff on a tour of northern locations. Two runs were despatched to Britain with spare parts for the Sabres based at North Luffenham. Two more North Stars went to Key West, Florida, to bring the personnel and equipment of No 404 Squadron and No 405 Squadron back to Greenwood on completion of *Operation CONVEX*. One flight went to No 6 Repair Depot at RCAF Station Trenton to pick up Dakota spares and transport them to RCAF Station Summerside in Prince Edward Island, and an aircraft was sent to Malton Airport near Toronto to pick up Orenda jet engines and eight personnel and take them to Churchill, Manitoba, where the engines were to undergo cold-weather trials. Finally, a special flight went to Washington and Mitchel Field, New York, to transport naval cipher equipment to Halifax and Rockcliffe.

April

April was another busy month for the squadron, which logged a total of 1,678 flying hours, including 969 on the Korean Airlift, 640 on domestic operations (of which about 100 hours was also training time), and sixty-nine hours mostly on training and testing. By the end of the month, the squadron had racked up a total of 23,505 flying hours on the Airlift. The unit completed its April quota of fifteen flights to Japan, with crews being absent from their Dorval base for an average of fifteen days, and the aircraft taking sixty-eight hours, on average, to return to McChord. During the month, the squadron had sixteen flight crews available, with four in slip positions and two on leave.

On the maintenance front, the squadron had a relatively trouble-free month on the Tokyo run with comparatively few delays for weather.

On 2 April, Flight Lieutenant Buchan and his crew departed McChord in NS17503, refuelled at Anchorage and headed for Shemya, which was socked in, so they attempted a GCA landing and then diverted to Adak, where they took a twelve-hour rest, having been on duty for nearly twenty-four hours, more than seventeen of them in the air. On 12 April, Flying Officer Strathy was seventy-five minutes outbound with NS17515 when he had to turn back to McChord with an unserviceable radio; within eighty minutes, the problem was fixed and the flight could leave again for Anchorage.

On 23 April, Wing Commander MacDonald and his crew left McChord for Japan with Wing Commander D.G.M. Nelson, the Senior Medical Officer of Air Transport Command, aboard. On their return to McChord, they conducted a shuttle run to Travis AFB.

Flying Officer Wolkowski and his crew, having left Dorval on 20 April, arrived at Haneda shortly after dawn on 26 April. As the aircraft approached the airport from the northeast, the early morning mists over Tokyo Bay were beginning to dissipate, revealing the oyster beds below. Some sixty miles to the west, Mount Fuji could be seen jutting through clouds tinged red by the rising sun. After landing, the crew met with the Detachment Commander and discussed the serviceability of NS17509 with the maintenance team. Airfield business complete, the officers were taken through the bustling streets of Tokyo to the Marunouchi Hotel in the heart of the city, a drive of about thirty minutes in a car recently acquired through the efforts of Flying Officer Timmins during his tenure as Detachment Commander. Corporal Thompson, the engineer, and Corporal Letourneau the air traffic assistant, were quartered at Ebisu Camp.

After checking into the hotel, which was managed by the Australian and British occupation forces, crew members cleaned up and repaired to the dining room for a leisurely breakfast, usually bangers and eggs. Meals and room cost $3.50 per diem, and a shop in the hotel basement provided a haircut and a very invigorating neck and scalp massage for fifteen cents. Afternoon tea was served in the dining room to the accompaniment of a Japanese string trio.

One of the squadron's more colourful captains, Flight Lieutenant Forbes Nelles, would look at the menu in the guests' dining room — which offered a choice of appetizers, about six entrées and several desserts — and solemnly declare that there was nothing on it that he didn't like. This caused a great deal of consternation among the Japanese waitresses as Nelles was quite serious about working his way through the entire bill of fare. When he felt the need of a little gastronomic diversion, Nelles would dine in the hotel's restaurant, which featured a Chateaubriand for four people. He had no trouble polishing it off by himself.

A day at the Marunouchi began with a discreet knock on the door, followed by two kimono-clad young women who would enter, place a steaming cup of tea and a couple of sweet biscuits on the night table, and quietly withdraw. This generally tided you over until you were ready to venture to the dining room for breakfast. Next, you would go shopping. A short walk from the hotel was the Ginza, the famous commercial street where vendors by the hundreds hawked a dazzling array of merchandise from shops, stalls and kiosks. The exchange rate was very favourable — 360 yen to one dollar Canadian or American.

Shopping forays on the Ginza and its side streets allowed many a squadron member to acquire a variety of wonderful items ranging from the ordinary to the exotic: fishing equipment, cameras and binoculars, silks, brocades and jewellery — especially pearls, for which a stop at world-famous Mikimoto's was a must. Specialty shops carried beautiful porcelain tea sets that wended their way to Canada to grace many Thunderbird homes. For the children, particularly at Christmas, there was an endless variety of toys to choose from. The Ginza also offered several large department stores and, a short distance away, the American Post Exchange (PX), which was with stocked with goods from the United States, and a cafeteria where you could lunch on North American delicacies such as hamburgers, hot dogs and Coke.

Japan is prone to earthquakes and the Tokyo area is no exception. One crew, just after their morning tea and cookies, felt the Marunouchi begin to shake. As it continued to rattle, the crew decided that they had better get out of the hotel; deciding to avoid the elevator, they hurtled en masse down the stairs and rushed outside to stand near the building waiting for the tremors to subside. In a few minutes, an Australian came out and suggested they would be safer inside, as parts of the building could easily become dislodged and fall into the street, posing a threat to life and limb. Taking his advice, the crew went back inside and discovered that the bar had suddenly opened, which gave them the equanimity they needed to wait for the end of the aftershocks. By the way, the hotel's drink prices were quite reasonable. A rum and Coke cost ten cents.

Many squadron members staging through Tokyo early in the Airlift made it a point to observe the arrival each morning of General MacArthur at his downtown headquarters in the Diaichi Building, a short walk from the Marunouchi, opposite the moat around the Imperial Palace of Emperor Hirohito. Hundreds of Japanese citizens would gather in advance of MacArthur's arrival and bow as he passed by in his car. It was an impressive sight.

Large areas of Tokyo had been devastated during the Second World War by American firebomb raids. Many of these mainly suburban areas had not been rebuilt, and the ruins were easily seen by anyone flying over or driving through the city. At this time, Japan was entering a period of intensive reconstruction, stimulated in part by the Korean War, and building sites dotted the urban landscape of Tokyo.

Getting around the city and its environs presented some interesting challenges. For short distances, you generally took a bicycle rickshaw, called a pedi-cab. Japanese taxis were in a class of their own, cars of late 1930s vintage with a coal-burner installed in the boot because of the gasoline shortage. Trucks were similarly equipped.

On the infrequent occasions when flights were delayed in Tokyo, crews had time to take short train trips to points of interest outside the city.[17]

Just before noon on 28 April, NS17511 captained by Flying Officer Wolkowski left Haneda for the nine-hour and ten-minute flight to Shemya. It was a routine flight for the most part, although the weather reports were far from encouraging: seven flights ahead of NS17511 had diverted to Adak, as Shemya was below landing limits. Through one of the vagaries of

Aleutian weather, the skies suddenly opened up over Shemya as the flight approached, and the whole desolate island could be seen. This condition lasted all of thirty minutes before cloud and fog closed in again; by then, luckily, NS17511 was safely on the ground. The crew (which included the author) were back at Dorval shortly after midnight on 2 May, having been away from base for fifteen days and having flown seventy-three hours.[18]

Most of the squadron's domestic operations in April centred on the spring re-supply of the Arctic weather stations, for which seven aircraft were used. Weather conditions and other high Arctic problems caused a five-day delay in the re-supply operation, which was scheduled to be complete by 21 April. Six trips, totalling 60,000 pounds of freight, were made to Resolute Bay from Dorval with stopovers at Churchill; eleven more runs conducted from Churchill airlifted an additional 71,000 pounds of cargo to Resolute Bay. From 7 April to 26 April, eighteen shuttles delivered 180,000 pounds of freight from Resolute Bay to Isachsen, a distance of 307 miles. During the same period, a similar number of shuttles airlifted an equal amount of cargo to Mould Bay, located 430 miles from Resolute Bay.

The author had returned from a trip to Tokyo, captained by Flying Officer Wolkowski, shortly before midnight on 4 April. A week later, on Good Friday, he learned that the next assignment was to Resolute Bay via Churchill in NS17504, again skippered by Wolkowski. The aircraft had just come off a maintenance cycle and was being ferried with its full load of cargo to replace another that was due for inspection back at base. After an overnight stop, the flight left Churchill at 0600 hours local time and arrived at Resolute Bay shortly before noon.

On 13 April, Easter Sunday, the crew made the one-hour forty-five minute shuttle run in NS17502 to Isachsen. After landing on the washboard-like ice strip, which had been cleared of snow by the weather station personnel, Wolkowski taxied the aircraft to the unloading point. The engines were left idling, as the ground temperature was -35°F with a 30-mph wind and, if the engines failed to start again, the crew would face an extended visit to this remote Arctic spot. The main cargo doors were swung open and the crew quickly dropped five tons of coal, packaged in 100-pound sacks, on the ground and shut the doors. After only twenty minutes at Isachsen, the aircraft was on its way back to Resolute Bay. The next day, the same aircraft was used to conduct another shuttle run to Isachsen, this time with a load of machinery and equipment.

On 15 April, NS17514 was brought out of Resolute Bay, departing at 0145 hours local time. The weather forecast was considerably off the mark. The flight, conducted at 7,000 feet, encountered both a high layer of cloud that obscured the sky, and a lower cloud deck that stretched almost to Churchill. The navigator had to rely on DR techniques as there were no fixing aids except the radio back-bearings taken on Resolute Bay early in the trip, and bearings on Churchill Radio as the flight neared its destination. Heading checks were not available for five hours of the five-hour-and-forty-five-minute flight. This meant the navigator had to rely on the "gyro log", in which the precession rates for the directional gyro had been recorded during previous flights. These precession rates were used to adjust the grid heading to keep the flight on track for Churchill, a procedure not particularly conducive to reducing the navigator's anxiety, given the state of gyro art at the time.

When it was finally possible to fix the aircraft's position, it was found to be, fortunately, not too far off track, and the flight arrived at 0730 local time. There was a twenty-five minute stop to fuel up and file a flight plan before departing for base, a five-hour and twenty-minute run. The final leg was routine, with arrival at 1420 local time. Five days later, as indicated earlier, the author was on his way to Tokyo with a crew under the same captain, Flying Officer Wolkowski.[19]

The squadron's other domestic chores in April included: seven freight runs to Goose Bay; picking up a Lancaster engine and equipment used in *Operation CONVEX* from Bermuda for delivery to Greenwood; airlifting fifty RCAF Staff College directing staff and students to Dartmouth for their Maritime tour and returning them to Toronto; taking a load of drop tanks for Sabre aircraft from St-Hubert to Bagotville; taking the Royal Canadian Legion Variety Show's cast of thirty-six entertainers and their 500 pounds of equipment to Greenwood for an evening performance and bringing them back to Dorval; and picking up thirty-five technicians with their equipment at Bagotville to accompany the national display of Sabre jets to Summerside, Halifax, Moncton, St-Hubert, Malton and North Bay before taking them home to Bagotville.

On the morning of 18 April, RCAF Station Lachine provided a Guard of Honour for Lord Trenchard, Marshal of the RAF, who was flying in to Dorval with Lady Trenchard. The next day, the guard was called out again for Air Chief Marshal Lloyd, Commander-in-Chief of RAF Bomber Command. On 20 April, the guard was on parade for the departure of Lord Trenchard, and on 22 April, the guard was again drawn up at Dorval for the arrival of Major-General Myers, Commander of USAF North-East Air Command, which was headquartered at St. John's, Newfoundland. On all these occasions, the Guard Commander was Flight Lieutenant Art James.

In April, the Medical Inspection Room (MIR), was relocated from the squadron's hangar at Dorval to a newly renovated building at the Lachine site. The building now housed a fifteen-bed hospital complete with pharmacy, an MIR, physiotherapy facilities, a diet kitchen and an operating room. Squadron Leader Beach, the Senior Medical Officer who was the medical representative on the re-supply operation out of Resolute Bay, would be severing his links with the squadron; he was being transferred to Winnipeg to take up the post of Staff Officer Medical Services at No 14 (Training) Group Headquarters. New additions to the station's hospital staff were a nursing sister, Flying Officer C.M. Trepanier, and medical assistants Aircraftsman 1st Class H.F. Adams and Aircraftsman 1st Class H.C. Erickson.[20]

On 18 March, the Minister of National Defence had circulated a memorandum to the Cabinet Defence Committee regarding the involvement of Canadian Pacific Airlines in the Korean Airlift. CPA was under contract to the Canadian government until 31 March 1952, to fly three and a half round trips a week between Vancouver and Tokyo, and MATS allocated this capacity as required to meet the needs of the United Nation's effort in Korea. At its 84th meeting, the Cabinet Defence Committee considered the question of whether to renew or terminate this

contract. Following a thorough airing of the subject, the Committee agreed to renew the contract for three months. CPA was to be informed that withdrawal of government support after that period was under consideration and possible arrangements for the period after 30 June were to be explored with the company.[21]

On 16 April, at a meeting in Washington, D.C., Air Commodore W.E. Bennett, the Air Member of the Canadian Joint Staff, discussed the possible termination of the CPA portion of the Korean Airlift with MATS Commander Major General J. Smith, and the Chief of Staff, Brigadier General W. Goss. As MATS resources were being heavily stretched in other theatres, USAF commitments to the airlift had been reduced as a matter of service policy. As a consequence, most of the airlift operations were being conducted by commercial carriers. Smith emphasized that all components of the airlift were essential to maintaining a delivery load of 2,000 tons a month. Any small reduction would have to be made up through other means. He foresaw no major change in the Pacific commitment before a possible cease-fire. The Commander stressed that any withdrawal or reduction of the CPA contribution would be viewed as a definite decrease in Canada's contribution to the United Nation's effort.[22]

In April, two more RCAF pilots were attached to the USAF on fighter operations in Korea and flew in actual combat. Flight Lieutenant L.E. Spurr reported on 10 April and would spend three months in Korea. Group Captain E.B. Hale, Commanding Officer of No 1 Fighter Wing at North Luffenham, arrived on 22 April and spent six weeks on combat operations.[23]

May–June

In May, the squadron logged 788 flying hours meeting the month's quota of fifteen round trips to Tokyo. There were four major delays. On 6 May, Flight Lieutenant Brown and his crew in NS17517 waited for thirty hours at Misawa for the Shemya weather to clear. On 12 May, Flight Lieutenant Gerding lost an engine on NS17515 shortly after taking off from Shemya for Elmendorf and returned to Shemya, where the flight was delayed for four days waiting for a new engine to be delivered, and for the detachment's technicians to make the repairs. A third delay occurred on 14 April at Haneda, when Flight Lieutenant Edwards and his crew were held up for nearly three days waiting for the weather to improve at Shemya, and having a fuel leak in NS17502 repaired. The last major delay was a three-day hiatus that began on 23 May at Haneda, where NS 17506, captained by Flight Lieutenant Butchart, had several mechanical defects repaired, and the crew had to wait for a late cargo of mail from Korea.

Of the 1,400 flying hours logged by the squadron in May, 570 were on domestic operations. On 4 May, four No 426 Squadron North Stars and two No 412 Squadron Dakotas airlifted the 250 men of an anti-aircraft artillery battery from Trenton to Goose Bay as part of an Air Defence Command anti-aircraft mobility exercise. On 6 May, NS17504, captained by Flying Officer Henry, was despatched to Churchill on a clean-up run at the end of the spring re-supply operation. This flight was weathered in at Churchill for two days before it could depart for Resolute Bay late in the afternoon of 9 May. Following a six-hour flight to Resolute and a three-hour stopover there, the crew headed back to Churchill. As the aircraft neared its destination, the crew were advised that ice fog had closed the airfield, and the flight had to divert to The Pas, extending the five-hour and twenty-minute trip from Resolute Bay by another two and a half hours. After the crew had spent nearly three hours on the ground, weather reports indicated that the fog was lifting, so they could return to Churchill.

Shortly before noon the next day, 11 May, the same crew left on a three-hour supply run to Coral Harbour, from where an overly encouraging and optimistic weather report had been received — no supply run had made it to the station for some time. Henry made four radio-range letdowns, overshooting on each occasion, before giving up his attempt to land. On the last pass, the aircraft was down to about twenty-five feet and the author briefly glimpsed radio masts off the starboard wingtip as the aircraft passed them. Climbing out and clearing cloud at 6,000 feet, the flight headed back to Churchill. Coral Harbour was fogged in the next day but, on 13 May, the crew was able to complete the mission, return to Churchill, and then leave for Montreal.[24]

On 7 May, a North Star picked up fifty University Reserve Flight Cadets from Vancouver and Edmonton and dropped them off at Saskatoon, London and Trenton for their summer RCAF training. The next day, thirty-nine members of the International Salvation Army Band, who had arrived from Britain by commercial air, were airlifted with their instruments from Dorval to Rockcliffe. Between 12 May and 19 May, a squadron aircraft again helped transport the National Sabre Display from St-Hubert to Toronto, North Bay and Bagotville.

Five ration runs to Goose Bay were conducted in May, of which one continued to Frobisher Bay. The 16 May flight to Goose Bay carried eighteen airwomen, the first female members of the peacetime force to be posted to RCAF stations in the near North. Three ration runs to Resolute Bay, including the delayed flight of 9 May, were made during the month.

In April, the newly formed No 4 (Transport) OTU had graduated its first course of Dakota first officers. By the end of May, the OTU's first two long-range training flights with the North Star were on their way to England, captained by Squadron Leader Michel, the OTU's Commanding Officer, and Flying Officer Quickfall. The OTU's captains' course included Flight Lieutenant Adamson of No 412 Squadron, and Flying Officer Budgeon and Flying Officer Sage of No 426 Squadron. Two of the student navigators, Flying Officer MacMillan and Flying Officer Quinn, would be assigned to No 426 Squadron on graduation from the OTU.

The check navigators on the two trips were Flight Lieutenant Knapper (an RAF exchange officer and the OTU's Chief Navigation Instructor) and Flying Officer Austin. Two of the five radio officers on the training flights were Flying Officer Filleul and Flying Officer Henry, who would soon join the Thunderbirds; their instructors were Flight Lieutenant Munock and Flying Officer Farrell. With one exception, the training runs were routed via Goose Bay, Keflavik, Prestwick, North Luffenham and London, returning to base by way of Prestwick and Goose Bay. The exception was the flight captained by Squadron Leader Michel, which made a stop at Narsarssuak (Bluie West 1) on the way over to check out the facilities on behalf of Air Transport Command.[25]

The first east-west transit of the Atlantic Ocean by jet aircraft took place on 14 July 1948, when a flight of six RAF Vampire fighters arrived at Goose Bay via Stornoway in the Outer Hebrides, Keflavik and Narsarssuak. Two days later, a large formation of USAF F-80s made the crossing for the first time from west to east, leaving from Goose Bay and using essentially the same routing.[26]

Between 20 July and 26 July 1950, Squadron Leader C.D. Bricker (then serving on exchange with a USAF F-84 fighter squadron at Shaw AFB, South Carolina) became the first RCAF pilot to fly a jet across the Atlantic, when his squadron flew as part of a larger formation to RAF Station Manston in Kent by way of Otis AFB, Massachusetts; Goose Bay; Narsarssuak; Keflavik; and Kinloss, near Inverness, Scotland. The USAF formation retraced its route to Shaw AFB five months later.[27]

When No 439 (Fighter) Squadron was formed at Uplands on 1 September 1951, equipped with the Canadair Sabre II, Squadron Leader Bricker became its first Commanding Officer. The squadron was slated to become part of No 1 (Fighter) Wing at North Luffenham, with No 410 Squadron, which had been transported by HMCS *Magnificent* in October 1951, and No 441 Squadron, which had gone overseas the same way in February 1952.[28]

For some time, planners at Air Force Headquarters had wrestled with the problem of getting RCAF squadrons flying the Canadair Sabre to Europe. During the Second World War, aircraft were routinely ferried across the North Atlantic to Prestwick from Dorval, with stops in Labrador, Greenland and Iceland, but the planners were acutely aware that each leg of the old ferry route was about 800 miles — just about as far as a Sabre II could fly with two standard 100-gallon drop tanks; depending on tail-winds, pilots could expect to arrive at each destination with only ten to fifteen minutes' worth of fuel left. Another serious planning consideration was the lack of alternate airfields for pilots confronted with deteriorating weather at Goose Bay, Narsarssuak or Keflavik.

Early in April 1952, two Sabres from No 439 Squadron flew from Uplands to St-Hubert, and then on to Goose Bay, a 792-mile run, where they refuelled and then returned to St-Hubert and Uplands. After these successful proving flights, Air Force Headquarters proceeded to authorize *Operation LEAP FROG I*, under command and control of Air Transport Command, which was tasked with providing logistics support aircraft — North Stars. The Task Force Commander in charge of *Operation LEAP FROG I* was Squadron Leader W.K. Carr of Air Transport Command Headquarters.

In accordance with Air Transport Command Operations Order 9/52, the task was divided into two phases. Phase I comprised the move of No 439 Squadron's ground crew personnel from Uplands to North Luffenham, to be carried out by three North Stars: one from No 412 Squadron and two from No 426 Squadron. The eighty-eight ground crew, each with 100 pounds of baggage, were divided among the three aircraft, which left Uplands on 23 May for Goose Bay, where they stayed the night. The following day, they flew directly to Prestwick, and they arrived at North Luffenham early on 25 May.

Phase II comprised the ferrying of No 439 Squadron's twenty-one F-86 Sabre II aircraft with sufficient maintenance personnel to take care of them during the trip. NS17502, NS17503, NS17504 and NS17511 from No 426 Squadron were assigned to transport the maintenance personnel, with five crews captained by Flight Lieutenant Brown, Flight Lieutenant Edwards, Flight Lieutenant Stuart, Flying Officer Husch and Flying Officer Wenzel. When Phase II began officially on 30 May with the send-off by Minister of National Defence Brooke Claxton at Uplands for the Sabres, which started departing at 0900 hours for the 304-mile run to Bagotville, some of the North Stars had already taken off so No 439 Squadron ground crews would be in place at Bagotville to prepare the Sabres for their next leg. The rest of the transports followed after to ensure that all the Sabres were safely on their way. This leap-frog procedure was repeated for each leg of the trip.

The squadron could not have completed the overseas legs without the wholehearted support of the USAF and the RAF, who provided servicing and fuelling facilities, accommodation, communications services, and search-and-rescue support. Near the mid-point of each over-water leg was a weather ship, or "ocean station vessel", with a powerful radio beacon that gave the radio compasses of the Sabres an excellent homing aid. Radar fixes were also available. The USAF Air-Sea Rescue Service kept Grumman SA-16s ("Duckbutts") circling designated positions one-quarter and three-quarters of the way along each over-water leg. Although their weak radio beacons were not much help to the Sabres as homing devices, the Duckbutts' mere presence reassured the pilots that, should they have the misfortune to come down in the sea or crash-land on the Greenland icecap, they might survive the experience.

At Goose Bay, operations briefings were conducted at the USAF facilities, using its scale model of Narsarssuak and its environs, and at both Narsarssuak and Keflavik, the operation depended almost entirely on USAF facilities and resources. At Kinloss, the RAF hosted the Sabres and the North Stars, and facilitated their passage to North Luffenham.

Weather problems at Goose Bay delayed the Sabres in Bagotville for three days. The North Stars captained by Edwards and Brown had gone ahead to Goose Bay, so they carried out weather reconnaissance flights for the Sabres on 31 May, 1 June and 2 June, when the Sabres were finally able to fly the 575 miles to Goose Bay safely. At that point, the whole operation ground to a halt again, this time for eight days, because of bad weather on the way to Bluie West 1, and low ceilings at the airfield.

On 10 June, the Sabres made it to Narsarssuak (Bluie West 1), a 777-mile flight. This airfield lay at the far end of a fifty-five-mile fjord liberally dotted with icebergs in summer, and a winding canyon with rock walls that rise several thousand feet in places. The runway started at the water's edge, gently sloping upwards and ending abruptly in an area covered with huge boulders. Aircraft usually took off heading downslope, towards the fjord. The weather was notoriously fickle, capable of changing in very short order from scattered cloud cover to zero visibility in fog, and again, the Sabres were held up, this time for two days.

On 12 June, the Sabres and support aircraft set out on the 754-mile run to Keflavik and made the crossing without undue delay or mishap. Two days later, the last overseas leg of 770 miles to Kinloss was flown with similar results, leaving only the 366-mile run to North Luffenham, which was carried out on 15 June. The new arrivals were welcomed to No 1 Fighter Wing by Group Captain Hale, just back from combat duty in Korea.

Technically, *Operation LEAP FROG I* ended on 18 June, when NS17504, captained by Flight Lieutenant Brown, returned to base. NS17511 skippered by Flight Lieutenant Edwards came in the next day, with Squadron Leader Carr aboard. He had accompanied Edward's crew since leaving Narsarssuak on 12 June.[29]

With the successful conclusion of *Operation LEAP FROG I*, a more ambitious ferrying effort was planned for early fall: *Operation LEAP FROG II*, in which three squadrons would move with their personnel and aircraft to continental Europe. *Op LEAP FROG II* would also come under the operational command and control of Air Transport Command, and the Thunderbirds would be tasked with providing logistics support.

Organization Orders issued by Air Force Headquarters authorized the activation of No 434 Squadron at Uplands, effective 1 June, and No 427 Squadron at St-Hubert, on 1 August. Both squadrons would proceed overseas as components of No 1 Air Division, RCAF.[30]

Pressing domestic and transatlantic requirements led Air Transport Command Headquarters to negotiate an agreement with MATS for a reduction in the squadron's Korean Airlift commitment. Starting in June, the unit would conduct eight, instead of fifteen, round trips per month from McChord to Japan. For the first time in nearly two years, flying hours spent on domestic operations far exceeded those on the Airlift. Of the 1628 flying hours put in by the squadron in June, 569 were used on the airlift and 988 hours on operations categorized as domestic. The remaining hours were mostly used for training and testing of aircraft. While the squadron's detachments remained in place at McChord, Shemya and Haneda, only one slip crew was positioned along the route and that was in Tokyo. The outbound crew would stay with the aircraft taking a crew rest at Shemya before pressing on to Tokyo. The inbound slip crew also took a crew rest in Shemya before proceeding to McChord. Elmendorf remained a refuelling stop for both outbound and inbound aircraft. A crew, on average, was away from McChord for eight days and back at their Dorval base in about 12 days. Apart from some minor delays for mechanical problems, the unit handily carried out its June airlift commitment.[31]

June saw No 426 Squadron busy with a variety of airlift assignments as well as *Op LEAP FROG I* and the Korean Airlift. On 5 June, NS17505, flown by Flying Officer Sage, went to Goose Bay to airlift soldiers assigned to *Operation ACK ACK MOBILITY*, most of whom returned to their garrisons by the regular service flights. From 5 June to 7 June, Squadron Leader Dickson in NS17509 was gone on a supply run to Resolute Bay, which included a para-drop at Isachsen. On 7 June, NS17512, captained by Flight Lieutenant Morrison, and NS17517, under Flying Officer Kuhn, flew to Greenwood where they picked up personnel and equipment from No 404 (Maritime Reconnaissance) Squadron, and then proceeded to St. Eval in Cornwall by way of Goose Bay and Prestwick. No 404 Squadron's Lancasters, which were already on their way, were to take part in NATO exercises. Kuhn and Morrison returned to base via London and Keflavik.[32]

On 14 June —Air Force Day — RCAF Station Lachine and RCAF Station St-Hubert held a joint program at Dorval organized by a committee chaired by Squadron Leader Foye of No 426 Squadron. The weather was excellent and thousands of spectators turned out to watch demonstration flights by jets, North Stars, a Chipmunk, a Bristol Freighter and a Dakota. A display area decorated with bunting was set up in B Bay of the No 426 Squadron hangar, and A Bay became a restaurant and rest area for visitors. All day, airmen escorted people through NS17514, which was parked in front of the hangar, and in mid-afternoon Flying Officer Spratt took NS17502 up for a short local flight with fifty passengers who had won tickets in a draw. By 1730 hours, the crowds had dispersed and the airmen started dismantling the displays, marking the end of a very successful day.

On Air Force Day, while some members of the squadron were hosting the festivities at Dorval, the rest were busy maintaining the operational tempo. At 1045 hours, their departure announced to the crowds on the public address system, Flying Officer Knight and his crew took off for Churchill and Resolute Bay in NS17512. About two hours and forty-five minutes out of Dorval, flying at the assigned altitude of 8,000 feet near James Bay, the aircraft ran into a line of thunderstorms. As well as turbulence and rain, the towering cumulo-nimbus clouds showered the aircraft with hailstones that damaged the radiators so badly that two engines started to overheat and had to be shut down. With the other two engines also showing signs of overheating, Knight reversed course and sent out a "Mayday" message to Ottawa Control.

As the fully loaded aircraft slowly lost altitude, stabilizing at about 2,500 feet, the navigator, Flying Officer Connolly, came forward to map-read and direct the flight back to base. All the way home, the crew watched carefully for high ground and lakes in which the aircraft might be ditched, as a successful crash landing would be impossible in the rugged terrain of northern Ontario. Some three hours after encountering the thunderstorms, NS17512 landed safely at Dorval after five hours and fifteen minutes of flying. Three days later, Knight and Connolly left again for Churchill and Resolute Bay, and this time the operation went off without a hitch.[33]

At 0930 on Air Force Day, Flight Lieutenant Allen and his crew in NS17522 left for Rockcliffe, where they picked up members of the Canada–United States Permanent Joint Board on Defence. (At this time, the Board comprised ten members, five from each country: a chairman, senior officers of the navy, army and air force, and a member of the foreign service as secretary. The chairman of the Board's Canada Section was General A.G.L. McNaughton, who held that appointment from August 1946 to 1959.) After embarking the Board members, the flight set a heading for Winnipeg, the first stop on an itinerary that included Vancouver, Alaska and the Yukon. Shortly after passing the Lakehead, General McNaughton asked if the flight could be diverted towards Fort Frances; the General, who was also chairman of the Canada Section of the International Joint Commission, wanted to see how much effluent was entering Canadian waters from pulp mills on the Minnesota side of the border. After making notes of the telltale streams of whitish discharge from the mills that had flowed to the Canadian side, the General indicated that course could be resumed for Winnipeg.

The flight arrived at Stevenson Field at 1720 hours, just as the Air Force Day activities there were winding down. After seeing their passengers' classified baggage — some 1,500 pounds of documents and other material packed in large canvas bags — safely into the custody of the Service Police, the crew made arrangements for the next day's flight.

By 0830 hours the next morning the aircraft was serviced and ready for departure, and a six-hour flight plan to Vancouver had been filed. As the crew went through their checklists, the VIP passengers arrived and started boarding — but their classified material had not been loaded. After a frantic but mercifully short search, the large canvas bags were found locked up in a detention cell at the guardhouse, the only place large enough to hold them that could be appropriately secured. Unfortunately, the keys were missing — a corporal on the evening shift had taken them home with him. As time was of the essence, a flight sergeant took a fire axe to the cell door, and the canvas bags were quickly delivered to the aircraft and loaded into one of its belly compartments. The aircraft was only ten minutes late in getting away.

After a routine flight to Vancouver, the crew had two days off before taking the Board members on to Juneau, Alaska, where they stayed for only thirty hours before continuing on to Elmendorf, where they arrived late in the afternoon of 18 June. As the North Star taxied behind the Follow-Me jeep, the crew broke out a pennant with four stars on it, denoting the rank of General McNaughton and, as the aircraft halted in its designated place, they saw hundreds of servicemen milling about and perched on every vantage point in the area. No, they weren't waiting to greet an obscure Canadian general, but a USO troupe with Gregory Peck and Anne Baxter, whose aircraft was expected on its way to Anchorage.

There was no doubt in anyone's mind as to who would take care of the classified material. Military Police arrived with a small armoured car to load the canvas bags onto a truck equipped with a machine-gun manned by a grim-looking gunner. The truck drove away surrounded by an siren-blaring escort of jeep-mounted MPs.

On 19 June, the Board moved on to Ladd Field at Fairbanks, and the following morning the aircraft was positioned at Eielson AFB some twenty miles distant. A motorcade brought the Board members from Fairbanks, and at 1350 hours NS17522 was on its way to Whitehorse, a two-and-a-half-hour run. Shortly after the passengers had disembarked, the canvas bags of classified material were unloaded into the back of a small pickup truck, and an Army sergeant sat on top of the pile. As the pick-up disappeared from view, the crew reflected on the stark contrast to the American approach. The next stop was Edmonton, and on 22 June the Board members were flown back to Rockcliffe and the aircraft returned to base.[34]

The Station Commander at Lachine, the newly promoted Group Captain Austin, captained NS17506 on a run to Resolute Bay on 19 June, returning to base the following day. The first officer on this trip was Group Captain G.G. Diamond, a future Air Officer Commanding, Air Transport Command.

The squadron's next major assignment was *Operation NUGGET*, which involved four aircraft and four crews, captained by Flight Lieutenant Edwards, Flight Lieutenant Wolkowski, Flying Officer Harrison and Flying Officer McLeod. *Operation NUGGET* was the airlift of 590 Auxiliary Air Force personnel from Winnipeg, Calgary and Saskatoon to summer training camps at Watson Lake and Whitehorse.

Early in June, Wing Commander MacDonald was promoted Group Captain and posted to Air Force Headquarters as Director of Air Plans and Programs. A farewell stag party was held for him on 20 June, although he would remain in command of No 426 Squadron until 28 August. With the periodic absence of Group Captain Austin, who was to take up the command of RCAF Station Comox, MacDonald was also acting CO of RCAF Station Lachine so, pending the arrival of a new Squadron Commander, Squadron Leader Dickson looked after the Thunderbirds' day-to-day affairs in the interim. Wing Commander W.H. Lupton, who had been posted from Training Command to Air Transport Command Headquarters, was designated to be the new commanding officer of No 426 Squadron pending completion of a North Star course at the OTU. He would take command officially on 8 September.

The squadron was advised that Flight Sergeant A.A. Drackley, a senior flight engineer, and Sergeant Senecal were to be posted to No 427 (Fighter) Squadron, which was being activated at RCAF Station St.-Hubert. Other personnel changes involved Flight Sergeant Preston and Leading Aircraftsman Forbes, who were posted to Goose Bay; Corporal Kirchner, who was posted to Comox; and Leading Aircraftsman Laturnus, who was posted to RCAF Station MacDonald, near Winnipeg.

Flying Officer Lepine returned to the squadron as Signals Officer after a stint at RCAF Station Lachine in the same role. Flying Officer Jim Kupkee was selected for a two-year assignment in Paris with the VIP Flight, flying in Dakotas as a radio officer. Flight Lieutenant Jack Egan was transferred to the Recruiting Unit at North Bay, and Flying Officer Dave Kuhn and Flying Officer Ted Orr were posted to the Flight Control Office. Flight Lieutenant Terry Createau, who had just been promoted, returned from the detachment at McChord and became a member of the Radio Officer instructional staff at the OTU. Flying Officer Charters proceeded to Shemya for three months as Detachment Commander, replacing Flying Officer Whitman. The unit also bid farewell to Flight Lieutenant Stuart, who was posted to a staff job at Air Force Headquarters. Flight Lieutenant Flewelling left on a posting to Goose Bay, and Flight Lieutenant Phillips joined the staff of the Recruiting Unit in Lethbridge, Alberta.

During June, several officers assigned to the squadron were under training at No 4 OTU: Wing Commander Lupton on the First Officer course, and Flight Lieutenant Hall, Flying Officer Casselman, Flying Officer Cook and Flying Officer Waddell on the captains' course. Navigators under instruction included Flying Officer Carmichael, Pilot Officer Lightstone and Pilot Officer Livock.[35]

For meritorious service on the Korean Airlift, the Queen's Birthday Honours List for 1952 included the names of fourteen officers and airmen who had served or were serving with the Thunderbirds. Wing Commander C.H. Mussells, DSO, DFC, CD, was appointed an Officer of the Military Division of the Most Excellent Order of the British Empire (OBE), and Wing Commander W.H. Lord was appointed a Military member of the Order (MBE). Awarded the Air Force Cross (AFC) were: Wing Commander H.A. Morrison, DSO, DFC; Squadron Leader J.D. Dickson, DFC, DFM; and Flight Lieutenant D.M. Payne, DFC. Flight Sergeant A.A. Drackley was awarded the Air Force Medal, and Warrant Officer 2nd Class A.L. Englebert would receive the British Empire Medal (BEM), Military Division. Recipients of the Queen's Commendation for Valuable Services in the Air were: Squadron Leader C.E. Endersbee; Squadron Leader R.E.D. Ratcliffe, DFC; Flight Lieutenant A. Finklestein, CD; Flight Lieutenant J.B. Miller; Flight Lieutenant W. Smith; Sergeant F.C.M. Bowman; and Corporal E.C. Grose.[36]

MAP 4: *North Star Operations in Canada, 1948–1962*

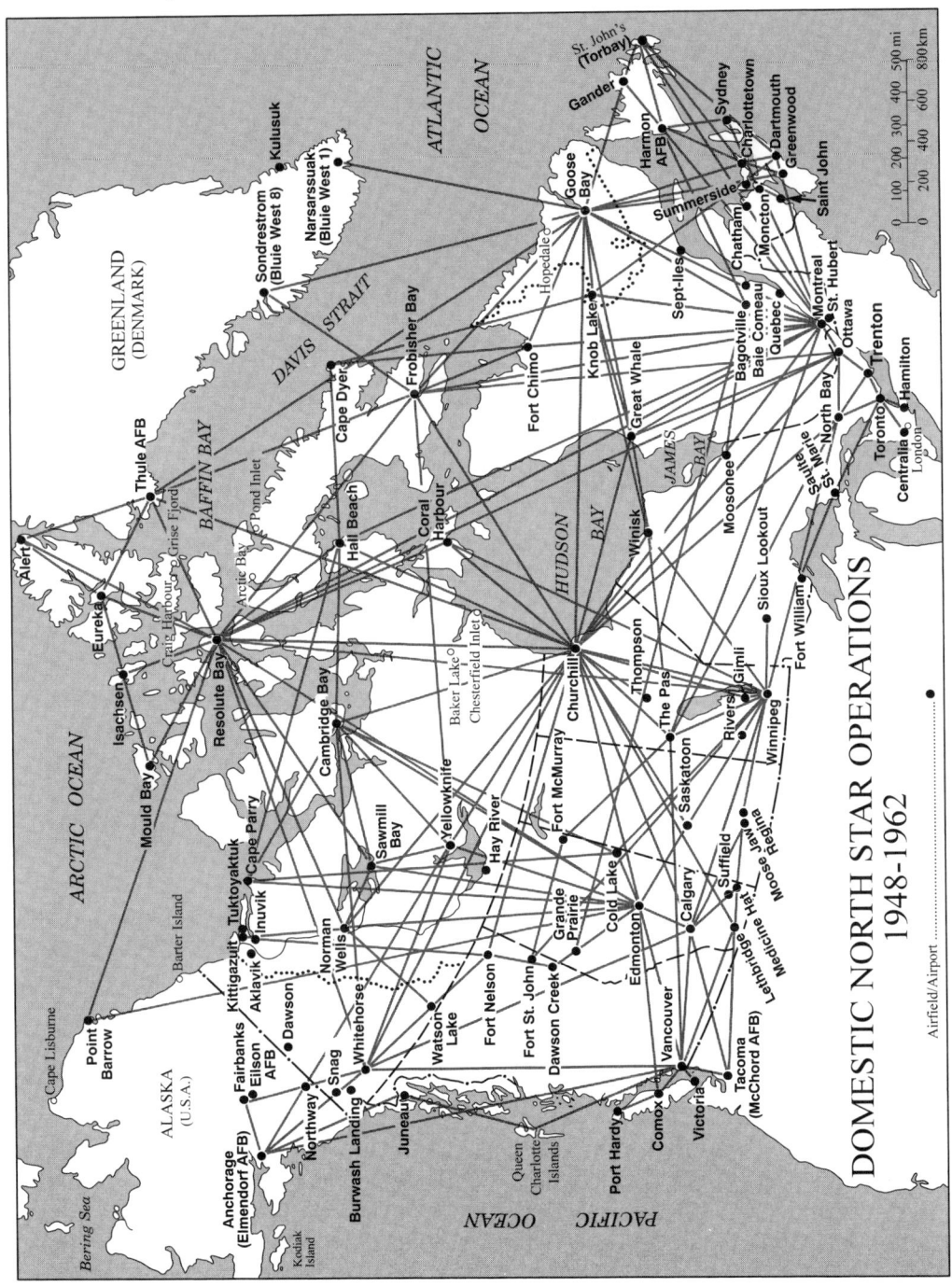

Maps by: Wm. Constable

PHOTO 105
F/O E.R. Wolkowski is checked out on a pedi-cab; Tokyo, 27 March 1952. (L. Motiuk Collection)

PHOTO 106
The author and F/O E.R. Wolkowski with the Japanese guards at the gate to the grounds of the Imperial Palace; Tokyo, 27 March 1952. (L. Motiuk Collection)

PHOTO 107
*Early morning tea service at the Marunouchi Hotel; Tokyo, April 1952.
(J. Henry Collection)*

PHOTO 108
*The string trio plays during afternoon tea service at the Marunouchi Hotel; Tokyo,
April 1952. (J. Henry Collection)*

PHOTO 109
No 426 Squadron's detachment at Shemya AFB; March 1952. The third man from the left in the middle row is LAC R. Nurse. (R. Nurse Collection)

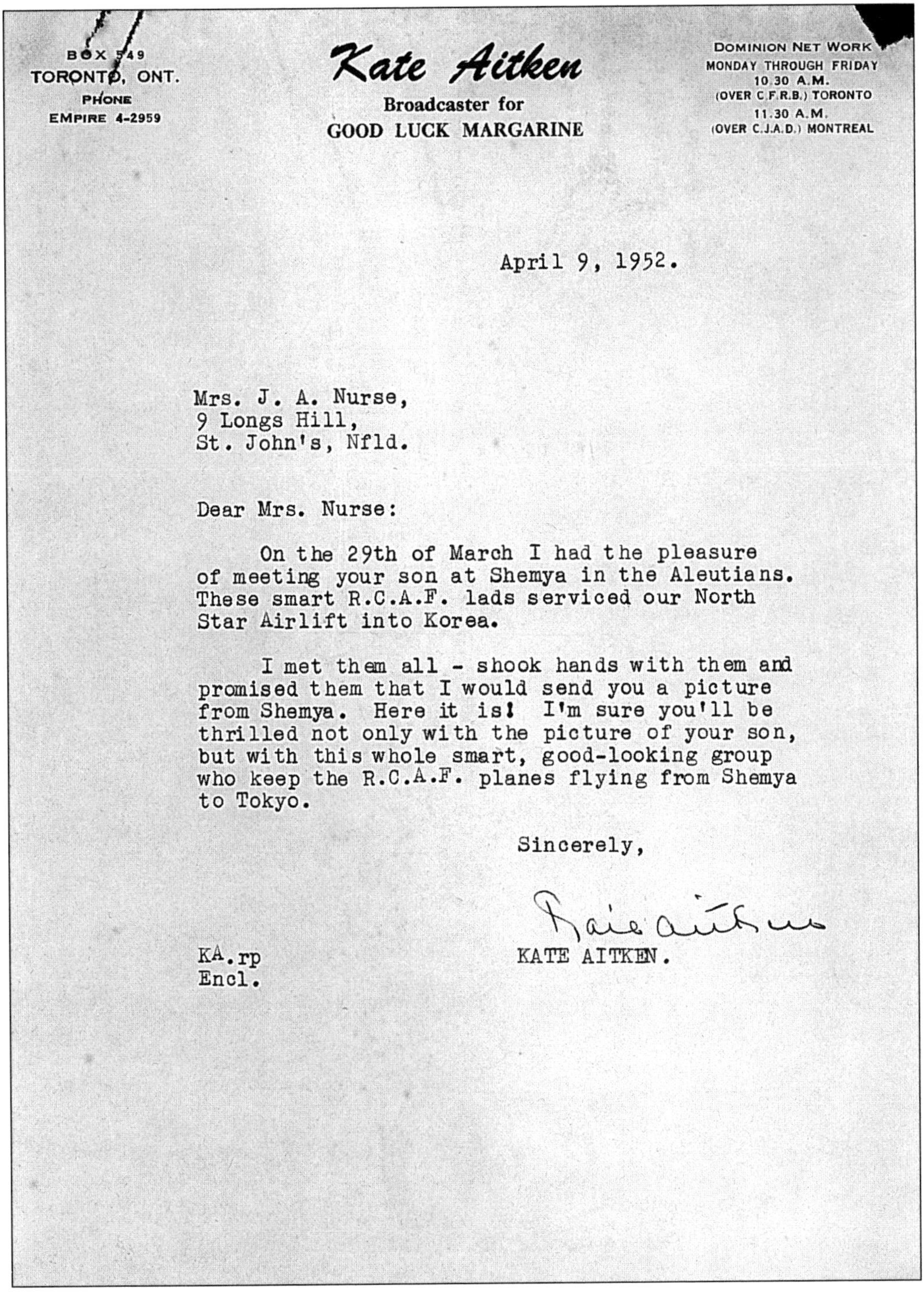

BOX 549	**Kate Aitken**	DOMINION NET WORK
TORONTO, ONT.	Broadcaster for	MONDAY THROUGH FRIDAY
PHONE	GOOD LUCK MARGARINE	10.30 A.M.
EMPIRE 4-2959		(OVER C.F.R.B.) TORONTO
		11.30 A.M.
		(OVER C.J.A.D.) MONTREAL

April 9, 1952.

Mrs. J. A. Nurse,
9 Longs Hill,
St. John's, Nfld.

Dear Mrs. Nurse:

On the 29th of March I had the pleasure of meeting your son at Shemya in the Aleutians. These smart R.C.A.F. lads serviced our North Star Airlift into Korea.

I met them all - shook hands with them and promised them that I would send you a picture from Shemya. Here it is! I'm sure you'll be thrilled not only with the picture of your son, but with this whole smart, good-looking group who keep the R.C.A.F. planes flying from Shemya to Tokyo.

Sincerely,

Kate Aitken

KATE AITKEN.

KA.rp
Encl.

PHOTO 110
Kate Aitken's letter to Mrs. J.A. Nurse, written after her trip to Tokyo with No 426 Squadron. (R. Nurse Collection).

PHOTO 111
No 426 Squadron North Stars at Resolute Bay during the spring re-supply of the Arctic weather stations; 2 April 1952. (DND PL54064)

PHOTO 112
A No 426 Squadron crew poses on the ramp used to unload supplies and equipment; Isachsen, Ellef Ringnes Island, 12 April 1952. From left: Sgt. G. Howard, F/L M.D. Broadfoot (Detachment Commander at Resolute Bay), F/L O.F. Bradley, F/O W.I. Butchart and F/O L.A. De Quoy. (DND PL54043)

PHOTO 113
An aerial view of Resolute Bay, NWT; 7 April 1951. (DND REA 636–1)

Lachine, July–December 1952

CHAPTER 14

LACHINE
JULY—DECEMBER 1952

The stalemate continued along the battlefront in Korea during the latter half of 1952. This period was characterized by stubborn fighting and seesaw battles for hill positions.

Meanwhile, the truce talks at Panmunjom were at an impasse on the issue of repatriating prisoners of war; by the fall, the talks were completely deadlocked and had to be recessed. In October and November, the Republic of Korea (ROK) units, which held the centre of the UN lines, were under heavy pressure from the Communist forces. The well-led and well-trained ROK troops were engaged in some of the war's fiercest actions in their sector of the front.

Early in December, US President-elect Dwight D. Eisenhower fulfilled a campaign pledge and made a short visit to Korea. Arriving at Suwon (or "K13" as it appeared on the military maps), Eisenhower embarked on a whirlwind tour of the areas behind the battlefront and met briefly with Dr. Syngman Rhee, the President of South Korea.[1]

Between July and December, nine RCAF fighter pilots flew combat operations with the USAF in Korea, spending four months in-country on average. They were Flight Lieutenant J.C.A. Lafrance, who arrived on 14 May; Flight Lieutenant E.A. Glover, 15 June; Flight Lieutenant R.E. Lowry and Squadron Leader J.D. Lindsay, 15 July; Squadron Leader E.G. Smith, 14 August; Wing Commander R.T.P. Davidson, 15 September; Flying Officer A. Lambros, 14 October; Squadron Leader A.R. MacKenzie, 15 November; and Flight Lieutenant F.W. Evans, 14 December. From time to time, Thunderbird crews would encounter the fighter pilots at the Marunouchi Hotel in Tokyo.[2]

Squadron Leader A.R. MacKenzie had been in Korea for a month and was on his fifth combat mission when he was shot down by friendly fire. He ejected safely but was captured and ended up spending two years in a Chinese prison camp.

On 26 June, the Cabinet reached some conclusions about the continued involvement of Canadian Pacific Airlines in the Korean Airlift, which was on the agenda for the Chiefs of Staff Committee meeting on 10 July. At the Cabinet meeting, Defence Minister Brooke Claxton stated that the RCAF was against continuing the CPA airlift, but the Army considered it necessary because large numbers of reinforcements would be needed in Korea should heavy fighting resume. Claxton understood that both the Minister of Transport and the Minister of Trade and Commerce wanted the contract extended, and Prime Minister St. Laurent noted that the Department of

External Affairs thought that a significant reduction in Canada's overall contribution to the UN forces would have an unfortunate effect on the negotiations, which seemed to be coming to a head. Taking CPA out of the Airlift would not only provoke a bad reaction in the United States, it would also be noticed in North Korea. After further discussion, the Cabinet approved the proposal to extend CPA contract for participation in the Korean Airlift for six months, beginning 1 July 1952.[3]

On 14 July, Organization Order 49/52 was issued, dealing with the formation of No 137 Transport Flight at Dorval, effective 1 August 1952, and subsequent move to 30 Air Materiel Base at Langar, a decommissioned RAF station on the Leicestershire-Nottinghamshire border. No 137 Transport Flight was to provide rapid re-supply and transport services between Langar and the units of 1 Air Division. To permit coordinated training of the new unit's aircrew and ground staff, and to ensure an efficient standard of transport operations, Air Force Headquarters decided that it would form at Dorval and come under the Station Commander at Lachine. No 4 (Transport) OTU would provide direction and, once the appropriate standard of efficiency had been attained in transport operations and maintenance, the flight would make the move overseas. No 137 Transport Flight was to be equipped with the twin-engine Bristol Freighter, of which it eventually acquired six, and be staffed by experienced Air Transport Command personnel.[4]

Between 24 June and 1 July, the squadron assigned four aircraft and eight crews to *Operation NUGGET*, airlifting 580 Auxiliary Air Force personnel of Tactical Air Group from their home stations in western Canada to summer training camps in Yukon Territory at Watson Lake and Whitehorse. As well as eight crews (captained by Flight Lieutenant Allen, Flight Lieutenant Edwards, Flight Lieutenant Lemieux, Flight Lieutenant Olsen, Flight Lieutenant Wolkowski, Flying Officer Budgeon, Flying Officer Harrison and Flying Officer McLeod), No 426 Squadron contributed four North Stars (NS17503, NS17504, NS17509 and NS17511). No 435 Squadron from Edmonton contributed four Dakotas and their crews. In five trips, the North Stars transported 250 Auxiliary personnel from Winnipeg to Watson Lake; three trips conveyed 165 airmen from Saskatoon to Whitehorse; and three trips carried another 165 airmen from Calgary to Watson Lake.

Airlift support for *Operation Nugget* resumed late in the afternoon of 4 July when Flight Lieutenant Edwards and an augmented crew left Montreal in NS17517 for Winnipeg. At 1250 hours the next day, the crew proceeded to Whitehorse with stops at Saskatoon, Edmonton and Watson Lake. On the 6th, the flight returned to Winnipeg after stopping at Watson Lake and Saskatoon on the way back. On the morning of 7 July Edwards went to Churchill, from where two freight runs were conducted to Resolute Bay. The flight returned to base at 1000 hours on 9 July. From 10-18 July Flying Officer Knight and his crew in NS17504 conducted several shuttle runs between Whitehorse and Watson Lake to Winnipeg, returning Auxiliary personnel to their home base. The squadron despatched two more aircraft: NS17511, captained by Flight Lieutenant Hall, and NS17510, skippered by Flying Officer Cook, to complete the personnel transfers from the summer camps to Saskatoon and Winnipeg. This was accomplished between 11-14 July. No 435 Squadron and four of its Dakotas were active during this phase of the operation.

Operation NUGGET continued in July under the new designation *Op SIGNPOST*, with the squadron tasked to airlift Air Defence Command personnel from St.-Hubert to Vancouver and Victoria. Three North Stars and crews captained by Squadron Leader Kightley, and Flying Officers

Harrison and Middleton were assigned to this airlift from 18 July to 20 July. Middleton went to Victoria, stopping at Winnipeg, Lethbridge and Vancouver before returning to base. Harrison's itinerary took him to Winnipeg, Edmonton and Vancouver, where he was tasked with a shuttle run to Tacoma, Washington, before returning to Montreal. Kightley's routing took him to Churchill and Lethbridge, Alberta, before he arrived at Victoria. He then headed back to base, making stops at Winnipeg and St-Hubert.

In July, two No 426 Squadron aircraft captained by Flight Lieutenant Herbert and Flying Officer Spratt flew to St. Eval, Cornwall, to provide logistics support from 3 July to 8 July to No 404 (Maritime) Squadron, which was deploying overseas for NATO exercises. No 426 Squadron also carried out six regular passenger and supply runs to Goose Bay and Resolute Bay, and several special flights to each location. From 15 to 17 July, NS17509 was used for a series of freight runs by two crews captained by Flying Officer Budgeon and Flying Officer Cook; the aircraft took an initial load from Dorval to Goose Bay, and then proceeded to Halifax. From Halifax, Budgeon and Cook each carried out two shuttle runs to Goose Bay and one to Frobisher Bay before returning home.

Between 18 July and 22 July, Flight Lieutenant Henry and his crew in NS17515 airlifted a load of freight to Churchill, where they picked up another load bound for Resolute Bay. From Resolute, the flight went on to Norman Wells, a four-hour and forty-five minute run, to deliver a loading ramp obtained in Churchill. At Norman Wells, the aircraft was loaded with 9,000 pounds of equipment belonging to No 408 (Photographic) Squadron that was delivered to Fort Nelson. From Fort Nelson, the aircraft returned to Churchill to drop off the ramp, and then returned to base.

On 22 July, Flying Officer Sage and his crew flew to Greenwood, where they loaded 10,000 pounds of supplies to Resolute Bay (via Goose Bay, Frobisher Bay and Churchill), for use in *Operation NANOOK*, a series of ice patrols and similar missions across the high Arctic conducted by Maritime Group out of Resolute Bay, flying Lancasters. On the return trip, Sage's flight was diverted to The Pas (as Churchill was closed by fog), where they had to wait three hours before Churchill opened up again. They returned to base after a delivery stop at Ottawa.[5]

Despite the vagaries of Aleutian weather, No 426 Squadron completed its July quota of eight round trips between McChord and Tokyo. When Flying Officer Knight and his crew brought NS17511 in to McChord on 26 July, the squadron had completed 405 round trips to Tokyo and two full years of operations on the Korean Airlift. Commenting on the anniversary, Minister of National Defence Brooke Claxton, made the following statement on 27 July:

> The operational record of 426 Squadron during its two years on the Korean Airlift merits the highest possible praise. I can think of no higher tribute than to say that squadron personnel have reduced a gruelling and extremely demanding task to the status of a purely routine operation. By their irreproachable record, all of the "Thunderbirds" have brought honour to their squadron, to the Air Force and to their country, while playing an important part in the combined struggle against aggression in Korea. My personal congratulations, and those of the Armed Services to 426 Squadron on the second anniversary of the commencement of their Korean airlift operations.[6]

August

In August, No 426 Squadron logged a total of 1,632 flying hours, including 419 on the Korean Airlift, 1,083 on domestic operations, and 130 on tests and training. Eight round trips to Japan were completed with only two major delays: NS17510 at McChord for thirty hours by an engine change, and the same aircraft at Misawa for sixty-five hours on the return trip by bad weather at Shemya.

The airlift of Air Defence Command personnel participating in *Operation SIGNPOST* continued from the latter part of July into early August. First, about eighty airmen were flown from Bagotville to St-Hubert, then three of five groups of Air Defence Command personnel at St-Hubert and Ottawa were flown to Winnipeg; and finally the other two groups at St-Hubert were flown to Vancouver and Victoria.

As it was summer, the squadron was also tasked with airlifting groups of air cadets to and from camp, and taking them on familiarization flights. A group of RAF cadets were taken on a western tour with stops at Lethbridge, Calgary, Edmonton and Winnipeg before returning to Montreal. American cadets touring the Montreal area were flown to RCAF Station Bagotville for a one-day visit.

In August, the squadron carried out a series of special assignments: airlifting the RCMP Band on a tour of the Atlantic Provinces that included St. John's, Torbay and Stephenville in Newfoundland, and Sydney, Nova Scotia; four trips from Malton Airport to North Bay to deliver Orenda jet engines; two shuttle runs transporting sailors from Halifax to Toronto to work at the RCN display at the Canadian National Exhibition; two trips to transport airmen from Bagotville to Toronto to work at the RCAF booth at the CNE; and four flights to take anti-aircraft gunners from Trenton to Kinross AFB, Michigan, near Sault Ste. Marie.[7]

In summer, the Arctic was a hive of activity, and the North Stars were heavily committed to provide airlift support. During August, four supply runs were conducted to Goose Bay, with one extending to Frobisher Bay. At the end of the month, the squadron made five flights between Churchill and Rockcliffe, bringing No 408 Squadron personnel and their equipment back to their home base. It was re-supply season in the high Arctic, so eight shuttle flights were conducted to Resolute Bay via Churchill. Two of these runs were made between 11 August and 17 August by Flying Officer Spratt and his crew in NS17517, who had Air Commodore Ripley with them as far as Churchill. Ripley was on a northern inspection tour, so that flight stopped at Goose Bay and Fort Chimo before heading to Churchill.

All through the 1950s, Resolute Bay on Cornwallis Island — "Miami North" — was the transportation hub of the Canadian Arctic, bustling with activity especially in spring and fall when the re-supply of the high Arctic weather stations was conducted, but also throughout the summer, when the weather stations' supplies were brought in by ship. For the personnel of these isolated weather stations, Resolute Bay felt like a city; it was the gathering and relay point for all weather information gathered in the Canadian Arctic, and the operations base for ice patrols and other reconnaissance flights, as well as the aerial photography that was so important to the mapping of the Arctic Islands. Resolute was also the base for the many non-military organizations conducting scientific research in the Arctic.

The normal strength of the RCAF detachment at Resolute was about twenty all ranks, and the Department of Transport weather station had six to eight people on staff, so the facilities were taxed to the maximum in summer, when construction, flying operations and ship re-supply were all going on at once. With the first snow flurries of autumn, however, the island population began to decline, and detachment life slowed down. The last week in September and the first week in October featured a final short burst of activity before winter: the autumn airlift to the satellite weather stations. The quiet of winter was broken only by itinerant RCAF and USAF aircraft until the airlift of supplies to the weather stations resumed in late March or early April. In winter, detachment personnel concentrated on clearing snow from the runway and campsite, and keeping their vehicles and equipment operating — no mean feat in the severe cold.

On 1 August 1952, an advance party from No 2 Construction Maintenance Unit (based in Calgary), a detachment of No 405 (Maritime) Squadron, and a working party from RCAF Station Lachine were in place at Resolute Bay. The Lachine working party was there to steam-clean thousands of fuel barrels before they were refilled. During the first week of the month, life was comparatively easy, with time to play softball in the evening — itself more a convention than a fact as the sun does not actually set until mid-August at latitude 74°43' North.

At 0230 hours on 7 August, the northern tranquillity was shattered by the arrival of four US Navy ships, including a tanker; within three hours, unloading was in full swing under beachmaster Flight Lieutenant Burn, and it continued around the clock until the job was done. At 0600 hours the same day, Flying Officer Knight and his crew arrived in NS17517 with thirty-one more men to help, a welcome sight as all personnel had been pressed into service.

On 8 August, NS17511 skippered by Flying Officer Waddell (with Group Captain Austin as First Officer) had to divert to Thule as the weather at Resolute Bay was down and its radio beacon had gone silent. The aircraft finally arrived at 1800 hours the next day, bringing twenty-two more men from No 2 CMU, whose very welcome arrival aggravated an acute housing problem.

On the morning of 10 August, Waddell and his crew conducted para-drops at Mould Bay and Isachsen, while back at Resolute, ice conditions forced the ships out of the bay for several days, which gave the detachment personnel time to recuperate, and to start sorting and checking the cargo. NS17517, captained by Flying Officer Spratt, arrived at 2020 hours on 13 August, bringing in eleven civilian construction workers. No 408 Squadron aircraft also dropped in periodically, adding their crews to the throng.

The supply ships returned on the morning of 16 August and, by 1800 hours the next day, had finished discharging their cargo, weighed anchor, and headed for home. The unloading crew — dubbed the "bull gang" — then started the brutal job of moving several thousand forty-five-gallon barrels of aviation gas, "mobile equipment" (i.e., motor vehicle) gas, and Diesel fuel from the beach to the camp. The bull gang laboured long and hard until this job, too, was done, and then started cleaning up the camp.

The No 405 Squadron personnel departed on 21 August. On 28 August, NS17502, captained by Flying Officer Middleton, took out thirty personnel from No 2 CMU, RCAF Station Rockcliffe and RCAF Station Lachine.

Air Commodore Ripley arrived at Resolute Bay at 1820 hours on 28 August in NS17506, captained by Flight Lieutenant Butchart. While he was at Resolute, Ripley flew on a mail-drop mission to Mould Bay, Isachsen and Eureka. (A drop would have been made at Alert, too, had the weather been better.) Following the mail drops, Ripley conducted a detailed inspection of the Resolute Bay detachment. On 31 August, he departed for Churchill, Yellowknife and Edmonton.[8]

On 21 August, Air Force Headquarters issued Organization Order 50/52, effective 1 October 1952, to authorize the formation of No 2 Fighter Wing at Grostenquin, France, as part of No 1 Air Division. No 2 Fighter Wing was to provide administrative and functional control of No 421 (F) Squadron from RCAF Station St-Hubert, Quebec; No 416 (F) Squadron from RCAF Station Uplands, Ontario; and No 430 (F) Squadron from RCAF Station North Bay, Ontario, all to be in place at Grostenquin with their Sabre aircraft by 31 October.

From 1 October to 27 November, 1952, before taking up the appointment of Director of Air Plans and Programs at Air Force Headquarters, Group Captain J.K.F. MacDonald would serve as No 2 Fighter Wing's first Commanding Officer.[9]

On 18 August, a conference was held at Air Transport Command Headquarters at RCAF Station Lachine to discuss *Operation LEAP FROG II*, the task of ferrying the three squadrons' Sabres to Grostenquin. The conference was opened by Air Commodore Ripley and chaired by Wing Commander Mussells, the designated Task Force Commander; his Operation Commander was Wing Commander J.F. (Stocky) Edwards, squadron commander of No 430 Squadron and a desert ace of the Second World War. Wing Commander J.R.D. Braham, Acting Senior Air Staff officer at Air Defence Command Headquarters, told the conference that each fighter squadron would have twenty-one aircraft, and the addition of three RAF Sabres to the operation brought the total number of aircraft involved in *Op LEAP FROG II* to sixty-six. A Wing Headquarters under Wing Commander Mussells was to be up and running by 1 September.[10]

On 26 August, Air Transport Command Headquarters laid out the roles and responsibilities for *Operation LEAP FROG II* in Operation Order 15/52: with the number of aircraft to be ferried reduced to sixty-three Sabres (three from the RAF, the rest Canadian), the operation would be conducted in two phases. In Phase 1, No 426 Squadron would airlift most of the ground crew personnel and their baggage (thirty-five men per day) to Grostenquin from North Bay, Uplands and St-Hubert, beginning at 0800 hours on 30 September. In Phase 2, the aircraft would be flown to their bases in Britain and France, and seventy-five maintenance support personnel and about ten administrative staff would be airlifted from Canada to Grostenquin. The overseas routing was Goose Bay to Narsarssuak (777 miles); to Keflavik (754 miles); to Prestwick (853 miles); and finally to Grostenquin (655 miles). Operation Order 15/52 included a route map showing where the USAF search-and-rescue Duckbutts would be operating, and where the Ocean Station Vessels *Bravo*, *Alpha* and *India* would be positioned.[11]

The squadron conducted five trips to Europe in August.

Between 8 August and 14 August, Flight Lieutenant Wolkowski and an augmented crew in NS17502 took a party of Air Defence Command personnel on an inspection tour of Britain and

France, following the routing to Prestwick set out for *LEAP FROG II* and ending up at North Luffenham. From there, the Air Defence Command group was flown to London, Paris (Orly) and Grostenquin before returning to Montreal. On 15 August, Squadron Leader Torontow headed for Europe in NS17506 with another augmented crew, transporting thirty-six veterans of the Dieppe Raid to France for the ceremonies marking the tenth anniversary of that event. Routed via Goose Bay and Keflavik, Torontow's flight stopped off in Paris, Brussels, Amsterdam and London before heading back home via Keflavik. Halfway to Keflavik, the crew were advised that the weather was down in Iceland, and Torontow brought the aircraft back to Prestwick. After an overnight stop, they set out again for Iceland, and arrived back at base on the morning of 20 August.

On 18 August, a flight went to Britain with a group of RAF cadets heading home after an extended visit to Canada. Two days later, another flight carrying RCAF personnel was despatched to Europe, and it stopped at North Luffenham, London and Paris before returning to base. Between 29 August and 3 September, Group Captain MacDonald skippered a passenger run to Europe in NS17510, with Wing Commander Lupton as First Officer. This flight stopped at Metz and Paris before heading to London, where the crew picked up a load of rockets before heading back to base.

In August, Flight Lieutenant Webb returned to Lachine from an exchange tour with a USAF C-97 squadron before moving on to his new assignment in the Training Branch at Air Transport Command Headquarters, and Squadron Leader Wallace, Staff Officer Pilot Training at Air Transport Command Headquarters, spent a week in Hagerstown, Maryland, taking a refresher course on the C-119 Flying Boxcar. (The first two Boxcars would soon be ferried by Air Transport Command crews to No 435 Squadron in Edmonton.) At Lachine, the new Station Commander, Wing Commander R.F. Douglas, arrived on 20 August from Brussels, where he had been the Air Attaché. The change of command would be official on 9 September.

At No 4 OTU, Chief Pilot Instructor (and former Thunderbird) Flight Lieutenant Rolly Lloyd was selected for training on the de Havilland Comet (the RCAF was acquiring two). Flight Lieutenant Al Kerslake was posted to the OTU to replace him, and Flying Officer Cliff Wenzel joined the training staff. Flight Lieutenant Barber was posted in from No 435 Squadron as Chief Navigation Instructor.

The No 426 Squadron students on the captains' course under Flight Lieutenant Quickfall and Flight Lieutenant Roane were Wing Commander Lupton, Captain Green (the USAF exchange officer), Flying Officer Kyle and Flying Officer McAninch. Slated to join the Thunderbirds were: Flying Officer Kowalik and Flying Officer McBride on the first officers' course; Flight Lieutenant Cox, Flying Officer Rhodes, Flying Officer Spikings and Flying Officer Woodhouse on the navigation course; and Flying Officer L.R.A. Brousseau, Flying Officer C.M. Knight and Flying Officer B.A. Rosenthal on the radio officers' course. Former Thunderbirds leaving the OTU were: Flight Lieutenant Buchan, to a staff assignment at Air Force Headquarters in Ottawa; and flight engineers Warrant Officer 2nd Class Baine, Sergeant Bowman and Sergeant Hoehn, who had been selected for the Comet course in England. Flight engineer replacements from the squadron were Flight Sergeant Smith, Sergeant Howard and Corporal Thompson.

In No 426 Squadron, Flight Lieutenant George Sweanor took over as the Senior Navigation Officer, and navigators Flight Lieutenant Doyle and Flying Officer Norton left to join No 137 (Transport) Flight, destined for Langar in England. Flying Officer Rosengren returned to base after a stint as Detachment Commander in Haneda, and was replaced by Flying Officer Norris. Flying Officer Simkins learned that he would become the next Detachment Commander at McChord. Flying Officer Fred Pearson and Flying Officer Marcel Brooks were posted from the Radio Section to No 137 (T) Flight. Finally, Flying Officer John Darwent was appointed Detachment Commander at Shemya, relieving Flying Officer Al Charters who, after three months, was more than happy to return to base.

Following the example of their wartime predecessors, the No 426 Squadron softball team finished the season on top of the four-team Lachine league.[12]

September

In a ceremonial parade held on 9 September, Wing Commander Douglas officially assumed command of RCAF Station Lachine, taking over from Group Captain Austin, who was posted to RCAF Station Comox as Station Commander. At the same time, Flight Lieutenant Timbrell, the Station Adjutant, was posted overseas to a similar position at 30 AMB Langar.

On Sunday, 14 September, a large contingent of airmen from units based at Lachine marched in the annual Battle of Britain parade in downtown Montreal.

Operationally, the twelve North Stars, sixteen flight crews and the maintenance staff of No 426 Squadron were truly stretched in September. Eight flights went out from McChord on the Korean Airlift, all on schedule with only a few minor delays, mainly for weather. A series of domestic specials were also carried out, including one to Greenland — on 10 September, Flying Officer Knight and his crew in NS17522 transported jet engines from the Canadair plant in Cartierville to Narsarssuak, to be in position in case any Sabres on *LEAP FROG II* needed an engine change after their first over-water crossing.

The six runs to Resolute Bay included the fall re-supply activities. Flying Officer Kuhn made the month's first flight of the month to Resolute on 4 September in NS17504, with Group Captain Austin as First Officer, Wing Commander Douglas as third pilot, and navigator Flying Officer Huard, who had USAF Captain Laudermilk with him to be checked out on high Arctic navigation techniques. On September 5, the No 1 engine in NS17504 malfunctioned on the way to Mould Bay, and the crew had to return to Resolute Bay for repairs. On September 6, their mission completed, Kuhn and his crew returned to base from Resolute Bay by way of Churchill. The last week of September featured the re-supply of the weather stations, completed by means of a series of shuttle runs from Resolute Bay to Isachsen and Mould Bay.

North Atlantic flying blossomed in September, with the overseas build-up of RCAF units. No 426 Squadron launched twelve flights to Europe during the month, with North Luffenham, London, Grostenquin and Paris as the principal destinations via Goose Bay, Keflavik and

Prestwick. Some aircraft also stopped at Narsarssuak on the outbound leg. Most of these flights were in direct support of *Operation LEAP FROG II*.

To provide logistics support for the fighter squadrons in Europe, the RCAF instituted two new scheduled service flights: SF51 (eastbound) and SF52 (westbound), with three round trips per week — a schedule No 426 Squadron maintained, with some variations, until 1961. The basic routing on the outbound leg was through Goose Bay and Keflavik to Prestwick or North Luffenham until Langar became fully operational, and through Keflavik and Goose Bay on the homeward leg. This routing was subject to modification, depending on the load and the weather.

On 13 September, two slip crews were positioned at Keflavik and one slip crew was placed at North Luffenham. Scheduled service between Dorval and Britain began on 18 September, with the despatch of the first Service Flight 51 and the arrival of the first Service Flight 52 at Dorval on 20 September. The average flight time for the round trip by North Star was thirty-four hours.[13]

Phase 2 of *Op LEAP FROG II* began on 28 September, with a formal send-off at RCAF Station Uplands for the three squadrons of No 2 Fighter Wing by Minister of National Defence Brooke Claxton. Following the ceremony, the three squadrons flew to Goose Bay, where they were to rendezvous with the No 426 Squadron North Stars that would shepherd the Sabres across the Atlantic. No 430 Squadron (commanded by Wing Commander J.F. Edwards) made the trip by way of North Bay and Bagotville, where they refuelled, and No 421 Squadron (commanded by Squadron Leader R.G. Middlemiss) went via St-Hubert. No 416 Squadron under Squadron Leader J. MacKay made the trip directly. The same day, No 426 Squadron despatched two North Stars from Dorval to Goose Bay. The aircraft and crews would be away from base for sixteen days.[14]

Wing Commander Lupton and his crew in NS17507 flew across to St. Hubert where they picked up a servicing team from No 421 Squadron and a load of Sabre spares for delivery at Goose Bay. Flying Officer Kuhn and his crew, in NS17516, headed first to North Bay to pick up servicing personnel from No 430 Squadron and aircraft spares destined for Goose Bay.

The Sabres made their first over-water crossing on 30 September, taking about ninety minutes to get to Narsarssuak. The North Stars followed the next morning. Kuhn and his crew continued on to Keflavik to drop off servicing personnel and spares, and Lupton returned to Goose Bay on a logistics run; both crews returned to Narsarssuak on 2 October. Meanwhile, the Sabres waited for a favourable weather forecast for Keflavik and on 3 October, after an early morning weather reconnaissance by Lupton and his crew, and a forecast of suitable limits at Keflavik — a ceiling of 2,000 feet and three miles visibility —the "Go" signal was given. No 416 and No 430 squadron got away easily and made their second over-water crossing in about ninety-six minutes. Just as No 421 Squadron was getting set to leave, however, word was received that the weather at Keflavik was expected to deteriorate, and it was decided that the aircraft should wait for a more favourable forecast. The weather stayed fine — CAVU (ceiling and visibility unlimited) all the way to and at Keflavik.[15]

The aircraft that arrived at Keflavik — No 416 and No 430 squadrons — were quickly refuelled and despatched on their last over-water leg, to Prestwick (a 100-minute run), there to remain until 11 October when the base at Grostenquin would be ready to receive them. Kuhn's aircraft remained at Narsarssuak while Lupton and his crew made a logistics run to Prestwick, returning on 4 October to Keflavik, where Lupton conducted one weather reconnaissance flight on 7 October and two more the day after. At Narsarssuak, Kuhn carried out a similar flight on the morning of 8 October, with Wing Commander Mussells, the Task Force Commander, aboard. With favourable actual and forecast weather conditions, No 421 Squadron took off for Keflavik, where they arrived without incident. With the departure of the Sabres, Kuhn set off for Keflavik and, after a brief stop, Prestwick, where No 421 Squadron rejoined the rest of the Wing on 9 October. Lupton then followed the group to Prestwick, while Kuhn and his crew made a series of runs to Grostenquin, Orly and London.[16]

On 11 October, the entire Wing made the trip to Grostenquin together, a seventy-five minute flight. The only real incident of *Operation LEAP FROG II* occurred on this leg, when a No 416 Squadron Sabre flamed out, forcing the pilot down in a farmer's field near North Luffenham.

The rest of the aircraft flew in to Grostenquin by squadron, at fifteen-minute intervals, and found a welcoming party that included Canada's ambassador to France, Georges-Phileas Vanier, whose message of 12 October to the Secretary of State for External Affairs reported the occasion in detail:

1. Our aircraft were given enthusiastic welcome yesterday on arrival at Grostenquin. They were received by representatives French Government, Ministry of Air, SHAPE and by Prefect Forbach, Mayors of Metz and Grostenquin, several Parliamentarians and many senior Allied air officers. General Norstad was also present and warmly congratulated our pilots. He expressed great satisfaction to me at having under his command this wing of the best jet fighters in the world. Of course the whole population of Grostenquin turned out also with the workmen.

2. Our Sabres arrived sharp on time in groups of four in beautiful formation and made perfect landings. This performance was splendid testimonial to the skill, training and efficiency of our pilots. All present were deeply impressed.

3. I lived one of the proudest moments of my mission in France when I saw our Sabres in the Lorraine sky.

4. Unfortunately one of the jets after taking off from Prestwick had to make a forced landing at Luffenham. The other three in the same group landed at Luffenham also and will be leaving today for Grostenquin. Please inform Minister of National Defence that his message was delivered and much appreciated.[17]

RCAF Station Grostenquin lay in the rolling hills of the Moselle region in eastern France, about twenty-five miles east-southeast of Metz. The first Canadian base to operate in continental Europe since the end of the Second World War, it came under the command of No 1 Air Division Headquarters, RCAF, in Paris (it later moved to Metz). No 1 Air Division would function operationally under the Commanding General of the 4th Allied Tactical Air Force.

Diplomatic niceties aside, No 2 Wing discovered on arrival that the station was still under construction. The roads were unfinished, the hangars were roofless, the quarters were heated only by Herman-Nelson generators, and the ramps were stacked with crated gear. Poor weather and lack of facilities prevented No 2 Wing from flying during its first week at its new home. The heavy rain caused floods that had wags calling the station "HMCS Grostenquin."[18]

On 12 October, Kuhn and his crew left Heathrow for North Luffenham, and the next day they headed home via Prestwick and Keflavik. Wing Commander Lupton left Heathrow on 13 October and returned to base by way of Keflavik and Goose Bay. Both crews were back at base on 14 October, their involvement in *Op LEAP FROG II* ended.

As the second phase of *LEAP FROG II* got under way, the squadron began the airlift of No 2 Wing personnel and their baggage to Grostenquin. Eight passenger flights went to Grostenquin between 1 October and 8 October, two from North Bay and three each from Uplands and St-Hubert.

Ten more service or special flights were despatched from Dorval during the month, five terminating at Grostenquin and five at North Luffenham. Follow-up support for No 2 Wing would continue in November.

On 25 October a debriefing conference on *Op LEAP FROG II* was held at Air Defence Command Headquarters, chaired by Wing Commander Braham. As well as a host of technical issues, the conference discussed the command and control of future ferry operations, a topic raised by Wing Commander Mussells, who thought it illogical for Air Transport Command Headquarters to be in charge of the *LEAP FROG* operations, recommending instead that such moves be handled entirely by Air Defence Command, with Air Transport Command cast only in the role of transport provider.[19]

In a letter to the Chief of the Air Staff, Air Commodore Ripley indicated that, although one of Air Transport Command's functions was to supply and control overseas ferry facilities, its involvement in the two *LEAP FROG* operations indicated too broad an interpretation of this role. *LEAP FROG* operations were movements of tactical formations from Canada to Europe, and Ripley thought that, in such operations, a tactical formation should be able to do its own detailed operational planning, and require only airlift services from Air Transport Command.

Ripley conceded that his staff officers had gained valuable planning experience, but pointed out that the experience would have been more valuable to the tactical formations involved. He argued that it was reasonable to assume that, in emergencies, tactical units would move often, and it was, therefore, not reasonable to assume that a Transport formation would direct or control these moves. Having ascertained that his opposite number at Air Defence Command agreed with him on this issue, Ripley sought early approval of a policy to make each tactical formation slated to move to Europe responsible for planning and executing its own move. This request was somewhat urgent, as *LEAP FROG III* was scheduled to begin on 1 March 1953, and had to be in the planning stage.

In reply to the Commander, Air Transport Command, Air Force Headquarters agreed to transfer operational control of future *LEAP FROG* moves from Air Transport Command to Air Defence Command.[20]

The squadron met its October quota of eight round trips to Tokyo with only a few minor delays for mechanical problems and bad weather in the North Pacific. On the domestic scene, three freight runs to Resolute Bay were conducted during the month, including one flight that stopped at Thule. Once in Resolute, each aircraft made shuttle runs to Isachsen and Mould Bay. Finally, the squadron carried out seven special domestic flights in addition to its other activities.

In a lengthy letter written in October to the Chief of the Air Staff, Air Commodore Ripley expressed concern about a government policy statement on Canadian participation in the Korean conflict that had been issued apparently in response to a UN request to its membership for a more equitable division of the operational burden. The government's position was that Canada was doing her share and was in no position to contribute more. As far as Air Force assets were concerned, Ripley wrote, Canada had offered full use of No 426 Squadron, which was operating under MATS since flying the North Pacific route seemed the most appropriate Korea-related mission for the North Star. Had No 426 Squadron been sent to Japan, it would probably have come under the UN Theatre Commander, as had the transport crews and aircraft supplied by other UN countries, which were integrated with the UN Air Forces rather than with MATS.

In his letter, Ripley emphasized that the trans-Pacific commitment had changed considerably since the winter of 1950–51. The supply situation had improved with the decrease in active military operations and increased use of larger aircraft more suitable to the mid-Pacific routes. Consequently, MATS had reduced movements over the North Pacific, and was now using mostly civilian contract carriers; in fact, the RCAF was the only military operator still flying the route on a scheduled basis. In Ripley's opinion, MATS was very concerned about developing a civilian airlift capability for national emergencies, and was therefore only too happy to use civilian carriers where possible to give them experience in the role. At the same time, some of these carriers obviously sought military work for their own advantage. With all these contributing factors, it seemed likely to Ripley that the RCAF was sometimes carrying cargo that was not really important enough to ship by air. He had received reports of cargo destined for sea shipment that was rerouted by air to make up aircraft loads.

In January, Ripley had received a letter from Air Force Headquarters in which he was advised to approach MATS to discuss reducing the RCAF commitment in light of the withdrawal of USAF aircraft. At the time, the Operations staff at Air Force Headquarters were told that the USAF aircraft were being taken off the North Pacific operation because of internal problems, but supply lines to Japan still needed to be maintained. As long as the UN was allocating the operational control of an RCAF squadron to MATS, that organization was more or less compelled to use it.

Ripley's official discussions with MATS confirmed this opinion. MATS would find itself in an awkward position if it declined a valuable UN contribution, while the US government was pressuring the UN for more assistance from other nations. As Commander, Air Transport Command, Ripley could get no formal acknowledgement from MATS at any level — McChord, Tokyo, Continental Division in San Antonio, or MATS Headquarters itself — that No 426 Squadron was no longer required on the Korean Airlift. That the unit was not carrying priority loads or that USAF units had been withdrawn from the North Pacific run did not in any way affect the issue.

Air Commodore Ripley discussed the squadron's cargoes with MATS officers at both Tokyo and McChord, correcting in the process some significant misunderstandings between the MATS Commander and the Canadian Army Liaison Officer in Tokyo. With other RCAF commitments increasing, Air Transport Command Headquarters made low-level arrangements with MATS to cut the squadron back from fifteen to eight North Pacific runs per month. The reduced schedule went into affect in June and was, in the Commander's view, subject to change. As Ripley saw it:

- A Canadian contribution to the UN (i.e., the services of No 426 Squadron) was not being used because of a local arrangement between the UN-delegated authority (MATS) and the RCAF; and
- The Canadian government was making public statements implying that the RCAF commitment, as offered, was used to the fullest extent possible, and that it could not be increased.

Ripley believed that, should any question arise as to the use of No 426 Squadron by MATS, that organization would be perfectly entitled to say that the commitment was reduced at the request of the RCAF. MATS could also assume that the Canadian government had agreed to the reduction in the RCAF commitment, and that the UN, too, was in the picture. Attention was drawn to the fact that RCAF operations in the North Pacific were not secret, as detailed reports containing information about the carriers and their loads were appearing in US aviation magazines.

Air Commodore Ripley sought policy guidance on the following points:

- Should the full operational capability of No 426 Squadron be returned to UN use at a moment's notice, if requested; and,
- Should he be satisfied with the present "old friend" basis regarding the level of operations in the North Pacific, or should he make it clear to MATS that, because the squadron had been officially offered to the UN, the UN agent — MATS — was responsible for any reduction in its employment, which should not be deemed to be a result of any Canadian request to reduce its contribution to the UN.

In closing, Ripley stated that Air Transport Command's dealings with MATS could be misinterpreted at the government level, and such misunderstandings could harm the excellent relationship between the RCAF and the USAF, something the RCAF could not afford. Any reduction in official co-operation between the RCAF and the USAF could, for example, seriously hinder the movement of fighter aircraft to Europe. If that happened, the RCAF would need to replace USAF services — which the RCAF just could not afford.[21]

In his reply to Air Commodore Ripley, the Chief of the Air Staff, Air Marshal Curtis, stated that he had spoken to the Minister about No 426 Squadron operations on the Korean Airlift, and the Minister was now fully aware that arrangements had been made with MATS to reduce the Pacific commitment from fifteen to eight trips per month, and had assured him that he would take this into account in any future discussions on the subject.

Curtis went on to say that, since the services of No 426 Squadron were first offered to the UN, circumstances had changed considerably. The increasing trans-Atlantic commitment in support of RCAF squadrons in Europe made it impossible ever to return the full operational capability of No 426 Squadron to the Korean Airlift. He felt sure that the government would readily appreciate this situation should conditions in Korea ever again necessitate a large-scale trans-Pacific airlift.

Since the existing arrangement with MATS was working so well, Curtis saw no reason to change it. MATS could be advised that, should circumstances in Korea deteriorate, the RCAF would be prepared to reinstate as many trips as possible. The number of trips was to be determined by Air Transport Command Headquarters and Air Force Headquarters, taking other current RCAF commitments into account.[22]

On 14 November, Group Captain R.W. McNair, the Air Attaché at the Canadian Embassy in Tokyo, wrote to the Chief of the Air Staff proposing that No 426 Squadron be taken off the Korean Airlift because not one single officer in Far East Air Forces Headquarters, even General Weyland, seemed to be aware that either the RCAF or Canadian Pacific Airlines was involved at all, let alone the extent of their efforts. McNair suggested that the current RCAF commitment of approximately 600 flying hours per month be reallocated to operations between Japan and Korea, a task in which the North Stars would be a great help to the 315th Air Division, which was responsible for airlift services in the theatre of operations. The Americans were known for a higher rate of turnover on the R&R system for combat troops and, although the existing airlift capability could operate at a higher tempo, it would strain both aircraft and crews.

In McNair's view, operating in-theatre would give Canadian flight crews and ground crews new and valuable experience. The North Star was considered ideal for the relatively short flights and could operate at a much higher utilization rate. With just four North Stars, something like 9,000 UN troops could be airlifted between Japan and Korea each month! McNair thought the aircraft could be maintained and operated by a detachment of not more than fifty tradesmen and five complete flight crews, little more than the personnel already tied up in the detachments at Haneda, Shemya and McChord — a wasteful arrangement for only eight trips per month. Major inspections could be done at Dorval, and the aircraft could carry useful loads between Japan and Vancouver on the rotation flights. As the North Star had proved itself mechanically reliable, it was reasonable to assume that a small stock of running spares would be sufficient at Tachikawa, the base for the proposed operation.

In addition to achieving a high utilization factor and broadening the experience of RCAF crews, in-theatre airlift operations would bring No 426 Squadron, the RCAF and Canada a lot of good publicity. On an average day, almost 4,000 UN personnel moved through the airports at Tachikawa and Seoul City, and many of these troops could travel by North Star, giving them personal contact with a major Canadian contribution to UN operations in Korea, which in turn would ensure increased importance and authority for any views Ottawa might wish to express on the Korean situation.[23]

On 21 November, the Charge d'Affaires at the Embassy, Arthur Menzies, sent Group Captain McNair's recommendations to the Under-Secretary of State for External Affairs with his endorsement. On 8 December, Charles Ritchie, the Acting Under-Secretary of State, wrote to the Chairman of the Chiefs of Staff Committee, drawing McNair's recommendations and Menzies' comments to his attention. On 16 December, Air Vice Marshal F.R. Miller, the Acting Chief of the Air Staff, wrote to the Chairman on McNair's proposal, saying that the RCAF had considered reassigning the North Stars before but, as RCAF participation in the Korean Airlift was a UN commitment and the aircraft were under the operational control of MATS, it was not advisable to make any change. He went on to say that the relatively short flights from Japan to Korea would give the flight and ground crews much less valuable experience and training than the trans-Pacific route did. Therefore, Miller concluded, the RCAF did not propose any changes in the assignment of No 426 Squadron.[24]

November

In November, No 426 Squadron made thirteen scheduled service flights (SF51/52) to Britain — so many that the squadron established a detachment at North Luffenham with Flying Officer Ray Langman in command.

Five flights to Resolute Bay were despatched during the month. On one run, Captain Green had to return to base in NS17515 with No 1 engine feathered. Setting off the next morning in the same aircraft, he had problems with No 1 engine again, and returned to Montreal to switch to NS17506, in which the flight was made without incident. The month's domestic schedule included six special flights, three of which were to Goose Bay.

The November commitment to conduct eight flights to Tokyo was fulfilled as usual, with one exception.

Flying Officer D.H. Kuhn left base in NS17511 on 8 November for the scheduled twelve-day trip to Japan. The crew included first officer Flying Officer J.F. Lambert, navigator Flying Officer D.G. Carmichael, radio officer Flight Lieutenant J. Egan, flight engineer Sergeant Boulet and air traffic assistant Leading Aircraftsman Robillard. Everything went routinely on the transit through Winnipeg and Edmonton, but as the flight approached Vancouver, the No 3 low-coolant warning light came on and, after watching the coolant temperature rise, the crew shut down the engine and feathered the propeller. They carried out a normal three-engine approach and landing. Boulet added coolant fluid, and the engine checked out on the run-up. The flight then went on to McChord, where a thorough maintenance check was carried out on No 3 engine, followed by an air test on the aircraft. With everything serviceable, the departed for Elmendorf AFB, the crew feeling confident that the No 3 engine problem was caused by the lack of coolant fluid, as nothing went wrong during the seven-hour flight.

At the weather briefing at Elmendorf, the crew learned that the forecast for Shemya was — as usual — down in fog and severe cross-winds. Departing Elmendorf, the aircraft climbed to its cruising altitude of 8,000 feet. As the flight passed King Salmon Radio and headed out over the Bering Sea, however, it ran into fairly heavy icing conditions as the aircraft bounced along the tops of the cumulus cloud. As the situation deteriorated, the radio officer tried to obtain clearance to climb to a higher altitude, but the atmospheric conditions and the ice on the aircraft interfered with radio transmission and reception.

With the situation becoming critical, Kuhn called for climbing power and began to climb out of the cloud, and at 12,000 feet the aircraft broke out into the clear and the very welcome moonlight. Not long after levelling out and before much of the ice could be shed, the No 3 coolant warning light began to flash again. As before, when the flash turned to a steady glow the coolant temperature began to rise and the engine had to be shut down, but with its massive load of ice, the could not maintain altitude and was forced to descend. Facing the prospect of four or five more hours of flying in icing conditions and a poor weather forecast at Shemya, Kuhn decided to divert to Cold Bay, a tiny station at the end of the Alaska Peninsula, about 200 miles to the south of the aircraft's position.

Flying Officer Carmichael came up with a heading and Kuhn made a descending turn to port, eventually finding better weather at a lower altitude, and Egan got clearance to proceed to Cold Bay. The weather was quite good for landing, except for the strong crosswind. On landing, Lambert helped to keep the wings level and to pin the nose wheel so Kuhn would have enough nose-wheel steering control. The aircraft rolled to an uneventful stop, and the crew were welcomed by a small USAF caretaker detachment and directed to the only accommodation available — an old Nissen hut. It was cold and miserable with a howling wind, and the small oil stove did them little good in the uninsulated metal building.

The next day, after a lot of checking by Sergeant Boulet in the teeth of the freezing wind, it was decided that No 3 engine had to be changed. It took three days to get a new engine and a couple of technicians flown in, and the engine change was performed outdoors in very nasty weather.

After a flight test, they took off for Shemya. Normally, the leg to Tokyo could be flown without refuelling, but not this time. After bucking headwinds for eleven and a half hours, Kuhn was forced to land at Misawa to take on fuel before carrying on to Haneda. By this point, the flight had taken ten days to cover a distance that normally took four to five days. After a two-day layover in Tokyo, Kuhn and his crew headed back to McChord. Shortly after leaving Elmendorf, No 2 engine began showing fluctuating RPM, which meant turning back. After yet another overnight stay, they were again on their way to McChord, and the day after that, the flight headed for Dorval via Vancouver, Edmonton and Winnipeg, arriving late in the evening of 28 November. Kuhn and his crew had been gone for nearly three weeks.[25]

On 11 November the customary tri-service Remembrance Day parade was held at the cenotaph in downtown Montreal, with RCAF Station Lachine units well represented. It was a cold day and greatcoats were very much in evidence.

No 426 Squadron aircraft logged 1,450 flying hours in November with a serviceability rate of 71 percent. As well as looking after its own North Stars, the squadron's Servicing Section cared for 205 aircraft that had visited Dorval.

Rejoining the squadron after completing his captaincy training at No 4 OTU was Flying Officer Bruce Ingall. Like the rest of the squadron, the Navigation Section found itself fully stretched in November, short of route-qualified navigators and required to call in ex-Thunderbirds serving in other commands. These veterans included Squadron Leader R.E.D. Ratcliffe, Squadron Leader E.J.J. Boland, Flight Lieutenant R.S. Reid and Flight Lieutenant J.W. (Jock) Rodger, who did an excellent job of familiarizing some of the newer navigators on the squadron's various routes. Three navigators — Flying Officer R.L. North, Flying Officer J.L. Belyea and Flying Officer D.H. Weir — went to Edmonton for the RCAF survival course and returned none the worse for a stint in the wintry bush. By November, three of the section's more senior navigators, Flying Officer J.L.A. DeQuoy, Flying Officer S.R. Langman and Flying Officer M. Majocha had already completed 1,000 flying hours in the year, considered the maximum, and were temporarily assigned to ground duties. Langman ended up as Detachment Commander job at North Luffenham.

The Radio Section faced a similar situation: many of the senior radio officers had reached the 1,000-hour mark and were grounded. No 435 Squadron in Edmonton was asked for reinforcements, and Flying Officer C.F.S. Grist, Flying Officer G.E. Taylor and Flying Officer A.D. Tompkins soon arrived to lend a hand. Leaving the squadron were Flying Officer E.J.M. Snelling, posted to No 412 Squadron; Flying Officer C.J.W. Gauthier, assigned to the Reserve Wing in Montreal, and Flying Officer J.P. Wilson, who became the Assistant Chief Administration Officer at RCAF Station Lachine.[26]

At about this time, the Department of National Defence, the Department of Transport and the USAF reached an agreement on operations at Torbay, Newfoundland. As of 1 November, the RCAF element there became a Station under Maritime Group Headquarters in Halifax to maintain the airfield and the RCAF-occupied buildings, to control station security, and to maintain the control tower. RCAF Station Torbay would also provide materiel accounting for all RCAF and Royal Canadian Air Cadet units in Newfoundland.[27]

As at Torbay, the RCAF element at Frobisher Bay was organized as a Station effective 1 December 1952, with responsibility for the control tower and ground-to-air communications. The Station Commander would also to be responsible for co-ordinating RCAF–USAF defence arrangements. The USAF was to provide housekeeping services, rations and quarters, and medical services for all personnel stationed at Frobisher Bay.[28]

December

At the end of November, Air Transport Command faced a critical shortage of ground crew, and immediately cut trans-continental flights by 50 percent and limited trans-Atlantic flights to one per week.[29] While these flight reductions did not affect the Korean Airlift commitment, other operational activities in December were curtailed by some 500 flying hours.

Two of the eight flights despatched to Tokyo from McChord encountered mechanical problems en route. On 3 December, Flying Officer Grant and his crew left Shemya for Haneda in NS17510 with thirty-five US Army paratroopers aboard. Before leaving Shemya, the crew had trouble with their nose-wheel steering, but the flight proceeded normally until an engine malfunctioned and had to be shut down and the propeller feathered — a situation that made some of the passengers uneasy. Since the flight had passed the point at which it was quicker to proceed at reduced airspeed to Japan than to return to Shemya, it was decided to head for Misawa, the nearest major airfield.

The navigator, Flying Officer Peter Sutherland, quickly worked out a revised heading and an ETA for the new destination. The radio officer transmitted a "Pan Pan Pan" message to alert Tokyo Airways to the existence of a problem that was not yet an emergency, but could become one. As the aircraft passed by Hokkaido, a USAF SA-16 search-and-rescue aircraft met them to provide an escort to Misawa, and arrangements were made for the passengers on arrival. It took until 7 December, three and a half days later, before the nose-wheel problem could be fixed so Grant could fly NS17510 on three engines to Haneda.[30]

Squadron Leader Torontow's flight of 4 December in NS17516 was the next one out of McChord. NS17516 was plagued by radio problems and, after some repairs at Elmendorf and more at Shemya, where an air test was carried out, Flight Lieutenant Milner, the Radio Officer, found the equipment functioning well enough to permit departure for Tokyo. Encountering stiff headwinds en route, Torontow decided to head for Misawa to refuel. The flight arrived at Haneda just before noon on 7 December.

Very early the next morning, Flying Officer Grant skippered NS17516 to Seoul City Airport (K16) with a load of Christmas comforts for Canadian troops and Squadron Leader Torontow and his crew aboard with Milner troubleshooting the radio problems, which were traced to faulty connections in the wiring. As soon as the cargo was unloaded, Grant flew the aircraft back to Haneda, where, after it was loaded and serviced, Flight Lieutenant J.N. Hall took it over for the flight back to McChord. Meanwhile, the Haneda detachment had changed the engine on NS17510, and both Grant's and Torontow's crews left for McChord, sharing the flying duties.[31]

The second delay occurred when Flying Officer Waddell in NS17511 was preparing to leave Elmendorf for McChord on 18 December. The Automatic Boost Control unit on the aircraft went unserviceable, causing a thirty-hour delay waiting for it to be fixed. This was only the second flight since the early days of the airlift on which the crew stayed with the aircraft, resting at Shemya and Haneda on the way out, and again at Shemya on the way back. The new schedule began with Serial 458 when Flying Officer Casselman left McChord on 5 December. After the departure of Grant and Torontow there would be no slip crew at Haneda, although the detachments at McChord, Shemya and Tokyo would remain. The round trip from McChord was expected to take six days, and each aircraft and its crew were away from Dorval for about ten days.[32]

On the domestic scene, Goose Bay was the destination of nine ration runs, and three special pre-Christmas trips were conducted to Resolute Bay by way of Winnipeg. The trips included landings at Churchill, Coral Harbour and Thule, and para-drops at Arctic Bay, Isachsen and Mould Bay.

The month started with some excitement at Resolute Bay, where a project supervisor from the Montreal firm Canadian Aviation Electronics Limited (CAEL) had become dissatisfied with an employee's work and relieved him of his duties. After brooding most of the evening, the employee picked up a .303-calbre rifle signed out to another member of the CAEL crew and took it to the supervisor's room at about 0130 hours. The men struggled and a shot was fired, missing the supervisor by inches. The detachment commander, Flight Lieutenant Wolkowski, proceeded cautiously to the scene with Sergeant Tresidder and found the employee subdued by the supervisor. Wolkowski separated the antagonists and placed the employee under close arrest on a charge of attempted murder.

There was no further trouble, but everyone was on edge; the prisoner, who had been given a sedative, was probably the only person who got any sleep that night. Two airmen were detailed to guard the prisoner in two-hour shifts until he could be turned over to the RCMP, and Wolkowski wrote a full report and sent it to RCMP detachment at Churchill and RCAF Station Lachine. SF 17, captained by Flying Officer McAninch, arrived from Churchill at 1500 hours on 3 December, and departed for Churchill again at 2000 hours as SF 18, with not only the prisoner aboard, on his way to RCMP custody at Churchill, but also the rest of the CAEL crew, who were heading home to Montreal.³³

Two flights to Britain were conducted in December. The first, to North Luffenham on 2 December, was carried out by Flying Officer Sage and his crew in NS17504 to pick up the three slip crews from Keflavik and North Luffenham; they returned to base four days later. On 16 December, Captain Green, the USAF exchange officer, took passengers and high-priority freight to North Luffenham in NS17503. That flight returned to base three days later.

The squadron handled one other assignment before the year ended. A double crew captained by Flying Officer Knight left base for McChord at 0940 hours on 23 December, stopping at Winnipeg and Edmonton on the way out. This special flight was taking wounded Canadian soldiers, accompanied by nurses, to hospitals closer to their home towns. On the return leg, the aircraft again landed at Edmonton and at Winnipeg, reaching Montreal shortly after midnight on Christmas Eve. Flight Lieutenant Butchart and his crew took over the aircraft, proceeding to Saint. John, New Brunswick, and Dartmouth, Nova Scotia, before returning to base at 0830 hours on Christmas Day.³⁴

After a busy year, the men of No 426 Squadron privileged to be at home in the Montreal area were more than content to spend a quiet Christmas with family and friends.

Chiefs of the Air Staff

PHOTO 114
Air Marshal R. Leckie (CAS 1 January 1944–31 August 1947) (DND PL 117339)

PHOTO 115
Air Marshal W.A. Curtis (CAS 1 September 1947–31 January 1953) (DND PL 110424)

PHOTO 116
Air Marshal C.R. Slemon (CAS 1 February 1953–31 August 1957) (DND PL 103213)

PHOTO 117
Air Marshal H. Campbell (CAS 1 September 1957–14 September 1962) (DND PL 110200)

Lachine, July–December 1952

AIR OFFICERS COMMANDING, AIR TRANSPORT COMMAND

PHOTO 119
Air Commodore A.D. Ross (AOC 16 August 1948–3 August 1951) (DND PL 104565)

PHOTO 118
Air Commodore L.E. Wray (AOC No 9 Transport Group 5 February 1946–31 March 1948; AOC Air Transport Command 1 April 1948–15 August 1948) (DND PL 108476)

PHOTO 120
Air Commodore R.C. Ripley (AOC 4 August 1951–17 November 1953) (DND PL 57066)

AIR OFFICERS COMMANDING, AIR TRANSPORT COMMAND

PHOTO 121
Group Captain Z.L. Leigh (Commanding Officer 18 November 1953–25 July 1954) (DND PL 142658)

PHOTO 122
Air Commodore H.M. Carscallen (AOC 26 July 1954– 5 August 1956) (DND PL 104080)

PHOTO 123
Air Commodore F.S. Carpenter (AOC 6 August 1956– 26 June 1961) (DND, No 426 Squadron)

PHOTO 124
Air Commodore R.J. Lane (AOC 27 June 1961– 27 December 1965) (DND PL 133650)

CHAPTER 15

LACHINE
JANUARY–JUNE 1953

By May 1952, the Korean Armistice Commission had reached agreements on all issues except the disposition of prisoners of war. Many prisoners held by UN forces did not wish to be repatriated, and the Chinese and North Korean negotiators contended that *all* prisoners should be returned to their country of origin, while the UN Command held that prisoners should be permitted to reject repatriation if they so decided. On 8 October, with negotiations completely deadlocked, the UN Command declared an indefinite recess in the truce talks.

Fighting continued in the hills along the 38th Parallel into 1953. On 11 February, Lieutenant General M. Taylor replaced Lieutenant General J.A. Van Fleet as Commander of the Eighth Army. Later that month, the UN Command again proposed an exchange of sick and wounded prisoners and, by the end of March, the Communists had agreed to the proposal. Between 20 April and 26 April, the first exchange of prisoners — *Operation LITTLE SWITCH* — took place at Panmunjom; 6,670 Chinese and North Korean prisoners, all of them sick or seriously wounded, were exchanged for 471 South Koreans, 149 Americans and sixty-four other UN personnel. On 27 April, the truce talks resumed at Panmunjom.[1]

While all this was taking place on land, the UN naval fleet blockaded the Korean coasts, denying the Communists effective use of the seas. Over three years of war, this fleet comprised sixteen aircraft carriers (thirteen American, one Australian, two British) as well as four battleships, eight cruisers and some eighty destroyers from the United States and ten other countries, including Canada, which maintained a three-destroyer task force.

Coastal bombardment by ships of the UN fleet, and strikes by carrier-based aircraft, severely restricted the movement of Communist troops and supplies by road and rail, and the stabilization of the battle line on the 38th Parallel permitted the UN air forces to concentrate on destroying Communist supply and communications facilities. Daylight raids were conducted against rail lines, highways, trains and truck traffic, while night-intruder operations attacked bridges and rail centres. The goal of this interdiction program was to prevent the Communists from building up enough troop strength and materiel to launch — let alone sustain — a major offensive. A bombing campaign was conducted against industrial targets and, by mid-1952, most of North Korea's hydroelectric power production was knocked out, and many of its remaining war industries crippled. Since November 1950, when Russian-built MiG-15 jet fighters began operating in Korean airspace from bases in China, in aerial dogfights alone the UN forces' F-86 Sabres had destroyed more than nine MiGs for every Sabre lost in action.[2]

Although disagreement on the issue of prisoner repatriation continued to dog the armistice negotiations through May 1953, Canadian troops fought their last major action of the Korean War on the night of 2–3 May, when the Communists attacked positions held by C Company of the 3rd Battalion, The Royal Canadian Regiment. In the ensuing battle, 3 RCR lost 26 killed, 27 wounded and seven taken prisoner.[3] During the last week of the month, Communist forces launched a major offensive designed to take dominant UN positions on ridges about ten miles northeast of Panmunjom.

The slow pace of the truce negotiations had a direct effect on the air war. Faced with the prospect of a protracted conflict, the UN Command decided to strike some previously untouched sensitive targets, including dams that were crucial to rice production in North Korea. As well as having a devastating economic impact, the destruction of the dams disrupted Communist plans for land operations by flooding out both rail and road networks.[4]

As the truce talks continued into June, Communist forces launched a total of 104 separate attacks on the UN lines.

Early in June, the Communists and the United Nations reached an accord that included the repatriation issue, but the Republic of Korea and its President, Syngman Rhee, still stood in the way of an armistice — it was politically difficult for Syngman Rhee to accept any agreement that left his country and people divided. The prospect of an armistice was almost destroyed on 18 June, when Syngman Rhee removed South Korean troops from General Mark Clark's UN command and ordered the release of about 27,000 anti-Communist Korean prisoners of war from camps in the Pusan area — an event described as a "mass escape". Most of the prisoners melted into the Korean population, and others joined the South Korean army. At this point, the Communist delegates halted peace negotiations as they doubted that South Korea would respect any armistice.

Required literally to make peace with his Korean ally, President Eisenhower dispatched his Assistant Secretary of State for Far Eastern Affairs, Walter S. Robinson, to Seoul. Robinson took twelve days to reach an agreement with Syngman Rhee, who agreed not to obstruct the armistice in exchange for Robinson's promise of a US–ROK mutual security treaty, and long-term economic aid. The Korean War effectively ended on 27 July at Panmunjom, where Lieutenant-General W.K. Harrison of the UN Command and General Nam Il of North Korea signed documents putting the truce into effect. Syngman Rhee supported the cease-fire and refrained from obstructing the armistice, as he had agreed, but he never ratified the truce, and neither did the government of South Korea.[5]

On the international scene, this period featured deepening chill in NATO-Soviet relations as the results of weapons research began to be known. On 3 October 1952, the first successful test of a British-designed and -constructed atomic weapon was conducted off the northwest coast of Australia, in the Monte Bello Islands, and a year later, the British tested a second weapon at the Woomera Rocket Range in Australia. On 1 November 1952, the Americans detonated the world's first thermonuclear explosion at Eniwetok Atoll in the South Pacific, and the Soviets followed suit on 12 August 1953. Earlier that year, the Americans had conducted a series of tests in the Nevada desert in which the first "tactical" nuclear weapon — an atomic artillery shell — was demonstrated; fired from a 280-mm gun that could handle both conventional and nuclear rounds, the shell detonated with a force equivalent to that generated by 3,000 tons of TNT. After this demonstration, the 280-mm gun was shipped to the Far East; the atomic ammunition followed, but was not delivered to Korea. Information about these shipments was allowed to fall into Communist hands, and some sources attribute the signing of the Korean armistice to this not-so-subtle American nuclear sabre-rattling. Another factor significant to the abrupt cessation of hostilities in Korea was Stalin's death on 5 March 1953, which produced significant unrest in the Communist world.[6]

A total of twenty-two RCAF fighter pilots served with the USAF in Korea, and nineteen of them flew combat missions. Of those nineteen, the following five pilots saw action with the USAF in 1953: Flight Lieutenant G.H. Nicholls (January–May), Flight Lieutenant R.D. Carew (February–July), Squadron Leader J. MacKay (March–July), Flight Lieutenant W.H.F. Bliss (April–August), and Squadron Leader W.H. Fox (May–October). The three pilots who served with the USAF but did not fly in combat were: Flying Officer J.D. Donald (April–May 1952), Flying Officer J.B. Mullin (June–October 1953), and Squadron Leader D. Warren (July–October 1953).[7]

The Queen's New Year Honours List for 1953 included the names of seven current or former members of No 426 Squadron, all of them cited for service on the Korean Airlift. Flight Lieutenant R.M. Edwards received the Air Force Cross, Corporal J.B.P.A. Trudel received the British Empire Medal, and the Queen's Commendation for Valuable Services in the Air was presented to Flight Lieutenant R.E. Burn, Flight Lieutenant E.R. Wolkowski, Flying Officer J.P. Wilson, Sergeant G. Howard and Sergeant L.C. Potekal. Fighter pilot Flight Lieutenant E.A. Glover, who flew with the USAF in Korea from June to October 1952, received the first Distinguished Flying Cross to be awarded to a member of the RCAF at a time when Canada was not formally at war. He was being recognized for exploits in Korea, including the destruction of three MiG-15s and damage to two more. He also received a DFC from the United States.[8]

In 1953, the RCAF Order of Battle increased by six squadrons: one transport, two fighter, and three all-weather fighter squadrons. On 1 January, No 422(F) Squadron was re-formed at RCAF Station Uplands under the command of Squadron Leader W.J. Buzza and initially flying the Canadair Sabre Mk II. On 1 March, No 444(F) Squadron was formed at RCAF Station St-Hubert under the command of Squadron Leader E.R. Heggtveit and flying the Sabre Mk IV. During the summer, both of these squadrons would go overseas to join No 4 Wing at Baden-Söllingen in West Germany, the move being carried out as *Operation LEAP FROG IV.*

The newly authorized all-weather fighter squadrons, developed for the air defence of North America, flew the AVRO CF-100 Mk IIIB — the Canuck, or "Clunk". The first of these units, No 445 AW(F) Squadron, was formed on 1 April at RCAF Station North Bay under Wing Commander G.E. Nickerson. The second, No 423 AW(F) Squadron, was re-formed at RCAF Station St-Hubert on 1 July under Wing Commander C.R.J. Lawler. The third, No 440 AW(F) Squadron, was re-formed at RCAF Station Bagotville on 1 October under Wing Commander C.A.G. Lawrence.[9]

The new transport unit, No 436 (T) Squadron, authorized by AFHQ Organization Order 15/53, was re-formed on 1 April at RCAF Station Lachine under Squadron Leader K.C.M. Dobbin and initially equipped with two Fairchild C-119Gs — Flying Boxcars. As part of Air Transport Command, No 436 Squadron would share the RCAF facilities at Dorval with No 426 Squadron and No 4 (T) OTU, and draw its personnel from Air Transport Command resources. To increase the supply of technicians qualified to maintain the C-119G, Air Transport Command Headquarters had arranged for training to be provided by Fairchild, and by the end of January 1953, about 120 tradesmen from No 4 (T) OTU and No 435 Squadron had completed sessions delivered at the factory.[10]

January

No 426 Squadron's northern operations for January included eight logistics runs to Goose Bay, three scheduled flights to Resolute Bay, a scientific exercise at the North Pole, and a special flight to Churchill. The first northern flight of the year was conducted by Flying Officer J. Grant and his crew, who left base on 3 January in NS17516, routed to Resolute Bay via Winnipeg, Churchill and Coral Harbour, and transporting Flight Lieutenant G.H. Knight to Resolute to replace Flight Lieutenant E.R. Wolkowski as Detachment Commander. Arriving at Resolute Bay at 1940 hours on 4 January, the crew were off again shortly before midnight to conduct para-drops at Arctic Bay, Craig Harbour and Pond Inlet before carrying on to Churchill.

Knight spent 5 January being briefed on the detachment and visiting the site's various facilities, and that evening the detachment personnel threw a farewell party for Wolkowski. The next day, Grant and his crew returned from Churchill at 1350 hours with another load of freight, and were on their way back to base two hours later with Wolkowski aboard.[11]

The squadron's first flight to the North Geographic Pole was carried out between 24 January and 29 January by Squadron Leader Cy Torontow in NS17517, to transport Dr. D.C. Rose of the Division of Physics at the National Research Council to the high Arctic to measure the ozone content of the atmosphere there, part of a study (the first of its type) being conducted by Dr. Rose in collaboration with his NRC colleagues Dr. Alexander E. Douglas and Dr. Gerhard Herzberg. The flight was planned by Squadron Leader Keith Greenaway of the Defence Research Board to take place when the moon was at a precise altitude between 85° and 90° North and, as this was the crew's first polar flight, Greenaway shared the navigation chores with Flight Lieutenant M. Majocha. The observers on the flight were Dr. O.M. Solandt, the Chairman of the Defence Research Board; Commissioner L.H. Nicholson of the RCMP; Major-General N.E. Rodger of the Canadian Army; Ivor Bowen, the Director of the Joint Intelligence Bureau; and Sir Archibald Nye, the High Commissioner for Great Britain.

The trip began in Ottawa, where NS17506 picked up the scientific team and senior officials. Leaving Ottawa at 1030 hours on 24 January, the flight was routed via Winnipeg to Churchill, where the party spent two nights. Departing Churchill at 0805 hours on 26 January, the flight then headed for Resolute Bay, where it stopped for five hours so the passengers could tour the facilities before going on to Thule. On 27 January at 1335 hours, NS17506 was on its way to the Geographic North Pole, a flight of four hours and twenty-one minutes.

Dr. Rose measured the ozone content of the atmosphere by taking ultraviolet spectrograms of sunlight reflected off the moon; later, he compared these spectrograms with others taken at Ottawa with the same instruments, with the moon at the same height above the horizon. The measurements showed that the atmosphere at the North Pole had about the same ozone content as the atmosphere at Ottawa.

With the sampling completed, a heading was set for Thule, a return run of five hours and nine minutes, where the party stayed overnight. At 1320 hours on 28 January, the party went on to Frobisher Bay, where they again spent the night. The flight returned to Ottawa at 1635 hours on 29 January, for a total distance flown from Ottawa of 7,364 miles, and a flight time of thirty hours and thirty minutes.[12]

As well as the northern flights, No 426 Squadron conducted two trips to Britain and four special flights in Canada in January, and completed the month's quota of eight round trips to Japan.

Air Commodore Ripley and officers of his staff carried out the annual inspection of RCAF Station Lachine on 21 January, and of the Dorval site the next day, which ended with the traditional mess dinner held by the station's officers to entertain the inspection party. At a CO's parade held on 30 January, Wing Commander H.W. Lupton presented the certificates of the Queen's Commendation for Valuable Services in the Air to Flight Lieutenant R.E. Burn and Sergeant G. Howard.[13]

Authorized by a 1952 organization order from Air Force Headquarters, No 3 Fighter Wing was forming at Zweibrücken, West Germany as part of No 1 Air Division, to provide administrative and functional control of No 413 (F) Squadron from RCAF Station Bagotville, Quebec; No 427 (F) Squadron from RCAF Station St-Hubert, Quebec; and No 434 (F) Squadron from RCAF Station Uplands, Ontario, which were to move to Zweibrücken by April 1953.

On 12 January, a small advance party led by No 3 Wing's Commanding Officer and Chief Administrative Officer, Group Captain A.C. Hull and Wing Commander J. Gellner, arrived at Zweibrücken to open the base. *Operation LEAP FROG III*, the move of the aircraft to Germany, was scheduled to take place in March, and planning was well advanced. Zweibrücken's first official landing was at 1307 hours on 27 January, when Flight Lieutenant Russ Roane brought in NS17507 from No 4 (T) OTU at Dorval.[14]

Early in the year, the Acting Chief of the Air Staff, Air Vice Marshal F.R. Miller, re-opened the issue of Canadian Pacific Airlines' contract to fly the Korean Airlift. In a letter to the Deputy Minister of National Defence, he expressed concern that the cost of the Canadian Pacific contract would be charged to the RCAF appropriation, as it had been three times already. The contract was not an RCAF requirement, so the RCAF budget did not provide for it, and the service had absorbed the cost so far only because some portions of the RCAF program had been delayed. Miller requested reconsideration of this matter at the appropriate levels, and the establishment of a policy on continuation of the Canadian Pacific contract into fiscal 1953–54, and administration of the contract by the RCAF. He emphasized that no provision had been made for the Canadian Pacific contract in the Defence estimates for 1953–54.

In his reply, the Deputy Minister asked the Chief of the Air Staff to raise the matter with the Chiefs of Staff Committee, as the Army was the service most concerned with keeping Canadian Pacific on the Airlift. The current contract was for three-and-a-half trips per week at $3.8 million per year, and Cabinet had decided to extend it to 31 March 1953.

On 28 January, the subject was discussed at the 533rd Meeting of the Chiefs of Staff Committee, where it was agreed that the Deputy Minister should undertake to work out the details of funding the Canadian Pacific contract. On 13 March, the Minister of National Defence wrote a memorandum to the Cabinet Defence Committee in which he advised them that the Air Transport Board recommended acceptance of the company's proposal, with a provision for a rate review at the end of six months. The proposal included a cancellation clause that permitted the government to cancel the contract any time — for a price. The Minister recommended also that any further contract with Canadian Pacific Airlines be entered into in accordance with the company's proposal.

On 5 May, Treasury Board approved a contract extension for the period from 1 April 1953 to 31 March 1954, providing for three westbound and two eastbound flights per week, with a payload of 8,700 pounds per trip at a rate of $2.59 per statute mile. This contract extension entailed an additional expenditure of $3,393,936 chargeable to the RCAF budget, which would be increased accordingly. The total cost of Canadian Pacific Airlines services on the Korean Airlift came to about $11.5 million.[15]

In a 20 January letter to the Chief of the Air Staff, Air Commodore Ripley inquired about the program to replace the Air Division's F-86E aircraft with Orenda-powered Sabres, which was planned for fall 1953. In his opinion, the overseas ferry phase of the replacement program could be done either by tactical moves like the *LEAP FROG* operations, or by ferry moves. Tactical moves would mean bringing the air and ground crews back to Canada for familiarization training; when they were all checked out on the new Sabres, they could then ferry them to Europe. Ferry moves would be smaller operations, conducted by a ferry organization established at Dorval. However the ferry phase was to be conducted, the replacement program would require Montreal-area storage space for up to twenty-five aircraft, and a team of five officers and twenty-five ground crew to maintain the aircraft in a state of readiness. Air Commodore Ripley also believed that accommodation for twenty-five officers and seventy-five airmen would be enough for either kind of move operation.

For *LEAP FROG*-type tactical moves, Ripley wrote, the operational responsibility should rest with Air Defence Command but, in accordance with existing policy, Air Transport Command should be responsible for ferry moves. To facilitate planning at Air Transport Command Headquarters, Ripley requested a complete delivery forecast for the new Sabre aircraft, by type, and confirmation that both hangar space and living quarters would be made available in the Montreal area.[16]

February

On 1 February, Air Marshal C.R. Slemon, CB, CBE, CD, was appointed Chief of the Air Staff, succeeding Air Marshal W.A. Curtis, who was retiring after having headed the RCAF since 1 September 1947.[17]

Operationally, February was a busy month for the squadron, with a commitment for eight trips on the Korean airlift, and three service flights to Resolute Bay.

The first flight to Resolute, captained by Flying Officer Waddell in NS17506, left Dorval on 3 February. It encountered mechanical difficulties about an hour after departure and returned to base for repairs. Six hours later, Waddell took off again for Winnipeg, where they stopped briefly before going on to Churchill. After a ten-hour crew rest, the flight proceeded to Coral Harbour and then to Resolute Bay, where they arrived at 0052 hours on 4 February. They were then scheduled to make an air drop at Isachsen, but the starter on No 3 engine malfunctioned. Waddell obtained permission to take off on three engines and ferry the aircraft to Churchill for repairs, which took six hours and twenty minutes; they arrived at 1940 hours on 6 February. Repairs were completed by the morning of 9 February, and the aircraft was brought back to base via Winnipeg the same day.

On the morning of 8 February, Air Commodore Ripley and several senior staff officers left Dorval for Resolute Bay to conduct an inspection in NS17514, captained by Flight Lieutenant Hall, which made its first stop at Ottawa to add Air Commodore Carscallen and Air Commodore Blaine from Air Force Headquarters to the inspection party. The flight carried on to Churchill, where it remained overnight, and departed the next afternoon. On the way to Resolute, the aircraft made a brief stop at Coral Harbour, and when the flight arrived at Resolute the airfield was closed because of blowing snow. Hall made one attempt to land before diverting to Thule. The flight left Thule at 0510 hours on 11 February, and arrived at Resolute Bay two hours and ten minutes later.

The inspection party was ready to leave after a complete tour of the detachment, including the beacon site, the water plant, and the Department of Transport facilities, but strong winds and blowing snow delayed their departure until the following morning. From Resolute Bay, the flight headed first for Edmonton, a run of seven hours and twenty minutes, and then returned to base on 14 February by way of Winnipeg and Ottawa.

The third trip of the month to Resolute Bay was carried out by Flying Officer Robert and his crew on 20–22 February in NS17515.

As well as three service flights to Resolute Bay and three to Goose Bay, the squadron's northern assignments in February included *Exercise BULL DOG*, an Army-Air Force training effort conducted from 15 February to 1 March near Churchill. The exercise scenario was an airborne assault on an enemy position, using Edmonton as the main base for operations and Churchill as the advanced base. With a company from the 1st Battalion, Royal 22e Régiment in the enemy role, the 1st Battalion, The Royal Canadian Regiment formed the assaulting force with airborne support elements.

On 14 February, three North Stars captained by Flight Lieutenant Wolkowski and Flying Officers Casselman and Waddell, departed for Churchill. The next morning, they loaded the troops and their equipment, and flew to Norman Wells, a flight of five and a half hours. On arrival, Wolkowski and Casselman were sent back to Dorval by way of Churchill, where they stayed the night. Waddell and his crew were routed back to Montreal by way of Fort Nelson, Edmonton and Winnipeg.[18]

The squadron made ten transatlantic flights in February. Four trips were made to transport Red Cross relief supplies for flood victims in the Netherlands. The first aircraft, NS17517, captained by Flying Officer Cook, left for Amsterdam on 5 February with a load of blankets, boots and clothing, and three Canadian Red Cross officials. Cook was followed by Flying Officer Raike in NS17503 on 12 February, Flight Lieutenant Gerding in NS17508 on 17 February, and Flight Lieutenant Adamson in NS17514 on 22 February.

Of the four service flights to North Luffenham via Keflavik, two included shuttle runs between North Luffenham and Zweibrücken. On the way home, one of these aircraft also stopped at Narsarssuak. The other two transatlantic runs were in direct support of *Operation LEAP FROG III*. Despatched toward the end of the month, these aircraft were routed via Goose Bay and Keflavik to Kinloss, Scotland, and returned to base by the same route.

On 8 February, NS17503, captained by Flight Lieutenant Gerding, was despatched to Toronto to pick up the directing staff and students of the RCAF Staff College; after a short stop at Cleveland, Ohio, to clear Customs, the aircraft headed for Maxwell AFB at Montgomery, Alabama, and then returned directly to Montreal. On 17 February, Flying Officer McAninch brought the Staff College directing staff and students back to Toronto in NS17510.

On 12 February, Captain Green and an augmented crew took NS17515 to Greenwood, where they conducted two shuttle flights to and from Jacksonville, Florida, to transport the personnel and equipment of No 404 (MR) Squadron and No 405 (MR) Squadron, which were slated to take part in an anti-submarine warfare exercise with the US Navy. From Jacksonville, the crew conducted a training run to Nassau in the Bahamas and then to Little Rock, Arkansas, before returning to base via Toronto on 18 February. Between 21 February and 24 February, Flying Officer McAninch conducted two shuttle runs between Jacksonville and Greenwood in NS17517 to bring the men and equipment of the two Maritime Reconnaissance squadrons back home.

The squadron conducted four other domestic runs in February, two of them flights to Victoria with several stops en route. The other two runs were logistics flights on behalf of Air Defence Command, one to Toronto, Bagotville and St-Hubert, and the other to Goose Bay, Greenwood, Stephenville and Bagotville.[19]

At a Squadron Commander's parade held on 6 February at RCAF Station Lachine, Flight Lieutenant E.R. Wolkowski received the certificate of the Queen's Commendation for Valuable Services in the Air from Squadron Leader V.J. Faurot, the station's Chief Administrative Officer. Similar certificates were presented by Wing Commander Lupton at a Commanding Officer's parade on 20 February to Flight Lieutenant J.P. Wilson and Sergeant L.C. Potekal.

On 10 February, Lupton officially opened the station skating rink. On 22 February, the new Station Theatre opened, a new endeavour operated by the Station Fund in a completely renovated building. The first show was *My Cousin Rachel*, screened for a large audience.

On 26 February, the first draft of airwomen posted overseas arrived for processing at No 1 Personnel Reception Centre, Lachine. The next day, reporters flocked to the station for the formal welcome by Wing Commander Lupton (as Acting Station Commander), and a formal parade was held on 28 February with a fly-past of jet aircraft and an address to the airwomen by Air Vice Marshal F.G. Wait, Air Member for Personnel. The parade was followed by a buffet lunch served in the Airwomen's Canteen, at which each airwoman received a cosmetic kit, compliments of "Charles of the Ritz" at the Ritz Hotel in Montreal. The guest list at lunch included Air Commodore R.C. Ripley (Air Officer Commanding, Air Transport Command, Wing Commander J.T. McCutcheon (Senior Personnel Staff Officer, Air Transport Command Headquarters), Group Captain Leduc (Senior Personnel Staff Officer, Air Defence Command Headquarters), and the mayors of Lachine and Montreal.[20]

March

The squadron's operational workload in March centred on providing air transport support to Canada's burgeoning military presence in western Europe, specifically *Operation LEAP FROG III*. The month's commitment of eight round trips to Tokyo under *Operation HAWK* was also fulfilled. Northern assignments included two flights to Goose Bay, one of them extended to Frobisher Bay, and two service flights and a special flight to Resolute Bay. Both service flights to Resolute involved an extra shuttle from Churchill, and the first nearly resulted in the loss of an aircraft.

Service Flight 17 arrived from Churchill at Resolute Bay at 0550 hours on 12 March. The aircraft was NS17517, captained by Flight Lieutenant Butchart. After embarking several passengers, the flight departed in twilight at 0714 hours on a shuttle run to Churchill, and at about 1030 hours Resolute Bay lost contact with the aircraft. Bases were notified to watch for NS17517, which was presumed lost or possibly forced down. At Dorval, Wing Commander Lupton dropped in at the office of Flight Lieutenant Burn, the Deputy Senior Navigation Officer, and said, "I think we've lost one of our aircraft."

This is what happened. During the cockpit crew's departure preparations, the Second Navigator instructed that the DGI (Directional Gyro Indicator, used instead of a magnetic compass) be set to the runway's true heading of 167°. This was the first mistake; the DGI should have been set to 262°, the *grid* heading of the departure runway, calculated by adding

95° West longitude to the true heading. The grid track to Churchill is 273°, which meant that, after takeoff, a minor heading alteration of eleven degrees, plus or minus an allowance for drift, would have had the aircraft heading south to its destination. The crew were fatigued, having been on duty for about twelve hours, and the pilots trusted their navigators, so the 95° error in the DGI setting was not detected. After takeoff, the aircraft must have turned about 106° to starboard and headed west instead of south, but the pilots, who both had extensive northern experience, did not question this drastic and very unusual heading — departures for Churchill on Resolute's south runway normally required only a minor change of heading.

Flight Lieutenant Burn had warned the experienced First Navigator on the flight that his Second Navigator was under instruction and should be supervised, but the First Navigator either disregarded or misunderstood the warning. Worse, he retired to the crew rest position without checking that the Second Navigator had the situation under control. From that point, the Second Navigator kept a DR plot based entirely on the flight plan to Churchill, which meant that each position report passed to the Radio Officer for transmission only maintained the mistake. Until sunrise, astro heading checks were restricted by twilight and ice crystal haze.

After flying a constant course for more than four hours, the captain asked why the sun was rising over the tail instead of the port wing tip, where it would have been if they had been heading south. They should have been approaching Churchill, but attempts to tune in on the Churchill radio beacon proved fruitless. Realizing they were in trouble, the captain got the First Navigator up from the crew rest area and put him to work. The First Navigator figured out what must have happened and calculated a rough DR position; their charts did not cover the area they were presumably over, so he drew a polar stereographic map on the back. By reconstructing the DR plot and plotting successive sunlines, combined with wind drift measurements, he eventually determined that the flight was northwest of the Beaufort Sea, some 500 miles north-northwest of Point Barrow and headed for the New Siberian Islands. Point Barrow is the most northerly settlement in Alaska, 1,200 miles west of Resolute Bay.

Course was altered for Point Barrow, the nearest airport available, where a powerful radio beacon helped bring the aircraft in. Coincidentally, the frequency of the Point Barrow radio beacon (281 kilocycles) was close to that of the Churchill beacon (236 kilocycles), and when the pilots did a radio-compass sweep they heard Point Barrow's identification letters instead of Churchill's. NS17517 landed at Point Barrow at 1612 hours Resolute Bay time, eight hours and fifty-eight minutes after departure, and the emergency was called off about two hours later.

Meanwhile, back in Ottawa, Air Commodore Carscallen, the Chief of Air Operations at Air Force Headquarters was on the telephone to Arctic expert Squadron Leader K.R. Greenaway at the Defence Research Board, demanding to know how the North Star could have ended up in Alaska after reporting progress on track for Churchill.

After the aircraft was refuelled, the flight took off for Edmonton even though the crew had been on duty for nearly twenty-four hours. The distance of 1,775 miles was covered in eight hours. After a rest, the crew received instructions from Air Transport Command Headquarters to go back to Churchill and complete the shuttle run to Resolute Bay. The flight arrived from Churchill at 1559 hours on 14 March, and left as S/F18 at 1832 hours for Dorval with stops at Churchill and Winnipeg.

A Board of Inquiry on the incident was held at RCAF Station Lachine, and there was talk in Air Transport Command of disciplinary action against the captain and both navigators. In the end, however, the matter was resolved discreetly. The Second Navigator was sent for a skills assessment at the Air Navigation School at Summerside; the assessment was negative, and he was released from the RCAF. The other actors in this drama carried on with their careers in a busy and expanding Air Force. The squadron's navigators did not forget, however, as they considered this incident a blot on a long, proud record of professional achievement. The grid-navigation portion of the syllabus at No 4 (T) OTU was beefed up, and pilots were lectured on the subject during both the First Officers' and Captains' courses.[21]

The second squadron flight to Resolute Bay in March was a special captained by Flight Lieutenant Gerding in NS17514, which arrived from Churchill at 1206 hours on 19 March, discharged its cargo, and was away again three hours later. On 25 March, Flying Officer Robert brought in SF17 at 1208 hours, with several technical staff officers from Lachine among the passengers. The aircraft returned to Churchill on a shuttle run and was back twenty-four hours later. The flight was turned around in two hours and was on its way back to Churchill and base, transporting a sick Eskimo child to Churchill for medical attention.

In March, a technical team installed new AN/FRN500 radio beacons at Eureka, Isachsen and Mould Bay, replacing battery-operated beacons that were unsatisfactory because of low power and unreliability.[22]

Support operations for *LEAP FROG III* got under way on 23 February, when Flying Officer Spratt and his crew in NS17503 departed Dorval for Kinloss, Scotland, by way of Goose Bay and Keflavik; two days later, they returned to base by the same route. On 27 February, Flying Officer Robert left St-Hubert in NS17514 with ground personnel from No 427 (F) Squadron bound for Kinloss. On its return to Dorval on 1 March, this flight made a straight run from Keflavik to Dorval in ten hours, bypassing Goose Bay.

Between 2 March and 6 March, four North Stars were despatched to Kinloss from Bagotville, Moncton, Ottawa and St-Hubert.

On 5 March, a cold and blustery day, the pilots of No 3 (F) Wing formed up with their Sabres on the tarmac at St-Hubert. The parade was inspected by Minister of National Defence Brooke Claxton, and Lord Ismay, the Secretary General of NATO, made a farewell address. The recently retired Chief of the Air Staff, Air Marshal W.A. Curtis, was also present to wish the Wing *bon voyage*. After a fly-past, No 413 (F) Squadron, commanded by Squadron Leader J.D. Lindsay, headed home to Bagotville, where Squadron Leader W.I. Gordon assumed the command two days later and led the unit overseas. No 434 (F) Squadron returned to Uplands.

The weather at Goose Bay was down with low visibility and snow, and it was not much better the next day. The bad weather did not prevent a North Star from leaving St-Hubert for Germany with an advance party from No 427 Squadron.

On 7 March, all three fighter squadrons of No 3 (F) Wing arrived at Goose Bay.

Two No 426 Squadron aircraft — NS17503, captained by Flying Officer Kyle, and NS17505, captained by Flying Officer Sage — were tasked as "mother ships" for the Sabre squadrons, and both North Stars and their crews would be away from base until 11 April. Kyle's aircraft left Ottawa for Bluie West 1 (Narssarsuak) with personnel from No 434(F) Squadron on board, and Sage headed for Goose Bay with a No 427 (F) Squadron servicing crew and two spare pilots. A third North Star — 17525, flown by Flying Officer Raike — went to Bagotville to pick up No 413 (F) Squadron's ground crew, and then proceeded to Goose Bay and Narssarsuak.

The weather cleared at Goose Bay, but not at Narssarsuak, where a persistent layer of cloud based at 500 feet lay along the fjord and held up the operation for six days. On 12 March, the Task Force learned that the weather ship Ocean Station Bravo, which was to provide a beacon on the *LEAP FROG* track, was 100 miles away from its position. Squadron Leader C.L.V. Gervais of No 427(F) Squadron and a wingman went up in their Sabres and tried homing in on Flying Officer Sage's North Star, which was circling the ship's assigned position. If Bravo was still off station on 13 March, the Task Force Commander intended to use NS17505 instead.

With No 427 Squadron in the lead, No 3 (F) Wing made the ninety-five minute crossing to Narssarsuak on 14 March, leaving only one of its forty-six Sabres in Goose Bay with mechanical problems. Although Ocean Station Bravo was still about forty miles off station, the Sabres had no navigation problems. NS17503, captained by Flying Officer Kyle, arrived later the same day, and departed again the next morning with a servicing crew bound for Keflavik, where they would prepare to welcome the Sabres after their second over-water leg. Sage arrived in Greenland on 15 March, and headed back to Montreal the next day to pick up more men and spare parts. NS17505 was back in Narssarsuak on 18 March.

Keflavik weather kept No 3 Wing cooling its heels at Narssarsuak for twelve days. When they arrived, a USAF F-84 pilot told the Canadians that he had been at Bluie West 1 waiting for decent weather in Iceland for fifty-one days! On 20 March, fourteen RAF Sabres under Squadron Leader Cole arrived from Goose Bay. (The RAF ferry operation was called "Bechers Brook." The USAF called their crossings "High Flight.")

On 28 March, the weather at Keflavik was adequate and No 3 Wing was finally able to leave for Iceland, but snow showers and reduced visibility were reported when the last section of No 427 Squadron was reaching the point of no return; on arrival, the four Sabres made it through a 500-foot ceiling with two miles of visibility. Twelve Sabres were stuck in Greenland, one requiring an engine change and the others caught by the weather, and the pilots planned to join the RAF Becher's Brook group scheduled to depart the next day, weather permitting. On 29 March, all twelve Sabres arrived at Keflavik, followed closely by a detachment of USAF F84s.

On 28 March, after conducting a weather flight in the Keflavik area, Sage and his crew in NS17505 headed for Bluie West 1 to pick up the rest of the servicing personnel and equipment. After a brief stop at Keflavik, they took their passengers and cargo to Prestwick and North Luffenham, and then returned to Keflavik, where they arrived on 30 March. On 3 April, they again flew to Prestwick, and then conducted two shuttle runs, one to Orly and the other to Zweibrücken, before returning to Keflavik on 5 April.

April

Most of No 3 Wing spent six days in Keflavik, grounded at first by bad weather in Scotland and later by bad weather in Iceland, but on 4 April *Operation LEAP FROG III* made it to Kinloss, battling head winds, and stopped for fuel. Three aircraft were left behind in Iceland. After refuelling, Squadron Leader Gervais led a section of six Sabres on to Prestwick, and the rest of the Wing followed on from Keflavik and Kinloss the next day, arriving at Prestwick without incident, but Squadron Leader Cole of the Becher's Brook operation had gone missing with his Sabre. No 3 Wing spent 6 April at Prestwick having new radio crystals installed in the Sabres to prepare them for operations in Europe.

At 0800 hours on 7 April, Prestwick received a message clearing the Sabres for the flight to Zweibrücken. At noon on the same day, two Air Division Expeditors arrived at Zweibrücken with a group of VIPs, including Mr. Chapdelaine from Bonn, and Air Vice Marshal H.L. Campbell, Air Commodore Hodson, Group Captain Cox, Wing Commander Ashman and Squadron Leader Cobus from No 1 Air Division Headquarters. After inspecting the Guard of Honour, the visitors were taken to lunch at the Zweibrücken Officers' Mess, as the Sabres were not expected to arrive until 1330 hours. After lunch, the visitors and station personnel gathered at No 1 Hangar to see the first aircraft arrive. Squadron Leader Gervais touched down at 1430 hours, followed in rapid succession by the rest of No 3 Wing's forty-five Sabres.

On 5 April, Sage and the crew of NS17505 did several shuttle runs, picking up and delivering personnel and equipment, first going to Kinloss, then back to Prestwick and on to Keflavik, and then North Luffenham, where they took a crew rest. They returned to Prestwick on 5 April, and on 7 April departed for Zweibrücken. On 8 April, they conducted a shuttle run to Laon and then flew to London, and on 10 April they returned to base via Lajes in the Azores, an eleven-hour direct flight. The crew were more than anxious to get home.

Meanwhile, Kyle and his crew in the second mother ship, 17503, were despatched from Prestwick on 5 April to North Luffenham, Zweibrücken and back to Prestwick. The next day, they flew to Kinloss, and on 7 April they went to Zweibrücken, where they spent the night. On 8 April, they flew to Grostenquin, Orly and London, and on 10 April, they went to North Luffenham to pick up personnel and equipment, which they delivered to London before departing for Lajes and home by the southern route, avoiding strong headwinds and bad weather on the northern route. The flight to Dorval from Lajes took eleven hours and ten minutes, and *Operation LEAP FROG III* was over for No 426 Squadron.

Between 9 March and 24 March, No 426 Squadron despatched seven other North Star flights in direct support of *Operation LEAP FROG III*: three from Ottawa, two from Moncton, and one each from Bagotville and St-Hubert. Three flights went to Orly, two to North Luffenham, one to Kinloss, and one to Keflavik by way of Bluie West 1.²³

As *Operation LEAP FROG III* wound down, Air Force Headquarters was planning a tactical move for the next Sabre Wing to proceed overseas: No 4(F) Wing, authorized by AFHQ Organization Order 27/53 to form as part of No 1 (RCAF) Air Division at RCAF Station Baden-Söllingen, near the east bank of the Rhine River and twelve kilometres west of the famous German resort town of Baden-Baden, with No 414 (F) Squadron from RCAF

Station Bagotville, Quebec; No 422 (F) Squadron from RCAF Station Uplands, Ontario; and No 444 (F) Squadron from RCAF Station St-Hubert, Quebec, all flying the Canadair Sabre Mk IV. An advance party from the Air Division was scheduled to go to the site on 18 April and stay there on temporary duty until the Wing activated, and the fighter squadrons would move to Europe in August.[24]

The squadron completed its April commitment of eight round trips to Tokyo, with only one significant delay. On 1 April, Flying Officer J.S. Middleton was taxiing NS17509 to the gas pits at Shemya when the crew noticed that No 3 engine was vibrating excessively; on inspection, they discovered that the propeller was loose. Both the engine and propeller had to be changed, delaying the flight for several days.[25]

It was re-supply time for the high Arctic weather stations.

On 7 April, Squadron Leader Torontow and his crew took out NS17510 on a special flight to Churchill and Resolute Bay. From Resolute, they flew to Isachsen and Mould Bay to test the runways, which they found fit for the re-supply operation, and then to Churchill by way of Coral Harbour. From Churchill, they conducted two shuttle runs to Resolute Bay carrying passengers, mail and equipment. On 12 April, they left Churchill for Dorval via Rockcliffe, where they stopped briefly.

On 13 April, two crews captained by Flight Lieutenant Hall and Flying Officer Budgeon were despatched in NS17510 to Resolute Bay to carry out a series of shuttle runs to the weather stations. By 25 April, when they returned to Dorval, the two crews had made twelve flights to Mould Bay, eight to Isachsen, and a special run to Alert and Eureka with a stopover in Thule. On 15 April, Flying Officer Ingall arrived at Resolute with NS17505, which he left with Budgeon and Hall, and took NS17510 back to base for a cyclical inspection check. On the same day, VC22109, a No 435 Squadron C-119, arrived from Edmonton via Churchill; it was the first RCAF C-119 to participate in the re-supply operation. Between 16 April and 21 April, it made twelve shuttles to Mould Bay and seven to Isachsen, with a side trip to Thule. Eventually, the RCAF's C-119s would take over most re-supply activities in the high Arctic.

On 16 April, Flying Officer Lambert and his crew in NS17511 arrived at Resolute Bay on a regular service flight that stopped at Winnipeg and Churchill on the way. During their stop at Churchill, they conducted a supply shuttle to Coral Harbour. On 20 April a USAF C54 arrived at Resolute Bay with a special load for No 426 Squadron to deliver to Alert. On 21 April, Wing Commander Lupton and his crew in NS17509 arrived at Resolute Bay, and then conducted supply runs to Isachsen and Mould Bay. They then went on to Thule, whence they departed for Alert and Eureka to drop off supplies and equipment before returning to Resolute Bay. On 23 April, NS17505 and VC22109 headed for Churchill and home to their respective bases, NS17505 making a para-drop at Arctic Bay first. On 25 April, Lupton and his crew airlifted another load of supplies and equipment from Churchill to Resolute Bay before returning to base.[26]

Other operations in April included six round trips to North Luffenham and, on the domestic scene, the first service flight to the Maritimes, called "the Blueberry", by Flying Officer Budgeon and his crew in NS17517. Departing Montreal on 6 April, it went to Halifax by way of Moncton, Summerside and Greenwood, and returned to Dorval via Summerside and Moncton. Other domestic flights included four trips to Goose Bay, of which one extended to Frobisher Bay and Greenwood, and one trip to Victoria.[27]

On 7 April, a team from RCAF Station Lachine won the Inter-Service Basketball championship, defeating RCAF Station St-Jean 107–106 in a two-game total-point series. The first game ended in a 53–53 draw, but the second produced a 54–53 victory for Lachine.

On 20 April, Air Vice Marshal C.E.N. Guest, the Commander-in-Chief RAF Air Transport Command, arrived at Dorval from Goose Bay in an RCAF North Star. He spent the next day in meetings with Air Commodore Ripley and his staff, and in the evening was entertained at a Mess Dinner held in his honour at RCAF Station Lachine. On 23 April, Group Captain Z.L. Leigh, the Chief of Staff at Air Transport Command Headquarters was at Dorval to greet Field Marshal Sir Bernard Montgomery, who was travelling with Major General J.P.E. Bernatchez, General Officer Commanding Quebec Command. The Field Marshal was scheduled take the liner *Empress of Scotland* to Europe the next day.[28]

May

In May, one of the squadron's nine round trips to Tokyo brought the first two Canadian Army prisoners of war home from Korea in NS17506, captained by Flight Lieutenant Schroder, which arrived at Dorval from McChord at 2150 hours on 11 May. Private A. Baker and Lance-Corporal P. Dugal of the Royal 22ᵉ Régiment were captured in November 1951 and June 1952 respectively, and recovered from the Communists in *Operation LITTLE SWITCH*.

The squadron completed its 500th round trip to Tokyo with the return of NS17510 to McChord at 0320 hours local on 3 June. Flying Officer W.F. Kyryluk and his crew completed the run in seven and a half days, having left McChord in NS17505 at 1915 hours on 25 May.[29]

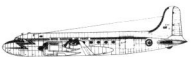

On 11 May, Squadron Leader C.F. Sanford and his crew in NS17509 made a special VIP run to Mexico. The wife of Mexico's Ambassador to Canada, Dr. José Manuel Alvarez del Castello, had died, and the RCAF had agreed to take the coffin home to Guadalajara, escorted by the bereaved ambassador and his brother.

The first stop was Ottawa, where an External Affairs briefer informed the crew that, for diplomatic reasons, the flight was not to land in the United States. Sanford agreed to do his best, but he had one problem: no letdown charts or local area maps for the destination airfield. They left Ottawa at 0700 hours the next day, and flew through bad weather all the way. Over Texas, they found thunderstorms and tornadoes and, as they were running low on fuel, they decided to land at the US Naval Air Station at Corpus Christi, where the ceiling was 300 feet with three-quarters of a mile visibility. The first leg of the flight had taken nine hours and forty minutes.

The flight received a courtesy clearance by US Customs, and the admiral in command of the base invited Dr. Alvarez del Castello to tea while the aircraft was being refuelled and the crew was getting a briefing on the leg to Guadalajara at Base Operations. The briefer told the crew that there was no airway to Guadalajara from Brownsville, Texas, so they should plan a direct flight from that point. Also, they would find only one radio aid en route: a Non-Directional Beacon (NDB) about halfway to Guadalajara. After forty-five minutes on the ground, the flight was on its way again. It was in cloud a good part of the trip.

Night had fallen and the weather had cleared as the aircraft neared Guadalajara, and the crew were able to pick up the weak NDB at the airfield. Sanford maintained his altitude of 10,000 feet to avoid the area's many hills. The next problem was contacting the tower: none of the crew spoke Spanish, and the air traffic controllers spoke no English. The runway lights were off, and the aircraft circled overhead transmitting fruitlessly until someone spotted a stream of cars heading for the airport — a local flight was coming in and, when the runway lights flashed on for it, Sanford seized his chance and landed. It was 2005 hours, and the flight had been airborne for four hours and forty minutes.

The crew were well cared for in Guadalajara. The local government paid to refuel the aircraft and, before they left, Dr. Alvarez del Catillo thanked them and expressed great satisfaction with all aspects of the trip. On the morning of 14 May, as Guadalajara lacked international flight-planning facilities, the crew filed a VFR direct flight plan to Montreal. As they approached Brownsville at 11,000 feet the aircraft was in solid cloud and the flight plan was changed to reflect IFR conditions. The aircraft remained in solid cloud all the way to Montreal. It was raining heavily at Dorval as Sanford landed, ten hours and forty minutes after leaving Guadalajara.[30]

The squadron carried out seven transatlantic flights in May: five to North Luffenham, one to Keflavik by way of Moncton and Goose Bay, and one to Iceland with stops at Narsarssuak on both the outbound and homeward legs of the journey. Both the Iceland trips were basically training flights. Three trips to Bermuda were also made, two from Dartmouth and one from Greenwood, in support of the Maritime Group and the RCN. All three flights returned to Dartmouth.

Ten flights were made to Goose Bay. One transported fifteen civilian geologists to Goose Bay, then proceeded to Fort Chimo to drop off nine RCN personnel, and finally made a ration and mail run to Frobisher Bay. Two flights brought the Legion Show and the RCAF Central Band to Goose Bay from Montreal.

And after all the activity and attention of April in Resolute Bay, only one service flight went to that destination in May.[31]

On 8 May, Wing Commander R.F. Douglas relinquished command of RCAF Station Lachine on retirement from the regular component of the RCAF. Temporary command of the station was assumed by Wing Commander R.I. Thomas, whose substantive appointment was as Chief Administrative Officer at RCAF Station Rockcliffe.[32]

Two of No 426 Squadron's flight engineers were cited for awards for meritorious service on the Korean Airlift. Sergeant W.S. McKnight received the Queen's Commendation for Valuable Services in the Air, and Corporal G.R. Reed was awarded the Air Force Medal. The citations were promulgated in the Canada Gazette on 30 May 1953 and in Air Force Routine Order 360/53, dated 12 June 1953.

On 29 May, a large crowd turned out at RCAF Station Uplands to see Squadron Leader Don Dickson and his crew bring in 5301, the first of the two forty-passenger de Havilland Comet 1As acquired by the RCAF, which thus became the first air force to use jet transport aircraft. At the same time, the RCAF also became the first operator of scheduled jet flights across the North Atlantic. Flight Lieutenant Rolly Lloyd captained the crew that brought in 5302, the second Comet, on 16 June. Both aircraft were assigned to No 412 Squadron at Uplands.

The Comet acquisition stemmed from a requirement first identified by RCAF planners in the late 1940s for a transport aircraft capable of high-speed, high-altitude, long-range operations: essential if the RCAF was to exercise its air defence squadrons, test the efficacy of the radar chain being constructed across the near north (the Pine Tree Line), and provide high priority transport, particularly for VIPs. Early in 1951, the Canadian government decided that the Comet was the aircraft to meet this requirement and, consequently, an order was placed with de Havilland in England that November for two aircraft, with delivery promised in early 1952.

The Comet was powered by four de Havilland Ghost turbojet engines, each rated at 5,000 pounds of thrust, and operated at a maximum altitude of 40,000 feet at a cruising speed of 455 miles per hour. Its range was about 2,500 miles with a capacity payload and standard fuel reserves, and its endurance was about eight hours. The first Comet flew on 27 July 1949, and deliveries to BOAC (British Overseas Airways Corporation) began in March 1952; the airline began commercial service with the aircraft in May 1952.

Canadian Pacific Airlines had ordered two of the forty-four-passenger version in 1950, for its Pacific routes. The first CPA Comet, CF-CUN (the *Empress of Hawaii*) was making a delivery and route-familiarization flight on 3 March 1953 when it failed to become airborne during a takeoff run at Karachi Airport and crashed, killing all eleven crew members.

In October 1952, about sixty flight crew and ground crew members of No 412 Squadron, many of them ex- Thunderbirds, were chosen to go to England for training on the Comet. The RCAF contingent included four crews: Squadron Leader J.D. Dickson, Flight Lieutenant L.W. Hussey, Flight Lieutenant W.R. Lloyd, and Flight Lieutenant C.S. Olsen (captains); Flight Lieutenant M.D. Broadfoot, Flight Lieutenant R.M. Edwards, Flight Lieutenant T.M. Hall and Flight Lieutenant R.G. (Herbie) Herbert (first officers); Flight Lieutenant C. Brown, Flight Lieutenant A. Martin, Flight Lieutenant W.D. Stewart and Flight Lieutenant H.J.A. Wright (navigators); Flight Lieutenant R.G. Chalk, Flight Lieutenant A.A. James, Flight Lieutenant J. Menton and Flight Lieutenant K.A. Wark (radio officers); Warrant Officer 2nd Class Cam Bain, Sergeant Fred Bowman, Sergeant Horace Easy and Sergeant Wally Hoehn (flight engineers); and Corporal Joe Bergin, Corporal Chuck Fortier and Corporal Ed Grose (transportation technicians). The thirty maintenance and servicing crew members were led by Flight Sergeant Capriano and Sergeant Sam Martin.

At first, only the pilots and some members of the ground crew were involved in the instruction program. The pilots received a two-week course at BOAC London on the theory of jet propulsion and high-level navigation, followed by an eight-week course at the de Havilland ground school in Hatfield. The next phase, flight and route training, was done with BOAC, and other flight crew members joined the pilots at this point. The airline's flight instruction included training runs to the Middle East, the Far East and South Africa. After a short break at home for Christmas, most of the men in the RCAF contingent were back in England in March 1953 to take delivery of two Comet 1As.

The Comet was grounded in January 1954, after several disastrous accidents that were later attributed to metal fatigue. In August 1956, the RCAF Comets were ferried back to Hatfield for extensive structural modifications by de Havilland. Flight Lieutenant Broadfoot headed a new group of No 412 Squadron personnel who brought the modified Comets, identified as Mk 1XBs, back into service. From 1 November 1957 to October 1963, when they were retired from the RCAF, the Comets performed admirably in the roles for which they had been acquired.[33]

On 11 June, Air Defence Headquarters issued general instructions for the movement to Europe of No 414, No 422 and No 444 squadrons, all flying Sabres. The move was tentatively scheduled to begin on 24 August, and the squadrons' pilots would fly their own aircraft. No 426 Squadron would airlift the ground staff from their parent stations to Paris in groups of thirty-five, beginning around 24 August, and departing each Monday, Wednesday and Friday until the airlift was completed — in about a month. From Paris, the ground crews were travel by rail to No 4 Wing Baden-Söllingen.[34]

The squadron dispatched eight trips to Tokyo in June. Shemya weather caused two of the outbound flights from Elmendorf to divert, one to Adak and the other to Cold Bay. Seven transatlantic flights to North Luffenham were made during the month. One of these flights, captained by Flying Officer Lambert in NS17509, had its No 4 engine fail shortly after leaving Keflavik, and Lambert turned back for an engine change. Two days later, the flight continued on to North Luffenham. Toward the end of the month, Squadron Leader Torontow captained a combination "training-and-backlog" special that covered the full European circuit from North Luffenham to Grostenquin, Baden- Söllingen, Zweibrücken, Orly and London before returning to North Luffenham and home to Dorval on the northern route. Finally, two trips to Keflavik were made in June, one a training run with a stop at Narsarssuak and the other to bring an engine for NS17509.

In Canada, No 426 Squadron conducted seven trips to Goose Bay in June, two of which made stops at Sept-Îles, and four service flights to Resolute Bay. One of the service flights delivered mail and supplies to Coral Harbour, made an air drop at Mould Bay, carried out a second shuttle run to Resolute Bay from Churchill and, then flew from Churchill to Coral

Harbour transporting 125 pounds of dynamite! Another of these flights carried a prisoner under close arrest on its return to base from Resolute Bay. In other domestic flights, a maritime shuttle was carried out with stops at Dartmouth, Greenwood, Torbay, Goose Bay, Gander and a return to Goose Bay before heading for base.

On 3 June, the squadron received notice from Air Force Headquarters that Flight Lieutenant J.S. Schroder had been selected for an exchange program for pilots with RAF Air Transport Command, and he was to be in Britain by 27 July. On 12 June, four wounded soldiers were airlifted from Tacoma on SF 8 to Dorval. Two of the soldiers were from Montreal and two came from the Québec City area.

On 17 June, Squadron Leader C.S. Olsen brought the Comet from Ottawa to Dorval, where it was displayed for the first time in Montreal. Air Commodore Ripley was on hand to meet the aircraft and greet Major-General Bernatchez, the General Officer Commanding, Quebec Command, and Commodore Earl of the RCN, who were on board. The next day, Squadron Leader Dixon took the Comet on to Torbay to pick up Air Commodore Ripley, Wing Commander Mussells and several staff officers, who had flown to Torbay on a North Star that blew its tires on arrival and was delayed for repairs.

On 24 June, Flying Officer D.T. Thompson proceeded to Shemya to take on the job of Detachment Commander, replacing Flying Officer J.A.F. Huard, who returned to Montreal on 3 July. On 25 June, the publicity director of the Unitarian Service Committee, a Miss Potter, arrived by scheduled service flight at McChord AFB for a visit. On 27 June, war correspondent Bill Boss departed for Haneda on NS17503, captained by Flight Lieutenant Morrison.[35]

MAP 5: *North Star Operations over the North Atlantic, 1948–1962*

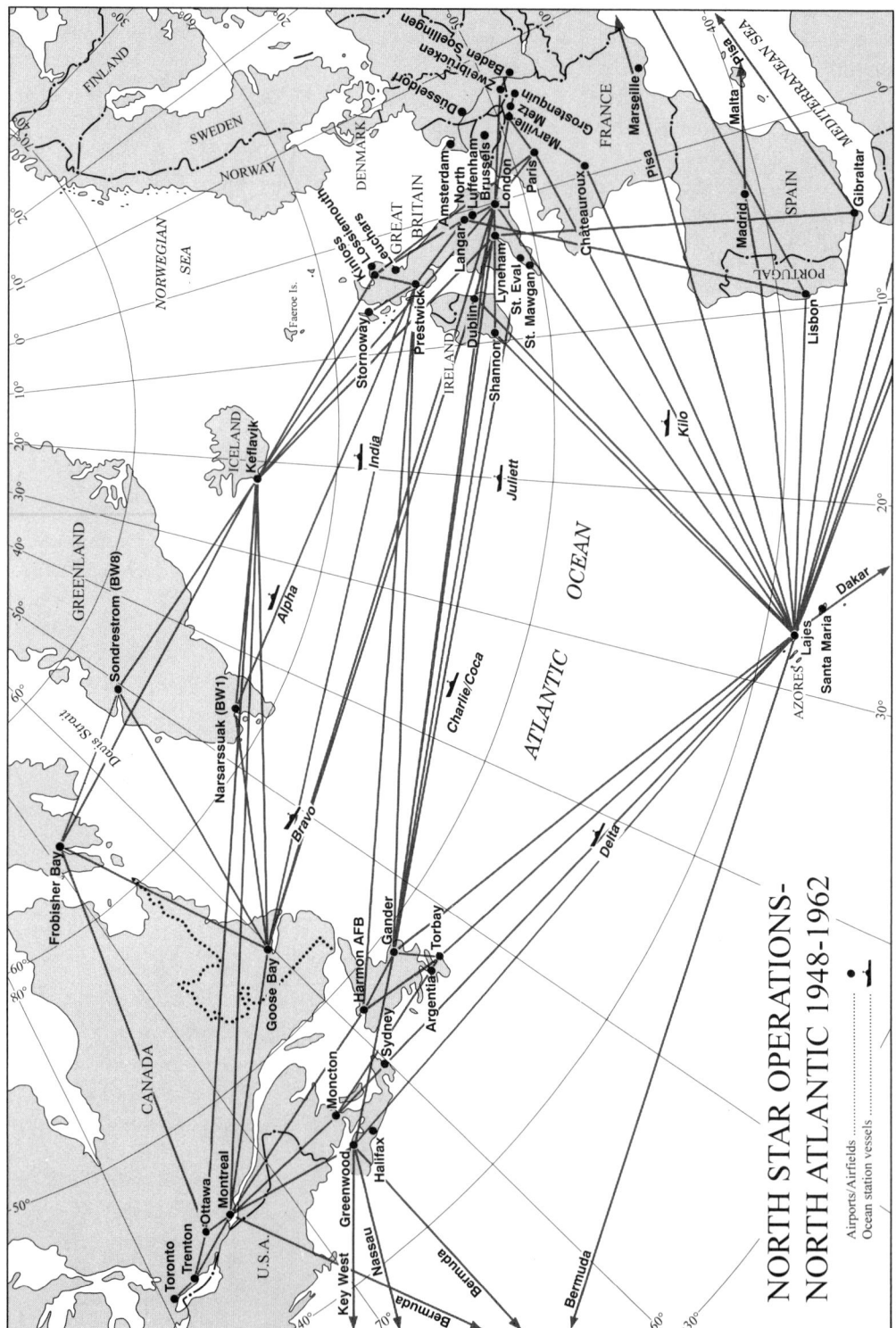

PHOTO 125
F/O R.B. Ingall in the Operations Room at Dorval, 13 February 1953. (DND PL55859)

PHOTO 126
Field Marshal Sir Bernard Montgomery arrives at Dorval, 23 April 1953. (D. Eagles Collection)

PHOTO 127
Cpl. Ernest Chevalier chats with F/O W.F. Kyryluk, who had recently captained No 426 Squadron's 500th mission on the Korean Airlift; Dorval, 10 June 1953. (E. Chevalier Collection)

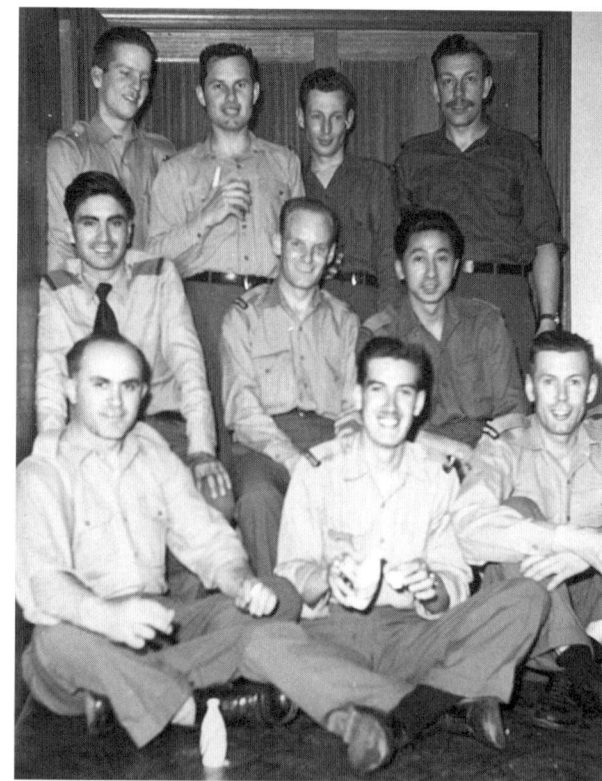

PHOTO 128
Members of No 426 Squadron's detachment in Tokyo relax at Ting's Restaurant; July 1953. From left: D'Aoust, Perras, Brooks; centre row: Robert, Chevalier, Ikebuchi; back row: Hall, Gauthier, Martin, Jamieson. (E. Chevalier Collection)

Lachine, July–December 1953

CHAPTER 16

LACHINE
JULY–DECEMBER 1953

On 2 July, Air Defence Command Headquarters in St-Hubert issued Operation Order 27/53 concerning the move from Canada to Baden-Söllingen, West Germany, of No 414 (F) Squadron, No 422 (F) Squadron and No 444 (F) Squadron: *Operation LEAP FROG IV*, the airlift of the personnel, baggage and equipment of all three squadrons, and the ferrying of sixty-five Sabre aircraft.

The first phase was the airlift of the ground crew, aircrew not involved in the ferry flights and their luggage. To meet this objective, the Station Commander at Lachine would despatch three North Star flights per week for three weeks commencing Wednesday, 12 August, with departures scheduled on Mondays from St-Hubert, Wednesdays from Bagotville and Fridays from Uplands — four North Star flights from each station. Each flight would take thirty-five passengers. The second phase was ferrying the Sabres, a task that included airlifting the jet fighters' support element. Three No 426 Squadron North Stars and their crews would participate in the airlift component of the ferry phase. One North Star would be in position at each base on 25 August to make the flight with the three fighter squadrons to Goose Bay on 26 August, arriving no later than the afternoon.

Wing Commander D.G. Malloy, the acting commanding officer of No 4 Wing since 3 May, was designated Task Force Commander. (On 8 July, Group Captain R.S. Turnbull would be appointed to the command of No 4 Wing, and Malloy would become Chief Operations Officer at No 4 Wing.) As Task Force Commander, Malloy would be responsible to the Commander, Air Defence Command, for the move as far as Kinloss, and to the Commander, No 1 Air Division, for the move from Kinloss to Baden. Under Malloy, Wing Commander J.F. Allan, the officer commanding No 414 (F) Squadron, was responsible for the actual movement of all Sabres being ferried in *Op LEAP FROG IV*; the Station Commander at Lachine was responsible for Phase 1, the airlift; and the Senior Transportation Captain, an officer appointed by the Station Commander, was responsible for the functional control of the transport aircraft employed in Phase 2.

The Sabres were to be routed to Baden-Söllingen through Goose Bay, Narsarssuak, Keflavik and Kinloss, with Leuchars (ninety-two miles to the south) as an alternate for Kinloss, and Zweibrücken as an alternate for Baden-Söllingen. The Sabres were to use only JP1 fuel on the over-water legs of the route, and the *LEAP FROG IV* flights would receive petrol, oil and lubricants (POL) from USAF stocks at Goose Bay and Narsarssuak, and from the RAF at Keflavik and Kinloss. On each over-water leg, an ocean station vessel would be in position at

375

the mid-point, and a Duckbutt would orbit at the one-quarter and three-quarters points. On the crossing to Narsarssuak, an extra Duckbutt would orbit at the entrance to Narsarssuak Fjord.[1]

On 8 July, Air Commodore Ripley wrote a letter to the Chief of the Air Staff in which he outlined an overseas ferry plan for Sabre Vs. From the Leap Frog and Becher's Brook operations, Air Transport Command had learned that such overseas moves required: a properly established ferry-training unit in Canada; a ferry squadron to be used only for ferrying jet aircraft; liaison detachments en route, with adequate accommodation and support backing for Sabre V aircraft; North Star support for all ferry operations; and monthly aircraft convoys to overcome problems arising from turnaround times and non-negotiable circumstances such as weather.

Ripley believed that the safest and most economical way to ferry Sabres across the North Atlantic was to form a "mobile ferry squadron" comprising at least fifty pilots selected to serve for six-month tours. With fifty pilots, ferrying operations would not be interrupted by annual leave, illness or attrition. Air Transport Command did not share in the belief, prevalent in some RCAF circles, that any pilot can ferry an aircraft: the Becher's Brook operations conducted by the RAF showed that only through strict selection of aircrew and rigid adherence to a preparatory training syllabus could trans-Atlantic ferry operations on the proposed scale be conducted successfully. The proposed mobile ferry squadron should also include at least forty airmen from a variety of trades.

Air Commodore Ripley concluded that the safest, most economical way for the RCAF to maintain a steady flow of Sabre aircraft to Europe was to integrate its ferry flights with the rest of the RAF Becher's Brook program. If that objective was to be realized, instruction in ferrying techniques would have to begin by 1 October 1953, which meant selecting suitable personnel and forming a training unit at St-Hubert immediately. A ferry squadron would have to be activated in September, under the command of an officer of at least Squadron Leader rank with ferrying experience on the proposed route. Liaison parties should be in position along the route by 1 November to learn the job from the RAF personnel already in place, and procurement action should be initiated for Sabre V pack-up kits at Goose Bay, Narsarssuak, Keflavik and Kinloss, the staging posts. Finally, organization establishments would have to be prepared, and logistics support arranged, for the duration of the operation.[2]

Following discussions between the commanders and the headquarters staff of No 1 Air Division and Air Transport Command, a joint overseas ferry plan was submitted to Air Force Headquarters. It had been agreed that the ferrying of aircraft should be placed on a proper continuing basis with minimum disruption to the Air Division's operational effectiveness, a priority that called for the formation of a ferry squadron at St-Hubert. It was recommended that the unit establishment be set up as follows:

- Ferry personnel: one Officer Commanding, thirty pilots, two administration officers and three aeronautical engineering officers to organize and conduct the ferry flights;
- Liaison personnel: four officers, eight senior technical NCOs and four supply technicians to operate the stop-over points; and
- Maintenance personnel: fifty ground crew technicians of all trades, including a Ferry Acceptance Flight of ten men, and two groups of twenty for *en route* ferry duties.

In the case of a ferry operation requiring more pilots than the ferry squadron could provide, the additional aircrew personnel should come from No 1 Air Division on temporary duty. (No 1 Air Division Headquarters agreed that ferry pilots should come from its resources and those of No 1 (Fighter) Wing, and that they would be employed on ferry duties for six months.)

It was also considered desirable, for personnel administration reasons, that pilots be transferred to the Ferry Squadron and assigned elsewhere in Canada on completion of their six months of ferry duty.[3]

An Organization Order drafted at Air Force Headquarters on 30 July and approved early in August authorized the formation of No 1 Overseas Ferry Unit (OFU) at RCAF Station St-Hubert effective 1 September 1953, under the control of the Air Officer Commanding, Air Transport Command, to perform the following tasks:

- to conduct post-acceptance air trials and pre-convoy inspections of F-86 aircraft assigned for delivery to No 1 Air Division;
- to carry out F-86 ferry operations to No 1 Air Division;
- to institute training programs as required to ensure the development and maintenance of a high standard of qualification of the unit's air and ground crews; and
- to supervise the activities of the unit's detachments located at the various staging posts.[4]

July

The third anniversary of the beginning of No 426 Squadron's participation in the Korean Airlift passed without fanfare. At 0800 hours on 21 July, Flying Officer E. Kowalik and his crew in NS17510 departed McChord for Elmendorf, where they took a twelve-hour crew rest as the weather was down at Shemya; the next day, Shemya was still below limits and the flight was diverted to Adak. On 23 July, Kowalik and his crew made it to Shemya, refuelled and pressed on to Haneda. On the return trip, they were held up for fourteen hours at Misawa to await better weather forecasts for Shemya and Adak, and arrived back at McChord on 27 July, marking the completion of three years of airlift activities on *Operation HAWK*. The July airlift commitment of eight round trips to Tokyo was met.[5]

During July, the squadron also completed eight trans-Atlantic flights to North Luffenham. On 8 July, the first flight in NS17505, captained by Flying Officer Casselman, proceeded directly from Goose Bay to North Luffenham, making the crossing in ten hours and fifty minutes. Flight Lieutenant Morrison and his crew made it to North Luffenham from Goose Bay on 26–27 July in ten hours and twenty-five minutes; on their return, they made a direct flight from Prestwick to Gander in ten hours and forty minutes. At the end of the month, Flying Officer Whitman conducted a special flight in NS17506 carrying passengers and cargo in support of *Operation LEAP FROG IV*.[6]

The squadron also despatched two flights to Goose Bay and four to Resolute Bay. The first trip to Resolute was conducted by Flying Officer Kyle and his crew between 12–17 July in NS17504, routed through St-Hubert, Greenwood, Goose Bay and Frobisher Bay. Kyle then proceeded to Churchill, where additional cargo was picked up for delivery to Coral Harbour and Resolute Bay. The flight then went directly to Winnipeg, and then returned to base by way of Ottawa. The second flight, in NS17509 captained by Flying Officer Raike, left base for Winnipeg on 14 July, with Wing Commander E.R. Johnston, the station commander at Lachine, aboard for the trip. That flight staged through Churchill and Coral Harbour on the way to Resolute Bay. On the return, the aircraft picked up four Eskimos and flew them to Winnipeg for medical treatment. The next Resolute Bay run was routed directly from Dorval through Churchill, and returned to base by the same route. Flying Officer Raike captained NS17525 on the month's last run to Resolute Bay. Leaving base on the morning of 28 July, the flight carried as passengers Group Captain Burbank, Director of Telecommunications Engineering at

Air Force Headquarters, and Maja van Steensel, a CBC correspondent. The flight proceeded via Winnipeg, Churchill and Coral Harbour to Resolute Bay, from where para-drops were carried out at Isachsen and Mould Bay. Returning to Churchill, Raike and his crew picked up more cargo for Resolute Bay. The aircraft returned to base via Thule and Goose Bay on 1 August.[7]

During July, two squadron aircraft carried out two shuttles each from Hamilton, Ontario, to RCAF Station Bagotville, airlifting personnel and equipment from No 424 "City of Hamilton" Squadron (Auxiliary) for an air-defence exercise. Fifteen members of 70th Observation Regiment, a Montreal artillery unit, were flown to Rivers, Manitoba, with sixty-five soldiers from 69th Observation Regiment and 133rd Locating Battery of Toronto, and then back to their home stations after a major exercise. An aircraft was despatched to The Pas to fly members of a Flin Flon unit, the 21st Field Engineer Squadron, to Vancouver. Personnel and equipment of No 403 (F) Squadron from Calgary and No 402 (F) Squadron from Winnipeg were flown to Rockcliffe to take part in deployment and air-defence exercises.

The squadron also conducted three shuttle runs in the Maritimes, airlifting Air Cadets and Army Cadets to their summer camps on several legs. Finally, the squadron carried out eight other passenger and logistics runs during the month, mainly in Eastern Canada.[8]

On 21 July, the RCAF lost a North Star: NS17501, which belonged to the Central Experimental and Proving Establishment at Rockcliffe, caught fire while it was being loaded for a northern flight; the fuselage was gutted and the cargo destroyed.[9]

On 24 July, a BOAC aircraft arrived at Dorval bringing Field Marshal Sir Bernard Montgomery, Lieutenant General G.G. Simonds and Major General S.F. Clark from England; Air Commodore Ripley was there to meet them.[10]

With the formation of No 436 (T) Squadron at Dorval, plans regarding the location of No 4 (T) OTU were finalized: instead of moving to RCAF Station Namao, the unit was to relocate to RCAF Station Trenton. Air Force Headquarters Organization Order 49/53 authorized the move, which became effective 1 September 1953.[11]

August

In August, the squadron's fleet of twelve North Stars were fully occupied, putting in nearly 1,600 flying hours, of which 1,500 were devoted to operations and nearly a quarter were used in eight round trips to Tokyo. Seven flights were despatched to North Luffenham and eight to Baden-Söllingen in direct support of *Operation LEAP FROG IV*. Of the Baden flights, three originated at Bagotville, three at Ottawa, and two at St-Hubert; base development at No 4 (F) Wing had progressed enough to permit personnel to arrive there by air instead of by rail from Paris as was done earlier.

During the month, the squadron made three trips to Resolute Bay, of which two were routed through Churchill and returned to base via Winnipeg. The third flight, carried out from 11–15 August in NS17503 and captained by Flight Lieutenant Wolkowski, transported Air Vice Marshal J.L.E.A. de Niverville (representing the Department of Transport), Air Commodore Ripley (Air Officer Commanding, Air Transport Command), Wing Commander Mussells (Senior Air Staff Officer, Air Transport Command Headquarters) and Wing Commander McVeigh (Senior Technical Staff Officer, Air Transport Command Headquarters) to the Arctic for a staff visit.

The flight proceeded to Resolute Bay through Winnipeg, Edmonton and Churchill; from there, it was routed to Frobisher Bay, where Air Commodore Ripley remained while the flight carried on to Goose Bay. Returning to Frobisher Bay on a logistics shuttle run, Wolkowski then took the flight to Churchill and returned to base after a brief stop at Rockcliffe, bringing two patients from Mould Bay who needed medical attention in Montreal.[12]

In mid-August, a devastating earthquake struck the region around the Greek island of Zakinthos in the Adriatic Sea, and the Canadian government arranged for an RCAF North Star to transport relief supplies to Greece for the Red Cross. At 1300 hours on 17 August, Squadron Leader Hare and his crew departed Montreal in NS17503 for Toronto, where they were joined by Red Cross representative L.A. Bjarnason and loaded about 9,000 pounds of supplies, including camp cots with sheets and pillow cases, canned meat, sugar and soap. Departing Toronto at 1650 hours, the flight proceeded to Gander, refuelled, and headed for Lajes where a twelve-hour crew rest was taken. Departing Lajes on the morning of 19 August, Hare stopped for fuel at Gibraltar and then pressed on to the airfield at Elevsis, about seventeen miles northwest of Athens. The aircraft and crew were met by the Canadian Ambassador and, after unloading the cargo, the flight proceeded to Athens. On the morning of 21 July, the aircraft was in position at Baden-Söllingen, where it was integrated into a *LEAP FROG* flight; departing that evening, the crew carried on to base, arriving at 1810 hours on 22 August after refuelling stops at Keflavik and Goose Bay, and a brief stop at Rockcliffe to drop passengers and cargo.[13]

On 19 August, No 1 Air Division issued Operation Order 25/53 concerning the part of *Operation LEAP FROG IV* that was under its authority. For operational reasons, instead of flying to Kinloss from Keflavik, the Sabres were to go to Lossiemouth, nine miles northeast of Kinloss. Leuchars remained the designated alternate, as it is ninety-four miles south-southeast of Lossiemouth and seven miles south of Dundee. The Sabres were not to arrive at Lossiemouth before 28 August, and their radios would be recrystallized for European operations there, before leaving for Baden-Söllingen. The Sabres' route to their destination would take them over Sculthorpe, Brussels and Luxembourg, a distance of 797 miles, and the alternate airfield for this final leg remained Zweibrücken. This stage of the operation would be supported by one Bristol Freighter from RCAF Station Langar.[14]

By 24 August, departure preparations for the three Sabre squadrons destined for No 4 (F) Wing were complete. The North Stars of No 426 Squadron had already started Phase 1 of the operation, the personnel airlift to Baden-Söllingen. No 414 (F) Squadron from Bagotville, commanded by Wing Commander J.F. Allan, and No 444 (F) Squadron from St-Hubert, led by Squadron Leader J. MacKay, flew in to RCAF Station Uplands to join No 422 (F) Squadron, under Squadron Leader W.J. Buzza, in a joint departure ceremony, at which the Chief of the Air Staff, Air Marshal C.R. Slemon would be on hand to wish the Wing "Godspeed".

On 26 August, three North Stars left Dorval to provide direct support for the overseas movement of the three Sabre squadrons. Flying Officer Kyle (the Senior Transportation Captain for the operation) and his crew positioned NS17515 at St-Hubert. Flying Officer Clifton in NS17525 proceeded to Ottawa, while Flying Officer Kowalik flew NS17506 to Bagotville. The following morning, the three aircraft headed for Goose Bay with servicing crews and spare parts aboard, with Kyle making a stop at Bagotville on the way. Wing Commander Malloy, the Task Force Commander, made the trip to Goose Bay with his staff in Kyle's aircraft.

Phase 2 of *Operation LEAP FROG IV* got rolling formally on 27 August, one day behind schedule. Goose Bay weather was warm and clear, but strong headwinds en route made it necessary for the St-Hubert and Uplands squadrons to refuel at Bagotville. Wing Commander Allan and the nineteen Sabres of his squadron were all down at Goose Bay by 1100 hours. On landing, the pilots burned off their excess JP4 fuel so their tanks could be filled to capacity with the heavier, longer-range JP1. The twenty-one Sabres of No 422 (F) Squadron were next to arrive, and the twenty-three Sabres of No 444 (F) Squadron, which had been delayed by poor visibility at St-Hubert, were the last to come in. By 1630 hours, sixty-three Sabres — two less than originally planned — were safely on the ground at Goose Bay.

On the morning of 28 August, Kowalik and his crew left Goose Bay for Narsarssuak, where they dropped off their passengers and cargo; the flight then returned to base via Goose Bay. Clifton made a similar run to Narsarssuak, returning to Goose Bay the following day. On 28 August, the Wing was ready to leave, but Wing Commander Malloy postponed their departure because of extremely strong headwinds on the leg to Greenland. Rain and low ceilings at Goose Bay again delayed departure on 29 August. On 30 August, between 1300 and 1500 hours, sixty Sabres and Clifton's North Star departed for Narsarssuak, rapidly vanishing into overcast skies. Two remained behind because of mechanical problems, which also meant that the Wing "clean-up man", Flight Lieutenant E.A. Glover, had to stay with them. The only accident of the whole operation occurred at Narsarssuak, where a Sabre suffered extensive damage running off the end of the concrete runway.

After conducting a weather reconnaissance for the Wing, Kyle returned to Goose Bay.

On 31 August, bad weather at Goose Bay prevented the last three Sabres from taking off, so they missed their rendezvous at Narsarssuak; Malloy decided to carry on to Keflavik with the other fifty-nine fighters and reform the Wing there.

Clifton and his crew proceeded to Keflavik with a support party aboard and, after discharging their passengers, returned to Narsarssuak, a four-hour trip. In the meantime, Kyle and his crew had left Goose Bay for Narsarssuak where they spent an hour on the ground and then took off again for Keflavik. On 1 September, Kyle returned to Goose Bay to pick up the remaining servicing personnel, who had seen Glover's three Sabres off to Greenland. After two hours on the ground, Kyle and his crew were airborne again, headed back to Narsarssuak. With Kyle on his way, Clifton embarked most of the servicing crew and headed for Lossiemouth. At Keflavik, Malloy decided to declare a day of rest and wait for Glover and the last three Sabres.

September

At 1400 hours on 2 September, Glover and his section of three Sabres arrived at Keflavik. With the Wing complete, all sixty-two aircraft were readied for departure, and Clifton returned to Iceland from Scotland while Kyle came in from Narsarssuak. The following day, they learned at the noon weather briefing that the ceiling at Lossiemouth had lifted to 2,000 feet and was improving; the go signal was given at 1325 hours and, two hours later, as the last of the Sabres were taking off at Keflavik, most of No 414 Squadron was on the ground at Lossiemouth. Wing Commander Allan's section had some anxious moments; his No 2 had an oxygen failure at the point of no return, and the section of four aircraft was forced to fly the leg at a much lower altitude than they planned, which meant faster fuel consumption. They landed at Lossiemouth with about four minutes of fuel to spare. The two North Stars arrived several hours after the Sabres.

By early afternoon on 4 September, all the Sabres were serviced and had had their radios recrystallized: fly-in day had arrived. The first aircraft landed at Baden-Söllingen at 1628 hours, and the rest followed in sections of three and four at five-minute intervals until 1840 hours, when all sixty-two Sabres were on the ground. The reception committee included Air Commodore K. Hodson, representing the Air Officer Commanding No 1 Air Division.

Clifton and his crew brought in their North Star two hours later. After a two-day rest, they left for home on 7 September by the northern route, after a brief stop at North Luffenham. Kyle, who had arrived at Baden-Söllingen well before the Sabres, returned to Lossiemouth to pick up the remaining servicing personnel. He was back at Baden on the afternoon of 5 September and, with his crew, took a two-day rest. Kyle departed Baden-Söllingen on the morning of 8 September and, after staging through North Luffenham, headed home to Dorval, arriving late the following afternoon.[15]

Early in September, while the mother ships captained by Flying Officer Kyle and Flying Officer Clifton were providing transport support for squadrons of No 4 Wing, No 426 Squadron despatched three final Phase 1 flights. Flying Officer Cook took NS17503 out of Bagotville on 2 September, proceeding to Baden-Söllingen through Goose Bay and Kelflavik and returning to base two days later via Keflavik. Flying Officer Roulston captained NS17516 out of RCAF Station Uplands on 4 September, and returned home by way of North Luffenham and Prestwick. On 7 September, Flight Lieutenant Wolkowski left St-Hubert in NS17521 on the last *LEAP FROG IV* shuttle run to Baden-Söllingen; on its return, the flight staged through North Luffenham.

As well as the *LEAP FROG* shuttles, the squadron also conducted eight trips to North Luffenham, two trips to Paris, and two trans-Atlantic flights in support of *Operation MARINER* in September. On 18 September, Flying Officer Nyhuus in NS17505, followed the next day by Squadron Leader Hare in NS17504, proceeded to Greenwood, where they picked up thirty-eight personnel from No 404 and No 405 (MR) Squadrons and airlifted them with their equipment to St. Eval in Cornwall by way of Gander, where they refuelled before making the ten-hour trans-Atlantic crossing. Both aircraft returned to base through North Luffenham by the northern route.

The squadron also made eight trips to Tokyo during September, with only one major delay: NS17506, captained by Flying Officer Roulston, lost an engine as the flight was approaching Tokyo, and it took seven days to complete the engine change as the replacement had to be brought in from McChord.

On 25 July, US Navy Task Force Nanook 53 left Halifax for Resolute Bay carrying 3,670 short tons of dry cargo and POL in drums, and 560,000 gallons of bulk POL, all to be stockpiled at the RCAF detachment[16] in preparation for the resupply of the Arctic weather stations to be conducted in late September. On 24 September, No 426 squadron despatched two crews, captained by Flight Lieutenant Sage and Flying Officer Cook, to conduct the resupply operation with one C-119 Flying Boxcar from No 435 Squadron. Before returning to base on 7 October, the two crews had completed: four shuttle flights from Churchill to Resolute Bay; four supply runs to Isachsen and three to Mould Bay from Resolute Bay; and two flights to Thule.[17]

A tragic acident occurred at Dorval on the evening of 29 September, when a crew captained by Flying Officer Ingall was preparing for a night exercise. When all the North Star's engines were running, the tractor-driver hauled the Auxiliary Power Unit away and parked the tractor off the port wing tip of the aircraft with its headlights on. Ingall then signalled the ramp crew to remove the chocks, and Aircraftsman 1st Class J.B. Pickard, an airframe technician, proceeded to comply. He removed the starboard chock, and then the one on the port side, and then started walking straight to the tractor. Noticing, to his horror, that Pickard was heading for the whirling propeller of the port outer engine, Ingall did the only thing he could: he told the flight engineer to engage the emergency idle cut-off switches. The engines shut down immediately, but the propeller was still rotating when Pickard walked into it. He was killed instantly. The coroner came and removed the body; the Board of Inquiry found the death to be accidental.[18]

October

On 1 October, administrative control of No 1 (F) Wing at North Luffenham was transferred from Air Force Headquarters to the Air Officer Commanding No 1 (RCAF) Air Division. pending its move to Marville in France, however, the Wing would remain under the operational control of the Air Officer Commanding-in-Chief, RAF Fighter Command. In August, Air Force Headquarters had given all its commands quotas to fill, so that the sixty-six airmen required to man the Overseas Ferry Unit at St-Hubert would be selected and transferred by 1 October; the instructions specified that the OFU was to be manned to 100 percent of its establishment, and that all its aircraft maintenance tradesmen had to have experience on F-86 aircraft.[19]

In a letter dated 9 October to the Chief of the Air Staff, Group Captain J.P. McCarthy, the Air Advisor in Tokyo, wrote that, in view of the cease-fire in Korea, the RCAF should reconsider some of its UN airlift commitments. He suggested increasing direct support to the 25th Canadian Infantry Brigade in Korea, to help Army commanders in the field deal with the problem of maintaining soldiers' morale during lulls in combat. Despite a chronic shortage of in-theatre airlift capacity, the Eighth Army leave policy called for two periods of R & R (Rest and Recuperation) per year, which meant that, every 12 days, the Canadian brigade had 280 soldiers entitled to a flight to Japan. The USAF aircraft used for airlift between Korea and Japan could meet about 75 percent of the Canadian requirement, but that left a shortfall of about fifty seats per week. To meet this need and to increase mail-delivery capacity, Group Captain McCarthy suggested extending RCAF trans-Pacific flights to Seoul but, like an earlier proposal from Group Captain McNair, it was turned down flat: the USAF was planning to phase out its North Pacific air transport operation and, should the northern route be closed down, the RCAF would also have to withdraw.[20]

In October, No 426 Squadron started operating on a new scheduled service to Britain: three departures for North Luffenham from Dorval per week, on Tuesday, Thursday and Saturday, not including special flights; slip crews were in position at Prestwick and Keflavik. The first month saw a total of sixteen round trips to North Luffenham completed: after refuelling in Goose Bay, thirteen flights landed first at Prestwick and three went directly to North Luffenham. Fourteen of these flights returned to base through Prestwick, Keflavik and Goose Bay; one stopped at Greenwood after leaving Goose Bay to drop off cargo, and one landed at Narsarssuak before heading for Montreal. Flying Officer Stevenson from the Radio Section was sent to North Luffenham to serve as the squadron's Detachment Commander.

The squadron completed its October quota of eight round trips to Japan. The western service, with stops at Winnipeg, Edmonton and Vancouver and connecting with the Tokyo run, left Montreal every four days, and the schedule gave slip crews a four-day rest period in Japan. Flying Officer Quinn took over the Tokyo detachment from Flying Officer Weir, who returned to the Navigation Section. Another navigator, Flying Officer North, was sent to head up the detachment at McChord.

The RCAF had taken delivery of most of the thirty-five Fairchild C-119s it had purchased by the end of August, and soon airlift tasks previously carried out by the Thunderbirds were taken over by C-119s flown by No 435 Squadron out of RCAF Station Edmonton. In particular, No 435 Squadron was handling more and more of the logistics flights to Resolute Bay, and was slated for most future spring and fall resupply operations in the high Arctic. Meanwhile, the C-119s flown by No 436 Squadron from Dorval were handling the bulk of the ration runs to Goose Bay. No 426 Squadron's participation in the October resupply activities was limited to one North Star and two crews. No 426 Squadron conducted two other flights to Resolute Bay, however. Between 13 October and 16 October, Flying Officer Kowalik and his crew in NS17503 conducted a shuttle run to Coral Harbour and Resolute Bay after staging through Winnipeg and Churchill. From 27 October to 30 October, the crew of NS17503, captained by Flight Lieutenant Sage, flew two shuttle runs to Resolute Bay from Churchill and another to Coral Harbour.[21]

Back at Dorval, Flying Officer Charchuk, Flying Officer Kronick and Flying Officer McDonald graduated from the North Star first officers' course at No 4 OTU and reported to the squadron, while Flight Lieutenant Evans and Flight Lieutenant Wynn completing the captains' course. Flying Officer Cook, an old hand at this type of work, was tasked with checking out all the unit's pilots on para-dropping techniques, and Flying Officer Casselman, an experienced North Star captain, was posted to No 4 OTU as a pilot instructor. Flying Officer Grant returned from the summer Bush Survival Course held near Fort Nelson, B.C.

At the Navigation Section, Flight Lieutenant Cox, an RAF exchange officer and the Deputy Senior Navigation Officer, was reassigned to No 435 Squadron and Flight Lieutenant Majocha took over his duties. Flying Officer Kilgour returned from survival training. Pilot Officer Brown and Pilot Officer Ramey reported in for flying duties from the Navigation Course at the OTU. Corporal Adams and Corporal Emery reported in to the Flight Engineering Section having completed their training course at the OTU. Corporal Sutton was away on the Bush Survival Course.²²

No 1 Overseas Ferry Unit started forming at RCAF Station St-Hubert on 1 September, and at the end of the month its first Officer Commanding, Squadron Leader R.G. Middlemiss, reported in from No 2 (F) Wing at Grostenquin, where he had commanded No 421 Squadron. In October, planning started in earnest for *Operation RANDOM*, the ferrying of Sabre V aircraft to Europe for the rearming of No 1 Air Division. At the end of the month, Wing Commander Mussells chaired a conference at Air Transport Command Headquarters to discuss the financial aspects of *Operation RANDOM* with the RAF liaison officers involved in the Becher's Brook ferry operation, who were based at Goose Bay, Narsarssuak and Keflavik. RCAF liaison officers newly assigned to Goose Bay, Narsarssuak, Keflavik and Kinloss also attended.²³

November

In a brief ceremony at Air Transport Command Headquarters on 5 November, Air Commodore Ripley officially relinquished the command to Group Captain Z.L. Leigh. After serving as Air Officer Commanding since 4 August 1951, Ripley was bound for Fontainebleau, France, to take up new duties at the headquarters of Allied Air Forces Central Europe.²⁴

The squadron's operational workload did not ease off in November. As well as three flights per week to North Luffenham, and the month's quota of eight flights to Tokyo, it despatched a northern run by Flying Officer Husch that included two shuttles from Churchill to Coral Harbour and Resolute Bay, from where a supply run was made to Isachsen. The Christmas supply and mail drops to stations in the eastern Arctic would be made by C-119s, but the North Stars still had the stations in the central Arctic, where drops were to begin on 7 December. Runs to the eastern Arctic would begin on 16 December.²⁵

Acting on an RCAF request, Canadair submitted a proposal to Air Force Headquarters for fitting twelve North Stars with seat rails and 100 rear-facing folding seats. The proposal was judged suitable, but the RCAF considered the $227,000 cost estimate excessive.²⁶

At 1005 hours on 30 November, Flying Officer Ingall and his crew left McChord in NS17504 on the first leg of their flight to Tokyo. The run to Anchorage took eight hours and fifteen minutes and, after refuelling, Ingall took off for Shemya; flight time on this leg was seven hours and twenty minutes, with arrival at 0110 hours Shemya time on 1 December. A fourteen-hour crew rest was taken at Shemya. At the weather briefing, in preparation for the Tokyo leg, the crew were advised that the winds at 10,000 feet at the beginning of the trip would be from the northwest at 35 mph, backing to the southwest at 60 mph by the mid-point. From there on, until the flight neared Japan, what was essentially a headwind was expected to moderate.

Flying Officer Y. Lafrenière, who was on his initial trip as first navigator, calculated the flight time to Matsushima to be nine hours and thirty-six minutes with a further sixty-one minutes to reach Tokyo. The aircraft carried a full fuel load of 2,950 Imperial gallons. After allowances were made for fuel to destination, an en-route reserve of 10 percent, fuel to alternate and forty-five minutes holding at destination Lafrenière determined there would be eighty-three gallons extra. The flight carried twenty US servicemen and mail.

NS17504 left Shemya at 1510 hours local, set course for Matsushima while climbing to 10,000 feet. After reaching cruising altitude, the first wind the navigator found was from the southwest, almost on the nose, at 25 mph. A fix taken half an hour later established that the wind speed had increased to 35 mph, after which the aircraft entered cloud, where the sole navigation aid was pressure pattern. Nearly three and a half hours after leaving Shemya, the flight passed Ocean Station Sugar, where the navigator obtained a radar fix, and track and ground speed checks; he also found that the wind at this point was from the west at 45 mph. Two hours after passing Sugar, the flight broke out on top of the cloud layer and Lafrenière was able to obtain a three-star fix, and to calculate the wind at 65 mph from the west. From an astro-fix an hour later, he found the wind-speed had increased to nearly 100 mph, and the ETA for Matsushima was set back by an hour and forty-two minutes. At this juncture, the aircraft went into cloud and stayed there for the next five hours.

During this period, the crew's only voice contact was with Buzzer Delta, a USAF B-29 weather aircraft that made a daily flight along the Kurile Islands to gather meteorological information, usually flying east from Japan at 17,000 feet and returning to base at the 10,000 foot level. When Ingall asked Buzzer Delta for wind information, he was told that it was from 240° at more than 115 mph — a problem, as there was a distinct possibility they would not reach the Japanese mainland. The one hope was that the headwinds would moderate as called for in the forecast.

Nearly ten hours into the flight, Ingall obtained a radar fix from the D/F station at Nemuro, on the easternmost tip of Hokkaido, that placed the aircraft on a bearing of 135° and 155 miles from the station. Some rapid calculations by Lafrenière determined that, since the last two fixes, the aircraft's average ground speed had dropped to about 115mph, not only because of the head winds, but also because the aircraft had lost airspeed because of moderate icing conditions encountered in cloud, and the captain had maintained a true airspeed of 230 mph only by increasing power periodically. When the ETA for Matsushima was recalculated, they found that the aircraft could not make it to the Japanese coast unless the headwinds abated. A Loran fix confirmed the accuracy of the range and bearing from Nemuro, and that the aircraft was on track for Matsushima.

Calling out on the VHF radio, Ingall was able to raise a radar station at Erimo on the south-central tip of Hokkaido; the fix he obtained indicated that the flight was at 289° and 173 miles from the station. When plotted, this finding put the aircraft's position on the western edge of Hokkaido rather than south of Erimo, which brought the captain vaulting out of his seat to the navigator's table, demanding, "What the hell is going on?" Lafrenière insisted that this radar fix must be wrong, since the Nemuro and Loran fixes indicated that the flight was heading directly for Matsushima; also, if the aircraft had passed over Hokkaido, the rise of land would have registered on the radar altimeter, since Lafrenière had maintained his pressure-pattern plot all along. Erimo Radar asked the North Star to make identification turns, first 50° to port and then 50° to starboard, and reported that the aircraft was on their radar screen. They gave another range and bearing, this time placing the North Star thirty-two miles south of the previous fix. This did not make much sense to Lafrenière, as the aircraft was heading west and therefore could not be south of Erimo's original fix.

Lafrenière was able to obtain another Loran fix that confirmed once more that the flight was definitely on track for Matsushima. About the same time, nearly eleven hours into the flight, the aircraft broke out of cloud and the crew could see the lights of the Japanese fishing fleet on the ocean below. The ground speed between the Nemuro fix and the one just obtained was calculated to be 200 mph, which meant that the headwinds had slackened substantially — from more than 100 mph to 30 mph. The revised ETA for Matsushima placed the flight at the airfield two hours and fifteen minutes later than the original estimate.

At 2148 hours, with the fuel gauges hovering on empty, the radar facility at Haramachi on the eastern coast of Honshu, fifty-six miles southwest of Matsushima, provided a range and bearing that placed the aircraft sixty-two miles east of Matsushima. The aircraft arrived over the airfield at 2210 hours and was on the ground with the engines off twenty-five minutes later, with an intense collective sigh of relief from the crew. Using a dipstick, the flight engineer checked the fuel tanks; when he took it out, he showed it to his crewmates: only the bottom was wet. As twelve hours and twenty-five minutes had elapsed since he first started the engines, Ingall doubted that enough fuel remained to carry out an overshoot and another circuit if one had been required. As well as the headwinds, increased power settings to maintain cruising speed in icing conditions accounted for higher than normal fuel consumption.

Fifty minutes after landing, the aircraft was refuelled and on its way to Tokyo, where it set down at 0100 hours on 3 December. During the debriefing at Haneda, the crew mentioned the Erimo incident and two USAF Intelligence officers were called in. After listening to the crew's account, the officers indicated this wasn't the first time such an incident had occurred, and offered the opinion that it was probably a Russian reconnaissance aircraft listening to the flight's conversation with Erimo on VHF and making the same identification turns to confuse both the radar station personnel and the flight crew.

After a five-day layover, Ingall and his crew departed Tokyo on 8 December in NS17525, arriving at McChord at 1020 hours the following day.[26]

December

The squadron's operational commitments for December totalled more than 1,400 flying hours. Unit taskings included: Service Flight 5/6, a weekly run to Whitehorse that staged through Uplands, Winnipeg, Edmonton, Watson Lake and Fort Nelson; and SF 7/8 and SF 9/10, weekly flights to Vancouver, with stops at Uplands, Winnipeg and Edmonton; from Vancouver these flights carried on to McChord AFB and Tokyo, returning to Dorval as SF 8 and SF 10. There were also three departures per week for North Luffenham — SF 51/52 on Tuesday, SF 53/54 on Thursday and SF55/56 on Saturday — with stops at Goose Bay and Prestwick outbound, and Prestwick, Keflavik and Goose Bay inbound. On top of its scheduled commitments, the unit made several domestic runs, including three to Resolute Bay.

Toward the end of the month, the squadron's long streak of good fortune ran out with the loss of two aircraft.[28]

Lachine, July–December 1953

On 8 December Flight Lieutenant J.P.H. Evans and his crew brought in NS17510 to Resolute Bay on *Operation SANTA CLAUS*, the delivery of mail and supplies for subsequent air-drop at RCMP outposts and weather stations in the high Arctic and, after a three-hour stop, they departed again for Churchill and Dorval. A week later, NS17521 captained by Flying Officer Cook arrived at Resolute Bay to carry out the air-drops at the various destinations across the North; on board were several Air Transport Command and RCAF Station Lachine personnel, including the Station Commander, Wing Commander E.R. Johnston; the Medical Officer, Flight Lieutenant Lee; the Protestant chaplain, Flight Lieutenant Neff; and the Roman Catholic chaplain, Captain Lord, all of them making a pre-Christmas staff visit. Flight Lieutenant Harvey, a Public Relations Officer, and a Mr. Brown from the British Broadcasting Corporation were also along to record a radio feature on the air-drops.

On 16 December, the temperature at Resolute Bay had dropped to -43°F, and all available Herman-Nelson generators were rounded up to blow heated air on the engines to warm them to the point at which they could build oil pressure. This procedure meant delaying take-off to 2100 hours. Once the engines were warm enough to run effectively, successful drops were carried out at Isachsen and Mould Bay while the Wing Commander Johnston and his party started their inspection of the detachment and its facilities.

The next day, Cook and his crew departed for Thule to conduct drops at Hendra Fjord, Alert and Eureka, but high winds prevented the drop at Alert. Flying Officer Kyle and his crew in NS17503 arrived from Churchill with a load of supplies for Resolute Bay. As soon as the aircraft was unloaded, it returned to Churchill for more cargo.

On 18 December, Cook and his crew left for Arctic Bay, Craig Harbour and Alert, but had to return to Resolute Bay with faulty gyros. In the meantime, NS17503 had returned from Churchill, so the load from NS17521 was transferred to NS17503 and Cook conducted successful air-drops at Arctic Bay and Craig Harbour. Kyle and his crew then took over NS17521 and left for Churchill and Dorval with the Station Commander and his party. The next day, Cook completed the air-drops, and all stations reported the job well done with little or no damage to the parcels. Cook and his crew then returned to base by way of Churchill.[29]

On 17 December, a meeting was held in Ottawa to discuss resupplying Resolute Bay and Eureka by sea in 1954, a joint undertaking by the Department of Transport and the RCAF. The meeting was chaired by the Department of Transport's Superintendent of Marine Services.[30]

On 18 December Squadron Leader C.E.L. Hare and his crew departed Dorval in NS17516 for McChord AFB, stopping at Uplands, Winnipeg, Edmonton and Vancouver en route. The flight left McChord on 20 December and arrived in Tokyo on the morning of 23 December. After a quiet Christmas in Tokyo, the crew picked up NS17505 from the inbound crew on 27 December for the return to base. The aircraft carried a cargo of mail, one USAF sergeant, and a crew of seven. At the briefing at the Haneda weather office, the crew learned that the weather en route and at Shemya was forecast to be marginal at best; in addition, even with a full

fuel load, the flight did not meet MATS regulations for an oceanic crossing. Therefore, Hare decided to proceed to Misawa, take on fuel and proceed to Shemya. The weather briefing received at Misawa was much the same as the one given at Haneda.

Squadron Leader Hare also decided that, to take advantage of a favourable tail-wind, the crossing should be made at an altitude much higher than the usual 9,000 feet. A flight plan to Shemya was filed at a cruising altitude of 23,000 feet, with Adak as the alternate airfield. Leaving Misawa late in the evening, the flight climbed out on course for Shemya with everyone aboard going on oxygen as the aircraft passed the 10,000-foot level. About two hours out of Misawa, the aircraft entered cloud, a condition that lasted for the rest of flight. The high static level made useful Loran readings unavailable, and navigator Flying Officer D. Weir had to rely on his DR plot and pressure-pattern position lines to calculate the aircraft's most probable position. Static also prevented radio officer Flying Officer A. Butt from communicating with Shemya, and contact was not established until about an hour out from the island.

The RCAF North Star was not a pressurized aircraft, and its Janitrol heater was not very reliable at high altitudes. The cabin heater, never particularly effective, often failed completely, and Sergeant Mansfield, the flight engineer, frequently left his position to restart the heater by hand. Without adequate heating, everyone aboard resorted to blankets and their Arctic gear to keep warm. Despite these efforts, the aircraft was uncomfortably cold for most of the flight.

As the aircraft passed over Occan Station Sugar, Weir obtained a fix that showed the aircraft to be on track for Shemya. About ninety minutes from destination, they began picking up weak signals from the island's radio beacon and, shortly thereafter, Hare began a slow descent towards Shemya. The crew were somewhat surprised, when well before ETA, the aircraft's radio compasses indicated "station passage" — they were flying over the radio beacon. Hare initiated a right-hand holding pattern, while Flying Officer T. Charchuk, the first officer, tried to unsuccessfully to contact Shemya on the VHF radio. After flying for several minutes on an outbound heading, the radio compasses again indicated passage over the beacon. At the same time, radio contact was established with Shemya, and the crew learned that the base had suffered a series of electrical failures and was operating on emergency power, and high winds at ground level had collapsed one of the communication towers. It was left to the navigator to come up with a new heading for Shemya.

Normally, when a beacon site has a power failure, the aircraft's radio compass needles will continue to rotate in search for the tuned frequency. This time, the aircraft's radio compasses remained steady, indicating a normal operating beacon. When the beacon signal was checked, it was determined two different codes were being transmitted on the same frequency, and one was coming from the Russians on the Kurile Islands, who were operating a very powerful radio beacon on the Shemya frequency. After the failure of the Shemya beacon, the aircraft's radio compass homed in on the Kuriles facility, which was how it came to produce the "station passage" indication. The Russians often increased their transmission power to harass air navigation along the Aleutian chain.

The weather was just about as bad at Adak, the alternate, so Squadron Leader Hare decided to land at Shemya. The weather for the approach was reported at: ceiling 200 feet; visibility one-half mile; temperature at 32°F; snow showers; and a 55- to 60-mph crosswind blowing at 90° to the runway. The runway surface was covered with one to two inches of wet snow, and braking action was assessed as "poor".

The Shemya runway is oriented east-to-west and parallel with the south shore of the island. Hare made three GCA approaches. On reaching minimums on the first approach, the aircraft was lined up on the centre line of the runway, but the strong crosswind from starboard put the aircraft's heading at about 30° greater than the runway direction. In the attempt to land, the flight was blown to port and a missed approach was initiated; during the overshoot, the aircraft drifted over some buildings. On the second GCA run, the same sequence of events took place except that the aircraft passed between two communications towers during the overshoot; the red obstruction lights on the top were visible above the aircraft. On the third GCA approach, the aircraft touched down on the runway, but the strong crosswind and wet snow surface made it very difficult to maintain control of the aircraft. The nose-wheel strut fractured, the North Star tilted on its nose, and at that point Mother Nature took over. With little braking action and a strong crosswind, the aircraft skidded off the side of the runway and down a steep slope, and came to rest in a gully. They were eight hours and fifty minutes out of Misawa.

As the aircraft slid to a stop, Charchuk and Mansfield were turning the engine switches off when they heard an engine overspeeding. Someone shouted that there may be a fire and for everyone to get out. Charchuk tried to slide his cockpit window open, but it was jammed shut. He then reached for the fire axe mounted on the face of the step to the cockpit, but got only a handful of snow, so he took down the fire extinguisher from behind his position and was about to smash the side window when the flight engineer yelled, "Don't! It might explode!" Charchuk dropped the extinguisher and decided his only exit route was through the crew rest area and into the main cabin. The cockpit was in an unusual position, with the floor slanting downward at a 30° angle, and twisted to starboard at about 45°.

The first officer got out of his seat, stepped past the flight engineer and headed for the main cabin, but the passage was partly blocked by radio equipment racks and other items. Fortunately, a v-shaped area at floor level was still relatively clear, and Charchuk crawled along the floor, calling for the rest of the cockpit crew to follow. He opened the starboard over-wing hatch and everyone slid down the wing to the snowy ground. Once outside, they noticed that the aircraft's navigation lights were flashing so, to prevent any spark that might ignite the fuel dripping from the wing tanks, the flight engineer returned to the cockpit and moved all the electrical switches to the "off" position.

Outside the aircraft, the storm continued to rage unabated, and the crew could hear the ocean waves crashing on the shore no more than a hundred yards away. To reach some sort of shelter, they climbed the steep, slippery slope of the gully onto the wet, snow-covered runway, crossed the runway and headed for the nearest building. It was a small hut, and inside they found a group of USAF personnel playing cards. One of the players glanced up at the crew, in their soaking wet battledress with their heads and faces covered with snow, and remarked, "Here are those drunken Canadians again."

Later that morning, activity on base slowly returned to normal with the passing of the storm. In the afternoon, Hare and his crew returned to the aircraft to retrieve their belongings and assess the damage to the aircraft. It was a write-off. The nose section was partially torn away forward of the wing, and twisted over. Three of the engines were still mounted with propellers attached; the propeller of No 1 engine had come off, and one of its blades pierced the captain's side of the cockpit right beside his headrest. The crew were shaken up but unhurt, and the cargo of mail was recovered intact. That aircraft was No 426 Squadron's only loss of the entire Korean Airlift.[31]

On 30 December NS17503, captained by Flight Lieutenant J.P.H. Evans, was prepared to leave Vancouver as SF10 for Edmonton, with a crew of eight and forty-six passengers. At the pre-departure weather briefing, the meteorologist suggested that Flight Lieutenant Evans might climb to cruising altitude on a westbound heading before proceeding east to Edmonton; heavy icing conditions were forecast en route below 10,000 feet. Evans elected to climb eastbound immediately after take-off, and at 10,500 feet, the starboard outer engine overheated and power had to be reduced. Unable to climb to their cruising altitude because of the heavy load of ice on the aircraft, the crew decided to return to Vancouver.

During the descent at Vancouver, more ice accumulated on the airframe making it necessary to use full power just to maintain a rate of descent of 500 feet per minute. An ILS (Instrument Landing System) approach was made to the Vancouver airport, where the ceiling was 500 feet with broken cloud and two miles of visibility. During the approach, the pilots' visibility was reduced considerably by ice on the windscreen, which fogged up as well; both the windscreen de-icer and heater systems were unserviceable. The captain's difficulties were considerably increased when the flight engineer lowered the flaps and reduced power without his instructions. The North Star stalled on final approach, and the nose-wheel and starboard wingtip struck the runway at the same time. The nose-wheel promptly collapsed, and the starboard wing fractured between No 3 engine and the fuselage, and was torn off. At this point, the aircraft rolled over coming to rest upside-down. Fortunately, fire did not break out, as the crash truck and the ambulance took three minutes to reach the scene. All fifty-four people aboard escaped, some of them with minor injuries. The aircraft was a write-off.

One of the passengers was Group Captain R.W. McNair, who was reading in the crew rest area when the aircraft crash-landed. He calmly made his way into the main cabin to help the crew evacuate the passengers, some of whom were suspended upside-down by their seat belts. After Evans had completed his check and left the aircraft, McNair returned to the wreck to verify that no one was left behind. He did this despite the danger of fire and the fact that his clothes were soaked in gasoline, and eventually received the Queen's Commendation for brave conduct.[32]

The squadron's eighth post-war Christmas passed quietly with many members on detachment or positioned with slip crews around the world from Japan to Britain. Those fortunate enough to be at home in the Montreal area were able to take part in the traditional holiday festivities at RCAF Station Lachine or simply stay home with their families and friends.

Lachine, July–December 1953

PHOTO 129
NS17505 parked in front of a hangar; Haneda AFB, summer 1953. (DND PL53223)

PHOTO 130
The crew of NS17503 at Athens Airport after delivering Red Cross relief supplies from Canada for earthquake victims; 19 August 1953. From left: S/L C.E.L. Hare (captain), F/L Evans, F/L Majocha, F/O Charters, Sgt. Harper, LAC Bereza and LAC Jobin. (M. Majocha Collection)

PHOTO 131
The remains of NS17505; Shemya AFB, 27 December 1953. (DND, No 426 Squadron)

PHOTO 132
Another view of the crashed NS17505; Shemya AFB, 27 December 1953. (T. Charchuk Collection)

Lachine, July–December 1953

PHOTO 133
Wreckage of NS17503; Vancouver Airport, 30 December 1953. (DND SD 3298–24)

PHOTO 134
The inverted fuselage of NS17503 at the crash scene; Vancouver Airport, 30 December 1953. All fifty-four people aboard escaped, some with minor injuries. (DND SD3298–25)

CHAPTER 17

LACHINE
JANUARY–JUNE 1954

In the spring of 1946, American and Canadian military planners drafted a Joint Security Plan that set a new priority for both nations' defence establishments: protecting the vital areas of Canada and the United States from air attack. The RCAF's mission was to co-operate with the USAF in an air-defence warning system complemented by the requisite communications, navigation and meteorological systems.

By the end of that year, the Canadian government had authorized its planners to proceed with detailed feasibility studies of long-range air-raid warning systems for the continent's main industrial areas to be installed on Canadian territory. Completed by the end of 1947, these studies brought the planners to the conclusion that a trans-continental radar chain in the far north would not be worth the effort of building it, as an interlocking grid of overlapping radar coverage would also be required to track incoming aircraft until they reached the main radar-control system far to the south. Despite the planners' conclusions, however, the idea of an Arctic radar chain survived in Canadian government and scientific circles.[1]

In 1946, an air attack on North America was the remotest of possibilities, as the United States held the monopoly on atomic weapons. That situation changed in September 1949, with the explosion of an atomic device by the Soviet Union and the appearance of long-range bombers in the Soviet air force, which meant that North America was now vulnerable to air attack from the Arctic.[2] In December 1949, American planners informed their Canadian counterparts that they were working on the assumption that, by mid-1954, the Soviets would possess an arsenal of 150 atomic bombs that could be delivered to North American targets by long-range bombers, merchant ships, or submarine-launched missiles capable of carrying their warheads 400 to 600 miles. Should the Soviets attack, the war would be lost in days.[3]

This analysis led to a series of scientific studies on radar warning systems conducted in Canada and the United States, which recommended the construction of three warning lines across Canada. The first of these was the Pinetree Line, which originated in an August 1951 Canada-U.S. agreement. The Pinetree Line was a warning and control system comprising thirty-three prime radars and six gap-filler radars that extended from Newfoundland to Vancouver Island. It was originally planned for the United States to cover American cities, but the agreement with Canada made it possible to extend radar coverage to include Canadian population centres. Under the joint financing arrangement, the United States paid roughly two-thirds of the cost of the radar installations in Canada. Completed in 1954, the Pinetree Line facilities could track hostile bombers and control and direct defending interceptor aircraft.

Most of the station personnel were American at first because Canada lacked trained radar operators, but it was agreed that, following consultation, Canada could eventually take the system over.[4]

Early in 1953, a Canada-U.S. Military Study Group was established to consider air defence in general and the feasibility of a Distant Early Warning (DEW) Line in particular. By the summer of that year, continental air defence was the subject of many studies conducted by both military and civilian groups working for the U.S. Department of Defense but, apart from the completion of the U.S. Permanent Radar Network and the Pinetree Line, very little had been done. Plans had been advanced for the construction of at least two continent-spanning radar chains: one across Canada at about 55° North latitude, and the other on the Arctic coast.[5]

Since 1951, a new form of aircraft detection technology had been under development at McGill University in Montreal; dubbed the McGill Fence, it was a radio-beam trip-wire, based on the Doppler principle, that detected aircraft flying across it. Although less sophisticated than search radar, the McGill Fence was not only cheaper to build, it was also Canadian technology, an important consideration for the Canadian government. The USAF had endorsed such a system for the trans-Canada line at the 55th parallel because it could be completed quickly and at relatively low cost, and in mid-October 1953, the Joint Military Study Group tabled a report in which Minister of National Defence Brooke Claxton recommended adding a McGill Fence-type warning line along the 55th parallel, and building it as a joint project.[6]

Claxton thought that Canada should build this warning line without American help, and found support for this approach in Canadian governmental circles. Quite apart from sovereignty issues — it would be entirely on Canadian territory — it would promote Canadian industry. In November 1953, therefore, the government initiated further feasibility studies for what became known as the Mid-Canada Line, and these studies were completed by June 1954. Consequently, on 19 November 1954, a joint U.S.–Canadian statement was made that Canada had undertaken to build the Mid-Canada Line.[7]

Construction began in 1955, and the Mid-Canada Line was fully operational in January 1958. Arranged along the 55th parallel from Labrador to the Alaska border, its radar sites included eight sector-control stations between Hopedale, Newfoundland and Dawson Creek, British Columbia and about ninety unmanned Doppler detection stations placed thirty miles apart. It cost nearly $225 million to build, and by early 1965, technological change had rendered it obsolete and slated for decommissioning.[8]

On 12 August 1953, the Korean War effectively over, President Eisenhower's National Security Council was deadlocked over competing priorities — should the United States improve defence or curtail expenditures? — when it received the shocking news that the USSR had detonated a hydrogen bomb. On 6 October, the National Security Council endorsed a paper that characterized the Soviet threat as "total", stated that the Soviet Union was capable of launching a nuclear attack on the United States, affirmed the priority of national defence over other goals, and recommended that efforts to improve continental defence be increased. Therefore, the paper's authors recommended, the United States and Canada should adopt a continental defence program put forward by scientists from the Lincoln Laboratories at the Massachusetts Institute of Technology, a project that would cost about $20 billion over five years. Much of this budget would be spent on Arctic early warning, and almost the entire expense would be borne by the United States.[9]

Like the Mid-Canada Line, the DEW Line project was recommended to the American and Canadian governments by the Military Study Group in June 1954, and on 19 November 1954, the two governments jointly announced that they had agreed to proceed with construction. Although both countries would participate, the U.S. would take full responsibility for construction and installation. On 20 May 1955, the text of the "5 May Agreement on Conditions to Govern the Establishment of a Distant Early Warning System in Canadian Territory" was tabled in the House of Commons.[10]

Apart from some early preliminary work (including an experimental station built near Herschell Island in the Yukon for feasibility tests), DEW Line construction began in the summer of 1955; on 15 May 1957 it was declared technically operational, and on 31 July it was fully operational. Of the fifty-eight stations sited more or less along the 70th parallel from Kulusuk on the east coast of Greenland to Cape Lisburne in Alaska, six were main stations spaced about 500 miles apart, and fifty-two were intermediate or auxiliary stations. Four of the main stations were in Canada, located at Cape Dyer, Hall Beach, Cambridge Bay and Cape Parry; the other two were in Alaska, at Barter Island and Point Barrow. To prevent an flanking attack on North America, the original plan included an extension of the DEW Line across the Pacific Ocean from Kodiak to Hawaii; eventually, the Pacific extension began at Umnak in the Aleutians and ended at Midway Island, and an Atlantic extension built by the USAF reached to Greenland, where two stations were built on the ice-cap. Manning was handled by the Americans, and many ex-RCAF personnel worked on the DEW Line.[11]

No 426 Squadron occasionally provided airlift support throughout the construction and operational phases of both the Mid-Canada Line and the DEW Line.

As the CF-100 Canuck began to roll off the assembly line at AVRO's Malton, Ontario plant in 1954, six RCAF squadrons were reformed as all-weather fighter units and added to the order of battle: No 419 Squadron at North Bay on 15 March, No 428 Squadron at Uplands on 21 June, No 425 Squadron at St-Hubert and No 432 Squadron at Bagotville on 1 October, No 409 Squadron at Comox on 1 November, and No 433 Squadron at Cold Lake on 15 November.

On 15 December, the Orenda Iroquois jet engine being developed for the AVRO CF-105 Arrow made its first test run. The Arrow was to be a replacement for the CF-100.[12]

Early in January, representatives of the USAF, the U.S. Navy and the U.S. Coast Guard came to Ottawa for a meeting with Department of Transport officials and senior RCAF officers to discuss weather ships in the Pacific, and points respecting the Korean Airlift were raised.

The military base at Shemya was slated for closure no later than 1 July 1954, and although the U.S. Civil Aeronautics Authority had yet to decide whether it would take over the airfield to support flights on the North Pacific route, and it was unlikely to do so. The airfields at Adak and King Salmon were to remain open, and Cold Bay was to be operated as a weather station. Because of its poor approaches, Adak was open only to supplementary traffic and not rated a good terminal in IFR weather conditions; moreover, the extended range to Haneda from this airfield made it unsuitable for regular North Star operations. For the North Star, Japan was beyond the safe range from either Cold Bay or King Salmon.[13]

Air Commodore F.S. Carpenter, the Chief of Air Operations at Air Force Headquarters, sought to clarify the issue of the pending de-activation of Shemya, so he contacted the Air Member of the Canadian Joint Staff in Washington, who obtained confirmation from USAF Headquarters that the base was indeed scheduled to be closed as of 1 July 1954. The Civil Aeronautics Authority was to advise the USAF by 1 April whether it would take over the airfield, but it looked unlikely; the CAA had never received a definite request to take it over, and the airfield was a costly proposition for which the CAA had no budget.

The rapidly deteriorating docks at Shemya, which came under the jurisdiction of the U.S. Navy, needed repairs urgently but the U.S.N. did not have the money to carry out the work. Consequently, the POL stocks and other supplies at Shemya were expected to fall below critical levels soon unless they were replenished. The USAF rationale for closing Shemya was that both Strategic Air Command and Alaskan Air Command considered it untenable in wartime operations. It was also learned that MATS was curtailing operations through Shemya and changing its focus to the mid-Pacific route.

Toward the end of January, Carpenter wrote a memorandum to Air Vice Marshal F.R. Miller, the Vice Chief of the Air Staff, informing him that Shemya was about to be deactivated, so the RCAF would be able to conduct a trans-Pacific airlift through the Aleutians after 1 July only at the risk of a high and fatal accident rate because the weather on the North Pacific route ranged from poor to extremely bad for most of the year. He stressed that the RCAF had been most fortunate in that it had not experienced more serious accidents on the northern route but, once the highly skilled GCA operators at Shemya were withdrawn, the route would be unsafe for RCAF operations and the Shemya area offered no suitable alternates. The North Stars simply did not have enough safe flight range to operate on the northern route without Shemya.

Although the RCAF had used the mid-Pacific route, staging through Honolulu, the route was not considered suitable for a scheduled service because of the vast distances involved and the limited range of the North Star. Flights could be delayed for days, particularly on the Honolulu-San Francisco leg, because of strong headwinds.

The pending closure of Shemya did not have the same effect on CPA operations, as the airline operated the DC-6B on the North Pacific route. This aircraft had a much greater range and speed than the North Star, and could quite safely fly from Tokyo through Honolulu and then directly to Vancouver.

In view of the political implications of withdrawing No 426 Squadron from the Korean Airlift, Carpenter said that such an action would have to be approved at a very senior level. On the other hand, the squadron's withdrawal from the airlift would release some 400 North Star flying hours every month for urgent tasks such as logistics support to the Air Division in Europe.

On 1 February, in a minute to Carpenter's 26 January memorandum, Miller stated that the AOC Air Transport Command had just told him that the USAF planned to stop using commercial contract carriers on the Pacific run as of 31 March, but MATS had asked for the RCAF schedule of eight trips per month to be maintained. Consequently, Miller asked the Commander to find out whether, as of 31 March, MATS would accept Canadian Pacific Airlines as the carrier on the eight trips per month previously conducted by the RCAF.[14]

On 22 February, in a further memorandum on Korean Airlift operations to the Vice Chief of the Air Staff, Carpenter informed him that CPA was using four DC-6B aircraft and one DC-6C, and had four DC-4s readily available. CPA was maintaining that the operations, communications and weather information from Shemya would be hard to replace, but the airline was working with another commercial carrier to use Cold Bay, and considered Vancouver-Cold Bay-Tokyo a practical alternative route. CPA did not anticipate any difficulty in handling an additional 60,000 pounds of cargo and passengers, the current RCAF monthly commitment, if they were given at least two weeks notice.

From the Canadian Joint Staff in Washington, Carpenter had learned that, as of 31 March, the USAF was terminating all U.S. civil carrier contracts, leaving MATS to handle the Americans' entire Pacific airlift requirement. All MATS aircraft and civil contract carriers were now using the mid-Pacific route. The USAF had also advised the Joint Staff that it did not object to the handover of No 426 Squadron's airlift commitment by a Canadian civilian carrier.

The USAF still planned to close Shemya on 1 July, and the CAA had yet to decide whether to take it over. Aviation fuel stocks at Shemya would be just about exhausted by 31 March, as the USAF had originally planned to close the base at that time and stocks had been allowed to run down. Because of political pressure, however, and the fact that Northwest Airlines had a CAA certificate to operate through Shemya until 1 July, the USAF was forced into a commitment to meet the airline's fuel requirements. Despite the exorbitant cost, therefore, General Nathan Twining, USAF Chief of Staff, ordered that enough aviation fuel was to be flown to Shemya to support limited civil operations until 1 July. After that date, the USAF would have no further interest in the continuance of Shemya and would not fly any more fuel to that location.

In light of all this information, Carpenter made two recommendations: first, that the RCAF component of the Korean Airlift be withdrawn as of 31 March or as soon after that date as practical, and, second, if politically expedient, that Canada maintain the same level of contribution to the Pacific airlift pool and that the present contract with CPA be renewed and expanded by the extent of the current RCAF contribution.[15]

An 11 March memorandum to the Minister, signed by Air Vice Marshal Miller for the Chief of the Air Staff, in essence restated the information provided by Air Commodore Carpenter. Canada's contribution to the Korean Airlift at the time comprised:
- eight monthly North Star trips carrying some thirty tons from Tacoma to Tokyo and return;
- twelve CPA DC-6B trips per month with a capacity of 600 passengers from Vancouver to Tokyo; and
- eight CPA DC-6B trips a month with a capacity of 400 passengers from Tokyo to Vancouver.

Miller recommended that, if it became possible to reduce the Canadian contribution to the trans-Pacific airlift, such reduction be made in the RCAF effort, and that the CPA contract be continued at either its current level or a lesser level that would still meet the Canadian obligation for trans-Pacific airlift.[16]

On 30 March, Brooke Claxton made two recommendations on Korean Airlift operations to the Cabinet Defence Committee: first, that if Canadian participation in the Korean Airlift could be reduced, the RCAF component should be withdrawn, and second, that the contract with CPA, which was due to expire on 31 March, be renewed at the best possible rate, but be subject to termination on short notice. At its 1 April meeting, the Cabinet Defence Committee approved the Minister's recommendations and decided that the CPA contract should be renewed for three months at a time.[17]

On 20 May, Chief of the Air Staff Air Marshal Slemon advised the Minister by memorandum that he had received definite information that the facilities at Shemya were to be closed gradually during June, so it would become impossible for the RCAF to operate through the area sometime before 1 July. As it would take five aircraft loads to bring in all personnel and equipment from the detachments along the airlift route, he thought that an order withdrawing the RCAF from the Korean Airlift as of 1 June should be given immediately. His recommendations to the Minister were that he approve the RCAF withdrawal effective 1 June, and that Canada advise the appropriate authorities that the Canadian contribution would be reduced by the amount of the present airlift: eight North Star return trips per month. Claxton approved the withdrawal on 25 May.[18]

On 26 May, Slemon sent the Minister a draft of a letter to be sent to Secretary of State for External Affairs Lester B. Pearson on No 426 Squadron's withdrawal from the Korean Airlift. The next day, Claxton informed Pearson that he had approved the discontinuance of No 426 Squadron operations on the trans-Pacific route, and had asked the Chief of the Air Staff to cease this operation effective 1 June and return the RCAF detachments to their parent bases. This meant a reduction in the overall Canadian airlift contribution to the trans-Pacific airlift by eight North Star return trips monthly, and the U.S. military components had been notified through service channels. The information was forwarded by Claxton so External Affairs could acquaint other agencies affected.[19]

While No 426 Squadron's future on the Korean Airlift was being decided, CPA's continued participation was being discussed. Negotiations were conducted as to the rate to be charged for the charter of aircraft between Vancouver and Tokyo and, as of early January 1954, no increase in weekly flights was contemplated.[20] The Chief of the General Staff, Lieutenant-General G.G. Simonds, wrote to Air Marshal Slemon on 22 January to raise an important issue: in the event of further hostilities in Korea, it would be necessary to transport reinforcements for the 25th Canadian Infantry Brigade Group to Japan as soon as possible, and airlift would be required for an advance party of 176 officers and men, followed by a main body of 1,475 more soldiers. The Army was allocated only 100 spaces per month on CPA flights to Tokyo, and Simonds doubted that this quota could be increased since, in an emergency, more space would be needed for U.S. troops. He wanted to know whether the RCAF could airlift the advance party immediately after the outbreak of an emergency in Korea, and what arrangements could be made to transport the main body to Japan rapidly. In his view, should the airlift of the main body take more than three weeks, it might be better to plan to send the reinforcements by sea.[21]

A month later, Slemon replied to Simonds that, with the long-range transport aircraft at its disposal, the RCAF could airlift only 50 percent of the reinforcements to Japan in the three-week period envisioned by the planners — 201 men in the first five days and a total of 825 men within three weeks. This could be done only by cancelling all other North Star flights during the deployment period, and only if suitable aerodromes were available in the Aleutians.[22]

With this reply in hand, Army Headquarters asked Air Force Headquarters to see what the commercial airlines could do: how much notice would they need, how much contract services would cost, and whether it would be possible to conduct the entire trooping program to Japan using commercial carriers. For planning purposes, the Army indicated that all the reinforcements would be concentrated in the Vancouver area ninety-six hours after notification of the emergency.[23]

Air Force Headquarters referred the matter to C.M. Drury, the Deputy Minister of National Defence, who wrote to J.R. Baldwin, the Chairman of the Air Transport Board, asking for the following information regarding the capability of the Canadian commercial air carriers to provide emergency airlift of Army reinforcements:

- time in days from receipt of notification to airlift 850 passengers from Vancouver to Tokyo, assuming Aleutian airfields would be available, as well as the associated cost; and
- time in days from receipt of notification to airlift 1,650 passengers from Vancouver to Tokyo, assuming Aleutian airfields would *not* be available, plus the associated cost.

Baldwin was advised that, if commercial air carriers were required, they would get at least seventy-two hours' warning.[24]

In his detailed reply of 25 May, Baldwin stated that the only commercial carriers in Canada capable of such an airlift were Trans-Canada Airlines, with eight aircraft (either Super Constellations or North Stars), and Canadian Pacific Airlines, with five DC6 and two DC4 aircraft. (The mix of aircraft TCA could provide depended on the delivery dates of the Super Constellations; until 15 June the company had only four, and after 15 October it would have eight.) Seventy-two hours after notification of an emergency, if Aleutian airfields were available, on or after 15 May the two companies would be able to airlift 884 passengers from Vancouver to Tokyo within thirty hours. Without Aleutian airfields, on or after 15 May, it would take at least seven days and seven hours for the two companies to airlift 1,663 passengers to Tokyo. After 15 October, with eight Super Constellations on TCA's inventory, the latter airlift could be carried out in four days and nine hours. The cost of the airlift on the northern route, carrying 884 passengers and using the Aleutian airfields, would be about $330,000; without the Aleutian airfields, using the mid-Pacific route and transporting 1,663 passengers, it would cost $754,000.[25]

Air Vice Marshal Miller sent a copy of Baldwin's letter to the Chief of the General Staff on 8 July, informing Lieutenant-General Simonds that the USAF base on Shemya was closed on 1 July, and any plans for airlifting reinforcements for the 25th Canadian Infantry Brigade Group should assume the use of civil carriers, which flew aircraft with more range than the North Star and were, therefore, less affected by the closing of Shemya.[26]

Since the Korean armistice was holding, the Cabinet had decided by September 1954 to reduce the Canadian contribution to the United Nations effort in Korea by about two-thirds, which meant a comparable reduction in the airlift contract with Canadian Pacific Airlines. At that time, Deputy Minister Drury wrote to Air Marshal Slemon directing him to maintain the current contract with CPA until 31 December 1954, and asking him to have Air Force Headquarters prepare a paper for the Cabinet Defence Committee recommending a contract reduction, beginning 1 January 1955, to one million dollars per year, to cover three Vancouver-to-Tokyo round trips by CPA per month in 1955. To establish a basis for the preparation of a new contract and the paper for the Defence Committee, Air Marshal Slemon wrote to Army Headquarters on 17 November asking what airlift support the Army needed for operations in Korea. With several months of rapid troop reductions behind it, the Canadian Army had only about 500 personnel in Korea by May 1955, and by June 1957 the last of them were back in Canada.

During this period, the Royal Canadian Navy presence was also reduced: two of the three destroyers in the Canadian squadron set sail for home on 26 September 1954, and the third left for Canada on 7 September 1955.[27]

January

On 8 January, the Department of Transport held a planning meeting in Ottawa on the re-supply program for the Arctic weather stations. All participating Canadian government agencies were represented, as were the U.S. Weather Bureau, the U.S. Navy and the U.S. Air Force. The 1954 program featured an important change: the Department of Transport would carry out the sea supply mission to Resolute Bay and Eureka, while the U.S.N. conducted the re-supply of Alert by sea as usual.[28]

No 426 Squadron carried out three runs to Resolute Bay in January. On 8 January, North Star 17516, captained by Flight Lieutenant Dick, departed base for Resolute Bay and, after an overnight stop in Churchill, it arrived at 1300 hours local time the next day. They brought with them a show troupe from Montreal and, after a late lunch, put on a ninety-minute performance for the personnel of the detachment and the weather station. At 1830 hours, with the troupe back aboard, the aircraft was on its way back to Churchill and Dorval. NS17525, captained by Flying Officer Paul, arrived on 13 January, and NS17512, captained by Flight Lieutenant Deeprose, came in on 27 January. Each flight was delayed for a day at Churchill by bad weather at Resolute Bay.[29]

Overseas runs in January included eight round trips to Tokyo and the three scheduled weekly flights to North Luffenham in support of No 1 Air Division in Europe. On a domestic run, the squadron transported the Royal Canadian Legion stage show from Montreal to Goose Bay.

On 18 January, No 4 (T) OTU began its long-planned move to RCAF Station Trenton, where it would continue to train crews on the North Star, the C-119 and the Dakota under the command of Squadron Leader P.L. Michel. Its Dorval offices were turned over to the Trade Training Unit.

On 20 January, Group Captain Z.L. Leigh, the commanding officer of Air Transport Command, conducted his annual inspection of RCAF Station Lachine with several officers of his staff. The Officers' Mess hosted the inspection party at a dinner on the evening of 21 January, and on 22 January they departed.[30]

On 25 January, Air Transport Command Headquarters issued Operation Order 2/54 regarding *Operation RANDOM*, the overseas ferry of about 500 F-86 Sabre fighters from Canada to Europe in convoys of about thirty aircraft every four weeks. Air Transport Command was to be responsible for co-ordinating the operation and had full operational control until the aircraft were delivered in Europe. The operation commander was to be Squadron Leader Middlemiss, the officer commanding No 1 OFU, based at St-Hubert. By the end of *Operation RANDOM* in 1957, more than 800 fighter jets had been ferried overseas.

A senior transport captain, appointed by the officer commanding No 426 Squadron, was to be responsible to the Operation Commander for the functional control of transport aircraft. In the original plan, the first convoy (scheduled to leave St-Hubert on 1 February) comprised twelve Sabre Vs, and subsequent monthly convoys would each total about thirty aircraft. For each convoy, North Star mother ships would airlift about forty maintenance technicians from Canada to Europe, and return the Sabre pilots and mobile parties to St-Hubert on completion of each operation. The routing overseas was from St-Hubert to Goose Bay, Narsarssuak, Keflavik, Kinloss and Luxembourg. On the last leg, all the fighters were to fly to the Luxembourg Radio Beacon and then alter course for either Grostenquin, Zweibrücken or Baden-Söllingen.³¹

February

Beginning in February, SF53 to North Luffenham was extended every second Saturday through one of the Wings of No 1 Air Division to Rabat-Salé in Morocco, provide air transport support for Sabres and their servicing crews when the Air Division's pilots flew to Rabat for gunnery practice. To make North Stars available for this support operation, the scheduled service flights to Resolute Bay were taken over by C-119s operating out of Churchill, and one of the weekly transatlantic runs would be made by a North Star configured to carry twenty-eight passengers per flight.³²

The first convoy of fourteen Sabre Vs departed St-Hubert for Goose Bay on 11 February as *Operation RANDOM 1*, with one North Star, captained by Flying Officer Clifton, detailed to transport two mobile parties and spares between the maintenance bases established at Goose Bay, Narsarssuak, Keflavik and Kinloss. Bad weather at Narsarssuak held up the operation for three days, and the convoy arrived at Keflavik on 15 February. Keflavik weather led to another delay, this time for six days; the Sabres were all airborne on 20 February but were recalled when conditions started to deteriorate rapidly. The convoy finally arrived at Keflavik on 22 February, Kinloss the next day, and reached their destination at No 4 (F) Wing Baden-Söllingen on the afternoon of 24 February.³³

No 426 Squadron despatched twenty scheduled flights in February, twelve to Britain and eight to Japan. On one of the runs to Japan, Sergeant J.G. Brogden was the flight engineer on NS17504, captained by Flying Officer Ken Roulston. The flight left Dorval on 16 February, stopped at Ottawa and Winnipeg, spent the night at Edmonton, and the next day continued on to Vancouver and McChord AFB, where the aircraft was loaded with priority freight. On 18 February, the crew departed for Elmendorf, where Brogden changed crews. (Flight engineers "slipped" at Elmendorf to carry out maintenance on North Stars transiting that base.)

On 22 February, Brogden joined Flying Officer Norris and his crew in NS17515, and the flight left for Shemya. The weather closed in shortly before arrival and, since they did not have enough fuel to make it back to Elmendorf, Norris had to land at the only available alternate, a USAF emergency strip at King Salmon. It was midnight when the flight arrived, after being airborne for twelve hours and ten minutes. The fuel truck had only about half the amount needed so Brogden and the transportation technician, Leading Aircraftsman J. O'Connor, had to hand-pump 1,300 gallons from 45-gallon drums, which first had to be dug out of the snowdrifts and rolled to the aircraft. Fuelling and other chores involved in putting the aircraft to bed took more than three hours, with the temperature a crisp -22°F.

Oiling had to wait for the morning because all the oil was congealed, and the drums had to be brought indoors to warm up. After four hours of rest, Brogden and O'Connor tried to get the

Herman Nelson heaters started, but to no avail; the temperature had dropped to -35°F which, with the wind at 25 miles per hour, meant a nasty wind-chill factor. Turning the propellers to break the frost seals, Brogden made ready to start the Merlins. He pressed the starter switch and, after some initial resistance, each engine in turn coughed, sputtered and burst into life. Once the engines were running smoothly, Brogden carried out the "boil-off". (When North Star aircraft were left out in sub-zero temperatures after a flight, gasoline had to be added to the oil in each engine to prevent it from congealing. The gasoline had to be "boiled off" before the aircraft could be ready for flight.)

Since Shemya was weathered in, the flight returned to Elmendorf. On 24 February, Norris and his crew headed back to Shemya and then, after a twelve-hour stopover, carried on to Tokyo. This last leg took twelve hours and five minutes, as the flight had to battle strong headwinds most of the way.

On 2 March, Norris and his crew, now flying NS17521, stopped off at Misawa to refuel — and stay, as the Shemya forecast placed it below limits. It snowed in the night, and Brogden was called out at three in the morning to move the aircraft out of the way of the snow blowers. By late morning on 5 March, Norris and his crew were on their way to Shemya but, ninety minutes into the flight, an engine had to be shut down and the propeller feathered. On returning to Misawa, the crew discovered that a plugged sump-pump filter was responsible for the engine problem, which was corrected. At the same time, a propeller de-icer and a nose heater were repaired.

The flight departed for Shemya again on 6 March, and made it this time. Shortly before arrival, however, No 2 engine developed a burnt valve and had to be shut down; this meant a block change, which was carried out by the detachment's maintenance personnel while the crew rested. On the morning of 8 March, after a flight test, the flight departed for Elmendorf, where Brogden slipped crews again; he returned to McChord on 9 March in NS17511, captained by Flying Officer Tapp. That flight left McChord on 11 March and, after stops in Vancouver, Edmonton, Winnipeg and Ottawa, arrived at Montreal late in the evening of 12 March. During this run to Japan, Brogden was away from base for twenty-four days and flew a total of 105 hours and 15 minutes.[34]

March

On 2 March, the Commanding Officer and Senior Supply Officer of RCAF Station Lachine, Wing Commander E.R. Johnston and Squadron Leader MacMillan, left on a trip to Japan and to visit the RCAF detachments en route. During the month, eight round trips to Tokyo and twelve to North Luffenham were completed.

On 9 March, Group Captain Leigh at Air Transport Command Headquarters forwarded the results of a review of the first ferry flight of *Operation RANDOM* to Air Force Headquarters. He indicated that, at the time, 108 brand-new Sabre Vs were at St-Hubert and four were at Goose Bay, all awaiting convoy to Europe, and almost all these aircraft needed at least five hours of shakedown flying before they could be considered ready for transatlantic ferry. He expected this aircraft backlog to continue for several months, since about twenty Sabres were coming off the Canadair assembly line every month, and added to the delivery pool. With the pilots available at No 1 OFU, Leigh considered it possible to convoy twenty-five aircraft per month.

In his view, there were three options. The first was to accept the backlog while making every effort to keep deliveries going as fast as possible. However, this course of action would delay No 1 Air Division's re-arming program and create storage problems at home. Leigh intended to store up to thirty aircraft at Goose Bay, allowing for the possibility of a double shuttle; the rest would remain on the airfield at St-Hubert. The second option was to bring enough pilots into No 1 OFU to permit the unit to convoy thirty or more aircraft per month. The third option was to supplement the planned ferry program by asking No 1 Air Division to provide enough pilots and ground crew to ferry twenty-five aircraft per month for two months — twenty-five pilots and forty ground crew. In this scenario, Air Transport Command would supply three North Stars: the one already allocated to *Operation RANDOM*, and two more.

Should the backlog figures be acceptable to Air Force Headquarters, Leigh recommended that the ferry operation continue as planned without augmentation by No 1 Air Division. This would allow conduct of *Operation RANDOM* by the Air Transport Command's current ferry aircrew and, keep the demand for North Star support to a minimum.

On 24 March, a second convoy of thirty-one Sabre Vs left St-Hubert for No 4 (F) Wing Baden-Söllingen, escorted by two North Star mother ships from No 426 Squadron. *Operation RANDOM 2* was delayed at Goose Bay for four days due to alternating doses of bad weather, first at the point of departure, then at the destination. On 28 March, the convoy reached Narsarssuak, where two Sabres had to be left behind with mechanical problems; Keflavik was reached the next day, and Kinloss on 30 March. Twenty-nine Sabres made it to No 4(F) Wing on 4 April after being held up by weather at Kinloss.[35]

In the fall of 1953, the Office of the Chief of the Air Staff asked Squadron Leader K.R. Greenaway of the Arctic Section of the Defence Research Board to suggest the best time of the year to visit the far north, as Defence Minister Brooke Claxton wished to see the northern territories and their waters. The trip was not to exceed four days and to include, if practicable, a flight to the North Pole.

On the morning of 26 March, Flying Officer R. Kyle and his augmented crew left Dorval in NS17518 and positioned their aircraft at Rockcliffe. The next morning, the crew embarked the following illustrious passengers: R.W. Douglas Stuart, the U.S. Ambassador to Canada; Leonard.W. Brockington of the Odeon Theatre chain and one of the "fathers" of the CBC; General A.G.L. McNaughton, Chairman of the Permanent Joint Board on Defence; Gordon Robertson, Deputy Minister of Indian Affairs and Northern Development; Dr. John A. Hannah, head of the University of Michigan and Manpower Advisor to the President of the United States; and, at Mr. Claxton's request, four RCAF musicians to provide entertainment at each stop. The flight then departed for Churchill where the Minister, who had been visiting western Canada with a party of industrialists, joined the northern tour group.

At 2215 hours on 28 March, the flight took off for the six-hour run to Resolute Bay, leaving behind one of the three pilots, Flight Lieutenant M.D. Broadfoot from No 412 Squadron, who had come down with the mumps. After two hours and twenty minutes to refuel and file a flight plan, the North Star departed for the North Geographic Pole at 0635 hours local time. Of the crew members, only the navigators, Squadron Leader Greenaway and Flight Lieutenant M. Majocha, had made a polar run before. Greenaway had been asked to join the crew not only to help with navigation, but also to brief the Minister and his party and act as their resource person. Throughout the high-latitude part of the flight, the sky was cloudless and visibility was excellent, so everyone could see the rugged terrain clearly. After reaching the North Pole, the flight returned to Resolute Bay by way of Ice Island T3. The trip took ten hours and fifty-five minutes.

After their arrival at Resolute at 1730 hours, the Minister and his party toured the Eskimo village, and that evening, after a new Odeon release (courtesy of Mr. Brockington) was shown in the canteen, a reception was held at which the musicians played and Mr. Claxton gave a speech. Early on the morning of 30 March, the flight left for Thule AFB, where the Minister's party spent six hours and toured the new base facilities. Late that afternoon, the aircraft departed for Goose Bay, arriving seven hours and forty-five minutes later. The next morning (31 March), the flight returned the passengers to Rockcliffe, and headed back to Dorval.

The distance flown from Ottawa was 8,609 miles, which was covered in a flight time of thirty-seven hours and fifty-five minutes. Brooke Claxton was the first Minister of the Crown to overfly the North Pole.[36]

April

At the end of March, the beginning of the re-supply of the Arctic weather stations was announced for 12 April. Three RCAF C-119s were to be positioned at Resolute Bay to carry out the task, and which would involve airlifting about 700,000 pounds of fuel and supplies into Mould Bay, Isachsen, Eureka and Alert.

Only two flights were required from No 426 Squadron. On 15 April, Flying Officer Wenzel brought in NS17502 and, after stopping long enough to unload cargo, returned to base; North Star captain Flight Lieutenant R. Raike came in on that flight to replace Flight Lieutenant J. Grant as the Detachment Commander. On 22 April, Flying Officer M. Casselman brought in NS17522 with Group Captain Leigh and an inspection party from Air Transport Command Headquarters aboard. Four hours after their arrival, the inspection party had completed its business and were on their way back to Dorval.[37]

In an organizational change that became effective on 1 April 1954, RCAF Station Rockcliffe was transferred from the jurisdiction of the Air Officer Commanding, Air Transport Command, to the Air Officer Commanding, Air Material Command, and the reporting relationships and status of all units on the station were redefined.[38]

The issue raised by Group Captain Leigh regarding the backlog of Sabre V aircraft in Canada led to a series of staff discussions between Air Force Headquarters, Air Transport Command Headquarters and No 1 Air Division Headquarters. These exchanges resulted on 2 April in No 1 Air Division Operation Order 59/54, in which the Air Division announced the formation of a Composite Squadron to help ferry the backlog of Sabre V aircraft from Canada. No 2 (F) Wing at Grostenquin was instructed to provide one Squadron Leader, twelve pilots experienced on the Sabre who had participated in at least one Leap Frog operation, and twenty ground crew. No 4 (F) Wing at Baden-Söllingen was also directed to contribute twelve Sabre pilots with Leap Frog experience.

The Composite Squadron of twenty-five aircrew and 20 ground personnel were to ferry twenty-five Sabre V aircraft from No 1 OFU at St-Hubert to Grostenquin as part of *Operation RANDOM*, which was scheduled to leave Canada in late May. Squadron Leader MacKay from No 2 (F) Wing was to command the unit, and conversion to the Sabre V was to be conducted at No 4 (F) Wing and include at least eight flying hours. Ground personnel were to receive technical training at Grostenquin and contact training at Baden-Söllingen.³⁹

In April, No 426 Squadron despatched thirteen flights to North Luffenham with two extensions to Rabat, and eight flights on the Korean Airlift to Tokyo. The squadron also provided transport support for *Operation RANDOM 3*. During the winter, thirty Sabre Vs had been ferried to Goose Bay, and twenty-eight of these aircraft were going to Europe.

On the morning of 20 April, Flying Officer Ingall and his crew left St-Hubert for Goose Bay in NS17506 with two ground support parties. That afternoon, the crew of NS17511, captained by Flying Officer McBride, proceeded to Goose Bay carrying the Sabre pilots and one Orenda engine. Twenty-eight Sabres set out from Goose Bay for Narsarssuak on 22 April, but two had to turn back due to mechanical problems. On 23 April, twenty-six Sabres made the double jump to Keflavik and Kinloss. The operation was mostly completed on 24 April with the delivery of eight aircraft to No 2 (F) Wing Grostenquin, eight to No 4 (F) Wing Baden-Söllingen and nine to Manchester; the tenth was delivered to Manchester three days later. Both NS17506 and NS17511 provided airlift support, and for once the weather co-operated, and the operation was carried out in five days.⁴⁰

May

In January 1954, the foreign ministers of the "Big Four" — the United States, the Soviet Union, Britain and France — met in Berlin to consider ways to reduce international tension. Although no progress was made on European issues, they did agree on a spring conference to consider Korea, where hostilities were winding down, and Indochina, where the French were fighting a bitter war against two enemies: the Communists and the Nationalists. The ministers agreed that for the Korean part of the conference, which was to be held in Geneva, representatives of the governments of North and South Korea, Communist China and the nations that had contributed troops to the UN forces should be invited. For the sessions on Indochina, only the three emerging states of Cambodia, Laos and Vietnam should be invited, along with the People's Republic of China, to meet with the Big Four. This decision created two Geneva Conferences.

The Korea session, which began on 26 April, made no headway, but the Indochina conference made considerable progress. The French were anxious to withdraw from Indochina, and had unilaterally recognized Cambodia, Laos and Vietnam as independent nations. On 7 May, during the protracted discussions in Geneva, the French stronghold of Dien Bien Phu, besieged since 20 November 1953, fell to the Viet Minh. An armistice was agreed to for each new state, in each case subject to the establishment of an international supervisory commission.

On 21 July, the co-chairmen of the conference, Anthony Eden of the United Kingdom and Viacheslav Mikhailovich Molotov of the USSR, invited Canada, India and Poland to designate representatives to form International Supervisory Commissions for Cambodia, Laos and Vietnam. On 27 July, Canada agreed to serve on the Commissions. Apart from providing representatives for each of the three Supervisory Commissions, India, Poland and Canada were to assign several military officers to inspection teams that were to monitor compliance with the cease-fire agreements in the field under the direction of the Supervisory Commissioners.

From 1 August to 6 August, the Indian government hosted a conference at which the Canadian Indian and Polish representatives studied the terms of the Geneva Accords. The conference set about determining how the functions of what were called the International Commissions for Supervision and Control (ICSC) might best be carried out. It was agreed that all the Commissions should be established by 11 August, and that a small tripartite advance party should proceed to Cambodia, Laos and Vietnam to prepare for the arrival of the Commissioners. It was also agreed that the three contributing countries should each despatch seventy-eight army officers, two for each of the twenty-six "fixed-site" inspection teams and one for each of the twenty-six mobile teams. The conference decided that the Commission for Vietnam would be based in Hanoi, the one for Cambodia in Phnom Penh, and the one for Laos in Vientiane, and an advance team of Canadian Army officers was flown from Korea to Hanoi in mid-August. They would soon be joined by seventy-one more officers airlifted from Canada by No 426 Squadron.[41]

Operationally, May was a busy month for the squadron. Twelve flights were despatched to North Luffenham, of which two were extended to Rabat, and the final eight trips on the Korean Airlift were conducted. The last departed Dorval on Saturday, 29 May.

Operation RANDOM 4 departed St-Hubert on two successive days. On 16 May, three RAF Sabre IVs and four T-33 Silver Stars left for Goose Bay, followed by one North Star carrying a ground crew party and spares. The next day, the main body of fifty-five Sabre Vs arrived at Goose Bay with the second North Star. Poor weather at Narsarssuak delayed the operation for three days, but on 22 May, fifty-four Sabre Vs, the three Sabre IVs and the four T-33s made the crossing to Greenland. One Sabre had mechanical problems and was left behind. The crossing to Keflavik was made the next day, and two unserviceable Sabre Vs remained at Narsarssuak. On 24 May the convoy was weathered in, and a T-33 was badly damaged when it was struck by a jeep. Fifty-eight aircraft reached Kinloss on 25 May, and they all reached their destinations the next day: forty Sabre Vs to Grostenquin, twelve Sabre Vs and the three Silver Stars to Zweibrücken, and the three Sabre IVs to RAF Station Kemble in Britain.[42]

On 27 May, having approved the withdrawal of No 426 Squadron from the Korean Airlift on 25 May, Minister of National Defence Brooke Claxton issued the following statement:

> The trans-Pacific airlift operation that the RCAF has been carrying out for almost four years in support of the United Nations effort in Korea is to finish shortly. A decision to end RCAF participation in the airlift has been made and it is expected that the final RCAF round trip to Japan will be made by a North Star leaving its home base at Dorval, outside Montreal, on Saturday, May 29.
> Requirement for air transport support of the UN operations in Korea has decreased and there has been a lessening of the overall airlift operations over the northern route. In consequence, the United States Air Force is reducing its facilities at Shemya Air

Force Base, in the Aleutians, which the RCAF North Stars have been using as a refuelling point. Unavailability of Shemya would make economic operation of the RCAF North Stars unfeasible over this run. Because of this, and the decreased requirement, the RCAF operation is being brought to an end.

Canadian Pacific Airlines will continue, for the time being at least, to operate its scheduled airlift flights to Korea, under charter to the Canadian government, as part of the Canadian contribution towards the UN effort in Korea. Operating with DC-6 aircraft having a longer range than the RCAF North Stars, CPA can continue to operate over the route without utilizing Shemya as a refuelling point. CPA is currently flying 3 ? round trips per week on the Korea airlift, between Vancouver and Japan, having begun its charter operations shortly after the RCAF.

The RCAF began its part in the Korea airlift on July 27, 1950. No 426 Squadron, acting on very short notice, flew out to McChord Air Force Base, outside Tacoma, in the State of Washington. It took with it its ground crew, administrative staff and ground servicing equipment.

The first North Star took off from McChord the evening of July 27, 1950, to begin the operation. The squadron went through a hectic period at first, maintaining a flight-a-day schedule with six aircraft on strength. The aircraft total was increased shortly afterwards, although the schedule still called for the maximum from personnel and equipment. This was during the early days of the airlift, when the situation in Korea called for a maximum effort to rush urgently needed supplies and equipment to the hard-pressed UN forces there.

As requirements eased the schedule was reduced to 15 round trips per month, and for the last year or so has stood at 8 round trips per month.

For the first year of its airlift operations the squadron was located at McChord Field. It then moved back to its normal home base at Dorval and has since continued to carry out its Korea airlift flights from there. Round trips have been made eight times a month between Dorval and Haneda airport in Japan. The cross-Canada portion of such flights has been utilized for domestic RCAF requirements and the aircraft have proceeded on to McChord from Vancouver, to take on their cargo for the trans-Pacific run.

While doing this, the squadron has carried out many other important commitments. These have included scheduled supply runs into the Arctic and the commencement of a scheduled trans-Atlantic service in support of the RCAF's Air Division in addition to numerous other special flights.

The Thunderbird Squadron has made more than 600 round-trips — 1200 Pacific crossings — and has flown more than 13,000 personnel, including many wounded. It has carried approximately 7,000,000 lbs of freight and mail and has chalked up 34,000 flying hours.

Most of 426 Squadron's flying during the airlift has been over the northern Pacific route, although some of the trips were made by way of the mid-Pacific through Hawaii and San Francisco, and on up to McChord.

Ground crew detachments have served at points along the route since the airlift started, to enable speedy and efficient servicing of the Merlin-powered North Stars. In addition to the Aleutians, such detachments have served at Haneda in Japan and at Honolulu, as well as at McChord Field.

The record set by 426 Squadron during its airlift operations is one of which the RCAF and all Canada can well be proud. It reputation for efficiency and safety was unsurpassed. Not a single life and not a single cargo was lost during the four years of operations.

The job represented a valuable and urgently required Canadian contribution to the cause in Korea. It was a gruelling job calling for the maximum from all those who took part, and this maximum was always forthcoming, under some of the world's worst flying conditions.

The RCAF North Stars which carry the blue and white United Nations emblem on their tail, indicating service on the airlift, are emblematic of a splendid service, in line with the very finest traditions of the Air Force.

To all those who have taken part in the RCAF's operations on the airlift I pass my personal congratulations for a demanding task done in proper Air Force fashion. I can give no higher praise than this.[43]

Brooke Claxton's long tenure as Minister of National Defence would end on 1 July; he had held the portfolio since early December 1946. He was succeeded by Ralph Campney.

The crew assigned to carry out Serial 599, the squadron's last run on the Korean Airlift, was captained by Flying Officer R.B. Ingall from Montreal, Quebec.[44] Before departing Dorval in NS17510 on Saturday, 29 May, the crew was briefed by Public Relations officers from Air Transport Command Headquarters, and Flight Operations assigned an arrival time back at base of 1430 hours on 9 June. On the way to McChord, the flight stopped at Winnipeg and Vancouver, dropping off and picking up passengers and freight.

Serial 599 began when Ingall and his crew left McChord in NS17510 at 1005 hours on 31 May. The cargo was high-priority freight and mail. Crew rests were taken at Elmendorf and Shemya, and the flight arrived at Haneda early on 3 June. After debriefing, the crew checked into their quarters at Ebisu Camp, the Australian Army-run establishment near the airport where the squadron's transient personnel had been quartered for the last several months. That afternoon, the crew went to the Canadian Embassy in Tokyo for a reception to mark the end of RCAF involvement in the airlift.

Flight Lieutenant Don Deeprose and his crew, who had arrived at Haneda on 30 May, took over NS17516 from Flying Officer Norm Paul on 4 June. Loaded with the detachment's equipment and stores, the flight to Shemya had to turn back shortly after departure because of a radio malfunction; the equipment was serviced and the flight resumed. The problems persisted, however, and this time Deeprose decided to land at Misawa, where the ground staff worked on the radios. The next day, after a thorough and successful air test, the flight departed for Shemya. On the way back to base, Deeprose stopped at Elmendorf, Vancouver and Edmonton, where crew rests were taken, but did not go to McChord. After Edmonton, he stopped briefly at Winnipeg and Ottawa before arriving in Dorval at 0100 hours on 10 June.

At 1515 hours on 4 June, Ingall and his crew departed Haneda for the nine-hour and forty-five minute run to Shemya, where they were able to put the aircraft in a hangar for the twenty-hour stopover. The hangar was available only because air traffic through Shemya had slowed to a trickle as the base prepared to close.

Serial 599 also did not return to McChord; instead, the flight was routed through Elmendorf, Vancouver, Saskatoon and Winnipeg, where crew rests were taken. On 8 June at Winnipeg, the crew were quartered at a local hotel, where they were able to get their dress uniforms pressed and brush themselves up for the next day's arrival ceremony at Dorval.

The equipment and stores carried by NS17510 were unloaded and transferred to another aircraft, and at 0745 hours, with just the crew aboard, Ingall left Winnipeg and headed for base; about an hour out of Montreal, the crew changed into their dress uniforms. At Dorval, personnel from all the units at RCAF Station Lachine were formed up in front of the hangar line in two squadrons facing each other, with enough space between them for the North Star to taxi to the back of the parade with its wingtips passing just over their heads. In command of the parade was Squadron Leader C.F. Sanford, the acting commanding officer of No 426 Squadron. Reporters were out in force, and the ceremony got full coverage.

At precisely 1430 hours, NS17510 was marshalled into place and the engines were shut down and the propellers dressed. The crew disembarked, lined up in front of the aircraft, and were inspected by Air Commodore C.L. Annis, the senior RCAF officer in the Montreal area. Returning to the dais in the company of acting station commander Wing Commander H.W. Lupton, Air Commodore Annis delivered a short address commending the Thunderbirds for their excellent job on the airlift. After the parade and press interviews, the crew and members of their families attended receptions organized at Lachine's various messes.

A historic chapter in the squadron's life had ended, but the future held many diverse and challenging tasks.

The RCAF participation in the Korean Airlift was over, but there was still some work to be done to close out operations along the route. At Shemya, the last detachment commander, Flying Officer Lafrenière (who had just taken over, on 3 May), set about with the squadron's servicing crew to pack up all the equipment and stores and prepare for the return to base.

After the detachment saw Ingall and Deeprose leave for home, there was still one aircraft out on the route: NS17509, captained by Flying Officer Paul. This aircraft arrived from Tokyo on 6 June carrying the slip crew, captained by Flight Lieutenant Baird, and the personnel of the squadron's Haneda detachment. On 7 June, the last items of equipment were loaded aboard NS17509 and the two flight crews and the twenty-four members of the Haneda and Shemya detachments said farewell to the nearly deserted Shemya Air Force Base. At 1715 hours, Paul lifted NS17509 off the runway and headed for Elmendorf, a seven-hour and forty-minute run. After a seventy-minute refuelling stop, Baird's crew worked the leg to Edmonton, a flight of seven hours and fifteen minutes. The stopover was nearly five hours long, and then the flight went on to Winnipeg, where it refuelled, and Montreal, where it arrived at 0655 hours local time on 10 June. At this point, the squadron's role in the Korean Airlift was really over, as the fourteen-member McChord detachment, with their equipment and stores, had been airlifted to base earlier through Vancouver.[45]

A total of 864 RCAF personnel were members of the Special Force that served in Korea and in support of Korean operations. This number included 764 members of No 426 Squadron, forty-four movement controllers, twenty-five nursing sisters (some sources give that figure as thirty-two), twenty-two fighter pilots and nine others. Between July 1950 and June 1954, No 426 Squadron logged some 34,000 flying hours and 6.3 million miles on the airlift, carrying 13,300 passengers, and 7 million pounds of freight and mail. Squadron members engaged in the Airlift received 23 awards.[46]

On 11 June, Air Force Day was observed at all RCAF units. It was service policy to invite the public to a display at only one Montreal-area station, and this year's venue was RCAF Station St-Hubert, with personnel and aircraft from RCAF Station Lachine. Throughout the day, people lined up to inspect a parked C-119 and many other aircraft exhibited on the hangar line. The flying display included jets, propeller-driven aircraft, and a C-119 dropping paratroopers on the airfield.

Operation RANDOM began at St-Hubert on 16 June with the departure for Goose Bay of five Silver Stars and one North Star carrying a maintenance team and spares. The next day, twenty-two Sabre Vs arrived to join them, but bad weather at Narsarssuak halted the operation for three days. On 21 June, one Sabre went unserviceable but twenty-one Sabres and all the Silver Stars made the crossing to Greenland. The next crossing was delayed for one day as available resources were stretched by a USAF High Flight operation, but this did not prevent a North Star from going on to Keflavik with the maintenance team. Twenty-one Sabres and four Silver Stars reached Keflavik on 23 June; the fuel tanks on one of the Silver Stars were not feeding properly, so the aircraft had to return to Narsarssuak. After refuelling, the Sabres and two Silver Stars carried on to Kinloss with their North Star mother-ship. The next day, all twenty-one Sabres were delivered to No 3 (F) Wing at Zweibrücken and the two Silver Stars to No 1 (F) Wing at North Luffenham. Two of the Silver Stars joined a High Flight convoy from Keflavik to Kinloss and made it to North Luffenham on 26 June.[47]

With the Korean Airlift ended, the North Stars were redirected to other operations. One area of attention was northern Canada, and flights to Resolute Bay increased. The first of these was captained by Flying Officer Kyryluk who brought in NS17521 late in the afternoon of 24 June. As well as several passengers and some high-priority freight, the flight brought in a batch of new movies, a definite morale-booster. The aircraft departed for base the following morning.

On 21 June, the station commander at Lachine, Wing Commander E.R. Johnston, returned to duty after nearly two months on sick leave. He was promoted to the rank of Group Captain at the end of the month, and would be transferred to Air Transport Command Headquarters in September to take up the post of Chief Staff Officer.[48]

Lachine, January–June 1954

PHOTO 135
The crew of NS17518, who flew Brooke Claxton and his party to the North Pole; Thule Air Base, 30 March 1954. From left: F/L A.O. Milner, Cpl. C.K.T. Hughes, F/O R.W. Livock, S/L K.R. Greenaway, F/L W. Butchart, F/O Kyle (captain), LAC R.G. Cornell, F/L M. Majocha, F/S J.R.H. Lohnes and F/O H.J. Filleul. (M. Majocha Collection)

PHOTO 136
Before departing for Ottawa, Minister of National Defence Brooke Claxton (fourth from left) and his party pose with the crew of NS17518; Goose Bay, 31 March 1954. (M. Majocha Collection)

PHOTO 137
F/O G.R.A. Kyle and S/L K.R. Greenaway on their way to the North Pole in NS17518; 29 March 1954. (K.R. Greenaway Collection)

Lachine, January–June 1954

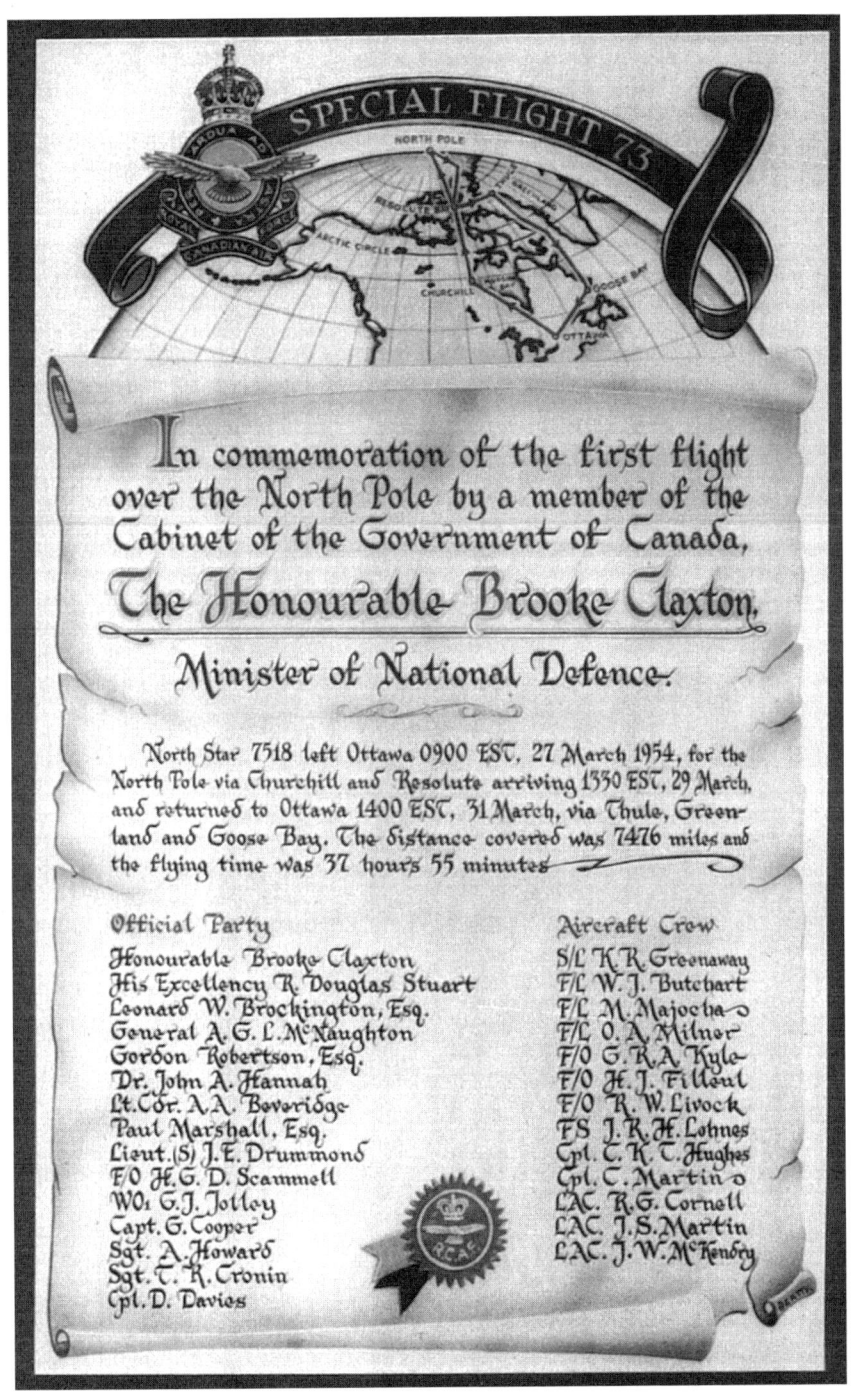

PHOTO 138
One of the certificates commemorating the flight of 29 March 1954 to the North Pole, sent by Minister of National Defence Brooke Claxton to the members of his official party and the crew of NS17518. The distance travelled on the flight is given in nautical miles. (M. Majocha Collection)

PHOTO 139
F/O G.H. McAninch (captain);
January 1954. (H. Filleul Collection)

PHOTO 140
F/O E.J. Kowalik (North Star captain);
May 1954. (M. Gee Collection)

Lachine, January–June 1954

PHOTO 141
During a Prestwick stopover, members of No 426 Squadron visit the battleship HMS George V; Garloch Head, Scotland; 30 May 1954. From left: F/L J. Shipton, F/L A. Finklestein, F/O B. Binette, F/L J. Lambert (Detachment Commander at Prestwick) and F/O W. Carss. (J. Shipton Collection)

PHOTO 142
The last members of No 426 Squadron's Shemya detachment; June 1954. Standing: fourth from left, LAC J. Ford; fifth from left, Sgt. G. Fleetham. (Y. Lafrenière Collection)

PHOTO 143
LAC J. Ford helps change an engine on the North Star that is bringing the Shemya Detachment home to Dorval; Edmonton, June 1954. (J. Ford Collection)

PHOTO 144
NS17510 (F/O R.B. Ingall, captain) taxis into position for the ceremony marking the end of No 426 Squadron's participation in the Korean Airlift; Dorval, 9 June 1954. (J. Shipton Collection)

Lachine, July–December 1954

CHAPTER 18

LACHINE
JULY–DECEMBER 1954

In addition to the three weekly service flights to Britain and the extensions to Rabat-Salé, No 426 Squadron's taskings for July 1954 included several domestic runs, many of which involved transporting Reserve personnel and Air Cadets to and from their summer camps, and five runs to Resolute Bay in support of the annual re-supply operation.

On the evening of 7 July, Flying Officer Husch arrived at Resolute Bay in NS17509 with twenty passengers, mail, and miscellaneous cargo. At noon the following day, the aircraft departed on a training trip to Mould Bay, Isachsen and Eureka, with mail drops at Isachsen and Eureka; after returning to Resolute Bay to refuel, the aircraft departed for Churchill and base that evening. The squadron's second flight of the month to Resolute Bay was NS17509, captained by Flight Lieutenant Baird, which arrived at 2030 hours on 12 July carrying Squadron Leader Day, fourteen ground crew personnel from No 405 (MP) Squadron at RCAF Station Greenwood, and aircraft spares for that unit, which was conducting ice-reconnaissance missions out of Resolute Bay. Baird returned to base through Churchill the next morning.

On 15 July, two more North Stars arrived from Churchill: at 1530 hours, NS17509, captained by Flight Lieutenant Deeprose, brought in much-needed canteen supplies, and some airmen for the Bull Gang that handled and cleaned the 3,000 fuel drums at the detachment; and NS17510, captained by Flight Lieutenant Kowalik, which arrived two hours later with an inspection party from the Department of Transport and Air Transport Command Headquarters. On 16 July, Deeprose and his crew left to conduct air drops at Eureka and Alert, but on the return to Resolute Bay they found the airfield fogged in and had to divert to Thule. Two days later, they made it back to Resolute, and then proceeded on a shuttle run to Churchill. Again returning to Resolute on 20 July, they unloaded their cargo and headed back to base. Kowalik took off for Churchill at 0630 hours on 16 July to bring back another load of supplies; on his return later that day, he too found the airfield fogged in and had to divert to Coral Harbour. The crew was able to complete the flight two days later and then head back to Dorval.

On 28 July, the supply vessel SS *Gander Bay* left the Port of Montreal, scheduled to arrive in Resolute Bay on 12 August with cargo for several northern points. During the summer, other vessels would follow. Flight Lieutenant Butchart of Air Transport Command Headquarters organized and assisted with the re-supply preparations, which included purchasing and loading the supplies; during the unloading operation at Resolute Bay, he would be the Beachmaster, one of the many officers and men sent to assist the detachment personnel under Flight Lieutenant Raike.

On 30 July at 1900 hours, NS17504 captained by Flight Lieutenant Clifton arrived at Resolute Bay carrying Wing Commander Lupton to inspect the detachment and its facilities.

Shortly before midnight, the RCN icebreaker HMCS *Labrador*, on her maiden voyage, dropped anchor in Resolute Bay, and her captain, Commander Leeming, came ashore in the morning by helicopter. Later in the day, fog prevented the ship's company from landing a shore party. After completing his inspection, Lupton left with Clifton at 1400 hours for Churchill and Dorval.[1]

The squadron handled two other assignments in July: providing transport support for *Operation RANDOM 6*, and providing logistics support following the initial delivery of Sabre jets to the air forces of Greece and Turkey.

Operation RANDOM 6 began on 15 July, when Flying Officer Joron and his crew took NS17504 to St-Hubert, where they embarked a ground crew support party and spare Sabre pilots with their luggage, plus a cargo of aircraft spare parts and equipment, and then departed for Goose Bay. At the same time, two RAF Sabre IVs and a spare RCAF Sabre V also left for Goose Bay by way of RCAF Station Chatham, where they refuelled. The next day, the rest of the convoy —eighteen Sabre Vs and five Silver Stars — departed St-Hubert for Goose Bay and, as the weather was favourable, the entire convoy completed the first over-water leg of the trip, from Goose Bay to Narsarssuak, the same day. Construction at Keflavik delayed their departure from Narsarssuak on 17 July, and then poor weather at Narsarssuak held them up for two more days. On 20 July, the entire convoy reached Keflavik, and eighteen Sabre Vs, two Sabre IVs and six Silver Stars — including one stranded at Keflavik during *RANDOM 5* — went on to Kinloss. On 21 July, the deliveries were made: fourteen Sabre Vs and one Silver Star to Zweibrücken, four Sabre Vs and two Silver Stars to Grostenquin, three Silver Stars to Baden-Söllingen, and the two RAF Sabre IVs to RAF Station Kemble. On 24 August, the North Stars picked up the Sabre pilots and the ground support teams and took them back to St-Hubert.[2]

The delivery of Sabre jets to Greece and Turkey was part of an aid program launched in 1953 under the NATO Mutual Assistance Program. An RCAF team of pilots and technical staff visited each country to train pilots and ground crew to fly and maintain the aircraft, which were flown to Europe by the RCAF Overseas Ferry Unit. Only the first delivery flights to the recipient countries were conducted by pilots from No 1 Air Division; subsequent deliveries were handled by Greek and Turkish pilots. Through the RCAF, Canada was responsible for the logistics support NATO provided for the 200 or so aircraft that were eventually delivered. On 15 July, Grostenquin despatched sixteen Sabres — eight for Greece and eight for Turkey — to Athens by way of refuelling stops at Istres, near Marseilles, and Ciampino in Rome. After stopping overnight in Athens, eight Sabres carried on to Eskisehir in Turkey.

On 23 July, NS17517 arrived from Dorval at Prestwick, where Flying Officer McAninch and the Prestwick slip crew took over and flew to North Luffenham. After dropping off cargo and passengers, the aircraft made the short hop to Langar to pick up technical representatives from Canadair and a load of Sabre spares, and then departed for Athens, an eight-hour run. In Athens, another slip crew took over the aircraft and flew it back to North Luffenham. On 26 July, NS17516 arrived in Athens with another load of Sabre spares and equipment, and McAninch and his crew took the aircraft on to Eskisehir, a flight of two hours and forty minutes. After unloading their cargo, the crew returned directly to North Luffenham, a trip that took ten hours and fifty minutes. The crew returned to Dorval on 31 July.[3]

On the morning of 26 July, RCAF Station Lachine received a distinguished visitor, Air Commodore H.M. Carscallen, the newly appointed Air Officer Commanding, Air Transport Command. He was greeted by a Guard of Honour, entertained that evening at a dining-in at the Officers' Mess, where a reception was held for him and Mrs. Carscallen the following evening.

August

On 2 August, NS17515 delivered a ground crew support party and a load of Sabre spares to Goose Bay in anticipation of *Operation RANDOM 7*, which began on 3 August with excellent weather all along the ferry route. The convoy of twenty-six Sabres completed the crossing in a record time of two days, making the double hop from St-Hubert to Goose Bay to Narsarssuak on 3 August and another double hop on 4 August, touching down first at Keflavik and then at Kinloss. At Narsarssuak, NS17515 brought in the ground support party shortly after the last Sabre touched down, and at Kinloss, it brought the support party in from Narsarssuak during the night of 4/5 August. The delivery flights were made on 5 August: ten Sabre Vs to Zweibrücken, eight to Grostenquin and two to Baden-Söllingen; and six Sabre IIs to North Luffenham. On the morning of 6 August, NS17515 departed Zweibrücken carrying No 1 OFU personnel bound for Montreal.[4]

At the end of the month, another spell of good weather across the North Atlantic permitted No 1 OFU to conduct *Operation RANDOM 8*, supported by No 426 Squadron with two North Stars. For the North Star crews, this Random was conducted in two phases: "Short Random" from Dorval to Keflavik, and "Long Random" to Europe. On 30 August, the North Stars flew two ground support parties from St-Hubert, one to Goose Bay and the other to Narsarssuak. The next day, a convoy of twenty-one Sabre Vs and four Silver Stars left St-Hubert for Goose Bay, where a twenty-second Sabre V joined the group. The same day, after refuelling, all twenty-six fighters made the hop to Narsarssuak. On 1 September, the entire convoy completed two over-water crossings, first to Keflavik and then on to Kinloss. One North Star then returned the support party from Keflavik to St-Hubert by way of Narsarssuak, while the other flew the second support party from Narsarssuak to Kinloss. On 2 September, twenty-one Sabres and two Silver Stars were flown to No 4 (F) Wing at Baden-Söllingen and two Silver Stars were delivered to Grostenquin. The next day, the twenty-second Sabre, which was held up at Kinloss for repairs, arrived at No 4 (F) Wing. NS17510 left Baden on 4 September with the Sabre pilots, and arrived back at Dorval on 5 September.[5]

In August, the three weekly service flights to Britain were despatched as usual. The unit was also tasked with several special domestic runs, and five flights to Resolute Bay. The northern flights were important because, for the first time, Canada was handling the sea supply missions to both Resolute Bay and Eureka. The first flight to arrive at Resolute Bay, on 3 August at 1930 hours, was NS17504, captained by Flight Lieutenant Clifton, transporting a construction maintenance unit, some telecommunications personnel and more airmen for the Bull Gang. At 0500 hours the next morning, Clifton and his crew departed to carry out paradrops at Mould Bay and Isachsen. On their return to Resolute Bay, they refuelled and then left at 1300 hours for home.

On the afternoon of 4 August, Flying Officer Husch brought NS17509 in to Resolute Bay with the rest of the Bull Gang and Squadron Leader MacMillan, the Senior Supply Officer from Lachine. The crew then went back to Churchill for more cargo, returning at 1600 hours the following day after a stop at Coral Harbour. At 1800 hours on 5 August, they were on their way back to base, carrying a No 405 Squadron crew who had run their Lancaster off the end of the runway on returning from an ice reconnaissance patrol several days earlier. (The Lancaster was salvaged, although its tail wheel was knocked off and its tail section was damaged.)

During the evening of 10 August, the Department of Transport icebreaker CGS *C.D. Howe* arrived in Resolute Bay, followed two days later by SS *Gander Bay* and the MV *Maruba* escorted by two more icebreakers, CG Ships *D'Iberville* and *N.B. MacLean*. Unloading started early on 13 August.

On 14 August, the squadron despatched two more flights to Resolute Bay: NS17515 captained by Flying Officer Paul, and NS17516 skippered by Flying Officer Joron. Both flights arrived in the afternoon of 15 August, having stopped at Churchill, discharged their cargoes, and departed for Montreal. The last squadron run to Resolute Bay involved NS17516, captained by Flying Officer Dunford, which arrived at 1700 hours on 26 August carrying Wing Commander W.K. Carr from Air Transport Command Headquarters, who was conducting a staff visit, and CBC reporter Maja van Steensel, who was a doing a story on the re-supply operation. The flight returned to Montreal the next morning.[6]

About this time, No 426 Squadron received another task, transporting Canadian personnel to Indochina to serve with the ICSC "truce teams". The RCAF was expected to be able to provide faster, cheaper service than commercial carriers.

In late August and into September, a series of special flights was conducted from Canada to Hanoi. The first aircraft out was NS17507, captained by Squadron Leader C.S. Olsen, which left Dorval for Ottawa on 26 August carrying two slip crews. In Ottawa, the flight picked up about 2,000 pounds of relief supplies destined for Calcutta to be distributed to flood victims in India. The next stop was Trenton to embark a small group of Army officers, who had come in from Kingston by bus. Leaving Trenton the next morning, the flight was routed through Gander to Lajes, where the slip crews were dropped off and Flying Officer L.A. Tapp and his crew were boarded. The flight refuelled at Gibraltar and Malta on the way to Nicosia, Cyprus, where Tapp's crew disembarked, and continued east, stopping at Basra in Iraq, Karachi in Pakistan, Calcutta where the Indian relief supplies were unloaded, and finally arrived in Hanoi on 1 September. On the return trip, the flight went by way of Manila, Tokyo, Wake Island, Honolulu, San Francisco and Vancouver.

The bruising pace of this round-the-world journey caused some anxious moments. On the Wake Island to Honolulu leg, all the engines suddenly quit — the fuel tanks feeding the engines had run dry because the crew were so tired they had fallen asleep at their stations. Jarred awake by the sudden quiet, the pilots and the engineer quickly switched to full tanks and, with some back-firing and sputtering, the Merlins were soon purring normally again. Olsen's crew took a three-day rest after arriving in Honolulu on 5 September, a period two of the crew members spent in hospital: the first officer had an ear infection and the navigator had a stomach ailment. Leaving Honolulu on 9 September, the flight refuelled at Travis AFB and carried on to Vancouver. At that point, it became a service flight, stopping off at Edmonton, Winnipeg and Ottawa on the way to Dorval, where it arrived on 11 September. The aircraft and its crew had been away for sixteen days, and logged a total of 110 flying hours.[7]

On 26 August, Flying Officer L.A. Tapp and his crew flew from Dorval to Lajes in NS17521, which was taken on to North Luffenham by a slip crew. At Lajes, Tapp and his crew boarded Olsen's aircraft as passengers for the trip to Nicosia, where they picked up NS17509 on 30 August for the flight to Hanoi. Leaving Hanoi on 2 September, NS17509 flew west by way of Calcutta and Karachi to Nicosia. On 7 September, Tapp and his crew left Nicosia in NS17525 and flew directly to North Luffenham, an eleven-hour and forty-minute trip. The next day, they departed for Keflavik, from where they made the direct ten-hour and twenty-five minute flight to Dorval on 9 September.[8]

On 27 August, NS17509, captained by Flying Officer R.G. Husch and his crew, left Montreal for Trenton. The next day they embarked a group of army officers and their equipment and proceeded to Lajes. On 30 August, the crew carried on to Nicosia in NS17525, stopping off to refuel at Gibraltar and Malta on the way. On 1 September, the crew took over NS17515 and, after several stops en route, reached Hanoi on 4 September, returning to Nicosia on 7 September. At Nicosia, the slip crew (captained by Flight Lieutenant T.D. Lamb, an RAF exchange officer) took over the flight to North Luffenham the next day and, on 9 September, proceeded to Keflavik. Both crews returned to Dorval in NS17510 on 11 September.[9]

Flying Officer Cook and his crew conducted the fourth flight to Hanoi in NS17515. Leaving Dorval on 29 August, the aircraft went first to Trenton to board eighteen army officers and their equipment. The flight then proceeded to Hanoi, using the route taken by Squadron Leader Olsen, and returned to base on 11 September through Karachi, Nicosia and North Luffenham.[10]

After years of putting up with loud noise in the North Stars, the RCAF finally decided in August 1954 to take a small step toward solving the problem: along with six spare power plants, Air Material Command took action to have the cross-over exhaust system developed by Trans-Canada Airlines installed on NS17518 and NS17520, along with six spare power-plants. Acquired as a trial project, the exhausts with supporting spares cost $127,310. NS17518 and NS17520, which belonged to No 412 (VIP) Squadron, were configured to carry passengers.[11]

September

On 7 September, Wing Commander P.S. Delaney (formerly Senior Personnel Staff Officer at Tactical Command Headquarters in Edmonton) arrived to take command of RCAF Station Lachine, and the formal change-of-command parade was held the next morning. The departing Station Commander was leaving to take up the post of Chief Staff Officer at Air Transport Command Headquarters, and the new CO led the parade in three cheers for him.

On 19 September, Battle of Britain Sunday was observed with church services and a parade in downtown Montreal. There was a full turnout of personnel from RCAF Station Lachine.[12]

During September, No 426 Squadron despatched only one flight to Resolute Bay: at 1430 hours on 9 September, Flying Officer Nyhuus and his crew arrived in NS17512 with a load of passengers and freight. Ninety minutes later, just as fog began to envelop the airfield, they left for a shuttle run to Churchill. Nyhuus was finally able to return to Resolute Bay at 1100 hours on 11 September, and he departed again two hours later for Churchill and Dorval. [13]

The next flight to Indochina left on 7 September, captained by Flying Officer Paul, who took NS17521 to Ottawa and Trenton first to embark the personnel assigned to the ICSC truce teams. The flight departed Trenton on 8 September and followed the route used by the previous flights, with rest stops at Lajes, Malta, Bahrain, Karachi and Calcutta, and arriving in Hanoi on 14 September. The flight then headed east to Manila, and returned to base on 23 September by way of Tokyo, Wake Island, Honolulu, Travis AFB and Vancouver. [14]

In a letter to Air Force Headquarters dated 8 September, Air Transport Command Headquarters recommended that Random operations be suspended from 1 December 1954 until mid-February 1955 for several reasons. The first and greatest was the winter weather, which tended to be severe with maximum danger of icing. Another reason was that the short winter days of the northern latitudes limited flying time for fighter aircraft. On the personnel front, most of the Ferry Unit's officers needed to prepare for the promotion exams for which they were eligible, and all the pilots had to complete their annual instrument re-checks before flying operations began again in the New Year. Finally, the first Sabre VIs were due to come off the Canadair production line in December, and pilots and ground crews alike needed considerable training before they could undertake to ferry the new aircraft. Air Transport Command was expecting to carry out four convoys before 1 December. [15]

On 14 September, the squadron despatched its sixth flight to Indochina transporting ICSC personnel. It began with captain Squadron Leader C.F. Sanford positioning NS17504 in Ottawa to load equipment and supplies for the Canadians serving with the truce teams, including a steel safe the size of a refrigerator and weighing more than a ton that was destined for the Canadian mission in Hanoi. The next morning, after embarking the passengers, the flight departed for Gander and Lajes, and then to Hanoi following the route taken by earlier flights, with crew rests at Malta, Basra and Karachi. On 20 September, during the Karachi-Calcutta leg, the flight ran into a series of violent thunderstorms with hail so severe that it stripped the paint off the spinners of the aircraft. The turbulence was so heavy that the safe looked likely to be shaken off its heavy wooden pallet, a matter of great concern to the crew because it would have broken through the flooring of the aircraft.

The Calcutta-Saigon leg on 21 September took NS17504 seven hours and fifteen minutes, and the flight arrived late in the afternoon. The passengers disembarked and the crew unloaded the cargo, which included several cases of Canadian apples. After refuelling, the flight took off again the next morning, heading for Hanoi to deliver the safe. They proceeded north at 8,000 feet just above a solid layer of cloud, which was worrisome because no radio beacons that could be used for navigation were operating along the route. When contact was established with a Hanoi radio facility, the crew received directions to the airport that, if followed, would have placed the aircraft over high ground to the north of the city and on a heading for China.

Acting on the navigator's ETA, Sanford reversed course and descended through cloud until he broke clear at about 1,500 feet. Luckily, the crew managed to identify the Red River, which flows by Hanoi, and locate the airport by its runway lights. Although he could not raise the control tower, Sanford decided to land anyway; on investigation, the crew found no one in the Tower or, indeed, anyone to meet the flight. This raised two problems: first, how to unload the safe and, second, how to refuel. Among the people in the airport was a Foreign Legionnaire, who provided some assistance. (The last French troops would leave Hanoi early in October.)

The flight engineer, Sergeant Leblanc, located a bowser with the right type of fuel, found a tractor and started it up, and towed the bowser to the aircraft. As the fuel flowed into the aircraft, Sanford noticed a well-armed, mean-looking security guard under the wing of the aircraft watching the proceedings while enjoying a cigarette. Calling out to Leblanc, Sanford asked him to tell the guard to put out his cigarette; Leblanc surveyed the situation and replied, "Sir, I suggest you tell him yourself." Sanford dropped the subject.

They also found a boom truck and used it to off-load the safe, which they left sitting on the tarmac. No member of No 426 Squadron ever heard what happened to it.

As no one was at the tower to accept a flight plan, Sanford simply took off again and headed for Clark Field, near Manila, hoping to establish radio contact en route. Over the next two hours, the radio officer made many attempts to contact Clark Field, all fruitless. Everyone was very tense, as the Communist Chinese had shot down an American aircraft earlier that day, so Sanford had no intention of arriving over a USAF base unannounced in the middle of the night. He decided to divert to Saigon.

The flight reached Saigon between midnight and dawn, and found the area under a mass of thunderstorms. Sanford managed to home in on the weak radio beacon, did a letdown in heavy turbulence, and landed in a torrential downpour. The crew had to spend the night in the aircraft as the rain did not even begin to let up until well into the forenoon.

On 23 September, the flight proceeded to Clark Field, a five-hour and ten-minute run. The next day, as the crew were preparing their flight plan for Tokyo, the Weather Office warned them that they would be skirting Typhoon Marie, thought to be moving north towards the East China Sea. The forecasters were wrong, and the North Star went right through the storm centre, encountering winds gusting up to 150 miles per hour with torrential rain and heavy turbulence. After a flight of eight and a half hours, the crew reached Haneda, where they decided to refuel and carry on immediately to Wake Island although the meteorologists did not think the typhoon would strike the Tokyo area. (The Haneda forecasters were wrong, too; Typhoon Marie did indeed hit Tokyo, and caused many deaths.) Once clear of Japan, however, the return to Dorval was routine, and the flight arrived in Montreal on 1 October by way of San Francisco and Vancouver. During this mission, Sanford's crew were away from base for sixteen days and logged 127 hours and thirty-five minutes of flying time.[16]

Flying Officer K. Roulston captained the next flight to Hanoi. On 22 September, NS17512 was positioned at Ottawa to embark the ICSC personnel, a group that included

Squadron Leader P.L. Michel, a former captain on the squadron and, until recently, the Officer Commanding No 4 (T) OTU. The hectic flight itinerary began the following day, with crew rests taken at Lajes, Malta, Basra, Karachi and Calcutta. On 29 September, the flight arrived at Hanoi, where it stopped briefly before carrying on to Manila. The next stop was Tokyo, and from there the flight returned to Dorval on 9 October by the mid-Pacific route through San Francisco to Vancouver.[17]

NS17510 was positioned at St-Hubert on 26 September for *Operation RANDOM 9*, to airlift a No 1 (OFU) ground crew party from there to Narsarssuak. The next day, twenty Sabre Vs and four Sabre IIs made the hop to Goose Bay, where they were delayed for two days by fog and low stratus at Narsarssuak. On 28 September, a second North Star brought another ground party from St-Hubert to Goose Bay. On 30 September, although the weather at Narsarssuak delayed their departure until late in the afternoon, the entire convoy of twenty-five made the crossing to Greenland; by late afternoon the next day, they made it to Keflavik. In Iceland, a Sabre left behind by a previous Random was added to the convoy, which was delayed on 1 October by the weather at Kinloss, and on 2 October by poor weather at Keflavik. On 3 October, all the Sabres made the hop to Kinloss, where the twenty-one Sabre Vs were immediately refuelled for the delivery flight to No 2 (F) Wing at Grostenquin; weather delayed the delivery of the four Sabre IIs to Ringway Airfield at Manchester until 4 October. The escort aircraft, NS17510, departed Grostenquin with the No 1 (OFU) personnel aboard on 5 October, and arrived at Dorval at 2200 hours on 7 October.[18]

October

Organization Order 52/54, issued by Air Force Headquarters on 7 October, authorized No 1 (F) Wing to move from North Luffenham to Marville, France, with effect from 15 November 1954 and to be completed by 1 April 1955. As well as Wing Headquarters, the move involved No 410, No 439 and No 441 squadrons, all fighter units. One consequence of the move was that the British terminus of the North Star service flights from Dorval moved to Langar, as did the fourteen-man squadron detachment.[19]

In October, the RCAF acquired twenty-five Kearfott N1 gyro-compass systems for its North Stars, Lancasters and C-119 Flying Boxcars. The gyro system precessed at less than one degree per hour, so it was a vast improvement over the erratic DG1, and it considerably enhanced the service's Arctic operational capability.[20]

In October, the squadron conducted several domestic runs, twelve flights to Britain and two trips to Resolute Bay.

The first trip to Resolute was on 15 October, when Flight Lieutenant Dick brought in NS17521 early in the morning, with Wing Commander Delaney, the Station Commander at Lachine aboard to inspect the detachment and its facilities; at 1700 hours, Dick left on a shuttle run to Churchill. He tried to return the next day but was forced back to Churchill by a blizzard at Resolute Bay. The weather eased up enough on 17 October to permit Dick and his crew to land at 1730 hours; two and a half hours later, with Delaney aboard, NS17521 departed for Churchill and base.

At 1500 hours on 19 October, a No 412 Squadron aircraft, NS17520 captained by Squadron Leader Lloyd, arrived at Resolute Bay carrying Air Commodore Carscallen and a party of officers from Air Transport Command Headquarters, including Flight Lieutenant G.R.A. Kyle, who was replacing Flight Lieutenant R.H.W. Raike as the Detachment Commander. After a tour of the facilities, Raike briefed the Air Commodore Carscallen and his party on activities at Resolute, and then entertained them at an informal dinner. The next morning, NS17520 departed for Churchill and Dorval with the visitors and Raike aboard.

On 26 October, Flying Officer Cook and his crew left Dorval for Winnipeg and Churchill in NS17516 for a re-supply clean-up operation that lasted eleven days and involved hauling equipment, rations and other supplies that had been misdirected during the August re-supply of the northern weather stations, or had simply not been delivered at all. On 27 October, the flight proceeded to Resolute Bay and then to Thule, where the crew spent the night. Early on 28 October, they conducted a supply run to Eureka, where they were held up by poor weather until the next day, when they returned to Resolute Bay.

On 30 October, Cook and his crew were sent to Alert to pick up a weather station staffer who was ill and bring him back to Resolute Bay. Alert was difficult enough to land at in summer, when the days are long, but as winter approached its problems were compounded by complete darkness and, on this particular occasion, by cloud cover.

During the four-hour flight, navigator Flying Officer Lafrenière noted that some of the mountain peaks were higher than his outdated maps indicated. When the aircraft arrived over Alert, the airfield radio operator informed the crew that the ceiling was about 1,000 feet; the gyros were set, and Cook began his letdown through cloud. As the aircraft passed through the 1,000 foot level, Cook still could not see a thing, but just when he was getting set to overshoot, he saw the runway off the port quarter, marked by flares placed on empty oil drums. Calling for gear and flaps down, Cook side-slipped the aircraft onto the runway and landed. It took about five minutes to load the patient and leave, but Cook made time to take the Alert radio operator to task; the ceiling was, in fact, much closer to 500 feet.

On the way back to Resolute Bay, the flight stopped briefly at Eureka to drop off some cargo. On arrival at Resolute, the patient was turned over to detachment members, and that evening, the crew treated Flying Officer Cook, a frugal individual, to a case of beer in the canteen.

On 31 October, Cook and his crew completed a supply run to Mould Bay. The next day, on their way to Churchill on a shuttle run, they were detailed to carry out a search for a party of Eskimos who had gone missing in the Coppermine area. After several unsuccessful hours of searching the frozen barrens along the coast south and west of Cambridge Bay, Cook and his crew headed for Churchill, where they arrived after nine hours and fifteen minutes of flying. The flight returned to Resolute Bay on 2 November.

On 3 November, supply runs were conducted to Alert, Eureka and Mould Bay; the next day, they went to Isachsen. On 5 November, the flight returned to Churchill by way of Arctic Bay, where they made an air drop. On 6 November, Cook and his crew returned to base via Winnipeg and Ottawa.[21]

November

On 5 November, *Operation RANDOM 10* got under way with a convoy of twenty-nine Sabre Vs and four Sabre IIs flying from St-Hubert to Goose Bay. Transport support for the mission was provided by two No 426 Squadron aircraft: NS17509, captained by Flying Officer Dunford, and NS17506, flown by Flying Officer Joron. Dunford arrived at Goose Bay with the first ground support party from St-Hubert shortly after the Sabres landed. Joron and his crew airlifted the second support party to Goose Bay the following day. Poor weather at Narsarssuak held up the movement of the convoy until 10 November; on 7 November, in the meantime, Joron brought the first support party to Narsarssuak.

Better weather on 10 November permitted thirty-two Sabres to make the crossing to Greenland (one Sabre II had to return to St-Hubert), and Dunford's crew took the second support party to Keflavik to wait for the convoy. For the next ten days, the Sabres were halted by poor weather at either the point of departure or the destination. On 12 November, Joron left for Montreal to pick up rations and supplies for the operation, returning to Goose Bay the next day. On 14 November, Joron and his crew left for Narsarssuak, but shortly after take-off they returned to Goose Bay with unserviceable compasses. The next day, with the problem rectified, they made it to Narsarssuak but found conditions of low ceilings and fog that meant a USAF SA-16 search and rescue aircraft had to escort the North Star up the fjord. Joron's crew conducted a shuttle run to Goose Bay on 19 November, returning to Greenland the next day.

Thanks to the Sabre pilots' initiative and the excellent maintenance work of the ground support party, *Operation RANDOM 10* was able to move on to Keflavik on 21 November. Twenty-nine Sabres made the crossing, and three aircraft stayed behind as spares. On 22 November, the weather was favourable and the twenty-nine Sabres made their final over-water hop to Kinloss, where they were held up again, this time by bad weather in continental Europe.

Shortly after departing Narsarssuak on 22 November with the first ground support party, Joron had to shut down his No 2 engine, dump fuel and turn back. The engine problem was fixed by the next morning, and the crew again set out for Kinloss, but on the way the flight encountered headwinds stronger than had been forecast, and had to divert to Keflavik for fuel. They took off again in marginal weather conditions, and arrived in Kinloss shortly before midnight.

An aircraft starter was needed at Narsarssuak and it fell to Dunford's crew to bring one in from Keflavik. Leaving early on the morning of 22 November, they made the four-hour crossing, unloaded the equipment, and got set to return to Iceland.

The runway at Narsarssuak was covered with hard-packed snow, so its edge was hard to see as it blended into the taxiway and parking area, but aircraft could take off in only one direction: down-slope towards the fjord. On receiving departure clearance, Dunford began his take-off roll, but as the aircraft rapidly accelerated, the crew suddenly spotted a snow-blower crossing the runway from left to right, heading right into the North Star's path. Dunford began to edge the aircraft to the right, hoping the snow-blower driver would see the North Star and stop. The aircraft was going too fast to stop but as yet had not accelerated enough to become airborne, so Dunford edged more to the right and, as the speed increased, both pilots pulled back on the control columns at the same time, and the North Star staggered into the air with its landing gear retracting. The snow-blower driver finally saw the aircraft as it passed over him.

Sergeant L. Larochelle, the flight engineer in Joron's crew, watched this departure from a spot to port of the aircraft and at right angles to the incident. Later, he recalled, "When the aircraft left the ground, it went into a slight starboard bank, the undercarriage buckled — the first movement in the retraction cycle — and the port gear skimmed over the top of the snow-blower while the starboard gear was obscured by the blower's cab."

The rest of the flight was uneventful. Since they were on the Short Random assignment, Dunford and his crew returned to base on 23 November, bringing with them the OFU's second support party.[22]

On 25 November, the convoy's three Sabre IIs were ferried to Manchester, and Joron and his crew conducted a shuttle run to Prestwick with six OFU pilots who were scheduled to catch SF52 for Dorval in preparation for *Operation RANDOM 11*. Returning the next day, Joron followed the twenty Sabre Vs that were delivered to No 4 (F) Wing Baden-Söllingen, and on 27 November, he returned to Kinloss with replacements for the six Sabre pilots who had gone home. On 28 November, the six Sabres left behind at Kinloss were flown to No 4 (F) Wing, where they were joined that evening by NS17506 with the first support party. On the afternoon of 29 November, Joron and his crew embarked the men from No 1 OFU and headed for North Luffenham, where the airfield was down in fog, so the flight had to divert to Prestwick. After refuelling, Joron headed for Keflavik and then directly to Dorval, where they arrived early in the evening of 30 November.[23]

The launch of *Operation RANDOM 11* was originally planned for 23 November, but this depended on timely completion of Random 10. The Random 11 convoy was to include twenty-eight aircraft (twenty-five Sabres and three Silver Stars), but with Random 10 held up by weather, Air Commodore Carpenter at Air Force Headquarters approved delaying Random 11 until February 1955.[24]

In November, as well as the three weekly service flights to Britain, the squadron carried out several domestic runs and some flights to the United States. Flying Officer Clifton captained the only squadron trip to Resolute Bay, where he arrived on 25 November, stopped briefly, and left for Churchill to pick up more cargo. He returned at 2200 hours the next day, unloaded, and immediately headed back to base via Churchill.[25]

On 26 November, Wing Commander Lupton departed Dorval in NS17512 with an augmented crew to conduct a combined training and logistics flight. The first stop was Churchill and, after unloading cargo and refuelling, the flight then proceeded to Thule. On 27 November, the crew headed for the North Pole and returned to Thule after a seven-hour flight. The next day's destination, Prestwick, was reached after the flight had been airborne for eleven hours and fifteen minutes. On 30 November, the flight stopped at Langar to pick up cargo for the Sabre aid program in Greece and Turkey, and continued on to Ciampino Airport in Rome for a crew rest. The next day, the flight headed for Eskisehir in Turkey and, after a brief stop, carried on to Athens. On 2 December, Lupton and his crew flew to Rabat-Salé, where they stayed the night; from Rabat, they returned to Langar on 3 December after a brief stop at Marseilles. After a twenty-four hour break at Langar, the crew left for London on 5 December and then continued on to Lajes. Departing Lajes the next day, the flight stopped for fuel at Harmon AFB and arrived at base on 7 December. Lupton and his crew were away for ten days and flew eighty-nine hours during that time.[26]

December

On 1 December, Flying Officer Paul positioned NS17511 in St-Hubert in preparation for a clean-up operation to end the year's Random flights. The purpose of the operation was to place any Sabres left behind into storage for the winter and pick up the Liaison Officers, pilots and servicing staff left along the ferry route to Europe. On 2 December, after picking up a small ground party, Paul and his crew left for Goose Bay and Narsarssuak. The flight was able to get away from Greenland for Keflavik on 5 December, making it to Kinloss on 7 December. The crew departed for Zweibrücken on 10 December, and headed back west through Prestwick to Keflavik two days later. On 13 December, they reached Narsarssuak and then went on directly to Dorval.[27]

On 3 December, NS17514 was despatched as a Christmas special to Indochina with an augmented crew captained by Flight Lieutenant W. Dick. The first stop was Ottawa, to pick up mail and supplies for the Canadian members of the ICSC truce teams, and the flight made it only as far as Harmon AFB the next day, as poor weather on the Atlantic coast closed both Gander and Torbay. On 5 December, the flight proceeded first to Argentia, where they took on fuel, and then made the seven-hour run to Lajes, where they stopped only enough to refuel and file a seven-hour flight plan for Port Lyautey, north of Rabat. From there, they flew another six hours to Malta, where they stopped for the night. On 7 December, the flight was on its way to Karachi by way of Nicosia and Basra, where they refuelled. They arrived in Calcutta on 9 December and Saigon the following day. Shortly after leaving for Hanoi on 10 December, an engine malfunctioned and had to be shut down, forcing the flight to return to Saigon, where the Hanoi cargo was unloaded, including a diplomatic bag and mail for the Canadian members of the truce team. Squadron Leader Michel, the Air Member of the Saigon truce team, made an arrangement with the French Air Force to have the Hanoi cargo delivered, and it was loaded into a Dakota that had clearly seen better days, accompanied by Flying Officer Haire. Meanwhile, Dick had obtained permission to ferry NS17514 on three engines to Singapore, three and a half hours away, where the maintenance facilities were thought to be better, especially as BOAC staged its North Stars (which it called Argonauts) through there. On 11 December, NS17514 went to Singapore and, with some use of local facilities, Sergeant G. Brogden and the crew's technicians restored the engine to serviceability. They returned to Saigon the next day.

Meanwhile, on 11 December, Haire was on his way to Hanoi with the four-man Dakota crew, all veterans of the war in Indochina and none able to speak English. During the flight, Haire somehow gleaned not only that the approach to Hanoi had to be made in a specific corridor in daylight at 10,000 feet, but also that the flight would reach Hanoi well after nightfall, and the crew had decided to press on anyway. On arrival, they found the city under curfew and blacked out, but they still managed to find the airport and land the Dakota without incident. Haire was welcomed by Squadron Leader Grant, a member of the truce team, who took custody of the cargo, arranged for Haire's accommodation, and conducted him on a tour of the city. Unlike Saigon, Hanoi was almost deserted except for soldiers on every street corner until about 0400 hours, when hundreds of peasants started their daily march to the rice fields carrying Ho Chi Minh banners. (Unlike the south, the north was a spartan society.) Haire returned to Saigon with the Dakota crew the next afternoon and rejoined his crew. That evening, they departed for Manila International Airport.

During the flight to Manila, the crew realized that one engine was burning too much oil. A detailed check conducted on arrival revealed that the aircraft needed a new engine, which had to be flown out from Canada. Eight days later, the crew was advised that MATS had delivered a new engine to Clark AFB, about fifty-five miles northwest of Manila International. The crew's transportation technician, Sergeant S. Rohatinsky, found a truck and, since an officer was required to sign for the engine, first officer Flight Lieutenant J. Wynn agreed to go with him to Clark. Despite reports of armed bandits on the road, they collected the engine and brought it to Manila without incident.

The engine change was executed quickly and professionally by Sergeant Brogden, assisted by the crew's technicians and using such tools and equipment as he could find. After a successful air test on 21 December, the crew departed for Guam, eight hour and five minutes from Manila, where they stopped for forty minutes to take on fuel and file a new flight plan and then took off for Wake Island. This leg took seven and a half hours. Seventy-five minutes after arrival at Wake, the flight took off again for the eleven-hour run to Honolulu, where they stopped for sixteen hours.

The crew were eager to get home for Christmas, but on 23 December the headwinds on the leg to San Francisco made that goal somewhat problematic. Indulging in some creative flight planning despite reservations from the navigators, Dick decided to push on. About an hour before they reached the point of no return, the USAF flight-following service radioed doubts as to whether the North Star would make it to San Francisco and, shortly before the aircraft reached PNR, the doubts became definitive advice to turn back. This they did, returning to Honolulu after nine hours and thirty minutes in the air.

Back at the hotel in Honolulu, Dick held a crew meeting, and the majority voted to press on after a minimum twelve-hour crew rest. Leaving on 24 December, they flew first to Travis AFB — eleven and a half hours — where they stopped for three hours and were ready to depart again, thinking they would make it home for Christmas. This was not to be, however; during take-off, an engine backfired and had to be shut down and the propeller feathered. When he got back on the ground, Dick informed the squadron that the aircraft needed another engine change. Much to the disappointment of the standby crew, they were called out and despatched to Travis AFB with the spare engine.

NS17512 and its crew arrived at Travis on Christmas Day. A quick offload was effected and Dick's crew were on their way home in that aircraft, leaving their own stricken aircraft with their colleagues. The round-the-world flight reached Dorval at 1430 hours on 26 December, eleven hours and five minutes out of Travis.[28]

On 3 December, the squadron despatched NS17515 to Resolute Bay to conduct the Christmas supply drops. Captained by Flying Officer Cook, the flight carried a media party escorted by Flight Lieutenant J.D. Harvey, the Public Relations Officer from Air Transport Command Headquarters. The journalists were Mr. White of *Time*, Mr. MacGillray of the *Montreal Gazette*, Mr. Rooke, a CBC producer, who came with a three-man TV crew, and Corporal Eagles, an RCAF photographer. The flight arrived at Resolute Bay in the afternoon of 4 December, returned immediately to Churchill for additional cargo, and was back at Resolute on 5 December.

The Christmas re-supply began with NS17515 making a drop at Mould Bay on 6 December. The aircraft lost an engine on the way, but made the drop and returned to Resolute Bay. On the ground, it was clear that NS17515 needed a new engine, so the squadron sent out a replacement: NS17521, captained by Flying Officer McBride, which arrived on the afternoon of 9 December. McBride took over NS17515 to ferry it back to Dorval, and was forced to abort a three-engine take-off when a strong cross-wind made the attempt too dangerous.

Taking advantage of the full moon, Cook and his crew boarded the journalists and left for Isachsen at midnight in NS17521. After unloading their cargo and giving the reporters time to record the operation, the crew returned to Resolute Bay early in the morning of 10 December. That afternoon, Cook made a supply drop at Craig Harbour, returned to Resolute Bay to pick up cargo, refuelled, and departed for Thule. The next day, he made successful air drops at Alert and Eureka and returned to Resolute Bay. The next day, he made drops at Arctic Bay and Pond Inlet, and overflew Thule to make additional drops at Alexandra Fjord, Alert and Eureka before returning to Resolute Bay. On 13 December, after making drops at Arctic Bay and Spence Bay, Cook and his crew carried on to Churchill, where they stopped briefly to refuel and take on cargo and passengers before heading back to Dorval. Cook and his crew were away from Montreal for ten days, during which they logged sixty-six hours and forty-five minutes of flying time.

Flying Officer Dunford and his crew brought in NS17517 to Resolute Bay on 13 December carrying eight ground crew members under Warrant Officer Jackson to repair NS17515, which turned out to need two engines changed. The technicians had to build wind shelters before they could start work, as the temperature ranged between -23°F (-30.5°C) and -37°F (-38.3°C). Work on the aircraft was completed on 16 December, but the run-up revealed several snags. The next day, after a successful air test, one unserviceable engine was loaded aboard NS17515, in which McBride and his crew departed Resolute Bay for Dorval at 2130 hours. The other unserviceable engine was taken to Winnipeg by a Flying Boxcar from No 435 Squadron, which had come to Resolute to deliver a backlog of 8,000 pounds of cargo from Churchill.[29]

In December 1952, Squadron Leader A.R. MacKenzie, one of twenty-two RCAF Sabre pilots serving in Korea with the Fifth US Air Force, was shot down and taken prisoner. In 1954, no one knew if he was still alive, as he was not released in the prisoner exchanges that followed the armistice of 1953. In May, Lester B. Pearson, the Secretary of State for External Affairs, left the Geneva Conference to return to Ottawa and, during his absence, Chester Ronning, the Canadian Ambassador to Norway, became the acting head of the Canadian delegation. The Geneva Conference was a valuable opportunity for the Canadian delegation to ask the Chinese informally about MacKenzie, his condition and possible return.

Ambassador Ronning not only spoke Chinese, he was personally acquainted with Chou En Lai, China's Foreign Minister and several members of the Chinese delegation in Geneva. When Ronning raised the matter of MacKenzie in a private conversation with Chou, he promised to make inquiries. Soon after, the Chinese told Ronning that MacKenzie was alive and would eventually be released, but it was November before the Department of External Affairs received word that MacKenzie would be set free, and he was finally escorted across the border at Hong Kong on 5 December. After several days under tight security, MacKenzie was taken by CPA to Vancouver by way of Tokyo. At Vancouver, he caught No 426 Squadron's scheduled service flight and on 11 December he was back in Montreal.[30]

Lachine, July–December 1954

In December, the squadron carried out domestic runs to Vancouver, Whitehorse and the Maritimes. Two flights were despatched to Bermuda to bring back Maritime Air Command personnel back to Greenwood and Summerside. Twelve scheduled service flights were conducted to Britain, and one of these came close to disaster.

Service Flight 52 left North Luffenham mid-morning on 23 December, refuelled at Prestwick, and carried on to Keflavik where the flight crew was changed. Aboard this flight was Squadron Leader G.W. Webb, the Command Check Pilot, who had been conducting instrument and route checks for pilots operating out of Langar, and was heading home for Christmas. He accompanied the crew during the pre-flight briefing. The Duty Meteorologist advised the crew that an extensive band of frontal weather lay across the route to Goose Bay, and heavy icing conditions in cloud had been reported. Since such conditions were normal for winter in the North Atlantic, these reports caused only mild concern.

One of the passengers was Squadron Leader A.J. Simpson, who was returning to Ottawa after attending NATO exercises in France. Sometime after the flight had left Keflavik, having nothing to do, he picked up a headset from the seat next to him and listened in on a conversation between the captain and the first officer, the gist of which was that they were encountering severe icing conditions that the de-icing equipment on the aircraft could not handle. Worried, Simpson woke Webb, who was napping in a seat opposite and said, "I think you had better listen to this."

Fifteen seconds after putting on the headset, Webb headed for the cockpit, where the situation was very serious: the aircraft was losing altitude and becoming difficult to control. The captain had decided to let the aircraft descend to sea level, where he assumed the air would be warmer, rather than risk damaging the engines by operating them at full power. Webb suggested in the strongest and most unequivocal terms that they should go immediately to maximum power and stay there in an attempt to gain altitude, rather than try to find warmer air below. The Merlins groaned their disapproval as they laboured under full power but, after some fine flying by the captain, the aircraft broke clear of cloud at 10,500 feet. It took some time for the aircraft to shed the load of ice that it had accumulated but the flight was out of danger. The rest of the trip to Montreal was routine.[31]

The annual conference of Commanding Officers and Officers Commanding was held at Air Transport Command Headquarters in Lachine between 13 December and 15 December, addressing a wide range of operational, technical and administrative topics. On 18 December, a fire in one of the airmen's barrack blocks destroyed one wing of the building and many airmen lost all their belongings; the same day, the squadron's annual Children's Christmas Party was held in the Drill Hall, with presents and candy for the children of all the station's service personnel.[32]

For the first time in several years, most of No 426 Squadron's personnel were home for Christmas. Only four crews were away: one in Keflavik, another at Prestwick, and two in San Francisco: one with an unserviceable aircraft and the stand-by crew sent out to help them.

The fourteen men of the North Luffenham detachment were also away from home. After church services on Christmas Day, in accordance with Air Force tradition, the officers served Christmas dinner to the airmen of RCAF Station Lachine. For New Year's Eve, the various mess committees organized parties and dances that were all well attended.

PHOTO 145
The west end of the runway at Gibraltar; September 1954. (J. Sare Collection)

MAP 6: *North Star Operations in Europe and the Mediterranean, 1948–1962*

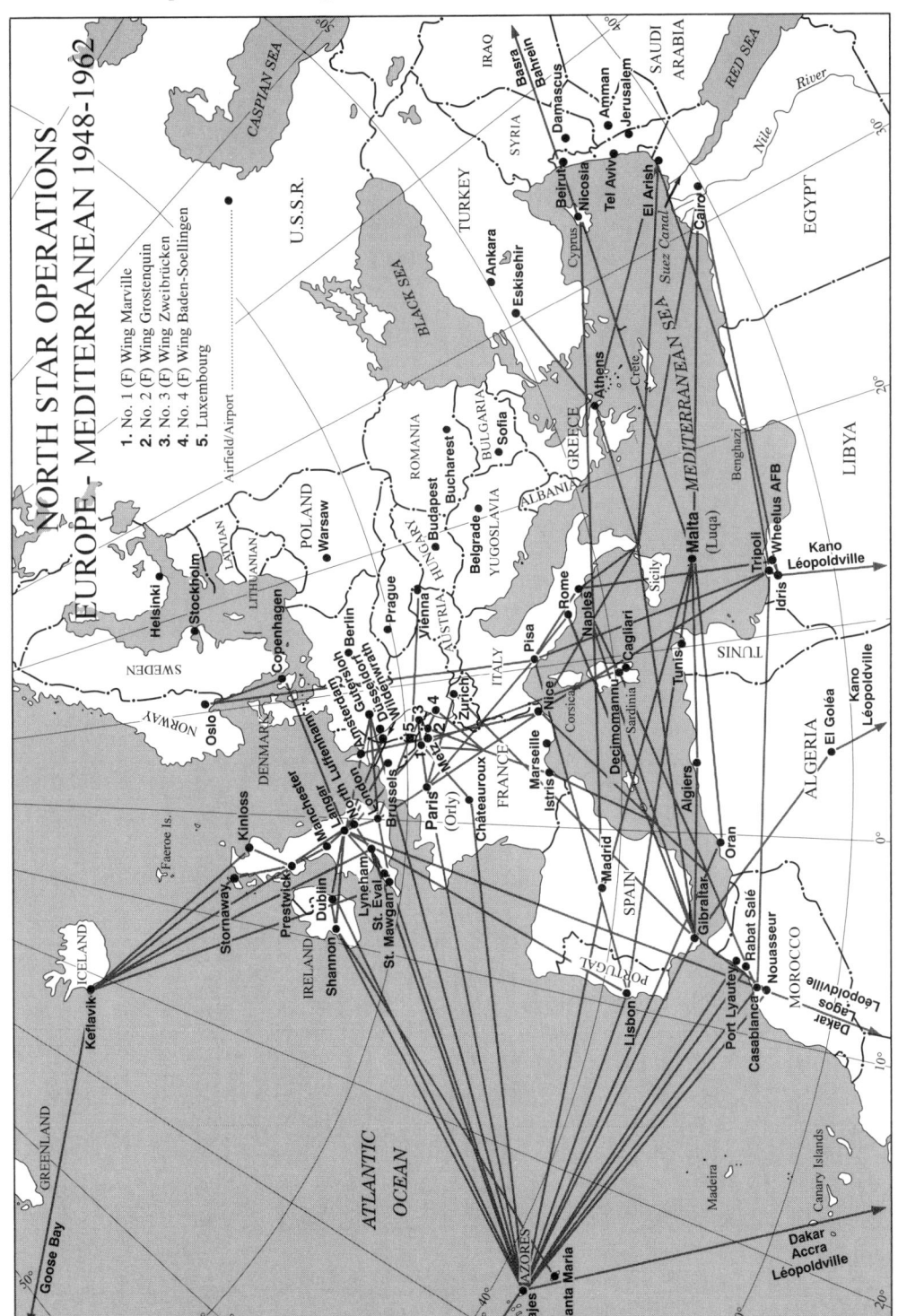

PHOTO 146
An aerial view of the Grand Harbour at Valetta; Malta, September 1954. (J. Sare Collection)

PHOTO 147
Boxes of equipment being loaded aboard a North Star for delivery to Turkey under the Mutual Aid plan; RCAF Station Langar, 15 July 1954. (National Archives of Canada PA166837)

Lachine, July–December 1954

PHOTO 148
Greek Minister of National Defence (in white suit) and other dignitaries pose with members of a No 426 Squadron crew; Athens, 20 July 1954. From left, front row: F/O R. Webber; F/O G. Brassard (RCAF Liaison Officer) and F/O Y. Lafrenière; back row: sixth from left, F/L J. Lambert (captain); eighth from left, F/O Ken Gray; and ninth from left, LAC O'Connor. (Y. Lafrenière Collection)

PHOTO 149
A North Star crew receives a weather briefing before leaving for Eskisehir, Turkey; Athens, 26 July 1954. From left: F/O E. Heikkila (navigator), an unidentified officer and F/O G.H. McAninch (captain). (E. Heikkila Collection)

PHOTO 150
Operation SANTA CLAUS: a para-drop from NS17515; Mould Bay, 6 December 1954. (D. Eagles Collection)

Lachine, 1955

CHAPTER 19
LACHINE, 1955

During 1955, the squadron had twelve North Stars on the inventory, with a monthly utilization rate of 130 hours. Squadron strength averaged 230, including ninety-three officers, a reduction of 265 personnel caused by the transfer of many administrative and technical support elements to RCAF Station Lachine. The year's operational commitments were both varied and wide-ranging. About 200 flights went to Europe: three weekly scheduled trips; escorts for nine fighter convoys across the North Atlantic, and several special runs. In Canada, the squadron operated regular flights to Vancouver, Whitehorse, the Atlantic provinces and the high Arctic. There were many special flights to destinations in the United States, and several trips to Indochina to exchange Canadian members of the ICSC truce teams. The squadron also launched several ambitious training flights, including runs to the North Pole.[1]

In accordance with a 1951 long-term plan to meet Canada's commitment to NATO, No 1 Fighter Wing was scheduled to move from North Luffenham to Marville, France. The airlift of the Wing, called *Operation RHUMBA QUEEN*, was carried out by four C-119s (two each from No 435 (T) Squadron and No 436 (T) Squadron) in conjunction with the North Star flights by No 426 Squadron. The C-119s departed Dorval on 4 January, arriving at North Luffenham on 9 January after being delayed en route for more than a week, mainly by bad weather; the aircraft had been routed through Goose Bay, Narsarssuak and Keflavik. Despite the delay, the entire airlift from North Luffenham to Marville — passengers and about 200 tons of freight — was completed in thirty-four round trips by 25 January. Three of the aircraft departed for Dorval the next day, arriving on 29 January; the fourth C-119 was held back to transport about twenty-four tons of wire cable from Villecoublay, on the southwestern outskirts of Paris, to Marville. That aircraft returned to Montreal on 1 February.

With the departure of No 1 Wing and the pending closure of RCAF Station North Luffenham, the destination of scheduled North Star flights to Britain from Dorval shifted to Langar. As a consequence, the detachment commanded by Flying Officer J. Forest would move to Langar in late March.[2]

The need to replace the Lancasters used for maritime reconnaissance was first raised at Air Force Headquarters in 1952. In 1953, the RCAF considered acquiring the Bristol Britannia transport and converting it to the long-range reconnaissance role; in the interim, twenty-five

Lockheed P2V–7 Neptunes were purchased for No 404 (MR) Squadron and No 405 (MR) Squadron at RCAF Station Greenwood. In late 1954, personnel from the Greenwood units went to the Lockheed plant at Burbank, California, for technical training on the new aircraft, and on 6 January, a No 426 Squadron North Star transported more personnel from both Greenwood squadrons for training at Lockheed. The Burbank-trained group eventually staffed the Neptune Conversion Unit at Greenwood.[3]

January

On the morning of 7 January, two North Stars left Dorval for Resolute Bay. The first aircraft, captained by Flying Officer Thompson, carried a troupe of twenty entertainers sponsored by Bell Canada; this flight stopped overnight at Churchill, went on to Resolute the next morning, and arrived at 1410 hours. The detachment personnel had built a special stage for the troupe's performance, which began at 1730 and ran for two and a half hours. It was thoroughly enjoyed by all those who were able to attend. The troupe departed at 2230 hours for the return to Churchill and Montreal.[4]

The second aircraft was NS17511 captained by Flight Lieutenant Deeprose, which left Montreal on a combined logistics and training run. Deeprose, one of the squadron's check pilots, was conducting a route check on two of the unit pilots, Flying Officer Holmes and Flying Officer Wood. After a flight of seven and a half hours, the aircraft arrived at Frobisher Bay where a crew rest was taken. On the morning of 8 January, the crew headed for Thule and, after refuelling, went on to Resolute Bay, where they arrived at 1710 hours. The next day (by the clock, that is; it was night according to the light conditions!), supply drops were carried out at Mould Bay, Isachsen and Eureka with the aircraft returning to Resolute Bay. On the climb-out from Mould Bay, a Public Relations photographer asked Deeprose to look back from the captain's seat. On doing so, Deeprose was immediately blinded by the light of a flashbulb popping off six feet from his eyes. Deeprose had to have First Officer Wood take control of the aircraft. Sometime during the fifteen minutes it took for him to regain his vision, Deeprose told the photographer in quite explicit language what a dumb thing he had done. On 10 January, the crew conducted a supply drop at Alert and then went to Thule where they remained overnight, returning to base the next day after a short stop at Churchill.[5]

On 20 January the squadron despatched a North Star to Knob Lake carrying a party of airmen who were tasked with reopening the Station Lachine Detachment at that location. Buildings at the site were to be reopened for future occupancy and the diesel equipment and telecommunication site had to be up and running. On 26 January, another North Star flew in the seven members of the Detachment, headed by Flying Officer F.R. Cleminson, a Radio Officer from No 408 Squadron. The Detachment would operate in support of the Mid-Canada line project. It maintained liaison with the field crews of Bell Telephone and the Iron Ore Company of Canada (IOC) and supplied telecommunication services for RCAF aircraft operating in the area. The Detachment's messing facilities were initially provided by the IOC.[6]

Flying Officer Paul and his crew carried out two supply runs from Churchill to Resolute Bay on 27 January and 29 January. The first was Service Flight 5 out of Dorval, and the second was a shuttle flight to help reduce the backlog of cargo that was accumulating at Churchill. Two augmented crews from the squadron, captained by Flight Lieutenant Tapp and Flying Officer Forest, left Dorval in NS17525 on 27 January on a combination logistics and training exercise. The flight stopped off at Churchill and continued on to Resolute Bay. After refuelling, the aircraft went to Thule where it stayed overnight. There was some difficulty in getting the North Star started the following day; as there was no hangar space, the crew had had to leave the aircraft out in the open with the temperatures hovering in the -40°F range. From Thule the crews headed for the North Geographic Pole, setting down at Resolute Bay after a nine and a half hour flight. It was a very uncomfortable trip as the cockpit heater was not working. Members of the crew manning the flight stations had to change positions frequently so they could warm up in the main cabin where the heaters were functioning. After a crew rest, the flight was back in Montreal early in the morning of 30 January, having stopped at Churchill on the way home.[7]

February

On 7 February, Flight Lieutenant Deeprose set off with an augmented crew in NS17521 on an extended training mission that would last twelve days. Although a payload was carried on several legs of the trip, the purpose of the mission was to have six relative newcomers to the squadron demonstrate their eligibility for upgrades of their respective categories. Two first officers were to be evaluated as to their potential as captains, and a determination was to be made whether the second navigator, radio officer, flight engineer and transportation technician were ready for operational rating. The other members of the thirteen-man crew were the five members of the check crew (including Deeprose), an aero-engine technician and an airframe technician.

The two first officers, Flying Officers Carss and Holmes, would exchange the positions of "acting captain" and co-pilot with each flight leg. Whoever was captain on a particular leg would make all the decisions and take all the action normally required of a line captain. In line with his responsibilities for the safety of the aircraft and those aboard, Deeprose would occupy the co-pilot's position for all take-offs and landings and whenever abnormal circumstances warranted. If he considered it necessary, he could override decisions made by an acting captain.

On leaving Dorval, the flight went to RCAF Station Downsview (in the northwestern outskirts of Toronto)[8] to pick up a load of freight for Churchill and Resolute Bay. With Carss as the Acting Captain on the flight to Churchill, the Second Navigator got to practice grid-navigation techniques. The aircraft was equipped with three gyro-driven instruments, two of which were electrically-powered, the J-2 and N-1 gyro/magnetic compass systems. By using a slaving switch each of the two systems could be operated as gyros only or used to stabilize their magnetic compasses. The third was a suction-driven instrument called the DGI (Directional Gyro Indicator). The Captain's instrument panel incorporated all three instruments, whereas the Navigator's panel displayed readouts of the Sperry Gyrosyn J-2 and the Kearfott N-1 only. The N-1 was a new state-of-the-art gyro-compass and NS17521 was the only aircraft in the squadron fleet in which this compass system had been installed. The degree of precession claimed by the manufacturer was one degree per hour and the crew were expected to test the N-1's suitability for installation in the fleet.

Shortly after 2200 hours, or six hours and ten minutes after leaving Downsview, the flight set down at Churchill The weather was clear and the temperature a frigid -35°F. As there was no hangar space, the aircraft had to be left in the open where it would cold-soak for about sixteen hours. Each engine's oil had to be diluted with gasoline to prevent it from congealing and the batteries were removed and stored in a warm place. Oil dilution in the North Star was done by activating four switches (one for each engine) on the switch panel above and forward of the captain's head. To adequately thin the oil for the next day's cold-engine start, one minute dilution was required for every 15°F below +32°F outside air temperature; therefore, on this occasion, a four-minute dilution was required before engine shut-down.

At the weather briefing the next day, it was noted that the outlook for Resolute Bay was less than promising. The forecast for the airfield at ETA was minimum landing limits, which were: overcast with a ceiling of 700 feet' visibility two miles in snow, occasionally one half mile in blowing snow; a surface wind 30 to 40° off the runway heading with a velocity of 30mph with occasional gusts of 40mph and a surface temperature of -40°F. Thule was the nearest alternate and the weather there was about the same as at Resolute Bay. Although the Acting Captain suggested that the flight cancel out to await better conditions, Deeprose disagreed. He thought the conditions were ideal for the Acting Captain to gain experience and demonstrate his ability. After all, such conditions would often be encountered. It was decided to press on.

Since there was a possibility that the flight might have to come back to Churchill, the flight engineers were instructed to fill the fuel tanks to the top, a total of 2,950 gallons. However, since this would put the aircraft 3,000 pounds over weight for take-off, the transportation technicians were instructed to unload that much cargo. After a last-minute check on the weather situation and the flight plan, the crew boarded the aircraft at 1700 hours local time. The aircraft was relatively warm since it had been ground-run by Holmes, the acting captain for that leg, and the flight engineers during an hour-long boil-off. Following the boil-off, the aircraft had its fuel tanks topped up.

Boiling-off was a procedure peculiar to the North Star, made necessary by the design of the engines' oil tanks. Oil diluted with gasoline tended to froth while recirculating through the tanks, and when the engines were at maximum or climbing power, the slipstream would suck the froth out through the oil-tank vent pipes. To prevent frothing, the oil had to be warm enough to evaporate — boil off — the gasoline. A boil-off was done by running the engines on the ground at climbing power for fifteen minutes for every minute of oil dilution after the temperature of the engine oil had reached 60°C. After the engines were started, the aircraft was taxied out to the runway, where another fifteen minute boil-off had to be carried out before the flight was ready to leave.

Departing at 1830 hours for the five-and-a-half-hour run, the aircraft climbed to 8,000 feet and headed north. As the trainees worked in the flight positions, their efforts were monitored by the check crew. Grid-navigation techniques were used, and both pilots maintained their own gyro logs, getting true heading information from the navigator. The radio officer received periodic weather reports for the destination and alternates, which were much as forecast except for surface winds at Resolute Bay they had strengthened to 35 mph with gusts of more than 45 mph and blowing some 50° off the runway heading. After four hours of flying in the clear, an undercast condition gradually developed so that, by the time the aircraft arrived over Resolute Bay, it was barely 1,000 feet above cloud.

Resolute Bay had two navigation beacons, one two miles south of the runway's south end and the other one mile north of the runway's north end. With one of the aircraft's two radio compasses tuned to the south beacon and the other tuned to the north beacon, a pilot could use the readings from these two instruments to make a reasonably precise instrument letdown to the runway. When a moderate or worse crosswind condition prevailed, however, an inexperienced pilot could easily go wrong and have to abort the letdown. Resolute Bay had but one runway— oriented north-to-south—and, under the current wind conditions, NS17521 would be landing south to north. Throughout the complicated fifteen-minute instrument letdown procedure, Holmes had trouble with the strong crosswind. Toward the end of the procedure, with the aircraft still descending south of the south beacon and outbound of it, the flight was off-track to the west.

Still off-track by several hundred yards as it passed abeam of the beacon, the aircraft broke out of cloud about 800 feet above the ground. Sighting the runway, Holmes "S-turned" the aircraft to gain alignment. He succeeded, but with the heavy turbulence buffeting the aircraft he had to crab 15 to 20 degrees to hold alignment. At that point, Holmes realized that he would not be able to land safely. At 300 feet and half a mile from the end of the runway, he called to the flight engineer, "Overshoot! Maximum power!" Observers on the ground watched the North Star disappear into the overcast as Holmes hauled it up to a safer altitude.

Knowing they had enough fuel in the tanks for only one more letdown and landing attempt before they would have to head back to Churchill, Deeprose changed seats with Holmes and took control of the aircraft. After a more effective instrument letdown, Deeprose managed to land the aircraft safely, despite poor visibility due to snow blowing across the runway.

After taxiing in and letting the oil cool below 60°C, Deeprose conducted a five-minute oil-dilution procedure before shutting down the engines. Most of the crew donned their Arctic gear and rode the Caterpillar tractor to the comfort of the all-ranks living accommodations, which combined both quarters and mess. The flight engineers and technicians had to stay behind for more than an hour, however, working in the wind at -40°F to complete the post-flight checks and ready the aircraft for its next departure. They covered the engines, refuelled the aircraft, checked the oil tanks and topped them up as required, removed the batteries, and lowered the flaps 15° to keep the blowing snow out of the control areas of the wing. Only after these chores were the engineers and technicians able to head for their quarters and a hot meal.

On 9 February, semi-blizzard conditions prevailed at Resolute Bay and the conditions forecast for Thule were even worse, so the proposed flight to the North Pole was delayed. The next morning, departure was scheduled for 1500 hours as the weather situation was more promising: the winds had moderated, the sky had cleared, the temperature was a brisk -35°F and the forecast for Thule was favourable. After an early lunch, Deeprose and the two aspiring captains went to the aircraft where the flight engineers were installing the batteries and the crew's two technicians were using two Herman Nelson gas-fired generators to blow heat through ducts into the tarpaulin-draped No 4 engine. Since the aircraft had cold-soaked for quite a while, the flight engineers considered it necessary to use both Herman Nelsons to warm each engine for at least ten minutes before trying to start them. At a signal from the cockpit, the ground crew disconnected the heat ducts, removed the tarpaulin draping the engine and rolled the Herman Nelsons to No 3 engine.

On receiving the "all clear", Carss (in the captain's seat) primed the engine, then hit the button to start No 4. After a couple of revolutions of the propeller the engine fired up, belched smoke and flame for a few seconds, and then settled into a smooth high-rev idle. They repeated the process until all four engines were idling contentedly, and it took about an hour for the oil to heat to 60°C. The next step was to boil off the gasoline that was injected into the oil after arrival to dilute it so it would be ductile on start-up. This took about ninety minutes, and the engines were then shut down and the fuel tanks topped up.

At this point, the rest of the crew boarded the aircraft and the main door was quickly shut, the engines restarted, and the aircraft taxied to the runway button for the pre-takeoff checks. All three gyros were carefully set — the DGI to the true heading (167°) of the departure runway and the N-1 and J-2 to the runway's grid heading of 262°. Shortly after 1500 hours, the flight was heading for the North Pole, 1,060 miles away. From there they would go on to Thule, a further 930 miles. The estimated flight time for the 1,990-mile trip was ten hours.

Discernable below the flight, as it headed toward the North Pole at 10,000 feet, was a rising solid layer of cloud, the tops of which were just a thousand feet below the aircraft as it neared the Pole. Five minutes before arriving over the Pole, the second navigator delivered a minute-by-minute commentary on the flight's progress, including a countdown of the last ten seconds. As the aircraft passed over the Pole, the crew could see only the brilliance of the stars and the glittering display of the Aurora Borealis. About a minute later, a 225° turn brought the aircraft back over the Pole and course was set for Thule. A heading check confirmed that the flight was on the correct southbound heading.

As the flight progressed, the cloud tops kept rising and, about forty-five minutes after leaving the Pole, the aircraft was in cloud. Carss and the second navigator discussed whether to climb to 15,000 to be above all cloud, or to remain at their current altitude of 10,000 feet. At the higher altitude, the whole crew would have to go on oxygen, and the oxygen masks available at the time were very uncomfortable. The check crew would have to get their oxygen from small, awkward, portable bottles. It was too cold for airframe icing, and the main disadvantages of staying in cloud were the lack of stars to navigate or check heading by, and the presence of static electricity that interfered with radio reception. It was decided to stay at 10,000 feet as the worse disadvantages would be encountered at higher altitudes.

After an hour in cloud, the second navigator was quite concerned about getting a heading check and some star shots to fix the aircraft's position, so Carss was asked to climb above cloud. All the crew members went on oxygen as the aircraft climbed to 1,000 feet above cloud and levelled off at 16,000 feet. As the second navigator prepared to take his observations from the astrodome, he found that his oxygen hose was not long enough, so he removed the mask and set it on the navigation table. The check navigator, who was now seated at the plotting table, also set aside his oxygen bottle and mask, although he took an occasional whiff of oxygen as he examined his colleague's chart work. After spending several minutes completing his observations, the second navigator resumed his position. He did not replace his oxygen mask while making his calculations, although from time to time he would take a few deep breaths from it before setting it aside.

The calculations did not work out as expected, so another set of star shots was taken, but the results of these observations, when plotted, were even more perplexing. The check navigator was consulted, and he then took several star sights before joining the second navigator to calculate the results. Finally, a heading-to-fly chit was prepared and passed to the pilots. Carss questioned the large course alteration requested, and the check navigator was instructed to take more sights. At this point, Deeprose, who had been watching the proceedings, came forward to speak to the pilot and asked what was happening. Carss explained that he had been asked to make an alteration to port of 87°, then went on to say that the navigators were surmising that something had set the gyros askew. A new series of star sights was taken and the results calculated, the navigators still working without wearing their oxygen masks. The alteration of heading given this time was similar to that passed to the pilots earlier. When asked whether he was sure about the heading change, the check navigator insisted the calculations were accurate.

In discussing whether to alter the heading as requested the two pilots were faced with a dilemma. If the navigators were right, the aircraft was now headed for Alaska but, if they were wrong, and heading was altered, the flight would find itself on the way to Spitzbergen or Murmansk. After several minutes of discussion, the pilots (who had both removed their oxygen masks to talk) concluded that the navigators must know what they were doing and agreed to alter heading as requested.

As Carss reached for the auto-pilot control knob, Deeprose stayed his hand and instructed both pilots to don their oxygen masks. After giving them a couple of minutes on oxygen, Deeprose then asked them to observe and evaluate the readings of the three gyro instruments; when they did so, it was apparent that the gyro readings did not vary enough to indicate that anything had gone askew. He also pointed out that the navigators had used very little oxygen while at 10,000 feet and had used it only occasionally since climbing to 16,000 feet, and concluded that they were all affected by anoxia, which had impaired their capability and judgement.

Advising Carss to hold the current heading, Deeprose spoke to the navigators but found them still convinced that their calculations were accurate; however, they also acknowledged their negligence with respect to their oxygen supply and readily agreed to take more star shots. Unfortunately, their new effort resulted in the same requirement for a near-90-degree course alteration. Despite some unease on the part of the pilots and over the navigators' objections, Deeprose ordered that the current heading be maintained.

The radio officer was asked to get bearings from any radio stations he could contact, but this proved fruitless. The flight continued for another hour or so before Holmes, in the co-pilot's seat, was able to tune in the Thule radio beacon on one of the radio compasses. After the RC's homing needle stabilized, it pointed almost straight ahead, indicating that the aircraft was close to the desired track to Thule. Even so, the navigators were still defensive when Deeprose asked them to take a heading check so that the DGI could be up-dated to True Heading. The check navigator took the sight and passed the newly determined True Heading to Carss, who reset the DGI accordingly. At this point, Deeprose replaced Holmes in the co-pilot's seat.

When Deeprose finally managed to contact Thule Approach Control, he was advised that Thule had the flight under radar surveillance, and that the aircraft should be turned onto a specified True Heading. Carss turned the aircraft onto the requested heading with reference to the DGI. A little later, Thule queried the aircraft's heading. Upon being told that it was the one requested, Thule replied: "You are not flying the heading requested. I assume you have had a gyro failure; I will bring you in using the "lost gyro" procedure. Are you familiar with that procedure?" Deeprose said he was, and the flight was then vectored in by radar to a landing after being airborne ten and a half hours. During the landing roll, Deeprose recorded the readings of the DGI, the J-2 and the N-1 gyros, and the navigators were told to do likewise. The DGI erred by nearly 80 degrees from the runway's published True Heading.

At 0300 hours, as soon as the engines were shut down, a mule (aircraft tractor) hooked up to the nose wheel and towed the North Star into a huge, warm hangar, so an oil dilution procedure was not required. This great service reflected the excellent relations between the RCAF and the USAF. In its operations around the world, No 426 Squadron depended heavily on the use of USAF (and, to a lesser extent, RAF) facilities.

After an early breakfast, the pilots, navigators and radio officers met in the mess lounge for a debriefing on the previous flight leg and a briefing on the next leg of the trip, to Prestwick. Both navigators were adamant something was wrong with the electrical circuits of the gyro compasses, and insisted that the flight not proceed until the circuits were thoroughly checked. This was a problem, since the nearest instrument technician was at Dorval. The pilots were equally convinced that the gyros were fine, and Deeprose ended the discussion by deciding the flight would depart for Prestwick at 2300 hours on 11 February.

After some sleep and a late dinner, the crew attended a weather briefing at 2130 hours. The weather forecast indicated that the flight would enter cloud at 2,500 feet after take-off, and climb through layered cloud until topping all cloud at 13,000 feet. These conditions would prevail until mid-flight, with clouds becoming broken to scattered until destination. For the 2,115-mile leg, a nine-hour flight plan at 15,000 feet was filed. Before take-off, the aircraft was carefully aligned with Runway 16 so that all the gyros could be set accurately — the DGI to the True Heading and the J-2 and N-1 to the runway's Grid Heading. Holmes, at the controls, climbed on course through 10,000 feet, where the crew was ordered to go on oxygen. On reaching cruising altitude, the flight was still in cloud and remained so for at least an hour. After this, the aircraft was in and out of the cloud tops for another thirty minutes before bursting out on top.

Shortly after take-off, Deeprose relinquished the co-pilot's position to Carss. About an hour into the flight, as the flight engineer checked the fuel gauges, Deeprose noticed that the fuel was much lower in No 4 Auxiliary tank than in its twin, No 1 Auxiliary. Deeprose and the flight engineer went to the main cabin, looked out the window and saw a tell-tale mist streaming from the trailing edge of the starboard wing. As the fuel was not coming from the filler cap on top of the wing, the flight engineer surmised that a malfunctioning valve was the most likely cause of the leak. Returning to the cockpit, Deeprose and the flight engineer noted that the tank was now nearly empty. Deeprose advised the flight engineer to transfer the remaining fuel into No 4 main tank and inform the pilots.

While the pilots were addressing this problem, the check navigator, after managing to take a star shot, had concluded that the gyros had again gone askew and asked for an 85° alteration to port. The pilots took one look at the heading chit and said there was no way they were going to alter heading without more heading checks. The pilots then told Deeprose that, despite the loss of fuel, the aircraft could still make it to Prestwick, with North Luffenham as an alternate. With all the uncertainty about the navigation, however, they recommended diverting to Keflavik, which was close to the original flight path. They considered the present heading good for the time being, and that they could confirm the aircraft's position when passing abeam of the Sondrestrom radio beacon. As the standby magnetic compass, which hung between the pilots' windscreens, seemed stable, they suggested that the navigators should stop using grid-navigation techniques and revert to regular navigation procedures using the J-2 magnetic compass as a directional reference, and leaving the N-1 in gyro mode so its accuracy could be assessed over the full duration of the flight. Deeprose approved this course of action.

Shortly after crossing the southeast coast of Greenland, the cloud tops dropped, allowing the flight to descend to 9,000 feet. After seven hours and thirty-five minutes airborne on the 1,315-mile leg, the flight landed at Keflavik at 0900 local time. Shortly after setting down, Deeprose checked the readings on the N-1 and noted that it was only 4° off the grid heading of the runway. This was remarkable accuracy, compared with other gyros in use at the time. He decided to take a twelve-hour crew rest, and to give the flight engineers and technicians enough time not only to get the aircraft ready for the 830-mile leg to Prestwick, but also to get the faulty fuel valve fixed, if possible.

Departing Keflavik on schedule at 2100 hours on 12 February, the flight landed at Prestwick four and a half hours later. After a two-hour stop, the aircraft was on its way to North Luffenham, where the crew took a twelve-hour rest. On 13 February, after picking up passengers and cargo, the flight left for Grostenquin and Zweibrücken, stopping for two hours at each fighter base before going on to Baden-Söllingen, where they took a thirty-six hour break. On 17 February, the flight was on its way to Rabat Salé with freight and a few passengers for the RCAF detachment in Morocco.

There was some excitement on this eight-hour leg. After encountering light turbulence near Gibraltar while flying in cloud, the flight blundered into a thunderstorm, in which the aircraft was thrown about in heavy turbulence and struck by lightning — a brilliant flash and loud boom that brought everyone up straight. Fortunately, everyone aboard was strapped in and there were no injuries.[9] When the aircraft was on the ground, a large tear was discovered in the fabric of the rudder, where the lightning bolt had left the aircraft. During the twelve-hour stopover, the engineers and technicians repaired the rudder and readied the aircraft for the next leg.

The six-hour flight to Lajes was routine, and the aircraft spent twenty-six hours on the ground there. Departure on the long over-water leg to Bermuda was scheduled for 2000 hours on 18 February. The navigators went to the Weather Office late in the afternoon, and returned to the quarters with the information that the headwind component forecast between Lajes and Bermuda was 35 mph. This meant that, with a full fuel load, the flight could tolerate only a -17 mph wind component, assuming that an airfield in the Bahamas was available as an alternate. On hearing the navigators' report, the two pilots were ready to cancel the weather briefing set for 1800 hours and delay the flight, but Deeprose disagreed. He thought they all should attend the weather briefing before deciding to cancel.

At the briefing, the meteorologist pointed out a large high-pressure area between the two islands and said that the headwind component at the 10,000-foot level averaged -35 mph, as the navigators had been told. Accepting the negative wind component at 10,000 feet, Deeprose asked the briefer, "What about the winds at 5,000 feet?" and the briefer replied that he was not authorized to forecast winds below the 10,000 foot level. When Deeprose asked whether he agreed that, with such a strong high pressure area straddling the flight path, the winds at the surface would be very light and the negative component at the 5,000 foot level would be about half that forecast for 10,000 feet, the briefer replied that he was not authorized to speculate.

Deeprose then said that, if he couldn't get a lower-level wind forecast, he'd make one himself. The meteorologist replied, "Fine," but refused to sign the flight plan. Deeprose announced that he would sign the flight plan himself, and the briefer informed him he could try, but the Base Operations Officer would not accept a flight plan without the briefer's signature on it. Deeprose was not concerned on this score, as USAF officers had no authority over RCAF crews and aircraft transiting their bases; USAF merely provided the RCAF with services, just as the RCAF provided services to transient USAF aircraft touching down at RCAF stations. An RCAF captain could sign off on his own flight plan, but if anything went wrong, the captain would be held accountable for the consequences.

The navigators strongly objected to leaving without a proper forecast wind, and Holmes and Carss were reluctant to override them. Deeprose pointed out that there was nothing unsafe in proceeding with the flight because, should the winds prove to be too strong before reaching the point of no return, the flight could simply return to Lajes. Deeprose then cut off the discussion by stating that the flight would depart at 2000 hours as planned.

On the basis of the "assumed wind," the navigators completed their calculations for a flight of ten and a half hours; the time to PNR was six hours. The pilots took the flight plan to Base Operations for filing, and the lieutenant on duty said he could not accept a flight plan not signed by the meteorologist. After some discussion, the lieutenant requested a ruling from his superior, a major, telling him that Deeprose was fully authorized by the RCAF to sign his own flight plans. The major instructed the lieutenant to accept the flight plan as presented, and help the crew on their way.

The flight departed as scheduled, climbed to 4,000 feet, and was soon cruising in the clear moonlight under brilliant stars. There were no navigation problems and the winds, as Deeprose had predicted, were light, with the headwind component averaging 14 mph. After being airborne for eleven hours, the flight landed in Bermuda early in the morning, and the crew took a thirty-hour rest.

On 19 February, the crew set off for Dorval on the last leg of their training mission. The last half of the five-hour flight was in cloud with the aircraft occasionally flying in moderate icing conditions. On arrival, the flight had to hold for fifteen minutes over the Montreal Radio Range so Carss could make a full instrument letdown before landing.

It was all good training.[10]

On 12 February, RCAF Station Lachine received a message from Resolute Bay that the power plant had burnt down at 0130 hours, and the detachment was left with only Herman Nelson generators to produce heat. The temperature was -40°F and the water supply was seriously affected: the lines had to broken and the pipes bled to keep them from freezing. Emergency equipment flown in from Churchill that evening included several oil-fired space-heaters and many spare parts; the same flight also brought a three-member Board of Inquiry. On 17 February, Squadron Leader Olsen arrived from Dorval with the spares required for repairs, three oil-fired high-speed air furnaces, and a plumber. The Board of Inquiry finished its work and left for Lachine with Olsen's aircraft on the morning of 18 February.[11]

Operation RANDOM 11 got underway on 16 February, when two North Stars were positioned at St-Hubert. On 18 February, NS17514 (captained by Flying Officer Reed), carrying No 1 Support Party, and NS17511 (captained by Flying Officer Major), with No 2 Support Party, followed a convoy of thirty-one jets to Goose Bay. On 19 February, Reed and his crew left Goose Bay at 0500 hours for Narsarssuak to position No 1 Support Party, and Major left at 0820 hours for Keflavik with No 2. During the afternoon, twenty-seven Sabres crossed to Greenland successfully. Two T-33s (to be used for training in case of weather delays) and three Sabre VIs were left behind, and the convoy picked up a Sabre II at Goose Bay.

The convoy went on to Keflavik on 20 February, leaving three Sabres at Narsarssuak. Reed and his crew left Greenland for Keflavik early that evening with a support party and, after a brief stop, carried on to Kinloss. The weather in Iceland was good, but a heavy snowfall and freezing temperatures at Kinloss delayed the convoy at Keflavik for a day.

Early on the morning of 21 February, an unfortunate accident occurred on the flight line at Keflavik, where most of the Sabres in the convoy were parked in an L formation. An airman from the support group was running up Sabre 23216 when the aircraft either jumped its sandbag chocks or pushed them aside. With the airman's hand frozen on the throttle at the full-open position, the aircraft started to move directly for the Terminal Hotel, which was full of transients. The Sabre then veered to the left, towards a hangar full of aircraft, then careered towards the Control Tower. It finally halted when it ran into a line of parked Sabres, ramming 23318, which caught fire and was destroyed, and 23356, which sustained a crumpled wing. Sabre 23216, too, caught fire and was badly damaged. No one was killed, and the airman in the cockpit suffered only minor bruises and shock; his crew mates had to crack open the canopy with a fire extinguisher and help him out.

Squadron Leader G.W. Webb came out from Air Transport Command Headquarters to carry out the investigation. One of his key recommendations, which was adopted throughout the RCAF, was to use steel chocks when running up a jet aircraft.[12]

Since Kinloss was forecast to be snowbound for a week, it was decided to route the operation through Prestwick. Twenty Sabres made the crossing on 22 February; the convoy being reduced by four Sabres: the three involved in the accident at Keflavik, and one that had turned back with an undercarriage that failed to retract after take-off. At Prestwick, a Sabre flown by Flying Officer C.R. Hallowell struck a seagull while in the circuit, and both the seagull and the aircraft were severely damaged. The collision shattered the canopy, punched a hole in the tailplane, and delivered a stunning blow to the front of the pilot's crash helmet, breaking his visor. Hallowell recovered from the ensuing dive and landed without further damage to himself or the aircraft.

On the morning of 22 February, Reed and his crew repositioned NS17514 at Prestwick, where they arrived from Kinloss at 0820 hours. That same morning, Major and his crew conducted a weather reconnaissance flight out of Keflavik for the convoy before heading for home. They left for Narsarssuak on 25 February, and departed for Goose Bay, St-Hubert and base on 1 March.

Part of *RANDOM 11* was held up at Prestwick for a week because of poor weather on the continent, but the weather was good enough on 26 February to deliver six serviceable Sabre IIs to Manchester. NS17514, too, went to Manchester, to bring the pilots back to Prestwick. The seventh Sabre II, the one damaged by the bird strike, went to Manchester on 2 March after receiving the attentions of a mobile repair party. The weather on the continent that day was good enough to permit the delivery of thirteen Sabre Vs: five to Grostenquin, and four each to Zweibrücken and Baden-Söllingen. NS17514 followed the Sabres to Grostenquin, where it remained overnight; the next day, it went on to Zweibrücken and Baden-Söllingen to pick up more Sabre pilots. On 4 March, Reed and his crew started the return trip, stopping at Zweibrücken and Prestwick on the way to Keflavik, where Flying Officer Webber and his slip crew took over to bring NS17514 and its passengers from No 1 OFU back to St-Hubert before returning to base.[13]

After the power plant fire at Resolute Bay, the detachment's main preoccupation (aside from clearing snow off the runway) was installing new furnaces. The cold — temperatures frequently dipped below -50°F — and high winds didn't help. On 22 February, SF5 captained by Flying Officer Joron brought in more Herman Nelsons, and Flight Lieutenant H. Hibbard, the new Detachment Commander, who would relieve Flight Lieutenant G.R.A. Kyle on 28 February. At 1730 hours on 27 February, NS17509 came in from Churchill and landed in a crosswind that sent it skidding off the runway. With bulldozers and digging, enough snow was cleared away from the North Star to permit it to taxi out under its own power. The next day, when the flight returned to base, Kyle was aboard.[14]

March

On 2 March, Brooke Claxton wrote a memorandum to the Cabinet Defence Committee in which he recommended that the Korean Airlift contract with Canadian Pacific Airlines (which would end on 31 March 1955) not be renewed, and the Army's personnel transport requirements after 1 April 1955 be met through the use of regular scheduled commercial flights. These recommendations were accepted on 3 March, at the Committee's 104th meeting.[15]

On 3 March, No 426 Squadron dispatched a special flight to airlift Maritime Air Command personnel involved in the Neptune patrol aircraft project from RCAF Station Greenwood to the Lockheed plant in Burbank, California. NS17512 (captained by Flying Officer Glover) was refuelled at Minneapolis on both the outbound and homeward legs of the trip, and Glover and his crew were back at Dorval on 6 March after thirty-two and a half hours of flying. This flight was the second to Burbank, the first having gone two weeks before and returned to Montreal via Vancouver and Winnipeg.[16]

Flying Officer Holmes and his crew brought NS17521 into Resolute Bay at 1615 hours on 10 March, bringing in several technical specialists from Air Transport Command Headquarters and RCAF Station Lachine to draw up the specifications for a new power plant, along with the Protestant padre from Lachine and the Roman Catholic padre from Churchill. That evening, Protestant service was held and Holmes departed on a shuttle run to Churchill; the next day, Father Lasser celebrated Mass in the morning, and Holmes and his crew returned from Churchill in the early evening and left again for home at 2130 hours, taking the technical team and the padres with them.[17]

In January, the Chief of Air Operations at Air Force Headquarters had issued Administrative and Logistics Order 1/55, implementing an agreement to allow RAF Fighter Command to examine the CF-100 Canuck IV to assess its potential value to the RAF. Air Defence Command was to provide three suitable crews, who were to report to Station St-Hubert on 1 February. These crews were to conduct shakedown flights on the three CF-100s and then proceed to Britain in March with a Random flight.[18]

On 21 March, Flying Officer J. Buechler and his crew positioned their North Star at St-Hubert for *Operation RANDOM 12*, but the weather at Goose Bay was unsuitable for jet ferry operations, so they returned to Dorval. This entire procedure was repeated again the next day, as the weather was still bad at Goose Bay. On 24 March, however, the Goose Bay weather cleared and the operation got under way. NS17521 captained by Flying Officer Grant provided some direct logistics support for *RANDOM 12*, stopping off first at Goose Bay and then proceeding to Narsarssuak and Prestwick on 27 March. From this point on, NS17521 became a regular service flight that returned to base on 3 April.

On 24 March, Buechler and his crew took NS17514 back to St-Hubert, embarked the first support group, and flew to Goose Bay, where the weather was still marginal. The three CF-100s and two T-33s (whose larger fuel loads gave them a wider choice of alternate airfields) managed the flight from St-Hubert, but the rest of the convoy (fourteen Sabre IIs and four more T-33s) did not arrive at Goose Bay until the following afternoon. They were followed by Flight Lieutenant Dick and his crew in NS17510 with the second support party from St-Hubert. The planned double jump to Greenland had to be cancelled, as the Duckbutts out of Narsarssuak were unserviceable.

With two more T-33s picked up at Goose Bay, the convoy numbered twenty-nine jet aircraft on 26 March when it made the first over-water crossing. At Narsarssuak, an unserviceable Sabre was left behind and two Sabre Vs were added, so the convoy had thirty aircraft for the second crossing to Keflavik, made that afternoon, with NS17510 and NS17514 following on. All thirty jets made the flight to Kinloss the next afternoon, still tailed by the two North Stars.

On 28 March, the two Sabre Vs in the convoy were delivered to No 2 Wing at Marville, and the seventeen Sabre IIs and eight T-33s destined for Greece and Turkey were flown to Ringway near Manchester, to be painted in camouflage colours and readied for delivery. The three CF-100s were ferried to the RAF Central Flying Establishment at West Raynham, Norfolk. Dick and his crew flew NS17510 to Manchester to pick up the ferry pilots and then went to Langar. Leaving Langar on 1 April, the crew returned to Dorval the next day by way of St-Hubert, where they dropped off the OFU personnel. Buechler's crew went to West Raynham with the CF-100s, and left again the next morning with the crews and went to Manchester, where they picked up more passengers, and then to London to stay the night. On 30 March, NS17514 left London for home by way of Langar, Prestwick and Keflavik, where a twelve-hour crew rest was taken, and arrived at base on 31 March after a stop at St-Hubert to disembark the ferry unit personnel and their equipment.[19]

April

April at RCAF Station Lachine began with Holy Week, featuring well-attended services at both the Protestant and Roman Catholic chapels and a series of presentations by guest speakers invited by the padres.

On 4 April, an augmented crew captained by Flying Officer Dunford left base in NS17521 to conduct a combined logistics and training flight. After a stop at Churchill to refuel and deliver and pick up cargo, the flight carried on to Resolute Bay, where a twelve-hour crew rest was taken. The flight then went to Thule by way of the North Pole. On 7 April, they made the long flight to Prestwick; and on 9 April they went to Langar to pick up cargo, and then flew to the Fighter Wings at Marville, Grostenquin, Zweibrücken and Baden-Söllingen, where the pilots practised approaches and landings. On 11 April, the flight went to Rabat-Salé and then carried on to Lajes, and the next day the long over-water leg to Kindley AFB in Bermuda was completed. Following a crew rest in Bermuda, the flight was back at base on 14 April.[20]

The spring 1955 re-supply of the weather stations from Resolute Bay coincided with Easter, and would be carried out by the C-119s of No 435 Squadron from Edmonton and No 436 Squadron from Dorval. The first C-119 arrived on 7 April, and work got under way the next day with shuttle runs to Isachsen and Mould Bay continuing steadily until 17 April. On the afternoon of 14 April, Air Commodore Carscallen and a group of his staff officers arrived from Air Transport Command Headquarters to conduct the AOC's annual inspection. Shortly after arriving in No 412 Squadron's NS17520 (captained by Flight Lieutenant R. Sturgess), Carscallen went to Isachsen with three of his party, returning several hours later. On 15 April, the AOC's party completed the inspection, toured the camp area and departed in NS17520 for Coral Harbour and Ottawa. The inspection team was very interested in the temporary arrangements made to supply the camp with water and heat after the power plant fire of 12 February.[21]

On 15 April, Flying Officer L. Joron and his crew went from base to RCAF Station Greenwood; the next day, they embarked personnel from No 404 and No 405 squadrons and airlifted them to Bermuda, where the Maritime Reconnaissance squadrons were scheduled to take part in a joint U.S.N.–R.C.N. anti-submarine warfare exercise. Joron and his crew returned to base on 17 April.[22]

That spring, No 1 Field Technical Training Unit was nearly finished training Turkish Air Force technicians to maintain Sabres. The seven airmen of this unit were originally scheduled to return to Canada and then go to Greece during the summer to give the same training program there, but Air Force Headquarters had decided that, on 15 April, they should go to Athens to work with the Hellenic Air Force until August.[23]

For No 426 Squadron, *Operation RANDOM 13* began on 19 April at 2000 hours, when No 1 OFU's second support party was in position at Goose Bay; the first support party was delivered to Narsarssuak early in the afternoon on 20 April. On 24 April, twenty jets — seventeen Sabre IIs and three T-33 Silver Stars — made the flight from St-Hubert to Goose Bay, where two Sabre IIs and a Silver Star were added to the convoy. The crossing to Greenland was made on 26 April and, once the jets had taken off, the support party was flown from Goose Bay to Keflavik.

With another Sabre II picked up in Greenland, the convoy now numbered twenty-four aircraft. On 27 April, it arrived safely in Keflavik, where one Silver Star went unserviceable, and the first support party went on to Kinloss by North Star. The next day, *RANDOM 13* was completed with a double hop to Kinloss and Manchester, where twenty Sabre IIs and three Silver Stars destined for Greece and Turkey were delivered to Ringway. NS17511 escorted the convoy to Ringway and picked up the pilots. Departing Manchester on 29 April, NS17511 then went to London for a one-day stop, and returned to Montreal on 1 May with the ferry unit personnel.[24]

A two-day AOC's inspection of RCAF Station Lachine began on 28 April with a parade and a briefing on the station's operations and administration. The next day, Air Commodore Carscallen and his staff inspected the facilities at Dorval, and a cocktail party in his honour was given at the Officers' Mess.[25]

Also on 28 April, Flying Officer Paul captained an augmented crew that left Dorval on an eight-day training flight routed through New Orleans, Bermuda, the Azores, Lisbon, Rome, Baden-Söllingen, Langar, Prestwick, Keflavik and Narsarssuak before returning to base.[26]

May

On 3 May, Flight Lieutenant W. Dick and his crew positioned NS17513 at Downsview, where they embarked the officers on course at the RCAF Staff College for a trip to Maxwell AFB near Montgomery, Alabama, by way of Cleveland, where they cleared Customs. Maxwell AFB was the scene of the annual joint study exercises the Staff College students conducted with their American counterparts on the Air Command and Staff College course at the USAF Air University. On 9 May, Dick and his crew flew the RCAF students to Eglin AFB, Florida, and back to Maxwell. On 12 May, they visited Keesler AFB, the site of the major USAF electronic and telecommunications training centre, and, after an overnight stop, they went on to New Orleans. On 14 May, the flight returned to Canada, dropping off the Staff College students and their Directing Staff at Downsview before heading for home.[27]

Operation RANDOM 14 began on 9 May, when Flight Lieutenant Jenkins and his crew in NS17516 airlifted one of the ferry unit's ground support teams and some aircraft spares to Keflavik, returning to Montreal two days later. Meanwhile, on 10 May, Flying Officer P. Culp, captain of NS17510, positioned a second ground support team at Goose Bay. A convoy of thirteen jets (seven new Sabre VIs, three Sabre IIs and three Silver Stars) left St-Hubert the same day for Goose Bay. The jets were quickly serviced and, having picked up another Sabre II, went on to Narsarssuak the same day. As soon as the jets departed, the support North Star followed.

The crossing to Keflavik was made on 12 May, with the convoy now up to fifteen aircraft including another Sabre II added at Narsarssuak. Jenkins switched to NS17514 at Dorval and made another shuttle run to Keflavik that coincided with the arrival of the convoy. High surface winds at Keflavik kept the jets grounded on 13 May, but this did not stop Jenkins from going to Goose Bay for another load of Sabre spares and equipment, which he brought back to Keflavik the following day. Meanwhile, Culp and his crew went to Kinloss with a ground support team, and the convoy of fifteen jets — minus one unserviceable Sabre VI and plus one Silver Star— made the crossing to Kinloss on 14 May. On 15 May, six Sabre VIs were delivered to Baden-Söllingen while the four Silver Stars and six Sabre IIs (including one added at Kinloss) were flown to Manchester. With the departure of the jets, Culp and his crew embarked the ground support team and positioned their North Star at Baden-Söllingen. They conducted a shuttle run to London the next day, departed for Keflavik on 18 May, and returned to Montreal on 19 May. Jenkins and his crew had left Keflavik on 15 May and made the trip back to base the same day, including a stop at Goose Bay.[28]

On 12 May, making the first of five shuttle runs, Flying Officer Glover and his crew arrived at Resolute Bay in NS17515 with construction engineering personnel from RCAF Station Lachine to carry out the plumbing and electrical phases of the power plant project. Over the next four days and as many shuttles, Glover and his crew hauled in the construction materials, leaving for the last time on 17 May. The evening before, Resolute received a Scandinavian Airlines DC6B that stopped for ninety minutes to check out the airfield facilities and file a flight plan before departing on a direct flight of eleven hours and fourteen minutes to Stockholm.[29]

June

On 6 June, Wing Commander A.J. Mackie was transferred from Air Force Headquarters to No 426 Squadron as the new Commanding Officer; Wing Commander Lupton was posted to the Canadian Joint Staff in Washington on 30 July 1955.[30]

At 1630 hours on 9 June, NS17515 (captained by Flying Officer Webber) arrived as SF5 in Resolute Bay with Escott Reid, the Canadian High Commissioner to India, aboard with Mr. Allesy, Chief Editor of the *Winnipeg Tribune*. During their stay they visited the Eskimo encampment and were briefed by Dr. Y.O. Fortier on *Operation FRANKLIN*. The visitors departed by North Star for Churchill the following morning.[31]

Another combined logistics and training flight with an augmented crew left Dorval for Churchill in NS17516 during the afternoon of 13 June. Captained by Flight Lieutenant McBride, the aircraft stopped at Churchill for thirty-five minutes before heading for Resolute Bay, where a sixteen-hour crew rest was taken. Departing early in the evening of 14 June, the flight went directly to Prestwick, a run of eleven hours and forty-five minutes. On 18 June, the crew stopped at North Luffenham, Marville and Grostenquin, ending up at No 3 Wing Zweibrücken. On 20 June, after a brief stop at Baden-Söllingen, the flight went on to Rabat-Salé in Morocco. The next day, the flight stopped at Lajes and, on 22 June, made the over-water hop to Bermuda, which took eleven hours and five minutes. The flight was back at base on 23 June.[32]

McBride and his crew had cleared the Air Division in advance of a massive NATO exercise called *CARTE BLANCHE* that was held in western Europe from 20 June to 28 June. All twelve squadrons of the Air Division took part in the exercise, which featured a huge allied armada of 3,000 aircraft. *CARTE BLANCHE* was the reason why no *RANDOM* operations were conducted in June.

Maritime warfare exercises in the Bermuda area resulted in the deployment of two Maritime Reconnaissance units from Greenwood to that island. On 24 June, NS17509 (captained by Flight Lieutenant W. Dick) went to Greenwood to pick up personnel and equipment bound for Bermuda. Two shuttle runs accomplished the task and the crew returned to Dorval on 26 June, having flown a total of twenty-three hours since their departure.[33]

The 1955 re-supply of the Arctic weather stations, *Operation NORS II*, was planned in January, at an interdepartmental conference organized by the Department of Transport. Air Transport Command was represented by Group Captain Johntson and Wing Commander McVeigh from Headquarters and Flight Lieutenant R. Raike from RCAF Station Lachine. the amphibious operation involved the Canadian Coast Guard icebreakers *C.D. Howe*, *N.B. MacLean* and *D'Iberville*, and two chartered vessels, the SS *Gander Bay* and the MV *Maruba*. The Resolute Bay Co-ordinator at Lachine would be Flight Lieutenant G.R.A. Kyle, and at Resolute the RCAF Beachmaster would be Flight Lieutenant J.R. Grant, assisted by Flying Officer R.W. Glover. All three officers were North Star captains. On 17 June, the Department of Transport issued Operation Order NORS II, which started the chain of events leading to the beginning of re-supply operations in August.[34]

On the afternoon of 24 June, Flying Officer Buechler brought NS17515 in at Resolute Bay from Churchill, having left Dorval the previous day. On board was Mr. Courtney, a British war correspondent, construction maintenance unit personnel, and members of the Bull Gang. Flight Lieutenant Kyle was also on the flight, having been in Dorval to iron out issues related to *NORS II*. That evening, Mr. Courtney showed films with commentary by himself.

The following afternoon, students on the Specialist Navigation Course at Winnipeg arrived in Resolute Bay as crew members on three different aircraft on a high Arctic navigation exercise: a Lancaster from No 408 (Photo) Squadron, a Neptune from No 405 (Maritime Reconnaissance) Squadron and a North Star from No 426 (Transport) Squadron captained by Flight Lieutenant Jenkins. Buechler and his crew left to carry out a shuttle run to Thule. Those not on duty that evening enjoyed an illustrated lecture by Mr. Courtney.

During the morning of 26 June, Neptune 24107 crashed on take-off. Premature selection of the undercarriage was considered to be the chief cause of the accident, in which no one was hurt and the aircraft suffered relatively light damage. The airfield, however, had to be closed until a Lorain crane could raise the Neptune, which was towed away from the runway with its undercarriage locked in position. A mobile repair party would restore the Neptune to flying condition so it could return to Greenwood.

While in Resolute Bay, Kyle and the other members of the detachment inspected the sea lines, the aviation gas and oil lines and the pump houses. On the afternoon of 27 June, Kyle returned to Montreal with Buechler, who had come back from Thule with NS17515. Jenkins left for base at midnight with the Neptune crew aboard.[35]

At the end of June, Air Force Headquarters announced that No 426 (T) Squadron would resume flights to Indochina in July in support of personnel changes on the truce teams. The operation, scheduled to end by October, was to include five round trips transporting passengers (about twenty-five truce team members per flight) and freight to and from Indochina. The flights were routed through Gander, Lajes, Gibraltar, Basra, Karachi and Calcutta, and back by the same route in reverse.[36]

July

In July, the overseas ferry of Sabre jets to No 1 Air Division resumed; the RCAF was running out of storage space for Sabre VIs fresh from the assembly line at Canadair. Four of the five RANDOM operations conducted in the second half of 1955 would be devoted entirely to Sabre VI aircraft.

On 1 July, Flying Officer Schwanky positioned NS17506 in St-Hubert, embarked a ground support team from No 1 OFU, and airlifted them to Goose Bay. The following morning, twenty-nine Sabre VIs of Operation RANDOM 15 made the hop to Goose Bay, followed by the second North Star assigned to the mission, there to remain for three days because the weather at Narsarssuak was unsuitable for jets. On 7 July, twenty-eight Sabres (one was unserviceable) made the crossing to Greenland, following NS17517 and a support team, and NS17506 flew to Keflavik. On 8 July, the jets crossed to Iceland, where the operation stalled again for a day because of fog at Kinloss. Kinloss was still closed on 10 July, so the convoy of twenty-eight Sabres was redirected to Prestwick. After refuelling, twenty-five Sabres carried on to Baden-Söllingen; the other three aircraft in the convoy had mechanical problems and could not be delivered until the following day. On 12 July, NS17517 brought most of the ferry pilots from Baden-Söllingen to London, where they spent the night; the flight continued to Keflavik the next morning, and arrived back in Montreal on 14 July.[37]

On 2 July, Flying Officer McBride and his crew left base in NS17504, stopped briefly in Ottawa to pick up passengers, and flew to Winnipeg where they embarked students from the Specialist Navigation Course and took them, first, to Churchill and then, the next day, to Resolute Bay, where the course members used NS17504 for more than seven hours of high-latitude training on 4 July and 6 July. On 8 July, they conducted two training flights, one seven hours and fifteen minutes long and the other lasting six hours and ten minutes. On returning to Resolute Bay, the aircraft was refuelled and the flight carried on through Churchill to Winnipeg to disembark the student navigators. After a rest stop, McBride and his crew returned to base on 10 July.[38]

The first of five flights to the Far East departed Dorval on 6 July: NS17525 (captained by Squadron Leader C.S. Olsen), carrying twenty-six Army officers and one RCAF officer assigned to truce teams in Indochina. After stops at Gander, Lajes, Gibraltar, Malta, Cyprus, Basra, Karachi and Calcutta, the flight reached Saigon early in the afternoon of 12 July. The crew and their passengers were transported by bus to the Majestic Hotel, where they were met by a crowd of young rowdies vociferously chanting opposition to the presence of the Truce Commission. As the front entrance was heavily guarded, the crew and the truce team members were spirited into the hotel through a back alley entrance. The demonstration broke up a little later and everyone was able to relax and get some rest. On 15 July, the flight left Saigon with twenty-five returning truce team members who were highly pleased to be headed home. Using the outbound route in reverse, the flight was back at Dorval on 23 July.[39]

At 1230 hours on 13 July, Flying Officer Webber and his crew arrived over Resolute Bay in NS17504 — having left base the previous day and stopped overnight at Churchill — and found the airfield below limits because of low ceilings and fog, so the flight was diverted to Thule. They returned the next morning, bringing in both RCAF Beachmasters and twenty airmen fresh out basic training for the Bull Gang being formed to steam-clean and store some 4,500 fuel drums at the beach. Webber and his crew quickly departed again for Churchill and Dorval. At Resolute Bay, the Beachmasters reviewed the plans for *Operation NORS II* and inspected the beach areas and the jetties; Flying Officer Glover would take over as Detachment Commander after this re-supply was completed.

On 17 July, NS17502 (captained by Flying Officer Schwanky) brought in a mobile repair party of fourteen technicians from No 6 Repair Depot at Trenton to repair the Neptune that crashed on take-off on 26 June.[40]

An Organization Order received at RCAF Station Lachine authorized the formation of No 2 Movements Unit (Air), effective 15 July 1955, to supervise and control the handling of all passengers, freight and mail arriving or departing from Lachine by service aircraft, and to provide "movement controllers air" (MCAs) for flying duties as specified by the Station Commander at Lachine. (The transportation technician trade had been redesignated MCA; it would eventually be known as "loadmaster".) The movements unit was also responsible for weighing Air Transport Command aircraft at Dorval, and for the Goose Bay detachment.[41]

Summer was Cadet season for the RCAF, and Lachine was involved as a collector unit and provider of air transport. On 15 July, twenty-eight Air Cadets began arriving from various Canadian cities in preparation for their 21 July departure by North Star on an overseas tour. Mr. Ross, Secretary of the Air Cadet League of Canada, and Wing Commander Scovill, Air Cadet Liaison Officer at Air Force Headquarters, were present to brief the Cadets before their departure. On 18 July, twenty-six more Air Cadets started assembling at Lachine, preparing to leave on 23 July for a tour of the United States. On 21 July, twenty-six U.S. Civil Air Patrol Cadets arrived at Lachine to begin a tour of Canada, and a reception was held for them at Dorval. On 26 July, thirty-six Air Training Corps Cadets from Britain arrived at Lachine to begin a tour of Canada and were welcomed with a reception at Lachine.[42]

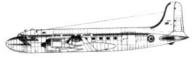

RANDOM 16, the month's second overseas ferry operation, got under way on 25 July, when two North Stars each embarked an OFU ground crew team and took them to Goose Bay.

The next day, Flying Officer Carss and his crew in NS17506 flew one team to Narsarssuak, and twenty-six Sabre VIs made the flight to Goose Bay, where they waited for three days for an improvement in the Greenland weather. A double hop to Greenland and Iceland was made on 30 July, and another to Kinloss and No 4 Wing Baden-Söllingen the next day. By 1 August, all twenty-six Sabres were delivered to No 4 Wing, twenty-five on 31 July and one the next day that had been delayed at Kinloss by hydraulic problems. North Star 17506 followed the Sabres from Keflavik to Baden-Söllingen and left for Langar and Prestwick on 2 August. An hour after departing for Keflavik, mechanical problems forced the aircraft to return to Prestwick. The flight finally made it to Iceland on 4 August and was back at base on 6 August.[43]

The second North Star flight to Saigon departed on 27 July with twenty-six truce team members and about 4,000 pounds of freight, baggage and mail. The flight followed the same route taken by Olsen's crew and was back in Montreal on 12 August.[44]

August

In August, the squadron was tasked with several domestic flights to transport reservists and cadets to and from exercises and summer camps.

On 10 August, RCAF Station Lachine took a break from its hectic round of activities for its Annual Sports Day at the Canadian National Railway Recreational Grounds adjacent to the station. All Regular Force personnel and their families were able to participate in a wide range of events that day.

At the end of the month, Lachine was given increased responsibility for the RCAF Detachment at Great Whale River, mainly in the areas of providing flying control services, radio communications and accommodation for transient personnel.[45]

After weeks of preparation, *Operation NORS II* began on 10 August with the arrival at Resolute Bay of the icebreakers *C.D. Howe* and the *N.B. MacLean*, and the departure of Flying Officer Carss and his crew in NS17525 from Dorval for Resolute with a load of cargo and twenty-five passengers, including Mr. Stark of the Department of External Affairs and Mr. English of the Department of Trade and Commerce, whom he picked up in Ottawa on the way. The next afternoon, NS17525 arrived in Resolute and off-loaded, and Carss then went on to Winnipeg to embark more passengers and continued to Churchill, where the flight remained overnight. On 12 August, Carss and his crew flew directly to Winnipeg, a seven-hour and forty-minute run, picked up more cargo and again stayed the night at Churchill. Meanwhile, at Resolute Bay, the *N.B. MacLean* started to discharge its cargo of lumber and empty drums brought from Thule for the U.S. Weather Bureau detachment.

On 13 August, Carss returned to Resolute Bay, embarked a full load of passengers (including Mr. Stark and Mr. English), and flew first to Coral Harbour and then to Churchill, where the airfield was below limits so the flight was diverted to The Pas, where it stopped for the night. After reaching Churchill the next day, the flight continued on to Winnipeg and returned to base on 15 August. At Resolute Bay, on the morning of 15 August, the *N.B. MacLean* departed for the convoy area in an attempt to help the *Gander Bay*, which was delayed with the other ships of the re-supply convoy by the ice in Baffin Bay and Lancaster Sound. On 16 August, the heavy ice conditions caused by high winds forced the *C.D. Howe* out of the bay at Resolute.

On 17 August, Group Captain Johnston arrived in NS17521 with an Air Transport Command Headquarters inspection team. After a briefing for the inspection team by the Detachment Commander, Flight Lieutenant Hibbard, and the Beachmasters on the shipping developments and outlook, Johnston and his crew toured the main camp, the beacon sites and the beach area. As the ice continued to keep the *C.D. Howe* out of the bay, the visitors were unable to witness unloading operations before the departure of the inspection team for Great Whale and Dorval on the morning of 18 August. The newly promoted Flight Lieutenant Glover officially took over that day as Detachment Commander.

On 25 August, the ships in the re-supply convoy reached Resolute Bay and unloading operations began; the cargo was ashore by 2 September and the bulk oil four days later. Also on 24 August, the service flight captained by Flying Officer Schwanky brought in Flight Lieutenant Coté and his crew from Greenwood to take their Neptune home. On 1 September, they test-flew the Neptune and then departed on the first leg to Churchill with the gear down for safety.

Anticipating the end of unloading operations, two North Stars (captained by Flight Lieutenant Jenkins and Flying Officer Charchuk) arrived at Resolute Bay on 1 September, and Jenkins departed that evening for Churchill and Montreal with Flight Lieutenant Hibbard and most of the Bull Gang. Charchuk followed him the next evening with a group of stevedores.[46]

Operation RANDOM 17 began for No 426 Squadron on 15 August with the despatch of two North Stars to St-Hubert, where they picked up two ground support teams and airlifted them to Goose Bay. On 16 August, Flying Officer Charchuk and his crew in NS17516 carried on to Narsarssuak with one team and twenty-four Sabre VIs made the hop to Goose Bay, where they were held up for two days by bad weather at Narsarssuak; on 19 August, conditions were ideal and they made the crossing, and Jenkins and his crew airlifted a ground support team to Keflavik and returned to base. The next day, the Sabres made the double hop to Keflavik and Kinloss, followed by Charchuk and his crew in NS17516. On 21 August, twelve of the Sabres were delivered to No 3 Wing and the other twelve went to No 4 Wing, and on 22 August, Charchuk flew from Kinloss to Prestwick to drop off the ground support team and carried on to Baden-Söllingen, where they spent the night. In the morning, Charchuk and his crew embarked the first contingent of ferry pilots, flew to Zweibrücken to pick up the rest at No 3 Wing, and then began the homeward journey by way of Prestwick and Keflavik, returning to Montreal on 24 August.[47]

The third aircraft to be despatched to Saigon was NS17504, which left Montreal on 17 August captained by Flying Officer L. Joron carrying twenty-five truce team members and about 3,500 pounds of baggage, mail and freight. Following the route taken by the previous two flights, it reached Calcutta on 23 August. The next day, the flight arrived in Saigon, disembarked the passengers, unloaded the cargo, and then began a week of waiting for the homeward-bound observers to arrive from their various posts and brief their replacements. This period was to be spent at Singapore, so Joron and his crew went there as soon as the aircraft was unloaded, and returned to Saigon on 31 August. The next morning, the flight departed with the homeward-bound truce team members, using the same airfields as it had on the outbound trip and reaching base on 7 September.[48]

September

Operation RANDOM 18 got under way on 7 September. Two North Stars flew across the St. Lawrence River to St-Hubert and each embarked a ground support team and flew to Goose Bay. The next morning, one of the support teams was transported to Narsarssuak by Flying Officer A. Ronning and his crew in NS17512. That same day, twenty-three Sabre VIs made the hop to Goose Bay. The aircraft were refuelled and two sections of four aircraft each were already on their way to Greenland when they were recalled; Narsarssuak had reported poor weather moving in. The expected conditions failed to materialize, but the convoy was held at Goose Bay on 9 September, as the weather at Narsarssuak went below limits for jet aircraft. Conditions improved on 10 September, and all twenty-three Sabres made a successful crossing to Greenland. The next day, twenty-three Sabres made the crossings to Keflavik and Kinloss and twenty-two made it to their destination, which was Zweibrücken. One Sabre was hung up at Kinloss with mechanical problems. This was the fastest crossing conducted by No 1 OFU to date, with the total flying time for the three crossings averaging five hours and fifteen minutes.

When the Sabres had departed from Goose Bay, the second North Star positioned a support team at Keflavik. Once the Sabres had left Greenland, Ronning and his crew took a ground support team to Kinloss. After the convoy departed from Keflavik, the team there was airlifted back to St-Hubert. Meanwhile, with the Sabres on their way from Kinloss to No 3 Wing, Ronning transported the second support team to Prestwick to link up with a service flight for the trip back to Montreal. After an overnight stop, Ronning and his crew went to Baden-Söllingen. The next morning, the flight returned to No 3 Wing to embark the ferry pilots and other passengers, and then headed for an overnight stop in London. On 14 September, the flight left London for Keflavik and Montreal, arriving back at base the following day.[49]

On 18 September, the now-traditional Battle of Britain Sunday observances were held in downtown Montreal. A contingent of airmen from RCAF Station Lachine attended church services and then marched in the commemorative parade.

The fourth aircraft to be despatched to Saigon — NS17521, captained by Flight Lieutenant Lamb with the new Squadron Commander, Wing Commander A.L. Mackie, as first officer — left base on 21 September carrying sixteen truce team members and nearly 5,000 pounds of baggage and freight. The route followed, both outbound and inbound, was the same as on previous flights, including a two-day pause at Singapore after arrival in Saigon on 28 September. The flight returned to Saigon on 1 October, embarked the tour-expired observers and started the long journey home, returning to base on 9 October.[50]

As the sea-borne *Operation NORS II* wound down, preparations were being made for the fall re-supply of the Arctic weather stations by air. Flying Officer Carss brought in NS17506 to Resolute Bay on the afternoon of 8 September, embarked forty passengers, returned to Churchill and then continued on to base. The departure of these passengers, and of 125 others airlifted out during the previous several days, greatly eased accommodation problems for the detachment.

Instructions had been forwarded from Air Transport Command Headquarters authorizing Scandinavian Airlines (SAS) to erect an antenna for the radio equipment the company had installed in Resolute Bay. Work on the antenna began on 9 September. The Department of Transport party finished putting up the antenna on 15 September and was airlifted out that day by NS17525, captained by Flying Officer Dunford. On the same flight were the personnel of the Construction Maintenance Unit, under Warrant Officer Nicholson, who had spent the summer completing a wide range of projects. Dunford returned from Churchill on 17 September to airlift out more personnel, including a team of geologists who had spent the summer surveying the Arctic islands.

On 20 September, Flying Officer Reed and his crew arrived at Resolute Bay in NS17502 with spares and equipment for the re-supply aircraft, which arrived shortly after, led by Squadron Leader R.K. Trumley and his three C-119s from No 436 (T) Squadron. The airlift operation swung into high gear the next day. The mission was expected to take forty trips: twenty-six to Eureka and the rest to Isachsen and Mould Bay. To clear up the re-supply backlog from Churchill, Reed conducted shuttle runs on 21 September and 22 September. Flying Officer Carss' arrival on 29 September in NS17502 coincided with the completion of re-supply operation and the rotation of personnel at the weather stations. After embarking twenty-nine passengers, the service flight returned to base after a stop at Churchill.[51]

During the Korean War, the South African Air Force flew USAF Sabre aircraft, which were returned when the Flying Cheetah Squadron went home. When the time came to replace its Vampires, South Africa bought thirty-four Canadair Sabre VIs. On 21 September, Group Captain R.D.P. Blagrave chaired a meeting at Air Force Headquarters to set up a ferry program to deliver the SAAF Sabres, the last of which was due off the production line in July 1956. As part of this program, twenty SAAF pilots would be attached to No 1 OFU at St-Hubert after being phased through the Sabre OTU at Chatham. The next day, Wing Commander G.J.J. Edwards chaired a meeting at Air Transport Command Headquarters to discuss the operational aspects of the South Africa ferry program. Several SAAF pilots trained at Chatham before the South Africans decided to transport the aircraft by sea and the mission was scrapped. The Sabres were readied for shipment at Canadair's Cartierville plant and arrived in South Africa in August 1956.[52]

October

Apart from the overseas and domestic service flights, the runs to Resolute Bay were high on the RCAF's priority list.

Flying Officer Reed arrived from Churchill at 1400 hours on 9 October in NS17525. Visibility was very poor in the blowing snow, and two passes were needed to get the aircraft on the ground. This particular flight brought in the foam glass insulation for the water pipeline at the detachment. The re-supply cleanup and the service flights due in on 13 October were delayed, as the conditions at the airfield were below operating limits. The next afternoon, Flying Officer Carss brought in NS17514 with Wing Commander Delaney and Flight Lieutenant Hibbard aboard to conduct a pre-AOC's inspection tour. Carss, who had returned to Churchill on a shuttle run, was prevented by heavy blowing snow from returning to Resolute Bay until 16 October; meanwhile, Delaney gave the camp and its buildings, the personnel and their quarters and the beacon sites a thorough going-over, and even visited the Eskimo camp. When Carss returned, he brought tools and spare parts for overhauling one of the main electrical generators. Carss and his crew departed for Churchill at 1600 hours with Delaney and Hibbard aboard. The aircraft was diverted to The Pas as Churchill was closed by weather, finally arriving in to Churchill on 17 October and then returning to base after stops at Winnipeg and Ottawa.

After a two-day delay due to weather, Air Commodore Carscallen and his Air Transport Command Headquarters party arrived at Resolute Bay on 27 October to make their semi-annual inspection of the airfield and its facilities. Shortly after his arrival at 1420 hours, Carscallen inspected the camp area and visited the Eskimo camp. The inspection party included the Protestant chaplain, Flight Lieutenant Hewitt, who held services in the library at 1800 hours. After an informal dinner, Flight Lieutenant Glover, gave a briefing on the detachment and its activities. Carscallen and his group departed the following morning for Montreal. Later that day, Flying Officer Webber brought in NS17521 from Churchill with several replacements for detachment staff, and departed a couple of hours later for more cargo. The staff replacements included Warrant Officer Johnson from CMU Calgary, to inspect the power plant, and Corporal Derash and an assistant, who were there to put the detachment members through a two-week ground defence course. Webber returned from Churchill on the afternoon of 29 October with the rest of the backlogged cargo destined for Resolute Bay. As soon as the aircraft was unloaded and refuelled, Webber embarked ten passengers and took off again for Churchill and base.[53]

Operation RANDOM 19 got under way on 20 October. The last Sabre ferry operation of the year, *RANDOM 19* was the clean-up *RANDOM*, in which all aircraft left behind during previous ferry flights would be delivered. Flying Officer T. Charchuk and his crew positioned NS17511 at St-Hubert, embarked a ground support party and headed for Goose Bay. The next morning, a convoy of twenty-two Sabre VIs and four Sabre IIs made the flight to Goose Bay; four more Sabre VIs would be added to the convoy as it progressed along the ferry route. A second support aircraft, NS17516, captained by Flying Officer P. Major, followed the jets to Goose Bay with another ground support party aboard. Poor weather at Narsarssuak held up the convoy at Goose Bay for two days, but this did not prevent Major from delivering a ground party there on 23 October.

On 24 October, the Sabres crossed to Greenland and Charchuk took a support party to Keflavik to wait for the convoy. Due to mechanical problems and the reduced daylight hours of those high latitudes, it took two days, 25 October and 26 October, for the entire convoy (now numbering thirty Sabres) to reach Keflavik. Most of the Sabres were able to carry on straight to Kinloss, and the rest made the crossing on 27 October. After refuelling, the four Sabre IIs continued to Manchester; the rest of the convoy's twenty-six Sabre VIs were delivered to Zweibrücken on 28 October. Charchuk and his crew left Keflavik for base that day, while Major went to Zweibrücken after stopping at Manchester to pick up Sabre pilots, and RAF Station Blackbushe in Hampshire to drop off passengers. On 30 October, Major returned to Blackbushe to re-embark his passengers and then went to Langar. The next day the flight left for Keflavik, where the crew took a twelve-hour rest, and returned to base on 1 November.[54]

November

Resolute Bay was the destination of two service flights in November. The first was carried out by Flying Officer L. Joron and his crew. On 9 November the flight stopped at Ottawa to pick up cargo and passengers and carried on to Rivers, Manitoba, where it stopped for the night. Proceeding to Winnipeg the next day, the flight was held up for two days as the weather at Churchill was below landing limits. On 12 November, an attempt was made to reach Churchill but the weather, which had been marginal at best, deteriorated as the flight progressed and Joron diverted to The Pas. The crew were able to reach Churchill the following morning, but the airfield was soon closed by blowing snow that grounded the flight for another two days. Finally, on 15 November, conditions at Churchill improved enough for the flight to continue to Resolute Bay, where it remained overnight. Joron returned to Churchill on 16 November, and went on to base the next day after a brief stop in Winnipeg.

The second run to Resolute Bay was made by Flying Officer Cline and his crew, who arrived in the afternoon of 24 November with supplies and eleven passengers, including Flight Lieutenant J. McDonald, Warrant Officer Clement and Warrant Officer Smith from Air Force Headquarters to check out the detachment's power and electrical installations. Also on board were Flying Officer Gagnon and four supply accountants from RCAF Station Lachine to compile inventories before a new accounting system was to be introduced. The last passenger was RCMP Constable R. Gibson, returning to his post after six weeks of leave. The service flight left for Churchill and base a couple of hours after its arrival. For the 1955 Christmas season, supply drops to the Arctic outposts would be carried out by C-119s from both Dorval and Edmonton.[55]

On 10 November Air Commodore Carscallen arrived at Lachine with a party of staff officers to inspect the station. The next day was Remembrance Day, and station personnel attended church services and participated in the parade held downtown.[56]

The fifth flight to Saigon left Montreal on 25 November with truce team members, baggage, equipment and mail. NS17521, captained by Squadron Leader Trotter, had an augmented crew aboard and the flight doubled as a training trip. The first stop was Gander and, since poor weather was forecast for both Gander and Lajes, the flight went next to Argentia, where it remained overnight. The aircraft left for Lajes the next morning and, after a refuelling stop carried on to Madrid where a crew rest was taken. This was the first visit of a squadron aircraft to Madrid, and they took the opportunity to check out the facilities should the need arise to use the airport again.

On 27 November, the flight departed Madrid for Malta, where it refuelled, and then carried on to Cyprus. On 29 November, it left Cyprus for Basra and Karachi, and finally arrived at Calcutta on 1 December. The next morning, the passengers and cargo were delivered to Saigon and the flight headed for Singapore and a three-day break. Since the journey back to Canada would be made by the mid-Pacific route, Manila was the next stop on 5 December, and the flight arrived in Tokyo on 7 December. Leaving Tokyo on 10 December, Trotter and his crew went to Wake Island, Honolulu and San Francisco, arriving in Vancouver on 14 December. The flight was back at base the next day.[57]

December

Early in December, the squadron was detailed to provide two aircraft to carry disaster relief supplies for flood victims in Pakistan and India. Flying Officer P. Major, with an augmented crew, left Montreal on 5 December with a full load of Red Cross blankets and other supplies as well as diplomatic mail for New Delhi. The flight was routed through Gander, the Azores, Lisbon, Malta, Nicosia and Bahrain, arriving at Palam Airport, New Delhi, on 9 December. After a three-day layover the crew returned to base on 16 December by way of Bahrain, Malta, Langar and Keflavik.[58]

The second aircraft, NS17525, with an augmented crew, was captained by Flying Officer J. Forest. It left Montreal for Karachi with a full load of Red Cross supplies on 7 December. Routed through Gander, Lajes, Gibraltar, Malta, Nicosia and Bahrain, the flight arrived at Karachi on 11 December. The crew took a three-day rest before the flight headed for home on 14 December via Bahrain, Malta, Langar and Keflavik, reaching Montreal on 17 December.[59]

The squadron carried out two service flights to Resolute Bay in December. On 15 December, Flying Officer Culp brought in NS17514 at 1630 hours, departing two hours later for Churchill for another load of supplies. On board was Flight Lieutenant Hibbard, who had come to meet with the Detachment Commander, Flight Lieutenant Glover, and Mr. E. Shea of the Department of Transport, based in Winnipeg, whose mission was to trace the source of static that was interfering with radio reception. The Protestant and Roman Catholic padres also visited the detachment and returned to Churchill with Culp. NS17514 was back at Resolute Bay the next day, departing nearly six hours later on only three engines because of mechanical difficulties. Hibbard was aboard the flight as it headed back to base.

NS17504 was the next squadron aircraft to arrive at Resolute Bay, coming in at 0600 hours on 19 December bringing an electrician from Churchill, Flight Sergeant Beaton, who determined that a loose connection in the power line leading to the runway was the cause of lighting difficulties. The flight departed for Churchill and base at 1830 hours with fifteen staff members, including Flying Officer Gagnon's supply accounting party.[60]

Most of the squadron members were back at base for Christmas, the most notable exceptions being a slip crew in Prestwick and the detachment at Langar. Air Commodore Carscallen concluded his Christmas greeting to all units with the following passage:

> I have recently visited most units in our Command. In every case, I have been most pleased with what I have seen, and what you have accomplished during the past year, and wish to extend sincere congratulations for your splendid efforts.[61]

Lachine, 1955

PHOTO 151
Sabre VIs on Operation RANDOM 14; Narsarssuak, Greenland, 11 May 1955. (D. Eagles Collection)

PHOTO 152
The crew of NS17504 on their way to Saigon; Gibraltar, 19 August 1955. From left, back row: F/O Dick Brown (navigator), F/L Roy Nurse (pilot), F/O Joe Sare (radio officer) and F/O Louis Joron (captain), unidentified; front row: F/O Cleve Knight (radio officer) and F/O Don Thompson (pilot). (J. Sare Collection)

PHOTO 153
Mould Bay, Northwest Territories, August 1954. USAF photo reproduced by permission

PHOTO 154
Isachsen, Northwest Territories, August 1954. USAF photo reproduced by permission

Lachine, 1955

PHOTO 155
Eureka, Northwest Territories, August 1954. USAF photo reproduced by permission

PHOTO 156
Alert, Northwest Territories, September 1955. USAF photo reproduced by permission

PHOTO 157
Thule AB, Greenland, September 1955. USAF photo reproduced by permission

PHOTO 158
Sondrestrom AB, Greenland, September 1955. USAF photo reproduced by permission

Lachine, 1955

PHOTO 159
Narsarssuak AB, Greenland, September 1955. USAF photo reproduced by permission

PHOTO 160
Fort Chimo, Québec, September 1954. USAF photo reproduced by permission

PHOTO 161
Goose Bay, Labrador, September 1955. USAF photo reproduced by permission

PHOTO 162
Gander, Newfoundland, June 1954. USAF photo reproduced by permission

Lachine, 1955

PHOTO 163
Torbay, Newfoundland, November 1955. USAF photo reproduced by permission

PHOTO 164
Ernest Harmon AFB, Newfoundland, June 1954. USAF photo reproduced by permission

PHOTO 165

NAS Argentia, Newfoundland, November 1955. USAF photo reproduced by permission

PLATE 1: *Squadron Crest, 1952–1962. (Courtesy of the Canadian Forces)*

PLATE 2: *"Habbaniya Departure" trooping run leaving Iraq for Lydda, Palestine enroute to base November 1945, by Don Connolly. (reproduced with permission)*

PLATE 3: *"Goose Bay Express" returning to Dartmouth October 1946, by Don Connolly. (reproduced with permission)*

PLATE 4: *"Haneda Approach" Korean Airlift flight arriving at Tokyo March 1952, by Don Connolly. (reproduced with permission)*

PLATE 5: *"Departing Bluie" Sabres of Operation Leap Frog 2 leaving Bluie west 1, Greenland for Keflavik, Iceland October 1952, by Don Connolly. (reproduced with permission)*

PLATE 6: *No 426 Squadron Standard, presented by the Honourable Pauline M. McGibbon, Lieutenant Governor of the Province of Ontario at CFB Trenton on 19 August, 1978. Emblazoned on the Standard are the squadron's five Major Battle Honours and three of its subsidiary Battle Honours. (Courtesy of the Canadian Forces)*

PLATE 7: *Operations Building, Shemya AFB; 1950. (J. Henry Collection)*

PLATE 8: *The runway at Shemya AFB: 10,000 feet long and 500 feet wide; summer 1950. (A.L. Quickfall Collection)*

PLATE 9: *Main Street, Shemya; autumn 1950. (A.L. Quickfall Collection)*

PLATE 10: *Transient Crew Quarters, Shemya AFB; winter 1950–51. (R.J. Brown Collection)*

PLATE 11: *Cliffs at Shemya; November 1950. (J. Henry Collection)*

PLATE 12: *Jack Blowers and George Howard (second and third from left) on the Shemya cliffs; November 1950. (A. St. Laurent Collection)*

PLATE 13: *F/O J. Henry; Shemya, autumn 1950. (J. Henry Collection)*

PLATE 14: *F/O Dick Spratt, F/O Syd Quickfall and F/O Danny Farrell; Shemya; autumn 1950. (A.L. Quickfall Collection)*

PLATE 15: *Derelict USAF search-and-rescue B-17; Shemya AFB, winter 1950–51. (A. St. Laurent Collection)*

PLATE 16: *An unseasonable snowfall; Haneda AFB, February 1951. From left: A. St. Laurent, J. Blowers and B. Cummings. (A. St. Laurent Collection)*

PLATE 17: *The entrance to Ebisu Camp; Tokyo, February 1951. (A. St. Laurent Collection)*

PLATE 18: *The front door of the Marunouchi Hotel, Tokyo; spring 1951. (J.–L. Denis Collection)*

PLATE 19: *Marunouchi Hotel staff in Japanese traditional dress; Tokyo, autumn 1950. (J. Henry Collection)*

PLATE 20: *F/O J.–L. Denis returns to Marunouchi Hotel after a shopping spree downtown; Tokyo, autumn 1951. (J.–L. Denis Collection)*

PLATE 21: *LAC A. St. Laurent shops for souvenirs near Ebisu Camp; Tokyo, autumn 1950. (A. St. Laurent Collection)*

PLATE 22: *NS17510 (F/O A.L. Quickfall, captain) makes a refuelling stop; Midway Island, 22 May 1951. (J.–L. Denis Collection)*

PLATE 23: *A gooney bird; Midway Island, 22 May 1951. (J.–L. Denis Collection)*

PLATE 24: *Drifters' Reef, the social centre on Wake Island; May 1951. (J.–L. Denis Collection)*

PLATE 25: *Transient quarters; Wake Island, February 1951. (J.–L. Denis Collection)*

PLATE 26: *F/O J.–L. Denis explores relics of the Second World War during crew rest; Wake Island, February 1951. (J.–L. Denis Collection)*

PLATE 27: *Hula dancers at the Moana Hotel, Honolulu; spring 1951. (Tim Timmins Collection)*

PLATE 28: *Canadian Press correspondent Bill Boss and the No 426 Squadron crew with whom he is flying home — Boss gave them the hats; Haneda AFB, 27 August 1951. From left: Bill McKnight (flight engineer), Jim Morrison (captain), Bill Boss, J.–L. Denis (navigator) and Russ Roane (pilot). (J.–L. Denis Collection)*

PLATE 29: *Members of the No 426 Squadron detachment working on North Star engine; Haneda AFB, October 1951. (Tim Timmins Collection)*

PLATE 30: *F/O Tim Timmins, the commander of No 426 Squadron's detachment at Haneda AFB, outside Operations tent at Ashiya before departing for Korea; October 1951. (Tim Timmins Collection)*

PLATE 31: *Members of No 426 Squadron's Haneda detachment in Seoul on a familiarization trip; October 1951. (Tim Timmins Collection)*

PLATE 32: *NS17504 being refuelled; RCAF Station Winnipeg, spring 1952. (J. Henry Collection)*

PLATE 33: *NS17504 at Churchill; May 1952. (J. Henry Collection)*

PLATE 34: *RCAF detachment buildings, Resolute Bay, NWT; October 1950. (DND RT–10–3)*

PLATE 35: *NS17504 being readied for departure at Resolute Bay, May 1952. (J. Henry Collection)*

PLATE 36: *NS17504 at The Pas after being diverted on a flight from Resolute Bay to Churchill; May 1952. (J. Henry Collection)*

PLATE 37: *Lancasters and a Mosquito in the dispersal area at Churchill; May 1952. (J. Henry Collection)*

PLATE 38: *From left: F/O Hugh Filleul, F/O Don Harrison and an unidentified companion take in the sights; Kamakura, Japan, June 1952. (J.–L. Denis Collection)*

PLATE 39: *F/L J. Sare (detachment commander) poses with children from a nearby Eskimo village; Resolute Bay, March 1957 (J. Sare Collection)*

PLATE 40: *Communications Flight C–119 and Dakota at Capodichino Airport; Naples, Italy, 13 November 1957. (J. Bugdale Collection)*

PHOTO 41: *NS17525 after an accident and fire; Athens, 21 June 1959. (L. Rodewolt Collection)*

PHOTO 42: *The burnt-out fuselage of NS17525; Athens, 21 June 1959. (J.A. Fullam Collection)*

CHAPTER 20

LACHINE, 1956

The 1956–1966 Long-Range Plan for the RCAF stated that the Canadian government would give priority to deterrent forces that would contribute most effectively to success in the initial phase of a global war. While "other forces" would be needed for operations in later phases, the importance of the initial phase and the limited resources available meant that these other forces necessarily were a lower priority for build-up. The plan offered no guidance for the development of forces for limited war supporting a United Nations action or other collective security operation.

For the RCAF, then, the top priority was air defence of the atomic-strike units based in the United States and western Europe, and the air defence forces comprised an early-warning system and an active air-defence system. In North America, the United States and Canada shared the responsibility for these systems, and the air defence of the region was co-ordinated with the U.S. Continental Air Defense Command.[1] Air defence of atomic-strike forces in western Europe was shared by several NATO countries, including Canada, whose contribution was the four fighter wings of No 1 (RCAF) Air Division.

The second priority went to such additional forces (and their support elements) that might be required for operations in the initial phase of an atomic war. These were the maritime air forces, which had to be effective in the early stages of hostilities to defend against a sea-borne atomic attack. The third and lowest priority for resources was any force (and its supporting elements) not directly involved in the first two priorities.

For both global and limited conflicts, the maintenance of an adequate air transport system was essential because, in modern warfare, personnel and materiel must often be transported quickly and at short notice, a task possible only with air transport; consequently, air transport was essential to the overall deterrent. The system might not contribute directly to vital military action during the initial phases of a conflict, but air transport was the only method with the flexibility and independence of action required to meet front-line emergency requirements for personnel and materiel. Also, it was the only form of transport that would be effective in certain kinds of disaster relief and rescue operations.

The RCAF air transport force was established to support other elements of the RCAF, other Canadian military forces, and other Canadian government departments and agencies as and when directed. In peacetime, air transport resources were allocated on a scale sufficient to support airborne training for the Canadian Army, and to meet urgent personnel and materiel requirements.

The essential elements of an air transport system are communications, ground support, and short-, medium- and long-range forces. In 1956, the RCAF air transport organization comprised four transport squadrons and one reconnaissance and survey squadron established for transport, troop-carrying, reconnaissance and photo-survey missions. The long-range transport squadron was No 426, the medium-range troop-carrying units were No 435 and No 436 squadrons, the special transport squadron was No 412, and the photo-survey reconnaissance squadron was No 408. The system also included No 1 Overseas Ferry Unit, which handled the trans-Atlantic delivery of jet-fighter and jet-trainer aircraft to No 1 Air Division.

The RCAF long-range plan did not envisage any major changes in the structure of Air Transport Command, but the relocation of Air Transport Command Headquarters and the selection of permanent locations for No 426 and No 436 squadrons were under active consideration. Although no increase in the number of air transport units was contemplated, the growing requirement for air transport was making it necessary to consider an increase in airlift capability. Apart from overseas requirements, the establishment of the Mid-Canada Line and the DEW Line was expected to entail a considerable demand for air transport.

By this time, the RCAF's long-range transport aircraft — the North Star — was considered obsolescent, although some of them would remain in service well into the 1960s. The RCAF Long-Range Plan conceded that the long-range fleet would have to be augmented and, eventually replaced. The construction of eight CL-44s at Canadair to replace the North Stars was already approved, and the goal was to acquire enough new aircraft to meet foreseeable air transport commitments and to provide for contingencies.[2]

In 1956, No 426 Squadron had twelve North Stars in its inventory, each with an assigned monthly utilization rate of 130 hours. Throughout the year, the squadron's primary destination was western Europe, with three scheduled flights per week to Langar, some of which extended to the fighter wings in France and Germany and the gunnery ranges in Morocco. The squadron also provided airlift support for seven *RANDOM* operations to Europe and two "reverse RANDOMs" to Canada, and transport support to *Operation NIMBLE BAT 1*, the first group of CF-100 Canuck all-weather fighters ferried to the Air Division. The year's work plan also included five truce team rotation flights to Indochina and back, and several ambitious long-range training flights.

In the last months of the year, events in the Middle East escalated into war between Israel and Egypt, with France and Britain intervening to defend their interests in the Suez Canal, and the United Nations was compelled to forestall involvement of the other great powers. Thus, No 426 Squadron was again tasked with missions in direct support of United Nations operations in the field.

January

The new year opened at Lachine with well-attended Sunday services at the station chapels, and dinner at the Airmen's Mess served to about 200 junior ranks by the Squadron Commander, Wing Commander Delaney, and twenty squadron officers and senior NCOs, followed by a lively sing-song in the lounge. The next day was the official New Year Levee, which attracted about 150 visitors to the Officers' Mess between 1200 and 1700 hours while the Air Officer Commanding, the Station Commander and several senior officers visited the messes at the Army's Quebec Command Headquarters, HMCS *Donnacona* and Air Defence Command Headquarters. Six other teams of six officers each visited other Navy, Army and Air Force messes in the greater Montreal area.

In January, as well as the scheduled and special flights, the squadron was tasked with delivering Red Cross supplies to India. On 9 January, Flying Officer Reed and his crew left Montreal in NS17525 for New Delhi, routed through Goose Bay and Narsarssuak (the weather at Keflavik was down) to Prestwick, Malta, Cyprus, Bahrain and Karachi, and arriving in New Delhi on 16 January. The crew returned to Dorval on 24 January via Bahrain, Cyprus, Malta, Langar and Keflavik.[3]

On 12 January, Flight Lieutenant Lamb brought in the first squadron flight of the year at Resolute Bay with nine passengers, including Flight Lieutenant Bradshaw, the Command Messing Officer, to inspect the messing facilities; Sergeant Haslem, a firefighter from RCAF Station Lachine, to conduct a fire inspection of the detachment buildings. The return flight to Churchill and base was delayed for nine hours because the oil lines on NS17514 had frozen. The lines had to be pre-heated before the engines could be started. On 26 January, Flying Officer Beuchler captained the next squadron flight, which brought in the new Detachment Commander, Flight Lieutenant J. Forest; a Construction Engineering party from Lachine led by Mr. Lockhart, to install a new boiler in the power plant; and several Air Transport Command supply technicians under Warrant Officer Desbiens to implement new accounting procedures for stores disbursed by the detachment. Buechler and his crew left the following morning for Coral Harbour and base.[4]

On 30 January, the squadron despatched a second flight to India with Red Cross supplies: North Star 17504, with an augmented crew captained by Squadron Leader Reid. This flight was routed via Lajes across the Mediterranean to Bahrain, Karachi and New Delhi, where it arrived on 4 February. Indian Customs officials held up the unloading of the cargo because the accompanying paperwork did not seem to be in order, but staff from the Canadian High Commission resolved the issue when Reid made it clear that he was quite prepared to take the cargo back. For the crew, the return flight was, in effect, a training exercise, with stops at Negombo in Ceylon, Singapore, Manila, Tokyo, Wake island and Honolulu, where they arrived on 14 February and got hung up for a week because of adverse headwinds. The flight made it to San Francisco on 21 February and returned to base the next day after a refuelling stop in Winnipeg.[5]

February

On 8 February, Flight Lieutenant J. Forest formally accepted the command of RCAF Detachment Resolute Bay from Flight Lieutenant R.W. Glover, who had completed nearly seven months in the post, and Flying Officer Ronning and his crew left Dorval in NS17502 for Resolute Bay via Ottawa and Winnipeg. On 9 February, NS17502 left Winnipeg, refuelled at Churchill and headed for Resolute Bay, but had to turn back after two and a half hours as the weather at Resolute Bay and Thule had gone below limits. The next day, Ronning and his crew airdropped medical supplies at Arctic Bay before carrying on to Resolute Bay, where they arrived at 1615 hours. Among the passengers they dropped off was Flight Lieutenant King, the Station Medical Officer from Lachine, who had come to conduct a medical inspection of the detachment.

At 1815 hours, Ronning and his crew departed on a shuttle run to Churchill for more supplies and equipment, and the detachment personnel gathered to see *The Eddie Cantor Story*, one of the new movies that came in on the North Star. NS17502 returned at 1525 hours on 11 February, and left again two hours later for Montreal, with Flight Lieutenant Glover and Flight Lieutenant King aboard.⁶

On 15 February, the year's first *Operation RANDOM* got off to a shaky start. Flying Officer Major and his crew positioned NS17512 at St-Hubert, embarked a ground support party and seven Sabre pilots, and headed for Goose Bay, where the pilots (with four others who had made the trip by T-33) were to test-fly sixteen Sabre VIs that had been in storage since November 1955. On 16 February it was snowing almost continuously, and the low ceilings and poor visibility delayed the test flights and the move of the main party from St-Hubert. The weather did not prevent Major and his crew from going on to Narsarssuak with technical personnel and spares, however, and that flight returned to Goose Bay the following day, and soon continued on to St-Hubert and Dorval.

Meanwhile, on 16 February, Flying Officer Ronning positioned NS17515, the second squadron aircraft assigned to the operation, at St-Hubert, but with the movement to Goose Bay scrubbed, he returned with his crew to Dorval. The next day, Ronning took NS17511 to St-Hubert, but the snow showers at Goose Bay were still delaying the operation so he returned to Dorval. On 18 February, the operation was still on hold, this time because of freezing rain in Montreal. The weather finally lifted on 19 February, and a convoy of fourteen Sabre VIs arrived at Goose Bay, followed from Dorval by Major in NS17512 while, Ronning went to St-Hubert to pick up the ground support crew; he then flew to Goose Bay as well.

With clear conditions at Goose Bay, the test flights of the stored Sabres were under way when Flight Lieutenant Himmelman, flying Sabre 23400, suffered an engine failure at 35,000 feet; unable to relight his engine, he had to make a forced landing — actually a Category A crash — on a frozen lake some eighty miles west of Goose Bay. Himmelman survived, and a Beaver from Goose Bay picked him up an hour later.

Operation RANDOM 20 was delayed for five days by a combination of snow at Goose Bay and poor weather with high surface winds in Greenland, but Major and his crew managed not only to position a ground support party at Narsarssuak on 21 February, but also to fly back to base via Goose Bay the same day. On 24 February, Ronning made a supply run to Montreal, returning to Goose Bay the following day.

On 25 February, the weather was finally suitable and the convoy of twenty-four Sabres made the crossing to Greenland; Ronning airlifted a ground support party from Goose Bay to Keflavik. He returned to Narsarssuak on the afternoon of 26 February.

High winds at Narsarssuak on 26 February prevented the Duckbutts from taking off, so the convoy crossing to Iceland was cancelled. The same conditions prevailed the next day, further delaying the operation. The weather was suitable on 28 February, but the departure of the USAF *High Flight* operation (due out first) was delayed, so *RANDOM 20* was scrubbed. On 29 February, twenty-one Sabres made the crossing to Keflavik, leaving three behind with a variety of mechanical problems. The Sabres were delayed again for the next two days by bad weather at both Keflavik and Kinloss, but Ronning took his North Star out of Narsarssuak on 2 March to airlift the ground support party to Kinloss. On 3 March, the weather was ideal, but a USAF C-124 had gone missing during the night and all available American aircraft —

especially the Duckbutts — were out searching for it. Lacking the Duckbutts, *RANDOM 20* was delayed yet again, for two more days.

Starting on 3 March, the support North Star conducted a shuttle run to Prestwick, returning to Kinloss the following morning. A second shuttle was carried out to Prestwick that afternoon with the flight coming back to Kinloss on the morning of 5 March. With the Duckbutts still searching for the missing C-124, arrangements were made with the RAF to position two Shackleton maritime patrol aircraft in their place. The arrangement worked out well and the convoy of twenty-one RCAF Sabres made the crossing to Kinloss on 5 March. The USAF *High Flight* operation followed the Sabres out of Keflavik. After being refuelled, the twenty-one Sabres were successfully delivered to No 3 Wing at Zweibrücken. NS17511 left Kinloss for Zweibrücken shortly after the convoy, leaving eight airmen behind in case the three Sabres in Greenland managed to cross to Kinloss.

Space on the scheduled North Star flights was fully booked, so Air Transport Command Headquarters directed that the ferry personnel should travel back to Montreal by commercial airlines, so on 7 March Ronning and his crew delivered nineteen ferry pilots and two technical representatives to London to catch a flight home. Ronning carried on to Prestwick to meet the eight airmen from Kinloss, who had come by rail, and the flight continued on to Keflavik, where a twelve-hour crew rest was taken. They then boarded the Keflavik ground support party and headed for Goose Bay and Dorval, arriving at base early in the evening of 8 March. The OFU personnel then made the trip across Montreal to St-Hubert by bus.[7]

On 22 February, Flying Officer Carss and his crew positioned NS17521 in Ottawa where they embarked Lieutenant-General Howard D. Graham, the Chief of the General Staff, with a party of twenty-seven Army officers from the Staff College in Kingston. The flight then proceeded to El Paso, a ten-hour run, where the Army officers were to visit U.S. Army establishments. On 25 February, Carss and his crew picked up the Staff College candidates for the return flight to Ottawa; Lieutenant-General Graham had left for Washington the previous day by commercial air. On the way, Carss was asked to stop in Toronto to allow Major-General Clark and four other officers to disembark, as it was closer to their destination than Ottawa; during his approach, the No 4 engine failed, which meant a three-engine landing and an engine change. It was after midnight so, rather than wait for a relief aircraft to come from Montreal (which would take four hours), the Army officers decided to stay the night in Toronto and continue their journey by commercial air the next day.[8]

The trans-Atlantic service flights from Dorval normally terminated in Langar, but they were often extended to the fighter wings in Europe to provide transport for Sabre squadrons conducting air-gunnery training at ranges in Morocco. The following is an account of a typical transport mission.

On 23 February, NS17515 (captained by Flying Officer Buechler) departed Dorval as SF 53/54 for Gander and Prestwick, where a slip crew took over. On 26 February, Buechler and his crew picked up NS17506 on its arrival from Canada and took it on, first, to Langar, and then to No 2 Wing at Grostenquin. The next morning, they loaded a cargo of Sabre spares and embarked a party of servicing personnel and proceeded to Rabat-Salé in Morocco, a flight of seven hours and fifteen minutes. Buechler returned to Grostenquin on 28 February, conducted another logistics run to Rabat-Salé on 29 February, and returned again to France on 1 March, stopping first at Istres, near Marseilles, where the Sabre squadrons stopped to refuel and service their aircraft on the way to and from Rabat-Salé; from Istres, they continued on to Marville and Baden-Söllingen. Still flying NS17506, Buechler and his crew began their homeward journey on 3 March, stopping at Marville, Langar and Prestwick before reaching Keflavik, where a slip crew took over the aircraft. On 5 March, an incoming crew turned over NS17521 to Buechler, who took it to Goose Bay and Dorval, arriving at base on the morning of 6 March.[9]

March

On 1 March, the Airmen's Mess at Lachine was the scene of the station's first ever junior ranks' black-tie dining-in, which attracted an attendance of 165 members and guests. The event was such a success that it was repeated on 8 March for a similar number of airmen who could not attend the first function, and who enjoyed themselves thoroughly despite the near-blizzard pounding Montreal most of the day. The Station Commander decided that more such events should be planned in the future.[10]

Shortly after midnight on 6 March, NS17502 (captained by Flight Lieutenant Jenkins) left Montreal with a load of medical supplies, bound for Karachi by the Mediterranean route. After passing through Gander, the Azores, Gibraltar and Malta, they arrived at Nicosia at 1300 hours on 9 May. With the insurgency in favour of *enosis* (political union with Greece) then under way, Cyprus was a known hot spot, and the crew were shaken by the sight that greeted them: a British civil airliner smouldering on the ramp in front of the terminal building. It was a Hermes, the civilian version of the RAF's Hastings transport. The crew had taxied it to the runway and were carrying out their run-up when they hit a snag serious enough to bring them back to the ramp to correct the problem. The passengers disembarked and, just as they entered the terminal — about twenty minutes after the engines had been started — something inside the aircraft exploded and set fire to the fuselage. The firefighters deployed immediately and succeeded in confining the fire so the cockpit, tailplane and wings were intact, and the fuel in the wing tanks did not ignite. No one was hurt, but if the flight had gone ahead as scheduled, the aircraft would have blown up in mid-air.

The next stop for Jenkins and his crew was Dhahran, on the Persian Gulf, and the flight arrived in Karachi on 10 March. Leaving the next day, the flight returned to base on 17 March via Bahrain, Malta, Langar, Keflavik and Goose Bay.[11]

The ration run conducted by the squadron to Goose Bay on 13 March carried thirty-two Royal Canadian Legion entertainers from Dorval. After presenting a lively performance that evening, the troupe was flown back to Montreal.

On 15 March, SF5, originating in Montreal, arrived at Resolute Bay on the coldest day of the year — temperature -62°F — with the Roman Catholic chaplain and Miss van Steensel of the CBC, who was making a return visit to this frozen outpost. In the morning, the padre said Mass while NS17504 returned to Churchill on a shuttle run. On Sunday, 18 March, the padre held several Masses and the North Star flight returned at 1300 hours, left again for Mould Bay with equipment and supplies, and returned at 1900 hours. Two hours later, the aircraft departed again for Churchill and base, taking the padre and the CBC reporter with it.

In late 1955, plans had been made for an early spring visit to northern Canada by Governor General Vincent Massey, who would spend sixteen days in the high Arctic and over-fly the North Pole. On top of their normally busy routine at Resolute Bay, Flight Lieutenant Forest and the detachment staff were tasked with preparing a reception for the Governor General and his entourage, who were due to arrive on 23 March. On 20 March, they installed a new flagpole next to the Operations building so the detachment could fly the Red Ensign (the Canadian national flag of the time) and the blue ensign of the RCAF at the same height. They also conducted a general clean-up and applied generous quantities of paint to the common areas of the detachment buildings.[12]

This was the first tour of the high Arctic for a Governor General of Canada, and the vice-regal party included prominent "resource persons": Dr. Graham Rowley, Secretary to the Advisory Committee on Northern Development, who was the subject-matter expert on introducing commercial and industrial activities to the north, and on the Eskimos, and Wing Commander K.R. Greenaway, to offer advice on geography, climate and navigation in high latitudes, and to help with the actual navigation during the tour.

The northern tour began on 20 March, with the departure of the vice-regal party from Ottawa for Great Whale River in No 412 Squadron's NS17520, captained by Wing Commander W.G.S. Miller. On 23 March, the weather at Resolute Bay was clear and the temperature a relatively balmy -15°F. The runway and taxi strip were scraped clean of snow in the morning, and everything was ready when the Governor General's aircraft arrived at 1930 hours, planning to stay three days. At 0755 hours the next morning, the Governor General left again in NS17520 for his flight over the North Pole, which would take ten hours and twenty-five minutes. On 26 March, the vice-regal party departed Resolute for the North Magnetic Pole and Cambridge Bay, arriving in Ottawa on 5 April.

A month before the tour, to ensure that it went off without a hitch, Miller and his crew had covered the entire route — including a flight to the North Pole from Resolute Bay on 28 February — in NS17513, the "Rockcliffe Ice Wagon", so named because the Central Experimental and Proving Establishment used it to research icing conditions. This aircraft was destroyed in a hangar fire at Dorval only a few weeks later.[13]

On 18 March, No 426 Squadron despatched a round-the-world training flight: NS17506, with an augmented crew co-captained by Flying Officer Dunford and Flying Officer Ronning.

The flight was routed via Gander and Lajes to Oran, Algeria; from there, it proceeded to New Delhi, stopping at Malta, Nicosia and Bahrain to refuel and rest. From India, the flight went on to Negombo in Ceylon, Singapore, Manila and Tokyo, where it arrived on 29 March. Easter was spent in Japan, and on Monday, 2 April, the flight departed for Wake Island and Honolulu, where the crew took a four day rest.

Their departure for Travis AFB, planned for 7 April, was cancelled because of adverse headwinds, and it wasn't until 11 April that the winds abated enough for the crew to file a flight plan to the mainland. Forty-five minutes into the flight, the aircraft lost No 1 engine and had to return to Hickam AFB. Station Operations at Dorval were informed, and Flying Officer Anderson and his crew left base at 1220 hours in NS17504 on 12 April with a replacement engine.

This crew arrived at Travis AFB sixteen and a half hours later (after fourteen hours and forty minutes in the air), having refuelled at Kansas City on the way, and a MATS flight took the engine on to Hickam. Anderson left Travis on 15 April on a direct flight to Montreal that took eleven and a half hours.

At 1420 hours on 15 April, its engine change completed, NS17506 made a short test flight, and four hours later, it was heading for Travis AFB, a flight of eleven hours and fifty minutes. The crew then took a sixteen-hour rest, and departed for Montreal shortly after midnight on 17 April. After eleven hours and fifty minutes in the air, the training flight was back at base, having been away for a month.[14]

Shortly before 0900 hours on 19 March, a fire alarm sounded in No 6 Hangar — the RCAF hangar — at Dorval, which housed the Unit Technical Stores of No 426 Squadron, and the Receipts and Issues Section and Stock Control Section of the Supply Branch of RCAF Station Lachine. The Air Movements Unit was also at risk, as it occupied a new Steelox building adjacent to the south end of the hangar. The fire had broken out above R&I Section in an area used for storing packing material, and it spread fast, destroying the hangar and most of its contents despite the combined efforts of the airport's Department of Transport firefighters, the RCAF firefighters from Lachine, and municipal fire crews from Dorval, Lachine and Montreal.

Property of the Department of Transport, the hangar dated from the earliest days of the Second World War and was built of heavy timber. Standing at the south end of a row of six hangars aligned on a north-south axis, its entire west side was flanked by a lean-to that housed the squadron and Supply Branch offices, and the heating plant. The interior of the hangar was divided into four large bays, of which A Bay was at the north end, closest to the seat of the fire. A Bay contained NS17513, the Rockcliffe Ice Wagon, which was being modified by Canadair personnel who were working in and around it.

Within three minutes of the fire alarm, the flames had engulfed A Bay and the Ice Wagon, and forced everyone to evacuate the area. The servicing and maintenance crews' first priority was to get the aircraft that were in the hangar for repairs out, and as the flames raged higher and higher they were moving aircraft — by hand. One of No 436 Squadron's C-119s, 22124, was being manhandled from the back of the hangar towards the doors, when its nose-wheel cocked and the crews had to stop moving it as its port wing would have jammed against the wall. The tractor that had just pulled C-119/22103 out of the hangar was hitched to 22124, but before the crews could finish extracting the second aircraft, NS17513 exploded in A Bay, blowing some of the hangar doors shut and jamming them solid; attempts to dislodge them were futile. By this time, the fire was so fierce and close that the tractor caught fire and the technicians had to flee the building. The entire hangar, its lean-to and the Air Movement Unit building were all destroyed.

NS17513 and C-119/22124 were both lost, but four other aircraft — NS17511, NS17521, C119/22103 and Expeditor 1519 — were saved through the courage, initiative and fast work of the ground staff. None of them was hurt.

No 426 Squadron lost some office equipment, but the classified files, operational records and publications in the Orderly Room, the Squadron Commander's office and the Adjutant's office were saved, including eighty-three log-books belonging to forty-one pilots, twenty-two navigators and twenty radio officers. From the Operations Office, however, only a cabinet drawer containing a variety of reports and background material was rescued, and nothing was salvaged from the Training Office, the Check Pilot's Office or the Flight Engineers' Section.[15]

On 20 March, a Board of Inquiry was convened at RCAF Station Lachine to investigate the fire under the chairmanship of Group Captain A.H. Jardine. The Board's findings and recommendations were in an extensive report submitted several weeks later, but it never identified the exact cause of the fire.[16]

To determine the extent of the damage caused by the hangar fire, Air Materiel Command Headquarters reviewed the supply of North Star spares, establishing that Air Transport Command operations could be supported at current flying rates. Problems did arise, but squadron operations were not noticeably affected.[17]

By the mid-1950s, as NATO expanded its air defence forces, modern all-weather interceptors were conspicuous by their absence. Therefore, to improve night and bad-weather combat capability, Canada agreed to provide four squadrons of CF-100 Canucks, replacing four of No 1 (RCAF) Air Division's interceptor–day-fighter units with the all-weather fighter units.

Air Force Headquarters Operations Order 1/56, issued on 29 March 1956, directed that, between November 1956 and August 1957, four of Air Defence Command's all-weather fighter squadrons were to move to No 1 (RCAF) Air Division, changing places with day-fighter units that would re-form in Air Defence Command as all-weather fighter squadrons. The operation was called *NIMBLE BAT.*

The move of No 445 AW(F) Squadron from RCAF Station Uplands in Ottawa to No 1 Wing at Marville was designated *NIMBLE BAT I* and scheduled for November 1956. No 445 was to replace No 410 (F) Squadron, which would move to Uplands (less personnel and equipment) to convert to the all-weather role. In similar fashion, *NIMBLE BAT 2*, slated for February 1957, would take No 423 AW(F) Squadron overseas from St-Hubert to No 2 Wing at Grostenquin, replacing No 416 (F) Squadron, which was to re-form as an all-weather unit at St-Hubert. The date set for the launch of *NIMBLE BAT 3* was May 1957, when No 440 AW(F) Squadron would move from Bagotville to No 3 Wing at Zweibrücken, replacing No 413 (F) Squadron, which was to re-form at Bagotville. *NIMBLE BAT IV*, the last of these operational moves, was the move of No 419 AW(F) Squadron in August 1957 from North Bay to No 4 Wing at Baden-Söllingen, replacing No 414 (F) Squadron, which was to become an all-weather fighter unit at North Bay.

Command of the four CF-100 squadrons participating in *Operation NIMBLE BAT* was vested in the Air Officer Commanding, Air Defence Command, until the first day of the month chosen for their departure. At that time, the Air Officer Commanding, Air Transport Command, would assume command, which he would retain until the squadrons arrived in Europe. The movement of the CF-100 convoys overseas would be handled in Air Transport Command by No 1 OFU, with air transport support by No 426 (T) Squadron. When they arrived at their overseas destinations, the Air Officer Commanding, No 1 Air Division would assume command of the squadrons.[18]

April

The 1956 spring re-supply of the Arctic weather stations, scheduled for April, was handled mostly out of Edmonton by the C-119s of No 435 Squadron. On 7 April, Resolute Bay had two power failures caused by strong winds (in the order of 85 mph) and blowing snow; fortunately, the weather cleared the next day, permitting the detachment staff to clear the runway. The re-supply flights began on 9 April and were completed by 28 April, despite several delays for bad weather. Two navigators, Flying Officer J.G. Fullam and Flying Officer G.H. Nishimura, and one radio officer, Flying Officer E.A. Barker, were seconded to the operation from No 426 Squadron.[19]

The squadron carried out one service flight to Resolute Bay in April. On 11 April, Flying Officer Joron and his crew left Montreal in NS17525 for Winnipeg by way of Ottawa, where they picked up passengers and freight. On 12 April, the flight continued on to Churchill, where it stopped briefly, and Resolute Bay. On 13 April, a storm grounded all flights and it wasn't until the following day that Joron was able to return to Churchill to pick up more cargo for the detachment. On the morning of 15 April, the crew set out for Resolute Bay and were three and a half hours into the journey when a radio message advised them that conditions at their destination had gone below limits; the flight returned to Churchill. On 17 April, the crew managed to complete the shuttle run and return to Churchill for another load of freight, completing the second delivery the next day. On 19 April, Joron left Churchill for Dorval, stopping at Winnipeg and Ottawa on the way.[20]

Operation RANDOM 21 actually got under way on 11 April, with the departure of four Sabre VIs from St-Hubert for Goose Bay, where they were positioned as spare aircraft; the pilots returned to Montreal on a scheduled North Star flight. The Sabre convoy was set to leave on 17 April, but it was delayed by bad weather at both Goose Bay and Narsarssuak. As usual, air transport support would be provided by No 426 Squadron, which despatched two North Stars; on the morning of 18 April, NS17517 departed St-Hubert for Goose Bay with No 2 Support Party and, after the departure of twenty-three Sabre VIs for Goose Bay, Flying Officer Culp embarked No 1 Support Party in NS17512 and followed the convoy.

Early the next morning, Culp and his crew transported a support party and two Sabre pilots, Flight Lieutenant Annis and Flying Officer Vaesen, to Narsarssuak, where they waited for the convoy; Annis and Vaesen were to join the convoy with two aircraft left behind on a previous *RANDOM*. Meanwhile, the other support party was flown to Keflavik in NS17517. On 20 April, the convoy of twenty-five aircraft arrived at Keflavik, and NS17512 proceeded to Kinloss with No 1 Support Party. On 21 April, the Sabres made the double jump to Kinloss and their destination, No 2 Wing at Grostenquin; once the Sabres were well on their way from Keflavik, No 2 Support Party boarded NS17517 for the trip back to Montreal. Culp and his crew proceeded from Kinloss to Prestwick where most of the support party was dropped off to catch a service flight back home. The flight then continued on to Grostenquin. On 23 April, most of the ferry pilots and some members of the support party boarded NS17512 for the trip back to Montreal. Staging through Langar and Keflavik, the flight was back at base early in the morning of 25 April.[21]

On 24 April, after an earthquake in Lebanon, NS17517 (captained by Wing Commander Mackie) departed Montreal for Beirut with a load of medicines and relief supplies provided by the Canadian Red Cross. The flight was routed through Goose Bay and Prestwick, Langar and Malta, and arrived in Beirut on 28 April. Leaving two days later, Mackie and his crew returned the way they came, reaching Dorval on 3 May.[22]

The RCAF had decided that its North Stars would be equipped with a lightweight, low-power, airborne search radar designated the AN/APS42 that could be used for navigation as well as for anti-collision warning, weather detection, and target identification. On 25 April, Flight Lieutenant Buchan and Flying Officer Major went to the Canadair plant at Cartierville to conduct airframe tests with the new radar mounted in the nose of NS17502, the first North Star to have this modification, which increased its length by sixteen and a half inches. Working with technicians from Canadair and CEPE, Buchan and Major carried out a series of ASI (Airspeed Indicator) calibrations, and over the next two days at Cartierville, they conducted further technical and airborne evaluations of the AN/APS42 prototype. With the prototype installed, NS17502 was turned over to the squadron on 1 May, and the squadron trained with the new equipment in the Montreal area from 9 May to 11 May. For each daily two-and-a-half-hour session, the aircraft was captained by Flying Officer Carss.[23]

May

On 1 May, the squadron despatched NS17517 to Malton Airport in Toronto to airlift the RCAF Staff College students to Maxwell AFB near Montgomery, Alabama. Captained by Flying Officer Anderson, the flight left Malton on 2 May for Maxwell by way of Cleveland, where the aircraft cleared Customs. On 8 May, the Staff College students were flown to Eglin AFB, Florida for a study visit, and then returned to Maxwell. The group's next trip was on 10 May, first to Patrick AFB and from there to MacDill AFB near Tampa, where the aircraft and its crew stayed the night. The next day, the students were flown to Miami, and on 13 May, they went back to Malton, after which the aircraft returned to Dorval.[24]

On 2 May, Air Commodore Carscallen arrived at Resolute Bay in a No 412 Squadron North Star for a brief visit and an inspection tour. The next day, the flight departed at 1100 hours for the North Pole and Alert, returning at 2130 hours. After a tour of the Eskimo village on 3 May, Carscallen and his party departed for Ottawa. The next visitor at Resolute was Wing Commander Delaney, the Station Commander at Lachine, who arrived on 14 May with the Roman Catholic padre from Lachine. Delaney had left Montreal on 13 May in NS17502 (the aircraft with the new radar), captained by Flying Officer Joron, bound for Great Whale, where he stopped for a brief inspection before heading for Churchill and Resolute. At Resolute Bay,

Delaney and his party carried out their semi-annual inspection of the quarters and the camp, and the padre said Mass. In the morning, the aircraft proceeded directly to Montreal, a ten-hour flight. The next squadron flight into Resolute Bay was NS17510, captained by Flying Officer Cline, which arrived on 24 May and was heading back to base only an hour and a half later.[25]

Air Commodore Carscallen inspection of Lachine on 11 May began with the Guard of Honour and the band in the morning, followed by a formal parade and inspection in the afternoon, and a cocktail party and buffet dinner at the Officers' Mess in the evening. The Air Commodore concluded the afternoon's parade and inspection with the following remarks:

> Wing Commander Delaney, Officers, NCOs, Airmen and Airwomen of Station Lachine, I would first like to compliment you on the excellent parade this afternoon. You have learned to do business on the parade ground as well as you fly aeroplanes. A few weeks ago I complimented you on your efforts as the result of the fire, today I would like to take the opportunity to compliment you on your efforts since the fire. I know it has been difficult with crowded conditions; unfortunately we are going to do it a bit longer.
>
> I would like to wish you the best of luck and thank you.[26]

On 18 May, Air Defence Command Headquarters issued Operation Order 6/56 concerning *Operation NIMBLE BAT*, the replacement of four Sabre units No 1 Air Division by CF-100 squadrons between November 1956 and August 1957, and the formation of four new all-weather fighter squadrons in place of the units going overseas. The immediate mission was to prepare No 445 AW(F) Squadron to move to Marville and to form a replacement unit. The build-up of the new unit would begin at RCAF Station Uplands on 1 August with the creation of a new flight in No 428 AW(F) Squadron, which would grow to squadron strength over the next three months. On 1 November, the date No 445 Squadron would leave Uplands, the new flight would become No 410 AW(F) Squadron.[27]

Operation RANDOM 22 got under way on 28 May, when NS17502 and NS17517 proceeded from Dorval to St-Hubert to pick up two ground support parties, and then airlifted them to Goose Bay, where the ground parties prepared for the arrival of twenty-five Sabre VIs. On 29 May, all the fighters made the hop to Goose Bay, averaging an hour and fifty minutes for the trip. On 31 May, Flying Officer Mace and his crew left for Narsarssuak in NS17517 with No 1 Ground support party, and NS17502 returned to base after dropping off the second support party at St-Hubert. The same day, the Sabre convoy flew to Greenland, averaging one hour and forty minutes, refuelled, and then made the crossing to Keflavik in an average time of ninety-five minutes. Mace and his crew followed them to Iceland shortly after the departure of the last Sabre section.

On 1 June, the convoy made the second double hop, from Keflavik to Kinloss (average flight time ninety-five minutes) where they refuelled, and then on to No 2 Wing Grostenquin (average flight time ninety-five minutes). Mace's North Star followed the Sabres to Grostenquin and departed for Montreal two days later with the ferry personnel.²⁸

June

On 1 June, a double crew captained by Flying Officer Ronning and Flying Officer McAlpine left base in NS17506 for Winnipeg to embark the Specialist Navigation Course candidates for the annual high Arctic exercise. Departing Winnipeg on 3 June, the flight proceeded to Churchill, where it stayed the night, and reached Resolute Bay the next day. On 5 June, Ronning and McAlpine carried out navigation exercises from Resolute Bay, each lasting seven hours and fifteen minutes. The next day, one of the engines backfired while NS17506 was taking off from Resolute, and the flight had to turn back on three engines. On 7 June, Flying Officer Culp and his crew brought in NS17517 to replace NS17506, which they took back to base on 9 June while Ronning and McAlpine resumed the navigation training in NS17517 with a flight of seven hours and ten minutes. On 10 June, another long-range exercise was completed, followed by an ice reconnaissance mission of six hours and ten minutes on 11 June. On 12 June, NS17517 returned to Dorval by way of Churchill and Winnipeg, where the student navigators disembarked.²⁹

On 1 June, Flying Officer John left Dorval in NS17511 for Prestwick on SF 53 to Langar. At Prestwick, they handed the the aircraft over to a slip crew for the leg to Langar, and on 3 June John and his crew took over the incoming NS17502, heading for Grostenquin via Langar. From Grostenquin, the crew left on a logistics run to Rabat-Salé the following morning, returning on 5 June to Zweibrücken and Grostenquin. On 6 June, John and his crew conducted another shuttle run to Morocco, returning the next day to Zweibrücken. On 9 June, the aircraft proceeded to Langar, where it became SF54, and headed for Prestwick and Keflavik, where Flying Officer John handed over NS17502 to a slip crew. On 11 June, John's crew took over NS17512 and returned to base.³⁰

On 8 June at Lachine, Air Transport Command Headquarters launched *Operation PETTICOAT*, a warm-up to Air Force Day in which about sixty wives of Montreal-area Air Transport Command personnel were taken on a tour of the station facilities, briefed on the work of the Command, given tea, and then taken for a half-hour flight around Montreal in NS17512, captained by Flight Lieutenant Grant. Air Force Day was celebrated on 9 June at St-Hubert, with the full participation of Lachine personnel and their families.³¹

The next round-the-world trip, designated Special Flight 160, varied from previous Thunderbird missions in one respect: the itinerary included Australia for the first time. The visit had a special purpose: the flight carried 6,500 pounds of radiation detection equipment for delivery to Australian researchers by Mr. A.N. Fordyce of the Defence Research Board, the flight's only passenger. The aircraft assigned to the mission was NS17525, in which the new APS42 search radar had been installed. The augmented crew of sixteen captained by Wing Commander Mackie included Squadron Leader J.D. Harvey and photographer Corporal D. Eagles from the Public Affairs Section at Air Transport Command Headquarters.

Special Flight 160 departed Dorval at 2300 hours on Saturday, 9 June, refuelled at Gander, and then carried on to Lajes, where the crew took a sixteen-hour rest. On 11 June, the flight halted briefly at Gibraltar to refuel and then went on to Malta. Leaving Malta on 14 June, the flight refuelled at Beirut and continued on to Bahrain. The search radar worked perfectly and proved to be an excellent en route navigation aid. The next refuelling stop was Karachi on 15 June, before the flight went on to the RAF base at Negombo, some twenty-five miles from Colombo, the capital of Ceylon. Again the search radar proved its worth, enabling the crew to pick their way around the towering formations of cumulo-nimbus cloud over the Indian Ocean. On 17 June, the flight left for Singapore, a run of eight hours and fifty minutes during which the APS42 helped the crew dodge most of the thunderstorms along the way. (Without it, the crew would have been forced to plough through the build-ups and hope for the best.)

Three hours after leaving Singapore on 20 June, the flight landed at Djakarta, Indonesia, where the Canadian ambassador, G.R. Heasman, treated the crew to lunch on the veranda of the terminal building. After only ninety-five minutes on the ground, and with the aircraft serviced, the crew were on their way to Darwin on the north coast of Australia. Mostly over water, this leg took eight and a half hours, with arrival at 0100 hours local on 21 June. The aircraft was serviced by Qantas Airways, which billeted the crew at its base camp at Berriman, a few miles from the airport. At 1615 hours, the flight left for Adelaide on Australia's south coast, where it arrived seven hours and thirty minutes later. At Adelaide, Mr. Fordyce handed over the cargo to the Australians and left the crew, heading to Melbourne to give a couple of lectures to the Australian equivalent of the Defence Research Board.

At noon on 22 June, the crew arrived in Sydney, where they stayed three days during which it rained most of the time. On 26 June, Mr Fordyce rejoined the crew, and the flight took off for home at 0810 hours, heading first to Nandi, in Fiji. Two active frontal weather systems lay across the flight path, and the radar equipment was put to good use taking the aircraft around the most active of the tropical storms. The flight arrived at Nandi shortly after sunset, having been airborne for eight hours and fifty minutes, and the crew spent two and a half days in in Fiji.

The flight left Nandi at 0800 hours on 29 June for Honolulu with a stop to refuel at Canton Island, which was administered jointly by Great Britain and the U.S., and used as a refuelling stop by most airlines flying the Pacific route to Australia. On leaving Nandi, the aircraft climbed to 13,000 feet (which meant going on oxygen) to get above most of the cloud and to give the navigator more advantage in directing the aircraft around the massive thunderheads produced by the active tropical front straddling the flight path. The flight to Canton Island took six hours and ten minutes, and the aircraft arrived at 1610 hours on 28 June. Having crossed the International Date Line en route, the crew had "lost" a day. After eighty minutes on the ground at Canton Island, the flight took off again for Hickam AFB, a nine-and-a-half-hour run; they arrived at 0400 hours on 29 June and were put up at the Moana Hotel on Waikiki Beach, where squadron personnel had been billeted during the days of the Korean Airlift.

The scheduled three-day stopover in Hawaii got stretched to six because of adverse winds on the way to the mainland. The flight finally left at 2140 hours on 5 July, made the crossing in ten hours and fifty minutes, and arrived at Travis AFB at 1030 hours on 6 July. After a short rest, the flight left again for Ottawa at 0145 hours on 7 July; time en route was ten hours and fifty-five minutes. After a brief stop at Uplands to disembark Mr. Fordyce, the flight landed at Dorval at 1820 hours the same day.

During the twenty-eight days it was away, Special Flight 160 operated out of eighteen different airports in both daylight and at night in a variety of weather conditions. It had logged a total of 126 flying hours.[32]

On 11 June, the Department of Transport issued Operation Order NORS56 concerning the annual re-supply of Resolute Bay and other Arctic outposts by the Coast Guard icebreakers and contract marine carriers.[33]

SF5, a cargo and passenger run, left Dorval for Resolute Bay on the morning of 13 June, with Flying Officer Schwanky as captain of NS17516. Stops were made at Uplands and Winnipeg and a crew rest was taken at Churchill. From Churchill, round trips were made to Resolute Bay on each of the next three days. On 17 June, the flight returned to Dorval by way of Winnipeg and Uplands, after four and a half days away from base and a total of fifty flying hours.[34]

The overseas movement of fighter jets continued in June. *Operation RANDOM 23* started on 14 June with the ferrying of two Sabre VIs from St-Hubert to Goose Bay as spare aircraft. On the afternoon of 19 June, Flying Officer Joron and his crew brought NS17516 across the St. Lawrence River to St-Hubert, picked up the ferry unit's No 2 Ground Support Party, flew them to Goose Bay, and returned to Dorval. On 20 June, twenty-eight Sabre VIs and two T-33 Silver Stars made the hop from St-Hubert to Goose Bay, with Air Commodore Carscallen flying with Flight Lieutenant J.C. Turner in Silver Star 21509. At this point, poor weather at Goose Bay and Narsarssuak held up the fighter convoy for eight days.

No 1 Ground Support Party left St-Hubert on 23 June and arrived in Greenland the next day. On 25 June, Goose Bay was clear but a cold front was approaching and Narsarssuak was forecast to go below limits for jet operations. NS17509 was despatched from Narsarssuak to carry out a weather check and report on conditions near the approaching front. Receiving a favourable report, the operation at Goose Bay was set in motion and the first Sabre section was launched. Shortly after the Sabres were airborne, advice was received that Duckbutt Tango of the search-and-rescue force was leaving its station for Narsarssuak, as it was running low on fuel after encountering heavy icing conditions. The Sabre section returned to Goose Bay and reports were soon received by the Operations staff that the weather was deteriorating rapidly in the fjord leading to Narsarssuak. The operation was stood down.

On 28 June, with favourable actual and forecast weather at Goose Bay and Narsarssuak, the first over-water crossing was launched, but not before NS17509 patrolled the fjord from Narsarssuak and radioed weather information to Goose Bay. The convoy's thirty jets made the crossing without incident. On 29 June, the prospects for a double jump to Keflavik and Kinloss looked promising and plans were made accordingly. The convoy crossed to Keflavik the next morning, refuelled, and continued on to Kinloss, with NS17509 following after. The next day, all thirty jets completed the last leg of their journey to No 1 Wing at Marville, and the North Star followed after a brief stop at Langar for some minor repairs. NS17509 departed Marville for Langar on 2 July with all the ferry pilots aboard; seventeen of them stayed at Langar to catch a later service flight back to Canada, and the rest stayed with the flight and were back at St-Hubert the following day.³⁵

A Red Cross blood donor clinic was held at No 4 Hangar at Dorval on 21 June. Three quarters of the aircraft technicians and associated trades made donations, for a total of 154 pints of blood.

On 26 June, No 436 Squadron personnel began the move to their new home at RCAF Station Downsview in Toronto.³⁶

SF5 to Resolute Bay was taken out by Flying Officer Joron on 27 June in NS17502. After a brief stop at Uplands, the flight continued on to Winnipeg where it remained overnight. The flight proceeded to Churchill the next day from where the crew made a ration run to Coral Harbour. The flight then returned to its point of departure. Joron and his crew left for Resolute Bay on the morning of 29 June carrying passengers, mail and general cargo. The next day, the crew carried out a para-drop at Isachsen and returned to Resolute Bay before departing for Churchill. On 1 July, a shuttle run was conducted to Resolute Bay with cargo that had been backlogged at Churchill. The next day, the flight returned to base after making stops at Winnipeg and Ottawa.³⁷

July

The first of five flights carrying replacements for tour-expired members of the ICSC truce teams in Indochina left Montreal on 6 July. NS17517, captained by Flight Lieutenant Carss, carried a crew of ten, twenty-four Army officers and one RCAF officer as passengers and Red Cross relief supplies for India. The routing was essentially the same as used on previous missions of this type, through Lajes, Malta, Bahrain, Karachi and Calcutta. The flight arrived in Saigon on 15 July. During the stopover at Calcutta the Red Cross flood relief supplies were turned over to the local authorities. As soon as the passengers and cargo were disembarked in Saigon, the flight left for Singapore to wait until the incoming Truce Team members had been briefed by those leaving for home. Carss and his crew flew back to Saigon on the morning of 19 July and embarked the returning officers. The flight then headed for Montreal, following the same route used outbound, and arrived at base on the morning of 25 July. The crew had been away for 19 days and put in 113 flying hours on the mission.³⁸

On 6 July, Flying Officer Byrne and his crew conducted an acceptance check of the APS42 installation in NS17521. A similar check was carried out on 19 July by Flying Officer McAlpine and his crew on NS17507. Canadair completed installing the radars in all of the RCAF's North Star fleet by 17 August.³⁹

The tempo of activity at Resolute Bay picked up dramatically in July as preparations were made for its annual re-supply by sea transport. Arriving from Station Comox by C-119 aircraft were personnel from No 407 (MP) Squadron who were assigned to ice reconnaissance duties. On 12 July, Flying Officer Webber brought in NS17502 from Churchill with passengers and cargo for the Detachment. Aboard was a Bell Telephone party which was to install new main telephone lines at Resolute Bay. Also aboard were Flying Officers Charchuk and Glover. Charchuk was designated as the new Detachment Commander while Glover was to be the Beachmaster for the following month's re-supply operation. After unloading, Webber returned to Churchill to conduct another shuttle run.

On 13 July, Glover and Flight Lieutenant Forest inspected the sector where the Bull Gang was to steam the fuel drums and the landing area on the beach. Working with Forest, Charchuk started to familiarize himself with his new responsibilities which were to last for the next six months. During the day, Flight Lieutenant Aitken brought in a No 407 Squadron Lancaster. Aitken was to be in charge of ice reconnaissance operations. Webber returned to Resolute Bay with more cargo at 1800 hours after dropping off mail and supplies at Coral Harbour en route. The flight left for Churchill two hours later where a short crew rest was taken. It arrived at Dorval shortly before midnight on 14 July, after stops at Winnipeg and Ottawa. Glover returned with the flight to Montreal and would be back at Resolute Bay on 29 July to take up his duties as Beachmaster.[40]

The RCAF Benevolent Fund, the St. George Kiwanis Club of Montreal and the squadron teamed up on 13 July to airlift one-year-old Luke Corbeil to the Mayo Clinic in Rochester, Minnesota. The baby, son of Corporal and Mrs. E.C. Corbeil, was born with a congenital malfunction of the heart requiring an operation using a mechanical heart, and the Mayo Clinic was one of only three hospitals in North America where such an operation had ever been done. Corporal Corbeil was one of No 426 Squadron's aero-engine technicians, and the flight was organized as a training trip. NS17512, captained by Flying Officer Buechler, left at 0800 hours for Duluth, where the flight cleared Customs and then went on to Rochester. After seeing the baby and his parents off to the hospital along with the RCAF and Kiwanis representatives, Buechler and his crew continued on to Regina to disembark several passengers. After remaining overnight there, the flight returned to Rochester after clearing Customs at Grand Forks, North Dakota. The two representatives were picked up and the flight returned to Montreal. Corporal and Mrs. Corbeil would remain in Rochester until the results of the operation could be known, which was expected to be in three weeks time. The operation was successful.[41]

The squadron's next service flight to Resolute Bay was taken out on 18 July by Flying Officer Anderson, who captained NS17516. The flight went directly to Winnipeg and then airlifted passengers and freight to Churchill, where it remained overnight, returning to Winnipeg the following day. On 20 July, the flight embarked the Bull Gang and cargo and proceeded to Resolute Bay, making a brief stop at Churchill en route. A shuttle run to Churchill was conducted the next day, with a crew rest taken at Resolute Bay. Proceeding to Winnipeg on the 22 July, the flight was back at base the next afternoon.[42]

Flying Officer Ronning and his crew left base for Prestwick on a regular service flight on 21 July. As slip crew, they took over NS17504 on 25 July and went to Langar. From there the flight was redirected to London to pick up 10,800 pounds of tents and Red Cross supplies to be airlifted to Athens for earthquake disaster relief. The cargo was delivered on 26 July, with the flight returning to Langar the next day after an eight-hour and fifteen-minute flight. On its return, NS17504 became a service flight and Ronning left for Prestwick and Keflavik on 28 July. At Keflavik the aircraft was turned over to a slip crew. Taking over NS17511 shortly before midnight on 29 July, Ronning and his crew were back at base at 0900 hours the following morning.[43]

Operation RANDOM 24 was launched on 23 July when Flying Officer Schwanky and his crew in NS17512 embarked the OFU's No 1 Support Party at St-Hubert and airlifted them to

Narsarssuak. The second support party was transported to Goose Bay by NS17511 the same day. On 24 July, fifteen Sabre VIs made the flight to Goose Bay, where they were joined by two spare aircraft to make the crossing to Narsarssuak. With good weather prevailing across the North Atlantic, the convoy proceeded to Keflavik on 25 July. At Goose Bay, the second support party was embarked on NS17511 and returned to Montreal. The next day, the Sabre convoy made the double hop to Kinloss and No 1 Wing in Marville. Schwanky and his crew in NS17515 followed the Sabres to Marville where they embarked all the Sabre pilots on 29 July, returning them to St-Hubert on 31 July.[44]

The second truce team rotation flight for the year was despatched to Saigon on 27 July: Flying Officer Webber and crew in NS17506 using the same route as the last flight. They reached Saigon on 5 August, disembarked their passengers and continued on to Singapore. On 9 August, the flight returned to Saigon to pick up the outgoing observers and then headed for Calcutta on the first leg back to base. The flight came back to Montreal on 15 August after being away for nineteen days, putting in a total of 115 hours and thirty-five minutes flying time.[45]

On 31 July, the incoming AOC, Air Transport Command, Air Commodore F.S. Carpenter, was received at Dorval by Air Commodore Carscallen and Wing Commander Delaney with a Guard of Honour. Carpenter would serve nearly five years with Air Transport Command. His previous appointment was Chief of Air Operations at Air Force Headquarters. He formally assumed his new responsibilities on 6 August.[46]

August

SF53 departed Dorval for Prestwick on 2 August with Flying Officer Major as captain of NS17502. On arrival, the flight was turned over to a slip crew, who left for Langar. Taking over NS17510 on 5 August, Major proceeded to Zweibrücken after making brief stops at Langar and Grostenquin. On 6 August, passengers and freight were airlifted to Rabat-Salé, the flight returning the next day to Marville before proceeding to Lahr, West Germany, some fifteen miles south of Strasbourg on the east bank of Rhine. On 8 August, Major and his crew carried out another shuttle to Rabat-Salé and on the following day returned to Marville before continuing on to Lahr. On 11 August, the flight was positioned at Langar and then carried on to Prestwick and Keflavik where the aircraft was turned over to a slip crew. Taking over inbound NS17511 on 13 August, Major and his crew returned to base.[47]

NS17502 left Dorval as SF5 on the morning of 8 August bound for Resolute Bay. The flight, which was captained by Flying Officer Schwanky, made stops at Ottawa and Winnipeg before proceeding to Churchill, where it remained overnight. On 9 August, the flight continued on to Resolute Bay. There Schwanky made two passes while trying to land in fog. Giving up the attempt, he diverted to Thule. The next day, the crew left Thule in another attempt to get their flight to Resolute Bay. While en route, the crew were advised that the ceiling at their destination had come down below prescribed landing limits and they had to turn back to Thule again.

On 11 August, the flight made it in to Resolute Bay, discharged its passengers and freight, and left for Churchill to conduct two more cargo runs. That evening, the Coast Guard icebreaker *C.D. Howe* arrived at Resolute Bay in advance of the re-supply convoy. Schwanky returned to Resolute Bay from Churchill on 12 August and again on 14 August with more cargo. The flight remained overnight. Air Commodore Carpenter arrived early that evening for a familiarization tour of the northern outpost; later, he and members of his staff were invited to a small reception aboard the *C.D. Howe*. Schwanky returned to Churchill on 15 August and was back at base the following day.[48]

Meanwhile, at Resolute Bay, Air Commodore Carpenter inspected the camp on 15 August and toured the Eskimo village, where he attended a double wedding celebrated by the Right Reverend D.B. Marsh, bishop of the Anglican diocese of the Arctic, who had come with the *C.D. Howe*. That evening's mess dinner, organized by Flight Lieutenant Forest, the Detachment Commander, was prepared by the detachment's chief cook, one of the best in the RCAF. (It was service policy to send its most talented chefs to isolated detachments such as Resolute Bay.) The main course was Arctic char, and the featured speaker was another passenger from the *C.D. Howe*, RCMP Superintendent Henry Larson, skipper of the RCMP ship *St. Roch* during her voyage through the Northwest Passage. Larson captivated his audience with stories of his adventures in the Arctic. With most of the members and guests in battledress, the dinner was on the casual side, but the setting bordered on the exotic; it was high summer, and the midnight sun glittered on the bay, where the *C.D. Howe* and the rest of the re-supply convoy rode at anchor surrounded by huge chunks of floating ice.

The discharge of cargo began early the next day and proceeded normally in good weather, with the Air Commodore observing. That afternoon, he departed for Montreal with his staff.[49]

At RCAF Station Lachine, 7 August was the annual sports day, starting on the parade square with roll call, after which everyone repaired to the CNR recreation grounds next to the station. The weather was excellent and everyone had a good time.

On 10 August, the station held a formal farewell for Air Commodore and Mrs. Carscallen at the Recreation Centre. The well-attended event was a fitting farewell to the popular out-going AOC and his wife.[50]

A special flight carrying a group of Canadian Air Cadets left Dorval on the evening of 12 August in NS17521 for an exchange visit to Britain. The augmented crew, captained by Squadron Leader Trotter, made a refuelling stop at Gander and then proceeded directly to London, a run of ten and a half hours. After a thirty-hour crew rest, the flight departed on the evening of 14 August for No 1 Wing at Marville. After picking up passengers and cargo the following afternoon, Trotter and his crew headed for base, making refuelling stops at Shannon and Gander. The flight was back at Dorval early in the afternoon of 16 August.[51]

The third flight to Saigon, carrying twenty-four Army officer replacements for the Canadian members of the ICSC truce teams in Indochina, left Dorval on 17 August in NS17504. The augmented crew, captained by Flight Lieutenant Culp, followed the route taken by previous flights.

Shortly after leaving Gander, the flight returned to point of departure after experiencing some mechanical difficulties. These were corrected at Gander by the flight engineers on the crew, Sergeant Chevalier and Sergeant Empey, and the flight was able to leave for Lajes on the morning of 19 August. Brief stops were made at Lajes and Gibraltar to refuel before carrying on to Malta where the crew took a short rest. On 21 August, the flight departed for Beirut and a two-day layover. Saigon was reached on the morning of 26 August and, after discharging their passengers, the crew left for Singapore. They returned two days later to pick up the homebound truce team members and returned to Dorval on 6 September. In the twenty days the crew were away from base, they logged 127 hours and forty-five minutes of flying time.[52]

On 19 August, Flying Officer Lebedis and his crew left base in NS17511 to carry out two supply runs to Resolute Bay. Routine stops were made at Winnipeg and Churchill before the flight arrived at destination the following day. On 21 August, the crew left for Churchill to carry out a shuttle run, returning to Resolute Bay later that evening. The next day, the flight returned to Dorval after a brief stop at Churchill. Aboard were Flying Officers Glover and Forest, fifteen stevedores and twenty-eight members of the Bull Gang. While at Resolute, Glover had acted as the Beachmaster for the re-supply operation. Forest had just completed a seven-month stint as Detachment Commander, relinquishing his acting rank of Flight Lieutenant. Forest spent the next year at Lachine as the Northern Detachment Co-ordinator, followed by a three-year assignment at Air Transport Command Headquarters, serving in the Air Transport Operations Centre.[53]

At Resolute Bay, the unloading of the re-supply convoy was completed by mid-day on 23 August and the convoy departed several hours later. A North Star on SF5 arrived from Dorval at dinner time and promptly left for Isachsen and Mould Bay to carry out para-drops at both locations, returning some six hours later. The next day, the flight left for Churchill with twenty-eight members of the Bull Gang. Twelve of the gang remained at Resolute Bay to assist in the cleanup after the re-supply operation.[54]

In August, the government approved a project for the manufacture of a number of long-range turbo-prop aircraft at Canadair Ltd. The new aircraft, destined for Air Transport Command, was to be a development of the Bristol Britannia and a Canadair design proposal to extend the capabilities of the CL-44 to meet RCAF requirements. This aircraft would become the CC-106 Yukon, and the RCAF would acquire twelve of them. Two would end up with No 412 Squadron in the VIP role, and the other ten would be assigned to No 437 Squadron, which would be reactivated at Trenton in October 1961.[55]

September

September was to be another busy month for the squadron. *Operation RANDOM 25* got under way on 4 September when Flying Officer Schwanky positioned NS17516 at St-Hubert and embarked a No 1 OFU ground support party and headed for Goose Bay. The next day twenty-five

Sabre VIs were ferried to Goose Bay. They made the hop to Narsarssuak on 6 September. The support North Star was repositioned in Greenland the following day. Poor weather delayed progress until 10 September, when the Sabre convoy was able to reach Keflavik. An additional Sabre, which had previously gone unserviceable at Narsarssuak, was added to the convoy. After the last Sabre had departed Greenland, Schwanky and his crew followed the convoy to Keflavik. The whole convoy made it to Kinloss the following day. On 12 September, the Sabre VIs were flown to the various fighter wings: nine were ferried to Marville, ten to Grostenquin, three to Zweibrücken and four to Baden-Söllingen. Leaving Kinloss, the North Star crew first stopped off at Marville to drop off the ground support party and then proceeded to pick up the ferry pilots at Grostenquin, Zweibrücken and Baden-Söllingen where a crew rest was taken. On 14 September, Schwanky returned to Marville, embarked nine of the OFU pilots and the ground party, and then went to London, where the flight remained overnight. On 15 September, Schwanky went to Lajes, returning to Montreal on 17 September.[56]

The squadron's next major task was the year's fourth truce team rotation flight to Indochina. Carrying twenty-two Army officers and one RCAF officer, the flight left Montreal on 7 September. The aircraft, NS17521, with a crew of ten, was captained by Flying Officer Buechler. The route followed was the same as that of the previous flight and it arrived at Saigon on 16 September at 1045 hours local. After a two-hour stop to disembark his passengers, Buechler proceeded to Singapore to await the completion of the Truce Team handover formalities. The crew returned to Saigon on the morning of 20 September at 0815 hours local, and then headed back to base, arriving in Montreal on 26 September. The flight was away for nineteen days, taking 117 flying hours to complete.[57]

On 8 September, Flight Lieutenant Carss and his crew left base in NS17510 for Winnipeg on a logistics run. From there the flight proceeded to Grand Forks, North Dakota to clear U.S. Customs before carrying on to Dickinson, North Dakota, to pick up the body of a Canadian airman who had died there and transport it to Patricia Bay, near Victoria, for burial. The flight then left for Sea Island, returning to base the next day.[58]

On 12 September, Flying Officer Byrne and his crew left base in NS17509 to conduct several shuttle runs to Resolute Bay, stopping at Ottawa, Winnipeg (where they spent the night) and Churchill on the way. At Resolute, they embarked thirty-two personnel from the CMU (Construction Maintenance Unit) and their equipment, and immediately left for Winnipeg, a direct flight. On 14 September, the aircraft was repositioned at Churchill and the next day completed another shuttle run to Resolute Bay, where more CMU personnel embarked with their equipment and were airlifted directly to Winnipeg. On 16 September, Byrne and his crew departed from Winnipeg for Churchill and Resolute Bay on their third supply run. After spending the night at Resolute, the crew returned to Winnipeg on 17 September and Dorval the day after.[59]

On 13 September, NS17512 (captained by Flying Officer Ronning) left Dorval as SF51, bound for Goose Bay with Air Commodore Carpenter and his executive assistant, Flight Lieutenant

Edwards aboard to accompany the crew on the Rabat extension. After a brief stop at Goose Bay to refuel and file a flight plan, the aircraft left for Prestwick, a nine-hour run. On arrival, SF51 was turned over to a slip crew, who took it on to Langar, and Ronning and his crew picked up NS17510, the next aircraft to arrive at Prestwick from Dorval on 16 September. Ronning proceeded to Zweibrücken by way of Langar, discharged passengers and cargo, and then took the flight on to Grostenquin, embarked a Sabre servicing crew, and flew them back to Zweibrücken, where aircraft and crew spent the night. The next morning, they embarked Carpenter and Edwards and left for Rabat-Salé, taking nearly seven hours to get there. On 18 September, Ronning and his crew went back to Zweibrücken to pick up more passengers and cargo, returning to Morocco the next day. On 20 September, the flight again returned to Zweibrücken, discharged passengers and cargo, and then proceeded to Langar. On the morning of 22 September, Ronning and his crew left for Prestwick and Lajes (where a rest stop was taken), and they were back at base the following day.[60]

On 5 September, RCAF Station Lachine provided a burial party for the funeral of Leading Aircraftsman Tieman of RCAF Station Greenwood, who was killed in a motorcycle accident. On Sunday, 9 September, the Protestant Chapel was the scene of three baptisms: John, son of Squadron Leader Harvey; Jacqueline, daughter of Flight Lieutenant Beath; and Robert Douglas, son of Flying Officer Long. On 23 September, Flight Lieutenant Hewitt the Protestant chaplain baptised Jack, son of Squadron Leader Trotter, and Rickey, son of Flying Officer Farmer.

On Battle of Britain Sunday, 16 September, a church parade was held at Lachine, and personnel from both Lachine and St-Hubert attended commemorative services in downtown Montreal: Protestants at St. George's Anglican Church on the corner of Osborne and Windsor streets, and Roman Catholics at St. James Basilica on Dorchester Street West. Following the services, a wreath was laid at the Cenotaph on Dominion Square, although the march-past and salute were cancelled due to inclement weather. That afternoon, Flight Lieutenant Hunt directed the Training Command Concert Band in a concert for personnel at RCAF Station Lachine.[61]

Preparations for the fall re-supply of the Arctic weather stations began as soon as the sealift to Resolute Bay was completed, and two C-119s from No 436 Squadron at Downsview arrived at the detachment on 25 September to carry out the airlift. On 27 September, Flying Officer Mace brought in SF5 in NS17512, having left base the previous day for Ottawa, Winnipeg and Churchill. As soon as NS17512 was unloaded, Mace departed on a shuttle run to Churchill. The same morning, Resolute received a visit from the RCN icebreaker HMCS *Labrador*, which sent a pair of helicopters to pick up the bags of mail (brought in by North Star) that were waiting for the crew.

On 28 September, Mace and his crew returned to Resolute Bay from Churchill by way of Coral Harbour, where they delivered cargo and mail. In the morning, the flight returned to Churchill, where it remained overnight. Leaving Churchill in the morning, the flight was back at base on 30 September, after stops at Winnipeg and Ottawa. Several days later, the fall airlift to the weather stations was completed.[62]

October

During October, two international crises — one in eastern Europe and the other in the Middle East — escalated into armed conflict.

The uprising in Hungary began on 23 October 1956 with a peaceful demonstration by university students demanding an end to Soviet occupation and the implementation of "true socialism". The police attempted to disperse the crowd by releasing tear gas and arresting some demonstrators, but when the students tried to free their comrades from custody and the police opened fire on the crowd. The next day, the demonstrations not only continued but grew to include workers, soldiers and townspeople as well as students, and the Central Committee of the Hungarian Communist Party responded by declaring a new government under Imre Nagy, a previous Prime Minister who had lost a struggle for power during the summer. The demonstrations continued, and on 25 October, Soviets tanks opened fire on protesters in Budapest's Parliament Square, leaving dozens of casualties. Over the next two and a half weeks, the people of Budapest flung themselves at the tanks while Imre Nagy proclaimed one liberal initiative after another, called for international support and asked the United Nations to intervene. Finally, on 4 November, Nagy announced Hungary's withdrawal from the Warsaw Pact, the Red Army rolled over the border, and the uprising was over.

Imre Nagy took refuge in the Yugoslav embassy, but the Soviets kidnapped him, tried him on charges of treason and "attempting to overthrow democratic state order", and hanged him. Two hundred thousand Hungarians fled across the Austrian border, and about 37,000 of them made their way finally to Canada.[63]

In the Middle East, the crisis was the result of enmity simmering between Israel and Egypt since the cease-fire agreement that ended the Israeli War of Independence in 1949. Egypt became a republic in 1953, and in 1954 Colonel Gamal Abd el-Nasser became Premier; in June 1956, he became President as well. At that time, Britain had withdrawn all its forces from the Canal Zone, in accordance with an agreement with Egypt concluded on 27 July 1954.

In October 1955, Egypt entered into an arms deal with Czechoslovakia that brought the Egyptians a significant quantity of modern weapons and significantly heightened tensions between Israel and Egypt. But the Suez Crisis was finally triggered by President Nasser's request, in June 1956, for financial support for the construction of the Aswan High Dam from the United States and Britain. The Americans' announcement that they would decline the request, made on 19 July, was followed closely by refusals from Britain and the World Bank. All three potential lenders were motivated mostly by concern over Egypt's close political and military ties with Czechoslovakia and the USSR. Nasser's fury at not receiving the money was merely added to his long-standing grudge over the foreign (i.e., French and British) ownership of the Suez Canal, and the announcement that Egypt was nationalizing the strategic waterway — huge surprise to the world — came on 26 October. The revenue from operating the Canal would finance the Aswan High Dam.

On its borders with Egypt and Jordan, the new state of Israel constantly had to deal with incursions by armed fedayeen, Arabs trained and equipped by the Egyptian intelligence services and sent to raid and disrupt life in the Israeli settlements. In 1950, as part of this ongoing struggle with Israel, Egypt prohibited ships bound for Israeli ports from using the Suez Canal. In 1956, Egyptian forces blocked the Straits of Tiran, the narrow waterway that is Israel's only outlet to the Red Sea. In response, Israeli troops invaded the Sinai Peninsula — Egyptian territory — on 29 October. Egypt struck back by blocking the Suez Canal by sinking forty ships that happened to be on their way through at the time. The next day, Britain and France offered to occupy the

Canal Zone temporarily, proposing a ten-mile buffer zone. President Nasser refused this offer, and on 31 October British aircraft based in Cyprus began to bomb Egyptian bases.

Meanwhile, the Egyptian Army east of the Canal was losing to the Israelis, who were on the east bank of the Canal by 4 November; the next day, British and French paratroopers landed at the north end of the Canal, and the Americans rejected a Soviet proposal that both great powers should intervene. While a bi-national commando brigade seized Port Said on the west side of the mouth of the Canal, a French infantry battalion took Port Fauad on the east side. Ismailia fell two days later. On 7 November, France and Britain ordered a ceasefire and all major fighting ended, although skirmishing continued for some days.

The entire world community — or that part of it represented at the United Nations — was genuinely afraid that the Suez Crisis would develop into another world war, especially when the Soviet Union announced that it would send "volunteers" to intervene if British, French and Israeli forces did not immediately withdraw from Egyptian territory. Neither the Security Council or the General Assembly of the United Nations could come to grips with the Suez Crisis when the fighting erupted, but on the night of 3–4 November, the General Assembly sat all night in emergency session to figure out how to implement a ceasefire so diplomacy could begin. During this session, the Canadian representative, Lester B. Pearson, introduced a draft resolution asking the Secretary General to submit a plan, within forty-eight hours, for an international emergency force under the UN flag to secure a ceasefire and monitor compliance with its terms. Early on 4 November, the Genral Assembly adopted Pearson's proposal, and Secretary General Dag Hammarskjöld responded later the same day. His recommendation was that a UN Command should be established immediately under Major-General E.L.M. Burns, the Canadian Army officer who had been the Chief of Staff of the UN Truce Supervisory Organization since 1954, when Canada's involvement in UN peacekeeping began. (UNTSO was established in 1948 to observe and report on any violation of the armistice between Israel and its neighbours.)

On 5 November, acting on the Secretary General's recommendations, a General Assembly resolution established a UN Command, with Major-General Burns serving as its Chief for the duration of the current emergency. He was authorized to assemble his force from contingents offered by countries that were not permanent members of the Security Council. Canada's offer of a large contingent was made on 4 November and formally accepted on 19 November.[64]

The squadron's operational taskings did not let up in October: they continued the schedule of three flights per week to Langar with frequent extensions to the wings in Europe, plus the service flights to Vancouver, Whitehorse and Goose Bay, numerous short domestic runs, and flights to the United States.

On 7 October, Flight Lieutenant Lewis and his crew took NS17511 to St-Hubert to carry out the service flight to Germany and to support *Operation RANDOM WEST 1*, the first "reverse Random", on the way home. The next morning, they embarked a Sabre ground party and flew to Keflavik by way of Goose Bay, where they stopped briefly. On 9 October, the flight reached Kinloss and disembarked the ground party, but bad weather delayed them there until 13 September, when Lewis completed the service flight portion of his mission with a flight to Zweibrücken. He returned to Kinloss the following day, and left again on 17 September with the Sabre ground party, following the twenty-two Sabre Vs of *RANDOM West 1*. The convoy reached Keflavik and, as the weather at Narsarssuak was excellent, refuelled and carried on to Greenland. The North Star with the ground party made it to Keflavik, but was held up there by a maintenance problem and finally reached Narsarssuak the following afternoon. The Sabre convoy reached Goose Bay on 19 September, refuelled and, after a short delay for Customs, left for St-Hubert. Still following the Sabres, Lewis and his crew left for St-Hubert by way of Goose Bay, where they, too, stopped briefly. After disembarking the ground party at St-Hubert, Lewis returned to Dorval.[65]

On 8 October, Flying Officer Major positioned NS17512 at Halifax; the next day, he embarked a group of Navy personnel and airlifted them to Bermuda for an exercise. The flight returned directly to Montreal on 10 October.[66]

Two service flights and a special to Resolute Bay were conducted in October. Between 11 October and 14 October, Flying Officer McLaughlin captained NS17516 on a scheduled run to Resolute Bay with stops at Ottawa, Winnipeg and Churchill, and returned to base on the same route. The Protestant chaplain from Churchill joined the flight north and held services in the detachment canteen during the stopover, and returned to his duty station on the homeward flight.

On 19 October, a special flight arrived from Dorval with a group of officers from Air Transport Command Headquarters, RCAF Station Lachine and No 408 Squadron, who were assessing accommodation and servicing facilities available for Shoran work to be done in the spring of 1957. "Shoran" was a highly accurate fixing aid No 408 Squadron used for its mapping missions in northern Canada.

The next scheduled service flight was carried out by Flight Lieutenant Carss and his crew in NS17510 between 24 October and 27 October. After stops at Ottawa and Winnipeg, the flight left for Churchill but had to return when the field there closed because of bad weather; on 25 October, the flight proceeded from Winnipeg to Resolute Bay by way of Churchill. The next day, Carss returned to Churchill, carried out a supply run from there to Coral Harbour, and then left for Winnipeg and base.[67]

On 27 October, Squadron Leader Cairns and his crew took NS17502 out on SF51 to Langar, where they arrived the next day. On 30 October, the first day of world-wide alarm over the Suez Crisis, Cairns and his crew went on a supply run to Zweibrücken, where the ground staff of No 3 Wing painted "Canada" in big, bold letters on both sides of the fuselage in anticipation of a diversion to airlift duties in the Middle East. Later that day, the flight went to No 4 Wing at Baden-Söllingen, and on the morning of 3 November it returned to Langar, where a slip crew took the aircraft back to base, where the Canada label was removed by the servicing crew. Cairns and his crew departed for Lajes on 3 November and were back at base the next evening.[68]

On 29 October, Flying Officer Joe Sare was the radio officer on the standby crew, so he was passing the evening quietly in the Officers' Mess at Lachine, where the standby captain, Flight Lieutenant Bill Lewis, found him to announce that the standby crew would be leaving the next morning on an International Red Cross mission to Vienna with a load of medical supplies for civilians injured in the Hungarian uprising. "What about passports?" asked Sare — at that time, External Affairs in Ottawa held all squadron passports and sent them out to the unit when they were needed. Lewis replied that there was no time to get them and, besides, External Affairs was making all the arrangements so they would not be needed.

The next morning, Lewis and his crew in NS17521 headed to Toronto to pick up their cargo and receive a warm send-off by the local Hungarian-Canadian community as they departed for Gander. After refuelling, the flight headed for Lajes and a short crew rest. On 1 November, they left Lajes early for RAF Station Lyneham, where they refuelled and took off for Vienna. They arrived at their destination late that afternoon in their best blues as they were expecting to be met by high-ranking officials, including the Canadian ambassador and the President of the Austrian Red Cross.

On their way into the terminal where the officials were waiting, Lewis and his crew were greeted by the police — politely, but the crew got the feeling that all was not well. Inside, the officials were engaged in heated debate, so the crew waited in the arrivals lounge near the KLM counter. After a few minutes, an elderly gentleman came out from behind the counter and, in perfect English, asked the crew to come with him. They hesitated, but then followed him into a large office, where the elderly gentleman asked whether they had any civilian clothes; when they gave him an affirmative answer, he advised them to change immediately, which they did. On their return to the lounge in mufti, the officials abruptly stopped arguing, smiles and handshakes broke out all around, and the Canadians were warmly welcomed.

Without knowing it, the crew had broken a 1955 peace protocol between the western allies and the USSR that prohibited the presence of foreign troops on Austrian soil. The Soviets obviously monitored the situation closely. The crew's passports were then requested and, alas, External Affairs had *not* arranged clearance into Austria for them. In their embarrassment and relief at the near-incident of the uniforms, the Austrian officials waived the requirement.

On 3 November, the crew left for Langar, where they spent a week on standby waiting for an assignment to airlift duties in the Middle East. On 10 November, Lewis and his crew took over NS17502 and set off for Dorval, where they arrived at 0600 hours the next day after stops at Keflavik and Goose Bay.[69]

Operation RANDOM 26, the last east-bound ferry mission of 1956, got under way on 30 October with the departure from St-Hubert of twenty-six Sabre VIs for Goose Bay, and NS17511 with the OFU support party not far behind. The next day's over-water crossing to Greenland was cancelled, not only because Narsarssuak was forecast to be below limits for jets but also because a signal came in from Air Force Headquarters, ordering engine modifications on all the Sabres. The operation halted at Goose Bay for a week, and on 6 November the Sabres were air-tested with the modifications complete. The next day, the convoy made the crossing to Greenland, followed by the North Star with the support party. Keflavik was below limits on 8 November, so all the aircraft completed their second over-water crossing the day after, and on 10 November the Sabres flew to Kinloss, refuelled, and were delivered to the fighter wings: one jet went to Marville, twelve to Zweibrücken and thirteen to Baden-Söllingen.

After picking up all twenty-six ferry pilots at the three wings and bringing them back to Langar, NS17511 went unserviceable. The pilots went on to Kinloss with NS17515, which took eleven of them home to Canada while the other fifteen stayed behind for *Operation RANDOM West 2* several days later. Its repairs completed, NS17511 became a service flight and returned to base.[70]

Lachine, 1956

On 30 October, Flight Lieutenant Lambeth and his crew positioned NS17510 at Uplands for *Operation NIMBLE BAT 1* while No 445 AW(F) Squadron prepared for its departure for No 1 Wing at Marville, and a farewell ceremony was held for its personnel. The next morning, Lambeth embarked a ground support party and a load of spares and took off for Goose Bay. On 1 November, No 445 Squadron's twenty CF-100 Mk 4Bs made the hop to Goose Bay, with an average flight time of two hours and ten minutes. Leaving Goose Bay the next day, the convoy made it safely to Keflavik, averaging three hours and forty minutes for the flight, with Lambeth and his crew following after with the support party.

During this crossing — as in others — the valves in the wingtip fuel tanks on the Canucks froze and seized, and the ferry crews were unaware of this situation when they arrived at Keflavik with full tip tanks. The frozen-valve problem probably arose from excess moisture in the fuel taken on at Goose Bay, which spent long periods in underground storage.

On 4 November, the CF-100s left Iceland to fly directly to Marville, and nineteen of the aircraft made the three-hour flight to their new home safely. Over Scotland, however, Flight Lieutenant J. Flanagan in Canuck 18395 felt his controls lock and, realizing that there was nothing he could do about it, ejected with his navigator, Flying Officer Earl Martin. Both survived, but the aircraft — the first of two to be lost in the four NIMBLE BAT operations — crashed near Perth. Lambeth brought the support North Star in at Marville several hours after the convoy.[71]

After completing their escort mission, Lambeth and his crew repositioned their aircraft at Langar on 5 November. The next afternoon, having picked up passengers and cargo, they headed for Grostenquin, where they joined two other North Stars for a mission to pick up equipment at Rabat-Salé and deliver it to Cagliari in Sardinia.

For several reasons (of which distance from the Air Division's bases in France and Germany was only one), the RCAF had decided to pull out of Morocco, and was in talks with the West Germans and Italians on establishing an air-gunnery range in Sardinia based on the airfield at Decimomannu, where the RCAF detachment would move from Morocco. That meant positioning the detachment's stores and equipment at Cagliari for the move to Decimomannu, some ten miles to the northwest.

With the Suez Crisis continuing, Lambeth and his crew were unclear on the route they were to take. On 7 November, their flight was finally despatched, first to London and then to Marseilles to refuel before heading for Rabat-Salé. On 9 November, the flight departed for Cagliari, where the aircraft was unloaded, and then proceeded to Langar, where a slip crew took over the aircraft. At 0100 hours on 11 November, Lambeth and his crew took over NS17514 and flew it to Keflavik, where they became passengers and the slip crew captained by Flying Officer Schwanky flew the aircraft back to base, arriving shortly before midnight.[72]

November

The UN General Assembly approved the United Nations Emergency Force (UNEF) concept quickly, and the advance elements of the force reached the staging area near Naples on 9 November; by the middle of the month, the first elements of the main body were on the ground near Ismailia in the Canal Zone. By 30 November, UNEF strength stood at about 2,900, and by 31 January 1957, it was more than 5,500 all ranks, not including 275 RCAF personnel in the Mediterranean area who provided communications and air transport support. Much of the responsibility for providing UNEF with strategic airlift would devolve upon No 426 Squadron and its North Stars, and it was a major undertaking. Twenty-four countries had offered contingents for UNEF, and the UN accepted troops from ten of them: Brazil, Canada, Columbia, Denmark, Finland, India, Indonesia, Norway, Sweden and Yugoslavia.

On 6 November, the armed services of Canada received their first official indication of the forces their government intended to offer, and with the receipt of detailed information the next day, planning began for *RAPID STEP*, the three-phased operation to deploy the Canadian contingent in the Canal Zone. *Operation RAPID STEP 1* was the build-up of the 1st Battalion, The Queen's Own Rifles of Canada, into a Battalion Group, and the airlift by No 426 Squadron of the Canadian Base Unit Middle East (CBUME) to the staging area. *RAPID STEP 2* was the despatch of second- and third-line support units, including a Signals Squadron, a Transport Company and an Infantry Workshop, and more CBUME personnel. *RAPID STEP 3* was the move to Egypt of the men and equipment of A Squadron, The Royal Canadian Dragoons (the Battalion Group's reconnaissance element), along with the last of the Army Service Corps administrators.

Early in November, Lieutenant-General Graham, the Chief of the General Staff, flew to New York with Air Marshal Slemon, the Chief of the Air Staff. They spent a day at United Nations Headquarters, discussing the size and composition of UNEF with Ralph Bunche, the Deputy Secretary General, and Lester Pearson. On 17 November, the two Chiefs of Staff went back to New York, this time accompanied by Colonel G. Leach, Group Captain R.A. Gordon and Squadron Leader D.R. Adamson, for more detailed discussions with UN officials on issues including the provision by Canada of an augmented air transport force for duties in the Middle East.

Major-General Burns and Lester Pearson had already worked out a draft of the UNEF establishment in which the Canadian Army contribution was identified as one battalion of infantry. On 18 November, however, the UN decided that UNEF should also have its own air element, and when Prime Minister Louis St. Laurent formally announced Canada's contribution to UNEF on 19 November, the RCAF commitment was twelve C-119 aircraft plus ground and support elements, and airlift services. Most of the C-119s were to come from No 435 Squadron, and No 436 Squadron would provide the remainder. No 426 Squadron would airlift soldiers to Naples as part of *Operation RAPID STEP*.[73]

On 7 November, the aircraft carrier HMCS *Magnificent* swung at anchor off Greenock, Scotland, waiting to pick up fifty RCAF Sabre Vs to return them to Canada, when she received a signal ordering her immediate return to Halifax. After a stormy passage, the carrier made port on 13 November and was immediately swarming with dockyard workers and RCN technicians converting her into a combination trooper and tank carrier. On 18 November, with *Maggie* ready for sea and some 950 soldiers airlifted in from Calgary waiting to embark with their weapons, vehicles and equipment, *Operation RAPID STEP* came to an abrupt halt, and remained in suspension for nearly a month. President Nasser, who was reluctant to have UN troops on Egyptian soil at all, was most resistant to the Canadian contingent — specifically, The Queen's Own Rifles of Canada, who were much too British for his taste.

Despite interventions from governments of India and the U.S. and Secretary General Dag Hammarskjöld in person, Nasser did not change his stance until 4 December, when

Major-General Burns informed the UN and Canada's ambassador in Cairo that he was being offered more infantry than UNEF needed, and the sophisticated Canadian forces should provide — as well as air transport — skilled support personnel such as signallers, engineers, logisticians, administrators and medics. This proposal was enough to mollify the Egyptians, as these second- and third-line troops would be less obvious than infantry, particularly in the Canal Zone.

On 10 December, therefore, the UN formally asked Canada to increase the proportion of maintenance, support and communications personnel in its contingent, and Acting Prime Minister C.D. Howe issued a press release announcing the government's agreement and listing the following additional units: a Signals Squadron (150 men), a RCEME Workshop (150 men) and two Transport platoons (120 men). When the airlift from Naples to Egypt was completed, an RCAF communication and observation detachment of 250 to 300 personnel would be formed to serve with UNEF. Altogether, the Canadian contingent in UNEF was expected to total more than 1,000 soldiers and airmen.

To deal with the uncomfortable fact that The Queen's Own Rifles of Canada would *not* go to Egypt, Mr. Howe concluded:

> Because of Canada's comparatively favourable position among the nations contributing forces to the UNEF, it is apparent that requirements for the support elements so necessary to round out and weld the UNEF into an effective and efficient force can best be supplied by Canada. The number of these specialists to be provided by Canada has now reached the point where we are about in balance, so far as numbers are concerned, with the other contributing nations. It is desirable from the UN point of view to preserve this balance and, as a result, it now appears doubtful whether an infantry unit will be required from Canada. For this reason it has been decided to return, at least for the time being, the 1st QOR of Canada to their home station. This will be done during the next few days. The members of this unit are to be commended for the speed and efficiency with which they prepared themselves for overseas service and for their exemplary conduct during these weeks of waiting in Halifax, and we all regret that changes in United Nations plans have not made it possible for the battalion to proceed overseas as originally planned.

The next day, The Queen's Own Rifles were ordered to return to Calgary and *Operation RAPID STEP 2* began. HMCS *Magnificent* had first to be unloaded and then reloaded with stores and equipment for the revised Canadian contingent, comprising 56 Canadian Signals Squadron from the Royal Canadian Corps of Signals, 56 Canadian Transport Company from the Royal Canadian Army Service Corps, and 56 Canadian Infantry Workshop from the Royal Canadian Electrical and Mechanical Engineers.

Men going to Egypt were granted Christmas leave, returning in time for the departure of HMCS *Magnificent* on 29 December; the carrier arrived at Port Said on 10 January. Eight days later, unloading was completed and the Canadian contingent was integrated into UNEF. *Maggie* sailed for Naples on 20 January.[74]

On 19 November, Air Commodore Carpenter placed selected crews, servicing personnel and C-119 aircraft on a twenty-four hour alert for extended operations in the Mediterranean area. At 0915 hours the next day, Carpenter departed from Uplands with a survey team of fifteen Air Force

officers in a No 426 Squadron freighter bound for Naples. As well as several staff officers from Air Transport Command Headquarters, the survey team included Group Captain H.A. Morrison, who would command the Air Transport Unit to be established at Capodichino Airfield, two legal officers from the Office of the Judge Advocate General at Air Force Headquarters, and a representative of Air Material Command. The survey team arrived at Capodichino at 2205 hours local on 21 November and were met by Colonel D. Douglas, the Military Attaché from the Canadian Embassy in Rome, and Colonel Folinea, the commander of Capodichino Airport. Soon after arriving, key members of Carpenter's party were in a formal meeting with Colonel Folinea, the UN representative in Naples, and the admiral commanding the nearby U.S. Navy base.

Carpenter's first objective was to find an airfield near Naples that No 435 Squadron could use as a base for the C-119s that would be airlifting UNEF troops and supplies to Egypt. His next priority was to get that facility ready so the C-119s could begin operating to and from Egypt immediately upon arrival. The upshot of that first meeting at Capodichino Airport was an offer of its facilities to the RCAF, backed up with offers of full co-operation from the U.S. Navy and the Italian Air Force to ensure that the RCAF could carry out its Mediterranean mission.

An Air Force Headquarters Organization Order, effective 22 November and considered supplementary to UNEF regulations, authorized the creation of an Air Transport Unit for the Canadian contingent in UNEF — ATU/CANUNEF —to execute such plans and carry out such tasks as might be assigned from time to time by the UNEF Commander, principally to direct and control the activities of No 114 Communications Flight at Capodichino Airport, and No 115 Communications Flight at Abu Suweir, seven miles west of Ismailia, Egypt. The commanding officer would be the senior RCAF officer serving with UNEF.

After two days on alert, the first C-119s left Canada for Naples on 21 November, and the first flight was ready to leave Capodichino for Egypt on 24 November but lack of clearances held it up for a day. No 435 Squadron and No 436 Squadron had moved twelve aircraft into an empty hangar at Capodichino Airport — some 6,700 miles from their previous base at Edmonton and Downsview, respectively — and got them operational within four days of receiving their orders. Capodichino thus became the European end of the emergency airlift to Egypt.

If the C-119s took the most direct route to Egypt, they would have to carry a great deal of fuel and less than the 12,000 pounds of cargo they were capable of airlifting. To get the most out of the Boxcar's payload capabilities, therefore, C-119 fuel was stored at the U.S. Navy base at Souda Bay on the island of Crete, which thus became an intermediate stop on the airlift route. In 1957, when Cairo became available as an alternate to Abu Suweir, the C-119s were able to fly direct, but with a reduced maximum payload of 9,500 pounds.

The North Stars of No 426 Squadron, still operating from Dorval, carried out the strategic airlift task directly, on behalf of UNEF.[75]

While No 426 Squadron's operations staff planned the involvement with UNEF, the unit continued to handle its more immediate commitments. On 1 November, Special Flight 1916 was

Lachine, 1956

despatched to Langar with high-priority cargo. NS17525, with an augmented crew, captained by Flight Lieutenant Misener, left base and proceeded to England, stopping only to refuel at Torbay and Lajes. On 6 November, the crew (now captained by Flying Officer Lebedis) took over NS17514 and left for Grostenquin and Marville before proceeding on 8 November to Rabat-Salé. On 9 November, they hauled a load of equipment and supplies was hauled to Cagliari and returned to Langar. On 10 November, Lebedis and his crew took NS17502 as far as Keflavik, where they turned the aircraft over to a slip crew, and the next day, they took over the next aircraft in, NS17509, and took it back to base by way of Goose Bay.[76]

On 2 November, the squadron dispatched its fifth observer-team rotation mission to Saigon. The flight was away for three weeks, being routed through Lajes, the Mediterranean, the Middle East and India and returning via Manila, Tokyo, Wake Island, Honolulu and San Francisco.[77]

On 5 November, Flying Officer Ronning and his crew left base for Goose Bay in NS17511 to position servicing personnel and spares for *Operation RANDOM West 2*. The flight reached Narsarssuak on 7 November, Keflavik on 9 November and Kinloss on 10 November. On 11 November, Ronning and his crew went on to the fighter wings, where they conducted several shuttle runs before returning to Kinloss on 18 November. *Operation RANDOM WEST 2* was originally scheduled to leave Kinloss on 17 November, but the convoy of sixteen Sabre Vs was delayed by the weather at Keflavik. The Sabres made the hop to Iceland on 18 November, and Ronning and his crew arrived from Kinloss with the support North Star on 19 November in the morning. The convoy made the trip's second over-water crossing, to Narsarssuak, that day, with NS17511 following with the servicing personnel and the Sabre spares. On 20 November, the Sabres made the double hop to Goose Bay and St-Hubert, and Ronning and his crew followed the convoy as far as Goose Bay and then returned directly to base on 21 November. The whole operation was carried off in near record time, just fifty-two hours from the Sabres departure from Kinloss to their arrival at St-Hubert.[78]

On 6 November, when the crisis in Egypt was peaking and the Hungarian uprising was in its last throes, Flight Lieutenant Carss took out NS17521 on a regular service flight to Prestwick. On 9 November he took over incoming NS17509 at Prestwick and took it to Langar, where he was ordered to wait, with NS17525 and one of the slip crews, while all the squadron's other North Stars and crews were recalled to base. On 13 November, Carss was asked to carry out a shuttle run to Kinloss to pre-position spares for *RANDOM WEST 2*, and from there he proceeded to Prestwick and Keflavik. After a short crew rest at Keflavik, the flight returned to base the following day.[79]

Remembrance Day was a cold, wet Sunday, and the annual commemorative parade in downtown Montreal was held during the afternoon. The only participants in the parade from Lachine and St-Hubert were bandsmen; everyone else was on duty because of the Suez Crisis.[80]

On 13 November, the Resolute Bay detachment received a message from Air Transport Command Headquarters advising that SF5, a North Star service, was postponed indefinitely;

the next day, the Detachment Commander mustered all hands in the canteen to explain Canada's role in Suez and squelch any rumours. Another message later that afternoon raised spirits with the announcement of a C-119 on a special flight that would arrive in several days.[81]

At 2005 hours on 12 November, the first North Star left for Naples on *Operation RAPID STEP*: Flight Lieutenant Major and his crew in NS17502, carrying a CBUME advance party of twenty-three officers and twelve other ranks to the staging area. Their passengers were on an urgent mission, so the crew stopped only long enough to refuel and file new flight plans at Gander, Lajes and Gibraltar, arriving at Capodichino twenty-nine hours and twenty minutes after leaving Montreal (flight time en route was twenty-five hours and ten minutes). A twenty-four hour crew rest was taken before Major and his crew started back for base on 15 November; they refuelled the aircraft at Gibraltar and took a twelve-hour crew rest at Lajes, where a slip crew took over NS17502 for the last leg of the trip to Montreal. Major picked up NS17504, the next homeward-bound squadron aircraft, and arrived back at base with it on 16 November. The crew were away from base a total of ninety-eight hours and ten minutes, including fifty hours and forty-five minutes of flying.[82]

Two and a half hours after Major's departure on 12 November, Flying Officer Byrne left Montreal in NS17504 with a second group of soldiers bound for Naples, and stopped briefly at Gander, Lajes and Gibraltar before arriving at Capodichino on 14 November. His elapsed time from departure until arrival was thirty hours, of which twenty-five hours were spent in the air. On 15 November, after twenty-four hours of rest, the crew returned to Lajes; the next day they were redirected to Langar, where a slip crew took over the aircraft as soon as it was loaded for the return trip to Canada, leaving Byrne and his crew at Langar as the slip crew. On 18 November, Byrne was assigned to take NS17516 as far as Lajes by way of St. Mawgan, where they took on extra fuel because of unfavourable winds. On 21 November, Byrne and his crew left Lajes for Montreal, where they arrived the next afternoon after a short crew rest in Gander.[83]

When SF51 departed Dorval for Langar at 1250 hours on 13 November, NS17520 was carrying two extra flight crews (captained by Flight Lieutenant McBurney and Flying Officer McLaughlin) and five squadron technicians all on their way to Naples. The captain, Flight Lieutenant Knight, took the aircraft to Lajes after a stop at Gander, and the flight left Lajes for Langar after a twenty-five minute stop with Flight Lieutenant Owston at the controls; it arrived at 1745 hours on 14 November. The next morning the two extra flight crews and the technicians boarded two Air Division Dakotas (634 and 944), captained by Flying Officer Thompson and Flying Officer Johnson, for the trip to Naples. McBurney and his crew left Naples in NS17515 on 23 November and headed for Lajes, where a slip crew took over the aircraft for the leg to Montreal. McBurney's crew returned directly to base from Lajes on 28 November, after a flight of twelve hours and fifty minutes.[84]

McLaughlin's crew left Naples for Gibraltar on 24 November. After refuelling, they set out for Lajes, but the field closed because of bad weather while the flight was en route, so it returned to Gibraltar. The next morning, the aircraft proceeded to Lisbon, which took two hours, and from there went to Santa Maria in the Azores, a four-hour hop, as Lajes was still weathered in. The crew refuelled and filed a direct flight plan to Montreal from Santa Maria. They arrived at destination eleven hours and thirty minutes later.[85]

On 15 November, Flight Lieutenant Lewis and his crew took out NS17512 and headed for Lajes as SF51; a slip crew then took NS17512 on to Langar, while Lewis and his crew waited six days for the next outbound flight. On 21 November, Lewis took over NS17517, a *RAPID STEP* flight, and headed for Naples via Gibraltar. The crew left Naples for Gibraltar on 24 November in NS17514, but the weather in the Azores area was unsuitable for the next two days so the flight went to Shannon on 26 November. There it was refuelled, and the crew pushed on to Keflavik for a short rest. On 27 November, the crew flew directly to Montreal, a flight of twelve hours and fifty-five minutes.[86]

On 19 November, with Parliament's consent to Canada's involvement in UNEF secured, *Operation RAPID STEP* got under way in earnest. On 21 November, Flight Lieutenant Lambeth positioned NS17514 at Downsview and embarked soldiers and their equipment and took off for Naples, pausing on the way only to refuel at Gander, Lajes and Gibraltar and arriving on 23 November. After a rest, the crew headed back to Gibraltar the next day. The winds on the southern route were unfavourable, so Lambeth headed for home by way of Langar, Keflavik and Goose Bay, and arrived at base on 27 November.[87]

On 22 November, the squadron despatched four *RAPID STEP* flights from Montreal to Naples within six hours. Flight Lieutenant Black and his crew took out NS17507, reached Naples the next day and, after a short crew rest, returned to base via Santa Maria shortly before midnight on 26 November. Next out was Flying Officer Reed's crew, who reached Naples in NS17521 on 23 November, left for Langar thirty-six hours later in NS17508, and returned to base on the morning of 27 November via Keflavik and Goose Bay. The day's third flight was NS17509 with Flight Lieutenant Major's crew, who arrived in Naples on 23 November, left again a day later, and returned to Montreal on 27 November by way of Gibraltar, Shannon and Keflavik. The last leg of their homeward journey took twelve hours.

The final departure for Naples on 22 November was Flight Lieutenant Carss and his crew in NS17515, who arrived on 23 November, took a twenty-four hour crew rest, and then were detailed to take NS17521 to Langar, where the aircraft was loaded with high-priority cargo bound for Canada. On 25 November, they took NS17521 to Prestwick, where a slip crew took it over for the flight back to base. On 29 November, Carss and his crew flew NS17507 (just in from Montreal) to Langar; the next day, they were assigned to NS17509, which they took to Lajes and then directly to Montreal, the last leg taking them twelve hours. They arrived at base on 1 December.[88]

Two more squadron flights left base for Naples on 23 November. Flight Lieutenant Nurse took out NS17511 and returned to base in NS17516 seven days later, and Flying Officer Ronning, who had returned home with his crew two days earlier from *Operation RANDOM WEST 2*, departed in NS17502, returning on 30 November in NS17507. Both aircraft were routed to and from Naples through Gander, Lajes and Gibraltar. The next flight to Naples, on 24 November, was captained by Flying Officer Byrne, who positioned NS17512 at Downsview to embark soldiers and their equipment, and left for Gander at 0900 hours the next morning. With poor weather prevailing in the Azores, the flight proceeded to Shannon, where the crew took a twelve-hour rest before continuing on to Naples. Byrne and his crew left Naples for Lajes in NS17517 on 27 November, and returned to base in NS17515 on the morning of 30 November.[89]

Before the end of the month, four more flights carrying soldiers and military equipment were despatched from Dorval to Naples. At 2040 hours on 26 November, Flying Officer McAlpine and his crew left for Italy; they returned on 1 December in NS17511. At 0140 hours on 27 November, Flight Lieutenant Owston took out NS17516, and he returned from Naples in NS17504 on 3 December. Three and a half hours after Owston's departure, Flight Lieutenant Misener and his crew in NS17507 headed for Harmon AFB (Gander was weathered in), refuelled and proceeded to Lajes; they returned to base in NS17510 on 3 December. Later in the morning of 27 November, Flight Lieutenant Schwanky set out for Naples in NS17515, and refuelled in Argentia as Gander was still closed. At Lajes, on the way home from Naples, Schwanky and his crew were detailed to take SF 51 to Langar; they returned to base on 8 December.[90]

On 28 November, SF5 (NS17508, captained by Flight Lieutenant Black) left Dorval for Churchill by way of Uplands and Winnipeg. It arrived at Resolute Bay the following afternoon, dropped off supplies and several visitors, and returned to Churchill for more cargo. Black and his crew left Churchill at 1015 hours on 30 November to carry out a supply drop at Spence Bay. After the drop, on the way to Resolute Bay, the aircraft developed an oil leak in No 1 engine and the propeller had to be feathered; this meant a three-engine landing at Resolute. The ground staff established that the engine had to be changed, and a message requesting a replacement engine was sent to Dorval. In the afternoon of 2 December, when Flight Lieutenant Lambert and his crew arrived with the new engine in NS17502, NS17508 was in the nose hangar with the affected components disconnected, ready for a quick engine change.

As soon as NS17502 had been serviced and the cargo (including the replacement engine) was unloaded, Black embarked his passengers and left on a direct flight to Winnipeg, where they picked up more cargo and took off for Churchill. On 4 December, Black and his crew conducted a shuttle run to Coral Harbour, returned briefly to Churchill, and departed for base via Winnipeg and Ottawa. Meanwhile, at Resolute Bay, NS17508 was test flown on 4 December, after the engine change, and found to be fully serviceable. Lambert took off at 1235 hours and flew directly to Montreal.[91]

During the fall of 1956, the planning staff at Air Force Headquarters discussed the future of No 1 OFU and the requirement to ferry fighter aircraft to the Air Division. By the end of 1956, according to Air Force Headquarters estimates, 300 Sabre VIs would have been ferried to Europe, and some thirty Sabre Vs returned to Canada. In 1957, there would be about sixty Sabre VIs to ferry to Europe, and sixteen Sabre Vs to be brought back. Planners believed that, subject to factory delays, these ferry operations should be completed without difficulty by July 1957, and until then, the current OFU establishment of forty-one officers and 108 airmen would be needed. However, if the OFU were to continue ferry operations to meet the replacement requirements of the overseas squadrons after July 1957, the unit establishment could be cut back to as few as sixteen officers and forty-four airmen, or even disbanded, which would mean finding another way to transport fighters to and from Europe — the Navy's new aircraft carrier, HMCS *Bonaventure*, perhaps, or an augmented No 129 Acceptance and Ferry Flight at RCAF Station Trenton.

The Air Operations Branch at Air Force Headquarters had postponed the third *RANDOM WEST* operation to spring 1957, not only because of the North Stars' higher-priority tasking in support of UNEF, but also because the USAF intended to phase out its base at Narsarssuak by 1 July 1957. To ensure adequate support to *RANDOM* flights moving through Narsarssuak up to 1 July, the USAF asked for an estimate of all the *RANDOM* flights, and let the RCAF know that it was prepared to discuss use of Sondrestrom Air Base for ferry flights after June 1957, if the ferry requirement was expected to continue, and provided that RCAF flights were co-ordinated with other activities planned for Sondrestrom.⁹²

December

As well as domestic and service flights to Langar and the fighter wings, the squadron flew eight *RAPID STEP* missions to Naples in December, all routed through Gander, Lajes and Gibraltar. The first out was captained by Squadron Leader Reid, who departed in NS17504 on 1 December, returning nine days later in NS17516. Flying Officer McAlpine left on 3 December in NS17511, and was back at base on 14 December. On 10 December, Flying Officer McLaughlin positioned NS17511 at Downsview, leaving the following day for Montreal after embarking soldiers and their equipment. He left for Naples on 12 December and returned to base on 22 December. Squadron Leader Hall departed in NS17516 on 11 December, returning to Montreal six days later. The next flight out was captained by Flying Officer Lebedis, who departed from Dorval at 2035 hours on 13 December and returned ten days later. Flight Lieutenant Lewis and his crew left base seventy minutes after Lebedis in NS17514 and were back home on 30 December after a seven-day layover in Naples. Flying Officer McAlpine took out his second flight of the month to Italy on 27 December, and returned to Montreal on New Year's Day. The last flight of the month to leave for Naples was captained by Flying Officer Byrne. He left base with his crew in NS17511 on 29 December and they arrived the next day at Capodichino, where the schedule gave them a seven-day layover; they were back at base on 8 January.⁹³

On 7 December, Flight Lieutenant Nurse took NS17515 to Greenwood; the next morning, he airlifted servicing personnel from the Maritime Patrol squadrons to Bermuda, and the flight returned to Montreal on 9 December. The reverse airlift was carried out on 14 December, when Flying Officer Reed positioned NS17509 in Bermuda; the next morning, the Greenwood airmen were transported to their home base, and Reed returned to Dorval.⁹⁴

Early in the morning of 8 December, Corporal J.M.E. Jobin, one of the squadron's flight engineers, was killed in an automobile accident on the road from Montreal to Québec City. He was buried with full military honours in Québec City on 12 December.⁹⁵

On 12 December, Squadron Leader Cairns took NS17521 out on SF 5 to Resolute Bay. The flight stopped at Ottawa, Winnipeg and Churchill, where radio problems developed that caused a delay of several hours. Cairns arrived at Resolute Bay at 2313 hours, followed closely by NS17512 with a double crew captained by Flight Lieutenant Owston and Flying Officer Byrne

as SF 2003 from Montreal with Christmas supplies to be para-dropped at several Arctic outposts. With his aircraft unloaded and serviced, Cairns departed for Churchill at 0238 hours on 14 December to pick up more cargo for Resolute Bay. That evening, NS17512 successfully carried out the first series of para-drops at Isachsen, Mould Bay and Sachs Harbour. Several minutes after its return, shortly after midnight on 15 December, Cairn's flight came in from Churchill.

At that point, a snag was discovered in the undercarriage of NS17512: the port oleo leg on the main undercarriage could not be inflated despite several attempts. Since Cairns was returning to Montreal, the crews decided to swap aircraft; consequently, NS17512 departed for Churchill and base at 0400 hours. Now a para-drop aircraft, NS17521 departed for Grise Fjord, where a drop was made, and then to Thule. Two sets of drops were made that day: the first at Sachs Harbour and the second a return trip to Grise Fjord, followed by a second run from Thule to Alexandra Fjord, Eureka and Alert. Leaving Thule on 16 December, the crew carried out drops at Arctic Bay, Pond Inlet and Clyde River before the flight landed at Frobisher Bay. After refuelling, the aircraft continued on to Goose Bay, and reached base on 17 December.[96]

On 19 December, Air Force Headquarters announced that 360 West German pilots would be coming to Canada to train with the RCAF. The final intakes of NATO aircrew to be trained in Canada would arrive by mid-1957, and the program would conclude a year later.[97]

On 21 December, the squadron despatched a special flight to Goose Bay and Frobisher Bay to complete the para-drops of Christmas supplies at Clyde River. On 26 December, Flying Officer Reed and his crew in NS17525 made the year's final run to Resolute Bay via Ottawa, Winnipeg and Churchill, arriving on 28 December. During the Resolute–Churchill leg of the return trip, para-drops were carried out at Isachsen and Arctic Bay, and the flight also stopped at Winnipeg and Ottawa before returning to base on 30 December.[98]

RCAF Station Lachine's annual children's Christmas party was held at the Recreation Centre on Saturday, 15 December, for some 700 children, with the civilian paymaster, Mr. Chrétien, in the role of Santa Claus. Soft drinks and ice cream were provided in plenty, and the entertainment included clowns. The next day was Sunday, and the children of the Protestant Chapel presented their Christmas Pageant at the Station Theatre in the afternoon.

Air Transport Command Headquarters and No 426 Squadron both held their Christmas parties at the Lachine on 20 December, and on Christmas Eve, half of the service personnel and all civilian employees were on leave. On Christmas Day, after church, the officers served dinner to about 200 airmen in the Airmen's Mess, and a lively sing-song was held; an enjoyable time was had by all. On New Year's Eve, all the civilian employees and RCAF personnel who had the duty over Christmas were on leave, and all the messes held dances and entertainment.

Lachine, 1956

Five squadron crews were out on the route at the end of the year: four on service flights at Langar and the Air Division, and one on a special flight to Naples.⁹⁹

In Naples, the RCAF Survey Team had signed a contract for the rental of accommodation in the Hotel Grilli, which would provide lodging and meals for flight crews and servicing personnel, and office space for RCAF administrators. The hotel also accommodated a Royal Canadian Army Postal Corps unit that operated a Field Post Office offering all the normal postal facilities. A teletype communications link was established between the RCAF Administrative offices at the hotel and the U.S. Navy National Circuits; this link provided three-hour service for messages between the Air Transport Unit in Naples and RCAF organizations in Canada. The RCAF contingent settled into its new surroundings, and soon were preparing to celebrate Christmas away from home. Mass was celebrated at the hotel on Christmas Eve, and Group Captain H.A. Morrison and Air Commodore Carpenter officially opened the airmen's lounge and wet canteen on Christmas Day. At noon, the officers and senior NCOs served a Canadian-style Christmas dinner with all the trimmings to the airmen. Before the meal, Air Commodore Carpenter gave an address in which he informed the gathering about the RCAF's reasons for being involved in UNEF, and thanked them for the excellence of their performance on the operation.

At 1300 hours, the senior NCOs entertained the officers in the Sergeants' Mess, which had been organized earlier in the month, and at 1430 hours the hotel staff served the officers and senior NCOs *their* Christmas dinner. Air Commodore Carpenter left for Dorval on 27 December, and the year ended for the ATU personnel with a USO variety show and a dinner of southern fried chicken.¹⁰⁰

PHOTO 166
Hangar fire; Dorval, 19 March 1956. (Jim Scrimger/D. Eagles Collection)

PHOTO 167
Aftermath of the hangar fire; Dorval, 19 March 1956. (Jim Scrimger/D. Eagles Collection)

PHOTO 168
Members of No 426 Squadron on the scene of the hangar fire; Dorval, 19 March 1956. From left: Sgt. Blier, F/L Tim Lamb, F/O Len Halpin and F/L Norm Paul. (L. Halpin Collection)

Lachine, 1956

PHOTO 169
Weather station personnel (geologists and radio operators) take the service flight to Resolute Bay with a load of assorted cargo; Churchill, spring 1956. (DND PL54030)

PHOTO 170
The crew of NS17525 before leaving on a round-the-world flight; Dorval, 9 June 1956. From left, back row: W/C Mackie (captain), F/O A.L. Anderson, F/L L.W. Schunk, F/O G. Serafimoff, F/O A.R. Greening, F/O D.M. Cameron, F/O C.F. Grist and F/L H.G. Maxwell; front row: Cpl. E. Bach, Sgt. W.T. Frame, F/S J.C. Trethowan, WO1 W.G. Jackson and LAC C.P. Barrett. (J.C. Trethowan Collection)

PHOTO 171
A stop on the round-the-world flight: members of NS17525's crew unload Defence Research Board equipment; Adelaide, Australia, 22 June 1956. (D. Eagles Collection)

PHOTO 172
W/C A.J. Mackie poses with the Deputy Lord Mayor of Sydney, Australia; 23 June 1956. (D. Eagles Collection)

Lachine, 1957

CHAPTER 21
LACHINE, 1957

Most of the logistics support provided in 1957 to the RCAF Air Division in Europe and UNEF in Italy and Egypt came in the form of three trans-Atlantic flights per week flown by No 426 Squadron; support to UNEF (including the rotation of the Canadian Contingent) consumed several special flights as well as about one-third of the weekly flights. During the year, the squadron was called on for air transport support to three *NIMBLE BAT*, four *RANDOM* operations and *JUMP MOAT 1*, the ferrying to Europe of CF-100s for the Belgian Air Force. The year's agenda also included five troop-rotation flights to Indochina and two flights to Australia to deliver the latest in Canadian-built radiation-detection instruments on behalf of the Defence Research Board.

Toward the end of the year, the RCAF's two Comets, which had been grounded since January 1954 for modifications, were ferried back from Britain to return to service; soon, No 412 Squadron was using them for overseas flights, thus easing the burden on the Thunderbirds. Finally, Air Transport Command inaugurated a schedule of trans-Canada service flights using C119s, further freeing the North Star fleet for longer-range missions. No 435 Squadron was tasked with the annual re-supply of the Arctic weather stations, while SF 5/6 to Resolute Bay remained a responsibility of No 426 Squadron.

The squadron's authorized strength for 1957 was 440 personnel, including ninety-six officers, 340 airmen and four civilians, and the inventory included twelve North Star aircraft with a utilization rate of 130 hours per month. The squadron received close support from No 2 Movements Unit (Air), with two officers, forty-seven airmen and two civilians, which supplied the "movement controllers (air)", better known as MCAs, for all squadron flights. At Capodichino were the UNEF Air Transport Unit (with ninety-six RCAF personnel — eleven officers and eighty-five airmen — and forty locally engaged civilians) and No 114 Communications Flight, with twenty-two officers and eighty-six airmen. Early in 1957, the allocation of C-119s to UNEF would be reduced from twelve to ten aircraft; later in the year, it would be further reduced to four. At Abu Suweir airfield in Egypt was No 115 Communications Flight, with eighty-one RCAF personnel — seventeen officers and sixty-four airmen — operating two Dakota and four Otter aircraft in direct support of UNEF.[1]

January

The squadron despatched its first overseas flight of the year on 3 January, when Flight Lieutenant Jenkins and his crew left base in NS17511 bound for Langar. The next morning, Flight Lieutenant McBurney took out NS17510 with three other crews aboard and headed for Gander;

on arrival, McBurney's crew and the crews captained by Flight Lieutenant Burnett and Flying Officer Schwanky disembarked to catch subsequent overseas flights. The fourth crew, captained by Flying Officer Reed, took NS17510 on to Prestwick and Naples. Burnett's and McBurney's crews proceeded as far as Lajes, where they took up slip crew positions before returning to Dorval. At Gander, Schwanky and his crew caught NS17512 and went directly to Naples by way of Lajes and Gibraltar, where they refuelled; they were back at base on 8 January.[2]

Subsequent to a decision made by the Department of National Defence the previous fall, representatives from Air Force Headquarters, Air Materiel Command Headquarters and the Royal Canadian Navy met in Ottawa on 7 January to finalize plans for the return of fifty-nine Sabre Vs to Canada by HMCS *Magnificent*, which was tentatively scheduled to arrive in Glasgow on 10 February and in Halifax, with her cargo, two weeks later.[3]

As well as nine more flights to Naples and twelve flights to Langar with several extensions to the wings in continental Europe, the squadron despatched three runs to Resolute Bay in January.

The first of these, between 9 January and 14 January, was captained by Flight Lieutenant Buechler in NS17514, and stopped at Ottawa, Winnipeg and Churchill, where Buechler carried out one shuttle to Coral Harbour and two to Resolute Bay. Flight Lieutenant Belair, Churchill's Roman Catholic chaplain, and a technical party from Lachine went to Resolute on the first shuttle and returned on the homeward leg of the second shuttle, along with two airmen bound for Dorval after completing six months of duty with RCAF Detachment Resolute Bay.

The second service flight was carried out between 18 January and 21 January by Flight Lieutenant Nurse and his crew in NS17525, going directly to Churchill and then to Resolute Bay, and returning to base by the same route. The passenger list included a troupe of twenty entertainers sponsored by the Bell Telephone Company; the Station Commander from Lachine, Wing Commander Delaney; reporters from the CBC and the *Montreal Star*; and several senior technical specialists. The flight arrived at 1730 hours on 19 January, and that night the Bell Troupe put on a show that started at 2100 hours and lasted until midnight, thoroughly pleasing the audience of RCAF and Department of Transport personnel, and employees of the U.S. Weather Bureau. Refreshments in the canteen followed the performance, and the flight departed again for Churchill and Montreal at 0215 hours.

Flight Lieutenant McBurney captained the third trip of the month to Resolute Bay. Carried out between 23 and 25 January in NS17525, this flight staged through Ottawa, Winnipeg and Churchill outbound, returning to base directly from Churchill.[4]

On the afternoon of 30 January, the squadron despatched three aircraft to Halifax: NS17502, NS17514 and NS17511 captained by Flight Lieutenant McBurney, Flight Lieutenant Owston and Flying Officer John respectively. In the morning, each aircraft embarked a full load of RCN personnel and airlifted them to Key West, Florida, for an exercise with the U.S. Navy; the average flight time en route was nine and a half hours. All three aircraft returned to base on 1 February.

On 31 January, Wing Commander Mackie and his crew positioned NS17521 at Greenwood; the next day, they embarked fifty-four servicing personnel from the Maritime Patrol squadrons, proceeded to Nassau, refuelled, and then carried on to Leeward Point Field near Guantanamo Bay, Cuba, where Neptune aircraft from Greenwood were involved in a test of submarine-detection devices with the U.S. Navy. The flight departed for Miami on 3 February and returned to base the following day.[5]

In January, the personnel of the Air Transport Unit had been at Capodichino for a month and were adapting well to their surroundings. On 6 January, they held a twelfth-day-of-Christmas party at the Grilli Hotel for seventy-five boys from a Naples orphanage, who each received lunch and a gift presented by Mr. G. de Siervo, the ATU's Italian Personnel Officer. From 9 January to 18 January, the unit hosted Wing Commander W.A. Bothwell, Staff Officer Accounts and Finance at Air Transport Command Headquarters. Wing Commander Edwards, Senior Air Staff Officer at Air Transport Command Headquarters, arrived in Naples on 11 January, flew to Egypt on a C-119 on 12 January, returned to Naples on 17 January, and left for Montreal the day after. On 18 January, Group Captain H.A. Morrison relinquished command at Capodichino and left for Air Transport Command Headquarters at Lachine to take up the appointment of Chief Staff Officer, and Group Captain W.P. Pleasance assumed the command, having been transferred from Air Force Headquarters. On 23 January, *HMCS Magnificent* arrived in the Bay of Naples, and Group Captain Pleasance and his Chief Administrative Officer, Squadron Leader Robertson, paid a formal call on the carrier's commanding officer, Captain A.B.F. Fraser-Harris, DSC and Bar. Four days later, the carrier sailed for Glasgow, where she would load fifty-nine Sabre Vs to be returned to Canada.[6]

The proposed introduction of the CC-106 transport (later known as the Yukon) and the continuing use by Air Transport Command units of temporary accommodation in eastern Canada required an action plan extending into the early 1960s. Reductions in the aircrew training requirements of the RCAF and NATO countries conducting flight training in Canada also meant organizational changes in Training Command. On 31 January, the Air Council met at Air Force Headquarters and approved the following recommendations in principle:
  a. Training Command would move its headquarters from Trenton to Winnipeg and re-form as Flying Training Command;
  b. 14 Training Group would move from Winnipeg to eastern Canada and re-form to take over responsibility for ground training;
  c. The Flight Instructors' School would moved from Trenton to Saskatoon;
  d. The Central Flying School would move from Trenton to Winnipeg;
  e. The RCAF stations at Lachine, Quebec; MacDonald, Manitoba; Claresholm, Alberta; and London and Aylmer, Ontario would close;
  f. Courses at the Advanced Flying Schools at RCAF Station Gimli and RCAF Station Portage La Prairie would be adapted to new requirements;

g. Air Transport Command Headquarters, No 426 (T) Squadron, No 2 Movements Unit and No 1 Personnel Reception Centre would move from Dorval and Lachine to Trenton;
h. No 436 (T) Squadron would stay at RCAF Station Downsview; and
i. No 1 Officers' School and No 1 Medical Selection Unit would move from London to RCAF Station Centralia, Ontario.[7]

February

During February, the squadron despatched four flights to Naples and eight runs to Langar, of which several were extended to the wings on the continent.

On 1 February, Squadron Leader V.A. Rutherford arrived in Capodichino from RCAF Station Trenton to take command of No 115 Communications Flight at Abu Suweir, replacing Squadron Leader J.S. Miller, who became Officer Commanding, No 114 Communications Flight, at Capodichino. On 14 February, Air Transport Command Headquarters' new schedule of service flights to Naples came into effect. SF53 would henceforth depart Dorval at 1100 hours every Thursday, heading for Capodichino by way of Gander, Lajes and Gibraltar, to arrive at 2130 hours on Friday. SF54 would depart Capodichino for Dorval at 1530 hours each Saturday, and return to base by the same route in reverse, arriving at 1630 hours on Sunday.[8]

On 9 February, *Operation NIMBLE BAT 2* — the move of No 423 AW(F) Squadron from St-Hubert to No 2 Wing at Grostenquin — got under way with two North Stars to provide air transport support. Having positioned NS17521 at St-Hubert on 9 February, Flying Officer Byrne and his crew departed for Goose Bay on 10 February with servicing personnel and aircraft spares; later the same day, Flying Officer Ronning brought NS17525 to St-Hubert to wait for the CF-100s to depart. On 12 February, all twenty-two of No 423 Squadron's aircraft left for Goose Bay followed by Ronning and his crew in NS17525; fuel troubles forced one of the fighters to land at Bagotville, but the rest of the convoy arrived in good order. On 13 February, twenty-one CF-100s left Goose Bay for Keflavik, and twenty arrived; one had to divert to Narsarssuak with a malfunctioning tip tank. Byrne and his crew headed for Keflavik, while Ronning proceeded to Narsarssuak with his load of servicing personnel so they could correct the problem. This they were unable to do, so they hangared the aircraft and boarded the North Star with the CF100 crew, and Ronning rejoined the convoy at Keflavik the following day. (The malfunctioning CF-100 would be ferried out in March during the year's first *RANDOM* operation.) Preceded by one North Star and followed by the other, the convoy took off for Kinloss on 15 February, and completed the final leg of the ferry operation on 16 February with the arrival at Grostenquin of the North Stars and twenty of No 423 Squadron's CF-100s. Both North Stars spent the night at the fighter base. Byrne and his crew departed for Lajes the next morning and were back at base on 18 February, and Ronning proceeded first to Langar, then carried on to Lajes, and arrived at Dorval shortly after Byrne's aircraft.[9]

Among several domestic missions, No 426 Squadron despatched three flights to Resolute Bay in February. Flight Lieutenant Owston and his crew took NS17525 as far as Churchill on 4 February, carrying on the next day to Resolute Bay, where they stopped only long enough to unload their cargo and refuel before heading directly back to Dorval, a flight of ten hours and fifteen minutes. On 13 February, Flying Officer Schwanky captained NS17515 on the next flight to Resolute Bay, by way of Ottawa, Winnipeg and Churchill, where they spent the night. The next morning, Schwanky was on the return leg of a shuttle run from Churchill to Coral Harbour when he had to turn back because the airfield at Churchill was weathered in. They finally made it back to Churchill on 15 February, and proceeded to Resolute Bay on 16 February. Among the passengers was Flight Lieutenant J. Sare, the new Detachment Commander, who was relieving Flight Lieutenant T. Charchuk.

On arrival, Schwanky received instructions to go to Cambridge Bay, pick up Dr. Hartley Zimmerman, the Chairman of the Defence Research Board, and his party, and fly them to Churchill. Schwanky took off for Cambridge Bay, completed the mission and returned to Resolute Bay on 17 February, thus completing a second shuttle run. The next day, the crew left again for Churchill, returning to Resolute Bay on 19 February with more cargo for the detachment. The flight then proceeded to Thule with cargo to be dropped at Arctic outposts. The flight was back at Resolute Bay on 20 February and then went to Churchill for yet more cargo, which was airlifted to Thule the following day. From Thule, the aircraft returned to Churchill and Winnipeg, and was back at base on 24 February.

The next service flight to Resolute Bay was NS17515, captained by Flying Officer McAlpine, which came in on schedule on 28 February, but was temporarily grounded soon after arrival with an electrical problem. Attempts to rectify the malfunction proved fruitless, so McAlpine obtained permission to return to base, and the flight departed Resolute Bay on 1 March for Churchill. After subsequent stops at Winnipeg and Ottawa, the aircraft was back at base on 3 March.[10]

On 18 February, Flying Officer McAlpine and his crew in NS17509 made a return flight of ten hours and twenty minutes each way to Guantanamo Bay, Cuba, to pick up the fifty-four airmen from Greenwood who had been working on a joint U.S.–Canadian test of submarine-detection equipment. On 19 February, the airmen were embarked at the U.S. Navy base and the flight proceeded to Greenwood by way of Bermuda, where it refuelled. McAlpine returned to base on 20 February.[11]

March

The squadron's assignments in March could be categorized as overseas, Arctic and domestic, if "domestic" includes destinations in the United States as well as Canada.

Of the month's eight scheduled flights to Langar, several involved extensions to the fighter wings. The squadron also conducted seven flights to Naples. All the overseas flights were carried out successfully despite a variety of maintenance and weather problems.

Operation RANDOM 27 was the overseas ferrying of twenty-two Sabre VIs and the CF-100 that was left at Narsarssuak during *NIMBLE BAT 2*, plus two F2H3 Banshees and two CS2F Trackers for the RCN, with air transport support by Flight Lieutenant Black and his crew in NS17521, and Flight Lieutenant Misener and his crew in NS17517. *RANDOM 27* was scheduled to start on 5 March, but poor weather at Goose Bay caused a day's delay; the twenty-two Sabre VIs were on their way from St-Hubert to Goose Bay by mid-morning of 6 March, followed closely by the North Stars with the ground parties. The second leg of the operation to Narsarssuak, where the CF-100 joined the convoy, was successfully completed on 7 March, and the entire group, followed by the North Stars, reached Keflavik without incident on 8 March and Kinloss on 9 March. On 10 March, the CF-100 rejoined No 423 Squadron at Grostenquin, and the Navy aircraft departed for the Royal Naval Air Station at Ford, near Portsmouth, where they would be used in the flying trials of Canada's new aircraft carrier, *Bonaventure*. The Sabres all went from Kinloss to Prestwick for storage.

From Kinloss, Black and his crew in NS17521 proceeded to Langar on 10 March to drop off maintenance personnel and spare parts, and repositioned at Prestwick on 11 March. On 12 March, they embarked all the Sabre pilots and headed for base by way of Keflavik, Goose Bay and St-Hubert.

Misener and his crew in NS17517 followed the Sabres to Prestwick, where they stayed the night; the next day, they returned to Kinloss and picked up the RCN and RCAF ground crews and followed the Navy aircraft to RNAS Ford, where their passengers left the flight, and then returned to Langar. On 12 March, Misener and his crew went to Lajes, and the next day they returned to Dorval by way of Halifax, where they dropped off RCN personnel, and St-Hubert, where the Ferry Unit ground crews disembarked.[12]

On 7 March, Flight Lieutenant Marshall and his crew took NS17511 on a special flight to Phillips Army Air Base. The next morning, they loaded a cargo of chemical warfare agents — both very secret and highly sensitive — and delivered it to the Defence Research Establishment at Suffield, Alberta. The flight took nearly ten hours and, when the cargo was unloaded, Marshall and his crew carried on to Winnipeg, a three-hour run. The flight returned to base via Ottawa on 9 March.

With the approach of spring, Arctic activity picked up and squadron taskings with it. No 408 Squadron was preparing for early completion of the aerial mapping of the Arctic Archipelago, and later in the year the DEW Line would be completed, and the radar system declared operational. Arrangements were being finalized for the spring re-supply of the Arctic weather stations, which was scheduled to begin in a few weeks, and several scientific projects marking the International Geophysical Year would require air transport support from the RCAF.

On 6 March, Flight Lieutenant Buechler and his crew left base in NS17504, bound for Resolute Bay via Ottawa, Winnipeg and Churchill; on the way back from Resolute to Churchill on 7 March, the crew made para-drops of supplies and mail at Pond Inlet and Arctic Bay. Flying Officer Charchuk, who had relinquished his acting rank on completion of his six months as Detachment Commander, took the flight home to Dorval.[13]

The next flight to Resolute Bay was captained by Flight Lieutenant McBurney in NS17510. The aircraft was positioned in Ottawa on 12 March to pick up special equipment for No 408 Squadron's aerial survey operations, and proceeded to Churchill the next day. On 14 March, they made a shuttle run from Churchill to Resolute Bay and back. They tried to make another shuttle run the next day, but strong crosswinds at Resolute Bay forced a diversion to Thule. On 17 March, they finally made it to Resolute Bay, unloaded their cargo, and left for Churchill. The aircraft returned to base by way of Winnipeg the next day.[14]

On 13 March, Air Commodore Carpenter opened No 2 Air Movements Unit's new home at Dorval. The Customs Service, the Department of Immigration and the Department of Transport were all represented among the invited guests.[15]

Two squadron aircraft were tasked for the next northern mission on 19 March, when Flight Lieutenant Black and his crew in NS17511, and Flight Lieutenant Misener and his crew in NS17514 went to Ottawa and loaded special equipment and general cargo for several locations. The next morning, both aircraft proceeded to Goose Bay and Frobisher Bay, going on to Thule on 21 March to drop off cargo. They then headed for Churchill, and Misener's crew made a shuttle run to Resolute Bay on 24 March, after which they returned directly to base, a flight of eight and a half hours. Black's aircraft developed mechanical difficulties, so he and his crew spent three days at Churchill repairing it, and returned to base on 24 March.[16]

On 26 March, an aircraft from No 4 (T) OTU — NS17507, captained by Flight Lieutenant Ingall — flew from RCAF Station Trenton to Churchill by way of Dorval and Ottawa, where it picked up passengers (including a Roman Catholic padre, Father Bélanger) and freight; the next day, it made a shuttle run to Resolute Bay, where Father Bélanger and twenty other passengers disembarked and the cargo was unloaded, and flew back to Churchill. On 28 March, Ingall and his crew flew another shuttle to Resolute Bay. The OTU aircraft was followed by NS17509 from No 426 Squadron, captained by Flying Officer McAlpine, which left Dorval on 27 March for Ottawa, Winnipeg, Churchill and Resolute Bay, arriving with mail, freight and passengers, including two DRB scientists, Dr. Thornsteinson and Dr. Tozer, who were involved in the International Geophysical Year project, and Flying Officer Forest, the Northern Detachment Co-ordinator from Lachine. After a two-hour stop, both North Stars returned to Churchill.

On 29 March, Ingall and his crew left Churchill for Trenton via Montreal and Ottawa, while McAlpine and his crew conducted a shuttle to Resolute Bay. The next day, McAlpine's crew conducted another shuttle, this time to deliver supplies and personnel of the Department of Transport and the US Weather Bureau, and taking Flying Officer Forest back to Churchill with them. On 31 March, they flew a third and final shuttle, airlifting more civilian staff and miscellaneous cargo to Resolute and immediately returning to Churchill. The next day, they returned to base, making scheduled stops at Winnipeg and Ottawa.[17]

Operation RAPID STEP 3 was the movement to Egypt of some Royal Canadian Ordnance Corps personnel for the CBUME, and No 56 Canadian Reconnaissance Squadron, Royal Canadian

Armoured Corps (drawn from The Royal Canadian Dragoons), with its equipment, scout cars and trucks. These elements were added to UNEF's Canadian contingent on 31 January at the specific request of the United Nations. HMCS *Magnificent* loaded the heavy equipment and vehicles at Saint John, departed Canada on 6 March, and began discharging her cargo at Port Said on 26 March. The first flight of Ordnance Corps personnel left Dorval for Naples on 7 March, and a North Star aircraft from Dorval was positioned at Uplands each day from 12 March to 14 March to airlift Recce Squadron personnel to Italy.[18]

On 28 March, a Canadair crew captained by W.S. Longhurst took the CL28 Argus out for its maiden flight. A development of the Bristol Britannia, the Argus would soon replace the Neptune as Canada's primary maritime patrol aircraft.

April

The spring re-supply of the Arctic weather stations began on 1 April, with the arrival at Resolute Bay of a C-119 carrying the No 436 Squadron advance party from Downsview led by Squadron Leader Smith. A second C-119 and a North Star came in on 3 April — the North Star returned to Dorval after dropping off its passengers and freight — and on 4 April, two more C-119s arrived, and the first C-119 shuttle went out to Mould Bay. The weather was excellent for flying, and the whole re-supply operation (including Alert, Eureka, Isachsen, Mould Bay and Thule) was finished in ten days. Then the C-119s returned to Downsview.

On 1 April, Flight Lieutenant Buechler and his crew left base in NS17502, bound for Goose Bay in support of the re-supply operation; the following day, they made a supply run to Thule and then headed for Churchill. Over the next several days, they made three more supply runs from Churchill to Thule and two to Resolute Bay. On completing the last run to Thule on 10 April, NS17502 stopped at Resolute Bay. It left the following morning with passengers bound for Churchill and Dorval.[19]

On 12 April, the next service flight arrived at Resolute Bay: NS17504, captained by Flight Lieutenant Marshall, with a group of technical officers from Lachine and the Roman Catholic and Protestant chaplains from Churchill, Flight Lieutenant Lord and Flight Lieutenant Perrier, who would spend the next two weeks, including Easter, at the detachment. Shortly after arriving, Marshall and his crew left on a shuttle run to Thule; the next morning, they returned to Resolute for a brief stop and then left again for Churchill and base.

The month's last North Star flight to Resolute Bay arrived on 27 April and immediately returned to Churchill on a shuttle run, taking the two chaplains home. After completing the shuttle at Resolute, the North Star returned to Dorval.[20]

In April, the squadron conducted nine flights to Langar, four to Naples, several domestic runs, and the flights required to provide air transport support for *Operation RANDOM 28*.

The pending USAF withdrawal from Narsarssuak forced Canadair to increase its production of Sabre VIs so the RCAF could get eighty of them to Europe before 30 June. Although the RCAF had accepted the USAF offer of occasional use of Sondrestrom, short-range aircraft such as the

Sabre could reach it from Goose Bay only in the best of conditions. When Danish facilities in Greenland turned out to be inadequate for RCAF flights, Air Force Headquarters planners had to reconsider the *RANDOM* program: the unit establishments of the squadrons in Europe were now complete, and the aircraft being ferried to the Air Division were going into storage. Furthermore, with most of the Sabres delivered, No 1 OFU was no longer required; future aircraft moves could be done by other means. For these reasons, the planners made several recommendations to the Operations Branch: specifically, after the June 1957 *RANDOM* operation, all new Sabre VI aircraft should be transported to Europe by ship, No 1 OFU should be disbanded, and the information required for reinstating overseas ferry operations should be retained at Air Transport Command Headquarters. The disbandment of No 1 OFU, effective 15 July 1957, was authorized by AFHQ Organization Order 8.9(L), dated 16 April 1957.[21]

Operation RANDOM 28 was originally scheduled to begin on 27 April, but it was advanced by four days to help compensate for the approaching loss of Narsarssuak. With Flight Lieutenant Lambert and his crew in NS17509 providing air transport support, the convoy of twenty Sabre VI aircraft made the hop from St-Hubert to Goose Bay on 24 April and, as the weather was good, all the aircraft made the first over-water flight to Narsarssuak the next day. On 26 April, the Sabres proceeded to Keflavik, refuelled, and carried on to Prestwick, and Lambert by-passed Iceland on a direct flight to Prestwick. From Prestwick, the North Star departed almost immediately for Langar with the ground party, who were to return to St-Hubert on SF 52. Lambert was back at Prestwick on 27 April, but had to return to Langar to rectify a mechanical problem. The next day, the repaired North Star flew back to Prestwick, picked up the Sabre pilots, and left for Keflavik, Goose Bay and Dorval, where it arrived on the afternoon of 29 April.[22]

On 15 April, Wing Commander Mackie assumed command of RCAF Station Lachine for the duration of Wing Commander Delaney's two-week UNEF familiarization tour. On 21 April, Easter Sunday, well-attended services were held at both the Protestant and Roman Catholic chapels, and on 26 April the renovated Airmen's Flight Club opened, with Air Commodore Carpenter to cut the ribbon and a guest list including Wing Commander Mackie and several senior NCOs.[23]

On 24 April, Air Marshal Slemon visited the ATU at Capodichino for two days with his wife and Group Captain Gillespie. At the same time, Group Captain Morrison from Air Transport Command Headquarters and Wing Commander Broadley from Air Force Headquarters were conducting a three-day staff visit to Capodichino and Abu Suweir.[24]

May

During May, another busy month, as well as many domestic runs, the squadron conducted five shuttle runs to Resolute Bay, one shuttle run to Thule, eight service flights to Langar, four service flights to Naples, and *Operation NIMBLE BAT 3* and *Operation RANDOM 29*.

On 1 May, a fire broke out in the furnace room of the Roman Catholic chapel at Lachine. The building suffered considerable smoke damage, but no one was hurt. On 17 May, Corporal G.R. Ohlson, one of the squadron's flight engineers, died suddenly at the Queen Mary Veterans' Hospital; on 21 May, he was buried in Montreal with full military honours. On 30 May, Air Commodore Carpenter conducted his inspection of RCAF Station Lachine, and was guest of honour that evening at a dance at the Officer's Mess.[25]

The squadron's northern flights began on 1 May, when Flight Lieutenant Schroder and his crew left base for Goose Bay in NS17510 carrying Air Commodore Carpenter and a party of senior officers, including Air Vice Marshal Bryans, Air Officer Commanding, Training Command. The flight proceeded to Frobisher Bay and Thule the next day, and arrived at Resolute Bay on 4 May with a USAF doctor and nurse who were returning an Eskimo baby who had been in Thule for medical treatment. During their visit to Resolute Bay, a No 408 Squadron Dakota took Carpenter and his party to visit a Shoran installation, and a North Star took them to Alert. The Air Commodore also managed to squeeze in a short hunting trip with two Eskimos and their dog team. On 6 May, the aircraft went to Churchill by way of Cambridge Bay, and on 7 May it returned to base via Great Whale and Ottawa.[26]

NS17509, captained by Flying Officer Ronning, was the next squadron aircraft to make a northern flight. It left base for Ottawa and Winnipeg on 3 May, stopped overnight at Churchill, and then proceeded to Resolute Bay. On 5 May, Ronning and his crew flew from Resolute directly to Ottawa, a run of eight hours and fifty minutes, dropped off passengers and priority cargo, and then returned to base.[27]

Flight Lieutenant Morrison captained NS17515 on the squadron's next flight to Resolute Bay. Departing from base on 8 May, Morrison went to Ottawa, where he embarked a CBC television crew assigned to cover the Shoran operation, Wing Commander Greenaway and Mr. Albrecht from the DRB, and Corporal Moodie of the RCMP, who was Corporal Gibson's replacement. Winnipeg was the next stop, and the flight remained there overnight. The next day, after Group Captain Richards, the Commander of Tactical Air Command, joined the flight, Morrison proceeded to Resolute Bay via Churchill. On 10 May and 11 May, Morrison and his crew returned to Churchill to bring back more priority cargo to Resolute Bay each day. On 12 May, the flight left for base via Churchill, Winnipeg and Ottawa.[28]

The next run to Resolute Bay departed base for Ottawa on 22 May. Among the passengers aboard NS17525 (captained by Flight Lieutenant Lambeth) were Colonel Folinea and Captain DeBeneditto of the Italian Air Force, from Capodichino. Leaving Ottawa the next morning, the flight stopped off at Winnipeg and Churchill before carrying on to Coral Harbour. On 24 May, Lambeth went to Resolute Bay, dropped off his passengers and cargo, and left for Churchill, where he picked up more supplies and a group of passengers — including Flight Lieutenant Horton and Flight Lieutenant Belair, Churchill's Protestant and Roman Catholic chaplains — and returned to Resolute Bay. The next day, Lambeth and his crew left for Dorval via Churchill and Ottawa, bringing with them the Italian officers and the tour-expired RCMP Corporal Gibson. During their visit at Resolute Bay, the Colonel Folinea and Captain DeBeneditto were taken to see a Shoran site by a No 408 Squadron Dakota and, as observers aboard a C-119, made the run to Mould Bay, where bad weather prevented them from landing.[29]

Flying Officer Ronning and his crew left Dorval in NS17517 on 28 May on the squadron's next northern flight. After stops at Goose Bay and Frobisher Bay, the flight carried on to Thule where a crew rest was taken. On 30 May, the crew proceeded to Churchill to pick up cargo, and then left for Thule. The following morning, Ronning departed for Montreal, making stops at Frobisher Bay and Rockcliffe on the way.[30]

Flight Lieutenant Marshall and his crew positioned NS17504 in Toronto on 4 May, and embarked the RCAF Staff College students and proceeded to Maxwell AFB at Montgomery, Alabama the next day. During the ten days they spent in the southern states, they conducted shuttle runs to Eglin and MacDill AFBs, and they returned to Dorval on 15 May by way of Downsview, where they dropped off the Staff College students.[31]

On 29 May, NS17511 left base for Winnipeg with two crews captained by Flight Lieutenant Black and Flight Lieutenant McBurney to pick up the candidates on the Specialist Navigation Course for the annual NAVARC exercise at Resolute Bay, where the flight headed via Churchill. On 1 June, they carried out the first navigation exercise, which was nearly eight hours long. The following morning, the flight proceeded to Ice Island T3, a seven-and-a-half-hour run. On 3 June, they went to the North Pole, a flight of ten hours and twenty minutes. Another long-range exercise was completed on 4 June, and the next day the course went to Alert. On 6 June, the aircraft flew to Winnipeg, a trip of eight hours and twenty minutes, and returned to Resolute Bay via Churchill. The students returned to Winnipeg on 7 June, and NS17511 was back at base the next day.[32]

On 9 May, the squadron despatched NS17516 and NS17506, captained by Flight Lieutenant Black and Flight Lieutenant Owston respectively, to Bagotville to provide air transport support for *Operation NIMBLE BAT 3*. The next day, the twenty-one CF-100 Mk IVBs of No 440 AW(F) Squadron left Bagotville for Goose Bay in convoy, followed by the North Stars carrying ground support personnel and aircraft spares. All the aircraft made an uneventful crossing to Keflavik the next day, and to No 3 Wing Zweibrücken on 12 May. Both North Stars proceeded to Langar on 14 May and returned to base the next day via Prestwick, Keflavik and Goose Bay.[33]

In preparation for *Operation RANDOM 29*, Flying Officer Byrne and his crew positioned NS17514 at St-Hubert, and on 21 May they embarked aircraft spares and a ground support party and flew them to Goose Bay. The following day, a convoy of sixteen Sabre VIs led by Squadron Leader Cuthbertson made the run from St-Hubert to Goose Bay, while the North Star carrying the ground party went on to Narsarssuak. On the morning of 23 May, fifteen Sabres made the crossing to Greenland; one aircraft aborted because of an unserviceable drop-tank feed. The aircraft of the convoy were all refuelled and made the second hop to Keflavik, still followed by the support North Star. The next day, the fifteen Sabres made the final over-water crossing to Prestwick, where the aircraft went into storage. After the last Sabre took off from Iceland, the North Star proceeded to Prestwick. Byrne and his crew embarked the ferry pilots on 26 May and headed for Keflavik, where the crew took a rest. The next day, the flight returned to base by way of Goose Bay and St-Hubert.[34]

On 25 May, Major-General Burns, the UNEF Commander, arrived at Capodichino to carry out a formal inspection of the RCAF facilities. He was greeted by an Italian Air Force guard of honour, which he inspected first, moving on to the RCAF parade drawn up in squadron formation under Squadron Leader Robertson. On completing his inspection, Major-General Burns spoke briefly to all RCAF personnel, thanking them for their excellent efforts on UNEF's behalf in the airlift from Naples to Egypt. The RCAF facilities at Capodichino Airport were inspected on 27 May, and those at the Grilli Hotel the next day before Major-General Burns' departure.[35]

June

In June, the squadron conducted four scheduled trips to Naples and twelve to Langar; of the latter, three were extended: one to Paris, one to Malta, and one — a combined logistics and training run captained by Wing Commander Mackie — to No 4 Wing at Baden-Söllingen and Naples. In addition to several domestic flights, the squadron made three trips to Resolute Bay, carried out a truce team-rotation mission to Saigon, and provided air transport support for the last *Operation RANDOM*.

The squadron's first scheduled flight of the month to Resolute Bay arrived on 6 June; NS17504 (captained by Flying Officer Mace) stayed the night and left for base the next morning, taking with it Flying Officer Charchuk, who had been in Resolute as District Returning Officer for the federal election. The next run to Resolute Bay was carried out by Flight Lieutenant Sled and his crew in NS17504 between 11 June and 14 June, who made the trip via Great Whale and Churchill. On 13 June, the flight proceeded to Alert, Thule and Churchill before returning to base.[36]

The movement of fifty-nine Sabre Vs from Glasgow to Canada, where most would find homes with RCAF auxiliary squadrons, was the last Red Ensign mission of the aircraft carrier *Magnificent*; as soon as the aircraft were unloaded at Halifax, she sailed for Plymouth, where she was paid off and returned to the Royal Navy on 14 June. Most of the ship's company travelled to the Harland & Wolff shipyard in Belfast, Northern Ireland, to join Canada's new carrier, HMCS *Bonaventure*. Commissioned on 17 January, she was then preparing to make her maiden voyage, to her new home port at Halifax.[37]

On 21 June, the Department of Transport issued Operations Order NOR57 on the re-supply of Resolute Bay and Eureka by the CCG icebreakers *C.D. Howe*, *N.B. McLean* and *Edward Cornwallis* (which was later replaced by the CCGS *D'Iberville*) accompanying the POL tanker *Sea Transporter* and the general cargo carrier *Knightsbridge*. *N.B. McLean* and *D'Iberville* would be loaded with frozen food, and Flying Officer Charchuk would be Beachmaster at Resolute Bay.[38]

Operation RANDOM 30, the last of the series, began on 24 June with a formal parade and send-off by Air Marshal Slemon and Air Commodore Carpenter. The weather was good for flying, and the convoy of twenty-four Sabre VIs and six T-33s, accompanied by Flying Officer Schwanky and his crew in NS17515, reached Goose Bay, refuelled and pressed on to Narsarssuak the first day. On 26 June, all the aircraft made the double hop to Keflavik and Prestwick. On 27 June, the Sabres went into storage, and the T-33s carried on to Marville and Baden-Söllingen, three to each destination. From Prestwick, Schwanky and his crew went first to Langar, and then followed the T-33s, ending up at Baden- Söllingen. On 29 June, Schwanky and his crew embarked three ferry pilots at Baden, headed to Marville to pick up three more, and then proceeded to Langar. The next day, they proceeded to Prestwick, embarked the rest of the OFU personnel, and then headed for Keflavik, where a crew rest was taken. On 1 July, Schwanky and his crew were back at base after refuelling at Goose Bay and dropping off their OFU passengers at St-Hubert.

From this point on, Air Transport Command involvement in the overseas ferrying of aircraft would be limited to air transport support; it would no longer plan and control ferry operations.[39]

On 26 June, the RCAF Air Weapons Unit at Decimomannu in Sardinia was officially activated, and No 439 (F) Squadron from Marville was the first unit to use the new NATO air weapons range. No 426 (T) Squadron would be tasked with providing logistics support for both the Air Weapons Unit and the fighter squadrons deployed there for training.[40]

The squadron's last flight of the month to Resolute Bay left base for Churchill on 26 June: Flight Lieutenant Misener and his crew in NS17511 stopped at Ottawa and Winnipeg en route to Churchill. With forty-two passengers aboard, including Bull Gang members, Construction Engineering personnel and Department of Transport staff, the flight arrived at Resolute Bay on 28 June, disembarked the passengers, and continued on to Alert and Eureka to drop off equipment and supplies before returning to Resolute Bay. The next day, Misener and his crew returned to Churchill for additional cargo. On 30 June, they flew to Resolute Bay, dropped off passengers and cargo, continued on to Alert, unloaded equipment and supplies, and returned to Resolute Bay. The next day, they left for Churchill and Winnipeg, and returned to base by way of Ottawa.[41]

The squadron's last major flight of the month was Special 179 to Saigon, the first of five trips (the other four were rotation flights). Squadron Leader Reid and his augmented crew were scheduled to depart Dorval in NS17502, but the failure of the J2 compass system held them up for several hours and, almost immediately after takeoff at 1730 hours, No 2 engine failed because of a faulty sump pump, and the flight returned to base. After a postponement to ensure all repairs were carried out satisfactorily, the flight departed for Gander the next day at 1400 hours, and the delay would have to be absorbed at the stop in Beirut if they were to benefit from the Middle East border-crossing arrangements made for them by the Department of External Affairs.

The routing on both outbound and return trips followed the now-established routine, with stops at Lajes, Gibraltar, Malta, Beirut, Bahrain, Karachi and Calcutta, and the flight reached Saigon on 6 July. After disembarking the ICSC observers, Reid and his crew prepared to fly to Hong Kong, where they would wait for several days while the homeward-bound truce team members assembled in Saigon and briefed their replacements. Following up on an offer issued by the Canadian legation in Saigon, quite a varied group of passengers from other embassies caught the flight to Hong Kong. The crew did not enjoy the trip as much as their passengers, however; both the radio officers came down with the 'flu, and Flying Officer Wipond had to be admitted to the RAF hospital.

On 12 July, the flight returned to Saigon, embarked the homeward-bound observers, and headed for Calcutta, encountering turbulence on the way as it ploughed through the considerable build-up of cumulus cloud. The APS42 search radar would have been useful, but it failed shortly after leaving Montreal and had been unserviceable ever since. The J2 compass system failed again on take-off at Saigon, but was repaired at Calcutta.

On 15 July, shortly after its arrival in Beirut, the North Star was struck in the nose section by a passenger ramp that the Karanack Servicing Company was moving near the aircraft. The collision smashed a radome, bent a scanner on the APS42, and warped the right panel of the door to the nose-wheel assembly. On receiving Karanack's damage report, Reid contacted base and asked for a nose section to be shipped as soon as possible; the arrangements were made through BOAC, and Karanack had the aircraft satisfactorily repaired by 17 July.

On 18 July, the flight left Beirut and pressed on to Lajes by way of refuelling stops in Malta and Gibraltar, putting in eighteen and a half hours of flight time. The crew took a rest on 19 July and the aircraft was back at base the next day.[42]

On 19 June, a UNEF C-119 flew to Belgrade, Yugoslavia on a mission to return to his family the body of a soldier who was killed by a land mine. The flight was conducted at the request of the Yugoslav government, and was thought to be the first time since the war that an RCAF aircraft had visited that country. The C-119 returned to Naples the following day.

On 22 June, the Central Command Band of the RCAF presented a concert at the Piazza del Plebiscito in Naples. The audience included Mayor Lauro, representatives of the Canadian Embassy, and members of the U.S. Navy, and the concert was followed by entertainment at the Officers' Mess and the Sergeants' Mess.[43]

On 30 June, No 408 Squadron was in the Arctic Archipelago when it completed the final flight of the aerial photographic survey of Canada. This project began during the 1920s and, as the main operational mission assigned to the fledgling RCAF during the Depression, was largely responsible for the survival of the Air Force as a separate service.[44]

July

On 1 July, the squadron despatched two overseas runs: Flying Officer McLaughlin and an augmented crew left for Australia in NS17504, while Flight Lieutenant Lambeth and his crew headed for Langar in NS17509. McLaughlin had left Gibraltar on 3 July, and was on his way to Malta when No 2 engine malfunctioned and had to be shut down; on landing, it was determined that the engine would have to be changed, but the nearest available spare engine was at Langar, so a message was sent. Lambeth had just brought in SF51, so he was detailed to take a spare engine to Malta, an errand he completed on 4 July. Under the supervision of the flight engineers, the engine on NS17504 was changed and the aircraft was test-flown the next day. On 6 July, McLaughlin resumed his flight to Australia, and Lambeth returned to Langar with the defective engine. The next day, Lambeth took out SF52 and headed for Lajes and Montreal, arriving at base on 9 July.[45]

The flight to Australia proceeded to Beirut and Bahrain and arrived in Bombay on 7 July. On the leg to Negombo the next day, the APS42 search radar failed and remained inert for the rest of the trip. The next stop was Singapore on 11 July. Two days later, the flight left for Djakarta and Darwin, and on 14 July it arrived in Adelaide, where Mr. Wright of the DRB (who had been with the flight since its departure from Montreal) turned over the cargo of radiation-detection equipment to the Australians. The next scheduled stops were Melbourne on 15 July and Sydney on 17 July. On 20 July, the flight left for Fiji, Canton Island, Honolulu and San Francisco, and it arrived at base eight days later.[46]

On 5 July, a Lockheed Hudson bomber converted into a civilian transport disappeared between Great Whale and Val d'Or, Quebec, triggering *Operation HAFFEY*, a major search-and-rescue effort. About eighteen aircraft (three civilian, the rest RCAF) were involved in the search, which was greatly hampered by poor weather. Among the passengers aboard the Hudson was an RCAF warrant officer, a member of the Construction Engineering Branch who was carrying blueprints and drawings for installations on the Mid-Canada Line. From 8 July to 12 July, No 426 Squadron contributed NS17506, captained by Flight Lieutenant Lewis, to the search, operating out of Val d'Or. (The author, then based at RCAF Station Trenton, was also a participant, flying with Dakota 692 and Dakota 663). Just as the SAR operation was beginning to wind down, the wreckage of the Hudson was found near the flight path to Val d'Or. There were no survivors.[47]

In July, the squadron carried out nine more service flights to Langar (of which one extended to Zweibrücken) and five trips to Naples.

On 9 July, Flying Officer Ronning and his crew left Dorval in NS17521 for Lajes where, as slip crew, they took over NS17515 on 12 July and proceeded to Naples. Shortly after taking off on 15 July, the No 3 engine malfunctioned and the flight returned to Naples, where the engine was quickly changed. After a successful test flight, the crew then headed for Cagliari where they remained overnight. The next morning, they went to Decimomannu, picked up some cargo, and headed for Gibraltar to refuel. Shortly after departure, No 2 engine had to be shut down, and the flight returned to Gibraltar where it was determined that another engine change was required. Another new engine was installed, and two test flights were carried out on 20 July. The first test flight indicated that there were still problems with the engine and, on further investigation on the ground, it was discovered that the coolant temperature valve had been reversed. The problem was rectified and the second test flight went smoothly. Ronning then set off for Lajes, where the aircraft was turned over to a slip crew. The next day, Ronning and his crew took over NS17525 and returned to base without further incident.[48]

On 11 July, heavy fog and rain at Resolute Bay kept SF 5 grounded at Churchill for two days. The fog lifted on 13 July, permitting Flight Lieutenant Buechler to bring his North Star into Resolute Bay. On board were twenty-three members of the Bull Gang and Flying Officer Charchuk, the Beachmaster for the re-supply operation. After disembarking the passengers and unloading cargo, the flight left for Churchill. The next day Buechler returned to Resolute Bay with more passengers and freight; after unloading, the flight left for Churchill and base. Meanwhile, in Montreal, the SS *Knightsbridge* and the SS *Sea Transporter* were being loaded with goods for the Arctic outposts. The icebreaker *D'Iberville* sailed from Montreal on 23 July, and reported that the ice situation in northern waters was the worst in fifty years, and both the Department of Transport and the Department of National Defence were monitoring events closely in the event that alternate supply action was necessary.[49]

The year's second flight to Saigon left Montreal on 18 July: an augmented crew captained by Flight Lieutenant Misener in NS17510, following the route taken by the earlier run to Indochina to arrive in Saigon on 27 July. Misener and his crew disembarked the truce team members, left for Hong Kong, returned to Saigon on 2 August, boarded the returning observers and departed for Calcutta and base, where the flight arrived on 10 August.[50]

On 18 July, the squadron held a going-away party at the Officers' Mess for three of its members: Squadron Leader Cairns, Flying Officer Parent and Flying Officer Yates.

On 24 July, No 412 Squadron conducted a special run to Resolute Bay carrying forty-two passengers, mainly members of the Bull Gang and several personnel from the Department of Transport and the US Weather Bureau, but also including Flying Officer McDonnell, the detachment's new second-in-command. In the morning, NS17518 left again for Churchill and Montreal. The regular service flight to Resolute Bay left Dorval on 25 July, a day late, after a delay for engine trouble. NS17515, captained by Squadron Leader Marshall, stopped at Winnipeg and remained overnight at Churchill. The next day, it carried on to Resolute Bay, where a cargo of rations and pipeline material was delivered. Two hours later Marshall and his crew left on a direct flight to Winnipeg that took nearly eight hours. On 27 July, the flight returned to Resolute Bay with more cargo after a stop at Churchill where it returned the following day. Another shuttle run was conducted to Resolute Bay on 29 July and, after discharging its cargo, the flight returned to Churchill. The next morning, Marshall and his crew left for base, making stops at Winnipeg and Ottawa en route.[51]

July was a busy month for No 419 AW(F) Squadron at North Bay, which was preparing for *Operation NIMBLE BAT 4*, its move with twenty-four CF-100 Mk 4Bs from North Bay to No 4 Wing Baden-Söllingen. During the afternoon of 30 July, an impressive farewell ceremony and parade were held, with the personnel of both the squadron proceeding overseas and of the new No 414 AW(F) Squadron, and the Training Command Band before an audience of about 700, including local dignitaries and several senior Air Force officers. That afternoon, NS 17521 (captained by Flight Lieutenant Kuhn) arrived at North Bay to provide transport support for the operation. The next day, after embarking servicing personnel, spare parts and baggage of the CF-100 crews, Kuhn left for Goose Bay.

August

Operation NIMBLE BAT 4 began at about 0400 hours on 1 August, when the first CF-100s started leaving for Goose Bay. At 0602 hours, the leader of Bravo 2 Section, Flight Lieutenant K. McNulty from Thorold, Ontario and navigator Flying Officer J. Wilding of Kingston, Ontario flying aircraft 18339, were near Sept-Îles, Quebec, when they experienced "control seizure" (a total loss of control) and peeled off from the formation, disappearing into cloud at 22,000 feet. Flying Officer Knight in 18406 of the same section circled the area for a while, squawking on the emergency frequency, and then continued on to Goose Bay. Search and Rescue units were alerted. Three aircraft of the convoy landed at Bagotville on the way to Goose Bay; two continued on later that afternoon and the third arrived at Goose Bay on 2 August.

The next day, nothing was heard from the missing aircraft and all the CF-100s were grounded for a special inspection. The search for the missing crew was discontinued on 9 August, when the remnants of one parachute and some maps were found. It was assumed that the aircraft had gone into the Moisie River.

After spending 3 August in thorough testing of all the aircraft, the convoy made a successful second hop to Keflavik on 4 August, followed by the North Star. On 5 August, the convoy and Kuhn and his crew completed the final leg to Baden-Söllingen without incident. With the support personnel aboard, Kuhn left for base on 7 August, stopped overnight at Keflavik, and arrived the next day at Dorval, via Goose Bay and St-Hubert.[52]

On 1 August, Flight Lieutenant L.T. Legaarden was transferred to RCAF Station Lachine as Officer Commanding, No 2 Movements Unit (Air), replacing Flight Lieutenant E.E. Mailloux who had been posted to No 436 Squadron at Downsview.

On 1 August, Flight Lieutenant Schroder and his crew took out NS17509 on the first service flight of the month to Langar. Eight other flights to Langar would be conducted during the month, with one extension to London and No 4 Wing carried out by Wing Commander Mackie. Four trips in August went to Naples.[53]

Also on 1 August, Flight Lieutenant Black left base for Australia with an augmented crew in NS17506, loaded with about 7000 pounds of DRB radiation-detection equipment for delivery to the Maralinga atomic test site in South Australia. The flight was routed through the Mediterranean and the Middle East to Bombay, then to Colombo, Singapore and Djakarta, arriving at Darwin on 13 August. The next day, the flight proceeded to Maralinga where the DRB's Mr. Andrew turned over the cargo to the Australian authorities. On 15 August, the aircraft left for Melbourne, continuing on to Sydney the following day. The crew started for home on 18 August, stopping at Fiji and Canton Island and reaching Honolulu on 22 August. Adverse headwinds delayed the flight for several days before it was able to leave for San Francisco early in the morning of 27 August. The flight took eleven hours and fifty minutes. After a two-hour stop, Black and his crew left for Winnipeg, a seven-hour and forty-five minute run, arriving at 0225 hours local time on 28 August. After a short rest, the crew left at 1210 hours for Ottawa to disembark Mr. Andrew. They then carried on to Dorval.[54]

The squadron's first flight of the month to Resolute Bay attempted to land on 7 August but poor weather and low ceilings caused the aircraft to divert to Thule. NS17507, with Air Commodore Carpenter and several Air Transport Command Headquarters staff officers aboard, arrived the following morning in marginal weather conditions of rain, low ceilings and poor visibility. Following his visit, the Air Commodore and his party departed on 9 August for Hall Beach and Churchill before returning to Dorval.[55]

On 8 August, NS17504, captained by Flying Officer John and carrying an augmented crew, departed Dorval on the next rotation flight to Saigon, using the same routing as the two previous flights. After arriving in Saigon on 19 August and disembarking the passengers, the flight carried on to Hong Kong. Flying Officer John and his crew returned to Saigon on 24 August and departed for Calcutta with the tour-expired observers. The flight was back in Montreal on 31 August after being away for twenty-three days, during which the crew put in 119 hours and forty minutes of flying time.[56]

On 12 August, Flight Lieutenant Buechler and his crew left base in NS17514 for Resolute Bay, making scheduled stops were made at Ottawa, Winnipeg and Churchill, where a crew rest was taken. After dropping off cargo at Coral Harbour the following morning, the flight headed north to Spence Bay, at the base of the Boothia Peninsula, where they made six para-drops before continuing on to Resolute Bay. The passengers on this flight included Squadron Leader Delmotte, who was to take over as Detachment Commander; only a week before, he had reported to RCAF Station Lachine and received a briefing on his new responsibilities. Shortly before midnight, when the cargo was unloaded and the aircraft refuelled, Buechler departed for Winnipeg, stopping at Churchill en route. The flight arrived at destination late in the afternoon of 14 August, picked up some priority cargo, and at 2220 hours left Winnipeg for Churchill, where a crew rest was taken.

Lachine, 1957

Meanwhile, at Resolute Bay, the weather had deteriorated considerably by late evening on 14 August, when the CCGS *C.D. Howe* arrived. The other ships of the re-supply convoy —the Coast Guard icebreakers *D'Iberville* and the *N.B. McLean*, the cargo carrier *SS Knightsbridge* and the tanker *SS Sea Transporter* — arrived the following morning. All the ships anchored in the bay except the *Sea Transporter*, which could not get into position to pump out her load of fuel because of adverse wind conditions. Discharge of cargo started with the frozen food, which was taken off the *N.B. McLean* in high winds and light snow. Despite the bad weather, the unloading proceeded quickly on 16 August.

Buechler and his crew returned to Resolute Bay on a shuttle run at 0310 hours on 17 August, bringing injectable gamma globulin from Winnipeg to treat about fifty Eskimos, mostly children, who had come down with measles and were hospitalized aboard the *C.D. Howe* to keep the disease from spreading. Two hours later, the flight was heading back to Churchill on a second shuttle run; it returned to Resolute Bay at 2050 hours, unloaded its cargo and left again for Churchill ninety minutes later. The flight was back at Resolute at 0255 hours on 18 August, and the crew took a ten-hour rest before departing for base via Winnipeg and Ottawa.

With the temperature below freezing and some improvement in the weather, the unloading proceeded briskly at Resolute Bay on 18 August. At noon, her Resolute Bay cargo discharged, the *D'Iberville* sailed for Eureka. By 20 August, all general cargo had been offloaded and the tanker had pumped most of the bulk fuel ashore. On 21 August, a Dakota from Churchill brought more gamma globulin for the measles patients aboard the *C.D. Howe*. On 22 August, Squadron Leader Delmotte assumed command of the detachment, the unloading of supplies was completed, and the measles patients were transferred from the *C.D. Howe* to two of the detachment's empty buildings. On 23 August, Flying Officer Mace and his crew in NS17512 arrived with a load of rations for Alert; after unloading and taking a short rest, they departed again for Dorval, nine hours and twenty minutes away, with a passenger list of stevedores. Its mission completed, the Department of Transport supply convoy headed south.[57]

With the City of Lachine planning to build a road through the middle of the station, Air Force Headquarters decided to accelerate its plans to move Air Transport Command units to Trenton. By mid-1959, Air Transport Command Headquarters, No 426 Squadron, No 1 Personnel Reception Centre and No 2 Movements Unit would all be at RCAF Station Trenton, and RCAF Station Lachine would be closed. No 426 Squadron Repair (second-line maintenance) would remain in No 4 Hangar at Dorval Airport until the new 426 Hangar planned for Trenton was completed in the fall of 1960. RCAF Station Trenton would be transferred to Air Transport Command, and the new hangar had to be ready to receive the CC-106 transport aircraft with which the RCAF planned to re-equip No 426 Squadron.[58]

In August, the Canadian Joint Staff in Washington advised Air Force Headquarters that the U.S. Chief of Naval Operations had approved a general plan for the use of the Naval Air Warfare Centre at Point Mugu, California for a CF-100 flight-test program. Point Mugu lay about sixty miles northwest of Los Angeles, and No 426 Squadron would provide air transport support for the deployment of CF-100 aircraft to the Naval Air Warfare Centre.[59]

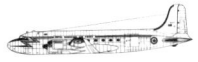

531

August was a busy month for the Air Transport Unit at Naples. On 2 August, C-119 flights between Capodichino and Abu Suweir were scheduled every three days. On 10 August, Flight Lieutenant A. Hicks, the runway expert from the Construction Engineering Branch at Air Force Headquarters, arrived to inspect the airfield at El Arish, about twenty-seven miles west of Rafah on the Gaza Strip, and make recommendations regarding improvements. UNEF planned to move No 115 Communications Unit from Abu Suweir to El Arish in the next few weeks.

On 15 August, Air Commodore Carpenter and a party of staff officers from Air Transport Command Headquarters left Dorval for Naples on SF53, arriving on 17 August. Carpenter and his party arrived at El Arish on 19 August, and then flew to Gaza by Otter for meetings at UNEF Headquarters. Back at Naples, a Commanding Officer's Parade was held at Capodichino on 22 August on the occasion of Air Commodore Carpenter's visit. The parade was attended by Colonel Folinea, commandant of the Italian Air Force Base, who came with a guard of honour of Carabinieri. Carpenter and his party left Naples on 24 August for Langar in NS17510, captained by Flying Officer Byrne, which departed the next morning for Lajes, via Valley, Wales, the ancestral home of the Carpenters. As usual, the Air Commodore was travelling with his bridge table, which he insisted on having aboard to help him while away the hours in the back of a noisy North Star. An excellent bridge player, Carpenter had little trouble mustering a foursome.[60]

The fourth rotation flight to Saigon left base on 29 August, used the same routing to and from Indochina as the previous three flights, and was back at base on 21 September.[61]

The last flight of the month to Resolute Bay arrived on 31 August, bringing with it Squadron Leader Thompson from Air Force Headquarters to inspect the detachment's radio installations, which had had some maintenance problems. NS17515 was quickly unloaded and refuelled, and left immediately for Churchill as the weather was deteriorating rapidly.[62]

September

On 1 September Air Marshal C.R. Slemon retired as the Chief of the Air Staff, and was succeeded by Air Marshal H.L. Campbell.[63]

In September, the squadron's main assignment was the rotation of the Canadian contingent in UNEF, which was scheduled to be completed by mid-November. This mission involved four regular scheduled flights and six special flights to Naples in September, so only four flights to Langar were carried out during the month. The squadron also had a variety of domestic runs to carry out, and two service flights to Resolute Bay, from where the fall re-supply of Alert, Eureka, Isachsen and Mould Bay was conducted by four Downsview-based C-119s from No 436 Squadron, which airlifted some 320,000 pounds of freight to the Arctic weather stations. At the end of the month the two RCAF Comets returned to Ottawa from Britain, the crews having completed the conversion phase of their training. Immediate plans for those aircraft included further training flights both in Canada and on the trans-Atlantic route to prepare the Comet crews for operational taskings by the end of October.[64]

In Egypt, the two-day operation to move No 115 Communications Flight from Abu Suweir to El Arish was completed on 5 September by aircraft and motor transport. Within a few months, the North Stars of No 426 Squadron would be operating into El Arish on a regular basis.⁶⁵

On 11 September, Flight Lieutenant Morrison and his crew in NS17510 left base for Resolute Bay, via Ottawa and Winnipeg, where the crew spent the night. On 12 September, they arrived at Churchill and conducted a shuttle run to Resolute Bay. On 13 September, they conducted another shuttle run to Resolute from Churchill, bringing members of the Bull Gang back with them on the return leg. On 14 September, Morrison and his crew returned to base via Winnipeg and Ottawa.

The second service flight to Resolute Bay was carried out by Flight Lieutenant Quickfall and his crew in NS17517 between 25 September and 29 September.⁶⁶

The rotation of the Canadian contingent in UNEF began on 13 September with the first special flight to Naples, conducted by Wing Commander Mackie and his crew in NS17512. The second flight was Flying Officer McAlpine and crew in NS17504 the next day. On 15 September, Flying Officer John and his crew brought NS17521 as far as Lajes, where they remained as a slip crew. Flights carrying fresh troops were despatched daily from 17 September to 20 September, captained by (in order of departure) Flying Officer Byrne (NS17517), Flying Officer Mace (NS17506), Flight Lieutenant Hamel (NS17504) and Flight Lieutenant Black (NS17512).⁶⁷

The new contingent moved in to relieve their predecessors on 19 September, when the first group of soldiers was flown from Naples to El Arish by way of a refuelling stop at Athens. The C-119 returned to Naples the next day, with troops returning to Canada. The rotation would be completed on 18 November, when the last draft left Naples for Canada. A total of 717 soldiers would be flown home and replaced by 678 from Canada.⁶⁸

October

Air Transport Command Headquarters cancelled SF53 and 54 for the duration of the UNEF rotation, and supplies and spares normally delivered to Naples and the Communications Unit at El Arish were airlifted on a space-available basis on the UNEF rotation flights. At the same time, Air Transport Command continued to provide logistics support to the Air Division. In October, No 426 Squadron despatched ten flights to Naples, of which two were routed through Langar, and two of the return flights also came through Langar. Four runs to Langar were conducted during the month, three by the southern route through Lajes and one routed by way of Keflavik. This last flight was used to check out new captains for the squadron; it went from Langar to Orly (Paris) and Northholt (London) before returning to base through Lajes. On top of all this, the squadron conducted a variety of domestic runs and despatched two service flights to Resolute Bay.⁶⁹

Flight Lieutenant McBurney captained NS17521 on the squadron's first flight of the month to Resolute Bay. Leaving base on 9 October, the flight picked up passengers and freight at Ottawa before going to Winnipeg. The next morning, McBurney and his crew departed for Churchill, picked up more cargo, and headed for Resolute Bay. After disembarking the passengers and unloading the freight, the flight left for Thule to drop off two scientists from an International Geophysical Year project, who had boarded in Ottawa. On 11 October, the flight returned to Churchill after a brief stop at Resolute Bay. The shuttle run returned to Resolute Bay the next day with several passengers, most of them RCA contractors and their staff. Shortly after arrival, the flight carried on to Thule to deliver a small load of scientific equipment. On 13 October, McBurney and his crew went directly to Churchill for a brief stop, carried on to Winnipeg, and returned to base the following day.

McBurney also captained NS17515 on the squadron's second flight of the month to Resolute Bay. Departing on 24 October, the flight was back at base on 27 October.[70]

On 2 October, Corporal Desroches from RCAF Station Lachine was killed in an automobile accident on Highway 11A near Ste-Thérèse. The funeral at Ste-Thérèse Cemetery was held on 7 October with a burial party and funeral parade mounted by Lachine personnel. On 11 October, Wing Commander Delaney handed over the command of the station to Wing Commander P.S. Turner at a parade that included a flypast of No 426 Squadron aircraft. Delaney was leaving for an assignment at No 1 Air Division Headquarters in Metz, and Turner was arriving from a stint in Moscow as Air Attaché at the Canadian Embassy.

On 21 October, the new Chief of the Air Staff, Air Marshal H. Campbell, paid a visit that included an inspection of the Guard of Honour that greeted him at Dorval, a tour of the RCAF facilities at Dorval and RCAF Station Lachine, accompanied by Air Commodore Carpenter and Wing Commander Turner, and stops at the Airmen's Flight Club and the Senior NCOs' Mess. That evening, a mess dinner was held in his honour at the Officers' Mess.[71]

November

In November, the rotation of the Canadian contingent in UNEF was completed, and the squadron conducted eight flights to Naples, including SF53/54, which Air Transport Command reinstituted 13 November. Bad weather, particularly at Lajes and Gibraltar, caused several last-minute route changes by the crews. Two flights that left Lajes for Naples refuelled at Port Lyautey instead of Gibraltar, which was closed for weather. Two flights went to Langar from Lajes and returned to base from Naples via Gibraltar, Shannon, Keflavik and Goose Bay. One flight went to Naples via Goose Bay, Prestwick and Langar, returning to base by way of Gibraltar and Lajes. And three flights used the southern route to and from Italy.[72]

In November, six flights went to Langar, five by the southern route; the sixth flight went to Langar by way of Gander and Shannon, returning by the northern route through Prestwick, Keflavik and Goose Bay. Another flight went to Marville, France and was routed through Gander and Shannon, returning to base by way of Lajes and Gander.[73]

The squadron despatched one other overseas flight from Dorval in November: the special taking Christmas comforts, gift parcels and mail to Indochina for the truce team members. Wing Commander Mackie and his augmented crew left Dorval in NS17504 on 14 November, bound for Gander and Lajes. The flight then proceeded to Saigon after making stops at Port Lyautey, Malta, Beirut, Bahrain, Bombay, Negombo and Singapore. It arrived at destination on 24 November, stopped only long enough to unload its cargo and immediately left for Hong Kong. Starting for base on 26 November, the flight proceeded to Tokyo, and then continued by way of Wake Island

and Midway to Honolulu, where it arrived on 29 November. Headwinds delayed departure for Travis AFB until 5 December, when Mackie and his crew were able to make the flight of eleven hours and forty minutes. The next day, the flight returned to base via Winnipeg, where it stopped to refuel.[74]

On the domestic scene, as well as three flights to Resolute Bay, the squadron conducted three shorter-range freight and passenger runs to northern destinations in November. The first of the shorter flights was to Knob Lake, Great Whale and Goose Bay; the next took in Knob Lake and Great Whale; and the third was routed through Goose Bay, Great Whale and Ottawa.[75]

The first Resolute Bay run involved delivering an engine for No 408 Squadron Lancaster KB 882. Flight Lieutenant Longworth and his crew positioned NS17521 in Ottawa on 5 November, loaded the spare engine and left for Churchill. Brake problems delayed the flight's departure from Churchill for Resolute Bay until the following day, and it stayed the night at the detachment. On 8 November, Longworth returned to base via Churchill and Ottawa, bringing with him the Detachment Commander from Resolute, Squadron Leader Delmotte, who was going to Montreal to organize the shipment of Christmas supplies.[76]

On 13 November, NS17506 (captained by Flight Lieutenant Black) departed for Resolute Bay via Ottawa and Churchill with Squadron Leader Delmotte, heading back to his command, and Miss Sutherland from the Northern Affairs Department, who was going to live at the Eskimo village near the detachment and supervise the school for a month. When the flight arrived at Resolute Bay on the afternoon of 14 November, one of the oleo legs developed problems and it was decided to fly the aircraft out to Churchill for repair. The flight left for Churchill several hours later and returned to base the next day by way of Winnipeg and Ottawa.[77]

On 28 November, Flight Lieutenant Buechler and crew left base for Resolute Bay in NS17517 with Group Captain Morrison aboard. Their first stop was Ottawa, where Air Vice Marshal Kerr and several staff officers from Air Force Headquarters joined the flight, and the flight spent the night at Winnipeg. The next day, they went on to Churchill and Resolute Bay. On 30 November, the flight proceeded to Thule from where they made two shuttle runs to Alert with special cargo and then returned to Resolute Bay. (Alert was a Signals Intelligence collection site that had been a joint Canadian–American weather station since 1950, and an experimental wireless station since 1956.) On 2 December, the flight left for Churchill and Winnipeg where it again spent the night, and it returned to base the following day via Ottawa, where the staff party disembarked.[78]

On 17 November, Flight Lieutenant Sled and his crew positioned NS17521 at Malton Airport, embarked a group of A.V. Roe technicians, and loaded CF-100 armament equipment bound for the Naval Air Warfare Center at Point Mugu, California, where missile-firing tests were to be conducted with CF-100s. The flight departed Malton on 19 November and proceeded to Point Mugu via Chicago and Amarillo, Texas. Sled and his crew returned to base on 21 November by way of Vancouver and Winnipeg.[79]

On 11 November, sixty officers and airmen from the ATU at Naples went to the Commonwealth War Cemetery at Cassino for a memorial service conducted by Flight Lieutenant E. Martin, the ATU's Protestant chaplain. On 15 November, Group Captain Pleasance went to Tunisia for the ceremonial unveiling of the Medjez El Bab Memorial by General Sir Kenneth Anderson, and to lay a wreath on behalf of Canada.[80]

On 25 November, Air Force Headquarters issued Operation Directive 100/57 concerning *Operation JUMP MOAT*, the delivery of fifty-three CF-100 Mk V aircraft to equip three new all-weather fighter squadrons of the Belgian Air Force under the NATO mutual aid program. The *JUMP MOAT* ferry flights would also be used increase the reserve of CF-100 4Bs in No 1 Air Division.

As set out in the Operation Directive, the mission was to deliver at least fourteen CF-100 Vs to Beauvechain Airport in Belgium on 20 December 1957, the remainder to be on the ground at Beauvechain by 30 June 1958. At the same time, at least nine CF-100 IVBs were to be delivered to the Air Division. Air Transport Command would be responsible for the first ferry operation, and Air Defence Command would handle all the rest. Air Transport Command would also provide airlift support for all the flights.

The first *JUMP MOAT* ferry operation was to be routed by way of Marville, France, where they would arrive no later than 18 December. The aircraft would then proceed to Beauvechain Airport to coincide with the official Belgian arrival ceremonies at 1500 hours on 20 December. All subsequent ferry operations from Keflavik were to proceed directly to Beauvechain. No 428 AW(F) Squadron, based at RCAF Station Uplands, was chosen to provide the ferry pilots and support personnel for the first flight.[81]

December

No 426 Squadron completed ten flights to Langar in support of the Air Division in December. One flight, from Ottawa to Marville, involved a Comet. Four flights were completed to Naples in support of UNEF.

In early December, the weather over the British Isles had deteriorated to the point that thick, heavy fog blanketed large areas of England, causing flight delays and route changes. Spells of poor weather at Gibraltar caused one flight heading for Naples to be routed from Lajes to Chateauroux, France and another to go by way of Gander, Shannon and Langar.[82]

Operation JUMP MOAT 1 began for No 426 Squadron on 2 December, when NS17506 airlifted a party of twenty-six technicians from Uplands and a load of immersion suits for the CF-100 crews to Goose Bay, and returned to Dorval. On 3 December, the route-support aircraft (NS17502, captained by Flight Lieutenant Lambeth) left Dorval for Uplands where the crew was briefed by Wing Commander Hall, who was in charge of the ferry operation. The next day the convoy of fifteen CF-100s left Uplands for Goose Bay, closely followed by the support North Star carrying a second party of aircraft technicians and a spare CF-100 crew. As the second party was not needed at Goose Bay, Lambeth went on to Keflavik to position the ground-support party at that airfield. The convoy arrived in Iceland without incident on 6 December.

Poor weather in Britain held up departure in Keflavik for a day, and the convoy and the support North Star made it to Langar on 8 December. Weather again delayed the operation, and it was not until 11 December that all the aircraft were able to make the short flight to Marville. On 13 December, the North Star was released and went on to Langar with some of the ground-support personnel aboard. The next day, Lambeth and his crew left for Lajes, and were back at base on 15 December after disembarking passengers at Uplands. The acceptance ceremony for the CF-100s took place at Beauvechain, Belgium, on 20 December, as planned.[83]

On 9 December, Flying Officer Byrne captained NS17514 to Goose Bay and the Mid-Canada Line Stations of Knob Lake and Great Whale to pick up personnel scheduled for Christmas leave and take them to Ottawa and Montreal. A similar flight was conducted by Flying Officer Mace in NS17511 on 27 December, to return personnel from Christmas leave and pick up those going on New Year's leave.[84]

Two service flights to Resolute Bay were completed in December. NS17515, captained by Flight Lieutenant Longworth, left base on 11 December and stopped at Ottawa, Winnipeg and Churchill before arriving in Resolute Bay on 13 December, carrying a TV crew, who immediately started shooting scenes for a movie called "Christmas at Resolute Bay", which was to be broadcast on the CBC on Christmas Day. CBC reporter Miss van Steensel, making her third visit to the detachment, had arrived for a week's stay to make recordings. After unloading and refuelling, the aircraft departed on a shuttle run to Churchill, and the film crew kept shooting scenes until Longworth returned the following afternoon. Two hours later, with the CBC crew on board, the flight was on its way back to Churchill, returning to base via Winnipeg and Ottawa on 15 December.

The next flight to Resolute Bay involved NS17509, captained by Flight Lieutenant Kuhn; it arrived on 18 December carrying Wing Commander Turner, the Station Commander at Lachine, and his Adjutant, Flight Lieutenant Woods, to conduct a staff visit, and a large amount of Christmas mail and other cargo for Resolute Bay and Alert. After a two-hour stop, Kuhn proceeded to Thule, returning the following day after failing (because of bad weather) to land at Alert. The flight returned to base on 21 December.[85]

Wing Commander Mackie decided that half of the squadron was to receive Christmas leave while the other half was to get New Year's leave, and the slip crews at Lajes and Langar were to be brought home just before Christmas so as many squadron personnel as possible could spend Christmas Day with their families. The service flight leaving Dorval on the 26 December would reposition two slip crews at Lajes and one at Langar.[86]

At Lachine, the airmen held a mess dinner on 4 December with Air Commodore Carpenter as guest of honour and Wing Commander Gallagher as guest speaker. The traditional well-attended children's Christmas party was held at the Recreation Centre on the afternoon of 14 December. On 20 December, the station's officers made their annual Christmas visit to the Senior NCOs' Mess. Reports indicated that everyone had a good time.

Christmas leave started on 23 December for half the service personnel, and Montreal had a green Christmas, sunny and mild. On Christmas Day, following crowded services at the station chapels, the officers at Lachine served Christmas dinner to about 100 airmen, and the Senior NCOs' made their annual pleasant visit to the Officers' Mess in the afternoon of 27 December.

In response to an urgent appeal from the Canadian Red Cross, NS17516 (captained by Flight Lieutenant McBurney) was despatched to Negombo, Ceylon, on the evening of 29 December with 8,100 pounds of Red Cross supplies for flood victims. The flight took the southern route through Lajes to Malta and Beirut, where the crew spent New Year's Day, and arrived on 3 January at Negombo, where its cargo was unloaded. The flight left for base on 6 January and returned by way of Bombay, Beirut, Naples and Lajes, arriving in Montreal on the evening of 11 January.[87]

AFHQ Organization Order 8.12, issued on 31 December 1957 with effect from 1 February 1958, authorized the creation of No 115 Air Transport Unit. to be based at El Arish, Egypt. With UNEF established and its airlift requirements considerably reduced, it no longer needed the RCAF to maintain and operate the Air Transport Unit and No 114 Communications Flight at Naples. Consequently, these units were to be disbanded, and No 115 Communications Flight would become No 115 Air Transport Unit Canadian/United Nations Emergency Force (No 115 ATU/CANUNEF), to execute such plans and carry out such tasks as the UNEF Commander might assign.

No 426 Squadron would soon be flying to El Arish instead of Naples to support UNEF.[88]

On 30 December, a highway accident on Metropolitan Boulevard in Pointe Claire claimed the life of Leading Aircraftsman Mayo, one of No 426 Squadron's aero-engine technicians, and caused serious injuries to Corporal Palagian, Leading Aircraftsman Jewison and Leading Aircraftsman Warner. The body of Leading Aircraftsman Mayo left Dorval for Winnipeg with a military escort on 3 January, and the funeral was held the following day.

On New Year's Eve the customary dances were held by all the messes. A very enjoyable time was had by all at these well-attended functions.[89]

PHOTO 173
Ed Jean and Stu Parmelee (pilots) in the door of NS17509 at Capodichino Airport; Naples, Italy, 13 November 1957. (J. Bugdale Collection)

PHOTO 174
F/O Al Campbell (navigator) at Capodichino Airport; Naples, Italy, 13 November 1957. (J. Bugdale Collection)

PHOTO 175
F/O Jim Bugdale (radio officer) in front of NS17509 at Capodichino Airport; Naples, Italy, 13 November 1957. (J. Bugdale Collection)

PHOTO 176
W/C A.J.P. Byford (Air Staff Officer, UNEF HQ, Gaza) discusses airlift matters with LGen E.L.M. Burns; March 1957. (A.J.P. Byford Collection)

Lachine, 1957

PHOTO 177
W/C Pete Delaney (Station Commander) presents W/C Al Mackie with the Sports Day Trophy won by No 426 Squadron; RCAF Station Lachine, 21 August 1957. (A.J. Mackie Collection)

PHOTO 178
During a round-the-world flight, F/L Pete Rawlyk (navigator) and companions head into the weather briefing at Luqa Airport; Malta, August 1957. (DND 426 Squadron)

Lachine, 1958

CHAPTER 22

LACHINE, 1958

During 1958, the squadron's main assignment was to carry out two scheduled flights to Europe per week in support of No 1 Air Division, of which most terminated at Langar but several went direct to to No 1 Wing at Marville. The squadron also conducted a weekly logistics flight to Egypt in support of UNEF. Previously terminating at Naples, these flights went to El Arish by way of Pisa and Athens after the Air Transport Unit closed and its four C-119s returned to Canada. The overseas missions also included troop rotation, disaster relief and a number of special flights. There was also a marked increase in domestic trips, including runs to the far north and the United States, and RCAF Programme Objectives called for procurement twelve CL-44 transports to replace the squadron's North Stars, the acquisition to begin late in the year.[1]

January

The squadron's first overseas flight of the year departed base for Langar on 2 January in NS17504, captained by Flight Lieutenant Owston. It carried two slip crews, one to be positioned at Lajes and the other at Langar.

The next day, a second special — Flight Lieutenant Buechler and his crew in NS17511 — was despatched to Negombo, Ceylon, with 8,350 pounds of Red Cross supplies for flood victims. The flight was routed to Negombo through the Mediterranean, the Middle East and Bombay, and arrived on 7 January; on the return trip, it stopped at Naples to pick up Air Transport Unit personnel and equipment returning to Canada. The flight was back at base on 16 January.[2]

As well as the scheduled flights, eight additional flights to Langar were despatched in January. One of these flights included a shuttle run to Paris and London, and two were routed back to base through Naples to bring more ATU personnel and equipment back to Canada; the Naples operation would close at the end of January, and RCAF holdings there were being progressively reduced.[3]

On 19 January, Air Commodore Carpenter arrived in Naples to inspect the operations at Capodichino and El Arish; he returned to Air Transport Command Headquarters a week later. On 23 January, the Italian officers and senior NCOs at Capodichino invited their RCAF counterparts to their messes for farewell parties, and Carpenter attended the officers' function to present the RCAF badge, suitably framed for hanging in the mess with an inscribed brass plate. On 24 January, the RCAF officers were the guests of honour at another farewell party,

this one in the Pax Room (a reception hall) at Allied Air Forces Southern Europe Headquarters in Naples, with a large attendance of American, British and Italian service personnel and civic officials.[4]

The flight that departed base in NS17515 for Langar and Naples on 23 January was captained by Flight Lieutenant Schroder, and arrived in Naples on 25 January. Between 27 January and 8 February, Schroder and his crew made five shuttle runs to El Arish, airlifting personnel and equipment for the Air Transport Unit and soldiers for UNEF. Meanwhile, on 29 January Group Captain Pleasance and most of his senior officers left Naples, and Squadron Leader Green assuming command of ATU Naples until 31 January, when the unit ceased to exist. Green stayed in Naples with several officers and fifteen airmen for nearly a month to deal with the last-minute supply and accounting problems. Schroder and his crew left Naples for Langar on 11 February and were back at base two days later.[5]

Domestic runs in January included a combined logistics and training flight in NS17516 captained by Flight Lieutenant Shunck. Leaving base on 17 January, the flight went to Churchill, Yellowknife, Calgary and the Lakehead, and was back at Dorval on 20 January.

On 27 January, Flight Lieutenant McBurney was returning to base in NS17502 after a routine service flight to Goose Bay when, shortly after departure, the crew noticed excessive oil loss in No 2 engine and the failure of the feathering mechanism, quickly followed by a complete loss of oil. The engine seized, causing the propeller shaft to shear and the engine to catch fire. McBurney immediately discharged all his bottles of bromide extinguisher and brought the fire under control. He returned to Goose Bay and made a successful three-engine landing. According to the accident report, the universal coupling in the drive to the auxiliary gearbox had failed, and the resulting vibration caused the failure of the stainless steel feathering line, which led to the loss of oil, the engine seizure, and the eventual failure of the propeller shaft. After an engine change and a flight test, the crew brought NS17502 back to base on 30 January.[6]

The squadron despatched a single service flight to Resolute Bay during the month; it arrived on 27 January, bringing in Squadron Leader W.P. Becker to replace Squadron Leader A.D.J. Delmotte as the Detachment Commander. Shortly after arrival, the flight left for Churchill on a shuttle run, returning the following day with more mail and supplies for the detachment. The flight returned to base on 29 January.[7]

February

In February, the unit despatched nine trips to Langar, three of which carried on to Naples. Two of these flights returned to base by way of Gibraltar and Lajes; after a shuttle run to El Arish, the other returned to Dorval by way of Langar and Lajes. Three more flights went directly to Naples by way of Lajes and Gibraltar and returned to base by the same route. The last flight of the month to leave Montreal for Europe went to Langar, Pisa, Naples and El Arish, and returned to base the same way.

Plans called for subsequent flights to El Arish to be staged through Pisa and Malta, and to go directly to Pisa and Langar on the return. This arrangement lasted only a short time, and Athens soon replaced Malta as the staging stop on the way to and from El Arish.[8]

Lachine, 1958

The squadron also kept busy on the domestic scene in February; as well as the scheduled runs, several special flights were conducted.

On 6 February, NS17504 (captained by Flight Lieutenant Hamel) and NS17506 (captained by Flight Lieutenant Stockdale) were positioned at RCAF Station Greenwood; the next morning, they embarked 108 personnel from No 404 (Maritime Patrol) Squadron and flew to Jacksonville, Florida (an eight-hour trip), refuelled, and then carried on for nearly five hours more to the U.S. Navy base at Guantanamo Bay, Cuba, where seven Neptunes from No 404 Squadron were deployed for an anti-submarine warfare exercise. On 9 February, both North Stars returned to Dorval, a direct flight of ten and a half hours.

At the end of the month, the squadron sent two aircraft to Guantanamo Bay to bring the personnel from No 404 Squadron back to Greenwood.[9]

On 15 February, the squadron despatched NS17509 (captained by Flight Lieutenant Ingram) and NS17514 (captained by Flight Lieutenant Owston) to Halifax; the next morning, they embarked eighty RCN personnel and airlifted them to the U.S. Naval Station Mayport in Jacksonville. Both aircraft returned to base on 17 February.[10]

Of the squadron's several northern flights in February, three went to Resolute Bay and one was a combined logistics and training run. This last flight left base on 8 February for Winnipeg and Edmonton, where forty-three candidates from the Survival School were embarked for the trip to Cambridge Bay, where the Arctic Survival Course was given. The flight returned to base by way of Yellowknife, Edmonton and Winnipeg.[11]

The month's first flight to Resolute Bay was in NS17504, captained by Flight Lieutenant Jackson, which left base on 12 February, arrived at Resolute Bay on 13 February, and proceeded the next day to Thule, where it made a shuttle run to Alert. Jackson and his crew left Thule on 15 February, arriving in Resolute Bay at 1730 hours and departing again for Churchill and Winnipeg two and a half hours later, taking with them Squadron Leader Delmotte, the outgoing Detachment Commander, and six airmen bound for Winnipeg. On 17 February, the flight was back at Churchill to conduct a shuttle run to Resolute Bay, where it landed in ice fog that created conditions of extremely poor visibility. The next morning, despite a temperature hovering around -50°F, the engines started easily (after an hour of warming with Herman-Nelson heaters) and the flight departed for Churchill. On 19 February, Jackson and his crew were directed to The Pas to take a patient to Winnipeg for treatment, after which they repositioned the aircraft at Churchill. On 20 February and 21 February, Jackson conducted shuttle runs to Resolute Bay, where the temperature stayed around -50°F, with brisk 30-mph winds from the north. The flight returned to base on 22 February.[12]

On 24 February, Flight Lieutenant Owston and his crew left base in NS17511 on the next flight bound for Resolute Ottawa, Winnipeg and Churchill, the flight arrived at destination the following day. On 26 February, they made a shuttle run to Alert with replacements for tour-expired personnel, and they were back at base on 1 March.

The month's last flight to Resolute Bay was NS17514, captained by Flight Lieutenant Sled, which left Dorval on 26 February and arrived at destination the next day after spending the night in Winnipeg. On 28 February, Sled and his crew returned to Churchill and conducted a shuttle run back to Resolute Bay. The flight departed early on 1 March and was back at base by midnight, after stops at Churchill, Winnipeg and Ottawa, for a total of slightly more than fifteen hours of flying time.[13]

March

In March, the squadron conducted thirteen scheduled overseas flights that stopped first at Langar; from there, four flights went on to El Arish in support of UNEF operations. All four returned to Canada by way of Langar.

The first flight to El Arish was captained by Flying Officer Johnston, who left for Pisa on 9 March in NS17516 and carried on to Naples the following day. On 11 March, the flight proceeded to El Arish and, on the return leg, landed at Wheelus AFB east of Tripoli, so the crew could assess the facilities for possible use as a staging point for troop-rotation flights to and from Egypt. The next day Johnston and his crew were back at Naples, where they embarked personnel, records and equipment from the ATU and returned to Langar by way of Pisa on 13 March.[14]

Flight Lieutenant Lambeth captained NS17502 on the next flight to El Arish, which left Langar on 15 March, stopped overnight at Pisa, and the next day proceeded to El Arish, where passengers and cargo were disembarked and the flight left again for Malta, where it spent the night. Lambeth carried on to Pisa in the morning, and returned to Langar on 18 March.

Wing Commander Mackie captained NS17511 on the month's third flight to El Arish, by way of Pisa and Malta on both the eastward and westward legs of the trip.

Flight Lieutenant Charchuk and his crew in NS17509 made the month's last trip to Egypt. Leaving Langar on 29 March, the crew flew to Malta via Pisa the first day, and made the run to El Arish on 30 March.. The return trip to Langar was made via Pisa.[15]

Operation JUMP MOAT 2 got under way on 3 March when a North Star was despatched to Uplands to airlift ground staff and spare parts to Goose Bay, where it was released on arrival to return to base. A second North Star was positioned at Uplands the following day to embark more ground staff and to accompany the convoy of sixteen CF-100 Mk Vs being ferried to Beauvechain in Belgium. The convoy left Uplands on 5 March and, after stops at Goose Bay and Keflavik, arrived at Beauvechain on the afternoon of 7 March. The escort North Star returned to base via Marville and Langar. More *JUMP MOAT* operations were planned for May and June.[16]

The squadron carried out two flights to Resolute w detachment members, including a badly needed Stationary Engineer) and freight. Three hours later, the flight left on a supply run to Thule and Alert, with a mail drop at Eureka, and then returned to Resolute. On 15 March, it left for base via Churchill, Winnipeg and Ottawa. The next flight into Resolute Bay was brought in on 25 March by Flight Lieutenant Hamel and his crew in NS17515 with no films or radio tapes aboard, disappointing the detachment staff, who would endure two more weeks without new entertainment. Two hours after arrival, the flight departed for Alert to drop off personnel, mail and supplies, and then headed for Thule, where the crew took a rest. On 27 March, the flight was back at Resolute Bay, where radio officer Flying Officer Sare acted as Deputy Returning Officer for those voting in the federal election. The aircraft returned to base the next day.[17]

As well as several domestic flights, the squadron despatched two combined logistics-training runs during the month. The first, captained by Flight Lieutenant Owston, left Dorval on 19 March in NS17516 and proceeded to Winnipeg and Vancouver; the next day, the crew carried on to Whitehorse, and to Saskatoon, where they stopped for the night. On 21 March, the flight returned to Dorval via Winnipeg. The next, more ambitious, run was captained by Flight Lieutenant Schunk in NS17504 and was routed by way of Ottawa, Lethbridge, Vancouver, Calgary, Edmonton and Comox, returning to Dorval on 24 March via Vancouver, Lethbridge and Ottawa.[18]

On 25 March, at Malton Airport, Janusz Zurakowski conducted the first flight of the AVRO CF-105 Arrow in Arrow 25201. This jet fighter-interceptor, scheduled to replace the CF-100 Canuck, was in the test-flight stage on 20 February 1959, when the Conservative government of John Diefenbaker cancelled the project.[19]

Also on 25 March, Flight Lieutenant Dick's crew had a fire in No 1 engine on NS17504, the squadron's training aircraft. Caused by a broken primer line, the fire occurred during start-up. The fire was quickly extinguished and there were no injuries.[20]

April

Thirteen flights were despatched to Langar in April, with four extensions to El Arish.

On 2 April, the squadron's Detachment Commander at Langar received a message from the aviation authorities in Malta regarding the staging of the unit's aircraft through Luqa airport: passing crews were giving the impression that the RCAF would be using Luqa regularly, but no arrangements had been made with the Maltese authorities, who wanted to know the duration and intensity of the commitment, and the name of the headquarters authorizing the flights. Air Transport Command Headquarters commented that it had understood that the Canadian Joint Staff in London had taken care of these formalities before approving the plan to stage through Luqa. At the end of the month, No 426 Squadron asked Air Transport Command Headquarters to substitute Athens for Malta on the El Arish itinerary, for the following reasons:
   a. Malta, which was enduring civil disturbances, lacked suitable overnight accommodations for crew and passengers;
   b. the current itinerary was too rushed, resulting in frequent late departures; and
   c. the route through Athens was shorter and permitted early-morning arrivals and departures at El Arish, improving the load factor by avoiding the heat of the day.[21]

On 1 April, a weekly run to the Maritimes was added to the squadron's schedule of domestic flights. Flying Officer Price took out the first flight in NS17525, which proceeded to Chatham, Greenwood, and Saint John and returned to base the same day.

Air Transport Command Headquarters directed that, effective 3 April, all service flights departing Langar would fly to Lajes via Shannon, recommended for some time as a refuelling stop by squadron captains who preferred its facilities and meteorology services to those available at St. Mawgan.[22]

At the Air Transport Command Conference held at Lachine on 28 February, it was announced that MCAs would be added to the strength of No 426 Squadron, beginning in April with an establishment of twenty-one MCAs — 1.75 per aircraft. On 8 April, Air Transport Command Headquarters authorization was received for the transfer of the MCAs from No 2 Movements Unit, to be operationally effective on the squadron on 14 April, the date Corporal D.K. Meldrum, Leading Aircraftsman J.L. Bissonnette, Leading Aircraftsman G.R. Brown, Leading Aircraftsman A.R. Burgess, Leading Aircraftsman G.R. Green, Leading Aircraftsman J.Y. Hould, Leading Aircraftsman D.N. Lethbridge, Leading Aircraftsman D.V. Mastrianni, Leading Aircraftsman W.J. Mulligan, Leading Aircraftsman C.W. Parker, Leading Aircraftsman D.K. Rice, Leading Aircraftsman M.E. Taylor and Leading Aircraftsman R.J. Wicks were taken on strength

The officer in command of No 2 Movements Unit was responsible for providing MCAs to fill the squadron's new billets, and the first thirteen men chosen were joined by others as MCAs became available. On 18 April, Leading Aircraftsman J.A. Hoffart, Leading Aircraftsman E.C. Meyers, Leading Aircraftsman W.D. Murphy and Leading Aircraftsman R.H. Tait were taken on strength for contact training while waiting for the MCA course at No 4 OTU in Trenton. The squadron opened a Movements office, and had equipment and supplies shipped in early so its new MCAs could start work on 14 April.[23]

Each year, the spring re-supply of the Arctic weather stations was an Air Transport Command responsibility involving the airlift of Department of Transport and US Weather Bureau personnel, equipment and supplies from Resolute Bay and Thule to Mould Bay, Isachsen, Eureka and Alert; the 1958 operation also included air-dropping supplies at Sachs Harbour. Planning for the 1958 re-supply operation began on 5 March, when Air Transport Command Headquarters issued Operations Order 9/58, specifying that No 435 Squadron at RCAF Station Namao was to provide three C-119 aircraft, six aircrews, supporting ground crew, and spare parts, and No 436 Squadron from Downsview was to supply two C-119 aircraft, four aircrews and spares.

Most of the materiel was shipped to Resolute Bay during the summer of 1957 during the brief period of open water, and stockpiled for the annual re-supply airlift. More equipment and supplies were shipped to Thule, and perishable goods such as fresh food went by rail to Churchill for airlift to Resolute Bay just in time for the main lift to the weather stations. Supplies to be air-dropped at Sachs Harbour were packed at Namao for airlift to Resolute Bay via Churchill.

The man in charge of the 1958 spring re-supply was Squadron Leader J.S. Miller of No 435 Squadron. The operation began on 7 April and was completed by 22 April, when participating aircraft and crews started heading for home. No 426 Squadron was not directly involved in this operation.[24]

Two flights were despatched from Dorval to Resolute Bay in April. The first was NS17506, captained by Flight Lieutenant Jackson, which left base on 9 April for Churchill via Ottawa and Winnipeg, and on 10 April arrived at Resolute, unloaded passengers, mail and cargo, and returned to Churchill. Three shuttle runs to Resolute Bay were carried out over the next three days, and the flight returned to Dorval on 16 April. The month's second run to Resolute Bay was conducted on 24 April by Flight Lieutenant Morrison in NS17515, which returned to Churchill for more cargo, delivered it to Resolute Bay on 26 April, and then returned to base.[25]

On 12 April, the squadron airlifted the Bell Telephone Show Troupe from Montreal to Knob Lake; the flight returned the following day. On 13 April, two North Stars went to Downsview, where they picked up sixty-three passengers from the RCAF Staff College and airlifted them to Dartmouth; the reverse airlift was carried out several days later.

At the end of the month, NS17506, captained by Flight Lieutenant Lynch, and NS17511, flown by Captain Taylor were positioned at Dartmouth to act as mother-ships for a group of RCN F2H3 Banshee jet fighters deploying to the US Naval Air Station at Key West for airborne intercept training. The next morning, both North Stars embarked maintenance crews and spare parts and proceeded to Charleston AFB in North Carolina, where they spent the night. On 2 May, the North Stars carried on to Key West, unloaded, and returned to Montreal.[26]

May

In May, fourteen scheduled flights went to Langar and five continued to El Arish. The original plan to stage the flights to and from Egypt through Malta was changed on 7 May, when Air Transport Command Headquarters approved a new schedule for SF53/54 that included an overnight stop at Pisa and a refuelling stop at Athens on the way to El Arish, and an overnight stay at Athens and a fuel stop at Pisa on the way back to Langar.[27]

On 6 May the squadron despatched NS17525 to Uplands for *Operation JUMP MOAT 3*, the delivery of eleven CF-100 Mk Vs to Belgium under the NATO Mutual Aid Agreement, and six CF-100 Mk IVBs to No 4 Wing in West Germany. In the role of mother ship, the North Star embarked maintenance staff and support equipment on 7 May and followed the convoy, first to Goose Bay and then to Keflavik. On 10 May, the CF-100s having been delivered to Beauvechain and Baden-Söllingen, the North Star headed for home by way of Langar, Shannon, Lajes, Gander and Ottawa.[28]

On 8 May, in the capacity of Acting Station Commander, Wing Commander Mackie held a CO's parade at Lachine in preparation for the Air Commodore's annual inspection, scheduled for 7 June. Another rehearsal parade was held two weeks later.

On 9 May, two North Stars captained by Flight Lieutenant Morrison and Flying Officer Johnston were despatched to Trenton for *Operation STAR FLIGHT*, another delivery of Mutual Aid aircraft to NATO allies: eight T-33 Silver Star Mk 3 jet trainers bound for Greece, and seventeen T-33s going to Turkey. Morrison and Johnston embarked their loads of maintenance personnel and aircraft spares and followed the convoy to Goose Bay. The weather was good, so the 998-mile run to Sondrestrom was made the next day. On 11 May, the convoy reached Keflavik — a distance of 827 miles — and then proceeded directly to Prestwick. On 12 May, the entire group arrived at Marville. On 15 May, Johnston and his crew positioned their aircraft at Decimomannu and, when the eight T-33s for Greece arrived, accompanied them to the military airport at Elevsis, near Athens. Morrison and his crew accompanied the remaining seventeen T33s from Marville to Eskisehir on 17 June. Johnston left Greece on 18 May and was routed back to base by way of Pisa, Marville, Lisbon, Lajes, Gander and Trenton, arriving in Dorval on 22 May. Morrison returned to base a day later by the same route.[29]

On 12 May, representatives of Canada and the United States signed the the North American Air Defence (NORAD) Agreement in Washington, formally establishing NORAD Command. The integrated NORAD Headquarters at Colorado Springs, Colorado was already at work; Air Marshal C.R. Slemon had taken up the duties of Deputy Commander there on 31 August 1957. On 21 May, the RCAF Support Unit Colorado Springs was formed to provide administrative services to the RCAF members on the NORAD staff.[30]

On 17 May, the first Canadair CP-107 Argus maritime patrol aircraft entered service with No 405 (MP) Squadron at RCAF Station Greenwood.[31]

The squadron completed three flights to Resolute Bay in May. The first, NS17517 (captained by Flight Lieutenant Stockdale), arrived from Churchill on 22 May carrying a Bell Telephone repair crew and 1,300 pounds of mail; on 23 May, it returned to Churchill, picked up more cargo and flew back to Resolute Bay, where the cargo was unloaded and the aircraft immediately left for Churchill again. Stockdale and his crew put in sixteen hours of flying time that day; they were back at Dorval on 24 May.[32]

On 28 May two flights were despatched to Resolute Bay. One was a normal scheduled flight in NS17506, captained by Flight Lieutenant Sled, which went to Churchill after stops at Ottawa and Winnipeg, and made one shuttle run to Resolute Bay per day from 29 May to 31 May. Sled and his crew returned to base on 1 June.

The second flight was a special in NS17509, co-captained by Flight Lieutenant Owston and Flying Officer Byrne, which went first to Winnipeg to embark Squadron Leader Cay, an RAF exchange officer teaching at the RCAF Central Navigation School, nineteen students on the Specialist Navigation Course, and thirteen airmen. After a stop at Churchill, the flight arrived at Resolute Bay on 30 May, and the students began their navigation exercises with a flight of seven hours and forty minutes on 31 May and a seven-hour exercise on 1 June. On 2 June, they flew to the North Pole, and returned to Resolute Bay via Thule. On 3 June, they made a training run to Alert, and returned to Resolute the following morning. After refuelling, the flight departed on a seven-hour navigation exercise that included overflying Sachs Harbour. On 5 June, the flight returned directly to Winnipeg, dropped off Squadron Leader Cay and the navigation students, and returned to base.[33]

On 3 June, NS17515 (captained by Flight Lieutenant McBurney) left base for Langar, the first of the month's twelve scheduled flights, of which four continued on to El Arish via Pisa and Athens. One other flight — NS17506, captained by Flying Officer Johnston — also went to Marville to embark personnel and equipment for airlift to the RCAF Air Weapons Unit at Decimomannu. That flight returned to Langar by way of Baden-Söllingen. All aircraft returning to base refuelled at Shannon before continuing on to Lajes.[34]

On 11 June, NS17502 (Flight Lieutenant Hamel) and NS17510 (Flight Lieutenant Stockdale) were despatched to the Key West Naval Air Station in Florida; their flight time averaged nine hours. The next morning, they embarked the party of RCN personnel involved in airborne intercept training with the Banshee fighters, and flew to Halifax via Charleston AFB, where they refuelled. Both aircraft were back at base on 13 June.[35]

In June, the Department of Transport issued Operation Order NORS58 concerning the re-supply of Resolute Bay and Eureka by a sea convoy comprising three Canadian Coast Guard icebreakers, one freighter and one tanker. All ships were to be loaded in Montreal and, depending on ice conditions, were scheduled to arrive at Resolute Bay in mid-August. Long-range ice-reconnaissance flights were to be conducted from Resolute by Lancasters of No 408 (R) Squadron; short-range ice-reconnaissance would be provided by helicopters flying from the icebreakers.[36]

The squadron conducted two service flights during the month to Resolute Bay. The first arrived on 19 June and left again the next day for Alert, where it was unable to land because of fog; instead, a para-drop was made at Lake Hazen on Ellesmere Island, and the flight returned to Resolute. After refuelling, the flight then departed for Churchill and base. The next flight in was NS17504 (captained by Flight Lieutenant Hamel), which reached Resolute Bay on 27 June, having left base the previous day with scheduled stops at Ottawa, Winnipeg and Churchill. Once the passengers had disembarked and all cargo destined for Resolute Bay was unloaded, the flight continued on to Alert. Hamel and his crew were back at Resolute the following morning, and then departed for Churchill and Winnipeg, where they picked up more cargo and passengers, and returned to Resolute Bay on 29 June, after a brief stop in Churchill. The next morning, Hamel and his crew made a shuttle run to Churchill, bringing more cargo and passengers back to Resolute Bay. On 1 July, the flight proceeded directly from Resolute Bay to Winnipeg and returned to base via Ottawa.[37]

On 24 June, Flight Lieutenant Lynch and his crew went to RCAF Station Uplands in NS17502 for *Operation JUMP MOAT 4*, the ferry of eleven CF-100s to Belgian Air Force and six to the Air Division; they embarked the servicing personnel and aircraft spares, and immediately left for Goose Bay. The next day, the convoy of CF-100s departed Uplands for Goose Bay, refuelled, and carried on to Keflavik, followed by Lynch and his crew in the North Star. Poor weather at Keflavik held up the operation until 28 June, when the aircraft destined for Belgium made a direct flight to Beauvechain, and the North Star followed the six bound for the Air Division to Zweibrücken. On 1 July, Lynch left for Beauvechain to pick up the ferry crews and, from there, the flight carried on to Brussels. On 3 July, the North Star flight was positioned at Langar from where it left the next day for Lajes. It was back at Dorval on 5 July.[38]

At RCAF Station Lachine, another practice parade was held on 4 June, and Air Commodore Carpenter arrived on 6 June to conduct his annual inspection, beginning with the Guard of Honour and the Dorval site in the morning, and moving on to Lachine in the afternoon, where the ceremonial parade and march-past were held before the inspection tour.

Air Force Day was 14 June, and Lachine co-operated with St-Hubert to present a number of activities and displays, several of them hosted by officers and airmen from Lachine. The weather was cool and so windy that some of the flying displays had to be cancelled.[39]

On 2 July, an RCMP truck ran over four Eskimo children at Resolute Bay, injuring two of whom seriously. Within four hours of a request for assistance from the USAF in Thule, the medevac aircraft arrived captained by the base commander himself, Colonel Shultz, who flew the injured children to Thule for treatment.

On 4 July, the Detachment Commander inspected all sections as part of a systematic clean-up of the RCAF facilities in preparation for the Air Commodore Carpenter's inspection on 20 August.

On 10 July, a US Navy Super Constellation brought a twenty-man technical team to Resolute Bay to erect a mooring mast for the US Navy blimp that was going to make a flight to Resolute from its base at Weymouth, Massachusetts. A site for the mast was selected, and construction began, with considerable blasting to sink suitable holes in the permafrost. Project completed, the Super Constellation left on 13 July.

At 1700 hours on 10 July, NS17515, captained by Flight Lieutenant Owston, arrived with Wing Commander Turner and fifty others on board, including members of the Bull Gang. The flight, which had left Dorval the day before for Winnipeg, had made stops at Churchill and Coral Harbour en route. The next morning, Owston and his crew departed for Churchill and

Winnipeg for more cargo and passengers, returning to Resolute Bay on 13 July. Shortly after its arrival the flight left to carry out supply drops at Isachsen and Mould Bay, after which it returned to Resolute. The next day Owston and his crew carried out a cargo run to Thule, where they stayed overnight. On 15 July, the flight proceeded directly to Churchill and then to Winnipeg, returning to base the following day.

The squadron's next flight to Resolute Bay was a special combined logistics and training run. Flying Officer Johnston departed Dorval in NS17514 on 18 July for Winnipeg and Churchill with an augmented crew. After an overnight stay in Resolute Bay, Johnston left on a direct flight to Cold Lake, Alberta on 20 July. After a brief stop, the crew made preparations to leave for RCAF Station Namao near Edmonton; however, during start-up, a severed primer line sprayed fuel over No 2 engine, starting a fire that was extinguished immediately. (The fire extinguisher on the engine worked, but the ground fire extinguisher could not be used because it had the wrong kind of nozzle.) A new engine was flown in, the damaged one was replaced, and the flight finally left for Namao and Winnipeg on 22 July, returning to base the following day.

The next scheduled flight to Resolute Bay arrived on 24 July; NS17502, captained by Flight Lieutenant Longworth, brought in passengers, mail, general cargo and Flying Officer Sare, the Beachmaster for the 1958 re-supply operation. The next morning, the flight proceeded to Churchill for more cargo, returning later in the day. Longworth and his crew departed for Dorval on 27 July.[40]

July

As well as many domestic runs, the squadron despatched fourteen scheduled flights to Langar and two overseas special flights: one to Prestwick and the other to Lyneham and Northolt. Five of the Langar flights went on to El Arish, and one was extended to the fighter wings and Decimomannu.[41]

SF 53 to El Arish on 14 July brought in Squadron Leader C.C. Cooling to replace Squadron Leader K.M. Ham in command of No 115 ATU. The formal change-of-command parade was held on 19 July, and Ham left the following day on SF 54 for Langar and Dorval. The same flight also brought Group Captain Morrison. the Chief Staff Officer at Air Transport Command Headquarters, for a stff visit.[42]

Operation Directive 125/58, issued by Air Force Headquarters on 18 July, dealt with *Operation JUMP MOAT 5*. The RCAF had planned to increase its reserve of CF-100 Mk IVBs in the Air Division by ferrying additional aircraft overseas. The mission was to deliver twelve to fifteen CF-100s to the fighter wings by 15 November; the aircraft were to be at RCAF Station Uplands by 30 September, and Air Transport Command would provide airlift support.[43]

On 19 July, a wings parade at RCAF Station Winnipeg marked the end of the NATO Aircrew Training Plan. From 1951 to 1958, some 5,575 pilots and navigators from ten countries had been trained to wings standard with RCAF trainees. Under separate agreements, training continued for nationals of Denmark, Norway, the Netherlands and West Germany.[44]

On 30 July, the DHC-4 Caribou prototype was test flown by G. Neal and D. Fairbanks at Downsview. The aircraft would soon join the Air Transport Command fleet.[45]

August

Resolute Bay was a hive of activity in August.

The US Navy blimp *ZPG-2*, which was to have arrived on 1 August, was held up at Akron, Ohio, for operational reasons, and on 4 August, the detachment was told that the re-supply convoy was several days ahead of schedule. On 7 August, therefore, the airship support party arrived by US Navy Super Constellation at 1900 hours, and the icebreaker CGS *C.D. Howe* dropped anchor in the bay at 2100 hours. *ZPG-2* flew in the next morning, with Wing Commander K.R. Greenaway aboard as Senior Navigator. On 9 August, the Super Constellation visited the American military and scientific station on Ice Island T3 during the day, and the blimp departed in the evening, passing overhead at 2200 hours en route to Churchill. The Super Constellation departed for home the next day.

On 11 August, the re-supply convoy called out No 408 Squadron's Lancaster FM212 to lead them to open water; the ships were about 450 miles to the east of Resolute Bay and almost stuck in solid ice. The Lancaster's crew found open water some forty miles to the north of the convoy's position, and informed the escorting icebreakers.

On 14 August, seventy more people arrived in Resolute Bay, straining the already tight housing situation. Captain Taylor brought in NS17502 at 1500 hours from Dorval and Churchill with mail, general cargo and several passengers, including Squadron Leader W.J. Kelley, the new Detachment Commander, relieving Squadron Leader Becker. Two hours later, Taylor and his crew departed for the DEW Line station at Hall Beach and then continued on to Churchill and Winnipeg. At 2200, Air Commodore Carpenter and his party (which included Air Vice Marshal C.L. Annis from Air Force Headquarters) arrived to a formal greeting on the tarmac.

The next day, 15 August, was the AOC's inspection of the Detachment, followed by a short fishing trip for the Air Commodore's party, and dinner aboard the *C.D. Howe*. Late that evening, the rest of the re-supply convoy arrived: the Coast Guard icebreakers *D'Iberville*, *Labrador* and *N.B. McLean*, the freighter *SS Brazilian Prince* with a full load of general cargo for Resolute Bay and the tanker *SS Sea Transporter*, with all the bulk fuel for next year's requirements at the RCAF, Department of Transport and US Weather Bureau establishments.

Air Commodore Carpenter and his party spent a good part of 16 August hunting walrus; in the evening, he inspected the detachment personnel at 1830 hours and then dedicated a new flag mast. His official business completed, the AOC was then free to enjoy a brief reception followed by a mess dinner. The entire inspection party left for Ottawa and Dorval the next morning.

Meanwhile, stevedores who had come in with the convoy were efficiently unloading the ships in clear, warm weather with little or no wind, while the fifty-eight airmen of the Bull Gang moved the cargo off the beach. The Bull Gang worked in two twelve-hour shifts organized by the Beachmaster, Flying Officer Sare.

On 20 August, a C-119 from No 4 (T) OTU at Trenton arrived to airlift 2,500 gallons of aviation fuel to Alert for use by the reconnaissance Lancasters of No 408 Squadron, and the detachment held a farewell party for Squadron Leader Becker in the evening.

On 21 August, Canso 11005 from RCAF Station Sea Island conducted a mercy flight, bringing an American meteorological observer with acute appendicitis from Isachsen to Thule via Resolute Bay. That evening, Captain Fournier of the *C.D. Howe* entertained Squadron Leader Becker and Squadron Leader Kelley at dinner aboard his ship; the convoy's load of more than 2,400 tons of cargo was nearly all ashore, so the ships were getting ready to leave Resolute Bay.

On 22 August, a No 435 Squadron C-119 airlifted forty-two stevedores from Resolute Bay to Churchill, a No 408 Squadron Lancaster left on a direct flight to Ottawa with Squadron Leader Becker aboard, and a No 412 Squadron North Star arrived in the afternoon, bringing thirty delegates to the British Commonwealth Scientific Conference to the detachment for a two-and-a half-hour visit, after which it departed again for Churchill. The next day, a C-119 from Trenton left on a direct flight to Montreal with forty-six passengers, including the last of the stevedores. With the stevedores gone, the canteen was able to resume beer sales.

On 24 August, a C-119 from CJATC Rivers departed Resolute Bay for Churchill and Montreal with thirty-seven Bull Gang members. The next day, two C-119s arrived, one from Edmonton and the other from Downsview, to airlift supplies and equipment to Alert in a series of shuttles. On 28 August, NS17509, captained by Flight Lieutenant Sled, arrived from Churchill as SF 5, having left Dorval the previous day and made stops at Ottawa and Winnipeg en route. The passengers included twenty-seven Army signallers — the Royal Canadian Corps of Signals would be taking over the wireless station at Alert from the RCAF on 1 September. After unloading, Sled and his crew left for Churchill, returning on 29 August with ten passengers and some 6,000 pounds of cargo. Next, the flight went to Isachsen, where Sled attempted to air-drop supplies, but the weather was below limits and the aircraft had to return to Resolute Bay. After refuelling, they left for Churchill at 2030 hours with thirty-six passengers. At Churchill, a fifteen-hour crew rest was taken and Sled returned to base on 30 August.

On 30 August, Flight Lieutenant Sierolawski brought in NS17502 with a load of water-line equipment for the detachment. After unloading, the flight left for Churchill. The same day, a C-119 took the Army signallers to Alert, and returned with a mixed load of Army and RCAF passengers. On 1 September, Sierolawski and his crew arrived back at Resolute Bay; two hours later, they took off again for Churchill, Ottawa and Montreal, taking with them an Eskimo girl who needed psychiatric treatment.[46]

The squadron's August workload included thirteen scheduled transatlantic trips, of which twelve went to Langar and one proceeded directly to Marville from Lajes, returning to base by the same route. Four of the Langar flights went on to El Arish via Pisa and Athens. The fifth carried out a series of shuttle runs, going first to Marville, then to Ramstein AFB (near Kaiserslautern), Baden-Söllingen, Decimomannu, Zweibrücken, Baden-Söllingen, Decimomannu, Baden-Söllingen and Marville, and returning to base via Shannon and Lajes.[47]

The month also included a flight to Saigon for the rotation of the ICSC truce teams. On this mission, Flight Lieutenant Kuhn captained NS17521, which carried an augmented crew and a group of about thirty Army officers. Leaving base on 8 August, the flight proceeded to Lajes and then to Saigon by way of Dakar, Lagos, Stanleyville, Nairobi, Aden, Karachi and Calcutta, arriving at its destination on 16 August. The next day, the flight proceeded to Hong Kong to wait while the homeward-bound observers briefed their replacements. On 26 August, when Kuhn returned to Saigon, the crew discovered a fuel leak on one of the engines; after several unsuccessful attempts to rectify the problem, it was determined that the engine had to be changed, and a message was sent to the squadron requesting a spare engine. On 1 September, to avoid the inevitable clearance issues, Kuhn took the flight to Singapore on three engines.

On 29 August, Wing Commander Mackie left base for Singapore with the spare engine in NS17511, making the trip via Travis AFB, Hickam AFB, Wake Island, Guam and Manila, and arriving on 2 September. Kuhn and his crew then took over NS17511, flew it to Saigon on 3 September, boarded the tour-expired observers, and departed for Montreal, taking the route used on the outbound journey, and arriving at base on 11 September after thirty-five days away from home. Meanwhile, the engine on NS17521 was changed and a test flight was carried out on 5 September. As everything checked out, Mackie and his crew set out for base, returning by way of Manila, Guam, Wake, Midway, Honolulu and San Francisco. The flight was back at base on 11 September, having been away for thirteen days; the crew had put in 120 flying hours.[48]

September

The first of the month's fifteen transatlantic flights was NS17525 (captained by Flight Lieutenant Longworth), which left base on 2 September bound for Langar carrying (among others) Flight Lieutenant Reid, who left the flight at Lajes to spend two months there as the squadron's Liaison Officer. Marville was the destination of three flights, two of which returned to base by way of Shannon and Lajes, the other proceeding to El Arish and returning by way of Athens, Pisa, Langar and Lajes. A special flight was despatched to Prestwick using the Goose Bay–Keflavik route outbound and returning through Shannon and Lajes.

One of three additional flights proceeding to Langar during the month provided air transport support for the Air Division's fighter squadrons going to Decimomannu, while another carried out SF 53/54 to El Arish. The first UNEF troop-rotation flight left El Arish on 17 September; seven such flights were carried out during the month. The aircraft were routed from Montreal to El Arish through Lajes, Gibraltar and Athens, returning to Canada by the same route.[49]

The squadron despatched two scheduled flights and one special flight to Resolute Bay during September. The first to arrive was NS17525, on 11 September, with passengers, freight and about 550 pounds of eagerly awaited mail. The flight remained overnight, as the crew planned an air-drop at Isachsen and a supply run to Mould Bay for the following day. The weather was below limits in the morning of 12 September, so the air-drop had to be delayed until 1400 hours, but after taxiing out for take-off the aircraft returned to the ramp with a malfunctioning engine. It was determined that an engine change was required and an "Operation Immediate" message was sent to base requesting a replacement engine. With an engine and other spares aboard, Flight Lieutenant Lynch and his crew left Dorval in NS17509 on the morning of 13 September and headed for Churchill. While Lynch was preparing to leave Churchill, mechanical problems with his aircraft forced a flight delay until the following morning. About an hour out of Resolute Bay, Lynch and his crew were advised that weather had closed Resolute and the flight was diverted to Thule. The airfield was closed again by weather on 15 September and another attempt by Lynch to get into Resolute the next day was unsuccessful and the flight returned to Thule again. The engine was finally delivered on 17 September. Several hours later, after boarding thirty-seven passengers, Lynch left for Churchill, returning to base the next day via Winnipeg and Ottawa. The engine on NS17525 was changed and the aircraft test-flown. It left Resolute Bay on 18 September for base via Churchill, Winnipeg and Ottawa.[50]

The squadron's next scheduled flight to Resolute Bay was NS17525, captained by Flying Officer Price, which arrived on 23 September with Wing Commander Turner, the Station Commander at Lachine; Wing Commander Songhurst, the Senior Technical Staff Officer at Air Transport Command Headquarters; and Group Captain Jacobsen of the Chief of the Air Staff Secretariat at Air Force Headquarters, to supervise preparations for the upcoming visit of the Honourable George R. Pearkes, Minister of National Defence, but with neither mail nor movies, much to the disappointment of the detachment personnel. The next day, Price and his crew made a supply run to Isachsen and Mould Bay, and a No 435 Squadron C-119 arrived with mail, films and spare parts for a No 408 Squadron Lancaster. Two other C-119s arrived, one from Edmonton and the other from Station Rivers, to start *Operation BOXTOP*, the fall resupply of the weather stations, which would involve a total of five C-119s and be completed by the end of the month.

On 25 September, Flying Officer Price and his crew left for Churchill, returning with more passengers and cargo for Resolute Bay. In the meantime, feverish preparations continued for the Minister's visit, which was scheduled for 1040 to 1500 hours on 26 September. The Minister's aircraft arrived at 1240 hours, two hours late and, since the departure time was not changed, the grand tour of Resolute Bay had to be considerably reduced. The Minister's party included Mr. F.R. Miller, the Deputy Minister; Air Marshal H. Campbell, the Chief of the Air Staff; Lieutenant-General S.F. Clark, the Chief of the General Staff; Major-General J.C. Jensen of the USAF; Captain Wilgress of the RCN; Mr. H.R.N. Roberts, the Minister's Executive Assistant, Wing Commander K.R. Greenaway and Wing Commander J.A. Wiseman of the RCAF; and Inspector Fitzsimmons of the RCMP. Two hours after the Minister's aircraft had departed, Price left for Churchill and base with Wing Commander Turner aboard.[51]

The late summer of 1958 ushered in significant changes to the RCAF. Its strength stood at about 51,000 all ranks, and Training Command was reduced by about 850 service and 330 civilian positions, mostly lost with the closures of the stations at London, Ontario, and Claresholm, Alberta, and the decrease in aircrew training brought by the end of the NATO-wide training scheme. At the same time, Maritime Air Command was building up with the introduction of the Argus, and its expansion created about 780 new positions that absorbed most of the Training Command losses; staff augmentation in the other commands accounted for the rest.

On 18 September, to accommodate the Air Transport Command units that were moving to Trenton, and the CC-106 Yukon transport, Treasury Board approved the construction of a 135-foot span-cantilever hangar, a control tower, and associated facilities, costing in the order of $6.4 million.

An Air Force Headquarters staff study found that the Canadian Army's requirement for air support focused primarily on air transport, not tactical support. The resulting conclusion was that a separate, independent Tactical Air Command was no longer justified, and the decision was made to disband Tactical Air Command Headquarters at Edmonton, and to reassign its functions to Air Transport Command, which would thus take over RCAF Station Namao and its lodger units, No 105 Communication & Rescue Flight and the Survival Training School, and assume administrative control of RCAF Station Whitehorse and the Canadian Joint Air Training Centre at Rivers, Manitoba. RCAF Station Namao would assume the administrative responsibilities of Tactical Air Command Headquarters Support Unit, and Training Command would assume control of the Tactical Air Command auxiliary units.[52]

On 23 September, Prime Minister John G. Diefenbaker announced that the RCAF would acquire BOMARC ground-to-air missiles. Early in the new year, the government would announce the termination of all contracts associated with the CF-105 Arrow.[53]

October

In October, the squadron despatched twenty transatlantic runs, including twelve UNEF troop-rotation flights to El Arish. Nine of these flights were routed by way of Lajes, Gibraltar and Athens; the other three went through Langar, Pisa and Athens, returning by the same route. Two flights to El Arish ran into mechanical difficulties. On 18 October, Flight Lieutenant Hutchinson, flying NS17414, lost an engine shortly after leaving Gibraltar, and returned to point of departure on three engines and had the defective engine changed. The next morning, after an air test, the flight resumed. NS17506 (captained by Flight Lieutenant Lynch) departed Langar on 1 November. Some fifty minutes into the flight, No 1 engine malfunctioned and had to be shut down. The flight returned to Langar where the engine was changed. After a test flight the following morning, Lynch and his crew departed for El Arish by way of Naples and Athens, returning to Langar by the same route. The troop rotation, completed on 31 October, took a total of nineteen flights.[54]

Langar was the destination of six other flights during the month. Three of them were extended to the fighter wings in Europe and the RCAF Air Weapons Unit at Decimomannu in Sardinia.

One aircraft was assigned to provide air transport support for *Operation JUMP MOAT 5*, escorting a convoy of fifteen CF-100 Mk 4B aircraft that left RCAF Station Uplands on 22 October to Baden-Söllingen by way of Goose Bay and Keflavik, arriving in Europe on 24 October.

At the end of the month Flight Lieutenant Charchuk captained a special logistics run in NS17510 to Gibraltar, after which the flight returned to base.

With No 426 Squadron so heavily commited to the UNEF troop-rotation task, the service flights to Resolute Bay were undertaken by C-119s from Downsview and Edmonton. The squadron did, however, conduct several other scheduled and special domestic flights.[55]

On 18 October, the 1,815[th] and last Canadair-built North American Sabre was delivered to the West German air force.

On 28 October, No 412 Squadron's C-5 (captained by Wing Commander W.K. Carr) departed Uplands on a round-the-world tour of allied and Commonwealth countries with Prime Minister Diefenbaker. The flight returned to Ottawa on 20 December.[56]

November

In November, the squadron carried out thirteen scheduled overseas flights, providing logistics support for the Air Division in Europe and UNEF in the Middle East. All these flights officially terminated at Langar, but four were extended to El Arish by way of Pisa and Athens, and one was directed to Marville and Baden-Söllingen to provide air transport support for the fighter squadrons going to the RCAF Air Weapons Unit at Decimomannu.

On 18 November, the squadron despatched NS17521, with an augmented crew and captained by Flight Lieutenant Jackson, on a flight that combined the functions of a Christmas run to Saigon and a round-the-world training tour. The flight headed first for Lajes, and then crossed Africa by way of Dakar, Lagos, Stanleyville, Nairobi and Aden. Proceeding through Asia via Bombay, Negombo and Singapore, the flight arrived in Saigon on 1 December. After unloading the mail, Christmas comforts and cargo for the ICSC truce teams, the flight left for Hong Kong. Crew and aircraft returned to base on 10 December, having stopped at Tokyo, Wake Island, Honolulu, San Francisco and Winnipeg en route.[57]

In June 1958, a detachment of about eighty RCAF personnel had replaced the A.V. Roe team airlifted to the Naval Warfare Center at Point Mugu, California, by No 426 Squadron in November 1957. Headed by Wing Commander F. Phripp and manned primarily by the Central Experimental and Proving Establishment at Rockcliffe, the RCAF detachment's mission was to test the Sparrow 2 air-to-air missile using CF-100 fighters. With the CF-105 program reduced to a bare minimum and facing cancellation, however, the RCAF detachment at Point Mugu was recalled to Canada, to set up at Cold Lake.

On 22 November, therefore, the squadron dispatched NS17516, captained by Flight Lieutenant Lambeth and carrying an augmented crew, to airlift the detachment and its equipment to Cold Lake. The first stage of the flight was the scheduled service run to Vancouver via Ottawa, Winnipeg and Namao; that completed, NS17516 headed for Point Mugu, where it arrived on 24 November. The next day, Lambeth and his crew embarked some forty passengers and their equipment, and the flight went on to Great Falls, Montana, where it stayed the night, and on 26 November, the flight carried on to Namao and Cold Lake. The next day, it returned directly to Point Mugu (a flight of seven hours and forty minutes); on 29 November, the crew embarked more passengers and freight, and on 30 November the flight returned to Cold Lake via Great Falls. As soon as the aircraft was unloaded, Lambeth and his crew returned to Point Mugu on a third shuttle flight. Departing on 1 December for Great Falls and an overnight stop, the flight arrived at Namao the next day, unloaded, and then left for Ottawa and base.[58]

The squadron made one scheduled flight to Resolute Bay during the month: NS17510, captained by Flying Officer Rodewolt, which departed Dorval on 26 November for Ottawa and Winnipeg. The next day, the flight proceeded to Resolute Bay after brief stops at Churchill and Coral Harbour. Rodewolt and his crew were back at Churchill on 28 November, and completed a shuttle run to Coral Harbour before heading for Winnipeg. The crew were back at base the following day. Another extended domestic flight left Dorval on 28 November in NS17506, captained by Flying Officer Lavigne. The flight was positioned at St-Hubert where it embarked the Bell Show Troupe and went on to Winnipeg. Fort St. John was the destination the next day, followed by Fort McMurray on 30 November. The troupe was airlifted to The Pas on 1 December, to Churchill on 2 December, to Great Whale on 5 December, and Winisk the following day. The flight returned to base on 7 December after dropping off the troupe at St-Hubert.[59]

On 11 November, personnel from Lachine and St-Hubert participated in the Remembrance Day ceremonies held at the Cenotaph in downtown Montreal; anyone not marching in the parade attended services at the chapels at Lachine.

On 21 November, the Sergeants' Mess held a dinner with Major-General Wilson of the USAF as guest of honour, accompanied by Colonel Payne and Major Murphy. His address to the gathering was a briefing on Strategic Air Command.[60]

December

In addition to a variety of domestic flights, the squadron carried out two scheduled runs to Resolute Bay in December. The first was taken out by Flying Officer Zbesheski and began by going to Ottawa and Winnipeg on 10 December, carrying several staff officers from Lachine. The next day, the flight carried on to Churchill, picked up more passengers and cargo, and headed for Resolute Bay. As soon as unloading was completed, Zbesheski and his crew returned to Churchill. On 12 December, a shuttle run was conducted to Resolute Bay, after which the flight departed for Churchill with the staff officers aboard. The crew were back at Dorval the next day, having stopped at Winnipeg and Ottawa on the way.

Flight Lieutenant Hutchinson in NS17515 brought in the last scheduled run of the year to Resolute Bay on 17 December, bringing a new teacher for the Eskimo village school, and his wife. The ground crews managed to unload and load the aircraft in a record forty minutes, enabling the flight to depart for Churchill only ninety minutes after arrival. Hutchinson and his crew were back at base on 18 December, after brief stops at Winnipeg and Ottawa on the way.[61]

During the month, the squadron sent two special flights to the Bahamas. On 5 December, Flight Lieutenant Lewis and his crew left Dorval in NS17502 and flew to Halifax, where they boarded a group of RCN personnel, and then to Greenwood, where they picked up a group of RCAF personnel. From Greenwood, the flight went directly to Bermuda, where it spent the night; the next day, it continued on to Nassau, where the passengers disembarked, and returned to Greenwood. It was back at base on 8 December.

On 11 December, Wing Commander Mackie departed base for Nassau in NS17525, a flight of nine hours and fifteen minutes, to pick up the sailors and airmen delivered there the week before. The flight left for Bermuda on 12 December, and returned to base the next day after disembarking its passengers at Halifax and Greenwood.[62]

December's workload also included twelve flights to Langar, four of which were extended to El Arish through Pisa and Athens, and, on 21 December, a special flight to Lajes — Flying Officer Johnston and his crew in NS17512 — to bring the slip crews and other RCAF personnel home for Christmas; that flight arrived at base early on Christmas Day.

On 27 December, Wing Commander Mackie took NS17502 to Lajes and Langar to reposition slip crews, and Flight Lieutenant Hutchinson and his crew took NS17512 to Lajes, where the aircraft was taken over by a slip crew who carried on to Langar. Mackie and his crew were back at base with NS17502 on 31 December; Hutchinson's crew took over NS17510 when it came in on 4 January, and went on to Langar and El Arish, returning to base on 10 January.[63]

An Air Council submission was prepared in December at Air Force Headquarters recommending the replacement of No 115 ATU's Dakotas and Otters with the DHC-4 Caribou, to improve operational effectiveness and safety.

At the A.V. Roe plant at Malton, the 692nd and last CF-100 Canuck rolled off the production line on 4 December.[64]

At El Arish on 15 December, a squadron of twelve United Arab Republic Air Force MiG 15s arrived and began operating from the airfield on a permanent basis. On 24 December, the the NCOs' Mess at No 115 ATU hosted Secretary-General Dag Hammarskjöld and Major-General E.L.M. Burns at a buffet luncheon; the next day, the Secretary General and the UNEF Commander were flown to Gaza. The traditional Christmas Day inter-mess visits were observed and dinner for the airmen was served by the officers and senior NCOs. On 31 December, an American entertainment group performed for the personnel of No 115 ATU, the Yugoslav battalion and the Indian signals detachment.[65]

RCAF Station Lachine held its usual array of well-organized Christmas parties between 16 December and 19 December. The Station Headquarters party was held in the north side of the Airmen's Mess on 17 December with an excellent turnout. On the afternoon of 22 December, the Sergeants paid their annual visit to the Officers' Mess.

On 23 December, Leading Aircraftsman J.G.A. Bélanger, who had died in a car accident at Centralia, Ontario, was buried at the Côte-des-Neiges Cemetery. RCAF Station Lachine provided a funeral party.

Christmas Day dawned clear and very cold and, after well-attended church services, the officers served Christmas dinner to some 125 airmen.

On 29 December, the officers visited the sergeants in their mess in the afternoon, and a good time was had by all. All the messes held parties and dances to bring in the New Year.[66]

PHOTO 179

The crew of NS17511 prepare to leave with Red Cross supplies for flood victims in Ceylon; Dorval, 3 January 1958. From left: F/O J. Bugdale and F/O J.C. Boutet; on ladder: F/O L. Landess, F/L J.J. Lynch and F/L T. Charchuk; and at the top: F/S A.G. Couillard, F/S E. Chevalier and LAC J.R. Conlin. (J. Bugdale Collection)

PHOTO 180

Operation STARFLIGHT: Mother ship NS17504 Prestwick Airport during a ferry flight with T–33 Silver Stars bound for Greece and Turkey; Glasgow, 12 May 1958. (DND PL 95790)

CHAPTER 23

LACHINE AND TRENTON, 1959

The squadron's first overseas departure of the year left Dorval at 2000 hours on 2 January, when NS17510, captained by Flying Officer Lavigne, departed for Langar with detachment personnel and slip crews aboard. From Langar, the flight proceeded first to Grostenquin and Zweibrücken, and then to Decimomannu, providing air transport support for the fighter squadrons carrying out air-firing exercises. Lavigne returned to Langar and was back at base on 15 January.

On the afternoon of 3 January, Flight Lieutenant Jackson left Dorval in NS17516 for Lajes and Baden-Söllingen. He returned to base on 8 January by way of Marville, Shannon and Keflavik, the last leg taking ten and a half hours.[1]

In January, ten more scheduled flights were despatched to Langar, and one went directly to Marville. Three of the flight extensions from Langar were to carry out SF 53/54 to El Arish, but only two were completed. The third, which was captained by Flight Lieutenant Lynch, had left Athens for El Arish on 19 January in NS17516. As the flight neared El Arish, the crew were advised that a severe sandstorm had hit the area, closing the field. Shortly after turning around and setting heading for Athens, No 3 engine malfunctioned and had to be shut down. The rest of the flight was completed on three engines and, on arrival, it was determined that an engine change was required. The squadron flew in a new engine that flight engineer Sergeant Demeter saw installed in place of the defective one, thus enabling the flight to leave for Pisa and Langar on 23 January.

Two other flight extensions from Langar went to the fighter wings and provided air transport support for the squadrons deployed to Decimomannu. Another flight was directed from Langar to Zurich. Flight Lieutenant Ingram and his crew, in NS17511, picked up a large, highly classified computer on 31 January and brought it back to Montreal by way of Gibraltar and Lajes.[2]

In 1959, the Resolute Bay Detachment continued to function as a major military air base in the Arctic under the control of RCAF Station Lachine. It was also a civil aerodrome, and the centre of administration and re-supply for the joint weather stations operated by the Department of Transport and the US Weather Bureau in the Arctic Archipelago. The civil importance of the airport was increasing with the beginning of oil exploration activities and the Polar Continental Shelf Project; Resolute Bay was a centre and re-supply base for these developments, which were expected to become very significant. The service commitment was also expected to increase during the year, as a result of activities planned by the Canadian Army and a possible winter survival course at Resolute Bay.

Plans were afoot to lengthen the runway from 5,400 to 6,500 feet and widen it from 125 to 220 feet. The overshoot area on Runway 17 was to be increased by 1,050 feet of gravel surface and that of Runway 35 by 1,000 feet. When re-survey of the runway heading was carried out, it was found to be 166° True–346° True — a one-degree correction — and action was taken amend all air publications and pilot handbooks accordingly. The approach and runway lighting was slated for improvement, and the parking area was to be expanded from 700 by 700 feet to 750 by 1,000 feet — big enough to accommodate nine C-119s instead of seven.[3]

In addition to a variety of domestic runs during the month, the squadron carried out its first scheduled flight of the year to Resolute Bay on 8 January, bringing the detachment its first mail in three weeks and Flight Lieutenant Renton, the Senior Medical Officer at Station Lachine, to make a staff visit. Once the aircraft was unloaded and refuelled, the flight left on a shuttle run to Churchill; it returned the following day, unloaded more cargo, and then left for Churchill and base. The next service flight arrived at Resolute Bay on 21 January, after weather delays of one day at Montreal and two days at Churchill. Shortly after its arrival on 25 January, the flight left to carry out an air-drop at Alexandra Fjord and then continued on to Thule. The sked brought Squadron Leader A.B. Singleton to the detachment to assume command on 27 January, and Flight Lieutenant Owston, the current Northern Co-ordinator at RCAF Station Lachine, for a staff visit. From Thule, the sked flight proceeded on a logistics run to Alert on 26 January, returned to Thule, and then proceeded to Resolute Bay. The next day, the flight left for Churchill and base with Squadron Leader Kelley, the out-going Detachment Commander, and the visitors aboard.[4]

At RCAF Station Lachine, Air Commodore Carpenter called muster parades of all personnel on 12 January and 13 January, at which everyone learned that the projected moving date for No 426 Squadron and Air Transport Command Headquarters to Station Trenton was to be 11 September 1959, and RCAF Station Lachine would then disband. At the same time, Training Command Headquarters would move from Trenton to Winnipeg, and No 14 Group Headquarters at Winnipeg would disband. During the month, RCAF strength was estimated at 51,092 personnel, comprising 9,483 officers and 41,609 other ranks, including 318 female officers and 2,441 airwomen.[5]

Under NATO Mutual Aid, Canada was making available twenty-five twin-engine Expeditor aircraft to France and Portugal. The aircraft were to be made ready by May, and Training Command was given the responsibility of delivering them. It was expected that the ferry operation would take place in late May or early June. The aircraft were to be fitted with 100-gallon overload tanks for the operation. Spares support was to be marshalled for shipment to reach France and Portugal by early May. No 426 Squadron was to provide air transport support for the operation.[6]

February

During the first two weeks of February the squadron completed the rotation of the personnel of the Reconnaissance Squadron serving with UNEF in Egypt. Flight Lieutenant Hutchinson captained the slip crew that was positioned at Athens on 31 January. Between 1 February and 15 February, they conducted seven shuttle runs from Athens, carrying replacements to El Arish and returning with soldiers whose tours had expired. During the rotation some of the squadron aircraft proceeding to and from Athens staged through Lajes and Gibraltar, while others went through Langar.[7]

On board the 8 February shuttle run to El Arish was Air Commodore Carpenter, making his annual visit to No 115 ATU; later in the day, he went on to Gaza for dinner with the UNEF Commander and his guests. The next day, No 115 ATU held a ceremonial parade and the Air Commodore inspected the airfield site; in the evening, he was guest of honour at a formal dinner in the officers' dining tent. On 10 February, the Air Commodore concluded his visit by inspecting the guard of honour before departing for Athens with Flight Lieutenant Hutchinson and his crew.[8]

As well as the seven troop-rotation flights, the squadron despatched nine overseas runs in February, eight to Langar and one directly to Marville. After the troop rotation was completed, two flights carried on to El Arish from Langar, and one was sent to the fighter wings and Decimomannu.

On the domestic scene, as well as scheduled runs, special flights to Vancouver, Cold Lake and Key West were conducted. Resolute Bay was the destination of two squadron flights, the first taken out by Flight Lieutenant Brown on 9 February in NS17516. The sked was delayed at Churchill on 10 February as weather conditions were below landing limits at Resolute Bay and both its alternates, Thule and Cambridge Bay. The flight arrived the following afternoon, and after unloading returned to Churchill to carry out a shuttle run. On 12 February, Brown was back at Resolute, making his landing in rapidly deteriorating weather conditions that closed the field shortly after his arrival. The flight was able to leave again on 14 February, and was back at base the next day. The second flight into Resolute Bay was captained by Flight Lieutenant Gill, who brought in NS17515 on 25 February and left for Churchill as soon as the aircraft was unloaded. The next day, Gill returned to Resolute Bay, leaving for Winnipeg and base on 27 February.[9]

The contract for the design and the manufacture of the A.V. Roe CF-105 Arrow was cancelled by the Canadian government on 20 February. The RCAF would strike the last of five CF-105s off its inventory on 22 July.[10]

On 10 March, Air Force Headquarters issued Organization Order 8.2, stating that, in accordance with the 1959–1963 Programme of Activities, RCAF Station Lachine was to disband and all its lodger units, including Air Transport Command Headquarters, would move to RCAF Station Trenton. Although the effective date for the move was 12 September 1959, Air Transport Command Headquarters would maintain a rear party at Lachine until the Department of Public Works was ready to hand it over to the Crown Assets Disposal Corporation, as the site would then be surplus to RCAF requirements.[11]

Thirteen flights were despatched to Europe in March, with ten staging through Langar and three proceeding directly from Lajes to Marville. There were four flight extensions during the month from Langar to El Arish.

One of the flights returning to base from Langar ran into some difficulties. Shortly after take-off on 6 March a fire warning light on NS17506, captained by Flight Lieutenant Charchuk, made it necessary to return to Langar. The ground staff checked out the aircraft and it departed the following day for Lajes, but it turned back again with the same problem. Another thorough check was completed, and this time the fault was attributed to a short in the electrical system. Following the check, the flight left for Lajes and returned to base without further incident.[12]

In March, the squadron carried out one combined logistics and training run to the north, two sked flights to Resolute Bay, and several domestic airlift assignments. Flight Lieutenant Gill captained NS17525 on the northern training flight, leaving base on 6 March for Churchill. It landed that day at Big Owl, a Mid-Canada Line air strip on the northwestern shore of James Bay, and at RCAF Station Winisk. The next day, the flight continued on to Whitehorse with an intermediate stop at Cambridge Bay. Gill and his crew returned to base on 9 March, making stops at Edmonton, Saskatoon, Winnipeg and Ottawa en route.[13]

The sked flight from Dorval arrived at Resolute Bay on 10 March, brought in by Flight Lieutenant Hutchinson in NS17504. The passengers included Wing Commander P.S. Turner, the Station Commander from Lachine; Wing Commander F.C. Jones, his Chief of Technical Services; and Squadron Leader T. Vanchuk, his Senior Supply Officer, to conduct a staff visit; Dr. Roots of the Continental Shelf Project with six members of his team; and Mr. Goodbrand from the headquarters of the Department of Transport Weather Service. As soon as the aircraft was unloaded, the flight departed again for Churchill and Winnipeg, returning to Resolute Bay on 12 March. The flight then continued on to Thule, and the next day made a supply run to Alert. After this, Hutchinson and his crew returned to Churchill via Resolute Bay. On 14 March, the flight was back at Resolute Bay dropping off passengers and cargo before continuing on to Thule. Another shuttle run was conducted to Alert on 15 March, after which the flight returned to Resolute Bay to pick up the staff officers from Lachine and the scientists. It then departed for Churchill and base, arriving back in Montreal on 17 March.[14]

On 24 March, Flight Lieutenant Brown arrived in NS17502 on the second sked flight of the month, unloaded, and returned to base by way of Churchill, Winnipeg and Ottawa.

On 13 March, RCAF Station Lachine provided a funeral party for Flight Lieutenant E.L. Fine, who died on 9 March in an accident at RCAF Station Gimli. The funeral went from Paperman's Funeral Home on Côte-des-Neiges Boulevard, Montreal, to the Beth Israel plot at Rue-de-la-Savanne Cemetery.[15]

April

On 1 April, the Officers' Mess at Lachine hosted veterans of the Second World War and guests from the aircraft industry at a mess dinner to celebrate the thirty-fifth anniversary of the RCAF and the fiftieth anniversary of powered flight in Canada.[16]

The squadron despatched seventeen overseas flights in April. Four were routed directly from Lajes to Marville, and three returned to base by the same route; the other came back by way of Langar. Of the eleven other flights to Langar, four were extended to El Arish and one went on to the fighter wings and Decimomannu. A logistics run in support of squadron operations was sent to Pisa by way of Gibraltar, returning to Montreal through Langar. An additional support flight went as far as Lajes before heading home.

Despite weather and maintenance problems, all flights but one were conducted on schedule. On 9 April, Flight Lieutenant Fawcett and his crew had just departed Zweibrücken for Langar in NS17506 when they noticed a slight tremor in the aircraft. A visual inspection revealed that the spinner on No 1 engine was vibrating violently and that the nose of the spinner had a hole in it. The propeller was promptly feathered and the engine shut down; Fawcett then brought the aircraft safely to Zweibrücken. On the ground, an inspection revealed that the nuts holding the backplate and spinner had pulled through the backplate. The aircraft was flown three and a half hours on three engines to Langar, where the necessary repairs were carried out. The flight then returned to base.[17]

In April, the squadron conducted three northern runs and a variety of scheduled and special domestic flights. The first northern run was carried out by Flight Lieutenant Nichol and his crew, who took out NS17517 to Resolute Bay. Leaving Dorval on 13 April, the flight stopped at Ottawa, Winnipeg and Churchill to pick up passengers and freight, and arrived at Resolute Bay at 1705 hours the following day. On board were Air Commodore H.H.C. Rutledge, Group Captain D.E. Galloway and four university professors who were on a northern familiarization tour and to observe the spring re-supply of the Arctic weather stations. The re-supply operation, under Squadron Leader J.S. Miller, had begun on 8 April and was being conducted using three C-119 aircraft, two from No 435 Squadron and one from No 436 Squadron. Four hours after their arrival, Nichol and his crew left for base via Churchill, Winnipeg, North Bay and Ottawa. The second logistics flight left Dorval for Churchill on 21 April in NS17517 captained by Flight Lieutenant McLaughlin. The crew proceeded to Frobisher Bay the next day, and returned to base on 23 April. Another North Star sked arrived in Resolute Bay on 28 April, unloaded, and promptly left for Churchill and Dorval.[18]

On 23 April, Air Transport Command Headquarters announced that Wing Commander C.H. Mussells, DSO, OBE, DFC, CD, of Montreal, had been appointed Officer Commanding the Central Flying School in Trenton. He was being replaced as Senior Air Staff Officer by Wing Commander G.J.J. Edwards, DFC, CD of Ottawa and Sudbury. Wing Commander Edwards came to Air Transport Command Headquarters from Edmonton where he had commanded No 435 Squadron.[19]

An Operational Requirements staff study of possible uses for the North Star in the 1961–1971 period found that the RCAF could employ a total of ten: eight for search-and-rescue, one for electronic countermeasures testing, and one for long-range navigation training. A submission recommending using the ten aircraft for the purposes indicated was being prepared for consideration by the Current Planning Committee. On receiving the Committee's agreement in principle, the submission would be forwarded to the Air Council for approval.[20]

The responsibility for the wireless station at Alert had passed from the RCAF to the Royal Canadian Corps of Signals on 1 September 1958. Although the station continued to be administered by the Canadian Army, it was to be manned by personnel from all three services until the Signal Corps could man it completely. The station's first major expansion was to be completed during the summer of 1959 but, by late April, the Quartermaster General was concerned that, if Treasury Board did not approve the plan soon, the target date of 1 November for project completion would not be met. Equipment had to be purchased in time for the summer's Montreal-to-Thule sealift, as all the material would have to be airlifted to Alert by mid-July. Project approval was finally received on 29 April, and Minister of National Defence George R. Pearkes advised the Chief of the General Staff the next day that he had obtained agreement in principle for the project after a meeting with the Prime Minister and the Ministers of Finance and Justice. The expansion of the wireless station, including an extensive antenna field two and a half miles south of Alert, would be completed during the summer of 1959.[21]

May

May was a busy month for the squadron and its twelve aircraft, which put in nearly 1,600 hours of relatively trouble-free operational flying. This attested to the superb efforts of the unit's servicing and maintenance crews, both at base and on detachment, who kept the North Star fleet operating at peak efficiency.

Fifteen flights to Europe and the Middle East were devoted to the support of the Air Division and UNEF in Egypt. Five of these flights staged through Lajes directly to Marville, and returned to base by the same route. The other ten flights went first to Langar; from there, four flights were directed to El Arish, and one went to Zweibrücken and the Air Weapons Unit at Decimomannu. In addition, a logistics flight in support of squadron operations was despatched as far as Lajes, from where it returned to base.[22]

Two of the flights returning home from Lajes in May were able to take advantage of favourable winds and make it to Dorval without an intermediate stop. On 6 May, Flight Lieutenant Sierolawski and his crew in NS17509 made the run in twelve hours flat; the next day, Flying Officer Johnston in NS17510 made the same flight in twelve hours and ten minutes.

Wing Commander Mackie and his crew left base for Langar on 28 April; two days later, they took over NS17512, which was positioned at RAF Station Gutersloh, twenty-four miles north of the group of Canadian Army bases around Soest, West Germany. On 1 May, they embarked the band of Princess Patricia's Canadian Light Infantry, which was beginning a tour of UNEF units, and flew to Egypt by way of Pisa and Athens, arriving at El Arish on 3 May. From El Arish, Mackie and his crew returned to Pisa, and from there their UN flight was extended to Copenhagen before carrying on to Langar and base.[23]

The month's domestic flights included the annual RCAF Staff College airlift to the Air University at Maxwell AFB in Montgomery, Alabama. On 3 May, Flight Lieutenant Fawcett in NS17502 and Flying Officer Zbesheski in NS17506 were in position at Malton Airport in Toronto to embark the directing staff and students, and the aircraft then left for Maxwell AFB. The next morning, the two aircraft took the entire Staff College group to Patrick AFB for a visit to Cape Canaveral and then back to Maxwell that afternoon. They went to Eglin AFB and back to Maxwell on 5 May, and departed for Montreal the following day.

On 9 May, the squadron despatched NS17502, captained by Flight Lieutenant Kuhn, and NS17521, flown by Flying Officer Hastie, to Maxwell AFB; they picked up staff and students and delivered them to Toronto the following afternoon, after which both aircraft returned to base.[24]

On 6 May, the squadron despatched the first of the month's several northern flights: NS17514, with two full flight crews captained by Flying Officer Rodewolt and Flying Officer Lavigne and a six-man servicing and maintenance crew. The first stop was Winnipeg, where on 7 May they embarked twenty-one staff and students from the Central Navigation School, including nine experienced officers on the Specialist Navigation Course, and proceeded to Churchill and Resolute Bay.

This was the Central Navigation School's annual long-range polar navigation exercise. Over the next five days, the North Star crews would alternate to carry out five reconnaissance and navigation exercises averaging seven hours and fifteen minutes each, and make three trips to the North Pole, all of which landed at Thule before returning to Resolute. The flying times for these polar flights were nine and a half hours, nine hours and forty minutes and ten hours and fifteen minutes respectively, and as each flight crossed the North Pole a canister containing the name of every person aboard was dropped from the aircraft.

On one of the reconnaissance exercises, the North Star flew over and around a Soviet ice station that was drifting about in the Canadian Sector. The navigators charted its exact position and estimated its movements and, when the radio officer contacted the station, the Soviet commander invited the crew to land on their 6,000-foot ice runway and have tea with his staff. The invitation was declined, however, and the flight returned to Resolute Bay.

With the completion of their scheduled exercises, the CNS staff and students were flown directly to Winnipeg on 13 May and the flight returned to Montreal the next day.[25]

As one squadron aircraft left with the CNS group, another arrived on a scheduled flight, bringing Corporal Moodie of the RCMP back to Resolute Bay after a two-month absence, and a variety of foodstuffs requested some time earlier through service channels, which would effect a marked improvement not only in the detachment's food services but also its morale. As soon as the sked was unloaded it left for Churchill and Montreal.

Resolute Bay had nearly a week of radio blackout and severely limited communications, which meant the detachment got quite a surprise on 16 May: a North Star due to land in twenty minutes with Air Commodore Carpenter and thirty visitors, including Group Captain G.A. Hiltz, Group Captain K.A.L. Schroeder and Wing Commander D.G. Malloy, James M. Minifee (the CBC's Washington correspondent) and a group of university professors. The visitors had come to Resolute to familiarize themselves with conditions in the high Arctic and the scientific and other activities being conducted there. The next evening, CHRB, the local radio station, hosted Mr. Minifee, who gave an interesting talk on recent events in Washington, and Air Commodore Carpenter, who commended the detachment personnel for their good work.

On 18 May, a search-and-rescue Lancaster arrived at Resolute Bay with Major-General W.J. Megill, General Officer Commanding, Prairie Command, who spent several days touring Alert and the weather sites before returning to Winnipeg.[26]

Early in the month, the Department of National Defence issued a statement by the Minister, George R. Pearkes, dealing with the late-May delivery under Mutual Aid arrangements of nineteen C-45 Expeditor aircraft to France and six to Portugal. The delivery also included ten spare engines (six to France and four to Portugal) and a one-year supply of other associated equipment. The Expeditors brought the total number of RCAF aircraft received by NATO countries since 1951 under Mutual Aid to 933. In service with the RCAF since 1943, the Expeditor was a twin-engine, twin-rudder aircraft with a passenger capacity of five. The aircraft going to Europe had been used to train students in aerial navigation.

The Expeditor was a military variant of the Beech-18, manufactured by the Beech Aircraft Corporation of Wichita, Kansas, and it entered RCAF service in 1940. By 1945, the RCAF had acquired two hundred and forty-seven Expeditors, and 147 were purchased after the war.[27] Affectionately known to those who flew it as the Bug-smasher, the Expeditor was used in the RCAF for multi-engine training, navigation training, search-and-rescue, and as a VIP transport.

The ferry flight — dubbed *Operation BEECHFLIGHT* — was the first mass transatlantic flight of Expeditors. The convoy commander was Wing Commander H.C. Forbell of St-Jovite, Quebec, with Squadron Leader B.H. Marfleet of Edmonton, Alberta as Deputy Commander and Squadron Leader L.S. Deyell of Lacombe, Alberta, as Flight Navigator. As in previous ferry operations, Air Transport Command provided airlift support.[28]

Operation BEECHFLIGHT was planned at Training Command Headquarters in Trenton under Wing Commander Forbell's direction. Early in May, Training Command pilots visited storage facilities at RCAF stations in western Canada, picked up twenty-six aircraft (the convoy would include one spare), and flew them to Trenton, where each one was fitted with an extra fuel tank, in the cabin. Each aircraft also had a complete navigation kit including a sextant and astro-compass. The plan called for the Expeditors to fly each route segment in sections of five, with each aircraft crewed by one pilot and one navigator (Training Command provided all the ferry crews). The operation's twelve-man technical support party was led by Squadron Leader C.E. Neyvatte and Warrant Officer 2nd Class J.B. Reardon.

Preparations for the operation included ditching drills in the station swimming pool, thorough crew briefings on North Atlantic weather conditions and the facilities and procedures they would encounter en route, and the positioning of liaison officers at each stop. Before leaving Trenton, the crews and technical staff discussed the fine points of asymmetric flight with a full 100-gallon long-range fuel tank in the cabin — there was some speculation that an engine failure on take-off might abruptly curtail budding Air Force careers. Some wives were heard to say that the whole thing seemed a bit dicey.

On 19 May, Training Command Headquarters issued a warning order announcing that *Operation BEECHFLIGHT* would launch the next day, and Flying Officer Johnston and his crew arrived from Dorval in NS17521 to be the mother ship for the operation.

On the morning of 20 May, the forecast was for VFR (visual flight regulations) flight conditions; at worst, the aircraft could be between cloud layers on the way to Goose Bay. And so the operation was launched: twenty-six Expeditors organized in four sections of five and one of six, taking off at one-hour intervals with an assigned block airspace to 10,000 feet, and followed by the North Star.

At 820 miles, the first leg of the operation to Goose Bay was the longest. The weather began to deteriorate as the convoy passed Montreal, and the sections soon encountered IFR (instrument flight regulations) conditions. Unable to maintain visual contact for formation flying, the crews promptly dispersed to ensure separation, and the twenty-six Expeditors were soon spread out, most of them in their block airspace but some outside, flying either just below cloud at 3,000 feet, or in cloud or between layers at 13,000 feet. All the aircraft made it to Goose Bay where the weather was clear, averaging six hours and forty-five minutes of flying time. On the ground, the servicing team (brought in by the North Star) got the Expeditors ready for their next departure. MATS had the task of providing air-sea rescue service from Goose Bay to Britain, and in their briefings the USAF officers assured the ferry crews that anyone who came down on the Greenland icecap would be picked up within thirty minutes.

In the morning, the convoy left for Frobisher Bay with VFR flight conditions holding for most of the leg, which averaged six hours, but weather held up the operation at Frobisher until 24 May. The aircraft crewed by Squadron Leader Marfleet and Flight Lieutenant Timmins went unserviceable at Frobisher Bay, and Marfleet and Timmins had to take over the spare aircraft. (A crew stayed at Frobisher Bay with the unserviceable aircraft which, once repaired, went back to Trenton.) The convoy departed for Sondrestrom, a four-hour leg, intending to refuel there and carry on to Keflavik.

Three sections refuelled at Sondrestrom and continued on to Keflavik, but shortly after departure, all crews encountered moderate to severe icing conditions over the Greenland icecap. The Bugsmasher was not known for its ability to perform in even light icing conditions, and the three sections could neither maintain safe altitudes nor hold formation. Despite the hazards, all the crews reached the east coast of Greenland, where they could descend over the water and shed the ice in the warmer air. Aware of the icing problem, the last two sections stayed at Sondrestrom, finally leaving on 27 May for Keflavik, where they rejoined the convoy after a routine flight averaging five hours and ten minutes. The support North Star, which stayed at Sondrestrom with the last two sections, followed them to Keflavik.

On the morning of 28 May, the convoy left Keflavik for Prestwick, a run averaging five hours and ten minutes. This was the only leg of the trip that was flown under clear skies. Radio silence from one of the Expeditors concerned the Scottish air traffic controller; perhaps it had gone down in the water. Later, the investigation established that the man in the right-hand seat — tired of the constant noise in his headset — had turned the radio off.

The final leg to Marville was completed on 29 May, with the Expeditors taking an average of four hours to make the flight. The first aircraft in the convoy left Prestwick at 0915 hours and the last departed some two hours later. The weather was poor, which meant some changes in assigned altitudes and some low flying over the continent. When the last Expeditor had taken off, the servicing personnel boarded the North Star, which then followed the convoy to Marville.

At Marville, the ferry crews handed over the Expeditors to the servicing crews, who removed their long-range tanks and navigation equipment. On 2 June, the North Star embarked the maintenance personnel and the ferry crews not required for the delivery flights and left for Lajes, where a slip crew took it over for the flight to Canada. The next day, Johnston and his crew took over NS17514 and returned to base.

On 3 June, the nineteen aircraft destined for France were flown to the French air force base at Chateaudun, forty-four kilometres south of Chartres, where Wing Commander Forbell turned them over to General Delfino. After the formalities were completed, two Air Division Dakotas returned the C-45 crews to Marville.

The six Expeditors destined for the Portuguese Air Force left Marville at 0930 hours on 4 June for the three-hour flight to Bordeaux, where they refuelled. The plan called for the aircraft to fly in formation in two sections, the first led by Wing Commander Forbell followed by Squadron Leader

Marfleet with the second. From Bordeaux, they were supposed to take the air route across Spain to Lisbon, but they learned at the Bordeaux weather briefing that severe weather associated with a frontal system made that route unsuitable. Consequently, they decided to file a VFR flight plan for a route over the Bay of Biscay, around Cape Finisterre and south to Lisbon.

Immediately after take-off, before the Expeditors could form up, they ran head-on into a formation of light military observation aircraft; after a few anxious moments, however, the Expeditors unscrambled themselves without incident, formed up, and flew west over the Bay of Biscay. The weather did not co-operate; to maintain contact, the formation had to fly very low, so low that the aircraft had to climb several times to clear shipping! The situation got so risky that Forbell chose to try VFR on top, so the formation climbed above cloud, but the cloud tops got higher and higher, and the formation was soon above 10,000 feet with no oxygen. Forbell decided to descend, but Marfleet kept his section at that altitude; consequently, the formation now had a high section and a low section, with Flight Lieutenant Timmins navigating for the high section. The sections lost contact, and Marfleet's group arrived at Lisbon fifteen minutes before Forbell and his three aircraft. Marfleet waited discreetly in the circuit until the Mission Commander could land, and then brought in his three aircraft. The flight time to Lisbon was five hours and forty-five minutes.

Wing Commander Forbell handed the aircraft over to the Portuguese Air Force at a ceremony on 5 May, but the Expeditor crews could not leave until 7 June — the Air Division Dakota that was to take them back to Marville blew a tire on landing. From Marville, the ferry crews caught a North Star service flight to Canada.

In the words of the Beechflight slogan, "You can't argue with success!"[29]

On 19 May, two special logistics and training flights were despatched to Victoria. Flight Lieutenant Charchuk and his crew took NS17517 by way of Trenton and Winnipeg, returning to base on 21 May through Vancouver and Winnipeg. Flight Lieutenant Sierolawski and his crew in NS17515 went to Victoria after a stop at Winnipeg, and returned to Dorval on 21 May via Vancouver, Edmonton and Québec City. The Edmonton-Québec leg was an eight hour run.[30]

On 25 May, Flight Lieutenant Brown took out NS17515 to Goose Bay and, after unloading, conducted a long range training flight to Winnipeg, a nine-and-a-half-hour leg. The flight returned to base the following day. On the same day, the Resolute Bay sked went out, proceeding to Churchill via Ottawa and Winnipeg and continuing on to Resolute the next day, bringing in several staff officers from Air Transport Command Headquarters. That flight departed again for Churchill as soon as the staff visits were complete, and the flight was back at base on 27 May.[31]

On 29 May, Flight Lieutenant Sierolawski and his crew left base in NS17509 for a special flight to take Wing Commander Sanford and a party of staff officers to the Arctic. The first destination was the DEW Line site at Hall Beach, a brief stop before going on to Resolute Bay, where they refuelled and carried on to Thule. The next day, the flight returned to Resolute Bay and then departed for Montreal, a flight of ten hours and forty minutes.[32]

June

The June operational commitments for the squadron's twelve North Stars totalled 1,650 flying hours. Overseas flights in support of No 1 Air Division and the Canadian brigade in Europe, UNEF in Egypt, and the truce teams in Indochina made up most of the commitment;

scheduled and special domestic flights made up the rest. The squadron would lose its fourth aircraft in an accident during the month.³³

Of the eight flights routed directly to Langar, four were extended to El Arish, and it was one of these that crashed at Athens. Two others went to Marville, and one was directed to Grostenquin and Athens. Six flights went directly from Lajes to Marville, and five of these returned to base by way of Langar. A fifth flight to El Arish was routed through Lajes, Nouasseur (an airfield near Casablanca) and Athens, returning to base by way of Athens, Pisa, Langar and Marville. The winds were so favourable on 3 June that Flight Lieutenant Sierolawski and his crew in NS17509 were able to make the flight from Lajes to Montreal in only twelve hours and fifty minutes.³⁴

Operation SILVER DOZEN, the ferry of twelve T-33 Silver Star jets from Trenton to No 4 Wing at Baden-Söllingen, was launched on 9 June and carried out by No 129 Acceptance and Ferry Flight, a unit subordinate to No 6 Repair Depot at Trenton. The jet convoy and its North Star escort left that morning for Goose Bay, a flight of two hours and forty-five minutes for the T-33s. On 12 June, after sitting out the weather for several days at Goose Bay, the convoy was able to leave for Sondrestrom, a hop of two hours and forty minutes for the Silver Stars. With good weather prevailing, the jets were refuelled and continued on for two hours to Keflavik, followed by the North Star. Another two-hour flight on 14 June brought the jets to Prestwick, where they refuelled, and one hour and forty minutes after their departure, they arrived at Marville. The next day, the convoy continued on to Baden-Söllingen. The flight crews and technical support personnel returned to Canada with the North Star.³⁵

As well as the two monthly sked flights to Resolute Bay, the squadron despatched a special northern logistics flight that delivered passengers and cargo and picked up a similar payload for the return flight. On 13 June, Flight Lieutenant Sierolawski and his crew positioned NS17509 at Rockcliffe, and then made a six-hour flight to Frobisher Bay. After thirty-five minutes on the ground the flight continued to Thule, which took four hours and twenty-five minutes, and then halted for thirteen hours for crew rest. Leaving just before noon on the 14 June, the flight proceeded to Resolute Bay, a trip of nearly three hours. Departing after an hour's stop, Sierolawski then headed for Uplands, arriving nine hours and ten minutes later. After a brief stop, the aircraft was back at base shortly after midnight.³⁶

The responsibilities of the Air Assessment Team — formed for reasons of economy as an integral part of No 4 OTU in August 1955 — had recently been expanded beyond Air Transport Command to include monitoring the operating standards of transport, communications and rescue flights, and Auxiliary units. To handle the increased workload, the team establishment was augmented to the point that it seemed most practical to organize a separate unit. Consequently, on 15 June 1959, Air Force Headquarters issued Organization Order 8.9.5 authorizing the formation of an Air Assessment Unit effective 12 September 1959.³⁷

On 16 June, Flying Officer Rodewolt and his crew departed Dorval in NS17510 for Lajes. Two days later, they took over NS17509 and proceeded to Marville, where they disembarked their passengers and unloaded their cargo. They then continued to Langar. On 19 June, Rodewolt took out NS17525 and positioned the aircraft at Pisa for the UNEF support flight to El Arish. Leaving Pisa on the evening of 20 June, the flight proceeded to Athens, a five hour run, refuelled and carried on to El Arish, and trip of nearly four hours. The flight arrived shortly after dawn on 21 May, spent four hours on the ground, and then left for Athens with about twenty passengers and a load of freight aboard. First officer Flight Lieutenant B. Genge was at the controls for this return leg.

By the time they were approaching Athens, Rodewolt and his crew had already been on duty for more than eighteen hours, and they were tired. When the control tower assigned the flight to one of Athens' relatively short runways, Flight Lieutenant Genge chose to make a straight-in approach, coming in over the water. With his depth-perception slightly put off by the water effect, Genge did not see the retaining wall in the undershoot area of the runway, forty-five feet from the button, until the aircraft was only 200 feet above touchdown. At that instant, Genge called for power off, and flight engineer Sergeant Demeter complied immediately, but the aircraft sank rapidly, possibly because of a downdraft. Genge took corrective action, but it was too late: the starboard undercarriage struck the retaining wall about four inches from the top, one tire bursting on contact and the other blowing when the aircraft thumped onto the runway and started to roll. The shock of the impact in the undercarriage was enough to start a substantial fuel leak from the starboard main-plane area, immediately aft of No 3 engine, and the fuel spraying from the broken fuel line was ignited by the sparks flying up from the starboard wheels, which were rolling on their rims.

Genge managed to halt the aircraft about one third of the way down the runway, and the other members of the crew got the passengers out through the rear cargo door, an eight-foot drop to the tarmac. Rodewolt left last, and only after checking to ensure everyone else was out. Within five minutes of touchdown, five crash vehicles were on the scene, and the fire was quickly extinguished, but NS17525 was a gutted write-off, and a large quantity of mail was lost. Of the passengers, several suffered sprains and bruises, and one broke a leg.

Shortly before midnight on 21 June, Flying Officer Lavigne and his crew departed Grostenquin in NS17510, bound for Athens to pick up Rodewolt and his crew. The pilots flipped coins to see which captain would work the return flight to No 2 Wing on 23 June, but the toss was fixed to ensure Rodewolt won. After a week spent at Grostenquin while the accident was investigated, Rodewolt and his crew proceeded to Marville where they caught a service flight for base on 1 July, reaching Montreal the following day.[38]

The first truce-team rotation flight of the year left base for Indochina on 23 June, with Flight Lieutenant Sled as captain of an augmented crew in NS17521. The flight was routed to Lajes and across Africa by way of Dakar, Lagos, Stanleyville and Nairobi to Aden. From there, the flight carried on to Karachi and Rangoon, and it arrived at Saigon on 3 July. The flight then proceeded to Hong Kong where the crew had to wait for ten days as there was some delay in bringing in the homeward-bound observers from their various posts so they could brief their replacements. Sled and his crew were back in Saigon on 13 July, embarked the returning team members, and departed for Rangoon. From Rangoon, the flight went to Bombay, Aden, and then across Africa to Lajes by the same route as it used on the outbound trip. The flight arrived at base on 21 July after an absence of twenty-eight days, the crew having put in 150 hours and fifteen minutes flying time on the operation.[39]

On 24 June, Flight Lieutenant Sierolawski and his crew left base in NS17514 as Special Flight 410, heading for Ottawa to pick up a group of Army and Air Force chemical warfare specialists and take them to Baltimore, where they loaded a consignment of nerve gas. The flight then departed under strict instructions to proceed directly to the Experimental Station at Suffield, a flight of nearly ten hours. The ground staff at Suffield looked like spacemen in the protective suits they wore to marshal the aircraft to a remote sector of the airfield — a bit strange, thought the crew, who had seen no special treatment or protective clothing at Baltimore. After an overnight stop, the flight left for Saskatoon, returning to base on 26 June after dropping off their passengers in Ottawa.[40]

On 18 June, Queen Elizabeth II and Prince Philip, Duke of Edinburgh, arrived at Torbay, Newfoundland to begin a forty-five day visit to Canada and the United States. The central event of this tour was the official opening of the St Lawrence Seaway, held at St-Lambert, Quebec on 26 June, at which the Queen presided with the President Dwight D. Eisenhower of the United States. On 1 July, Her Majesty was in Ottawa to unveil the Commonwealth Air Force Memorial, which commemorates the 798 men and women of the Commonwealth air forces who lost their lives in Canada and adjacent lands and waters during the Second World War, and who have no known graves.[41]

July

On 1 July, joint RCN-RCAF Maritime Commands were established on the Atlantic and Pacific coasts, and on 2 July, Minister of National Defence George R. Pearkes announced that the eight fighter squadrons of No 1 Air Division in Europe would re-equip with the Lockheed F-104, to be built under licence by Canadair at its Cartierville plant.[42]

Totalling all domestic and overseas runs, the squadron was committed to 1,700 hours of operational flying in July. As well as special flights, this total included four scheduled transatlantic flights per week in support of the Air Division and 4 Brigade, the Canadian Army formation in central northern Germany. Four of the overseas flights were extended to El Arish in support of the UNEF in Egypt, and one was extended to the fighter wings and and the Air Weapons Unit at Decimomannu. The initial destination for twelve of the European runs was Langar, and six flights proceeded directly to Marville from Lajes, and one went to London.

There was one incident during the month: on 14 July, Flight Lieutenant Charchuk had just taken off from Langar in NS17504 when the aircraft hit a flock of gulls. Charchuk made a quick circuit and landed the aircraft, and a thorough check found no damage. The flight then left for Lajes and base.[43]

Flight Lieutenant McLaughlin and his crew in NS17517 were assigned to transport the luggage for part of that summer's royal tour. Leaving Dorval on 17 July, the flight went to Winnipeg, refuelled, and carried on to Vancouver. The next morning, the aircraft went first to Patricia Bay (near Victoria) to pick up its cargo, and then to Whitehorse, a run of five hours and ten minutes. In the afternoon of 20 July, the flight went to Edmonton, a trip that took four hours and forty minutes, refuelled, and departed for Montreal, arriving eight hours and forty-five minutes later.[44]

At 1820 hours on 25 July, one of No 412 Squadron's Comets arrived at RCAF Station Trenton with the Queen and Prince Philip, who were greeted by Air Vice Marshal J.G. Bryans (AOC Training Command) and Mrs. Bryans; Group Captain and Mrs. D.J. Williams, and Mayor and Mrs. Ross Burtt of Trenton. The royal party then departed by limousine to spend the weekend at Batterwood, Governor General Vincent Massey's home in Port Hope, while RCAF Station Trenton accommodated and entertained the forty-four members of the royal staff.[45]

On 27 July, the squadron despatched Flight Lieutenant Longworth and his crew on a special flight to Resolute Bay in NS17508, bound for Churchill via Ottawa and Winnipeg. The flight arrived at Resolute Bay the next day, dropped off some of its passengers and cargo, and continued to Thule. On 29 July, the flight returned to Churchill on a shuttle run after a stop at Resolute. On 30 July, Longworth and his crew were back at Resolute, where they remained overnight. The flight departed for base the following morning, making stops at Churchill, Winnipeg and Ottawa on the return and putting in fourteen hours and twenty-five minutes flying time in the process.[46]

During the month, five C-119s and crews from No 435 and 436 Transport Squadrons carried out *Operation BOXTOP*, the airlift of equipment, materials and supplies for the wireless station project from Thule to Alert. The airlift operation was completed on 30 September.[47]

Flight Lieutenant Fawcett captained an augmented crew in NS17521 on the squadron's second flight of the year to Saigon. On the morning of 28 July, the flight departed Dorval for Lajes with the outward-bound truce team members and their equipment; the next day, the flight reached Dakar, where it was held up for several days with mechanical problems. Leaving Dakar on 3 August, the flight crossed Africa, making stops at Lagos, Stanleyville and Nairobi before proceeding to Aden, Bombay and Rangoon, and reaching Saigon on 8 August. After disembarking the passengers and unloading their equipment, the flight then left for Hong Kong, but problems with No 4 engine appeared shortly after departure; the engine had to be shut down, and the aircraft had to return to Saigon. By 11 August, the flight engineers were able to rectify the problem and the flight went on to Hong Kong. After a six-day stay, it returned to Saigon on 17 August to pick up the homeward-bound observers. Leaving several hours later, the flight followed the same route as it had taken outbound, arriving back at base on 26 August. This mission took twenty-nine days to complete, during which the crew put in 142 hours and thirty minutes of flying time.[48]

August

By August, preparations for the move of Air Transport Command units to Trenton and the closure of RCAF Station Lachine were well advanced, with even the family moves carried out with minimal disruption to flying operations. Air Force Headquarters sent out an advisory to the effect that, as of 1 September, all transatlantic service flights would originate and terminate at Trenton instead of Dorval. On 5 August, Group Captain H.A. Morrison and Wing Commander H. Lisson of Air Transport Command Headquarters visited RCAF Station Trenton to discuss the move.[49]

Operational commitments in August for the squadron's North Star fleet totalled some 1,530 hours. The transatlantic schedule called for four flights per week in support of the fighter wings and the brigade in Europe, and there was also the weekly UNEF flight to El Arish. Apart from the Saigon run, there was only one major delay in the transatlantic schedule during the month. Flight Lieutenant Rodewolt and his crew were heading for Lajes and Langar in NS17508 when they were held up for two days at Gander with mechanical problems before being able to continue the flight.[50]

On the domestic scene, the squadron made many move-related flights to Trenton. Domestic schedules were maintained, including two runs to Resolute Bay, and several special flights were conducted.

The squadron also provided airlift support for *Operation SECOND SILVER DOZEN*, the delivery of eleven T-33 Silver Stars to Europe by No 129 Acceptance and Ferry Flight from Trenton. To provide airlift support for the operation, Flight Lieutenant Sierolawski and his crew were despatched on 9 August to position NS17509 in Trenton. The Silver Star convoy proceeded to Goose Bay the next morning, followed by the North Star with the ground support staff. On 11 August, the convoy made the hop to Sondrestrom, refuelled, and continued on to Keflavik. Two days later, the convoy and its mother-ship were at Prestwick, which they left on 15 August for No 4 Wing at Baden-Söllingen. The following morning, Sierolawski and his crew, with the ferry pilots and ground staff aboard, flew to Lisbon, refuelled, and continued on to Lajes. The flight arrived in Trenton and disembarked the ferry personnel on 18 August, and returned to Dorval the next day.[51]

On 9 August, the service flight to El Arish brought in Flight Lieutenant W.J. Davidge, a former pilot with No 426 Squadron who was taking up flying duties with No 115 ATU. A week later, Wing Commander R.H. Manson arrived on SF 53 from Air Force Headquarters to take command of No 115 ATU, formally accepting the handover from Squadron Leader C.C. Cooling on 20 August. Cooling departed on SF 54 for Canada on 23 August, having been posted to No 121 Communications Unit at Sea Island, near Vancouver.[52]

September

On 1 September, elements of No 426 (T) Squadron moved from RCAF Station Lachine to No 9 Hangar at RCAF Station Trenton, premises formerly occupied by the Flying Instructors' School. Advance elements of No 1 Personnel Reception Centre and No 2 Air Movements Unit also moved from Lachine on the same date. At the formal handover parade on 10 September, control of RCAF Station Trenton was transferred from Training Command Headquarters to Air Transport Command Headquarters, and its role changed from training to transport operations, housing No 426 (T) Squadron, No 4 (T) OTU, No 1 PRC, No 2 AMU, No 102 Communications Unit (KU), No 4 Flight Technical Training Unit and the Air Assessment Unit. Training Command Headquarters moved to Winnipeg, leaving the Training Standards Establishment, the School of Instructional Technique and the School of Meteorology at Trenton as lodger units.

The hand-over parade was made up of two squadrons, a 100-man guard of honour and a colour guard commanded by the Station Commander, Group Captain D.J. Williams. Air Vice Marshal J.G. Bryans of Training Command took the salute on the first march-past and addressed the parade. Air Commodore Carpenter of Air Transport Command took the salute on the second march-past.[53]

At Trenton, No 426 Squadron had all its operational and administrative elements on the same site, and did not have to conduct its flying activities in an essentially civilian environment as it had at Dorval, a Department of Transport airport — the airfield at Trenton was strictly military. The small neighbouring towns of Trenton and Belleville, too, were very different from sprawling, cosmopolitan Montreal, so squadron personnel and their families enjoyed much closer relationships. On the operational side, however, the flight crews did not find much difference, and they adjusted to their new surroundings quickly. The squadron's operational commitments meant that crews continued to spend about sixty percent of their time away from base.

In September, Trenton saw a wide variety of activities. From 10 September to 12 September, the Golden Hawks (the RCAF aerobatic team, operating for the occasion from Trenton) performed at the Canadian International Air Show in Toronto with the USAF Thunderbirds. On 14 September, the Royal Marines Band played at the station under the direction of Lieutenant Colonel V. Dunn. Battle of Britain Sunday was marked on 20 September with services at the Roman Catholic chapel and the Station Theatre. On 25 September, the West German Minister of Defence, F.J. Strauss paid a two-hour visit with Lieutenant General J. Kammhüber, West Germany's Chief of the Air Staff, and several senior military and civilian officials who were touring Canada. On 26 September, the Golden Hawks were formally disbanded in a parade held at 1000 hours at No 9 Hangar, with Air Marshal H. Campbell, Air Vice Marshal J.G. Bryans, Air Commodore Carpenter in attendance, and all the Golden Hawk pilots, ground staff and aircraft. The aerobatic team was reactivated, again under the name Golden Hawks, in 1960, and finally disbanded in 1964.

At 1000 hours on 30 September, Minister of National Defence George R. Pearkes arrived at the station to make several presentations to Air Transport Command personnel at a parade held in his honour, and to attend an informal reception and luncheon at the Officers' Mess. After lunch, the Minister and his party departed by car to visit No 26 Central Ordnance Depot at Coburg.[54]

The squadron's flying commitments for September totalled nearly 1,500 hours. There were many shuttles between Dorval and Trenton in connection with the move, but most of the domestic runs were the skeds to the Atlantic provinces, the north and the west coast. Two flights a week went overseas via Langar in support of the fighter wings and the brigade in Europe. One flight was extended to Grostenquin and the Air Weapons Unit at Decimomannu, returning first to Marville and then Langar and Trenton. There was also a weekly UNEF support flight to El Arish, and the rotation of the Canadian contingent in UNEF, which began out of El Arish on 18 September and was completed by the end of October. The troop-rotation involved airlifting 530 fully equipped soldiers from Trenton to El Arish, and bringing an equivalent number home to Canada. Eight troop-rotation flights were completed in September, and eleven more in October.[55]

Most of the troop-rotation flights to and from El Arish were routed by way of Lajes, Nouasseur and Wheelus AFB near Tripoli. The author's first operational flight after his return to the squadron began with a delay. Following an 0930 briefing, the crew (captained by Flying Officer Lavigne) boarded NS17504 and started the engines, but while the crew were going through the checks, they discovered that the APS42 search radar was unserviceable and had to shut down the engines. After an hour of work, the maintenance staff got the radar serviceable again and the flight left Trenton for Gander shortly before noon, carrying a load of high-priority freight bound for Langar. The flight of five hours and twenty minutes to Gander was uneventful, and after the fifty-minute stop the aircraft was refuelled and a flight plan filed to Lajes. The author got to navigate this leg under the watchful eye of the check navigator, Flight Lieutenant P. Rawlyk. All navigators new to the squadron had to complete two overseas runs under supervision before they were allowed to proceed on their own. (As a matter of squadron policy, all flight crew — not just new arrivals — were given flight checks and route checks each year and when circumstances warranted.)

The weather was good on the way to Lajes, and the 1,527-mile leg was completed in seven hours and fifteen minutes. The route featured several fixing aids, including astro, Loran, pressure pattern, radar fixes, and radio bearings, especially when the flight passed over Ocean Station Delta, near the mid-point of the leg. As the flight neared the Azores, the navigator could also obtain Consol position lines, an electronic aid introduced by the Germans during the Second World War and used extensively by aircraft and submarines for distances up to 1500 miles. Consol was further developed after the war, and the approach to Europe had five stations near the coast: Bush Mills in Northern Ireland, Stavanger in Norway, Seville and Lugo in Spain, and Ploneis in France. Consol was a simple, reliable aid for obtaining position lines, requiring only a receiver that covered the frequency band from 200 to 400 kilocycles; in a North Star, the radio compass was used. (In North America, the system was called Consolan and there were stations at Atlantic City and Nantucket.)

The crew was alerted at 0430 hours on 22 September, and the flight left two hours later for Nouasseur in NS17517, carrying twenty-eight soldiers and their equipment. The 1,154-mile flight was completed in six hours. After a four-hour stop to conduct a DI (Daily Inspection), refuel, file a flight plan and feed the passengers, the flight continued to Wheelus AFB, passing over Morocco, Algeria and Tunisia on the way. (For passengers, the trip from Trenton to El Arish was an exhausting forty-hour ordeal, including about thirty-two hours in the air.) The run to Wheelus took six hours and twenty minutes, dodging thunderstorms all the way. After arrival at 0300 hours local, the flight was turned over to a slip crew, who carried on to El Arish, but the crew were not to enjoy their rest: shortly after dawn, the sound of the USAF F-100 Super Sabres cutting in their afterburners on take-off made sleep impossible. The stifling heat at Wheelus made it necessary to conduct flying exercises very early in the day.

The crew was alerted for its flight at 0100 on 25 September, and NS17504 came in from Nouasseur an hour later. Shortly after take-off at 0325, No 2 engine malfunctioned and was shut down, and Lavigne decided to dump fuel outside Tripoli harbour and the flight returned to Wheelus. Once the aircraft was on the ground, the passengers — all soldiers — were disembarked and it was determined that an engine change was required. A Bristol Freighter from Langar arrived early in the evening of 26 September with a spare engine and several technicians to carry out the replacement.

NS17504 was still not ready when the next flight from Nouasseur arrived shortly after midnight on 27 September, so Lavigne took over NS17508 for the run to El Arish. Leaving at 0325, the trip took six hours. The flight across Libya and Egypt was uneventful, and the grim reminders of the Second World War were visible on the ground. There was a two hour stopover at El Arish before the flight headed back to Wheelus, with twenty-eight tour-expired Canadian soldiers happy to be heading home. The return trip took five hours and forty-five minutes, and the aircraft was turned over to a slip crew on arrival.

The crew was alerted at 0430 hours on 28 September and left Wheelus in NS17504 at 0610 hours for Nouasseur. The weather was clear with headwinds, and it took seven hours and ten minutes to reach destination. As the winds to Lajes were unfavourable, placing the crew over the eighteen-hour limit of duty time, the flight was delayed until 0600 hours the following morning. The run to Lajes took six hours and fifteen minutes, and a slip crew took over the aircraft on arrival. After a two-day layover, Lavigne picked up NS17515 and left Lajes for Gander shortly after midnight on 2 October. With a forty-mph headwind component, the flight proceeded initially to Torbay, but the weather en route was good and, after over-flying Torbay, the flight arrived at Gander after nine hours and ten minutes. From Gander, it took six hours and ten minutes to reach Trenton.[56]

The Advanced Research Projects Agency (ARPA), part of the US Department of Defense, was conducting a program to design a satellite-based system to detect and track inter-continental ballistic missiles by following the heat generated by the launch vehicle and the radiation from the warhead caused by atmospheric friction as it re-entered the atmosphere. DND was asked to take part in this program, not only because Canada was a formal partner in the defence of North America through NORAD, but also because DND already had an active program, the Canadian Research and Armament Development Establishment (CARDE) at Valcartier, near Quebec City, where studies of atmospheric composition were being conducted using infrared equipment mounted on high flying balloons. More important, Canada had CF-100 Canuck fighters, which could reach 45,000 feet carrying large tip-tanks fitted with instruments to measure solar radiation in the infrared bands of interest.

Arrangements were made to have these specially equipped CF-100s conduct flights to measure radiation during the missile's re-entry phase, beginning in 1960. This Canadian project, called *Operation LOOKOUT*, would provide valuable information for the Americans' satellite-borne detection and tracking system design project.

On 21 September, Air Force Headquarters issued Operation Order 443/59 covering RCAF participation in *Operation LOOKOUT*, assigning the detection task to the CEPE detachment at CARDE. An RCAF team of two flight crews, twenty-four airmen and two CF-100 fighters would go with two CARDE scientists to Ascension Island in the South Atlantic, about 5,000 miles downrange from Cape Canaveral. No 426 Squadron would provide airlift support for this operation.[57]

On 22 September, *Operation WESTERN WEAL* started at Trenton. This ferry convoy consisted of twenty-two T-33 Silver Stars, some for the Air Division and some to be delivered to NATO air forces as Mutual Aid. The operation was conducted by No 129 Acceptance and Ferry Flight under the command of Squadron Leader J. Cuthill. Flight Lieutenant Robertson and his crew in NS17516 provided airlift support. The first flight to Goose Bay was made during the morning without any hitches; the North Star followed the convoy with a ground support party of twenty-seven airmen and a load of aircraft spares. Weather delayed the convoy's departure for Sondrestrom until 26 September, when the jets made the double hop that took them to Keflavik. The final over-water leg to Prestwick was completed on 28 September, and on 30 September, the Silver Stars proceeded to Marville. The North Star was routed to Zweibrücken to carry out a logistics flight for the Air Division to Elmas (Cagliari), returning the same day to Grostenquin.

On 2 October, five T-33s went to Decimomannu, where they refuelled and carried on to the Hellenic Air Force Base at Elevsis, near Athens. Another flight of five Silver Stars, led by Flight Lieutenant W. Clarke, was delivered to the Portuguese Air Force at Lisbon. The North Star that had been positioned at Marville went to Elevsis, picked up the flight crews, and then made the short flight to Athens. On 3 October, Robertson and his crew conducted a shuttle run to Pisa, returning to Athens the same day. On 4 October, the flight proceeded first to Pisa and then to Marville, where the ferry flight support staff boarded. The next stop was Lisbon, where Clarke and the other ferry pilots boarded, and then the flight carried on to Lajes, where Robertson turned over his aircraft to the slip crew, who took it back to base. On 9 October, Robertson and his crew took over NS17506 and returned to Trenton.[58]

October

The squadron's domestic and overseas flying commitments for October totalled nearly 1,650 hours, the transatlantic schedule focusing on the needs of the fighter wings and the brigade in Europe. The UNEF support flights to El Arish from Langar were supplemented by the rotation of troops serving with the Canadian contingent in UNEF, which was completed during the month.

Mechanical difficulties plagued two flights. On 6 October, Flight Lieutenant Lynch and his crew were departing Nouasseur for Wheelus AFB in NS17506 when a problem appeared in the No 3 engine. Lynch returned to Nouasseur and flight engineer Sergeant Dahr corrected the malfunction, enabling the flight to continue. On 12 October, the crew were departing Nouasseur for Lajes, heading home in NS17515, but had to turn back only ninety minutes later: No 3 engine was malfunctioning, and Sergeant Dahr again fixed the problem so the flight could continue to Lajes. On 28 October, Flying Officer Whillans and his crew were leaving Gander for Lajes in NS17509 when they, too, had engine problems and had to turn back after only thirty-five minutes. They set out again the next day, and were out nearly two hours before they had to turn back. Following an engine change and a flight test, the crew departed for Lajes on 30 October, without incident.[59]

In October, about eighty percent of the spares required by the fifty T-33s delivered to NATO allies under Mutual Aid (eighteen to France, twenty-two to Turkey, five to Greece and five to Portugal) were available from stock. On 28 October, the cargo carrier *Port Said* sailed from Montreal with more than 100 tons of materiel, including fifty tons destined for Turkey, and twenty-five tons each for Greece and Portugal. The thirty-five-ton load of materiel for France would be shipped out in the *Waldemar Peter*, which sailed from Montreal on 5 November.[60]

November

It was announced in November that Squadron Leader J. Maitland, the Squadron Operations Officer, would be the new Squadron Commander, replacing Wing Commander A.J. Mackie who had held the appointment for four years. Mackie would become the Chief Operations Officer at RCAF Station Trenton.

On 4 November, DND's first large electronic computer entered service with the RCAF: the IBM 705 Mk. III, installed at Air Material Command Headquarters at Station Rockcliffe.

On 15 November, the CC-106 Yukon flew for the first time at Cartierville, a test run of two hours and ten minutes that included a series of stalls and speed runs, with Bill Longhurst and Scotty McLean at the controls; they reported that the aircraft performed satisfactorily throughout. Another test run was completed before the first official flight, on 18 November, which was witnessed by the Chief of the Air Staff, and on 24 November, the aircraft formally entered RCAF service. Yukon 15501, the first on the RCAF inventory, was used for test and development. Canadair's largest aircraft yet, the Yukon went into operational service in 1961.[61]

The squadron's flying commitments for November amounted to nearly 1500 hours. In addition to various domestic scheduled and routine flights, the squadron carried out two transatlantic sked runs per week during November in support of the fighter wings and the brigade stationed in Europe. Another weekly flight went to El Arish in support of UNEF. With the semi-annual UNEF troop-rotation completed, the squadron began its first trooping operation with the brigade in Germany: seventeen flights, including nine in November and eight in December, in which 475 soldiers were airlifted to Europe and 476 were repatriated to Canada. The rotation flights operated to and from RAF Station Gutersloh.[62]

On 17 November, NS17512 left Trenton with an augmented crew captained by Flight Lieutenant Stockdale on the annual Christmas re-supply airlift to Saigon. The flight went by way of Harmon AFB and Lajes to Dakar, and crossed Africa to Kano, Nairobi and Aden. From Aden, the next stops were Bombay and Rangoon, and the aircraft reached Saigon on 26 November. Departing Saigon on 28 November, the flight headed east to Djakarta, Indonesia, and then to Australia, where it arrived at Sydney on 29 November after a stop at Darwin. Leaving Sydney on 2 December, it arrived at Honolulu the next day, via Fiji and Canton Island. Adverse headwinds delayed the flight at Honolulu for seven days, and it wasn't until 11 December that the crew could leave for San Francisco, a run of eleven hours and ten minutes. The flight was back at base on 13 December after a stop in Winnipeg. The mission took twenty-six days to complete, and the crew put in 138 hours and ten minutes of flying during the trip.[63]

From 24 November to 27 November, Air Transport Command held its annual Commanding Officers' Conference at RCAF Station Trenton. The conference opened with a briefing on the new IBM computer at Air Materiel Command Headquarters, and closed with a formal ball at the Officers' Mess on 27 November, with Air Marshal Campbell and Mrs. Campbell as guests of honour.[64]

At the end of November, the Air Council approved a plan to provide No 1 Air Division with strategic lift of all air-transportable equipment direct from Canada as of 1 June 1961, with the introduction of the CC-106 Yukon to operational service.[65]

December

The squadron's flying commitments for December were much the same as for the previous month. Two weekly scheduled flights went to Langar, one per week went to El Arish, and eight troop-rotation flights to and from Gutersloh were conducted. On the domestic scene, as well as the scheduled flights, the squadron despatched a special flight to airlift an entertainment troupe sponsored by Canadair to two Mid-Canada Line stations.

On 18 December, Flight Lieutenant Longworth and his crew positioned NS17515 at Cartierville, embarked the troupe, and set off for The Pas, where the entertainers performed for the personnel of Cranberry Portage, a Mid-Canada Line station thirty-six miles southeast of The Pas. The next day, the flight went to Fort McMurray in northern Alberta, and the troupe put on a show for the personnel of Station Stony Mountain, which lay twenty-four miles south of Fort McMurray near the town of Anzac. The flight returned the troupe to Montreal on 20 December and then carried on to Trenton.

Aircraft returning to base just before Christmas brought back the slip crews and detachment personnel, who would be repositioned on the first flights departing on overseas runs after Christmas Day.[66]

On 18 December a commemorative wings parade was held at Winnipeg for the last group of pilots and navigators to train under the original NATO program. Air Marshal C.R. Slemon presented flying badges to fifty pilots and navigators, including forty Canadians, seven from the Netherlands and three from Norway, who completed their training at Gimli, Portage la Prairie and Winnipeg.[67]

Christmas 1959 was the first squadron personnel spent at Trenton with family and friends. As usual, church services were well attended, and designated officers served Christmas dinner to the airmen and airwomen living in quarters. The next day, Squadron Leader Maitland captained the first overseas flight, heading for Langar and El Arish. The year ended with dances and parties at all the messes on the station.

PHOTO 181
Operation BEECHFLIGHT: From left: F/L Tim Timmins, S/L Brian Marfleet and mission commander W/C Harry Forbell are met by Portuguese civil and military officials on delivery of Expeditors; Lisbon, Portugal, 5 June 1959. (Tim Timmins Collection)

PHOTO 182
The passenger terminal sign comes down in preparation for the move to RCAF Station Trenton; Dorval, 18 August 1959. From left, top: LAC C.Y.G. Dumont, LAC Dan Spivak and LAC H.F. Branch; bottom: LAC C.P. Barrett and F/S J.J. McWilliams. (DND PL 115825)

Lachine and Trenton, 1959

PHOTO 183
Engine-bay personnel move a Merlin engine to a truck for the move to Trenton; Dorval, 18 August 1959. From left: LAC A.E. Corbin, LAC M. Firestone, LAC A. Coen and LAC E. Ralph. (DND PL 115828)

PHOTO 184
The last pay-day before the move to Trenton; Dorval, 20 August 1959. (DND PL 115833)

Chapter 24

Trenton, 1960

The squadron was busy in 1960, logging more than 22,000 flying hours with twelve North Stars. The largest new commitment was the squadron's second major United Nations effort, this time in Africa. The year's workload also comprised troop-rotation missions, the provision of airlift support to a defence research project in the South Atlantic, an important disaster relief operation, and a host of domestic flights, including trips to northern bases. The squadron lost its fifth North Star in an accidental fire during the year.

January

January commitments, totalling well over 1,450 flying hours, included a variety of domestic scheduled and special runs in addition to eight overseas flights to Langar, of which four were extended to El Arish.

The first overseas run left Dorval on 2 January, with Flight Lieutenant Lynch and his crew in NS17512; at Lajes, this flight was turned over to a slip crew, and Lynch and his crew took the next aircraft in and proceeded to Langar and El Arish.[1]

On 3 January, NS17506, captained by Flight Lieutenant Nichol, departed for Langar. The next day Flight Lieutenant McLaughlin and his crew (including the author as navigator) left base for Lajes and Langar in NS17515. Half an hour after departure, the APS42 search radar went unserviceable, but there were no other problems for the rest of the flight to Gander and then to Lajes. On the morning of 6 January, McLaughlin took over NS17508 (brought in by Flight Lieutenant Gill) for the seven-and-a-half-hour leg to Langar. The weather was good en route and the aircraft had a serviceable radar, and the flight arrived at destination in the middle of the afternoon. On 8 January, NS17510 arrived at Langar with Flight Lieutenant Price and his crew, and departed again that evening with McLaughlin for the five-hour night flight to Pisa, with a marginal weather forecast at the destination and the prospect of a diversion to Marseilles; the weather improved as the flight neared Pisa, however, and the aircraft arrived well after midnight. The crew checked in the Albergo dei Cavaliere and then headed to the railway station — the only place selling food at that time of night — for some large Italian sandwiches and beer.

Departure was at 1350 hours on 9 January for the four-and-a-half-hour flight to Athens, where the crew secured the aircraft and proceeded downtown to the Hotel National, a forty-minute taxi ride from the airport. The next morning, they departed at 1000 hours in NS17510 for the four hour run to El Arish. The search radar was not working, which complicated matters as the flight neared destination — an active Egyptian anti-aircraft gunnery range lay just west of the airfield. The weather forecast was off, and the flight descended through considerable turbulence as it passed in and out of cloud. While the aircraft was being unloaded and serviced, most of the crew took the seven-mile jeep ride to No 115 ATU, which had a base camp at a place called Marina for its proximity to the Mediterranean. Marina was about thirty miles from the Canadian Army camp at Rafah, itself about 100 miles east of the Suez Canal. From El Arish, it was sixty miles to UNEF Headquarters at Gaza, which was seven miles inland.

The role of No 115 ATU was to provide UNEF with reconnaissance and transport services in support of its task of keeping the peace between the United Arab Republic and Israel. The unit had seven aircraft: three Dakotas, used mainly for transport, and four Otters, intended for reconnaissance but also used for shorter transport flights. ATU strength fluctuated around 100 personnel, including nineteen officers.

After lunch at the mess, crew members visited the Egyptian-managed Post Exchange to buy souvenirs — the number of camel saddles brought back to Canada can only be guessed at — and met a large group of Egyptian soldiers on the road back to the airfield, members of units involved in the manoeuvres the Egyptian Army had been conducting in the area for two months. At 1605 hours, the flight left El Arish for Athens carrying passengers, mail and general cargo.

As the aircraft neared Athens, it encountered plenty of layered cloud containing several embedded thunderstorms. Athens Air Traffic Control had stacked incoming aircraft in holding patterns between 6,000 to 18,000 feet over the Kavouri Radio Beacon; Control then brought them down progressively from their assigned altitudes until they were cleared to approach the airfield. Starting out at 10,000 feet, NS17510 was brought down and then granted permission to make an approach. Breaking out of cloud, McLaughlin lined up with the runway in use and switched on the landing lights. At that that very moment, the landing lights of another aircraft came on at the other end of the runway. McLaughlin immediately called the tower and asked if the other aircraft was landing. After several moments of panic and noise from the tower an excited Controller shouted "Overshoot, Overshoot!" He didn't say *which* aircraft should overshoot, so both did. The captain of the other aircraft, a Lufthansa Constellation, called the tower and requested permission to land but, as he had brought his aircraft down through the stack from 18,000 feet without clearance so he could make his ramp time, the North Star was given clearance to land first. As the Constellation was landing, the controller asked its captain to report to the tower.

At 1300 hours on 11 January, the flight left for Pisa, a five-hour trip. On arrival, the crew went into town for dinner, but it began to snow heavily and, when they returned to the airfield, they found the aircraft covered with freezing slush. They decided to cancel the flight, as Pisa had no de-icing alcohol or equipment; it was the first snow the area had seen in six years. The next morning, the crew waited for the sun to melt the snow enough so it could be swept off, and departed for Langar at 1015 hours. The radar set was not working, which was unfortunate as it would have been useful in the cloud through which the flight approached St-Tropez. The aircraft flew into the base of a thunderstorm, hitting an abundance of hail and turbulence; with a brilliant flash, a bolt of lightning struck, entering from the nose-wheelwell area and passing through the fuselage, exiting at the tail. A quick check found no apparent damage, although both crew and passengers were shaken up.

Once out of cloud, the flight was over France and in the clear, and the crew could see that, for the first time in many years, the ground from the Riviera to the Channel was completely covered in snow. On arrival at Langar after a flight of five hours and forty-five minutes, the aircraft was checked more thoroughly for damage caused by the lightning bolt, and a hole about the size of a football was found at the base of the vertical stabilizer in front of the rudder. The maintenance personnel repaired the damage for the return to base.

McLaughlin and his crew left Langar for Shannon in NS17514 at 1910 hours on 13 January. This leg took two hours and ten minutes, and the aircraft had a serviceable radar. While the aircraft was being refuelled, a flight plan was filed for Santa Maria since the weather at Lajes was forecast to be below limits; but an hour and a half out of Santa Maria, the flight plan was changed to Lajes. The weather was good throughout the six-and-a-half-hour flight, but the landing run was rough because of strong crosswinds and surface turbulence.

The crew enjoyed their four-day layover, which they spent on an American base well-equipped for the crews of the aircraft streaming back and forth across the North Atlantic. It had messes and sports facilities, including bowling alleys and a gym; a well-stocked PX and "package stores" (which actually sold liquor); a theatre showing the latest movies; and purveyors of those personal services that military people depend on, namely barbers, dry cleaners, cobblers and coin-laundry operators. The transient quarters were spartan but adequate, and the Officers' Club offered good meals and entertainment, including slot machines and all-night poker for those so inclined. Regular services were held at the Protestant and Roman Catholic chapels, and these were well attended.

The crew was alerted for the return flight to Canada at 0230 hours on 18 January. The forecast called for a headwind component at 8,000 feet of thirty miles per hour, with a flight time to Gander of eight and a half hours and marginal weather reported for most of Newfoundland. Leaving Lajes in NS17502, the flight climbed through cloud to 8000 feet and was in the clear until close to destination. The headwinds moderated, and the flight reached Gander an hour earlier than planned; descending through cloud, the aircraft picked up a heavy load of ice on the approach to the airport. As the aircraft was readied for another take-off, a flight plan was filed for Trenton with departure at 1300 hours. Five minutes from Buchans, No 1 engine malfunctioned and was shut down. The aircraft was in cloud and picking up ice, with not enough power to climb. McLaughlin declared an emergency and headed for Harmon AFB. After landing, it was determined that an engine change was required.

At Operations, McLaughlin contacted Squadron Leader Maitland in Trenton and advised him of the flight's situation, and Maitland replied that he would see how he was fixed for engines as the squadron had had several failures recently. A new engine was flown in on 19 January and quickly installed. The aircraft was test-flown, and the crew prepared to continue the flight to Trenton. The winds picked up, however, and soon the crosswind component exceeded the safety margin, so the flight was cancelled until the following morning. Departure the next day was at 1315 hours, and the flight finally arrived at Trenton after four hours and ten minutes.²

The squadron despatched three aircraft on 7 January: NS17510 (Flight Lieutenant Price), bound for Langar, NS17516 (Flight Lieutenant Fawcett) to Downsview to pick up equipment for *Operation LOOKOUT* and take it to Québec City, and NS17521 (Flight Lieutenant Kuhn) to Québec City to provide airlift support for the CARDE Detachment's 7,000-mile flight to Ascension Island.

On 8 January, the detachment's two CF-100s left Québec City for Patrick AFB; Canuck 18439 with Flight Lieutenant O.M. Sweetman (the Detachment Commander, as pilot) and Flying Officer K. Peters (navigator), and Canuck 18453 with Flight Lieutenant G. Brown (pilot) and Flying Officer J. Watson (navigator), followed by a C-119 loaded with scientific equipment, and Fawcett and Kuhn in their North Stars with detachment personnel and more equipment. After a brief stop at Patrick AFB, the jets went on to Ramey AFB in Puerto Rico. Fawcett left his cargo at Patrick AFB and returned to Trenton the following day. Kuhn's North Star and the C-119 arrived at Ramey AFB on 10 January, their second stop en route to Ascension Island.

Late in the afternoon of 11 January, Kuhn and his crew left for Piarco, Trinidad, a flight of nearly four hours, and the CF-100s arrived the next day, followed by a KC-97 refueller from Plattsburg AFB in upstate New York. The CF-100s could not be refuelled in the air so they refuelled from the KC-97 on the ground, thus avoiding the risk of taking on contaminated fuel. Leaving late in the afternoon of 12 January, Kuhn went to Belém, a city on the coast of Brazil just south of the equator near the mouth of the Amazon. The jets left Piarco on the morning of 13 January, and were the first CF-100s to cross the equator at 1245 GMT as they neared Belém. After being refuelled, the jets carried on to Recife, followed by the KC-97, the North Star and the C-119.

At 2320 hours on 14 January, Kuhn took off for Ascension Island, 1,426 miles almost due east of Recife. The flight took seven hours and twenty-five minutes. Some nine hours later, having disembarked the passengers and unloaded the cargo, the flight returned to Recife, arriving at 2200 hours on 15 January. The next morning, the CF-100s made the hop to Ascension Island; Brown took three hours and fifteen minutes to make the crossing and Sweetman ten minutes longer. The CF-100s were the first jets to land at Ascension Island, and the crossing was considered to be the longest over-water flight ever made by an AVRO CF-100. The CARDE Detachment operated for eleven months on the island, where the first of many missile nose-cone intercepts was made on 24 February.

On 19 January, Kuhn and his crew proceeded directly to Piarco from Recife, the flight taking ten hours and twenty-five minutes. The next day, they headed for Patrick AFB, a run of eight hours and forty minutes. Kuhn returned to Trenton on 21 January after a stop at Ottawa to drop off passengers.[3]

On 8 January, Flying Officer Zbesheski and his crew positioned NS17502 at St-Hubert, where they embarked a CBC entertainment troupe, who gave two weeks of daily performances for the military and civilian staff based at Seven Islands, Knob Lake, Great Whale, Winisk, Churchill, Winnipeg, Resolute Bay, Alert and Thule. The flight returned to base on 22 January.[4]

On 17 January, NS17516 (captained by Flight Lieutenant J. Morrison) was dispatched to Winnipeg; the next day, the flight embarked the Specialist Navigation Course from the Central Navigation School for a nineteen-day tour of American industrial and military establishments at Dayton, Ohio; Cedar Rapids, Iowa; Burbank, California; Nellis AFB, Nevada; and Mather AFB and Castle AFB in California. The flight returned to Winnipeg on 4 February and was back at base the following day.[5]

During the month, one flight was despatched to Resolute Bay. NS17514, captained by Flight Lieutenant Hutchinson, left base on 18 January for Winnipeg and Churchill and proceeded to Resolute Bay the next day carrying passengers, mail and general cargo. The flight continued on to Thule on 20 January and the following day carried out a supply run to Alert, before returning to Resolute Bay and Churchill. From there, the flight returned to Trenton on 22 January after a stop at Winnipeg.[6]

On 21 January, Flight Lieutenant Lynch and his crew took NS17511 to Dartmouth, where they embarked RCN personnel and their equipment the following morning and then left for Bermuda, a trip that took nearly five hours. After disembarking the passengers and unloading the cargo, Lynch and his crew returned to Trenton, a six-hour run.[7]

A Treasury Board submission was raised in January to cover the procurement of four C130B Lockheed prop-jet transport aircraft at an estimated cost of $14.5 million. The plan was to procure the aircraft through the USAF, with all spending taking place between 1 April 1959 and 31 March 1960.[8]

February

The squadron's flying commitments for February totalled nearly 1,500 hours, and included eight scheduled service flights to Langar, four of which were extended to El Arish and one to the fighter wings and Decimomannu. In addition, between 8 February and 21 February, elements of the Canadian Army were rotated between Trenton and El Arish, an operation requiring five flights staged through Wheelus AFB, Nouasseur and Lajes. One logistics flight in support of squadron operations was sent to Lajes.

One of the overseas flights encountered some difficulties. On 24 February, NS17502, captained by Flight Lieutenant Pelletier, was en route from Shannon to Santa Maria in the Azores when No 4 engine failed. Having passed the critical point at which it is quicker to continue to destination than to return to the point of departure, the crew carried on to Santa Maria on three engines. What would have been a six-hour flight (in normal circumstances) took eight hours and twenty minutes. The next day, having dropped off their cargo, the crew conducted a three-engine ferry flight to Lajes, taking an hour and twenty-five minutes to make the crossing. After an engine change, the aircraft was returned to base.[9]

A wide range of scheduled and special flights were carried out in February, including five to Resolute Bay, of which three were extended to Alert and Thule. SF5, captained by Flight Lieutenant McBurney, arrived at Resolute Bay on 16 February. On board NS17512 was a diverse group of passengers including: Miss van Steensel and Mr. Derbyshire of the CBC; Squadron Leader G. Stantial, who headed Food Services at Air Transport Command Headquarters; Flight Lieutenant Belair, the Roman Catholic chaplain from Churchill; Captain J. Clark, the new commander of the signals station at Alert; and an RCMP constable. After dropping off the passengers and cargo destined for Resolute Bay, the flight continued on to Thule. The next day the flight made the run to Alert, returned to Resolute and continued on to Churchill, where it remained overnight. The service flight was back at base on 18 February after a stop in Winnipeg.[10]

Between 3 February and 6 February, Flight Lieutenant Charchuk and his crew in NS17502 carried out an air transport support flight on behalf of Maritime Command; proceeding to Greenwood and Halifax, they airlifted RCAF and RCN personnel and their equipment to Bermuda for a joint and combined naval exercise, and returned to base on 6 February after a stop at Greenwood. Another domestic flight involved the transport of cadets from the *Collège militaire royal* at St-Jean, Quebec, to Victoria for the annual sports meet with the cadets of Royal Roads Military College. On 17 February, Flight Lieutenant Gill and his crew took NS17508 to St-Hubert, embarked the cadets and flew them to Victoria; they were back at base on 21 February.[11]

As the result of apparent surplus of spare engines and a shortage of major overhaul items (such as crankcases) for the Merlin 622 Repair and Overhaul Program, Air Materiel Command Headquarters was given authority to cannibalize fifty repairable and time-expired engines. Consequently, only fifty-four spare engines were available to support the sixteen RCAF North Stars, in which sixty-four engines were installed.[12]

March

March flying commitments for the squadron totalled 1,400 hours, and saw the reduction of the RCAF fleet (and the squadron's inventory) by one North Star, due to an accident.

Of the twelve service flights despatched to Langar, four were extended to El Arish and two went to the fighter wings; from there, the service flights provided air transport support for the fighter squadrons going to the Air Weapons Unit at Decimomannu. On 6 March, Flight Lieutenant Hutchinson and his crew in NS17521 made a special overseas run to Rabat, Morocco, where they delivered eight medical personnel and some 6,650 pounds of medical supplies for subsequent transport to Agadir, which had been hit by an earthquake.[13]

Two homeward-bound flights ran into difficulties during the month.

When NS17512 came in at Langar on 2 March, an inspection revealed that the up-lock pins to its main landing gear were sheared. (Up-lock pins were made of soft metal. They normally held the gear in the "up" position and, should their control cables pins break, the undercarriage could be lowered by applying hydraulic pressure to break the pins, thus allowing the undercarriage to drop into position and lock.) During servicing, however, the maintenance crew inadvertently replaced the sheared pins with some made of high-tensile steel that could not be sheared by hydraulic pressure. Flight Lieutenant R. Hayes and his crew then took over the flight and headed for Shannon to refuel before carrying on to Lajes, and the undercarriage failed to come down during the approach to the airport. Flight engineer Sergeant J. Moric opened a hatch in the cockpit, crawled into the hydraulic compartment in the belly of the aircraft and discovered that the rod to the undercarriage lever was broken; Moric activated the selector with a pair of pliers, thus causing the undercarriage to lower. After a successful landing, the damaged rod was replaced, the proper pins were installed, and the aircraft was put up on jacks and for retraction tests on the undercarriage. As everything checked out, Hayes and his crew were able to leave for Lajes the following day.[14]

On 11 March, Flight Lieutenant Charchuk and his crew had refuelled NS17515 at St. Mawgan and were on their way to Lajes with a full load of expired ordnance, mainly rockets, when the flight encountered some heavy weather, including thunderstorms. Considering the build-up of static electricity and the possibility of a lightning strike, Charchuk asked that all electrical equipment be shut down. Only the radios had been turned off when a bolt of lightning hit the nose in a brilliant flash and passed through the aircraft. After a few anxious moments, the crew checked the aircraft, found no apparent damage, and continued on to Lajes. All the electrical equipment was affected by the lightning strike, but everything came back on, even the search radar; on the ground, however, inspection of the aircraft revealed that the lightning had taken eight to ten inches off the vertical stabilizer. The damage was repaired and the aircraft was flown back to base.[15]

Arrangements were completed in March for provision of extensive RCAF air and materiel support to the Department of Mines and Technical Surveys for the Polar Continental Shelf Project during the spring and summer of 1960. The RCAF would provide personnel and cargo airlift through Churchill and Resolute Bay, and POL, rations and quarters at Resolute on a Treasury-recoverable basis, at an estimated cost of $80,000. One of the more specialized tasks associated with the Polar Continental Shelf Project was the transport of a S55 helicopter from Downsview to Isachsen by a No 436 Squadron C-119.[16]

The squadron despatched four northern flights in March. Between 6 March and 12 March, Flight Lieutenant J. Morrison and his crew in NS17517 airlifted a group of Air Defence Command personnel from St-Hubert on a tour of northern stations, part of the Arctic Indoctrination Course; they visited Knob Lake, Cape Dyer, Hall Beach, Cambridge Bay and Cape Parry, and the flight returned to base by way of Cold Lake and St-Hubert. The next Arctic run was SF 5/6 (Flight Lieutenant Gill and his crew in NS17508), which arrived at Resolute Bay on 8 March without the expected consignment of beer, provoking the usual grumbling. Gill and his crew then proceeded to Thule, carried out a supply run to Alert, and then briefly returned to Thule before going on to Resolute Bay. On 10 March, Gill and his crew returned to base via Churchill and Winnipeg. On 15 March, Flight Lieutenant Pelletier arrived at Resolute in NS17515 with a load of passengers, mail and cargo; after a two-hour stop, the flight left for Churchill, and it was back at Trenton the following day.

The unit's last northern flight of the month took place between 21 March and 25 March. Flight Lieutenant Hutchinson and his crew left Churchill in NS17502 on 22 March, made a brief stop at Hall Beach to drop off cargo, and then continued on to Resolute Bay and Thule. The next day, they made a supply run to Alert, returned to Thule, and then took off for Resolute Bay, where the weather went below limits, so Hutchinson had to return to Thule. On 24 March, the flight made it in to Resolute, and then took off again for Churchill, Winnipeg and Trenton.[17]

In addition to a number of scheduled and special flights conducted in March, the squadron carried out three flights in support of RCN exercises being conducted off Bermuda. On 5 March, Flight Lieutenant Longworth and his crew in NS17514 embarked a group of sailors and their equipment, and airlifted them to Bermuda; the next day a similar group was returned to Halifax, and the flight returned to base. On 21 March, two flights — NS17504 (Flying Officer Whillans) and NS17516 (Flight Lieutenant Pelletier) — went from Trenton to Bermuda; the next day, they airlifted two groups of sailors to Halifax, and returned to base.[18]

On 24 March, the maintenance staff were working on NS17509 in No 9 Hangar at Trenton. Technicians were in the wheelwell to remove the accumulated grease and oil from the connecting points to the oxygen tank and the lines leading into the aircraft. The pressurized tank had not been shut off before it was disconnected, and spontaneous combustion created by the sudden release of oxygen against the grease on the fittings started a fire. The maintenance crew quickly attached a nose tow-bar to the aircraft and dragged it out of the hangar but, by the time the fire was extinguished, the aircraft was a write-off; the squadron was lucky to have saved the hangar. NS17509 was the aircraft that clipped a mountain-top in Japan in April 1951, during the Korean Air Lift.[19]

April

April's flying commitments for the squadron's eleven North Stars totalled nearly 1,500 hours. Twelve flights were despatched to Langar in support of the Air Division and 4 Brigade in Europe. Two of these flights were extended to Baden-Söllingen and Decimomannu and another four to El Arish. The first of these arrived on 4 April with Wing Commander Manson, the commanding officer, who was returning to No 115 ATU after a period of leave.[20]

On 7 April, No 115 ATU drilled with the bagpipers of the 4th Battalion, Kumaon Regiment (part of the Indian contingent in UNEF) to prepare for the parade to be held during the forthcoming visit by Air Commodore Carpenter, and the first Sabena DC-7 arrived to begin the airlift of Scandinavian troops to and from the Sinai; the troop-rotation took until 15 May. On 10 April, SF 53 brought the Air Commodore to El Arish with his aide, Flight Lieutenant L. Skaalen, and Carpenter hosted a mess dinner in the evening. The next morning, a "medals parade" was held, during which Carpenter presented the UNEF medal to twenty-five officers and airmen of No 115 ATU. The parade was followed by a briefing by the Section Commanders and the Air Commodore's inspection of the unit.

Carpenter left on 12 April to visit UNEF Headquarters and other sites in the area, returning to the ATU on 15 April, when he visited the NCOs' Mess and attended an all-ranks turkey dinner and party held in the Airmen's Club with a Brazilian dance band. On 16 April, the year's first major sandstorm passed through El Arish; visibility was limited to fifty feet, with winds up to sixty miles per hour; that evening, the Air Commodore officially opened the officers' new dining room. The next day, Carpenter departed for Langar and Trenton on SF 54.

The month's fourth flight into El Arish came in on 24 April and departed for base after a four-hour stop.[21]

The annual spring re-supply of the Arctic bases was carried out in April by four C-119 aircraft from No 435 Squadron and No 436 Squadron, which airlifted 694,000 pounds of equipment and supplies. The month's three service flights to Resolute Bay, conducted by No 426 Squadron, were supplemented by two No 4 OTU training flights from Trenton.

The first squadron run to Resolute Bay — Flight Lieutenant Gawne and his crew in NS17521 — arrived on 5 April, bringing in Flight Lieutenant Skuce from Trenton to handled the detachment's flying control duties during the re-supply operation. Gawne then proceeded to Thule, conducted a supply run to Alert and returned to base on 8 April via Resolute Bay, Churchill and Winnipeg. The next squadron flight to Resolute was conducted by Flight Lieutenant Rayson and his crew in NS17511, who arrived on 12 April with a group of VIPs to observe the re-supply operation; when the aircraft was unloaded, Rayson returned to Trenton. The squadron's third flight of the month to Resolute came in on 19 April; NS17521 (captained by Flight Lieutenant Hayes) remained overnight and left the next day on a supply run to Thule and Alert. The flight then returned to Resolute Bay and departed for base on 20 April. The first No 4 OTU flight arrived on 22 April carrying 7,500 pounds of freight destined for Alert. The next flight came in on 24 April, carrying an RCMP party of eight, including Inspector Larsen, who was nearing retirement, and his replacement, Inspector Fraser, to conduct an inspection tour of police detachments in the north.[22]

Northern units would soon be re-supplied by C-130B Hercules aircraft, but if Resolute Bay was to support the new aircraft, it obviously needed more POL storage tanks. The station already had three 200,000-gallon tanks and, by 1961, one of them would be required for "turbo" (turbine fuel); in 1962, a new 3½-inch pipeline for turbo would be installed from the dock to the tank farm. Until the new facilities could be installed, both turbo and "avgas" (aviation fuel) would be piped through the existing avgas line. The cost of construction was estimated at $225,000, and a Treasury Board submission would be made in late April 1960.

A second Treasury Board submission was prepared, seeking approval for the construction of terminals to support overseas air transport operations serving Marville and Baden-Söllingen from Trenton. The estimated cost for these new facilities was $532,000.[23]

No 426 Squadron carried out a variety of scheduled and special flights in April, including a special to the United States. Squadron Leader Maitland and his crew (including Group Captain Williams, the Station Commander at Trenton, as first officer) departed Trenton on 10 April in NS17504 for Winnipeg and Edmonton, where they spent the night. On 11 April, the flight went on to Vancouver and then to the Lockheed plant at Burbank, California. The purpose of the flight was to airlift some forty RCAF engineers from Lockheed, where they were working on the F-104 Starfighter contract, to Ottawa. The engineers were embarked on 13 April, and Maitland then proceeded to George AFB, northeast of Los Angeles, to refuel. The direct flight to Ottawa took ten hours and twenty minutes and, after disembarking the passengers, Maitland and his crew returned to Trenton.[24]

May

In May, the squadron returned to its established strength of twelve North Stars with the receipt of a replacement for NS17509, the aircraft lost in the fire in March. Flying commitments for the month totalled 1660 hours, including ten flights despatched in support of the Air Division and 4 Brigade in Europe. Nine of these flights had their initial destination as Langar and one went directly to Marville from Lajes. One of the Langar flights was extended to the fighter wings to provide airlift support to the squadrons going to Decimomannu. Another four flights, two scheduled and two specials, were extended from Langar to El Arish in support of UNEF in Egypt.

Two special flights were conducted on 9 May to airlift the band of The Royal Canadian Dragoons from RAF Station Gütersloh in Germany to El Arish. During its sixteen-day tour, the band visited all UNEF units to an enthusiastic reception, particularly at the isolated desert outposts where No 115 ATU aircraft took them. The other two despatched to El Arish in May went via Lajes and Pisa; one returned to base by way of Langar and the other through Gibraltar and Lajes.[25]

On 22 May, the squadron despatched NS17512, captained by Flight Lieutenant Pelletier, to Summerside to provide airlift support for a Maritime Command operation. Embarking ground personnel and equipment, the flight proceeded directly to Keflavik, a run of nine hours and five minutes. Pelletier and his crew returned to Summerside on 27 May in a ten-hour-and-thirty-five-minute flight. After a short stop to unload passengers and equipment, the crew left for Trenton.[26]

Domestic flying commitments in May included the airlift of the RCAF Staff College course from Toronto to Maxwell AFB and back, and four scheduled and one special flight to Resolute Bay. Three of the scheduled runs were extended to Alert. The special, NS17506 (captained by Flight

Lieutenant McNair) went to Winnipeg on 8 May. Embarking the students of No 12 Specialist Navigation Course and staff members of the Central Navigation School (including the Officer Commanding, Wing Commander K.R. Greenaway), the flight proceeded to Resolute Bay the following day. The first of several long-range northern flying exercises began on 10 May with a nine-and-a-half-hour flight that ended in Thule, and the return to Resolute Bay on 11 May was combined with another training exercise. Flights to the North Pole were carried out on 12 May and 13 May, taking ten hours and five minutes and ten hours and fifteen minutes respectively. Shortly after returning from the second flight to the North Pole, the aircraft left Resolute Bay for Winnipeg, a run of eight hours and forty-five minutes. After a twelve-hour crew rest, the flight returned to base on 14 May.[27]

On 21–22 May, the south coast of Chile from Concepción to Isla de Chiloé was devastated by a series of major earthquakes, and every coastal town between the 36th and 44th parallels (a distance of some 500 miles) suffered at least some damage. Reports at the time indicated that more than 5,000 people were killed or missing, two million left homeless, and property damage was estimated at more than half a billion dollars. A series of aftershocks between 21 May and 20 June added to the damage and loss of life.[28]

As part of the massive international humanitarian aid and relief operation that was immediately mounted, Canada made an initial commitment to airlift about 50,000 pounds of medical and other supplies, involving five squadron aircraft that would return to base on completion of the operation. On 26 May, the squadron was placed on standby for a mission dubbed *Operation AMIGO*, for which seven crews, five aircraft and twenty maintenance personnel were selected; on arrival in Chile, the aircraft and crews were to be placed at the disposal of the Chilean Disaster Committee in Santiago. As the USAF was also mounting a sizeable relief mission, the North Stars were routed through USAF bases in Charleston, South Carolina; Tocumen (a civil airport) or Albrook AFB in Panama; and then on to Lima, Peru and Santiago, Chile.

Operation AMIGO began on Saturday, 28 May, and at 1300 hours, Wing Commander Maitland lifted off in NS17512 and set heading for Charleston AFB. It was Air Force Day at RCAF Station Trenton and many spectators thought the North Star was part of a display until the announcer told the crowds that the aircraft was leaving on a disaster relief mission to Chile. Fifteen minutes later, Flight Lieutenant J. Morrison took off in NS17502 and also set course for Charleston AFB. Each aircraft carried 10,000 pounds of Red Cross relief supplies for the earthquake victims, accompanied by two Canadian Red Cross officials: Reuben C. Bates, Assistant National Commissioner and Richard H. Gluns, the National Director of Public Relations.

Both aircraft refuelled at Charleston AFB and continued on to Panama, where the crews took a rest. They were in Lima on 30 May, and they reached Santiago the following day. On 31 May, Flight Lieutenant H.M. Smith left base at 2000 hours in NS17508, bound for Uplands to pick up a load of Red Cross supplies. At 2230 hours, Flight Lieutenant R.R. Hayes in NS17517, with relief supplies and two slip crews captained by Flight Lieutenant J. Lynch and Flight Lieutenant J.S. Parmelee, left Trenton for Charleston AFB. Smith departed Uplands for Charleston at 0915 hours on 1 June, and Flight Lieutenant R.J. Robertson left Trenton for Charleston at 1200 hours in NS17515.

June

Hayes' aircraft (with the author as navigator) was routed south from Trenton via Watertown and Syracuse, New York. After dodging a number of thunderstorms during the initial stages of the flight, the aircraft found clear weather as it headed for Charleston AFB, where it arrived at 0240 hours. The aircraft was refuelled, the crews had an early breakfast, and a flight plan of eight hours and fifteen minutes to Albrook AFB in Panama was filed. The flight departed at 0435 hours, passed over Miami at dawn, and flew over central Cuba, although attempts to get clearance to fly over Cuba were hampered by poor communications. At 9,000 feet, the flight had no trouble skirting the heavy cumulus build-ups and the occasional thunderstorm along the track. By the time the flight had passed the western tip of Jamaica, it was clear skies over the Caribbean to destination. On landing at Albrook at 1250 hours, the aircraft was turned over to Flight Lieutenant Lynch and his crew, who took the aircraft on to Lima. At this point, Flight Lieutenant Parmelee and his slip crew left the aircraft.

NS17508 (captained by Flight Lieutenant Smith) arrived at Albrook AFB from Charleston early on 2 June in a violent thunderstorm. At 0500 hours, Hayes and his crew were alerted to take the aircraft on its next leg to Lima. Fully loaded with relief supplies, the flight left Albrook at 0750 hours for the seven-hour-and-thirty-five-minute leg to Lima. They encountered some thunderstorm activity and heavy cumulus build-ups over the Gulf of Panama, and these conditions lasted as far as landfall at Esmeraldas, Ecuador. After passing over the steamy jungles of the coastal plain and crossing the equator, the flight's next checkpoint was Guayaquil. The aircraft entered Peruvian airspace and flew over the semi-arid northern regions and the towns of Talara and Trujillo. The flight path then paralleled the coast until at 1525 hours and their arrival at Lima, where the captain made an instrument landing.

On the morning of 2 June, Robertson brought NS17515 in at Albrook and turned the aircraft over to Smith, who then departed for Lima. Robertson and his crew remained in Panama until 6 June, when the operation was being wound down and the aircraft began returning to base.

At 0830 hours on 3 June, Hayes and his crew departed for Lima in NS17515 on the flight of eight hours and five minutes to Santiago, following two other squadron aircraft — NS17508 (captained by Lynch) and NS17517 (flown by Parmelee) — which had left for Santiago about an hour earlier. The flight south paralleled the coast of Peru and Chile, and Hayes arrived at 1630 hours, making an instrument landing. Santiago airport was crammed with dozens of aircraft from the United States and all over South America.

The new arrivals were met by Mr. Murdock from the Canadian Embassy and Wing Commander Bell, who had left the party of Minister of External Affairs Howard Green, who had been on a South American tour when the earthquake struck, to co-ordinate Canadian relief activities. As Spanish was the only language spoken on the air traffic control network south of Santiago, a Chilean Air Force pilot was seconded to each North Star crew. Following a preliminary briefing on the relief operation and a meal at the Chilean Air Force mess, the crews were taken to a hotel in downtown Santiago.

Maitland and Morrison had both arrived in Santiago late in the morning of 31 May, and the next day, they each took their aircraft to Puerto Montt with a full load of relief supplies. When the aircraft were unloaded, they embarked evacuees from the disaster area and took them to Santiago. It was late fall, and the temperature was a cool 40° F with winds and heavy rain showers. Maitland's passengers were a large group of orphan boys escorted by two priests, who sat toboggan-style on the floor in four rows, holding ropes threaded through the D-rings fitted to the cargo floor.

As Maitland prepared to start the engines, his movement controller, Leading Aircraftsman Murphy, came to the flight deck to say that he had boarded ninety-two youngsters and two priests, but there were four more boys shivering in the cold at the bottom of the boarding ladder and had had no room for them, although the aircraft was well within its weight limit. Maitland went to the rear of the aircraft with his Chilean liaison officer, Squadron Leader Manuel Villalobos, and as they arrived at the cargo door they saw the two priests climbing down the boarding ladder. When Villalobos asked what they were doing, the priests replied that they were getting off so that the four boys on the ground could board. Struggling with the lumps in their throats, the crew members boarded all the boys with the two priests and took off for Santiago, where they arrived three bumpy hours later. Every youngster aboard was airsick during the flight.

On 2 June, Maitland and Morrison took their aircraft to Antofagasta, a coastal city four hours north of Santiago, where the aircraft were loaded with bedding and clothing donated to the relief effort by local people. Each crew conducted a second run to Puerto Montt the next day.

At this stage of the operation, the USAF was withdrawing most of its C-124s from the operation; the Soviets had just shot down Gary Powers' U-2, and major elements of the USAF strategic airlift capability were required elsewhere. This precipitated a call to Wing Commander Maitland from Howard Green, who instructed Maitland to stay in Chile, with his crew and aircraft, and airlift the C-124 loads from Santiago to Puerto Montt. Green advised Maitland that he would clear the matter with his colleague, the Minister of National Defence.

At 1245 on 4 June, Hayes and his crew departed in NS17515 on the three-hour-and-thirty-five-minute flight to Puerto Montt, with Lieutenant Sergio Berriosa of the Chilean Air Force as liaison officer, a 10,000-pound load of Red Cross supplies, and two priests bound for the disaster area. Their actual destination was a new landing strip eight miles west of Puerto Montt that was completed only a week before the earthquake and was undamaged; unfortunately, it had no approach or landing aids, or lighting.

The flight climbed to 8,000 feet and proceeded to destination, flying between cloud layers. During the flight, first officer Flight Lieutenant P. Hope asked if someone could bring him a cup of coffee, and the flight engineer, Sergeant C. Lalande, went back to the crew rest area and set about heating some water. While he was at it, he got into a conversation with the younger priest, and the elder priest came into the cockpit and had the functions of the various instruments and equipment explained to him by Flight Lieutenant Hope and the author. When he asked if there were any Catholics on the crew and was told that there were, he presented the first officer and the author with medallions blessed by the Pope but, as he handed them over, the engines suddenly started to sputter and quit. The thought that passed through the author's mind was, "Holy Father, we need you now!" but Lalande, on hearing the sputtering, dashed back to the cockpit and in a flurry switched them from empty fuel tanks to the full ones. The engines were soon purring contentedly again and the flight continued without further incident.

The weather was relatively clear as the flight arrived at the airfield, and the North Star landed by leapfrogging the USAF C-124 Globemaster parked at the approach end of the runway. (The heavy C-124 would have sunk into the wet gravel had it left the concrete runway.) The North Star was quickly unloaded and promptly filled again with evacuees, and the aircraft took off at 1715 hours, leapfrogging another C-124 parked at the other end of the runway. The three-hour return flight to Santiago was routine, and two other relief flights to Puerto Montt were carried out on 4 June by Lynch in NS17508 and Parmelee in NS17517.

On 5 June, Flight Lieutenant Morrison and his crew, who had been in Chile since the start of the operation, departed in NS17517 for Lima and Panama; the aircraft was going back to base for maintenance. Flight Lieutenant Lynch and his crew returned as far as Lima, where they were positioned as a slip crew. Morrison continued on to Panama, where he turned over the aircraft to Flight Lieutenant Robertson, who flew it back to base.

Squadron aircraft conducted three relief flights on 5 June. Flight Lieutenant Smith and his crew took NS17515 to Victoria, a small inland town two hours and fifteen minutes flying time south of Santiago to deliver a complete thirty-bed hospital unit, including a fully equipped operating room and a generating plant. Two flights went to Puerto Montt, one captained by Flight Lieutenant Parmelee in NS17502, and the other by Flight Lieutenant Hayes and his crew in NS17512, who left Santiago at 0950 hours and headed south with 12,000 pounds of emergency food supplies.

The weather at Puerto Montt was poor with low ceilings and frequent squalls with heavy rain showers. A descent below cloud was made using the APS42 radar and the radio compass tuned to the low-frequency beacon at Puerto Montt. Letting down over Lago Lianquihue and the town, the aircraft broke clear south of Puerto Montt over a large body of water called the Seno de Reloncavi. The ceiling was a ragged 600 feet, and Hayes reversed course over the water to come back over the town; from there, he made a timed run of two and a half minutes on a heading of 279° magnetic. Seconds after the end of the timed run, the airfield was spotted and Hayes landed, again clearing a C-124 sitting at the approach end of the runway. He parked the North Star on the wet gravel and the local workers took about ninety minutes to unload the aircraft in chilly, damp conditions. As more evacuees were embarking for the return flight, there was a stir of excitement as a woman gave birth under the wing of the aircraft; mother and child both boarded for the flight to Santiago. The return flight took three hours, arriving at 1805 hours.

On 6 June, Smith and his crew in NS17515 made one relief flight to Puerto Montt, and at 0910 hours Hayes and his crew in NS17508 left for Lima on the first leg back to base, carrying a US Army field hospital unit comprising ten doctors, sixteen nurses and several medical assistants who were not needed in the disaster area. The flight took seven hours and forty minutes to reach Lima, where it was turned over to Flight Lieutenant Lynch and his crew. The author had some trouble explaining to the Peruvian authorities what an RCAF aircraft was doing bringing US military personnel into the country, but that hurdle was cleared, and arrangements were made to settle the Americans at the Hotel Crillon for a rest, as Lynch had scheduled a midnight departure to Panama.

On 7 June, Maitland and his crew conducted a relief flight to Puerto Montt in NS17515, and Parmelee proceeded on a similar flight to Victoria in NS17502. At 2150 hours, Parmelee left in NS17512 from Santiago for Lima, where the aircraft was turned over to Hayes and his crew, who were alerted at 0500 hours on 8 June to take the flight out to Panama. Parmelee and his crew had twenty-six passengers, including a pregnant evacuee and her two children. Departure was at 0800 and the expected flight time was seven hours. After climbing through the overcast, the flight encountered no weather problems as it headed north. Arriving at Albrook at 1500 hours, the aircraft was turned over to Flight Lieutenant Lynch for the return to base with Parmelee and his crew.

The squadron's last two flights to Puerto Montt were carried out by the Squadron Commander and his crew on 8 June and 9 June. Departing Lima in NS17502 at 1815 hours on 11 June, Smith arrived at Tocumen seven hours and fifteen minutes later, and turned the aircraft over to Flight Lieutenant Hayes, who had been alerted with his crew at 0100; they then took the long bus ride to the civil airport to file a flight plan for Charleston AFB. NS17502 was airborne at 0445 hours with twenty US Army passengers, mainly medical personnel, who were returning from relief work in Chile. As the flight neared Cuba, it was decided to carry on directly to Andrews AFB near Washington, DC, their passengers' destination, and the flight plan was changed accordingly. Good weather prevailed, and Hayes set down at Andrews at 1500 hours after being airborne for ten hours and fifteen minutes. A two-hour-and-thirty-five-minute flight plan was filed for Trenton, and NS17502 was back at its home base at 1910 hours.

Wing Commander Maitland and his crew left Santiago in NS17515 on 11 June for Lima, where they remained overnight. At 1225 hours the next day, the crew proceeded to Panama, the flight taking seven hours and five minutes. There the aircraft was refuelled, Smith and his crew were boarded, and a direct flight plan was filed to Trenton. Departing at 2250 hours on 12 June, the aircraft arrived at base at 1035 hours the next day after a flight of eleven hours and forty-five minutes.

Maitland's arrival ended a very successful operation, which could not have succeeded without the flight engineers and maintenance staff who kept the aircraft fully serviceable while they were away from base. During *Operation AMIGO*, some 50,000 pounds of medical and relief supplies were airlifted from Canada to Santiago. While in Chile, the squadron carried an estimated 165,000 pounds of supplies to Puerto Montt and Victoria, including about 15,000 pounds of bedding and clothing from Antofagasta to Santiago. In addition, approximately 400 evacuees were airlifted from the disaster areas to Santiago. Squadron aircraft put in a total of 414 hours of flying time during the operation.[29]

The squadron's flying commitments for June (apart from *Operation AMIGO*) totalled 1,700 flying hours. The unit conducted twelve overseas flights, of which nine went to Langar and three ended at Marville. Five of the flights to Langar were extended to El Arish, and one was extended to the fighter wings and Decimomannu. A sixth flight to El Arish was routed by way of Lajes, Gibraltar and Pisa. On the domestic scene, in addition to a variety of scheduled and special flights, four northern runs to Resolute Bay and Alert were carried out during the month.[30]

July

In July, the squadron started out by meeting a variety of domestic flying commitments and conducting airlift support activities on behalf of the Air Division in Europe and UNEF in Egypt. By mid-month, however, the service flights to Europe were suspended so the squadron's aircraft could be committed to a new UN operation in central Africa; service to the Middle East was not affected.

Seven overseas flights had Langar as their initial destination with four extensions to El Arish and one to the Fighter Wings and the Air Weapons Unit at Decimomannu. One flight went directly to Marville from Lajes, returning to base by way of Langar.[31]

A fifth flight to El Arish was routed by way of Lajes, Gibraltar and Pisa, returning to base by the same route. On 10 July, shortly after NS17504 had departed El Arish, No 4 engine backfired and Flight Lieutenant Smith had to return too point of departure. On 12 July, the crew conducted a three-engine ferry to Malta. The engine was changed the next day, the aircraft was flight tested and it then returned to El Arish. The next day, Smith and his crew left for Pisa, Langar and base. Arriving at El Arish on the 17 July service flight was Wing Commander R.K. Trumley, the new CO of No 115 ATU. The handing over ceremony and presentation of medals on 20 July was cancelled because of heavy flying commitments in connection with the movement of Swedish troops who were being reassigned to the Congo. Wing Commander Manson left for Canada on 24 July on relinquishing command of No 115 ATU.[32]

The squadron conducted two service flights to Resolute Bay and Alert during the month. Flight Lieutenant Spencer brought NS17516 into Resolute Bay on 5 July. On board were General Hilmy, delegate of the United Arab Republic, and Group Captain Williams. The visitors were accorded a brief tour of the facilities and hosted at a mess dinner that evening. Poor weather at Alert prevented the service flight's departure for that destination until the following morning. After returning to Resolute Bay later in the day, Spencer and his crew picked up passengers, mail and other cargo and departed for Churchill and Trenton. The second flight to Resolute was carried out by Flight Lieutenant Hastie in NS17506. Leaving base on 11 July, the flight proceeded to Winnipeg, picking up passengers, mail and cargo, and continued on to Churchill. Unable to get into Churchill because of weather, the flight returned to Winnipeg. The next day the weather situation cleared sufficiently for the flight to make a scheduled stop at Churchill and proceed to Resolute Bay. Taking off for Alert shortly before midnight, the Captain had to feather No 1 engine and return to Resolute Bay. After the Flight Engineer and servicing personnel had worked on the aircraft, the flight was able to leave on the afternoon of 13 July for Alert and then proceed to Thule. Returning to Resolute Bay the next day, Hastie and his crew left for Churchill and Trenton.[33]

The colonial independence movement peaked in 1960 with the acceptance into the United Nations of seventeen new African member states. One of these states was the Congo, where the first government was formed on 24 June with Joseph Kasavubu as President and Patrice Lumumba as Prime Minister. A Treaty of Friendship between the Congo and the outgoing colonial power, Belgium, was signed on 29 June, and on 30 June King Baudouin of Belgium was in Léopoldville to proclaim independence. Tribal violence erupted at once, and on 5 July, law and order broke down completed with the mutiny of elements of the 25,000-member *Force publique* (a native paramilitary force) against their Belgian officers. The government of Belgium began flying in troops to protect Belgian citizens, and tried to persuade Prime Minister Lumumba to invoke the Treaty of Friendship and seek aid from the Belgian forces in the Congo. (By 19 July, Belgian strength in the Congo totalled about 10,000 all ranks.)

On 10 July, Lumumba announced that, as the situation was calming down, the new Congolese government could bring matters under control without help. On 11 July, several unrelated events set off a new round of mutinies and even more violence. Belgian authorities ordered all Europeans out of the port city of Matadi, and then launched a combined assault by aircraft and warships that cost many lives. Exaggerated reports of this action immediately spread through the country on the Congolese Army radio network, sparking violence in areas that had been quiet. News of Belgian paratroopers being dropped at several widely separated points spread fear and terror, and inspired attacks on Europeans. Finally, Moise Tshombe announced the secession of the mineral-rich province of Katanga.

On 12 July, President Kasavubu and Prime Minister Lumumba flew to Elizabethville in Katanga in an attempt at reconciliation, but their aircraft was denied permission to land on orders from

Tshombe's Minister of the Interior. Belgian troops were still in charge of the Elizabethville airport, and this incident caused a break in relations between the Congolese government and Belgium.

On 12 July, realizing that the internal security situation was well beyond its control, the Congolese government requested a UN security force. Unanimously approved by the Security Council on 14 July, the UN mission dubbed the *Opération des Nations Unies au Congo* or ONUC was formed under the command of Major-General Carl von Horn of Sweden, then the Chief of Staff of the UN Truce Supervisory Organization in the Middle East. Major-General von Horn arrived in the Congo on 18 July, delayed for several days by aircraft problems. The security force numbered 1,200 troops on 15 July, increased to more than 14,000 within a month, and eventually reached a maximum strength of 20,000 soldiers from thirty-five countries. Most ONUC troops came from the African states of Ethiopia, Ghana, Guinea, Liberia, Mali, Morocco, Nigeria, Sudan, Tunisia and the United Arab Republic. Non-African countries contributing military contingents included Canada, India, Indonesia, Ireland, Pakistan and Sweden.[34]

The possibility of Canada making a contribution to ONUC was first raised in the House of Commons on 12 July, and Prime Minister Diefenbaker replied that, "… until the United Nations plans have been formulated, there is no question of requests for assistance from member governments." Replying to a second question, the Prime Minister stated that the Army's stand-by battalion "is available, but subject to the direction of the government." At Army Headquarters, the Directorate of Military Operations and Planning was already developing a possible contribution under the authority of the Chairman of the Chiefs of Staff Committee, Air Marshal F.R. Miller.[35]

On 13 July, Chief of the General Staff Lieutenant-General S.F. Clark called a meeting of the Army Council in Ottawa to consider recommendations to be made to the Minister of National Defence, in the event of a request from the UN for a Canadian contingent for ONUC. On 14 July, Prime Minister Diefenbaker answered another question in the House of Commons by stating that the government had granted the Secretary-General's initial request for two Army officers — Colonel J. Berthiaume and Major W. King — to be redeployed from UNTSO to the Congo, and for RCAF aircraft and crews to ferry food, military personnel and supplies.[36]

On 14 July, the Army and RCAF intelligence directors briefed the Chief and Vice Chief of the Air Staff on the Congo situation, saying that they considered it serious enough to warrant a warning order to Air Transport Command, and a review of plans in view of a potential Congo airlift. On 15 July, the UN requested food, and the Vice Chief of the Air Staff alerted Air Transport Command, authorizing the preparation of four North Stars for an airlift of food — pending a Cabinet decision. (Several countries, including Canada, were mustering food aid to counter shortages looming in the Congo, the results of an almost complete breakdown of the transportation system, one of the most important effects of the disorders.) The next day, Parliament announced that the RCAF would airlift 20,000 pounds of canned pork and 20,000 pounds of whole milk powder to the Congo, and the North Stars were also authorized to evacuate refugees, provided priority was given to Canadians.

The food shipments arrived at Trenton on 17 July and 18 July, and the aircraft were loaded, crewed and ready to go at noon on 18 July, when the Chief of the Air Staff received authority to proceed from the Department of External Affairs through Minister of National Defence George Pearkes. Forty-five minutes later, NS17511 (Squadron Leader M. Hlady), NS17516 (Flight Lieutenant R.T.L. Gill), NS17508 (Flight Lieutenant E.M. Spencer) and NS17517 (J.S. Walton) began departing at half-hour intervals for Léopoldville. The route took them through Gander, Lajes, Nouasseur, Dakar and Lagos, and three North Stars reached Léopoldville on 21 July.

Spencer's aircraft had an engine malfunction as it neared Dakar and it had to remain there for several days pending repairs. Among them, the four aircraft delivered 23,584 pounds of pork, 20,570 pounds of milk powder, and six RCAF technicians.[37]

The UN made two separate requests regarding the four North Stars: first, that they stay overseas for thirty days to provide airlift between Europe and the Congo, and second, on 20 July, that aircraft authorized to transport refugees could instead carry food. Parliament granted both requests on 21 July, placing the four North Stars at the disposal of the UN Commander for thirty days.[38]

The squadron's North Stars flew into N'Djili, Léopoldville's major international airport, which lay fifteen miles southeast of the city. With a 15,420-foot concrete runway (one of the world's longest), a modern terminal building and high-pressure hydrant refuelling, N'Djili could handle every type of aircraft then in service. The UN Commander immediately committed the North Stars to internal airlift, and on 23 July, three North Stars carried out a three-hour shuttle to Luluabourg in the interior of the Congo, east of Léopoldville, ferrying Tunisian troops and their equipment out and bringing back refugees from the violence, many of them missionaries. The next day, each aircraft carried out two additional shuttle flights, taking more Tunisian troops to Luluabourg and again returning with refugees.[39]

At this point in the operation, the North Stars were authorized to transport only supplies and equipment. On 23 July, after receiving reports that RCAF aircraft were airlifting troops in the Congo, the Ministers of External Affairs and National Defence wired the Canadian representative in Léopoldville as follows:

> From now on, use of RCAF North Stars is to be restricted to the transport of supplies and equipment for the UN force from Pisa to Léopoldville by shuttle service for a period of 30 days from 21 July. The use of these aircraft for the transportation of troops is not authorized by the Cabinet and is to cease forthwith.

By the time the restriction filtered through the ONUC command structure, however, the North Stars had airlifted some 240 Tunisian soldiers from Léopoldville to Luluabourg.[40]

On 20 July, Air Commodore F.S. Carpenter left for the Congo with Wing Commander J.O. Maitland to survey the UN airlift requirement while Maitland organized accommodations for slip crews and servicing personnel, and quick turnaround facilities for squadron aircraft at N'Djili. The first leg of their trip took them to UN Headquarters in New York for a brief meeting with Secretary-General Dag Hammarskjöld to discuss the situation in general terms, and more detailed discussions with Dr. Ralph Bunche, Hammarskjöld's special representative for the Congo, and his busy staff.

For diplomatic and other reasons, the UN did not maintain dossiers on countries that might become international hot spots, so only sketchy information was available in New York on the Congo's transportation infrastructure. Dr. Bunche suggested that Carpenter and Maitland go to Paris to interview a French diplomat who had just returned from a posting as chargé d'affaires in the Congo, so the two RCAF officers left New York on an Air France flight that evening, arrived at Orly the next morning, and arranged to meet the diplomat. Unfortunately, the diplomat knew a great deal about the political reasons for the upheaval in the Congo, but nothing of practical value about air operations such as fuel distribution and quantity, navigational aids, air traffic control, or meteorological services. He did know, however, that Belgium's national airline, Sabena, operated transport and general utility aircraft across the Congo.

Carpenter and Maitland left Paris on the evening of 22 July by Air France, heading for Brazzaville, across the Congo River from Léopoldville, where they chartered a small aircraft to fly to N'Djili. (The only commercial aircraft operating into or out of the Congo were Belgian.) The situation at Léopoldville verged on the chaotic. Brian Urquhart (later Sir Brian), of Dr. Bunche's New York staff was sharing a temporary office in a downtown hotel with Major-General von Horn and his Acting Chief of Staff, Colonel J. Berthiaume of the Royal 22e Régiment. There was no telephone service to the interior, and the trains were running, but not co-ordinated. Barge traffic on the Congo River had almost stopped, and the harbour at Matadi, 160 miles downstream from Léopoldville near the Atlantic coast, was silting up and would soon be unusable; it required constant dredging, and such work had stopped.

Carpenter soon discovered that ONUC had little need for additional external airlift capability; the urgent requirement was for airlift *within* the Congo — a task for which both Bunche and von Horn had wanted to use the North Stars. There was also an urgent need for air transport staff, and the UN officials asked Carpenter to take charge.

The Democratic Republic of the Congo is a huge country — 902,274 square miles, nearly one quarter the size of Canada — and the interior was sprinkled with airports. The population was then about 14 million, including about 113,000 Europeans. Sabena did, indeed, operate a significant number of aircraft into and inside the Congo, including its new Europe-based Boeing 707s, which had evacuated thousands of Belgians in only eight days. Inside the Congo, Sabena operated a mixed bag of aircraft: DC4s, C-119s, some Otters and Beavers, and a few helicopters. On their second day in Léopoldville, Carpenter sent Maitland to N'Djili to meet with the Sabena flight crews and reassure them of continued employment by the UN, and to take over the best hangar at the airport. Meanwhile, Carpenter had arranged to have all Sabena's local aircraft painted white and labelled "Air Congo", a task accomplished with enthusiasm by Sabena's remaining headquarters staff, who wished to keep their aircraft intact and flying.

Arrangements for the internal airlift by Air Congo, training standards for the flight crews, fuel problems throughout the country, hangar and passenger facilities at all the airports, and the issue of navigation and landing aids, were among many urgent air transport issues. By the time he left for Canada, Carpenter concluded that ONUC immediately needed an RCAF officer with an extensive transport background. On 1 August, Carpenter briefed the Minister of National Defence on the type and disposition of troops and aircraft authorized by Cabinet so far. As a result of Carpenter's work in the Congo, the UN asked Canada to provide an Air Commander and an Air Staff to organize and conduct ONUC air operations. Until these officers could be selected and deployed, Wing Commander Maitland carried out some of the functions of an Air Commander, and Flying Officer G. Bussieres, the navigator in Squadron Leader Hlady's crew, took on administrative and translation duties on behalf of the squadron crews. Bussieres became an assistant to the Air Commander before leaving on 9 September to rejoin the squadron in Trenton.[41]

On 21 July, Flight Lieutenant Charchuk departed Trenton in NS17502 for Gander and Lajes, where a slip crew took over for the rest of the trip to Europe. On 24 July, Charchuk took over NS17515 and left for Dakar with a spare engine for NS17508; the engine was changed and NS17508 was test flown the next day. Flight Lieutenant Spencer and his crew left for Nouasseur and Lajes in NS17515 while Charchuk and his crew departed for Accra and Léopoldville in

NS17508; its cargo of food was delivered on 26 July. Two days later, Charchuk left for Dakar in NS17511, taking twelve hours and forty minutes to complete the flight. The crew's next stop was Lajes, and they were back at base on 1 August.[42]

Flight Lieutenant Lavigne and his crew left base on 21 July in NS17504, carrying twenty-six maintenance personnel and 3,500 pounds of spares to support an anticipated airlift from Pisa to Léopoldville. The flight proceeded to Lajes and Gibraltar, and then carried on to El Goléa, an airfield in north-central Algeria used by Air France. From there, the flight proceeded to Kano in Nigeria, and it reached Léopoldville on 24 July. The crew were kept on stand-by status until 3 August, when they took out NS17516 to Dakar, a twelve-hour flight. Leaving Dakar the next day in NS17504, the crew were back in Trenton on 5 August.[43]

August

On 1 August, after many requests from the UN for help in providing ONUC with a reliable internal airlift capability, the Prime Minister advised the House of Commons that the RCAF was in the process of acquiring two de Havilland DHC-4 aircraft — Caribou — to be used for airlifting supplies to the deployed elements of the Canadian contingent. The plan was to have the two Caribou in the Congo by 15 August; a third aircraft would depart in September, and a fourth in October. The government was also in a position to provide six or seven RCAF officers to organize the ONUC Air Transport Force.[44]

An organization order issued by Air Force Headquarters on 2 August authorized the formation of an RCAF Air Transport Unit (Congo) to be based in Léopoldville, and initially equipped with the four Caribou aircraft, to be employed in support of the Canadian contingent. The order also stated that four North Star aircraft were committed to provide airlift from Pisa to Léopoldville for ONUC until 20 August, and that the RCAF was to arrange airlift into Léopoldville as required in support of the Canadian contingent. Should these commitments mean that the Air Transport Unit needed a North Star Flight, the order provided for it. Operational control of the Caribou aircraft was vested in the Air Officer Commanding, Air Transport Command. Until 20 August, the North Stars were under the operational control of Major-General von Horn, the ONUC Commander.[45]

Aircrew and ground crew for the Caribou unit were selected and began arriving at the de Havilland plant at Downsview on 4 August for training on the aircraft. By 12 August, six pilots and thirty-five technicians had completed the factory phase of their training. With the procurement of short-term spares, the unit was ready to leave Downsview for the Congo on 15 August, escorted by an Argus from Greenwood. Because the Caribou unit was offered to the UN as part of the ONUC Air Transport Force, it had to remain in Canada until the UN asked for it formally. The aircraft and their crews and ground personnel were moved to Trenton and prepared to leave on short notice.

The question of the Caribou unit proved troublesome, as Canada had offered the aircraft on 30 July without consulting the UN. In New York, officials' first reaction to the offer was favourable, considering the need, but the Secretary-General eventually turned it down. Canada was told that it was not politically advisable to increase the Canadian contingent in ONUC by 100 men, as the Soviet Union had already lodged a strong protest against the deployment of Canadian Army signallers and would probably object even more strenuously to aircrews. It is more likely that the UN Secretariat resented the way the offer was made — that is, without consultation and prior announcement. RCAF efforts to change the Secretary-General's mind proved fruitless, and the first two Caribou were eventually reassigned to No 115 ATU at El Arish, replacing two Dakotas.[46]

Wing Commander W.K. Carr, the commanding officer of No 412 Squadron, was on leave in late July when he received a phone call from the office of the Chief of the Air Staff: he was promoted Group Captain, and ordered to go to the Congo "for a few weeks temporary duty." Actually, he was the new ONUC Air Commander. He left Ottawa on 3 August for New York, where he was supposed to be briefed by a UN staff officer before departing for Brussels that afternoon. The briefer failed to show up, and Carr left on schedule. At Brussels, he was met by the Air Attaché from the Canadian Embassy, who told him that he was booked on a Sabena DC-7 flight for Léopoldville via Lisbon, leaving immediately. Proceeding as ordered with precious little indication of what his duties entailed, Carr arrived in Léopoldville on 5 August. There he met with Wing Commander Maitland and was brought up to date on the Congo situation.

On 2 August, Flight Lieutenant J. Morrison and his crew in NS17512 departed Trenton for Léopoldville with four members of Carr's new staff: Wing Commander H.B. Russell of No 4 OTU, Squadron Leader D. Harrison and Flight Lieutenant J. Forest of the Air Operations Staff at Air Transport Command Headquarters, and aeronautical engineer Flight Lieutenant W.R. Pearson. The North Star was also carrying a 1,000-kw single sideband (SSB) transmitter (at 5,422 pounds, it was nearly a full load in itself) and seven communications technicians. The SSB equipment could be used only for voice communications and was not considered secure, but once installed, it would provide a direct voice link between Trenton and Léopoldville. The flight also carried two additional crews captained by Flight Lieutenant E.J. McLaughlin and Flight Lieutenant R. Sierolawski.

On reaching Lajes, McLaughlin's crew took over, and flew the aircraft to Nouasseur and then to Dakar, where the flight arrived on 3 August. Flight Lieutenant Walton and his crew were waiting for the aircraft, having made the twelve-hour run from Léopoldville in NS17508 the previous day. Taking over NS17512 on 4 August, Walton returned to Léopoldville by way of Accra. In the meantime, Sierolawski departed Dakar for Lajes in NS17516 with McLaughlin and his crew aboard. The aircraft had been flown in from Léopoldville the previous day by Flight Lieutenant Lavigne.[47]

Since the Canadian government did not seem willing to allow the North Stars to operate on an internal airlift, Air Marshal Miller (the Chairman of the Chiefs of Staff Committee) asked on 1 August for their return to Canada to assist in the airlift of the Canadian contingent to the Congo. As ONUC had no immediate requirement for external airlift, the UN Secretariat agreed. After meetings with Group Captain Carr and some of the Air Commander's staff, Wing, Commander Maitland prepared to return to Trenton. Flight Lieutenant Gill and his crew left Léopoldville on 3 August in NS17515, taking twelve hours and fifteen minutes to reach Dakar. A run of eight hours and fifteen minutes the next day brought them to Lajes. On 5 August, they made a direct flight to Trenton that took twelve hours and fifteen minutes. Squadron Leader Hlady and his crew departed Léopoldville on 4 August for Dakar in NS17504. At Dakar, the aircraft was handed over to Flight Lieutenant Lavigne, who took it on to Lajes. Hlady took over NS17512, which was brought in from Léopoldville on 5 August by Flight Lieutenant Walton, and departed for Lajes. After a four-day layover, Hlady returned to base on 10 August. Walton and his crew remained in Dakar in a slip position for the Congo airlift, leaving for Lajes on 12 August. He then returned to base on 14 August after a direct flight to Trenton.[48]

Shortly after the special meeting of the Army Council on 13 July, Canada received a UN request for a communications organization like the one deployed with UNEF, a technical and specialist logistics support organization, less the vehicle maintenance unit, like the one in UNEF — or both.

The Army Council met the next day to discuss a paper prepared on 17 July by the Directorate of Operations and Planning, that laid out the situation from the Army's perspective. Not knowing the exact UN requirements, the planners considered that the most likely signal support for the Congo force would be a modified brigade squadron of about five officers and 183 men. The problem of the Army's contribution was addressed at Cabinet meetings on 19 July and 21 July, where it was agreed to prepare a detachment of signallers and sufficient Royal Canadian Army Service Corps personnel to staff four logistics depots in the Congo. Everyone to be deployed had to be fully immunized, a process that would take three weeks.[49]

At Army Headquarters, planning for the deployment of signallers began on 20 July. They were to be concentrated at Barriefield Camp, near Kingston, and the troops with all their equipment were to be airlifted to the Congo from Trenton. The code name *MALLARD* was assigned to the operation, and the dispatch of the first troops was scheduled for 11 August. Establishments were being prepared for a proposed Canadian contingent that included a reconnaissance party of six officers and ten other ranks, commanded by Colonel A. Mendelsohn of the Royal Canadian Electrical and Mechanical Engineers; a signals squadron of eight officers and 110 other ranks; and thirty-nine officers and 314 men for several logistics depots. When the Minister of National Defence received requests from Army Headquarters to authorize the concentration of the soldiers selected for the Congo, but these requests were refused on the grounds that the warning orders could not go out until Canada's contribution to the ONUC ground forces was announced in the House of Commons.

The Cabinet met on 28 July to consider a revised request from the UN for signallers, and approved a maximum Canadian contribution of 500 all ranks, including no more than 200 signallers. On 30 July, the Prime Minister announced the deployment and, on 1 August, Parliament approved an authorizing resolution, and the departure of Colonel Mendelsohn and his advance party for the Congo. The advance party arrived by Air France at Brazzaville on the morning of 1 August, with two primary goals: to determine general personnel and equipment requirements and, in particular, to justify sending a headquarters unit for the Army component of the Canadian contingent.[50]

Preliminary planning figures for the Army airlift were delivered in late July to the Congo Co-ordinator at Air Force Headquarters, Air Commodore W.W. Bean, who had to tell the Canadian Joint Staff in Washington unofficially that the North Stars could not lift 500,000 pounds of heavy Army equipment and the USAF might be asked to help. It wasn't until 10 August that Air Force Headquarters was able to notify the Joint Staff regarding the size, weight, numbers and destination of the heavy equipment involved. On the basis of this information, informal talks were initiated with the USAF, but no formal request could be made until the Army confirmed load priorities and destinations — information that was not immediately forthcoming, due mainly to the confused situation in the Congo. Matters were clarified when Air Force and Army planners met in Ottawa on the morning of 12 August, and the conclusions were relayed to the Joint Staff by phone. Air Commodore R.A. Cameron was thus able to inform the appropriate officials in Washington and New York of the Army's airlift requirements.

CJS(W) advised Air Force Headquarters on 13 August that MATS had authorized the Trenton-to-Congo airlift using its C-124 Globemasters. A meeting was arranged at McGuire AFB in New Jersey, where representatives from Army Headquarters in Ottawa and Air Transport Command Headquarters finalized the details. Consequently, a MATS airlift was arranged to transport the Army's heavy equipment, beginning 18 August and to be completed by the end of the month.[51]

The original Canadian Army contingent comprised two units: 57 Canadian Signals Squadron and Canadian Headquarters, ONUC, which formed on 27 July. The Headquarters was to provide administrative facilities such as quartermaster, food service and a medical section, and carry on its strength all Canadian personnel on the ONUC Headquarters staff. Two separate units were not really needed, and the Headquarters element was disbanded by October, when the Signals Squadron was designated 57 Canadian Signals Unit, with all Canadian Army personnel in the Congo on its strength. *Operation MALLARD* began on 28 July, and signallers began arriving at Barriefield Camp on 31 July. Air Force Headquarters was advised that the first group of signallers and their equipment would be ready to leave for the Congo on 9 August.[52]

No 426 Squadron had scheduled twenty-three flights to the Congo to airlift an estimated 193 personnel and 209,000 pounds of cargo for the Army, and thirteen RCAF personnel, two Canadian Press correspondents and 7,600 pounds of cargo for the Air Force. Flights were scheduled to leave Trenton on 9 August, initially at twelve-hour intervals, and then at the rate of one per day until 29 August. Fourteen flights by USAF Globemasters were scheduled to airlift forty-three soldiers accompanying 358,000 pounds of Army radio equipment and trucks that the North Stars could not carry, and 10,900 pounds of freight for the RCAF. This portion of the airlift was dubbed *MATS MALLARD*, and the flights were scheduled to leave Trenton daily, beginning on 18 August.

To enable No 426 Squadron to carry out its flying commitments over the next several months, the established flying hours for the North Stars were increased from 130 to 200 per month, and twenty-five hours were added to the interval between aircraft inspections. More air and ground crew personnel were brought in to handle the extra workload, and the squadron's North Star fleet was increased to thirteen aircraft. Direction was received from the Air Commodore Carpenter that the squadron detachment in Léopoldville would be fourteen strong, like the detachment at Langar.[53]

In August, the squadron was able to despatch two flights to Langar. The first was taken out by Flying Officer Zbesheski who departed in NS17506 on 4 August, returning to base nine days later. This was the first of several flights during the month on which, returning to Trenton from Lajes, the crews were able to bypass Gander and other intermediate points. On his return, Zbesheski took thirteen hours and forty-five minutes to complete the last leg of the flight. The second run to Langar was captained by Flight Lieutenant Longworth, who left Trenton in NS17507 on 23 August and was back at base on 4 September. On 6 August a special logistics run was sent to Lajes carrying slip crews, maintenance personnel and aircraft spares for the Congo operation. Service flights in support of UNEF in Egypt were continued during the month, with four runs to El Arish completed.[54]

Serial 1 of *Operation MALLARD* got under way at 1600 hours on 9 August, when Flight Lieutenant Spencer and his crew left Trenton for Léopoldville in NS17516 carryng nine signallers, including Major R.C. Bindoff, the officer commanding 57 Signals Squadron, who came in from Kingston by bus earlier in the day. As cargo, the aircraft carried two jeeps and miscellaneous stores. During *Operation MALLARD*, the 7,280-mile flights to the Congo were routed by way of Gander, Lajes, Dakar and Accra, and the return flights staged through Dakar and Lajes. Barring delays for weather or mechanical problems, it took a flight about forty-one hours to reach Léopoldville, of which thirty-four hours were in the air. Crews slipped at Lajes, Dakar and Léopoldville and were usually away from base six to eight days. The round trip for an aircraft normally took four days. Army and RCAF liaison officers were positioned in Lajes, Dakar and Accra.[55]

Between 9 August and 29 August, the squadron had conducted twenty-two round trips between Trenton and Léopoldville. During that period, a total of 200 military passengers (194 soldiers and six RCAF personnel), 173,332 pounds of stores, six jeeps and three trailers were airlifted to the Congo. That this intensive phase of the Congo airlift was carried out as scheduled was due in no small measure to the professionalism and dedication of the servicing and maintenance crews at base and along the route, who often worked around the clock to keep the aircraft moving.

There was one minor incident at Lajes on 15 August: NS17515 was parked at the ramp when it was clipped by a USAF C-118 operated by a US Navy MATS crew; two feet of the starboard wingtip and aileron on the rear side were damaged. The damage was quickly repaired and the aircraft was able to leave with minimal delay.[56]

Additional flights to Léopoldville included three specials. Two of these were carried out in response by Canada to a UN request to airlift medical supplies and forty-four World Health Organization staffers and other UN personnel from Pisa to Léopoldville. The first was carried out by a squadron aircraft that had returned to Langar from El Arish and was preparing to leave for base; on 10 August it was redirected to Pisa, where it picked up passengers and cargo and proceeded to Léopoldville by way of Wheelus AFB and Kano. On arrival at Léopoldville, *MALLARD 9*, instead of returning to base, was despatched to Pisa on 17 August by way of Kano and Wheelus AFB. The flight returned by the same route. The third special left Trenton on 11 August, carrying seven communications technicians and 11,000 pounds of SSB equipment and aerials.[57]

The *MATS MALLARD* flights from Trenton began on 18 August, and the thirteenth and last departed 30 August. Nine went to Léopoldville, and one flight each went to Coquilhatville, Elizabethville, Luluabourg and Stanleyville. The C-124 Globemasters carried 404,625 pounds of cargo, consisting of heavy signals equipment, five ½-ton signals vans with their trailers, thirteen 1½-ton trailers, and thirteen 2½-ton trucks. This portion of the airlift was completed on 2 September.

For three and a half years, MATS dedicated a substantial portion of its air transport fleet to flying the Congo airlift which the USAF codenamed *Operation NEW TAPE*. By January 1964, when the airlift concluded, MATS had conducted 2,128 *NEW TAPE* missions, transporting 63,798 personnel and 18,593 tons of cargo.[58]

MALLARD 22 left Léopoldville on 29 August carrying the slip crew and ten members of the ground crew; en route, it picked up the Army and RCAF liaison officers at Accra, Dakar and Lajes, the two slip crews from Dakar, and the slip crew from Lajes. The aircraft was back at base two days later, ending this phase of the Congo airlift.[59]

The squadron's UN commitments took precedence over domestic assignments, including flights to the Arctic, so during this period service to Resolute Bay and Alert was provided by No 435 Squadron and No 436 Squadron, flying C-119s. By mid-month, the re-supply convoy was in the harbour at Resolute Bay, and the cargo was being discharged ashore under the supervision of the Beachmaster, Flight Lieutenant W.T. Owston.

On 16 August, Resolute Bay received an unusual visitor: the American nuclear-powered attack submarine USS *Seadragon*, which surfaced late in the afternoon just outside the harbour. The submarine's captain, Commander G.P. Steele, announced its presence by inviting Squadron Leader Milliken (the Detachment Commander), Flight Lieutenant Owston, and Mr. Paul Adams, the Executive Officer of the US Weather Bureau, to dinner aboard the boat that evening. The guests travelled out to the submarine in the *C.D. Howe*'s launch, offered by the skipper, and at dinner they were introduced to Commodore O.C.S. Robertson of the RCN, a member of the Joint Staff in Washington. *Seadragon*'s mission was to collect oceanographic and hydrographic data during a transit of Barrow Strait, Viscount Melville Sound and McClure Strait. On 21 August, *Seadragon* completed the first submarine transit of the Northwest Passage.[60]

September

Despite the collapse of plans to deploy a Caribou unit to the Congo, the RCAF contribution to that operation was significant. On 1 September, the Canadian government granted a formal request from the UN for two North Star flights per week between Pisa and Léopoldville, but only for a ninety days; after that, the commitment would be reviewed. The Congo airlift lasted until the end of June 1964.[61]

On 1 September, SF 51/52 between Canada and Europe was reinstated, so the month's flying commitments for No 426 Squadron's thirteen North Stars totalled nearly 2,100 hours. As well as domestic assignments, the unit conducted ten overseas flights in support of the Air Division, six UNEF runs to El Arish and eight flights to the Congo. Most flights to and from Léopoldville were routed through Pisa, Idris (Tripoli) and Kano, thus establishing Pisa as an air transport hub for UN operations in Africa and the Middle East. Toward the end of the month, the squadron despatched two flights to start the 4 Brigade troop-rotation between Canada and Germany, operating into and out of RAF Station Gütersloh or RAF Station Wildenrath; by the first week of December, a total of thirty trooping flights would be completed, with 832 soldiers repatriated to Canada and 1,020 soldiers airlifted to Germany.[62]

Of the ten flights that terminated at Langar in September, five were extended through Pisa to El Arish and one proceeded to El Arish by way of Lajes and Pisa.

On 9 September, Flight Lieutenant Hastie and his crew brought in NS17517 at Pisa from Langar, heading for the Congo, and the aircraft was redirected on arrival to El Arish. The next day, they embarked a load of cargo for El Arish and a mixed group of passengers, including a Scandinavian entertainment group comprising a male trio and four female vocalists. The first obstacle on the run to Athens was the swarm of aircraft departing Rome after the close of the XVII Olympiad, taking tens of thousands of spectators home to destinations all over the world. The North Star flight was first cleared by Rome Air Traffic Control to 7,000 feet and then to 9000, and then 11,000 and then 13,000 feet; after a while, clearance was given to descend to 7,000 feet. Before long, instructions were received to climb back up to 13,000 feet.

The aircraft started out by flying through an area of heavy cumulus build-ups and thunderstorms, encountering rain squalls, a lot of turbulence and some icing. Most of the passengers suffered at least some nausea, but one of the Swedish musicians was so sick he had to be put up in the crew rest. Luckily, the radar set was working and the author was able to steer the aircraft around the heaviest of the build-ups. As the flight neared Greece the weather improved and the aircraft was cleared down for an overnight stop at Athens.

On 11 September, after arriving at El Arish, the entertainers boarded an Otter for the short run to Gaza, where they were scheduled to perform for the peacekeepers for the next sixteen days. Hastie and his crew returned to Langar on 12 September, and were redirected again; on 14 September, they departed for Decimomannu. On 16 September, they made a passenger and cargo run to Grostenquin, returned to Langar, and then began the trip back to base.[63]

On 14 September, Flight Lieutenant J. Hutchinson (who was posted from No 426 Squadron to No 115 ATU on 10 July) was near El Arish in an Otter with Flying Officer Bob Arnold, familiarizing himself with the various desert landing strips, when an Egyptian pilot in a MiG 15 buzzed the Otter several times. Making its final pass after the Otter had landed, the fighter suddenly disappeared about 100 feet off its starboard wingtip: the MiG had struck the ground and disintegrated. Later, the servicing crew painted a MiG 15 silhouette on the door to the captain's position.[64]

On 23 September, Flight Lieutenant Longworth and his crew arrived at El Arish in NS17510, which had mechanical problems that prevented it from departing on schedule. Longworth and his crew left in NS17518, which came in on 27 September, and the incoming crew took over NS17510 when it was serviceable again. On 28 September, two Caribou aircraft arrived at El Arish with three officers to train the flight crews and twenty technicians to maintain the new aircraft. These were the aircraft and personnel originally slated for duty in the Congo.[65]

The squadron was able to resume some service flights to the Arctic in September, and three were conducted to Resolute Bay. On 1 September, Flight Lieutenant W. Owston assumed command of the detachment, replacing Squadron Leader S.E.M. Milliken. On 6 September, Flight Lieutenant Culp brought in NS17511, leaving several hours later with forty-five passengers on a direct flight to Winnipeg, a run of seven hours and forty-five minutes; the next day, the flight departed for Resolute via a scheduled stop at Churchill, where the aircraft ran into a flock of ducks that knocked out the starboard outer engine during the final approach. On the morning of 8 September, Culp and his crew ferried the aircraft to Trenton on three engines, a flight that took six hours and forty-five minutes.

Flight Lieutenant Walton captained NS17511 on the next run to Resolute Bay, which arrived on 13 September, stopped briefly, and carried on to Alert. The next day, Walton proceeded to Thule, returned to Resolute Bay, and then left for Churchill. A shuttle run to Resolute Bay was completed on 15 September, after which the flight returned to base. The next squadron run to Resolute was carried out by Flight Lieutenant Sierolawski in NS17517 and, shortly after its arrival on 20 September, the flight proceeded to Alert with passengers and cargo. The next day, Sierolawski and his crew returned to Resolute after a brief stop at Thule. On 22 September, the flight left for Trenton, stopping at Churchill and Winnipeg en route. During September two C119s of No 435 Squadron flew 190 hours, airlifting 348,000 pounds of cargo on the fall re-supply of the Arctic weather stations.[66]

On 27 September, Flight Lieutenant J. Morrison captained NS17502 on a positioning flight to RCAF Station Chatham; the next day, maintenance personnel and spare parts were embarked for the RCAF Sabre team going to an air-weapons meet at Nellis AFB, near Las Vegas, Nevada. The flight proceeded first to Bunker Hill AFB, near Kokomo, Indiana (a flight of six hours and ten minutes), refuelled and carried on to Nellis, where it arrived eight hours and fifty minutes later. On 29 September, the aircraft flew to El Paso, embarked a group of Army officers the next day and airlifted them to Trenton, a flight of nine hours and five minutes.[67]

Late in September, two C-119s were despatched from Downsview to the Congo to provide internal airlift support until the UN could organize a civil air transport fleet. Leaving base on 24 September, the two aircraft were routed to Léopoldville by way of Gander, Lajes, Dakar and Lagos. Their main task was to transport heavy vehicles and equipment for the UN and, by early October, the C-119s were operating as far east as Albertville, well into the interior. Before returning to Canada on 6 December, the two aircraft had transported nearly 375,000 pounds of cargo and 100 passengers as well as 5,400 pounds of baggage and mail.[68]

By September, in addition to Group Captain Carr as Air Commander, the staff of ONUC Headquarters in Léopoldville included eight RCAF officers on its Air Staff, which eventually became international. The Air Staff was responsible for organizing and directing all flying in an area about a quarter the size of Canada, with an Air Transport Force comprising thirteen types of aircraft flown by military and civilian crews from Argentina, Brazil, Denmark, Ethiopia, India, Norway, Sweden and Yugoslavia. Some of the flight crews arrived ready to fly all the various types of UN aircraft, but others were unfamiliar with transport planes, so ONUC had to establish a training program. As well as the Congo's unstable political situation, the Air Staff had to cope with maintenance and supply shortages, language barriers and inadequate aircrew training, and conduct operations over unexplored territory with very few navigation aids.

For the first several weeks in the Congo, the RCAF staff officers, flight crews and ground staff worked around the clock to keep troops, official UN passengers and vital freight moving from the main staging area at Léopoldville into the interior. Crews were often despatched to airfields with marginal facilities and unknown hazards, including potential hostilities. Despite the various obstacles, the Air Staff rapidly established regular air service between the Congo's major cities, the country's only reliable means of transport and supply in the almost complete breakdown of road, rail and river transportation.[69]

Early in the RCAF involvement in the Congo, it was clear that the planning and technical staff at Air Transport Command Headquarters needed a telecommunications link with the ONUC Air Staff, so Air Force Headquarters directed Air Materiel Command to provide a direct high-frequency voice circuit between Trenton and Léopoldville. One of the first members of the Air Staff was Flying Officer J.G.J. Lee, a telecommunications officer, who arrived in Léopoldville on 21 July with the first RCAF aircraft despatched to the Congo. He supervised the siting and assembly of the SSB radio equipment that arrived (with the seven technicians) on 4 August. Permission had to be obtained from the Congolese authorities (not an easy matter), to locate the transmitter-receiver and antennae on a parcel of land at N'Dolo, Léopoldville's secondary airport, which lay about seven miles south of the city and was considered suitable only for UN helicopter operations.

The Congo call sign was heard for the first time at Trenton in the evening of 10 August, and two-way communication was established within twenty-four hours, using temporary antennae. By 17 August, up to five hours per day of voice communication was achieved.

On 13 August, the arrival from Trenton of more SSB equipment, including a more powerful transmitter and more efficient antennae, coincided with the arrival of two more telecommunications specialists from Air Materiel Command Headquarters in Ottawa: Flying Officer W.D. McNeil and Flight Sergeant F.E. Collins, to supervise the SSB facility, and the new equipment produced an immediate improvement in radio performance. By mid-September several more Air Materiel Command personnel had arrived in Léopoldville to help operate this communications link, which was eventually manned by two officers, three senior NCOs, six aircraftsmen and one civilian, a rather lonely group as they were housed in a villa miles from their colleagues in Léopoldville. The Trenton end of the link was supervised by Squadron Leader W.H. Holmes, the officer commanding the Telecommunications Maintenance Unit at No 6 Repair Depot. A telephone link between Trenton and Ottawa was added later, so Air Force Headquarters could communicate directly with the RCAF detachment in Léopoldville.[70]

At the end of September, Group Captain Carr prepared a "Consolidated Report ONUC Air Operations," and sent a copy to Air Marshal Campbell, the Chief of the Air Staff. ONUC strength then stood at 16,628 personnel from thirty countries. This total included the 330 members (from ten countries) of the Air Staff and the Air Transport Force, which were expected to increase by 100 to 150 personnel; the Air Transport Force was carrying approximately eighty percent of the total internal airlift requirement and, since its creation, had carried nearly 10,000 tons of freight and several thousand passengers. The key positions on the Air Staff were occupied by officers from NATO countries, especially Canadians; this was done to ensure that operations would be conducted in compliance with ICAO standards. NATO standards prevailed in logistics and maintenance matters.

Group Captain Carr sought clarification from UN Headquarters and the Canadian government regarding the doubtful status of the RCAF telecommunications personnel sent to Léopoldville to install the SSB facility; from the UN point of view, the SSB installation existed only to support the RCAF service flights from Pisa to Léopoldville. After considerable procrastination at the UN, and an implied threat by Group Captain Carr to send the RCAF signallers and technicians home, it was agreed that it was in the UN's best interests to complete the facility. At the same time, the UN accepted a RCAF proposal that the Air Transport Force also required SSB installations with a telephone patch at Stanleyville and Kamina. These facilities would not only give the Air Staff the control necessary to conduct air operations, it would also provide a reliable communications link from the Congo to Europe and North America.

The SSB facility at N'Dolo was, at best, an intermittent operation because of major structural problems such as a makeshift aerial array and a power supply that lacked output controls. Flying Officer Lee informed Group Captain Carr that he had found a more powerful SSB that the Belgians had left behind, and the Air Staff could acquire it if suitable inducements were offered to some Congolese government officials. With Carr's agreement, the N'Dolo radio station and airport were closed to UN internal fixed-wing operations, and Lee managed the installation of a fully functioning SSB facility with an extensive antenna farm at N'Djili. A secure source of electricity was obtained at no cost to the UN by tapping into the airport's main power supply — without the knowledge of the Congolese officials. The N'Djili SSB facility would stand the ONUC Air Staff in good stead over the months to come.

The Congo's only military air station of significant size was Kamina, so that was where the Air Transport Force established its main maintenance base, where all second-line and some third-line repair and maintenance were carried out. UN policy did not cover aircraft spares, so a special policy had to be developed, and attempts to get an IBM system from Canada were unsuccessful; instead, an unautomated Indian supply organization was provided. The local IBM representative was capable of organizing and providing the required services on a contract basis, as long as an RCAF specialist was available to set the ground rules. This situation resulted in a request forwarded to Air Force Headquarters in Ottawa through New York for a squadron leader supply officer to be deployed for about two months.

Under Carr's direction, the ONUC Air Staff rewrote the Air Transport Command Air Staff Instructions for the Air Transport Force, and prepared special Air Transport Captain's examinations based on the exams for the RCAF Green Ticket (IFR Instrument Rating). These Congo examinations were co-ordinated through the local ICAO Mission with a view to issuing a special UN Air Transport Licence. The RCAF technical exams on the C-119, C-47 and Otter were accepted, and included in the upgrading syllabus. A considerable amount of air and ground crew training had to be undertaken, particularly on Dakotas, helicopters and light aircraft. Another special request went to New York, this time to carry Wing Commander Russell, an expert training trouble-shooter, as supernumerary to the Air Staff until mid-November.

On the subject of clothing, Carr reported that the RCAF uniforms and the bush jackets they were issued when they came to the Congo were completely unsuitable in local conditions: most days, the noon temperature ran to 105°F, and the humidity was always above sixty percent, usually running from ninety to ninety-five percent. Carr suggested that RCAF personnel be permitted to wear khaki cotton shirts (with appropriate national markings) with locally available Dacron shorts, knee socks and low-cut suede boots. Black shoes were unbearable and nylon shirts hopeless, and the state of local laundry services meant that, whatever uniform was approved, its owner would have to wash it himself.

Reporting on communications and radio facilities, the Air Commander opined that the basic facilities for control and navigation of air traffic throughout the Congo were excellent — when they worked. At the end of September, about ninety percent of such facilities were off the air because almost all the Belgian controllers and technicians had left the country. ICAO had launched a crash program to reactivate them, but progress was disappointing. Also, internal and external commercial and military air operators throughout the Congo tended to consider the ONUC Air Commander the only competent authority for air operations matters; therefore, to help overcome the Congo's many problems in this area, Carr was instrumental in securing authority for ICAO to hire the necessary specialists from outside the Congo; UN Headquarters in New York relayed the hiring authority to ICAO in Montreal. It was felt, however, that, unless positive results were achieved in short order, ONUC would have little chioce but to hand over the air navigation facilities to the Congolese authorities until qualified civilians could be secured. Since few of the contributing nations had suitable military specialists in the field, the Air Staff had prepared a tentative plan to provide the minimum number necessary to operate and maintain air navigation facilities at eleven major airfields. The Congo had more than 330 airfields, including 150 that could take a DC-4.

Meteorological facilities in the Congo were quite good before independence, and most of the operators were Congolese. The complete breakdown in civil communications had resulted in an almost total lack of meteorological data, however, and temporary arrangements had been made with the World Meteorological Organization to permit their observers to pass meteorological observations over military links. The WMO provided pamphlets in French on meteorological trends in the Congo, and these were translated into the various languages of the Air Transport Force for use in crew briefings.

The UN Air Transport Force was still a long way from the disciplined, proficient, efficient organization of the Air Staff's dreams, but they were making progress, much of it directly attributable to the efforts of RCAF personnel. Carr concluded that their morale was excellent and none had been involved in local incidents, saved from danger (at worst) and embarrassment (at best) by professionalism, training, their natural response to discipline, and a good deal of common sense. He believed that the United Nations would be in the Congo for a long time, and that the requirement for air transport under UN control would increase.[71]

October

The squadron's fleet of North Stars was reduced in October to its normal establishment of twelve aircraft, but the month's flying commitment was increased to 2,340 hours. Fourteen troop-rotation flights were despatched in October, ten operating into Gütersloh and four into Wildenrath. Most of these flights proceeded to and from their West German staging points, using Lajes to refuel and make a crew change; when flights encountered strong headwinds, refuelling stops were made at Shannon. Thirteen other overseas flights were completed during the month, all initially proceeding to Langar in support of No 1 Air Division and becoming UN flights on departure from Langar for Pisa. All the flights stopped at Pisa, and nine departed from there for Léopoldville in support of ONUC, and four became scheduled UNEF flights to El Arish. A variety of domestic runs rounded out the squadron's October commitments.[72]

On 11 October, George Randolph Pearkes retired as Minister of National Defence, and was replaced by Douglas Harkness.[73]

November

In November, RCAF strength stood at 50,342 personnel, including 9,344 officers (9,014 male and 330 female), and 40,998 other ranks (38,369 airmen and 2,629 airwomen). This total did not include the 775 Flight Cadets enrolled in the Regular Officer Training Plan.[74]

By November, the RCAF supply staff had arranged user trials of a nylon-cotton twist fabric designed for wear in tropical climates, and the plan was to issue bush-pattern uniforms made of this material to some of the RCAF personnel in the Congo. The fabric of bush uniforms they were currently wearing was suitable for many climates, but not the heat and humidity of the Congo.[75]

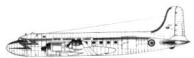

Most of No 426 Squadron's November flying schedule was devoted to overseas commitments, and the month's taskings for the unit's twelve North Stars totalled 2,230 flying hours. The squadron conducted thirteen scheduled runs to Langar in support of the Air Division and 4 Brigade, but all these aircraft went on to Pisa, becoming scheduled UN flights. Nine flights went to Léopoldville and returned to Pisa before departing for Langar and Trenton. The other four flights went to El Arish, returning to Pisa. Three continued to Langar, and one was redirected to Copenhagen to transport tour-expired Scandinavian military personnel from both UNEF and ONUC. The 4 Brigade troop-rotation continued in November with ten flights staged into and out of RAF Station Gütersloh. There were also two special runs to deliver Christmas supplies, the first to Saigon with 7,600 pounds of cargo for the Canadians serving with the ICSC, and the second to the Congo with 11,000 pounds of cargo for the Canadian contingent in ONUC.[76]

During the month, Group Captain Carr was replaced as Air Commander at ONUC Headquarters by Group Captain C.G.W. Chapman, DSO, CD, the Commanding Officer of RCAF Station Penhold and a former CO of No 426 Squadron. Group Captain Chapman was promoted Air Commodore in an acting capacity for the assignment. On his return to Canada, Carr became Station Commander at Namao.

No 115 ATU at El Arish acquired a third Caribou aircraft during November, which brought the unit establishment to three Caribou and two Otters. Another important aircraft delivery took place that month: the fourth C-130B Hercules to No 435 Squadron at Namao. All local and domestic training for the initial Hercules crews was completed during the month, and transatlantic training was scheduled to begin in December.[77]

On the domestic scene, several scheduled runs were made, but only one scheduled northern flight. Flight Lieutenant Rayson and his crew left base on 7 November in NS17510, waited one day at Churchill for the weather to improve, and reached Resolute Bay on 9 November, stopping only long enough to drop off passengers and cargo before going on to Thule.

The squadron airlifted the Chief of the Air Staff, the Chief of the General Staff, and the Deputy Minister of National Defence and their assistants to Alert on 11 November for an official visit, and brought them back to Thule the following day. The same aircraft made a second flight to Alert on 13 November, and then made a brief stop at Resolute Bay before carrying on to Churchill. The next day, Rayson and his crew returned to Trenton after a brief stop in Winnipeg.[78]

A special flight transported a Royal Roads Military College party of thirty-one cadets and faculty from Victoria to Colorado Springs and back. Another flight embarked directing staff and students from the National Defence College at Kingston and took them to New York for a tour of UN Headquarters, and back to Trenton.[79]

On 23 November, the first Hercules arrived at Resolute Bay from Churchill, captained by Wing Commander C.C.W. Marshall, the Commanding Officer of No 435 Squadron. The aircraft was loaded not only with the entire backlog of cargo that had been awaiting shipment to Resolute Bay, but also with enough fuel for the direct flight back to Edmonton. With its increased range, speed and carrying capacity, the Hercules would soon replace both the C-119 and the North Star as the main transport aircraft in the high Arctic.[80]

December

In December, No 426 Squadron was committed to 2,180 operational flying hours, mostly on overseas runs. Thirteen scheduled flights went to Langar in support of the Air Division and 4 Brigade, and all the aircraft went on from England to Pisa, where they received airlift taskings in support of UNEF and ONUC: four scheduled runs went to El Arish, and nine were despatched to Léopoldville. Early in the month, two flights to and from Gütersloh completed the 4 Brigade troop-rotation that began in September.⁸¹

Three aircraft were despatched to South America on two special airlift missions. On 7 December, Flying Officer Zbesheski and his crew positioned NS17508 at HMCS *Shearwater*, the RCN air station outside Dartmouth, Nova Scotia, where ten Royal Netherlands Navy personnel had been training with the RCN since August, preparing for the handover of seventeen CS2F-1 Tracker carrier-borne anti-submarine search and attack aircraft to the Dutch through NATO Mutual Aid. (Since 1956, de Havilland in Toronto had built ninety-nine Trackers for the RCN under licence from Grumman Aircraft of Bethpage, Long Island.) The first five Trackers were handed over in an official ceremony in Halifax on 5 December.

On 8 December, the Trackers began the journey to Curaçao in the Dutch West Indies, flown by RCN crews and loaded with Canadian and Dutch naval air personnel and aircraft spares. A North Star mother ship followed the Trackers first to the Quonset Point Naval Air Station in Rhode Island, where they refuelled, and then to Norfolk, Virginia, where they spent the night. The next day, all aircraft proceeded to Jacksonville, where the Trackers refuelled again, and then carried on to Homestead AFB in Florida. On 10 December, the convoy (followed by the North Star) flew to Port au-Prince, Haiti, via Nassau, in the Bahamas, and the next day the Trackers were delivered to the Dutch authorities in Curaçao. On 14 December, when all the transfer arrangements were completed, Zbesheski and his crew boarded the RCN air and support crews and left for Bermuda. The next day, the flight dropped off the passengers at Shearwater and returned to base.⁸²

For the return airlift for *Operation LOOKOUT*, two North Stars from No 426 Squadron and a C-119 from No 436 Squadron at Downsview were assigned. On 7 December, Flying Officer K. Whillans and his crew in NS17510 positioned the aircraft at RCAF Station Greenwood; the following morning, they boarded personnel from the Maritime Patrol squadrons and a load of aircraft spares and headed for Shearwater, where some RCN personnel joined the flight. The aircraft then departed for Kindley AFB in Bermuda, where the passengers disembarked; they were involved with joint Canadian–U.S. anti-submarine exercises. On 9 December, Whillans left Bermuda and positioned his aircraft at Ramey AFB in Puerto Rico.

On 9 December, Flight Lieutenant H. Gawne and his crew in NS17504 left Trenton for Patrick AFB in Florida, where they spent the night; the next day, they brought NS17504 in at Ramey AFB. On the morning of 11 December, Gawne left for Zanderij Airport, some thirty miles due south of Paramaribo, Surinam, to find out whether the airport facilities could handle the CF-100s, which were scheduled to stop there on way back to Canada from Ascension Island; after a couple of hours on the ground, Gawne's flight continued to Belém.

Whillans left Ramey shortly after Gawne for the five-hour flight to Atkinson Field in British Guiana, twenty-five miles south of Georgetown, which was checked as a possible alternate for the CF-100s. Two hours later, NS17510 was on its way to Belém, arriving shortly after sunset in hot, very humid conditions. The crew changed into civilian clothes, the better to maintain the fiction of a civil operation for the sensitive South American authorities.

Before noon on 12 December, both North Stars left within ten minutes of each other for the five-and-a-half-hour flight to Recife. The aircraft dodged thunderstorms and a lot of heavy cumulus cloud, and found clear weather as they passed by Natal, a war-time departure point for Ferry Command flights to Africa. At Recife, the crews found that their transportation and accommodation had been arranged by Pan American Airways, which had the contract to staff the missile range stretching from Cape Canaveral to Ascension Island. The crews were booked into a hotel on a beach, but the shark fins slicing through the water told them that swimming was out of the question.

At 2135 hours on 13 December, Gawne and his crew departed for Ascension Island, followed ten minutes later by Whillans in NS17510. The flight took seven hours and the author, who was with Whillans' crew, was able to use the leg to rate the new LDG1 (low-drift gyro), a new compass system by Sperry. Six and a half hours into the flight, the island appeared on the radar, and the flight arrived shortly after sunrise. Following breakfast and several hours sleep, Whillans' crew toured the island with Flight Lieutenant Sweetman, the local RCAF detachment commander. A British dependency, Ascension is a volcanic island of thirty-eight square miles that was used as a refuelling base for American aircraft during the Second World War. Most of the 200 residents of Georgetown, the island's only village, were employees of the British Cable and Wireless Company who spent only specified periods on the island. Although some of the lower hills were planted with grasses and shrubs, most of the island's vegetation was found on Green Mountain, a huge elliptical crater that rose 2,817 feet above the sea, which supported a farm where vegetables, poultry and cattle were raised to supply Georgetown. The mountain also had cabins that provided the inhabitants with some relief from the drab landscape below.

At 0230 hours on 15 December, Gawne and his crew left with a load of equipment and passengers for the six-and-a-half-hour flight back to Recife. The CF-100s left at 0630 hours, and Whillans followed a half hour later after loading the rest of the equipment required for the trip, including the APUs (auxiliary power units). Shortly after the flight reached its cruising altitude of 7,500 feet, Ascension Radar called and asked the North Star to relay a message to the CF-100s, which were then at 33,000 feet, "395 nautical miles from Ascension, on track." The message was passed on. The weather was excellent, and at 1225 hours local NS17510 reached Recife for an overnight stop.

On 16 December, NS17504 departed Recife at 0305 hours for the five-hour run to Belém, arriving before the two CF-100s. After refuelling, the three aircraft departed for Zanderij, a run of three hours and twenty minutes for the North Star but only an hour and forty-five minutes for the jets. As Whillans got ready to depart, NS17510 developed a hydraulics problem and had to go back to the dispersal area. A rubber gasket had split, spilling most of the aircraft's hydraulic fluid, and flight engineer Sergeant Burton took about three hours to fix it. The flight got away at 1145 hours, dodged many thunderstorms during the flight of eight hours and thirty-five minutes, and arrived at Zanderij well after nightfall. The nearest town offering accommodation was Paramaribo, nearly forty miles away by road.

Gawne left at 0840 hours the next day for Ramey AFB, followed by the CF-100s and Whillans an hour later. On 18 December, Gawne proceeded to Patrick AFB, followed by the jets and Whillans. On the morning of 19 December, the CF-100s departed Patrick for Québec City, a flight of three hours and twenty minutes, followed NS17510 with ten ground crew technicians and a load of classified equipment. The North Star arrived at Québec City at 1700 hours, and Whillans and his crew found the freezing temperature (normal for Québec in December) a bit of a shock after ten days in the tropics. After attending the reception for the CF-100 crews and ground personnel, Whillans' crew headed for the tourist home in town that was booked for them, and

NS17510 headed back to base in the morning. Gawne and his crew left Patrick AFB in NS17504 on 20 December, proceeded first to Québec City to drop off equipment and then to Ottawa to disembark passengers, and returned to base later that evening.

This ended Phase 1 of *Operation LOOKOUT*; Phase 2 and Phase 3 would be conducted from Patrick AFB in 1961.[83]

On 23 December, the RCAF's fourth CC106 Yukon was delivered for inspection to CEPE at Uplands. It was to be used for cold-weather trials at Churchill beginning early in the new year.[84]

With the approach of Christmas, slip crews and personnel on detachment came home with flights returning from overseas. Following well-attended religious services on Christmas Day, Trenton's officers served the traditional turkey dinner to all the airmen and airwomen living on the station. On the first flights after Boxing Day, slip crews and detachment personnel were again repositioned at Lajes, Langar and Léopoldville. The busy year ended at RCAF Station Trenton with a gala New Year's Ball at the Officers' Mess and well-attended parties and dances at the Sergeants' Mess and the Airmen's Club.

MAP 7: *Operation Amigo, 28 May–12 June 1960*

Trenton, 1960

PHOTO 185

Operation AMIGO: The crew of NS17502 looks at the flight plan for the first leg to Chile, where they are to deliver disaster relief supplies. From left: F/O A.B. Cole (radio officer), Capt. B.T. Saunders (USAF exchange officer, pilot), F/L J.R. Morrison (captain), F/O J.B. Bussières (navigator) and Sgt. J. Sopaz (flight engineer). RCAF Station Trenton, 28 May 1960. (DND PL 118676)

PHOTO 186

Arrival of Service Flight 53; El Arish, Egypt, 21 August 1960. (L. Motiuk Collection)

PHOTO 187
The RCAF camp at the marina; El Arish, Egypt, 21 August 1960. (L. Motiuk Collection)

PHOTO 188
No 426 Squadron North Stars at N'Djili Airport; Léopoldville, Congo, July 1960. (L. Milberry Collection)

Trenton, 1960

PHOTO 189
NS17517 being serviced en route to the Congo; Idris (near Tripoli), Libya, autumn 1960. (DND PL 146104)

PHOTO 190
No 426 Squadron maintenance personnel change an engine on a North Star; Kano, Nigeria, 21 December 1960. At far right: Dennis Smith. (D. Smith Collection)

PHOTO 191
No 426 Squadron North Stars on the flight line; RCAF Station Trenton, 27 December 1960. (L. Milberry Collection)

Trenton, 1961

CHAPTER 25

TRENTON, 1961

RCAF strength at the start of the year stood at 50,467 personnel, including 9,377 officers (9,046 male and 331 female), and 41,030 other ranks (38,409 airmen and 2,621 airwomen), but not including the 776 Flight Cadets enrolled in the Regular Officer Training Plan. During the same period the total number of personnel under the operational control of Air Transport Command was 7,618. This total was made up of 894 officers, 4,996 other ranks and 1,728 civilians.[1]

The role of Air Transport Command was to train, support and control the forces provided to meet RCAF air transport and area reconnaissance commitments. The Command's organization at the start of 1961 included:
- Air Transport Command Headquarters at Trenton.
- Five air stations:
  - RCAF Station Downsview
  - RCAF Station Goose Bay
  - RCAF Station Hamilton
  - RCAF Station Namao and
  - RCAF Station Trenton, which was responsible for RCAF Detachment Resolute Bay.
- Five operational squadrons:
  - One special transport squadron, No 412 (T) Squadron at RCAF Station Uplands.
  - One long-range transport squadron, No 426 (T) Squadron at Trenton.
  - Two troop-carrier squadrons:
    – No 435 (T) Squadron at Namao and
    – No 436(T) Squadron, Downsview.
  - One area reconnaissance squadron, No 408 (R) Squadron at RCAF Station Rockcliffe.
- One operational training unit, No 4 (T) OTU at Trenton.
- One air transport unit, No 115 ATU, El Arish.
- One ground unit, RCAF Unit Fort Churchill.
- Four movement units, and five movement detachments;
  - No 1 Mov. Unit (Air), Namao with a Sea Island Detachment;
  - No 2 Mov. Unit (Air), Trenton with detachments at Dorval, Gander and Winnipeg;
  - No 3 Mov. Unit (Air), Uplands with a detachment at Greenwood; and
  - No 7 Mov. Unit (Air), Downsview.
- Auxiliary Units:
  - Hamilton: No 16 Wing Headquarters,
  - No 424 Squadron,

- No 4006 Medical Unit, and
- No 3050 Technical Training Unit.
- London: No 4004 Medical Unit.
- Ottawa: No 4007 Medical Unit.
- Toronto: No 14 Wing Headquarters,
- No 400 Squadron,
- No 411 Squadron, and
- No 4005 Medical Unit.

New transport aircraft recently phased in or added to the Air Transport Command inventory included the Canadair CC-106 (Yukon), the Lockheed C-130B (Hercules), the Canadair CC-109 (Cosmopolitan), and the De Havilland DHC-4 (Caribou). The Grumman SA-16 (Albatross), another new acquisition, was for search and rescue.

The RCAF Program of Activities for the 1961–1966 period called for the deployment of twelve CC-106s to replace sixteen of the RCAF's seventeen North Stars. Eight of the new aircraft would go to No 426 Squadron, two to No 412 Squadron as VIP aircraft, and two to No 4 OTU as trainers, deliveries to be completed by the end of 1961. Eleven North Stars would be redeployed, six to search-and-rescue units, two to the Central Navigation School, one to CEPE, and two to reserve; the other five North Stars would be sold through Crown Assets Disposal, and the C-5 would remain with No 412 Squadron. Associated with the introduction of the CC-106 was the construction at Trenton of a 600,000-gallon POL facility and an intermediate six-bay cantilever hangar, the extension of the main runway from 8,000 to 10,000 feet with a 500-foot overrun at each end, the strengthening of the taxiways, and the hardening of the ramps. The hangar was scheduled to be completed in January, and to be ready for occupancy shortly thereafter.

The new aircraft brought other changes to Air Transport Command. An Air Transport Operations Centre would be added to Air Transport Command Headquarters to direct and control air transport operations in peace and war, and air terminal units and detachments would be formed at the main and secondary terminals to handle freight and passengers.

At the beginning of the year, Air Transport Command held an inventory of 140 aircraft of sixteen different types: seventeen North Stars (including the C-5), six Lancasters, two Comets, four C-130B Hercules, three CC-106s, nineteen C-119 Boxcars, twenty-one Dakotas, ten Cosmopolitans, twenty-nine Expeditors, four Caribou, four Albatross, twelve Otters, five T-33 Silver Stars, two Sikorsky H34A helicopters, and one Vertol H21A helicopter.[2]

No 426 Squadron establishment for most of 1961 stood at 131 personnel: 103 officers and twenty-eight airmen. The greater efficiency of the CC-106 meant that the squadron required fewer aircraft and flight crews to accomplish its tasks, so the establishment was scheduled to shrink to ninety-one personnel (seventy-one officers and twenty airmen) by the end of the year. A thirteenth North Star was added to the squadron inventory in May, and the utilization rate was set at 130 hours of flying time per month per aircraft; the year's flying commitments added up to about 20,000 hours. RCAF Station Trenton provided centralized support services, especially aircraft repair, maintenance and servicing.[3]

It was a busy year of considerable change, in which the squadron's re-equipment program would be dropped and it would start moving back to the Montreal area. The primary missions continued to be the provision of airlift support to the Air Division and 4 Canadian Infantry Brigade in Europe, UNEF in the Middle East, and ONUC in the Congo. The squadron would also conduct troop-rotation and disaster-relief operations, and a wide range of scheduled and special domestic flights across Canada and to the far north.

January

January flying commitments totalled 1,600 hours, mostly on overseas missions. Nine flights were dispatched to Europe, six went to El Arish and nine to Léopoldville.

On the domestic scene, five service flights and one special flight were sent to Resolute Bay. The special flight to Resolute brought in spare parts and a crew to repair a C-119 that had been on training mission when its starboard engine failed, and it had to land with that engine shut down and the propeller feathered. On inspection, a rupture was found in an oil tank and several panels inside the wing were bent. A scheduled flight on 25 January brought in Flight Lieutenant V.E. Cottrell to replace Flight Lieutenant Owston in command of the detachment, which at that time stood at fifty-one personnel: two officers, forty-six airmen and three civilians.[4]

The squadron airlifted the staff and students from the National Defence College at Fort Frontenac on their annual tour of Canadian and US military bases, conducted between 22 January and 10 February. At the end of the month, twenty-two RCAF personnel were flown from Ottawa to George AFB in California to attend a CF-104 course.

Several crews ran into difficulties during the month.

On 15 January, No 3 engine failed on NS17510 shortly after Flight Lieutenant Misener left Churchill for Trenton; Misener turned back to Churchill, unloaded his passengers and cargo, and took the aircraft back to base on three engines.

On 24 January, Flight Lieutenant Mahoney left Trenton at 1740 hours taking SF 51 to its first stop at Gander. Half an hour into the flight the radios failed, so Mahoney had to dump fuel and return to base. The problem was rectified, the flight departed again at 1930 hours — and, forty-five minutes later, the radios failed again: this time, the dynamotor unit that supplied the transmitter with high-voltage power had shorted out and caught fire. Again the fuel was dumped, and the flight returned to Trenton. The cargo was moved to another aircraft, the standby crew called out (Mahoney and his crew would have exceeded their eighteen hours of duty time if they tried again), and SF 51 departed for a third time at 2200 hours.

On 28 January, soon after leaving Kano for Léopoldville in NS17511, Flight Lieutenant Peterson and his crew noticed fuel venting from the aircraft. The flight returned to Kano, the problem was fixed, and the crew took off again for Léopoldville.[5]

At Trenton, Wing Commander Maitland met with the Operations Staff at Air Transport Command Headquarters to discuss placing shuttle crews at Kano for a month at a time. As this system would bring aircraft back to base at least one day sooner and reduce crew time on the route by two days, it was implemented in February.

No 426 Squadron's tests of the Sperry LDG1 low-drift gyro were going well, with the equipment producing good results especially in the north.[6]

Because of slippages in engine deliveries and the need for mandatory modifications, delivery of the CC-106 was delayed for about a month. Rolls-Royce was having trouble achieving acceptable oil-consumption and vibration levels during acceptance testing of its Tyne engine, and the rejection rate was high. The flight and testing program had been revised in light of the new delivery dates, and crew training was now scheduled to commence on 15 March, intensive flying trials on 21 April, and operational suitability trials by mid-June. The introduction of the aircraft to service was already nearly six months late.[7]

In January, the RCAF signed an agreement with the US Army for logistics support of the RCAF detachment at Pisa, including services such as station-level materiel, communications, motor vehicle maintenance, rations and quarters, and personal laundry.[8]

February

During February the squadron's twelve aircraft were tasked with missions adding up to 1,680 hours of operational flying. Eight overseas flights terminated at Langar, six more proceeded to El Arish, and ten went to Léopoldville. Three of the El Arish flights were troop-rotation runs originating in Calgary, where the squadron despatched three aircraft: the first on 30 January and the other two on 1 February and 3 February. The troops were airlifted to Trenton and then proceeded by service flight to the Middle East.

On 3 February, No 426 Squadron moved from No 9 Hangar to No 10, the new cantilever hangar, and experienced all the problems associated with operating from a facility that the contractors had yet to finish building.

On 6 February, Flight Lieutenant Mahoney and his crew were two hours out of Pisa and bound for Langar in NS17515 when they encountered radio problems, and Mahoney returned to Pisa. Two days later, an hour after departure the radios failed again, and the flight turned back to Pisa. On 9 February, Mahoney and his crew left Pisa for the third time, bound for Langar in NS17506, and their No 3 engine malfunctioned and had to be shut down. They finished the flight on three engines.[9]

Flight Lieutenant R. Sierolawski brought in NS17521 to El Arish on the morning of 14 February, bringing Air Commodore Carpenter to No 115 ATU to conduct his annual inspection. A guard of honour greeted the Air Commodore, who inspected them before proceeding to the camp at Marina. That evening, the Officers' Mess hosted Colonel Fosberry, the commandant at Rafah, at a "dining-in", and at 0900 hours the next morning the unit paraded to the music of the band of a Rajput regiment from the Indian contingent, and Air Commodore Carpenter presented twenty UNEF medals and one Canadian Forces Decoration. The ceremonial part of his visit completed, Carpenter was then flown to Gaza for meetings with UNEF officials. On 18 February, the Air Commodore was back at El Arish for dinner and a show at the Airmen's Mess, and he left for Trenton the next day on SF 54.[10]

At 1000 hours on 18 February, Flight Lieutenant Robertson and his crew took NS17516 out on a typical overseas run. As SF 51, the aircraft left Trenton for the five-hour flight to Gander, where it arrived on schedule. During the ninety-minute stop, the aircraft was refuelled and a flight plan filed for Lajes. Taking off at dusk, the aircraft climbed to its cruising altitude of 9,000 feet and levelled off for the flight to Lajes, above most of the weather. On this flight, the author shared the navigation duties with Flying Officer G. Hyslop, a recent arrival on the squadron who was being given a route check. Just past Ocean Station Delta, the aircraft ran into an active frontal zone, and was blown to starboard off track as it ploughed through an area of heavy cloud. After six hours and forty minutes in the air, SF 51 arrived at Lajes at 0200 hours local and was turned over to the slip crew for the trip to Langar.

After a two-day layover, Robertson's crew was alerted at 0215 hours on 21 February for a scheduled departure at 0500 hours: Flight Lieutenant Fawcett and his crew had brought in NS17515 as SF 61, a troop-rotation flight to Léopoldville. While the aircraft was on the ground, the soldier passengers stretched their legs and ate a hot meal before boarding for the next leg of their journey. The flight departed at 0445 hours and proceeded on the ten-hour-and-ten-minute run to Pisa via Lisbon and Madrid. The weather was good en route, and SF 61 arrived at 1800 hours. It was turned over to the slip crew at Pisa for the trip to Kano, with a refuelling stop at Idris.

At 1645 hours on 23 February Robertson and his crew departed in NS17502 for the four-hour flight to Idris as SF 59, a mixed passenger and cargo run to Léopoldville. After an eighty-minute refuelling stop at Idris, the flight left for Kano; as it crossed the Sahara, a region almost totally devoid of navigation aids, the navigators fixed the aircraft's position by taking star sights through a thin overcast. The flight of seven hours and ten minutes arrived in Kano at 0525 hours, and the shuttle crew took over as the flight was serviced and readied for its departure to Léopoldville. Robertson's crew, like other transient crews operating into and out of Kano, were quartered at the Central Hotel, several miles from the airport, a facility that is best described as "adequate". Most of the crew were up by early afternoon and took a walk along a dusty road to the nearby Kano Club, a dismal structure featuring a couple of bars and a swimming pool that was the principal social centre for Europeans (mostly British) who either had business interests in the area or were employed by the Nigerian government.

At 2230 hours, the crew headed back to the airport by bus. The rainy season was about three months away, and the whole region lay under a sort of dust haze. NS17502 returned from its run to Léopoldville, and Robertson took it over for the flight to Idris. The fifteen passengers included two English stenographers employed by the UN, and thirteen soldiers — six Swedes, three Norwegians, one Dane, two Malaysians and one Egyptian — all heading home from the Congo. The aircraft was also carrying mail and miscellaneous cargo. The flight departed shortly after midnight on 25 February, and Hyslop performed the navigation duties on this leg. About six hours into the flight, after a favourable weather forecast for Pisa was obtained, it was decided to overfly Idris and, after being airborne for eleven hours, the flight arrived at Pisa at 1200 local and was turned over to Flight Lieutenant Nichol and his crew for the return to base.

On 28 February, Robertson's crew learned that their aircraft (which was at Léopoldville) needed an engine change, and would be delayed by two days. On 2 March, SF 58 — a troop rotation flight from El Arish — came in, and Robertson took it over and filed a flight plan of five hours and fifteen minutes for Lisbon. Departing at 2310 hours in excellent flying conditions — a full moon and no weather — NS17508 headed towards Marseilles and Barcelona with gasoline fumes emanating from mid-section of the aircraft and gradually filling the fuselage. It turned out that fuel had been splashed on some of the baggage at El Arish. At 0330 hours, Robertson landed at Lisbon in a light mist; soon, the airfield was closed by fog. The fog lifted shortly after sunrise, and Robertson was able to take NS17508 on to Lajes, departing at 0735 local and arriving at destination five hours later. At Lajes, the aircraft was turned over to a slip crew for the rest of the flight to Trenton.

After a two-day layover, Robertson's crew was alerted at 0200 hours on 5 March for the trip home. Taking over NS17521, which had arrived from Langar as SF52, they departed for Gander at 0455 hours. The aircraft ran into some weather and icing on the way, avoiding the worst of it by judicious use of radar. After seven hours and thirty-five minutes in the air, the flight arrived at Gander where the ceiling was low enough that Robertson was brought in by GCA. After eighty minutes on the ground to refuel, the flight left again for Trenton, where low ceilings and freezing rain had been reported. The flight was in cloud by the time it reached Charlottetown, and began picking up ice in the Fredericton area. At 8,000 feet over the Eastern Townships of Quebec, the aircraft started bouncing through the cloud tops and was soon above the weather. On the approach to Trenton, where the ceiling was 600 feet and the visibility three miles, the flight got a radar descent, and was down at 1715 hours, ending a trip of six hours and fifteen minutes.[11]

On 5 September 1960, President Joseph Kasavubu of the Republic of the Congo dismissed his Prime Minister, Patrice Lumumba. Two days later, the dismissal was revoked by a motion of the Congolese Chamber of Representatives. Within the fortnight, Colonel Joseph Mobutu launched a successful coup, temporarily deposing the President, and Lumumba took refuge in his Léopoldville home guarded by ONUC troops. On 27 November, Lumumba slipped through the defensive perimeter around his house and fled; four days later, Mobutu's soldiers caught him and three of his parliamentary associates near Port Francqui in Kasai Province. On 2 December, Lumumba was returned to Léopoldville and imprisoned, and in January 1961, he was put aboard an Air Congo C-54 with an armed escort to be flown to Elizabethville, the capital of Katanga, on the orders of President Kasavubu, who had been restored to power.

On 10 February, it was announced that Lumumba had escaped, and the news of his death came three days later. Despite claims by the Katangan government that he had been killed by hostile villagers, the view was widely held both in the Congo and abroad that this was a case of political murder. In November 1961, a UN Commission of Inquiry would report that Lumumba was murdered on 17 January in a villa near Elizabethville shortly after his arrival, probably in the presence of Katanganese authorities.

Lumumba's transfer to Elizabethville and subsequent death only added to the serious political divisions wracking the Congo. Disorders throughout the country, which had increased as the political crisis deepened, were punctuated by open clashes between well-armed supporters of the central and regional government factions. By February the 24,000-strong *Armée nationale congolaise* had been split, half under the command of General Mobutu in Léopoldville and the other half under General Lundula in Stanleyville. All over the country, intertribal warfare began breaking out as central authority decreased and political differences became more acute. The chaos was increased by the appearance of several self-declared provinces where local chiefs embarked on campaigns against rival tribes to consolidate claims over disputed territory. At UN Headquarters in New York, delegates began demanding the resignation of Secretary-General Hammarskjöld over the Lumumba affair, and several national contingents were withdrawn from the ONUC force, bringing it down to 15,000 all ranks, including only 10,000 combat troops — hardly adequate to the task of maintaining law and order in an enormous underdeveloped country heading into a civil war.¹²

At Trenton, meanwhile, the author visited the Operations Staff at Air Transport Command Headquarters in his capacity of Squadron Senior Navigation Officer on 15 February to obtain Emergency Evacuation Routes for extracting all Canadian personnel from the Congo should the need arise. Flight plans were prepared and emergency map orders completed. On 16 March, a new shuttle crew (skippered by Captain B. Sanders, a USAF exchange officer) left Trenton for Nigeria; during their month at Kano, they would conduct the ONUC shuttle flights to and from Léopoldville.¹³

In accordance with the 1961–1966 Program of Activities and as part of changes in the logistic support of No 1 Air Division, No 5 Movements Unit was to move from No 30 AMB Langar to No 1 (F) Wing at Marville, continuing its original role and gradually taking over the duties of No 6 Movement Unit in Paris, which would be disbanded in December 1961. The relocation date of 15 May would provide air movement facilities at the European terminus when CC-106 operations were due to begin. Starting in June, most North Star flights for the Air Division would proceed directly from Lajes to Marville, which meant routing the UN service flights to and from El Arish and the Congo by way of Lajes and Pisa.¹⁴

No 426 Squadron's domestic flying commitments for February included a weekly service flight to Resolute Bay and Alert.

On 4 February, two North Stars were assigned to airlift eighty students and directing staff from the Army Staff College at Fort Frederick in Kingston, from Trenton to Churchill and return. On 16 February, one aircraft was despatched from Trenton to Victoria to pick up thirty-nine faculty and cadets from Royal Roads Military College, and transport them to St-Hubert and back. From 17 February to 26 February, a North Star took a CBC troupe featuring the McGill Chorus on a tour of northern bases, stopping at Seven Islands, Knob Lake, Great Whale, Winisk and Churchill. On 24 February, the RCAF Central Band was flown from Ottawa to the Maritimes to present concerts at Greenwood, Summerside and Dartmouth; the band returned to Ottawa on 26 February. On 25 February, a North Star flew to Bermuda to pick up twenty-four RCN and RCAF personnel and airlift them to Dartmouth. On 27 February, two North Stars went to Toronto, embarked seventy-six students and directing staff from the RCAF Staff College, and flew them to St-Hubert and Québec City. That flight returned to Toronto the following evening.¹⁵

On 27 February and 28 February, two conferences were held at Air Transport Command Headquarters in Trenton to discuss the spring airlift to the Joint Arctic Weather Stations and the Army resupply of Alert (*Operation BOXTOP*). The airlift to the weather stations from Resolute Bay was scheduled to commence on 10 April, with two C-130B Hercules from No 435 Squadron. The Hercules would carry all the cargo except fuel to the satellite stations until 20 April, when they were scheduled to proceed to Thule to start airlifting building materials and fuel to Alert for the Department of Transport. On 21 April, the C-119s were to move to Resolute Bay to continue the airlift to the weather stations. Once the Department of Transport airlift from Thule to Alert was completed, *Operation BOXTOP* would start. *Operation ROVING DEPOSIT*, using Dakota aircraft from Namao, would deliver technicians and miscellaneous cargo to the satellite stations.[16]

March

Squadron taskings during March totalled nearly 1,560 flying hours.

In addition to a variety of domestic special and scheduled flights, the squadron despatched nine trips to Langar in support of Canadian forces in Europe, and five to El Arish and eleven to Léopoldville for the UN.

On 22 March, Flying Officer Zbesheski and his crew were returning to Pisa from El Arish when they and their aircraft were redirected to Copenhagen to airlift Scandinavian personnel home at the end of their six-month UN tour; after disembarking the passengers, the flight carried on to Langar. Shortly after leaving Pisa for Idris in NS17510 on 27 March, Flight Lieutenant Genge encountered mechanical problems and turned back to Pisa, where the servicing crew fixed the problem. After an air test, the flight was resumed. The same day, Flight Lieutenant Lavigne and his crew in NS17504 were flying to El Arish as SF 57, with a group of Canadian soldiers aboard, when an engine backfired shortly after leaving Argentia for Lajes. Flying on three engines, Lavigne returned to Argentia, where the aircraft was found to need an engine change. Trenton was advised, and the standby crew captained by Flight Lieutenant Swan were called out. They left base at 0230 hours on 28 March in NS17521 as a replacement aircraft for NS17504. On Swan's arrival at Argentia, the passengers from SF 57 and their equipment were embarked on NS17521, and Lavigne was quickly on his way to Lajes. As Swan and his crew prepared to ferry NS17504 to Trenton on three engines, weather closed the field. The crew sat it out for thirty-six hours before they could leave for home.[16]

On 3 March, the first CC-106 — RCAF No 15927 — was delivered to Trenton, still with the unmodified engines that were to be removed by a Canadair Mobile Repair Party and returned to Cartierville. The aircraft's modified engines were to be delivered by the end of the month. Although this was the sixth CC-106 accepted by the RCAF it was the first available for training. Two were in the Integrated Test Flight Program at Canadair, CEPE had one at Churchill for climatic trials and another at Uplands for telecom trials, and a fifth had been delivered to Timmins Aviation for conversion to a passenger transport.[18]

On 15 March, the AOC's Conference commenced at Trenton, with Lieutenant-General J.W. Kelly of MATS and Air Marshal Sir Denis Barnett of RAF Air Transport Command to meet with Air Commodore Carpenter to discuss matters of mutual interest. It was the first tri-lateral meeting of the commanders of the American, British and Canadian air transport organizations.[19]

On 26 March, one of those rare occasions when most of No 426 Squadron's personnel were at at base, a dinner and social evening were held at the Officers' Mess, and the occasion was used to make presentations to several officers and their wives who were leaving the squadron. Flight Lieutenant Mike Rayson, an exchange officer from the RAF, was returning to England; Flying Officer Barry Browning, a navigator, was leaving the service for medical reasons; and Flight Lieutenant J. Lynch, a squadron captain, had been appointed Flight Safety Officer at RCAF Station Trenton.[20]

On the international scene, Canada sent a delegation to Geneva to attend a fourteen-state conference on Laos; there was a move to reactivate the International Commission for Supervision and Control, composed of India, Canada and Poland. In case the Canadian representatives had to go to Laos, Air Transport Command Headquarters placed a No 435 Squadron Hercules on standby on 29 March; the Hercules could accomplish the mission much faster than a North Star. The proposed flight was to be routed from Edmonton to Vientiane by way of Anchorage, Tokyo and Manila.[21]

In March, the RCAF announced that Resolute Bay would be required as a base for northern operations for the foreseeable future. The formal statement was necessary because the Department of Northern Affairs and National Resources was initiating a move to Radstock Bay on Devon Island, and Treasury Board was withholding approval of Resolute Bay projects pending a decision on moving the base about seventy miles to the east.[22]

On 28 March, the RCAF received its first delivery of CF-104 Starfighters manufactured by Canadair at Cartierville.[23]

At the end of the month, arrangements were made for the squadron to airlift a group of fifteen CBC entertainers to El Arish to perform for the troops on UN duty. On the way back to Canada, they would stop in Europe to put on the show for Air Division personnel and the soldiers of 4 Brigade.[24]

April

On 1 April, all the auxiliary squadrons of the RCAF were transferred to Air Transport Command: No 400, No 401, No 411, No 424, No 438, No 442 and No 443 from Air Defence Command, and No 402, No 403, No 406 and No 418 from Training Command.[25]

The squadron's flying commitments for April totalled 1,560 hours, the same as in March. Nine flights were despatched to Langar in support of units in Europe; one of these proceeded to Marville and carried out two shuttle flights from there to the Air Weapons Unit at Decimomannu. Five flights — including the one that airlifted the CBC troupe — went to El Arish. Ten flights went to Léopoldville.

On 10 April, Flight Lieutenant McNair and his crew were returning from the Congo via Pisa to Langar in NS17508 when it had a malfunction in No 1 engine, which had to be shut down. Flying on three engines, they were nearing Langar when they were advised that the field was fogged in, and diverted to Bruntingthorpe, ten miles south of Leicester. The aircraft was flown out to Langar the next morning on three engines, and the aircraft returned to base once the engine was changed.[26]

On 7 April, Lieutenant-General P.S. Gyani, the UNEF Commander, came to El Arish to inspect No 115 ATU. After the inspection of the fifty-man guard of honour and the presentation of UNEF medals to twenty-four unit members, the General inspected the airport and the camp at Marina, where the Officers' Mess hosted him at lunch before his departure for Gaza. On 12 April, the Scandinavian troop rotation began through El Arish. On 17 April, the CBC troupe put on a two-hour show featuring Tommy Hunter and the Rhythm Pals, Joyce Hahn, Sandra Lee, Terry Moore, Denyse Ange and Peter Appleyard, with Gordie Tapp as master of ceremonies.[27]

On 7 April, the squadron received a new task from AFHQ: airlifting equipment and baggage to Laos for a new truce team. A crew was put on standby and flight plans were prepared.

The next day, the author (who had canvassed the squadron's various sections) gave Wing Commander Maitland three potential names for the CC-106: Chinook, Voyageur and Yukon. Wing Commander Maitland forwarded the names to Air Force Headquarters, and the Chief of the Air Staff chose Yukon.

On 8 April, Flying Officer Zbesheski and his crew left base in NS17510 and flew to St-Hubert, where they embarked a group of officers from Air Defence Command Headquarters for an eight-day tour of northern bases and DEW Line sites, including Knob Lake, Cape Dyer, Hall Beach, Cambridge Bay, Churchill, Cape Parry and Cold Lake.[28]

On 11 April, Air Commodore Leonard Birchall, the Chief of Operations at Air Force Headquarters, called Air Commodore Carpenter to ask him to prepare a plan to airlift a large contingent of Indian troops and their equipment: 1,500 soldiers, about 350 tons of freight, twenty-six Jeeps, eight motorcycles and eight recoilless guns from Dar-es-Salaam, Tanganyika, to Kamina in the Congo. The author prepared routing to and the time required to reach Dar-es-Salaam by North Star and delivered it to the Squadron Commander for an urgent meeting at Air Transport Command Headquarters.

The draft plan required four aircraft, six flight crews and eighteen ground crew personnel. The aircraft were to be routed to Dar-es-Salaam by way of Gander, Lajes, Idris and Khartoum, and the flight time en route was expected to total forty-one hours and thirty minutes. The route distance between Dar es Salaam and Kamina was 960 miles, at a safety altitude of 11,700 feet, and a North Star would take ten hours to make the round trip. To airlift everything, the North Stars would have to make ninety-three round trips: at four trips per day, that would come to twenty-four days — or, more realistically, thirty days — of full serviceability and about 1,300 flying hours to complete the operation.

Another plan was drafted based on three Hercules from No 435 Squadron, with all six of the unit's available flight crews, two technical officers and twenty airmen to provide ground services, and one officer, six senior NCOs and six transportation technicians to organize an air terminal. The Hercules would do the round trip from Dar-es-Salaam to Kamina and back in six and a half hours, and the entire operation in nineteen days. The Hercules and North Star plans were both finalized and forwarded to AFHQ on the very day the request was received. No 426 Squadron selected personnel for the operation, but did not put them on standby yet. The aircraft earmarked for the operation were checked, the map kits were prepared and the flight plan folders were made ready.

Two days later, the flap was over, and the incident became another planning exercise. At the same time, however, the squadron was advised that a second aircraft might be required to take the truce team personnel to Laos — subject to an agreement by the Conference in Geneva on the function of the ICSC in Laos.[29]

On 12 April, Major Yuri Gagarin of the Soviet Union orbited the Earth for 108 minutes in the satellite Vostock 1, thus becoming the first man in space.[30]

On 13 April, directing staff and students from the RCAF Staff College visited Trenton for a series of briefings on Air Transport Command and its operations, led off by Air Commodore Carpenter and the Chief Staff Officer, Group Captain G.J.J. Edwards. The briefings were followed by a tour of the new cantilever hangar that was to house the CC-106 Yukon.[31]

On 14 April, Chief of the Air Staff Air Marshal H. Campbell arrived at Trenton at 1030 hours to address students from the Canadian Army Staff College at Fort Frontenac, and the transfer of Air Commodore Carpenter to Air Force Headquarters as Chief of Training was announced. Carpenter would replace Air Commodore Rutledge, who was retiring, and the new Air Officer Commanding, Air Transport Command would be Air Commodore R.J. Lane, DSO, DFC and Bar, CD, currently serving at Air Force Headquarters as Chief of Plans and Intelligence. On receipt of new orders two augmented crews were placed on standby to fly Canadian truce team members to Laos. On 18 April, their standby was extended from twenty-four hours to five days.[32]

The high Arctic resupply operation was in full swing during April, supported by scheduled flights to Resolute Bay by No 426 Squadron. Between 14 April and 23 April, two No 435 Squadron Hercules airlifted 1,100 tons of cargo from Resolute Bay to the Arctic weather stations. From 21 April to 30 April, two Hercules transported about 1,000 tons of POL from Thule to Alert. Meanwhile, ski-equipped Dakota aircraft airlifted about 110 tons of supplies from Resolute Bay to the Royal Canadian Engineers survey parties at work across the north.[33]

On 21 April, His Excellency Mario Rodriguez, the Ambassador of Chile to Canada arrived at RCAF Station Trenton to present Chilean Air Force wings to No 426 Squadron personnel who had participated in *Operation AMIGO*. The Chilean government originally intended to present medals, but the idea was nixed somewhere in Ottawa's more ethereal circles — the thinking was that the crews were only doing their jobs, and that merited no special recognition. The government of Chile insisted on doing something in formal recognition of the squadron's contribution to the relief effort, and Canada finally agreed that the presentation of "honorary wings" would serve the purpose.

Due to persistent rain showers, the one hour-ceremony took place in the spacious new cantilever hangar, and at 1430 hours Flight Lieutenant J. Morrison had all available participants in *Operation AMIGO* paraded before the reviewing stand. The Ambassador delivered a speech of welcome from the Chilean Air Force and thanked the Canadian government and the RCAF for the assistance rendered in the aftermath of the earthquakes. The presentation of wings was next, with Wing Commander Maitland receiving the first set. The proceedings received excellent coverage from the newspapers and local radio and television stations. That evening, a celebratory dinner dance was held in the Officers' Mess. Another presentation was held later for *Operation AMIGO* personnel who were away from Trenton on 21 April.[34]

All squadron flight crew members were subject to annual proficiency checks, and the author had arranged checks for several navigators over a three-week period beginning 24 April. That day, SF 57 (a troop-rotation flight) was scheduled to leave Trenton for El Arish. The assigned aircraft was NS17521, captained by Flight Lieutenant H.M. Smith. The first officer, Flying Officer Ian Banyard, was receiving his captaincy check, while Flying Officer G. Hyslop was being flight-checked as a navigator. At 1000 hours, as Smith started up No 4 engine, it caught fire; it was shut down immediately, and the aircraft's fire extinguishers activated while the servicing crew standing by for start-up deployed their portable extinguisher. At the same time, the author helped the thirty-three soldiers aboard the aircraft to disembark as quickly as possible — a shaky beginning to their long journey. A suitable interval was allowed to elapse after the fire was put out before the soldiers were brought back to the aircraft to retrieve their luggage and equipment.

Cargo and passengers were switched to NS17517 and the flight left for Gander at 1205 hours. The weather en route was good, but it was snowing at Gander on arrival and the flight was brought in by GCA. Departure for Lajes was delayed a couple of hours for de-icing; the snow was freezing on the aircraft. Some thirty minutes after departure the aircraft entered an active frontal zone, and it was in cloud for more than an hour, picking up a good deal of ice. Once clear of the front, however, the rest of the flight was routine, and at 0610 hours the aircraft came in at Lajes, where a slip crew took it over.

On 30 April, after a four-day layover, the author joined a crew skippered by Flight Lieutenant Longworth, who took over NS17508 from Wing Commander Maitland to continue SF 51 to Langar. Departure was at 0440 hours, and the navigator, Flying Officer W. Hamilton, received a check on this leg. The weather en route presented no problems, and the flight arrived at Langar at 1355 hours. After a two-hour stop, the flight continued to Pisa as SF 59; arrival was at 2140 hours after being airborne for four hours and forty minutes. The Detachment Commander at Pisa was Flight Lieutenant Ray Griffiths, one of the squadron's navigators, and he came to pick up the author and take him to the Mediteranneo Hotel, where Flight Lieutenant Smith and his crew were staying. The author was to join them for the next day's flight to Kano.

On May Day, the Italian Communist Party held parades and demonstrations of solidarity in every city and major town in the country. Like the RCAF personnel at Pisa, the Americans based nearby at Camp Darby (Headquarters, 8th Logistics Command) were under orders to keep a low profile. At 1430 hours, Smith's crew boarded a bus for the airport. A three-hour-and-fifty-minute flight plan was filed to Idris, and the crew were away in NS17508 at 1750 hours. With a bright moon and no weather, it was a routine flight to Idris, where they arrived at 2140 hours local, but as soon as the aircraft was shut down a problem surfaced: a hydraulic leak that flight engineer Sergeant C. Lalande tried to fix. After three and half hours, Smith decided to call it a day and the crew proceeded to quarters provided by the RAF. A short time later, Lalande informed the captain that the problem could be rectified within two hours, and preparations were made to leave for Kano.

Departure was at 0345 hours local on 2 May, and dawn found the aircraft winging its way at 10,000 feet over one of the world's most desolate and inhospitable regions: thousands of square miles completely devoid of vegetation or signs of life. The sun slowly rose and was soon a blazing fireball broiling the aircraft until the cockpit was uncomfortably hot. One hour out of Kano, the desert was left behind and the countryside was sprinkled with villages. As the flight passed over Zinder in French West Africa (now Niger), Smith began his descent, and the arrival at Kano was at 0945 hours local, after a seven-hour run. The passengers disembarked and were taken for a hot meal while NS17508 was serviced, and Flight Lieutenant Robertson and his shuttle crew took over for the leg to Léopoldville.

At midnight, the author proceeded to the airport with Smith's crew, who were taking over the flight that Robertson brought in from Léopoldville at 0020 hours. One of the passengers aboard the aircraft was Captain Gerald Bélanger of the Royal Canadian Corps of Signals, who was pinned down with his detachment at their office in Matadi on 4 March during a fire-fight between the ONUC Sudanese soldiers guarding the post and Congolese troops who had taken over the city. The action left one Sudanese soldier dead and four wounded, and Bélanger survived by sheltering in a gully. After this incident, the Canadian signallers at Matadi were withdrawn by air to Léopoldville.[35]

The author joined Robertson's crew for the bus ride to the hotel, and at noon he took the walk to the Kano Club with navigator Flying Officer Paul Roberge. As on previous visits to Kano, three lepers sat in the shade of a tree with their begging bowls, and a young woman with her child asked for money at a crossroads. Each beggar received a contribution, and the navigators went back to the hotel to try to get some rest. The outside temperature was well over 110°F.

The next inbound flight was due in by midnight, and the shuttle crew headed for the airport where a six-hour flight plan was filed to Léopoldville. SF 61 left at 0155 hours on 4 May in NS17511, and Robertson climbed to the flight's cruising altitude of 8,000 feet. The author conducted a flight check on Flying Officer Roberge, and the radar set came in handy as there were many thunderstorms to avoid along the track. The arrival at Léopoldville was at 0750 hours, and while the aircraft was being serviced, a flight plan was filed for the return to Kano. As the thirty-four passengers (including twenty-nine Canadians) were boarding, a crusty RC Sigs Staff Sergeant remarked that he would never have believed he would ever see the day when he'd be glad to see the Air Force. After six months in a jungle post, he would probably have walked out if pointed in the right direction. Squadron crews quickly realized that no-one ever missed or was late for a homeward-bound flight from the Congo.

SF 62 was away at 1040 hours on 4 May. It climbed out over Léopoldville, crossed the Congo River, over-flew Brazzaville and headed north to Kano at 9,000 feet. Some of the thunderstorm activity encountered on the way down had subsided, but the flight had to skirt some heavy cumulus build-ups as it approached Kano. On arrival at 1640 hours, the slip crew took over the flight and Robertson and his crew caught a bus for the Central Hotel.

Early in the morning of 5 May, Wing Commander Maitland brought in NS17512 and handed it over to Robertson's crew for the shuttle to Léopoldville. Robertson returned to Kano at 2200 hours after a rough trip either going through or dodging a succession of thunderstorms along track, with a coffin aboard: an Indonesian soldier who had accidentally shot and killed himself.

The body was being returned to Indonesia for burial. The cargo also included the personal effects of a Swedish officer who was shot and thrown into a crocodile-infested river by the Congolese. The flight with its twenty-nine passengers was away at 0125 hours on 6 May. Wing Commander Maitland climbed NS17512 to 11,000 feet and set heading for the flight of six hours and fifty minutes to Idris. The author used this leg to conduct a flight check on the navigator, Flying Officer Bill Watt. It was a clear, moonlit night and the trip was routine, arriving at Idris at 1000 hours. After a one-hour refuelling stop, the flight continued to Pisa, which took four hours and fifteen minutes; arrival was at 1330 hours local.

The author left Maitland's crew and was quartered at Camp Darby. On 10 May, he joined Flight Lieutenant Scott's crew for the night flight to Langar in NS17515, conducting flight checks on Flight Lieutenant Jarvis and Flying Officer Niehaus en route. On joining Flight Lieutenant Mahoney's crew on 14 May, the author proceeded to Wildenrath in NS17504. The next day, the thirty-six-man band of the Royal Canadian Dragoons were embarked, and the flight for Pisa, where it refuelled, and continued on to Athens. On 16 May, the flight arrived at El Arish, disembarked the band, and returned to Athens, and the following day, Mahoney and his crew headed for Marville via Pisa. On 20 May, Mahoney took NS17510 out to Lajes at 0455 hours, and the author carried out a navigation check on Flight Lieutenant Griffiths during the flight, which should have taken eight and a half hours but extended to ten hours because of an Air Force Day parade at Lajes that left incoming aircraft stacked in holding patterns to 30,000 feet. The flight landed at 1200 hours.

A twelve-hour crew rest was taken, and the crew was alerted at midnight for the return to base. Departure was at 0215 hours 21 May. The weather was good en route, but at destination and the alternates it was somewhat uncertain. After seven hours and fifty-five minutes, the flight landed at Gander. Forty-five minutes later, SF 52 was on its way to Trenton, a run of six hours, arriving at base at 1400 hours.[36]

Operation LOOKOUT continued from April to June, with the RCAF CF-100 crews based at Patrick AFB in Florida observing American rocket launchings and measuring infra-red radiation.[37]

On 25 April, the Air Transport Command Band left Downsview for Europe to begin a tour of units in No 1 Air Division, giving concerts for civilians living near the bases and performing on the radio. The band was then airlifted to Britain for engagements at Langar, Nottingham and London, and returned to Canada on 5 June.

The second CC-106 aircraft (RCAF Registration 15928) was delivered to Station Trenton on 27 April. This aircraft also had unmodified engines that had to be removed and returned to Canadair. With modified engines installed, the aircraft was to be used in the training program.[38]

May

On 1 May No 415 (MP) Squadron was re-formed at Summerside, PEI, equipped with the Canadair CL-28 Argus aircraft. Its first commanding officer was Wing Commander S.S. Mitchell.[39]

During May domestic and overseas tasking for the squadron's fleet of thirteen North Stars totalled 1,650 flying hours. Overseas runs included nine to Langar in support of the Air Division and 4 Brigade, and five UNEF support flights to El Arish. On the return leg, one of these latter flights involved airlifting the band of the Royal Canadian Dragoons from El Arish to West Germany. Of the ten flights to Léopoldville, eight were logistic support missions and two were troop-rotation flights.[40]

As in previous years, the squadron was tasked with providing an aircraft and crew to take the Specialist Navigation Course from the Central Navigation School on its annual polar exercise. Consequently, on 7 May, Flight Lieutenant E. Fawcett and his crew positioned NS17516 at Winnipeg, and the next day embarked Wing Commander K.R. Greenaway (Officer Commanding, Central Navigation School), several directing staff, and the students of No 13 Specialist Navigation Course. The flight proceeded first to Churchill, stopped there briefly, and then continued to Thule. On 9 May, the exercise moved to Resolute Bay, the base for a series of polar flights, and on 10 May an eight and a half hour training flight around Baffin Island was carried out. On 11 May, the first North Pole trip was conducted, with the aircraft routed by way of Isachsen, position 87°N 145°W, the Pole, and directly back to Resolute Bay; that flight took ten hours and twenty minutes. A similar flight taking ten hours and fifteen minutes was carried out the next day, routed to the Pole via 87°N 130°W, and back to base by way of 87°N 65°W. Fawcett and his crew returned the navigators and their students to Winnipeg on 13 May, and were back at Trenton the following day.

The squadron carried out one other northern flight in May. Wing Commander Maitland and his crew took out NS17511 on 28 May and proceeded on a supply run to Churchill, Resolute, Alert and Thule, returning to base from Thule on 30 May, a run of nine hours and forty minutes.[41]

A submission was prepared in May by Air Force Headquarters which sought authority of the Governor General in Council to transfer Harvard Mk II aircraft spares worth $100,000 to Turkey as Mutual Aid, in response to a request to support the forty Harvards transferred to Turkey as Mutual Aid in 1958.[42]

At a meeting of the Air Council held on 17 May, it was agreed that the four CF-100 squadrons of No 1 Air Division should be disbanded in 1963.[43]

By the end of the month, the RCAF had accepted its ninth CC-106 from Canadair. Two of the aircraft — 15921 and 15922 — were on loan to Canadair; 15555 was at Timmins Aviation for fitting up as a special transport; 15924 was at CEPE for flight trials; 15930 was assigned to No 4 OTU; and 15925, 15926, 15927 and 15928 were assigned to No 426 Squadron. Trouble with the compass system was delaying the IFR clearance for the CC-106, and much depended on securing that clearance: unless it came through soon, the purchase of fifteen aircraft by commercial carriers would be cancelled. This was a $120-million deal backed by the Canadian government.[44]

On 29 May, Air Force Headquarters announced the promotion to Acting Air Commodore of Group Captain H.A. Morrison, DSO, DFC, AFC, CD, the commanding officer of the Central Experimental and Proving Establishment in Ottawa. He had been selected to replace Acting Air Commodore C.G.W. Chapman, DSO, CD as the Air Commander at ONUC Headquarters in Léopoldville. On his return to Canada, Chapman would take up his previous appointment as Station Commander at Penhold.[45]

At the end of May, advice was received from No 1 Air Division to the effect that administrative officials in France had ordered the enforcement of more rigid controls on passengers and crews on RCAF flights arriving in France from other parts of Europe. All civilians (including RCAF dependants) and all non-Canadian NATO military personnel would require passports, and all arriving passengers and crews would be required to complete and submit the Landing Card that was being distributed to all air movements units by the Air Division. Only Canadian military and naval personnel in uniform would be permitted to continue using their identity card and orders as travel documents. This procedure did not affect transatlantic flights.[46]

At the same time, Air Force Headquarters announced that arrangements had been made to have the Canadian Army conduct small-arms training for RCAF personnel deployed in the Congo, using the 9-mm Browning automatic pistol and the 9-mm Stirling submachine-gun, both Army issue.[47]

June

The squadron's June flying commitments totalled nearly 1,700 hours.

Overseas flights included eight in support of Canadian forces in Europe, most of which were routed directly to Marville instead of Langar. Of the sixteen UN flights, six went to El Arish and ten to Léopoldville. Two flights on their way back to Pisa from Kano were redirected to carry out special runs: one to Wildenrath to take some Canadian soldiers home, and the other to Baden-Söllingen to support the deployment of a fighter squadron to the Air Weapons Unit at Decimomannu. From there, the crew conducted a passenger and cargo run to Grostenquin before positioning at Langar for the return to Trenton.[48]

On 9 June, RCAF Station Trenton celebrated the official opening of No 10 (Cantilever) Hangar and the christening of the CC-106. Chief of the Air Staff Air Marshal H. Campbell and Mrs. Campbell arrived from Ottawa at 1200 hours, accompanied by Air Vice Marshal W.A. Orr (Air Member Personnel), Air Commodore Whiting (Chief of Construction Engineering) and several Montreal-based representatives of Canadair and Rolls-Royce. The author was assigned to escort Mrs. Campbell to Air Commodore Carpenter's residence and to hand over the "christening chit" for the CC-106, which — following Air Marshal Campbell's choice — would be called the Yukon.

At 1500 hours, the guests of honour and spectators took their places in the stands erected for the event near No 10 Hangar. The ceremony began with a parade of aircraft — the CC-106, a Hercules, a Caribou, a Cosmopolitan, an Albatross and an Otter — from which the marching contingents and the colour party emerged onto the tarmac. After inspecting the parade and giving his speech, the Air Marshal declared No 10 Hangar officially open and the colour party escorted a CC-106 as it was towed out of the hangar to the dais where Mrs. Campbell performed the naming ritual in Navy fashion: by smashing a bottle of champagne on the nose. That done, the parade was dismissed, followed that evening by a well-attended reception and buffet dinner at the Officers' Mess.[49]

Two important announcements concerning RCAF air defence were made on 12 June: Canada was to take over the eleven stations of the Pinetree Line from the Americans, and purchase sixty-six McDonnell F-101B Voodoo supersonic jet fighters. On 24 July, the Pinetree Line station at Beausejour, Manitoba, was the first formally handed over to the RCAF. The Voodoo acquisition was a more complex matter, however. Its top speed was more than 1,200 miles per hour, and it was fully effective only when equipped with nuclear weapons. Four RCAF home-defence squadrons were slated for disbandment before year's end, and No 425 AW(F) Squadron at St-Hubert had been de-activated on 1 May in preparation for conversion to the Voodoo aircraft; on 15 October, it was re-activated at Namao, having completed crew training, and thus became the first RCAF squadron to fly the Voodoo aircraft. In July 1962, after serving as a training unit to convert four other squadrons to the new aircraft, No 425 moved to RCAF Station Bagotville. As the CF-101B entered service, three Canuck squadrons were disbanded: No 428 AW(F) Squadron at Uplands on 31 May; No 433 AW(F) Squadron at North Bay on 31 July; and No 432 AW(F) Squadron at Bagotville on 15 October.[50]

On 23 June, a formal farewell mess dinner was held for Air Commodore F.S. Carpenter at the Officers' Mess, and on 27 June a formal change-of-command parade was held at Trenton for the transfer of Air Transport Command from Air Commodore Carpenter to Air Commodore Lane. Carpenter had served as Air Officer Commanding, Air Transport Command since 6 August 1956.[51]

In addition to the usual range of scheduled and special domestic flights, No 426 Squadron took part in *Operation HOPPER STOPPER* at the request of the government of Saskatchewan, which was so plagued by grasshoppers and cutworms that crop failures were imminent. In seventeen flights — six by Hercules, three by North Star, and eight by C-119 Boxcar, Air Transport Command airlifted 330,807 pounds of insecticide from Toronto to Regina. The two C-119s from No 435 Squadron at Namao also airlifted 23,968 pounds of insecticide from Toronto to Lethbridge for the Alberta government.[52]

During the last week in June, while Flight Lieutenant Adam and his slip crew were on a layover in Marville, flight engineer Sergeant George Brasseur and transportation technician Corporal Vern Downey were in a serious car accident. They had been to Verdun with Sergeant Frank Campbell, an airframe technician stationed at Marville, travelling in Campbell's Volkswagen. On the way back to base, a large car attempting to pass the Volkswagen sideswiped it, knocking the little car right off the road and into a tree. Thrown out of the car, Sergeant Brasseur was knocked out and badly bruised. Sergeant Campbell suffered a broken leg and other injuries, and Corporal Downey was killed outright.[53]

On 29 June, Wing Commander K. Trumley, commanding officer of No 115 ATU at El Arish, left for Canada on SF 58 on posting to Air Force Headquarters. His replacement, Wing Commander H.R. Knight, did not arrive until 26 July, so Flight Lieutenant Read was Acting CO in the interim.[54]

At the end of June, plans were finalized for the redeployment of sixteen North Star aircraft released from the transport role. Two were to go to CEPE in Ottawa, one for Electronic Countermeasures and the other to the National Aeronautical Establishment. Four would be allocated for training: two at No 4 OTU at Trenton for crew training, and two to the Central Navigation School in Winnipeg for navigation training. Five North Stars would be transferred to search and rescue duties: two with No 111 KU at Winnipeg, and three with No 107 RU at Torbay. One North Star would be kept in reserve, and four would eventually be declared surplus to requirements. The tentative schedule for the release of the North Stars was as follows:
- two from No 412 Squadron between 1 January and 1 April 1962;
- six from No 426 Squadron between 1 January and 1 June 1962; and,
- six from No 426 Squadron between 1 June and 1 September 1962.

The last two North Stars were already at No 4 OTU, where they would remain.[55]

July

The squadron's domestic and overseas flying commitments for July totalled nearly 1,750 hours. Scheduled overseas runs included nine in support of the Air Division and 4 Brigade in Europe, which staged through Lajes and Marville. One special to Northolt, near London, brought thirty-five Air Cadets to Britain for an exchange visit, and an equal number of Air Training Corps cadets went to Canada on the return flight. Sixteen flights were carried out during the month in support of UN operations: five to El Arish and eleven to Léopoldville. On 8 July, a flight to El Arish ran into some difficulties: NS17504 (captained by Wing Commander Maitland) had its No 1 engine fail shortly after leaving Pisa, and Maitland returned to base on three engines. The Servicing Detachment rectified the problem, and the flight resumed in the morning.[56]

On top of its international commitments, the squadron completed a variety of scheduled and special flights within North America. The seasonal large-scale movement of regular and reserve personnel from all three services, and of cadets to and from training and duty stations, contributed significantly to the increased workload.

In addition to the monthly scheduled flights to the north, a special was despatched to Alert. Squadron Leader Marshall and his crew left Trenton on 28 July in NS17508 for Frobisher Bay, flight of a six and a half hours. After the aircraft was refuelled, the flight carried on to Alert which took six hours and ten minutes more. As soon as the passengers and cargo were unloaded, Marshall proceeded to Thule (two hours and twenty minutes), where a crew rest was taken. On 30 July, the flight returned directly to Trenton, taking eleven hours to complete the trip.[57]

Trenton, 1961

The crisis that arose over Berlin in 1961 was to have a significant impact on Canada's armed forces in general and No 426 Squadron in particular. On 2 June, President John F. Kennedy of the United States went to Vienna for two days of meetings with Soviet Premier Nikita Krushchev, who again declared his intention (first expressed in 1958) to make a separate treaty with East Germany by the end of the year if the Soviet plan for Berlin was not accepted. He made it plain that the separate treaty would abrogate the four-power agreements under which Britain, France and the United States were guaranteed access to West Berlin. The three Western powers responded that no treaty entered into unilaterally by the Soviets could nullify their responsibilities and rights in West Berlin, including the right of unobstructed access.

In 1961, West Berlin was the main exit point for refugees from East Germany, and the flow of emigrants was reaching serious proportions. About 103,000 people left East Germany for the West between January and June 1961, compared with 199,000 for the whole of the previous year. By early August 1961, the stream of refugees into West Berlin had topped 3,000 per day. In years past, emigrants from the east were mostly young people of working age, but now an increasing proportion of those leaving the German Democratic Republic were professionals and students whose skills were urgently required for the country's internal development. East Germany's faltering economy, already critically short of manpower, may have been the primary reason for the measures taken to curtail movements into West Berlin.

Early in July, the German Democratic Republic began restricting the movements of the 52,000 East Germans who worked in West Berlin, and they were eventually directed to jobs in the East German economy. On 13 August, all movement stopped between East and West Berlin, and barriers appeared on the boundary between the two parts of the city, and between West Berlin and the surrounding East German territory. Named the Berlin Wall, this barrier effectively sealed the East Germans' best escape route, halting the mass movement of the people to the West. On 20 August, the West Berlin garrison was increased by 1,500 fresh American troops and armoured fighting vehicles for both the U.S. and British contingents. Wih the Wall in place, Berlin gradually settled down to an uneasy and sometimes dangerous truce, and the crisis did not ease appreciably until the following spring.[58]

August

The August flying commitments for the squadron's thirteen North Stars came to about 1,700 hours. As well as a variety of domestic scheduled and special runs, the unit despatched twenty-six international flights, including nine routed to Marville in support of Canadian forces in Europe, and seventeen UN flights staged through Pisa: six to El Arish in support of UNEF, and eleven to Léopoldville on behalf of ONUC.[59]

The convoy of ships laden with cargo for the resupply of Resolute Bay and the Joint Arctic Weather Stations sailed from Montreal on 30 July and 31 July. While the convoy was en route, the eight-day airlift of fuel and supplies from Thule to Alert in support of the Army signals unit

(*Operation BOXTOP 5*) commenced on 2 August, with two Hercules from No 435 Squadron airlifting about 600 tons of cargo from Thule, where it was landed from the ships by a detachment of Canadian soldiers flown in for the job. The Hercules also transported some of the 400 tons of Department of Transport supplies to Alert. Completed by 10 August, *Operation BOXTOP 5* eased some of the airlift requirement that would have been necessary in the fall of 1961 and the spring of 1962. The resupply convoy reached Resolute Bay on 13 August, discharged its cargo by 23 August, and then sailed for Montreal.[60]

During the month, 1,000 soldiers had to be airlifted to Newfoundland to fight severe forest fires. Air Transport Command assigned ten aircraft to this operation, including North Stars from No 426 Squadron and No 4 OTU, C-119s from No 436 Squadron, and Hercules from No 435 Squadron. Helicopters from Chatham, Greenwood and Trenton were also deployed to take soldiers and other firefighters to the fire lines, survey the fire to ensure the best deployment of firefighters, and evacuate people from threatened areas.[61]

Several transfers from the squadron provided the occasion for a farewell party at the Officers' Mess on 5 August. Pilots Flight Lieutenant D. Kuhn and Flight Lieutenant M.G. (Mac) Morrison and navigator Flying Officer J. Bourgeois were transferred to Air Transport Command Headquarters. Flight Lieutenant J. Coates, the squadron's Radio Leader, was posted to No 2 Air Observer School at Winnipeg. The author, too, was posted out, heading for the RCAF Staff College in Toronto for the next one-year course.[62]

The NATO countries responded to the construction and closure of the Berlin Wall with a display of force. MATS supported the deployment of the Combined Air Strike Force to NATO bases in Europe between 4 September and 7 September, and the sudden appearance of 170 tactical fighters with nuclear-delivery capability may have changed Krushchev's mind with respect to a separate treaty with the German Democratic Republic — on 17 October, he withdrew the threat during a speech in Moscow. The build-up of American forces in Europe continued with the airlift by MATS of nearly 10,000 soldiers and some 2,380 tons of cargo between 31 October and 27 November. MATS was also tasked to move sixty F-104 Starfighters to West Germany during November.[63]

In a statement to the House of Commons on 7 September, Prime Minister John Diefenbaker announced that the Government of Canada, after consultation with allied governments in NATO, had concluded that certain measures should be taken to strengthen Canada's preparedness for defence both at home and overseas. The government had decided to increase the overseas and naval forces assigned to NATO as follows:
- to bring the crews of HMC ships up to strength for a prolonged emergency, the present establishment was to be increased by 1,749 officers and ratings;

- the 4th Canadian Infantry Brigade in Europe was to be strengthened by 1,106 officers and other ranks, with 1,515 reinforcements readily available in Canada; and
- No 1 Air Division in Europe was to be strengthened by 250 officers and airmen.

To allow for the strengthening of 4 Brigade and No 1 Air Division, and for future increases, the establishment deployed in Europe was raised from 12,000 all ranks to 14,000 by Order-in-Council. The increases to NATO-assigned forces were to be accomplished by transferring fully trained personnel from the home establishment.

In order to improve the general military effectiveness of Canadian forces at home, particularly those earmarked for the strategic reserve and available for use in Europe, the government intended to increase the Army by 8,950 officers and other ranks, and the Air Force by 989 personnel. To make this increase legal under the *National Defence Act*, an Order-in-Council raised the combined regular establishment of the Canadian Army, the Royal Canadian Navy and the Royal Canadian Air Force from 120,000 to 135,000 soldiers, sailors and airmen.[64]

September

The squadron's domestic and international commitments for September totalled nearly 1,850 hours. Nine scheduled flights went to Marville, and sixteen flights staged through Pisa for the UN: six flights to El Arish, and and ten to Léopoldville. Only one overseas flight encountered trouble. On 21 September, Squadron Leader Marshall was leaving Lajes for Gander in NS17515 when the No 1 engine failed shortly after take-off, compelling him to turn back on three engines. Following an engine change, the flight returned to base.[65]

The Berlin Crisis focussed attention on Canada's rather frugal strategic airlift capability. The teething troubles that normally accompany the introduction of a new aircraft meant that it would be several months before the Yukons would be fully operational with crews and support systems. Thus, for long-range transport, the RCAF had only No 426 Squadron and its obsolescent North Stars to handle the continuing urgent requirement to support No 1 Air Division and 4 Brigade in Europe, and the Canadian contingents in UNEF and ONUC. In these circumstances, No 426 Squadron had to be retained in the transport role, but with the Yukons coming on strength, Trenton had no room for North Stars. At the same time, it did not make sense to break up No 426 Squadron, and have part of it operating Yukons from Trenton and another part flying North Stars from somewhere else. In a submission to the Air Council, Air Commodore Lane had recommended the retention of No 426 Squadron as a North Star unit, located at St-Hubert. He also recommended reforming No 437 Squadron and equipping it with the Yukon.

There was historical precedent for activating No 437 Squadron as a long-range transport unit: its motto was *Omnia passim* — "anything, anywhere". Formed in England in September 1944, No 437 Squadron became part of No 120 (Transport) Wing on 17 September 1945 when the wing was formed as part of No 46 Group, RAF Transport Command. No 120 Wing comprised No 435 Squadron at Down Ampney, Gloucestershire, and No 436 and No 437 squadrons at Odiham, Hampshire. No 120 Wing Headquarters moved from London to Odiham on 7 October 1945, and its Dakota aircraft provided airlift support for Canadian units assigned to the Occupation force in Germany. The wing was commanded by Group Captain R.J. Lane from 15 January to 12 June 1946, and disbanded on 30 June 1946.

The Air Council approved the recommendation to retain No 426 Squadron and move it to St-Hubert. The move would take place as soon as possible after No 437 Squadron became fully operational with the Yukon. On 28 September, Minister of National Defence Douglas Harkness announced this plan in the House of Commons.[66]

When the UN made an urgent appeal for additional airlift, the Canadian government responded by offering (after some delay) two C-119s with flight crews and ground support personnel. The Cabinet Decision was rendered on 23 September, and the next morning two No 436 Squadron C119s departed for the Congo, accompanied by a No 435 Squadron Hercules carrying two extra crews, servicing personnel, spare parts and ground handling equipment. Routed by way of Torbay, Lajes, Nouasseur, Dakar and Lagos, the C-119s arrived at Léopoldville on 1 October.

The No 436 Squadron detachment at Léopoldville, which was commanded by Flight Lieutenant R.R. Flynn, was mainly involved in transporting vehicles to destinations in the Congo. This operation began to wind down toward the end of November, when spare crews and servicing personnel began returning to Canada on the North Star flights. Both C-119s departed Léopoldville on 29 November, returning to Canada by way of Kano, Idris and Pisa and arriving at Downsview on 5 December.[67]

On 18 September, UN Secretary-General Dag Hammarskjöld died in an air crash in the jungle about ten miles from N'dola airport in Northern Rhodesia. He was going to a meeting with Moise Tshombe in the hope of negotiating a cease-fire between the UN and the forces of Katanga. Hammarskjöld's replacement as the UN Secretary-General was U Thant from Burma.[68]

During the fall resupply of the Joint Arctic Weather Stations, which took place in last two weeks of September and first part of October, nearly 780,000 pounds of cargo were airlifted to Isachsen, Mould Bay, Eureka and Alert by two C-130s (Hercules) and two C-119s (Boxcars) from No 435 Squadron based at Station Namao. In carrying out this operation, the Hercules logged 167 flying hours and the Boxcars a total of 125 hours.[69]

October

The squadron's workload eased somewhat during October, with a flying commitment of 1,680 hours. Aside from the scheduled and special domestic runs, the unit was tasked with twenty-five overseas flights, nine to Marville and the sixteen to Pisa. From Pisa, five flights proceeded to El Arish and eleven went to Léopoldville.

The 7 October flight to El Arish brought two senior officers from Air Transport Command Headquarters — Group Captain W.H. Schroeder, the Chief Staff Officer, and Wing Commander Butcher, Senior Personnel Staff Officer — to inspect No 115 ATU's facilities at the Marina and the airport, and to visit UNEF Headquarters in Gaza. Both departed for Trenton by SF 58 on 12 October.[70]

Air Force Headquarters Organization Order 8.9.1 was issued on 3 October to incorporate those organizational changes occasioned by the activation of No 437 (T) Squadron, equipped with

Yukon aircraft, and the decision to make No 426 Squadron self-supporting as a lodger unit at St-Hubert, which was not an Air Transport Command station, sometime after 1 January 1962. The squadron's role was to provide air transport as directed by the Air Officer Commanding, Air Transport Command, and to carry out air evacuation from isolated units from time to time. For command and control, the Commanding Officer was the Station Commander at Trenton, and officer appointed to command No 426 Squadron was designated "Officer Commanding". Control was to be exercised by the Air Officer Commanding, Air Transport Command, through the Commanding Officer, RCAF Station Trenton.

On 19 October, Wing Commander J.O. Maitland, CD, was appointed Officer Commanding, No 437 (T) Squadron. The following day, Wing Commander A.J. Mackie, DFC, CD, became Officer Commanding, No 426 (T) Squadron for the second time. The formal change of command was scheduled for the end of November, so Squadron Leader J.R. Marshall was acting OC until then.[71]

Immediately after the government decided to increase the size of the RCAF, No 1 Air Division and Air Transport Command were expanded: 208 airmen went to Europe on restricted transfers (without dependants), the imminent repatriation of 200 airmen from Europe was cancelled, and 350 airmen were posted to Air Transport Command units at RCAF Station Trenton to meet the increased commitments in the North Star and Yukon programs. Most of these airmen were experienced aircraft tradesmen, and some of those posted to Air Transport Command were later transferred to St-Hubert with the move of No 426 Squadron.[72]

November

November's flying commitments for the squadron's thirteen North Stars totalled nearly 1,700 hours. Most of the effort was on overseas commitments, with nine scheduled flights terminating in Marville in support of the Air Division and 4 Brigade, and fifteen flights staging through Pisa in support of UN operations. Five UN flights went to El Arish, and ten went to Léopoldville.[73]

On 8 November, a special flight was despatched to the Caribbean: Flight Lieutenant Smith and his crew in NS17521, taking a load of relief and Red Cross supplies for the victims of a devastating hurricane from Downsview to Belize City in the British Honduras via an overnight stop at New Orleans. After unloading at Belize City the next day, Smith and his crew returned to New Orleans. On 10 November, after taking on another load of supplies, the flight was positioned in Mexico City, where more relief supplies were loaded for delivery to Belize City the following day, after which the flight proceeded to New Orleans. Smith and his crew were back in Trenton on 12 November.[74]

During the month, the Congolese seized one of the first Yukons to arrive in Léopoldville, mistaking it for a Soviet aircraft. Consequently, the Canadian government barred the Yukon from Congo operations, and the RCAF had great difficulty obtaining permission to resume Yukon flights on the Congo run.[75]

Upon assuming command of No 426 Squadron at the end of the month, Wing Commander Mackie appointed Squadron Leader J.R. Marshall as the Squadron Operations Officer and Squadron Leader H.G. Herbert as Aircrew Leader. The squadron's primary role would be to carry out scheduled flights on behalf of the UN in the Middle East and Africa; its secondary role would be to conduct routine scheduled flights to fulfill domestic commitments. Planning was under way for January's move to St-Hubert.

December

Squadron taskings during December totalled 1,453 flying hours, mostly on scheduled overseas runs. Eight overseas flights were routed to Marville in support of No 1 Air Division and 4 Brigade. Of the fifteen UN flights, five went to El Arish and ten to Léopoldville. A special flight was despatched to airlift the personnel and equipment of No 407(MP) Squadron from RCAF Station Comox to Ballykelly, Northern Ireland; on completion of the deployment exercise, personnel and equipment were airlifted back to Comox.[76]

On 13 December, an advance party headed by Flight Lieutenant B.V. Genge moved to St-Hubert to arrange for the squadron's re-location, which was scheduled for 3 January 1962.

All flight crews and detachment personnel were returned for Christmas. Due to a staggered system of time off, the squadron ceased operations for only one day — Christmas Day. The unit's personnel spent Christmas quietly with family and friends. Church services were well attended and, in keeping with Air Force tradition, designated officers served Christmas dinner to the airmen and airwomen living in quarters.

On 28 December, Flight Lieutenant Schwanky and his crew in the first post-Christmas North Star left Trenton for Pisa with the slip crews and detachment personnel ready to resume UN operations. Those at Trenton on New Year's Eve attended the parties, dances and entertainment organized by all the messes on the station.[77]

PHOTO 192

Ambassador Mario Rodriguez of Chile presents the author with Chilean Air Force aircrew wings; RCAF Station Trenton, 21 April 1961. (L. Motiuk Collection)

PHOTO 193
Sgt. W. Wiser supervises Air Congo workers fuelling a North Star at N'Djili Airport; Léopoldville, Congo, 26 May 1961. (DND PL 124720)

Part V

Disbandment

St-Hubert, January–October 1962

CHAPTER 26

ST-HUBERT
JANUARY—OCTOBER 1962

The conduct of operational suitability trials that led to the introduction of the CC-106 Yukon into RCAF service was the responsibility of Yukon Flight, an *ad hoc* sub-unit formed early in 1961 as part of No 426 Squadron under the command of Squadron Leader W.R. Lloyd. Yukon Flight became the nucleus of No 437 Squadron on that unit's re-formation on 1 October 1961.

The first overseas trial of the Yukon began on 10 August 1961, when Squadron Leader Lloyd and his crew in Yukon 15930 departed Trenton for No 1 Wing at Marville, a direct night flight arriving in the morning with an escort of by two fighters ceremonially scrambled by the Air Division. By October, the number of Yukon flights had increased to six per month, and on 13 October, the first Yukon flight to Léopoldville was despatched: Yukon 15930, captained by Squadron Leader Hlady. Staging through Marville to Pisa, the flight then proceeded directly to Léopoldville, a run of ten hours and fifty minutes, with the return taking ten hours and fifteen minutes. The second flight, in November, was the one temporarily seized by the Congolese authorities.[1]

January

On 4 January, Yukon 15927, captained by Squadron Leader Lloyd, was the year's first scheduled flight to arrive at Marville from Trenton. At this early stage of Yukon operations, flights to Marville averaged ten hours outbound and eleven hours for the return to Trenton, and were despatched at the rate of one passenger run and three freight runs per week. Capable of airlifting up to 120 people on a passenger flight and about 25,000 pounds of cargo on a freight run, the Yukon had more than three times the capacity of the North Star, and did not need two refuelling stops en route. By March, the Yukons would be making most of the passenger and freight runs to Europe in support of No 1 Air Division and 4 Brigade, which came to at least twenty-three flights per month.

Consequently, the primary role of No 426 Squadron's twelve North Stars became airlift support for UNEF in the Middle East and ONUC in the Congo. In Canada, the squadron continued to be tasked with a variety of scheduled and special flights, including service to the far north. The squadron's monthly flying commitments were reduced by about twenty-five percent from levels assigned for the previous year, and this reduced level would be maintained until the end of August, when the squadron was disbanded.[2]

Immediately after the New Year holiday, No 426 Squadron set about completing the move to St-Hubert: on 3 January and 4 January, twenty-two truckloads of equipment and four aircraft loaded with equipment and personnel were despatched. The last two squadron North Stars left for their new base on 5 January, and on 6 January, the squadron was fully operational at its new base with no disruptions in its schedule.[3]

During the month, the squadron flew a total of 1,228 hours, including 1,006 hours on regular scheduled flights.

The month's overseas taskings included five flights to El Arish and eleven to Léopoldville. Complications arose when the French authorities — suspecting that RCAF aircraft on ONUC missions were entering French airspace — refused to grant permission for RCAF aircraft to overfly French territory, which meant re-routing and rescheduling all flights to Léopoldville. The Canadian Ambassador in Paris was told that the decision was made at the highest levels, but was not directed at Canada. In the end, after diplomatic negotiations, the flights were allowed to continue on their original routes.[4]

The 20 January flight to El Arish brought Air Commodore R.J. Lane to No 115 ATU to conduct his annual inspection, accompanied by his Executive Assistant, Squadron Leader D.C. MacKenzie. After a greeting from the commanding officer, Wing Commander H.R. Knight, the Air Commodore inspected a guard of honour commanded by Flight Lieutenant G.U. Springer, and then proceeded to the Marina for an informal luncheon at the Officers' Mess. That evening, the Air Commodore was guest of honour at a mess dinner attended by General Gyani, Commander UNEF, and his aide, Captain Mickelson; Colonel Stevenson, Commander CBUME and Acting Chief of Staff, UNEF; Group Captain Langstaff, Canadian Air, Military and Naval Attaché in Cairo; Wing Commander Sanford, Air Staff Officer at UNEF HQ, Gaza; and Lieutenant Colonel Pierce-Goulding, Chief Logistics Officer, UNEF HQ. On 24 January, Air Commodore Lane inspected No 115 ATU, commencing at 0830 hours with a parade at the airport, at which thirty-three officers and airmen received UNEF medals. Following the parade the Air Commodore went first to the headquarters building for a meeting with Wing Commander Knight, and then to the Marina to inspect the domestic facilities. Air Commodore Lane and Squadron Leader MacKenzie departed El Arish by North Star on SF 318, at 0900 hours on 25 January.[5]

January's domestic flights included the weekly trans-Canada run originating at St-Hubert and proceeded to Trenton, Winnipeg, Edmonton, Vancouver and Comox, the new western terminus of the air transport system, which was still on a trial basis. From Comox, the flight proceeded to Port Hardy and Vancouver. The four-day flight returned to base by way of Edmonton, Winnipeg and Trenton. A scheduled seven-day northern flight was taken out on 11 January by Flight Lieutenant Gawne in NS17504. After positioning at Trenton the flight left for Winnipeg, Churchill, Resolute Bay, Alert and Thule, then returning to Resolute Bay before leaving for Churchill and Winnipeg. From there, the flight continued to Edmonton and Whitehorse, and returned to base by way of Edmonton, Winnipeg and Trenton.[6]

At the end of 1961, No 413 AW(F) Squadron at Bagotville became the fourth and last of the nine CF-100 units in Canada to be disbanded; by March 1962, No 409 Squadron at Comox, No 410 Squadron at Uplands, No 414 Squadron at North Bay, and No 416 Squadron and No 425 Squadron at Bagotville would be re-equipped with the CF-101B Voodoo. The reorientation of Air Defence Command was completed with the creation of two new units equipped with the nuclear-capable Boeing CIM-10B Bomarc surface-to-air missile: No 446 (SAM) Squadron, activated at North Bay on 28 December 1961, and No 447 (SAM) Squadron, formed at La Macaza, Quebec, on 15 September 1962. At the end of the year, No 419, No 423, No 440 and No 445 AW(F) squadrons, all in No 1 Air Division, were all disbanded.[7]

February

In February, No 426 Squadron flew a total of 1,220 hours, including 1,177 hours on routine service flights.

Overseas runs included five to El Arish and eleven to Léopoldville. While at El Arish on 3 February, a squadron aircraft conducted several shuttles to Beirut to facilitate the rotation of Canadian troops, who were airlifted to Canada by Yukon. UN aircraft were still not permitted to fly over French territory, and all North Stars returning to Canada from Pisa were routed over Spain.

As well as the weekly scheduled flights to the west coast, the squadron carried out a northern run to Resolute Bay, Alert and Whitehorse, and on 3 February, cargo and passengers were airlifted for Maritime Command from Greenwood to Jacksonville, Florida. A second Maritime Command support flight was carried out on 15 February, leaving HMCS *Shearwater* for Bermuda and Jacksonville and returning to Greenwood.[8]

On 2 February, NS17520, captained by Flight Lieutenant T. Merrick of No 412 Squadron, crashed at Hall Beach, North West Territories. About two minutes after take-off, when the aircraft had reached 1,000 feet, the No 2 engine began to run rough and the oil pressure dropped to zero. Thirty seconds later, No 3 engine malfunctioned the same way, and No 4 engine soon began to siphon oil. Forced to carry out a wheels-up landing, Merrick attempted an approach to the Hall Beach runway but the visibility was so poor that he could not see it clearly, so he crash-landed NS17520. No one aboard was hurt, and all passengers and crew members were evacuated without difficulty. The aircraft was scrapped.[9]

On 20 February, the launch from Cape Canaveral of NASA astronaut John Glenn was observed from 40,000 feet by CF-100 crews deployed on *Operation LOOKOUT*, who also measured the infra-red rays and radiation emissions associated with the rocket launch, in co-operation with USAF U-2s flying above them and C-119s flying below.[10]

In his address to the AOCs' Conference at the end of February, Air Vice Marshal D.M. Smith (Vice Chief of the Air Staff) touched on several issues pertaining to Air Transport Command. The RCAF air transport capability had its nerve centre at the Air Transport Operations Centre, the focal point of communications and the source of command and direction for all components of the transport system, to which two new types of long-range aircraft had been introduced. For the Yukon, twelve had been ordered, all necessary tests were completed, eight were already delivered, and regular services had been inaugurated. Some problems had appeared in engines and airframes, but that situation was improving, and did not affect the operation of the aircraft. Four Hercules aircraft had been procured, and authority was being sought for the acquisition for two more, thus providing six aircraft against the requirement for a long-range bulk carrier. So far, the Hercules had been used almost exclusively on Arctic flights and trans-Atlantic operations, but the plan for transporting the new CF-104 Starfighter called for packing them into the Hercules. Since the Hercules was the most suitable replacement for both the North Star and the C-119s, the real requirement was for a fleet of at least thirty-two.

In his remarks, the Air Vice Marshal mentioned that the retention of the North Star as a transport aircraft was one result of the Berlin Crisis of 1961, and that the RCAF fleet could be maintained until 1966 — although a need for the indefinite retention of No 426 Squadron had yet to be identified. At that time, the North Stars were operating out of Pisa to support UN operations in the Middle East and the Congo.[11]

March

During March, No 426 Squadron logged 1,387 flying hours, almost all on scheduled domestic and overseas missions. Of the sixteen flights conducted in support of UN operations, five went to El Arish and eleven to Léopoldville. On 18 March, Flight Lieutenant Walton captained a flight extension from Pisa to Stockholm, taking thirty-four Swedish soldiers and airmen who had departed Léopoldville on 16 March home to Stockholm with as few stops as possible. Domestic commitments included the weekly flight to Comox and the northern run to Resolute Bay, Alert and Whitehorse.[12]

April

No 426 Squadron logged a total of 1,081 flying hours in April, including 720 hours on operations out of Pisa.

On 2 April, Flight Lieutenant Johnston left St-Hubert on the last scheduled flight to Comox and Port Hardy. On 9 April, Flight Lieutenant Owston departed base bound for the DEW Line to take a party from Air Defence Command on a tour of sites including Hall Beach, Cambridge Bay and Cape Parry, and returning to base by way of Cold Lake. On 16 April, Flight Lieutenant Gawne and his crew positioned their North Star at Trenton, where they joined a convoy of ten C-45 Expeditors as mother ship for the ferry flight routed to the French Air Force base at Chateaudun through Goose Bay, Frobisher Bay, Sondrestrom, Keflavik, Prestwick and Marville. That mission took two weeks to complete. From Pisa, the squadron conducted sixteen UN flights during April: five to El Arish and eleven to Léopoldville.[13]

May

On 5 May, the Honourable Paul Comptois, Lieutenant-Governor of Quebec, came to RCAF Station St-Hubert to present colour standards to No 401 Squadron and No 438 Squadron, both Auxiliary units. The military and civilian dignitaries in attendance included the Chief of the Air Staff, Air Marshal Hugh Campbell; and the Air Officer Commanding, Air Defence Command, Air Vice Marshal W.R. MacBrien.[14]

On 6 May, two complete crews captained by Flight Lieutenant Walton and Flight Lieutenant Price left base for Winnipeg in NS17516; the next morning, after embarking Central Navigation School instructors and the students of No 14 Specialist Navigation Course, the flight proceeded to Resolute Bay via Churchill. Over the next several days, a series of long-range navigation exercises — not including an overflight of the North Pole — was conducted from Resolute Bay. The North Star returned to St-Hubert on 15 May after disembarking the CNS staff and students at Winnipeg.[15]

During May, No 426 Squadron logged a total of 1,085 flying hours. Its overseas commitments were all UN-related, with five flights to El Arish and eleven to Léopoldville. On 9 May, a flight to El Arish from Pisa brought in a CBC entertainment troupe featuring the cast of *The Tommy Hunter Show*, who visited all the UNEF contingents and helped celebrate Canada Day at Camp Rafah on 19 May. On 24 May, the troupe left for Pisa and their return flight to Canada. On 14 May, Flight Lieutenant Schroder and his crew airlifted the thirty-six-man band of The Royal Canadian Dragoons from RAF Station Gütersloh to Athens and El Arish. The band played for the Canada Day festivities at Camp Rafah and then toured the other UNEF units. Restrictions on overflights of French territory were rescinded on 16 May, permitting the North Stars to go back to using the inland route from Kano to Léopoldville. On 25 May, Flight Lieutenant Gawne carried out a special UN flight, airlifting passengers and cargo from Pisa to Oslo and Stockholm and returning to Pisa the following day.[16]

By mid-May, the placement of liaison officers at Goose Bay, Sondrestrom, Keflavik, Prestwick and Chateaudun was arranged in preparation for *Operation WESTERN WEAL*, the ferrying of fifty T-33 Silver Star jets to Europe, where they were to be given to several NATO countries under the Mutual Aid agreement. As ten aircraft were going to Greece, the flight crews would need to fly back to Canada from Athens. About 130 RCAF personnel were involved in WESTERN WEAL.

The first convoy of twelve Silver Stars left Trenton for Goose Bay on 23 May, followed by NS17510, captained by Flight Lieutenant McBurney, carrying a servicing crew and spare parts. On 24 May, the jets made two hops, to Sondrestrom and Keflavik, and on 25 May the entire convoy arrived at Prestwick where the operation was held up for several days by weather and maintenance problems. On 28 May, the Silver Stars flew to Marville and Chateaudun, followed by McBurney. The next day, the ferry pilots boarded the North Star and McBurney returned to Marville to pick up the servicing crew. On 30 May, the flight departed for Canada by way of Shannon, Keflavik, Goose Bay and Trenton, where the ferry personnel were dropped off, and arrived back at St-Hubert in the afternoon of 31 May. Three more ferry flights were scheduled to complete the delivery of the fifty Silver Stars.[17]

June

In June, pilots began training at Cold Lake with the CF-104 Starfighter, the new strike reconnaissance aircraft with which eight fighter squadrons in Europe were to be re-equipped. The first graduates would emerge from this conversion programme in November. Between December 1962 and March 1964, the Starfighter was introduced to the six strike-attack squadrons — No 421, No 422, No 427, No 430, No 434 and No 444 — and the two strike reconnaissance squadrons — No 439 and No 441.[18]

During the month of June, No 426 Squadron logged a total of 1,537 flying hours, a marked increase over the last few months. Domestic taskings accounted for most of the increase. Seventeen UN flights were completed, including six to El Arish and eleven to Léopoldville.

On 11 June, Flight Lieutenant Schwanky and his crew positioned NS17516 in Trenton to be the mother ship for another convoy of Silver Stars going to Europe. The following morning, the twelve jets departed for Goose Bay followed by the North Star with the servicing crew and spare parts. The convoy made the double hop to Sondrestrom and Keflavik on 13 June and went on to Prestwick the next day. On 18 June, they convoy reached Marville, refuelled, and carried on to Chateaudun. On 20 June, Schwanky and his crew embarked the ferry pilots, flew to Marville, boarded the servicing crew, and departed for Keflavik, where they spent the night. The next day, the flight proceeded to Trenton, dropped off the ferry personnel. Schwanky and his crew were back at St-Hubert on 22 June.[19]

July

By July, the future of No 426 Squadron was a topic of serious consideration. The situation in and around Berlin had eased considerably and many RCAF long-range airlift commitments had been transferred to the Yukon fleet.

The squadron's taskings in July totalled 1,351 flying hours, most of it on overseas missions. Sixteen UN flights were conducted from Pisa: five to El Arish and eleven to Léopoldville. On 21 July, in response to a UN request received by the Canadian Permanent Mission in New York, Flight Lieutenant Schwanky and his crew in NS17504 left Léopoldville for Kano, the first leg of a flight to Tunis repatriating the bodies of seven Tunisian soldiers killed in the Congo. The next day they completed their mission to Tunis and departed for Pisa. On 29 July, Flight Lieutenant Walton captained NS17521 on a special UN flight to Copenhagen and Oslo, first to take forty-four Danish soldiers home and then to pick up forty-five Norwegian soldiers and bring them to Pisa for the flight to the Congo.[20]

On 3 July, the squadron provided a mother ship for the third convoy of twelve Silver Stars bound for Chateaudun. Leaving Trenton the next day, the convoy was routed by way of Goose Bay, Sondrestrom, Keflavik, Prestwick and Marville, arriving at Chateaudun on 9 July. The North Star returned to Trenton on 11 July with the ferry pilots and the servicing crew. The fourth convoy of *Operation WESTERN WEAL* left Trenton on 23 July, again supported by a North Star mother

ship carrying the servicing crew and spare parts and using the same route to Chateaudun. From the French base, the convoy proceeded to Athens, where the North Star picked up the ferry pilots and servicing crews for the trip back to Canada.[21]

On 31 July, an amendment to AFHQ Organization Order 8.21(L) bluntly stated that, as part of the government's austerity program, No 426 Squadron would be disbanded with effect from 31 August. The unit's fate was not announced until 15 August, when Air Commodore Lane visited St-Hubert to deliver the sad news at an all-ranks assembly at the Station Theatre, explaining the decision as one result of government direction to effect economies and reduce federal spending.

RCAF commitments for North Star transport out of Pisa for the United Nations could not be terminated as of 31 August, however. Operations at Pisa were not wound up until mid-September.[22]

August

Despite No 426 Squadron's pending disbandment, its domestic and overseas flying commitments in August totalled 1,375 flying hours, including sixteen scheduled UN flights from Pisa: five to El Arish and eleven to Léopoldville. On 16 August, Flight Lieutenant McAlpine captained NS17521 on a special flight from Pisa to Oslo to repatriate the bodies of several Norwegian soldiers killed while on duty with UNEF in the Middle East. From Oslo, the flight proceeded to Shannon and base by way of Gander and Trenton.[23]

On 1 August, a North Star departed St-Hubert for HMCS *Shearwater*; the next morning, the band of HMCS *Stadacona* boarded the flight, which then for Kingston, Jamaica, where the band performed in the island nation's independence celebrations. The flight returned to base on 10 September after airlifting the band back to *Shearwater*.

On 17 September, almost all the squadron's officers had received their transfer instructions: most of them were going back to Trenton, either to No 437 Squadron or to No 4 OTU. By 29 September, transfer instructions for most of the airmen had arrived, with the majority going to Air Transport Command units at Trenton and Namao, or to No 412 Squadron at RCAF Station Uplands.[24]

September

On 29 August, Air Transport Command Headquarters issued Organization Directive 15/62 regarding the disbandment of No 426 Squadron. Although the effective date was 31 August, a rear party was to remain at St-Hubert until all squadron business was completed — but no later than 1 November 1962. Since flights from Pisa were slated to continue until 9 September, that element of the squadron had to remain intact until then, but as a particularly far-flung element of the No 426 (T) Squadron Rear Party (St-Hubert). After 9 September, the Pisa component would be reduced to the small number required to close out the squadron facilities there. This group, too, was officially part of St-Hubert rear party.[25]

On the evening of 29 September, the airmen held an all-ranks party to mark the closing of the unit. Wing Commander Mackie took this opportunity to make a short, moving speech thanking the airmen for their hard work, their many hours of extra duty and devotion to the task.

The end of the month was the last official day of No 426(T) Squadron, disbanded for the second time in seventeen years. The last domestic flight to return to base was a Whitehorse trip captained by Flight Lieutenant Adam and flown in NS17516. Operations on all domestic routes ceased on 30 September, but UN commitments had to continue. On 31 September, the Squadron Commander sent his last official message to Air Transport Command Headquarters:

> To AOC, Officers and men of ATCHQ from CO, Officers and men of 426(T) Squadron. It is with deep regret that this message is sent as it constitutes the last official dispatch by 426(T) Squadron. From the early days of 9(T) Group through to the present the officers and men of 426(T) Squadron have endeavoured to uphold the fine tradition of RCAF and help build a military transport reputation. Any success achieved in this endeavour could not have been possible without the whole hearted support, guidance, cooperation and understanding of all members of ATCHQ. As we now individually take up our new tasks spread throughout the RCAF we extend to the entire command, good luck and a prosperous future.
>
> Signed,
>
> A.J. Mackie

As of 1 September, the squadron rear party headed by Wing Commander Mackie reported to the Commanding Officer of RCAF Station St-Hubert.

On 7 September, the officers of the Thunderbird Squadron held a disbandment dinner with Group Captain G.J.J. Edwards, DFC, CD, the Deputy Air Officer Commanding, Air Transport Command, as guest of honour, and Group Captain W.B. Hodgson, the Station Commander at St-Hubert, and other senior officers also in attendance.

The last flight to Léopoldville left Pisa on 9 September and arrived back at base on 16 September.[26]

During the month, the responsibility for the operation of North Star aircraft after the disbandment of No 426 Squadron was assigned to No 4 OTU at Trenton. To handle this task, the OTU formed a North Star Flight affectionately known as No 213 Squadron (half of No 426), with three North Stars, about forty aircrew and supporting maintenance crews. A fourth North Star was added in October. As well as domestic assignments, the North Star Flight conducted a weekly run from Pisa to El Arish in support of UNEF. The Yukons took over the Léopoldville run in September, carrying out two flights per month from Pisa that also handled UNEF traffic between Trenton and Pisa. The Yukon runs to the Congo continued until June 1964.

In all, a total of 392 North Star and Yukon trips to the Congo carried some 2,000 tons of freight and 12,000 passengers.[27]

October

On 19 October, the last North Star at St-Hubert was ferried out to the airfield at Mountain View, near Trenton, for disposal. The disbandment of the No 426 Squadron Rear party on 31 October ended another chapter in the unit's proud history. By its pioneering flights to all points of the globe, No 426 Squadron helped pave the way for modern air transport, and laid the foundations of Canada's present-day military air transport operations.

Phoenix-like, No 426 Squadron was reactivated yet again, at Trenton in May 1971 — but the Diary of a Transport Training Squadron is another story.[28]

St-Hubert, January–October 1962

PHOTO 194
F/L Doug McBurney and W/C Al Mackie unpack; RCAF Station St-Hubert, January 1962. (A.J. Mackie Collection)

PHOTO 195
W/C A.J. Mackie and S/L J.R. Marshall discuss the administrative details of settling in at a new location; RCAF Station St-Hubert, January 1962. (A.J. Mackie Collection)

PHOTO 196
NS17517, one of the last North Stars to fly to the Congo, is marshalled into position at N'Djili Airport; Léopoldville, 28 August 1962. (DND PL 140337)

PHOTO 197
The last No 426 Squadron flight into Léopoldville: F/L Danny Mahoney (at the bottom of the stairs) and his crew disembark from NS17521; 8 September 1962. Second from left: Sgt. E. Empey (flight engineer). (C. Empey Collection)

EPILOGUE

EPILOGUE

The North Star era in the RCAF ended on 8 December 1965, in No 10 Hangar at RCAF Station Trenton, where the aircraft was ceremonially retired from service. The guests of honour were NS17508 and NS17515 (on display) and Air Marshal W.A. Curtis, who was, first, Air Member and then Chief of the Air Staff during the period of the North Star's acquisition by the RCAF.

On arrival at No 10 Hangar, Air Marshal Curtis inspected the Guard of Honour commanded by Flying Officer A. Slater. After welcoming remarks by the Station Commander, Group Captain E.M. Butcher, the Air Marshal was introduced to the assembled guests and the flights on parade by Air Commodore R.J. Lane, Air Officer Commanding Air Transport Command. Air Marshal Curtis then spoke on the proud history and achievements of the North Star, and finished by accepting the aircraft log of NS17515 from Flight Lieutenant J.A. McNair, a long-serving North Star captain, and flight engineer Sergeant V.P. Pawliuk. The station band — including pipes and drums — then played "Auld Lang Syne" and "O Canada", and the ceremony was over.

The last North Star to fly domestic and overseas missions was NS17515. The final overseas run, conducted from 3 October to 24 October, visited all four Fighter Wings, Decimomannu and El Arish. The last domestic flight, on 18–19 November, went to RCAF Station Namao.

Shortly after the retirement ceremony, NS17515 was flown to RCAF Station Rockcliffe to join the National Aeronautical Collection. It has stood on the tarmac outside the Canada Aviation Museum for nearly forty years now, and it needs extensive renovation before it is fit for display.[1]

PHOTO 198

The Guard of Honour presents arms during the ceremony marking the retirement of the North Star from service; RCAF Station Trenton, 8 December 1965. (DND Z–10578–1)

PHOTO 199

Air Marshal (Ret'd) W.A. Curtis accepts the log book of NS17515 from F/L Bud McNair and Sgt. Paul Pawliuk during the North Star's retirement ceremony; RCAF Station Trenton, 8 December 1965. (DND Z–10578–4)

NOTES & REFERENCES

NOTES

CHAPTER 1: FROM BOMBING TO TRANSPORT, 25 APRIL 1945–25 JUNE 1945

1. No 426 Squadron ORB, 25 April 1945; RCAF Station Linton ORB, 25 April 1945; No 6 Group ORB, 25 April 1945; DHist 181.003 (D1605): Wangerooge; DHist Day Raid Report 43, 25 April 1945; *Bomber Command War Diaries*, p. 700.
2. No 426 Squadron ORB, 25 April 1945.
3. *RCAF Official History Vol 3*, pp. 106–108; Stacey, *Arms, Men and Governments*, pp. 54–55.
4. *RCAF Official History Vol 3*, pp. 108–111; Stacey, *Arms, Men and Governments*, pp. 56–57.
5. *RCAF Official History Vol 3*, pp. 113–114; Stacey, *Arms, Men and Governments*, p. 60.
6. *RCAF Official History Vol 3*, pp. 115–116.
7. *Ibid.*
8. *RCAF Official History Vol 3*, pp. 116–117.
9. *RCAF Official History Vol 3*, pp. 117, 195, 917; Stacey, *Arms, Men and Governments*, p. 61. For details on Tiger Force see DHist 94/168, File 2/44: *RCAF Planning For Tiger Force* by T.W. Melnyk, and DHist 74/711: *Policy and Participation By The RCAF In The War Against Japan* by I. Cuiciura.
10. *RCAF Official History Vol 3*, p. 118.
11. DHist 181.009 (D6223): ROYCANAIRF Message C261, 19 April 1945.
12. DHist 181.009 (D6223): ROYCANAIRF Message C261, 19 April 1945; AFHQ Ottawa Message A514X351, 20 April 1945.
13. DHist 181.009 (D6223): Air Ministry Letter MS275/45, 652/DG/DGO, 27 April 1945.
14. DHist 181.009 (D6223): RCAF/OSHQ Letter TS.100-1-15 (AOC-in-C), 7 May 1945.
15. DHist 181.009 (D6223): RCAF/OSHQ Message C328, 19 May 1945.
16. DHist 181.009 (D6223): RCAF/OSHQ Message C328, 19 May 1945; No 62 Base ORB, 15 May 1945.
17. No 426 Squadron ORB, 26–30 April 1945.
18. No 426 Squadron ORB, 1–4 May 1945; RCAF Station Linton ORB, 4 May 1945; No 62 Base ORB, 1–4 May 1945.
19. No 426 Squadron ORB, 5–7 May 1945; RCAF Station Linton ORB, 5–6 May 1945; No 62 Base ORB, 5–6 May 1945.
20. No 426 Squadron ORB, 8–9 May 1945; RCAF Station Linton ORB, 8–9 May 1945; No 62 Base ORB, 8–9 May 1945.
21. RCAF Station Linton ORB, 10 May 1945.
22. No 426 Squadron ORB, 12–14 May 1945; RCAF Station Linton ORB, 12–14 May 1945.
23. RCAF Station Linton ORB, 15–16 May 1945; DHist 181.009 (D799): HQBC BC/S 30033/6/Org, 18 May 1945.
24. DHist 181.009 (D799): HQBC 30033/6/Org, 18 May 1945; DHist 181.009 (D5757): OSHQ Planning Paper No 2, 15 May 1945; RCAF Station Linton ORB, 18–19 May 1945.
25. No 425 Squadron ORB, 20 May 1945; RCAF Station Linton ORB, 20 May 1945; No 62 Base ORB, 20 May 1945; Motiuk, *Thunderbirds at War*, p. 492.
26. No 426 Squadron ORB, 23–25 May 1945; RCAF Station Linton ORB, 23–25 May 1945; No 62 Base ORB, 25 May 1945.
27. Motiuk, *Thunderbirds at War*, p. 493.

28. Kostenuk and Griffin, *RCAF Squadron Histories and Aircraft*, pp. 21, 82; Halpenny, *Action Stations 4: Military Airfields of Yorkshire*, pp. 65–71.
29. No 426 Squadron ORB, 26–31 May 1945.
30. DHist 181.002 (D264): OSHQ Planning Paper No 2, 2 June 1945.
31. DHist 181.009 (D799): Minutes of meeting held at HQTC, 8 June 1945.
32. DHist 181.009 (D799): HQTC LM/585/Org 3 "Transfer of RAF Station Tempsford to No 47 Group, 11 June 1945".
33. DHist 181.009 (D6223): Second Meeting of Combined Staffs, 18 June 1945.
34. DHist 181.009 (D799): HQTC LM/612/Org 3 "Transfer of 426 (RCAF) Squadron from RAF Station Driffield to RAF Station Tempsford, 22 June 1945"; No 4 Group Administrative Order No 9/45, 22 June 1945; No 426 Squadron Movement Order No 2, 22 June 1945.
35. DHist 181.009 (D799):13th Meeting Phase Two Planning Working Committee, 26 June 1945.
36. *Ibid.*
37. *Ibid.*
38. No 426 Squadron ORB, 1–25 June 1945.

CHAPTER 2: FORMATION AND TRAINING, 26 JUNE 1945–SEPTEMBER 1945

1. No 426 Squadron ORB, 26 June 1945.
2. Bowyer, *Action Stations No 6*, pp. 52–53, 245–251; Falconer, *RAF Bomber Airfields of World War II*, pp. 72–76.
3. No 426 Squadron ORB, 27–30 June 1945.
4. No 426 Squadron ORB, 1 July 1945.
5. No 426 Squadron ORB, 2–4 July 1945; DHist 181.003 (D5089): 14th Meeting, Planning Working Committee, 4 July 1945.
6. No 426 Squadron ORB, 6 July 1945; Stephens, *The Canadian Entertainers of World War II*, p. 56.
7. No 426 Squadron ORB, 8–9 July 1945.
8. No 426 Squadron ORB, 10–12 July 1945.
9. No 426 Squadron ORB, 13–14 July 1945.
10. No 426 Squadron ORB, 16 July 1945.
11. No 426 Squadron ORB, 17–18 July 1945; Gurney, "Recollections of Trooping".
12. Gurney, "Recollections of Trooping".
13. Chant, *Aircraft of World War II*, pp. 90–91; Lloyd, *Liberators, America's Global Bomber*, pp. 377, 379, 388, 396–399; Thetford, *Aircraft of the Royal Air Force Since 1918*, pp. 182–187; Freeman, *Profile Aircraft: Consolidated B-24J Liberator*, pp. 9–11.
14. Chant, *Aircraft of World War II*, p. 90; Thetford, *Aircraft of the Royal Air Force Since 1918*, pp. 186–187.
15. Gurney, "Recollections of Trooping".
16. No 426 Squadron ORB, 19 July 1945.
17. No 426 Squadron ORB, 20 July 1945; DHist 181.009 (D546): Transport Command Operation Instruction No 57, 20 July 1945; No 4 Group signal AO120, 19 July 1945.
18. No 426 Squadron ORB, 25 July 1945; Stephens, *The Canadian Entertainers of World War II*, p. 55.
19. No 426 Squadron ORB, 27–29 July 1945.
20. No 426 Squadron ORB, 30–31 July 1945.
21. No 426 Squadron ORB, 1–2 August 1945.
22. *RCAF Official History Vol 3*, p. 907; Harries and Harries, *Soldiers of the Sun*, pp. 451–453, 456–461.

Notes & References

23. No 426 Squadron ORB, 6–8 August 1945.
24. No 426 Squadron ORB, 9–12 August 1945.
25. No 426 Squadron ORB, 13–15 August 1945.
26. DHist 181.009 (D799): ROYCANAIRF message 16 August 1945.
27. No 426 Squadron ORB, 18–20 August 1945
28. No 426 Squadron ORB, 24 August 1945.
29. No 426 Squadron ORB, 29 August 1945.
30. No 426 Squadron ORB, 30–31 August 1945.
31. No 426 Squadron ORB, 1–3 September 1945.
32. No 426 Squadron ORB, 4–5 September 1945.
33. No 426 Squadron ORB, 9–12 September 1945.
34. DHist 181.009 (D546): Transport Command Operation Order No 12/1945, 14 September 1945.
35. Jacobson, *426 Squadron History*, p. 62.
36. No 426 Squadron ORB, 21 September 1945; No 426 Squadron ORB, 30 September 1945, Jacobson, *426 Squadron History*, p. 62.
37. DHist 181.009 (D753): Organization, Transport Squadrons, Minutes of Conference No 3, 22 September 1945.
38. DHist 181.009 (D546): Transport Command Operation Order No 13/1945, 21 September 1945.
39. No 426 Squadron ORB, 23–26 September 1945.
40. DHist 181.009 (D546): No 47 Group Operation Order No 21/45, 28 September 1945.
41. No 426 Squadron ORB, 30 September 1945.
42. Gurney, "Recollections of Trooping"; Conversations and correspondence with H.E. Miskiman.

Chapter 3: Trooping Operations, RAF Transport Command, 1 October 1945–6 January 1946

1. DHist 181.009 (D546): No 47 Group Operation Order No 21/45, 28 September 1945; No 426 Squadron ORB, 1 October 1945.
2. No 426 Squadron ORB, 2–3 October 1945.
3. No 426 Squadron ORB, 4–5 October 1945.
4. No 426 Squadron ORB, 6–7 October 1945.
5. No 426 Squadron ORB, 10–12 October 1945.
6. No 426 Squadron ORB, 17–18 October 1945.
7. No 426 Squadron ORB, 19–20 October 1945.
8. No 426 Squadron ORB, 21 October 1945.
9. No 426 Squadron ORB, 23–24 October 1945; Gurney, "Recollections of Trooping".
10. No 426 Squadron ORB, 25 October 1945.
11. No 426 Squadron ORB, 26–28 October 1945.
12. No 426 Squadron ORB, 29–31 October 1945; DHist 181.003 (D51): Progress Report, 31 October 1945.
13. No 426 Squadron ORB, 1 November 1945.
14. Gurney, "Recollections of Trooping"; Conversations and correspondence with H.E. Miskiman.
15. Gurney, "Recollections of Trooping".
16. No 426 Squadron ORB, 2–3 November 1945.
17. No 426 Squadron ORB, 4 November 1945.
18. No 426 Squadron ORB, 9 November 1945; Gurney, "Recollections of Trooping".

19. No 426 Squadron ORB, 12 November 1945.
20. Gurney, "Recollections of Trooping".
21. No 426 Squadron ORB, 18–20 November 1945.
22. No 426 Squadron ORB, 26 November 1945; Vincent, *Canada's Wings Vol 2*, p. 155.
23. DHist 181.009 (D799): Letter, Wing Commander P.J. Grant to RCAF Overseas Headquarters, 28 November 1945.
24. DHist 181.009 (D799): ROYCANAIRF London to AFHQ Ottawa Message C.723, 28 November 1945.
25. No 426 Squadron ORB, 30 November 1945; DHist 181.003 (D51): Progress Report, 30 November 1945; Conversations with G. Webb.
26. Jacobson, *426 Squadron History*, p. 63; Conversations and correspondence with H.E. Miskiman.
27. No 426 Squadron ORB, 1 December 1945.
28. DHist 181.009 (D799): AFHQ Message CX371, 5 December 1945.
29. No 426 Squadron ORB, 6–7 December 1945.
30. Gurney, "Recollections of Trooping".
31. DHist 181.009 (D799): ROYCANAIRF London to AFHQ Message C.735, 8 December 1945.
32. DHist 181.009 (D799): AFHQ Message CX375, 8 December 1945.
33. No 426 Squadron ORB, 9–10 December 1945.
34. DHist 181.009 (D799): Letter, S.2-3-426 (AOC-in-C), 10 December 1945.
35. DHist 181.009 (D799): Letter, S.2-3-426 (D/AOC-in-C), 10 December 1945.
36. No 426 Squadron ORB, 11 December 1945.
37. No 426 Squadron ORB, 13 December 1945.
38. DHist 181.009 (D799): Letter, Air Ministry ACAS(P) 9915, 14 December 1945.
39. DHist 181.009 (D1501): Organization LM/Org. 3. (No 977), 18 December 1945.
40. No 426 Squadron ORB, 22 December 1945.
41. No 426 Squadron ORB, 27 December 1945.
42. No 426 Squadron ORB, 28 December 1945.
43. DHist 181.009 (D799): Letter, 426S/102/1/Org., 29 December 1945.
44. "Disbandment of 426 (RCAF) Squadron W.E.F. 31/12/45", *Maple Leaf*, 29 December 1945.
45. No 426 Squadron ORB, 31 December 1945.
46. DHist 181.003 (D51): Progress Report, 31 December 1945; No 426 Squadron ORB, 31 December 1945.
47. Jacobson, *426 Squadron History*, p. 65.
48. Conversation with J.F. Green; DHist 181.003 (D4437): Letters to Mr. G. Stronach and Miss L. Frasken, 426 S/706/1/P1, 9 January 1946.
49. DHist 181.003 (D4437): Letter to Overseas Headquarters 426S/S.6/5/Air, 9 January 1946; DHist 181.009 (D799): Postagram, Air Ministry to Transport Command A800701/0.A.6, 16 January 1946; Letter, Overseas HQ to Air Ministry S.2-3-426 (DAS/Org), 22 January 1946; Letter, Air Ministry to Overseas HQ 51/965/H.0.3., 18 February 1946; Postagram, Air Ministry to Transport Command A808270/0.A.6., 26 February 1946.

Chapter 4: Dartmouth, August–December 1946

1. Kostenuk and Griffin, *RCAF Squadrons and Aircraft*, pp. 34–36, 167; Christie, *Ocean Bridge*, p. 291. No 12 Squadron was redesignated as No 412 (Composite) Squadron on 1 April 1947, then as No 412 (Transport) Squadron on 1 April 1949. Wing Commander W.H. Swetman DSO, DFC served as the commanding Officer from 1 April 1947 to 12 August 1949; he was Commanding Officer of No 426 Squadron from 18 August 1943 to 4 April 1944.

2. *RCAF Official History Vol 2*, pp. 649–650.
3. Christie, *Ocean Bridge*, pp. 291–292; Kostenuk and Griffin, *RCAF Squadrons and Aircraft*, p. 70; Leigh, *And I Shall Fly*, pp. 145–146; *RCAF Official History Vol 2*, p. 650.
4. Kostenuk and Griffin, *RCAF Squadrons and Aircraft*, p. 71; Leigh, *And I Shall Fly*, p. 146.
5. Leigh, *And I Shall Fly*, pp. 146–147.
6. Kostenuk and Griffin, *RCAF Squadrons and Aircraft*, pp. 58, 74; For a full account of RAF Ferry Command see Christie's *Ocean Bridge*.
7. Kostenuk and Griffin, *RCAF Squadrons and Aircraft*, pp. 73, 209; Leigh, *And I Shall Fly*, pp. 147–158.
8. DHist 181.009 (D5345), Organization Order 317, 1 November 1945. Kostenuk and Griffin, *RCAF Squadrons and Aircraft*, p. 71.
9. DHist 181.009 (D5430), Organization Order 328, 15 April 1946; Kostenuk and Griffin, *RCAF Squadrons and Aircraft*, pp. 73, 209.
10. DHist **[need reference no]**, RCAF Directorate of Public Relations, Release No 6988, 31 May 1946.
11. DHist 181.009 (D5418), Organization Order 331, 10 July 1946; DHist 181.009 (D5420), Organization Order 332, 10 July 1946; Kostenuk and Griffin, *RCAF Squadrons and Aircraft*, pp. 70, 185–191.
12. Chant, *Aircraft of World War II*, p. 113; Gordon, *Of Men and Planes*, pp. 109, 111; Gradidge, *The Douglas DC3 and its Predecessors*, pp. 40–42; Pearcy, *The Dakota*, pp. 143–148; Pearcy, *Dakota at War*, pp. 93–98; Pearcy, *Sixty Glorious Years*, pp. 82–89; Thetford, *Aircraft of the Royal Air Force Since 1918*, pp. 151–152.
13. No 426 Squadron Diary, 1–6 August 1946.
14. No 426 Squadron Diary, 7 August 1946.
15. No 426 Squadron Diary, 12–14 August 1946.
16. No 426 Squadron Diary, 26 August 1946.
17. No 426 Squadron Diary, 31 August 1946.
18. No 426 Squadron Diary, 30 September 1946.
19. No 426 Squadron Diary, 1–3 October 1946.
20. No 426 Squadron Diary, 1–30 November 1946.
21. No 426 Squadron Diary, 1–31 December 1946.

Chapter 5: Dartmouth and Dorval, 1947

1. No 426 Squadron Diary, 1–31 January 1947.
2. National Archives RG25 Vol 22551, Lachine Organization Order No 767, Letter 192-10-5/56 DOE, 2 December 1946.
3. No 426 Squadron Diary, 1–28 February 1947.
4. No 426 Squadron Diary, 1–31 March 1947.
5. Conversations with C.W.G. Chapman.
6. No 426 Squadron Diary, 1–11 April 1947.
7. No 426 Squadron Diary, 13–15 April 1947; Milberry, *The Canadair North Star*, p. 29.
8. No 426 Squadron Diary, 1–30 April 1947.
9. No 426 Squadron Diary, 1–31 May 1947.
10. No 426 Squadron Diary, 1–30 June 1947.
11. No 426 Squadron Diary, 3 July 1947; conversations with C.W.G. Chapman.
12. Conversations with C.W.G. Chapman.
13. No 426 Squadron Diary, 1–31 July 1947.

14. No 426 Squadron Diary, 18 August 1947; conversations with C.W.G. Chapman.
15. No 426 Squadron Diary, 26–28 August 1947; Milberry, *The Canadair North Star*, p. 237.
16. No 426 Squadron Diary, 1–31 August 1947.
17. No 426 Squadron Diary, 1–30 September 1947.
18. Claxton, *Canada's Defence*, p. 1.
19. No 426 Squadron Diary, 1–31 October 1947.
20. No 426 Squadron Diary, 1–30 November 1947.
21. No 426 Squadron Diary, 1–31 December 1947.

Chapter 6: Dorval, 1948

1. Milberry, *The Canadair North Star*, p. 10.
2. Christie, *Ocean Bridge*, pp. 92, 94 and 289; Milberry, *The Canadair North Star*, p. 12.
3. Christie, *Ocean Bridge*, pp. 289–290.
4. Christie, *Ocean Bridge*, p. 290; Milberry, *The Canadair North Star*, p. 12.
5. Milberry, *The Canadair North Star*, pp. 15–16.
6. *Ibid.*, pp. 16, 33.
7. *Ibid.*, p. 15.
8. *Ibid.*, p. 20.
9. *Ibid.*, p. 33.
10. Milberry, *The Canadair North Star*, pp. 20–23; "New Aircraft For Old", *Canadian Aviation*, August 1946, pp. 34–35, 58.
11. Milberry, *The Canadair North Star*, pp. 23–24.
12. Glenn, "TCA/Air Canada's New Fleet Decisions", *CASI Log*, December 1999, pp. 26–27; Milberry, *The Canadair North Star*, pp. 32–34; "Canadair History Highlights", *Canadian Aviation*, February 1948, pp. 19, 32, 58.
13. Milberry, *The Canadair North Star*, pp. 26–27.
14. *Ibid.*, p. 27.
15. Milberry, *The Canadair North Star*, p. 29; Molson and Taylor, *Canadian Aircraft Since 1909*, pp. 298–304.
16. Milberry, *The Canadair North Star*, pp. 244–245; RCAF Engineering Orders, EO 05-5A-2; Webb, ATCHQ EO 05-5A-1; Keith, "Versatile Canadair Four", *Canadian Aviation*, February 1948, pp. 14–16; "Flight in the Canadair Four", *Canadian Aviation*, February 1948, pp. 17–18, 32; "Transport Aircraft Specifications", *Canadian Aviation*, October 1947, pp. 36, 39; Bridgeman, Janes' 1949/50, pp. 97C-98C; Molson and Taylor, *Canadian Aircraft Since 1909*, pp. 298–304.
17. Milberry, *Sixty Years: The RCAF and CF Air Command*, p. 444.
18. No 426 Squadron Diary, 1–31 January 1948.
19. Fuller et al., *125 Years of Canadian Aeronautics*, p. 255.
20. No 426 Squadron Diary, 1–29 February 1948.
21. No 426 Squadron Diary, 1–31 March 1948.
22. Kostenuk and Griffin, *RCAF Squadrons and Aircraft*, p. 209.
23. Milberry, *The Canadair North Star*, p. 42; Conversations with C.W.G. Chapman.
24. No 426 Squadron Diary, 1–30 April 1948.
25. *Encyclopaedia Britannica*, 1957 ed., "Israel", Vol 12, p. 732.
26. Milberry and Halliday, *RCAF at War*, p. 392; Humphries, "Buzz Beurling Remembrance", *Airforce*, April 1995, p. 43; Halliday, "Buzz Beurling", *Sentinel*, January 1968, pp. 44–45; Clare, "Eagle For Hire", *Maclean's*, May 15, 1948, pp. 7–8, 58–61.

Notes & References

27. No 426 Squadron Diary, 1–31 May 1948.
28. Milberry, *The Canadair North Star*, pp. 42, 46; "North Star Rates Approval of Experts After 2,000 Crossings of Atlantic", *Canadian Aviation*, January 1948, pp. 32, 42.
29. DHist 630.013(D3) Report on Operation PLAINFARE by Major W.B.T. Gillis; DHist 630.013(D4) Report on Visit to Germany by W/C D.I. McMonnies and Major J.W.B. Marshall; Eayrs, *In Defence of Canada: Growing Up Allied*, pp. 38–51; Holmes, *The Shaping of Peace* Vol 2, pp. 101–104; Warnock, *Partner to Behemoth*, pp. 9–11; Cameron, "No. 46 Group", *RAF Quarterly*, Autumn 1972, pp. 172–173; "Operation Plainfare", *Canadian Aviation*, December 1948, pp. 16–17, 40; Gunston, "Berlin Airlift Recalled", *Airforce* 12/4 (1989), pp. 14–15.
30. No 426 Squadron Diary, 1–30 June 1948.
31. Milberry, *Sixty Years: the RCAF and CF Air Command*, p. 243.
32. No 426 Squadron Diary, 1–31 July 1948.
33. No 426 Squadron Diary, 1–31 August 1948.
34. Air Transport Command Diary, 22 September, 25–27 September, 1 October 1948.
35. No 426 Squadron Diary, 1–30 September 1948.
36. Air Transport Command Diary, 1–31 October 1948; No 426 Squadron Diary, 1–31 November, 1948.
37. Air Transport Command Diary, 16 November 1948; No 426 Squadron Diary, 16 November 1948; Milberry, *Sixty Years: The RCAF and CF Air Command*, pp. 251–252.
38. Air Transport Command Diary, 1–30 November 1948; No 426 Squadron Diary, 1–30 November 1948.
39. Kostenuk and Griffin, *RCAF Squadrons and Aircraft*, pp. 163–164, 208.
40. Milberry, *Sixty Years: The RCAF and CF Air Command*, p. 232.
41. Fuller et al., *125 Years of Canadian Aeronautics*, p. 257; No 426 Squadron Semi-Annual Historical Record, 1 December 1948–31 May 1948, p. 1; ATCHQ Semi-Annual Historical Record, 1 December 1948–31 May 1949, p. 1.

Chapter 7: Dorval, 1949

1. Ellis, *Canada's Flying Heritage*, pp. 347, 350; Milberry, *The Canadair North Star*, p. 141.
2. Air Transport Command Headquarters Semi-Annual Historical Record, December 1948–May 1949, p. 2.
3. Keith, R.A., "GCA-RCAF", *Canadian Aviation*, July 1949, pp. 18–19, 47–49.
4. Milberry, *The Canadair North Star*, pp. 239–240.
5. No 426 Squadron Semi-Annual Historical Record, December 1948–May 1949, p. 3; Air Transport Command Headquarters Semi-Annual Historical Record, December 1948–May 1949, p. 2.
6. Kostenuk and Griffin, *RCAF Squadrons and Aircraft*, pp. 208–210.
7. McKay, *Canadian Foreign Policy*, 1945–1954, pp. 192–194. Also see: Eayrs, *In Defence of Canada: Growing up Allied*; Holmes, *The Shaping of Peace*, Vol 1 (eds. Munro and Inglis); Pearson, *Mike: The Memoirs of The Right Honourable Lester B. Pearson*; and Fry, *Freedom and Change, Essays in Honour of Lester B. Pearson*.
8. Air Transport Command Headquarters Semi-Annual Historical Record, December 1948–May 1949, p. 3.
9. Milberry, *The Canadair North Star*, pp. 82–84; Keith, R.A., "CP Air Lines Spreads its Wings", *Canadian Aviation*, September 1949, pp. 18–21; Wicker, F.J., "Navigating Across The Pacific", *Canadian Aviation*, October 1949, pp. 28, 58, 60 and 62.
10. No 426 Squadron Semi-Annual Historical Record, December 1948–May 1949, pp. 4–5; Air Transport Command Headquarters Semi-Annual Historical Record, December 1948–May 1949, pp. 3–4.
11. Holmes, *The Shaping of Peace*, Vol 2, pp. 103–104; Eayrs, *In Defence of Canada: Growing Up Allied*, p. 51; Cameron, "46 Group", *RAF Quarterly*, Autumn 1972, p. 173.

12. No 426 Squadron Semi-Annual Historical Record, December 1948–May 1949, p. 5; Air Transport Command Headquarters Semi-Annual Historical Record, December 1948–May 1949, p. 4 and Appendix A: "South Atlantic Training Flight, 426 Squadron", pp.1–8.
13. Milberry, *The Canadair North Star*, pp. 84–90; Keith, R.A., "CP Air Lines Spreads Its Wings", *Canadian Aviation*, September 1949, pp. 18–21; Wicker, F.J., "Navigating Across The Pacific", *Canadian Aviation*, October 1949, pp. 28, 58, 60 and 62.
14. No 426 Squadron Semi-Annual Historical Record, June–November 1949, pp. 1–2; Air Transport Command Headquarters Semi-Annual Historical Record, June–November, pp. 1–2.
15. No 426 Squadron Semi-Annual Historical Record, June–November 1949, pp. 2–4; Air Transport Command Headquarters Semi-Annual Historical Record, June–November 1949, pp. 2–3.
16. No 426 Squadron Semi-Annual Historical Record, June–November 1949, p. 4.
17. Air Transport Command Headquarters Semi-Annual Historical Record, June–November 1949, p. 3, Appendices C1 and C2.
18. Hailey, A.F., "Eagle With Tattered Wings", *Canadian Aviation*, September 1949, pp. 14–15, 48–49.
19. Milberry, *The Canadair North Star*, pp. 63–64; Milberry, *Sixty Years: The RCAF and CF Air Command*, pp. 278–279; Keane, T., "The AVRO Jetliner", *Airforce*, 20/2 (1996), pp. 10–13.
20. Fuller et al., *125 Years of Canadian Aeronautics*, pp. 261, 265; Kostenuk and Griffin, *RCAF Squadrons and Aircraft*, pp. 115, 179.
21. Air Transport Command Headquarters Semi-Annual Historical Record, June–November 1949, p. 5; No 426 Squadron Semi-Annual Historical Record, June–November 1949, pp. 6–7.
22. *Encyclopaedia Britannica*, 1957 ed., "Europe, After World War II", Vol 8, p. 886, "Mao Tse-Tung" Vol 14, p. 834; Eayrs, *In Defence of Canada: Growing Up Allied*, pp. 385–386; Mackay, *Canadian Foreign Policy*, pp. 43, 337.
23. *Encyclopaedia Britannica*, 1957 ed., "Atomic Explosions", Vol 2, pp. 650–651; Eayrs, *In Defence of Canada: Growing Up Allied*, pp. 385, 389; Emme, *The Impact of Air Power*, pp. 511, 634–635.
24. Air Transport Command Headquarters Semi-Annual Historical Record, June–November 1949, p. 7, Appendix K1; Johnson, *Trenton: 50 Years of Airforce*, pp. 5–6, 31.
25. Air Transport Command Headquarters Semi-Annual Historical Record, June–November 1949, Appendix M.
26. No 426 Squadron Semi-Annual Historical Record, June–November 1949, p. 8; Milberry, *Sixty Years: The RCAF and CF Air Command*, pp. 216–217; Ripstein, H.B., "No 1 Radar and Communications Wing", *Roundel* 3/4 (March 1951), pp. 40–46.
27. Air Transport Command Headquarters Semi-Annual Historical Record, June–November 1949, p. 15.
28. Kostenuk and Griffin, *RCAF Squadrons and Aircraft*, p. 208.
29. No 426 Semi-Annual Historical Record, June–November 1949, p. 4.
30. No 426 Semi-Annual Historical Record, December 1949–May 1950, p. 1; Air Transport Command Headquarters Semi-Annual Historical Record, December 1949–May 1950, pp. 1–4.

Chapter 8: Dorval, January–June 1950

1. ATCHQ Semi-Annual Historical Record, December 1949–May 1950, P. 4 and "General Points of Interest and Recommendations On The First Round The World Flight In North Star 17518, 28 February, 1950," pp. 1–14; 426 Squadron Semi-Annual Historical Record, December 1949–May 1950, p. 2; Munro and Inglis, *Mike: The Memoirs of The Right Honourable Lester B. Pearson*, Vol 2, pp. 107–120, 145–147.
2. National Archives of Canada, RG 24, Vol 18, 115, RCAF File 976-3 "Search and Rescue – Operations – Aircraft Cases, Memorandum from W/C W.H. Swetman to CAS, 21 January 1950.
3. ATCHQ Historical Record, December 1949–May 1950, p. 5 and Appendix A, ATC Operational Order 1/50.

Notes & References

4. Conversations with G.W. Webb and A.L. Quickfall; 426 Squadron Semi-Annual Historical Record, December 1949–May 1950, p. 2; Jacobson, 426 Squadron History, pp. 72–73; Milberry, *The Canadair North Star*, p. 141.
5. ATCHQ Historical Record, December 1949–May 1950, p. 6 and Appendix B.
6. Milberry, *The AVRO CF–100*, pp. 15–16.
7. ATCHQ Historical Record, December 1949–May 1950, p. 8 and Appendices I, J; MacKay, Canadian Foreign Policy, pp. 235–237.
8. ATCHQ Historical Record, December 1949–May 1950, p. 8.
9. *Ibid*.
10. Eayrs, *In Defence of Canada: Growing Up Allied*, p. 272.
11. Milberry, *Sixty Years: the RCAF and CF Air Command*, pp. 215–216.
12. Clearwater, *U.S. Nuclear Weapons In Canada*, pp. 95, 110–111; Septer, "Broken Arrow", *Airforce* 24/4, pp. 12–16; Pugliese, "The Downing of U.S. Bomber 2075", *Ottawa Citizen*, 13 February 2000, pp. C3–C4.
13. ATCHQ Historical Record, December 1949–May 1950, Appendix A.
14. ATCHQ Historical Record, December 1949–May 1950, p. 12; 426 Squadron Semi-Annual Historical Record, December 1949–May 1950, p. 3.
15. ATCHQ Historical Record, December 1949–May 1950, p.13.
16. ATCHQ Historical Record, December 1949–1950, Appendix S.
17. ATCHQ Historical Record, December 1949–May 1950, p. 14.
18. Kostenuk and Griffin, *RCAF Squadrons and Aircraft*, pp. 89–90, 157.
19. ATCHQ Historical Record, December 1949–May 1950, p. 18 and Appendix W.
20. ATCHQ Historical Record, December 1949–May 1950, p. 19 and Appendix B.
21. ATCHQ Historical Record, December 1949–May 1950, p. 19 and Appendix AA.
22. ATCHQ Historical Record, December 1949–May 1950, p. 19–20; Appendix Y, RCAF Tactical Group Plan For Operation "Blackboy" Airlift, 14 pages.
23. ATCHQ Historical Record, December 1949–May 1950, p. 20.
24. No 426 Squadron Semi-Annual Historical Record, December 1949–May 1950, p. 6; Conversations with T. Plunkett.
25. No 426 Squadron Semi-Annual Historical Record, December 1949–May 1950, p. 6.
26. ATCHQ Historical Record, December 1949–May 1950, p. 22.
27. No 426 Squadron Semi-Annual Historical Review, June–November, 1950, p.1
28. McKay, *Canadian Foreign Policy, 1945–1954*, pp. 294–298; Bercuson, *True Patriot*, pp. 207–208.
29. Bercuson, *True Patriot*, pp. 207–208; Holmes, *The Shaping of Peace*, p. 149; Mackay, *Canadian Foreign Policy*, pp. 294–296, 298; Munro and Inglis, *Mike*, Vol 2, pp. 147–148.
30. Pearson, *Canada and the Korean Crisis*, p. 11.
31. Bercuson, *True Patriot*, p. 208; Mackay, *Canadian Foreign Policy*, pp. 294–295, 298.
32. No 426 Squadron Semi-Annual Historical Record, June–November 1950, p.1.

CHAPTER 9: DORVAL AND McCHORD AFB, JULY–AUGUST 1950

1. No 426 Squadron Semi-Annual Historical Record, June–November 1950, pp. 1–2; Conversations with M.D. Broadfoot, L.P. Rodrique and G.W. Webb.
2. Milberry, *The Canadair North Star*, pp. 185–186; Conversations with E.C. Grose.
3. Bercuson, *True Patriot*, p. 209; Mackay, *Canadian Foreign Policy*, p. 299; Pearson, *Canada and the Korean Crisis*, pp. 10–11.
4. Thorgrimson and Russell, *Canadian Naval Operations in Korean Waters*, pp. 3–5.

5. ATC Historical Record, June–November 1950, Appendix K: C15–64–2 (AMOT) dated 12 July 1950.
6. Military Airlift Command, *Anything, Anywhere, Anytime*, p. 74.
7. Pearson, *Canada and the Korean Crisis*, pp. 12, 28.
8. Bercuson, *True Patriot*, p. 209; Conversations with A.J.P. Byford and E.C. Grose.
9. ATC Historical Record, June–November 1950, Appendix K: TS 7–1 dated 16 July 1950.
10. *Ibid.*
11. ATC Historical Record, June–November 1950, Appendix K: S 4–3–7 (C Staff O) dated 18 July 1950.
12. Bercuson, *True Patriot*, pp. 209–210; National Archives, RG 24 Vol 923, C500–104, Extract from the Minutes of the 65th Meeting of the Cabinet Defence Committee July 19, 1950.
13. Pearson, *Canada and the Korean Crisis*, pp. 12–13, 28–29.
14. ATC Historical Record, June–November 1950, Appendix K: CAS Directive, Serial No 1, dated 20 July 1950.
15. ATC Historical Record, June–November 1950, p. 4; No 426 Squadron Semi-Annual Historical Record, June–November 1950, p. 2; Conversations with W.H. Swetman.
16. National Archives, RG 24, Interim Access 184, 500–4 Vol
17. ATC Historical Record, June–November 1950, Organization Order 39/50, 895-9/426 (DOE) dated 24 July 1950; Organization Order 40/50, 895-5/56 (DOE) dated 24 July 1950; Organization Order 1/50, Formation of Rear Party 426 Transport Squadron, dated 24 July 1950.
18. ATC Historical Record, June–November 1950, S4-1-6 (SSSO/S1) Minutes of Meeting Held at AMCHQ 24 July 1950.
19. ATC Historical Record, June–November 1950, 4-3-14 (SO Ops) dated 24 July 1950, RCAF Air Transport Command Operation Order 17/50 dated 24 July 1950.
20. ATC Historical Record, June–November 1950, pp. 4–5, No 426 Squadron Semi-Annual Historical Record, June–November 1950, p. 2.
21. Montreal *Daily Star*, Wednesday 26 July, 1950 p. 21; Montreal *Gazette*, Wednesday 26 July, 1950 p. 3; Toronto *Globe and Mail*, 26 July, 1950, p. 1; Squadron Activities 25 June to 25 July 1950, pp. 2–3 and, No 426 Squadron Semi-Annual Historical Record, June–November, 1950, p. 2.
22. Conversations with M.D. Broadfoot.
23. Report on 426 Squadron Activities, 25 July to 25 August 1950, p. 1; No 426 Semi-Annual Historical Record, June–November 1950, p. 2; Conversations with H.G. Graves and E.C. Grose.
24. Tacoma *News Tribune*, Thursday 27 July 1950, p. 1; Montreal *Daily Star*, Friday, 28 July 1950, p. 3; Conversations with H.R. Graves.
25. Conversations with H.R. Graves, E.C. Grose, J.P. McDonald and, D.I. Shade.
26. Conversations with M.D. Broadfoot.
27. No 426 Squadron Operations Record, July 1950; Extracts from the log-books of, E.C. Grose, A.L. Quickfall, and J.W. Santarelli.
28. No 426 Squadron Operational Record, August 1950.
29. Pearson, *Canada and the Korean Crisis*, pp. 31–35.
30. No 426 Squadron Semi-Annual Historical Record, June–November 1950, p. 3.
31. Munro, "Trans-Pacific Airlift Greater Than Berlin", Ottawa *Citizen*, 18 August 1950, p. 3; Conversations with H.R. Graves; No 426 Squadron Operations Record, August 1950.
32. Milberry, *The Canadair Sabre*, pp. 17–18, 337.
33. Pearson, *Canada and the Korean Crisis*, p. 35.
34. Munro, "Trans-Pacific Airlift Greater Than Berlin", Ottawa *Citizen*, 18 August 1950, p. 3; No 426 Squadron Operations Record, August 1950.
35. No 426 Squadron Semi-Annual Historical Record, June–November 1950, p. 3; Conversations with H.G. Graves and J.P. McDonald.

36. No 426 Squadron Report of Squadron Activities, 25 July–25 August 1950, p. 1.
37. No 426 Squadron Report of Squadron Activities, 25 July–25 August 1950, pp. 2–5.
38. ATC Historical Record, June–November, 1950, pp. 6–7; ATCHQ Letter 24-4-1 (CSO) dated 16 August 1950, "Radio Aids to Navigation".

CHAPTER 10: MCCHORD AFB, SEPTEMBER–DECEMBER 1950

1. Air Transport Command, *Weather Manual*; D. Connolly, "Remembering the Korean Airlift", *Airforce* 7/4 (December 1983), pp. 4–5, 17–18; J. Shipton, personal memoir; Torontow, C. "Remembering the Airlift", *Airforce* 19/4 (Winter 1995–96), pp. 6–8; Torontow, *Up, Up and Oy Vay*, pp. 104–106; No 426 Squadron Semi-Annual Historical Record, June–November 1950, Report on 426(T) Squadron Activities from 25 July to 25 August 1950, pp. 1–2; Author's personal notes and conversations with M.D. Broadfoot, A.J.P. Byford, D. Connolly, L.P. Rodrique, J. Shipton, A.J.S. Timmins, and G.W. Webb.
2. No 426 Squadron Semi-Annual Historical Record, June–November 1950, p. 3; National Archives, RG 24, Vol 22517, Air Transport Command; ATC Historical Record, June–November 1950, pp. 7–8.
3. No 426 Squadron Operations Record, 9 September 1950; Log-book entries of Flying Officer A. Finkelstein; Correspondence and conversations with D.I. Shade.
4. Air Transport Command Historical Record, June–November 1950, Appendix K: Letter 41-3-1 (AOC) dated 12 September 1950; Archives, Air University, Maxwell AFB, K3629, frames 460, 461.
5. Carew, *The Korean War*, pp. 80, 85–87, 119–120; Fehrenbach, *This Kind of War*, pp. 258–266, 267–284; Melady, *Korea: Canada's Forgotten War*, p. 58; Stairs, *The Diplomacy of Constraint*, pp. 113–115, Wood, *Strange Battleground*, p. 42. Also see: Alexander, *Inchon To Wonsan*; Langley, *Inchon Landing: McArthur's Last Triumph*; Sheldon, *Hell or High Water*.
6. No 426 Squadron Semi-Annual Historical Record, June–November 1950, p.4.
7. No 426 Squadron Operational Record, September–October 1950; Conversations with D.M. Payne; *The RCAF Overseas: The Sixth Year*, pp. 165–166.
8. Air Transport Command Historical Record, June–November 1950; Operation Order 20/50, 4-3-8 (SO Ops) 29 September 1950.
9. Fehrenbach, *This Kind of War*, pp. 288, 291–292, 295, 298; Pearson, *Documents on the Korean Crisis*, pp. 3, 7.
10. No 426 Squadron Operational Record, October 1950; Conversations with J. Shipton.
11. Air Transport Command Press Release No 3, dated 2 October 1950.
12. No 426 Squadron Semi-Annual Historical Record, June–November 1950, p. 4; Report of Squadron Activities 25 September–25 October 1950, p.2.
13. Air Transport Command Historical Record, June–November 1950, Annex K: Organization Order 3/50, 2-1-23 (AOC) dated 18 October 1950.
14. Armed Forces Public Information Office, Seattle, Washington: Press release dated 20 October 1950.
15. Correspondence and conversations with P. Tutt; Anchorage *Daily Times* 1 November 1950, p. 1, and 2 November p. 1; Anchorage *Daily News*, 2 November 1950, p. 1; No 426 Operations Record, October 1950.
16. No 426 Squadron Operational Record, November 1950.
17. Air Transport Command Historical Record, June–November 1950, p. 11; Appendix B: "Proposed North Star Allocations", 1026DO (STSO) dated 6 November 1950.
18. Air Transport Command Historical Record, June–November 1950, p. 11; Appendix O: Minutes of Commanding Officers' Conference 20–21 November 1950, S41-1-3 dated 24 November 1950.
19. ATC Historical Record, June–November 1950: press release; No 426 Squadron Semi-Annual Historical Record, June–November 1950, p. 6; Wood, *Strange Battleground*, p. 47.
20. Conversations with and log-book entries by J.L. Denis.

21. Bercuson, *True Patriot*, p. 221; Wood, *Strange Battleground*, p. 49.
22. Bercuson, *True Patriot*, p. 221; Fehrenbach, *This Kind of War*, pp. 708–709; Wood, *Strange Battleground*, pp. 49–52.
23. ATC Historical Record, June–November 1950, p. 13; No 426 Squadron Semi-Annual Historical Record, June–November 1950; Report of Squadron Activities 25 October–25 November 1950, pp. 3–4.
24. No 426 Squadron Semi-Annual Historical Record, December 1950–May 1951, p.1.
25. No 426 Squadron Operations Record, December 1950.
26. No 426 Squadron Semi-Annual Historical Record, December 1950–May 1951, p. 1; ATC Historical Record, December 1950–May 1951, p. 1; Report of Squadron Activities, 25 November–25 December 1950, p.1.
27. No 426 Squadron Operations Record, December 1950; Report of Squadron Activities, 25 November–25 December 1950, p.1.
28. ATC Historical Record, December 1950–May 1951, p.1.
29. ATC Newsletter, January 1951, p. 5.
30. AFHQ Directorate of Public Relations, Press release 7788, 18 December 1950.
31. Archives, Air University, Maxwell AFB, 1705th Air Transport Wing, K3629, Frames 489, 490; Conversations with H.G. Graves.
32. Fehrenbach, *This Kind of War*, pp. 407–408, 709.

CHAPTER 11: McCHORD AFB, JANUARY–JUNE 1951

1. Fehrenbach, *This Kind of War*, p. 709.
2. Wood, *Strange Battleground*, pp. 56, 58, 62–63.
3. No 426 Squadron Operational Record, January 1951.
4. No 426 Squadron Semi-Annual Historical Record, December 1950–May 1951, pp. 2–3.
5. Conversations with J.-P. Rodrique.
6. Air Transport Command Newsletter, January 1951, p. 23.
7. No 426 Squadron Semi-Annual Historical Record, December 1950–May 1951, pp. 2–3; Air Transport Command Newsletter, January 1951.
8. Air Transport Command Newsletter, January 1951, p. 6.
9. Air Transport Command Headquarters Historical Record, December 1950–May 1951, pp. 2–3; Operation Order 1/51, 24-3-5 (SO Ops) dated 5 January 1951; Appendix D: "Minutes of Canada-United States Meeting, 11 January 1951"; Appendix E: "Minutes of Conference *Operation RESUPPLY*, 4-3-8 (SO Ops) dated 22 January 1951"; Operation Order 2/51, C4-3-1 (AOC) dated 22 January 1951.
10. Air Transport Command, *Weather Manual*, Chapter 206 "Tropical Weather" and Chapter 208 "Weather in the Pacific".
11. Eayres, *In Defence of Canada: Growing Up Allied*, pp. 209–210; Stairs, *The Diplomacy of Constraint*, pp. 173–175; MacKay, *Canadian Foreign Policy, 1945–1954*, pp. 305–309.
12. Denis, "A Flight to Remember", *Airforce* 24/2 (Summer 2000), pp. 18–19; Conversations and correspondence with R.M. Edwards; No 426 Squadron Operational Record, February 1951.
13. Air University Archives, Maxwell AFB, 1705th Air Transport Wing, K3629, Frame 516; No 426 Squadron Operational Record, February 1951.
14. No 426 Squadron Operational Record, February 1951; Conversations with M.D. Broadfoot, J. Shipton.
15. Air University Archives, Maxwell AFB, 1705th Air Transport Wing, K3629, Frame 537.
16. *Encyclopaedia Britannica*, 1957 ed., "Korean War", Vol 13, pp. 488–489; Fehrenbach, *This Kind of War*, pp. 415–420; Wood, *Strange Battleground*, p. 68.
17. Berton, "Milk Run To Korea", *Maclean's*, May 15, 1951, pp. 20–21, 36, 39.

18. Connolly, "Remembering the Korean Airlift", *Airforce* 7/4 (December 1983), p. 4; Conversations with D. Connolly, C.F. Sanford and G. Webb.
19. No 426 Squadron Semi-Annual Historical Record, December 1950–March 1951; Air Transport Command Headquarters Historical Record, December 1950–May 1951, pp. 4–5; Air Transport Command Newsletter, March 1951, p. 17.
20. Air Transport Command Newsletter, March 1951, pp. 17–20.
21. Air Transport Command Newsletter, March 1951, p. 9; RCAF Station Lachine File No 093-17523: "Accident Report"; Milberry, *The Canadair North Star*, p. 237.
22. Air Transport Command Newsletter, March 1951, pp. 9–11.
23. Halliday, "In Korean Skies", *Roundel*, December 1963, pp. 14–20.
24. Fehrenbach, *This Kind of War*, pp. 444–445; Wood, *Strange Battleground*, pp. 68–69.
25. Conversations with W.R. Lloyd and A.S. Logan.
26. Logan, "Cherry Blossoms in the Cockpit", *Airforce* 21/1 (Spring 1997), pp. 32–34; Conversations and correspondence with R.M. Edwards; No 426 Squadron Operational Record, April 1951; No 426 Squadron Semi-Annual Historical Record December 1950–May 1951, p. 5; *Canada Gazette* dated 3 January 1953; AFRO 10/53 dated 9 January 1953. Many flight personnel, including the author, believed that NS17509's brush with the trees affected the fuselage rigging so that, with comparable power settings, the aircraft flew five knots faster than any other North Star in the fleet.
27. Air University Archives, Maxwell AFB, 1705th Air Transport Wing, K3629, Frames 578–579; No 426 Squadron Operational Record, April 1951.
28. No 426 Squadron Semi-Annual Historical Record, December 1950–May 1951, p. 5; Air Transport Command Historical Record, December 1950–May 1951, p. 5; Air University Archives, Maxwell AFB, 1705th Air Transport Wing, K3629, Frame 578; Wood, *Strange Battleground*, pp. 89–90.
29. Air Transport Command Headquarters Historical Record, December 1950–May 1951, p. 5; Air Transport Command Operation Order 9/51, 960 Resupply (SASO) dated 3 April 1951; Letter 40-R.10 (SO Ops) dated 3 April 1951, Runway and Approach Lights, Resolute Bay.
30. Air Transport Command Headquarters Historical Record, December 1950–May 1951, p. 7; Air Transport Command Newsletter, April 1951, p. 5.
31. No 426 Squadron Operational Record, May 1951; No 426 Squadron Semi-Annual Historical Record, December 1950–May 1951, p. 6; *Canada's Army in Korea*, p. 22; Wood, *Strange Battleground*, pp. 97–98; Conversations with C.F. Sanford.
32. No 426 Squadron Semi-Annual Historical Record, December 1950–May 1951, pp. 6–7; DHist 181.001 (D12) "Pacific Airlift".
33. Air Transport Command Newsletter May 1951, p. 1.
34. Air Transport Command Headquarters Historical Record, December 1950–May 1951, p. 7.
35. No 426 Squadron Operations Record, June 1951; Operations Report 26 May–25 June 1951; No 426 Squadron Semi-Annual Historical Report, June–November 1951, pp. 1–2.

CHAPTER 12: LACHINE, JULY–DECEMBER 1951

1. *Encyclopaedia Britannica*, 1957 ed., "Armistice Negotiations", Vol 13, p. 491; Fehrenbach, *This Kind of War*, pp. 710–711; Stairs, *Diplomacy of Constraint*, pp. 156–167.
2. Kostenuk and Griffin, *RCAF Squadrons and Aircraft*, pp. 163, 169, 179, 210, 213; Milberry, *60 Years: The RCAF and CF Air Command*, p. 470; Milberry, *The Canadair Sabre*, pp. 33–36.
3. DHist 181.005 (D1780) "426 Squadron Establishments"; AFHQ Organization Order 71/51, 895-9/426 (DOE) dated 13 June 1951.
4. The author made his first run to Tokyo with Flying Officer Broadfoot's crew. It was a memorable learning experience.

5. Olsen, "Shemya, Where Are You?", 426 (Thunderbird) Squadron Association 50th Anniversary Booklet, June 1992, pp. 39–41.
6. Lévesque, *Memoirs*, pp. 106–107; Conversations and correspondence with J. Denis and R. Edwards. René Lévesque would later enter provincial politics and become the first Parti Québécois premier of Quebec.
7. The author participated in the 21 July exercise. The navigator was positioned in the astrodome, standing on a stool and hanging on to a safety strap, when he called for evasive manoeuvres as the fighter planes came in on the attack.
8. Some years after the original banner was destroyed in a hangar fire, the Squadron Association had a reproduction made; on 1 June 1996, at the association's Biennial Reunion in Montreal, Colonel David Eberly (US Defence and Military Attaché in Ottawa) presented it to Brigadier-General Bert Proulx (Commander, Air Transport Group), who accepted it on the Thunderbirds' behalf.
9. No 426 Squadron Semi-Annual Historical Record, June–November 1951, p. 3.
10. Author's notes and log-book entries.
11. Greenaway, *Arctic Air Navigation*, pp. 34–35; *Observer Training Manual*, Vol 1: "Gyro Steering", pp. 114.01–114.03, and Vol 2: "Directional Gyro Indicator", pp. 212.01–212.05.
12. *Observer Training Manual*, Vol 1: "Grid Navigation Technique", pp. 115.01–115.23.
13. *Observer Training Manual*, Vol 3: "AN/APN 2 Rebecca and Eureka Mark 4", pp. 319.02–319.09.
14. Author's notes and log-book entries; Conversations with C.S. Olsen.
15. No 426 Squadron Semi-Annual Historical Record, June–November 1951, p. 4.
16. No 426 Squadron Operations Record, October 1951; Conversations with J. Lindgren.
17. Conversations with M.D. Broadfoot; Author's notes and log-book entries.
18. Williams, *Flying Through Fire*, pp. 19–20, 216–224.
19. No 426 Squadron Operations Record, September–October 1951; Author's notes and log-book entries; Conversations with M.D. Broadfoot.
20. No 426 Squadron Semi-Annual Historical Return, June–November 1951, pp. 6–7.
21. Graham, *The Price of Command*, pp. 151–157; Foster, *Meeting of Generals*, p. 327; MacDonald, *The Trial of Kurt Meyer*, pp. 3–8; Margolian, *Conduct Unbecoming*, pp. 44–56; Neillands and De Norman, *D–Day 1944*, p. 236; Stacey, *The Victory Campaign*, pp. 76, 128–133, 153.
22. MacDonald, *The Trial of Kurt Meyer*, pp. 15–36; Margolian, *Conduct Unbecoming*, pp. 57–116.
23. Foster, *The Meeting of Generals*, p. 400–402, 417, 459, 463–485, 488–489, 490, 494–495; MacDonald, *The Trial of Kurt Meyer*, pp. 78, 81, 86; Vokes and MacLean, *Vokes: My Story*, pp. 202–208; Margolian, *Conduct Unbecoming*, pp. 157–170.
24. MacDonald, *The Trial of Kurt Meyer*, pp. 201–202; Olsen, "426 Goes Global", 426 (Thunderbird) Squadron Association 50th Anniversary Booklet, June 1992, p. 35.
25. Foster, *The Meeting of Generals*, pp. 508, 511; Macdonald, *The Trial of Kurt Meyer*, pp. 202–204; Olsen, "426 Goes Global", 426 (Thunderbird) Squadron Association 50th Anniversary Booklet, June 1992, pp. 36–37; Conversations with C. Baine and C.S. Olsen.
26. Conversations with C. Baine and C.S. Olsen.
27. ATC Newsletter, October 1951, pp. 18–21.
28. Author's notes and log-book entries; Correspondence and discussions with T. Potekal and P. Tutt; No 426 Squadron Operations Record, November 1951. The first officer on the flight was Flying Officer Butchard and the air traffic assistant was Corporal Letourneau. Two USAF officers were aboard, catching a lift to Elmendorf.
29. No 426 Squadron Semi-Annual Historical Return, June–November 1951, pp. 7–9.
30. No 426 Squadron Operation Report, November 1951; No 426 Squadron Semi-Annual Historical Return, June–November, 1951, pp. 7–9.
31. No 426 Squadron Semi-Annual Historical Return, December 1951–May 1952, pp. 1–2.

32. No 426 Squadron Operation Report, December 1951; Conversations and correspondence with R.M. Edwards.
33. No 426 Squadron Operation Report, December 1951; No 426 Squadron Semi-Annual Historical Return, December 1951–May 1952, pp. 1–2.
34. No 412 Squadron Operational Record, December 1951; Author's notes and log-book entries; Conversations with D.J. Connolly.

CHAPTER 13: LACHINE, JANUARY–JUNE 1952

1. Fehrenbach, *This Kind of War*, pp. 615–616, 711; Wood, *Strange Battleground*, p. 191; Halliday, "In Korean Skies", *Roundel*, December 1963, p. 18.
2. Halliday, "In Korean Skies", *Roundel*, December 1963, pp. 18–20.
3. Historical Record 30 AMB, Langar, Notts., Period: Organization to 30 November 1952, pp. 1–17 [National Archives of Canada RG 24, Vol 22826, Folder 79.1]; DHist 79/429, Vol 5, Item 7 for week ending 23 February, 1952; Halpenny, *Action Stations 2*, pp. 125–127.
4. Kostenuk and Griffin, *RCAF Squadrons and Aircraft*, p. 197; Milberry, *The Canadair Sabre*, p. 53.
5. RCAF Organization Order 6/52, 895-22/4 (DOE) 1 March 1952 [National Archives of Canada, RG 24, Vol 22760, Folder 60-8]; DHist 79/429, Vol 5, Item 1 for week ending 10 April 1952.
6. Milberry, *Sixty Years: The RCAF and CF Air Command, 1924–1984*, p. 280; Kostenuk and Griffin, *RCAF Squadrons and Aircraft*, pp. 191–192.
7. HQ Military Airlift Command, *Anything, Anywhere, Anytime*, pp. 74–80; Conversations with G.W. Webb.
8. No 426 Squadron Operations Record, December 1951 and January 1952; Operations Record Summary, January 1952, pp. 1–3; Conversations with D.J. Connolly; Author's notes and log-book entries. Nearly fifteen years after these events, the author made the crossing from Tokyo to Elmendorf in a CF-106 Yukon transport; the flight time was nine hours and fifteen minutes.
9. No 426 Squadron Semi-Annual Historical Return, December 1951–May 1952, pp. 2–3 [National Archives of Canada, RG 24, Vol 22687, Folder 2, 44.13]; No 426 Squadron Operations Record, January 1952.
10. No 426 Squadron Operations Report, February 1952; DHist 704-5-1 (Vol 1): *Exercise Sundog III*.
11. No 426 Squadron Semi-Annual Historical Return, December 1951–May 1952; DHist 79/429 Vol 5, Air Force Historical Data for the week ending 16 February 1952, p. 1.
12. No 426 Squadron Semi-Annual Historical Return, December 1951–May 1952, p. 3.
13. Author's notes and log-book entries; No 426 Squadron Semi-Annual Historical Return, December 1951–May 1952, pp. 3–4.
14. No 426 Squadron Operations Report, March 1952; No 426 Squadron Operations Record, February, March 1952; Author's notes and log-book entries. In-flight engine stoppages (the result of fuel transfers by the flight engineers), while infrequent, were more frequent than was generally thought at the time, and rarely if ever discussed among the crews. A similarly hair-raising incident, involving two engines, occurred while the author was on a mission to Chile eight years later.
15. No 426 Squadron Operations Record, March 1952; Conversations with R. Burn. Also aboard this flight were Flight Lieutenant Ray Boucher and Flying Officer Ron Button, on a familiarization trip to Tokyo.
16. Correspondence and conversations with D. Connolly and R. Nurse; No 426 Squadron Semi-Annual Historical Return, December 1951–May 1952, p. 5.
17. Connolly, "Remembering the Korean Airlift", *Airforce* 7/4 (December 1983), pp. 4–5, 17–18; Correspondence and conversations with R.M. Edwards and J. Shipton; Conversations with M.D. Broadfoot, D. Connolly and A.J.S. Timmins; Author's notes and log-book entries.
18. No 426 Squadron Operations Record, April 1952; Author's notes and log-book entries. The first officer on this flight was Flying Officer Bruce Ingall, who was captain of the squadron's last flight of the Airlift. The radio operator was Flying Officer Brooks.

19. No 426 Squadron Semi-Annual Historical Return, December 1951–May 1952, pp. 5–6; Author's notes and log-book entries.
20. No 426 Squadron Semi-Annual Historical Return December 1951–May 1952, pp. 5–6; Air Transport Command Monthly Newsletter, pp. 5–8; No 426 Squadron Operations Report April 1952.
21. Memorandum S-15-64-2 dated 17 April 1952 and Memorandum S-15-64-2 (CAS) dated 25 April 1952 [National Archives of Canada, Interim Access 184, ATIP, 500-4 Vol, Transportation—General]
22. Letter S-4-1-1/5 Vol 2 (AFCS) dated 16 April 1952 [National Archives of Canada, Interim Access 184, ATIP, 500-4 Vol, Transportation—General]
23. DHist 111, 21.01 (D10), Statistics–Korean Operations, Annex B.
24. Author's notes and log-book entries.
25. Air Transport Command Monthly Newsletter, June 1952, pp. 13–15; Conversations with D. Farrell.
26. Milberry, *Sixty Years: The RCAF and CF Air Command*, p. 243.
27. Milberry, *The Canadair Sabre*, p. 103.
28. Kostenuk and Griffin, *RCAF Squadrons and Aircraft*, pp. 163, 195, 197.
29. No 426 Squadron Operations Record, May–June 1952; Reports by Squadron Leaders W.K. Carr and C.D. Bricker, L.G. Tibbles and Flying Officer S.G. Snell [National Archives of Canada, Box 3531 (Interim 217) 960—Leap Frog 1]; Childerhose, C. "Operation Leap Frog", *Airforce* 5/4 (December 1981), pp. 10–11, 38.
30. DHist 79/429 Vol 5, Items of Interest: Week Ending 15/22 May 1952.
31. DHist 111.21.01 (D10) Korean Airlift Operations Report June 1952.
32. No 426 Squadron Operations Record, June 1952; No 426 Squadron Semi-Annual Historical Return, June–November 1952.
33. Air Transport Command Monthly Newsletter, June 1952; p. 1; No 426 Squadron Operations Record, June 1952; Conversations with D. Connolly.
34. No 426 Squadron Operations Record, June 1952; Swettenham, *McNaughton*, Vol 3, pp. 164–165, 210–211; Author's notes and log-book entries. After this trip, the author completed the Navigation Instructors' Course, and was then posted to the Air Navigation School at RCAF Station Summerside.
35. No 426 Squadron Semi-Annual Historical Return, June–November 1952; Air Transport Command Monthly Newsletter, June 1952, pp. 1, 5–7.
36. *Canada Gazette*, June 5, 1952.

CHAPTER 14: LACHINE, JULY–DECEMBER 1952

1. *Encyclopaedia Britannica*, 1957 ed., "Korean War", Vol 13, pp. 487–491; Fehrenbach, *This Kind of War*, pp. 676–678, 711.
2. Stuebing, "Korea's MiG Alley Recalled", *Airforce*, 7/3 (September 1983), pp. 2, 10, 25; DHist 111.21.01 (D10), Statistics—Korean Operations.
3. National Archives of Canada, RG 24, Vol 923, C-500-104, TS500-204, dated 10 July, 1952.
4. DHist, 79/103, AFHQ 532-3TD 74(DOE), dated 14 July 1952; Milberry, *Sixty Years*, p. 458.
5. No 426 Squadron Semi-Annual Historical Return, June–November 1952; No 426 Squadron Operations Record, July 1952.
6. DHist, "Pacific Airlift", monograph, p. 5.
7. No 426 Squadron Operations Record, August 1952.
8. Air Transport Command Newsletter, April 1952 (August–September activities at Resolute Bay were covered in pp. 9–11 of this issue); No 426 Squadron Operations Record, August 1952.
9. DHist, 79/429 Vol 5, AFHQ Historical Data, 21 August 1952, p. 3.
10. National Archives of Canada, RG 24, Box 3531, 960 Leap Frog 2, Vol 1, Interim 217: Minutes of Conference, 18 August 1952.

11. National Archives of Canada, RG 24, 83/84 (216) Box 3531, 960 Leap Frog 2, Air Transport Command Operation Order 15/52, 26 August 1952.
12. Air Transport Command Newsletter, August 1952; No 426 Squadron Operations Record, August 1952.
13. No 426 Squadron Operations Record, September 1952; No 426 Squadron Semi-Annual Historical Return, June–November 1952; Air Transport Command Newsletter, September 1952.
14. Milberry, *The Canadair Sabre*, pp. 104–105; Childerhose, "Operation Leap Frog", *Airforce* 5/4 (December 1981), pp. 11, 38.
15. No 426 Squadron Operations Record, September–October 1952; No 421 Squadron History, p. 43; Childerhose, "Operation Leap Frog", *Airforce* 5/4 (December 1981), p. 38.
16. Milberry, *The Canadair Sabre*, pp. 104–105; No 421 Squadron History, p. 43; No 426 Squadron Operations Record, October 1952.
17. No 421 Squadron History, p. 43; National Archives of Canada, RG 24, Box 3531, 960 Leap Frog II, Vol 2, Message No 922, October 12, 1952.
18. No 421 Squadron History, p. 46; Childerhose, "Operation Leap Frog", *Airforce*, Vol 5, No 4 (December 1981), p. 38.
19. No 426 Squadron Operations Record, October 1952; National Archives of Canada, RG 24, Box 3531, 960 Leap Frog II, Vol 2, S960-111, Minutes of a debriefing conference on Leap Frog 2 held at Air Defence Command Headquarters on 25 October 1952.
20. National Archives of Canada, RG 24, 83–84/216 Vol 3531, 960 Leap Frog III, Letter S960 Leap Frog III (AOC) dated 28 October 1952; AFHQ Letter S96–110, dated 17 November 1952.
21. National Archives of Canada, RG 24, Interim Access 184, ATIP, Transportation Generally: Korean Airlift 500-4 Vol, Letter to Chief of the Air Staff from Air Commodore Ripley, dated 11 October 1952.
22. National Archives of Canada. RG 24, Interim Access 184, ATIP, Transportation Generally: Korean Airlift, 500-4 Vol, Letter to Air Commodore Ripley from Chief of the Air Staff dated 1 November 1952.
23. National Archives of Canada. RG 24, Interim Access 184, ATIP, Transportation Generally: Korean Airlift 500-4 Vol, Letter to Chief of the Air Staff from Group Captain McNair dated 14 November 1952.
24. National Archives of Canada. RG 24, Interim Access 184, ATIP, Transportation Generally: Korean Airlift 500-4 Vol; Despatch 1234 to Secretary of State for External Affairs from Chargé d'Affaires, Canadian Embassy, Tokyo dated 21 November 1952; Letter 4606-c-12-40 to Chairman, Chiefs of Staff, from Acting Under-Secretary of State for External Affairs dated 8 December 1952; Letter to Chairman, Chiefs of Staff from Air Vice Marshal Miller dated 16 December 1952.
25. Correspondence and conversations with D. Kuhn.
26. Air Transport Command Newsletter, November 1952, pp. 1, 7–9.
27. DHist, 79/429 Vol 5, Air Force Headquarters Historical Data, 6 November 1952.
28. *Ibid.*, 29 November 1952.
29. *Ibid.*
30. No 426 Squadron Operations Record, December 1952; Conversations with P. Sutherland.
31. No 426 Squadron Operations Record, December 1952; Conversations with O. Milner and P. Sutherland.
32. No 426 Squadron Operations Record, December 1952.
33. RCAF Detachment Resolute Bay Daily Diary, 1–3 December 1952.
34. *Ibid.*

CHAPTER 15: LACHINE, JANUARY–JUNE 1953

1. Fehrenbach, *This Kind of War*, pp. 676–688; Warnock, "Significant Events April 1953" in *The U.S. Air Force's First War: Korea 1950–1953*.
2. *Encyclopaedia Britannica*, 1957 ed., "Korean War", Vol 13, pp. 490–491.
3. Wood, *Strange Battleground*, pp. 225–236.

4. Warnock, "Significant Events May 1953" in *The U.S. Air Force's First War: Korea 1950–1953*.
5. Fehrenbach, *This Kind of War*, pp. 688–693; Wood; *Strange Battleground*, pp. 245–257; Warnock, "Significant Events, June–July 1953" in *The U.S. Air Force's First War; Korea 1950–1953*; *Encyclopaedia Britannica*, 1957 ed., "Korean War", Vol 13, p. 491.
6. Eayrs, *In Defence of Canada: Growing Up Allied*, pp. 262–266; *Encyclopaedia Britannica*, "Atomic Explosions—Post World War II Period", Vol 2, pp. 650–651; Fehrenbach, *This Kind of War*, pp. 685–687; Stairs, *The Diplomacy of Constraint*, pp. 277–279.
7. DHist 111.21.01 (D10), "Korean Airlift"; Kostenuk and Griffin, *RCAF Squadrons and Aircraft*, p. 232.
8. *Canada Gazette* for 1 January, published 17 January and 17 March 1953.
9. Kostenuk and Griffin, *RCAF Squadrons and Aircraft*, pp. 181–182, 196, 202–203.
10. Kostenuk and Griffin, *RCAF Squadrons and Aircraft*, p. 192; DHist 79/429, Vol 5, Air Force Headquarters Historical Data, 27 February 1953.
11. No 426 Squadron Operations Record, January 1953; National Archives of Canada, RG 24, Vol 22798, 72/2, RCAF Detachment Resolute Bay Daily Diary, 4–6 January 1953.
12. Conversations and correspondence with K.R. Greenaway; Rose, "Ozone Over The North Pole", *The Arctic Circular* 6/5 (1953), p. 57; RCAF Detachment Resolute Bay Daily Diary, 26 January 1953. On 22 May 1953, Squadron Leader Greenaway was presented with the Trans-Canada (McKee) Trophy for 1952 for his work in navigation techniques for the North, and the development of the Twilight Computer.
13. RCAF Station Lachine Daily Diary, entries for 21, 22 and 30 January 1953.
14. DHist, 3 Wing (PRF).
15. National Archives of Canada RG 24, Interim Access 184, 500-4, Vol: Transportation Generally, Korean Airlift: Memorandum S60-CPA Ltd. (DAF), dated 16 January 1953; Letter CSC 7-10-5 dated 23 January 1953; Memorandum S500-104 (CAS) dated 28 January 1953; MND Memorandum to Cabinet Defence Committee dated 13 March 1953; Treasury Board Minute, TB450149 dated 5 May 1953.
16. National Archives of Canada, RG 24, Vol 3531, Letter S960 Leap Frog III (AOC) dated 20 January 1953.
17. Kostenuk and Griffin, *RCAF Squadrons and Aircraft*, p. 207.
18. No 426 Squadron Operations Record, February 1953, pp. 22–23; "Exercise Bull Dog", *Arctic Circular* 7/4 (1954), p. 54.
19. No 426 Squadron Operations Record, February 1953; No 426 Squadron Semi-Annual Historical Return, December 1952–May 1953.
20. RCAF Station Lachine Daily Diary, entries for 6, 10, 22 and 26–28 February 1953.
21. RCAF Detachment Resolute Bay Daily Diary entries for 12 March and 14 March 1953; Conversations and correspondence with navigators J. Beath, R. Burn, D. Connolly, K.R. Greenaway and G. Sweanor; Conversations and correspondence with flight engineer R. Lohnes.
22. DHist 79/429, Vol 5, Air Force Headquarters Historical Data Report, 12 March 1953.
23. No 426 Operations Record, March 1953, pp. 29–44; No 426 Squadron Semi-Annual Historical Return, December 1952–May 1953, p. 1; DHist 78/475, Diary No 427(F) Squadron pp. 2–7; DHist 3 Wing (PRF); Kostenuk and Griffin, *RCAF Squadrons and Aircraft*, pp. 169, 186, 190, 217; National Archives of Canada, RG 24, Box 3531, 960 Leap Frog III, Vol 1: Report on Operation Leap Frog III at Prestwick.
24. DHist 79/429 Vol 5, Air Force Headquarters Historical Data, 16 April 1953; DHist 4 Wing PRF; Kostenuk and Griffin, *RCAF Squadrons and Aircraft*, pp. 171, 181, 202.
25. RCAF Accident Report, 1 April 1953: Accident No 304055.
26. No 426 Squadron Operations Record, April 1953, pp. 50–54, 56; RCAF Detachment Resolute Bay Daily Diary, 8–25 April 1953.
27. No 426 Squadron Operations Record, April 1953.
28. RCAF Station Lachine Daily Diary, 20–21 April 1953; No 426 Squadron Semi-Annual Historical Return, December 1952–May 1953, p. 2.

Notes & References

29. Wood, *Strange Battleground*, pp. 224–225; No 426 Squadron Semi-Annual Historical Return, December 1952–May 1953, p. 2; No 426 Squadron Operations Report, April–May 1953; Conversations with A. DeQuoy.
30. Conversations with C.F. Sanford; No 426 Squadron Semi-Annual Historical Return, December 1952–May 1953, p. 2; No 426 Squadron Operations Record, May 1953, p. 66.
31. No 426 Squadron Operations Record, May 1953.
32. RCAF Station Lachine Daily Diary, 8 May 1953.
33. Childerhose, "Comet Operations in the RCAF", *Aircraft*, August 1958, pp. 8–10, 70; Milberry, *Air Transport in Canada*, pp. 241, 267, 426–428; Donald, *The Encyclopedia of Civil Aircraft*, pp. 366–373; Conversations with M.D. Broadfoot.
34. National Archives of Canada, RG 24, Box 3531, 960 Leap Frog IV, Instruction 501-7 (DPC) dated 11 June 1953.

CHAPTER 16: LACHINE, JULY–DECEMBER 1953

1. National Archives of Canada, RG 24, Box 3531, 960 Leap Frog IV, Air Defence Command Operation Order 27/53, 2 July 1953.
2. National Archives of Canada, RG 24, Box 3103, S-895-100-63/14, Letter S960 (Air Officer Commanding) dated 8 July 1953 to Chief of the Air Staff.
3. National Archives of Canada, RG 24, Box 3103, CanAirDiv message to Air Force Headquarters AO-524 dated 17 July 1953.
4. National Archives of Canada, RG 24, Box 3103, S8950101 DOE dated 30 July 1953; Air Force Headquarters Letter S895-101 (DAF) dated 14 August 1953 to Canadian Joint Staff, Washington.
5. No 426 Squadron Operations Record, July 1953.
6. *Ibid*.
7. Conversations with A.J.S. Timmins; No 426 Squadron Operations Record, July 1953.
8. No 426 Squadron Operations Record, July 1953; No 426 Squadron Semi-Annual Historical Return, June–November 1953, pp. 2–5.
9. RCAF Accident Report on Accident No. 307061, dated 21 July 1953.
10. No 426 Squadron Semi-Annual Historical Return, June–November 1953, p. 5.
11. DHist 79/429 Vol 5 Air Force Headquarters Historical Data, 6 July 1953.
12. No 426 Squadron Operations Record, August 1953.
13. No 426 Squadron Operations Record, August 1953, p. 42; Conversations with M. Majocha, who was the navigator on this crew, of which the other were: Flight Lieutenant Evans (first officer), Flying Officer Charters (radio officer), Sergeant Harper (flight engineer), and Leading Aircraftsman Bereza and Leading Aircraftsman Jobin (transportation technicians).
14. National Archives of Canada, RG 24, Vol 3531, Interim 217, 960 Leap Frog IV, Operations, 1 Air Division Operation Order 25/53 dated 19 August 1953.
15. No 426 Squadron Operations Record, August 1953; No 426 Squadron Semi-Annual Historical Return, June–November 1953; pp. 5–7; National Archives of Canada, RG 24, Vol 22824, 78.3, No 4 (F) Wing Historical Record Return, July–August 1953; Waterman, "The Story of Leap Frog IV", *Roundel*, Vol 6, No. 2, (February 1954), pp. 11–19; Log-book entries by T. Potekal, the flight engineer in Flying Officer Kyle's crew.
16. DHist 79/429, Vol 6, Air Force Headquarters Historical Data, 7 August, 1953.
17. No 426 Squadron Operations Record, September 1953.
18. DHist 86/235 Aircrew Transfer Ledger; Conversations with B. Ingall and R. Smith.
19. DHist 79/429, Vol 6, Air Force Headquarters Historical Data, 10 and 27 August 1953.

20. National Archives of Canada, RG 24, Interim Access 194, 500-4 Vol, Transportation Generally: Korean Airlift, Canadian Embassy letter S18-3 (AAT) dated 9 October 1953 and Minutes 2 to 5 thereto.
21. Milberry, *Sixty Years: The RCAF and CF Air Command 1924–1984*, p. 458; DHist 79/429, Vol 6, Air Force Headquarters Historical Data, 28 August 1953; No 426 Squadron Operations Record, October 1953; National Archives of Canada, RG 24, Vol 22518, Air Transport Command Newsletter, October–November 1953.
22. National Archives of Canada, RG 24, Vol 22518, Air Transport Command Newsletter, October–November 1953.
23. National Archives of Canada, R24, Interim 126, File 895-63/14, C960 Random, Minutes of Conference dated 29 October 1953.
24. No 426 Squadron Semi-Annual Historical Return, June–November 1953.
25. No 426 Squadron Operations Record, November 1953; DHist 79/429, Vol 6, Air Force Headquarters Historical Data, 26 November 1953.
26. DHist 79/429, Vol 6, Air Force Headquarters Historical Data, 27 November 1953.
27. Conversations and correspondence with Y. Lafrenière; No 426 Squadron Operations Record, November–December 1954.
28. DHist 181.005 (D2118), Air Transport Command Airlift Requirements, October 1953–March 1954.
29. National Archives of Canada, RG 24, Vol 2298, File 72/2, RCAF Detachment Resolute Bay Daily Diary, December 1953.
30. DHist 79/429, Vol 6, Air Force Headquarters Historical Data, 21 December 1953.
31. RCAF Accident Report on Accident No 312061, dated 27 December 1953; Log-book entries by Squadron Leader C.D.W. Hare (courtesy, L. Milberry); National Archives, RG 24, Vol 22551, RCAF Station Lachine Daily Diary, December 1953; No 426 Squadron Semi-Annual Historical Return, December 1953–May 1954; Conversations and correspondence with T. Charchuk. Sgt D. Mansfield was the flight engineer on this crew, and Leading Aircraftsman D.F. Marentette was its transportation technician. Squadron Leader Hare was later killed in a crash of a CF-100 Canuck all-weather fighter.
32. RCAF Accident Report on Accident No 312067, dated 30 December 1953; Conversations with Y. Lafrenière and G. Webb. The first officer of this crew was Flying Officer M.A. Lavoie and the navigator was Flying Officer Ted Simkins.

Chapter 17: Lachine, January–June 1954

1. Eayrs, *In Defence of Canada: Peacekeeping and Deterrence*, p. 356; Bercuson, *True Patriot: The Life of Brooke Claxton*, p. 222.
2. Mackay, *Canadian Foreign Policy*, pp. 234–235.
3. Eayrs, *In Defence of Canada: Peacekeeping and Deterrence*, p. 359.
4. Mackay, *Canadian Foreign Policy*, p. 235; National Archives of Canada, http://www.pinetreeline.org/misc/other/misc5a.html, p. 3; Nicks, Bradley and Charland, *Air Defence of Canada*, pp. 33–35.
5. Bercuson, *True Patriot: The Life of Brooke Claxton*, pp. 261–263.
6. Eayrs, *In Defence of Canada: Peacekeeping and Deterrence*, pp. 368–369; Bercuson, *True Patriot: The Life of Brooke Claxton*, pp. 263–264.
7. Bercuson, *True Patriot: The Life of Brooke Claxton*, pp. 263–264; Eayrs, *In Defence of Canada: Peacekeeping and Deterrence*, pp. 368–371; Mackay, *Canadian Foreign Policy*, pp. 246–247.
8. "The Mid-Canada Line", http://www.magmacom.com/~lwilson/mcl.htm; French, "The Mid-Canada Line" Part 1: *Roundel*, 10/3 (April 1958), pp. 2–5, 31–32; Part 2: *Roundel*, 10/4 (May 1958) pp. 10–15.
9. Eayrs, *In Defence of Canada: Peacekeeping and Deterrence*, pp. 360–361, 363–364; Swettenham, *McNaughton*, p. 186.
10. Eayrs, *In Defence of Canada: Peacekeeping and Deterrence*, pp. 370–372.

Notes & References

11. Nicks, et al, *Air Defence of Canada*, pp. 39–40; "The DEW Line Sites in Canada, Alaska and Greenland", http://www.magmacom.com/-lwilson/dewline.htm; Dewitt and Leyton-Brown, *Canada's International Security Policy*, pp. 86–87; "Agreement between Canada and the United States on the establishment of a Distant Early Warning System in Canadian Territory", *The Arctic Circular*, 9/2 (1958), pp. 23–31.
12. Kostenuk and Griffin, *RCAF Squadrons and Aircraft*, pp. 162, 177, 184–185, 187, 189–190.
13. National Archives of Canada, RG 24, Interim Access 184 ATIP, 500-4 Vol, Transportation Generally—Korean Airlift, Memorandum W/C W.B.M. Millar to CA Ops, dated 14 January 1954.
14. National Archives of Canada, RG 24, Interim Access 184 ATIP, 500-4, Vol, Transportation Generally—Korean Airlift, Memorandum S500-104 (CAOps) dated 26 January 1954, Korean Airlift Operations; Minute 2 to CAOps from VCAS, dated 1 February 1954.
15. National Archives of Canada, RG 24, Interim Access 184 ATIP, 500-4, Vol, Transportation Generally—Korean Airlift, Memorandum S-500-4 TD 42 (CAOps) dated 22 February 1954.
16. National Archives of Canada, RG 24, Interim Access 184 ATIP, 500-4, Vol, Transportation Generally—Korean Airlift, Memorandum S-500-4 (VCAS) dated 11 March to Minister.
17. National Archives of Canada, RG 24, Interim Access 184 ATIP, Vol, Transportation Generally—Korean Airlift, S-500-4 TD42A (CAS) 30 March 1954, Memorandum to Cabinet Defence Committee—Korean Airlift Operations; Memorandum to Minister S-500-4 (CAS) dated 20 May 1954.
18. CAS Memorandum to Minister S500-104 (CAS) dated 20 May 1954.
19. National Archives of Canada, RG 24, Interim Access 184 ATIP, Vol, Transportation Generally—Korean Airlift, S500-104 (CAS) Memorandum to Minister dated 26 May 1954; Claxton letter to Pearson dated 27 May 1954.
20. National Archives of Canada, RG 24, Vol 1754, Canadian Pacific Airlines, Letter B.18-2-20 dated 7 December 1953 from W.F. Murphy, Aircraft Division, Department of Defence Production to Deputy Minister, Department of National Defence, Letter B18-2-20 dated 8 December 1953 from A.B. Belyea, Aircraft Division, Department of Defence Production to R.W. Ryan, Vice President, CPA; Letter 001 Canadian Pacific Airlines, Vol 5 (DAF) dated 6 January 1954 to Deputy Minister, Department of Defence Production from Deputy Minister, Department of National Defence.
21. National Archives of Canada RG 24, Vol 923 C-500-104, Korean Airlift, Letter HQ TS 5800-151/TD296 (QMG) dated 22 January 1954.
22. National Archives of Canada, RG 24, Vol 923 C-500-104, Korean Airlift, Letter TS 500-204 TD36 (CAS) dated 22 February 1954.
23. National Archives of Canada, RG 24, Vol 923 C-500-104, Korean Airlift, Letter HQ TS 5800-151/TD296 (MOV 1) dated 17 March 1954.
24. National Archives of Canada, RG 24, Vol 923 C-500-104, Korean Airlift, Letter TS 500-200 TD77 dated 4 May1954.
25. National Archives of Canada, RG 24, Vol 923 C-500-104, Korean Airlift, Air Transport Board letter dated 25 May 1954.
26. National Archives of Canada, RG 24, Vol 923 C-500-104, Korean Airlift, Letter TS 500-204 TD77 (VCAS) dated 8 July 1954.
27. National Archives of Canada, Interim Access 184 ATIP, 500-4 Vol, Transportation Generally—Korean Airlift, Minute 2 to VCAS dated 10 November 1954, and letter S500—104 (CAOps) to Chief of the General Staff dated 17 November 1954; Stairs, *The Diplomacy of Constraint*, p. 296; Thorgrimsson and Russell, *Canadian Naval Operations in Korean Waters, 1950–1955*, pp. 129–133; Wood, *Strange Battleground*, pp. 254–257.
28. DHist 79/429 Vol 6, AFHQ Historical Data Report, 8 January 1954.
29. National Archives of Canada, RG 24, Vol 22798, File 72/2, RCAF Detachment Resolute Bay Daily Diary, January 1954.
30. National Archives of Canada, RG 24, Vol 22551, RCAF Station Lachine Daily Diary, 18, 20–21 January 1954.
31. National Archives of Canada, RG 24, Box 3535 HQ 960 Pt.3, ATCHQ Operation Order No 2/54.

32. DHist 79/429, Vol 6, AFHQ Historical Data Report, 4 February 1954.
33. No 426 Squadron Semi-Annual Historical Return, December 1953–May 1954; National Archives of Canada, RG 24, Box 3535, HQ960 Pt.2, Memorandum S960-100 Random (DAO) dated 21 October 1954; DHist 181.003 (D240) Operation Random.
34. Notes and log-book entries from J.G. Brodgen; Milberry, *Sixty Years: The RCAF and CF Air Command, 1924–1984*, pp. 398–400.
35. National Archives of Canada, RG 24, Box 3535 HQ Pt.2, Pt.3, Letter C960 Random (OC) dated 9 March 1954, Memorandum S960-100 Random (DAO) dated 21 October 1954; DHist 181.003 (D240) Operation Random.
36. Correspondence and conversations with and log-book entries from K.R. Greenaway, H.J. Filleul and M. Majocha; National Archives of Canada, RG 24, Vol 22798, File 72/2, RCAF Detachment Resolute Bay Daily Diary, 29–30 March 1954; National Archives of Canada, RG 24, Vol 22551, RCAF Station Lachine Daily Diary, 26 March 1954; Bercuson, *True Patriot: The Life of Brooke Claxton*, p. 266.
37. DHist 79/429, Vol 6, AFHQ Historical Data Report, 30 March 1954; National Archives of Canada, RG 24, Vol 22798, File 72/2, RCAF Detachment Resolute Bay Daily Diary, 15 and 22 April 1954.
38. DHist 79/429, Vol 6, AFHQ Historical Data Report, 18 January 1954.
39. National Archives of Canada, RG 24, Vol 3535, Interim 226, HQ960 Random Pt 1, Operation Order 59/54, S4-2-35 (SASO) dated 2 April 1954.
40. National Archives of Canada, RG 24, Box 3535, HQ 960 Pt.2, Memorandum S960-100 Random (DAO) dated 21 October 1954.
41. Eayrs, *In Defence of Canada, Indochina: Roots of Complicity*, pp. 58–70, see also chapters on ICSC Cambodia, Laos and Vietnam; Holmes, Canada and the Search for World Order, 1943–1957, Vol 2, pp 193, 351; pp 144, 156–160, 195, 204, 296 (on Korea), pp. 202, 213 (on Indochina), pp 200–220, 331, 392 (on Control Commissions); Mackay, Canadian Foreign Policy, 1945–1954, pp 322–334; Stairs, The Diplomacy of Constraint, pp 280–296 (on Geneva Conference).
42. National Archives of Canada, RG 24, Box 3535, HQ960 Pt.2, Memorandum S960-100 Random (DAO) dated 21 October 1954; DHist 181.003 (D240) Operation Random.
43. DHist 111.21.01 (D10) Korean Airlift, AFHQ Message PR269 dated 27 May 1954; Figures in the Minister's statement rounded by the PR Branch.
44. The crew of Serial 599 on the Korean Airlift comprised Flying Officer B.R. Ingall of Montreal, Quebec (captain); Flying Officer R.E. Schwanky of Moose Jaw, Saskatchewan (first officer); Flying Officer R.W. Livock of Vankleek Hill, Ontario (first navigator); Flying Officer J. Knox of Halifax, Nova Scotia (second navigator); Flying Officer R.S. MacKenzie of Port Morien, Nova Scotia (radio officer); Sergeant R. Mansfield of Vancouver, British Columbia (flight engineer); and Corporal J. List of Regina, Saskatchewan (movement controller).
45. Conversations with and log-book entries from D. Deeprose, B. Ingall, and R. Livock; National Archives of Canada, RG 24, Vol 22551, RCAF Station Lachine Daily Diary, 9 June 1954; Montreal Daily Star, June 10, 1954, p. 1. Air Commodore Annis served for a time during the war as Commanding Officer of RCAF Station Linton-on-Ouse, where No 426 (Bomber) Squadron was based.
46. DHist 111.21.01 (D10) Korean Airlift; Conversations with C. Mills.
47. DHist 181.003 (D240) Operation Random.
48. National Archives of Canada, RG 24, Vol 22798, File 72/2, RCAF Detachment Resolute Bay Daily Diary, 21 June 1954; No 426 Squadron Semi-Annual Historical Return, June–November 1954.

Chapter 18: Lachine, July–December 1954

1. National Archives of Canada, RG 24, Vol 22551, RCAF Station Lachine, July 1954; RG 24, Vol 22798, RCAF Detachment Resolute Bay Daily Diary, July 1954.
2. DHist 181.003 (D240), Operation Random; Conversations with and log-book entries from L. Joron.

Notes & References

3. Milberry, *The Canadair Sabre*, pp. 138–139, 319–320; Conversations with and log-book entries from E. Heikkila.
4. DHist 181.003 (D240), Operation Random.
5. *Ibid.*
6. National Archives of Canada, RG 24, Vol 22798, RCAF Detachment Resolute Bay Daily Diary, August 1954; No 426 Squadron Semi-Annual Historical Return, June–November 1954.
7. Conversations with and log-book entries from C.S. Olsen and J. Forest. The crew on the first flight to Hanoi were: Squadron Leader C.S. Olsen (captain), Flying Officer Forest (first officer), Flying Officer R. North (navigator), Flying Officer O. Milner (radio officer), Warrant Officer II Jackson and Flight Sergeant Barber (flight engineers), Corporal Thivierge and Leading Aircraftsman Lecouffe (transportation technicians), and Flight Sergeant Dan (security).
8. Conversations with and log-book entries from C.V. Bennett, W. Carss and E. Heikkila. The crew on this flight were: Flying Officer L.A. Tapp (captain), Flying Officer W. Carss (first officer), Flying Officer E. Heikkila (navigator), Flying Officer Makarchuk (radio officer), Sergeant Millette and Corporal C.V. Bennett (flight engineers), and Leading Aircraftsman Derocher (transportation technician).
9. Conversations with and log-book entries from P. Major and H. Filleul. The crew on this mission were: Flying Officer R.G. Husch (captain); Flying Officer P. Major (first officer); Flying Officer P. Sutherland (navigator); Flying Officer H. Filleul (radio officer); Flight Sergeant Harper and Corporal Thompson (flight engineers), and Leading Aircraftsman W. Bereza (transportation technician).
10. No 426 Squadron Semi-Annual Historical Return, June–November 1954.
11. DHist 79/429 Vol 7, AFHQ Historical Data, 19 August 1954.
12. National Archives of Canada, RG 24, Vol 22551, RCAF Station Lachine Daily Diary, September 1954.
13. National Archives of Canada, RG 24, Vol 22798, RCAF Detachment Resolute Bay Daily Diary, September 1954.
14. Conversations with and log-book entries from T. Sutton.
15. National Archives of Canada, RG 24, Box 3535, HQ960 Pt. 2, Letter S960 Random SASO dated 8 September 1954.
16. No 426 Squadron Semi-Annual Historical Return, June–November 1954; Conversations with and log-book entries from C.F. Sanford. The other members of the crew were: Wing Commander W.G.S. Miller and Flying Officer Kline (first officers), Flying Officer Pete Woodhouse (navigator); Flying Officer Bob Rose (radio officer), Sergeant Harry Leblanc (flight engineer), Sergeant Carl (communications technician), Sgt Belanger (electrical technician), Corporal Parmenter and Corporal Goulet (transportation technicians), and Leading Aircraftsman South. Wing Commander Miller became Commanding Officer of No 412(Transport) Squadron on 8 January 1955.
17. The crew members of NS17512 were: Flying Officer Roulston (captain); Flying Officer D. Schwanky (first officer), Flight Lieutenant J. Beath (navigator), Flying Officer A. McKay and Flying Officer J. Sare (radio officers); Flight Sergeant R. Lohnes (flight engineer), and Leading Aircraftsman J.D. Budnick (transportation technician). Log-book entries from J. Sare and conversations with J. Beath.
18. National Archives of Canada, RG 24, Box 3535, HQ960 Pt. 2, Memorandum S960–100–Random (DAO) dated 21 October 1954; DHist 181.003 (D240) Operation Random.
19. National Archives of Canada, RG 24, Vol 22820, Item 77.6, Organization Order 52/54, 895-59/1 (DOE) dated 7 October 1954.
20. DHist 79/429, Vol 7, AFHQ Historical Data, 28 October 1954.
21. National Archives of Canada, RG 24, Vol 22798, File 72/2, Daily Diary RCAF Detachment, Resolute Bay, October–November 1954; Conversations with and log-book entries from Y. Lafrenière.
22. Correspondence with and log-book entries from G. Brodgen, flight engineer on Dunford's crew.

23. National Archives of Canada, RG 24, Vol 3535, HQ960 Pt. 3, Memorandum S960-100-Random (DAO) dated 1 November 1954; No 426 Squadron Semi-Annual Historical Return, June–November 1954; Conversations with and log-book entries from L. Joron. Crew members of NS17506 were: Flying Officer Doug Wood (first officer), Flying Officer Merv Hunter (navigator), Flying Officer Red Manley (radio officer), Sergeant Larry Larochelle and Corporal Joe Jobin (flight engineers); Leading Aircraftsman Lorne Ridley (transportation technician).

24. National Archives of Canada, RG 24, Box 3535, HQ960 Pt. 2, Memorandum S960-100 Random (DAO) 29 November 1954.

25. No 426 Squadron Semi-Annual Historical Return, June–November 1954; National Archives of Canada, RG 24, Vol 22798, File 72/2, RCAF Detachment Resolute Bay Daily Diary, November 1954.

26. Wing Commander Lupton's log-book entries provided by R. Lupton; Conversations with J. Beath and A.N. Ronning, who also provided log-book entries. The crew members of NS17512 were: Wing Commander H.W. Lupton (captain), Squadron Leader Broadley and Flying Officer A.N. Ronning (first officers), Flight Lieutenant J. Beath, Flying Officer A. Campbell and Flying Officer P. Sheppard (navigators), Flying Officer Rose and Flying Officer MacKenzie (radio officers), Sergeant Evans and Sergeant Murray(flight engineers), and Leading Aircraftsman Slade (transportation technician).

27. Log-book entries provided by W. Carss. Crew members of NS17511 were: Flying Officer Paul (captain), Flying Officer Carss (first officer), Flying Officer Cameron (navigator), Flying Officer Hopkins (radio officer), Sergeant Taylor (flight engineer) and Leading Aircraftsman Graham (movement controller).

28. Conversations with and correspondence and log-book entries from G. Brogden, T. Charchuk, W. Dick, M. Gordon and D. Haire. The crew members of NS17514 were: Flight Lieutenant W. Dick (captain), Flight Lieutenant J. Wynn and Flying Officer T. Charchuk (first officers), Flying Officer G. Brassard and Flying Officer M. Gordon (navigators), Flying Officer A. Butt and Flying Officer D. Haire (radio officers), Sergeant G. Brogden (flight engineer), Sergeant S. Rohatinsky (transportation technician), Flight Lieutenant E. Harris (Medical Officer, RCAF Station Lachine), Warrant Officer 1st Class E. Ellias (senior airframe technician), Corporal Boucher (electrical technician), and Leading Aircraftsman D. Cameron (telecommunications technician). On arrival, Wing Commander Lupton met the crew and drove Flight Lieutenant Dick to his home at the Temporary Married Quarters in Lachine. Dick's wife had been ill for several days and neighbours were looking after their five-year-old son and one-year-old daughter.

29. National Archives of Canada, RG 24, Vol 22798, File 72/2, RCAF Detachment Resolute Bay Daily Diary, December 1954; Log-book entries provided by E. Heikkila.

30. Stairs, *The Diplomacy of Constraint*, pp 211–295; Conversation with A.R. MacKenzie.

31. Simpson, "A.J. Lucky", *Airforce* 15/4 (January–March 1992), pp. 21–22; Conversations with G.W. Webb.

32. National Archives of Canada, RG 24, Vol 22551, RCAF Station Lachine Semi-Annual Historical Return, December 1954–May 1955.

Chapter 19: Lachine, 1955

1. DHist 181.005 (D468), 426 Squadron Establishments.

2. RCAF Station Lachine Semi-Annual Historical Return, December 1954–May 1955; National Archives of Canada, Vol 22707, File 46.4, No 426 Squadron.

3. Milberry, *Canada's Air Force at War and Peace*, Vol 3, pp. 410–411; RCAF Station Lachine Semi-Annual Historical Return, December 1954–May 1955.

4. RCAF Station Lachine Semi-Annual Historical Return, December 1954–May 1955; RCAF Detachment Resolute Bay Daily Diary, 8 January 1955.

5. RCAF Detachment Resolute Bay Daily Diary 8–9 January 1955; Conversations with and log-book entries from D. Deeprose.

6. RCAF Station Lachine Semi-Annual Historical Return, December 1954–May 1955; Conversations with F.R. Cleminson.

Notes & References

7. RCAF Detachment Resolute Bay Daily Diary, 27–29 January 1955; Conversations with and log-book entries from J. Forest and M. Gordon. The crew of 17525 consisted of Flight Lieutenant L.A. Tapp and Flying Officer J. Forest (captains); Flying Officer Anderson and Flying Officer Cline (first officers); Flying Officer A. Campbell, Flying Officer M. Gordon, Flying Officer H. Graham and Flying Officer R. Greening (navigators); Flying Officer D. Cameron and Flying Officer D. Yates (radio officers); and Sergeant D. Mansfield and Corporal E. Ruth (flight engineers).
8. This airfield, which was also the home of the De Havilland Aircraft Co. of Canada, is now completely surrounded by the city of Toronto.
9. It would be more than a year before North Stars were fitted with radar that permitted the crews to pick out and fly around thunderstorms.
10. Notes and log-book entries provided by D. Deeprose; Conversations with and log-book entries from W. Carss. In addressing the navigators' performance with the squadron's Navigation Leader, Deeprose recommended that the check navigator's competency and attitude be reassessed and the second navigator fly another check mission, as he was put in an awkward predicament by the requirement to satisfy the check navigator as well as the pilots. Within a month, both Carss and Holmes were upgraded to captain, the second navigator was on operational status, and the check navigator had been assigned to other duties. The second radio officer, the flight engineer and the transportation technician had also achieved operational status.
11. RCAF Station Lachine Semi-Annual Historical Return, December 1954–May 1955; RCAF Detachment Resolute Bay Daily Diary, 12–17 February 1955.
12. DHist 181.003 (D240) *Operation RANDOM*; AFHQ Memorandum S960–100 RANDOM (DAO) dated 22 February 1955, Progress Report *Operation RANDOM II*; Milberry, *The Canadair Sabre*, pp. 192–193, 364; Log-book entries provided by P. Major and M. Gordon; Conversations with G.W. Webb. The crew of NS17511 consisted of Flying Officer Major (captain); Flying Officer Lambert (first officer); Flying Officer Griffiths (radio officer); Corporal Ruth (flight engineer); Leading Aircraftsman Durelle and Leading Aircraftsman Stewart (transportation technicians).
13. DHist 181.003 (D240) Operation Random.
14. National Archives of Canada, RG 24, Vol 22798, File 72/2, RCAF Detachment Resolute Bay Daily Diary, 18–28 February 1955.
15. National Archives of Canada, RG 24 Interim Access 184ATIP, 500–4 Vol, Transportation Generally—Korean Airlift, Record of Cabinet Defence Committee Decision, 3 March 1955.
16. No 426 Squadron Semi-Annual Historical Return, December 1954–May 1955; Log-book entries from G. Brassard.
17. National Archives of Canada, RG 24, Vol 22798, File 72/2, RCAF Detachment Resolute Bay Daily Diary, 10–11 March 1955.
18. National Archives of Canada, RG 24, Vol 3535, HQ960–Pt.3, Administrative and Logistics Order 1/55.
19. DHist 181.003 (D240) Operation Random; Log-book entries from W. Dick, D. McBurney and Y. Lafrenière.
20. National Archives of Canada, RG 24 Vol 22798, File 72/2, RCAF Detachment Resolute Bay Daily Diary, 5 April 1955; Log-book entries from P. Major. The crew of NS17521 consisted of Flying Officer Dunford, Flying Officer Major and Flying Officer McLaughlin (pilots); Flying Officer Brown, Flying Officer Hunter and Flying Officer Serafimoff (navigators); Flight Lieutenant Fontaine and Flying Officer MacDonald (radio officers); Flight Sergeant Harper and Corporal Lacroix (flight engineers); and Leading Aircraftsman Downey (transportation technician).
21. National Archives of Canada, RG 24, Vol 22798, File 72/2, RCAF Detachment Resolute Bay Daily Diary, 7–17 April 1955.
22. Log-book entries from G. Brogden.
23. DHist 79/42 Vol 7, AFHQ Historical Data, 21 April 1955.
24. DHist 181.003 (D240) Operation Random.
25. RCAF Station Lachine Semi-Annual Historical Return, December 1954–May 1955.

26. No 426 Squadron Semi-Annual Historical Return, December 1954–May 1955.
27. No 426 Squadron Semi-Annual Historical Return, December 1954–May 1955; Log-book entries from W. Dick.
28. DHist 181.003 (D240) Operation Random; Harvey, J.D. "Random 14", *Roundel*, Vol 7 No 9 (October 1955), pp. 32–36; Log-book entries from A. Ronning.
29. RCAF Detachment Resolute Bay Daily Diary, 12–17 May 1955.
30. RCAF Station Lachine Semi-Annual Historical Return June–December 1955.
31. RCAF Detachment Resolute Bay Daily Diary, 9–10 June 1955.
32. Log-book entries from L. Leclair.
33. Log-book entries from W. Dick.
34. DHist 71/200 Northern Re-supply 1955.
35. RCAF Detachment Resolute Bay Daily Diary, 24–27 June 1955.
36. RCAF Press Release No 8547, 28 June 1955.
37. Milberry, *The Canadair Sabre*, pp. 222–223; DHist 181.003 (D240) Operation Random; Log-book entries provided by M. Gordon. The crew of NS17506 comprised Flying Officer Schwanky (captain); Flight Lieutenant Misener (first officer); Flying Officer Gordon (navigator); Flying Officer Turner (radio officer); Corporal Lacroix (flight engineer); Leading Aircraftsman Angers (movement controller air).
38. RCAF Detachment Resolute Bay Daily Diary, 3–8 July 1955; Log-book entries from J. Sare.
39. Jacobsen, *426 Squadron History*, pp. 88–91; Conversations with and log-book entries from C.S. Olsen; ATCHQ press release No 146, dated 5 July 1955. The crew of NS17525 consisted of Squadron Leader C.S. Olsen (captain); Flying Officer A.W. John and Flying Officer D.M. Dunford (first officers); Flight Lieutenant R.T. Barnette and Flying Officer L.J. Halpin (navigators); Flying Officer C.F. Grist and Flying Officer G.L. Lewis (radio officers); Flight Lieutenant E.E. Mailloux (air movements officer); Sergeant A.L. Murray and Sergeant W.T. Frame (flight engineers); and Flight Lieutenant P. King (Senior Medical Officer, RCAF Station Lachine).
40. RCAF Detachment Resolute Bay Daily Diary, 14–17 July 1955.
41. RCAF Station Lachine Semi-Annual Historical Return, June–December 1955.
42. *Ibid.*
43. DHist 181.003 (D240), Operation Random; Log-book entries from W. Carss and L. Leclair. The crew of NS17506 comprised Flying Officer Carss, Flying Officer McAlpine, Flying Officer Fullam, Flying Officer Herrington, Flying Officer Hagstrom, Sergeant Leclair and Leading Aircraftsman St. Amour.
44. No 426 Squadron Semi-Annual Historical Return, June–November 1955.
45. RCAF Station Lachine, Semi-Annual Historical Return, June–December 1955; No 426 Squadron Semi-Annual Historical Return, June–November 1955.
46. DHist 71/200 Northern Resupply 1955; RCAF Detachment Resolute Bay Daily Diary, 10 August–2 September 1955; Log-book entries from T. Charchuk.
47. DHist 181.003 (D240) Operation Random, Log-book entries provided by T. Charchuk.
48. No 426 Squadron Semi-Annual Historical Return, June–November 1955; Conversations with and log-book entries from L. Joron. The crew of NS17504 comprised Flying Officer L. Joron and Flying Officer D. Thompson (captains); Flight Lieutenant R. Nurse (first officer); Flight Lieutenant H. Morrison and Flying Officer D. Brown (navigators); Flying Officer C. Knight and Flying Officer K. Griffiths (radio officers); Sergeant L. Larochelle and Sergeant D. Mansfield (flight engineers); and Sergeant J. Letourneau (movement controller air). Flying Officer J. Sare accompanied the flight as far as Malta, where he caught it again on its way back to base.
49. DHist 181.003 (D240) Operation Random; Milberry, *The Canadian Sabre*, p. 192; Log-book entries from A. Ronning. The crew of NS17512 comprised Flying Officer A. Ronning (captain); Flight Lieutenant Lewis (first officer); Flying Officer Ramey (navigator); Flying Officer Cameron (radio officer); Corporal Poirier (flight engineer); and Corporal Stevenson and Corporal Morin (movement controllers air).

50. No 426 Squadron Semi-Annual Historical Return, June–November 1955; Log-book entries from A.L. Mackie.
51. RCAF Detachment Resolute Bay Daily Diary, 8–29 September 1955.
52. Milberry, *The Canadair Sabre*, p. 322; National Archives of Canada, RG 24, Box 3535, 960 Random, Vol 4, Minutes of Meeting Held at AFHQ, 21 September 1955; RG 24, Vol 3535, HQ960–Pt.3, Minutes of Conference, 22 September 1955.
53. RCAF Detachment Resolute Bay Daily Diary, 9–29 October 1955.
54. DHist 181.003 (D240) Operation Random; Conversations with and log-book entries from T. Charchuk and P. Major. The crew of NS17516 comprised Flying Officer Major (captain); Flight Lieutenant Cairns (first officer); Flying Officer Cameron (navigator); Flying Officer Grist (radio officer); Corporal Lacroix (flight engineer); and Leading Aircraftsman Grahame and Leading Aircraftsman Geneaux (movement controllers air). The first officer on NS17511 was Flying Officer Misener.
55. RCAF Detachment Resolute Bay Daily Diary, 15–16 and 24 November 1955; Conversations with and log-book entries from L. Joron.
56. RCAF Station Lachine Semi-Annual Historical Return, June–November 1955.
57. Conversations with and log-book entries from D. McBurney. The crew of NS17521 included Squadron Leader Trotter (captain); Flying Officer McBurney and Flying Officer Reed (first officers); Flight Lieutenant McClintlock, Flying Officer Nishimura and Flying Officer Wynyk (navigators); and Flight Lieutenant Lindgren and Flight Lieutenant Hopkins (radio officers).
58. No 426 Squadron Semi-Annual Historical Return, December 1955–May 1956; Log-book entries from P. Major, W. Carss and B. Lahey. The crew of NS17502 comprised Flying Officer Major (captain); Flying Officer Carss and Flying Officer Mace (first officers); Flying Officer Knox and Flying Officer Lahey (navigators); Flying Officer Cameron and Flying Officer Grey (radio officers); Corporal Poirier (flight engineer); and Corporal Jobin (movement controller air).
59. Conversations with and log-book entries from J. Forest. The crew of NS17525 comprised Flying Officer Forest (captain); Flight Lieutenant Marshall and Flying Officer Schwanky (first officers); Flying Officer Fullum and Flying Officer Ramey (navigators); Flying Officer Landess and Flying Officer McKenzie (radio officers); Corporal Sayers (flight engineer); and Corporal Kenney (movement controller air).
60. RCAF Detachment Resolute Bay Daily Diary, 15, 16 and 19 December 1955.
61. ATCHQ Press Release No 188, 21 December 1955.

Chapter 20: Lachine, 1956

1. On 12 May 1958, the North American Air Defence Command (NORAD) was established by an agreement signed in Washington, D.C. by Canada and the United States.
2. DHist 73/438, Long-Range Plan for the RCAF, 1956–1966. The RCAF eventually acquired twelve copies of the Canadair CL-44, a redesign of the Bristol Britannia transport. Designated the CC-106, the first of these aircraft made its maiden flight on 15 November 1959.
3. Conversations with and log-book entries from F. King. The first officer on this flight was Flight Lieutenant J. Wynn.
4. National Archives of Canada, Vol 22798, RCAF Detachment Resolute Bay Daily Diary, January 1956.
5. Conversations with and log-book entries from L. Byrne, W. Crosby and J. Sare. The crew of NS17504 comprised Squadron Leader Reid (captain); Flying Officer Byrne and Flying Officer McAlpine (first officers); Flight Lieutenant Morson, Flying Officer Ducie and Flying Officer Graham (navigators); Flying Officer Sare and Flying Officer Herrington (radio officers); Flight Sergeant Lohnes and Corporal Crosby (flight engineers); and Flight Lieutenant Tobin, Flying Officer Laforest, Sergeant Thompson, Corporal Williams and Leading Aircraftsman Smith.
6. National Archives of Canada, RG 24, Vol 22798, RCAF Detachment Resolute Bay Daily Diary, 8–11 February 1956; Log-book entries from J. Fabi and A. Ronning.

7. DHist 181.003 (D240) *Operation RANDOM*; Log-book entries from L. Leclair, P. Major and A. Ronning. The crew of NS17512 consisted of Flying Officer Major (captain); Flight Lieutenant Black (first officer); Flying Officer Serafimoff (navigator); Flying Officer Wicks (radio officer); Corporal. Stevens (flight engineer); Aircraftsman 1st Class Frost and Leading Aircraftsman Martel (movement controllers air). The crew of NS17511 comprised Flying Officer Ronning (captain); Flight Lieutenant Cairns (First officer); Flying Officer Fullam (navigator); Flying Officer Lewis (radio officer); Sergeant Frame and Corporal Leclair (flight engineers); and Aircraftsman 1st Class Nelson (movement controller air).
8. No 426 Squadron Semi-Annual Historical Return, December 1955–May 1956.
9. Log-book entries from H Cram, the flight's first officer, and F. King, the radio officer.
10. National Archives of Canada, RG 24, Vol 22551, RCAF Station Lachine Daily Diary, March 1956.
11. Correspondence with and log-book entries from G. Brogden.
12. National Archives of Canada, RG 24, Vol 22798, RCAF Detachment Resolute Bay Daily Diary, March 1956.
13. Notes from K.R. Greenaway; National Archives of Canada RG 24, Vol 22798, RCAF Detachment Resolute Bay Daily Diary, February–March 1956.
14. Log-book entries from C.L. Empey, E. Hiekkila, B. Lahey and A. Ronning. Conversations with B. Lahey and A. Ronning. The crew of NS17506 included Flying Officer Dunford and Flying Officer Ronning (captains); Flight Lieutenant Cairns (first officer); Flying Officer Heikkila and Flying Officer Lahey (navigators); Flying Officer Cave and Flying Officer Wicks (radio officers); Sergeant LaRochelle and Sergeant Mansfield (flight engineers); and Corporal O'Conner (movement controller air). C.L. Empey was a member of the crew of NS17504.
15. National Archives of Canada, RG 24, Vol 21991, C-66-100-D18-1 Board of Inquiry Report, Exhibit U "426 (T) Squadron Items Salvaged from #6 Hangar Offices and Sections". While the report indicates that the squadron's operational records were saved, from mid-1953 to March 1956 and beyond, these records range from sparse (at best) to non-existent; therefore, the squadron's operational history has been recreated in part from other sources, principally the log-books of former squadron members.
16. National Archives of Canada, RG 24, Vol 21991, C-66-100-D18-1, Board of Inquiry Report; Milberry, *The Canadair North Star*, p. 169.
17. DHist 79/429, Vol 7A, Air Force Headquarters Divisional Items of Interest, AMTS, 23 March 1956.
18. National Archives of Canada, RG 24, 1983–84/216, HQ-S-960-100 Air Force Headquarters Operations Order 1/56 dated 29 March 1956; Kostenuk and Griffin, *RCAF Squadrons and Aircraft*, pp. 163–164, 169–175, 177, 182, 196, 203; Milberry, *The AVRO CF-100*, pp. 139–140.
19. National Archives of Canada, RG 24, Vol 22798, File 72-2, RCAF Detachment Resolute Bay Daily Diary, April 1956; DHist 71/203, Spring Re-supply 1956.
20. Log-book entries from E. Chevalier and D. McBurney.
21. DHist 181.003 (D240), *Operation RANDOM*; Log-book entries from G. Brogden.
22. Log-book entries from E. Chevalier and A. Mackie.
23. DHist 79/429 Vol 7A, Air Force Headquarters Divisional Items of Interest; Training Command Observer Training Manual Vol III: "Electronic Aids to Navigation" 321.01-321.28; Log-book entries from B. Carss, E. Chevalier, and P. Major.
24. No 426 Squadron Semi-Annual Historical Return, December 1955–May 1956; Log-book entries from G. Brogden.
25. National Archives of Canada, RG 24, Vol 22798, File 72-2, RCAF Detachment Resolute Bay Daily Diary, May 1956; No 426 Squadron Semi-Annual Historical Return, December 1955–May 1956; Log-book entries from G. Brogden, F. King and J. Trethowan.
26. National Archives of Canada, RG 24, Vol 22551, RCAF Station Lachine Daily Diary, May 1956.
27. National Archives of Canada, RG 24, *Operation NIMBLE BAT*, 1983–84/216, File HQ-S-960-100, ADCHQ Operations Order 6/56 dated 18 May 1956.
28. DHist 181.003 (D240) *Operation RANDOM*; No 426 Squadron Semi-Annual Historical Return, June–November 1956.

29. Log-book entries from L. Byrne, B. Doucette, F. King, A. Ronning and J. Sare.
30. Log-book entries from T. Charchuk, W. Crosby and L. Halpin.
31. National Archives of Canada, RG 24, Vol 22551, RCAF Station Lachine Daily Diary, June 1956; Log-book entries from C. Empey.
32. Harvey, J.D. "426 Squadron Round The World Trip", pp 1–22; Log-book entries from A.J. Mackie and J. Trethowan; No 426 Squadron Semi-Annual Historical Return, June–November 1956; Air Transport Command Headquarters Public Relations Releases 211–223, dated 10 June 1956. The crew of NS17525 comprised Wing Commander A.J. Mackie (captain); Flight Lieutenant L.W. Schunk and Flying Officer H.L. Anderson (first officers); Flying Officer R. Greening and Flying Officer G. Serafimoff (navigators); Flying Officer D.M. Cameron and Flying Officer F.S. Grist (radio officers); Flight Sergeant J.C. Trethowan and Sergeant W.T. Frame (flight engineers); Leading Aircraftsman C.P. Barrett (movement controller air); Flight Lieutenant H.G. Maxwell (Pilot); Warrant Officer 1st Class W.G. Jackson, Sergeant D. Biddle, and Corporal E. Bach (Maintenance Team).
33. DHist 71/203 Re-supply Operations 1956.
34. National Archives of Canada, RG 24, Vol 22798, RCAF Detachment Resolute Bay Daily Diary, June 1956; Log-book entries from G. Brogden and R.E. Schwanky. The crew of this service flight included Flying Officer R.E. Schwanky (captain); Flying Officer Blackburn (first officer); Flying Officer Brassard and Flying Officer Ginrich (navigators); Flight Lieutenant Coates (radio officer); Sergeant Brogden (flight engineer); and Sergeant Adams (movement controller air).
35. DHist 181.003 (D240) *Operation RANDOM*; No 426 Squadron Semi-Annual Historical Return, June–November 1956; Log-book entries from J. Sare.
36. National Archives of Canada, RG 24, Vol 22551, RCAF Station Lachine Daily Diary, June 1956.
37. National Archives of Canada, RG 24, Vol 22798, RCAF Detachment Resolute Bay Daily Diary, June–July 1956; Log-book entries from W. Crosby.
38. Air Transport Command Headquarters Press Release No 231 dated 6 July 1956; No 426 Squadron Semi-Annual Historical Return June–November 1956; Log-book entries from W. Carss, L. Halpin, P. Major and T. Sutton. The crew of NS17517 comprised Flight Lieutenant Carss (captain); Flight Lieutenant J. Hamel and Flight Lieutenant P.J. Major (first officers); Flying Officer L. Halpin and Flying Officer F. Lisgo (navigators); Flying Officer E. Barker and Flying Officer L. Landess (radio officers); Flight Sergeant J. Lohnes and Sergeant T. Sutton (flight engineers); and Leading Aircraftsman W. Nelson (movement controller air).
39. Log-book entries from L. Byrne and E. Heikkila; DHist 79/429, Air Force Headquarters Divisional Items of Interest 24 August 1956.
40. National Archives of Canada, RG 24, Vol 22798, RCAF Detachment Resolute Bay Daily Diary, July 1956; Log-book entries from G. Brogden.
41. Air Transport Command Headquarters Press Release No 241 dated 12 July 1956; Log-book entries from F. King; No 426 Squadron Semi-Annual Historical Return, June–November 1956; Conversations with L. Leclair. Corporal Corbeil became a flight engineer and flew with the squadron for several years in that capacity. His son became a successful Quebec businessman.
42. RCAF Detachment Resolute Bay Daily Diary, July 1956; Log-book entries from C. Lalande.
43. No 426 Squadron Semi-Annual Historical Return, June–November 1956; Log-book entries from A. Ronning and J. Sare.
44. DHist 181.003 (D240) Operation RANDOM; Log-book entries from J. Fabi and R.E. Schwanky. The crew of NS17512 included Flying Officer Schwanky (captain); Flight Lieutenant Longworth (first officer); Flying Officer Fabi (navigator); Flying Officer Wicks (radio officer); Corporal Jobin (flight engineer); and Leading Aircraftsman Barrett and Leading Aircraftsman Conway (movement controllers air).
45. Log-book entries from L. Leclair.
46. RCAF Station Lachine Daily Diary, 31 July 1956; Kostenuk and Griffin, *RCAF Squadrons and Aircraft*, p. 209.

47. Log-book entries from P. Major.
48. National Archives of Canada, RG 24, Vol 22798, File 72-2, RCAF Detachment Resolute Bay Daily Diary, August 1956; Log-book entries from R.E. Schwanky.
49. National Archives of Canada, RG 24, Vol 22798, File 72-2, RCAF Detachment Resolute Bay Daily Diary, August 1956; Correspondence and conversations with J. Beath.
50. National Archives of Canada, RG 24, Vol 22551, RCAF Station Lachine Daily Diary, August 1956.
51. No 426 Squadron Semi-Annual Historical Return, June–November 1956; Log-book entries from J. Fabi.
52. No 426 Squadron Semi-Annual Historical Return, June–November 1956; Log-book entries from E. Chevalier, B. Doucette, C. Empey, and J. Sare.
53. National Archives of Canada, RG 24, Vol 22798, File 72-2, RCAF Detachment Resolute Bay Daily Diary, August 1956; Log-book entries from J. Trethowan.
54. National Archives of Canada, RG 24, Vol 22798, File 72-2, RCAF Detachment Resolute Bay Daily Diary, August 1956.
55. DHist 79/429, Vol 7A, Air Force Headquarters Divisional Items of Interest, 31 August 1956.
56. DHist 181.003 Operation RANDOM; Log-book entries from F. King and R.E. Schwanky. The crew of NS17516 included Flight Lieutenant Hamel (first officer); Flying Officer Duce (navigator); Flying Officer King (radio officer); Corporal Dyer (flight engineer), and Leading Aircraftsman Lewis and Leading Aircraftsman Tasker, (Movement Controllers).
57. No 426 Squadron Semi-Annual Historical Return, June–November 1956; Log-book entries from D. McBurney and H. Stevens. The crew of NS17521 included Flight Lieutenant McBurney and Flight Lieutenant Longworth (first officers); Flying Officer Gingrich and Flying Officer Wynyk (navigators); Flight Lieutenant Fontaine and Flight Lieutenant McDonald (radio officers); Sergeant. Stevens and Corporal John (flight engineers); and Corporal Stevens and Leading Aircraftsman Whincup (Movement Controllers).
58. Log-book entries from W. Carss and J. Trethowan.
59. National Archives of Canada RG 24, Vol 22798, File 72-2, RCAF Detachment Resolute Bay Daily Diary, September 1956; Log-book entries from L. Byrne.
60. No 426 Squadron Semi-Annual Historical Return, June–November 1956; Log-book entries from A. Ronning. The crew of NS17512 and NS17510 included Flying Officer Ronning (captain); Flight Lieutenant Misener (first officer); Flying Officer Nunney (navigator); Flying Officer Wicks (radio officer); and Sergeant. Larochelle (Flight Eengineer).
61. National Archives of Canada, RG 24, Vol 22551, RCAF Station Lachine Daily Diary, September 1956.
62. National Archives of Canada, RG 24, Vol 22798, RCAF Detachment Resolute Bay Daily Diary, September–October 1956; Log-book entries from G. Brogden.
63. *Britannica Book of the Year*, 1958, pp. 329–330; Holmes, *The Shaping of Peace*, pp. 370–376; http://www.whitepinepictures.com/seeds/iii/sidebar.html.
64. *Britannica Book of the Year*, 1958, pp. 440–441, 473–474; *Encyclopaedia Britannica*, "Suez Canal", Vol 21, 1958, pp. 516–519; Fry, *Freedom and Change* (see also: Alistair Buchan, *Concepts of Peacekeeping*, pp. 16–25; E.L.M. Burns, *Pearson and the Gaza Strip*, 1957, pp. 26–42); Holmes, *The Shaping of Peace*, pp. 183–185, 189, 246–248; 289, 292, 337, 348–379; Westwood, *The History of the Middle East Wars*, pp. 30–61; National Archives of Canada, RG 24, Box 17872, File 870-100-76/9 (Army Headquarters), Palestine Question—1947 to the Suez Crisis.
65. DHist 181.003 (D2198), Report on *RANDOM West 1*; Conversations with and log-book entries from J. Lynch.
66. Log-book entries from P. Major.
67. Log-book entries from B. Carss, J. Lynch and G. McCormick; National Archives of Canada, RG 24, Vol 22798, File 72-2, RCAF Detachment Resolute Bay Daily Diary, October 1956.
68. Correspondence with and log-book entries from G. Brogden.

Notes & References

69. Air Transport Command Headquarters Press Release No. 252 dated 30 October 1956; Conversations with J. Sare; Log-book entries from J. Sare and T. Sutton. The crew of NS17521 included Flight Lieutenant W.M. Lewis (captain); Flying Officer R. Mace (First officer); Flying Officer H.J. Graham (navigator); Flying Officer J. Sare (radio officer); and Sergeant. T. Sutton (flight engineer).
70. DHist. 181.003 (D240) *Operation RANDOM*.
71. DHist. 79/429, Vol 7A, Divisional Items of Interest 2, 9 November 1956; Milberry, *The Avro CF-100*, pp. 139–140; Log-book entries from L. Halpin.
72. Conversations with and log-book entries from L. Halpin.
73. National Archives of Canada, Box 17872, File 870-100-76/9 (Army Headquarters), Palestine Question—1947 to the Suez Crisis; DHist 112.3M2 (D527), Report on Operation Rapid Step dated 1 April 1957; DHist 79/429, Vol 7A, Air Force Headquarters Divisional Items of Interest, 23 November 1956; Graham, *Citizen and Soldier*, pp. 231–235; Gaffen, *In The Eye of the Storm*, (see Chapter 2, "United Nations Emergency Force 1", pp. 39–64).
74. Kealy and Russell, *A History of Canadian Aviation*, pp. 96–98; Holmes, *The Shaping of Peace*, Vol 2, pp. 365–368; Graham, *Citizen and Soldier*, pp. 233–235; DHist. 112.3M2 (D527) "Report on Operation Rapid Step As It Affected the Canadian Army"; DHist 653.003 (D27), Memorandum for the Prime Minister, Canadian Contribution to UNEF; National Archives of Canada, RG 24, Interim 217, 900-960-5, United Nations Emergency Force: Press Release issued by the Secretary of State For External Affairs, 10 December 1956; RG 24 Vol 17872, 870-100-76/9, Army Headquarters Palestine Question–1974 To The Suez Crisis, dated 12 June 1961; Granatstein, *Canada's Army*, "Waging War and Keeping the Peace", pp. 344–347.
75. National Archives of Canada, RG 24, Vol 22794, File 70.9 (ATU); DHist 79/429, Vol 7A, Air Force Headquarters Divisional Items of Interest 23 November 1956; DHist Air Transport Command Headquarters Operations Document, Item No 4, 1960; Conversations with R.M. Edwards.
76. No 426 Squadron Semi-Annual Historical Return, June–November 1956; Log-book entries from F. King.
77. No 426 Squadron Semi-Annual Historical Return, June–November 1956.
78. DHist 181.003 (D2198) RCAF Report on Reverse RANDOM Operation October–November 1956; Log-book entries from A. Ronning.
79. No 426 Squadron Semi-Annual Historical Return, June–November 1956; Log-book entries from B. Carss.
80. RCAF Station Lachine Daily Diary, November 1956.
81. National Archives of Canada, RG 24, Vol 22798, RCAF Detachment Resolute Bay Daily Diary, November 1956.
82. Conversations with and log-book entries from P. Major; Log-book entries from M. Gordon. Flight Lieutenant Major's crew included Flight Lieutenant Longworth (first officer); Flying Officer Gordon (navigator); Flying Officer Callaghan (radio officer); Corporal. Ohlson (flight engineer); and Leading Aircraftsman Burgess (Movement Controller).
83. Conversations with and log-book entries from G. Brodgen and L. Byrne. Log-book entries from J. Fabi, and G. McCormick.
84. No 426 Squadron Semi-Annual Historical Return, June–November 1956; Log-book entries from D. McBurney, J. Sare and T. Sutton. Flight Lieutenant McBurney's crew included Flight Lieutenant Hamel (first officer); Flying Officer Boutet (navigator); Flying Officer Sare (radio officer); and Sergeant Sutton (flight engineer).
85. Log-book entries from J. Lynch.
86. Log-book entries from E. Chevalier and E. Heikkila.
87. Log-book entries from F. King.
88. Log-book entries from B. Carss, B. Lahey, C. Lalande, P. Major, R. Sierolawski, and H. Stevens.
89. Log-book entries from B. Doucette, A. Ronning, G. Brogden, and L. Byrne.
90. Log-book entries from G. Brogden, L. Leclair, G. McCormick and R.E. Schwanky.

91. National Archives of Canada, RG 24, Vol 22798, File 72-2, RCAF Detachment Resolute Bay Daily Diary, November–December 1956; Log-book entries from H. Stevens.
92. National Archives of Canada, RG 24, Interim 74, HQ-C-960-100-RANDOM: File S960-100 RANDOM (DPRM), Min(3) Sabre Situation/CF-100, Wing Commander G.T. Doucet, 5 Sep 56; Min.(4), Wing Commander G. Broadley, 7 Sep 56; Min.(5), Squadron Leader W.J. Buzza, 11 Sep 56; 1 Overseas Ferry Unit—Supporting Data, 18 Oct 56 and Min.(2), 24 Oct 56; Memorandum S960-100 RANDOM (DOE), 1 Overseas Ferry Unit, 1 Nov 56; Memorandum S960-100 RANDOM (Org M), 1 Overseas Ferry Unit, 2 Nov 56; Memorandum S960-100 RANDOM (C/Mat) Westbound RANDOM—Residual Aircraft, 26 Nov 56 and Min.(2) Squadron Leader D.R. Adamson, 28 Nov 56; Letter USAF Central Co-ordinating Staff—Canada, Letter to CAS/Air Force Headquarters, Attn. Group Captain R.A. Gordon from Colonel W.A. Trippet, USAF.
93. Log-book entries from: L. Byrne, G. Brogden, H. Cram, B. Doucette, M. Gordon, B. Lahey, C. Lalande, J. Sare, R. Sierolawski, and T. Sutton.
94. Log-book entries from E. Chevalier and G. McCormick.
95. National Archives of Canada, RG 24, Vol 22551, RCAF Station Lachine Daily Diary, December 1956; Conversations with L. Leclair.
96. No 426 Squadron Semi-Annual Historical Return, December 1956–May 1957; National Archives of Canada, RG 24, Vol 22798, File 72-2, RCAF Detachment Resolute Bay Daily Diary, December 1956; Log-book entries from L. Byrne and E. Heikkila.
97. Milberry, *Sixty Years: The RCAF and CF Air Command 1924–1984*, p. 471.
98. Log-book entries from E. Chevalier; National Archives of Canada, RG 24, Vol 22798, File 72-2, RCAF Detachment Resolute Bay Daily Diary, December 1956.
99. No 426 Squadron Semi-Annual Historical Return, December 1956–May 1957; National Archives of Canada, RG 24, Vol 22551, RCAF Station Lachine Daily Diary, December 1956.
100. National Archives of Canada, RG 24, Vol 22794, File 70.9 (ATU), Daily Diary November–December 1956.

Chapter 21: Lachine, 1957

1. DHist 73/430 RCAF Program of Activities 1957–1960.
2. No 426 Squadron Semi-Annual Historical Return, December 1956–May 1957; Log-book entries from E. Chevalier, B. Doucette, C. Empey, B. Lahey, D. McBurney and R.E. Schwanky.
3. DHist 79/429, Vol 7A, Divisional Items of Interest, 10 January 1957.
4. National Archives of Canada, RG 24, Vol 22798, File 72/2, RCAF Detachment Resolute Bay Daily Diary, January 1957; Log-book entries from G. Brogden, C. Empey and J. Fabi.
5. No 426 Squadron Semi-Annual Historical Return, December 1957–May 1957; Log-book entries from B. Lahey, T. Latham, A. Mackie and J. Sare.
6. Kealy and Russell, *A History of Canadian Naval Aviation*, pp. 98–99; National Archives of Canada, RG 24, Vol 22794, File 70.9, ATU Daily Diary, January 1957. During the war, Group Captain Pleasance commanded RCAF Station Linton-on-Ouse, where No 426 Squadron was based.
7. DHist 79/429, Vol 7A, Divisional Items of Interest, 7 February 1957.
8. National Archives of Canada, RG 24, Vol 22794, File 70.9, ATU Daily Diary, February 1957.
9. DHist 79/429, Vol 7A, Divisional Items of Interest, 18 January, 22 February 1957; National Archives of Canada, RG 24, Vol 17752, 810–144, Vol 2, Operations Summary February 1957; Log-book entries from G. Brogden, J. Bugdale, L. Byrne, C. Empey, J. Fabi, M. Gordon, E. Heikkila, F. King, B. Lahey, C. Lalande, T. Latham, L. Leclair, J. Lynch, D. McBurney, A. Ronning, and J. Trethowan.
10. No 426 Squadron Semi-Annual Historical Return, December 1956–May 1957; National Archives of Canada, RG 24, Vol 22798, File 72/2, RCAF Detachment Resolute Bay Daily Diary, February 1957; Log-book entries from B. Lahey, J. Sare, R.E. Schwanky, and H. Stevens.

11. No 426 Squadron Semi-Annual Historical Return, December 1956–May 1957; Log-book entries from R. Sierolawski.
12. Kealy and Russell, *A History of Canadian Naval Aviation*, pp 105–106; DHist 181.003 (D240) Operation Random; National Archives of Canada, RG 24, Vol 17752, 810–144 Vol 2, Operations Summary; Log-book entries from J. Lynch and R. Sierolawski.
13. National Archives of Canada, RG 24, Vol 22798, File 72/2, RCAF Detachment Resolute Bay Daily Diary, March 1957; Log-book entries from B. Doucette, C. Empey, E. Heikkila and M. Gordon.
14. *Ibid.*; Log-book entries from M. Gordon and L. Leclair.
15. National Archives of Canada, RG 24, Vol 22551, RCAF Station Lachine Daily Diary, 13 March 1957.
16. National Archives of Canada, RG 24, Vol 22798, File 72/2, RCAF Detachment Resolute Bay Daily Diary, March 1957; Log-book entries from G. Brogden, J. Fabi and E. Heikkila.
17. *Ibid.*; Log-book entries from B. Ingall and F. King.
18. DHist 112.2M2 (D527), Report on Operation Rapid Step 1, April 1957.
19. National Archives of Canada, RG 24, Vol 22798, File 72/2, RCAF Detachment Resolute Bay Daily Diary, April 1957; Log-book entries from J. Fabi and T. Latham.
20. *Ibid.*; Log-book entries from B. Lahey and H. Stevens.
21. National Archives of Canada, RG 24, Interim 74, HQ-C-960-100-Random, AFHQ Letter to Chief Central Co-ordinating Staff, 3 January 1957; AFHQ Memorandum DTRMO to CA Ops, 8 March 1957; RG 24, Box 3551, 960–100 Despatch, Canadian Ambassador to Denmark to Secretary of State for External Affairs, 20 March 1957; RG 24, Vol 22792, File 70-3, Letter 895-63/14 (DOE), 16 April 1957.
22. DHist 181.003 (D240) Operation Random.
23. National Archives of Canada, RG 24, Vol 22551, RCAF Station Lachine Daily Diary, April 1957.
24. National Archives of Canada, RG 24, Vol 22794, File 70.9, ATU Daily Diary, April 1957.
25. National Archives of Canada, RG 24, Vol 22551, RCAF Station Lachine Daily Diary, May 1957.
26. National Archives of Canada, RG 24, Vol 22798, File 72/2, RCAF Detachment Resolute Bay Daily Diary, May 1957; Log-book entries from B. Lahey.
27. Log-book entries from C. Lalande and A. Ronning.
28. National Archives of Canada, RG 24, Vol 22798, File 72/2, RCAF Detachment Resolute Bay Daily Diary, May 1957; Log-book entries from J. Fabi.
29. National Archives of Canada, RG 24, Vol 22798, File 72/2, RCAF Detachment Resolute Bay Daily Diary, May 1957; Log-book entries from R. Sierolawski.
30. Log-book entries from C. Empey and A. Ronning.
31. Log-book entries from E. Chevalier.
32. National Archives of Canada, RG 24, Vol 22798, File 72/2, RCAF Detachment Resolute Bay Daily Diary, May–June 1957; Log-book entries from G. Brogden, J. Lynch and D. McBurney.
33. Kostenuk and Griffin, *RCAF Squadrons and Aircraft*, p. 196; Log-book entries from B. Doucette, F. King and C. Lalande.
34. DHist 181.003 (D240) Operation Random; Log-book entries from L. Byrne and B. Doucette.
35. National Archives of Canada, RG 24, Vol 22794, File 70.9, ATU Daily Diary, May 1957.
36. National Archives of Canada, RG 24, Vol 22798, File 72/2, RCAF Detachment Resolute Bay Daily Diary, June 1957; Log-book entries from F. King.
37. Kealy and Russell, *A History of Canadian Naval Aviation*, pp 99–100; Fuller, Griffin & Molson, *125 Years of Canadian Aeronautics*, p 283.
38. DHist 71/204 Northern Re-supply 1957.

39. *The Orenda*, Vol 3, No 12, June 28, 1957, pp 1, 4–5; Milberry, *The Canadair Sabre*, pp 224; Log-book entries from R.E. Schwanky. The crew of NS17515 on this operation comprised Flying Officer Schwanky (captain), Flying Officer Johnston (first officer); Flying Officer Nishimura and Flying Officer Bourgeois (navigators), Flying Officer Burger and Flying Officer Schaapman (radio officers), Corporal Chartrand (flight engineer), and Leading Aircraftsman Tait (movement controller air).
40. DHist 79/429 Vol 7A, Divisional Items of Interest, 13 June 1957; Milberry, *The Canadian Sabre*, p 167.
41. National Archives of Canada, RG 24, Vol 22798, File 72/2, RCAF Detachment Resolute Bay Daily Diary, June 1957; Log-book entries from B. Lahey.
42. No 426 Squadron Semi-Annual Historical Return, June–November 1957; Log-book entries from J. Lynch. The crew of Special Flight 179 comprised Squadron Leader J.C. Reid (Captain); Flight Lieutenant W.T. Owston (co-captain), Flight Lieutenant J.J. Lynch (first officer); Flight Lieutenant H. Hibbard and Flying Officer J.S. Boutet (navigators); Flying Officer G.F. Smyth and Flying Officer N. Wipond (radio officers); Sergeant J.C. Poirier and Sergeant J.H. Chambers (flight engineers), and Leading Aircraftsman J.W. MacDonald (movement controller air).
43. National Archives of Canada, RG 24, Vol 22794, File 70.9, ATU Daily Diary, June 1957.
44. Fuller et al., *125 Years of Canadian Aeronautics*, p 283.
45. Log-book entries from J. Fabi and J. Hutchinson.
46. Log-book entries from J. Fabi. The crew of Special Flight 288 comprised Flying Officer McLaughlin (captain), Flight Lieutenant Hamel (co-captain), Flight Lieutenant Gill (first officer), Flying Officer Fabi and Flying Officer Kilgour (navigators), Flight Lieutenant Coates and Flying Officer Perron (radio officers), Sergeant Adams and Sergeant Stevens (flight engineers), Corporal Teasdale (movement controller air), Sergeant Braine (airframe technician), and Corporal Marquis (radio technician).
47. No 426 Squadron Semi-Annual Historical Return, June–November 1957; DHist 79/429, Vol 7B, Divisional Items of Interest, July 1957; Log-book entries from T. Latham and L. Leclair; Author's notes and log-book entries.
48. Log-book entries from C. Lalande and A. Ronning.
49. DHist 79/429 Vol 7B, Divisional Items of Interest, 19 and 26 July 1957; National Archives of Canada, RG 24, Vol 22798, File 72/2 RCAF Detachment Resolute Bay Daily Diary, July 1957.
50. No 426 Squadron Semi-Annual Historical Return June–November 1957; Log-book entries from L. Byrne and G. McCormick. The crew of NS17510 on this flight included Flight Lieutenant Misener (captain), Flying Officer Byrne (co-captain), Flight Lieutenant Ingram (first officer), Flight Lieutenant McCormick and Flying Officer Greening (navigators), Flying Officer Callaghan and Flying Officer Turner (radio officers), Sergeant Slaunewhite and Corporal Dahr (flight engineers), and Leading Aircraftsman Mulligan (movement controller air).
51. National Archives of Canada, RG 24, Vol 22798, File 72/2, RCAF Detachment Resolute Bay Daily Diary, July 1957; Log-book entries from G. Brogden.
52. National Archives of Canada, RG 24, Vol 22677, Operational Record No 419 AW(F) Squadron, July–August 1957; Kostenuk and Griffin, *RCAF Squadrons and Aircraft*, p 177; Conversations with and log-book entries from L. Leclair.
53. Log-book entries from G. Brogden, N. Campbell, B. Doucette, B. Lahey and A. Mackie.
54. National Archives of Canada, RG 24, Vol 17752, ATC Operational Review, August 1957; Log-book entries from T. Latham, R.E. Schwanky and R. Sierolawski. The crew of NS17506 on the mission to Australia included Flight Lieutenant Black (captain), Flying Officer Schwanky (co-captain), Flight Lieutenant Sierolawski (first officer), Flight Lieutenant Rawlyk and Flying Officer Nunney (navigators), Flying Officer Latham and Flying Officer Landiss (radio officers), Flight Sergeant Coulliard and Sergeant Luhtala (flight engineers), Leading Aircraftsman Parker (movement controller air), Flight Lieutenant McGregor (aeronautical engineer), and Flight Sergeant Brownrigg and Sergeant McPherson (technicians).
55. National Archives of Canada, RG 24, Vol 22798, File 72/2, RCAF Detachment Resolute Bay Daily Diary, August 1957.

Notes & References

56. Log-book entries from J. Bugdale and C. Lalande.
57. National Archives of Canada, RG 24, Vol 22798, File 72/2, RCAF Detachment Daily Diary, August 1957; No 426 Squadron Semi-Annual Historical Return June–November 1957; Log-book entries from B. Doucette, L. Leclair and H. Stevens.
58. DHist 79/429 Vol 7B, Divisional Items of Interest, August 1957.
59. *Ibid.*
60. No 426 Squadron Semi-Annual Historical Return, June–November 1957; National Archives of Canada, RG 24, Vol 22794, File 70.9, Air Transport Unit Daily Diary, August 1957; Log-book entries from L. Byrne, B. Lahey and L. Rodewolt.
61. National Archives of Canada, Vol 17752, 810–144, Operational Review, August 1957.
62. National Archives of Canada, RG 24, Vol 22798, File 72/2, RCAF Detachment Resolute Bay Daily Diary, August 1957.
63. Fuller, et al. *125 Years of Canadian Aeronautics*, p. 285.
64. National Archives of Canada, RG 24, Vol 17752, Operational Review, January–December 1957; DHist. 79/429, Vol 7B, Divisional Items of Interest, August 1957.
65. National Archives of Canada, RG 24, Vol 22794, File 70.9, ATU Daily Diary, September 1957.
66. Log-book entries from R. Sierolawski. The crew of the service flight included Flight Lieutenant Morrison (captain), Flight Lieutenant Sierolawski (first officer), Flight Lieutenant Rawlyk (navigator), Flight Lieutenant Fowler and Flying Officer Psaila (radio officers), and Flight Sergeant Coulliard (flight engineer). Log-book entries for the 25 September flight were provided by B. Doucette and C. Lalande.
67. No 426 Squadron Semi-Annual Historical Return, June–November 1957. Log-book entries from H. Cram, B. Doucette, A. Mackie, J. Hutchinson, C. Lalande, J. Fabi, L. Byrne, H. Zbesheski, N. Campbell and J. Trethowan.
68. National Archives of Canada, RG 24, Vol 22794, File 70.9, ATU Daily Diary, September 1957.
69. National Archives of Canada, RG 24, Vol 17752, 810–144, Operational Review, October 1957; Log-book entries from: G. Brogden, J. Bugdale, L. Byrne, N. Campbell, B. Doucette, J. Fabi, J. Hutchinson, B. Lahey, C. Lalande, T. Latham, L. Leclair, D. McBurney, K. Reid, L. Rodewolt, R. Sierolawski, D. Woodman and H. Zbesheski.
70. National Archives of Canada, RG 24, Vol 22798, File 72/2, RCAF Detachment Resolute Bay Daily Diary, October 1957; Log-book entries from B. Doucette, J. Fabi and D. McBurney.
71. National Archives of Canada, RG 24, Vol 22551, RCAF Station Lachine Narrative Report, October 1957.
72. National Archives of Canada, RG 24, Vol 17752, 810–144, Operational Review, November 1957; Log-book entries from G. Brogden, J. Bugdale, E. Chevalier, C. Empey, J. Hutchinson, B. Lahey, C. Lalande, T. Latham, K. Reid, L. Rodewolt, R. Sierolawski and H. Zbesheski.
73. Log-book entries from G. Brogden, J. Bugdale, N. Campbell, E. Chevalier, J. Lynch and R. Sierolawski.
74. Log-book entries from B. Doucette, L. Leclair, A. Mackie and D. Woodman.
75. Log-book entries from L. Byrne, B. Doucette, C. Lalande and T. Latham.
76. National Archives of Canada, RG 24, Vol 22798, File 72/2, RCAF Detachment Resolute Bay Daily Diary, November 1957; Log-book entries from L. Leclair and D. Woodman.
77. Log-book entries from B. Lahey.
78. National Archives of Canada, RG 24, Vol 22798, File 72/2, RCAF Detachment Resolute Bay Daily Diary, November–December 1957; Gray, Alert, pp. 11–17; Log-book entries from L. Byrne, J. Fabi, J. Sare and J. Trethowan.
79. Milberry, *The AVRO CF-100*, pp. 99–100; Log-book entries from G. Brogden, J. Fabi and T. Latham.
80. National Archives of Canada, RG 24, Vol 22794, File 70.9, ATU Daily Diary, November 1957.
81. National Archives of Canada, RG 24, 83-84/216, S960-100 (Jump Moat), 25 November 1957; DHist. 79/429, Vol 7B, Divisional Items of Interest, 24 October 1957.

82. National Archives of Canada, RG 24, Vol 17752, 810–144, Operational Review, December 1957; Log-book entries from: G. Brogden, J. Bugdale, L. Byrne, N. Campbell, E. Chevalier, B. Doucette, C. Empey, J. Fabi, J. Hutchinson, B. Lahey, C. Lalande, T. Latham, L. Leclair, J. Lynch, D. McBurney, G. McCormick, K. Reid, L. Rodewolt, R. Sierolawski, and H. Zbesheski.
83. Milberry, *The AVRO CF-100*, pp. 151–152; National Archives of Canada, RG 24, ATIP Interim 263, 960–100 "Jump Moat: Report on Operation", 3 January 1958; RG 24, 83-84/216 Operation Jump Moat, ADC Operation Order 25/57; AFHQ Directive 100/57, 25 November 1957; DHist 79/429, Vol 7B, Divisional Items of Interest, December 1957; Log-book entries from J. Hutchinson.
84. No 426 Squadron Semi-Annual Historical Return, December 1957–May 1958; Log-book entries from: C. Empey and K. Reid.
85. National Archives of Canada, RG 24, Vol 22798, File 72/2, RCAF Detachment Resolute Bay Daily Diary, December 1957; Log-book entries from: B. Lahey, C. Lalande, T. Latham and G. McCormick.
86. No 426 Squadron Semi-Annual Historical Return, December 1957–May 1958.
87. No 426 Squadron Semi-Annual Historical Return, December 1957–May 1958; Log-book entries from G. Brogden, B. Lahey, T. Latham and D. McBurney.
88. National Archives of Canada, RG 24, Vol 22794, File 70.9, 115 ATU, El Arish, AFHQ Organization Order S895-127 (DOE), 31 December 1957.
89. National Archives of Canada, RG 24, Vol 22551, RCAF Station Lachine Daily Diary, December 1957.

Chapter 22: Lachine, 1958

1. DHist 73/430 RCAF Program of Activities, 1958–1962.
2. No 426 Squadron Semi-Annual Historical Return, December 1957–May 1958; Log-book entries from J. Bugdale, L. Byrne, T. Charchuk, E. Chevalier, J. Fabi and J. Lynch.
3. Log-book entries from G. Brogden, J. Bugdale, L. Byrne, N. Campbell, B. Doucette, C. Empey, J. Hutchinson, B. Lahey, C. Lalande, L. Leclair, G. McCormick, K. Reid, L. Rodewolt, R. Sierolawski, J. Trethowan and D. Woodman.
4. National Archives of Canada, RG 24, Vol 22794, File 70.9, ATU Daily Diary, January 1958.
5. National Archives of Canada, RG 24, Vol 22794, File 70.9, ATU Daily Diary, January 1958; Log-book entries from J. Hutchinson and G. McCormick.
6. RCAF Accident Report 801092; Log-book entries from D. McBurney.
7. National Archives of Canada, RG 24, Vol 22798, File 72/2, RCAF Detachment Resolute Bay Daily Diary, January 1958.
8. No 426 Squadron Semi-Annual Historical Return, December 1957–May 1958; Log-book entries from G. Brogden, E. Chevalier, T. Charchuk, B. Doucette, D. McBurney; K. Reid, R. Sierolawski, D. Woodman and H. Zbesheski.
9. No 426 Squadron Semi-Annual Historical Return, December 1957–May 1958; National Archives of Canada, RG 24, Vol 17752, Operations Summary, 810-144, Vol 2, February 1958; Log-book entries from B. Lahey and T. Latham.
10. No 426 Squadron Semi-Annual Historical Return, December 1957–May 1958; Log-book entries from J. Bugdale, T. Charchuk, J. Fabi, and D. Woodman.
11. No 426 Squadron Semi-Annual Historical Return, December 1957–May 1958.
12. National Archives of Canada, RG 24, Vol 22798, File 72/2, RCAF Detachment Resolute Bay Daily Diary, February 1958; Log-book entries from N. Campbell and C. Empey.
13. National Archives of Canada, RG 24, Vol 22798, File 72/2, RCAF Detachment Resolute Bay Daily Diary, February 1958; Log-book entries from J. Bugdale, B. Doucette and B. Lahey.
14. No 426 Squadron Semi-Annual Historical Return, December 1957–May 1958; Log-book entries from N. Campbell, J. Hutchinson, B. Lahey, L. Leclair, K. Reid, R. Sierolawski, J. Trethowan and D. Woodman.

Notes & References

15. No 426 Squadron Semi-Annual Historical Return, December 1957–May 1958; Log-book entries from T. Charchuk, J. Fabi, A. Mackie and L. Rodewolt.
16. National Archives of Canada, RG 24, Vol 17752, File 810-144, Vol 2, Operational Summary, March 1958; No 426 Squadron Semi-Annual Historical Return, December 1957–May 1958.
17. National Archives of Canada, RG 24, Vol 22798, File 72/2, RCAF Detachment Resolute Bay Daily Diary, March 1958; No 426 Squadron Semi-Annual Historical Return, December 1957–May 1958; Log-book entries from G. Brogden, E. Chevalier, G. McCormick and J. Sare.
18. No 426 Squadron Semi-Annual Historical Return, December 1957–May 1958; Log-book entries from T. Charchuk, K. Reid and L. Rodewolt.
19. Milberry, *Sixty Years of RCAF and CF Air Command, 1924–1984*, pp. 317–318, 471; Fuller et al, *125 Years of Canadian Aeronautics*, pp. 285, 287.
20. No 426 Squadron Semi-Annual Historical Return, December 1957–May 1958.
21. No 426 Squadron Semi-Annual Historical Return, December 1957–May 1958; Log-book entries from G. Brogden, L. Byrne, N. Campbell, P. Dragojevich, J. Fabi, J. Hutchinson, B. Lahey, T. Latham, L. Leclair, K. Reid, D. Woodman and H. Zbesheski.
22. No 426 Squadron Semi-Annual Historical Return, December 1957–May 1958; Log-book entries from G. Brogden.
23. No 426 Squadron Semi-Annual Historical Return, December 1957–May 1958.
24. DHist 71/204 Northern Re-supply 1958, Operation Order 9/58; DHist 71/205 Report on Spring Re-supply of Arctic Weather Stations, 25 May 1958; National Archives of Canada, RG 24, Vol 22798, File 72/2, RCAF Detachment Resolute Bay Daily Diary, April 1958.
25. No 426 Squadron Semi-Annual Historical Return, December 1957–May 1958; National Archives of Canada, RG 24, Vol 22798, File 72/2, RCAF Detachment Resolute Bay Daily Diary, April 1958; Log-book entries from N. Campbell.
26. No 426 Squadron Semi-Annual Historical Return, December 1957–May 1958; Log-book entries from J. Fabi, J. Lynch and L. Rodewolt.
27. No 426 Squadron Semi-Annual Historical Return, December 1957–May 1958; Log-book entries from J. Bugdale, N. Campbell, P. Dragojevich, B. Doucette, C. Empey, J. Fabi, B. Lahey, J. Lynch, G. McCormick, L. Rodewolt, J. Sare, R. Sierolawski, J. Trethowan, D. Woodman, H. Zbesheski.
28. No 426 Squadron Semi-Annual Historical Return, December 1957–May 1958; DHist 79/429, Vol 7B, May 1958.
29. Milberry, *The Canadair North Star*, pp. 174–175; No 426 Squadron Semi-Annual Historical Return, December 1957–May 1958; Log-book entries from N. Campbell and L. Rodewolt.
30. Halliday, *Chronology of Canadian Military Aviation*, p. 130; DHist 79/429, Vol 7B, Divisional Items of Interest, 29 May, 1958.
31. Milberry, *Sixty Years of RCAF and CF Air Command, 1924–1984*, p. 471; Halliday, *Chronology of Canadian Military Aviation*, p. 130.
32. No 426 Squadron Semi-Annual Historical Return, December 1957–May 1958; National Archives of Canada, RG 24, Vol 22798, File 72/2, RCAF Detachment Resolute Bay Daily Diary, May 1958; Log-book entries from K. Reid.
33. No 426 Squadron Semi-Annual Historical Return, December 1957–May 1958; National Archives of Canada, RG 24, Vol 22798, File 72/2, RCAF Detachment Resolute Bay Daily Diary, May 1958; Log-book entries from L. Byrne and T. Latham.
34. Log-book entries from N. Campbell, P. Dragojevich, C. Empey, J. Fabi, J. Hutchinson, B. Lahey, C. Lalande, D. McBurney, K. Reid, L. Rodewolt, D. Woodman, H. Zbesheski.
35. Log-book entries from J. Bugdale and L. Rodewolt.
36. DHist 71/205, Operation Order NORS58.
37. National Archives of Canada, RG 24, Vol 22798, File 72/2, RCAF Detachment Resolute Bay Daily Diary, June 1958; Log-book entries from J. Fabi and J. Sare.

38. DHist 79/429, Vol 7B, AFHQ Divisional Items of Interest, July 1958; Log-book entries from E. Chevalier and J. Lynch; National Archives of Canada, RG 24, Vol 17752, 810-144 (Vol 3).
39. National Archives of Canada, RG 24, Vol 22551, RCAF Station Lachine Daily Diary, June 1958.
40. National Archives of Canada, RG 24, Vol 22798, File 72/2, RCAF Detachment Resolute Bay Daily Diary, July 1958; Log-book entries from B. Doucette, G. McCormick, L. Rodewolt and J. Sare; RCAF Accident Report 807087, 20 July 1958.
41. Log-book entries from J. Bugdale, L. Byrne, E. Chevalier, P. Dragojevich, C. Empey, J. Hutchinson, B. Lahey, C. Lalande, T. Latham, J. Lynch, A. Mackie, K. Reid, J. Sare, R. Sierolawski, J. Trethowan, D. Woodman and H. Zbesheski.
42. National Archives of Canada, RG 24, Vol 22794, File 70.9, Historical Narrative, No 115 ATU, July 1958.
43. National Archives of Canada, RG 24, Box 3549, Jump Moat, S-960-100 (Part 2).
44. Halliday, *Chronology of Canadian Military Aviation*, p. 130.
45. Fuller et al. *125 Years of Canadian Aeronautics*, p. 285.
46. DHist 71/205 Northern Re-supply 1958, Beachmaster's Report; National Archives of Canada, RG 24, Vol 22798, File 72/2, RCAF Detachment Resolute Bay Daily Diary, August–September 1958; Milberry, *Sixty Years of RCAF and CF Air Command, 1924–1984*, p. 471; Gray, *Alert: Beyond the Inuit Lands*, pp. 15–17; Log-book entries from J. Hutchinson, B. Lahey, C. Lalande, and R. Sierolawski.
47. Log-book entries from J. Bugdale, N. Campbell, E. Chevalier, W. Dick, P. Dragojevich, J. Hutchinson, C. Lalande, T. Latham, L. Leclair, J. Lynch, K. Reid, and D. Woodman.
48. Log-book entries from B. Doucette, A. Mackie and H. Zbesheski; Conversations with B. Doucette and D. Kuhn.
49. National Archives of Canada, RG 24, Vol 22794, File 70.9, No 115 ATU Historical Narrative, September 1958; Log-book entries from J. Bugdale, N. Campbell, T. Charchuk, B. Doucette, P. Dragojevich, C. Empey, J. Hutchinson, B. Lahey, C. Lalande, J. Maitland, G. McCormick, K. Reid, R. Sierolawski, S. Walton, D. Woodman and H. Zbesheski.
50. National Archives of Canada, RG 24, Vol 22798, File 72/2, RCAF Detachment Resolute Bay Daily Diary, September 1958, Log-book entries from E. Chevalier and B. Lahey.
51. National Archives of Canada, RG 24, Vol 22798 File 72/2, RCAF Detachment Resolute Bay Daily Diary, September 1958; Log Book entries provided by L. Leclair.
52. DHist 79/429, Vol 8, AFHQ Divisional Items of Interest, September–October 1958.
53. Halliday, *Chronology of Canadian Military Aviation*, p. 130.
54. National Archives of Canada, RG 24, Vol 17752, AFHQ Operational Summary, October 1958; RG 24, Vol 22794, File 70.9, No 115 ATU Historical Narrative, October 1958; Log-book entries from J. Bugdale, N. Campbell, T. Charchuk, B. Doucette, P. Dragojevich, J. Hutchinson, C. Lalande, B. Lahey, L. Leclair, J. Lynch, J. Maitland, L. Rodewolt, S. Walton, D. Woodman and H. Zbesheski.
55. DHist 79/429, Vol 8, Divisional Items of Interest, October 1958; National Archives of Canada, RG 24, Vol 22798, File 72/2, RCAF Detachment Resolute Bay Daily Diary, October 1958; Log-book entries from N. Campbell, T. Charchuk, E. Chevalier, P. Dragojevich, C. Empey, J. Hutchinson, J. Lynch, H. Zbesheski.
56. Fuller et al. *125 Years of Canadian Aeronautics*, p. 285; Milberry, *Sixty Years of RCAF and CF Air Command 1924–1984*, p. 471.
57. Log-book entries from T. Charchuk, N. Campbell, E. Chevalier, B. Doucette, P. Dragojevich, J. Hutchinson, B. Lahey, C. Lalande, L. Leclair, A. Mackie, M.G. Morrison, K. Reid, S. Walton, D. Woodman, and H. Zbesheski.
58. Milberry, *The AVRO CF-100*, pp. 99–101; Log-book entries from J. Lynch, K. Reid and D. Woodman.
59. National Archives of Canada, RG 24, Vol 22798, File 72/2, RCAF Detachment Resolute Bay Daily Diary, November 1958; Log-book entries from P. Dragojevich, J. Maitland and J. Sare.
60. National Archives of Canada, RG 24, Vol 22551, RCAF Station Lachine Daily Diary, November 1958.

61. National Archives of Canada, RG 24, Vol 22798, File 72/2, RCAF Detachment Resolute Bay Daily Diary, December 1958; Log-book entries from J. Hutchinson, L. Leclair, M.G. Morrison, D. Woodman and H. Zbesheski.
62. Log-book entries from B. Lahey, A. Mackie, L. Rodewolt and S. Walton.
63. Log-book entries from E. Chevalier, B. Doucette, P. Dragojevich, C. Empey, J. Hutchinson, B. Lahey, C. Lalande, L. Leclair, J. Lynch, J. Maitland, D. McBurney, M.G. Morrison, K. Reid, L. Rodewolt and J. Sare.
64. DHist 79/429, Vol 8, AFHQ Divisional Items of Interest, December 1958; Milberry, *Sixty Years of RCAF and CF Air Command, 1924–1984*, p. 471; Fuller et al. *125 Years of Canadian Aeronautics*, p. 285.
65. National Archives of Canada, RG 24, Vol 22794, File 70.9, No 115 ATU Historical Narrative, December 1958.
66. National Archives of Canada, RG 24, Vol 22551, RCAF Station Lachine Daily Diary, December 1958.

CHAPTER 23: LACHINE AND TRENTON, 1959

1. Log-book entries from N. Campbell and J. Sare.
2. Log-book entries from G. Bussieres, T. Charchuk, B. Doucette, P. Dragojevich, B. Hoy, B. Lahey, C. Lalande, J. Lynch, J. Maitland, J. Moric, K. Reid, S. Walton, D. Woodman, and H. Zbesheski.
3. National Archives of Canada, RG 24, Vol 22798, File 72/2, RCAF Detachment Resolute Bay Historical Return, Report January–July 1959.
4. *Ibid.*, January 1959.
5. National Archives of Canada, RG 24, Vol 22551, RCAF Station Lachine Daily Diary, January 1959; DHist 79/429, Vol 9, AFHQ Divisional Items of Interest, 16 January 1959.
6. DHist 79/429 Vol 9, AFHQ Divisional Items of Interest, 30 January 1959.
7. National Archives of Canada, RG 24, Vol 22794, File 70.9, Historical Narrative No 115 ATU El Arish, February 1959; Log-book entries from J. Hutchinson and M.G. Morrison.
8. National Archives of Canada, RG 24, Vol 22794, File 70.9, Historical Narrative No 115 ATU El Arish, February 1959.
9. Log-book entries from G. Bussieres, N. Campbell, E. Chevalier, C. Empey, B. Hoy, W. Lupton, J. Lynch, A. Mackie, J. Maitland, D. McBurney, J. Moric, K. Reid, L. Rodewolt, J. Sare, S. Walton, D. Woodman, and H. Zbesheski.
10. Fuller, et al., *125 Years of Canadian Aeronautics*, p. 287; Milberry, *Sixty Years: The RCAF and CF Air Command 1924–1984*, p. 471.
11. National Archives of Canada, RG 24, Vol 27551, File 15.3, AFHQ Organization Order 8.2 dated 10 March 1959.
12. Log-book entries from G. Bussieres, T. Charchuk, B. Doucette, P. Dragojevich, C. Empey, B. Hoy, B. Lahey, C. Lalande, L. Leclair, W. Lupton, J. Moric, M.G. Morrison, L. Rodewolt, R. Sierolawski, J. Sare, D. Woodman, H. Zbesheski.
13. Conversations with and log-book entries from G. Bussieres.
14. National Archives of Canada, RG 24, Vol 22798, File 72/2, RCAF Detachment Resolute Bay, Historical Return, March 1959; Log-book entries from N. Campbell and J. Hutchinson.
15. National Archives of Canada, RG 24, Vol 22551, RCAF Station Lachine Daily Diary, March 1959.
16. *Ibid.*, April 1959.
17. Log-book entries from G. Bussieres, N. Campbell, B. Doucette, P. Dragojevich, C. Empey, B. Hoy, B. Lahey, C. Lalande, W. Lupton, J. Moric, M.G. Morrison, A. Mackie, K. Reid, L. Rodewolt, J. Sare, R. Sierolawski, D. Woodman, and H. Zbesheski.
18. National Archives of Canada, RG 24, Vol 22798, File 72/2 RCAF Detachment Resolute Bay, Historical Return, April 1959; Log-book entries from B. Hoy and M.G. Morrison.

19. ATC Headquarters press release dated 23 April 1959.
20. DHist 79/429, Vol 9, AFHQ Divisional Items of Interest, 24 April 1959.
21. Gray, *Alert: Beyond the Inuit Lands*, pp. 16–17.
22. National Archives of Canada, RG 24, Vol 17752, AFHQ Operations Summary, 810-144-Vol 3, May 1959; Log-book entries from G. Bussieres, N. Campbell, E. Chevalier, B. Doucette, P. Dragojevich, C. Empey, B. Hoy, B. Lahey, L. Leclair, W. Lupton, D. McBurney, G. McCormick, J. Moric, K. Reid, L. Rodewolt, J. Sare, S. Walton and D. Woodman.
23. Log-book entries from W. Lupton, A. Mackie, R. Sierolawski and D. Woodman.
24. Log-book entries from P. Dragojevich, B. Hoy, B. Lahey and H. Zbesheski.
25. National Archives of Canada, RG 24, Vol 22798, File 72/2, RCAF Detachment Resolute Bay Historical Return, May 1959; Log-book entries from M.G. Morrison; Correspondence and conversations with and log-book entries from L. Rodewolt; Conversations with K.R. Greenaway.
26. National Archives of Canada, RG 24, Vol 22798, File 72/2, Vol 22798, RCAF Detachment Resolute Bay Historical Return, May 1959.
27. Milberry, *Air Transport in Canada*, Vol 1, p. 183; Milberry, *Sixty Years: The RCAF and CF Air Command, 1924–1984*, p. 284.
28. National Archives of Canada, RG 24, Vol 17910, 900-960-5, Vol 3, Statement by the Hon. George R. Pearkes, Minister of National Defence, Department of National Defence Press Release, May 1959.
29. Morrison, "Bugsmashers, Ho!" *Airforce* 20/3 (Fall 1996), pp. 24–26; DHist 79/429, Vol 9, AFHQ Divisional Items of Interest, 12 June 1959; Halliday, *Chronology of Canadian Military Aviation*, p. 132; Milberry, *Sixty Years: The RCAF and CF Air Command, 1924–1984*, p. 471; Correspondence and conversations with and log-book entries from A.J. Timmins; Conversations with and log-book entries from B. Doucette and C. Lalande.
30. Log-book entries from T. Charchuk and R. Sierolawski.
31. Log-book entries from P. Dragojevich and J. Moric.
32. National Archives of Canada, RG 24, Vol 22798, File 72/2, RCAF Detachment Resolute Bay, Historical Return, May 1959; Log-book entries from R. Sierolawski.
33. National Archives of Canada, RG 24, Vol 17752, AFHQ Operations Summary, 810-144-Vol 3, Reports and Returns, June 1959.
34. Log-book entries from G. Bussieres, E. Chevalier, N. Campbell, P. Dragojevich, C. Empey, J. Hutchinson, B. Lahey, C. Lalande, L. Leclair, W. Lupton, J. Lynch, J. Moric, M.G. Morrison, K. Reid, L. Rodewolt, R. Sierolawski and S. Walton.
35. National Archives of Canada, RG 24, Vol 22773, File 65.2, Folder 6, No 6 Repair Depot Semi-Annual Historical Return, June 1959; Canadian Aviation Museum, Log No. 277, F/L J.F. Dyer.
36. Log-book entries from G. Bussieres, K. Reid and R. Sierolawski.
37. DHist 79/429, Vol 9, AFHQ Divisional Items of Interest 19 June 1959.
38. DHist 79/429, Vol 9, AFHQ Divisional Items of Interest, 26 June 1959; Correspondence and conversations with and log-book entries from L. Rodewolt; RCAF Report on Accident No 906087, 21 June 1959, File 093-17525; Log-book entries from W. Lupton and K. Reid; Conversations with D. Woodman. The navigator on this flight was Flying Officer André Fullam, and the radio officer was Flying Officer Ivor Allen. The author was on the No 4 OTU flight to Athens at the end of August that brought back two of the engines salvaged from the wreck of NS17525.
39. Log-book entries from B. Hoy.
40. Milberry, *The Canadair North Star*, p. 170; Log-book entries from N. Campbell and R. Sierolawski.
41. *Encyclopaedia Britannica Book of the Year*, 1960, pp. 2, 4, 16–17, 137; Halliday, *Chronology of Canadian Military Aviation*, p. 132.
42. Fuller et al, *125 Years of Canadian Aeronautics*, p. 287; Halliday, *Chronology of Canadian Military Aviation*, p. 132.

Notes & References

43. Log-book entries from G. Bussieres, N. Campbell, T. Charchuk, E. Chevalier, B. Doucette, P. Dragojevich, C. Empey, J. Hutchinson, B. Lahey, C. Lalande, L. Leclair, W. Lupton, J. Lynch, D. McBurney, J. Moric, M.G. Morrison, L. Rodewolt, S. Walton, D. Woodman and H. Zbesheski.
44. Milberry, *The Canadair North Star*, p. 170; Log-book entries from C. Lalande (flight engineer) and K. Reid (navigator). Other members of the crew were Flying Officer G. Martin (first officer), Flying Officer E. Decaux (radio officer) and Leading Aircraftsman Falardeau (movement controller air).
45. National Archives of Canada, RG 24, Vol 22574, RCAF Station Trenton Narrative Report, July 1959. Air Vice Marshal Bryans was AOC Training Command, and Group Captain D.J. Williams was the Station Commander at Trenton.
46. Log-book entries from M.G. Morrison.
47. National Archives of Canada, RG 24, Vol 17752, AFHQ Operations Summary, 810-144-Vol 3, Reports and Returns July, August, September 1959.
48. Conversations with and log-book entries from P. Dragojevich (radio officer) and K. Reid (navigator). Other crew members were: Flight Lieutenant McLaughlin and Flight Lieutenant Robertson (pilots), Flying Officer Niehaus (navigator), Flying Officer Wickstrom (radio officer), Sergeant Kondra and Corporal Harriman (flight engineers), and Leading Aircraftsman Falardeau (movement controller air).
49. National Archives of Canada, RG 24, Vol 22574, RCAF Station Trenton Narrative Report, August 1959; DHist 79/429 Vol 9, AFHQ Divisional Items of Interest, 21 August 1959.
50. Log-book entries from G. Bussieres, E. Chevalier, B. Hoy; B. Lahey, C. Lalande, L. Leclair, W. Lupton, J. Lynch, J. Moric, M.G. Morrison, L. Rodewolt, D. Woodman and H. Zbesheski.
51. National Archives of Canada, RG 24, Vol 22773, File 65.2 Folder 6, No 6 Repair Depot Semi-Annual Historical Return, August 1959; Conversations with and log-book entries from R. Sierolawski; Log-book entries from H. Zbesheski.
52. National Archives of Canada, RG 24, Vol 22798, File 70.9, No 115 ATU Historical Narrative, August 1959.
53. National Archives of Canada, RG 24, Vol 22574, RCAF Station Trenton Narrative Report, September 1959.
54. *Ibid.*
55. National Archives of Canada, RG 24, Vol 17752, AFHQ Operations Summary, 810-144-Vol 3, Reports and Returns, September 1959; Halliday, *Chronology of Canadian Military Aviation*, p. 133; RG 24, Vol 22794, File 70.9, No 115 ATU Historical Narrative, September–October 1959; Log-book entries from G. Bussieres, T. Charchuk, E. Chevalier, B. Doucette, P. Dragojevich, C. Lalande, L. Leclair, W. Lupton, J. Lynch, A. Mackie, J. Maitland, J. Moric, M.G. Morrison, L. Motiuk, K. Reid, L. Rodewolt, D. Woodman and H. Zbeskeski.
56. *Observer Training Manual*, Vol 3, "Electronic Aids to Navigation", Chapter 3.04, Consol; Author's notes and log book entries. The members of the flight crew were: Flying Officer J. Lavigne (captain), Flight Lieutenant V. Peterson (first officer), Flight Lieutenant L. Motiuk (navigator), Flight Lieutenant P. Rawlyk (check navigator), Flying Officer S. Sanderson (radio officer), Corporal E. Gauthier (flight engineer) and Leading Aircraftsman B. Lloyd (movement controller air).
57. National Archives of Canada, RG 24, Vol 22799, CEPE/CARDE Detachment, Narrative Report September 1959; Canada Aviation Museum, Log 0407, Captain O.M. Sweetman; Milberry, *Canada's Air Force at War and Peace*, Vol 3, pp. 287–289.
58. National Archives of Canada, RG 24, Vol 22773, File 65.2 Folder 6, 6 Repair Depot Narrative Report, September 1959; Conversations with and log-book entries from W. Clarke and D. Woodman; DHist 79/429, Vol 9, AFHQ Divisional Items of Interest, 9 October 1959.
59. National Archives of Canada, RG 24, Vol 17752, AFHQ Operations Summary, 810-144-Vol 3, Reports and Returns October 1959; Log-book entries from G. Bussieres, T. Charchuk, E. Chevalier, P. Dragojevich, C. Empey, B. Hoy, J. Hutchinson, C. Lalande, L. Leclair, J. Lynch, J. Moric, M.G. Morrison, L. Motiuk, K. Reid, R. Sierolawski, S. Walton and H. Zbesheski.
60. DHist 79/429, Vol 9, AFHQ Divisional Items of Interest, 23 October 1959.

61. Halliday, *Chronology of Military Aviation*, p. 133; Milberry, *Sixty Years: The RCAF and CF Air Command, 1924–1984*, p. 314; DHist 79/429, Vol 9, AFHQ Divisional Items of Interest, 13 and 30 November 1959.
62. National Archives of Canada RG 24, Vol 17752 AFHQ Operations Summary, 810-144-Vol 3, Reports and Returns, November 1959; Log-book entries from G. Bussieres, B. Doucette, M. Gordon, J. Hutchinson, C. Lalande, L. Leclair, W. Lupton, J. Lynch, A. Mackie, J. Maitland, J. Moric, M.G. Morrison, L. Motiuk, K. Reid and S. Walton.
63. Log-book entries from T. Charchuk and B. Hoy. Crew of NS17512 were: F/L Stockdale, Captain; F/Ls Charchuk and Nichol, 1st Officers; F/L Hoy and F/O McMann, Navigators; F/L Lashley and F/O De Caux, Radio Officers; Sgts Brasseur and Porier, Flight Engineers; LAC Tait, Movement Controller Air; Sgt. Darresse and Cpl Mathieu, Technicians.
64. National Archives of Canada, RG 24, Vol 22574, File 21-3, RCAF Station Trenton Narrative Report, November 1959.
65. DHist 79/429, Vol 9, AFHQ Divisional Items of Interest, 4 December 1959.
66. Log-book entries from G. Bussieres, E. Chevalier, B. Doucette, P. Dragojevich, C. Empey, D. Kuhn, C. Lalande, W. Lupton, A. Mackie, D. McBurney, J. Moric, L. Motiuk, K. Reid, J. Sopaz, S. Walton and D. Woodman.
67. Halliday, *Chronology of Canadian Military Aviation*, p. 133.

CHAPTER 24: TRENTON, 1960

1. National Archives of Canada, RG 24, Vol 17752, AFHQ Operations Summary, January 1960; Log-book entries from G. Bussieres, T. Charchuk, B. Doucette, B. Hoy, L. Leclair, W. Lupton, J. Lynch, L. Motiuk, and H. Zbesheski.
2. Burge and Lindsay, "Somewhere East of Suez", *Roundel* 12/2 (March 1960), pp. 4–10; Author's notes and log-book entries.
3. Milberry, *Canada's Air Force*, Vol 3, pp. 287–289; Milberry, *The AVRO CF-100*, pp. 136–138; Morrison, "South Atlantic Lookout", *Roundel*, 12/3 (April 1960) pp. 2–3; Canada Aviation Museum, Log 0407 Captain O.M. Sweetman; DHist 79/429, Vol 10, AFHQ Divisional Items of Interest, 8 and 15 January 1960; Fuller et al, *125 Years of Canadian Aeronautics*, p. 289; Halliday, *Chronology of Canadian Military Aviation*, p. 133; Log-book entries from E. Chevalier and D. Kuhn.
4. Conversations with and log-book entries from P. Dragojevich and H. Zbesheski.
5. Conversation with K. Greenaway and log-book entries from C. Empey.
6. Log-book entries from J. Hutchinson and K. Reid.
7. Log-book entries from C. Lalande and J. Lynch.
8. DHist 79/429 Vol 10, AFHQ Divisional Items of Interest, 29 January 1960.
9. National Archives of Canada, RG 24, Vol 17752, AFHQ Operations Summary, February 1960; RG 24, Vol 22794, File 70.9, Historical Narrative, No 115 ATU El Arish, February 1960. Log-book entries from G. Bussieres, B. Doucette, P. Dragojevich, B. Hoy, J. Hutchinson, C. Lalande, L. Leclair, W. Lupton, J. Lynch, J. Maitland, J. Moric, M.G. Morrison, K. Reid, J. Sopaz and D. Woodman.
10. National Archives of Canada, RG 24, Vol 22798, File 72/2, RCAF Detachment Resolute Bay, Historical Record, February 1960; Log-book entries from G. Bussieres, T. Charchuk, P. Dragojevich, C. Empey, J. Hutchinson, D. Kuhn, D. McBurney, and S. Walton.
11. Author's log-book entries.
12. DHist 79/429, Vol 10, AFHQ Divisional Items of Interest, 5 February 1960.
13. National Archives of Canada, RG 24, Vol 17752, AFHQ Operations Summary, March 1960; RG 24, Vol 22794, File 70.9, Historical Narrative, No 115 ATU El Arish, March 1960. Log-book entries from G. Bussieres, T. Charchuk, B. Doucette, P. Dragojevich, J. Hutchinson, D. Jones, C. Lalande, L. Leclair, W. Lupton, J. Lynch, J. Maitland, K. Reid, J. Sopaz, R. Sierolawski, S. Walton, H. Zbesheski.
14. Conversations with R. Hayes and J. Moric; Log-book entries from J. Moric.

15. Conversations with and log-book entries from T. Charchuk and W. Lupton.
16. DHist 79/429, Vol 10, AFHQ Divisional Items of Interest, 11 March 1960.
17. National Archives of Canada, RG 24, Vol 17752, AFHQ Operations Summary, March 1960. Log-book entries from C. Empey, J. Hutchinson, C. Lalande, J. Moric and L. Motiuk.
18. Log-book entries from J. Moric, K. Reid and J. Trethowan.
19. Conversation with J. Lynch, then the squadron's Flight Safety Officer, who observed the incident from the window of his office in No 9 Hangar.
20. National Archives of Canada, RG 24, Vol 17752, AFHQ Operations Summary, April 1960; Log-book entries from G. Bussieres, T. Charchuk, B. Doucette, C. Empey, M. Gordon, B. Hoy, J. Hutchinson, D. Kuhn, L. Leclair, W. Lupton, J. Lynch, J. Moric, K. Reid, S. Walton and H. Zbesheski.
21. National Archives of Canada, RG 24, Vol 22794, File 70.9, Historical Narrative, No 115 ATU El Arish, April 1960.
22. National Archives of Canada, RG 24, Vol 17752, AFHQ Operations Summary, April 1960; RG 24, Vol 22798, File 72/2, RCAF Resolute Bay Detachment, Daily Diary, April 1960; Log-book entries from; B. Doucette, C. Empey, B. Hoy, D. Jones, L. Leclair and C. Lalande.
23. DHist 79/429, Vol 10, AFHQ Divisional Items of Interest, 14 April 1960.
24. Conversation with, and log-book entries from J. Maitland; Log-book entries from G. Bussieres.
25. National Archives of Canada, RG 24, Vol 17752, AFHQ Operations Summary, May 1960; RG 24, Vol 22794, File 70.9, Historical Narrative, No 115 ATU El Arish, May 1960; log-book entries from G. Bussieres, T. Charchuk, B. Ducette, B. Hoy, J. Hutchinson, C. Lalande, L. Leclair, W. Lupton, J. Lynch, J. Moric, L. Motiuk, R. Sierolawski, J. Sopaz, J. Trethowan and S. Walton.
26. Log-book entries from B. Doucette.
27. National Archives of Canada, RG 24, Vol 22798, File 72/2, RCAF Resolute Bay Detachment, Daily Diary, May 1960; Correspondence and conversations with K.R. Greenaway; Log-book entries from T. Charchuk, D. Jones, L. Leclair, J. Lynch, J. Moric, M.G. Morrison, D. Woodman and H. Zbesheski.
28. *Encyclopaedia Britannica Book of the Year*, 1961, P. 619.
29. National Archives of Canada, RG 24, Vol 17752, AFHQ Operations Summary June 1960; Howard Green, "Canada and Latin America: Report to the House of Commons by the Secretary of State for External Affairs, on May 30, 1960", Statements and Speeches, No 60/20, pp. 3–4; DHist 75/351: News Release, 27 May 1960; Red Cross News Service 28 May 1960; News Release 1 June 1960; Fuller et al, *125 Years of Canadian Aeronautics*, p. 160; Halliday, Chronology of Canadian Military Aviation, p. 134; "Canadian Aid For Chile", *Roundel*, Vol 12, No 6, July–August 1960, p. 12; Maitland, J. "Fasten Your Seat Belts (Rope)", 426 Thunderbird Squadron Association, 9th Biennial Association Brochure, June 1992, pp. 48–49; Captain's report, conversations with and log-book entries from J. Lynch; Conversations with and log-book entries from J. Maitland; Log-book entries from G. Bussieres, B. Doucette, C. Empey, B. Hoy, C. Lalande, R. Parmelee, J. Sopaz, D. Woodman; Author's notes and log-book entries. **The following crews deployed on** *Operation AMIGO*: Wing Commander J. Maitland (captain) with Flight Lieutenant V. Peterson (first officer), Flight Lieutenant B. Hoy (navigator), Flying Officer D. Woodman (radio officer), Sergeant M. Demeter (flight engineer) and Leading Aircraftsman W.D. Murphy (MCA); Flight Lieutenant J.R. Morrison (captain) with Captain B. Saunders, USAF (first officer), Flying Officer G.B. Bussieres (navigator), Flying Officer A.E.B. Cole (radio officer), Sergeant J. Sopaz (flight engineer) and Leading Aircraftsman K.F. Ulmer (MCA); Flight Lieutenant R.R. Hayes (captain) with Flight Lieutenant P.F. Hope (first officer), Flight Lieutenant L. Motiuk (navigator), Flying Officer L. Landess (radio officer), Sergeant C. Lalande (flight engineer) and Leading Aircraftsman R.L. Bryson (MCA); Flight Lieutenant J.J. Lynch (captain) with Flight Lieutenant R. Lehman (first officer), Flight Lieutenant F.G. Hannington (navigator), Flying Officer J.A.C. Belanger (radio officer), Sergeant R.K. Turner (flight engineer) and Leading Aircraftsman J.A. Hoffart (MCA); Flight Lieutenant J.S. Parmelee (captain) with Flight Lieutenant D. Spence (first officer), Flying Officer H.J. Neihaus (navigator), Flying Officer P. Psaila (radio officer), WO2 T.F. Kelly (flight engineer) and Leading Aircraftsman G. Falardeau (MCA); Flight Lieutenant H.M. Smith (captain) with Flight Lieutenant B.V. Genge (first officer), Flying Officer L.F. Friedel (navigator),

Flying Officer R.W. Doucette (radio officer), Sergeant T.B. Dyer (flight engineer) and Leading Aircraftsman G. Tanner (MCA); and Flight Lieutenant R.J. Robertson (captain) with Flying Officer G.M. Martin (first officer), Flying Officer L.G.E. Bourgeois (navigator), Flight Lieutenant J.M. Coates (radio officer), Sergeant C. Empey (flight engineer) and Leading Aircraftsman R.G. Lloyd (MCA).

30. National Archives of Canada, RG 24, Vol 17752, AFHQ Operations Summary, June 1960; Log-book entries from G. Bussieres, T. Charchuk, B. Doucette, C. Empey, D. Jones, D. Kuhn, L. Leclair, J. Lynch, M.G. Morrison, L. Motiuk, R. Sierolawski, J. Sopaz, S. Walton, D. Woodman and H. Zbesheski.

31. Log-book entries from B. Doucette, J. Hutchinson, D. Jones, L. Leclair, J. Maitland, J. Moric, L. Motiuk, K. Reid, J. Sopaz and H. Zbesheski.

32. National Archives of Canada, RG 24, Vol 22794, File 70.9, Historical Narrative No 115 ATU, July 1960; Log-book entries from J. Moric and H. Zbesheski.

33. National Archives of Canada, RG 24, Vol 22798, File 72/2, RCAF Detachment Resolute Bay, Historical Record, July 1960; Log-book entries from G. Bussieres and J. Moric.

34. Gordon, UN in the Congo, pp. 6–24; Gaffen, *In the Eye of the Storm: A History of Canadian Peacekeeping*, pp. 217–222; Britannica Book of the Year, 1961, pp. 187–190, 698; DHist 73/299 Congo Republic, Background Information.

35. CHC Debates, 12 July 1960, 6101; Saywell, Canadian Annual Review for 1960, pp. 113–116, 117.

36. Gaffen, *In the Eye of the Storm*, p. 219; von Horn, *Soldiering for Peace*, p. 131; DHist. Report No 8, Canada and Peacekeeping Operations, The Congo, 1960–64, p. 6; DHist 73/297, The Army Council, 13 July 1960.

37. National Archives of Canada, RG 24, 1983–84/216, Vol 3532, 960–Mallard, Memorandum to CAS, 19 August 1960 and CAS Memorandum to Minister, Congo Airlift–Progress Report; RG 24, Vol 17910, 900–960–7, Canlift Message PR192, 19 July 1960; RG 24, Vol 17831, File 810-53 Congo, Status Report on Congo Activities 22 August 1960; Conversations with and log-book entries from G. Brasseur, G. Bussieres, W. Hamilton, M.G. Morrison and D. Woodman. **The following crews departed for the Congo on 18 July 1960:** Squadron Leader L.M. Hlady (captain) with Flight Lieutenant M.G. Morrison (first officer), Flying Officer B. Neihaus (navigator), Flying Officer A.R. Woodman (radio officer), Sergeant B. Frame (flight engineer) and Leading Aircraftsman W.D. Murphy (MCA); Flight Lieutenant R.T.L. Gill (captain) with Flight Lieutenant W.J. Scott (first officer), Flight Lieutenant W. Thompson (navigator), Flying Officer B.R. Woods (radio officer), Sergeant G. Brasseur (flight engineer) and Leading Aircraftsman G.R. Brown (MCA); Flight Lieutenant E.M. Spencer (captain) with Flight Lieutenant G.C. Jutras (first officer), Flying Officer W.D.M. Hamilton (navigator), Flying Officer A.E.B. Cole (radio officer), Sergeant W. Kondra (flight engineer) and Leading Aircraftsman R. Bryson (MCA); and Flight Lieutenant J.S. Walton (captain) with Flying Officer C.H. Parent (first officer), Flying Officer N.M. Davidson (navigator), Flying Officer I. Allen (radio officer), Sergeant A. Dahr (flight engineer) and Leading Aircraftsman K. Ulmer (MCA).

38. National Archives of Canada, Vol 17831, File 810-53 Congo, Status Report on Congo Activities, 22 August 1960.

39. DHist 73/299 Congo Republic, Background Information; Conversations with and log-book entries from M.G. Morrison; Log-book entries from G. Brasseur and D. Woodman.

40. National Archives of Canada, RG 24, 1983–84/216, Vol 3522, 960–Mallard, Memorandum to CAS on Operation Mallard, 19 August 1960; DHist Report No 8, Canada and Peacekeeping Operations, The Congo 1960–64, p. 12; Hilliker and Barry, *Canada's Department of External Affairs*, Vol 2, pp. 176–177.

41. von Horn, *Soldiering for Peace*, p. 137; DHist. 73/299 Congo Republic, Background Information; Bowdery, "A Year in the Congo", *Roundel* 13/7 (September 1961), p. 2; DHist. Report No. 8, Canada and Peacekeeping Operations, The Congo 1960–64, p. 12; National Archives of Canada, RG 24, Vol 17831, File 810-53 Congo, Status Report on Congo Activities, 22 August 1960; correspondence and conversations with J. Maitland; Log-book entries from G. Bussieres.

42. Log-book entries from T. Charchuk and W. Hamilton.

Notes & References

43. National Archives of Canada, RG 24, Vol 17831, File 810-53 Congo, Status Report on Congo Activities, 22 August, 1960; Log-book entries from C. Empey.
44. DHist Report No 8, Canada and Peacekeeping Operations, The Congo 1960–64, pp. 12, 16.
45. DHist. 79/113, AFHQ Organization Order 8.13 dated 2 August 1960.
46. National Archives of Canada RG 24, 1983–84/216, Vol 3532, Memorandum to CAS dated 19 August 1960; DHist Report No 8, Canada and Peacekeeping Operations, The Congo 1960–64, pp. 15–16.
47. Correspondence and conversations with LGen W.K. Carr; DHist 75/380 RCAF News Release No 60, 2 August 1960; National Archives of Canada RG 24, 1983–84/216, Vol 3532, 960–Mallard, CAS Memorandum to Minister, Congo Airlift–Progress Report; RG 24, Vol 17831, File 810–53 Congo, Status Report on Congo Activities 22 August 1960; DHist Report No 8, Canada and Peacekeeping Operations, The Congo 1960–64, p. 14; Log-book entries from R. Sierolawski and S. Walton.
48. National Archives of Canada, RG 24, Vol 17831, File 810–53 Congo, Status Report on Congo Activities, 22 August 1960; DHist. Report No 8, Canada and Peacekeeping Operations, The Congo 1960–64 p. 12; Log-book entries from G. Brasseur, M.G. Morrison, S. Walton and D. Woodman.
49. DHist Report No 8, Canada and Peacekeeping Operations, The Congo 1960–64, pp. 7–10. The required immunizations were for cholera (three shots, seven days apart), yellow fever (one shot that took twenty-one days to become effective), smallpox, polio, plague, and a booster of the TABTD combination (typhoid type A and type B, tetanus and diphtheria).
50. *Ibid.*, pp. 8, 11, 13.
51. National Archives of Canada, RG 24, 1983–84/216, Vol 3532, 960–Mallard, Memorandum to CAS dated 19 August, 1960.
52. National Archives of Canada, RG 24, Vol 18482, Folder 1, War Diary of No 57 Canadian Signal Squadron; DHist. 144.9.009, 57 Canadian Signal Unit in the Congo; King, "UN Commander Honours Canadian Signal Unit in Congo", *Canadian Army Journal*, Vol 17 No. 1 (1963), pp. 92–95; Stetham, "Signal Squadron in the Congo", *Canadian Army Journal*, Vol 17, No. 2 (1963), pp. 110–120.
53. National Archives of Canada, RG 24, vol 17831, File 810–53 Congo, Status Report on Congo Activities, 22 August 1960; RG 24, 1983–84/216, Box 3551, File QH–S–960–100 Mallard, Memorandum to CAS dated 27 July 1960 and Aide-Mémoire to CAS from A/C Bean, Congo Co-ordinator, 8 August 1960.
54. National Archives of Canada, RG 24, Vol 22794, File 70.9, Historical Narrative, 115 ATU El Arish, August 1960; Log-book entries from W. Dick, C. Empey, C. Lalande, W. Lupton, L. Motiuk, K. Reid and H. Zbesheski.
55. Log-book entries from B. Doucette and L. Leclair; National Archives of Canada, RG 24, Vol 18482, Folder 1, War Diary of No 57 Canadian Signal Squadron, 9 August 1960; DHist. Report No 8, Canada and Peacekeeping Operations, The Congo 1960–64, p. 16.
56. DHist Report No 8, Canada and Peacekeeping Operations, The Congo 1960–64; p. 16; National Archives of Canada, RG 24, 1983–84/216, Vol 3532, 960–Mallard, CAS Memorandum—Congo Airlift, Progress Report; and Message LASOP 8/1497 dated 15 August to Canairlift from Liaison Officer, Lajes, Log-book entries from L. Byrne, T. Charchuk, E. Chevalier, D. Jones, J. Lynch, J. Moric, M.G. Morrison, R. Parmelee, K. Reid, R. Sierolawski, J. Sopaz, and D. Woodman.
57. National Archives of Canada, RG 24, 1983–/216, Vol 3532, 960–Mallard, Memorandum to CAS dated 19 August 1960; Canairlift Message AO923 dated 17 August 1960; Coughlin, "Candid Congo", *Roundel* 16/1 (January–February 1964), p. 12.
58. DHist Report No 8, "Canada and Peacekeeping Operations: The Congo, 1960–1964", pp. 16–17; Military Airlift Command, *Anything, Anywhere, Anytime*, p. 99.
59. Message CY47 Leo to Canairhead dated 29 August 1960.
60. National Archives of Canada, RG 24, Vol 22798, File 72/2, RCAF Resolute Bay Detachment Daily Diary, August 1960.
61. DHist Report No. 8, Canada and Peacekeeping Operations: The Congo, 1960–1964, pp. 24–25.

62. Halliday, *Chronology of Canadian Military Aviation*, p. 134; National Archives of Canada, RG 24, Vol 17752, AFHQ Operations Summary, September 1960; Log-book entries from L. Byrne, G. Bussieres, E. Chevalier, W. Dick, B. Doucette, C. Empey, B. Hoy, W. Lupton, J. Maitland, J. Moric, M.G. Morrison, K. Reid, R. Sierolawski, D. Woodman and H. Zbesheski.
63. National Archives of Canada, RG 24, Vol 22794, File 70.9, Historical Narrative, No 115 ATU El Arish, September 1960; Log-book entries from C. Lalande; Author's notes and log-book entries.
64. Conversations with and log-book entries from J. Hutchinson.
65. National Archives of Canada, RG 24, Vol 22794, File 70.9, Historical Narrative, No 115 ATU El Arish, September 1960; Log-book entries from M.G. Morrison.
66. National Archives of Canada, RG 24, Vol 22798, File 72/2, RCAF Resolute Bay Detachment, Daily Diary, September 1960; Log-book entries from L. Byrne, K. Reid, R. Sierolawski, J. Trethowan and S. Walton.
67. Author's notes and log-book entries.
68. Milberry, *Sixty Years: The RCAF and the CF Air Command 1924–1984*, p. 327.
69. National Archives of Canada, RG 24, Vol 17831, File 810–53 Congo; Bowdery, "A Year in the Congo", *Roundel* 13/7 (September 1961), pp. 2–4; Correspondence and conversations with J. Maitland and, J.A. Forest. As well as G/C W.K. Carr, the following RCAF officers served on the Air Staff at ONUC Headquarters: W/C H.B. Russell, S/L D. Harrison, Flight Lieutenant J.A. Forest, Flight Lieutenant H.J. King and Flight Lieutenant J.R. Pelletier (Pilots); Flight Lieutenant W.R. Pearson (Aeronautical Engineer); Flying Officer J.G.J. Lee and Flying Officer W.B. McNeil (Telecommunications Engineers); and Flying Officer T.C. Hamilton (Supply Officer).
70. National Archives of Canada, RG 24, 1983–84/216, Vol 3532, File 960–Mallard, CAS Memorandum to Minister; RG 24, Vol 17831, File 810–53 (Congo), Memorandum to A/CAS, RCAF Personnel Congo, 21 September 1960; DHist. 73/299, Congo Republic Background Information; DHist. 75/380, UN Air Operations Force in the Congo; Bowdery, "A Year In The Congo", *Roundel* 13/7 (September 1961), pp. 2–4; Coughlin, "Candid Congo", *Roundel* 16/1 (January–February 1964), pp. 12–14; Conversations with W.K. Carr.
71. Carr, G/C W.K.,"Consolidated Report ONUC Air Operations" dated September 1960; Conversations with W.K. Carr.
72. National Archives of Canada, RG 24, Vol 17752, AFHQ Operations Summary, October 1960; Log-book entries from G. Bussieres, E. Chevalier, W. Dick, B. Doucette, C. Empey, M. Gordon, B. Hoy, D. Jones, D. Kuhn, C. Lalande, W. Lupton, J. Lynch, J. Maitland, D. McBurney, L. Motiuk, K. Reid, R. Sierolawski, J. Trethowan, S. Walton and H. Zbesheski.
73. Fuller, et al, *125 Years of Canadian Aeronautics*, p. 289.
74. DHist. 79/429, Vol 10, AFHQ Divisional Items of Interest, 25 November 1960.
75. *Ibid*.
76. National Archives of Canada, Vol 17752, AFHQ Operations Summary, November 1960; Log-book entries from G. Bussieres, L. Byrne, T. Charchuk, E. Chevalier, W. Dick, B. Doucette, C. Empey, D. Jones, L. Leclair, M.G. Morrison, L. Motiuk, K. Reid, R. Sierolawski, J. Trethowan and S. Walton.
77. National Archives of Canada, Vol 17752, AFHQ Operations Summary, November 1960.
78. National Archives of Canada, RG 24, Vol 22798, File 72/2, RCAF Detachment Resolute Bay Historical Record, November 1960; Log-book entries from B. Hoy.
79. National Archives of Canada, RG 24, Vol 17752, AFHQ Operations Summary, November 1960.
80. National Archives of Canada, RG 24, Vol 22798, File 72/2, RCAF Detachment Resolute Bay Historical Record, November 1960.
81. National Archives of Canada, RG 24, Vol 17752, AFHQ Operations Summary, December 1960; Log-book entries from T. Charchuk, B. Doucette, C. Empey, D. Jones, L. Leclair, W. Lupton, J. Lynch, M.G. Morrison, R. Sierolawski, J. Sopaz, S. Walton and D. Woodman.
82. Hotson, *The De Havilland Canada Story*, pp. 129–130; Kealy and Russell, *A History of Canadian Naval Aviation*, pp. 61, 65; Log-book entries from L. Byrne and H. Zbesheski.

83. Canadian Aviation Museum, Log 0407, Operation Lookout, Captain O.M. Sweetman; National Archives of Canada, RG 24, Vol 17752, AFHQ Operations Summary, December 1960; RG 24, Vol 22799, CEPE CARDE Detachment Narrative Report, December 1960–May 1961; Milberry, *The Avro CF–100*, pp. 136–137; Morrison, "South Atlantic Lookout", *Roundel* 12/3 (April 1960), pp. 2–3; *Encyclopaedia Britannica*, 1957 edition, "Ascension"; Vol II, p. 499; Log-book entries from W. Lupton; Author's notes and log-book entries.
84. DHist. 79/429, AFQH Divisional Items of Interest, Vol 10, 30 December 1960.

CHAPTER 25: TRENTON, 1961

1. DHist. 79/429, Vol 11, AFHQ Historical Data, Divisional Items of Interest, 6 January 1961.
2. DHist. 73/430 RCAF Program of Activities, 1961–1966, Chapter 7, Section 1, Air Transport Command; Conversations with J. Lynch.
3. *Ibid.*
4. National Archives of Canada, RG 24, Vol 17,752, File 810-144, AFHQ Operational Summary, January 1961; RG 24, Vol 22798, File 72-2, Historical Record, RCAF Detachment, Resolute Bay, January 1961; Log-book entries from T. Charchuk, E. Chevalier, C. Empey, C. Lalande, L. Leclair, J. Lynch, J. Maitland, D. McBurney, J. Moric, K. Reid, J. Sopaz and D. Woodman.
5. National Archives of Canada, RG 24, Vol 17,752, File 810-144, AFHQ Operational Summary, January 1961; Log-book entries from J. Moric, J. Sopaz and D. Woodman; Author's notes; Training Command, *Observer Training Manual* (1961), "Communications Equipment".
6. Author's notes.
7. DHist. 79/429, Vol 11, AFHQ Historical Data, Divisional Items of Interest, January 1961.
8. *Ibid.*
9. National Archives of Canada, RG 24, Vol 17,752, File 810-144, AFHQ Operational Summary, February 1961; Author's notes; Log-book entries from G. Bussieres, T. Charchuk, E. Chevalier, P. Dragojevich, C. Empey, D. Jones, C. Lalande, L. Leclair, W. Lupton, L. Motiuk, J. Sopaz, S. Walton and H. Zbesheski.
10. National Archives of Canada, RG 24, Vol 22794, File 70.9, Historical Narrative, No 115 ATU, February 1961.
11. Author's notes and log-book entries.
12. Gordon, *UN In The Congo*, pp. 86–87, 95–96, 103–110; Gaffen, *In The Eye of the Storm: A History of Canadian Peacekeeping*, pp. 227–228; *Britannica Book of the Year: 1962*, pp. 177, 179, 511, 682, 694–695.
13. Author's notes.
14. DHist. 79/429, Vol 11, AFHQ Historical Data, Divisional Items of Interest, February 1961.
15. National Archives of Canada, RG 24, Vol 17,752, File 810-144, AFHQ Operational Summary, February 1961.
16. DHist. 79/429, Vol 11, AFHQ Historical Data, Divisional Items of Interest, March 1961.
17. National Archives of Canada, RG 24, Vol 17,752, File 810-144, AFHQ Operational Summary, March 1961; Log-book entries provided by T. Charchuk, D. Jones, C. Lalande, J. Maitland, M.G. Morrison, J. Moric, S. Walton, D. Woodman and H. Zbesheski; Author's notes.
18. DHist. 79/429, Vol 11, AFHQ Historical Data, Divisional Items of Interest, March 1961.
19. Author's notes.
20. *Ibid.*
21. *Britannica Book of the Year: 1962*, pp. 349, 388; Author's notes.

22. DHist. 79/429, Vol 11, AFHQ Historical Data, Divisional Items of Interest, March 1961; Honderich, *Arctic Imperative*, p. 81.
23. Halliday, *Chronology of Canadian Military Aviation*, p. 135.
24. DHist. 79/429, Vol 11, AFHQ Historical Data, Divisional Items of Interest, March 1961.
25. Halliday, *Chronology of Canadian Military Aviation*, p. 135.
26. National Archives of Canada, RG 24, Vol 17752, File 810-144, AFHQ Operational Summary, April 1961; Log-book entries from G. Bussieres, P. Dragojevich, C. Empey, D. Jones, C. Lalande, L. Leclair, J. Lynch, J. Maitland, L. Motiuk, K. Reid, D. Woodman and H. Zbesheski.
27. National Archives of Canada, RG 24, Vol 22794, File 70.9, Historical Narrative 115 ATU, April 1961.
28. Author's notes; Log-book entries provided by H. Zbesheski.
29. National Archives of Canada, RG 24, 1983–84/216 Box 3532, 960—Mallard, ATCHQ Letter 960-100-Congo, dated 11 April, 1961 to CAS on C-130 and North Star airlift plans; Author's notes.
30. *Britannica Book of the Year: 1962*, p. 447.
31. Author's notes.
32. *Ibid.*
33. National Archives of Canada, RG 24, Vol 17752, File 810-144, AFHQ Operational Summary, April 1961.
34. ATC Public Relations Press Release No. 3 dated 21 April 1961; *The Trentonian*, 22 April 1961; Author's notes.
35. DHist Report No. 8, Canada and Peacekeeping Operations, pp. 28–29. Gaffen, *In The Eye Of The Storm*, p. 228; Author's notes and log-book entries.
36. Author's notes and log-book entries.
37. Halliday, *Chronology of Canadian Military Aviation*, p. 135.
38. DHist 79/429, Vol 11, AFHQ Historical Data, Divisional Items of Interest, April 1961.
39. Halliday, *Chronology of Canadian Military Aviation*, p. 136.
40. National Archives of Canada, RG 24, Vol 17,752, File 810-144, AFHQ Operational Summary, May 1961; Log-book entries from G. Bussieres, D. Jones, C. Lalande, L. Leclair, W. Lupton, J. Maitland, J. Moric, M.G. Morrison, L. Motiuk, R. Sierolawski and S. Walton.
41. Conversations and correspondence with K.R. Greenaway; Log-book entries from C. Empey and J. Maitland.
42. DHist 79/429, Vol 11, AFHQ Historical Data, Divisional Items of Interest, May 1961.
43. *Ibid.*
44. DHist 79/429, Vol 11, AFHQ Historical Data, Divisional Items of Interest, May 1961; Author's notes.
45. Author's notes.
46. DHist 79/429, Vol 11, AFHQ Historical Data, Divisional Items of Interest, 2 June 1961.
47. *Ibid.*
48. National Archives of Canada, Vol 17,752, File 810–144, AFHQ Operational Summary, June 1961; Log-book entries from G. Bussieres, T. Charchuk, C. Empey, C. Lalande, L. Leclair, W. Lupton, J. Lynch, J. Moric, L. Motiuk, S. Walton and H. Zbesheski.
49. Author's notes.
50. *Canadian Annual Review for 1961*, p. 146; Nicks et al., *Air Defence of Canada, 1948–1997*, pp. 168–169; Halliday, *Chronology of Canadian Military Aviation*, pp. 135–137.
51. Kostenuk and Griffin, *RCAF Squadrons and Aircraft*, p. 209; Author's notes.

Notes & References

52. National Archives of Canada, RG 24, Vol 17752, File 810-144, AFHQ Operational Summary, June 1961; Halliday, *Chronology of Canadian Military Aviation*, p. 136; Fuller et al., *125 Years of Canadian Aeronautics*, p. 291.
53. Author's notes; Conversation with G. Brasseur.
54. National Archives of Canada, RG 24, Vol 22794, File 70.9, Historical Narrative, 115 ATU, June 1961.
55. DHist. 79/429, Vol 11, AFHQ Historical Data, Divisional Items of Interest June 1961.
56. National Archives of Canada, Vol 17,752, File 810-144, AFHQ Operational Summary, July 1961; Log-book entries from G. Bussieres, P. Dragojevich, C. Empey, D. Kuhn, W. Lupton, J. Maitland, M.G. Morrison, L. Motiuk and H. Zbesheski.
57. Log-book entries from C. Empey, J. Maitland, M.G. Morrison and R.E. Schwanky.
58. *Britannica Book of the Year: 1962*, pp. 87, 90–91, 379, 382–383; Hilliker and Barry, *Canada's Department of External Affairs, Vol 2: 1946–68*, pp. 160–166; *Canadian Annual Review for 1961*, pp. 144–147, 166–168.
59. National Archives of Canada, RG 24, Vol 17,752, File 810-144, AFHQ, Operational Summary, August 1961; Log-book entries from G. Bussieres, P. Dragojevich, C. Lalande, L. Leclair, W. Lupton, M.G. Morrison, R.E. Schwanky, S. Walton and H. Zbesheski.
60. DHist. 79/429, Vol 11, AFHQ Historical Data, July–August 1961.
61. Halliday, *Chronology of Canadian Military Aviation*, p. 136.
62. uthor's notes.
63. Military Airlift Command, *Anything, Anywhere, Anytime*, pp. 99; Hilliker and Barry, *Canada's Department of External Affairs, Vol 2: 1946–68*, p. 162.
64. *Canadian Annual Review for 1961*, pp. 358–359.
65. National Archives of Canada, RG 24, Vol 17,752 File 810-144, AFHQ Operational Summary, September 1961; Log-book entries from C. Empey, D. Kuhn, C. Lalande, L. Leclair, J. Maitland, J. Moric, R.E. Schwanky and S. Walton.
66. DHist 79/429, Vol 11, AFHQ Historical Data, Divisional Items of Interest, 29 September, 1961; Kostenuk and Griffin, *RCAF Squadrons and Aircraft*, pp. 191–193, 221; *The Trentonian*, 29 September 1961, p. 1; Conversations with R.J. Lane and J.O. Maitland.
67. RG 24, Vol 22709, No 436 Squadron Daily Diary, September–December 1961; DHist. Report No 8, "Canada and Peacekeeping Operations: The Congo", p. 30.
68. DHist 73/299, Congo Republic: Background Information; *Britannica Book of the Year: 1962*, pp. 179, 508, 693–695; Gordon, *UN In The Congo*, pp. 127–129; Gaffen, *In the Eye of the Storm: A History of Canadian Peacekeeping*, pp. 237–238.
69. National Archives of Canada, RG 24, Vol 17,752, File 810-144, AFHQ Operational Summary, October 1961.
70. National Archives of Canada, RG 24, Vol 17,752, File 810-144, AFHQ Operational Summary, October 1961; RG 24, Vol 22794, File 70.9, Historical Narrative, No 115 ATU, October 1961. Log-book entries from P. Dragojevich, C. Empey, C. Lalande, L. Leclair, J. Maitland, J. Moric, M.G. Morrison, R.E. Schwanky and S. Walton.
71. Kostenuk and Griffin, *RCAF Squadrons and Aircraft*, pp. 185, 193; AFHQ Organization Order 8.9.1, File 895-9/426 (DOE) dated 3 October 1961.
72. DHist 79/429, Vol 11, AFHQ Historical Data, Divisional Items of Interest, 20 October 1961.
73. National Archives of Canada, RG 24, Vol 17,752, File 810–144, AFHQ Operational Summary, November 1961; Log-book entries from C. Empey, C. Lalande, L. Leclair, W. Lupton, J. Lynch, D. McBurney, A. Mackie, R.E. Schwanky, S. Walton and H. Zbesheski.

74. Log-book entries from J. Moric.
75. Directorate of History, Report No. 8, "Canada and Peacekeeping Operations: The Congo", p. 31.
76. National Archives of Canada, RG 24, Vol 17,750, File 810-144, AFHQ Operational Summary, December 1961: RG 24, Vol 22687, No 426 Squadron Semi-Annual Historical Return, December 1961–May 1962; Log-book entries from C. Empey, C. Lalande, W. Lupton, J. Lynch, J. Moric, R.E. Schwanky, S. Walton and H. Zbesheski.
77. National Archives of Canada, RG 24, Vol 22687, No 426 Squadron Semi-Annual Historical Return, December 1961–May 1962.

CHAPTER 26: ST-HUBERT, JANUARY–OCTOBER 1962

1. Conversations with and log-book entries from W.R. Lloyd. The crew of the 30 August flight also included pilots Flight Lieutenant B. Carss and Flight Lieutenant R. Longworth, and navigators Flight Lieutenant P. Rawlyk, Flying Officer G. Nishimura and Flying Officer I. McMann. Entries regarding the first flight to Léopoldville taken from the log-book of P.H. Hope provided by the RCAF Memorial Museum.
2. DHist. R S7 437, ATC News Release 4 January 1962; National Archives, RG 24, Vol 17, 752, File 810-144, AFHQ Operational Summary, January–August 1962; Milberry, *The Canadair North Star*, p. 184. The crew of Yukon 15927 included: Wing Commander J.O. Maitland, officer commanding No 437 Squadron; pilot Flight Lieutenant A.R. Lehman; navigators Flight Lieutenant R.T.A. Barnett, Flight Lieutenant R.W. Griffiths and Flying Officer J.L. Kubas; radio officers Flight Lieutenant R. McKenzie and Flying Officer J. Chandler; flight engineers Sergeant B. Nott and Sergeant B. Dyer; transportation technician Leading Aircraftsman L. Gerow, and flight steward Corporal W.W. Hubbard.
3. National Archives of Canada, RG 24, Vol 22687, File 44-13, No 426 Squadron Semi-Annual Historical Return, January 1962.
4. National Archives of Canada, RG 24, Vol 22687, File 44-13, No 426 Squadron Semi-Annual Historical Return, January 1962; DHist. Report No 8, "Canada and Peacekeeping Operations", p. 31; Log-book entries from L. Leclair, W. Lupton, S. Walton and H. Zbesheski.
5. National Archives of Canada, RG 24, Vol 22794, File 70.9, No 115 ATU Historical Narrative, January 1962.
6. DHist. 79/429, Vol 12, AFHQ Historical Data, Items of Divisional Interest, January 1962; National Archives of Canada, RG 24, Vol 22687, File 44-13, No 426 Squadron Semi-Annual Historical Return, January 1962; Log-book entries from C. Empey, M.G. Morrison and H. Zbesheski.
7. Kostenuk and Griffin, *RCAF Squadrons and Aircraft*, pp. 162–163, 169, 171, 173, 177, 182, 184, 196, 203–205; Halliday, *Chronology of Canadian Military Aviation*, pp. 136–138.
8. National Archives of Canada, RG 24, Vol 22687, File 44-13, No 426 Squadron Semi-Annual Historical Return, February 1962; Log-book entries from C. Empey, C. Lalande, M.G. Morrison, R.E. Schwanky and H. Zbesheski.
9. RCAF Aircraft Accident Record, Accident No 202009 dated 2 February 1962; DHist. 79/429, Vol 12, AFHQ Historical Data, Items of Divisional Interest, February 1962.
10. Fuller et al., *125 Years of Canadian Aeronautics*, p. 293; Halliday, *Chronology of Canadian Military Aviation*, p. 138; *Britannica Book of the Year 1963*, p. 751.
11. National Archives of Canada, RG 24, Vol 17829, 840-105 Vol 9, VCAS address to AOCs' Conference.
12. National Archives of Canada, RG 24, Vol 17,752, File 810-144, AFHQ Operational Summary, March 1962; RG 24, Vol 22687, File 44-13, No 426 Squadron Semi-Annual Historical Return, March 1962; Log-book entries from C. Empey, C. Lalande, W. Lupton, J. Trethowan, S. Walton, H. Zbesheski.
13. National Archives of Canada, RG 24, Vol 17,752, File 810-144, AFHQ Operational Summary, April 1962; RG 24, Vol 22687, File 44-13, No 426 Squadron Semi-Annual Historical Return, April 1962; Log-book entries from L. Leclair and R.E. Schwanky.

14. National Archives of Canada, RG 24, Vol 22564, RCAF Station St-Hubert Historical Record, May 1962.
15. National Archives of Canada, RG 24, Vol 22687, File 44-13, No 426 Squadron Semi-Annual Historical Return, May 1962; Conversations and correspondence with K.R. Greenaway; Log-book entries from S. Walton.
16. National Archives of Canada, RG 24, Vol 17752, File 810-144, AFHQ Operational Summary 1962; RG 24, Vol 22794, File 70.9, Historical Narrative No 115 ATU, May 1962; RG 24, Vol 22687, File 44-13, No 426 Squadron Semi-Annual Historical Return, May 1962; Log-book entries from R.E. Schwanky and H. Zbesheski.
17. DHist. 79/429, Vol 12, AFHQ Historical Data, Divisional Items of Interest, 18 May and 25 May 1962; National Archives of Canada, RG 24, Vol 22687, File 44-13, No 426 Squadron Semi-Annual Historical Return, May 1962; Log-book entries from D. McBurney.
18. Halliday, *Chronology of Canadian Military Aviation*, p. 139; Kostenuk and Griffin, *RCAF Squadrons and Aircraft*, pp. 179, 181, 186, 188, 190, 195, 197, 202.
19. National Archives of Canada, RG 24, Vol 17752, File 810-144, AFHQ Operational Summary, June 1962; RG 24, Vol 22687, File 44-13, No 426 Squadron Semi-Annual Historical Return June–October 1962; Canadian Aviation Museum, Log 0407: Captain [?] O.M. Sweetman; Log-book entries from D. McBurney, C. Empey, C. Lalande, W. Lupton, R.E. Schwanky and S. Walton.
20. DHist. 79/429, Vol 12, AFHQ Historical Data, Vol 12, Divisional Items of Interest July 1962; National Archives of Canada, RG 24, Vol 17752, 810-144, AFHQ Operational Summary, July 1962; RG 24, Vol 22687, File 44-13, No 426 Squadron Semi-Annual Historical Return June–October 1962; Log-book entries from C. Empey, C. Lalande and S. Walton.
21. National Archives of Canada, RG 24, Vol 22687, File 44-13, No 426 Squadron Semi-Annual Historical Return, June–October 1962.
22. National Archives of Canada, RG 24, Vol 22794, File 70.9, AFHQ 895-9/426 (DOE) dated 31 July 1962, Organization Order 8.21 (L); RG 24, Vol 22687, File 44-13, No 426 Semi-Annual Historical Return, June–October 1962; RG 24, Vol 22564, RCAF Station St-Hubert Historical Record 15 August 1962.
23. National Archives of Canada, RG 24, Vol 17752, 810-144, AFHQ Operational Summary, August 1962; RG 24, Vol 22687, File 44-13, No 426 Squadron Semi-Annual Historical Return, June–October 1962; Log-book entries provided by: C. Empey, W. Lupton, S. Walton and H. Zbesheski.
24. National Archives of Canada, RG 24, Vol 22687, File 44-13, No 426 Squadron Semi-Annual Historical Return, June–October 1962.
25. ATCHQ Organization Directive 15/62 dated 29 August 1962.
26. National Archives of Canada, RG 24, Vol 22687, File 44-13, No 426 Squadron Semi-Annual Historical Return, June–October 1962. Log-book entries from C. Empey.
27. Milberry, *Sixty Years: The RCAF and CF Air Command*, p. 328.
28. National Archives of Canada, RG 24, Vol 22687, File 44-13, No 426 Squadron Semi-Annual Historical Return, June–October 1962.

EPILOGUE

1. Milberry, *The Canadair North Star*, pp. 237—238; *Trentonian*, 10 December 1965, pp. 1–2; RCAF Station Trenton Brochure, "North Star Retirement"; Conversations with and log-book entries from P. Pawliuk.

REFERENCES

OFFICIAL HISTORIES

Appleton, T.E. 1968. *Usque Ad Mare: A History of the Canadian Coast Guard and Marine Services*. Ottawa: Queen's Printer, 318 pp.

Bernier, Serge. 2000. *Canadian Military Heritage, Volume III: 1972–2000*. Montreal: Art Global for the Department of National Defence, 254 pp.

Canada. Army. General Staff, Historical Section. 1956. *Canada's Army in Korea*. Ottawa: Queen's Printer, 108 pp.

Canada. Royal Canadian Air Force. Air Historian's Office. 1949. *The RCAF Overseas: The Sixth Year*. Toronto: Oxford University Press, 537 pp.

Canada. Department of National Defence. Directorate of History and Heritage. 2002. *Canada and the Korean War*. Ottawa: Department of National Defence, 158 pp.

Cowdrey, A.E. 1987. *The United States Army in the Korean War: The Medics' War*. Washington, D.C.: Center of Military History, United States Army, USGPO, 391 pp.

Douglas, W.A.B. 1986. *The Official History of the Royal Canadian Air Force, Volume II: The Creation of a National Air Force*. Ottawa: University of Toronto Press for the Department of National Defence and the Canadian Government Publishing Centre, 797 pp.

Farrar-Hockley, A. 1990. *The British Part In The Korean War.* Volume 1: *A Distant Obligation*. London: HMSO, 512 pp.

———. 1995. *The British Part In The Korean War*. Volume 2: *An Honourable Discharge*. London: HMSO, 534 pp.

Field, J.A. 1962. *History of United States Naval Operations: Korea*. Washington, D.C.: USGPO, 499 pp.

Futrell, R.F. 1983. *The United States Air Force in Korea 1950–1953*. Washington, D.C.: USAF Office of Air Force History, USGPO, 823 pp.

Gough, T.J. 1987. *U.S. Army Mobilization and Logistics in the Korean War: A Research Approach*. Washington, D.C.: Center of Military History, United States Army, USGPO, 126 pp.

Greenhous, Brereton and Hugh A. Halliday. 1999. *Canada's Air Forces 1914–1999*. Montreal: Art Global for the Department of National Defence, pp.158.

Greenhous, Brereton and Stephen J. Harris, William C. Johnson and William G.P. Rawling. 1994. *The Official History of the Royal Canadian Air Force*. Volume 3: *The Crucible of War, 1939–1945*. Ottawa: University of Toronto Press for the Department of National Defence and the Canadian Government Publishing Centre, 1,096 pp.

Kealy, J.D.F. and E.C. Russell. 1965. *A History of Canadian Naval Aviation, 1918–1962*. Ottawa: Naval Historical Section, Department of National Defence.

Schnabel, J.F. 1992. *United States Army in the Korean War, Policy and Direction — The First Year*. Washington, D.C.: Center of Military History, United States Army, USGPO.

Stacey, Charles Perry. 1960. *The Victory Campaign: The Operations in North West Europe, 1944–1945*. Ottawa: Queen's Printer.

———. 1970. *Arms, Men and Governments: The War Policies of Canada, 1939–1945*. Ottawa: Queen's Printer.

Thorgrimsson, Thor and E.C. Russell. 1965. *Canadian Naval Operations in Korean Waters, 1950–1955*. Ottawa: Queen's Printer.

United States. United States Air Force. Military Airlift Command. 1991. *Anything, Anywhere, Anytime: An Illustrated History of Military Airlift Command, 1941–1991*. Scott Air Force Base, Illinois: Headquarters Military Airlift Command.

Westover, Capt. J.G. 1955. *Combat Support in Korea*. Washington, D.C.: Combat Forces Press.

Wood, Herbert Fairlie. 1966. *Strange Battleground: The Operations in Korea and Their Effects on the Defence Policy of Canada*. Ottawa: Queen's Printer.

CANADIAN GOVERNMENT PUBLICATIONS

Greenaway, Keith R. 1951. *Arctic Air Navigation*. Ottawa: King's Printer for the Defence Research Board.

Griffin, J.A. 1969. *Canadian Military Aircraft, 1920–1968*. Ottawa: Canadian War Museum.

Johnston, H., and N. Steinhaur. 1957. *Weather Ways*. Ottawa: Queen's Printer.

Pearkes, G.R. 1960. *Statements on Defence Policy*. Ottawa: Queen's Printer for the Department of National Defence.

Pearson, L.B. 1950. *Canada and the Korean Crisis*. Ottawa: King's Printer.

Pearson, L.B. 1951. *Documents on the Korean Crisis*. Ottawa: King's Printer.

Senate of Canada. Special Committee on National Defence. February 1986. *Report on Military Air Transport*. Ottawa: Department of Supply and Services.

CANADIAN GOVERNMENT DOCUMENTS

Canada. Royal Canadian Air Force. Air Transport Command. 1963. *Navigation Manual*. RCAF Station Trenton: No 4 (T) Operational Training Unit.

———. No 426 (Thunderbird) Squadron. Operations Record Book. 14 October 1942–31 December 1945. National Archives of Canada, RG24, Volume 22686 and Volume 22687.

———. No 426 Squadron. Operations Record Book. 15 October 1942–31 December 1945. National Defence Headquarters, Directorate of History and Heritage, microfilm.

———. RCAF Station Linton-on-Ouse. Operations Record Book. 18 June 1943–15 October 1945. National Archives of Canada, RG24, Volume 22838.

———. No 62 (Beaver) Base. Operations Record Book. 18 June 1943–31 August 1945. National Archives of Canada, RG24, Volume 22842.

———. No 6 (RCAF) Group, Bomber Command, RAF. Operations Record Book. 25 October 1942–1 November 1945. National Archives of Canada, RG24, Volume 22846.

———. Air Transport Command. 1952. *North Star Engineering Orders*, E0 05-5A-1.

———. Air Materiel Command. 13 February 1958. *RCAF Engineering Orders*, E0 05-5A-2, "Description and Maintenance Instructions North Star 1 and 1M", Canada Aviation Museum, 871 pp.

———. Air Transport Command. 1964. *Weather Manual*. No 4 (T) Operational Training Unit, RCAF Station Trenton, Ontario.

———. Training Command. 1958. *Observer Training Manual*, Volume 1: *DR Navigation*. RCAF Station Trenton, Ontario: Training Command Headquarters, various paging.

———. Training Command. 1958. *Observer Training Manual*, Volume 2: *Allied Subjects*. RCAF Station Trenton, Ontario: Training Command Headquarters, various paging.

———. Training Command. 1958. *Observer Training Manual*, Volume 3: *Electronic Aids To Navigation*. RCAF Station Trenton, Ontario: Training Command Headquarters, various paging.

———. Training Command. 1960. *Observer Training Manual*, Volume 6: *Supplementary Electronic Theory for Observers*. Ottawa: Queen's Printer, various paging.

———. Training Command. 1961. *Observer Training Manual*, Volume 4: *Communications Equipment*. Ottawa; Queen's Printer, various paging.

———. Training Command. 1964. *Weather Guide*: TC-110: RCAF Station Winnipeg: Training Command Headquarters, various paging.

Diefenbaker, John G. "Western Policy and International Law", *Statements and Speeches*, No 61/9. Ottawa: Department of External Affairs.

Green, Howard. "Canada and Latin America", *Statements and Speeches*, No. 60/24. Ottawa: Department of External Affairs.

Nesbitt, W.B. "The Situation in the Congo", *Statements and Speeches*, No. 61/4. Ottawa: Department of External Affairs.

UNPUBLISHED SOURCES

Chapman, Group Captain C.W.G. "Post War: RCAF Museum Interview". Videotape made available to the author by C.W.G. Chapman, Ottawa, Ontario.

Ciuciura, Ivan. 1974. "Policy and Planning for Participation by the RCAF in the War Against Japan". Kingston: Queen's University, MA Research Paper, 103 pp. (DHIST 74/711).

Gurney, Wing Commander, R.J. "Recollections of Trooping, No 426 Squadron: Tempsford, July–December 1945". Personal memoir made available by the author, R.J. Gurney of Dunrobin, Ontario.

Melnyk, T.W. 1978. "RCAF Planning for Tiger Force". Ottawa: National Defence Headquarters, Directorate of History, 89 pp. (DHIST 94/168 File 2/44).

Shipton, Flight Lieutenant, J.S. Personal memoir made available by the author, J.S. Shipton of Nepean, Ontario.

SOURCES ON AIRFIELDS, AIRCRAFT AND EQUIPMENT

Baglow, Bob. 1985. *Canucks Unlimited: Royal Canadian Air Force CF-100 Squadrons and Aircraft, 1952–1963*. Ottawa: Canuk Publications, 124 pp.

Bowyer, M.J.F. 1983. *Action Stations 6: Military Airfields of the Cotswolds and the Central Midlands*. Cambridge, UK: Patrick Stevens, 311 pp.

Chant, Chris. 1999. *Aircraft of World War II*. Etobicoke, Ontario: Prospero Books, 320pp.

Donald, David (ed.). 1999. *The Encyclopedia of Civil Aircraft*. Toronto: Prospero Books, 816 pp.

Donald, David (ed.). 1999. *The Encyclopedia of Civil Aircraft*. Etobicoke, Ontario: Prospero Books, 816 pp.

Dow, James. 1979. *The Arrow*. Toronto: James Lorimer, 160 pp.

Ellis, Frank H. 1954. *Canada's Flying Heritage*. Toronto: University of Toronto Press, 1954, 398 pp.

Falconer, Jonathan. 1992. *RAF Bomber Airfields of World War II*. London: Ian Allan, 128 pp.

Falconer, Jonathan. 1993. *RAF Fighter Airfields of World War II*. London: Ian Allan, 128 pp.

Freeman, R.A. 1981. *Aircraft Profile No 19: Consolidated B-24J Liberator*. Windsor, Berkshire: Profile Books, 11 pp.

Fuller, G.A., J.A. Griffin and K.M. Molson. 1983. *125 Years of Canadian Aeronautics: A Chronology 1840–1965*. Willowdale, Ontario: Canadian Aviation Historical Society, 328 pp.

Glenn, C.H. "TCA/Air Canada's New Fleet Decisions 1943–1984: Were They Wise Decisions?" *CASI Log* 7/5 (December 1999), pp. 26–33.

Gordon, John. 1968. *Of Men and Planes, Volume III: The RCAF*. Ottawa, Ontario: Love Printing Service, 206 pp.

Gradidge, J.M.G., et al. 1984. *The Douglas DC-3 and Its Predecessors*. Tonbridge, Kent: Air-Britain Publications, 672 pp.

Gray, David R. 1997. *Beyond The Inuit Lands: The Story of Canadian Forces Station Alert*. Ottawa: Borealis Press, 197 pp.

Gunston, Bill (ed.) 1998. *The Encyclopedia of Modern Warplanes*. Etobicoke, Ontario: Prospero Books, 288 pp.

Halpenny, B.B. 1981. *Action Stations 2: Military Airfields of Lincolnshire and the East Midlands*. Cambridge, UK: Patrick Stevens, 217pp.

———. 1982. *Action Stations 4: Military Airfields of Yorkshire*. Wellingborough, UK: Patrick Stevens, 216 pp.

Hotson, Fred W. 1983. *The De Havilland Canada Story*. Toronto: CANAV Books, 244 pp.

International Civil Aviation Organization. 1958. *Location Indicators: Doc 7910*. Montreal: ICAO, various paging.

———. 2001. *Location Indicators, Doc 7910/102*. Montreal: ICAO, various paging.

Jockel, J.T. 1987. *No Boundaries Upstairs: Canada, the United States, and the Origins of North American Air Defence*. Vancouver: University of British Columbia Press, 160 pp.

Kostenuk, Samuel and John Griffin. 1977. *RCAF Squadrons and Aircraft: 1924–1968*. Toronto: Samuel Stevens, 255 pp.

Langeste, Tom (ed.) 1995. *Words on the Wing*. Toronto: Canadian Institute of Strategic Studies, 330 pp.

Lloyd, Alwyn T. *Liberator: America's Global Bomber*. Missoula, Montana: Pictorial Histories Publishing, 548 pp.

Milberry, L. 1981. *The AVRO CF-100*. Toronto: CANAV Books, 204 pp.

———. 1982. *The Canadair North Star*. Toronto: CANAV Books, 252 pp.

———. 1986. *The Canadair Sabre*. Toronto: CANAV Books, 372 pp.

———. 1997. *Air Transport In Canada*. Toronto: CANAV Books, 2 volumes, 1040 pp.

Milberry, L. (ed.) 1984. *Sixty Years: The RCAF and CF Air Command 1924–1984*. Toronto: CANAV Books, 480 pp.

Milberry, L., and H. Halliday. 1990. *The Royal Canadian Air Force at War: 1939–1945*. Toronto: CANAV Books, 480 pp.

Molson, K.M., and H.A. Taylor. 1982. *Canadian Aircraft Since 1909*. Stittsville, Ontario: Canada's Wings, 530 pp.

Pearcy, Arthur. 1972. *The Dakota: A History of the Douglas Dakota in RAF and RCAF Service*. London: Ian Allan, 320 pp.

———. 1982. *Dakota at War*. London: Ian Allan, 127 pp.

———. 1995. *Sixty Glorious Years: A Tribute to the Douglas DC-3 Dakota*. Osceola, Wisconsin: Motorbooks International, 160 pp.

Render, Shirley. 1999. *Double Cross: The Inside Story of James A. Richardson and Canadian Airways*. Toronto: Douglas & McIntyre, pp. 334.

Smith, David J. 1989. *Britain's Military Airfields, 1939–1945*. Wellingborough, UK: Patrick Stevens, 249 pp.

Thetford, Owen. 1988. *Aircraft of the Royal Air Force Since 1918*. London: Putnam, 685 pp.

The Timechart Company. 2001. *The Time Chart of Aviation History*. London: TTC, 144 pp.

Vincent, C.R. 1975. *Canada's Wings*, Volume 2: *Consolidated Liberator and Boeing Fortress*. Stittsville, Ontario: Canada's Wings, 246 pp.

Williams, G. 1995. *Flying Through Fire: FIDO, The Fogbuster of World War Two*. Stroud, Gloucestershire: Allan Sutton, pp. 228.

Other Sources

Alexander, Bevin. 1986. *Korea: The First War We Lost*. New York: Hippocrene Books, 558 pp.

Alexander, J.E. 1996. *Inchon To Wonsan: From the Deck of a Destroyer in the Korean War*. Annapolis, Maryland: United States Naval Institute Press, 228 pp.

Appelman, Lt. Col. Roy E. 1987. *East of Chosin: Entrapment and Breakout in Korea, 1950*. College Station, Texas: Texas A & M University Press, 399 pp.

———. 1990. *Escaping the Trap: The U.S. Army X Corps in Northeast Korea, 1950*. College Station, Texas: Texas A & M University Press, 411 pp.

———. 1990. *Ridgeway Duels For Korea*. College Station, Texas: Texas A & M University Press, 665 pp.

Bailey, Sydney D. 1992. *The Korean Armistice.* New York: St. Martin's Press, 312 pp.

Barclay, Brig. C.N. 1954. *The First Commonwealth Division: The Story of the British Commonwealth Land Forces in Korea, 1950–1953.* Aldershot, UK: Gale & Polden, 236 pp.

Bercuson, D.J. 1993. *True Patriot: The Life of Brooke Claxton, 1898–1960.* Toronto: University of Toronto Press, 363 pp.

———. 1999. *Blood on the Hills: The Canadian Army in the Korean War.* Toronto: University of Toronto Press, 269 pp.

Bergot, Erwan. *Battalion de Corée : Les voluntaires français 1950–1953.* Paris: Presses de la Cité, 294 pp.

Berebitsky, William. 1996. *A Very Long Weekend: The Army National Guard in Korea, 1950–1953.* Shippensburg, Pennsylvania: White Mane Publishing, 293 pp.

Biderman, A.D. 1963. *March to Calumny: The Story of American POWs in the Korean War.* New York: MacMillan, 326 pp.

Blair, Clay. 1987. *The Forgotten War: America in Korea, 1950–1953.* New York: Times Books, 1,136 pp.

Bland, Douglas. 1987. *The Administration of Defence Policy in Canada 1947 to 1985.* Kingston, Ontario: Ronald P. Frye & Co., 252 pp.

Breuer, W.B. 1996. *Shadow Warriors: The Covert War in Korea.* New York: John Wiley & Sons, 260 pp.

Britannica Book of the Year 1958. Toronto: Encyclopaedia Britannica Inc., 778 pp.

Brown, W.L. 1961. *The Endless Hours: My Two and a Half Years as a Prisoner of the Chinese Communists.* New York: W.W. Norton, 254 pp.

Brune, L.H. (ed.) 1996. *The Korean War: Handbook of the Literature and Research.* Westport, Connecticut: Greenwood Press.

Bruning, J.R. 1999. *Crimson Sky: The Air Battle For Korea.* Dulles, Virginia: Brassey's, 231 pp.

Bussey, Lt. Col. C.M. 1991. *Firefight at Yechon: Courage and Racism in the Korean War.* New York: Brassey's, 264 pp.

Cagle, M.W., and Manson, F.A. 1957. *The Sea War in Korea.* Annapolis, Maryland: United States Naval Institute Press, 555 pp.

Carew, Tim. 1967. *The Korean War: The Story of the Fighting Commonwealth Regiments 1950–1953.* London: Pan Books, 319 pp.

Chen, Jian. 1994. *China's Road to the Korean War: The Making of Sino-American Confrontation.* New York: Columbia University Press, 339 pp.

Christie, Carl A. 1995. *Ocean Bridge: The History of RAF Ferry Command.* Toronto: University of Toronto Press, 458 pp.

Clearwater, J. 1999. *U.S. Nuclear Weapons In Canada.* Toronto: Dundurn Press, 299 pp.

Coates, K.S., and W.R. Morrison. 1992. *The Alaska Highway in World War II: The U.S. Army of Occupation in Canada's Northwest.* Toronto: University of Toronto Press, 309 pp.

Collins, J. Lawton. 1969. *War in Peacetime: The History and Lessons of Korea.* Boston, Massachussets: Houghton Mifflin, 416 pp.

Cotton, J. and I. Neary (eds.) 1989. *The Korean War in History.* Atlantic Highlands, New Jersey: Humanities Press, 187 pp.

Cox, David. 1986. *Trends in Continental Defence: A Canadian Perspective.* Ottawa: Canadian Institute for International Peace and Security (Occasional Paper No 2), 50 pp.

Cuthbertson, Brian. 1977. *Canadian Military Independence in the Age of the Superpowers.* Toronto: Fitzhenry and Whiteside, 282 pp.

Deane, Philip. 1976. *I Should Have Died.* Don Mills, Ontario: Longmans, 182 pp.

Delmas, Claude. 1982. *Corée 1950 : Paroxysme de la guerre froide.* Brussels: Éditions Complexe, 191 pp.

Dewitt, D.B., and D. Leyton-Brown. 1995. *Canada's International Security Policy.* Scarborough, Ontario: Prentice-Hall, 504 pp.

Dorr, R.F. and Warren Thompson. 1994. *The Korean Air War*. Osceola, Wisconsin: Motorbooks International, 192 pp.

Eayrs, James. 1964. *In Defence of Canada: From the Great War to the Great Depression*. Toronto: University of Toronto Press, 382 pp.

———. 1965. *In Defence of Canada: Appeasement and Rearmament*. Toronto: University of Toronto Press, 261 pp.

———. 1972. *In Defence of Canada: Peacemaking and Deterrence*. Toronto: University of Toronto Press, 448 pp.

———. 1980. *In Defence of Canada: Growing Up Allied*. Toronto: University of Toronto Press, 431 pp.

———. 1983. *In Defence of Canada: Indochina — Roots of Complicity*. Toronto: University of Toronto Press, 348 pp.

Emme, E.M. 1959. *The Impact of Air Power*. Princeton, New Jersey: Van Nostrand, 914 pp.

Encyclopaedia Britannica. 1957. Toronto: Encyclopaedia Britannica Inc.

Evanhoe, Ed. 1995. *Dark Moon: Eighth Army Special Operations in the Korean War*. Annapolis, Maryland: United States Naval Institute Press, 193 pp.

Evans, D.K. 1984. *Sabre Jets Over Korea: A Firsthand Account*. Blue Ridge Summit, Pennsylvania: Tab Books, 251 pp.

Farrar-Hockley, Capt. A. 1955. *The Edge of the Sword*. London: The Companion Book Club, 286 pp.

Fehrenbach, T.R. 1964. *This Kind of War: Korea — A Study In Unpreparedness*. New York: Giant Cardinal, 747 pp.

———. 1966. *Crossroads in Korea: The Historic Seige of Chipyong-Ni*. New York: MacMillan, 96 pp.

———. 1969. *The Fight for Korea from the War of 1950 to the Pueblo Incident*. New York: Grosset-Dunlap, 165 pp.

Foot, Rosemary. 1985. *The Wrong War: American Policy and the Dimensions of the Korean Conflict, 1950–1953*. Ithaca: Cornell University Press, 290 pp.

———. 1990. *A Substitute for Victory, The Politics of Peacemaking at the Korean Armistice Talks*. Ithaca: Cornell University Press, 273 pp.

Foster, Tony. 1986. *Meeting of Generals*. Toronto: Methuen, 559 pp.

Fry, M.G. 1975. *Freedom and Change: Essays in Honour of Lester B. Pearson*. Toronto: McClelland and Stewart, 258 pp.

Gaffen, Fred. 1987. *In The Eye of the Storm: A History of Canadian Peacekeeping*. Toronto: Deneau & Wayne, 302 pp.

Gardam, John. 2000. *Canadians in War and Peacekeeping*. Burnstown, Ontario: General Store Publishing, 237 pp.

———. 1994. *Korea Volunteer*. Burnstown, Ontario: General Store Publishing, 262 pp.

Gardner, Lloyd C. (ed.) 1972. *The Korean War*. New York: Quadrangle Books, 242 pp.

Goodman, Allan E. 1978. *Negotiating While Fighting: The Diary of Admiral C. Turner Joy at the Korean Armistice Conference*. Stanford, California: Hoover Institution Press, 476 pp.

Gordon, K. 1962. *UN In The Congo: A Quest For Peace*. Washington, D.C.: Carnegie Endowment for International Peace, 184 pp.

Gosfield, Frank and B.J. Hurwood. 1969. *Korea: Land of the 38th Parallel*. New York: Parent's Magazine Press, 265 pp.

Graham, Dominic. 1993. *The Price of Command: A Biography of General Guy Simonds*. Toronto: Stoddart, 345 pp.

Graham, Howard. 1987. *Citizen and Soldier: Memoirs of Lieutenant-General Howard Graham*. Toronto: McClelland and Stewart, 304 pp.

Granatstein, J.L. 2002. *Canada's Army: Waging War and Keeping the Peace*. Toronto: University of Toronto Press, 519 pp.

Grey, Jeffrey. 1988. *The Commonwealth Armies and the Korean War: An Alliance Study.* Manchester, UK: Manchester University Press, 224 pp.

Guttmann, Allen. 1967. *Korea and the Theory of Limited War.* Boston, Massachussets: D.C. Heath, 118 pp.

Guttmann, Allen (ed.) 1972. *Korea, Cold War and Limited War.* Lexington, Massachussets: D.C. Heath, 285 pp.

Halliday, Hugh A. 2000. *Not in the Face of the Enemy: Canadians Awarded the Air Force Cross and Air Force Medal 1918–1966.* Toronto: Robin Brass Studio, 284 pp.

Halliday, J., and B. Cummings. 1988. *Korea: The Unknown War.* New York: Pantheon Books, 224 pp.

Hallion, R.P. 1986. *The Naval Air War in Korea.* Baltimore, Maryland: Nautical and Aviation Press of America, 244 pp.

Hammel, E.M. 1981. *Chosin: Heroic Ordeal of the Korean War.* Novato, California: Presidio Press, 457 pp.

Hastings, Max. 1987. *The Korean War.* London: Michael Joseph, 476 pp.

Harries, Meirion and Susie Harries. 1991. *Soldiers of the Sun: The Rise and Fall of the Imperial Japanese Army.* New York: Random House, 604 pp.

Heinl, Col. R.D. 1968. *Victory at High Tide: The Inchon-Seoul Campaign.* Philadelphia: Lippincott, 315 pp.

Heller, Francis H. 1977. *The Korean War: A 25-Year Perspective.* Lawrence: Regents' Press of Kansas, 251 pp.

Hendrie, Andrew. 1997. *Canadian Squadrons in Coastal Command.* St. Catharines, Ontario: Vanwell Publishing, 208 pp.

Hepenstall, Robert. 1995. *Find the Dragon: The Canadian Army in Korea 1950–1953.* Edmonton, Alberta: Four Winds Publishing Co., 380 pp.

Higgins, M. 1951. *War in Korea: The Report of a Woman Combat Correspondent.* Garden City, New York: Doubleday, 223 pp.

Higgins, Trumbull. 1960. *Korea and the Fall of MacArthur.* New York: Oxford University Press, 229 pp.

Hilliker, J. and D. Barry. 1995. *Canada's Department of External Affairs*, Volume 2: *Coming of Age 1946–1968.* Montreal & Kingston: McGill-Queen's University Press, 496 pp.

Hockney, B. and M. Gates. 2002. *Nadir To Zenith: An Almanac of Stories By Canadian Military Navigators.* Picton, Ontario: Hockney and Gates Printcraft, 399 pp.

Holmes, John W. 1979. *The Shaping of Peace, 1943–1957: Canada and the Search for World Order.* Volume 1. Toronto: University of Toronto Press, 349 pp.

———. 1982. *The Shaping of Peace, 1943–1957: Canada and the Search for World Order.* Volume 2. Toronto: University of Toronto Press, 443 pp.

Honderich, J. 1987. *Arctic Imperative: Is Canada Losing the North?* Toronto: University of Toronto Press, 258 pp.

Hopkins, W.B. 1986. *One Bugle, No Drums: The Marines at Chosin Reservoir.* Chapel Hill, North Carolina: Algonquin Books, 274 pp.

Hoyt, Edwin P. 1984. *The Pusan Perimeter: Korea 1950.* New York: Stein and Day, 310 pp.

———. 1984. *On To The Yalu.* Briarcliff Manor, New York: Stein and Day, 297 pp.

———. 1985. *The Bloody Road to Panmunjom.* New York: Stein and Day, 320 pp.

———. 1990. *The Day the Chinese Attacked: Korea 1950.* New York: McGraw-Hill, 245 pp.

Huston, James A. 1989. *Guns and Butter, Powder and Rice: US Army Logistics in the Korean War.* Selinsgrove: Susquehanna University Press, 429 pp.

Jackson, Robert. 1997. *Air War Korea, 1950–1953.* Osceola, Wisconsin: Motorbooks International, 160 pp.

Jacobsen, Capt. Ray. 1985. *426 Squadron History.* Belleville, Ontario: Hangar Bookshelf, 187 pp.

James, D. Clayton. 1993. *Refighting the Last War Command and Crisis in Korea.* New York: MacMillan, 282 pp.

Jockel, J.T. 1994. *Canada and International Peacekeeping.* Toronto: Canadian Institute of Strategic Studies, 83 pp.

———. 1999. *The Canadian Forces: Hard Choices, Soft Power.* Toronto: Canadian Institute of Strategic Studies, 132pp.

Johnson, Major E.A. (ed.) 1981. *Trenton: 50 Years of Air Force.* CFB Trenton: Trenton 50th Anniversary Committee, 160pp.

Kaufman, Burton I. 1986. *The Korean War: Challenges in Crisis, Credibility and Command.* Philadelphia: Temple Press, 381 pp.

———. 1999. *The Korean Conflict.* Westport, Connecticut: Greenwood Press, 193 pp.

Kim Chum-kon. 1980. *The Korean War 1950–1953.* Seoul: Kwangmyong Publishing Co., 604 pp.

Kim, Myung-Ki. 1991. *The Korean War and International Law.* Claremont, California: Paige Press, 291 pp.

Kinkead, Eugene. 1959. *In Every War But One.* New York: W.W. Norton, 219 pp.

Knox, D. 1985. *The Korean War, Pusan to Chosin: An Oral History.* New York: Harcourt Brace Jovanovich, 697 pp.

———. 1988. *The Korean War, Uncertain Victory: The Concluding Volume of An Oral History.* New York: Harcourt Brace Jovanovich, 516 pp.

Kwak Tae-Hahn, et al. (eds.) 1984. *Korean Reunification: New Perspectives and Approaches.* Seoul: Kyungman University Press, 525 pp.

Langley, Michael. 1979. *Inchon Landing: MacArthur's Last Triumph.* New York: Times Books, 182 pp.

Large, Lofty. 1988. *One Man's War in Korea.* Wellingborough, UK: William Kimber, 175 pp.

Lawson, Don. 1964. *The United States in the Korean War.* New York: Abelard-Schuman, 159 pp.

Leckie, Robert. 1962. *Conflict: The History of the Korean War 1950–1953.* New York: G.P. Putnam's Sons, 448 pp.

———. 1987. *La guerre de Corée.* Paris: Laffont, 519 pp.

Lee, Chae-Jin (ed.) 1991. *The Korean War: 40-Year Perspectives.* Claremont, California: Keck Centre for International and Strategic Studies, 131 pp.

Leigh, Z. Lewis. 1985. *And I Shall Fly.* Toronto: CANAV Books, 212 pp.

Lévesque, Rene. 1986. *Memoirs.* Toronto: McClelland and Stewart, 368 pp.

MacDonald, LCol. B.J.S. 1954. *The Trial of Kurt Meyer.* Toronto: Clarke, Irwin, 216 pp.

Mackay, Robert A. 1970. *Canadian Foreign Policy 1945–1954: Selected Speeches and Documents.* Toronto: McClelland and Stewart, 407 pp.

Maloney, S.M. 1997. *War Without Battles: Canada's NATO Brigade in Germany 1951–1993.* Toronto: McGraw-Hill Ryerson, 525 pp.

Margolian, H. 2000. *Conduct Unbecoming: The Story of the Murder of Canadian Prisoners of War In Normandy.* Toronto: University of Toronto Press, 298 pp.

McLin, Jon B. 1967. *Canada's Changing Defence Policy 1957–1963: The Problems of a Middle Power in Alliance.* Toronto: Copp Clark, 251 pp.

Meador, D.J. 1998. *The Korean War in Retrospect: Lessons for the Future.* New York: University Press of America, 200 pp.

Melady, John. 1983. *Korea: Canada's Forgotten War.* Toronto: Macmillan, 215 pp.

Merrill, John. 1989. *Korea: The Peninsular Origins of the War.* Newark: University of Delaware Press, 235 pp.

Meyers, Edward C. 1991. *Thunder In The Morning Calm: The Royal Canadian Navy in Korea 1950–1955.* St. Catharines: Vanwell Publishing, 248 pp.

Middleton, Harry J. 1965. *The Compact History of the Korean War.* New York: Hawthorn Books, 255 pp.

Milberry, L. 1987. *Canada's Air Force Today.* Toronto: CANAV Books, 152 pp.

———. 2000. *Canada's Air Force at War and Peace.* Toronto: CANAV Books, Volume 1: 296 pp; Volume 2: 256 pp.

———. 2001. *Canada's Air Force At War and Peace.* Volume 3. Toronto: CANAV Books, 526 pp.

Morton, Desmond. 2003. *Understanding Canadian Defence.* Toronto: Penguin/McGill Institute, 234 pp.

Mousset, Paul. 1951. *Paralléle 38*. Paris: Gallimard, 294 pp.

Munro, J.A., and A.I. Inglis (eds.) 1973. *Mike: The Memoirs of the Right Honourable Lester B. Pearson*. Volume 2: 1948–1957. Toronto: University of Toronto Press, 344 pp.

Murphy, E.F. 1992. *Korean War Heroes*. Novato, California: Presidio Press, 304 pp.

Neillands, Robin and R. De Norman. 1993. *D-Day, 1944: Voices From Normandy*. London: Weindenfeld-Nicolson, 252 pp.

Nicks, D., J. Bradley and C. Charland. 1997. *Air Defence of Canada, 1948–1997*. Ottawa: Commander Fighter Group, Air Command, 207 pp.

Noble, Harold J. 1975. *Embassy at War*. Seattle: University of Washington Press, 328 pp.

No 412 (Transport) Squadron. *1936–1995*. Paducah, Kentucky: Turner Publishing Co., 112 pp.

No 421 (Tactical Fighter) Squadron. 1982. *421 Squadron History*. Stittsville, Ontario: Canada's Wings, 105 pp.

No 440 Squadron. 1983. *440 Squadron History*. Belleville, Ontario: Hangar Bookshelf, 103 pp.

O'Rourke, G.G., and F.T. Woodbridge. 1998. *Night Fighters Over Korea*. Annapolis, Maryland: United States Naval Institute Press, 208 pp.

Paige, Glenn D. 1968. *The Korean Decision: June 24–30, 1950*. New York: The Free Press, 394 pp.

Real, John R. 1964. *The Pearson Phenomenon*. Toronto: Longmans, 210 pp.

Rempel, R.A. 1987. *Canada's Defence Policy and NATO's Northern Flank*. Winnipeg, Manitoba: Thesis presented to the University of Manitoba, 327 pp.

Richter, Andrew. 1996. *The Evolution of Strategic Thinking at the Canadian Department of National Defence 1950–1960*. Toronto: York Centre for International and Strategic Studies, 36 pp.

Ridgway, Matthew B. 1967. *The Korea War*. Garden City, New York: Doubleday, 291 pp.

Roberts, Leslie. 1959. *There Shall Be Wings: A History of the Royal Canadian Air Force*. Toronto: Clarke, Irwin, 290 pp.

Saywell. John T. 1961. *Canadian Annual Review for 1960*. Toronto: University of Toronto Press, 401 pp.

———. 1962. *Canadian Annual Review for 1961*. Toronto: University of Toronto Press, 476 pp.

Sheldon, Watt. 1968. *Hell or High Water: MacArthur's Landing at Inchon*. New York: MacMillan, 340 pp.

Spurr, Russell, 1988. *Enter The Dragon: China's Undeclared War Against the U.S. In Korea, 1950–1951*. New York: Newmarket Press, 335 pp.

Stairs, Denis. 1974. *The Diplomacy of Constraint: Canada, the Korean War, and the United States*. Toronto: University of Toronto Press, 373 pp.

Stephens, W. Ray. 1993. *The Canadian Entertainers of World War II*. Oakville, Ontario: Mosaic Press, 116 pp.

Stewart, Col. James T. 1957. *Airpower: The Decisive Force in Korea*. New York: Van Nostrand, 310 pp.

Sweanor, George. 1981. *It's All Pensionable Time*. Toronto: Gesnor Publications, 333 pp.

Swettenham, John. 1969. *McNaughton*. Volume 3: 1944–1966. Toronto: Ryerson Press, 396 pp.

Vokes, MGen Chris, with John P. MacLean. 1985. *Vokes: My Story*. Ottawa: Gallery Books, 233 pp.

von Horn, C. 1966. *Soldiering for Peace*. London: Cassell, 372 pp.

Warnock, John W. 1970. *Partner to Behemoth: The Military Policy of a Satellite Canada*. Toronto: New Press, 340 pp.

Westwood, J. 1956. *The History of the Middle East Wars*. North Dayton, Massachussets: World Publications Group, 216 pp.

Whelan, R. 1990. *Drawing the Line: The Korean War 1950–1953*. Boston: Little, Brown, 428 pp.

Whiting, Allen S. 1960. *China Crosses the Yalu: The Decision to Enter the Korean War*. New York: MacMillan, 219 pp.

APPENDICES

Appendix A: Glossary

APPENDIX A

GLOSSARY

ACRONYMS AND ABBREVIATIONS

ADC: Air Defence Command
AFB: Air Force Base
AFHQ: Air Force Headquarters
AirDiv: No 1 (RCAF) Air Division, Europe
AOC: Air Officer Commanding
AOC-in-Chief: Air Officer Commanding in Chief (RAF)
ANS: Air Navigation School
CAdO: Chief Administrative Officer
CAS: Chief of the Air Staff
CCG: Canadian Coast Guard
CEPE: Central Experimental and Proving Establishment
CFR: Commissioned from the Ranks
CFS: Central Flying School
CGS: Chief of the General Staff
CNS: Central Navigation School
COpsO: Chief Operations Officer
CPA: Canadian Pacific Airlines
CP: Critical Point
Dak: Douglas DC–3 Dakota
DND: Department of National Defence
DOT: Department of Transport
DR: Dead Reckoning
EAC: Eastern Air Command
EFTS: Elementary Flying Training School
FE: Flight Engineer
FIDO: Fog Investigation and Dispersal Organisation

FIS: Flying Instructors' School
GCA: Ground-Controlled Approach
Herc: Lockheed C-130 Hercules
HMCS: His (or Her) Majesty's Canadian Ship
ICAO: International Civil Aviation Organization
ICSC: International Commission for Supervision and Control
IFS: Instrument Flying School
MAC: Maritime Air Command
MAP: Ministry of Aircraft Production
MedA: Medical Assistant
MiG: Soviet jet fighter built by **Mikoyan-Gurevitch**
MIR: Medical Inspection Room
MO: Medical Officer
NAAFI: Navy, Army and Air Force Institute
Nav: Navigator
No 1 Wing: No 1 (F) Wing, Marville
No 2 Wing: No 2 (F) Wing, Grostenquin
No 3 Wing: No 3 (F) Wing, Zweibrücken
No 4 Wing: No 4 (F) Wing, Baden-Söllingen
NWAC: North West Air Command
OC: Officer Commanding
OFU: Overseas Ferry Unit
Ops: Operations
OTU: Operational Training Unit
POL: Petrol, Oil and Lubricants
RAAF: Royal Australian Air Force
RAF: Royal Air Force

733

RCAC: Royal Canadian Air Cadets
RCAF: Royal Canadian Air Force
RCEME: Royal Canadian Electrical and Mechanical Engineers
RCMP: Royal Canadian Mounted Police
RCN: Royal Canadian Navy
RD: Repair Depot
Recce: Reconnaissance
RNZAF: Royal New Zealand Air Force
RO: Radio Officer
RTB: Return to Base
SBA: Standard Beam Approach
SFTS: Service Flying Training School
Sqn: Squadron
Stn: Station
SWO: Station Warrant Officer
TAC: Tactical Air Command
T-Bird: Lockheed T-33 Shooting Star or Silver Star
TC: Training Command
TCA: Trans-Canada Airlines
u/s: Unserviceable
USAF: United States Air Force
USN: United States Navy
VCAS: Vice Chief of the Air Staff
V-E Day: Victory in Europe Day
VIP: Very Important Person
V-J Day: Victory in Japan Day
WAC: Western Air Command
WEE: Winter Experimental Establishment
w/o: Write-off

Phonetic Alphabet

In 1957, all three of Canada's armed services adopted the following ICAO alphabet:

Alpha	Foxtrot	Kilo	Papa	Uniform
Bravo	Golf	Lima	Quebec	Whisky
Charlie	Hotel	Mike	Romeo	X-Ray
Delta	India	November	Sierra	Yankee
Echo	Juliet	Oscar	Tango	Zulu

Repair Categories for Crashed Aircraft

A: Category A crash, usually a write-off.
B: Category B crash, serious, requiring major repairs.
C: Category C crash, minor, requiring repairs that can be done locally.
D: Category D crash, very minor damage.

Appendix A: Glossary

RANK STRUCTURE

ROYAL AIR FORCE (RAF) AND ROYAL CANADIAN AIR FORCE (RCAF)		UNITED STATES AIR FORCE (USAF)
* Marshal of the RAF (MRAF)		
* Air Chief Marshal (ACM)		General
Air Marshal (AM)		Lieutenant General
Air Vice Marshal (AVM)		Major General
Air Commodore (A/C)		Brigadier General
Group Captain (G/C)		Colonel
Wing Commander (W/C)		Lieutenant Colonel
Squadron Leader (S/L)		Major
Flight Lieutenant (F/L)		Captain
Flying Officer (F/O)		First Lieutenant
Pilot Officer (P/O)		Second Lieutenant
* Warrant Officer (WO)	† 1st Class (WO1)	Warrant Officer
	† 2nd Class (WO2)	
Flight Sergeant (F/S)		Master Sergeant
		Technical Sergeant
Sergeant (Sgt.)		Staff Sergeant
Corporal (Cpl.)		Sergeant
Leading Aircraftsman (LAC)		Corporal
Aircraftsman 1st Class (AC1)		Private 1st Class
Aircraftsman 2nd Class (AC2)		Private

(* *RAF only* / † *RCAF only*)

WORDS AND PHRASES

Apron: Concrete or asphalt area around a hangar used for moving and parking aircraft.

Blues: RCAF winter uniforms.

Bowser: Fuel tanker truck.

Boxcar: Fairchild C-119 transport, also called the "Dollar-19".

Bugsmasher: Beech C-45 Expeditor, also called the Exploder.

Button: Approach end of a runway.

Cannibalize: Remove usable parts and components from a damaged aircraft for use on another aircraft.

Chief of the General Staff: Most senior officer of the Army.

Chock: Steel, wood or rubber wedge placed under the wheel of a parked aircraft to prevent it from rolling forward.

Circuits and bumps: Approaches and landings done for practice.

Clag: Thick layer of overcast cloud.

Clamped in: Condition of an airport when low cloud or fog prevents safe landings (also "socked in").

Clunk: AVRO Canada CF-100 Canuck all-weather jet fighter.

Cocoon: Coat an aircraft with airtight rubber or plastic to protect it during shipment or in storage.

Critical point: The point along track between base and destination at which it would take as long to return to base as it would to proceed to destination at a reduced ground speed.

Dead reckoning: Calculating the ground position of an aircraft from its air position and an estimation of the wind effect.

Ditch: Make a controlled emergency landing into water.

FIDO equipment: System of pipes to distribute high-octane gasoline along runways, warm the fuel, and burn the resulting vapour to generate sufficient heat to dispel heavy fog.

Feather: Turn the blades of a propeller into the wind to shut down the engine and eliminate drag.

Fitter: Aero-engine technician.

Fix: In navigation, to ascertain one's position on a map.

Flight: Largest sub-unit in a squadron.

Flight deck: In a large aircraft, the interior space containing the crew positions for the pilot, co-pilot, navigator, radio officer and flight engineer.

George: Auto-pilot.

Green Ticket: Card identifying the bearer as an instrument-rated pilot.

Jam: Disrupt a radio transmission of any kind (including radar) by broadcasting a stronger signal of the same frequency and amplitude.

Jump-seat: Spare seat installed for an observer out of the crew's way on the flight deck.

L-14: Document for recording technicians' line-servicing actions on a given aircraft on a given day.

Leg: Stage of a long flight.

Let-down: Steady, controlled descent by an aircraft; often refers to the descent to a landing.

Let-down chart: Navigation document describing the instrument approach and landing procedures for a specific airport.

Mayday: Radio codeword indicating distress.

On top: Flying above cloud.

On track: In air navigation, flying on the planned route.

Overshoot: Abort landing approach and climb away.

Padre: Military or naval chaplain.

Point of no return: Point along track beyond which an aircraft cannot return to its starting point without over-reaching the limits of its endurance.

Prang: Crash an aircraft.

Rigger: Airframe technician specializing repair and maintenance of aircraft structures, flight controls, fuel systems, hydraulics and pressurization.

Snag: Mechanical or electrical fault in an aircraft that renders it or any part of its equipment unsafe in flight.

Stall: Abrupt loss of lift; "stalling speed" is the speed at which the wings cease to produce enough lift to overcome drag.

Tannoy: British-made public-address system.

Tarmac: Asphalt-paved ramp area of the hangar line on an air base (from "tarred macadamized surface").

Undershoot: Touch ground short of the intended landing spot.

Vamp: DH 100 Vampire, a pioneering fighter built in Britain and assembled in Canada by DeHavilland; the first jet aircraft in operational service with the RCAF.

Visibility (Vis): In meteorology, the distance a person with average vision can see in current weather conditions.

White-out: Dangerous atmospheric condition in which blowing snow on the ground combines with overcast conditions to obscure the horizon and obliterate visual references to the ground.

Wings: RCAF badge indicating aircrew specialty.

Zero-zero: "Zero visibility, zero ceiling" — thick fog.

Zulu time: Radio codeword for Greenwich Mean Time, now called Universal Co-ordinated Time.

Primary References:

Kostenuk and Griffin, *Canadian Military Aircraft*, pp. 682–686.

Langeste, *Words on the Wing*, passim.

Appendix B

Schedule of Operations

Schedule of Operations — Trooping

Date/1945	Liberator MK.VI/MK.VIII	Captain	Duty (LTT)	Depart Base (GMT)	Return To Base (GMT)
30 September	VI KL641/A	F/L K.W. Warner	1	1830	
30 September	VI KK341/P	F/O H.E. Miskiman	3	1955	
1 October	VI KL658/B	F/L J.H. Badgely	5	1610	
2 October	VI KL670/G	F/L C.W. Crawford	7	1600	
2 October	VI KL619/H	F/L D. Harrison	9	1600	
3 October	VI KL639/F	F/L R.J. Roach	11	1620	
4 October	VI KL663/C	F/L R.J. Traill	13	1555	
4 October	VI KL621/D	F/L J.M. Reilly	15	1550	
5 October	VI KL618/K	F/L F.R. McGill	17	1700	
6 October	VI KK340/R	F/L G.E. Seward	19	1555	
6 October	VI KK374/T	F/L L.R. Pattee	21	1550	
7 October	VI KK267/0	F/L D.E. Merriam	23	1655	
7 October	VI KL641/A	F/O W.A. Craig	2		1350
7 October	VI KK341/P	F/L L. Greenburgh	4		1450
8 October	VI KL625/V	F/L J.A. Elviss	25	1610	
8 October	VI KK255/Q	F/L L.B. Wyman	27	1622	
9 October	VI KH381/W	F/O N.A. Noel	29	1620	
9 October	VI KL658/B	F/L A. Paruk	6		1048
9 October	VI KL619/H	F/L D.K. Horner	10		1128
10 October	VI KL647/M	F/L R.H. Fraser	31	1450	
10 October	VI KK341/P	F/L G.R. Guess	33	1355	
10 October	VI KL670/G	F/L K.W. Warner	8		0955
10 October	VI KL639/F	F/L D. Harrison	12		0945
11 October	VI KH333/J	F/O G.S. Galley	35	1405	
12 October	VI KL641/A	F/O H. Niblett	37	1425	

Date/1945	Liberator MK.VI/MK.VIII	Captain	Duty (LTT)	Depart Base (GMT)	Return To Base (GMT)
12 October	VIII KG983/Y	F/L H.A. Lutes	39	1440	
12 October	VI KL621/D	F/L J.H. Badgely	16		1415
13 October	VI KL658/B	F/L A.J. Mackie	41	1355	
13 October	VI KL663/C	F/O N.A. Noel	14		1410
13 October	VI KL618/K	F/L R.J. Roach	18		1455
13 October	VI KK340/R	F/L C.W. Crawford	20		1315
14 October	VI KL670/G	F/L C.E. Goodwin	45	1400	
15 October	VIII KH179/HW	F/L T.W. Lloyd	43	1005	
15 October	VI KL639/F	F/L L. Greenburgh	47	1435	
15 October	VI KK267/O	F/L R.J. Traill	24		1505
15 October	VI KK255/Q	F/O H.E. Miskiman	28		1425
16 October	VI KL621/D	F/O W.A. Craig	51	1530	
16 October	VI KL625/V	F/L F.R. McGill	26		1315
16 October	VI KH381/W	F/L J.M. Reilly	30		1740
17 October	VI KL650/J	F/L G.S. McDonald	49	1130	
17 October	VI KL618/K	F/L W.J. Cameron	53	1415	
18 October	VI KL647/M	F/L G.E. Seward	32		1400
18 October	VI KK340/R	F/O H.J. Oliver	55	1400	U/S Melsbroek Cancelled
18 October	VI KL619/H	F/L A. Paruk	57	1445	
19 October	VI KK267/O	F/O G. Rubenck	59	1410	U/S Melsbroek Cancelled
19 October	VI KL641/A	F/L L.R. Pattee	38		1100
20 October	VI KL663/C	F/L L.W. Barclay	61	1425	
20 October	VI KK255/Q	F/O G. More	63	1330	
20 October	VI KH333/JW	F/L D.E. Merriam	36		1335
21 October	VI KL625/V	F/O N.A. Noel	65	1340	U/S Melsbroek Cancelled
22 October	VI KL670/G	F/L J.A. Elviss	46		1325
22 0ctober	VI KH381/W	F/L J.F. Lambert	69	1414	No load Cancelled
22 October	VI KL647/M	F/O J.S. Wright	67	1510	U/S Melsbroek Cancelled
22 October	VI KK341/P	F/L L.B. Wyman	34		1410
23 October	VI KK340/R	F/O H.J. Oliver	56	Cancelled	1610
23 October	VI KL647/M	F/O J.S. Wright	68	Cancelled	1550
23 October	VI KH381/W	F/L J.F .Lambert	70	Cancelled	1537
24 October	VI KK267/O	F/O G. Rubenck	60	Cancelled	1600

Appendix B: Schedule of Operations

Date/1945	Liberator MK.VI/MK.VIII	Captain	Duty (LTT)	Depart Base (GMT)	Return To Base (GMT)
24 October	VI KL641/A	F/O A.B. Cronje	71	0925	
25 October	VI KK340/R	F/L F.A. Keetley	73	0900	
25 October	VI KL647/M	F/O D.T. Cook	75	0925	
26 October	VIII KH179/HW	F/L R.H. Fraser	44		1335
26 October	VI KL639/F	F/O H. Niblett	48		1525
26 October	VI KL650/J	F/L H.A. Lutes	50		1505
26 October	VI KL618/K	F/L G.R. Guess	54		1405
27 October	VI KL621/D	F/L C.E. Goodwin	52		0950
27 October	VIII KH329/Z	F/O H.J. Oliver	77	1130	
27 October	VI KK267/O	F/O J.S. Wright	79	0815	
27 October	VI KH381/W	F/L G.B. McDormund	81	0840	
27 October	VIII KG983/Y	F/L A.J. Mackie	40		0555
27 October	VI KL619/H	F/L L. Greenburgh	58		1415
27 October	VI KL663/C	F/L T.W. Lloyd	62		1450
28 October	VI KK255/Q	F/L G.S. McDonald	64		1425
28 October	VI KL625/V	F/O N.A. Noel	66	Cancelled	1350
28 October	VI KK341/P	F/O G. Rubenck	83	0950	
29 October	VI KL658/B	F/L W.J. Cameron	42		0950
29 October	VI KL670/G	F/L C.W. Crawford	85	0810	
29 October	VI KH333/JW	F/L J.R. Ketcheson	87	1110	
30 October	VI KL625/V	F/L K.W. Warner	89	0750	
31 October	VI KL618/K	F/L D.R. Horner	91	0945	
31 October	VIII KH179/HW	F/L D. Harrison	93	1205	
1 November	VI KL639/F	F/L N.K. Stansfield	95	1435	
1 November	VI KL621/D	F/L T.P. Flint	97	1430	
1 November	VI KL647/M	F/L A. Paruk	76		1535
2 November	VI KL650/J	F/L R.J. Traill	99	1400	
2 November	VI KL619/H	F/O H.E. Miskiman	101	1400	
2 November	VI KH381/W	F/O G. More	80		1625
2 November	VI KK267/O	F/O G.S. Galley	82		1545
3 November	VI KL663/C	F/L J.F. Lambert	103	1755	
3 November	VI KL658/B	F/L F.R. McGill	105	1400	
3 November	VI KK341/P	F/O A.B. Cronje	84		1527
4 November	VI KK255/Q	F/L G.E. Seward	107	1440	
4 November	VI KL647/M	F/L J.A. Badgley	109	1430	
6 November	VI KH381/W	F/L R.J. Roach	111	1050	
6 November	VI KK341/P	F/L J.H. Reilly	113	1045	
6 November	VI KK267/O	F/L L.R. Pattee	115	1358	
6 November	VI KL641/A	F/O D.T. Cook	72		1515
7 November	VI KL618/K	F/L F.A. Keetley	92		1445

Date/1945	Liberator MK.VI/MK.VIII	Captain	Duty (LTT)	Depart Base (GMT)	Return To Base (GMT)
7 November	VI KL670/G	F/L L.W. Barclay	86		1605
7 November	VIII KH179/HW	F/O J.S. Wright	94		1440
7 November	A/C Not Available		117/118	Cancelled	
7 November	A/C Not Available		119/120	Cancelled	
8 November	VI KL639/F	F/L G.B. McDormund	96		1255
8 November	VI KL650/J	F/O G. Rubenck	100		0930
8 November	VI KK374/T	F/O K.W. Warner	22		0950
8 November	VI KL625/V	F/L T.P. Flint	90		2100
8 November	A/C Not Available		121/122	Cancelled	
8 November	A/C Not Available		123/124	Cancelled	
9 November	VI KL641/A	F/L J.A. Elviss	125	1355	
9 November	VIII KH181/LW	F/L L.B. Wyman	127	1350	
10 November	VI KL618/K	F/L A.J. Mackie	129	1415	
10 November	VI KL650/J	F/L G.R. Guess	131	1420	
11 November	VI KL686/MW	F/L H.A. Lutes	133	1415	
11 November	VI KL639/F	F/L C.E. Goodwin	135	1405	
11 November	VI KH333/KH	F/L D. Harrison	88		1255
11 November	VI KL663/C	F/L C.W. Crawford	104		2215
11 November	VI KL658/B	F/O H.J. Oliver	106		0731
11 November	VI KL647/M	F/L G.E. Seward	110		1035
12 November	VIII KH179/HW	F/L G.W. Lloyd	137	1345	
12 November	VI KK374/T	F/L L. Greenburgh	139	1450	
13 November	VI KL625/V	F/L G.S. McDonald	141	1425	
13 November	VI KL621/D	F/L F.R. McGill	98		1423
14 November	VI KK341/P	F/O H.E. Miskiman	114		1305
14 November	VI KL619/H	F/L R.J. Traill	102		2240
14 November	VI KK255/Q	F/L D.K. Horner	108		1940
14 November	VI KK267/O	F/L J.A. Badgley	116		1500
14 November	VI KL658/B	F/L M.C. Butler	143	1540	
14 November	VI KH333/JW	F/L W.J. Cameron	145	1500	
15 November	VI KL670/G	F/O A.B. Cronje	147	1400	
15 November	VI KL647/M	F/O G. More	149	1525	
15 November	VI KK340/R	F/O H. Niblett	74		1445
15 November	VI KH381/W	F/L J.F. Lambert	112		1640
16 November	VI KL618/K	F/L R.H. Fraser	130		1410
16 November	VI KL686/MW	F/L R.J. Roach	134		1815
16 November	VI KL663/C	F/L A. Paruk	151	1725	
16 November	VI KL621/D	F/O G.S. Galley	153	1405	U/S Cairo
17 November	A/C Unserviceable		155/156	Cancelled	
17 November	VI KL619/H	F/O D.T. Cook	157	1930	

Appendix B: Schedule of Operations

Date/1945	Liberator MK.VI/MK.VIII	Captain	Duty (LTT)	Depart Base (GMT)	Return To Base (GMT)
17 November	VIII KH181/LW	F/L J.R. Christopher	128		1525
17 November	VIII KH179/HW	F/O W.A. Craig	138		0905
18 November	A/C Not Available		159/160	Cancelled	
18 November	A/C Not Available		161/162	Cancelled	
18 November	VIII KH329/Z	F/L N.K. Stansfield	78		1350
18 November	VI KK374/T	F/L J.M. Ketcheson	140		1445
19 November	VI KL625/V	F/O N.A. Noel	142		0145
19 November	VIII KH179/HW	F/L G.E. Seward	163	1420	
19 November	VI KK340/R	F/L L.W. Barclay	165	1730	
20 November	Weather Conditions		167/168	Cancelled	
20 November	Weather Conditions		169/170	Cancelled	
20 November	VI KL641/A	F/L D.E. Merriam	126		0450
20 November	VI KL670/G	F/L H.A. Lutes	148		1625
21 November	Weather (fog)		171/172	Cancelled	
21 November	Weather (fog)		173/174	Cancelled	
22 November	VI KK267/O	F/L G.B. McDormund	177	1515	
23 November	VI KL647/M	F/L L.R. Pattee	150		1618
23 November	VI KH333/JW	F/L J.A. Elviss	146		1205
23 November	VI KL619/H	F/L L.B. Wyman	158		1930
23 November	VIII KH181/LW	F/L T.P. Flint	175	1100	
23 November	VI KL686/MW	F/L K.W. Warner	179	1350	
23 November	VI KL618/K	F/O G. Rubenck	181	1355	
23 November	VIII KH179/HW	F/L L. Greenburgh	164		1325
24 November	VI KK374/T	F/L D. Harrison	183	1400	
24 November	VI KK255/Q	F/O F.J. Oliver	185	1349	
24 November	VI KL658/B	F/L C.E. Goodwin	144		1335
24 November	VI KK340/R	F/L G.R. Guess	166		1425
25 November	VI KL639/F	F/L A.J. Mackie	136		1405
25 November	VI KH381/W	F/O J.S. Wright	187	1410	
26 November	VI KK341/P	F/L F.R. McGill	189	0850	
26 November	VI KK341/P		190	Castel Benito (Cancelled)	A/C Accident
26 November	VI KL658/B	F/O H.E. Miskiman	191	1400	
26 November	VIII KH224/NW	F/L J.A. Badgley	193	1630	
27 November	VIII KH181/LW	F/L G.S. McDonald	176		0735
27 November	VI KL686/MW	F/O A.B. Cronje	180		1000
27 November	VI KL641/A	F/L R.J. Traill	195	1505	
27 November	VI KL625/V	F/L D.K. Horner	197	1425	

Date/1945	Liberator MK.VI/MK.VIII	Captain	Duty (LTT)	Depart Base (GMT)	Return To Base (GMT)
28 November	VI KL618/K	F/L J.D. Matheson	182		0130
28 November	VIII KH329/Z	F/O H. Niblett	199	1420	
28 November	VI KL918/X	F/L J.F. Lambert	201	1425	
29 November	VI KK255/Q	F/L C.W. Crawford	186		1345
29 November	VI KK374/T	F/O G. More	184		1315
29 November	VI KL619/H	F/L R.J. Roach	203	1422	
29 November	VIII KH179/HW	F/L R.H. Fraser	205	1430	
30 November	VI KL670/G	F/L J.M. Ketcheson	207	1415	
30 November	VI KK340/R	F/L F.A. Keetley	209	1425	
30 November	VI KH381/W	F/O G.S. Galley	188		1100
1 December	VI KN833/OW	F/O N.A. Noel	211	1525	
1 December	VI KL686/MW	F/L J.R. Christofer	213	1415	
1 December	VI KL658/B	F/O D.T. Cook	192		1255
2 December	VI KK267/O	F/L M.C. Butler	178		1240
2 December	VI KL663/C	F/L L.W. Barclay	152		1540
3 December	VI KL618/K	F/L D.E. Merriam	215	0716	
3 December	VI KH181/LW	F/L J.J. O'Flynn	217	0600	
3 December	VIII KH333/JW	F/O K.M. Yeats	219	1240	
3 December	VI KL639/F	F/L H.A. Lutes	221	1200	
4 December	VI KH381/W	F/L J.A. Elviss	223	1205	
5 December	Wx Conditions		225/226	Cancelled	
5 December	Wx Conditions		227/228	Cancelled	
5 December	VI KL619/H	F/L K.W. Warner	204		1750
5 December	VIII KH224/NW	F/L C.E. Seward	194		1800
6 December	Wx Conditions		229/230	Cancelled	
6 December	Wx Conditions		231/232	Cancelled	
8 December	VI KL658/B	F/L L.R. Pattee	233	1210	
8 December	VI KK374/T	F/L L.B. Wyman	235	1530	
8 December	VI KK255/Q	F/L C.E. Goodwin	237	1220	
8 December	VIII KH224/NW	F/L N.K. Stansfield	239	1700	
8 December	VI KL625/V	F/L T.P. Flint	198		1535
8 December	VI KG918/X	F/O G. Rubenck	202		1645
8 December	VIII KH179/HW	F/L F.R. McGi11	206		1547
8 December	VI KN833/OW	F/L D.K. Horner	212		1627
9 December	Wx Conditions		241/242	Cancelled	
9 December	Wx Conditions		243/244	Cancelled	
9 December	VI KL670/G	F/O H.J. Oliver	208		1445
9 December	VI KL663/C	F/L G.R. Guess	Trainer		1700
11 December	VI KL647/M	S/L A.J. Mackie	245	1155	
11 December	VI KL663/C	F/L C.W. Crawford	247	1210	

Appendix B: Schedule of Operations

Date/1945	Liberator MK.VI/MK.VIII	Captain	Duty (LTT)	Depart Base (GMT)	Return To Base (GMT)
11 December	VI KN833/OW	F/L C.S. McDonald	249	1300	
11 December	VI KL686/MW	F/L G.B. McDormund	214		1630
11 December	VI KL639/F	F/L D. Harrison	222		1355
12 December	VI KH381/W	F/O H.E. Miskiman	224		1455
12 December	VI KK340/R	F/O J.S. Wright	210		1530
12 December	VI KG918/X	F/O A.V. Cronje	251	1352	
13 December	VIII KH179/HW	F/L G.R. Guess	253	1318	
13 December	VI KL625/V	F/L J.D. Matheson	255	1350	
13 December	VI KL619/H	F/O G.B. Galley	257	1420	
13 December	VI KL650/J	F/L R.J. Roach	132		1535
13 December	VI KL641/A	F/L G.W. Lloyd	196		1520
13 December	VIII KH329/Z	F/L J.M. Ketcheson	200		1605
14 December	VI KL670/G	F/O D.T. Cook	259	1550	
14 December	VI KL658/B	F/O N.A. Noel	234		1710
14 December	VIII KH224/NW	F/O H. Niblett	240		1510
15 December	VI KL639/F	F/L M.C. Butler	261	1430	
15 December	A/C U/S		263/264	Cancelled	
15 December	A/C U/S		265/266	Cancelled	
15 December	VI KK374/T	F/L J.A. Badgley	236		1545
15 December	VIII KH333/JW	F/L A. Paruk	220		1115
15 December	VI KK255/Q	F/L R.J. Traill	238		U/S Tunis
16 December	VIII KH329/Z	F/L L.W. Barclay	269	1320	
16 December	VI KL647/M	F/L D.E. Merriam	246		1235
16 December	VI KL663/C	F/L F.A. Keetley	248		1610
17 December	VI KH381/W	F/O W.A. Craig	267	1208	
17 December	VI KL650/J	F/L D.K. Horner	271	1215	
17 December	VI KK340/R	F/L C.E. Seward	273	1335	
17 December	VI KN833/OW	F/O K.M. Yeats	250		1510
17 December	VI KL619/H	F/L R.H. Fraser	258		1450
18 December	Wx Conditions		275/276	Cancelled	
20 December	VI KL658/B	F/O G. More	277	1330	
20 December	VI KK267/O	F/L L. Greenburgh	279	1310	
20 December	VI KL686/MW	F/O G. Rubenck	281	1340	
20 December	VI KL647/M	F/O H.J. Oliver	283	1600	
20 December	VIII KH181/LW	F/O H.A. Lutes	218		2045
20 December	VI KL670/G	F/L L.R. Pattee	260		2120
20 December	VI KL639/F	F/L J.F. Lambert	262		2125
22 December	VIII KH179/HW	F/L J.A. Elviss	254		1300
22 December	VI KL625/V	F/L L.B. Wyman	256		1405
22 December	VIII KH329/Z	F/L C.E. Goodwin	270		1330

Date/1945	Liberator MK.VI/MK.VIII	Captain	Duty (LTT)	Depart Base (GMT)	Return To Base (GMT)
22 December	VI KK340/R	F/L J.J. O'Flynn	274		1345
22 December	VIII KH333/JW	F/L C.B. McDormund	Trainer		1615
23 December	VI KL650/J	F/L C.W. Crawford	272		1210
27 December	VI KH381/W	F/O A.V. Cronje	268		2230
27 December	VI KL686/MW	S/L A.J. Mackie	282		1810
29 December	VI KL658/B	F/L J.D. Matheson	278		1220
29 December	VI KK267/O	F/O G.S. Galley	280		1630
29 December	VI KL647/M	F/O D.T. Cook	284		1635
31 December	VI KL621/D		154		U/S Cairo
31 December	VI KK341/P		190		U/S Castel Benito
31 December	VI KK255/Q		238		U/S Tunis
31 December	VI KG918/X		252		U/S Shaibah
1 January 1946	VI KL618/K	F/L Hogarth (RAF)	216		1356

Trooping Operations — Summary

1945 Month	Scheduled Flights	Cancellations			Outbound – Departures					Inbound – Arrivals		
		No A/C Available	A/C U/S	Weather	Base	RTB A/C U/S	RTB No Load	Duty Carried Out	Pax Carried	A/C Left U/S On Route	Duty Carried Out	Pax Carried
October	47				47	4[2]	1[3]	42	1,043		29	752
November	58	7		4	47	–	–	47	1,205	1[4]	45	1,134
December	38[1]		2	7	29	–	–	29	520	3[5]	40	813
	143	7	2	11	123	4	1	118	2,767	4	114	2,699

* NOTES:
 1 One trainer included
 2 4 A/C returned to base (RTB) after unserviceabilities rectified
 3 One A/C RTB — no load
 4 An A/C left unserviceable (31 Dec 45) at Castel Benito
 5 3 A/C left unserviceable (31 Dec 45) at Cairo West, Shaibah and Tunis

Appendix C

RCAF-MATS Airlift Agreement

HEADQUARTERS
MILITARY AIR TRANSPORT SERVICE
ANDREWS AIR FORCE BASE
WASHINGTON 25, D.C.

28 Jul 1950

SUBJECT: RCAF participation in USAF MATS Far East Airlift

TO: Air Officer Commanding
Royal Canadian Air Force Transport Command
Rockcliffe, Ontario, Canada

1. With reference to the RCAF Transport Command participation in the USAF MATS airlift to the Far East, the following suggestions for establishment of a modus operandi are submitted for your concurrence, in the absence of a formal agreement on this matter between our respective Governments.

2. Based upon conversations between officers of our respective commands in this headquarters on 20 July 1950, it is presently understood that the RCAF will provide:

   a. The 426th Heavy Transport Squadron, RCAF, to be based at McChord Air Force Base, Tacoma, Washington, to be manned at an approximate strength of 50 to 60 officers and 200 enlisted personnel, and to be equipped with six (6) Northstar aircraft. The RCAF Squadron strength in personnel and/or aircraft is subject to future augmentations as resources may become available for that purpose.

   b. Aircraft spares and equipment to be delivered to McChord Air Force Base, and consisting at the outset of approximately 100,000 pounds of material which will be airlifted when the RCAF squadron is deployed to McChord Air Force Base.

   c. Emergency and arctic survival equipment for the RCAF aircraft employed, except that parachutes will not be carried.

d. Supply and other support required by the RCAF squadron and available from Canadian or Empire sources.

e. Reimbursement for logistic support provided the RCAF squadron from US. sources at established rates. Appropriate reimbursement documents will be furnished RCAF by USAF requesting payment for aircraft fuels, lubricants, spare parts, etc. In the event RCAF personnel are not in possession of personal funds to insure "pay as you go" status, USAF will request appropriate reimbursement for rations and billets and other USAF local supply support items and services furnished. It is contemplated that the detailed procedures to be employed in accounting for reimbursable support furnished will be made the subject of a separate communication at an early date.

3. It is agreed that MATS will provide, or will arrange for other U.S. agencies to provide, the following at McChord Air Force Base and enroute USAF bases:

a. Logistical support to include housing, food services, medical care, ground handling equipment, use of shop facilities and equipment, fuel, lubricants, and such other supply support as may be required but not readily available from Canadian sources.

b. Complete crew briefings at McChord Air Force Base and enroute bases, and such qualified USAF personnel as may be available to augment RCAF crews to provide route checks on the initial trips.

c. Preparation of manifests and supervision of aircraft loading except that RCAF airplane captains will be responsible for proper loading of aircraft.

4. It was further understood that:

a. The personnel of the RCAF Squadron would be sufficient to provide:

(1) Two (2) crews for each aircraft, including flight attendants (traffic clerks).
(2) Maintenance personnel for RCAF aircraft, sufficient to perform all maintenance and inspections.
(3) Internal administration of RCAF squadron.
(4) Augmentation to the MATS traffic section at McChord Air Force Base by RCAF flight attendants when not operationally engaged.
(5) An aircraft maintenance detachment at the Far East terminus of the route (five (5) enlisted personnel), and possibly two (2) mechanical specialists at each of the enroute stations if determined by the RCAF Squadron Commander to be required.
(6) One field grade officer to act a liaison with the Continental Division, MATS, to be located as desired by the Commander, Continental Division.

Appendix C: RCAF-MATS Airlift Agreement

b. The six (6) Northstar aircraft:

   (1) Would complete approximately eight (8) round trips per month, initially.
   (2) Would have a capacity for 33 passengers or 10,000 pounds of cargo on the critical leg, and a maximum capacity of 44 passengers or 13,244 pounds of cargo.
   (3) Would not be used for evacuation of medical patients due to cabin noise.
   (4) Would be permitted to return to base from adjacent stations on three engines in event of abort.

c. That channels of communication would be through the Commander of the Continental Division, MATS, unit at McChord Air Force Base on operational matters, and direct to RCAF agencies on RCAF technical and internal administrative matters, with information copies to MATS Commanders on any matters in which they have an interest.

d. The RCAF Squadron Commander will exercise responsibility for disciplinary control over all RCAF Squadron personnel wherever they may be located along the route.

e. The RCAF Squadron Commander will keep the Commander of the Continental Division, MATS, unit at McChord Air Force Base constantly informed regarding:

   (1) The personnel strength of the RCAF Squadron, both actual and forecast or programmed for the foreseeable future.
   (2) Any actual or predicted change in the numbers or capabilities of aircraft committed to the operation.
   (3) Any other developments or predictions which might have an affect upon the capabilities of the RCAF Squadron.

Laurence S. Kuter
Major General, USAF
Commanding

Appendix D

Nominal Roll—Operation HAWK

No 426 Squadron Personnel Posted to McChord AFB Effective 25 July 1950

Number	Rank	Name	Branch	Home
Aircrew Officers				
19523	W/C	C.H. Mussells	GL/P	Montreal, QC
19984	S/L	H.A. Morrison	GL/P	Lauder, MB.
19812	S/L	J.D. Dickson	GL/P	Hammond River, Kings Co. N.B.
20756	S/L	J.H.C. Lewis	GL/P	Naniamo, BC
2366	F/L	C.E. Emond	AIR/P	Ottawa, ON
6552	F/O	A. Finkelstein	AIR/NO	Ottawa, ON
23526	F/L	C.E. Endersbe	AIR/RO	Pontiac, SK
26384	F/L	R.E. Churchill	AIR/P	Edmonton, AB
9550	F/L	P.F. Lee	AIR/RN	Belleville, ON
30261	F/O	J.M. Latter	AIR/RO	Herring Cove, NS
20142	F/L	A.J.P. Byford	AIR/P	Ottawa, ON
17706	F/L	R.E.D. Ratcliffe	AIR/NO	Kingston, ON
20405	F/O	W. Smith	AIR/RO	Montreal, QC
20160	F/L	W.R. Lloyd	AIR/P	Regina, SK
30518	P/O	D.H. Kuhn	AIR/P	Dartmouth, NS
20024	F/L	E.J. Boland	AIR/RN	Montreal, QC
30473	F/O	N.E. Bohn	AIR/RO	Montreal, QC & UK
RAF54395	F/L	R. Coates	AIR/P	UK
27799	F/O	D.G. Scott	AIR/P	Russell, ON
RAF	F/L	A. Knapper	AIR/NO	UK
30266	F/O	T.E. Richardson	AIR/RO	Whitby, ON
25662	F/L	J.A. Watt	AIR/P	Montreal, QC & Rapid City, MB.
205006	F/O	J.C. Henry	AIR/P	Kirkland Lake, ON

Number	Rank	Name	Branch	Home
17599	F/O	A.S. Logan	AIR/NO	Pictou, NS
25663	F/O	G.W. Fisher	AIR/RO	Vancouver, BC
17600	F/O	J.B. Miller	AIR/P	Gainsboro, SK
4140	F/L	C.E. Goodwin	AIR/P	Moose Jaw, SK
30443	F/O	J.A. Gauthier	AIR/NO	Ottawa, ON
20193	F/O	D.G. Selby	AIR/RO	Font Hill, ON
30087	F/O	A.L. Quickfall	AIR/P	Victoria, BC
16610	F/L	H.J. Weeden	AIR/NO	Halifax, NS
17318	F/O	J.W. Santarelli	AIR/RO	Toronto, ON
20333	F/L	K.T. Wallace	AIR/P	Toronto, ON
25486	F/O	E.R. Wolkowski	AIR/P	Tiny, SK
30241	F/O	J.W. Rodger	AIR/NO	Montreal (Verdun), QC
25667	F/O	C.G. Jessup	AIR/RO	Cache Bay, ON
30018	F/O	R.M. Edwards	AIR/P	St. James, MB
15053A	CAPT	T.J. Upton	USAF/PILOT	Monéssen, PA USA
12982	F/O	B.L. Ray	AIR/NO	Vancouver, BC
30282	F/O	A.J.S. Timmins	AIR/RO	Pakenham, ON
26365	F/O	D.M. Payne	AIR/P	London & Toronto, ON
30335	F/O	M.W.E. Inglis	AIR/P	Montreal, QC
20265	F/O	R.S. Reid	AIR/RN	Toronto, ON
30232	F/O	A.F. Fielman	AIR/RO	Rosenfeld, MB
30000	F/O	M.D. Broadfoot	AIR/P	Tisdale, SK
30153	F/O	P.M. Lemieux	AIR/P	Maniwaki, QC
30427	F/O	E.H. Moberg	AIR/NO	Saskatoon, SK
30265	F/O	J.S. Shipton	AIR/RO	Montreal (Verdun), QC

Crewmen

Number	Rank	Name	Branch	Home
21735	SGT	H.F. Smith	AETech 3	Craik, SK
21603	SGT	A.A. Drackley	AETech 3	Birsay, SK
22690	SGT	E.S. Barber	AETech 3	Carberry, MB
23776	LAC	J.A.A. Guenet	AETech 3	Montreal, QC
25233	LAC	G.R. Reed	AETech 3	North Bay, ON
23592	CPL	W.J. Hoehn	AETech 3	Gravelbourg, SK
367	FS	C.W. Baine	AETech 3	Vancouver, BC
22554	SGT	F.S.M. Bowman	AETech 3	Hamilton, ON
22902	CPL	T.C. Harper	AETech 3	Chatham, NB
22223	CPL	W.S. McKnight	AETech 3	Saskatoon, SK
23636	CPL	T.W. Brodie	AETech 3	Bracebridge, ON
2348	SGT	J.K. Robertson	AETech 3	Winnipeg, MB

Appendix D: Nominal Roll—Operation HAWK

Number	Rank	Name	Branch	Home
Air Traffic Assistants				
22461	FS	J.W. Whalen	ATA 3	Kars & Ottawa, ON
7705	CPL	J.E. Nadeau	ATA 3	St. Honore, QC
19212	LAC	J.A.A. St. Laurent	ATA	Levis, QC
12305	LAC	R.G. Rogers	ATA	Kelowna, BC
19123	LAC	H.R. MacDonald	ATA	Picton, NS
17675	LAC	J.L. Lakteigne	ATA	Bathurst, NB
16396	LAC	E.C. Grose	ATA	Thorold (St. Catherines), ON
25348	CPL	J.G. Gallipeau	ATA	Winnipeg, MB
16417	LAC	D.W. Towe	ATA	Christopher Lake, SK
16411	LAC	W.D. Verch	ATA	Eganville, ON
12443	LAC	F.E. Everatt	ATA	Flintoft, SK
16430	LAC	D.S. Wood	ATA	St. Catherines, ON
Flight Control				
20336	F/L	J.P. McDonald	AIR/P	Vancouver, BC
901 ATHU Officer				
26389	F/L	H. Brisebois	AIR/RO	Ottawa, ON
AERO Engine Technicians				
20639	FS	H.V. Hogarth	AETech 3	Ottawa, ON
6589	SGT	A. Bradley	AETech 3	Stittsville, ON
9829	SGT	A.C. Craig	AETech 3	Winnipeg, MB
21334	SGT	G.L. Read	AETech 3	Winnipeg, MB
7823	CPL	M. Soame	AETech 3	Ottawa, ON
7629	CPL	J.A.R. Berube	AETech 3	Montreal, QC
21778	CPL	G.W. Fleetham	AETech 3	Oakville, ON
23275	CPL	J.H. MacLeod	AETech 3	Montreal, QC
19259	LAC	M.R. Howse	AETech 1	Wesleyville, NF
23582	LAC	J.P. Thompson	AETech 2	Montreal, QC
23147	LAC	T.G.S. Thompson	AETech 3	Winnipeg, MB
24781	LAC	M. Storos	AETech 3	Winnipeg, MB
23958	LAC	C.H. Taylor	AETech 3	Hazenmore, SK
25387	LAC	J.A.N. Paquette	AETech 3	St. Jean, QC
23715	LAC	J.L.N. Larochelle	AETech 3	St. George, QC
25554	LAC	D.I. Shade	AETech 3	Coventry, England
18360	LAC	A.B. Zion	AETech 3 (P)	Ottawa, ON
18813	LAC	S.R. Ettienne	AETech 3	Sydney, NS

Number	Rank	Name	Branch	Home
14600	ACI	R.C. Offerdahl	AETech 1	Winfield, BC
18989	LAC	J.H. Nickel	AETech 2	Toronto, ON
25747	LAC	M.M. Steff	AETech 3(P)	Wood Mountain Station, SK
23778	LAC	F.C. Helynck	AETech 3	Montreal, QC
22159	LAC	J.R. Ramsay	AETech 3	Newcastle, NB
28773	ACI	R.M. Pentney	AETech 1	Montreal, QC
14430	ACI	M.L. Carnegie	AETech 1	Winnipeg, MB
28683	LAC	L.G. Constantine	AETech 1	St. John's, NF
13522	LAC	J.J. Monchamp	AETech 3	St. Norbert, MB
27991	ACI	W. Blotniuk	AEATech 1	Lachine, QC
28601	ACI	R.S. Beattey	AETech 1	Arvida, QC
28282	LAC	J.P. Mayville	AETech 1	Montreal, QC
25278	LAC	W.E. Luhtala	AETech 3	Malartic, QC
24505	LAC	L. Myrhaugen	AETech 3	Swift Current, SK
27906	LAC	J.N. Lauzon	AETech 3 (P)	Montreal, QC
27201	LAC	J.J. Hazel	AETech 3	Montreal, QC
14794	ACI	T.A. Crawford	AETech 1	Ganges, BC
17621	ACI	J.F. Roberge	AETech 1	Montreal, QC
28794	ACI	R.W. Gray	AETech "S"	Pointe Claire, QC
15949	LAC	R.G. Rooke	AETech 3	Montreal QC
17597	ACI	J.J. Hebert	AETech 1	Montreal, QC
24938	LAC	J.B. Caya	AETech 3	Montreal, QC
18375	ACI	J.A. Galipeau	AETech 1	Cache Bay, ON
17603	ACI	J.E. Poirier	AETech 1	St. Georges, QC
26544	LAC	J.G.R. Dubois	AETech 3	Trewdale, SK
24478	LAC	T. Bryant	AETech 3	Shediac, NB
18596	LAC	K.V. Morrow	AETech 3	Moncton, NB
15736	LAC	J.J.M. Kaye	AETech 3	Montreal, QC
23057	LAC	J.H.L. Millette	AETech 3	Montreal, QC

Master Aircraft Technicians

4234	WOI	E. Edey	MATech 4	Calgary, AB
345	FS	R.H. Wilson	MATech 4	Vancouver, BC
2195	FS	W.R. Ruffell	MATech 4	Victoria, BC
2414	FS	A.L. Engelbert	MATech 4	Toronto, ON

Airframe Technicians

1023	SGT	W.J. Purcell	AFTech 3	Moncton, NB
21948	SGT	J.I. James	AFTech 3	Coleman, AB
2451	SGT	J.A. Chalin	AFTech 3	Verdun, QC

Appendix D: Nominal Roll—Operation HAWK

Number	Rank	Name	Branch	Home
25710	CPL	R.K. Ellery	AFTech 3	Winnipeg, MB
21397	CPL	W.J. Widger	AFTech 3	Calgary, AB
23680	CPL	A.W. Bock	AFTech 3	Meadow Lake, SK
25060	CPL	G.J. Shane	AFTech 3	Ottawa, ON
10297	CPL	H.G. MacLean	AFTech 3	Toronto & London, ON
2452	CPL	J.P. Senecal	AFTech 3	Montreal, QC
21713	CPL	J.T. Callaghan	AFTech 3	Renfrew, ON
25399	LAC	E.B. Ferguson	AFTech 3	Norwood, ON
21918	LAC	C.E. Veno	AFTech 3 (P)	Berwick, Kings Co. NS
14068	LAC	W.T. Frame	AFTech 3	Lenore, MB
24199	LAC	W.G. Perrement	AFTech 3	Lethbridge, AB
12344	LAC	B.D. Emery	AFTech 3	Victoria, BC
23272	LAC	J.G. Frappier	AFTech 3	Albion, RI, USA
26840	LAC	C.L. Riseley	AFTech 3	Toronto, ON
26573	LAC	J.A. Beaudry	AFTech 3	Aylmer, QC
18164	ACI	J.A. McGovern	AFTech 1	Montreal, QC
28848	ACI	J.L.O. Leblanc	AFTech 1	Buctouche, NB
16321	ACI	P.J. Rooney	AFTech 1	Prescott, ON
17064	ACI	C.A. Guillet	AFTech 1	Ottawa, ON
28964	ACI	C.A. Lagroix	AFTech 1	Martintown, ON
28612	ACI	J.A. Tanguay	AFTech 1	LaSarre, QC
28219	ACI	A.A. McLaughlin	AFTech 1	St. Stephen, NB
21455	LAC	E.W. Bell	AFTech 3	Saskatoon, SK
24127	LAC	J.E. Mailly	AFTech 3	Three Rivers, QC
26309	LAC	J.V. Ringuette	AFTech 3	Levis, QC
25965	LAC	L.F. Wedgewood	AFTech 2	Wellwyn, SK
19499	ACI	J.V. Jacques	AFTech 1	Montreal, QC
29301	LAC	D.A. Kirkman	AFTech 1	Montreal, QC
28869	ACI	P.J. Moring	AFTech 1	Cap Rouge, QC
16917	ACI	F.J. Smith	AFTech 1	Halifax, NS
19383	LAC	W.B. Reay	AFTech "S"	Amherst, NS

LINE CREW

Number	Rank	Name	Branch	Home
24851	CPL	W.P. Shields	AETech 3	Winnipeg, MB
16492	LAC	D.H. Wood	AETech 3	Willowdale, ON
24070	LAC	H.R. Claveau	AETech 3	Quebec City, QC
17530	ACI	T.J. McGrath	AETech "S"	Quebec City, QC
18830	LAC	F. Ford	AETech 2	Sydney, NS
18127	LAC	G.T. Walsh	AETech 1	St. John's, NF

Number	Rank	Name	Branch	Home
Tool Crib				
21715	SGT	T.J. Banks	AFTech 3	Lethbridge, AB
Paint Shop				
22032	CPL	J.W. Wilson	AFTech 3	Toronto, ON
Hydraulic Shop				
21871	CPL	J.C. Brooks	AFTech 3	Victoria, BC
Maintenance Control				
20743	FS	F.J. Hill	AFTech 3	Ottawa, ON
21582	SGT	T.C. Casbolt	AFTech 3	Glace Bay, NS
23067	CPL	J.H. Cooper	AFTech 3	Winnipeg, MB
Photo Section				
16842	LAC	R.M. Ritchie	Photo 2	Montreal, QC
Workshops				
22897	SGT	L.G. McLeod	MW 3	Sackville, NS
24441	CPL	T.W. O'Bee	MW 3	Vancouver, BC
23159	LAC	J.H. Hillman	MW 3 (P)	Vancouver, BC
15885	LAC	F.T. Lyons	MW 3	Sudbury, ON
24491	LAC	J.E. Paquette	MW 3	Montreal, QC
28228	ACI	J.S. Lipari	MW 1	Montreal, QC
17977	LAC	G.J. Racine	MW 2 (P)	Quebec City, QC
Motor Transport				
7864	SGT	S.E. James	METech 3	Ottawa, ON
24973	CPL	N.J. Patton	OpMME 3	Montreal, QC
Engine Bay				
21392	SGT	S.T. Patterson	AETech 3	Lethbridge, AB
26558	CPL	J.P. Aveline	AETech 3	St. Adele, QC
18935	LAC	P. Taylor	AETech 3	Lincoln, UK
16118	LAC	R.A. Arnott	AETech 3	Montreal, QC
26110	LAC	Z.J. Medzwiecki	AETech 2	Montreal, QC

Appendix D: Nominal Roll—Operation HAWK

Number	Rank	Name	Branch	Home
Modification Section				
21029	SGT	C.J. Tian	AFTech 3	Regina, SK
Carpenter Shop				
22600	CPL	W.A.C. Doyle	AFTech 3	Souris, MB
Stores Liaison				
1528	FS	J.E. Wood	AFTech 3	Ottawa, ON
Radar Technicians				
25354	LAC	J.M. Sparling	RdrTech 1	Toronto, ON
15773	LAC	D.D. Green	RdrTech 1	Richmond, ON
17761	AC1	E.D. Pitre	RdrTech 1	Montreal, QC
Clerk Adm.				
21405	SGT	G.A. Nicholls	Clk Adm 3	Calgary, AB
21629	SGT	G.E. Perry	Clk Adm 3	Montreal, QC
18293	AC1	J.G. Roy	Clk Adm 1	Armagh, QC
Safety Equipment				
6567	SGT	G.H. Moodie	SETech 3	Ottawa, ON
22945	CPL	W.F. Magdalinski	SETech 3	Gurnsey, SK
18882	LAC	R.M. MacLeod	SETech 3	Moncton, NB
19025	LAC	R.H. Fougere	SETech 1	Antigonish, NS
28815	AC1	K.R. Clay	SETech 1	Sault Ste. Marie, ON
Communication Technicians				
22151	FS	D.S. Farmer	ComTech 4	Andover, MB
26829	SGT	J.H. Guindon	ComTech 3	Sudbury, ON
26282	LAC	K.G. Porter	ComTech 3	Yarmouth, NS
25134	LAC	J.G. Ladouceur	ComTech 3	Vankleek Hill, ON
22813	LAC	J.P. Quinn	ComTech 3	Buckingham, QC
24752	LAC	J.L. Pelletier	ComTech 2	Montreal, QC
25712	LAC	A.C. Springate	ComTech 2 (P)	Glamorganshire, UK
22812	LAC	P.M. Logan	ComTech 1	Morinville, AB
17405	AC1	J.B. Garceau	ComTech 1	Montreal, QC
18307	AC1	J.P. Caron	ComTech 1	Quebec City, QC

Number	Rank	Name	Branch	Home
Supply Technicians				
10756	FS	A. MacAulay	ST 3	Montreal, QC
22063	CPL	J.C. Jobin	ST 3	Montreal, QC
22073	CPL	R.C. Verney	ST 3	Ottawa, ON
16347	LAC	J.L. Coailler	ST 2	Montreal, QC
28478	LAC	J.G. Foley	ST 1	Bridgewater, NS
28961	AC1	L.R. Ducharme	ST 1	Hull, QC
29449	AC 1	J.D. Smith	ST 1	Picton, ON
Instrument Technicians				
9572	WO2	J.S. Cates	MIETech 4	Chemainus, BC
22946	FS	E.E. Brason	ITech 3	Winnipeg, MB
24992	CPL	A.P. Marshall	ITech 3	Victoria, BC
27032	CPL	J.H. Dash	ITech 3	Regina, SK
23842	CPL	A.C. Cowtan	ITech 3	Ottawa, ON
24370	CPL	M.N. MacKeracher	ITech 3	Eston, SK
16378	LAC	D.N. Stead	ITech 2	Montreal, QC
24912	LAC	K.O. Sollows	ITech 2	Port Maitland, NS
16336	LAC	J.E. Labonte	ITech 2	Parent, QC
18816	LAC	R.P. Riseley	ITech 2	Toronto, ON
17053	AC1	H.S. Tigges	ITech 2	Ottawa, ON
19284	LAC	H.G. Kirchner	ITech 1	Vancouver, BC
16078	LAC	J.A. Menard	ITech 2	Montreal, QC
Electrical Technicians Aero				
26702	FS	H. Moores	ETech (A) 3	North Sydney, NS
22347	SGT	R.E. Auger	ETech 3	Sudbury, ON
23312	CPL	W.R. Peterson	ETech 3	Hamilton, NS
25347	CPL	G.M. Dupuis	ETech 3	Riviére-du-Loup, QC
24503	CPL	L. Mancuso	ETech 3	Toronto, ON
22944	CPL	J. Rogina	ETech 3	Saskatoon, SK
22468	LAC	J.C. Mayer	ETech 3	Ottawa, ON
16576	LAC	J.D. Thompson	ETech 3	Three Rivers, QC
16600	LAC	B.R. Price	ETech 3	Canterbury Stn., NB
13155	LAC	H. Rizon	ETech 2	Vegreville, AB
16532	LAC	C.R. Reynolds	ETech 2	Chatham, ON
19064	LAC	R.M. Michaud	ETech 2	Montreal, QC
27986	AC1	L.H. Horrocks	ETech 1	Montreal, QC

Appendix D: Nominal Roll—Operation HAWK

Number	Rank	Name	Branch	Home
16533	LAC	W.W. Pinsonneault	ETech 2	Chatham, ON
28506	AC1	R.W. Nurse	ETech 1	St. John's, NF
13386	AC1	J. Evans	ETech 1	Blue Ridge, AB

Supply Officer

9647	F/L	V.W. Duke	SUP	Medicine Hat, AB

Signals Officer

20132	F/L	A.B. Stuart	Tech/Sigs	Edmonton, AB

Engineering Officers

1874	S/L	W.H. Lord	Tech/AE	Ottawa, ON
2469	F/O	H.G. Graves	Tech/AE	McCreary, AB
30218	F/O	G. Kreklewetz	Tech/AE	Theodore, SK

Medical Assistant

25997	CPL	G.A.M. Normandin	Med A2	Montreal, QC

Clerk Accountants

21538	FS	L.S. Hall	Clk Acct 3	Hamilton, ON
19239	LAC	F.B. Ruel	Clk Acct 2	Sherbrooke, QC
25321	LAC	L. Leclerc	Clk Acct 3	Montreal, QC
28057	AC1	L.A.L. Lamire	Clk Acct 1	Ottawa, ON
15899	LAC	J.G.R. Leboeuf	Clk Acct 3	Montreal, QC

List of Abbreviations of Branch or Trade

GL/P	General List Pilot
AIR/P	Aircrew Pilot
AIR/RN	Aircrew Radio Navigator
AIR/NO	Aircrew Navigation Officer
AIR/RO	Aircrew Radio Officer
Tech/AE	Aero Engineer Officer
Tech/Sigs	Signals Officer
SUP	Supply Officer
MATech	Master Aircraft Technician
MIETech	Master Instrument & Electrical Technician
AETech	AERO Engine Technician
AFTech	Airframe Technician
ComTech	Communication Technician
Rdr Tech	Radar Technician
ETechA	Electrical Technician Aero
ITech	Instrument Technician
MW	Metal Worker
SETech	Safety Equipment Technician
ST	Supply Technician
ATA	Air Traffic Assistant
Clk Adm	Clerk Administrative
Clk Acct	Clerk Accountant
Med A	Medical Assistant

Nominal Roll of Station Rockcliffe Personnel Posted to McChord AFB
Effective 5 August, 1950

Number	Rank	Name	Home
2458	SGT	M.H. Dixon	Montreal, QC
22550	CPL	W.J. Emery	Ottawa, ON
26398	LAC	J.B. Boudreau	Bathurst, NB
23143	LAC	D.J. Fletcher	Toronto, ON
24360	LAC	C.A. Magnes	Lockwood, SK
24049	LAC	D.W. Holmes	Ottawa, ON
12428	LAC	G.A. Seymour	Eriksdale, MB
25100	LAC	E.A. Hall	Victoria, BC
28052	AC1	M.C. Lang	Ottawa, ON
14092	AC1	J.G.B. Lafleche	Winnipeg, MB
28216	AC1	D.J. Banes	Kitchener, ON
26266	LAC	W.F. Presley	Ottawa, ON
16592	LAC	M.W. Leedham	St. Williams, ON
28923	AC1	R.A. Pinkham	Halifax, NS
28933	AC1	S.C. Rideout	St. John's, NF
25987	LAC	J.A.G. Archambault	Montreal, QC
28982	LAC	J.P. Hunt	Toronto, ON
28638	AC1	R.L. Meloche	River Carnard, ON
20850	SGT	G.L. Capuano	Montreal, QC
21139	CPL	C.H. Baker	Ottawa, ON
24436	LAC	F.W. McNiven	Guelph, ON
26118	LAC	R.B. Blais	Sudbury, ON
25306	LAC	M.M. Gordon	Edmonton, AB
27739	LAC	H.N. Rees	Vancouver, BC
16198	LAC	F.J.O. Labreche	Ottawa, ON
22311	LAC	J.P. Rogan	Vancouver, BC
16933	AC1	J.L. Schingh	Ottawa, ON
27275	LAC	R.R. Dupleix	Vancouver, BC
29354	AC1	W.A. Hynes	Clarenville, NF
29100	AC1	D.J. Annesley	Bury, QC
12635	LAC	R.C. Dolye	New Westminster, BC
17331	LAC	J.E.M. Gendron	Three Rivers, QC
26773	LAC	J.L. Beauchamp	Buckingham, QC
15624	LAC	G.E.M. Stephens	Madawaska, ON

Appendix D: Nominal Roll—Operation HAWK

Number	Rank	Name	Home
2338	SGT	R.A. Englebert	Manitou, MB
21970	CPL	R.E. Mohr	Regina, SK
13057	LAC	V. Pawliuk	Vegreville, AB
15618	LAC	L.W. Reid	Sherbrooke, QC
2501	SGT	A.G. McGregor	Toronto, ON
21164	SGT	A. Danforth	Ottawa, ON
12839	LAC	H.L. Hurl	Marquis, SK
26846	LAC	D.M. Babcok	
26061	LAC	H. Parkinson	Ottawa, ON

Personnel Returning to McChord

Personnel at Tokyo

Number	Rank	Name
26563	CPL	J.W. Beatty
21582	SGT	T.C. Casbolt
23082	LAC	J.E. Desrosiers
4234	WO1	E. Edey
23143	LAC	D.J. Fletcher
21778	CPL	G.W. Fleetham
23272	LAC	J.G. Frappier
22202	CPL	L.J. Garding
17405	AC1	J.B. Garceau
20743	FS	F.J. Hill
18882	LAC	R.A. McLeod
24436	LAC	F.E. McNiven
23237	CPL	J.A. McEvoy
24199	LAC	W.G. Perrement
25934	LAC	C.P. Quinton
21013	SGT	A.F. Routledge
22944	CPL	J. Regina
25554	LAC	D.I. Shade
22432	LAC	T.H. Stephens
23958	LAC	C.H. Taylor
16576	LAC	J.D. Thompson

Personnel at Anchorage

Number	Rank	Name
26773	LAC	J.L. Beauchamp
21913	CPL	R.S. Blanchard
24452	LAC	R.B. Calaway
21106	CPL	J.C. Coutts
	LAC	J.W. Good
14105	LAC	W.D. Gordon
25097	LAC	R. Grainger
26488	SGT	J.W. Hilker
23772	CPL	H. Hodgson
23778	LAC	F.C. Helnyck
21448	CPL	N. MacLeod
2408	FS	J.H. Oldham
23153	CPL	J.G. Pearse
25387	LAC	J.A. Paquette
2442	SGT	J.B. Reardon
21078	CPL	J.C. Skinner
22032	CPL	H.W. Wilson

Appendix E: Korean Airlift—Schedule of Operations

APPENDIX E

KOREAN AIRLIFT—SCHEDULE OF OPERATIONS

NOTE: The squadron's "Operations Record" regarding the airlift for the period June 1952–June 1954 was either incomplete or segments were missing entirely. The schedule for this period of time was, for the most part, reconstructed using log book entries provided by former squadron members or their families.

GMT	Greenwich Mean Time used for departures from and arrivals at McChord AFB.	
Local Time	McChord AFB (GMT -8 hours)	
RTB	Return to Base	
NR	Northern Pacific Route: McChord, Anchorage, Shemya, Tokyo–return to base by way of Shemya and Anchorage.	
SR	Southern or Mid–Pacific Route: Northern Route to Tokyo–return to base by way of Wake Island, Honolulu and Travis AFB (San Francisco)	

Location Indicators:

TCM	Tacoma (McChord AFB)
ANC	Anchorage (EDF-Elmendorf AFB)
SYA	Shemya AFB
HNA	Tokyo (Haneda Air Base)
HIK	Honolulu (Hickam AFB)
VR	Vancouver
XD	Edmonton
WG	Winnipeg
UL	Montreal (Dorval)

Serial	Departure	A/C	Captain	RTB	Remarks
1	28–7–50	17511	S/L H.J.C. Lewis	31–7–50	NR RTB Via Adak
2	28–7–50	17507	S/L J.D. Dickson	31–7–50	NR RTB Via Adak
3	28–7–50	17502	F/L A.J.P. Byford	1–8–50	NR RTB Via ANC
4	2–8–50	17517	F/O J.B. Miller	13–8–50	NR
5	2–8–50	17517	W/C C.H. Mussells	8–8–50	NR (Slip Crew ANC)
6	4–8–50	17507	F/L R. Coates	14–8–50	NR
7	6–8–50	17511	S/L H.A. Morrison	15–8–50	NR
8	8–8–50	17514	F/L A.J.P. Byford	16–8–50	NR
9	10–8–50	17517	S/L H.J.C. Lewis	17–8–50	NR
10	12–8–50	17502	F/L J.A. Watt	20–8–50	NR

Serial	Departure	A/C	Captain	RTB	Remarks
11	14–8–50	17504	F/L J.R. Bell	20–8–50	NR
12	15–8–50	17507	F/L G.W. Allen	22–8–50	NR
13	15–8–50	17516	S/L J.D. Dickson	21–8–50	NR
14	16–8–50	17502	F/L G.W. Webb	22–8–50	NR
15	16–8–50	17511	F/O D.M. Payne	23–8–50	NR
16	17–8–50	17504	W/C C.H. Mussells	24–8–50	NR
17	19–8–50	17515	F/O J.B. Miller	25–8–50	NR
18	20–8–50	17516	F/L R. Coates	25–8–50	NR
19	21–8–50	17507	S/L H.A. Morrison	28–8–50	NR
20	22–8–50	17511	F/L A.J.P. Byford	29–8–50	NR
21	23–8–50	17517	S/L H.J.C. Lewis	30–8–50	NR
22	25–8–50	17502	F/L J.A. Watt	2–9–50	NR
23	26–8–50	17515	F/L J.R. Bell	1–9–50	NR
24	26–8–50	17514	F/L G.W. Allen	2–9–50	NR
25	28–8–50	17517	F/L G.W. Webb	4–9–50	NR
26	30–8–50	17516	F/O J.B. Miller	7–9–50	NR
27	31–8–50	17514	W/C C.H. Mussells	5–9–50	NR
28	31–8–50	17502	F/L R. Coates	7–9–50	NR
29	1–9–50	17514	F/O R.M. Edwards	7–9–50	NR
30	2–9–50	17511	F/L A.J.P. Byford	9–9–50	NR
31	3–9–50	17516	S/L H.J.C. Lewis	10–9–50	NR
32	4–9–50	17507	F/L J.R. Bell	12–9–50	NR
33	5–9–50	17517	F/L J.A. Watt	14–9–50	NR
34	7–9–50	17502	F/L G.W. Allen	14–9–50	NR
35	8–9–50	17504	F/L G.W. Webb	15–9–50	NR
–	9–9–50	17515	W/C C.H. Mussells	10–9–50	2 engine failure–land at Sandspit–RTB on 3 engines
36	10–9–50	17507	F/O J.B. Miller	18–9–50	NR
37	11–9–50	17515	W/C C.H. Mussells	20–9–50	NR
38	13–9–50	17502	F/L R. Coates	23–9–50	NR
39	15–9–50	17516	F/O R.M. Edwards	23–9–50	NR
40	17–9–50	17511	F/O D.M. Payne	25–9–50	NR
41	19–9–50	17515	S/L H.J.C. Lewis	26–9–50	NR
42	20–9–50	17514	F/L A.J.P. Byford	28–9–50	NR
43	22–9–50	17516	F/L J.R. Bell	29–9–50	NR
44	23–9–50	17504	F/L J.A. Watt	30–9–50	NR
–	24–9–50	17512	S/L H.A. Morrison	5–10–50	Survey run SR
45	25–9–50	17511	F/L G.W. Allen	2–10–50	NR
46	26–9–50	17517	F/L R. Coates	4–10–50	NR
47	27–9–50	17510	F/L G.W. Webb	6–10–50	NR
48	28–9–50	17514	F/L W.R. Lloyd	6–10–50	NR

Appendix E: Korean Airlift—Schedule of Operations

Serial	Departure	A/C	Captain	RTB	Remarks
49	29–9–50	17515	F/O R.M. Edwards	8–10–50	NR
50	30–9–50	17516	F/O D.M. Payne	7–10–50	NR 17504 Mech. problems out of SYA
51	1–10–50	17504	F/O J.B. Miller	9–10–50	NR Mech. problems out of Base
52	2–10–50	17511	F/L J.R. Bell	15–10–50	NR
53	2–10–50	17517	S/L J.D. Dixon	11–10–50	NR
54	3–10–50	17515	F/L J.A. Watt	14–10–50	NR
55	4–10–50	17502	F/L A.J.P. Byford	14–10–50	NR
–	5–10–50	17516	F/L G.W. Allen	9–10–50	SYA–Ferry 17504
56	7–10–50	17507	F/O M.D. Broadfoot	15–10–50	NR Engine–ANC
57	8–10–50	17511	F/L G.W. Webb	15–10–50	NR
58	9–10–50	17510	F/L W.R. Lloyd	18–10–50	NR
59	10–10–50	17522	F/O R.M. Edwards	18–10–50	NR
60	11–10–50	17512	F/O D.M. Payne	19–10–50	NR
61	12–10–50	17523	F/O J.B. Miller	20–10–50	NR
62	13–10–50	17507	F/O G.W. Allen	21–10–50	NR
63	15–10–50	17512	S/L H.J.C. Lewis	21–10–50	NR
64	16–10–50	17517	F/L C.E. Goodwin	24–10–50	NR
65	17–10–50	17522	F/L K.T. Wallace	25–10–50	NR
66	18–10–50	17502	F/L J.R. Bell	27–10–50	NR
67	20–10–50	17510	F/L A.J.P. Byford	27–10–50	NR
68	20–10–50	17507	F/O M.D. Broadfoot	27–10–50	NR
69	21–10–50	17509	F/L G.W. Webb	29–10–50	NR
70	22–10–50	17512	F/L W.R. Lloyd	29–10–50	NR
71	23–10–50	17508	F/O R.M. Edwards	4–11–50	NR RTB via Yokota
72	24–10–50	17522	F/O J.B. Miller	5–11–50	NR RTB via Yokota
–	25–10–50	17517	F/O D.M. Payne	26–10–50	Ferry A/C to ANC
73	28–10–50	17511	F/L G.W. Allen	7–11–50	NR RTB via Yokota
74	30–10–50	17512	F/L R. Coates	6–11–50	NR RTB via Yokota
75	30–10–50	17507	F/O D.M. Payne	8–11–50	NR RTB via Yokota
76	31–10–50	17505	F/L K.T. Wallace	9–11–50	NR
77	1–11–50	17507	F/L C.E. Goodwin	9–11–50	NR
78	2–11–50	17506	S/L H.J.C. Lewis	13–11–50	NR RTB SR
79	3–11–50	17510	F/L G.W. Webb	11–11–50	NR
80	4–11–50	17523	F/L W.R. Lloyd	17–11–50	NR
81	6–11–50	17516	F/O M.D. Broadfoot	13–11–50	NR
82	6–11–50	17502	F/L J.R. Bell	17–11–50	Survey flight SR RTB NR
83	6–11–50	17502	F/O R.M. Edwards	19–11–50	Double crew to HNA RTB NR
84	8–11–50	17512	F/L J.A. Watt F/O J.B. Miller	18–11–50	Survey flight double crew SR HNA RTB NR

Serial	Departure	A/C	Captain	RTB	Remarks
85	9–11–50	17510	F/L R. Coates	14–11–50	NR
86	10–11–50	17523	F/L G.W. Allen	20–11–50	NR
87	12–11–50	17509	F/O D.M. Payne	21–11–50	NR
88	14–11–50	17511	F/L K.T. Wallace	22–11–50	NR
89	15–11–50	17505	F/L C.E. Goodwin	21–11–50	NR
90	16–11–50	17506	F/L G.W. Webb	24–11–50	NR
91	17–11–50	17507	S/L H.J.C. Lewis	23–11–50	NR
92	18–11–50	17511	F/O M.D. Broadfoot	25–11–50	NR
93	19–11–50	17523	F/L A.B. Hammond	29–11–50	NR
94	21–11–50	17522	F/L R. Coates	30–11–50	NR
95	21–11–50	17517	F/L J.A. Watt	1–12–50	NR
96	23–11–50	17507	F/O J.B. Miller	01–12–50	NR
97	23–11–50	17505	F/L C.E. Emond	02–12–50	NR
98	24–11–50	17508	F/L C.E. Goodwin	03–12–50	NR
99	25–11–50	17506	F/L G.W. Allen	06–12–50	NR
100	27–11–50	17523	F/L W.R. Lloyd	05–12–50	NR
101	29–11–50	17505	F/O M.D. Broadfoot	15–12–50	NR HNA RTB SR
102	1–12–50	17516	F/L A.B. Hammond	13–12–50	SR Wake RTB SR
–	1–12–50	17516	S/L H.J.C. Lewis	12–12–50	Extra crew to Wake RTB SR
103	1–12–50	17516	F/L G.W. Webb	14–12–50	Extra crew to Wake SR HNA RTB SR
104	4–12–50	17506	F/L C.E. Emond	20–12–50	NR Ashiya RTB SR
105	5–12–50	17512	F/L J.R. Bell	19–12–50	NR HNA RTB SR
106	8–12–50	17523	F/O J.B. Miller	17–12–50	NR HNA RTB SR
107	8–12–50	17509	F/L C.F. Sanford	15–12–50	NR HNA RTB SR
108	8–12–50	17502	F/L H.T. Giles	16–12–50	NR HNA RTB SR
109	9–12–50	17506	F/L R. Coates	18–12–50	NR HNA RTB SR
110	9–12–50	17522	F/L K.T. Wallace	18–12–50	NR HNA RTB SR
111	9–12–50	17517	F/L W.R. Lloyd	21–12–50	NR HNA RTB SR
112	10–12–50	17516	F/L C.E. Goodwin	22–12–50	NR HNA RTB SR
113	11–12–50	17507	S/L J.D. Dickson	21–12–50	NR Ashiya RTB SR
114	14–12–50	17509	F/O A.L. Quickfall	23–12–50	NR HNA RTB SR
115	14–12–50	17511	Capt. T.J. Upton	23–12–50	NR Itami RTB SR
116	15–12–50	17502	F/L G.W. Webb	23–12–50	NR HNA RTB SR
117	16–12–50	17506	F/L C.F. Sanford	23–12–50	NR Itami RTB SR
118	17–12–50	17516	F/L H.T. Giles	23–12–50	NR HNA RTB SR
119	17–12–50	17510	F/O M.D. Broadfoot	23–12–50	RTB twice on 3 engines NR HNA RTB SR
–	19–12–50	17511	F/O R.M. Edwards	23–12–50	Special to SYA–Kodiak RTB
120	19–12–50	17505	F/O J.B. Miller	23–12–50	NR HNA RTB NR

Appendix E: Korean Airlift—Schedule of Operations

Serial	Departure	A/C	Captain	RTB	Remarks
121	19–12–50	17517	F/L R. Coates	23–12–50	NR HNA RTB NR
122	30–12–50	17510	F/L J.R. Bell	7–1–51	NR HNA RTB SR
123	30–12–50	17512	F/L W.R. Lloyd	7–1–51	NR HNA RTB SR
124	1–1–51	17511	F/L C.E. Emond	7–1–51	NR HNA RTB SR
125	1–1–51	17511	F/L K.T. Wallace	11–1–51	Slip crew at ANC NR HNA RTB SR
126	1–1–51	17502	F/O R.M. Edwards	13–1–51	Return twice HNA–radios NR HNA RTB SR
127	2–1–51	17511	F/L C.E. Goodwin	10–1–51	Slip crew at SYA HNA RTB SR
128	3–1–51	17517	F/O M.D. Broadfoot	15–1–51	Return twice HIK–engines NR HNA RTB SR
129	4–1–51	17512	F/L C.F. Sanford	6–1–51	Slip crew at Wake RTB SR
–	4–1–51	17512	Capt. T.J. Upton	5–1–51	Slip crew at HIK RTB SR
130	5–1–51	17516	F/L G.W. Allen	19–1–51	NR HNA RTB SR
131	7–1–51	17504	F/O A.L. Quickfall	20–1–51	NR Itami RTB SR
132	8–1–51	17505	F/L R. Coates	20–1–51	NR HNA RTB SR
133	10–1–51	17507	F/L C.E. Snider	21–1–51	NR Itami RTB SR
134	12–1–51	17502	F/L C.F. Sanford	23–1–51	Return SYA–engine NR Itami RTB SR
135	14–1–51	17510	Capt. T.J. Upton	25–1–51	NR HNA RTB SR
136	15–1–51	17511	F/L W.R. Lloyd	26–1–51	NR Itami RTB SR
137	16–1–51	17509	F/L C.E. Emond	28–1–51	NR HNA RTB SR
138	18–1–51	17504	F/L G.W. Webb	30–1–51	Return Wake–engine NR Itami RTB SR
139	20–1–51	17516	F/O J.B. Miller	1–2–51	NR HNA RTB SR
140	22–1–51	17517	F/O R.M. Edwards	1–2–51	NR HNA RTB SR
141	23–1–51	17510	F/L R. Coates	2–2–51	NR Itami RTB SR
142	24–1–51	17506	F/L C.E. Snider	4–2–51	NR Itami RTB SR
143	26–1–51	17509	S/L J.D. Dickson	6–2–51	NR Itami RTB SR
144	28–1–51	17502	Capt. T.J. Upton	8–2–51	NR HNA RTB SR
145	30–1–51	17505	F/L W.R. Lloyd	10–2–51	NR HNA RTB SR
–	31–1–51	17517	F/L C.E. Goodwin	3–2–51	Special to HIK–RTB
146	31–1–51	17512	F/L K.T. Wallace	11–2–51	NR HNA RTB SR
147	2–2–51	17506	F/L G.W. Webb	12–2–51	NR HNA RTB SR
148	4–2–51	17511	F/O J.B. Miller	14–2–51	NR Itami RTB SR
149	6–2–51	17509	F/L C.E. Goodwin	18–2–51	NR Itami RTB SR
150	7–2–51	17512	F/O R.M. Edwards	19–2–51	NR Itami RTB SR
151	8–2–51	17502	F/O M.D. Broadfoot	19–2–51	NR HNA RTB SR
152	10–2–51	17504	F/L C.E. Snider	24–2–51	NR Itami RTB SR

Serial	Departure	A/C	Captain	RTB	Remarks
153	12–2–51	17510	F/L R.J. Brown	27–2–51	NR HNA RTB SR
154	13–2–51	17505	F/L J.A. Watt	27–2–51	NR Itami RTB SR
155	14–2–51	17511	F/L P.L. Michel	27–2–51	NR Itami RTB SR
156	16–2–51	17506	F/O A.L. Quickfall	6–3–51	NR Itami RTB SR
157	18–2–51	17509	F/L J.R. Bell	6–3–51	NR HNA RTB SR
158	20–2–51	17516	W/C C.H. Mussells	6–3–51	NR Itami RTB SR
159	21–2–51	17512	F/O J.B. Miller	6–3–51	NR Itami RTB SR
160	22–2–51	17502	F/L G.W. Webb	6–3–51	NR Itami RTB SR
161	23–2–51	17506	F/L C.E. Goodwin	7–3–51	NR Itami RTB SR
162	26–2–51	17517	F/O M.D. Broadfoot	8–3–51	NR HNA RTB SR
163	28–2–51	17509	F/L C.E. Emond	12–3–51	NR Itami RTB SR
164	1–3–51	17516	F/L W.R. Lloyd	13–3–51	NR Itami RTB SR
165	3–3–51	17504	F/L C.E. Snider	14–3–51	NR Itami RTB SR
166	4–3–51	17502	F/L P.L. Michel	17–3–51	NR HNA RTB SR
167	8–3–51	17511	F/L C.F. Sanford	18–3–51	NR HNA RTB SR
168	9–3–51	17517	F/O A.L. Quickfall	6–3–51	NR Itami RTB SR
169	10–3–51	17507	F/L C.S. Olsen	22–3–51	NR Itami RTB SR
170	12–3–51	17504	F/O M.D. Broadfoot	24–3–51	Return HIK–engine NR HNA RTB SR
171	14–3–51	17511	F/O R.M. Edwards	26–3–51	NR Itami RTB SR
172	15–3–51	17515	F/L C.E. Emond	28–3–51	NR Itami RTB SR
173	16–3–51	17506	F/L W.R. Lloyd	30–3–51	NR Itami RTB SR
174	18–3–51	17505	F/L R.J. Brown	1–4–51	NR Itami RTB SR
175	20–3–51	17516	F/L J.A. Watt	13–4–51	NR Itami RTB SR
176	22–3–51	17507	F/O A.L. Quickfall	13–4–51	NR Itami RTB SR
177	24–3–51	17517	F/O J.B. Miller	13–4–51	Return HNA/Wake NR Itami RTB SR
178	26–3–51	17504	F/L C.S. Olson	13–4–51	NR Itami RTB SR
179	28–3–51	17502	S/L J.D. Dickson	13–4–51	NR Itami RTB SR
180	30–3–51	17511	F/O M.D. Broadfoot	14–4–51	NR Ashiya RTB SR
181	3–4–51	17517	F/L C.E. Goodwin	18–4–51	NR Ashiya RTB SR
182	4–4–51	17510	F/L C.E. Snider	16–4–51	NR Ashiya/Itami RTB SR
183	6–4–51	17507	F/L P.L. Michel	20–4–51	NR Itami RTB SR
184	8–4–51	17512	F/L C.E. Emond	23–4–51	NR HNA RTB SR
185	10–4–51	17506	F/L R.J. Brown	25–4–51	NR Itami RTB SR
186	12–4–51	17516	F/O R.M. Edwards	5–5–51	NR HNA RTB SR
187	14–4–51	17509	F/L J.W. Borden	26–4–51	Return HIK–engine NR Itami RTB SR
–	14–4–51	17509	F/L J.A. Watt	8–5–51	Double crew to SYA, NR Ashiya incident 19 April, RTB SR
188	15–4–51	17502	F/O J.B. Miller	29–4–51	NR Ashiya RTB SR

Appendix E: Korean Airlift—Schedule of Operations

Serial	Departure	A/C	Captain	RTB	Remarks
189	18–4–51	17510	F/O M.D. Broadfoot	30–4–51	NR Itami RTB SR
190	20–4–51	17517	F/L C.E. Goodwin	1–5–51	NR Itami RTB SR
191	22–4–51	17507	F/O W.J. Buchan	11–5–51	NR Ashiya RTB SR
192	24–4–51	17515	F/L E.F. Nelles	11–5–51	NR Ashiya RTB SR
193	26–4–51	17502	F/O R.G. Herbert	14–5–51	NR Ashiya RTB SR
194	28–4–51	17505	F/L C.E. Snider	17–5–51	Return HNA/Itami NR Itami RTB SR
195	30–4–51	17510	F/L P.L. Michel	16–5–51	RTB #1 engine U/S NR Ashiya RTB SR
196	2–5–51	17515	F/L C.E. Emond	19–5–51	NR Ashiya/Itami RTB SR
197	4–5–51	17505	F/L R.J. Brown	19–5–51	NR Ashiya/Itami RTB SR
198	6–5–51	17505	F/L C.F. Sanford	20–5–51	**NR HNA–Pusan RTB SR**
199	8–5–51	17510	F/O J.B. Miller	23–5–51	Return HNA–engine NR Itami RTB SR
200	10–5–51	17512	F/L W.R. Lloyd	24–5–51	NR Itami RTB SR
201	12–5–51	17505	F/O A.L. Quickfall	26–5–51	NR HNA RTB SR
202	14–5–51	17502	F/O R.M. Edwards	29–5–51	NR HNA RTB SR
203	16–5–51	17504	F/L C.S. Olson	29–5–51	NR HNA RTB SR
–	18–5–51	17511	F/O R.G. Herbert	20–5–51	SPL to HIK and return
204	18–5–51	17515	F/L E.F. Nelles	30–5–51	NR HNA RTB SR
205	20–5–51	17510	F/L C.E. Snider	1–6–51	NR HNA RTB SR
206	22–5–51	17512	F/O R.G. Herbert	2–6–51	NR HNA RTB SR
207	24–5–51	17506	F/L K.T. Wallace	4–6–51	NR HNA RTB SR
208	26–5–51	17504	F/O J.B. Miller	6–6–51	NR HNA RTB SR
209	28–5–51	17510	F/L W.R. Lloyd	6–6–51	NR HNA RTB SR
210	30–5–51	17515	F/L J.A. Watt	9–6–51	SYA #1 eng./HIK–fuel NR HNA RTB SR
211	31–5–51	17504	F/O A.L. Quickfall	7–6–51	SYA return NR HNA RTB SR
212	2–6–51	17507	F/L R.J. Brown	12–6–51	**NR HNA/Kimpo RTB SR**
213	3–6–51	17506	F/L P.L. Michel	11–6–51	NR HNA RTB SR
214	4–6–51	17517	F/L C.S. Olsen	12–6–51	NR HNA RTB SR
215	5–6–51	17505	F/L E.F. Nelles	14–6–51	SYA return NR HNA RTB SR
216	6–6–51	17504	S/L C.F. Sanford	15–6–51	NR HNA RTB SR
217	7–6–51	17507	F/L C.E. Snider	19–5–51	NR Itami RTB SR
218	8–6–51	17512	Maj. T.J. Upton	19–6–51	NR HNA RTB SR
219	9–6–51	17515	F/O R.G. Herbert	19–6–51	NR HNA RTB SR
220	10–6–51	17511	F/O K.T. Wallace	19–6–51	NR Itami RTB SR
221	11–6–51	17505	F/L W.R. Lloyd	19 6 51	NR HNA RTB SR
222	12–6–51	17506	F/L J.A. Watt	18–6–51	NR HNA RTB SR
223	13–6–51	17517	F/L G.W. Webb	20–6–51	NR HNA RTB SR

Serial	Departure	A/C	Captain	RTB	Remarks
224	14–6–51	17504	F/O A.L. Quickfall	19–6–51	TCM return NR HNA RTB SR
–	15–6–51	17515	F/O R.M. Edwards	16–6–51	Special to SYA
			All flights RTB NR		
–	UL 28–6–51	17510	F/L R.J. Brown	10–7–51	Slip Crew SYA (USAF C–54), Travis Shuttle
–	UL 28–6–51	17510	F/L C.E. Snider	9–7–51	Slip Crew HNA (N.W. Airlines)
–	UL 30–6–51	17507	F/L W.J. Buchan	6–7–51	Slip Crew SYA, Travis Shuttle
225	1–7–51	17510	F/L J.A. Watt	9–7–51	
226	3–7–51	17507	F/L K.T. Wallace	12–7–51	
227	5–7–51	17505	F/O M.D. Broadfoot	14–7–51	RTB Misawa, Travis Shuttle
228	7–7–51	17517	F/L C.S. Olsen	18–7–51	
229	9–7–51	17510	F/O A.L. Quickfall	24–7–51	
230	13–7–51	17511	F/L W.R. Lloyd	25–7–51	
231	11–7–51	17505	F/L J.B. Miller	25–7–51	
232	15–7–51	17517	F/L R.G. Herbert	26–7–51	Travis Shuttle
233	17–7–51	17515	F/L G.W. Allen	28–7–51	
234	20–7–51	17506	F/L W.J. Buchan	2–8–51	
235	19–7–51	17511	F/L D.M. Payne	1–8–51	
236	25–7–51	17512	F/L G.M. Stuart	4–8–51	
237	26–7–51	17506	F/O M.D. Broadfoot	3–8–51	
238	27–7–51	17515	F/O E.R. Wolkowski	6–8–51	Travis Shuttle
239	29–7–51	17504	F/L J.A. Watt	7–8–51	
240	31–7–51	17512	F/L R.M. Edwards	11–8–51	Travis Shuttle
241	2–8–51	17510	F/O A.L. Quickfall	12–8–51	
242	4–8–51	17504	F/L C.S. Oslen	14–8–51	
243	6–8–51	17507	F/L C.E. Goodwin	15–8–51	
244	8–8–51	17505	F/L R.G. Herbert	17–8–51	
245	10–8–51	17510	F/L W.R. Lloyd	21–8–51	
246	13–8–51	17517	F/L J.B. Miller	22–8–51	
247	14–8–51	17505	F/L W.J. Buchan	26–8–51	
248	16–8–51	17517	F/L G.W. Allen	26–8–51	
249	18–8–51	17507	F/O M.D. Broadfoot	28–8–51	
250	20–8–51	17514	F/L J.R. Morrison	30–8–51	
251	22–8–51	17515	F/O E.R. Wolkowski	1–9–51	
252	24–8–51	17504	F/L E.F. Nelles	3–9–51	
253	26–8–51	17514	F/O R.M. Edwards	4–9–51	
254	29–8–51	17505	F/L C.E. Goodwin	6–9–51	A/C U/S Delay 24 hrs
255	30–8–51	17504	F/O A.L. Quickfall	8–9–51	
256	1–9–51	17502	F/L D.M. Payne	11–9–51	
257	3–9–51	17505	F/L G.M. Stuart	12–9–51	
258	5–9–51	17510	F/L C.S. Olsen	15–9–51	

Appendix E: Korean Airlift—Schedule of Operations

Serial	Departure	A/C	Captain	RTB	Remarks
259	7–9–51	17502	F/O M.D. Broadfoot	16–9–51	
260	9–9–51	17506	F/L J.R. Bell	20–9–51	
261	11–9–51	17510	F/L R.G. Herbert	22–9–51	
262	13–9–51	17507	F/L G.W. Allen	23–9–51	
263	15–9–51	17506	F/O D.G. Scott	24–9–51	
264	17–9–51	17509	F/O E.R. Wolkowski	28–9–51	
265	19–9–51	17507	F/L W.R. Lloyd	30–9–51	
266	21–9–51	17517	F/L R.J. Brown	1–10–51	
267	24–9–51	17504	F/L J.B. Miller	2–10–51	RTB U/S
268	25–9–51	17514	F/O J.C. Henry	4–10–51	
269	27–9–51	17505	F/L J.R. Morrison	6–10–51	
270	29–9–51	17502	F/L W.J. Buchan	8–10–51	
271	1–10–51	17504	F/L G.M. Stuart	10–10–51	
272	3–10–51	17511	F/O M.D. Broadfoot	17–10–51	U/S ANC
273	5–10–51	17505	F/L J.R. Bell	14–10–51	**HNA–Kimpo (K14)**
274	7–10–51	17502	F/L G.W. Allen	17–10–51	
275	9–10–51	17507	F/L R.G. Herbert	18–10–51	
276	11–10–51	17511	F/L C.E. Goodwin	21–10–51	
277	13–10–51	17506	F/O D.G. Scott	22–10–51	
278	15–10–51	17510	MAJ. R.H. Ralph	24–10–51	
279	18–10–51	17506	F/L W.R. Lloyd	26–10–51	
280	19–10–51	17512	F/L G.M. Kightley	28–10–51	
281	21–10–51	17510	F/O J.C. Henry	30–10–51	
282	23–10–51	17517	F/L J.R. Morrison	1–11–51	
283	25–10–51	17512	F/L G.M. Stuart	3–11–51	
284	27–10–51	17505	F/L W.J. Buchan	5–11–51	
285	29–10–51	17517	F/O E.R. Wolkowski	8–11–51	
286	31–10–51	17515	F/O A.L. Quickfall	9–11–51	
287	2–11–51	17507	F/L R.J. Brown	13–11–51	
288	4–11–51	17504	F/L J.R. Bell	15–11–51	
289	6–11–51	17505	F/L R.E. Churchill	17–11–51	
290	8–11–51	17506	F/L G.W. Allen	19–11–51	
291	10–11–51	17515	F/L R.G. Herbert	23–11–51	**HNA–Itazuki–Kimpo**
292	12–11–51	17510	F/L C.E. Goodwin	21–11–51	
293	14–11–51	17504	F/O D.G. Scott	27–11–51	
294	16–11–51	17502	F/L E.F. Nelles	27–11–51	
295	18–11–51	17510	F/O R.M. Edwards	27–11–51	
296	20–11–51	17517	F/L W.J. Buchan	29–11–51	
297	22–11–51	17502	F/L J.R. Morrison	1–12–51	
298	24–11–51	17509	F/O E.R. Wolkowski	3–12–51	

Serial	Departure	A/C	Captain	RTB	Remarks
299	26–11–51	17517	F/O A.L. Quickfall	6–12–51	
300	28–11–51	17506	MAJ. R.H. Ralph	7–12–51	
301	30–11–51	17505	F/L E.J. Trotter	9–12–51	Stall out off Vancouver Island (icing)
302	2–12–51	17509	F/L P.L. Michel	12–12–51	
303	4–12–51	17515	S/L C. Torontow	16–12–51	**HNA–Iwakumi–Kimpo**
304	6–12–51	17505	F/L R.G. Herbert	15–12–51	
305	8–12–51	17512	F/L G.M. Kightley	17–12–51	
306	10–12–51	17515	F/L R.J. Brown	19–12–51	
307	13–12–51	17504	F/L G.M. Stuart	21–12–51	U/S engine RTB 24 hr. delay
308	14–12–51	17512	F/L G.W. Allen	23–12–51	
309	16–12–51	17510	F/L J.R. Bell	23–12–51	SPL run Great Falls, San Diego
310	18–12–51	17504	F/O J.C. Henry	28–12–51	
311	20–12–51	17517	F/O D.G. Scott	30–12–51	
312	22–12–51	17510	F/O R.M. Edwards	31–12–51	
313	24–12–51	17511	F/L E.F. Nelles	2–1–52	
314	26–12–51	17517	F/L W.J. Buchan	5–1–52	
315	28–12–51	17506	F/O E.R. Wolkowski	8–1–52	
316	30–12–51	17511	F/L J.R. Morrison	11–1–52	
	30–12–51	17514	F/L E.J. Trotter	9–1–52	Special to HNA, lose engine SYA
317	2–1–52	17515	F/O A.L. Quickfall	15–1–52	
318	4–1–52	17506	S/L G.M. Kightley	15–1–52	
319	6–1–52	17503	F/L R.G. Herbert	15–1–52	
320	8–1–52	17508	F/L G.M. Stuart	18–1–52	
321	11–1–52	17503	F/L G.W. Allen	21–1–52	Mechanical problems, ANC
322	12–1–52	17509	S/L C.E. Goodwin	22–1–52	
323	14–1–52	17508	F/L C.S. Olsen	25–1–52	
324	16–1–52	17512	F/O D.G. Scott	27–1–52	
325	18–1–52	17515	F/O J.C. Henry	29–1–52	
326	20–1–52	17505	F/O R.M. Edwards	29–1–52	U/S Nosewheel, SYA
327	22–1–52	17509	F/L R.J. Brown	31–1–52	
328	24–1–52	17510	F/O A.L. Quickfall	2–2–52	
329	26–1–52	17512	F/O E.R. Wolkowski	5–2–52	
330	28–1–52	17510	F/L J.R. Bell	6–2–52	
331	30–1–52	17514	F/L W.J. Buchan	8–2–52	
332	2–2–52	17505	F/L E.J. Trotter	10–2–52	Delay–Mech. Problems
333	3–2–52	17517	F/L W.R. Lloyd	12–2–52	
334	5–2–52	17506	F/O D. Harrison	14–2–52	
335	7–2–52	17514	F/O W.V.C. Strathy	18–2–52	
336	9–2–52	17517	F/L R.G. Herbert	18–2–52	

Appendix E: Korean Airlift—Schedule of Operations

Serial	Departure	A/C	Captain	RTB	Remarks
337	11–2–52	17506	F/O R.A. Roane	22–2–52	
338	13–2–52	17511	F/L G.M. Stuart	24–2–52	
339	15–2–52	17502	S/L G.M. Kightley	26–2–52	
340	17–2–52	17511	F/O J.C. Henry	29–2–52	
341	19–2–52	17502	F/O R.M. Edwards	29–2–52	
342	22–2–52	17504	F/O E.R. Wolkowski	2–3–52	
343	23–2–52	17503	F/O A.L. Quickfall	3–3–52	Fuel Leak–ANC
344	26–2–52	17509	F/L E.J. Trotter	8–3–52	
345	27–2–52	17512	F/L G.W. Allen	8–3–52	
346	29–2–52	17505	F/L W.J. Buchan	9–3–52	Divert to Adak
347	2–3–52	17503	F/O D.H. Kuhn	12–3–52	Engine change–ANC
348	4–3–52	17512	F/O D. Harrison	16–3–52	
349	6–3–52	17514	F/O W.V.C. Strathy	17–3–52	SYA to Base 11+ 35
350	8–3–52	17505	F/L R.J. Brown	17–3–52	
351	10–3–52	17506	F/L J.R. Morrison	19–3–52	SYA–Engine change/ SYA RTB 13 + 00
352	12–3–52	17514	F/L G.M. Stuart	21–3–52	
353	14–3–52	17517	F/O R.A. Roane	22–3–52	
354	16–3–52	17504	F/L R.G. Herbert	25–3–52	
355	18–3–52	17506	F/O J.C. Henry	29–3–52	
356	20–3–52	17517	F/L G.W. Allen	29–3–52	
357	22–3–52	17504	F/O E.R. Wolkowski	1–4–52	Travis Shuttle
358	24–3–52	17511	F/O P.M. Lemieux	2–4–52	
359	26–3–52	17503	F/O D. Harrison	6–4–52	
360	28–3–52	17509	F/O G.H. Knight	7–4–52	
361	30–3–52	17511	F/O C.L. Wenzel	9–4–52	
362	2–4–52	17503	F/L W.J. Buchan	10–4–52	
363	4–4–52	17509	F/L R.J. Brown	14–4–52	
364	6–4–52	17505	F/L A.F. Gerding	15–4–52	
365	8–4–52	17510	F/O D.H. Kuhn	17–4–52	
366	10–4–52	17505	F/O R.A. Roane	19–4–52	
367	12–4–52	17515	F/O W.V.C. Strathy	22–4–52	RTB–Radios U/S
368	14–4–52	17510	F/L R.G. Herbert	23–4–52	
369	16–4–52	17506	S/L E.F. Nelles	25–4–52	
370	18–4–52	17515	F/O J.C. Henry	27–4–52	
371	20–4–52	17511	W/C J.K. MacDonald	28–4–52	Travis Shuttle
372	22–4–52	17506	F/O E.R. Wolkowski	1–5–52	
373	24–4–52	17509	F/L G.W. Allen	3–5–52	SPL San Diego–Lindberg Field
374	26–4–52	17511	F/O G.H. Knight	6–5–52	RTB Via Misawa
375	28–4–52	17517	F/O R.A. Spratt	8–5–52	RTB via Misawa

Serial	Departure	A/C	Captain	RTB	Remarks
376	30–4–52	17509	F/L R.J. Brown	16–5–52	
377	2–5–52	17512	F/O P.M. Lemieux	11–5–52	
378	4–5–52	17517	F/L A.F. Gerding	16–5–52	Engine problems–SYA
379	6–5–52	17515	F/O C.L. Wenzel	17–5–52	
380	8–5–52	17512	F/L G.M. Stuart	17–5–52	
381	10–5–52	17515	F/O R.M. Edwards	19–5–52	
382	12–5–52	17502	F/O D. Harrison	21–5–52	
383	14–5–52	17514	F/O R.A. Roane	23–5–52	
384	16–5–52	17506	F/O W.V.C. Strathy	27–5–52	
385	18–5–52	17514	F/L J.R. Morrison	28–5–52	
386	20–5–52	17502	F/O W.I. Butchart	29–5–52	
387	22–5–52	17506	F/O D.H. Kuhn	31–5–52	
388	24–5–52	17509	F/L G.W. Allen	2–6–52	
389	26–5–52	17517	F/O D. McLeod	6–6–52	
390	28–5–52	17512	F/O J.C. Henry	7–6–52	
391	30–5–52	17509	S/L C. Torontow	5–6–52	
392	2–6–52	17517	F/O R.A. Spratt	5–6–52	
393	2–6–52	17510	F/O G.H. Knight	10–6–52	
394	6–6–52	17514	F/O D. Harrison	18–6–52	Divert to Adak
395	10–6–52	17506	F/O B.J. Budgeon	18–6–52	
396	14–6–52	17515	F/L W.I. Butchart	22–6–52	
397	18–6–52	17502	F/O M.D. Broadfoot	30–6–52	
398	22–6–52	17514	F/O G.F. Sage	2–7–52	
399	26–6–52	17517		–7–52	
400	–6–52			–7–52	
401	2–7–52	17510	F/O C.L. Wenzel	14–7–52	
402	6–7–52	17515	F/L P. Lemieux	15–7–52	
403	13–7–52	17508	F/L R.M. Edwards	22–7–52	
404	14–7–52	17505	S/L C. Torontow	23–7–52	
405	18–7–52	17511	F/O G.H. Knight	26–7–52	
406	24–7–52	17503	F/L C.S. Olsen	3–8–52	
407	–7–52			–8–52	
408	30–7–52	17505	F/O R.H. Cook	7–8–52	
409	2–8–52	17510	F/L D. Harrison	10–8–52	
410	6–8–52	17515	F/L J.N. Hall	14–8–52	
411	10–8–52	17504	F/O D. McLeod	19–8–52	
412	14–8–52	17503		–8–52	
413	20–8–52	17510	F/O G.G. Waddell	26–8–52	
414	22–8–52	17514	F/O B.J. Budgeon	31–8–52	
415	26–8–52	17509	F/O G.H. Knight	3–9–52	

Appendix E: Korean Airlift—Schedule of Operations

Serial	Departure	A/C	Captain	RTB	Remarks
416	30–8–52	17511	F/O C.L. Wenzel	6–9–52	
417	2–9–52	17515	F/O G.R.A. Kyle	10–9–52	
418	6–9–52	17505	F/L W.I. Butchart	15–9–52	
419	10–9–52	17502	F/O R.A. Spratt	18–9–52	
420	14–9–52	17506	F/O E.R. Wolkowski	22–9–52	
421	–9–52			–9–52	
422	–9–52			–10–52	
423	26–9–52	17510	F/O J.S. Middleton	6–10–52	
424	30–9–52	17505	F/L J.N. Hall	7–10–52	
425	4–10–52	17504	F/L A.F. Gerding	15–10–52	
426	6–10–52	17506	F/O D. McLeod	14–10–52	
427	–10–52			–10–52	
428	–10–52			–10–52	
429	19–10–52	17517	F/O J.M. Robert	28–10–52	
430	22–10–52	17505	F/O G.R.A. Kyle	30–10–52	
431	–10–52			–11–52	
432	30–10–52	17516	F/O L.A.R. Tapp	7–11–52	
433	3–11–52	17504	F/O B.J. Budgeon	10–11–52	
434	6–11–52	17503	F/O G.F. Sage	19–11–52	
435	11–11–52	17511	F/O D.H. Kuhn	23–11–52	
436	14–11–52	17506	S/L G.H. Kightley	21–11–52	
437	18–11–52	17509	F/L W.I. Butchart	28–11–52	
438	23–11–52	17504	F/O G.H. Knight	2–12–52	
439	26–11–52	17505	F/L A.F. Gerding	10–12–52	
455*	28–11–52	17525	F/L J.N. Hall	10–12–52	**HNA–Seoul City Airport (K16)**
456	1–12–52	17510	F/O J. Grant	11–12–52	(K16 with Grant's Crew)
457	4–12–52	17516	S/L C. Torontow	11–12–52	
458	5–12–52	17511	F/O M.G. Casselman	15–12–52	
459	12–12–52	17516	F/O G.G. Waddell	20–12–52	
460	13–12–52	17509	F/O G.R.A. Kyle	19–12–52	
461	20–12–52	17515	F/L A.L. Quickfall	26–12–52	
462	23–12–52	17515	F/O J.S. Middleton	29–12–52	
463	28–12–52	17515	F/O J.M. Robert	3–1–53	
464	29–12–52	17525	F/O R.H. Cook	4–1–53	
465	5–1–53	17525	F/L A.F. Gerding	14–1–53	
466	7–1–53	17516	F/O R.B. Ingall	13–1–53	
467	–1–53			–1–53	
468	20–1–53	17515	F/O R.A. Spratt	26–1–53	
469	21–1–53	17509	F/O R.H.W. Raike	27–1–53	

* Numbering changed (no reason given)

Serial	Departure	A/C	Captain	RTB	Remarks
470	23–1–53	17506	F/O J.M. Robert	28–1–53	
471	29–1–53	17606	F/O G.L. McAninch	12–2–53	
472	30–1–53	17504	F/L J.R. Morrison	5–2–53	
473	6–2–53	17504	F/L G.F. Sage	16–2–53	
474	7–2–53	17505	F/L R.A. Spratt	13–2–53	
475	13–2–53	17505	F/O G.R.A. Kyle	23–2–53	
476	14–2–53	17509	F/L W.I. Butchart	21–2–53	
477	–2–53			–2–53	
478	22–2–53	17509	F/O E.R. Wolkowski	1–3–53	
479	–2–53			–3–53	
480	2–3–53	17504	F/L A.F. Gerding	11–3–53	
481	3–3–53	17504	F/O R.A. Cook	9–3–53	
482	10–3–53	17504	F/O J.R. Grant	16–3–53	
483	11–3–53	17510	F/O B.J. Budgeon	17–3–53	
484	18–3–53	17509	F/L J.S. Schroder	27–3–53	
485	19–3–53	17510	F/O J.F. Lambert	25–3–53	
486	26–3–53	17509	F/O J.S. Middleton	8–4–53	
487	27–3–53	17517	F/O R.B. Ingall	2–4–53	
488	2–4–53	17515	F/O E.R. Wolkowski	15–4–53	
489	3–4–53	17511	F/O M.G. Casselman	9–4–53	
490	8–4–53	17506	F/O R.H.W. Raike	16–4–53	
491	11–4–53	17515	F/O G.L. McAninch	19–4–53	
492	15–4–53	17516	F/L J.R. Morrison	25–4–53	
493	20–4–53	17514	F/L G.F. Sage	28–4–53	
494	23–4–53	17503	F/L W. Dick	1–5–53	
495	27–4–53	17515	F/L A.F. Gerding	6–5–53	
496	1–5–53	17515	F/L J.S. Schroder	10–5–53	
497	5–5–53	17506	F/O R.T. Whitman	14–5–53	
498	9–5–53	17504	F/O R.G. Husch	18–5–53	
499	13–5–53	17516	F/O L.A.R. Tapp	22–5–53	
500	26–5–53	17505	F/O W.F. Kyryluk	3–6–53	Designated as Trip 500
501	19–5–53	17505	F/L D.F. Deeprose	26–5–53	
502	21–5–53	17509	F/O M.G. Casselman	30–5–53	
503	29–5–53	17510	F/O R.H.W. Raike	8–6–53	
504	3–6–53	17506	F/O G.L. McAninch	11–6–53	
505	6–6–53	17515	F/O E.R. Wolkowski	14–6–53	
506	11–6–53	17517	F/O J.N. Hall	19–6–53	
507	14–6–53	17504	F/O R.B. Ingall	26–6–53	
508	19–6–53	17504	F/O G.R.A. Kyle	27–6–53	
509	22–6–53	17510	F/L A.F. Gerding	5–7–53	

Appendix E: Korean Airlift—Schedule of Operations

Serial	Departure	A/C	Captain	RTB	Remarks
510	27–6–53	17503	F/L J.R. Morrison	6–7–53	
511	30–6–53	17525	F/O R.T. Whitman	12–7–53	
512	4–7–53	17517	F/O W.F. Kyryluk	15–7–53	
513	8–7–53	17515	F/O R.G. Husch	19–7–53	
514	13–7–53	17511	F/L W. Dick	20–7–53	
515	16–7–53	17510	F/L D.F. Deeprose	22–7–53	
516	21–7–53	17510	F/O E.J. Kowalik	27–7–53	
517	24–7–53	17509	F/O R.B. Ingall	3–8–53	
518	28–7–53	17517	S/L C. Torontow	6–8–53	
519	–7–53			–8–53	
520	1–8–53	17504	F/L G.F. Sage	10–8–53	
521	5–8–53	17505	F/O G.R.A. Kyle	16–8–53	
522	9–8–53	17511	F/O R.W. Norris	18–8–53	
523	13–8–53	17516	F/O J.M. Robert	23–8–53	
524	17–8–53	17509	F/L G.H. Knight	26–8–53	
525	20–8–53	17516	F/L D.F. Deeprose	27–8–53	
526	25–8–53	17504	F/O W.F. Kyryluk	4–9–53	Crosswinds SYA, blow 3 tires on landing
527	30–8–53	17505	F/O J.F. Lambert	7–9–53	
528	2–9–53	17511	F/O J.H. Nyhuus	11–9–53	
529	6–9–53	17509	F/O R.G. Husch	15–9–53	
530	10–9–53	17503	F/L A.F. Gerding	19–9–53	
531	14–9–53	17512	F/O J.M. Robert	27–9–53	
532	18–9–53	17506	F/L K.C. Roulston	28–9–53	
533	22–9–53	17510	F/O E.J. Kowalik	30–9–53	
534	26–9–53	17504	F/O R.W. Norris	5–10–53	
535	30–9–53	17511	F/O D.F. Clifton	9–10–53	
536	5–10–53	17521	F/O R.B. Ingall	13–10–53	
537	8–10–53	17509	F/L A.F. Gerding	18–10–53	
538	12–10–53	17512	F/L D.F. Deeprose	20–10–53	
539	16–10–53	17506	F/O R.H. Cook	24–10–53	
540	20–10–53	17510	F/O K.D. McBride	28–10–53	
541	24–10–53	17521	S/L G.F. Sanford	2–11–53	
542	28–10–53	17504	F/O J.F. Lambert	10–11–53	
543	–10–53			–11–53	
544	2–11–53	17511	F/O J.H. Nyhuus	9–11–53	
545	5–11–53	17509	F/L W. Dick	14–11–53	
546	9–11–53	17512	W/C H.W. Lupton	18–11–53	
547	13–11–53	17521	F/O N.F. Paul	28–11–53	
548	17–11–53	17506	F/O J.M. Robert	26–11–53	

Serial	Departure	A/C	Captain	RTB	Remarks
549	21–11–53	17503	F/O R.G. Husch	30–11–53	
550	25–11–53	17505	S/L C.E.L. Hare	4–12–53	
551	30–11–53	17504	F/O R.B. Ingall	9–12–53	
552	3–12–53	17525	F/O G.L. McAninch	10–12–53	
553	6–12–53	17516	F/O D.F. Clifton	15–12–53	
554	9–12–53	17512	F/O N.F. Paul	18–12–53	
555	14–12–53	17510	F/O J.F. Lambert	22–12–53	
556	18–12–53	17506	F/O R.W. Norris	24–12–53	
557	20–12–53	17516	S/L C.E.L. Hare	(27–12–53)	Crash at SYA 17505
558	27–12–53	17509	F/O R.H.W. Raike	5–1–54	
559	31–12–53	17504	F/O J.H. Nyhuus	9–1–54	
560	5–1–54	17512	F/L D.F. Deeprose	12–1–54	
561	7–1–54	17502	F/O C.L. Wenzel	15–1–54	
562	10–1–54	17512	F/O E.J. Kowalik	19–1–54	
563	14–1–54	17516	F/O L.A.R. Tapp	23–1–54	
564	18–1–54	17510	F/O R.B. Ingall	29–1–54	
565	21–1–54	17525	F/O R.H. Cook	31–1–54	
566	26–1–54	17521	F/O G.H. McAninch	3–2–54	
567	29–1–54	17504	F/O R.G. Husch	5–2–54	
568	4–2–54	17511	F/O R.H.W. Raike	13–2–54	
569	7–2–54	17516	F/O G.R.A. Kyle	17–2–54	
570	11–2–54	17525	F/O J.F. Lambert	20–2–54	
571	14–2–54	17515	F/O N.F. Paul	24–2–54	
572	18–2–54	17504	F/L K.C. Roulston	6–3–54	
573	21–2–54	17515	F/O R.W. Norris	9–3–54	
574	–2–54			–3–54	
575	28–2–54	17511	F/O H.A. Pecht	15–3–54	
576	–3–54			–3–54	
577	–3–54			–3–54	
578	8–3–54	17516	F/O E.J. Kowalik	17–3–54	
579	14–3–54	17525	F/O D.F. Clifton	22–3–54	
580	19–3–54	17521	F/O R.H. Cook	26–3–54	
581	22–3–54	17515	F/O R.G. Husch	30–3–54	
582	25–3–54	17504	S/L G.F. Sanford	3–4–54	
583	28–3–54	17525	F/O R.B. Ingall	6–4–54	
584	2–4–54	17511	F/O N.F. Paul	9–4–54	
585	4–4–54	17510	F/O J.A. Forest	13–4–54	
586	8–4–54	17516	F/O J.F. Lambert	16–4–54	
587	11–4–54	17515	F/O W. Dick	21–4–54	
588	–4–54			–4–54	

Appendix E: Korean Airlift—Schedule of Operations

Serial	Departure	A/C	Captain	RTB	Remarks
589	22–4–54	17509	F/L J.G. Wynn	30–4–54	
590	23–4–54	17525	F/O R.H. Cook	4–5–54	
591	29–4–54	17512	F/O D.F. Clifton	7–5–54	
592	2–5–54	17516	F/O L.A.R. Tapp	11–5–54	
593	6–5–54	17507	F/O E.J. Kowalik	15–5–54	
594	9–5–54	17510	F/O K.D. McBride	18–5–54	
595	13–5–54	17506	F/L K.C. Roulston	21–5–54	
596	16–5–54	17509	F/L T. Lamb	26–5–54	
597	27–5–54	17507	F/L D.F. Deeprose	10–6–54	To Dorval via ANC–VR–WG
598	30–5–54	17516	F/O N.F. Paul	10–6–54	To Dorval via ANC–XD–WG
599	31–5–54	17510	F/O R.B. Ingall	9–6–54	To Dorval via ANC–VR–WG

APPENDIX F

SQUADRON COMMANDERS

W/C D.R. Miller
(DND, PL 110912)

Wing Commander Donald R. Miller, AFC, CD
Squadron Commander 25 May–11 December 1945

Born in Saskatoon, Saskatchewan in 1913, Donald R. Miller was educated at Bedford and City Park Collegiate. In 1935, he left for England, where he joined the RAF, trained as a pilot and, after the war broke out, flew on operations with an RAF night-fighter squadron. Posted to Canada in 1941, he served as a squadron commander at No 32 Service Flying Training School, RAF Station Moose Jaw. Still with the RAF, he was transferred to Ferry Command in 1943, operating between Dorval, Britain and Africa. In 1945, he returned to England to join No 525 Transport Squadron, based at RAF Station Lyneham, where he became Squadron Commander. On transferring to the RCAF on 7 May 1945, he was given the task of re-forming No 426 Squadron as a transport unit. On his return to Canada in 1946, he attended the RCAF Staff College, after which he held a series of appointments including command of No 406 (City of Saskatoon) Auxiliary Squadron, RCAF Station Uplands at Ottawa, and RCAF Station Fort Nelson in British Columbia. He retired from the service in 1964 at the rank of Group Captain.

W/C J.F. Green
(DND, No 426 Squadron)

Wing Commander John Frederick Green, DFC
Squadron Commander 12 December 1945–1 January 1946

John Frederick Green was born in St. Thomas, Ontario, on 23 October 1907, and educated at Ridley College School and the University of Toronto. He was a sales representative for Hudson Motors before enrolling in the RCAF on 8 May 1940, and he trained as a pilot at No 3 Elementary Flying Training School (London, Ontario) and No 6 Service Flying Training School (Dunville, Ontario). He received his wings on 3 July 1941 and was assigned to Eastern Air Command, where he served with No 145 (BR) Squadron flying Ventura aircraft out of Dartmouth on anti-submarine patrols over the North Atlantic. While with No 145 Squadron, he served both as a Flight Commander and as Squadron Commander, was Mentioned in Despatches, and received the Distinguished Flying Cross. On proceeding overseas during the summer of 1945, he joined No 426 Squadron as a Flight Commander. On 12 December 1945, he was appointed Squadron Commander only to oversee the disbandment of the squadron at the end of the year. He left the RCAF on repatriation in 1946, and returned to civilian life in St. Thomas.

W/C C.A. Willis
(DND, PL 121404)

Wing Commander Charles Albert Willis, DFC, CD
Squadron Commander 1 August 1946–28 February 1947

Charles Albert Willis enrolled in the RCAF at Halifax on 4 April 1938, trained as a pilot, and received his wings at Trenton on 17 June 1939. He was assigned to No 8 (BR) Squadron, Eastern Air Command, flying Delta and Bolingbroke aircraft on anti-submarine missions out of Sydney, Nova Scotia, and served as its Squadron Commander from June 1941 to May 1943. Soon after Japan entered the war, No 8 Squadron was transferred to Western Air Command and based at Sea Island, British Columbia; it operated in Alaska from June 1942 to March 1943, and then returned to Sea Island.

Willis proceeded overseas in 1943, and commanded No 404 (Coastal Fighter) Squadron from 8 September 1943 to 30 March 1944, when he was shot down and taken prisoner. During his time with No 404 Squadron, he flew Bristol Beaufighters out of Wick, Scotland, against enemy shipping along the coasts of Norway and the Netherlands, earning the Distinguished Flying Cross. After repatriation to Canada, he commanded No 164 (Transport) Squdron, based at Dartmouth, from 30 April to 1 August 1946. When the squadron was reorganized into two transport units, he assumed the command of the Dartmouth element, renamed No 426 (T) Squadron, and served in that capacity until 28 February 1947.

After leaving No 426 Squadron, Willis attended the RCAF Staff College and then, from September 1947 to August 1949, served on the staff at Air Force Headquarters. From September 1949 to May 1951, he was on the staff at Air Materiel Command Headquarters, after which he was transferred to No 2 Manning Depot at St-Jean, Quebec, where he served until September 1952, when he was posted to RCAF Station Bagotville. His next appointment was to the staff at Air Defence Command Headquarters, where he served from May 1954 to May 1960, when he was posted for the last time, to RCAF Station Winnipeg. Wing Commander Willis retired from the service in February 1965.

Wing Commander Cecil G.W. Chapman, DSO, CD
Squadron Commander 1 March 1947–17 February 1949

Cecil George William Chapman was born on 17 August 1918 in Hillsborough, New Brunswick, and graduated from the University of New Brunswick in electrical engineering. He enrolled in the RCAF at Fredericton on 5 June 1939 and trained as a pilot at the Calgary Flying Club, receiving his wings on 30 October 1939. He then attended No 1 Wireless School in Montreal, and was assigned as a General List Signals Officer to No 120 (BR) Squadron at Sea Island, British Columbia. Following the Specialist Navigation Course at No 1 Navigation School in Rivers, Manitoba, he was posted to No 5 (BR) Squadron at Dartmouth, Nova Scotia, where he served as Squadron Navigation Officer until his transfer to Eastern Air Command Headquarters as the Command Navigation Officer. He later flew on anti-submarine operations with No 162 (BR)

Appendix F: Squadron Commanders

W/C C.G.W. Chapman
(DND, PL 110363)

Squadron, which operated Consolidated Canso flying boats out of various bases in the Maritime provinces, Iceland and northern Scotland. He commanded No 162 Squadron from September 1943 to September 1944, and was appointed to the Distinguished Service Order for carrying out a successful attack on a German submarine in the North Atlantic. On leaving the squadron, he was seconded to Coastal Command Headquarters at Northwood, Middlesex.

On repatriation to Canada in 1945, he seved as Secretary to the Postwar Planning committee at Air Force Headquarters until selected for the 1946 course at the RCAF Staff College. Upon graduation, he was appointed to the command of No 426 (T) Squadron. In 1949, he was transferred overseas to join the Directing Staff at the RAF Staff College. He returned to Canada in December 1950 with an appointment to the Directorate of Air Operations at Air Force Headquarters; later, he became Director of Operational Requirements. From 1953 to 1957, he commanded RCAF Station Greenwood, and from there he went to the Canadian Joint Staff Headquarters in Washington, D.C., as Chief Staff Officer, an appointment he held until 1959, when he was posted to the command of RCAF Station Penhold in Alberta. In the fall of 1960, he was appointed Air Commander at the headquarters of the Opération des Nations Unies au Congo in Léopoldville, in which capacity he served a six-month tour, returning to Penhold in 1961. Two years later, he was appointed Air and Military Attaché to Sweden and Finland at the Canadian Embassy in Stockholm, where he served until September 1966. Group Captain Chapman retired from the RCAF in June 1967.

W/C C.H. Mussells
(DND, PL 110962)

Wing Commander Campbell Haliburton Mussells, OBE, DSO, DFC, CD
Squadron Commander 18 February 1949–31 March 1951

C.H. Mussells was born in Montreal on 20 June 1920, and educated at Westmount High School and McGill University. He enrolled in the RCAF in January 1940 and trained as a pilot. After several years of instructional duties in Canada, he was posted overseas, where he served with No 405 (Pathfinder) Squadron. For his wartime services, he was appointed to the Distinguished Service Order and awarded the Distinguished Flying Cross.

After the war, he attended the RCAF Staff College in Toronto and served on the staff at Air Force Headquarters until his appointment in February 1949 to the command of No 426 (T) Squadron. In June 1952, he was appointed to the Order of the British Empire for his part in the Korean Airlift (*Operation HAWK*). On leaving the squadron in March 1951, he was named Senior Air Staff Officer at Air Transport Command Headquarters, where he served until April 1954, when he was posted to the Central Flying School at RCAF Station Trenton as Officer Commanding.

Mussells was promoted Group Captain in 1957 and posted to the command of RCAF Station Uplands, in which capacity he served until June 1961 when he became Director of Air Defence Requirements at Air Force Headquarters. He commanded RCAF Station Cold Lake from

November 1961 until February 1962, when he returned to Air Force Headquarters as the Chief of Operational Requirements. In December 1963, he was transferred to the Canadian Joint Staff in London to attend the year-long course at the Imperial Defence College. Upon successful completion of this course, he was assigned to No 1 Air Division Headquarters as the Senior Air Staff Officer. In October 1967, he was promoted Air Commodore and appointed Director of Exchange Services at Canadian Forces Headquarters. He was assigned to the staff of the National Defence College in July 1971, and he retired from the Canadian Armed Forces in October 1975.

*W/C J.K.F. MacDonald
(DND, PL 110812)*

Wing Commander John Kennedy Francis MacDonald, DFC, CD
Squadron Commander 1 June 1951–28 August 1952

Born on 5 January 1917 in Antigonish, Nova Scotia, John K.F. MacDonald was educated at Morrison School and St. Francis Xavier University, graduating with a B.A. in 1936. He joined the RCAF in November 1938 and trained as a pilot, receiving his wings at Camp Borden on 5 September 1939. During the war, he served for three years with RCAF Coastal Command units on both the east and west coasts of Canada and in Alaska. In June 1943, he proceeded overseas and began a tour of operations flying Halifax bombers over Europe in April 1944. Shot down over France in July 1944, he evaded capture and returned to England to resume flying duties, soon taking command of No 432 Squadron at East Moor. He received the Distinguished Flying Cross on completion of his tour of operations, and was appointed to the command of RCAF Station Middleton St. George.

He returned to Canada during the summer of 1945, posted to Dartmouth to command No 662 (Heavy Bomber) Wing, which was training for operations in the Pacific. After V-J Day, he served as Deputy Air Staff Officer at No 2 Air Command in Winnipeg until March 1947, when he went to the RCAF Staff College in Toronto. From the fall of 1947 until 1950 he held senior staff positions at North West Air Command Headquarters at Edmonton, and then at Air Transport Command Headquarters at Lachine, where he was Senior Personnel Staff Officer. In 1951, he took over command of No 426 (T) Squadron, and in 1952 he was appointed Director of Air Plans and Programs at Air Force Headquarters. After a jet refresher course at RCAF Station Chatham, flying T-33s and Sabres, he proceeded overseas to command No 3 (F) Wing at Zweibrücken from May 1956 to July 1960. He was then transferred to the Directorate of Air Policy at Air Force Headquarters.

In 1963, he attended the National Defence College, followed by an assignment in 1964 as Director Senior Appointments (Air Force) at Air Force Headquarters. Promoted to Air Commodore in 1965, he served on the Training Command Planning Group and as Chief of Staff Support Services at Training Command Headquarters in Winnipeg. From January 1967 until his retirement in 1970, he commanded the Maritime Operations Test and Evaluation Unit.

Wing Commander Hugh William Lupton, AFC, CD
Squadron Commander 8 September 1952–20 July 1955

Born and educated in Regina, Saskatchewan, Hugh William Lupton joined the RCAF in June 1940, trained as a pilot at Dunville, Ontario, and as an instructor at Trenton, and served as an instructor at No 6 Service Flying Training School at Yorkton, Saskatchewan, from April 1941

*W/C H.W. Lupton
(DND, PL 142854)*

to November 1944, when he received the King's Commendation for Valuable Services in the Air and the Air Force Cross. In March 1945, after a three-month instrument flying course, he was posted overseas as an instructor.

Lupton continued instructing after the war, serving at the Instrument Flying School at Trenton and as an exchange officer with the RAF at the Empire Flying School in Hullavington, Wiltshire. Returning to Canada in July 1949, he joined the instructional staff at the Central Flying School at RCAF Station Trenton. In June 1950, he was posted to Training Command Headquarters, where he served as a staff officer until his transfer to Air Transport Command Headquarters at Lachine in June 1952. In September, he assumed command of No 426 Squadron, an appointment he held until July 1955.

From No 426 Squadron, Wing Commander Lupton was posted to the Canadian Joint Staff in Washington, where he served as an exchange officer at USAF Headquarters on the Air Standardization Co-ordinating Committee. Posted to Toronto in September 1958, he attended the RCAF Staff College until June 1959, when he was assigned to Air Force Headquarters as a staff officer in the Air Plans Directorate. In July 1961, he was promoted Group Captain and transferred to Air Transport Command Headquarters as Senior Air Staff Officer, in which capacity he served until July 1965. His next posting was to Ramstein Air Base in West Germany, at the headquarters of the 4th Allied Tactical Air Force.

In 1967, Group Captain Lupton completed the National Defence College course at Fort Frontenac in Kingston, where he then served on the Directing Staff until his retirement from the Canadian Armed Forces in 1975.

*W/C A.J. Mackie
(DND, PL 112534)*

Wing Commander Allan James Mackie, DFC, CD
*Squadron Commander 21 July 1955–3 November 1959,
20 October 1961–1 September 1962*

Allan James Mackie joined the RCAF at Regina on 14 April 1941, trained as a pilot, and obtained his wings at No 11 Service Flying Training School at Yorkton, Saskatchewan on 30 December 1941. Arriving in England early in 1942, he completed operational training and in February 1943 was posted to the Middle East to fly Liberators on bombing missions in North Africa, Italy and the Balkans, first with No 178 Squadron, RAF, and later while attached to the 9th Air Force, USAAF. For his services with the 9th Air Force, he received the U.S. Distinguished Flying Cross. On leaving No 178 Squadron in November 1943, he was posted to a Heavy Conversion Unit in Egypt where he served as an instructor until September 1944. After a period of staff duties at Abu Suweir, he returned to Britain in February 1945, where he joined No 246 Squadron, an RAF transport unit flying Liberators from Lyneham to India and the Middle East. In June 1945, he was posted to No 426 Squadron to fly trooping runs to India. In January 1946, after the first disbandment of No 426 Squadron, he was posted to No 120 (RCAF) Wing at Odiham.

Mackie was repatriated in July 1946 to join the staff of No 2 Air Command in Winnipeg. In October 1946, he was assigned to North West Air Command for duties at No 3 (LF) Loran Slave Station at Dawson Creek, British Columbia. In 1947, he was posted to No 9 (T) Group Headquarters at Rockcliffe in January, and then to No 412 Squadron in March. He joined No 435 Squadron in Edmonton in April 1948, and in September 1950 he proceeded to Toronto to attend the RCAF Staff College. In July 1951, on completion of the course, he was posted to Air Force Headquarters, where he served on the staff until June 1955, when he was appointed to the command of No 426 Squadron. In November 1959, he was sent to England to attend the Joint Services Staff College at Latimer, and he returned to RCAF Station Trenton in March 1960 as Chief Operations Officer. From May to November 1961, he served as Air Operations Officer with the ONUC Air Transport Force in the Congo, and on his return to Canada he again took command of No 426 Squadron, which he held until its second disbandment at St-Hubert in September 1962. Wing Commander Mackie was then transferred to Air Force Headquarters, where he served as a staff officer, first in the Plans Division and later in the Personnel Branch. He retired from the Canadian Armed Forces in October 1968.

W/C J.O. Maitland
(DND, No 426 Squadron)

Wing Commander John Oliver Maitland
Squadron Commander 4 November 1959–18 October 1961

John Oliver Maitland was born in Moose Jaw, Saskatchewan, in May 1920, and educated in Winnipeg, where he joined the RCAF in November 1940, He trained as a pilot, receiving his wings at No 34 Service Flying Training School in Medicine Hat, Alberta, in August 1941. He was then posted overseas to No 23 Operational Training Unit at Pershore, and in December 1941 he and his crew ferried a new Wellington bomber to Shallufa, Egypt, where they joined No 70 Squadron, RAF. Maitland then completed a tour of operations, flying bombing missions against targets in North Africa and the Greek islands.

Maitland returned to No 23 OTU at Pershore as an instructor in October 1942, and in June 1943 he was repatriated to Canada, posted to No 45 Group, RAF Transport Command, at Dorval. On successful completion of training as a captain of transatlantic flights at North Bay, Ontario, he proceeded to No 113 Wing South Atlantic for duties as a check pilot on various aircraft, including those being ferried to Africa. For his services with No 113 Wing, Maitland received the King's Commendation for Valuable Services in the Air. During the summer of 1944, he returned to North Bay as an instructor with No 313 Ferry Training Unit.

In October 1945, he was transferred to No 2 Air Command, RCAF, in Winnipeg, where he served until 1949. He was then assigned to a staff position at North West Air Command Headquarters in Edmonton. In 1953, after two years in command of the search-and-rescue unit at Edmonton, he went to Toronto to attend the RCAF Staff College. He served in the Directorate of Plans and Programs at Air Force Headquarters from 1954 to 1958, when he was posted to No 426 Squadron, becoming Squadron Commander in November 1959. In October 1961, he was posted to the command of No 437 (T) Squadron at RCAF Station Trenton, an appointment he held until 1964 when he became the station's Chief Operations Officer. In 1967, he was posted to Canadian Forces Base Borden as Deputy Base Commander, and he retired from the Canadian Armed Forces in 1969.

APPENDIX G

HONOURS AND AWARDS

OBE: Officer of the Order of the British Empire
MBE: Member of the Order of the British Empire
BEM: British Empire Medal
AFC: Air Force Cross
AFM: Air Force Medal
Queen's Commendation: Queen's Commendation for Valuable Services in the Air

Service Number	Rank	Name	Trade	Honour or Award	Gazette or AFRO Date
22554	Sgt	Bowman, F.M.	FE	Queen's Commendation	13 June 1952
17486	F/L	Burn, R.E.	N	Queen's Commendation	9 January 1953
19812	S/L	Dickson, J.D.	P	AFC	13 June 1952
21603	F/S	Drackley, A.A.	FE	AFM	13 June 1952
30018	F/L	Edwards, R.M.	P	AFC	9 January 1953
23526	S/L	Endersbe, C.E.	RO	Queen's Commendation	13 June 1952
2414	F/S	Englebert, A.L.	MA Tech	BEM	13 June 1952
6552	F/L	Finklestein, A.	N	Queen's Commendation	13 June 1952
16396	Cpl.	Grose, E.C.	ATA	Queen's Commendation	13 June 1952
J13738	F/L	Harrison, D.	P	AFC *	26 July 1946
25880	Sgt.	Howard, G.	FE	Queen's Commendation	9 January 1953
1874	S/L	Lord, W.H.	Tech/AE	MBE	13 June 1952
J15174	S/L	McCutcheon, J.T.	P	AFC *	26 July 1946
22223	Sgt.	McKnight, W.S.	FE	Queen's Commendation	12 June 1953
17600	F/L	Miller, J.B.	P	Queen's Commendation	13 June 1952
19984	S/L	Morrison, H.A.	P	AFC	13 June 1952
19523	W/C	Mussells, C.H.	P	OBE	13 June 1952
26365	F/O	Payne, D.M.	P	AFC	5 June 1952
23347	Sgt.	Potekal, L.C.	FE	Queen's Commendation	9 January 1953

NOTE: * Awards earned on trooping operations. All other awards were earned on *Operation HAWK*.

Service Number	Rank	Name	Trade	Honour or Award	Gazette or AFRO Date
17706	S/L	Ratcliffe, R.E.D.	N	Queen's Commendation	13 June 1952
25233	Cpl.	Reed, G.R.	FE	AFM	12 June 1953
20405	F/L	Smith, W.	RO	Queen's Commendation	13 June 1952
24068	Cpl.	Trudel, J.B.P.A.	Tech/AE	BEM	9 January 1953
25597	F/O	Wilson, J.P.	RO	Queen's Commendation	9 January 1953
25486	F/L	Wolkowski, E.R.	P	Queen's Commendation	1 January 1953

INDEX

INDEX

A
Air Assessment Unit 573, 577
Abu Suweir (Egypt) 513, 516, 521, 532–533
Acceptance and Ferry Flight (No 129, Trenton) 506, 573, 577, 580
Accra 604, 606, 608
Adak (Alaska) 134, 190, 210, 227, 311–312, 370, 377, 388, 397
Adam, F/L B.A. 641, 660
Adams, ACI H.E. 314
Adams, Corporal 384
Adams, Paul 610
Adamson, F/L (S/L) D.R. 316, 360, 500
Adelaide (Australia) 486, 527
Aden 555, 576, 582
Adenauer, Chancellor Konrad 144
Advanced Research Projects Agency 580
Agattu (Alaska) 286
Airborne Brigade Group 182
Air Cadets 86, 103, 111–114, 116, 117, 280, 334, 337, 378, 457, 491
Air Congo 604
aircraft:
  AVRO C-102 Jetliner, 141
  AVRO CF-100 Canuck 161, 166, 356, 397, 450, 561, 590
  AVRO CF-105 Arrow 397, 547, 558–559, 565;
  Beech Aircraft C-45 Expeditor 570;
  Bristol Freighter 332, 579;
  Canadair CL-28 (CP-107) Argus 520, 550, 557, 638;
  Canadair DC-4M North Star 63, 77, 95–99, 103, 115, 132, 171, 179, 423, 474, 642, 663;
  Canadair F-86 Sabre 192, 558
  Canadair CF-104 Starfighter 575, 595, 633, 656, 658;
  Canadair CL-44 (CC-106) Yukon 474, 492, 515, 531, 543, 557, 582, 619, 628, 632, 638–640, 653;
  Consolidated Liberator B. Mk.VI, 18–20;
  de Havilland Comet 337, 369, 513, 532;
  de Havilland DHC-4 Caribou 553, 605, 616;
  de Havilland DH-100 Vampire Mk.1, 100;
  de Havilland Vampire Mk. III, 121;
  de Havilland CS2-F Tracker 617;
  Douglas C-47 Dakota 64;
  Douglas C-124 Globemaster 598, 607–608;

Fairchild C-119 Flying Boxcar 302, 383;
Grumman SA-16 Albatross (Duckbutt) 318;
Lockheed C-130B Hercules 591, 595, 616;
Lockheed P2V-7 Neptune 440;
McDonnell F-101B Voodoo 641;
MiG-15 Jet Fighter 353, 561, 611;
North American F-100 Super Sabre 579
Air Defence Command (RCAF) 315, 342, 370, 482, 536, 593, 633–634, 656
Air Division (No 1 RCAF) 301, 304; Org. Order 25/35 Leap Frog IV, 379; 382, 405; Op. Order 59/54, Composite Squadron, 406; 473, 481–482, 543, 575, 577, 580, 605, 607, 616, 638–639, 647, 653
Air Division (315th USAF) 344
Air France 607
Air Force Day 319–320, 412, 485, 552
Air Force Headquarters: 377, 502, 507–508;
  Air Council 515, 561, 582, 639, 645;
  Logistics Order 1/55, RAF CF-100 evaluation 450;
  Op. Directive 125/58, Jump Moat 553;
  Op. Order
    1/50, Arctic Re-supply 161,
    1/56 Nimble Bat 481,
    100/57 Jump Moat 536,
    443/59 Lookout 580;
  Org. Order
    50/52 No 2(F) Wing 336,
    27/53 No 4(F) Wing 365,
    49/53 No 4(T) OTU relocation 378,
    52/54 No 1(F) Wing 426,
    8.12 No 115 ATU 538,
    8.2 ATC Unit relocation 565,
    8.9.5 Air Assessment Unit 573,
    8.9.1 437 Squadron 646,
    8.2.1(6) 426 Squadron 659
airlift operation (planning) 135–136
Air Materiel Base 301
Air Material Command (RCAF) 132, 141, 169, 185, 406, 481, 582, 592, 612–613
Air Movements Unit (No 2), 457, 513, 419, 519, 529, 531, 548, 577
Air Movements Unit (No 5, Langar) 631
Air Movements Unit (No 6, Paris) 631

Air Navigation School 363
air reconnaissance 244
Air Traffic Handling Unit No 901 (Rockcliffe) 102, 165, 186
Air Training Corps (UK, cadets) 642
Air Transport Board 358, 400
Air Transport Command (RCAF): 62, 103, 110, 116, 165, 182–183, 185, 194; Org. Order 3/50, 220; 224, 229, 257; Org. Order 49/52, 332; 336, 341, 376–377, 384, 405–406, 412, 419, 424, 427, 433, 450, 455, 461–462, 474, 477, 481–482, 485–486, 492, 497, 501, 503, 513, 516, 525, 530–531, 533, 536 547–549, 557, 564–565, 570, 576–578, 582, 602, 606–607, 612, 614, 625, 631–633, 638, 641, 644, 647, 656, 659
Air Transport Force (Congo) 613–614
Air Transport Tactical Development Unit 20
Air Transport Unit (ATU/CAN UNEF) 502, 513, 531, 543
Air Transport Unit (No 115, El Arish) 538, 561, 565, 577, 588, 600, 605, 616, 628, 634, 642, 646, 654, 656
Aitken, Kate 310
Akron (Ohio) 554
Alaskan Air Command 398
Albertville (Congo) 612
Albrecht, Mr. 522
Albrook AFB 596–597, 599
Alert (NWT) 161, 261, 336, 366, 387, 402, 406, 419, 427, 432, 440, 483, 508, 520, 524, 531–532, 537, 545–546, 548, 551, 554–555, 564, 566–569, 576, 591 593–594, 601, 611, 632, 635, 639, 642–644, 646, 654–655
Alexander of Tunis, Viscount 145, 149, 172, 173, 260, 288
Alexandra Fjord (NWT) 432, 508, 564
Alford, Surgeon LCdr 121
Allan, F/L E.A. 27, 42
Allen, F/L G.W. 139, 143, 147, 191, 218, 277, 280, 304, 320, 332
Allan, W/C J.F. 375, 379–381
Allesy, Mr. 454
Allied Air Forces Central Europe 384
Allied Air Forces Southern Europe 554
Allied Tactical Air Force (No 4) 340
Allister, Major 113
Alliston, F/O (F/L) T. 77, 87, 91, 100, 101, 110, 111, 118
Almond, MGen E.M. 216

789

Alvarez del Castello, Ambassador Dr. José Manuel 367–368
Amchitka (Alaska) 286
Amsterdam (Schiphol Airport) 149, 167, 337, 360
Anchorage (Elmendorf AFB) 134, 185, 189–190, 209, 212, 222, 227–228, 264, 276–277, 286–287, 291, 293–294, 304, 306, 308, 311, 315, 321, 345–346, 348, 370, 377, 384, 403–404, 410–411
Anderson, F/L E. 75, 79
Anderson, F/O H. 480, 483, 489
Anderson, Gen. Sir Kenneth 536
Andrew, Mr. 530
Andrews AFB 183, 599
Annis, A/C (AVM) C.L. 411, 554
Annis, F/L R.H. 482
Antofagasta (Chile) 598
Antung (Manchuria) 256
Aquitania (Cunard Liner) 289
Arctic Bay (NWT) 229, 305, 348, 356, 366, 387, 427, 432, 508, 518
Arctic Re-Supply 161, 165, 167–168, 171, 173, 263, 284, 313–314, 387, 482, 494, 520, 523, 548, 590, 616, 632, 635, 646
Arctic Weather Stations 401, 611, 632, 646
Argentia NAS 430, 464, 632
Armée nationale congalaise 630
Arnold, F/O Bob 611
Ascension Island 580, 589–590, 617–618
asco-gyro system 281, 363, 442
Ashdown, W/C H.C. 46
Ashiya (Japan) 243, 257, 262
Ashman, W/C R.A. 365
Aswan High Dam 495
Athens 420, 429, 452, 489, 533, 547, 556, 573, 581, 588, 611, 638, 657–659
Atkinson Field (British Guiana) 136, 617
Attlee, Prime Minister Clement 174
Attu (Alaska) 212
Auckland (New Zealand) 137
Austin, W/C (G/C) G.S. 292–293, 308, 321, 338
Austin, F/O R.J. 316
Australia 174, 485
Austrian Red Cross 498
AVRO Canada Limited 161, 166, 535, 559, 561

B

Badgely, F/L J.A. 31, 36, 39, 48
Bahrain 424, 464, 475, 480, 486, 488, 527, 534
Bain, J. 98

Baine, WO2 C.W. 189, 289–290, 337, 369
Baird, F/L T,.M. 411, 419
Baker, Pte. A. 367
Baker, Cpl. 290
Baker Lake (NWT) 90
Baker, R. 98
Baldwin, J.R. 400–401
Ballerini, F/O B.S. 47
Ballykelly (Northern Ireland) 648
Baltimore 575
Banks, F/O (F/L) E.L. 82, 85, 89, 120, 137–138, 140, 142, 167, 225, 229, 244, 254–255, 264
Banks, Sgt. 290
Banyard, F/O I.S. 636
Barber, Sgt. (F/S) E.S. 189, 222
Barber, F/L R.R. 337
Barbey, RAdm. D.E. 224
Barker, F/O E.A. 482
Barnett, AM Sir Denis 632
Barrett, W/C 109
Barriefield Camp (Kingston) 607–608
Barrow, Sgt. 290
Barter Island (Alaska) 121, 397
Bascomb, F/L S.A. 110, 119, 130
base: No 63 Leeming, 5,6;
    No 62 (Beaver) Linton-on-Ouse 7, 113, 145
Basra (Iraq) 422, 426, 430, 456, 464
BAT Flight: Bramcott 17; Wymeswold 17
Bates, Reuben C. 596
Battle of Britain Sunday 116, 284, 338, 423, 460, 494, 578
Bayliss, F/O (F/L) R.C.M. 90, 141
Bayne, F/O R.J. 141
Baynton, S/L W.L. 255,
Beach, F/L (S/L) A.M. 220, 314
Bean, A/C W.W. 607
Beath, F/L J. 494
Beaton, F/S 464
Beaudet, Captain 33
Beauvechain (Belgium) 536–537, 546, 549, 552
Becker, S/L W.P. 544, 554
Beirut (Lebanon) 483, 486, 492, 526–527, 555
Beko, LAC 160
Belair, F/L 514, 522, 591
Belanger, Father 519
Belanger, Capt. Gerald 637
Bélanger, LAC J.G.A. 561
Belanger, Cpl. J.H. 137
Belém 590, 617–618
Belgium 601–602
Belgian Air Force 513, 552
Belgrade 526
Belize City (British Honduras) 647
Bell, LAC E.W. 192

Bell, W/C J.F.M. 597
Bell, F/L J.R. 139–141, 147, 168, 191, 219, 222, 284, 286
Bell Telephone 440, 488, 550
Belyea, F/O J.L. 346
Bennett, Col. T.A. 188, 193, 221, 243, 293
Bennett, A/C W.E. 315
Bergin, Cpl. Joe 369
Berlin Airlift 109, 111, 116–118, 135, 180
Berlin Wall 633–635, 656, 658
Bermuda (Kindley AFB) 170, 255, 247–248, 451–453, 497, 507, 517, 560, 591, 593, 617, 631, 655
Bernatchez, Brig. (MGen.) J.P.E. 171, 367, 371
Berriosa, Lt. Sergio 598
Berthiaume, Col. J. 602, 604
Berton, Pierre 251
Beurling, G.F. (Buzz) 105
Big Owl (Ontario) 566
Bilik, F/O P. 255
Bindoff, Maj. R.C. 608
Binette, F/O J.J.C. 290
Bion, F/O 116
Birchall, G/C (A/C) L.J. 170, 634
Bishop, F/L (S/L) A.W. 107, 170
Bishop, F/L L.M. 79–80, 83
Bissonnette, LAC J.L. 548
Bjarnson, F/O D.H. 37
Black, F/L C.K. 505–506, 518–519, 523, 530, 533, 535
Blackburn, S/L A.P. 119
Blagrave, G/C R.D.P. 461
Blaine, A/C D.S. 359
Bliss, F/L W.H.F. 355
Blowers, Sgt. 249
Boby, F/O (F/L) J.H.C. 77, 103, 110, 111, 118, 139
Bocking, W/C A.I. 118, 135
Bohn, F/O N.E. 143, 189
Boland, F/L (S/L) E.J.J. 141, 189, 229, 255, 346
Bolte, General 138
Bombay 530, 576, 582
Bomber Mail 95
Bond, Colonel 118
Bordeaux (France) 571–572
Boss, Bill 371
Bothwell, W/C W.A. 515
Bouchard, L. 85–86
Boulet, Sgt. 345–346
Bourgeois, F/O J. 642
Boville, B. 221
Bowen, Ivor 356
Bowhill, ACM Sir Frederick 95
Bowman, Sgt. F.S. 189, 322, 337, 369
Boyce, F/L A.J. 64–65
Boyd, F/L 104

Boyd, F/O J. 86
Boyle, F/O J. 3
Boyle, G/C N.J. 170
Bradford, F/L A.J. 121
Bradshaw, F/L K.T. 475
Braham, W/C J.R.D. 336, 341
Brasseur, Sgt. George 641
Bray, F/L N. 102
Brazzaville (Republic of Congo), 604, 607
Breadner, AM L.S. 4, 61, 62
Bricker, S/L C.D. 316–317
Brisbane (Australia) 137
Brisbois, F/L H. 185
British Cable and Wireless Company 618
British Commonwealth Scientific Conference 555
British Overseas Airways Corporation (BOAC) 132, 288, 290, 369, 370, 430
Broadfoot, F/O (F/L) M.D. 179, 187, 189, 217, 219, 228, 241, 249, 251, 275–278, 283–284, 286, 290, 307, 369–370, 405
Broadley, W/C G. 521
Brock, Captain J.V. 180
Brockington, L.W. 405–406
Brodeur, F/L P.V. 117
Brogden, Sgt. J.G. 403–404, 430–431
Broken Arrow 165
Bromiley, Col. Richard F. 214, 221, 228, 242–243, 260
Brooks, F/O M. 252, 254, 338
Brousseau, F/O L.R.A. 337
Brown, Colonel 242–243
Brown, F/L C. 369
Brown, F/L C.A.T. 565–566, 572
Brown, LAC C.W. 137
Brown, F/L G. 589
Brown, Cpl R.J. 81
Brown, F/O (F/L) R.J. 84, 87–89, 91, 99, 100, 110, 112, 120–121, 137, 140–141, 243, 250, 253, 257, 265, 276, 292, 315, 317
Browning, F/O Barry 633
Brownridge, S/L D.D. 27
Brush, Robert R. 98
Brussels 337, 552
Bryans, AVM J.G. 522, 576–578
Buchan, F/L W.J. 265, 277–278, 308, 311, 337, 483
Buchans (Newfoundland) 107, 589
Buckle, G/C N.R. 40
Budgeon, F/O B.J. 248, 316, 332, 333, 366, 367
Buechler, F/O H.M. 255,
Buechler F/O (F/L) L.W. 451, 455, 475, 477, 489, 493, 514, 518, 520, 528, 530, 535, 543

Bunche, Dr. Ralph 603
Bunker Hill AFB 612
Burbank, G/C S.R. 377
Burgess, LAC A.R. 548
Burn, F/L R.E. 309, 355, 361–362
Burnet, F/O A.G. 90
Burnett, F/L A.H. 514
Burns, MGen (LGen) E.L.M. 496, 500–501, 524, 561
Burns, F/O L.S. 255
Burns, F/O V. 42
Burton, Sgt. 618
Burtt, Mayor Ross 576
Burwash Landing (Yukon) 107
Bury, S/L G.J. 141
Busk, A/C 104
Bussieres, F/O G. 604
Butchart, F/L W.I. 315, 336, 349, 361, 419
Butcher, W/C (G/C) E.M. 646
Butler, F/L M.C. 42
Butt, F/O A. 388
Buxton, F/O C. 86
Buzden, LCdr. John 280
Buzza, S/L W.J. 355, 379
Byford, F/L (W/C) A.J.P. 139, 167, 181, 187 189–190, 229, 244
Byrne, F/O L.F. 488, 493, 504–505, 507, 516, 533, 537, 550

C

Cabinet Defence Committee 182, 248, 314, 358, 399, 401, 450
Cagliari (Sardinia) 499, 503, 527, 580
Cahill, W/C J.E. 46
Cairns, S/L N.D. 497, 507, 528
Cairo 170
Cairo West, 35, 50
Calcutta 422–424, 426, 430, 456, 459, 464, 488, 490, 526, 528, 530, 555
Calgary (Alberta) 169, 321, 334, 378
Cambridge Bay (NWT) 120, 397, 427, 479, 517, 522, 545, 565–566, 593, 634, 656
Cameron, Brig. H.L. 224
Cameron, G/C (A/C) R.A. 170, 607
Cameron, F/L W.J. 37
Camire, F/O J.W.J.P. 290
Campbell, Flight Officer A.L. 31, 36, 47
Campbell, Sgt. Frank 641
Campbell, AVM (AM) H.L. 365, 532, 534, 557, 578, 582, 602, 613, 635, 640, 656
Campbell, F/L J.B. 119
Campbell-Rogers, F/L I.F. 84, 111
Campney, Hon. Ralph 260, 410
Canada Carries On series 65
Canada House (Tempsford), 17, 20, 39, 40, 42, 47

Canada-United States Military Study Group 396
Canada-United States Permanent Joint Board on Defence 138, 320
Canadair Limited 97, 98, 115, 404, 424, 456, 461, 480, 520, 575, 582, 640
Canadian Arsenals (Staff Houses) 85, 87, 111, 251
Canadian Armament and Research Development Establishment (CARDE) 580, 589
Canadian Army 473, 563, 568, 591, 607
Canadian Army Special Force (25th Cdn. Inf. Bde.) 191, 220–221, 225–226, 250, 251, 260, 382, 400–401
Canadian Army Staff College 293, 308, 477, 631, 635
Canadian Aviation 131
Canadian Aviation Electronics Ltd. 348
Canadian Base Unit Middle East (CBUME) 500, 504, 519
Canadian Coast Guard Service(CCGS): C.D. Howe 422, 455, 458–459, 490–491, 524, 531, 554, 610; D'Iberville 422, 455, 524, 528, 531, 554; N.B. MacLean 422, 455, 458, 524, 531, 554; Edward Cornwallis 524; Labrador 554
Canadian Corps of Commissioners 113
Canadian Defence Liaison Staff (London) 290, 547
Canadian Government Trans-Atlantic Air Service 95
Canadian Headquarters (ONUC) 608
Canadian Infantry Brigade Group (No 4) 575, 610, 615–616, 653
Canadian Infantry Brigade (27th) 274
Canadian Infantry Workshop (No 56) 501
Canadian International Air Show 578
Canadian Joint Air Training Centre (Rivers, Manitoba) 133, 147, 169, 288, 293, 302, 306, 463, 555, 558
Canadian Joint Staff (Washington) 399, 607, 610
Canadian Legion Memorial Building (Montreal) 148
Canadian National Exhibition 334
Canadian Pacific Airlines (CPA) 134, 137, 192, 273, 314–315, 331–332, 344, 358, 369, 398–401, 432, 450
Canadian Red Cross 291, 379, 475, 483, 488, 538, 543, 596
Canadian Reconnaissance Squadron (No 56) 519, 564
Canadian Sector (Arctic) 569
Canadian Signals Squadron (No 56) 501

Canadian Signals Squadron (No 57) 608
Canadian Signals Unit (No 57) 608
Canadian Transport Company (No 56) 501
Canadian Vickers 96
Canton Island 137, 486, 527, 530, 582
Cape Perry 165
Cape Parry (NWT) 397, 593, 656
Cape Dyer (NWT) 397, 593, 634
Cape Canaveral 568, 580, 618, 655
Capodichino airfield (Naples) 502, 504–507, 513, 515–516, 521–522, 532, 538, 543
Capreol, Lee, 108
Capriano, F/S 369
Carew, F/L R.D. 355
Carl, Cpl. 291
Carling, F/L H.E. 112, 118, 134
Carmichael, F/O D.G. 322, 345–346
Carnegie, AVM 82
Carpenter A/C F.S. 398–399, 429, 490–491, 493–494, 501, 509, 519, 521–522, 524, 530, 532, 534, 537, 543, 552, 554, 564–545, 569, 577–578, 594, 603–605, 608, 628, 632, 634–635, 640–641
Carr, S/L (G/C) W.K. 317, 422, 558, 605, 612–616
Carrol, C.A. 251
Carscallen, A/C H.M. 359, 361, 421, 427, 452–453, 462–464, 483–484, 487, 490–491
Carss, F/O (F/L) W.B. 441–448, 458, 461–462, 477, 483, 488, 493, 497, 503, 505
Casey, F/L W.P. 79
Casselman, F/O M.G. 322, 348, 360, 377, 383, 406
Cassino (Italy) 536
Castel Benito (Tripoli) 18, 24, 35, 50
Cay, S/L 550–551
Central Experimental and Proving Establishment (Rockcliffe/Uplands) 86, 129, 378, 479, 559, 580, 619, 632, 640, 642
Central Flying School (Trenton) 567
Central Air Command (RCAF): 102, 132; Band 83
Central Navigation School 550, 569, 590, 595, 639, 642, 657
Central Ordnance Depot (No 26 Coburg) 578
Chabot, Cpl. K.F. 137
Chambers, F/O L. 77
Chandler, F/O P.J.L. 255
Chapdelaine, Mr. 365
Chapman, W/C (G/C) C.G.W. 75, 77–81, 83–84, 86–87, 89–91, 101–106, 108–109, 111–116, 118–120, 122, 130, 616, 640

Charchuk, F/O (F/L) T. 383, 388–389, 459, 461–463, 488, 489, 517–518, 524, 528, 546, 558, 566, 572, 575, 591–592, 604
Charleston AFB 549, 551, 596–597, 599
Charters, F/O A.L. 255, 322, 338
Chateaudun (France) 571, 656–659
Chaulk, F/L R.G. 369
Chesterfield Tobacco Company 222
Chevalier, Sgt E. 492
Chief Mathais 263
Chiefs of Staffs Committee 182, 331, 345, 358
Chile 596–600
Chilean Air Force 597, 636
Chilean Disaster Committee 596
Chou En Lai 432
Chrétien, Mr. 508
Chrismas, F/O W.C. 83
Christmas 47, 68, 92, 122, 151, 228, 294–295, 349, 390, 434, 464, 537–538, 560–561, 583, 619, 648
Churchill (Manitoba) 74, 84, 90–91, 105, 107, 138–139, 147, 167–168, 171, 229, 245, 275, 281, 293–294, 306–307, 313, 315–316, 320, 333–334, 336, 338, 348–349, 356, 359–361, 363, 366, 370, 377–379, 382–384, 402–403, 405, 419–420, 422, 427, 429, 432, 440–441, 449, 451, 456–458, 461–464, 482–483, 485, 488–489, 493–494, 497, 506–508, 514, 517–519, 522, 524, 528, 530, 534, 544, 546, 550, 552, 554–557, 559, 569, 576, 590–591, 594, 601, 611, 616, 627, 631–632, 634, 639, 654, 657
Churchill, F/L R.E. 290, 291, 294
Churchill, Prime Minister Winston 7
Clark, F/O Bob 121
Clark Field (Philippines) 425, 431
Clark, Capt. J. 591
Clark, Gen. Mark W. 301, 354
Clark, MGen. (LGen) S.F. 378, 477, 557, 602, 616
Clarke, S/L D.R.L. 16
Clarke, F/L W. 581
Claveau, LAC René 193
Claxton, Hon. Brooke 88, 107, 122, 144–145, 149, 166–167, 181, 186, 224, 226, 248, 260, 263, 295, 303, 314, 317, 331, 333, 339, 363, 396, 399–400, 405–406, 408–410, 450
Clement, W/O 463
Clements, F/L R.S. 64
Clements, G/C W.I. 168, 194, 280
Cleminson, F/O F.R. 440
Clifton, F/O (F/L) D.F. 380–381, 403, 419–421, 429

Cline, F/O W.A. 463, 484
Clough, F/O W.J. 100
Clyde River (NWT) 508
Coates, F/L J. 644
Coates, WO2 J.S.L. 137
Coates, F/L R. 143, 147, 169, 171, 185, 191
Cobus, S/L A.E. 365
Cochrane, AM Sir Ralph A. 17, 38, 40, 49
Cohen, Leonard 105
Cold Bay (Alaska) 210, 276, 309, 346, 370, 397, 399
Cole, S/L 364–365
Collège militaire royal 591
Collins, Sgt. F.E. 613
Colombo (Ceylon) 157, 530
Colorado Springs 616
Commonwealth Air Force Memorial 575
Communications Flight No 114 (Capodichino) 502, 513, 516, 538
Communications Flight No 115 (Abu Suweir) 502, 513, 516, 532–533, 538
Communications and Rescue Flight (No 105 Namao) 557
Communications Unit (No 102 Trenton) 577
Communications Unit (No 121 Sea Island) 577
Comptois, Hon. Paul 656
Congo (Democratic Republic of the) 601, 604
Connolly, F/O Don 252, 254, 291, 295, 320
Continental Shelf Project 566, 593
Cook, F/O D.T. 48
Cook, F/O R.H. 322, 332–333, 360, 381–383, 387, 423, 427, 431, 432
Cooling, S/L C.C. 553, 577
Cooper, Mr. 133
Copenhagen 568, 615, 632, 658
Coquilhatville (Congo) 609
Coral Harbour (NWT) 90, 112, 275, 307, 315–316, 348, 356, 359, 366, 370–371, 377, 379, 383–384, 419, 421–422, 452, 458, 475, 488–489, 494, 506, 514, 517, 522, 530, 552, 559
Corbeil, Cpl E.C. 489
Corpus Christi NAS 367–368
Costello, A/C M. 132, 171
Coté, F/L J.Y.A. 459
Cottrell, F/L V.E. 627
Courrier, Cpl. 291
Courtney, Mr. 455
Coutts, Cpl. 291
Cowan, F/L S.F. 78, 79, 80, 82, 87, 90, 100, 104–106, 107, 109, 110, 114

Cowell, C. 186
Cox, F/L 337, 383
Cox, G/C R.M. 365
Craig, S/L F.Y. 139, 141
Craig Harbour (NWT) 356, 387, 432
Craig, F/O W.A. 32, 46
Crawford, F/L G.W. 31
Crawley, Al 105
Creeper, F/L J.E. 84
Crerar, Gen. H.D.G. 66
Creteau, F/O (F/L) T.P.L. 255, 322
Cronje, F/O A.B. 27, 48
Cronk, Cpl. 173
Crown Assets Disposal Corporation 565
Culp, F/O (F/L) P.S. 453, 464, 482, 485, 491
Cumming, F/O R.J. 143
Cunningham, LCol. 114
Cunningham, Gen. Sir Allan 105
Cunningham, F/L J.E. 39
Curaçao (Dutch West Indies) 617
Curtis, AM W.A. 102, 111, 119, 144–145, 164, 166, 180–182, 186, 214, 224–225, 301, 344, 359, 363, 665
Cuthbertson, S/L D.R. 523
Cuthill, S/L J. 580
Cyprus 496
Czechoslovakia 495

D

Dagg, F/L A.G. 83
Dahr, Sgt. A. 581
Daines, Lt. D.B. 186
Dakar 136, 170, 555, 559, 574, 576, 582, 602, 606, 608, 646
Dalton, F/L J.T. 141
Dar-es-Salaam (Tanganika) 634
Darwent, F/O John 338
Darwin (Australia) 486, 527, 582
Davidge, F/L W.J. 577
Davidson, W/C R.T.P. 331
Davison, F/O A.M. 15, 47
Day, S/L W.S. 419
de Seversky, Major Paul 108
de Niverville, AVM J.L. 108, 378
de Havilland Aircraft Co. 136, 370, 617
de Siervo, G. 515
De Quoy, F/O J.L.A. 346
De Benedito, Capt. 522
De Merlis, Guy 250
Decimomannu (Sardinia) 499, 525, 527, 550–551, 553, 556, 558, 568, 575, 578, 581, 592, 595, 600, 611
Deeprose F/L D.F. 402, 410–411, 419, 440–448
Defence Research Board 356, 362, 405, 485, 517, 519, 522, 527, 530
Defence Research Establishment (Suffield) 108, 518, 575

Dekoyer, G. 134
Delaney, W/C P.S. 423, 462, 474, 483–484, 490, 514, 521, 534
Delfino, Gen. 571
Delhi 157
Delmotte, S/L A.D.J. 530, 535, 544–545
Demeter, Sgt. 563, 574
Deneau, F/O V.M. 280
Denis, F/O J.-L. 225, 243, 248, 279, 281
Denomy, F/L B.C. 112, 121, 140
Department of External Affairs 525
Department of Mines and Technical Surveys 593
Department of Munitions and Supply 97
Department of National Defence 528
Department of Northern Affairs and National Resources 633
Department of Public Works 565
Department of Transport 387, 401, 419, 421, 455, 457–458, 461, 480, 487, 519, 524, 528, 531, 548, 551, 554, 563, 566, 644
Derash, Cpl. 462
Derbyshire, F/O (Mr.) T.J. 64–68, 112, 591
Desautels, LCol. P.M. 108, 186
Desbeins, W/O 475
Desroches, Cpl. 534
Deyell, S/L L.S. 570
D-Day 288
Dhahran (Saudi Arabia) 478
Diaichi Building (Tokyo) 312
Diamond, G/C G.G. 321
Dick, F/L W. 402, 426–427, 430–431, 451, 453–454, 547
Dickson, F/L (S/L) J.D. 78, 84, 90–92, 100, 103, 107, 112, 114–115, 119–121, 138–139, 142, 149, 163, 166, 170–171, 189–190, 219, 257, 279, 284, 321, 322, 369, 371
Dickson, AVM W.F. 44, 46
Diefenbaker, Prime Minister John G. 558, 602, 607, 644
Dien Bien Phu 407
Dieppe Raid (10th Anniversary) 337
Dinsmore, S/L 21, 22
Directional Gyro Indicator 361
Directorate of Air Transport Command (AFHQ) 61, 62
disaster relief:
  Agadir, Morocco 592;
  British Honduras 647
  British West Indies 283;
  Calcutta 422;
  Chile 596–600;
  Greece 379, 489;
  India 464, 475, 488;
  Italy 291–292;
  Lebanon 483;
  Netherlands 360;
  Pakistan 464;
Distant Early Warning (DEW) Line 396–397, 474, 518, 556
Djakarta (Indonesia) 486, 527, 530, 582
Dobbin, S/L K.C.M. 356
Doherty, F/L 45
Donald, F/O J.D. 355
Dorchester Penitentiary 289
Dorval airport (Montreal) 74, 75, 83, 85, 91, 103, 105–107, 109, 112–114, 117, 119, 121, 135, 137–138, 145, 147, 149, 159, 167, 172–173, 184–185, 187, 193, 223, 244, 253, 264, 275, 279, 281, 283, 287–295, 304, 306, 308, 311, 313–314, 317, 333–334, 339, 346, 348–349, 357–358, 360–361, 367–368, 371, 377–378, 380, 382–383, 386,–387, 402, 410–411, 420–421, 423, 426–427, 432, 440–441, 448–453, 455, 460, 476, 478, 480, 484–487
Douglas, Dr. A.E. 356
Douglas Aircraft 96
Douglas, Col. D. 502
Douglas, W/C R.F. 337–338, 368
Downey, Cpl. Vern 641
Doyle, F/L G.W. 338
Doyle, G/C M.G. 29, 46
Drackley, Sgt. (F/S) A.A. 137, 322
Drury C.M. (Bud) 279, 400–401
Dubbo (Australia) 137
Duccet, Major 105
Duckbutt 318, 376
Dugal, LCpl. P. 367
Duke, F/L V.W. 174
Dulles, John Foster 242
Dunford, F/O D.M. 422, 428–429, 432, 451, 461, 479
Dunlap, AVM C.R. 138
Dunn, LCol. V. 578
Dunphy, S/L W.H. 102
Dupuis, Cpl. 291
Durand, Paul 193, 225

E

Eagles, Cpl. D. 431, 485
Earl, Cdre. P. 371
Eastern Air Command (RCAF) 6, 64
Easy, Sgt. Horace 369
Ebisu Camp, 190, 311, 410
Eckblow, Mr. 108
Eden, Sir Anthony 306, 407
Edey, WO1 E. 218
Edwards, W/C (G/C) G.J.J. 461, 515, 567
Edwards, W/C J.F. 336, 339

Edwards, F/O (F/L) R.M. 136, 187, 222, 241, 248, 257–259, 278–279, 294, 305, 315, 317, 321, 332, 355, 369, 494
Egan, F/L Jack 322, 345–346
Eglin AFB 483, 568
Egypt 495
Egyptian Army 588
Eielson AFB 164, 222, 321
Eisenhower, President Dwight D. 331, 354, 575
El Adem (Tobruk) 38
El Aouina (Tunis) 36, 46, 47, 50
El Arish (Egypt) 532–533, 538, 543–544, 546–547, 549, 553, 556, 558, 561, 563, 568, 573–574, 577–579, 583, 587–588, 595, 600, 608, 610–611, 627–629, 632–634, 636, 638–640, 642–643, 645–647, 654–660
El Goléa (Algeria) 605
El Paso 477
Electric Boat Company 98
Elevsis airfield (Greece) 379, 550, 581
Elizabethville (Congo) 601, 609, 630
Elliott, S/L G.E.F. 20
Elmas Airfield (Cagliari) 580
Elviss, F/L J.A. 21, 42
Ely, F/L E.B. 3
Emery, ACI (Cpl.) 102, 384
Emond, F/L C.E. 242, 262
Empey, Sgt. C. 492
Empress of France 302
Endersbe, F/L (S/L) C.E. 139, 254
Englebert, WO2 A.I. 322
English, Mr. 458
Eniwetok Atoll 354
entertainment (Britain):
  W-Debs 16;
  All Clear Show 22;
  Airscrews 25;
  Westernaires 25;
  Thunderbird Orchestra 39;
  Flying Home Troupe 45
entertainment (Canada):
  Montreal Troupe, Goose Bay 310;
  Legion Variety Show, Greenwood 314;
  Legion Show, Goose Bay 368;
  Montreal Troupe, Resolute Bay 402;
  Legion Stage Show, Goose Bay 402;
  Bell Canada Troupe, Resolute Bay 400;
  Royal Canadian Legion, Goose Bay 478;
  Bell Canada Troupe, Resolute Bay 514;
  Bell Canada Troupe, Knob Lake 549;
  Bell Canada Troupe, Northern Bases, 559;
  Canadair Troupe, Northern Bases 583;
  CBC Troupe, Northern Bases 590
entertainment (Europe/Middle East):
  Scandinavian Group, El Arish 610;
  CBC Troupe, El Arish 633–634;
  CBC Troupe, El Arish 657
Equipment Depot No 1, Weston 83
Equipment Depot No 5, Moncton 81, 83
Erickson, ACI H.C. 314
Erimo (Hokkaido) 385
Eskisehir (Turkey) 420, 429
Eureka (NWT) 161, 167, 261, 284, 336, 363, 366, 387, 401, 419, 421, 427, 432, 440, 461, 508, 520, 524, 531–532, 546, 548, 551, 646
Evans, F/L F.W. 331
Evans, F/L J.P.H. 383, 390
Evill, AM Sir Douglas 4
exercise:
  Sweet Briar 145, 158, 160, 162, 164, 169;
  Buckreadie 169;
  Sundog II, 245;
  Sea Green 261;
  Sundog III, 307;
  Bull Dog 359;
  Carte Blanche (NATO) 454

F

Fairbanks (Alaska) 134, 209, 257, 321
Fairbanks, D. 553
Fairchild Aircraft 302
Far East Airlift Task Force 214
Farmer, F/O D.S. 494
Farnborough Air Show 179
Farrell F/O D.C. 241, 316
Fasken, Lorna 50
Faurot, S/L V.J. 361
Fawcett, G/C G.M. 260
Fawcett, F/L W.J.E. 567–568, 576, 589–590, 629, 639
Fayid (Egypt) 157
Federal Republic of Germany 144
Ferguson, LAC Bert 192
FIDO 286
Field Engineer Squadron (21st, The Pas) 378
Fieldman, F/O A.F. 187
Filleul, F/O H.J. 316
Fine, F/L E.L. 566
Finklestein, F/O (F/L) A. 222, 248, 254, 322
Fisher, F/O G. 84, 160, 255
Fisher, S/L G.C. 255
Fisher F/O (F/L) G.W. 80, 160, 255
Fitzgerald, S/L C.J. 16
Fitzsimmons, Inspector 557
Flanagan, F/L J. 499

Fleishman, F/L H.E. 17
Fleming, F/L J.C. 290
Fleming, F/O S.B. 301
Flemming, LAC L.M. 137
Fletcher, Captain 17
Flewelling, F/L G.W. 322
Flight Technical Training Unit (No 4) 577
flood relief:
  Winnipeg 104; 171
  Vancouver 106;
  British Columbia 107, 173;
Flying Instructors School 577
Flying Cheetah Squadron 461
Flynn, F/L R.R. 646
Folinea, Col. 502, 522, 532
Forbell, W/C H.C. 570–572
Forbes, LAC 322
Forbes, F/O T.S. 100
Force publique (Congo) 601
Forde, F.M. 145
Fordyce, A.N. 485–487
Forest, F/O (F/L) J.A.R.J. 439, 440, 464, 475, 479, 489, 491–492, 519, 606
Forrest, F/L D.G. 89, 115
Forsythe, Mrs. 100
Fort Chimo, 80, 110, 148, 294, 305, 307
Fort Lewis, 221, 225, 252, 260
Fort Nelson (British Columbia) 105, 122, 333, 360, 383, 386
Fort Norman (NWT) 138
Fort St. John (British Columbia) 140
Fort William (Ontario) 288
Fortier, Cpl. Chuck 369
Fortier, Dr. Y.O. 454
Fosberry, Col. 628
Foster, MGen. H.W. 288
Foulkes, LGen. Charles 149, 164
Fournier, Capt. 554
Fox, S/L W.H. 355
Foye, S/L S.H. 319
Franklin, B. 96, 97
Franks, W/C W.R. 99
Fraser, Inspector 594
Fraser, F/L R.H. 36
Fraser-Harris, Capt. A.B.F. 515
Frederkiewicz, Dr. A. 78
French Air Force 430, 571, 656
French, W/C D.T. 168
Frobisher Bay (NWT) 109, 134, 162, 165, 244, 255, 275, 279, 293–294, 305, 308, 333, 347, 357, 361, 377, 379, 440, 508, 522, 571, 573, 642, 656
Fukuoka (Japan) 134
Fullam, F/O J.G. 482
Fulton, Sgt. 112
Fusiliers de Sherbrooke 288

G

Gagarin, Maj. Yuri 635
Gagnon, F/O Paul 252, 254
Gagnon, F/O R.E. 463–464
Galen, F/L H.J. 82
Galipeau, F/O J. 136
Gallagher, S/L (W/C) N.J. 137, 537
Galley, F/O C.S. 48
Galloway, W/C (G/C) D.E. 135, 567
Gander airport (Newfoundland) 65, 66, 83, 108, 138, 157, 292, 371, 377, 379, 381, 422, 456, 463–464, 477, 480, 486, 491, 504–505, 507, 602, 608, 627, 630, 636, 638, 659
Gardiner, LAC R.E. 47
Gardner, W. 186
Garnett, S/L W.M. 280
Gates, F/O C.R. 77
Gauthier, F/O C.J.W. 254, 347
Gauthier, F/O J.A. 187
Gawne, F/L H.G. 594, 617–619, 654, 656–657
Gaza 532, 588
Gellner, W/C J. 357
Genge, F/L B.V. 574, 632, 648
Geoffrion, F/S J.D. 38
George AFB 595, 627
Georgetown (Ascension Island) 618
Gerding, F/O (F/L) A.F. 255, 315, 360, 363
German Democratic Republic 144
Gervais, S/L C.L.V. 364–365
Gibb, G/C R.F. 104, 116, 121, 138, 194
Gibraltar 141, 157, 170, 292, 379, 423, 456, 664, 492, 505, 527, 556, 558, 605
Gibson, Cpl. 522
Gibson, Hon. Colin 63, 107
Gibson, Constable R. 463
Gilbert, F/O A.A. 140
Giles, F/O (F/L) H.T. 64, 68, 73–75, 79–81, 84, 87, 90, 91, 101–104, 106, 108–114, 118, 120, 136, 139, 147, 149, 157, 229, 244, 255
Gill, F/L R.T.L. 565–566, 587, 591, 593, 602, 606
Gill, F/L W. 46
Gillespie, G/C W.L. 521
Gilmour, F/L J.H. 115
Gilmour, F/O (F/L) R.A. 108, 132
Glenn, C. 98
Glenn, John 655
Glover, F/O C.E. 21, 35, 36
Glover, F/L E.A. 355, 380
Glover, F/O (F/L) R.W. 331, 450, 454, 457, 459, 462, 464, 475–476, 488, 492
Gluns, Richard, H. 596
Glustien, F/O A. 136, 149, 191

Godwin, A/C H.B. 22, 26, 28, 34, 42, 45, 48
Golden Hawks 578
Goldsmith, F/O J. 100
Goodbrand, Mr. 566
Goodman, F/L G.M. 39, 45
Goodwin, F/L C.E. 249
Goodwin, RAdm. Hugh H. 250, 259
Gordon, S/L W.I. 363
Goss, Col. (BGen.) Wentworth, 279, 315
Gouin, W/C W.P. 222–223
Graham, MGen. (LGen.) H.D. 138, 477, 500
Grand Prairie (Alberta) 140
Grant, F/O (F/L) J.R. 255, 276, 347–348, 356, 383, 406, 455, 485
Grant, W/C P.J. 32, 37, 39, 40, 41, 45, 89
Grant, S/L W. 116
Grassi, F/O C.A. 35, 37
Graves, F/O H.G. 188, 192
Great Whale River (Quebec) 458–459, 479, 483, 522, 524, 535, 537
Great Falls (Montana) 559
Green, Captain 337, 345, 349, 360
Green Lt. Col. 280
Green, LAC G.R. 548
Green, Hon. Howard 597–598
Green, S/L (W/C) J.F. 27, 32, 37, 39, 41, 44–48, 50
Green, S/L R.H. 544
Greenaway S/L (W/C) K.R. 356, 362, 405, 479, 522, 554, 557, 596, 639
Greenburgh, F/L L. 32, 39, 45, 47
Greenock (Scotland) 500
Greenway, F/L M. 25
Greenway, F/L P.F. 244
Grenfell Mission (Labrador) 85, 100
Griffiths, F/O G.F.T. 290
Griffiths, F/L R.W. 636, 638
Grise Fjord (NWT) 508
Grist, F/O C.F.S. 347
Grose, LAC (Cpl) E.C. 189, 322, 369
ground controlled approach (GCA) 108, 110, 113, 115, 117, 118, 130–135, 137, 173
Ground Observer Corps 274
group (RAF):
    No 3 Bomber Command 15;
    No 4 Transport Command 6, 7, 16;
    No 38 Transport Command 10;
    No 46 Transport Command 645;
    No 47 Transport Command 10, 31, 35;
    No 48 Transport Command 32, 35, 50
group (RCAF):
    No 1 Air Defence 121, 148;
    No 6 Bomber Command 3;

No 9 Transport 62–64, 81, 89, 103;
No 10 Central Command 132;
No 11 North West Air Command 132;
No 12 North West Air Command 191;
No 14 Training 274, 314, 564;
Maritime 132, 333, 347;
Tactical Air 132, 273, 332
group (USAF):
    61st Troop Carrier 188, 214, 254;
    62nd Troop Carrier 214, 254;
    92nd Bombardment 222
Groz, F/L E.J. 75, 77, 85, 86, 102, 116, 117, 121
Grumman Aircraft 617
Guadalajara (Mexico) 368
Guam 180, 431, 556
Guantanamo Bay (Cuba) 515, 517, 545
Guennette, LAC 160
Guess, F/L G.R. 37
Guest, AVM C.E.N. 367
Guillet, LAC 291
Gurney, F/O R.J. 43
Gyani, LGen. P.S. 634
gyro-magnetic compass systems 441

H

Habbaniyah (Iraq), 35, 41
Haire, F/O D. 430
Hale, F/L H. 64, 65
Hale, G/C E.B. 315, 318
Haley, F/L P. 258
Hall Beach (NWT) 397, 530, 554, 572, 593, 634, 655–656
Hall, F/L (S/L) J.N. 322, 332, 348, 359, 366, 507
Hall, W/C L.A. 536
Hall, F/L T.M. 369
Hallowell, F/O C.R. 449
Hamel, F/L J.C.C. 533, 545–546, 551–552
Hamilton (Mount Hope airport) 293
Hamilton Standard 303
Hamilton, F/O W.D.M. 636
Hamm, S/L K.M. 553
Hammond, F/L A.B. 106, 107, 115, 118, 119, 137–140, 141, 148, 149, 158–160, 227, 229
Hamsley, Mr. 120
Hannah, Dr. John A. 405
Hannifan, J.G. 242
Hanoi 408, 422–423, 430
Haramachi (Honshu) 386
Hare, S/L C.E.L. 379, 381, 387–389
Harkness, Hon. Douglas 615, 646
Harland & Wolff (Belfast) 524
Harmon AFB (Stephenville) 158, 171, 181, 360, 429, 506, 582, 589
Harris, MRAF Sir Arthur 77

Harris, W.L. 98
Harrison, F/L (S/L) D. 31, 37, 309–310, 321, 332–333, 606
Harrison, LGen. W.K. 354
Harvey, A/C 26
Harvey, F/L (S/L) J.D. 387, 431, 486–494
Haslem, Sgt. 475
Hastie, F/O (F/L) J.W. 569, 601, 610–611
Hawtrey, G/C R.C. 260
Hayes, F/L R.R. 592, 594, 596–600
Heasman, Ambassador G.R. 486
Heggtveit, S/L E.R. 355
Hellenic Air Force 452, 581
Henderson, Sir Arthur 144, 145, 283
Hendra Fjord (NWT) 387
Hendrick, A/C M.M. 224, 301
Henry, General 138
Henry, F/O D.A. 255
Henry, S/L D.W. 143, 184
Henry, F/O (F/L) J.C. 315, 333
Herbert, S/L H.G. 647
Herbert, F/L R.G. 277, 279, 291, 333, 369
Herzberg, Dr. G. 356
Hewitt, F/L W.C. 462, 494
Hibbard, F/L H. 449, 459, 462, 464
Hickey, F/O J.C. 136
Hicks, F/L A. 532
Hill, WO1 173
Hill, F/S E.J. 132
Hill, W/C V.R. 131
Hilmy, General 601
Hiltz, G/C G.A. 569
Himmelman, F/L R.D. 476
Hiroshima 22, 134
Hlady, S/L M. 602, 604, 606, 653
HMCS (His/Her Majesty's Canadian Ship):
 Swansea 142;
 Athabaskan 180, 182;
 Cayuga 165, 180, 182;
 Sioux 180, 182;
 Magnificent 274, 302, 317, 500–501, 514–515, 520, 524;
 Donnacona 280, 474;
 Cornwallis 307;
 Labrador 420, 494;
 Bonaventure 506, 518, 524;
 Shearwater 617, 655, 659;
 Stadacona 659
HMS (His/Her Majesty's Ship) Glasgow 143
Hobbs, F/O C.A. 37
Hodgins, F/O G.C. 173
Hodgkinson, S/L B.B. 31, 37
Hodgson, G/C (A/C) K.L.B. 21, 365, 381
Hodgson, G/C W.B. 660

Hoehn, Sgt. Wally 289–290, 337, 369
Hoffart, LAC J.A. 548
Hogarth, F/L 49
Hogarth, F/S H. 148
Hollies, S/L J.H. 116
Hollinghurst, ACM 144, 145
Holloway, F/L P.W. 78, 100
Holmes, Cdr. 114, 121
Holmes, S/L A.R. 21, 26
Holmes, F/O G.G. 441–448, 450
Holmes, John, 180–181, 192
Holmes, S/L W.H. 613
Homestead AFB 617
Hong Kong 134, 157, 432, 525, 528, 530, 555, 559, 574
Honolulu (Hickam AFB) 137, 157, 217, 222, 241–243, 245–246, 248, 253, 256–257, 264, 280, 303, 422–424, 431, 464, 480, 486, 527, 530, 535, 556, 559, 582
Hope, Bob (comedian) 222, 294
Hope, F/L P.F. 598
Hopkins, Lt. (RCN) 121
Horton, F/L 522
Houde, Mayor Camille 86
Houghton, RAdm. E.L. 138
Hould, LAC J.Y. 548
House, J.S. 130
Howard, Sgt. G. 337, 355, 357
Howe, Hon. C.D. 95–97, 501
Huard, F/O J.A.F. 338, 371
Hubbard, F/O T.H. 43
Hull, G/C A.C. 357
Hungarian-Canadian Community (Toronto) 498
Hungary 495
Hunt, F/L C.O. 494
Hunter, Tommy 634, 657
Hurley, A/C J.L. 144, 145
Husch, F/O (F/L) R.G. 308, 317, 384, 419, 421, 423
Hussey, F/L L.W. 295, 369
Hutchinson, F/L A.P.R. 560–561, 564–566, 590, 592–593, 611
Hyslop, F/O G. 629, 636

I

Ice Island (T3) 406, 523, 554
Idris airport (Tripoli) 629, 632, 636, 638
Imperial Defence College 140, 141
Imperial Palace (Tokyo) 312
Inch'on (Korea) 216
Indochina 407, 439, 474, 488, 490–491, 493, 502, 534, 574
Ingall, F/O (F/L) Bruce 346, 366, 382, 384–386, 407, 410–411
Ingram, F/L W.H. 545, 563
Institute of Aviation Medicine 99, 102
International Civil Aviation Organization (ICAO) 79, 133, 141, 613–614

International Commissions for Supervision and Control; 407–408; truce teams 422, 424–425, 430, 439, 455–456, 463–464, 488, 491, 493, 503, 525, 534, 555, 559, 633, 635
International Geophysical Year 518–519, 534
International Red Cross 497
Iron Ore Company 440
Isachsen (NWT) 161, 165, 218, 223, 261, 284, 313, 319, 335–336, 338, 348, 359, 363, 366, 378, 382, 384, 387, 406, 419, 422, 427, 440, 452, 461, 488, 492, 508, 520, 532, 548, 553, 555–557, 593, 646
Ismailia (Egypt) 496, 499–500, 502
Ismay, Lord 363
Israel 105, 495
Istres-le-Tube 18, 37, 43, 420, 478
Itami (Japan) 241, 248, 250
Itazuki (Japan) 291
Iwakuni (Japan) 291, 294
Iwo Jima 217

J

Jackson, Warrant Officer 432
Jackson, F/L Ken 545, 549, 559, 563
Jacksonville NAS 360, 545, 655
Jacobsen, G/C G.F. 557
James, F/O (F/L) A.A. 229, 244, 314, 369
James, AVM A.L. 167, 186
Jardine, G/C A.H. 481
Jarvis F/L 638
Jeffs, W/C 100
Jenkins, F/L S.H. 453, 455, 478, 513
Jensen, MGen. J.C. 557
Jensen, F/L M.G. 39, 45
Jessup, Philip 135
jet trans-Atlantic crossings:
 east–west 110, 316;
 west–east 111, 316
jet-stream (low-level) 209, 287
Jewison, LAC 538
Jobin, Cpl. J.M.E. 507
John, F/O A.W. 485, 514, 530, 533
Johnson, W/O 462
Johnson, F/O C.R. 67, 75, 78, 79, 105
Johnson, AM G.O. 5, 6, 10, 23, 38, 40, 42–44, 46, 49
Johnston, W/C (G/C) E.R. 377, 387, 404, 412, 455, 459
Johnston Island 222, 246
Johnston, F/O (F/L) Jasper 546, 550–551, 553, 560, 568, 570–571
Johnston, F/L W.J. 64, 82, 89, 90, 101, 102, 108, 122
Johnsville NAS 307
Joint Arctic Weather Stations 245

Jolicoeur, F/O J.A. 74, 75, 79, 91, 105–107, 129
Jones, W/C F.C. 566
Jones, F/L P.A. 116
Jordan 495
Joron, F/O L.J.E. 420, 422, 428, 449, 452, 459, 463, 482–483, 487–488
Juneau (Alaska) 321

K

Kaesong (Korea) 273
Kamina (Congo) 614, 634
Kammhüber, LGen. J. 578
Kano (Nigeria) 582, 605, 609, 627, 629, 631, 637, 657–658
Karachi 157, 422–424, 426, 430, 456, 464, 475, 478, 486, 488, 555, 574
Kasavubu, Joseph 601
Katanga Province (Congo) 601
Kearfott NI gryo-compass 426
Keefer, W/C G. 116
Keesler AFB 453
Keflavik (Iceland) 110–111, 114, 136, 244, 290, 294, 316–318, 336–340, 360, 364–365, 375–376, 379–381, 384, 386, 402–403, 405, 407–408, 412, 421, 426, 428, 433, 446, 448, 451–454, 456, 459–460, 463–464, 476–478, 482, 484, 487, 489–490, 493, 496–497, 499, 516, 518, 521, 523, 550, 552, 558, 573, 575, 577, 580, 595, 656–658
Keller, MGen. R.F.L. 288
Kelley, S/L W.J. 554
Kelly, Dr. 113
Kelly AFB 228, 292, 302–303
Kelly, LGen. J.W. 632
Kennedy, President John F. 643
Kennedy, G. 86
Kennedy, F/O R.M. 112
Kennedy, A/C W.C. 280
Kerr, AVM J.G. 535
Kerslake, F/L E.C. 337
Ketcheson, F/L J.R. 48
Key West NAS 307, 310, 549
Kieth, L.A. 131
Kightley, F/L (S/L) G.M. 255, 306, 332
Kilgour, F/O J.G. 383
Kim Il Sung 218
Kimpo Air Base 255, 264, 284, 291, 294
King, S/L 20
King Baudouin 601
King George VI, 307
King, F/L P.A.M. 475–476
King Salmon (Alaska) 397, 403
King, Maj. W. 602
King, Prime Minister William Lyon Mackenzie 4, 145, 187

Kingston (Jamaica) 283, 659
Kinloss (Scotland) 318, 360, 363, 365, 375–376, 384, 402, 405, 407–408, 412, 421, 428–429, 448–449, 452, 456, 458–460, 463, 476–477, 482, 484, 487, 493, 496, 498, 503, 516, 518
Kinross (Michigan) 138, 334
Kipp, S/L R.A. 121
Kirchenner, LAC (Cpl) 160, 322
Kittigazuit (NWT) 120
Knapper, F/L A. 185, 229, 316
Knight, F/O C.M. 337
Knight, F/O (F/L) G.H. 248, 291, 310, 320, 333, 349, 356, 504
Knight, W/C H.R. 642, 654
Knight, F/O J.R. 529
Knob Lake (Quebec) 440, 535, 537, 593, 634
Knowles, S/L C.R. 73, 75, 78, 80, 86–88, 90, 100, 103–104, 106–108, 110–112, 114
Kodiak (Alaska) 209
Korean Airlift 219, 224, 254, 260, 274, 275, 280–281, 283, 291, 294, 308, 314–315, 319, 331–332, 343, 355, 358, 369, 377, 389, 397–400, 408–411, 450, 486, 593
Korean Armistice Commission 253
Korean War 174, 181, 222, 251, 252, 255–256, 262, 273, 331, 396, 461
Kotze, Major 138
Kowalik, F/O (F/L) E.J. 337, 377, 380, 383, 419
Kreklewetz, F/O G. 188
Kristofferson, BGen. Henry C. 214, 215, 243
Kronick, F/O W.I. 383
Krushchev, Premier Nikita 643
Kuhn, F/O (F/L) D.H. 187, 189, 222, 308, 319, 322, 338–341, 345–346, 529, 537, 555, 569, 589–590, 644
Kunce, F/O V. 254
Kupkee, F/O J.E. 322
Kuter, LGen. Laurence S. 183, 243
Kwajalein 180
Kyle, F/O (F/L) G.R.A. 337, 364–365, 377, 380–381, 405, 427, 449
Kyryluk, F/O W.F. 367, 412

L

Labatts 259
Lafrance F/L C.A. 331
Lafrenière, F/O Y. 385–386, 411, 427
Lagos (Nigeria) 555, 559, 574, 576, 602, 646
Lahr (West Germany) 490

Lajes (Azores) 108, 110, 157, 292, 379, 422–424, 426, 447, 453, 456, 464, 479, 486, 488, 492, 504–505, 507, 556, 577–578, 581–582, 591, 602, 605–606, 608–609, 629–630, 632, 636, 646
Lake Hazen (NWT) 551
Lalande, Sgt. C. 598, 637
Lamb, F/L T.D. 423, 460, 475
Lambert, F/L J.F. 33, 345, 366, 370, 506, 521
Lambeth, F/L D.L.F. 499, 505, 522, 526–527, 536–537, 546, 559
Lambros, F/O A. 331
Landreville, Cpl. 100
Lane, WC (A/C) R.J. 141, 157, 170, 635, 641, 645, 654, 659
Langlie, Governor A.B. 260
Langlois, Mr. 108
Langman, F/O Ray 255, 345–347
Langstaff, G/C W.C. 654
Lanteigne, LAC 229
Larochelle, Sgt. L. 428
Larson AFB, 284
Larson, Supt. Henry 491, 594
Lasser, Father 350
Latter, F/O J.M. 187
Laturnus, LAC 322
Laudermilk, Captain 338
Lauro, Mayor 526
Lavigne, F/O Y.J. D.B.P. 559, 563, 569, 574, 578–579, 605–606, 632
Law, F/L A.A.S. 74
Lawlor, W/C C.R.J. 356
Lawrence, W/C C.A.G. 356
Le Droit 250
Le Blanc, R.G. 17
Leach, Col. G. 500
Lebedis, F/O S.T. 492, 503, 507
Leblanc, Cpl. P. 160
Leblanc, Sgt. 425
Leboldus, S/L M.J. 265
Leckie, AM Robert 5, 10, 40, 42, 43, 44
Ledoux G/C H.C. 361
Lee, F/O C. 115
Lee, F/O J.G.J. 612–613
Lee, F/L P.E. 131
Lee, F/L R.H. 387
Lee, F/L Ted 255
Leeming, Cdr. J.M. 420
Leeward Point Field (Cuba) 515
Legaarden, F/L L.T. 529
Leigh, S/L (G/C) Z.L. 61, 78, 186, 306, 308, 367, 402, 404, 406
Leiskam, F/O 27
Lemieux, F/O (F/L) P.M. 187, 332
Léopoldville (Congo) 601–602, 604–606, 609, 617, 627, 629–630, 632, 653–660

Lepine, F/O J.H.C.A. 322
Lethbridge (Alberta) 225, 333, 334, 547
Lethbridge, LAC D.N. 548
Letourneau, Corporal 311
Leuchars (Scotland) 375
Levesque, F/L J.A.Omer 255–256
Lévesque, Réne 278–279
Lewis, S/L J.H.C. 141, 143, 174, 187, 189–190, 219, 227
Lewis, S/L W.H. 67, 109, 114, 116, 117, 120
Lewis, F/L W.M. 496–498, 505, 507, 527, 560
Libby, Admiral 138
Lightstone, F/O M. 322
Lilly, A.J. 98, 132, 179, 192
Lima (Peru) 596–600
Lindgren, F/O J.E. 290
Lindsay, S/L J.D. 331, 363
Lingham, S/L H.T. 35
Lisbon 453, 464, 504, 572, 577, 581
Lisson, W/C H. 577
Livock, F/O R.W. 322
Lloyd, AVM (ACM) Hugh 5, 314
Lloyd, F/L (S/L) W.R. 189, 227–228, 257, 277–278, 290, 337, 369, 427, 653
Locating Battery (No 133, Toronto) 378
Lockhart, Mr. 475
Lockheed Aircraft Corporation 440, 450, 595
Logan, F/O (F/L) A.S. 149, 254, 257–259, 290
Lomas, F/O L.J. 135
London (Heathrow) 111, 290, 319, 338, 340–341, 365, 460, 477, 491
Long, F/O 494
Longhurst, W.S. 520, 582
Longworth, F/L R. 535, 537, 553, 556, 576, 583, 593, 608, 611, 636
loran:
    AN/APN 4, 195;
    AN/APN 9, 195, 243
Lord, Captain 387
Lord, S/L (W/C) W.H. 181, 183, 188, 194, 322
Lord, F/L W.J.F.H. 520
Lossiemouth (Scotland) 379–381
Lowe, Frank 105
Lowery, F/L R.E. 331
Lowry, S/L R.H. 219
Loynes, F/L W. 85, 88, 110
Luluabourg (Congo) 603, 609
Lumumba, Patrice 601, 630–631
Lund, W/C F. 67
Lundula, Gen. Victor 630
Lupton, W/C W.H. 321, 322, 337, 339–340, 357, 361, 366, 411, 419–420, 429, 454
Lutes, F/L H.A. 32

Lydda (Palestine) 35
Lynch, F/L J.J. 549, 552, 556, 558, 563, 581, 587, 591, 596–600
Lyons, Sgt. M.M. 43

M

M.V. Maruba 422, 455
MacArthur, Gen. Douglas 174, 180, 216, 218, 226, 256, 312
MacBrien, G/C (AVM) W.R. 121, 148, 656
MacDill AFB 483
MacDonald, LAC H.R. 189
MacDonald, W/C (A/C) J.K.F. 170, 222, 251, 255, 257–258, 263, 265, 274, 279, 291, 294, 308, 311, 321, 336–337
MacDonnell, Sgt. H.T. 250
MacDougall, G/C 108
Mace, F/O E.R. 484, 494, 524, 531, 537
MacGillray, Mr. 431
MacIntyre, LAC M.D. 263
MacKay, S/L J. 339, 355, 379, 407
MacKell, F/L A.F. 8, 9, 21
MacKell, A/C D.E. 137, 144
MacKenzie, S/L A.R. 302, 331, 432
MacKenzie, S/L D.C. 654
Mackie, F/L (W/C) A.J. 39, 44, 47, 73–75, 454, 460, 483, 486, 515, 521, 524, 529, 533–534, 537, 546, 549, 556–561, 568, 581, 647, 659–660
MacMillan, S/L M.B. 404, 422
MacNeil, F/O R.J. 244
Madigan Hospital (Fort Lewis) 252
Madrid 464
Magdalinski, Cpl. Pat 192
Mahoney, F/L D.C. 627–628, 638
Mailloux, F/L E.E. 529
Maintenance Command (RCAF) 86, 116, 117, 121, 132
Maitland, S/L (W/C) J.O. 581, 583, 589, 595–600, 603–604, 606, 627, 634, 636–639, 642, 647
Majocha, F/O (F/L) M. 346, 356, 383, 405
Major, F/O (F/L) P.J. 448–449, 462, 464, 476, 483, 490, 497, 504–505
Malik, Yakov 135, 174, 273
Mallinson, S/L J.D. 39
Malloy, W/C D.G. 375, 380, 569
Malta (Luqa airport) 36, 157, 170, 422–424, 430, 456, 464, 475, 478, 480, 483, 486, 488, 492, 544, 546–547, 600
Manchester (Ringway airport) 407, 426, 429, 451–452, 454, 463
Manila 422, 424–426, 430, 464, 480, 556
Manning Depot 273

Mansfield, Sgt. 388–389
Manson, W/C R.H. 577, 594, 600
Mao Tse-Tung 144
Maple Leaf 48
Maralinga (Australia) 530
Marcus Island 245
Marfleet, S/L B.H. 570–572
Maritime Air Command (RCAF) 450, 557, 591
Maritime Commands (RCN-RCAF) 575
Marriott, F/L H.W. 37
Marseilles 429
Marsh, Rt. Rev. D.B. 491
Marshall, W/C C.C.W. 616
Marshall, F/L (S/L) J.R. 518, 520, 523, 528, 642, 645, 647
Marshall, F/O S.R. 220
Martin, F/L A. 369
Martin, F/L E. 536
Martin, F/O Earl 499
Martin, Sgt. Sam 369
Marunouchi Hotel (Tokyo) 191, 279, 331
Massey, Governor General Vincent 479, 576
Matadi (Congo) 601, 604
Mather, F/O A.T. 135
Matheson, F/L J.D. 39, 48
Matsushima (Honshu), 190, 211, 285, 308, 385–386
Mauripur airfield (Karachi) 35
Maxwell AFB 360, 483, 523, 568, 595
Mayo, LAC 538
Mayo Clinic (Rochester) 489
McAllard, W/C 104
McAlpine, F/O (F/L) W.E. 485, 488, 506–507, 517, 519, 533, 659
McAninch, F/O G.L. 337, 349, 360, 420
McBride F/O (F/L) K.D. 337, 407, 432, 456
McBride, Nursing Sister M.F. 34, 39
McBurney, F/L D.C. 504, 513–514, 519, 523, 533, 538, 544, 551, 557
McBurney, AVM R.E. 132
McCallum, S/L J.D. 110
McCarthy, S/L J.C. 73, 86
McCarthy, G/C J.P. 382
McCarthy, G/C W.V. 21
McChord AFB 183–185, 188–195, 209, 213–216, 218, 219, 223, 228–229, 242, 249–250, 253, 259–260, 262, 263–265, 275–279, 281, 283–284, 287, 291, 293–294, 305–306, 309, 311, 319, 333–334, 338, 348–349, 367, 371, 377, 381, 383–384, 386–387, 403–404, 410–411
McCord, J.E.D. 242
McCormick, G/C G.E. 261–262

McCoy, F/O (F/L) K.A. 88, 140
McCutcheon, S/L (W/C) J.T. 15, 17, 20, 27, 31, 103, 109, 361
McDonald, F/L J. 463
McDonald, F/L J.P. 188, 260, 262
McDonnell F/O 528
McDormund, F/L C.B. 47
McDougall, G/C G.S. 11, 16, 22, 25
McEwen, AVM C.M. 99, 140
McGill, F/L F.R. 36, 39
McGovern, F/S 48
McGovern, Major 218
McGuire AFB 607
McIntosh, F/O G.G.D. 140
McIvor, F/L D. 37
McKinney, Capt. G.H. 21, 24
McKinnon, W/C M.B. 185
McKinnon, S/L T.J. 224
McKnight, F/L A.C. 173
McKnight, Sgt. W.S. 222, 281, 369
McLaughlin, F/O (F/L) E.J. 497, 504, 507, 526–527, 567, 576, 587–589, 606
McLean, S/L C.D. 66, 67, 74, 117, 132
McLean, John 221
McLean, Scotty 582
McLeod, LAC 112
McLeod, Mr. 118
McLeod, F/O D. 321, 332
McLeod, F/L R.D. 23
McLeod, F/L S.C. 24, 25
McLeod, F/L T.M. 31
McMillan, F/O R.B. 316
McNair, F/L J.A. 596, 633
McNair, W/C (G/C) R.W. 219, 221–222, 224, 229, 244, 265, 344, 382, 390
McNaughton, Gen. A.G.L. 138, 158, 320–321, 405
McNeely, F/L J.E. 173
McNeil F/O W.D. 613
McNutty, F/L K. 529
McVeigh, W/C C.H. 378, 455
Medjez El Bab Memorial (Tunisia) 536
Megill, MGen. W.J. 569
Melbourne (Australia) 486, 527
Meldrum, Cpl. D.K. 548
Memorial Gates (Trenton) 144
Mendelsohn, Col. A. 607
Menton, F/L J. 369
Menzies, Arthur 344
Merriam, F/L D.E. 46
Merrick, F/L T. 655
Meyer, F/L 32, 36
Meyer, Standartenführer Kurt 288–290
Meyers LAC E.C. 548
Miall, S/L E. 131
Michaud, F/O J.W. 143

Michel, F/L (S/L) P.L. 67, 73, 77–80, 84, 85, 90, 100, 103, 110, 111, 121, 129, 243, 257, 293, 316, 402, 425, 430
Mickelson, Capt. 654
Middle East 495
Middlemiss, S/L R.G. 339, 384, 402
Middleton, AVM E.E. 83, 84, 86, 105, 107, 112, 113, 132
Middleton, F/O J.S. 229, 290, 333, 366
Middleton, W/C R.B. 17, 21
Mid-Canada Line (McGill Fence) 396, 440, 474
mid-Pacific route 245, 399
Midway Island 246, 535, 556
Military Air Transport Service (MATS) 115, 161, 180–186, 190, 192, 214, 220, 227, 228, 242, 243, 250, 279, 292, 302, 310, 314–315, 319, 342–345, 388, 398–399, 430, 480, 571, 607–608, 632
Millard, G/C V.S.J. 260
Miller, S/L B.G. 110
Miller, W/C D.R. 9, 15–17, 20, 23–25, 27, 28, 31, 32, 34, 36, 39–42, 45, 46
Miller, S/L E.C. 88
Miller, AVM (AM) F.R. 186, 280, 345, 358, 398–399, 401, 557, 606, 616
Miller, F/L Gordie 108
Miller, F/O (F/L) J.B. 166, 179, 190, 191, 219, 223, 249, 256, 261, 277, 283, 290, 322
Miller, S/L J.S. 516, 548, 567
Miller, W/C W.G.S. 479
Milliken, F/O (S/L) S.E.M. 99, 610–611
Mills, F/L J.G. 73, 75, 79, 86, 87, 91, 92, 99–101, 103–105, 108
Milner, F/L O.A. 348
Mingan (Quebec) 148
Minifee, James M. 569
Ministry of Aircraft Production 10
Miryang River (Korea) 241
Misawa (Honshu) 134, 185, 189, 212, 219, 277–278, 315, 346, 348, 377, 388, 404, 410
Misener, F/L H.M. 503, 506, 518–519, 525, 528, 627
Miskiman, F/O H.E. 28, 39
Mistral 43
Mitchel Field (New York) 147
Mitchell, W/C S.S. 638
Moana Hotel (Honolulu) 245, 486
Moberg, F/O E.H. 187
Moberly, Cpl. 291
Mobutu, Col. (Gen.) Joseph 630
Moisie River (Quebec) 529
Molotov, V.M. 407

Moncton (New Brunswick) 73, 83, 114, 148, 255, 289, 365, 368
Mont Joli (Quebec) 81, 172
Mont Bello Islands (Australia) 354
Montgomery, Field Marshal Sir Bernard 65, 367, 378
Montgomery, F/O N.C. 248
Moodie, Cpl. 522, 569
Moore, Capt. K.A. 24, 33
More, F/O G. 47
Moric, Sgt. J. 592
Morphee, AVM A.L. 67, 79
Morrier, Ron 86
Morris, F/O J. 32
Morrison, S/L (G/C) H.A. 113–116, 118–121, 140, 145, 146, 148, 157, 163, 166, 167, 170, 187, 216–217, 219, 322, 502, 509, 515, 521, 535, 553, 577, 640
Morrison, F/L J.R. 281, 304, 307, 309, 319, 371, 377, 522, 533, 549–550, 590, 593, 596–600, 606, 612
Morrison, F/L M.G. 644
Morrison, F/L W.A. 37
Morton, MGen. R.O.G. 186, 280
Moss, F/L 106
Mould Bay (NWT) 161, 165, 167, 218, 223, 257, 261, 284, 313, 335–336, 338, 348, 363, 366, 370, 378, 382, 387, 406, 419, 422–423, 427, 431, 440, 452, 461, 479, 492, 508, 520, 522, 532, 548, 553, 556–557, 646
Mountain Home AFB 303
Movement Controllers Air 457
Mulligan, LAC W.J. 548
Mullin, F/O J.B. 355
Munnock, F/O (F/L) J. 254, 316
Murdock, Mr. 597
Murphy LAC W.D. 548, 598
Murray, F/L R. 105, 107, 108
Musk Calf (Loran) Chain 120
Mussells, S/L (A/C) C.H. 100, 130–132, 134, 136, 149, 159–161, 167, 168, 174, 181–184, 186–188, 190–193, 213, 216, 219–221, 224–225, 228, 242–243, 251, 257–258, 260–263, 280, 322, 336, 340, 341, 371, 378, 384, 567
Myers, MGen. 314

N

N'Djili airport (Léopoldville) 603, 613
N'dola airport (Northern Rhodesia) 646
N'Dolo airport (Léopoldville) 612–613
NAAFI 7, 22
Nagasaki 22, 180
Nagy, Imre 495
Nairobi 555, 574, 576, 582
Nakamura, LAC 242

Nam Il, General 354
Nandi (Fiji) 137, 486, 527, 582
Naples 505, 509, 516, 521, 524, 529, 531, 533, 543, 546
Naples (Capodichino airfield) 502, 504–507, 513, 515, 521–522, 532–533, 538
Narsarssuak, Greenland (Bluie West 1) 111, 316, 318, 336, 338–340, 364, 375–376, 380, 402–403, 405, 407–408, 412, 421, 426, 428, 430, 448, 450–453, 456, 458–460, 462, 464, 475–476, 482, 484, 487, 490, 493, 498, 503, 507, 516, 518
Nassau (Bahamas) 360, 515, 617
Nasser, Col. Gamal Abdel 495–496, 500
Natal (Brazil) 136, 170, 617
National Aeronautical Establishment (Ottawa) 642
National Defence College 105, 119, 147, 168, 194, 242, 305, 310, 616
National Research Council 103, 169, 283, 356
Naval Air Warfare Center (Point Mugu) 531, 535, 559
Neal, G. 553
Neff, F/L J.S. 387
Negombo (Ceylon) 480, 486, 534, 538, 543
Nelles, F/L E.F. 264, 289–290, 294, 311
Nellis AFB 292, 612
Nelson, W/C W.G.M. 311
Nemuro (Hokkaido) 304, 385–386
New Delhi 464, 475, 480
Newfoundland 132
Newsom, W/C W.F.M. 83, 108, 114
New Zealand 174
Neyvatte, S/L C.E. 570
Nice (France) 170
Nichol, F/L L.G. 567, 587, 629
Nicholls, F/L G.H. 355
Nicholson, W/O 461
Nicholson, Commissioner L.H. 356
Nickerson W/C G.E. 356
Nicosia (Cyprus) 422–423, 430, 456, 464, 475, 478, 480
Niehaus, F/O H.J. 638
Nightingale, J. 261
Nishimura, F/O G.H. 482
Nixon, F/O G.W. 301
Noel, F/L N.A. 33
Noland, W/C M.J. 118
Nonamaker, F/L E.P. 24
Norfolk (Virginia) 617
Norman Wells (NWT) 138, 333, 360
Normandin, Pierre 250
Norris, F/O R.W. 338, 403–404
North American Air Defence (NORAD) 550, 580

North Atlantic Treaty Organization (NATO): 133, 167, 223, 274, 284, 333, 473, 481;
 Aircrew Training, 553, 583;
 Exercise Carte Blanche 454;
 Mutual Aid 420, 536, 549–550, 564, 570, 580–581, 617, 657;
 Secretary General 363
North East Air Command (USAF) 245
North Geographic Pole 356–357, 405, 429, 439, 441, 451, 479, 483, 523, 551, 569, 596, 639, 657
North Korea 174
North Nova Scotia Highlanders 288
North, F/O R.L. 346, 383
North West Air Command: Band 225, 273
North West Airlines 265, 399
Northwest Highway System 164
North West Staging Route 140
Norton, F/O E.W. 290, 338
Nouasseur (Morocco) 573, 578–579, 581, 591, 602, 604, 606, 646
Nurse, F/L R.D. 505, 507, 514
Nye, Sir Archibald 356
Nyhuus, F/O J.H. 381
Nymark, F/O R.W. 136

O

O'Brecht, F/O E.T. 24
O'Connor, LAC J. 403
O'Neil, F/L P.E. 134
Observation Regiment:
 No 40, No 60, 281;
 No 69, No 70, 378
Ocean Station Vessels:
 Sugar 211, 217, 285, 304, 385, 388;
 Uncle 246;
 Nan 246;
 Papa 309;
 Bravo 336, 364;
 Alpha 336;
 India 336;
 Delta 579, 629
Octagon Conference 4
Ohakea (New Zealand) 137
Ohlson, Cpl. G.R. 521
Okinawa 134, 222
Oliver, MGen. 140
Oliver, F/O H.J. 32, 47
Olsen, F/L (S/L) C.S. 257, 276–277, 280–283, 289, 290, 332,369, 371, 422–423, 448, 456
operation:
 Ack Ack Mobility 319;
 Amigo 596–600, 635–636;
 Annex 27, 36, 40;
 Bechers Brook (RAF) 364–365, 376, 384;

Beechflight 570;
Beefsteak 64;
Beetle 120, 130, 159;
Black Boy 172;
Box Top 557, 576, 632, 644;
Brix 164–165;
Cariberg 105;
Convex 307, 310, 314;
Eagle 133, 140, 141;
Franklin 454;
Haffey 527;
Hawk 186–187, 189, 219, 223, 262, 264, 275, 293, 361, 377;
High Flight (USAF) 364, 412, 476–477;
Hopper Stopper 641;
Jump Moat 513, 536, 546, 549, 552–553, 558;
Leap Frog 317–318, 336–341, 355, 360–361, 364, 375, 377–381;
Little Switch 353, 367;
Lookout 580, 617–619, 638, 655;
Mallard 607–609;
MATS Mallard 608–609;
Mariner 381;
Metropolis 147;
Mobility 138, 143, 145, 162;
New Tape (MATS) 609;
Nanook 333;
Nimble Bat 474, 481–482, 499, 513, 516, 518, 521, 523, 529;
Nugget (Signpost) 321, 332, 334;
Orient 120, 121;
Petticoat 485;
Random: 384, 402–406, 408, 412, 420–421, 424, 426, 428, 429, 448–450, 452–456, 457, 459–460, 462–463, 474, 476, 482, 484, 487, 489, 492, 496, 498, 503, 505, 507, 513, 518, 520–521, 523–524;
Rapid Step 500, 504–505, 507, 519;
Red Ramp 171–173;
Re-Supply (Arctic) 167–168, 171, 173, 218, 223, 263, 284, 313–314, 401, 406, 427, 452, 455, 457–458, 461–462, 487–488, 491, 524, 548, 551, 594, 609, 611;
Rhumba Queen 439;
Santa Claus 387;
Silver Dozen 573;
Second Silver Dozen 577;
Star Flight 550;
Tiger (Mould) 5;
Western Weal 580, 657
operation orders:
 Air Defence Command: No 27/53 Relocation to Baden-Söellingen 375;

Index

Air Division (No 1): No 25/53 Leap Frog IV, 379;
Air Transport Command:
  No 9/50 Arctic Re-supply 165, 167;
  No 17/50 Hawk 185;
  No 20/50 Arctic Re-supply 218;
  No 24/50 Airlift 421 Squadron 229;
  No 6/51 Air Evac Canadian Casualties 251;
  No 7/51 Sea Green 252;
  No 9/51 Arctic Re-supply 261;
  No 13/51 Deployment 405 Squadron 263;
  No 9/52 Leap Frog I, 317;
  No 15/52 Leap Frog II, 336;
  No 2/54 Random;
  No 9/58 Re-supply 548;
  North West Air Command No 7/49 Eagle 133;
  RAF Transport Command No 12/45, No 13/45, No 75/45, trooping 25, 27, 45
Operational Training Unit (Transport): 426 Squadron 184;
  North Star 224; No 4, 302, 316, 332, 337, 378, 383, 402, 425, 519, 548, 554, 573, 577, 594, 642, 644, 659
Operational Training Unit (Fighter) 114, 116, 461
Oran (Algeria) 480
Orenda jet engine 225, 397
Orr, F/O E.D. 322
Orr, AVM W.A. 640
Orr, S/L W.L. 99, 102, 106
Osaka (Japan) 134
Oslo 657–659
Otis AFB 317
Overseas Ferry Unit (No 1) 377, 382, 383, 405, 420–421, 424, 426, 429, 460–461, 482, 489, 498, 506, 521
Owston, F/L W.T. 504, 506–507, 514, 517, 523, 543, 545–546, 550, 552–553, 564, 609–611, 627, 656
Oxspring, S/L R.W. 110

P

P'yongyang 226
Palagian, Cpl. 538
Palmer, G/C 15
Palmer, F/L D.L. 42
Palmyra Is. 137
Pan American Airways 245, 618
Pangborn, Capt. Clyde 95
Panmunjom 273, 331, 353–354
Paramaribo (Surinam) 617–618
Parent, F/O 528
Paris 301, 337, 338, 340, 365, 381
Parker, LAC C.W. 548
Parks, S/L (W/C) E.E. 88, 170
Parks, W/C W.F. 131
Parmelee F/L J.S. 596–600
Pary, F/O 109
Pate, F/L W.G. 85
Patricia Bay (Victoria) 334, 360
Patrick AFB 483, 568, 589–590, 617–619, 638
Patrick, F/L G.W. 115
Pattee, F/L L.R. 43
Paul, Joan 98
Paul, F/O N.F. 402, 410–411, 422, 430, 440, 453
Payne, F/O (F/L) D.M. 149, 166, 168, 190, 217–219, 244, 277–278, 290, 322
Pearkes, Hon. George R. 557, 568, 570, 575, 578, 602, 604, 607, 615
Pearson, F/O F.L. 291, 338
Pearson, Hon. Lester B. 157, 163–164, 174, 400, 432, 496, 500
Pearson, F/L W.R. 606
Pelletier F/O Joe 591, 593, 595
Pelletier, LAC Lionel 193
People's Republic of China 144
Perkins, LAC 113
Perrier, F/L 520
Personnel Reception Centre, Bournemouth 16
Personnel Reception Centre: No 1 (Lachine) 361; (Trenton) 577
Peters, F/O K. 589
Peterson, S/L H.V. 27, 48
Peterson, F/L V. 627
Phillips Army Air Base 518
Phillips, F/L H.G. 322
Phnom Penh (Cambodia) 408
Phripp, W/C F. 559
Piarco airport (Port of Spain) 170, 590
Pickard, ACI J.B. 382
Pierce-Goulding, LCol. 654
Piette, F/O D.E. 65
Pinetree Line 395
Pinsonneault, Cpl. 291
Pirie, AVM G.C. 5
Pisa 544, 574, 588, 610, 628–629, 632, 636, 638, 643, 645, 648, 653, 656–657, 659
Plant, AVM J.L. 186
Plattsburg AFB 590
Pleasance, G/C W.P. 7, 114, 131, 134, 141, 515, 536, 544
Plunkett, Sgt. Thomas 172
Pody, Dr. 113
Point Barrow (Alaska) 362, 397
Poling, LCol. 109
Pollard, W/C M.E. 170
Pond Inlet (NWT) 356, 432, 508, 518
Poona (India) 33
Port Fauad (Egypt) 496
Port Francqui (Congo) 630
Port Hardy (Vancouver Island) 292, 654, 656
Port Lyautey (Morocco) 430, 534
Port Radium (NWT) 138
Port Said (Egypt) 496, 501, 520
Portal, MRAF Sir Charles 4
Port-au-Prince (Haiti) 617
Portuguese Air Force 571–572, 581
Potekal, Sgt. L.C. 355, 361
Potter, Miss 371
Power, Hon. C.G. 3, 145
Powers, Gary 598
Pratt and Whitney:
  Montreal 77, 79;
  Hartford 171
Pressanges, A/C 26
pressure-pattern 284
Preston, F/S 322
Prestwick airport (Scotland) 316, 336–340, 365, 377, 383, 386, 420, 429, 433, 446, 449–450, 453, 456, 458–459, 475, 477–478, 482, 485, 489, 494, 503, 523, 550, 553, 556, 571, 577, 580, 656–658
Price, LAC 291
Price, F/O (F/L) Reg 547, 557, 587, 589, 657–658
Prince Bernhart 137, 167
Prince Philip 575–576
Princess Patricia's Canadian Light Infantry (PPCLI) 133, 169, 191, 226, 241, 568
prisoners of war (Canadian) 367
Puerto Montt (Chile) 597–599
Pusan 216, 259, 262

Q

Qantas Airways 486
Queale, F/L (S/L) L.W. 139, 160, 163, 166, 262
Queen Elizabeth II 292, 575–576
Queen Mary (Cunard Liner) 65
Queen Mary Veteran's Hospital 521
Queen's Own Rifles 288, 500–501
Quickfall, F/O (F/L) A.L. 143, 160, 187, 189, 256, 264, 277–278, 288, 306, 316, 337, 533
Quinn, F/O C.E. 316, 383
Quonset Point NAS 617

R

Rabat Salé 18, 403, 408, 419, 429, 446, 451, 454, 478, 485, 490, 494, 499, 503, 592
Radar and Communications Unit, No 1 (St-Hubert) 147
radio beacons 363
Rafah (Gaza Strip) 532, 588, 628, 657

Raike, F/O (F/L) R.H.W. 360, 377, 406, 419, 427, 455
Ralph, Maj. R.H. 291
Ralston, Hon. J.L. 105
Ramey AFB (Puerto Rico) 136, 590, 617–618
Ramey, P/O K.E. 384
Ramstein AFB 555
Rangoon (Burma)157
Ratcliffe, F/L (S/L) R.E.D. 140, 189, 229, 278, 290, 322, 346
Rawlyk, F/L P. 579
Ray, F/O B.L. 189
Rayson, F/L M. 594, 616, 633
RCMP Band 133, 334
Reardon, WO2 J.B. 570
Recife (Brazil) 590, 618
Reed, F/O 449, 461–462, 475, 505, 507–508, 514
Reed, Cpl. G.R. 369
Reedy, E.F. 133
Reeves, S/L W.D. 121
Regina 104, 489, 641
Reid, Escott 454
Reid, S/L J.C. 475, 507, 525–526
Reid, F/L Ken 556
Reid, F/O (F/L) R.S. 141, 346
Remembrance Day: 90, 120, 293, 346, 463, 503, 560
Renton, F/L A.J. 564
Repair Depot No 6, Trenton 79, 310, 457, 573
repatriation policy 25
Repatriation Depot, Torquay 16
Resolute Bay (NWT): 138–139, 146, 165, 167–168, 170–171, 183, 223, 229, 244–245, 254, 261, 275, 279, 282–284, 290, 293–294, 307–308, 313, 315–316, 320, 332–336, 338, 345, 356–357, 359, 361–363, 366, 371, 377, 379, 382–384, 386–387, 402–403, 405–406, 412, 419, 421–422, 424, 426–427, 429, 431–432, 440–443, 448–452, 455–459, 461–464, 475, 479, 482–485, 487–494, 497, 503, 506, 508, 514, 517–519, 521–522, 524–525, 528, 530–535, 537, 544–546, 549–554, 556, 558–560, 563–565, 569, 572–573, 576, 590–591, 593–595, 601, 609–611, 616, 627, 632–633, 635, 639, 643–644, 654–657
Revington A/C A.P. 280
R-Day (reversion) 66
Rhéame, S/L E. 47
Rhee, Dr. Syngman 331, 354
Rhodes, F/O M.A. 337
Rice, LAC D.K. 548
Richards, G/C H.G. 522

Richardson, F/O J. 142
Richardson, F/O T.E. 187, 248, 281
Richer, W/C J.A.D.B. 108, 114, 167
Ridgeway, Gen. Matthew B. 230, 256, 263, 301
Ripley, A/C R.C. 280, 283, 291–292, 294–295, 308, 334, 336, 341–344, 357–358, 359, 361, 367, 371, 376, 378, 384
Ritchie, Charles 345
Rizum, LAC Harry 192
Roach, F/L R.J. 31, 48
Roane, F/O (F/L) R.A. 281, 337, 357
Robb, Lord 145
Roberge, F/O J.E.L.P. 637
Robert, F/O J.M. 255, 363
Roberts, Glenda 99
Roberts, H.R.N. 557
Robertson, G/C 104
Robertson, F/O D.F. 115
Robertson, Gordon 405
Robertson, S/L G.L. 515, 524
Robertson, W/C J.H. 113
Robertson, Cdre. O.C.S. 610
Robertson, F/L R.J. 580–581, 596–600, 629–630, 637
Robillard, LAC 345
Robinson, Walter S. 354
Rockliffe Ice Wagon 479–480
Rockingham, Brig. J.M. 260, 262
Rodewolt, F/O (F/L) L.R. 559, 569, 574, 577
Rodger, F/O (F/L) J.W. 141, 254, 346
Rodger, MGen. N.E. 356
Rodrique, F/O J.A.L.P. 119, 132, 140, 242, 248, 254
Rodriquez, Ambassador Mario 635
Rohatinsky, Sgt. S. 431
Rolls-Royce Company 96, 185, 193, 229, 628, 640
Rome (Ciampino airport) 292, 420, 429, 453
Ronning, F/O A.N. 460, 475–477, 479, 485, 489, 493, 503, 505, 516, 522, 527
Ronning, Ambassador Chester 432
Roots, Dr. 566
Rose, Dr. D.C. 356–357
Rosengren, F/O A.L. 255, 338
Rosenthal, F/O B. 337
Rosenthal, S/L L.A. 115, 116, 120–121
Ross, Colonel 113
Ross, A/C A.D. 113, 114, 119, 120, 129, 131, 140, 146, 148, 160, 161, 168–170, 171, 183, 186–187, 213–215, 219, 223–224, 228, 242, 245, 260–262, 265, 279
Ross, G. 85, 86, 457
Roulston, F/O (F/L) K.C. 381, 403, 425

Roundel 119
Rouse, F/L C.V. 3
Rowley, Dr. Graham 479
Royal Air Force (RAF):
  Central Flying Establishment 451;
  Ferry Command 95;
  Fighter Command 382, 450;
  Staff College (Bracknell) 130
Royal Canadian Air Force (RCAF):
  Air Transport Unit (Congo) 605;
  Air Weapons Unit (Decimomannu) 525;
  Band 79, 80, 88, 105, 279, 288, 293, 368, 526, 529;
  Benevolent Fund 489;
  Flyers 101;
  green ticket 100, 614;
  Regular Officer Training Plan 615;
  Staff College (Toronto) 75, 78–79, 103, 113–114, 119, 139, 229, 260, 314, 360, 453, 483, 523, 549, 568, 595, 631, 635, 644;
  strength 169, 615, 625;
  Survival Training School 122, 383, 545, 557;
  uniforms 614
Royal Canadian Army Postal Corps 509
Royal Canadian Army Service Corps 607
Royal Canadian Corps of Signals 555, 568
Royal Canadian Dragoons 500, 595, 638–639, 657
Royal Canadian Electric and Mechanical Engineers 607
Royal Canadian Horse Artillery 260
Royal Canadian Legion 314
Royal Canadian Navy 401, 518
Royal Canadian Ordnance Corps 519
Royal Canadian Regiment 191, 245, 354, 360
Royal Marines Band 578
Royal Military College 166,308
Royal Navy 524
Royal Navy Air Station (Ford) 518
Royal Netherlands Navy 617
Royal Roads Military College 631
Royal 22nd Regiment 191, 278, 360, 367
Royal Tour 284, 288, 290, 292–293, 576
Royal Wedding Anniversary 104
Royal Winnipeg Rifles 288
Rubenck, F/O G. 33, 47
Ruffell, F/S Bert 192
Russell, W/C H.B. 606, 614
Rutherford, S/L V.A. 516
Rutledge, G/C (A/C) H.H.C. 113, 567, 635

S

Sabena Airlines 603–604
Sachs Harbour (NWT) 508, 548, 551
Sage, F/O G.F. 316, 319, 333, 349, 364–365, 382–383
Saigon 425, 430, 456–461, 463–464, 488, 490–493, 503, 524–526, 528, 530, 532, 534, 555, 559, 574, 576, 582, 616
Saint John (New Brunswick) 349, 520
Sampson, G/C F.A. 26
San Francisco (Travis AFB) 137, 157, 163, 214, 217, 222, 227, 243, 246, 257, 275, 303, 422, 424–426, 431, 464, 480, 486, 527, 530, 535, 556, 559
Sand Point NAS 224
Sandspit (Queen Charlotte Islands) 213
Sanford, F/L (W/C) C.F. 64–68, 75, 78, 79, 81, 90, 102, 103, 105, 106, 110, 112–114, 116, 118, 129, 229, 242, 252–253, 261, 367, 411, 424–425, 572, 654
Santa Maria (Azores) 504–505, 589, 591
Santarelli, F/O J. 116, 139, 189
Santiago (Chile) 596–600
Sare, F/O (F/L) J. 497–498, 517, 546, 553, 554
Sasebo (Japan)180
Saunders, Capt. B. 631
Sawmill Bay (NWT) 107, 121, 138
Scandinavian Airlines 454, 461
School of Instructional Technique 577
School of Meteorology 577
Schroder, F/L J.S. 367, 371, 522, 529, 544, 657
Schroeder, G/C K.A.L. 569
Schunk, F/L L.W. 544, 547
Schwanky, F/O (F/L) R.E. 456–457, 489–490, 493, 499, 506, 514, 517, 524, 648, 658
Scott, F/O (F/L) D.G. 187, 283, 291
Scott, F/L W.J. 638
Scovill, W/C T.T. 457
Seaforth Highlanders of Canada 281
search radar (APS 42) 146, 483, 486, 488, 526–527, 587
Selby, F/O D.G. 141, 149
Senecal, Sgt. 322
Seoul: 241, 251; City Airport 348
Seward, F/L G.E. 36, 42
Shade, LAC D.I. 213
Shanghai 134
Shannon 505, 547, 556, 589, 591, 615, 657, 659
Shaw AFB 316
Shaw, F/L E.H. 105, 106
Shaw, W/C R.O. 169, 223
Shea, E. 464

Sheahan, F/L G.L. 73, 74, 75, 79, 82, 84, 91, 104, 110, 111, 115, 136, 145
Shelfoon, W/C 109
Shemya AFB, 134, 185, 189, 212, 217, 227, 242–243, 265, 275–279, 283–286, 291, 294–295, 304–306, 308–312, 315, 319, 334, 338, 345–348, 366, 371, 377, 384, 387–389, 397, 399, 403–404, 410–411
Shipton, F/O (F/L) J.S. 187, 219, 254
Shultz, Col. 552
Sierolawski, F/L R. 555, 568, 572–575, 577, 606, 611, 628
Silver, F/O D.J. 255
Silverman, F/S 173
Simkins F/O E. 255, 338
Simonds, LGen. Guy 251–252, 378, 400–401
Simpson, S/L A.J. 433
Sinai Peninsula 495
Sinclair, Sir Archibald 3
Singapore 157, 430, 460–461, 464, 480, 486, 488, 490, 492–493, 527, 530, 534
single sideband 606, 613
Singleton, S/L A.B. 564
Skaalen, F/L L. 594
Skinner, F/O W. 32
Skuce, F/L E.B. 594
Skull Cliff (Alaska) 120
Sled, F/L J.E. 524, 535, 545, 550, 555, 574
Slemon, A/C (AM) C.R. 5, 78, 359, 379, 399–401, 500, 521, 524, 532, 550, 583
Sloan, F/L T. 86
Smith, F/S 337
Smith, W/O 463
Smith, AVM D.M. 656
Smith, S/L E.G. 331
Smith, F/L E.W. 157
Smith, Sgt. H.F. 229
Smith, F/L H.M. 596–600, 636, 647
Smith, MGen. Joseph 315
Smith, F/O J.A. 107
Smith, Brig. J.D.B. 149
Smith, Sgt. R.T. 136
Smith, F/O (F/L) W. 139, 189
Smith, F/O (F/L) W.H. 75, 76, 77, 79, 82, 87, 117, 136
Snelling, F/O E.J.M. 255, 347
Snider, F/L C.E. 79–82, 84, 101, 103, 111, 121, 129, 229, 249–250, 259, 265, 276
Soame, Cpl. Maurice 192
Solant, Dr. O.M 356.
Sondrestrom Air Base (Greenland) 446, 507, 520, 550, 571, 573, 577, 580, 656–658

Songhurst, W/C F.E. 557
Souchen, F/O (F/L) D.W. 229, 332
Souda Bay (Crete) 502
South African Air Force 461
Soviet Ice Station 569
Special Operations Executive 15
Specialist Navigation Course 118, 290, 456, 485, 523, 569, 590, 596, 639, 657
Spector, F/L H. 191, 254
Spence Bay (NWT) 432, 506, 530
Spencer, F/L E.M. 601–604, 608
Sperry Gyroscope Company 133, 628
Spikings F/O H.A. 337
Spratt, F/O R.A. 248, 290, 319, 333–334, 363
Springer, F/L G.U. 654
squadrons (RAF):
  No 53 Merrifield 49;
  No 54 Odiham 110;
  No 76 Holme 3;
  No 102 Bassingbourn 46, 50;
  No 138 Tempsford 15;
  No 161 Tempsford 15;
  No 347 Elvington 3;
  No 511 Lyneham 31;
  No 525 Lyneham 9, 15
squadrons (RCAF):
  No 12 (Communications) Rockcliffe 61, 62;
  No 13 (Operational Training) Sea Island 61;
  No 124 (Ferry) Rockcliffe 62;
  No 164 (Transport) Moncton 61, 63;
  No 165 (Transport) Sea Island 61, 62;
  No 168 (Transport) Rockcliffe 62, 78, 96;
  No 170 (Ferry) Winnipeg 62;
  No 400 (City of Toronto) Auxiliary Toronto, 293, 633;
  No 401 (City of Westmount) Auxiliary, St-Hubert 63, 99, 147, 283, 633, 656;
  No 402 (City of Winnipeg) Auxiliary, Winnipeg 378, 633;
  No 403 (City of Calgary) Auxiliary, Calgary 378, 633;
  No 404 (Coastal Fighter) Banff 4; (Maritime Patrol) Greenwood 261, 307, 319, 333, 360, 404, 452, 545;
  No 405 (Pathfinder) Gransden Lodge 9, 130; (Maritime Patrol) Greenwood 168, 261, 279, 307, 360, 419, 440, 452, 455, 550;
  No 406 (City of Saskatoon) Auxiliary, Saskatoon 633;

No 407 (General Reconnaissance) Chivenor 4, 5; (Maritime Patrol) Comox 488–489, 648;
No 408 (Bomber) Linton-on-Ouse 3, 6, 7; (Photographic) Rockcliffe 129, 145, 162, 169, 244–245, 282, 333–334, 440, 455, 497, 518–519, 522, 526; (Reconnaissance) 551, 554–555, 557;
No 409 AW(F) Comox 397, 455;
No 410 (Fighter) St-Hubert 121, 223, 261; North Luffenham 274, 317, 426, 481; Marville AW(F): Uplands 455;
No 411 (County of York) Auxiliary, Toronto 633;
No 412 (Transport) Rockcliffe 78, 118, 170, 183, 245, 288, 317, 369, 423; Uplands 492, 555, 558, 576, 605, 659;
No 413 (Photographic) Rockcliffe 100, 169; (Fighter) Bagotville 274, 308; Zweibrücken 357, 363–364, 481; AW(F) Bagotville 655;
No 414 (Photographic) Rockcliffe 110, 169; (Fighter) Bagotville 365; Baden Söellingen 370, 375, 379–380, 481; North Bay 529, 655;
No 415 (Maritime Patrol) Summerside 638;
No 416 (Fighter) Uplands 264, 287, 336; Grostenquin 339–340; St-Hubert/Bagotville 655;
No 418 (City of Edmonton) Auxiliary, Edmonton 633;
No 419 AW(F) North Bay 397, 481, 529; Baden-Soëllingen 573, 655;
No 420 (City of London) Auxiliary, London, 293;
No 421 (Fighter) Chatham 143, 223, 229; Odiham 244, 274; St-Hubert 293, 336; Grostenquin 339–340, 384, 658;
No 422 (Coastal) Pembroke Docks 4, 6, 9, 11, 22–24; (Fighter) Uplands 355, 366, 370, 375, 379–380; Baden-Soëllingen 381, 658;
No 423 (Coastal) Castle Archdale 4, 6, 9, 11, 23–24; AW(F) St-Hubert 481, 516; Grostenquin 518, 655;
No 424 (City of Hamilton) Auxiliary, Mount Hope 293, 378, 633;
No 425 AW(F) St-Hubert 397, 441; Namao 655;
No 426 (Bomber) Linton-on-Ouse 3, 5, 8; (Transport) Driffield 9–10; Tempsford 11, 22, 23, 25, 31, 34–35, 40, 42, 44, 50;

Dartmouth 63, 65, 68, 73–75; Lachine/Dorval 76, 78–83, 87–89, 91–92, 100–101, 103–104, 106, 109, 112, 114, 116, 119, 121–122, 130–132, 138, 140, 145, 149; McChord AFB 188, 218, 221, 226–227, 243, 248, 250–253, 261; Lachine/Dorval 275, 280, 283, 287, 291, 293–294, 303, 305–306, 308, 310, 315, 317, 319, 333–334, 342–345, 360–361, 366, 370, 377–378, 384, 386, 397–398, 400, 402–403, 407–408, 411, 429, 433, 439, 455, 474, 481–482, 500, 508, 513, 517, 521, 524, 531, 533, 536, 555, 558, 560, 564–565, 568, 572, 575–578; Trenton 580–583, 587, 591–592, 594–595, 600, 608, 610, 615–616, 631, 634–635, 639, 641–648; St-Hubert 653–660;
No 427 (Fighter) St-Hubert 318, 322; Zweibrücken 357, 363–364;
No 428 AW(F) Uplands 397, 536, 641;
No 430 (Fighter) North Bay 336; Grostenquin 339–340, 658;
No 431 (Bomber) Croft 3;
No 432 (Bomber) East Moor 263; AW(F) Bagotville 397, 641;
No 433 AW(F) Cold Lake 397, North Bay 641;
No 434 (Fighter) Uplands 318; Zweibrücken 357, 363–364, 658;
No 435 (Transport) Odiham 26; Edmonton 63, 112, 130, 138, 145, 183, 245, 251, 302, 366, 383, 439, 452, 482, 500, 502, 513, 548, 555, 557, 567, 594, 609, 611, 616, 633–635, 644, 646;
No 436 (Transport) Dorval 302, 356, 378, 383, 439, 452, 461, 474, 488; Downsview 494, 500, 502, 520, 529, 532, 548, 567, 576, 593–594, 609, 612, 644, 646;
No 437 (Transport) Trenton 492, 645–646, 653, 659;
No 438 (City of Montreal) Auxiliary, St-Hubert 63, 147, 656;
No 439 (Fighter) Uplands 274, 317; North Luffenham 318, 426; Marville 658;
No 440 AW(F) Bagotville 356, 481, 523, 655;
No 441 (Fighter) St-Hubert 302, 317; North Luffenham 426; Marville 658;

No 442 (City of Vancouver) Auxiliary, Vancouver 633;
No 443 (City of New Westminister) Auxiliary, Vancouver 274, 442;
No 444 (Fighter) St-Hubert 355, 366, 370, 375, 379–380; Baden-Söellingen 381, 658;
No 445 AW(F) North Bay 356, 481; Marville 499, 655;
No 446 (SAM) North Bay 655;
No 447 (SAM) La Macaza 655
Spurr, F/L L.E. 315
SS Brazilian Prince 554
SS Gander Bay 419, 422, 455, 459
SS Knightsbridge 524, 528, 531
SS Sea Transporter 524, 528, 531, 554
St. Laurent, LAC J.A.A. 189, 291
St. Laurent, Prime Minister Louis 120, 142, 145, 174, 180–182, 191, 288, 331, 500
St. Lawrence Seaway 575
St. Eval (Cornwall) 263, 319, 333, 381
Stacey, Flight Officer F.W. 25, 31
Stalin, Josef V. 355
Stanleyville (Congo) 555, 559, 574, 576, 609, 613
Stantial, S/L G. 591
Stark, Mr. 458
stations (RAF):
 Abingdon 179;
 Bassingbourn 21, 34, 179;
 Bircham Newton 17;
 Blackbushe 463;
 Bückeburg 289;
 Driffield 7, 9, 10;
 Gutersloh 568, 582, 595, 610, 615–616, 657;
 Kemble 408, 420;
 Langar 301;
 Lyneham 108, 110–111, 136, 141, 170, 289, 498, 553;
 Manston 317;
 Melsbroek 28;
 Merrifield 20, 24;
 North Luffenham 274;
 Northolt 17, 140, 150, 553;
 Odiham 17, 44, 223, 244;
 Shaibah 28, 50;
 Speke 33;
 St. Mawgan 18, 24, 547;
 Tain 22;
 Tempsford 10, 11, 15;
 Wildenrath 610, 615, 638, 640;
 Wünstorf 289
stations (RCAF):
 Bagotville 308, 316–317, 334, 339, 357, 360, 363–365, 375, 378–380, 397, 481, 523, 641;
 Camp Borden 118;

Swan, F/L R.M. 632
Sweanor, F/L G.J. 338
Sweetman, F/L O.M. 589, 618
Swetman, W/C (G/C) 105, 108, 114, 121, 133, 134, 140, 141, 160, 183, 186, 229
Swift, F/S 218
Sydney (Australia) 486, 527, 530
Sydney (Nova Scotia) 293, 334

T

Tachikawa AFB 250, 284
Tactical Air Command (RCAF) 522, 557
tactical nuclear weapons 354
Taegu 257, 262
Tait, LAC R.H. 548
Tapp, Gordie 634
Tapp, F/O (F/L) L.A.R. 404, 422–423
Taylor, Cpl. 291
Taylor, D. 86
Taylor, F/O G.E. 347
Taylor, LGen. M. 353
Taylor, LAC M.E. 548
Taylor, Capt. R. 549, 554
Technical Services Unit (No 314) 301
Tedder, Lord 145, 147
Telecommunications Maintenance Unit (6RD Trenton) 613
Tesidder, Sgt. 348
Teslin (Yukon) 138
The Pas (Manitoba) 88, 315, 333, 378, 458, 462–463, 545
Thomas, W/C R.I. 229, 280, 368
Thompson, S/L B.R. 532
Thompson, F/O D.L. 280
Thompson, F/O D.T. 371, 440
Thompson, Cpl. J.G. 291, 311
Thompson, F/L J.H. 47
Thompson, LAC J.P. 193
Thompson, LAC T.G. 192
Thorn, James 145
Thornsteinson, Dr. 519
Thornton, G.B. 242
Thule (Greenland) 161, 171, 257, 335, 348, 357, 359, 366, 387, 406, 419, 429, 432, 440, 443, 445, 451, 457, 490, 508, 517, 519–522, 534, 537, 545–546, 552–553, 556, 564, 566, 572–573, 576, 591, 593–595, 611, 616, 635, 639, 642–644, 654
Thunderbird Club 262
Tieman, LAC 494
Tiger Force 4–8, 16, 23
Tigges, Cpl. 291
Timbrell, F/O (F/L) E.S. 229, 338
Timlick, F/L H.B. 33
Timmins, F/O (F/L) A.J.S. 187, 290, 311, 571–572
Tocumen airport (Panama) 596

Tofino (Vancouver Island) 292
Tokyo (Haneda AFB) 134, 157, 185, 189–193, 211, 213, 217–219, 221–223, 227, 241, 243, 245, 248–250, 256–257, 259, 262, 264, 275–278, 283–285, 291, 293–295, 303–304, 309, 311–313, 315, 333, 338, 342, 344, 346–348, 361, 366, 370, 377–378, 381, 383–384, 386–387, 401, 404, 407–408, 410–411, 422, 424–426, 432, 464, 480, 534, 559
Tompkins, F/O A.D. 255, 347
Tongabatu 137
Torbay airport (St. John's) 148, 166, 169, 280, 293–294, 347, 371, 642, 646
Toronto 80, 88, 103, 107, 138, 187, 281, 283, 291, 293–294, 314, 316, 334, 360, 379, 477, 483, 631, 641
Torontow, F/L (S/L) C. 86, 280, 294, 337, 348, 356, 366, 370
Tozer, Dr. 519
Traill, F/L R.J. 46, 47
Training Command (RCAF)132, 169, 171, 557, 564, 570, 577, 633
training flights:
 long-range (Edmonton) 102, 103;
 trans-Atlantic 104, 107–111, 115, 116;
 South Atlantic 131, 135, 137, 139–141, 143;
 training proposals 146–147, 160;
 Europe-South Atlantic 170;
 1950 itineraries 171;
 Europe, Africa, Middle East 173;
 Britain, South Atlantic 179, 183;
 planned 223;
 special Pacific 257
Training Standards Establishment 577
Trans-Canada Airlines 61, 80, 88, 95–98, 104, 114, 119, 129, 146, 159, 229, 254, 401
Transport Aircraft Modification Unit (RAF) 15
Transport Command Development Unit (RAF) 20
Transport Command Headquarters (RAF) 10, 20, 21, 46
Transport Flight (No 137 Langar) 301, 332
Tremblay, Sgt. 167
Trenchard, MRAF Lord Hugh 314
Trepanier, F/O C.M. 314
Trepanier, S/L H.R.R. 119, 141
troop rotation 591, 610, 615, 617
Trotter, F/L (S/L) E.J. 292, 295, 303–306, 463, 491, 494
Trudel, Cpl. J.B.P.A. 355
Truman, President Harry S. 144, 163, 174, 218, 256, 273

Trumley, S/L (W/C) R.K. 461, 600
Truscott, G/C G.G. 17
Tshombe, Moise 601
Tunis 658
Tunisian troops 603
Tuplin, WO2 J.C. 3
Turkish Air Force 452
Turnbull, W/C (G/C) R.S. 115, 375
Turner, F/L J.C. 487
Turner, W/C P.S. 534, 537, 552, 556–557, 566
Tutt, F/O P.M. 222
Twinning, Gen. Nathan 399

U

United Services Institute (Montreal) 102
United Nations: Emergency Force (UNEF) 500, 520, 532–533, 538, 543, 546, 558, 564, 575, 577–578, 594–595, 607–608, 615–616, 653, 656–657, 659–660;
 General Assembly 248, 496, 499;
 Korea (Air Forces) 256, 273, (Army) 256, 273, (Naval) 353, (Command) 273, 301, 353–354, 496;
 Opération des Nations Unies au Congo (ONUC) 602, 604–606, 612, 614–616, 631, 653–654, 656;
 Secretariat 605–606;
 Secretary General (Trygve Lie) 174, 180–182, 192, (Dag Hammarskjöld) 496, 500, 631;
 Security Council 174, 180;
 Truce Supervisory Organization (UNTSO) 496, 602
United States:
 Air Force 520, 578, 598, 607;
 Army, 8th (Korea) 226, 230, 353;
 Camp Darby (HQ 8th Logistics Command) 636, 638;
 Chief of Naval Operations 531;
 Civil Aeronautics Authority 397–399;
 Continental Air Defense Command, 473;
 Department of Defence 580;
 Field Hospital Unit (Chile) 599;
 National Security Council 396;
 Navy Blimp ZPG-2, 554;
 Navy Task Force (Nanook 53) 382;
 Strategic Air Command 398;
 Weather Bureau Detachment (Resolute Bay) 458, 519, 528, 548, 554, 563, 610
Unruh, F/O W. 255, 290
Upton, Capt. (Maj.) T.J. 185, 264
Urquhart, Sir Brian 604
USNS General Edwin P. Patrick 260

Index

Centralia 82, 113, 170, 259, 280, 287, 294, 306;
Chatham 229, 244, 420, 547;
Charesholm 557;
Clinton 77–78, 254;
Cold Lake 397, 553, 559, 593, 634, 656–657;
Comox 338, 397, 488, 648, 654, 656;
Dartmouth 73, 75–76, 79, 84–85, 114, 121, 160, 293, 307, 349, 371, 497, 518;
Down Ampney 64;
Downsveiw 441, 488, 612, 646;
Edmonton 102–103, 107, 109, 114, 117, 130, 138, 158–159, 162, 164, 166, 260, 264, 273, 287–288, 295, 321, 332–334, 336, 346, 349, 360, 362, 366, 379, 383, 386–387, 390, 403, 410–411, 452, 654;
Gimli 138–139, 556;
Goose Bay 61, 64, 67–68, 73–75, 78–82, 84–85, 88–91, 95, 100, 105, 107–112, 114, 132, 136, 148, 150, 163, 165, 167–168, 170–171, 183, 244, 255, 289–290, 305, 307–308, 310, 315–319, 333–334, 336, 338–339, 348, 360–361, 364, 368, 371, 375–377, 379–381, 383–384, 386, 402–403, 405–408, 420–421, 426, 428, 430, 448, 450–454, 456, 458–460, 462, 475–476, 478, 482–484, 487, 496, 498–499, 503, 508, 516, 518, 520–524, 535, 537, 544, 552, 558, 573, 577, 580, 656–657;
Greenwood 82, 106, 122, 168, 252, 261, 263, 275, 279–280, 294, 307, 314, 319, 360, 371, 377, 381, 383, 419, 433, 440, 450, 494, 507, 517, 545, 550, 617, 655;
Lachine 76, 87, 144, 172, 184, 193, 219, 223–224, 243–245, 254–255, 265, 274–275, 279, 293–294, 301–302, 314, 321, 335, 337–338, 346, 349, 356–357, 362, 367–368, 387, 402, 412, 421, 423, 439, 450, 454–455, 457–458, 460, 463, 481, 491, 494, 497, 508, 521, 530–531, 534, 552, 561, 563–566, 577;

Langar (No 30 Air Materiel Base) 332, 379, 439, 497, 499, 503, 505, 518, 521, 524–525, 527, 534, 543–544, 547, 549, 552–556, 560, 578, 600, 608–609, 632–633, 636, 638, 639, 640;
Linton-on-Ouse 3, 6, 8;
MacDonald 322;
Namao 378, 383, 482, 548, 557, 559, 616, 641, 646, 659;
North Bay 288, 316, 336, 339, 397, 481;
Penhold 616, 640;
Rockcliffe 66, 78–79, 86, 100–101, 105, 111, 129, 132, 140, 142, 145, 157, 163, 165, 167, 179, 185, 223, 244–245, 263, 275, 279, 288, 295, 306, 320–321, 334–335, 368, 378–379, 405–406;
Saskatoon 170, 288, 332, 547;
Sea Island (Vancouver) 106–107, 134, 137–139, 160, 187, 191–192, 220, 226, 252, 254, 261, 264, 306, 320, 322, 333, 334, 346, 373, 383, 386, 387, 389, 403–404, 408, 410–411, 422–426, 432–433, 464;
St-Hubert 89, 100, 114, 117, 147, 294, 316–318, 332–334, 336, 339, 357, 360, 363, 365–366, 375, 377–380, 397, 402, 404–405, 412, 420–421, 426, 428, 448, 450, 452–453, 456, 459–462, 476, 481–482, 484–485, 489, 496–498, 503, 521, 523, 552, 559, 590, 593, 631, 634, 647–648, 654, 656–660;
Summerside 118, 252, 261, 290, 293, 363, 638;
Trenton 79, 82, 100, 119–120, 135, 138, 144–145, 171, 293–294, 302, 308, 310, 315, 334, 378, 422–424, 457, 519, 527, 531, 557, 564–565, 576–578, 582, 590, 593, 595–597, 600, 602, 606, 611, 613, 616–617, 619, 626, 628–633, 635–636, 638–640, 642, 647–648, 653–654, 656–660;
Uplands (Ottawa) 76, 293, 366–367, 369, 375, 378–380, 397, 481, 487–488, 536, 552, 558–559;

Whitehorse 103, 107, 111, 114, 121, 130, 138, 158, 306, 321, 332, 386, 433, 547, 558, 566, 576, 654–656, 660;
Winisk 566;
Winnipeg 84, 86, 90–91, 104, 106–107, 114, 129, 138–139, 159, 171–173, 187, 264, 274–275, 288, 308, 320–321, 333–334, 346, 348–349, 356, 359, 362, 366, 377–379, 383, 386–387, 410–411, 423, 427, 455–456, 458, 462–463, 485, 488, 493, 553, 559, 564, 593, 601, 611, 642, 654, 657
Stead, LAC Don 193
Steele, Cdr. G.P. 610
Steinhardt, Ambassador L.A. 168
Stevens, AVM 32
Stevenson, Col. 654
Stevenson Field (Winnipeg) 187
Stevenson, G/C J.G. 186
Stevenson, F/O W.D. 383
Stewart, F/L W.D. 369
St-Tropez 588
Stitt, W/O A.P. 43
Stockdale, F/L J.W. 545, 550–551, 582
Stocker, F/O R.W. 39
Stockholm 656–657
Stopps, Ralph G. 96, 97
Stornaway, (Scotland) 111, 316
Straits of Tiran 495
Strang, Sir William 84
Stranks, Cpl. 291
Stratemeyer, LGen. G.E. 301
Strathy, F/O W.V.C. 255, 311
Strauss, F.J. (Minister of Defence) 578
Stronach, G. 50
Sturgess, F/L R. 452
Stuart, F/L A.B. 188
Stuart, F/L G.M. 225, 255, 278, 284, 292–293, 309, 317
Stuart, Ambassador R.W. Douglas 405
Suez Canal 495, 588
Suez Crisis 495–496, 499, 503
Suffield (Alberta) 108, 518
Sullivan, F/O D.J. 309
Supply Depot (No 312) 301
Supreme Headquarters Allied Powers in Europe (SHAPE) 248
Supreme Headquarters Allied Expeditionary Force (SHAEF) 288
Sutherland, Miss 535
Sutherland F/O P.B. 347
Sutton, Cpl. 384
Suwon (K13) 259, 331

805

Index

USNS Marine Adder 260
USNS Private Joe Martinez 226
USO: Troupe 321; Variety Show 509
USS President Jackson 260
USS Seadragon 610

V

Vaesen, F/O M.R. 482
Val d'Or (Quebec) 527
van Steensel, Maja 378, 422, 479, 537, 591
Van Benthuysen, Lr.Col. Max E. 280
Van Camp, G/C W.C. 263
Van Fleet, LGen. James A. 256, 353
Vanchuk, S/L T. 566
Vanier, Ambassador Georges-Phileas 340
VE-Day 7, 79
Verner, G/C J.A. 170
Victoria (Chile) 599
Victory Loan 33, 37
Victory Aviation (Toronto) 95
Vienna 497–498
Vientiane (Laos) 408
Viet Minh 407
Villalobos, S/L Manuel 598
Villecoublay (France) 439
Vinnicombe, S/L H.C. 108, 120
Vokes, MGen. Chris 288–289
von Horn, MGen. Carl 602–605
Vrooman, F/L E.G.F. 260

W

Waddell, F/O G.G. 322, 348, 359–360
Wait, A/C (AVM) F.G. 132, 186, 361
Wake Island 157, 217, 227, 241–242, 245, 248–249, 256, 264, 422, 424, 431, 464, 480, 534, 556, 559
Walker, LGen. Walton H. 216, 230
Wallace, F/L (S/L) K.T. 222, 265, 276, 337
Wallace, F/O R.R. 47
Walsh, General 138
Walshe, F/O Ted 255
Walt, LAC 222, 281
Walton, F/L J.S. 602, 606, 611, 656–658
Wangerooge 3
Wark, F/L K.A. 369
Warner, LAC 538
Warner, F/L K. 20, 22, 23, 28, 37
Warren, S/L D. 355
Warsaw Pact 495
Waterton, S/L W.A. 161
Watkins, G/C F.H. 65
Watson, F/O J. 589
Watson Lake (Yukon) 138, 158, 321, 332, 386
Watt, F/L J.A. 83, 102, 139, 187, 223, 244, 256–258, 264, 275, 278, 279
Watt, F/O W.D. 638

Watts, S/L J.V. 111, 119, 139
Webb, F/O (S/L) G.W. 118, 141, 145, 148, 159, 163, 167, 179, 183, 191, 227, 242, 252, 302, 337, 433, 449
Webber, S/L 135
Webber, F/O R.O. 449, 454, 457, 462, 488–490
Weeden, F/O (F/L) H.J. 139, 149, 217
Weir, F/O D.H. 346, 383, 388
Wenzel, F/O C.L. 317, 337, 406
Werl (West Germany) 289
West Germany 644
Westell, Sgt, W.A. 66
Wheelus AFB (Tripoli) 546, 578–579, 591, 609
Whillans, Dr. 242
Whillans, F/O K.M. 581, 593, 618
White, Mr. 431
Whitehorse (Yukon) 547, 566, 576
Whiting, A/C R.B. 640
Whitman, F/O R.T. 322, 377
Whitney, RAdm. John P. 250
Whitten, MGen. L.P. 148
Whittington, F/O G.C. 136
Wicks, LAC R.J. 548
Widger, Cpl. 91
Wilding, F/O J. 529
Wilgress, Capt. V.J. 557
Wilkins, G/C F.S. 66
Williams, G/C D.J. 576–577, 595, 601
Williams, F/L G.W. 149
Williams, S/L M.W. 78, 81, 88, 102, 106
Williamstown (Australia) 137
Willis, W/C C.A. 63, 64–68, 73, 74, 75
Willis, W/C D.A. 111, 115
williwaw 210
Wilson, MGen. 560
Wilson, S/L E.A. 108, 172
Wilson, F/O (F/L) J.P. 255, 347, 355, 361
Wilson, F/O R.K. 290
wing (RCAF):
  No 1 Fighter (North Luffenham) 274, 293, 302, 315, 317–318, 338–340, 345, 349, 360, 364–365, 367–368, 270, 376–378, 381–383, 386, 403–403, 407–408, 412, 420–421, 423, 426, 429, 439, 446; (Marville) 451, 478, 488, 490, 493, 499, 525, 536, 543, 550, 571, 573, 578, 580, 595, 600, 631, 640–643, 647, 653, 656–658;
  No 2 Fighter (Grostenquin) 336, 338, 370, 384, 403, 406–408, 420–421, 426, 446, 449, 451, 478, 481–482, 484, 493, 516, 578, 580;

  No 3 Fighter (Zweibrücken) 357, 360, 364–365, 370, 403, 408, 412, 420, 446, 449, 451, 454, 459–460, 463, 477, 481, 493, 496–497, 523, 567–568;
  No 4 Fighter (Baden-Söellingen) 370, 375, 378–379, 381, 420–421, 429, 446, 449, 451, 458–460, 478, 525, 529, 551, 595, 640; No 7 Photographic (Rockcliffe) 86;
  No 120 Transport (Odiham) 35, 45, 48–49, 645
wing (USAF): 1705th Air Transport (McChord) 214, 229, 249–250, 274, 279–280
Winter Experimental Establishment (Edmonton) 117
Wipond, F/O N. 526
Wiseman, W/C J.A. 557
Witt, Brigadeführer Fritz 288
Wolkowski, F/O (F/L) E.R. 140, 187, 278, 304, 311–313, 321, 332, 336, 348, 355, 356, 360–361, 378–379, 381
Wolmi-do Island (Korea) 216
Woodhouse, F/O D.P. 337
Woods, F/L N.C. 537
Woomera Rocket Range (Australia) 354
World Health Organization (WHO) 609
World Meteorological Organization (WMO) 617–619
Wortman, F/O F.B. 255
Wray, A/C (AVM) L.E. 63, 74, 75, 79, 84, 91, 101, 103, 108, 113
Wright, Mr. 527
Wright, F/L H.J.A. 369
Wright, S/L G.G. 136
Wright, F/O J.S. 33, 35, 43, 45
Wynn, F/L J.G. 383, 431

Y

Yates, F/O C.D. 528
Yellowknife (NWT) 336, 544
Yokota AFB 221
Young, F/L J.H. 17

Z

Zakinthos Island (Greece) 379
Zanderij airport (Surinam) 617–618
Zbesheski, F/O H.V. 560, 568, 590, 608, 617, 632, 634
Zimmer, Cpl. P. 137
Zimmerman, Dr. Hartley 517
Zurakowski, Janusz 547
Zurich 563